FOR REFERENCE

Do Not Take From This Room

GREENLEAF LIBRARY
COPPER MTN. COLLEGE
JOSHUA TREE, CA

ENCYCLOPEDIA
of AMERICAN
FOREIGN POLICY

ADVISORY BOARD

Elizabeth Cobbs Hoffman
San Diego State University

Nick Cullather
Indiana University

Chester Pach
Ohio University

William O. Walker III
Florida International University

ENCYCLOPEDIA
of AMERICAN
FOREIGN POLICY

Second Edition

VOLUME 2
E – N

*Alexander DeConde, Richard Dean Burns,
and Fredrik Logevall, Editors in Chief*

Louise B. Ketz, Executive Editor

CHARLES SCRIBNER'S SONS

GALE GROUP
THOMSON LEARNING

New York • Detroit • San Diego • San Francisco
Boston • New Haven, Conn. • Waterville, Maine
London • Munich

Copyright © 2002 by Charles Scribner's Sons

Charles Scribner's Sons
An imprint of the Gale Group
300 Park Avenue South
New York, NY 10010

All rights reserved. No part of this book may be reprinted or reproduced or utilized in any form or by any electronic, mechanical, or other means, now known or hereafter invented including photocopying and recording, or in any information storage or retrieval system, without permission in writing from Charles Scribner's Sons.

1 3 5 7 9 11 13 15 17 19 20 18 16 14 12 10 8 6 4 2

Printed in the United States of America

Library of Congress Cataloging-in-Publication Data

Encyclopedia of American Foreign Policy : studies of the principal movements and ideas / editors, Alexander DeConde ... [et al.]--2nd ed.
    p. cm.
Includes bibliographical references and index.
ISBN 0-684-80657-6 (set : alk. paper) -- ISBN 0-684-80658-4 (v. 1) -- ISBN 0-684-80659-2 (v. 2) -- ISBN 0-684-80660-6 (v. 3)
    1. United States--Foreign relations--Encyclopedias. 2. United States--Foreign relations--Philosophy--Encyclopedias. I. DeConde, Alexander.

E183.7 .E52 2002
327.73'003--dc21
                                                                                                          2001049800

The paper used in this publication meets the requirements of ANSI/NISO Z3948-1992 (Permanence of Paper)

Contents

ECONOMIC POLICY AND THEORY	1
David Shreve	
ELITISM	17
Alan K. Henrikson	
EMBARGOES AND SANCTIONS	33
Jerald A. Combs	
ENVIRONMENTAL DIPLOMACY	49
Kurk Dorsey	
EXCEPTIONALISM	63
Trevor B. McCrisken	
EXTRATERRITORIALITY	81
Jules Davids and Jonathan M. Nielson	
FOREIGN AID	93
Katherine A. S. Sibley	
FREEDOM OF THE SEAS	111
Armin Rappaport and William Earl Weeks	
GENDER	123
Laura McEnaney	
GLOBALIZATION	135
Thomas W. Zeiler	
HUMANITARIAN INTERVENTION AND RELIEF	151
Darlene Rivas	
HUMAN RIGHTS	173
T. Christopher Jespersen	
IDEOLOGY	187
Jennifer W. See	
IMMIGRATION	203
Roger Daniels	
IMPERIALISM	217
David Healy	
INTELLIGENCE AND COUNTERINTELLIGENCE	225
John Prados	
INTERNATIONALISM	241
Warren F. Kuehl and Gary B. Ostrower	

Contents

INTERNATIONAL LAW	259
Christopher C. Joyner	
INTERNATIONAL MONETARY FUND AND WORLD BANK	283
Francis J. Gavin	
INTERNATIONAL ORGANIZATION	299
Inis L. Claude, Jr., and Klaus Larres	
INTERVENTION AND NONINTERVENTION	315
Doris A. Graber	
ISOLATIONISM	337
Manfred Jonas	
JUDICIARY POWER AND PRACTICE	353
Terrence R. Guay	
LOANS AND DEBT RESOLUTION	365
Richard W. Van Alstyne and Joseph M. Siracusa	
MANDATES AND TRUSTEESHIPS	381
Edward M. Bennett	
MILITARISM	387
William Kamman	
THE MILITARY-INDUSTRIAL COMPLEX	403
James A. Huston	
MOST-FAVORED-NATION PRINCIPLE	417
Justus D. Doenecke and Michael R. Adamson	
MULTINATIONAL CORPORATIONS	429
Burton I. Kaufman	
THE MUNICH ANALOGY	443
Joseph M. Siracusa	
NARCOTICS POLICY	455
William O. Walker III	
THE NATIONAL INTEREST	473
H. W. Brands	
NATIONALISM	485
Lawrence S. Kaplan	
NATIONAL SECURITY COUNCIL	499
Anna Kasten Nelson	
NATIVISM	511
Geoffrey S. Smith	
NAVAL DIPLOMACY	529
William R. Braisted	
NEUTRALISM	543
T. Michael Ruddy	
NEUTRALITY	559
Thom M. Armstrong	
NORTH ATLANTIC TREATY ORGANIZATION	573
Klaus Larres	
NUCLEAR STRATEGY AND DIPLOMACY	595
Kenneth J. Hagan and Elizabeth Skinner	

CONTENTS OF OTHER VOLUMES

VOLUME 1

PREFACE	xiii
CHRONOLOGY OF AMERICAN FOREIGN POLICY, 1607–2001	xvii
Richard Dean Burns and Louise B. Ketz	
AFRICAN AMERICANS	1
Brenda Gayle Plummer	
ALLIANCES, COALITIONS, AND ENTENTES	13
Warren F. Kimball	
AMBASSADORS, EXECUTIVE AGENTS, AND SPECIAL REPRESENTATIVES	29
Kenneth J. Grieb	
ANTI-IMPERIALISM	49
Robert Buzzanco	
ARBITRATION, MEDIATION, AND CONCILIATION	61
Calvin D. Davis	
ARMED NEUTRALITIES	73
Ian Mugridge	
ARMS CONTROL AND DISARMAMENT	79
Richard Dean Burns	
ARMS TRANSFERS AND TRADE	105
Michael T. Klare	
ASYLUM	117
Michael Dunne	
BALANCE OF POWER	131
A. E. Campbell and Richard Dean Burns	
THE BEHAVIORAL APPROACH TO DIPLOMATIC HISTORY	141
J. David Singer	
BIPARTISANSHIP	155
Randall Woods	
BLOCKADES	171
Frank J. Merli and Robert H. Ferrell	
THE CHINA LOBBY	185
Warren I. Cohen	
CIVIL WAR DIPLOMACY	193
Kinley Brauer	
COLD WAR EVOLUTION AND INTERPRETATIONS	207
Walter L. Hixson	
COLD WAR ORIGINS	223
Anders Stephanson	
COLD WARRIORS	241
Andrew J. Rotter	
COLD WAR TERMINATION	257
Thomas R. Maddux	
COLLECTIVE SECURITY	273
Roland N. Stromberg	
COLONIALISM AND NEOCOLONIALISM	285
Edward M. Bennett	
CONGRESSIONAL POWER	293
Robert David Johnson	
CONSORTIA	313
Warren I. Cohen	
THE CONSTITUTION	323
David Gray Adler	
CONTAINMENT	345
Barton J. Bernstein	
CONTINENTAL EXPANSION	365
David M. Pletcher	
THE CONTINENTAL SYSTEM	377
Marvin R. Zahniser	
COVERT OPERATIONS	387
John Prados	
CULTURAL IMPERIALISM	397
Jessica C. E. Gienow-Hecht	
CULTURAL RELATIONS AND POLICIES	409
Akira Iriye	

DECISION MAKING	427	PHILANTHROPY	141
Valerie M. Hudson		James A. Field, Jr., and Tim Matthewson	
DEPARTMENT OF DEFENSE	439	POST–COLD WAR POLICY	153
Steven L. Rearden		Richard A. Melanson	
DEPARTMENT OF STATE	451	POWER POLITICS	169
Jerry Israel and David L. Anderson		Thomas H. Etzold and Robert L. Messer	
DETERRENCE	463	PRESIDENTIAL ADVISERS	179
David Coleman		Albert Bowman and Robert A. Divine	
DEVELOPMENT DOCTRINE AND MODERNIZATION THEORY	477	PRESIDENTIAL POWER	195
Nick Cullather		Alexander DeConde	
		THE PRESS	221
		Ralph B. Levering and Louis W. Liebovich	
DICTATORSHIPS	493	PROPAGANDA	239
David F. Schmitz		Kenneth A. Osgood	
DISSENT IN WARS	505	PROTECTION OF AMERICAN CITIZENS ABROAD	255
Russell F. Weigley and David S. Patterson		Burton F. Beers	
DOCTRINES	521	PROTECTORATES AND SPHERES OF INFLUENCE	265
Marc Jay Selverstone		Raymond A. Esthus	
DOLLAR DIPLOMACY	543	PUBLIC OPINION	275
Eugene P. Trani		Melvin Small	
DOMINO THEORY	551	RACE AND ETHNICITY	289
Edwin Moïse		John Snetsinger	
		REALISM AND IDEALISM	311
		Norman A. Graebner	

VOLUME 3

OIL	1	RECIPROCITY	329
David S. Painter		Robert Freeman Smith	
OPEN DOOR INTERPRETATION	21	RECOGNITION	345
William Appleman Williams		Paolo E. Coletta	
OPEN DOOR POLICY	29	REFUGEE POLICIES	357
Mark Atwood Lawrence		David M. Reimers	
ORGANIZED LABOR	45	RELIGION	371
Elizabeth McKillen		Leo P. Ribuffo	
OUTER SPACE	61	REPARATIONS	393
Roger Launius		Carl P. Parrini and James I. Matray	
PACIFISM	73	REVISIONISM	407
Charles Chatfield		Athan G. Theoharis	
PAN-AMERICANISM	83	REVOLUTION	425
Thomas M. Leonard and Thomas L. Karnes		Jeremi Suri	
PARTY POLITICS	99	SCIENCE AND TECHNOLOGY	443
Fredrik Logevall		Ronald E. Doel and Zuoyue Wang	
PEACEMAKING	113	SELF-DETERMINATION	461
Berenice A. Carroll		Betty Miller Unterberger	
PEACE MOVEMENTS	129	SPECIAL-INTEREST LOBBIES	483
Robert H. Ferrell		William Slany	

SUMMIT CONFERENCES 501	**THE VIETNAM WAR AND ITS IMPACT** . . . 597
Theodore A. Wilson	*Larry Berman and Jason Newman*
SUPERPOWER DIPLOMACY 513	**WILSONIANISM** 617
Vojtech Mastny	*Tony Smith*
TARIFF POLICY 531	**WILSONIAN MISSIONARY DIPLOMACY** . . . 627
Thomas W. Zeiler	*Roger R. Trask*
TELEVISION 547	
Chester Pach	**EDITORS AND ADVISERS** 637
TERRORISM AND COUNTERTERRORISM . . . 563	**CONTRIBUTORS** 639
Brian Michael Jenkins	**INDEX** 643
TREATIES 571	
J. B. Duroselle and Ian J. Bickerton	

Encyclopedia of American Foreign Policy

Economic Policy and Theory

David Shreve

Merging in numerous ways, economic theory has often been linked to U.S. foreign policy. When the United States began its life as a fledgling exporter of raw materials vitally dependent upon connections to Liverpool merchants, crude economic theories accompanied virtually all deliberations and pronouncements on foreign affairs. As the nation grew in size, population, and wealth, this connection became less apparent and, indeed, far less critical or commonplace. By most estimates, foreign trade rarely exceeded 5 percent of the American gross national product. Moreover, after significant growth and increasing specialization in export markets in the late nineteenth century, levels of international market integration that prevailed in 1914 were equaled again only in the 1990s, albeit with far less market segmentation than in the earlier period. The information gaps of that earlier period have almost completely disappeared.

Only when it emerged as a world power following the two world wars did the United States again endeavor to combine the latest in economic theory with virtually all of its foreign policy concerns. The rise of professional economics had much to do with this resurgence; so did the demands for the cooperation and rebuilding made virtually indispensable by both economic depression and destructive and widespread conflict. Institutionalization of professional economic advice, most of which followed the Great Depression and World War II in the twentieth century, brought economic theory into the limelight, where it joined readily and quite seamlessly with heightened international concerns for peace and prosperity. Here it began by acknowledging as well the growing awareness that domestic prosperity was at least partly hinged to global prosperity.

The adaptable theories of giants such as the British economists Adam Smith and David Ricardo notwithstanding, economic theory previously had been applied only loosely to U.S. foreign policy concerns or, as it was in the early Republic, only in forms of a largely prescientific character, too amorphous and philosophical to construct a lasting bond or significant transgenerational analysis. Here it had often reflected little more than a concern for how one might either tease out the factors behind international commercial advantage or better discern both commercial limits and commercial potential in world markets. Falling loosely under the rubric of "mercantilism," such concerns seldom reflected anything approaching a scientific method or cognizance of recent or past advances in economic theory, and they seldom attracted those social scientists interested in testing the theoretical challenges of pioneers such as Smith and Ricardo. Smith's suggestion that political economists must find a theory that comports with maximum wages and modest profits, for example, along with Ricardo's critique of landlord-based economic exploitation, remained obscured by conventional analyses designed mostly to promote commercial interests.

Despite this tendency toward limited, mostly superficial economic analysis of international affairs, discussions of monetary policy in the early Republic often veered into the analysis of international factors and approached levels of sophistication unmatched by many twentieth-century analysts. In some ways, for example, late nineteenth-century U.S reliance on a gold standard with fixed exchange rates represented a departure from an earlier, more flexible bimetallic monetary policy—to which the nation would ultimately return. The alteration, in 1834, of Alexander Hamilton's 15:1 silver-to-gold valuation of the dollar—to a 16:1 ratio—largely kept silver dollars out of circulation, limited the worldwide potential of later Nevada silver discoveries, and signaled the advent of a more restrictive, even emasculating, U.S. monetary policy. Ceding control of domestic monetary policy to the vagaries of international gold flows, and the overall level of international commerce to the total gold supply, policymakers had essentially ignored existing economic theory, however immature, in favor of economic policy handcuffs.

But talk of trade clearly occupied the minds of far more policymakers and economic theorists than did international currency analysis. Smith's theories, principally those found in his groundbreaking synthesis published in 1776, *An Inquiry into the Nature and Causes of the Wealth of Nations,* focused attention squarely on international trade, proffering an analysis designed to integrate trade policy and consumer welfare. Smithian analysis of how to pay for war (taxation versus borrowing)—designed to make its costs more obvious and disabling—also filtered into a great number of American foreign policy debates and was digested and considered fully by both late eighteenth- and early nineteenth-century American leaders. David Ricardo's early nineteenth-century postulates regarding comparative advantage—the notion that two nations may gain through trade even if one can produce everything more efficiently than the other—had percolated, as well, into policy circles in both Great Britain and the United States. Few of these theories, however, found anything but temporary or comparatively insecure footholds in the policy arena until the mid-twentieth century.

From the American economists who toiled for the Strategic Bombing Survey during World War II to those serving today as consultants on currency stabilization, economic theory has now permeated virtually every conceivable foreign policy analysis and situation. It no longer remains confined principally to questions of international commercial advantage or even international trade. At the same time, its chief occupation has most often been limited to three major areas: trade policy, international monetary policy, and policies for international growth and development (for developed, developing, and undeveloped nations). Since the breakdown of the Bretton Woods system for international currency stabilization in the early 1970s, monetary policy has become much more newsworthy; much more often the subject of policy discussions, high and low; and has increasingly become the preoccupation of many skilled economists and specialized policy advisers. Likewise, growth and development policy also increased in significance in the late twentieth century, albeit mostly as a result of both increasing numbers of American, European, and East Asian multinational corporations and increasing emphasis on development that emerged along with post–World War I and post–World War II rebuilding efforts. As the welfare of these companies came to depend increasingly on rising prosperity abroad, and as altruism merged increasingly with self-interest in prominent rebuilding or relief efforts, more people naturally came to ask how such prosperity should be created or sustained.

Analysis of trade policy, however, continues to engage economic theorists more than any other large foreign policy concern. Indeed, a great number of international monetary policy analyses are, in effect, designed to explain how international money affects international trade.

INTERNATIONAL TRADE

Although Adam Smith (1723–1790) is regarded today as the progenitor of "laissez-faire" economic theory—where self-interest, limited government, and the unbridled profit motive converge to produce the ideal political economy—his economic theory really began on much more limited grounds.

Beginning with the overarching belief that the best political economy produced a regime of high wages and low prices—and modest profits—Smith created what many regard as the first modern economic theory, a theory constructed squarely upon a critique of British international trade in the late eighteenth century. When Smith spoke of restraint in critical terms, for example, he most often referred to import restrictions, not restraint of the individual and his single-minded pursuit of wealth. With much of Smith's general theory lost to the questionable interpretation of his lofty, somewhat more malleable rhetoric, one is left mostly with a trenchant special theory. Like the French Physiocrats who preceded him, Smith constructed his theory upon the notion that government promotion of trade most often came at the expense of groups or individuals who were less powerful but more significant, economically, than the commercial exporters favored by such promotion. For the Physiocrats, these individuals were farmers; for Smith, consumers.

Thus began both a long-running debate on the economic merits of free trade versus protectionism and trade promotion, and on a course of theoretical formulations built partly on the criticism of policies that favored commercial interests over agricultural counterparts. Placing the con-

JOHN MAYNARD KEYNES AND BRETTON WOODS

Although the area around Bretton Woods, New Hampshire, possesses one of the least reliable climates anywhere in the United States, it was chosen as the site of the 1944 international conference for post–World War II international economic planning precisely because it promised a potentially pleasant climate. "For God's sake do not take us to Washington in July," wrote the British economist John Maynard Keynes to the American Harry Dexter White in May 1944, "which would surely be a most unfriendly act." White, who had joined the Treasury department in 1934 and had become Treasury Secretary Henry Morgenthau's chief planner for postwar international economic policy was Keynes's chief intermediary with the Roosevelt administration. The "White Plan" for postwar international economic cooperation, leaked by the London *Financial News* in April 1943, became the principal blueprint which guided postwar planning in general and the Bretton Woods conference in particular. Lord Keynes was the chief British spokesperson, a confidant of White's, and, as it turned out, chiefly responsible for choosing the site of the conference.

Convened on 1 July 1944, and held at the Mount Washington Hotel at Bretton Woods, this groundbreaking conference opened only a short distance from the peak of the highest summit in the American Northeast. On 12 April 1934, the weather observatory on its summit recorded a sustained wind gust of 231 miles per hour, a record that has yet to be equaled anywhere on the planet. It is a place reckoned by many to be one of the windiest places on earth, and attracts a multitude of visitors today, many drawn by the strange lure and challenge of unpredictable conditions. Snow has fallen on the peak in every month of the year, and temperatures below freezing are not uncommon at any time.

There is little doubt that Keynes, who suffered from heart ailments and who would die of a heart attack in 1946, preferred the chance of a blustery climate in July to the potential for oppressive heat and humidity in the nation's capital. And though the conference concluded by eschewing Keynes's plea for both an international reserve currency (that he had given the name "bancor") and an international overdraft fund, it was the masterful British economist who ensured that the more than seven hundred delegates from forty-four nations would meet to plan the postwar international economic order in the Presidential Range of New Hampshire's White Mountains.

sumer at the heart of his theory, rather than the producers favored in eighteenth-century British policy, Smith ensured that such consumers would always be represented in subsequent economic theory related to international trade. Favors granted by governments to resident exporters, Smith pointed out, might well benefit those producers only at the expense of resident consumers, leaving almost everyone less well off. Hereafter, these consumers would be removed from trade policy calculations only by ignoring relevant and advancing economic theory. Freer trade—perhaps anticipating the theory of the "second-best" enunciated by James Edward Meade and Richard Lipsey in the 1950s and the "scientific tariff" theories promulgated by Harry G. Johnson in the 1970s, became a means to improve domestic purchasing power for the first time under Smith's formulation.

Although it ultimately came to be submerged within later economic theories that often ignored its most immediate postulates, Smith's analysis was highly regarded in the early American republic. Indeed, Thomas Jefferson—attracted, perhaps, to Smith's reshaping of physiocratic, agrarian-centered critiques of commercial subsidy—regarded it as the paragon of contemporary political economy. Smith's trade theories would also help establish a general pattern for regional political battles in the early nineteenth century (for example, the 1828 "Tariff of Abominations"). Vice President John C. Calhoun's challenge to American protectionism, nascent despite its implicit connection to the special interests of southern slaveholders, may well have anticipated both the consumer-based populism in the American South during the late nineteenth and early twentieth centuries and the underconsumptionist economic theories of the mid-twentieth-century followers of John Maynard Keynes. His focus on the costs of effective and proposed U.S. tariffs was constructed squarely, if unwittingly, on the back of Smith's trade theory.

If Smith pointed economic theory toward the potential general benefits of freer trade—couched within a broader, somewhat more ambivalent philosophical treatise—then David Ricardo (1772–1823) transformed it into a more single-minded pursuit of improved economic analysis. Ricardo's masterpiece, *The Principles of Political Economy and Taxation,* first published in 1817, contributed greatly to the analysis of wage determination, pricing, and tax policy. But most famously, perhaps, it also gave us the law of comparative advantage. Explaining how a nation may gain by importing a good even if that good can be produced at home more efficiently (by allowing it to devote more resources to the production of goods at which it is most efficient), Ricardo revealed previously unrecognized advantages to a regime of freer trade. He also suggested the kind of rigorous analysis upon which all subsequent theory of international economics would have to rest. Indeed, few economists can yet escape Ricardian challenges, especially in the ongoing analysis of price determination and the relative importance of wage and profit levels. And though policymakers tend to conform to the characterization of the nineteenth-century British prime minister Benjamin Disraeli—encouraging free trade as an expedient rather than a principle—it is also likely that they can seldom avoid beginning the analysis of any trade policy regime without the admonishments of both Adam Smith and David Ricardo.

INTERNATIONAL TRADE THEORY: FROM TRAILBLAZERS TO TWENTIETH-CENTURY PROFESSIONALS

The British philosopher and economist John Stuart Mill (1806–1873) updated (and endorsed) much of Ricardo's analysis with his 1848 publication, *Principles of Political Economy.* The first to emphasize that allocation of resources and distribution of income are two somewhat distinct roles performed by modern market systems, Mill parted company with earlier classical economists by suggesting that policy could indeed shape the distribution of income. The late nineteenth-century (principally 1871–1877) analyses of William Stanley Jevons (1835–1882) in England, Karl Menger (1840–1921) in Austria, and Leon Walras (1834–1910) in Switzerland saw the emergence of the marginalist school of economic theory. Reorienting economic analysis away from theories of price determination that had relied exclusively upon supply-side factors or the costs of production, the marginalist school significantly updated the analyses of Smith and Ricardo and the classical economic theory built upon their writings. Beginning their theory of prices (and therefore of production and allocation as well) with consumer behavior and consumer choice, the marginalists moved economic theory closer to the consumer-centered philosophy espoused, but never developed systematically or mathematically, by Smith. Walras would do this to great effect, for example, with his creation of demand functions, mathematical functions that for the first time expressed the quantities of a given product or service as they were determined collectively by consumer income, consumer preference or taste, product price, and product price relative to other related goods or services.

Until the assiduous efforts of Alfred Marshall (1842–1924) on behalf of the discipline and profession in England, however, economics was the vocation of few in academe, public policy was constructed with little or no professional economic advice, and international trade theory in particular had progressed only a little past its Smithian and Ricardian foundations. Academic chairs in political economy had been established early in the nineteenth century, but throughout much of that century most were either vacant or held as a secondary occupation. Jevons, Menger, and Walras, in fact, all worked in professions outside of academe before being appointed to chairs in political economy at universities in England, Austria, and Switzerland. Jevons's government post as an assayer in Sydney, Australia, appears to have convinced him, in fact, that public officials required more—and more consistently offered—professional economic policy advice. Despite their later association with schools of free-market or even anti-government economic analyses, the progenitors of the marginalist revolution gravitated to economic theory out of concern for public policy, much of which centered on international affairs and international trade. Like Jevons, Menger, and Walras, the first professional economists found themselves holding academic chairs in political economy; the fledgling science and public policy were undeniably woven together. Until the twentieth century, however, the designation implied no distinct body of knowledge or craft. In Ireland, for example, it fell initially under the instruction of law, changing soon after into a course of study geared principally to business or industrial management.

Professor of political economy at the University of Cambridge from 1885 to 1908, Marshall began his teaching career in 1868 at St. John's College, Cambridge, as a lecturer in moral sciences. When he retired from teaching in 1908 to devote his final years to writing, he had succeeded in establishing a new honors examination (tripos) in economics and politics (1903) at Cambridge, had bequeathed to economic analysis the critical distinction between the short run and the long run (in what he called "period analysis"), and had established political economy as a distinct subject worthy of widespread study and generous public attention. The London School of Economics opened in 1895, and Oxford University offered its first diploma in economics in 1903, attesting to the rising popularity and increased relevance of economic study. Marshall's direct contribution to international trade theory was limited to his analysis of two-country trade with intersecting "offer curves" and its concomitant analysis of demand elasticity (how the increase of goods offered by one nation might affect the quantity of goods offered by a trading partner). The term "elasticity," so widely used by economists today to denote the ratio of change between dependent and independent variables, was Marshall's invention. More significantly, his attention to the professional standing of economists, his willingness to engage in policy debate and to observe real economic conditions and changes, and his conscious linking of modern economic analysis to classical foundations paved the way for the most significant twentieth-century breakthroughs in international trade theory.

Marshall's major work devoted to international trade issues, *Industry and Trade,* published in 1919, may well have lacked theoretical consistency or structure precisely because it considered so closely recent trends and activities in British and world trade networks. Indeed, his attention to the practical reach of modern economics led to the frequent inclusion in all of his writings of cautionary notes on what might or might not be successfully "impounded" in analytic assumptions about dynamic economic processes. These caveats remain significant today. For Marshall, any accurate depiction of dynamic economic processes required more information than was ever possible to obtain, an insight proved increasingly sound by the limitations and shortcomings of the newest and most ambitious computer-generated models.

Marshall also created a theoretical path that tended to consolidate and synthesize previous lines of economic analysis constructed upon a classical and orderly market-clearing conception of the economic world. As economic science matured and academic posts in political economy proliferated around the turn of the twentieth century, a classical consensus emerged, much of it constructed upon Marshall's edifice. With his *Theory of International Trade, with Its Application to Commercial Policy,* published in 1936, Gottfried Haberler introduced an expansive reformulation of this emerging consensus by fitting it with the dynamic language of general equilibrium analysis. The benefits of free trade could subsequently be viewed in terms of both direct and indirect effects, bringing free trade theory closer to real world phenomena. And though German historical economists and American institutional economists, such as Thorstein Veblen, pointed dramatically to the ways in which economic reality differed widely from the behavior predicted by classical economic theory, they offered no compelling theoretical substitute.

Only the economic dislocations of World War I and the onset of the Great Depression compelled economists to urge greater caution and to force the construction of new theoretical pathways, many of which highlighted and served questions of international trade. That levels of international trade had declined so precipitously during the Great Depression—by two-thirds in nominal dollar terms and by one-third in real, inflation-adjusted terms—made it virtually impossible to consider new economic ideas without an unwavering focus upon international trade.

The principal economists of this interwar period nudged theory onto different planes and punctured much of the prevailing orthodoxy regarding general economic adjustment, unemployment and investment, and the influence of money and interest rates. Free markets were judged increasingly as artifacts of the imagination and as abstractions toward which behavior was often inclined but seldom made manifest without significant gyrations, fits and starts, or failings of even the simplest economic prophecy. Free trade orthodoxy, however, proved to be something else; it depended in part upon a free market framework for much of its explanatory power, yet it also came to be viewed increasingly as a sphere of potentially unrestricted behavior existing atop a large assortment of thoroughly regulated or more artificially cultivated domestic economic affairs. In the face of rising skepticism toward the usefulness of the free market abstraction, and rising trade protectionism—the first significant departure from freer trade since the beginning of the nineteenth century—the tenets of the prevailing free trade orthodoxy emerged virtually unchanged.

In 1921 the American economist Frank Knight (1885–1972) published *Risk, Uncertainty, and Profit*, in which he distinguished between insurable risk that could be mostly ascertained and uninsurable uncertainty that proved impossible to predict. Almost ten years later the Swedish economist Gunnar Myrdal (1898–1987) published *Monetary Equilibrium* (1930), in which he introduced the terms "ex ante" and "ex post," underscoring both the distinction and the relation between expectations and outcomes and the unpredictable ways in which savings equaled investment. And in 1936 the British economist John Maynard Keynes, a former student of Alfred Marshall's, published *The General Theory of Employment, Interest, and Money*, in which he questioned both the microeconomic and the automatic and instantaneous market-clearing foundations of inherited classical theory.

Yet, despite increasingly numerous challenges of this kind, the implications and tendencies of inherited theory on questions of international trade remained virtually untouched. After extensive involvement with the German reparations question after World War I, as well as the debate surrounding the British return to the gold standard in 1924, Keynes had surely proven his interest in international affairs. Later in his career he looked increasingly to the United States for the most practical and noteworthy application of his increasingly refined economic principles. And Keynes's *General Theory* did carry implications for how nations might best effect freer trade and how domestic policy formulation should account for the dislocations and perturbations introduced by an increasingly open and free international trade network. But these implications were in no way an assault upon the general free trade consensus. Indeed, few direct theoretical challenges to free trade emerged in the late twentieth century, despite recurring offensives launched by politicians and various labor movements, and the relatively desperate reaction to economic recession.

From the General Agreement on Tariffs and Trade (GATT), signed in Geneva, Switzerland, on 1 January 1948, through the seven GATT revisions and negotiating rounds beginning in 1955 (and within World Trade Organization negotiations after 1994), free trade resumed its ascent in policy-making circles. Crafted as a means to expanded multilateral trade in the post–World War II era, GATT began with nine signatories (including Cuba) and expanded to include 128 by 1994; in 1995 it was subsumed under the newly formed World Trade Organization. Pausing only for the briefest moments during late twentieth-century recessions that paled in comparison with the calamity of the 1930s, free trade-centered theory found itself with fewer and fewer detractors and policy once again conformed generally to theory.

Implications of **The General Theory** Despite the perceptible ascendancy of Keynesian economics in the second half of the twentieth century, many of the questions raised by Keynes in *The General Theory* remain unsettled. His own followers, for example, continue to argue over whether Keynes described an economy that commonly achieved equilibrium—albeit at unacceptably low levels of output from time to time—or one characterized by continuous oscillations around a stable point or plateau. Few would argue, however, that Keynes did not describe an economy that converged on equilibrium—whether it could ever reach that point or not—by means of changes in income and output rather than through rapid and responsive price adjustments. Indeed, as Janos Kornai later explained, such tendencies may well be universal in modern, mass-production economies, whether capitalist or not. In Kornai's formulation, when confronted with underutilization and excess capacity, Western capitalist economies produced unemployment, whereas the command economies of the East, former and present, produced shortages of consumer goods. Under both schemes, price adjustments played no significant role. This may explain in part why officials in the People's Republic of China have in recent decades been so eager to learn Keynesian economics. Although Keynes left much of the explanation of sticky prices to his successors, he noticed the obvious way in which interest rates, wages, and commodity prices responded in Great Britain and abroad. And since they moved too slowly, haltingly, or imperceptibly to clear markets effectively enough to secure full employment, this led Keynes to his revolutionary conclusions regarding effective demand and the causes of economic stagnation or recession.

Ironically, regarding trade among nations, Keynes had first overlooked this kind of adjustment. The Swedish economist Bertil Ohlin (1899–1979) did much to establish his reputation by disputing Keynes's rendering of the post–World War I German reparations problem, which Keynes had couched solely in terms of relative price changes. Although prejudiced somewhat by his belief that geographic endowments ordained Germany to lead the European economy, Keynes also believed that Germany faced a double burden under its requirement to pay reparations as determined under the armistice. First, it had to tax its citizens to pay for reparations, and second, it had to cheapen its export prices relative to its import prices by lowering wages at home (to effect export surpluses needed to transfer marks to foreign reparations creditors). Ohlin noted that the first burden would likely remove all necessity for the second; new German taxes sent abroad would simultaneously lower German demand and increase the demand of Germany's foreign creditors. And this would effect higher levels of German exports and lower levels of German imports without any relative change in the levels of German wages or export goods.

While Keynes eventually termed the debate "muddled" due to his insistence on the genuine possibility that creditor nations might entomb the German payments in hoarding or newly erected import barriers—a possibility largely ignored by Ohlin—the latter's argument had made its mark. Indeed, not long afterward, Keynes moved swiftly through a series of theoretical gyrations—building on and then dispensing with the quantity theory of money; finishing his *Treatise on Money* (1930) by reemphasizing in part his reparations policy argument and, at the same time, orienting himself more toward a general theory built upon a closed, static economy that underscored Ohlin's emphasis upon output or demand changes. Here, currency transfer and associated international trade problems diminished in importance and could be solved with less restricted currencies or special taxes on income from foreign lending. Free trade theory could march on not because it guaranteed the most efficient placement of all resources or global full employment, but because it only helped, and could largely be ignored if one could both loosen the "furtive Freudian cloak" of the gold standard-based, fixed exchange rate regime and focus instead on the stabilization of demand at home. Within a few years of the publication of the *Treatise*, Keynes encouraged President Franklin D. Roosevelt to make the currency and exchange policy of the United States "entirely subservient" to the aim of raising output and employment.

Heckscher-Ohlin, Factor-Price Equalization, and Real Free Trade Patterns If the abstract economic advantage of free trade had been well established by the late 1930s, the way in which free trade actually worked required additional explanation. Building upon "The Influence of Trade on the Distribution of Income," an article written in 1919 by his teacher, Eli Heckscher (1879–1952), Bertil Ohlin undertook analyses that would consolidate more completely the preeminence of the free trade persuasion in the process. Heckscher, under whom Ohlin had studied from 1917 to 1919 at the Stockholm School of Economics and Business Administration, and whom Ohlin succeeded in 1930, envisioned his article as a minor updating of classical Ricardian theory, which had, like Ricardo's Law of Comparative Advantage, done nothing to address the reasons for the existence of such advantage. Using both Heckscher's paper and his own graduate research, Ohlin staked out a theoretical position that began to explain the existence of comparative advantage, suggested the stringent real world requirements for the exploitation of free trade principles, and in part revived location theory, a substantial part of Adam Smith's cosmology that had been lost to most economists outside of the German historical school. Walter Isard's subsequent work in the economics of location and in regional economic studies, reflected principally in his 1956 publication *Location and Space Economy*, followed in part this theoretical pathway reopened chiefly by Bertil Ohlin.

As illustrated in Ohlin's *Interregional and International Trade* (1933)—for which he won the 1977 Nobel Prize—the Heckscher-Ohlin theorem explained how a nation will tend to have a relative advantage producing goods that require resources it holds in relative abundance (and an advantage importing those goods that require relatively scarce resources). If a nation possesses a relatively greater abundance of labor than its trading partners, for example, it will most frequently export products derived most intensively from labor, rather than capital, inputs.

In 1922, Ohlin had submitted a paper to Francis Edgeworth (1845–1926), Drummond professor of political economy at Oxford and Keynes's coeditor of the *Economic Journal*, in which he introduced the mathematical outlines of what would become the Heckscher-Ohlin theorem. Though Keynes responded to Edgeworth's request for comment with a curt "This amounts to nothing and should be refused," it was one of Keynes's foremost American disciples, Paul Samuelson, who further refined the Heckscher-Ohlin theorem. It soon became a staple of virtually all general economics texts, including Samuelson's own best-selling work, first published in 1948.

Samuelson's *Economic Journal* article, "International Trade and the Equalization of Factor Prices," also published in 1948, underscored and refined Ohlin's theoretical work. In this article, Samuelson exploited Heckscher-Ohlin to provide a polished mathematical explanation for how free trade might well serve as a substitute for the free mobility of capital and labor. He extended the theorem to reveal how the change in price of an internationally traded commodity effects a similar change in the income of the factor (labor or capital) used most intensively in producing it. From this followed what he termed the factor-price equalization theorem: as free trade narrows differences in commodity prices between nations, it must also, under the same conditions, narrow differences in income accruing to the factors of production. Thus, free trade naturally lessens the differences and resulting imbalances introduced by immobile or relatively immobile workers, factories, or natural resources.

By dropping one modifying assumption of Ohlin's theory after another (zero transportation costs and import duties, flexible exchange rates, immobile capital, etc.), Samuelson revealed both the positive force and efficiency of a hypothetical free trade regime and the stringent conditions necessary to carry out such a regime. Indeed, as the empirical work of Wassily Leontief revealed, Heckscher-Ohlin did not always fit the real world. Building on his groundbreaking work in input-output studies, Leontief noted in his "Domestic Production and Foreign Trade: The American Capital Position Re-Examined" (1954) that American exports tend to be labor intensive while American imports are mostly capital intensive, results in direct opposition to those suggested by the Heckscher-Ohlin theorem. Likewise, when put to the test, the purchasing power parity theory—developed principally by another of Ohlin's Swedish professors, Gustav Cassel (1866–1945)—appears to have equal difficulty fitting real world conditions. Relating free trade flows to international currency matters, purchasing power parity suggests that the purchasing powers of currencies in equilibrium would be equivalent at that rate of exchange. The exchange rate between any two national currencies should, in other words, adjust to reflect differences in price levels in the two nations.

The chief factors that account for the breakdown of purchasing power parity—currency speculation in foreign exchange markets, an abundance of goods and services that are not traded internationally, the extensive trading of financial assets, and the difficulty with which both general domestic and comparable international price levels are determined—also account in part for the potential invalidity of the Heckscher-Ohlin theorem. That Leontief found an apparent contradiction in the U.S. example may only suggest that its economy is both more varied and complex than that of most other nations, and that its behavior consistent with the Heckscher-Ohlin pattern may simply be more readily found within its regional, as opposed to international, trading networks.

Such theoretical insights proved to make Samuelson a virtually indispensable economic policy adviser. Indeed, as chairman of the task force advising president-elect Kennedy in 1960–1961 on economic policy (and Kennedy's first choice for chairman of the Council of Economic Advisers), Samuelson may well claim paternity of Kennedy's efforts on behalf of free trade. The Trade Expansion Act (TEA) of 1962, the first significant American legislative sponsorship of free trade since the 1934 Reciprocal Trade Agreements Act, bore the stamp of Samuelson's theoretical work and policy advice. Well aware of the elusive conditions under which an ideal free trade regime might be enacted, Samuelson provided a sound theoretical footing for the pragmatic approach reflected in the TEA, one of President Kennedy's few major legislative victories. Giving rise to the so-called Kennedy Round of GATT negotiations, which reduced import duties on industrial goods worldwide by approximately 35 percent (and by a remarkable 64 percent for American-produced goods), the TEA also included new restrictions on textile imports. A historic milepost on the road to greater trade liberalization, the TEA nonetheless reflected a pragmatic appraisal of real-world economic conditions and policy limitations. Trade liberalization for manufactured goods was likely impossible without the textile industry protections.

Lingering Theoretical Challenges Appointed to teach international economics at the London School of Economics in 1947, James Edward Meade (1907–1995) launched a book project to help him better grasp the ideas he hoped to convey to his new students. The resulting *Theory of International Economic Policy,* published in two volumes (*The Balance of Payments* in 1951; *Trade and Welfare* in 1955), attempted to integrate domestic and international policy, pre-Keynesian price effects with Keynesian income effects, and abstract free trade patterns with real world tendencies that often included or necessitated trade control. Recognizing and underscoring the notion that legitimate government assistance (international market research, for example) is often difficult to distinguish from subsidized trade protection, Meade discovered the "theory of second best." In Meade's formulation, abstract free trade models may well produce less than optimum outcomes, given real world conditions or tendencies. His theory of the second best revealed how a free trade regime might countenance alternative policies that diverged from absolute free trade principles, protecting the authentic gains from freer trade in the process. Subsequent to Meade's discovery, few criticisms of free trade outcomes found anything but a loose theoretical foothold, especially so if the free trade regime itself became the object of criticism. After Meade, few of these criticisms represented broad theoretical challenges to the growing free trade orthodoxy but were, instead, reminders that imperfect conditions and irrational economic behavior had to be accommodated—or isolated and marginalized—within the prevailing regime.

The chief ongoing quarrel with increased trade liberalization appears to be a criticism of theorists and policymakers who conflate international free trade with domestic free markets, or international trade with international capital flows. With the recent advent of policy initiatives such as Trade Related Investment Measures (TRIMs), it has become easier to make such a conflation. Promulgated by the World Trade Organization, TRIMs are measures that force nations to compensate foreign investors for rules imposed after their initial investment (such as minimum wage increases). But free trade need not imply a policy of strict noninterference on the part of national governments (or even international organizations); some, like Charles Kindleberger, have suggested that government-sponsored domestic prosperity may even be a prerequisite for the enlargement of free trade networks abroad. If such enlargement requires that one prosperous nation serve as a lender or buyer of last resort, and be willing to sacrifice parts of some internationally exposed markets in the process, then this may well be the case.

As free trade theory and policy burnished their standing among policymakers worldwide in the last quarter of the twentieth century, economic circumstances continued to raise nagging questions. The distributional effects of trade often appeared to undermine general prosperity; protectionist regimes often appeared beneficial if introduced skillfully enough to avoid retaliation; free trade appeared to undermine environmental protection in developing nations. The Prebisch-Singer theory arose directly in response to rising distributional problems, particularly those that surfaced in the southern hemisphere. Named for Raul Prebisch (1901–1986), professor of economics at the University of Buenos Aires and the first director-general of the UN Conference on Trade and Development, and Hans W. Singer, German-born UN economist who had trained under both Joseph Schumpeter and Keynes, the Prebisch-Singer theory suggested that international free trade reinforced harmful economic development practices in the developing and least developed countries. Because colonialism had produced unsustainable economic structures in these nations based on the encouragement of exports—most of which were inexpensive raw materials—Prebisch and Singer argued that trade protection and import substitution strategies were necessary if these developing nations were to strike out onto a sustainable path of growth and prosperity.

An agreement to set up a common raw materials price support fund of $750 million, after deliberations at the fourth UN Conference on Trade and Development, came as a direct result of Prebisch-Singer. Prebisch later suggested, however, that he was motivated primarily by the promise of industrialization, well suited to policies of import substitution but not, perhaps, to the labor surpluses so evident in the developing economies. Noticing later that increased wealth and increased demand for imports in developed nations might well improve the terms of trade for developing countries, Singer also modified his theoretical conclusions and policy recommendations. The slow maturation of the Latin American economies in the early post–World War II period, combined with rising American and European prosperity in the 1950s and 1960s (especially the latter decade), perhaps masked the ways in which protectionism and import substitution may have easily become self-defeating strategies. These developing nations matured and came to depend increasingly upon external markets and capital only a few years before the stagflation, oil price hikes, and higher interest rates of the 1970s obliterated gains on both sides.

The apparent success of East Asian protectionist regimes in the late twentieth century and the onslaught of developing world environmental crises also cast doubt upon the superiority and applicability of free trade theory. But here, as well, theorists have largely acknowledged that protectionist regimes can flourish only when foreign sources of prosperity offer forbearance and accommodation in place of retaliation or increasing autarky. Absent undemocratic political systems and regressive fiscal and monetary policies, most theorists have also inferred that global free trade need not prevent environmental stewardship, just as it need not prevent lessened inequality within or between nations. Most have concluded that it is economic growth itself and the associated capital intensity that bring pressure on the natural environment. Free trade has essentially been implicated, then, in environmental crises as little more than the handmaiden of economic growth. If free trade is not distinguished from the absolute free market, however, such theoretical conclusions often remain opaque and virtually incomprehensible. And since the theoretical gains from freer trade tend to be as regressive as the theoretical gains from economic growth in general, the conflation of free trade with laissez-faire only serves to make trade theory even more ambiguous. Linking trade theory to development and growth theory, Gunnar Myrdal and others urged deliberate policy initiatives, without which lessened inequality and growth would prove unattainable. Failing to make that distinction, they argued, would place "second best" policy and the progressive, compensatory measures it often required beyond reach and would render free trade incapable of fulfilling its modest theoretical promise.

INTERNATIONAL MONETARY POLICY

International monetary policy attracted few economic theorists before the twentieth century. Only when historic mercantilist concern for the accumulation of specie, and the rapid adjustment of interest rates under the gold standard, gave way to greater concern for mass unemployment did it begin to garner much theoretical attention. Before that, few who suffered at the hands of recurring gold outflows and restrictive domestic monetary policy were in any position of influence to either arrest such trends or call for new policies and theory with which to assail or question the prevailing regime. Exchange rates and gold reserves were defended at almost any cost, interest rates moved precipitously to reverse potentially large capital outflows, and investment planning could proceed under the assumption of minimal or virtually nonexistent exchange rate risk. However secure it rendered investment planning, this approach often proved that it would require, above all else, the willingness to sacrifice output in the name of exchange rate stability. As industrialization reconstituted American and European labor markets, this approach also implied recurring episodes of mass unemployment.

Much as it had with international trade theory, the shock of world war and the Great Depression gave great impetus to change. And just as these events compelled economists to rethink the theories that had somehow prevented them from capturing or explaining real world tendencies in international trade, so they forced economists to train their sights anew on questions of international money. The Baring-Argentine financial crisis of 1890 and the U.S. depression of 1890s had also focused much attention on international currency problems, but economic theorists were as yet unequipped to respond directly or forcefully. It was not until the later crises and the even more widespread economic calamity of the 1930s that economic theory began to respond with analyses directed at international monetary policy. It was at this time that the United States, for example—closely following its European counterparts—began to compile international balance of payments accounts, records of its transactions with the rest of the world. It was also at this time that Keynes and others began to urge new ways of conducting international monetary transactions, actively seeking theoretical insights by which changes could be guided and accommodated. "To close the mind to the idea of revolutionary improvements in the control of money and credit," Keynes warned, "is to sow the seeds of the downfall of individualistic capitalism."

To Keynes, the early twentieth century had proven the extent to which nations would resort to currency devaluation as a lever to improve their balance of trade, seldom improving in the process either their own terms of trade or the opportunities inherent in a flourishing and expanding trade network. As balance of payments accounting had become more common, many Western nations had come to believe that unilateral currency devaluation would, in the absence of reciprocal action, improve the terms of trade. It would make a nation's own exports cheaper in terms of foreign currency and would, of course, make imports equally more expensive. It was not uncommon to find, however, the price of imports rising under such an initiative to the point where the aggregate value of imported goods continued to outpace the value of the higher, newly attained level of exports. Abba Lerner, in his 1944 publication *The Economics of Control,* introduced what eventually came to be called the Marshall-Lerner criterion, a theoretical rule with which one could determine the positive or negative outcome of such a devaluation. Assuming that factors such as supply constraints do not enter into the picture, Lerner showed that if the price elasticity of exports plus the price elasticity of imports is less than 1, then the increased cost of the imports exceeds the value of the growth in exports. Moreover, if a nation began with a large sum of foreign liabilities denominated in foreign currency, devaluation of its own currency might well add terrific sums to its net interest payments. With competitive devaluation added to the mix as a likely outcome, perhaps only after an interval of unilateral manipulation and worsening results, the terms of trade could seldom be rendered any more reliable or propitious. Global trade diminution became an increasingly likely outcome.

With a little prodding from Bertil Ohlin and others, Keynes's theoretical insight here was to recognize that in modern industrial economies, monetary policy would simply have little effect in restoring balance through price deflation. It would regulate external balance, instead, by causing unemployment, lower incomes, and decreased imports. He then seized upon the notion that exchange rate mechanics mattered far less than international liquidity. Though gold, the pound sterling, and the U.S. dollar had all proved somewhat useful in attempts at securing substantial international reserves with which to conduct increasing levels of trade, even the highly regarded British and American currencies remained vulnerable to the deflationist tendencies Keynes so abhorred.

Bretton Woods and the Triffin Dilemma As the end of World War II approached, Keynes and many of his American counterparts began planning for the postwar period. The Bretton Woods conference of 1944 convened with a sharp focus on both the monetary fragility of the interwar period and the theoretical prescriptions of Keynes and his growing legion of American disciples. The conference proved successful in reorienting the world's economic exchange system away from the constraints of the gold standard. Exchange rates were fixed and pegged, and could be adjusted within limits only during periods of "fundamental disequilibrium." Because Keynes and the head of the U.S. delegation, Treasury assistant Harry Dexter White, hoped to insulate government domestic policies from the misdeeds of currency speculators, Bretton Woods called for explicit capital controls. It also created the International Monetary Fund (IMF), an organization designed to provide a cushion of international reserves to nations caught in a persistent current account deficit. The IMF would also serve as the final arbiter of fundamental disequilibrium.

In the end, however, Keynes's preoccupation with international currency reserves gave way to the overriding American concern for exchange rate stability. His proposal for an International Clearing Union, under which international liquidity could be expanded without reliance upon a single currency, never came to pass, mostly due to widespread fears that it would prove to have an inherent inflationary bias. It included provisions for bank "credits," extended to surplus states, and an artificial bookkeeping currency he called a "bancor," to maintain exchange rate stability. Overdraft provisions (up to $26 billion initially for member states) were proposed as well, to prevent contractionary domestic policy measures or competitive devaluations undertaken in the defense of embattled currencies. The IMF, however, acknowledging part of Keynes's theoretical contribution, did arrange for lending quotas (based mostly on the relative value of recent trading levels). In theory, these might have been utilized for both reconstruction and investment, and like the Clearing Union, could become a means to increased international liquidity. Unprecedented inflation in the immediate postwar years, however, altered the real value of IMF quotas to the point that short-term currency stabilization proved to be the only feasible activity. And since the Bretton Woods system came to be anchored upon the U.S. dollar (pegged to gold at $35 per ounce) rather than any type of new reserve asset, international liquidity would also depend in large measure upon worldwide confidence in a currency destined to wind up in a precarious overhang or glut position. Indeed, generous Marshall

Plan assistance, combined with larger than anticipated Cold War military outlays, quickly transformed a dollar shortage expected to last for some time into a dollar glut. By about 1953 the dollar gap or shortage had disappeared.

Although the modest U.S. payments deficits of the mid-1950s represented little more than a sensible response to varying levels of worldwide savings and investment requirements, Yale economist Robert Triffin noted that the dollar's unique position in the fixed exchange rate Bretton Woods system posed a fundamental dilemma. As the anchor of the system and the chief reserve asset, the flow of dollars into foreign accounts would necessarily outpace the flow of other currencies into American hands. Yet, despite the salutary effect such reserves would have on international trade in general, Triffin speculated that confidence in the dollar as a store of value would decrease as its numbers and its role as a reserve asset increased. Dollar accumulations overseas would engender an increasingly risky situation governed by a self-fulfilling prophecy. The implication of this dilemma was that international liquidity depended upon either a return to the Keynesian approach and a new independent reserve asset, or an end to fixed exchange rates pegged to the dollar value of gold.

Although the Lyndon Johnson administration tried to move in the direction of the former option, by introducing special drawing rights (informally, "paper gold") into IMF operations, they failed to catch on as a source of genuine, day-to-day international liquidity. Previously, John Kennedy's undersecretary of the Treasury for International Monetary Affairs, Robert Roosa, had arranged for a series of mostly stopgap measures designed to ease the dollar overhang and stanch the attendant gold outflow. Negotiated offsets (purchase of U.S. goods by nations receiving U.S. military aid), swap arrangements (U.S. agreement to exchange U.S.-held foreign currencies for dollars at a future date to protect foreign banks otherwise reluctant to hold large sums of dollars), and the December 1961 "General Arrangements to Borrow" (a large, short-term borrowing arrangement that gave Great Britain and the United States additional IMF resources to avert a speculative currency crisis) were among the measures employed by Roosa and his successor in the Johnson administration, Frederick Deming. Afterward, the only remaining questions concerned the way in which the world would manage the departure from the Bretton Woods system and the nature of the floating exchange rate system certain to take its place.

The end came quite abruptly after a decade of patchwork revisions, holding operations, and stopgap measures. President Nixon's decision of 15 August 1971, to end the guaranteed conversion of U.S. dollars into gold at $35 per ounce, announced after a series of Camp David meetings with top-level economic advisers, effectively ended the Bretton Woods international monetary regime.

Floats, "Dirty Floats," and the Tobin Tax
While floating exchange rates theoretically promised greater scope for expansionary domestic policies—part of Keynes's hope for the Bretton Woods blueprint—large, speculative movements in currency value and rapid, unsettling episodes of capital flight remained distinct possibilities. Indeed, financial transactions soon dwarfed those in goods and services in the post–Bretton Woods era; potentially large and rapid movements became all the more likely. But the demand for reserves did diminish along with the adoption of floating exchange rates, and increased capital mobility opened up the potential for other, more varied types of reserves in general. Nations also adapted, instinctively, by accepting floating exchange rates but with currency management intact. Few currencies were ever allowed to float freely, and instead central bankers most often practiced a "dirty float"; large swings were to be checked by rapid central bank buying and selling in currency markets. This is why Barry Eichengreen has suggested that the Mexican peso crisis of 1994–1995 was "the last financial crisis of the nineteenth century," resembling in a fundamental way the Baring crisis of 1890. In both cases, central bankers rallied around the system by rallying around a besieged currency (and, coincidentally, a Latin American nation).

With ample room for speculation and capital flight, however, theorists have more recently come to question the stability of the prevailing system. Currencies have likely become more volatile, capital flight has become an increasing malady, and trade has lost ground to multinational production due to the increasing currency market volatility. It is in this context that economists have debated the potential for capital controls and, as James Tobin often described it, the means by which policymakers might potentially throw a little "sand in the gears," reducing volatility in the process. Chief among the theoretical contributions or policy proposals here is the international currency transactions tax, or "Tobin tax." Proposed initially by the Yale economist James Tobin, such a tax would be small (typically proposed at 0.1 percent) and placed upon all international currency transactions. Theoretical debate on the Tobin tax has thus far focused upon the potential for offsetting effects. Would a transactions tax decrease volatility by increasing the costs to speculators, or would it increase volatility by reducing the total number of transactions, producing "thinner," more vulnerable markets in the process? Because it would not distinguish between speculative transactions and those conducted on behalf of trade, would the transactions tax reduce levels of trade as it reduced speculation, or would it increase trade by reducing currency market volatility? If introduced, could the tax be applied widely enough (that is, fairly and equitably) by wedding it to the policies of developed nations, or would it be difficult to enforce uniformly, and therefore conducive to avoidance and resulting misallocation?

Although free trade remains a contentious political idea, economists have increasingly devoted their attention to the related problems of capital flows, currency speculation, and international monetary instability. And though many economists predicted at the time that the end of fixed exchange rates would give nations the freedom to create fiscal and monetary policies of their own choosing (unencumbered by exchange rate parity concerns), few remained as sanguine by the end of the twentieth century. Introducing foreign trade and capital movements into a closed economy model, Robert Mundell described in the 1960s and 1970s how a floating exchange rate regime would, by connecting government fiscal stimulus with higher interest rates, capital inflows, and currency appreciation, automatically render fiscal stimulus ineffective. The currency appreciation, he argued, would lower net exports to the point where any fiscal stimulus that gave rise to them in the first place would be completely eliminated. Despite its less suitable conformity to large, as opposed to small, open markets, the apparent lack of correlation between government deficits and interest rates, and the numerous real world examples of currency appreciation tied to comparatively low interest rates, Mundell's pessimistic appraisal of modern fiscal policy remains the dominant analysis for floating exchange rate regimes.

DEVELOPMENT AND GROWTH THEORY

Economic growth theory remains the most difficult to master of all modern economic theories. It requires advanced mathematical skills (differential calculus) and, as a result, also introduces assumptions and limitations very difficult to account for or envision. Even if one excludes the possibility of perpetual disequilibrium—however close it may come to a precarious balance—the passage from one equilibrium state to another typically excludes any notion that underlying conditions may change with time as external variables exert change upon them. To do otherwise would be to require mathematical reasoning so complex and fragile that it would likely render all resulting models completely impractical by exposing them to the hidden, often increasing feedback effects of the most minute errors.

Although he was a leading biographer of John Maynard Keynes and a promoter of Keynesian economics, Roy F. Harrod was also among the first to leave behind Keynes's theoretical focus on a static economy. Although Keynes avoided taking a similar step on his own because he wanted to focus on existing problems of underutilization rather than apparent ongoing cycles of growth and recession, Harrod was more interested in the latter, effectively inventing growth economics in the process. His 1939 *Economic Journal* article, "An Essay in Dynamic Theory," gave rise to growth theory by introducing the notion of a steady-state equilibrium growth path from which actual growth most often diverged. Harrod also revealed how such a divergence fed upon itself, widening the gap between steady-state and actual economic trajectories.

Recognizing only a few years later (1946) that investment created additional productive capacity capable of being exploited only when further increments of investment gave rise to new income, Evsey D. Domar developed a simple model corroborating Harrod's theory. Known thereafter as the Harrod-Domar model of dynamic equilibrium, this model and accompanying theory were adopted by the International Bank for Reconstruction and Development (World Bank) immediately after World War II, setting the stage for the pending marriage of growth theory and third world economic development. Although intended for use in the analysis of advanced, developed economies like that of the United States, the World Bank quickly adopted it as a way to determine the amount of aid required to lift poor nations onto a more prosperous growth path. Aware in the 1950s that his model was being applied without questioning the relationship between aid and investment—or inequality, consumption, and investment—Domar disavowed its use. As decolonization proceeded apace after World War II, however, it was inevitable that growth theory would come to be employed in this fashion.

Nicholas Kaldor and Joan Robinson, both, like Harrod, among the first in the Keynesian camp, endeavored to highlight the importance of income distribution to economic growth. Mostly due to his 1960 presidential address to the American Economic Association, "Investment in Human Capital," Theodore W. Schultz publicized the work begun in the 1950s by Jacob Mincer and popularized the notion that education and training were as critical to development as technology and industrialization. Hollis Chenery, Simon Kuznets, and Irma Adelman all questioned the notions that growth depended solely upon industrial development and that growth automatically engendered greater equality, lessened poverty, and promoted a self-sustaining pattern of development. Kuznets's famous "inverse U relationship"—between national income per capita and inequality, positive in poor nations and negative in advanced national economies—sparked numerous rounds of debate, including Adelman's study of semideveloped nations that contradicted Kuznets's assertion.

Until Raul Prebisch, Hans Singer, Dudley Seers, and others criticized the assumption that poor nations were simply primitive versions of their more advanced, wealthier counterparts, however, few of these theoretical developments questioned the theoretical claim that investment in machinery, however effected, automatically engendered growth. Although Prebisch in particular seemed enamored of the possibilities for industrialization of the developing world and import substitution policy, he placed equal, if not overriding, emphasis on the elimination of unemployment, poverty, and inequality as a prerequisite for industry-led growth. Developing world debt crises of the 1970s and 1980s, evident in nations that had adopted the Prebisch-Singer theory and government intervention designed to implement it, spawned an even more vigorous countermovement marked by criticism of government intervention.

The "total factor productivity growth" approach, developed principally out of Robert Solow's groundbreaking work in capital theory in the 1950s, also questioned the primacy of capital formation in general or investment as a simple means to economic growth. Solow developed, for example, "vintage" models of growth that underscored not just the size of a given nation's capital structure, but also its age or vintage. The newer the technology, the greater its productive capacity, and—following Albert O. Hirschman on the "unbalanced" character of economic growth—the greater its linkage to key industries—on both the input and output sides. Research and development, scientific advances, and the processes of technology diffusion—all seemingly outside the scope of economic policy—evidently played as significant a role as policy itself. Vigorous debate on this issue ensued, most notably due to the emergence of empirical studies suggesting that government policy and high investment often appeared to spell the difference between nations that grew more or less rapidly. Joseph Schumpeter's earlier suggestion that oligopoly allowed firms to compete on the basis of technological innovation rather than price hinted at the role conceivably played by policy and burgeoning investment. Much like Kindleberger's lender of last resort—a nation that could afford to liberalize trade and share the wealth—Schumpeter's oligopoly capitalist could provide room for full employment and rising shares to labor as well as produce the profit margins with which to assume risky research or investment outlays. Unmitigated free market competition, it seems, would be incapable of the same. Amartya Sen posed theories of development, social choice, and inequality that suggested similar conclusions. Clarifying the conditions under which collective decisions can best reflect individual values and stressing the way in which poverty and inequality restrict economic choice and freedom, Sen forced economists and policymakers to consider general welfare and development in terms beyond reported changes in per capita income or gross national product.

Economic theory has for centuries remained a significant part of foreign affairs related to trade, money, and development. This is especially so for the foreign affairs of the United States, less dependent on international trade than many other nations but connected vitally to all by virtue of its dominant currency and ascendant role in international economic institutions. Since the emergence of stagflation in the 1970s, its history of adapting foreign policy to advances in theory has been marked by both indecision and a willingness to countenance only the most confident and simplistic versions of new economic theory. The debt crises of the 1980s and monetary turmoil of the 1990s did little to alter this course. And though heterodoxy remained distant and beyond the ken of most policymakers, the foreign affairs of the United States remained wedded integrally to the counsel of economists, both active and defunct.

BIBLIOGRAPHY

Bordo, Michael D., and Barry Eichengreen, eds. *A Retrospective on the Bretton Woods System.* Chicago, 1993. A collection of essays examining the origins, operations, and legacy of the Bretton Woods international monetary system.

Dornbusch, Rudiger, "Expectations and Exchange Rate Dynamics." *Journal of Political Economy* (December 1976). Influential article examining the potential volatility of a regime of floating exchange rates.

Gardner, Richard N. *Sterling-Dollar Diplomacy: The Origins and Prospects of Our International Order.* New ed. New York, 1980.

Haberler, Gottfried. *Theory of International Trade, with Its Application to Commercial Policy.* Translated by Alfred Stonier and Fredric Benham. London, 1965. First work to place Ricardian trade theory in a general equilibrium framework.

Harrod, Roy. *The Dollar.* 2d ed. New York, 1963. History of the post–World War II transition from dollar shortage to dollar glut.

James, Harold. *International Monetary Cooperation Since Bretton Woods.* Washington, D.C., and New York, 1996. Detailed history of international monetary affairs from the 1970s.

Keynes, John Maynard. *The Collected Writings of John Maynard Keynes.* Edited by Donald E. Moggridge. 30 vols. London and New York, 1971–1989. Although other volumes in this set are also relevant to studies of international economic policy and theory, volumes 5, 7, 25, and 26 are particularly useful.

Kuznets, Simon. *Growth, Population, and Income Distribution: Selected Essays.* New York, 1979. Essays on the origins of inequality, including the inverse-U relationship theory.

Lerner, Abba. *The Economics of Control.* New York, 1970. Reprint of 1944 publication in which Lerner introduced the Marshall-Lerner criterion for analyzing the effect of exchange rate changes on the balance of payments.

Marshall, Alfred. *Industry and Trade: A Study of Industrial Technique and Business Organization and of Their Influences on the Conditions of Various Classes and Nations.* London, 1919. Influential British economist's last work. Less well organized than his more famous text, but brimming with questions and observations that became critical parts of modern trade theory.

Meade, James. *Theory of International Economic Policy.* 2 vols. London, 1966. British economist's Nobel Prize-winning study of international trade that integrates Keynesian and pre-Keynesian analyses, domestic and international economic policy. First published in 1951 and 1955.

Myrdal, Gunnar. *International Economy: Problems and Prospects.* Westport, Conn., 1978. Analysis of international trade and money with an emphasis on developing world economic problems. An update of Harrod's analysis of departures from equilibrium and their essentially cumulative effects.

Ohlin, Bertil. *Interregional and International Trade.* Cambridge, Mass., 1967. Work in which the Nobel prize-winning economist introduced the Heckscher-Ohlin theory of international trade.

Pitchford, John D. *The Current Account and Foreign Debt.* London and New York, 1995. Concise analysis of international payments operations and problems.

Ricardo, David. *Works and Correspondence: Principles of Political Economy and Taxation.* Vol. 1. Edited by Piero Sraffa. First volume of a ten-volume collection of Ricardo's writings. Edited over 30 years by an influential Cambridge economist whose fear of teaching was so profound that the editorship of this series and other smaller tasks had to be invented (principally by John Maynard Keynes) to keep him on the Cambridge faculty.

Samuelson, Paul. "International Trade and the Equalization of Factor Prices." *Economic Journal* (June 1948). A corroboration and updating of the Heckscher-Ohlin theory of international trade.

Sapsford, David, and John-Ren Chen, eds. *Development Economics and Policy.* New York, 1998. Recent survey of development economics theory and related policy applications.

Seers, Dudley, and Leonard Joy, eds. *Development in a Divided World.* New York, 1970; Harmondsworth, U.K., 1971. Collection of essays documenting developmental economic problems unique to developing nations.

Singer, Hans Wolfgang, and Sumit Roy. *Economic Progress and Prospects in the Third World: Lessons of Development Experience Since 1945.* Aldershot, U.K., and Brookfield, Vt., 1993.

Smith, Adam. *An Inquiry into the Nature and Causes of the Wealth of Nations.* Edited by Kathryn Sutherland. New York, 1998. Arguably the first scientific analysis of domestic and international economic affairs, first published in 1776.

Thomas, Brinley. *Migration and Economic Growth: A Study of Great Britain and the Atlantic Economy.* 2d ed. Cambridge, 1973. History of the U.S. trade network with Great Britain, with emphasis on European demography and migration.

Tobin, James. "A Proposal for International Monetary Reform." *Eastern Economic Journal* (winter 1978): 153–159. Seminal article in which the Tobin international currency transactions tax was first proposed.

Treverton, Gregory F. *The Dollar Drain and American Forces in Germany: Managing the Political Economics of Alliance.* Athens, Ohio, 1978. History of U.S. efforts to manage the post–World War II dollar glut in one European country.

Triffin, Robert. *Gold and the Dollar Crisis: The Future of Convertibility.* New Haven, Conn., 1961. Influential book examining the unique and potentially troublesome role of the U.S. dollar in the Bretton Woods system. Introduced the "Triffin dilemma."

See also FOREIGN AID; INTERNATIONAL MONETARY FUND AND WORLD BANK; TARIFF POLICY.

ELITISM

Alan K. Henrikson

A theory of wide-ranging importance in historical and political thought, elitism as applied to foreign policy seeks to explain how that policy is made—by whom, in whose interest, in what manner, for what purpose, and with what results, including possible benefits for the policymakers themselves. A causal relationship generally is posited, or at least implied, between the composition of the policymaking group and the content and consequences of the policy it makes. Typically, the explanation of policy is to be found in the machinations of persons belonging to or admitted to a small coterie representing a wider privileged class, at the very top levels of society—an elite. A recurrent issue in elite analysis is that of whether the elite consists principally of the decision makers themselves or whether the elite is instead mainly the socially superior part of a community from which decision makers are drawn. The former view, which tends to be that of diplomatic historians and other scholars who focus on particular events, emphasizes the *actors* who are involved. The latter view, which tends to be that of sociologists and political scientists who compare overall patterns and may be interested in predicting, as well as explaining, public policy, emphasizes the *structures* that produce policy decisions. Common to most elite analyses is an assumption that there is some connection between actors, or power holders, and the structures, or social and governmental frameworks.

The English word "elite," adapted from the French *élite*, derives from the Latin *eligere*, a verb meaning to pick out, choose, or select. There is thus a meritocratic element in the concept. The exclusiveness of an elite group, especially in a nominally "classless" country such as the United States, with a republican form of government and democratic social institutions, is not based merely on birth or on wealth. It is, in principle, based as well on individual merit and on achievement—the person's intelligence and skill, courage and energy, and, of particular relevance in foreign policymaking, expertise and experience. Like wine, diplomats and other statesmen are often thought to get better as they grow older, achieving the status of "wise men." The role of women in the foreign policy elite, as it is sometimes called, has not been equal, though there is a trend toward greater representation of women in international service.

The broad sensibility needed for foreign policymaking in the United States and elsewhere was usually thought to owe something to an individual's family background. In the late nineteenth century a wealthy family could embark on a grand tour of Europe, and even around the world, that would expand a young person's horizons and permanently inform his or her outlook. Before (and even after) passage of the 1924 Rogers Act—which combined the U.S. diplomatic service and the less elitist consular service and established a merit-based classification system for officers—the American foreign service was, as the historian Martin Weil entitled his 1978 book, "A Pretty Good Club." This almost familial milieu was well described in many diplomatic memoirs and biographies, for example that of Ambassador Joseph Clark Grew by Waldo H. Heinrichs, Jr. (1966). Increasingly, however, the knowledge and skills needed for the practice of diplomacy and for international policymaking generally include a firm grasp of economics and an acquaintance with science as well as working proficiency in languages besides English and French. This may entail specialized study and preparation at postgraduate schools of international relations or equivalent professional training.

In the United States, international service was further democratized by the Foreign Service Act of 1946, as well as the reforms proposed by the Commission on the Organization of the Executive Branch of Government (Hoover Commission) in 1949 and by a committee formed under President Henry M. Wriston of Brown University in 1954. These reforms were aimed partly at familiarizing the domestically based civil service with the world and partly at preventing the foreign service from losing contact with American life. "Wristonization," as the effort was informally called, resulted in some integration of qualified members of the domestic civil service into the foreign service, though not at the expense of the latter's sense of itself as a select profession.

CLASSICAL AND NEW ELITE THEORY

Although the idea probably always has been present in some form, elitism emerged as a recognizable and clearly defined part of Western political thought in the late nineteenth and early twentieth centuries. The leading contributors to the theory were Gaetano Mosca, Vilfredo Pareto, and Robert Michels. These writers attacked classical democratic thought and also Aristotle and Karl Marx. Majority rule, they insisted, is impossible. Every society is divided into those who rule and those who are ruled; and the rulers constitute only a small minority of any society. Aristotle's classification, which divided political systems into three types (rule by one, rule by a few, and rule by the many), does not fit reality either, for no man is capable of ruling by himself, and the many, too, lack the ability to govern. It is the few, under any political system, who exercise effective control. And Marx, with his emphasis on a class struggle that in the end (following the victory of the working class) leads to social harmony in a classless society, was also wrong. History features a continuing struggle among elites. That struggle will never end, and a classless society cannot be created. Moreover, to the pioneers in the development of elitist theory, Marx placed too much emphasis on economics and not enough on politics, which could be autonomous.

Classical elitist theory did not maintain merely that the active, socially recognizable people in a country made its important decisions—whether from within offices of government, from somewhere behind the scenes, or from completely outside the state apparatus. It emphatically asserted that the common man, however numerous within a society in absolute or relative terms, did not. Analysts of elites, who generally focus on the distribution of power rather than on the allocation of values, or on property and other wealth forms, differ somewhat over the degree of participation in government or, more generally, the political process that is necessary for a member of the elite accurately to be judged a member of what Mosca characterizes as "the ruling class." A society's elite is usually thought to be a stable entity, self-sustaining and constant over time. Yet the actual group that is in office can change markedly and very quickly. The concept of an elite therefore may need to be understood as encompassing all those who *might* govern as well as those who in fact *do* govern.

However "elite" is precisely understood, elitist theory is clear in the basic point that a minority, rather than the masses, controls things. The general population of a country—the common man—is ineffective. Even in societies with elections and other democratic mechanisms, it is posited, the ruling elite functions in a way that is largely independent of control by a popular majority. However, it made need a justifying doctrine. That the elite ordinarily functions according to a "political formula," in Mosca's term, is what makes its rule effective and acceptable to the masses. Thus, in theory, there can be a democratic elitism, however paradoxical that may seem.

A "new elite paradigm," building on the work of Mosca and other classical theorists, emerged in the 1980s and 1990s among comparative political sociologists. It drew attention to the occurrence, and the important effects, of divisions that may arise within the elite of a society. Its central proposition, as stated by John Higley and Michael Burton (1989), is as follows: "A *disunified* national elite, which is the most common type, produces a series of *unstable regimes* that tend to oscillate between authoritarian and democratic forms over varying intervals. A *consensually unified* national elite, which is historically much rarer, produces a *stable regime* that may evolve into a modern democracy, as in Sweden, or Britain, or the United States, if economic and other facilitative conditions permit."

In the United States, normally, internal and external conditions have favored consensual unity within the nation's elite. Of course, the American Revolution and, later, the Civil War, are the major exceptions to this generalization. During those periods, divisions ran so deep as to produce counter-elites. As the political sociologist Barrington Moore, Jr., and the political historian C. Vann Woodward have shown, the reconciliation between North and South that occurred following post–Civil War Reconstruction was in significant part a result of a complex bargain between the elites in formerly opposed geographical sections. After the late nineteenth century, issues of foreign policy have on occasion divided the American elite as well. A by-product of this has been a widening of participation in the national debate over foreign policy. That this amounts to a "democratization" of American foreign policymaking, however, is highly disputable.

FROM IMPERIALISM TO REVISIONISM

American thinking about the relationship of elites to foreign policy began to develop around the year 1900 during the debate over imperialism. Most elite theorists, or commentators applying elite theory, have viewed policy from the Left, although not all have done so. There is also a conservative, or Rightist, elitism, sometimes politically ideological but more often having a traditional religious or cultural perspective on matters of public life. Such conservative elitists have been somewhat less inclined to address issues of foreign policy.

Most American critics having a view of society as headed, if not actually led, by elites have stressed the influence of business groups. These were seen to have had a role in causing the U.S. war with Spain and the subsequent effort to dominate the Philippines. A few denunciators of such overseas ventures, including socialists such as Daniel De Leon and Eugene V. Debs and populist reformers like William Jennings Bryan, openly blamed imperial expansion on the greed of the commercial and moneymaking classes and on trusts and syndicates looking for new fields to exploit. Most opponents of imperialism at the time did not fully develop such a radical view, but an English writer, John A. Hobson, supplied a theoretically coherent version of it in *Imperialism* (1902). He interpreted the imperialist dynamic as being the result of a capitalist drive for greater profits than were available at home and also for security for investments made in overseas territories. In studying the American reaction to not only U.S. but also British imperial engagements such as that against the Boers in southern Africa, the historian Ernest R. May, in *American Imperialism: A Speculative Essay* (1991), surmises that Americans, "already disillusioned by the Philippine war and concerned about the growing power of trusts, probably found Hobson's arguments especially attractive."

Putting the whole subject in a broad comparative frame from a transnational perspective, the Norwegian political sociologist Johan Galtung, in the essay "A Structural Theory of Imperialism" (1971), interprets imperialism not so much as the result of the drives or motives behind it as the product of a structured, collaborative relationship between elites. He abstractly outlines one elite "center" inside the imperial power and another, smaller center inside the colonial country. He then theorizes that imperialism succeeds when the relationship between the two elites is "harmonious," or smoothly functioning and mutually profitable, but that it is bound to fail if it is not. Galtung's theory helps to account for the breakdown of British control over southern Africa. It also helps to explain the failure of the United States to achieve "harmony" with the Philippines, whose native leadership in large part refused to collaborate with American authorities and henceforth were subdued by military force. What is pertinent here is that a significant part of the American "center" also refused to enter into such a collaborative relationship, one of imperialism.

It has been shown that in the United States those who most prominently opposed U.S. territorial expansion in Asia following the Spanish-American War were themselves in many cases members of the American elite, if not mainly from the ruling political class or dominant economic group. Many were of an older type, for whom the early American Republic rather than the current and purportedly liberal British Empire was an appropriate model for the country. In *Twelve Against Empire* (1968), Robert L. Beisner observes that the leading anti-imperialist figures he studied generally "all shared the same biases and for the most part cherished the same conservative vision of an ideal American society." They were "elitists," he emphasized, and as such "they were not so much interested in conserving a system of economic privilege for themselves as in defending a style of life and a social tone against the leveling influences of *arriviste* businessmen and the democratic masses." Most of these, being themselves white, Anglo-Saxon, and Protestant (later to be called the WASP type), had long been concerned that increased immigration, from sources other than certain countries in western Europe, might alter the racial and religious character of American society. Taking over the Catholic Philippines wold only add to this perceived risk.

Previously, Ernest May notes, the American elite as a whole had been "overwhelmingly anticolonialist." In the late 1890s, however, the nation's ruling classes began to divide, with some, mostly of a younger generation, identifying with England's liberal imperialists and becoming enthusiasts for a similar high-minded American imperial expansion. The split between imperialists and anti-imperialists cost the American elite some of its influence and also its control over public opinion. May writes: "In 1898–1899, this not only made for an intra-elite debate about whether the United States should or should not acquire colonies; it legitimated a much wider public debate. Less educated and less cosmopolitan Americans could speak with greater freedom because they could take sides with one set of opinion leaders against another." Arguably the elite division had a permissive effect, allowing persons who previously had been merely "talkers" to become, if not real authorities, then frequently quoted "advisers."

In that era there were few American scholars who systematically employed elitist theory, or at least an awareness of the role of leadership groups, in attempting to comprehend the structure of American society. One who did was the pioneering sociologist Edward A. Ross. "Every editor, politician, banker, capitalist, railroad president, employer, clergyman, or judge has a following with whom his opinion has weight. He, in turn, is likely to have *his* authorities," Ross observed in *Social Psychology* (1908). "The anatomy of collective opinion shows it to be organized from centers and subcenters, forming a kind of intellectual feudal system."

Much more broadly, a Progressive outlook, shared by Charles A. Beard and other historians as well as by leftist and reform-minded politicians, disposed Americans to detect "hidden" influences responsible for the country's social direction and political decisions—for example, in permitting monopolies to operate. With the beginning of World War I in July 1914, explicit arguments about the class or group domination of American public life gained greater prominence. When the war started, President Woodrow Wilson asked Americans to be "impartial in thought as well as in action." Congress's declaration of war in April 1917—at the president's own request and following repeated protestations of U.S. neutrality—was something that required an explanation.

Critics on the Left, many of them strongly opposed to the war decision on grounds that it was inimical to the interests of the workingman or out of an ideological pacifism, supplied an explanation that stressed the malign influence of an economic elite. The centers of it were seen to be located on the East Coast, in the financial and industrial elites of New York and other Europe-oriented cities. Particular individuals such as J. P. Morgan, the Rockefellers, and the Du Ponts were named. Somewhat more generically defined groups, notably international bankers and the munitions makers—or, simply, "Wall Street" and war-profiteering "merchants of death"—were identified as being responsible for causing the country to join in the European carnage. They were thought to favor the overly ambitious peace-making efforts led by President Wilson and his friend Colonel Edward M. House, along with his group of experts called the Inquiry, that resulted in the Treaty of Versailles and the League of Nations Covenant, which many feared would be an "entangling alliance."

This interpretation of history, with its emphasis on economic factors, resembled Marx more than Mosca, Pareto, or Michels. Also unlike those European theorists who accepted the idea of a permanent ruling class, the American accusers of the "interests" did not regard elite domination of society and determination of national policy as inevitable. The "people"—who, in the view of critics, had been, or at least should have been, opposed to intervention in the war because it meant suffering and loss rather than profit for them—could and should be put in control.

A number of writers during the 1920s were participants in a "revisionist" historiography that challenged official explanations of the war and the claim that U.S. intervention was caused by Germany's assault on America's maritime rights. Further, these writers augmented what was essentially an economic conspiracy theory by finding other, noneconomic forces at work: British propaganda, pro-British official bias, and Wilsonian idealism. Harry Elmer Barnes, C. Hartley Grattan, and others whose work is assessed by Warren I. Cohen in *The American Revisionists: The Lessons of Intervention in World War I* (1967) accorded considerable weight to the activities of political leaders, above all President Wilson himself and even certain diplomats, such as his ambassador to the Court of St. James's, Walter Hines Page, who was known for his Anglophile tendencies.

World War I revisionism became politically relevant during the 1930s as many Americans grew alarmed about the fateful course that American foreign policy might take. The 1929 stock market crash and the ensuing Great Depression reinforced doubts about America's private economic leadership. Barnes, Grattan, and Beard, who turned his attention from domestic history to current foreign policy, stressed the inability of banking and commercial elites to redefine the American "national interest" to suit themselves and their international connections. A Senate investigating committee, headed by North Dakota Republican Gerald P. Nye and consisting mainly of isolationists, publicized this general historical interpretation—the "devil theory" of war, as Manfred Jonas called it in *Isolationism in America, 1935–1941* (1966). The Neutrality Acts of 1935, 1936, and 1937, the major policy expressions of the isolationism of the time, were designed to keep the United States out of future wars by placing restrictions on three dangerous parts of the American elite that had gotten the country into the last war: international bankers, armaments manufacturers, and presidents of the nation.

The other side of anti-elitism is populism, a belief not just in the political rightness of majority rule but also in the people's inherent goodness and wisdom. In 1937, Representative Louis Ludlow, Democrat of Indiana, proposed an amendment to the U.S. Constitution that would require a popular referendum before Congress could declare war. The premise of Ludlow's scheme, one of many of the same type made during the interwar period, was that only small groups would seek American intervention in foreign wars. The people, if asked to decide, would guard against this. The Ludlow amendment gained considerable support, which increased after an American gunboat, the USS *Panay,* was sunk by Japanese bombers on the Yangtze River in December 1937. But it never came to a final vote in the House of Representatives.

As elitist theories began almost to make policy, two revisionists grew unhappy with them. Walter Millis argued that the American people, rather than their leaders, had made war possible in 1917–1918. Charles Beard recognized that the people as a whole had become dependent on wartime purchases by the Allied powers. He continued to fear the influence of bankers and politicians, but he also feared that of farmers and other large groups having a stake in foreign trade. Logically but unrealistically, Beard called for a sharp reduction in U.S. dependence on such trade and for a more concentrated economic development of America, a doctrine called "continentalism." He imagined that this could be done through a more equitable division of wealth and thus a more widely exercised purchasing power. Determined to stay out of war, he would, if necessary, use state power to scrap the capitalist system.

This emphasis on the people, and their economic needs, became background discussion as the events leading to U.S. involvement in war commanded immediate attention. As Nazi Germany overran France and as the United Kingdom and the United States began to coordinate their naval operations, Beard, for one, became convinced that President Franklin D. Roosevelt was masterfully engineering the entry of the United States into another world war by dramatizing incidents in the Atlantic. In *Back Door to War: The Roosevelt Foreign Policy, 1933–1941* (1952) another revisionist, Charles Callan Tansill, saw the biggest "incident" of all, the Japanese attack on Pearl Harbor on 7 December 1941, as the culmination of Roosevelt's strategy. In Tansill's view, the president provoked a war in the Pacific that he could not obtain in the Atlantic in order to cloak his domestic political failures and come to the aid of the British Empire.

During the period of America's involvement in World War II, the influence of economic interpretations of U.S. government policy and action fell off considerably, as military imperatives dominated official thinking and conduct. To be sure, there were those who suspected the motives, short-term and especially long-term, of the corporate "dollar a year" men who went to Washington to manage war production. The accomplishments of American industry during the war, under relatively little state supervision, did restore much of the reputation that American business had lost. Major decisions, however, were made by the president and his closest advisers, notably the secretary of war, Henry L. Stimson, and the senior military leadership, including General George C. Marshall. New government entities such as the Office of Scientific Research and Development, headed by Dr. Vannevar Bush of the Massachusetts Institute of Technology, significantly contributed to the war effort by managing the contracts for the secret production of new weapons including the atomic bomb. Diplomacy during the war was conducted mostly by President Roosevelt himself at leaders' conferences with his British and Soviet counterparts, Winston Churchill and Joseph Stalin. The State Department under Cordell Hull was somewhat eclipsed, though it did concentrate on postwar planning.

FROM MCCARTHYISM TO THE NEW LEFT

In order to shape a better world order, what could be considered a series of elite groups assisted the Department of State in its planning process. The most central of these, the Inquiry-like War and Peace Studies project of the Council on Foreign Relations in New York, which received support from the Rockefeller Foundation, became part of a civilian advisory committee that reported directly to Assistant Secretary of State Leo Pasvolsky in Washington, D.C. Among the subjects addressed by the various study groups under the aegis of the Council on Foreign Relations was the structure for a new international organization to replace the League of Nations, which was generally thought to have failed. This blueprinting effort contributed to what eventually became the Charter of the United Nations.

The influence of the council's War and Peace Studies project should not be exaggerated. By 1944 the memoranda of the project, which previously had been circulated confidentially to the State Department, were made available to the general membership of the council for private reading. "Such indications that the ideas produced by the studies staff did not need to be kept secret," comments Robert D. Schulzinger in an irreverent but informed assessment, *The Wise Men of Foreign Affairs: The History of the Council of Foreign Relations* (1984), "demonstrated both the Council's success in raising issues of international cooperation and collective security and the drab conventionality of its approach."

In Washington, what has been called a revolution in foreign policy—the Truman Doctrine, Marshall Plan, and North Atlantic Treaty Organization—took place, with a fair measure of bipartisan congressional support for the Democratic administration under Harry S. Truman. The quick succession of World War II by the Cold War did not permit relaxation. Many wartime military chiefs entered the national leadership structure, including George C. Marshall, who served President Truman as his personal representative to China and subsequently became secretary of state and then secretary of defense. Marshall was emblematic of the new place of the "warlords," in the lexicon of the radical sociologist C. Wright Mills (*The Power Elite*, 1956), who argued that the military had moved alongside the big corporations and the machinery of the state itself in America's "higher circles." General Marshall did indeed wield enormous organized power in what some scholars, including the historians Daniel Yergin and Melvyn Leffler, have characterized as the American "national security state."

Perhaps most exemplary of the elite type, as some perceived it, was Secretary of State Dean Acheson, whose aristocratic manner represented "the British accent" in American diplomacy, as the historian John T. McNay suggests in *Acheson and Empire* (2001). An Episcopal bishop's son from Connecticut who became a Washington lawyer, Acheson wrestled with "a conflict that would be evident throughout his life: an intellectual attachment to democratic values pitted against a personal elitism that caused him to view with condescension 'the vulgar mass of humanity,'" as Walter Isaacson and Evan Thomas put it in *The Wise Men* (1986), describing Acheson and a circle of friends who epitomize the style and outlook that dominated American foreign policy after the war. Sartorially elegant, meticulously mustached, and verbally fastidious, Acheson would later title his memoir *Present at the Creation* (1969), compounding the impression he perhaps inescapably gave of arrogance. He was elitism's very embodiment—Groton, Yale, Scroll and Key, Harvard Law School, Covington & Burling, and then the cabinet, to which, however, he did not seem particularly to aspire but, rather, only to deserve.

In part because of his manner, Acheson was a red flag to some politicians, notoriously Joseph R. McCarthy, the junior Republican senator from Wisconsin, who accused Acheson of "coddling" communists in the State Department. McCarthy was among the conservatives who believed that the setbacks the United States experienced internationally in the early years of the Cold War—the "loss of China" to communism in 1949 and the near collapse of South Korea when invaded by North Korea in 1950—were the result of high-level policy mistakes. Imagining "a great conspiracy on a scale so immense as to dwarf any previous venture in the history of man," the senator found the answer in "the traitorous actions by those who have been treated so well by this nation."

With his accusing finger pointed at Acheson and even the respected General Marshall, as well as more vulnerable officials, McCarthy carried out an anticommunist campaign that was, in its social-psychological basis as well as in its rhetorical method, anti-elitist. To the extent that it was grounded, it was based on populism, a conviction that "the people," the majority of the U.S. population that lived outside centers of sophistication, properly should rule but were losing their ability to do so. McCarthyism reflected what the historian Richard Hofstadter has termed "the paranoid style" in American politics. To be sure, McCarthy's credibility was in question. To accuse the highest authorities in the land of treason, as he did, required a temerity that could only be justified by the actual truth of the charges. McCarthy's ultimate inability to produce significant proof finally undermined his crusade, but not before it had cost some of the expert "China hands" in the State Department their jobs and, moreover, cautioned many other members of the educated upper class to think twice about entering government service or any other form of public life. It was more comfortable, and safer, for those who were securely employed to remain in good positions in industry, finance, and academe—the institutional niches of the "silent" generation.

McCarthyism failed partly because it did not offer a substitute elite. It merely threatened the existing one, which, entrenched in institutions, survived. The administration of John F. Kennedy brought into government a younger generation that had come of political age during World War II but had not been responsible for political decisions during the conflict. Kennedy nonetheless drew heavily on older leaders of what was called by the journalist Richard A. Rovere the "American Establishment," seeking counsel and reassurance during events such as the perilous 1962 Cuban Missile Crisis. As Leonard Silk and Mark Silk authoritatively recount in *The American Establishment* (1980), this notion of an Establishment— the word derives historically from the establishment of a state church, the Church of England—had been popularized in Britain in the 1950s by the historian A. J. P. Taylor and the journalist Henry Fairlie. The "heart" of the American Establishment was the New York financial and legal community, in the view of the Harvard historian Arthur M. Schlesinger, Jr., who served as a special assistant in the Kennedy White House. The Establishment's "front organizations" were the Rockefeller, Ford, and Carnegie foundations along with the Council on Foreign Relations, as he noted in his memoir *A Thousand Days*. Its "organs" were the *New York Times* and the journal *Foreign Affairs*.

Curiously, President Kennedy, though himself unmistakably a member of the American upper class (Boston branch, Irish Catholic), did not personally know many bankers, industrialists, leaders of the bar, university presidents and deans, foundation officials, generals, and others who constituted America's nonpolitical, institutional leadership. Nor was he very familiar with the New York financial and legal community, at the Establishment's center. It thus was a measure of that elite's power that a significant number of Establishmentarians entered his cabinet. He filled the position of secretary of state, for example, with Dean Rusk, a former senior State Department official who had been president of the Rockefeller Foundation, on whose board were a number of older Establishment figures including Robert A. Lovett and John J. McCloy, both of whom were assistant secretaries of war during the Roosevelt administration. Perhaps the best example of an Establishment man who entered the new administration was Douglas Dillon, who became secretary of the Treasury. Dillon, son of Clarence Dillon of the New York banking house of Dillon, Read and Company, had served as undersecretary of state in the outgoing Eisenhower administration. An internationalist more than a partisan, he easily made the transition from a Republican to a mainly Democratic cabinet.

The American Establishment, though "predominantly Republican," acknowledged Schlesinger, "possessed what its admirers saw as a commitment to public service and its critics as an appetite for power which impelled its members to serve Presidents of whatever political faith." Presidents Roosevelt and Truman both "had drawn freely upon them," as Schlesinger shrewdly explained, "partly to avail themselves of Establishment competence, partly to win protective coloration for policies which, with liberals in front, would have provoked conservative opposition. It was never clear who was using whom; but, since it *was* never clear, each side continued to find advantages in the arrangement."

President Kennedy, as the journalist David Halberstam observed in a similarly knowing but more critical account, *The Best and the Brightest* (1972), "believed in the Establishment mystique." At the beginning of the 1960s, there was little criticism from outside the Establishment or dissension within it either. "Rarely had there been such a political consensus on foreign affairs," Halberstam commented. Containment was good, communism was dangerous, and foreign aid bills, required to keep the Third World from going communist, could be politically debated in Congress. "Besides," Halberstam noted of Kennedy, "he was young, and since his victory over Nixon was slimmer than he had expected, he needed the backing of this club, the elitists of the national security people. And he felt at ease with them," more so than he did with liberal "Democratic eggheads" with causes to push.

The American foreign policy consensus fractured when the Vietnam War began, as did the Establishment, although the cause-and-effect relationship is uncertain. Never a perfectly solid or solitary monolith, the Establishment began to fall apart, its cracks widening to open spaces for other, new participants to enter. Teaching then at Harvard University, the historian Ernest May remembers, "I thought I saw in progress in the mid-1960s something similar to what had taken place in the late 1890s," when the American elite had split over imperialism and the Philippine conflict. At the start of the Kennedy administration there had been a near consensus about the need, in the words of Kennedy's inaugural address, to "pay any price, bear any burden . . . support any friend, oppose any foe." But the televised hearings conducted by Foreign Relations Committee Chairman Senator J. William Fulbright and teach-ins at Harvard and many other universities throughout the country were evidence of serious division within the American foreign policy elite. However, that this dissension in elite circles was, as May suggests, responsible for "bringing in its train a great expansion of the public prepared to argue opinions" is not a total explanation. An alternative view would assign more autonomy to the American public itself, enabled by television and other media to be more attentive, while coming to doubt the justice and wisdom of the war being conducted in their name. The massive public reaction to the apparently successful North Vietnamese Tet offensive in January 1968, which caused President Lyndon B. Johnson to decide against running for another term and to opt for a partial bombing halt and peace talks, would tend to support this view.

Coinciding with, and to a considerable degree a part of, these events was the emergence of a political New Left and a corresponding revisionist historiography, which challenged the very premises of American foreign policy, then and earlier. Locating the causes of the Cold War and the later Vietnam struggle less in external threats to the United States than in factors within it, including the influence of powerful elites, the new revisionists dominated academic discussion for a time and also shaped the public debate. The seminal work was William Appleman Williams's *The Tragedy of American Diplomacy* (1972), an idiosyncratically radical critique of U.S. foreign policy and its leadership as being inherently expansionist, using the "open door" principle both as an ideological motivation and as a diplomatic instrument—in the manner of Mosca's "political formula"—in carrying out American imperialism. Other writers, including those in the Williams-influenced "Wisconsin school," did monographic work on particular periods. The Vietnam War itself was subjected to detailed New Left analysis, with researchers finding precise evidence of American corporate and other elite manipulation of U.S. policy, implicating, for example, the Firestone Tire and Rubber Company and the Roman Catholic Church. While sometimes lacking historical perspective and interpretive balance, these studies had a powerful effect in discrediting the foreign policy of the United States and also those, members of various elites, involved in making it.

FROM GEOPOLITICS TO TRILATERALISM

The ambivalence regarding Vietnam of many in the American Establishment itself as well as in the American electorate was evident in the election in November 1968 of Richard M. Nixon, a Californian Republican semi-outsider and former hardline cold warrior, to the presidency. Declaring the purpose of "peace with honor," President Nixon and his national security adviser, Henry Kissinger, a refugee from Nazi Germany who became a celebrated professor of government at Harvard, carried out a strategy of gradual withdrawal of U.S. ground forces ("Vietnamization") while using air strikes to demonstrate America's will, even while engaged in peace talks with representatives of Hanoi in Paris. The effort was institutionally and politically very complex, requiring emotional balance as well as brain power.

In order to help hold the government and country together, and possibly also to gain personal reassurance as well as policy confirmation, Kissinger in particular cultivated the elite, among whom, however, he carefully picked and chose. "On a personal level I can never forget the graceful—I might almost say gentle—way in which Dean Acheson welcomed me to Washington when I arrived as national security adviser, and the wisdom and patience with which he sought thereafter to bridge the gap between the perceptions of a Harvard professor and the minimum

>
>
> ### KISSINGER'S "WISE MEN" (AND WOMEN)
>
> "Some of my education was supplied by consulting many men and women who had been prominent in the Eisenhower, Kennedy, and Johnson administrations. For the entire postwar period foreign policy had been ennobled by a group of distinguished men who, having established their eminence in other fields, devoted themselves to public service. Dean Acheson, David K. E. Bruce, Ellsworth Bunker, Averell Harriman, John McCloy, Robert Lovett, Douglas Dillon, among others, represented a unique pool of talent—an aristocracy dedicated to the service of this nation on behalf of principles beyond partisanship. Free peoples owe them gratitude for their achievements: Presidents and Secretaries of State have been sustained by their matter-of-fact patriotism and freely tendered wisdom. While I was in office they were always available for counsel without preconditions; nor was there ever fear that they would use governmental information for personal or political advantage. Unfortunately, when I came into office they were all in their seventies."
>
> — Henry Kissinger, White House Years (1979) —

requirements of reality," as Kissinger recalled in *White House Years* (1979). He was particularly gratified when Ambassador David K. E. Bruce, scion of an old Maryland family who had served as U.S. representative in London, Paris, and Bonn, agreed, at the age of seventy-two, to represent the Nixon administration in the difficult peace negotiations with the North Vietnamese in France. "We were on a long road, certain to be painful," Kissinger wrote. "But with David Bruce as a companion its burdens would be more bearable. And any effort to which he was willing to commit himself had a strong presumption of being in the national interest." The importance of the sustainment that Kissinger, an immigrant to America, received from his association with Establishment figures like the aristocratic Bruce, who seemed to represent as well as recognize the U.S. national interest, was surely profound, if difficult to estimate precisely.

With the very different administration of Jimmy Carter, an almost complete outsider from Plains, Georgia, who had been a submarine officer in the U.S. Navy and a pro–civil rights governor of his home state, the Establishment seemed to have lost out. This would be a mistaken impression. In an attempt to formulate a completely new, post-Vietnam foreign policy consensus for the country on a different basis from the essentially power-oriented, "geopolitical" focus of the Nixon and subsequent Gerald Ford presidencies, President Carter emphasized human rights, nuclear disarmament, and "interdependence."

This last was a concept associated with the Trilateral Commission, a nongovernmental group of North American, European, and Japanese leaders who were focusing not on East-West competition but on North-South cooperation. Intellectually, its approach appealed to Carter. The initiative (and the resources) for the formation of this elite group came from David Rockefeller, chairman of Chase Manhattan Bank and the Council on Foreign Relations, following his return from a Bilderberg Conference in Holland early in 1972. With Zbigniew Brzezinski of Columbia University as executive secretary, the Trilateral Commission enlisted some 145 "commissioners"—bankers, industrialists, labor leaders, lawyers, politicians, academics—from the three Trilateral regions. Among the politician members invited (co-opted, a skeptic might say) to join the U.S. group was James E. Carter, Jr., as his name then was listed. Carter was grateful for the chance. As he wrote in his campaign autobiography, *Why Not the Best?* (1976), "Membership on this commission has provided me with a splendid learning opportunity, and many of the other members have helped me in my study of foreign affairs." As Leonard and Mark Silk reported, when Carter became president, some 40 percent of the U.S. members of the Trilateral Commission became members of his administration (the co-optation was mutual).

One of these was the New York corporate lawyer and former high-ranking Defense Department official Cyrus R. Vance. "If, after the inauguration," President Carter's closest aide from Georgia, Hamilton Jordan, had injudiciously said in a widely quoted statement, "you find Cy Vance as secretary of state and Zbigniew Brzezinski as head of national security, then I would say we failed." Indeed, it did seem as if the Carter people had been forced to give in. "There can be no doubt today," commented Robert A. Manning in the nonestablishment journal *Penthouse,* "that David Rockefeller and his Trilateral Commission have succeeded in seizing control of America's foreign policy." Such fears should have been partially laid to rest, commented the Silks, when National Security Affairs Adviser Brzezinski and Secretary of State Vance started feuding over arms control and other issues.

These internal differences within the Carter administration notwithstanding, the Trilateral concept, and the international associations that came with it, broadened the purview of American foreign policy, making it more truly global. In place of the shifting "triangular" diplomacy handled, sometimes arbitrarily, by Nixon and Kissinger alone in a way that seemed to place America's relations with Moscow and Beijing on the same, or even higher, plane than its established relations with London, Paris, Bonn, Rome, Ottawa, and Tokyo, there would now be a new emphasis on working with neighboring Canada, the western European powers, and Japan in a more structured and reliable trilateral formation. The policy aim was to coordinate the decisions of the so-called industrial democracies so as not only to stabilize their own economies but also to enable them to grow consistently in order to absorb more of the primary and other products of developing countries. Newer issues such as protection of the global environment and the universal promotion of human rights also were placed on the agenda. That radical critics of Trilateralism, such as Holly Sklar and others (1980), saw it as "elite planning for world management" bothered but did not deter David Rockefeller and his fellow commissioners, outside government or in.

FROM REAGANISM TO CLINTONISM AND BACK TO BUSHISM

The Iranian Revolution in 1979 and particularly the Soviet invasion of Afghanistan at the end of that year brought the U.S. government suddenly back to geostrategic thinking and produced a shift in elites. The holding of U.S. embassy personnel as hostages by young Islamic militants in Tehran seemed to immobilize the Carter administration. Carter's defeat in the election of 1980 by the conservative former Republican governor of California, Ronald Reagan, replaced talk of "interdependence" with assertions of "strength," a readiness to defend U.S. interests around the world—unilaterally, if necessary. The relevant elites for Reagan were not international bankers in New York, Frankfurt, or Tokyo but the very rich businessmen in California who, remaining behind the scenes (as his "kitchen cabinet"), had long financed and in other ways facilitated the actor-politician's career. This West Coast elite expected, and got, a resolute defense of the Free World against Soviet-supported insurgencies and a worrisome Soviet arms buildup. In the important field of economic policy, the ideology of the "magic of the marketplace" replaced technocratic discussion of international "policy coordination."

Within the broader American Establishment, there was considerable repositioning, not just between coasts. Long-established organizations of business leaders like the Conference Board and the Business Roundtable gained in influence. Among the policy-oriented research institutes, those like Brookings, being moderately liberal, were overshadowed somewhat by the newer and highly energized conservative American Enterprise Institute and Heritage Foundation. The Hoover Institution, situated on the campus of Stanford University, also gained in status and influence. While not dominant in the actual policymaking process, within government itself, these conservative think tanks assisted the Reagan administration by providing informed, articulate commentary useful in the national debate over foreign policy, defense strategy, and economic philosophy. President Reagan, the "great communicator," was able through his skillful use of the media to express much of his message to the American public directly. It was simplified but well crafted for mass effect.

The "CNN factor"—twenty-four-hour-a-day worldwide cable TV—emerged as an actual historical force during the subsequent presidency of George H. W. Bush. When the Iraqi army invaded Kuwait, when anarchy broke out in Somalia, and when internecine violence began in Yugoslavia, CNN was there, and its reports commanded American and worldwide attention. There was speculation, exaggerated but perhaps having an element of truth, that media moguls such as CNN's owner, Ted Turner, were capable of setting the agenda of American foreign policy, presumably to improve their outlets' ratings and increase their profits. Although assimilable to the general idea of corporate capitalism, the notion of a distinct "media elite" emerged to compete with old theories about the influence of traditional establishments in America.

The rise in importance of the media—particularly "new news" sources including talk radio, cable TV, and the fledgling Internet—did create a new competitiveness among would-be opinion leaders within the government or outside it. Even the dignified Council on Foreign Relations was prompted to engage in public "outreach," in the form of traveling panels and radio programs. It also gave its journal, *Foreign Affairs,* a more polished look. The council had been startled when, as he began his run for the presidency, George Bush resigned his council membership. He also ceased participating in the Trilateral Commission. Having formerly been U.S. permanent representative to the United Nations, chief of the U.S. Liaison Office (ambassador) in Beijing, and director of the Central Intelligence Agency, these were natural affiliations for him to have. But it was no longer clear that such connections were needed by political aspirants, or even advantageous for them.

The emergence of Bill Clinton, from Hope, Arkansas, was further evidence of uncertainty and flux among American elites. He himself was a mixture of backgrounds and influences. A man of modest beginnings but prodigious energy and ability, he graduated from Georgetown University in Washington, interned there in the office of Senator William Fulbright, won a Rhodes Scholarship to Oxford, and completed his education at Yale Law School. He then returned to Arkansas and rose smoothly to its governorship. Except for longtime "Friends of Bill" (many of them fellow lawyers by training), new acquaintances made in Hollywood and in salons in Georgetown, and comradely relations with his fellow governors, he was relatively independent of powerful interest groups and even the national Democratic Party.

His administration, in its composition, was intended to "look like America" and, owing to the large number in it of women, African-Americans, and Hispanics, it did somewhat. The impression it gave of diversity was reduced, however, by the reality that many of its inner figures had received their educations at the same few institutions, principally Harvard, Yale, and Stanford. Like President Clinton himself, nearly all were government-focused. As Thomas R. Dye observed in *Who's Running America? The Clinton Years* (1995), "Almost all top Clinton officials are lawyers, lobbyists, politicians, and bureaucrats; very few have any background in business, banking, the media, or the military."

The Clinton administration at the outset emphasized the essential connectedness—the "inextricable intertwining," in a phrase used by Secretary of State Warren Christopher—of foreign affairs and domestic affairs. The main practical effect of this doctrine, which seemed to reject the idea that foreign policy required specialized geopolitical understanding, was aggressive trade promotion. This effort was led by Secretary of Commerce Ron Brown, who went abroad with retinues of American business leaders, and by President Clinton himself, who pressed for the negotiation of multilateral trade accords including the North American Free Trade Agreement (NAFTA), the Asia Pacific Economic Cooperation (APEC) arrangement, the World Trade Organization (WTO), and, prospectively, a Free Trade Area of the Americas (FTAA). The increasing stake of the United States in large overseas markets and investment outlets powerfully conditioned the Clinton administration's policy. In dealing with the People's Republic of China, for instance, President Clinton ultimately "de-linked" the issue of human rights and that of the extension of most-favored-nation trading rights, which were made permanent. This surely reflected the ever-enlarging American economic interest specifically in China but, more generally, a globalizing world economy. Many elite interests were subsumed in this Open Door–like expansionism.

The administration of Texas governor George W. Bush, the first son of a former president to become president himself since John Quincy Adams followed John Adams and a reminder of the curious "dynastic" factor in America's open and democratic politics, was even more conspicuously committed to the defense of America's business interests. A businessman himself, President Bush had only limited personal experience in foreign affairs except with bordering Mexico. In Texas it was said that his worldview was formed by the Midland Petroleum Club, though the example of his father's rich international involvement must have somewhat informed it too. A kind of political throwback, he surrounded himself with (or was surrounded by) many of his father's former advisers. The person he selected as vice president, Richard Cheney, formerly a White House chief of staff and also secretary of defense, was chairman of the Halliburton Corporation, a Houston-based oil-equipment firm. Cheney was a proponent of an energy policy that emphasized increasing supply rather than energy conservation or environmental protection, and no doubt influenced the president's quickly made decision to withdraw from the Kyoto Protocol on global warming. President Bush's remark,

"We will not do anything that harms our economy because first things first are the people in America," somewhat masked his solicitude for corporate interests. So, too, did his blunt denunciation of the 1972 Anti-Ballistic Missile Treaty, though negotiated by a Republican administration, as "a relic of the past." He surely was reinforced in his suspicion of the restrictive ABM Treaty by the man he appointed as secretary of defense, Donald Rumsfeld, another corporate CEO who had been White House chief of staff and secretary of defense. Most pertinently, as chairman of a bipartisan commission that in 1998 had produced the Rumsfeld Report, the new secretary was a strong advocate of building a national missile defense (NMD) system, if necessary with the United States doing so alone.

Environmentalist associations and arms control groups at home and abroad weighed in heavily against what seemed a hard-right political turn, which the uncertain outcome of the November 2000 U.S. presidential election did not seem to warrant. The popular majority, which the Democratic candidate Al Gore had won, clearly had not chosen such a radical departure. The president seemed to be a captive of his Texas cowboy persona, perhaps of defensive feelings about having been established in office by the U.S. Supreme Court and of the interested elites in the Bush camp.

Viewed from many perspectives, especially from outside the country, the younger Bush was initially perceived as the most divisive president of the United States since Ronald Reagan. Foreign opinion, including the influence of European and other elites, had an impact on U.S. decision making. Not merely President Bush's trip to Europe in June 2001 to meet his counterparts in NATO and the European Union but also the media-reported popular reactions abroad to the stark positions he had taken brought about immediate adjustments in at least the presentation of his policies.

This responsiveness was something new. In Galtung's transnational scheme of analysis, the "center" in America was being harmonized with, and to some extent by, "centers" of influence within Europe. The intra-institutional processes of the NATO alliance and also of the increasingly structured U.S.–European Union relationship described by Éric Philippart and Pascaline Winand as an "Ever Closer Partnership" (2001), as well as the interpersonal chemistry of relations at the leadership level, made the new president, and administration, much more sensitive to foreign, particularly European, opinion. This was evident not just with regard to foreign and security policy matters, including global warming and military defense, but also cultural and moral matters, such as the death penalty.

For elite theory, as applied to international relations, this pattern of development is instructive. The intellectual and social division over policy issues may increasingly become cross-national, with elites in one country joining with elites in other countries to influence the publics, as well as the governments, within. The American "foreign policy elite" has always been internationally minded to a degree, though actual contact with its counterparts elsewhere has been limited. In an age of nearly instant global communication, with travel and networking made easier than ever before, it is likely to become more even globalist in outlook. In the process of globalization, the elite itself may be globalized.

THE FUTURE OF AMERICAN FOREIGN POLICY: ELITISM VERSUS PLURALISM

The idea that a cosmopolitan elite has controlled, even actually dominated, American foreign policy and diplomacy is a difficult thesis to evaluate. The subject is an elusive one. Part of the reason is the uncertain relation of elites to institutions, of actors to structures. There is a continuing debate among sociologists, political scientists, and other commentators on American social patterns between those who see power as founded on and inhering in institutions, including, but not limited to, the formal institutions of government, and whose leadership almost by definition constitutes the elite, and those who see power as requiring actual participation in decision making, which can be somewhat extra-institutional. Institutions and their representatives may not in fact be actively involved in important historical events. Outside forces, including a variety of organized groups and even unassociated individuals, may at times participate in them very effectively. The former, institution-oriented view, stressing positional power and latent influence, sometimes is called the "elitist" school. The latter, more group-oriented view, requiring actual involvement and impact to prove the reality of power, is commonly known as the "pluralist" school.

C. Wright Mills believed that "great power" —such as foreign policy entails—must be institutionalized and, more specifically, that America's leaders are institutional elites because they are the ones who possess formal authority in the country. Among scholars who later emphasized this was Thomas Dye, whose book *Who's Running America? Institutional Leadership in the United States* (1976) and its sequel volumes attested to this view in detail, "naming names." Somewhat similar, though concentrating on persons occupying powerful institutional positions who come to government and other command positions from what is regarded as the "upper class," was G. William Domhoff, whose book *Who Rules America?* (1967) and other studies carried on a more radical tradition. Both were basically on the "elitist" side. The opposing view, that mere potential control and formal authority are not enough, and that an examination of actual decisions made in America shows a wider variety of participants, was perhaps most influentially stated by Robert A. Dahl in numerous works, including *Who Governs?* (1961), a study of local politics in New Haven, Connecticut. This, the "pluralist" view, resists the argument that there is a single power structure, describing instead a basic competition for power and control.

Such an approach offers not a hierarchical model of American politics but a polyarchical model, suggesting that different groups of individuals exercise power in different sectors of society, that they acquire power in different ways, and that the interplay among them has an indeterminate outcome. It should be noted that neither the so-called elitists nor the so-called pluralists see the mass of the population as capable of leadership. This basic point is shared with Mosca, who posits a permanently ruling minority of variable composition. Elitism theorists see groups as being socially and in other ways interlocked, operating in monopolistic or at least oligopolistic fashion. Pluralism theorists see intergroup dynamics, much less constrained by social and other structures, as the essence of American policymaking. According to the pluralists, the public, though incapable of directing itself, can maintain its freedom and thereby preserve American democracy by choosing among rival elites that compete for its favor.

A question that has not adequately been addressed in most of the pertinent sociological and political scientific literature is whether the making of foreign policy is essentially different from the making of domestic policy. There is some evidence, to be sure, of a difference between elite opinion and mass opinion with regard to foreign policy, especially now that the Cold War international consensus has somewhat broken down. Eugene R. Wittkopf and Michael A. Maggiotto have found (1983) that elite views among Americans tend to be more "accommodationist" as well as "internationalist," and American mass, or public, opinion tends to be more "hard-line" and "isolationist." Nonetheless, it still may be supposed that "politics stops at the water's edge," and that such internal differences, involving opinion only, make little difference, on the traditional premise that foreign policy—the actual management of it—is an elite preserve.

In general, it still is true in the United States that foreign affairs is an elite sphere, with those in office running things. The federal government is recognized constitutionally as the nation's "one voice" in speaking to the world. Increasingly, however, America's international relations, which include more than policymaking and formal diplomacy, are coming to involve and affect a much wider array of direct participants, official and unofficial. This may challenge the institutionalized elite character of U.S. foreign policy and its conduct. It may be that the only way the American foreign policy elite, or Establishment, can retain its historical and accustomed control will be to continue to outcompete the growing list of participants by concerting more closely with elite counterparts in other centers, through interallied consultation and meetings such as those of the Group of Eight. The more that transnational "civil society" penetrates the global plane of power and influence, however, the more the making of foreign policy in the United States is likely to become pluralistic, and anti-elitist.

BIBLIOGRAPHY

Acheson, Dean G. *Present at the Creation: My Years in the State Department.* New York, 1969. An ornately written, historically informative public autobiography of an American diplomatic exemplar.

Beisner, Robert L. *Twelve Against Empire: The Anti-Imperialists, 1898–1900.* New York, 1968. An elegant set of biographical sketches, well compared and contrasted, of members of a mostly conservative elite opposed to U.S. imperial expansion.

Cohen, Warren I. *The American Revisionists: The Lessons of Intervention in World War I.* Chicago, 1967. The best treatment of the subject.

Dahl, Robert A. *Who Governs?* New Haven, Conn., 1961.

Domhoff, G. William. *Who Rules America?* Englewood Cliffs, N.J., 1967.

Dye, Thomas R. *Who's Running America? Institutional Leadership in the United States.* Englewood Cliffs, N.J., 1976.

———. *Who's Running America? The Clinton Years.* 6th ed. Englewood Cliffs, N.J., 1995.

Galtung, Johan. "A Structural Theory of Imperialism." *Journal of Peace Research* 8 (1971): 81–117. A seminal essay, powerfully reinterpreting imperialism as a set of interconnected center-periphery relationships.

———. *The True Worlds: A Transnational Perspective.* New York, 1980. A full development of Galtung's complex model of the international system, aimed at transforming it.

Gill, Stephen. *American Hegemony and the Trilateral Commission.* Cambridge, 1990. A well-constructed study of the Trilateral Commission that is also an attempt to develop "a historical materialist theory of international relations."

Halberstam, David. *The Best and the Brightest.* New ed. New York, 2001. Originally published in 1972. A sprawling but scintillating journalistic treatment of U.S. policymaking during the Vietnam War, with numerous short biographies.

Heinrichs, Waldo H., Jr. *American Ambassador: Joseph C. Grew and the Development of the United States Diplomatic Tradition.* Boston, 1966. Rightly described as a majestic diplomatic biography dealing with institutions and policies as well as its central figure and other persons.

Higley, John, and Michael G. Burton. "The Elite Variable in Democratic Transitions and Breakdowns." *American Sociological Review* 54 (1989): 17–32. A statement of the "new elite paradigm," emphasizing the importance of elite divisions and elite settlements.

Hofstadter, Richard. *The Paranoid Style in American Politics and Other Essays.* New York, 1965. A distinguished American political and intellectual historian's critique of "conspiracy" theorizing in the United States, and also of "pseudo-conservatism."

Isaacson, Walter, and Evan Thomas. *The Wise Men: Six Friends and the World They Made.* New York, 1986. An admiring group biography of Averell Harriman, Robert Lovett, Dean Acheson, John McCloy, George Kennan, and Charles Bohlen—"two bankers, two lawyers, two diplomats"—by two editors of *Time.*

Jonas, Manfred. *Isolationism in America, 1935–1941.* Ithaca, N.Y., 1966. The best analytical treatment of isolationist thinking, with a focus on isolationist leaders rather than on American isolationist opinion or organization.

Kissinger, Henry A. *White House Years.* Boston, 1979. Inscribed "To the memory of Nelson Aldrich Rockefeller," his early patron, the first of Kissinger's monumental volumes recording his central role in U.S. foreign policymaking.

Leffler, Melvyn P. *A Preponderance of Power: National Security, the Truman Administration, and the Cold War.* Stanford, Calif., 1992.

May, Ernest R. *American Imperialism: A Speculative Essay.* Chicago, 1991. A new edition of his 1968 book, with an introduction by the author that includes a retrospective assessment of relevant scholarship.

McNay, John T. *Acheson and Empire: The British Accent in American Foreign Policy.* Columbus, Mo., 2001. Acheson's affinity for imperial-style international relations, owing in part to his family background, is shown to go beyond the secretary of state's clothing and mannerisms.

Mills, C. Wright. *The Power Elite.* 2d ed. New York, 1999. Originally published in 1956. The controversial work that introduced this phrase to the American language.

Mosca, Gaetano. *The Ruling Class: Elementi di Scienza Politica.* Edited and revised by Arthur Livingston and translated by Hannah D. Kahn. New York and London, 1939. The major statement of classical elitist theory, including the "ruling class" concept progressively developed by the Italian jurist-politician.

Philippart, Éric, and Pascaline Winand, eds. *Ever Closer Partnership: Policy-Making in US-EU Relations.* Brussels, 2001.

Rovere, Richard H. *The American Establishment and Other Reports, Opinions, and Speculations.* New York, 1962.

Schlesinger, Arthur M., Jr. *A Thousand Days: John F. Kennedy in the White House.* Boston, 1965. A politically partisan but highly professional and polished account of foreign policy, mainly during the brief Kennedy presidency.

Schulzinger, Robert D. *The Wise Men of Foreign Affairs: The History of the Council on Foreign Relations.* New York, 1984. The first scholarly study of the council to make use of its archives, but not governed by an "inside" perspective.

Silk, Leonard, and Mark Silk. *The American Establishment.* New York, 1980. A clearly written, informative, and balanced interpretation.

Sklar, Holly, ed. *Trilateralism: The Trilateral Commission and Elite Planning for World Management.* Boston, 1980. Somewhat amateurish in part, and to be handled with care, but a collection of radically oriented essays that is a repository of interesting information.

Weil, Martin. *A Pretty Good Club: The Founding Fathers of the U.S. Foreign Service.* New York, 1978.

Williams, William Appleman. *The Tragedy of American Diplomacy.* Rev. ed. New York, 1972. A search for the roots of U.S. foreign policy, found to be involved with the Open Door principle. A New Left classic.

Wittkopf, Eugene R., and Michael A. Maggiotto. "Elites and Masses: A Comparative Analysis of Attitudes Toward America's World Role." *Journal of Politics* 45 (1983): 303–334.

Yergin, Daniel. *Shattered Peace: The Origins of the Cold War and the National Security State.* Boston, 1977.

See also AMBASSADORS, EXECUTIVE AGENTS, AND SPECIAL REPRESENTATIVES; IMPERIALISM; ISOLATIONISM; REVISIONISM; TELEVISION.

EMBARGOES AND SANCTIONS

Jerald A. Combs

For most of America's history, the word "embargo" was used to refer specifically to a prohibition on the departure of ships or exports from a nation's own ports, whereas the words "boycott" and "nonimportation" were used to describe prohibitions of imports or ship entries, and "nonintercourse" was used to describe a total prohibition of trade with a nation. But the word "embargo" also was used generically to refer to all stoppages of trade.

Since World War II, the growth of modern economic institutions and relations has afforded governments, especially rich and powerful ones like that of the United States, an arsenal of commercial weapons extending far beyond an outright stoppage of trade, including denial of aid and loans, commodity dumping, import and export limitations, revocation of most-favored-nation (MFN) trade status, and freezing assets. As those means increased, the word "embargo" seemed less applicable to the wide range of economic coercive measures that the United States, the United Nations, and other entities were using to accomplish noneconomic goals. The preferred term now is "sanctions." In eighteenth-century Europe, an embargo was generally a prelude to a formal declaration of war. A civil embargo prohibited a nation's own ships from leaving port; a hostile embargo affected all ships in the port, foreign or domestic. Neutral ships caught in the embargo might even be forced into the service of the belligerent nation. The right to do this was called the power of angary. By imposing an embargo before declaring war, a nation could keep friendly ships from falling into the hands of the enemy and hold enemy ships hostage for future contingencies.

European powers rarely resorted to an embargo as a weapon in itself rather than as a prelude to war, although there were two exceptions to this in the sixteenth century: a French grain embargo against Spain and a threatened Turkish wheat embargo against Venice. In most cases, European nations had little incentive to consider a broader use of embargoes because geographical proximity made conventional military attacks easy and effective. Besides, the seventeenth and eighteenth centuries constituted the age of mercantilism, in which people believed that national power depended upon exports exceeding imports. Thus, most diplomats expected an embargo of long duration to hurt the embargoing nation more than its enemy. An extreme example of this philosophy was Great Britain's famous blockade of Napoleonic France, which was not designed to starve France but to compel it to accept British imports or receive no trade at all.

THE REVOLUTIONARY WAR ERA

The United States was the first modern nation to make significant use of the embargo as a substitute for, rather than a prelude to, war. Being three thousand miles from the centers of European power, the United States was not in imminent danger of invasion if it resorted to economic warfare, and for most of its early history, the United States had a small army and only a moderate-sized navy. America also had been a colony whose major physical ties to the mother country had been those of trade. Since the American colonies were of value to England primarily as economic entities that provided between a third and a sixth of the entire trade of the empire, it stood to reason that the colonists would think first of commercial measures if they were seeking to coerce the mother country. They were convinced especially that the West Indies were dependent upon imports of American food and lumber for survival. They reasoned, then, that an embargo would be a formidable weapon against any nation with colonies in those islands.

But Americans were reluctant to resort to a complete embargo. They had economic interests and mercantilist ideas of their own that militated against such a measure. In the decade preceding the American Revolution, the colonists wielded economic weapons against many of Britain's unpopular measures, but in each case the chosen weapon was a boycott rather than an embargo. In fact, when George Mason proposed that Virginia embargo certain exports to protest the Townshend Acts of 1767, his fellow members of the Virginia legislature specifically rejected the idea, adopting nonimportation and nonconsumption resolutions instead. Similarly, the Continental Congress, meeting in 1774 to respond to the Coercive Acts, quickly adopted nonimportation. But the Virginia delegation insisted that any embargo be delayed until September 1775, by which time the Virginia planters could sell off their tobacco crop. Congress agreed. Then, when actual warfare broke out in April, the members moved immediately to forbid all exports without congressional permission. The embargo was soon lifted when Congress found that it was hurting America more than Britain. After a lengthy debate, America's ports were thrown open to all nations except Britain, and Congress was soon begging the French for naval help to get American ships out of their home ports.

Despite this failure, most members of Congress were still convinced that the United States could wield economic weapons effectively. They remembered that the British had repealed the Stamp Act and Townshend Acts at least partly in response to boycotts, and they were convinced that, during and after the war, foreign nations would pay a high price to divert American trade from Britain to themselves. When Congress appointed Benjamin Franklin as minister to France, it instructed him and his colleagues to offer only American trade as bait for France to enter the war as an ally of the United States. Although quickly enough disabused of the hope that France would accept so little for so much, Americans continued to believe that once the war was over, European powers would scramble over one another to offer concessions for access to American markets and goods. But when peace was restored, Europeans returned to their mercantilist systems and closed the United States out of most colonial markets. So, once again Americans contemplated commercial retaliation.

Because the Articles of Confederation left trade regulation in the hands of the individual states, it was found impossible to coordinate any retaliatory policy. The Constitutional Convention at Philadelphia met in part to correct the situation.

But southerners were fearful that the commercial Northeast, using its greater population for voting advantage in Congress, would wield the weapon of commerce too freely. The South demanded that any navigation law should require a two-thirds vote of each house for passage. Ultimately, the convention reached a compromise. The Constitution would permit the federal government to levy taxes on imports; taxes on exports would be constitutionally prohibited. Exports could be embargoed, but they could not be taxed.

Despite this evidence of southern opposition to export taxes, several southern leaders still believed devoutly that economic sanctions could be America's primary diplomatic weapon. The leaders in this movement were Secretary of State Thomas Jefferson and James Madison. When the first Congress met after ratification of the Constitution in 1789, Madison used his position as a leader of the House of Representatives to begin a campaign for a broad use of commercial weapons that would last for more than twenty years. Angry at Britain for closing American ships out of the British West Indies and for refusing to sign a trade treaty with the United States, Madison told Congress that America could force Britain into a more amenable posture by threatening to divert American trade from Britain to France. He did not propose anything so drastic as an embargo at this point; he merely called for higher duties on imports from unfriendly nations than from friendly nations. The shipping interests and their congressional representatives had been strong supporters of commercial retaliation against Britain during the hard times of the Confederation period, but now, in a time of rising prosperity, they changed their minds. Led by Secretary of the Treasury Alexander Hamilton, they defeated Madison's proposals in session after session. Hamilton and his supporters thought British trade too valuable to the United States to risk using it as a diplomatic weapon, and they feared that British retaliation would hurt America far more than America could hurt Britain.

When war broke out between Great Britain and revolutionary France in 1793, Madison and Jefferson saw a new chance for the use of economic sanctions, and introduced discriminatory duties against England in the House. Hamilton and his followers in Congress rallied against the proposals, with Fisher Ames of Massachusetts complaining that "Madison & Co. now avow . . . that we will make war, not for our commerce, but with it; not to make our commerce better, but to make it nothing, in order to reach the tender sides of our enemy, which are not to be wounded in any other way." Ames and his fellow Federalists argued for military preparedness and negotiation rather than commercial retaliation. They succeeded until early 1794 in putting off Madison's proposals, but when the British suddenly swooped down on American ships trading in the French West Indies and captured more than 250 of them, Madison and the Republicans introduced even more stringent measures, such as sequestering British debts and stopping all trade with England.

Compelled by the public's outrage to do something, the Federalists agreed on a short-term general embargo as the least harmful alternative. By embargoing all ships, foreign and domestic, in American harbors, the measure would ostensibly affect all nations alike, thus avoiding a direct challenge to Great Britain. It also could be defended as a traditional precautionary step in case of war, and the Federalists could deny that it had anything to do with the Republican campaign for commercial coercion. Thus, with mixed motives, Congress passed a joint resolution in March 1794, laying a hostile embargo for thirty days. This was later extended for another month, and President Washington was empowered to resume the embargo if the public safety required it.

The Federalists then resumed their crusade to strengthen the army and navy and thwart the rest of the Republican program for commercial retaliation against Britain. They sidetracked the bill for sequestering British debts, and Vice President John Adams cast the tie-breaking vote in the Senate against a total prohibition of British trade, imports as well as exports, which had passed the House. Meanwhile, the Federalists persuaded Washington to send John Jay to England as a special envoy to negotiate with the British and head off the war crisis. When Jay returned with a treaty promising not to interfere in any way with Anglo-American trade in exchange for a minimum of British concessions, the Republicans cried that using America's commercial weapons would have been far more effective than exchanging them for so little. After a bitter battle, the Federalists got the treaty ratified by the narrowest of margins in 1796. On the heels of that victory, they then elected John Adams to the presidency over his Republican rival, Thomas Jefferson.

Adams, however, found the French as bitter about Jay's Treaty as the Republicans. The French counted on Americans as carriers of their commerce because the British had swept the seas clear of most French ships. The Americans, by compromising with the British rather than fighting for America's neutral rights, hurt French trade as badly as their own. The French responded by capturing American ships, claiming the right to do to the Americans whatever the Americans allowed the British to do to them. The Federalists and Adams were less reluctant to oppose the French revolutionaries than they had been to resist the British, but they used the same techniques they had used in the Jay's Treaty crisis: military preparations and negotiation. Their only concession to Republican theories of commercial retaliation was an embargo on French trade passed in July 1798, after negotiations had broken down over the XYZ affair. Even this was clearly a precautionary war measure rather than a substitute for a military response. Ultimately, Adams made peace with France, splitting the Federalist Party and enabling Jefferson to defeat him for the presidency in 1800. The embargo would soon receive its supreme test as a substitute for war.

THE EARLY REPUBLIC

The Treaty of Amiens (1802) brought a temporary peace to Europe, which allowed President Jefferson to concentrate on domestic programs and to purchase the Louisiana Territory. Then, the Napoleonic Wars resumed, and Jefferson found himself in the same predicament his predecessors had faced. Once again the belligerents interfered with American trade and captured American ships. In the early years of the wars, British offenses were more numerous and blatant than those of the French, often taking place within sight of the American coast and involving the impressment of American seamen and the raiding of U.S. commerce. Jefferson began his program of retaliation with the Nonimportation Act of 1806, barring certain British imports. It was more a gesture to demonstrate American determination on the eve of negotiations than an all-out attempt to coerce Britain, and the Republican negotiators, James Monroe and William Pinckney, did no better than their Federalist predecessor, John Jay. Jefferson and his secretary of state, Madison, rejected the treaty their negotiators sent back from Britain because it failed to prohibit impressment. The envoys were instructed to renegotiate the treaty, eliminating the excessive appeasement of Britain. Such a task, Monroe and Pinckney realized, was hopeless.

Meanwhile, another event drove Jefferson and Madison toward stronger measures. On 22 June 1807, a British vessel, the HMS *Leopard,* fired on an unsuspecting U.S. naval ship, the USS *Chesapeake.* The British attackers then mustered the crew of the *Chesapeake* and removed four men who were alleged to be British deserters. This violation of American sovereignty brought a loud outcry even from many Federalists, and Jefferson could easily have had a declaration of war. He delayed six months, until he received news of a British order in council barring all nations from trading with any part of Europe except the Baltic area. At the same time, he learned that France had begun capturing American ships in enforcing Napoleon's Berlin Decree. Jefferson then called upon Congress not for war but for an embargo. He and his followers in Congress defended the move on two separate grounds. On the one hand, it would be a proper precautionary move in case of war; on the other, it might in itself coerce Great Britain. Thus, he appealed to two very different groups. Those who wanted war should have been put on their guard by the fact that the administration secured a rejection of the original plan to embargo foreign as well as domestic ships, and specifically refused to place a time limit on the measure. But the two disparate groups were united for the time being by the ambiguity of the measure. The Senate passed the Embargo Act in a single day in December by a vote of 22 to 6; a few days later the House did the same by a two-to-one margin.

As the months wore on, America's ardor for war cooled. Jefferson was soon left with no alternatives but to continue the embargo as the sole coercive weapon or to abandon the measure entirely, in a humiliating retreat. He decided to continue the embargo. But, as he introduced supplementary measures designed to close loopholes in the law, the Federalists leaped to the attack. Between the embargo and the supplementary laws there was no connection, declared Barent Gardenier, representative from New York. One was a prelude to war, preventing ships from going out and being captured; the other, a measure of coercion in itself. Gardenier and his fellow Federalists insisted that only French influence could inspire so foolish and wicked a measure as a permanent embargo. Jefferson was strong enough in Congress to override these objections and force through stringent enforcement acts, including elaborate bonding procedures, precautionary seizures, and general search warrants. But the unpopularity of the embargo, especially in New England, led to widespread defiance, smuggling, and criticism. As a result, the Federalists' electoral vote in 1808 was triple that of 1804, and their share of the House of Representatives was doubled.

The embargo was no more successful abroad than it was popular at home. France, of course, was unaffected by the embargo, since its trade had already been substantially cut off by the British blockade. British trade was affected. The embargo substantially reduced American exports to Britain, and the Nonimportation Act of 1806, which unlike the embargo was directed explicitly at Great Britain, reduced British exports to the United States. This affected Britain's foreign exchange, and gold began leaving the country. The price of gold rose from 8 shillings per ounce in 1807 to 110 shillings per ounce in 1813, embarrassing the Treasury and precipitating discontent over wages and prices. In most other areas, the Embargo Act and the Nonimportation Act did not wound Britain severely. The stoppage of America's cotton exports was actually welcomed by many British merchants, who had warehouses so full they had been worried about a glut. It did harm many workers in the textile industry, setting off a riot of weavers in Yorkshire; but they were not people with much political leverage.

Meanwhile, the revolutions in Spain and the Spanish colonies in Latin America opened new markets and sources of supply for Britain, which helped compensate for the loss of trade with the United States. The Nonimportation Act of 1806 was no more effective than the embargo, since it exempted cheap textiles and manufactured goods, those things the United States needed most from Britain but also the goods Britain most needed to export. The sight of British ships arriving in American ports with these goods galled the American merchants, whose own ships were rotting at the wharves. They were not much consoled that the embargo forced British vessels to leave in ballast. In the West Indies, too, the embargo failed. It hurt the French West Indies more than the British because the British had ships to supply their islands, while the French did not.

As the failure of the embargo abroad became apparent and disaffection at home continued to rise, the Republicans had to retreat. During Jefferson's lame duck period, he abandoned his direction of Congress, which promptly replaced the Nonimportation Act and the Embargo Act with the Nonintercourse Act of 1809. This act reopened trade with all nations except Britain, France, and their dependencies. But the purposeful vagueness as to just which nations would be considered British or French dependencies, and the lack of a navy to enforce these regulations outside U.S. territorial waters, made the new law an invitation to smuggling. It, too, was soon abandoned and was replaced by Macon's Bill Number Two (1810), throwing trade open to all nations with the promise that the United States would cut off trade with the enemy of any nation that would respect America's neutral rights. When Napoleon promised to respect those rights, Madison, Jefferson's successor, cut off trade with Britain, despite the fact that Napoleon never actually lived up to his promises. When economic weapons again failed to coerce Britain, Madison recommended, and Congress declared, war. Actually, Britain had finally abandoned some of its orders in council before the American declaration. But news of the repeal failed to reach the United States before Congress voted. When the news did arrive, Madison refused to consider peace unless impressment also was eliminated. So the war went on.

Ironically, two months before the United States declared war, Congress had laid yet another embargo on Great Britain. It was specifically a measure to prepare for war, and it expired shortly after the war began. But Madison was not satisfied. He pushed another embargo through Congress in 1813. This had little effect on the southern states because the British were already blockading them; but in New England, which the British left unblockaded as a mark of favor to the section most opposed to the war, the embargo hit hard, increasing discontent and leading to threats of secession. Madison and his followers refused to admit the uselessness of the measure until the defeat of Napoleon in 1814 opened the markets of Europe to the British and destroyed what little leverage the embargo had.

In the euphoria of what Americans considered a victorious and glorious defense against Britain in the War of 1812, the American people nearly forgot the humiliations they had suffered in the commercial warfare period and the early fighting. Republican partisans cast the blame for the failure of the embargo on the Federalists and the New Englanders who had defied the law, saying that only such subversion prevented the measure from coercing Britain. But this rhetoric did not erase America's bitter memories of its attempts at economic sanctions, and it would be many years before the United States tried them again.

THE CIVIL WAR

For decades after the War of 1812, peace in Europe gave the United States a chance to expend its diplomatic energies on westward expansion, where it did not need economic weapons. Population pressure and diplomatic maneuvering were often adequate, and where they failed, outright military action was possible because these areas were physically contiguous. Not until the Civil War was the weapon of economic sanctions once again taken up, this time by the Confederacy. The South was convinced that "cotton was king" and essential to both British and French industry. After the North instituted a blockade of the entire Confederacy, the South decided to enhance that blockade by embargoing exports of cotton. The Confederacy urged southerners not to plant cotton until the war was over, and they burned more than two and a half million bales. Unfortunately for the South, the bumper crop shipped in 1860 had already given Great Britain an oversupply of cotton, and cotton factors actually welcomed the shortage as a chance to reduce their supplies. Shortages did begin to occur by 1862. Four hundred thousand workers lost their jobs. Many of these workers advocated British intervention on behalf of the South to restore the cotton supplies; but their political impotence, the increasing supplies of cotton from Egypt, and the growing realization that the South would lose the war doomed their efforts. As the war went on, even southerners found the embargo too painful, and they cooperated in running more than a million and a half bales of cotton through the northern blockade. Once again an economic sanction had proved to be a disastrous failure.

THE EARLY TWENTIETH CENTURY THROUGH THE INTERWAR YEARS

From the Civil War until after the United States emerged from World War II as the most powerful economy in the world, America used economic sanctions more sparingly. Gone was the confidence that economic sanctions could substantially affect a powerful enemy. In this period, sanctions were used more as a gesture than as a weapon. They might be used to indicate moral disapproval or to keep the United States out of foreign wars. They might be used as a warning of firmer measures to come, or as a futile substitute for war when armed force was impolitic. But

Americans no longer regarded economic sanctions as an extraordinarily potent weapon in their foreign policy armory.

In 1898, Congress passed a joint resolution granting the president authority to bar the export of coal or war matériel from American seaports during the Spanish-American War. This embargo was merely an adjunct to war, not an important weapon in itself. President Theodore Roosevelt stretched the authority of this law in 1905 to keep weapons from falling into the hands of revolutionaries in the Dominican Republic, where the United States had taken control of the customs. In 1912, when the government of Francisco I. Madero protested American shipments of arms to Mexican rebels, Congress gave President William Howard Taft more specific authority to handle the situation than it had delegated to Roosevelt. It amended the 1898 resolution to provide that when there existed in any Western Hemisphere country conditions of domestic violence promoted by U.S. arms, the president should proclaim that fact. This would make exports of arms or munitions illegal except as the president provided. In effect, this gave the president the right to provide arms to whichever side he favored. Taft used this authority to embargo all arms to Mexico, but when a revolt broke out against the reviled Victoriano Huerta, President Woodrow Wilson lifted the embargo so that arms could be shipped to Huerta's opponents. When the United States recognized the government of Venustiano Carranza, it restored the embargo but made American arms available to Carranza's forces near the U.S. border. Then Pancho Villa began raiding in the area, so Wilson sent General John J. Pershing across the border after him and removed the exemption to the embargo. Thus, the United States had begun a regular use of arms embargoes as a means of controlling or manipulating domestic revolutionary situations in the Western Hemisphere, as well as using them to prevent aid to nations with which it was at war.

During this same period, U.S. businesses began serious overseas operations and another kind of embargo made its appearance—the capital embargo. Throughout most of American history, capital embargoes applied only to loans involving the public sale of foreign bonds and were quite informal. The government had only to recommend against a loan, and foreign bonds would not find purchasers because prospective buyers knew that the government would not enforce payment if the borrowing country should default. Thus, Taft's secretary of state, Philander C. Knox, discouraged a loan to China during the revolution of 1911, and Wilson discouraged a consortium seeking to reorganize a loan to China in 1913. Wilson also advised against loans to the belligerents during World War I but reversed that policy in 1916. In March 1922 the State Department made its informal policy official by announcing the hope that American corporations contemplating loans would check with the department first.

Just prior to World War I, Wilson dusted off the idea of a broader use of economic sanctions as a means of forcing the British to reduce their interference with American shipping to the European continent. In September 1916, he persuaded Congress to pass a law permitting him to ban imports and deny clearance for any departing vessels. After his reelection in November of that year, he hinted to the British that he might use that authority to embargo arms or deny clearance to vessels refusing to carry goods for firms blacklisted by the British. Since the British blockade had already cut off trade to Germany, any embargo would hurt only the Allies, thus paralleling the situation in Jefferson's day. Wilson never actually exercised his authority because he was more concerned with German submarine warfare than with the British blockade or blacklist. He did not want to find himself in the position of Jefferson and Madison, locked in a dispute with both belligerents at the same time or allied with the wrong nation because it capitulated more quickly to U.S. sanctions.

With the entry of the United States into the war, Congress embargoed all supplies to the Central Powers by passing the Trading with the Enemy Act of 1917. This embargo was wielded against the neutral powers of Europe, driving them into agreements to limit trade with the Central Powers in exchange for vitally needed goods from the United States. These agreements, along with blacklisting and limits on coal supplied to ships seeking refueling at U.S. ports and bases directed against firms within neutral countries suspected of trading with the enemy, tightened the economic noose that the Allied blockade and American embargo placed around the Central Powers and contributed substantially to the Allied victory in World War I.

After the war there arose in the United States a general revulsion against American involvement in world politics, and the policy of using economic sanctions as an alternative to political or military entanglements came to play an important part in

ON SANCTIONS

Historians, analysts, and politicians differ passionately about the efficacy and morality of America's record in using sanctions, as one can readily see from the following quotations:

"A nation that is boycotted is a nation that is in sight of surrender. Apply this economic, peaceful, silent, deadly remedy and there will be no need for force. It is a terrible remedy. It does not cost a life outside the nation boycotted, but it brings a pressure upon the nation which, in my judgment, no modern nation could resist."

—*Woodrow Wilson, quoted in Hufbauer, Schott, and Elliott, vol. 1, p. 9.*—

"We use sanctions so often—nearly 100 times this century—that they have become America's grand diplomatic experiment. This experiment, repeated many times, shows [that sanctions do not work and are America's folly]. . . . A nation boycotted is not in sight of surrender: recall North Korea, Cuba, and Iran. . . . In achieving 'high' foreign policy goals, sanctions are not a substitute for force, but they can be a prelude to force—consider Iraq, Haiti, Bosnia. . . . Contrary to [Woodrow] Wilson's belief, economy sanctions have turned out to be an offer that nearly every target can refuse—not only powerful China, but also powerless Panama."

—*From Gary C. Hufbauer, "Economic Sanctions: America's Folly," in Singleton and Griswold, pp. 91–92.*—

"Sanctions can offer a nonmilitary alternative to the terrible options of war or indifference when confronted with aggression or injustice."

—*National Conference of Catholic Bishops, quoted in Haass, p. 2.*—

"[Sanctions] do not work. . . . it is important for us to recognize as a nation the enormous value of having American businesses engaged around the world. To recognize that engagement does more to encourage democracy and freedom, to open up societies, to create opportunities for millions of people who up until now have not been able to participate, than just about anything else we can do."

—*Richard B. Cheney, "Defending Liberty in a Global Economy," quoted in Singleton and Griswold, p.27.*—

"It is indisputable that the myriad pressures generated by the many forms of sanctions imposed on South Africa forced the previously immovable and inflexible system of apartheid to recognize the necessity of change."

—*Jennifer Davis, "Sanctions and Apartheid: The Economic Challenge to Discrimination," in Cortright and Lopez, p.181.*—

"The economic sanctions continued to strangle the people of Iraq, and the country has been pushed to the verge of collapse, placing the life of its civilian population in great peril."

—*Bashsir Al-Samarrai, "Economic Sanctions Against Iraq: Do They Contribute to a Just Settlement?" in Cortright and Lopez, p. 135.*—

---

the debate over the shaping of a new foreign policy for the United States. As a kind of prelude, Congress made two minor gestures in 1922. It expanded the arms embargo of 1912, which had previously applied only to Western Hemisphere countries, and permitted the president to embargo arms to countries where the United States exercised extraterritorial jurisdiction whenever there existed conditions of civil violence. This law was directed primarily at China. Also in 1922, the State Department recommended against credits to Soviet Russia because that nation refused to pay its war debts. But neither this capital embargo nor the refusal to recognize the Bolshevik regime hindered American trade with the Soviets.

Consideration of a broader use of the arms embargo began later in the 1920s. Some influential Americans wanted the president to have authority to embargo arms and munitions to any aggressor nation. They saw this measure as a chance for the United States to cooperate with the League of Nations. They were fearful that America's traditional policy of neutrality, which insisted on a neutral's rights to trade with all belligerents, would undermine any system of collective sanctions the league might undertake. Conversely, American cooperation in those sanctions would strengthen the league and the system of collective security immeasurably. Thus, they argued for a discretionary embargo, which would allow the president to embargo arms to aggressor nations but to supply arms to the victims of that aggression.

The movement for cooperation with the league ran head-on into a growing countermovement inspired by disillusionment with World War I and a belief that American involvement in the war had been manipulated by munitions makers and other so-called merchants of death. This countermovement, too, called for an arms embargo, but its advocates insisted that the embargo be impartial. The purpose should be to keep the United States out of any future wars, not to deter future wars by the threat of collective sanctions against aggressors. This debate created a groundswell of support for some sort of arms embargo. By the mid-1930s, only a few congressional voices, along with the weapons manufacturers themselves, still called for adherence to America's traditional policy of enforcing a neutral's right to trade with belligerents in any commodities whatever.

Although the debate over arms embargoes began in 1928, Congress did not pass the first Neutrality Act until 1935. Henry Stimson, secretary of state in the late 1920s, favored a discretionary embargo to strengthen collective security but received little support from President Herbert Hoover. Without strong administration backing, the measure failed. Hoover was particularly adamant against imposing economic sanctions on Japan for its aggression in Manchuria, sanctions strongly favored by Stimson. Instead, Hoover forced Stimson to retreat to an ineffective policy of refusing to recognize any gains Japan might make, a policy ironically known as the Stimson Doctrine.

Franklin D. Roosevelt came to the presidency pledged to Stimson's policy of discretionary embargoes. Such an embargo actually passed the House in 1932. But when it encountered opposition in the Senate, Roosevelt consented to an impartial embargo, a complete negation of collective security. When his own advisers, including Secretary of State Cordell Hull, objected to his concession, Roosevelt agreed to drop the whole matter, and the embargo died.

The issue was revived during the next congressional session, however. Bolivia and Paraguay were engaged in the Chaco War, and the administration wanted to cooperate with the League of Nations in an arms embargo against both nations. Roosevelt could have supported a general impartial embargo on all warring nations; one was already before the Senate. But he still hoped for a discretionary embargo, and so he settled for a specific resolution embargoing arms to Bolivia and Paraguay only. This was the first time the United States had adopted an embargo avowedly for the purpose of stopping a war between two countries, and in that way it could be seen as a step toward collective security. In fact, it strengthened the concept of an impartial embargo because it stopped arms to both countries. The widely publicized Nye Committee hearings and the publication of several best-selling books further strengthened the concept of an impartial embargo by promoting the idea that American economic interests, particularly the munitions makers, had been responsible for America's entry into World War I. Perhaps even more important in the movement for an impartial embargo were the growing crises in Europe and Asia, as Japan, Germany, and Italy engaged the other powers in an arms race and embarked on campaigns of territorial expansion. Many hoped that the United States could escape the coming conflagration by embargoing arms and thus not repeating the supposed error of becoming involved in World War I.

The result of this growing movement was the Neutrality Act of 1935. Rejecting an administration bill allowing discretionary embargoes, Congress instead passed a mandatory impartial embargo on arms to belligerents, closed American ports to belligerent submarines, and prohibited Americans from taking passage on belligerent liners. The administration managed to limit the act to six months' duration, and then to use it for its own purposes. When Italy attacked Ethiopia, Roosevelt, to show America's displeasure with Italy, put the Neutrality Act into effect and declared a further "moral embargo" on any trade with the belligerents that was not covered by the Neutrality Act. Although supposedly impartial, the actions hurt only Italy. The United States had no trade with Ethiopia, and Ethiopia had no passenger liners to suffer from a prohibition against American passengers.

Although these actions may have given America some spiritual satisfaction, they had little effect on the course of world events. American businesses defied the moral embargo, and the League of Nations embargo omitted oil from the list of prohibited exports. Since oil was Italy's most vital need, the conquest of Ethiopia continued apace. This failure notwithstanding, Congress renewed the Neutrality Act in 1936 and added a provision prohibiting loans to belligerents. The administration and the business community managed to stave off a movement for an impartial general embargo rather than a mere arms embargo, but sentiment for a general embargo gained considerable strength as the year wore on.

When civil war broke out in Spain later in 1936, Congress honored the administration's request to embargo arms to that country. As Germany and Italy began to provide massive support for Francisco Franco, liberals put considerable pressure on the U.S. government to lift the embargo and supply the Loyalists. But the embargo remained. The advocates of collective security had been defeated again.

In 1937, congressional pressure to expand the arms embargo to a general embargo applying to all belligerents frightened many businessmen, and they sought a way to sidetrack the issue. Presidential adviser Bernard Baruch came up with a suggestion of "cash-and-carry," arguing that as long as American goods were purchased and transported by belligerents, the capture or sinking of the goods would not affect the United States. In return for other concessions, the administration succeeded in making the cash-and-carry principle discretionary, to be instigated with the rest of the Neutrality Act only at the option of the president. Roosevelt was also willing to accept cash-and-carry because he realized it would favor Britain and France; Great Britain controlled the seas and could ensure that only Allied ships would reach the United States to take advantage of the offer. The Neutrality Act of 1937 passed Congress just one day before the expiration of the act of 1936 and was flown to the presidential yacht in the Gulf of Mexico for Roosevelt's signature.

The Neutrality Act of 1937 was the highwater mark for advocates of an impartial neutrality; the decline of the movement had already begun. American sentiment was heavily against Franco's forces, and many regretted the embargo on arms to his opponents. Then, in 1937, Japan renewed its war against China. By rights, Roosevelt was supposed to embargo arms and loans to both nations and, if he chose, to establish the cash-and-carry policy. But both of these actions would favor Japan, since China needed the arms and credits, whereas Japan needed neither. Also, Japan was a sea power capable of taking advantage of the cash-and-carry policy. Roosevelt avoided this dilemma by pointing to the technicality that no official declaration of war had been made. Thus, he refused to invoke the Neutrality Act, enabling private loans and arms to continue to flow to China. Roosevelt followed this action with his famous quarantine speech and then imposed a moral embargo on exports of aircraft to Japan. Although isolationism remained strong and Roosevelt was forced to retreat from his quarantine policy, the American people generally accepted his tacit ignoring of the Neutrality Act. The United States was beginning to use sanctions as weapons against aggressors rather than as a means of avoiding conflicts.

WORLD WAR II

In 1938 Roosevelt failed to secure revision of the Neutrality Act. It was not until Germany invaded Poland in 1939, setting off World War II, that Congress revised the act. Even then, Roosevelt had to disguise his actions by claiming that the arms embargo actually endangered the peace of the United States. He also offered to bar American ships from designated war zones. He was thus able to persuade Congress to place arms on the same cash-and-carry basis as other commodities. He then went on to greater aid measures, such as the destroyer deal and lend-lease.

But while Roosevelt turned from sanctions toward measures of positive aid to Europe, in Asia his administration moved toward a more pointed use of embargoes against Japan. Japan relied heavily upon American oil and metals to supply its war effort in China. Any threat to stop those exports would have a significant impact on Japanese plans. The swing of public opinion and the revision of the Neutrality Act in 1939 allowed Roosevelt to take some action on behalf of China. So, in May 1939 the United States notified Japan that it was withdrawing from the 1911 Treaty of Commerce. According to terms of the treaty, in six months the United States would be free to limit or terminate exports to Japan. Roosevelt hoped this would give the Japanese pause, but Japan continued its war in China. The U.S. government hesitated to implement sanctions for fear that they would drive Japan to replace the embargoed items by invading new sources of supply. This would most likely be Southeast Asia, where French, British, and Dutch colonies were supplying those same vital materials to America's allies in Europe. The six-month period of grace passed, then a year, with no sanctions applied.

In July 1940, a cabinet change in Japan signaled a more aggressive Japanese policy in Southeast Asia. With that, the United States imposed an embargo on aviation gasoline and high-grade scrap iron to Japan. This embargo affected only a fraction of exports to Japan, and the U.S. government went to some lengths to justify the embargo on the grounds of American domestic needs rather than any displeasure with Japan. Still, the embargo signaled the Japanese that the United States would oppose any moves against Southeast Asia.

Instead of backing down, Japan accelerated its search for more secure sources of vital raw materials. It extorted concessions from the Dutch East Indies, coerced Vichy France into allowing Japanese occupation of northern Indochina, and began negotiations for an alliance with Germany and Italy. The United States responded with a complete embargo on scrap iron, but this was followed the very next day by the formal announcement of the Axis pact. The United States continued to expand its embargo, extending it to tools, iron, steel, copper, bronze, and many other critical metals. When the United States intercepted Japanese messages detailing plans for further expansion in Southeast Asia and reports arrived that Japanese transports were moving on southern Indochina, Roosevelt decided on a last-ditch gamble to stop Japanese expansion. He issued an order freezing all Japanese assets in the United States. Only a special license from the U.S. government could release Japanese assets to pay for American exports, including, most critically, oil. When the British and Dutch joined the oil embargo, it cut off the vital Southeast Asian sources of raw materials as well. With only a two-year supply of petroleum, Japan either had to give up the war in China or secure its own sources of supply. Japan first tried diplomacy, but negotiations with the United States failed, and Japan declared war. During World War II, the United States used the 1917 Trading with the Enemy Act to impose a complete embargo on the Axis powers.

COLD WAR SANCTIONS

The United States emerged from World War II as the only great power whose economy had escaped the conflict relatively unscathed. Consequently, it was a potential reservoir for rebuilding war-torn nations and was often the sole supplier of critical goods. Such economic power inevitably made economic sanctions an attractive option for the United States in the Cold War, despite the dismal record of embargoes in American history. Economic sanctions were often the only recourse for the United States when fear of nuclear war or other political constraints put limits on the use of military force.

In 1948, the United States began a campaign of economic sanctions against the Soviet Union that would last more than fifty years. In March of that year, the Department of Commerce announced restrictions on exports to the Soviet Union and its European allies. Congress formalized these restrictions in the Export Control Act of 1949. Originally, Congress intended this act as a temporary measure to keep arms and strategic materials out of the hands of potential enemies, but the outbreak of the Korean War in 1950 made the Cold War more rigid and the measure became permanent. In 1951, the United States attempted to strengthen these sanctions with the so-called Battle Act. According to this act, the United States would refuse assistance to any nation that did not embargo strategic goods, including oil, to the Soviet Union and nations subject to its influence. Under pressure from its allies, the United States accepted many exemptions from this act and it was not notably effective.

For many years, the embargo on the Soviet Union was quite severe. The embargo on Eastern European countries was less stringent, in hopes of driving a wedge between the Soviet Union and its allies. Two of the most independent East European nations, Poland and Romania, were given particularly mild treatment. With the growing détente of the 1970s, trade restrictions on the Soviet Union and its allies were increasingly lightened, most notably in the permission granted the Soviets to purchase large amounts of American wheat when Soviet crops failed in 1973. But restrictions were tightened again after the Soviet invasion of Afghanistan in December 1979. In 1983, Ronald Reagan approved the National Security Decision Directive 75, which set the policy of using economic pressure to limit the foreign policy and military options of the Soviets. This stricter regime of sanctions led to considerable conflict with America's allies on the Coordinating Committee for Multilateral Export Controls (COCOM), especially over the export of oil and gas equipment.

When the Soviet Union collapsed in 1991, a major debate broke out over the contribution that the campaign of economic sanctions had made toward the fall of the Soviet empire. Many former officials in the Reagan administration credited sanctions with a significant role in the disintegration of the Soviet economy and therefore of the

Soviet Union itself. On the other hand, the leading work on the effectiveness of economic sanctions—Hufbauer, Schott, and Elliott, *Economic Sanctions Reconsidered* (vol. 1, p. 137)—concludes that although the United States did succeed in denying some arms and key technologies to the Soviets, the collapse stemmed from internal inefficiencies rather than U.S. economic sanctions.

Ironically, the most effective use of economic sanctions made by the United States during the Cold War in Europe was against its own allies, Great Britain, France, and Israel, during the Suez Crisis of 1956. When those three powers concerted to invade Egypt in response to Egyptian nationalization of the Suez Canal, President Dwight Eisenhower not only warned them to retreat, he began a massive sell-off of British pounds and embargoed U.S. oil shipments to the three nations. For one of the few times in history, sanctions stopped a military invasion in its tracks.

During the Cold War in Asia, the United States imposed embargoes on North Korea, China, and North Vietnam. These were severe embargoes established under the Trading with the Enemy Act. The embargo of China and North Korea began in 1950, during the Korean War. Secretary of State John Foster Dulles insisted that the embargo continue after the war, but America's allies protested, arguing that such trade should be under the same regulation as trade to Eastern Europe. The United States used the Battle Act to prevent this, but in 1957 gave way to allow its allies to trade with China and North Korea. The United States, however, maintained its own unilateral embargo until 1969, when the administration of Richard M. Nixon lifted restrictions on most trade to China except for strategically important goods. The economic effect of the embargo on China was minimal because China itself chose to restrict imports to what it could pay for with its few exports. China found all the imports it needed in Europe anyway.

The United States reimposed some sanctions on China after the Tiananmen Square massacre of 1989. President George H. W. Bush suspended arms and some commercial contracts but maintained China's most-favored-nation status. Congress, however, continuously threatened to remove that status in order to apply pressure against China over its record on human rights. Using the Jackson-Vanik Amendment to the Trade Act of 1974, which was originally designed to force the Soviet Union to permit Jewish emigration, Congress required the president to certify annually that China was respecting human rights before he could renew its MFN status. Ultimately, in 1999, President Bill Clinton narrowly succeeded in convincing Congress to grant China permanent MFN status and permit China to join the World Trade Organization. Clinton argued that the best way to influence China was to keep it engaged in the world economy and polity. The likelihood that the United States would resort to economic sanctions to influence China's human rights policy in the near future diminished as a result of this decision, but the United States continues to hold out the possibility of sanctions against China's nuclear proliferation policies by restricting Chinese access to advanced technologies.

While the United States relaxed its harsh economic sanctions against China a few years after the Korean War, it maintained those sanctions against North Korea because of human rights violations, a nascent nuclear building program, and a continuing military threat to South Korea. In 1994, North Korea's concessions on its nuclear program led the United States to lessen the restrictions and offer some aid. A famine in North Korea and the growing détente between North and South Korea have brought some increase in that aid, but U.S. sanctions against North Korea were still quite severe at the turn of the century.

Economic sanctions accompanied America's war against North Vietnam just as they did previous U.S. conflicts. The Eisenhower administration suspended all export licenses for North Vietnam in 1954, shortly after the Geneva Convention temporarily divided Vietnam in two. President Lyndon Johnson extended those sanctions to a prohibition of all commercial and financial transactions with North Vietnam when the war escalated in 1964. Although the peace agreement signed in 1973 included a provision for renegotiating economic ties, the final conquest of South Vietnam by North Vietnam in 1975 resulted in an extension of the sanctions to all of Vietnam. President Jimmy Carter moved toward easing those restrictions, but he was thwarted first by congressional opposition and then by Vietnam's occupation of Cambodia. Thus, sanctions remained in place until February 1994, when Bill Clinton ended the nineteen-year trade embargo.

America's Cold War embargoes and sanctions in the Western Hemisphere were somewhat different from those in either Europe or Asia. Rather than being attempts to punish military adventures or to slow the arms buildups of major powers, the United States used sanctions to destabilize weaker regimes that were too friendly to the Soviet Union or otherwise threatened stability and U.S. interests in the Western Hemisphere.

The United States levied the most stringent and long-lived of its sanctions against Cuba. In 1962, following the embarrassing defeat at the Bay of Pigs, President John F. Kennedy expanded a set of piecemeal sanctions that had been imposed on Cuba after its 1959 revolution by using congressional authorization to embargo all trade with Cuba. The United States then brought pressure on the Organization of American States and the NATO allies to follow suit, especially by threatening to deny aid to, and penalize companies of, nations continuing to trade with Cuba. The OAS did embargo trade except for food and medical supplies, but there was considerable leakage. More important, the Soviets granted large subsidies to keep the Cuban economy afloat, primarily by trading oil to Cuba for sugar on extremely favorable terms.

The fall of the Soviet Union and the elimination of its subsidies devastated the Cuban economy. Some in the United States thought that the end of the Cold War should lead to a termination of the Cuban embargo as well. But others, especially the Cuban exile lobby in Florida, thought that the end of Soviet subsidies provided a chance to tighten the embargo and finally oust Castro. Presidents George H. W. Bush and Bill Clinton, with an eye on Florida's twenty-five electoral votes, tightened restrictions on U.S. foreign subsidiaries trading with Cuba, on the grounds that Cuba needed to improve human rights on the island. The U.S. Congress went even further. In 1996, it passed legislation sponsored by Senator Jesse Helms and Representative Dan Burton to apply economic sanctions to any U.S. ally that continued to trade with Cuba. President Bill Clinton threatened to veto the legislation until Cuba shot down two civilian planes being flown toward Cuba by anti-Castro Cuban exiles. The furor this created in the midst of the 1996 presidential election brought Clinton to sign the Helms-Burton Act, but bitter protests from America's allies and Clinton's own inclinations caused the president to suspend the most onerous provisions of the act indefinitely. America's allies continued to simmer over this attempt to force their participation in the U.S. embargo of Cuba, especially because the United States was passing similar legislation to coerce an expansion of existing embargoes against Libya and Iran. In the annual votes of the UN General Assembly that urged the United States to abandon its sanctions against Cuba, the United States found itself increasingly alone. Meanwhile, Castro hung on to power and continued to defy the United States.

Sanctions against other Latin American nations during the Cold War were somewhat more effective. When President Rafael Trujillo of the Dominican Republic tried to have President Romulo Betancourt of Venezuela assassinated in 1960, the United States limited the Dominican sugar quota and successfully pressed two-thirds of the OAS members to vote for an embargo on oil, trucks, and spare parts to Trujillo. The sanctions did play a part in the fall of Trujillo's regime, but the assassination of Trujillo and subsequent threats of military force against his successors played a larger part.

Sanctions also played a minor part in the military coup that ousted Joao Goulart of Brazil in 1964. They destroyed the viability of Salvador Allende's government in Chile, which made it easier for the Chilean military, with U.S. support, to overthrow Allende in 1973. Sanctions helped to strangle the economy of Nicaragua under the Sandinistas and secure the election of the opposition UNO party favored by the United States in 1990. Finally, the denial of aid and loans to Manuel Noriega's government in Panama sowed much discontent, paving the way for the U.S. invasion of Panama and the arrest of Noriega in 1989. Thus, economic sanctions against regimes in Latin America during the Cold War had a more obvious effect than they did in Europe or Asia, primarily because those regimes were already weak and unstable, and received little outside help from the Soviet Union. But, even then, sanctions in Latin America most often required covert activities and military action to succeed fully.

Because the United States had fewer vital interests in Africa than in Europe, Asia, or Latin America, there were fewer instances of American economic sanctions. The United States did institute sanctions against Angola and Ethiopia in the 1970s to counter Soviet influence. But in the two major instances of embargoes and sanctions, South Africa and Rhodesia, the United States was a reluctant and partial participant in UN sanctions rather than an initiator of them. This was because the human rights objectives of the sanctions, with which the United States for the most part sympathized, threatened America's Cold War interests in the strategic materials supplied by South Africa and Rhodesia. In both cases, therefore, the United States supported limited sanctions as a moderate alternative to the more militant actions demanded by a majority of United Nations members.

From 1951 to 1962, the United States embargoed any arms to South Africa that could be used domestically to support apartheid; it extended that embargo to all arms in 1962. The United States and its allies, Britain and France, voted consistently against attempts by the United Nations to apply further sanctions, however. Jimmy Carter tightened arms sanctions slightly, but Ronald Reagan reversed course with his policy of "constructive engagement." Reagan specifically undercut a concerted UN move to impose wider sanctions on South Africa in support of the independence of Namibia by tying any action on Namibia to the exodus of Cuban troops from Angola. Congress, however, steadily pressed for tighter sanctions and, in 1986, overrode Reagan's veto to extend sanctions beyond arms to loans, new investments, and many imports. Combined with the sanctions of the United Nations and the refusal of many private banks to roll over South African loans, these economic pressures contributed significantly to the internal pressures from black anti-apartheid rebels that finally brought the white regime to accept a new constitution installing majority rule in the 1990s.

In Rhodesia, when Ian Smith declared independence from the British Commonwealth in 1965 as a means of maintaining white rule, the United States followed the lead of Great Britain in the United Nations. The United States first joined a 1966 embargo on oil, arms, and spare parts along with a boycott of major Rhodesian products; it then moved on to a complete embargo in 1968. While responding to these initiatives of the United Nations, the United States voted against proposals that called on Britain to use force against Rhodesia. The United States cast its first veto ever in the Security Council to defeat such a measure in 1970. In 1971, a coalition of conservative legislators led by Harry F. Byrd, Jr., sponsored an amendment forbidding the United States to boycott products from noncommunist countries unless it also boycotted such products coming from communist nations. Because the United States was importing much of its chromium from Russia instead of its usual supplier, Rhodesia, the Byrd amendment opened the door once again to imports of Rhodesian chromium. Although South Africa and Portugal had tacitly defied the embargo to the point that Rhodesia's exports and imports were almost back to the pre-embargo level by 1972, the American action was the first formal defiance of United Nations economic sanctions. This congressional action seriously embarrassed the United States in the United Nations until 1977, when the Carter administration secured the repeal of the amendment and reinstituted the sanctions. By 1979, Smith had succumbed and agreed to majority rule.

SANCTIONS AND HUMAN RIGHTS, TERRORISM, AND NUCLEAR PROLIFERATION

The Carter administration enhanced the use of sanctions for human rights purposes in areas outside Africa as well. Secretary of State Henry Kissinger and the administration of Gerald Ford resisted a 1973 congressional initiative that would have denied aid to nations that violated human rights, but Carter was more favorable to this tactic. With Carter's support, Congress attached riders to military aid bills denying aid to South Korea, Chile, Uruguay, the Philippines, Brazil, El Salvador, Guatemala, Nicaragua, Paraguay, Ethiopia, Argentina, and Zaire. Carter used his presidential prerogative to expand further the list of nations denied security aid on human rights grounds to include Bolivia, Haiti, and Iran. Reagan reversed course on this and vetoed legislation that tied aid to human rights, but with the end of the Cold War, the United States once again adopted sanctions on human rights grounds, most notably against China, Iraq, and Serbia.

In the 1970s, the United States also began using sanctions specifically against terrorism. Congressional legislation in 1976 and 1977 prohibited aid and exports to nations abetting terrorism. At the behest of Congress, the State Department began issuing lists of nations supporting terrorism. These lists included Libya, Syria, Iraq, Cuba, South Yemen, and Iran.

In the same decade, the United States and many other nations began using sanctions to discourage the proliferation of nuclear weapons. These sanctions sought to stop trade in items related to nuclear weapons with nations that refused to sign the Non-Proliferation Treaty. The nations most affected were Brazil, Argentina, India, Pakistan, and Iraq.

POST–COLD WAR SANCTIONS

With the end of the Cold War, the United States had greater success in persuading other nations to join it in imposing sanctions against terrorism, nuclear proliferation, and violations of human rights. Rival powers on the UN Security Council no longer automatically vetoed sanctions that affected their respective allies. The two most prominent crises in which broad multilateral sanctions played a major role were the Gulf War of 1991 and the meltdown of the former Yugoslavia. Sanctions in these cases succeeded in devastating the economies of the two rogue nations at the center of the crises, Iraq and Serbia. But in the end it took military force to compel the leaders of those countries to make major changes of policy.

When Iraq invaded Kuwait in 1990, the United States and the UN Security Council sanctioned all Iraqi trade and financial aid. But Saddam Hussein defied the bans and received substantial supplies through sympathetic Palestinians in Jordan. He also made a firm peace with Iran, thus securing his borders. As Saddam showed no signs of relenting on Kuwait, President George Bush began pushing his allies for military action. Many American leaders, including the former chairman of Reagan's joint chiefs of staff, Admiral William Crowe, argued that continuing sanctions might well force Saddam to settle without further bloodshed. Bush's own joint chiefs, led by General Colin Powell, were also reluctant to go to war, but were willing to do so if overwhelming force were used to avoid another Vietnam. Bush agreed, and the resulting Operation Desert Storm routed Saddam's army. But the allied armies stopped before taking Baghdad or capturing Saddam himself. They then signed an agreement with Saddam that restored Kuwait's border and permitted inspections to ensure the dismantling of all Iraqi weapons of mass destruction.

Saddam defied those agreements, and the United States and the United Nations continued their sanctions to try to bring him into line. Nevertheless, Saddam held out for more than a decade while the sanctions regime slowly declined. The United States and its allies exempted some Iraqi oil from the sanctions under strict controls to see that the money was used for humanitarian purposes within Iraq and to compensate Kuwait for war damages. But Saddam managed to divert some of that aid to maintaining his regime. He also smuggled oil, with the cooperation of Iran and others, to keep himself afloat. Meanwhile, Russia, France, and other nations pressed for further loosening or even ending the sanctions, on the grounds that Saddam had sufficiently conformed to his agreements and that the embargoes bore most heavily on innocent civilians.

Multilateral sanctions also played a major part in the Balkan crises of the 1990s. After the death of Tito, Slobodan Milosevic began appealing to Serbian nationalism as a substitute for the collapsing communist ideology that previously had sustained his position. As a result of growing Serb militancy, Slovenia, Croatia, and then Bosnia declared their independence. Milosevic used his control of the Yugoslav army and heavy weapons to invade Bosnia and Croatia in support of the Serb inhabitants of those areas. He then expelled or massacred all non-Serbs in the conquered areas, in a program dubbed "ethnic cleansing." The Croats and Muslims often returned the favor of ethnic cleansing when they had the chance, but the imbalance of power gave them fewer of those opportunities.

The United States under George H. W. Bush left the Europeans to furnish a few thousand UN troops to deliver humanitarian aid to besieged areas while America led the Security Council to impose an economic blockade of Serbia. By 1994, the blockade had worn Milosevic down to the point that he deserted the Bosnian Serbs and joined the embargo against them in hopes of getting the sanctions lifted against Serbia. But the Bosnian Serbs refused to quit. In July 1995, they brushed aside a UN force protecting the sanctuary of Srbrenica, massacred the adult males, and brutalized many others. Finally, the United States and NATO began a major bombing campaign that, combined with pressure from a rejuvenated Croat army, forced Milosevic to the peace table. At Dayton, Ohio, in November 1995, Bill Clinton succeeded in hammering out a peace agreement to be enforced by an enlarged UN contingent to which the United States would contribute one-third of the troops.

Milosevic, however, began a similar ethnic cleansing program in Kosovo in 1998. Despite the reluctance of Russia, the NATO allies restored sanctions against Milosevic. They eased them when he agreed to negotiate with the Kosovar Muslims, but nothing came of the talks, and Milosevic resumed military activities in Kosovo. It was clear to all that mere sanctions would not change Milosevic's policy, so NATO resorted to threats, and finally the use of force. A devastating ten-week bombing campaign ultimately brought Milosevic to retreat from Kosovo in favor of a UN peacekeeping force that included U.S. troops.

THE EFFECTIVENESS OF U.S. SANCTIONS IN HISTORICAL CONTEXT

The United States also imposed economic sanctions in cases far less serious than Iraq and Serbia after the Cold War. It was imposing sanctions against forty different nations as of 1999. Certainly, the United States was using sanctions more often than any other nation. In fact, many critics believed that its use of sanctions had gotten out of hand. *Economic Sanctions Reconsidered,* a major compilation of case studies by Gary Clyde Hufbauer, Jeffrey J. Schott, and Kimberly Ann Elliott concerning economic sanctions as exercised throughout the world in the twentieth century, concludes that sanctions worked only about one-third of the time, usually when they were exercised decisively rather than gradually, had multilateral rather than mere unilateral support, and were directed at rather weak and unstable regimes (vol. 1, p. 93). Truly altering a nation's fundamental political or military policy most often required military force. The history of sanctions in American history as narrated here seems to bear out that analysis.

On the other hand, sanctions have served purposes beyond the most ambitious one of changing another nation's fundamental policy decisions. Sanctions have signaled to adversaries, allies, and America's domestic constituencies the seriousness of an issue. They have prepared domestic constituencies for the possibility of armed conflict by making clear that all peaceful options were being tried before resorting to war. They have weakened the economies of adversaries in ways that interfered with their preparations for conflict. And they have served as an object lesson for future adversaries. Fidel Castro and Saddam Hussein demonstrated that determined regimes can survive powerful sanctions for an extended period of time, but the ravages on their economy certainly ensure that no nation will risk such sanctions lightly in the future.

Nevertheless, sanctions also have produced nationalist reactions in target nations that stiffened rather than weakened resistance to America's foreign policy goals. Moreover, even friendly nations often refuse to go along with U.S. sanctions, and the economic effect is simply to transfer commerce from the United States to other countries. In the end, then, sanctions are a tempting means for the U.S. government to try to coerce cooperation with its policies by means short of war and to signal its determination at home and abroad, but in the absence of the threat or use of military force, embargoes and sanctions do not often succeed in changing a nation's fundamental policies, and they impose costs on the initiator as well as the object of such measures.

BIBLIOGRAPHY

Combs, Jerald A. *The Jay Treaty: Political Battleground of the Founding Fathers.* Berkeley, Calif., 1970. Deals with the struggle between Madison and Hamilton over economic retaliation, culminating in the embargo of 1794 and Jay's Treaty.

Cortright, David, and George A. Lopez. *The Sanctions Decade: Assessing UN Strategies in the 1990s.* Boulder, Colo., 2000. Surveys of U.S. and UN sanctions against Iraq, Yugoslavia, Haiti, Libya, Sudan, Afghanistan, Cambodia, Angola, Sierra Leone, Somalia, Liberia, and Rwanda. The authors argue that sanctions are a valuable tool and can work if they are carefully designed to include carrots as well as sticks.

Cortright, David, and George A. Lopez, eds. *Economic Sanctions: Panacea or Peacebuilding in a Post–Cold War World.* Boulder, Colo., 1995. A collection of essays with contrasting views on the efficacy and morality of sanctions. There are specific case studies of the sanctions against Iraq, Serbia, Haiti, and South Africa.

Day, Erin. *Economic Sanctions Imposed by the United States against Specific Countries: 1979 Through 1992.* Washington, D.C., 1992. A reference work compiled by the Congressional Research Service.

Divine, Robert A. *The Illusion of Neutrality: Franklin D. Roosevelt and the Struggle over the Arms Embargo.* 2d ed. New York, 1979. An excellent account of the sanctions contained in the Neutrality Acts of the 1930s.

Gibbons, Elizabeth D. *Sanctions in Haiti: Human Rights and Democracy under Assault.* Westport, Conn., 1999. Documents the impact of sanctions on unintended victims, the general population.

Gilbert, Felix. *To the Farewell Address: Ideas of Early American Foreign Policy.* Princeton, N.J., 1961. A brilliant exposition of American ideas of economic warfare during the nation's formative years.

Haass, Richard N., ed. *Economic Sanctions and American Diplomacy.* New York, 1998. An outstanding group of essays covering the post–Cold War sanctions against China, Cuba, Haiti, Iran, Iraq, Libya, Pakistan, and the former Yugoslavia.

Hanlon, Joseph, ed. *South Africa: The Sanctions Report. Documents and Statistics.* London, 1990. A collection that spells out the economic impact of sanctions on South Africa.

Heinrichs, Waldo. *Threshold of War: Franklin D. Roosevelt and American Entry into World War II.* New York, 1988. A good discussion of Roosevelt's use of sanctions against Japan before World War II.

Hufbauer, Gary Clyde, Jeffrey J. Schott, and Kimberly Ann Elliott. *Economic Sanctions Reconsidered.* 2d ed. 2 vols. Washington, D.C., 1990. An encyclopedic work that contains case studies of most of the twentieth-century sanctions discussed in this essay.

Jensen, Merill. *The Founding of a Nation: A History of the American Revolution, 1763–1776.* New York, 1968. A good account of pre-Revolution economic action.

Kunz, Diane B. *Butter and Guns: America's Cold War Economic Diplomacy.* New York, 1997. Contains much on sanctions since 1945.

May, Ernest R. *The World War and American Isolation, 1914–1917.* Cambridge, Mass., 1959. An excellent account of how Woodrow Wilson dealt with the Allied embargo against Germany before World War I.

Moore, John Bassett. *A Digest of International Law.* 8 vols. Washington, D.C., 1906. A good reference source for early American precedents.

Owsley, Frank L., and Harriet C. Owsley. *King Cotton Diplomacy: Foreign Relations of the Confederate States of America.* 2d ed. Chicago, 1959. The most complete work on King Cotton diplomacy during the Civil War.

Perkins, Bradford. *Prologue to War: England and the United States, 1805–1812.* Berkeley, Calif., 1961. The best work on the economic measures leading to the War of 1812.

Preeg, Ernest H. *Cuba and the New Caribbean Economic Order.* Washington, D.C., 1993. Details the problems with the unilateral U.S. embargo against Cuba.

———. *Feeling Good or Doing Good with Sanctions: Unilateral Economic Sanctions and the U.S. National Interest.* Washington, D.C., 1999. An opponent of unilateral economic sanctions examines the U.S. embargoes against Cuba, Iran, Vietnam, Myanmar, and China.

Singleton, Solveig, and Daniel T. Griswold, eds. *Economic Casualties: How U.S. Foreign Policy Undermines Trade, Growth, and Liberty.* Washington, D.C., 1999. A collection of passionate essays by politicians and analysts opposed to sanctions.

Spivak, Burton. *Jefferson's English Crisis: Commerce, Embargo, and the Republican Revolution.* Charlottesville, Va., 1979. The best work on Jefferson's embargo.

Waldmeir, Patti. *Anatomy of a Miracle: The End of Apartheid and the Birth of a New South Africa.* New York, 1997. Recounts the successful use of sanctions in South Africa.

See also BLOCKADES; CONTINENTAL SYSTEM; ECONOMIC POLICY AND THEORY; FREEDOM OF THE SEAS; NAVAL DIPLOMACY; OIL

Environmental Diplomacy

Kurk Dorsey

Environmental diplomacy can be broken into two general categories: conventions regulating the use of natural resources, and conventions regulating pollution. In each case, the central problem is that political boundaries rarely reflect biological boundaries, so that as national economies consume resources and produce pollution, they spread environmental problems far beyond their national boundaries. The sheer size of the U.S. economy has given it both the power to degrade the environment around the world and the influence to push diplomatic efforts to protect the environment. For most of its history, the United States has been one of the leading nations in the field of environmental diplomacy, but at the end of the twentieth century the United States found itself more often on the outside, as global discussions produced treaties that were increasingly unacceptable to the U.S. government. This loss of leadership has coincided with a shift away from bilateral treaties, first to small multilateral treaties and then to conventions that are open to every nation. That shift has been a logical reaction to an increasing international awareness that some of the biggest threats to human society come from global environmental problems, but it has meant that the United States has been less able to shape the course of events to its liking.

Environmental diplomacy has almost always been a secondary, or even tertiary, goal of U.S. foreign policy. Simultaneously, though, it is often the product of intense domestic political pressure, as nongovernmental organizations (NGOs) have done a masterful job of putting their members' concerns on the diplomatic agenda. As such, it usually reflects the primary diplomatic and domestic goals of the time. Hence, in the twentieth century, such trends and policies as progressivism, the Good Neighbor Policy, containment, détente, and environmentalism, as well as the state of the national and world economy, all played crucial roles in shaping specific treaties. In addition, the increase in scientific knowledge as well as public awareness of and faith in that science were crucial elements in shaping the course of environmental diplomacy during the twentieth century. The United States has almost always been a strong proponent of using science as an impartial tool in international environmental protection, particularly in moving away from static treaties to dynamic bodies that can address changing problems. Finally, one must acknowledge that just as there are formal and informal forms of diplomacy, so too are there formal and informal kinds of environmental diplomacy. While the focus here is largely on conventions and treaties, it should be remembered that the sheer appetite of the United States for imported goods created an unintended international environmental impact that might actually be greater than that generated by formal environmental diplomacy.

THE UNITED STATES–CANADA BILATERAL RELATIONSHIP

Although the term "environmental diplomacy" is a creation of the late twentieth century, the United States has in fact been negotiating access to natural resources since its independence from Great Britain. One could certainly interpret westward expansionism as environmental diplomacy, as the United States strove to acquire the most valuable resource of all, relatively untapped land and the various forms of mineral and living wealth that came with it. More obviously, repeated deals with Great Britain between 1783 and 1910 were a sustained effort to secure access to the grand fisheries off Newfoundland, including those for cod and several other species. These two efforts were, in a way, complementary, as fishing was dear to the New England states and landed expansion was perhaps more appealing in the South and West. In any case, the efforts of the United States and its northern neighbor to work out fisheries deals were the start of a long and generally fruitful history of bilateral cooperation on both resource use and pollution control.

John Adams and his son, John Quincy Adams, personified the New England obsession with access to the Grand Banks. At the urging of the elder Adams, the Treaty of Paris of 1783, which ended the revolutionary war, ensured that U.S. fishermen would have the liberty to fish within three miles of British territory in North America, as well as the right to continue to catch fish on the high seas. Throughout the nineteenth century, the two nations continued to struggle over these fisheries, with special difficulty interpreting the meaning of the 1783 treaty.

Not accidentally, the next attempt to regularize fishing relations came during the younger Adams's term as secretary of state (1817–1825). The Treaty of Ghent (1815), which ended the War of 1812, had not reopened Newfoundland's inshore fisheries to the United States, but many New England fishermen pressed their luck by returning to their old haunts, and as a consequence often found their vessels confiscated. Tension forced the two nations to negotiate a new convention in 1818, which explicitly spelled out which areas were open to U.S. fishermen and which were closed, as well as shore points that could be used for drying and curing fish. Great Britain agreed that these limited areas would be open to the United States forever.

It turned out that "forever" was also open to interpretation, so the Grand Banks dispute did not go away. In the 1850s, the British threatened again to close the inshore fisheries; in the ensuing Marcy-Elgin Agreement of 1854 they traded access to all of Newfoundland's waters for a reciprocity deal between the United States and British North American colonies. After the Civil War, the United States repudiated Marcy-Elgin, and negotiations opened once again. The Treaty of Washington (1871) not only resolved the Alabama Claims but also settled questions of duties on fish products and access to Newfoundland's shoreline. Congress eventually abrogated this treaty in 1885, opening the way for yet another agreement, this one emerging from the Joint High Commission meetings in 1888. Because of congressional intransigence, this agreement was never formalized, but the two sides agreed to abide by it for many years, until in 1905 Newfoundland imposed its own set of restrictions on American fishermen.

Finally, in 1907, Great Britain and the United States agreed in principle to arbitration. In 1909 they sent the matter to the Permanent Court of Arbitration at The Hague, as each side presented lengthy arguments to justify either expanded or restricted U.S. access. After months of deliberation, the court issued a complex ruling that resolved the outstanding disagreements and left London with the right to make reasonable regulations. Apparently, "reasonable" has not become the subject of any serious dispute since then.

This fisheries dispute consumed a remarkable amount of time for the young United States, reflecting the importance of both the North Atlantic Triangle (Great Britain, the United States, and Canada) and the raw materials involved. The terms of discussion were quite traditional, as negotiators never considered conservation of the cod and other valuable species, nor did they really address the problem of shifting technology. In a sense, the diplomats could not create a permanent solution because the environment, the technology, the fishing patterns, and the markets that shaped human fishing were all interconnected and all changing constantly. In short, they were trying to create static solutions to dynamic problems. This has been a recurrent shortcoming of environmental diplomacy.

Such problems were not insoluble though, as the North Pacific Fur Seal Convention revealed. The North Pacific fur seal first drew the attention of Europeans when Russian explorers encountered it in the Bering Sea in the late 1700s. The seals breed on rookery islands, with the vast majority using the Pribilof Islands of Alaska, although they spend about three-quarters of their lives on the high seas. They became the subject of intensive hunting early in the 1800s, when sea otter populations crashed, and it turned out that the thick coats that kept them warm in the ocean were quite appealing to people.

Russian management of the seals, limited though it was, sufficed as long as the seals were remote from centers of human habitation and Russia could claim both the breeding islands and the seas around them. When Russia sold Alaska to the United States in 1867, at the same time that British Columbia was rapidly gaining population, hunting of fur seals became a diplomatic issue. The U.S. government leased the Pribilofs and their inshore waters to a private company for twenty years and limited that company to 100,000 skins per year. Both the government and the stockholders profited immensely until the early 1880s. By then, sailors out of Victoria, as well as a few from U.S. ports, had begun to kill large numbers of seals on the high seas. The response of the U.S. government was to accuse Canadian sealers of piracy and seize their ships, arguing that it owned not only the seals but also the eastern Bering Sea. Such an argument did not get very far in London, where the British generally showed restraint despite their strong support for freedom of the seas. Neither side wanted to back down, nor could either justify military action.

The first move toward compromise, in 1891, was crucial for two reasons. First, the two nations agreed to arbitrate their dispute if necessary; second, they appointed a four-member scientific committee to study the issue during a visit to the Bering Sea. The scientists, like the diplomats, failed to find any common ground beyond the obvious conclusion that fur seal numbers were declining. Still, their very presence—coupled with an 1892 joint scientific commission to study the fisheries along the U.S.–Canadian border—showed that the United States and the British Empire were beginning to consider that science might offer solutions to disputes over use of resources. Given the deadlock, the two nations were headed for arbitration. In 1893, after weeks of arguing and the production of sixteen volumes full of documents, arbitrators created a buffer zone and a closed season meant to protect the seals from pelagic hunting.

Although at first the ruling settled the U.S.–Canadian disagreement, the solution turned out to be temporary, as again shifting behavior and populations left a static agreement behind. Canadian sealers responded by crossing the ocean and demolishing the small Japanese and Russian herds, after which they then began to leave the industry; in response, the Japanese government lifted limits on its pelagic sealers, who promptly crossed the Pacific and took large numbers of Pribilof seals, as they were not bound by the arbitrators' ruling. The seal population continued to decline; the herd that once numbered 2.5 million was slipping toward 200,000 early in the twentieth century.

After many starts and stops, in 1911 the United States, Great Britain, Japan, and Russia worked out a deal that allowed some flexibility. The key component was a ban on pelagic sealing, which U.S. scientists had shown unequivocally to be the cause of the decline of the seal herd. In exchange, Canada and Japan received a fixed percentage of the skins harvested from the Pribilofs each year, and they allowed the United States to decide how many, if any, seals were to be taken. In effect, the United States had purchased the other nations' right to catch seals on the high seas. They had been willing to sell in part purely because of economics, but also because the United States had pressed hard that pelagic sealing was both immoral and scientifically indefensible.

The North Pacific Fur Seal Convention was one of the first great successes in environmental diplomacy. The species rebounded quickly to more than two million individuals; all four sides were reasonably happy with the deal; and all agreed that they were willing to conserve the species. The convention broke down in 1941 on the eve of World War II, but after the war international management resumed and continues today, even though the harvest for the fur trade has ended.

In the use of science as a tool of, and conservation as a goal of, diplomacy, the fur seal negotiations proved to be something of a harbinger for North American diplomacy. In 1906, Secretary of State Elihu Root proposed that the United States and the British Empire resolve three outstanding issues: the Newfoundland fisheries, boundary waters control, and inland fisheries. On the third issue he specifically proposed that the protection and conservation of the fisheries should be a central goal. After much fruitless haggling—a facet of environmental diplomacy just as any other kind of diplomacy—Great Britain and the United States signed a treaty to regulate the fisheries along their common border; this brief treaty stood out for its emphasis on a joint regulatory committee based on a scientific understanding of the fisheries. Years later, Congress killed the treaty by failing to enforce it, but it lived on as a model for later agreements.

Attempts to apply the model to just the sockeye salmon fishery in the Northwest began with frustration but eventually met with success. Scientists and regulators met often, proposed solutions frequently, and watched them collapse consistently. On some occasions the culprits were Americans, other times they were Canadians; sometimes they were fishermen, other times diplomats. In 1929, Ottawa rejected a salmon treaty; in 1930, the U.S. Senate returned the favor. Disagreements arose over two main issues: the division between U.S. and Canadian catches and the waters to be covered. Finally, in 1937, after some minor modifications, the Senate reversed course and approved the 1930 treaty, which established the International Pacific Salmon Fisheries

Commission. This commission involved Canadians and Americans in scientific research as a central tool in managing and allocating the catch of this most valuable fish species. In 1985 it was replaced by the Pacific Salmon Treaty, designed to address problems that had not been imagined in the 1930s, such as renewed political clout among the First Nations and greater foreign fishing on the high seas. Still, the startling protest by Canadian salmon fishers in July 1997, when they blockaded a ferry bound for Alaska and burned an American flag, demonstrated that diplomatic solutions rarely met everyone's requirements.

In the wake of Root's 1906 initiative, in 1909 Canada and the United States signed the Boundary Waters Treaty, which formed the International Joint Commission (IJC), with powers to regulate pollution, rivers, and the like. The treaty created a system of arbitration to find those solutions that eluded the members of the IJC. Water pollution, though, remained a low priority. On a few occasions, the two nations have established measures to reduce pollution in the Great Lakes, with a 1972 water quality agreement standing out as the most important.

Over time, the IJC found itself moving into air pollution issues, including most famously the Trail Smelter case. The Trail Smelter opened for business in 1927 and quickly earned a reputation for ruining agriculture on both sides of the British Columbia–Washington border. The smelter's owners offered to pay for damages, but they could not agree on terms with U.S. farmers, who in turn called in the Department of State. In 1941, after years of haggling, the IJC crafted an agreement to resolve the dispute based on "the polluter pays" principle. For many years, the Trail Smelter case appeared, like the fur seal arbitration case, to be a symbol of the ability of Canada and the United States to resolve their differences amicably. In recent years, however, critics have noted that diplomats and regulators deliberately kept the ruling narrow so that it would not impact other sources of transborder pollution. For example, the historian John Wirth noted that the Trail Smelter case, rather than being a victory, in fact impeded international efforts to control pollution for thirty years.

While the Trail Smelter case focused on a Canadian pollution source, a quick study of wind currents and the U.S.–Canadian boundary would suggest that the vast majority of transborder air pollution runs north, not south. As fate would have it, the industrial heartland of the United States was not only built above a belt of sulfurous coal but under wind currents that run right into the most populated parts of Canada. Nature in turn left eastern Canada especially vulnerable to acid rain—there was very little limestone to act as a natural buffer, especially in lakes and ponds popular with both locals and tourists, and the forests were easily damaged by sustained pollution. By the 1970s, Canadian politicians were complaining loudly about acid rain and calling for the U.S. government to control industrial emissions, especially from the Ohio Valley. The Reagan Administration addressed acid rain with great reluctance, suggesting first that the scientific evidence was unclear, then in 1982 simply declaring that acid rain was not an issue. In 1987, Ronald Reagan and Canadian Prime Minister Brian Mulroney announced a treaty to coordinate joint research into acid rain. Still, no steps to curb acid rain were put in place until after passage of the U.S. Clean Air Act of 1990, which mandated a reduction in sulfur dioxide emissions.

The bilateral Canadian-American relationship has also addressed wildlife protection in North America. Most famously, in 1916 the two countries signed the Migratory Bird Treaty (MBT), which protected most species of birds that lived north of the Rio Grande. The MBT divided birds into three categories: game, insectivorous, and others. Game birds could be hunted during specific seasons; insectivores were permanently protected; and those listed in the third category got protection just because they were popular. Like the fur seal treaty before it, the MBT succeeded because it combined solid science, economics, and appeal to people's fundamental ideas about aesthetics. The rationale for protecting birds was that they were beautiful *and* useful.

Still, the treaty stirred controversy because its motivation was largely domestic. Conservationists had pushed through Congress a law to protect migratory birds in 1913, but most of them believed that the Supreme Court would declare it to be unconstitutional. With Root's support, they focused on the idea that the treaty clause of the Constitution in Article 6 trumped the Tenth Amendment's notion that residual powers were reserved to the states, and they began to push for treaties with other countries to protect migratory birds. That they settled for the adjective "migratory" suggested that they were still very conscious that the states had the right to protect birds that did not migrate across state lines. As in the fur seal convention, the animals' movements were central to their presence on the diplomatic agenda. When in 1920 the Supreme Court ruled on the treaty's enabling legislation in *Missouri* v. *Holland,* Justice Oliver Wendell Holmes placed wildlife protection squarely in the lap of the federal government, and it has not left there since.

Since 1920, the MBT has served as the basis for bird protection throughout the United States and Canada, since the enabling legislation has been updated frequently, and it has also served as a model for three other bilateral treaties. In 1936 the United States and Mexico signed a Migratory Bird Treaty that had been on the conservationists' wish list since 1913. That treaty did little to change U.S. law, although it did add birds of prey to the protected lists, and its main value was to export U.S. ideas about bird conservation to Mexico. In 1972 the United States signed a similar deal with Japan in order to protect birds in the Pacific. And in 1976 the Soviet Union joined the club with an agreement to protect birds that migrated in the northern Pacific.

A few conclusions can be drawn from the U.S.–Canadian environmental connection. First, one can well ask about the treaties that ought to have been executed but never were. The fisheries of the Great Lakes were the scene of intense competition, but only the failed treaty of 1908 attempted to regulate them in any way. Rather than make a sustained effort to work with fishermen to create a sustainable fisheries regime on the lakes, the two governments dropped the issue and focused on local regulations that were doomed to failure. Simply put, there was no strong lobbying group or government agency committed to freshwater fisheries conservation, and now there is no commercial fishery of consequence on the lakes and many native species have been severely depleted.

Second, many treaties that are completed often are held up by strong economic opposition, sometimes until it is too late. It usually takes some dire emergency to move these treaties forward at the last moment. The fur seal convention could have been completed years earlier, but stubbornness in Ottawa and Washington prevented leaders from making a few minor sacrifices until it was almost too late for the species. The water quality agreements in the Great Lakes came long after the International Joint Commission had declared all of the boundary waters far too polluted to drink—only a catastrophe like the fire on the Cuyahoga River compelled the two sides to take any serious action. No doubt, much of the opposition to cleaning up the lakes came from the industrial concerns that would be forced to change their ways.

Third, by comparison, there have been very few treaties to regulate the environment between Mexico and the United States. In part, this trend reflects the smaller border between the two and perhaps some environmental differences in the borderlands and their species. But it also reflects differences in levels of competition—Canada and the United States were similar enough societies to demand the same goods from the same source—and deep diplomatic suspicion. The Mexican War and U.S. opposition to the Mexican Revolution, not to mention deep religious and cultural differences, left Mexico uncooperative and the United States aloof. The great differences between U.S. relations with Mexico and those with Canada suggest that environmental diplomacy requires a great deal of goodwill and trust. For all of their disagreements and harsh comments, the United States and Canada have fundamentally trusted one another since Canadian Confederation in 1867. The same certainly cannot be said about Mexico and the United States. One need look no further than the sorry state of the rivers shared by Mexico and the United States to see how far these two neighbors have to go to bring their relationship to a standard that Canada and the United States have shared for years. The signing of the North American Free Trade Agreement in 1992 and the subsequent creation of the Commission for Environmental Cooperation may well result in a leveling of the environmental relationship among the three countries, but it is not clear what the level will be.

Fourth, two large countries can solve a number of problems with bilateral diplomacy, but even then there are limits to what they can do. Just because of sheer land mass, the United States and Canada are in a position to create and solve important environmental problems in a way that is probably unique. And yet, for all of their efforts to protect birds, they really cannot save the scores of species of neotropical migrants that winter in Latin America without cooperation from at least a dozen nations. Likewise, a solution to the sealing crisis eluded them until they satisfied Japan. In short, bilateral diplomacy normally tackles relatively easy questions; as a consequence, when an environmental problem involves more countries, the diplomacy becomes significantly more important and more complex.

EARLY MULTILATERAL CONVENTIONS

While there had been a handful of multilateral conservation agreements before 1940, none were so sweeping as that year's Convention on Nature Protection and Wildlife Preservation in the Western Hemisphere (CNP). U.S. scientists and conservationists conceived the CNP in the 1930s as a means to spread what they considered to be obvious ideas about conservation. Each nation, they proposed, ought to set aside national parks, national reserves, natural monuments, and wilderness areas, all of which already had been established in some form in the United States. They also thought that each signatory ought to protect endangered species and migratory birds, which revealed the convention's roots in the early conservation movement. The scientists worried, despite the Good Neighbor Policy, that Latin American governments might well suspect their motives. Therefore, at the 1938 meeting of the Pan-American Union, delegates sympathetic to the idea created a study committee of Latin Americans. They came back in 1940 with a draft treaty full of ideas suggested first by the U.S. scientists. The Pan-American Union's official stamp was sufficient to give the CNP legitimacy.

By 1942 nearly every nation in the Western Hemisphere had signed on, even though few of them were in a position to fulfill its terms. There were relatively few scientists in Latin America, few conservation nongovernmental organizations such as the National Audubon Society, and few parks or reserves already established. In the face of these difficulties, only Costa Rica did much to set aside large tracts of land. Even the United States failed to take the convention very seriously, as it did not move to protect endangered species as a group until 1966. Granted, the outbreak of World War II distracted attention from nature protection, but the war also served as a catalyst to sign the treaty as a show of unity and cooperation.

While the CNP was not the first environmental treaty to draw in dozens of countries, it provides an excellent example of the two fundamental difficulties of multilateral environmental diplomacy. First, it is a challenge to coordinate policies for countries with vastly different levels of economic development. Not surprisingly, the United States and Guatemala had very different attitudes toward conservation of land and wildlife, based on differences in industrialization, population, wealth, and landmass. Some citizens of Latin American states suspected that part of the U.S. agenda was keeping their nations in a state of economic subservience, while the U.S. scientists and conservationists who created the convention believed that they were simply passing on the wisdom that they had learned the hard way, as well as ideas that were inherently good in any society. Later in the century, differences among rich and poor societies along the same lines would hamstring other efforts to protect the environment.

Second, enforcement mechanisms are usually the first thing to be dropped from such a treaty. Most governments in the Western Hemisphere were willing to say that nature protection was a valuable goal. Few were willing to be held to any specific promises. None would accept the possibility of penalties for failing to live up to the CNP. This pattern repeated itself for the next sixty years. The rhetoric of environmental protection has been unusually appealing, but few governments will sacrifice their sovereignty over internal resource decisions or forgo the possibility of economic development for the sake of environmental protection. If forced to choose between signing an environmental protection convention with real teeth or risking public censure for failing to sign such an agreement, most governments will take the risk of criticism. If anything, the United States was just as reluctant as any country to risk its sovereignty, even though it often had the least distance to go to live up to its obligations.

The reluctance of the United States to push for strong enforcement mechanisms—and the implications of that policy—can be seen most clearly in the long efforts to control whaling. By the early twentieth century, the vast majority of whaling was confined to Antarctic waters, with whales being caught and then brought back for processing to shore stations in such remote places as South Georgia Island. There whalers could be tightly controlled by licenses issued by the European colonial governments. Two technological innovations in the 1920s, the stern slipway and condensers for producing freshwater at sea, allowed whalers to process whales at sea on large floating factory vessels. Whaling companies in Norway and Great Britain quickly worked out the logistics for expeditions involving a floating factory and up to a dozen smaller whale catchers, which could stay at sea for months at a time, catching whales, processing them for their oil, and then delivering the oil to any port in the world. In short, because they could operate on the high seas and fly any flag they chose, they were extremely difficult to regulate.

In 1931, after two years of discussion, the League of Nations produced the Geneva Convention for the Regulation of Whaling as a first step toward international control of the industry. The twenty-six signatories, including landlocked Switzerland, agreed that all whaling vessels would be licensed, that calves and nursing females would be protected, and that they would conduct more scientific research. Despite sponsorship by the suspect League of Nations and the limited nature of U.S. whaling operations, the United States participated in the drafting of the convention, signed it, and ratified it in 1935, all because doing so was an easy way to placate domestic conservation interests.

The 1931 convention did nothing to address the real problem, which was massive exploitation of a finite number of whales. Only a huge glut in whale oil, which was used mainly for margarine, curtailed whaling operations in the early 1930s. In fact, the British and Norwegian whaling companies did more than any government to regulate whaling and save whales by their own private agreements to limit production. The problem was that they could not work with other foreign companies, especially those from Germany and Japan, that were pursuing whaling for national reasons as much as private economic gain.

Over the objections of industry, the United Kingdom and Norway called another conference on whaling in 1937 to craft a tougher convention. They set an open season for Antarctic whaling, created rules for efficient use of whale carcasses, and banned the hunting of certain endangered species. The United States, led by Dr. Remington Kellogg, took an active role, even though U.S. companies contributed only 3 percent to the world's whaling catch. Germany was also an active participant, which was a victory, but Japan refused to abide by the 1937 convention or any of its subsequent protocols. Not only were the signatory nations unable to do anything about Japanese whaling, they faced strong internal pressure from their own whalers who wanted the same freedom from regulation that the Japanese had.

Attempts to rectify the problems of the 1937 convention came to a halt when World War II erupted, and yet the war also played an important role in shuffling the interests of the nations involved in whaling diplomacy. On one hand, Japan and Germany found themselves at the mercy of the victorious Allies. On the other hand, the United States found itself somewhat unwillingly thrust into the position of global leadership. And most whaling ships found themselves on the bottom of the ocean floor. In short, the opportunity was there for a recasting of global whaling operations.

Under Kellogg's influence, the United States, a nation that neither caught nor consumed baleen whales, decided to seize that opportunity. With the reluctant compliance of Norway and the

REMINGTON KELLOGG

Remington Kellogg may have been the single most influential person in the history of efforts to regulate whaling, and he is therefore an excellent example of how one person can—and sometimes cannot—shape environmental diplomacy. In 1930, after receiving his Ph.D. from the University of California for his work on whale fossils, Kellogg worked at the Smithsonian Institution as a curator of mammals. As such, he was the closest thing that the Department of State could find to an in-house expert to send to the League of Nations meeting on a whaling convention. For the next thirty-five years, Kellogg served the cause of international conservation as an adviser to the Department of State, a delegate to the IWC meetings, and chair of the commission. The State Department took no step on whaling matters without consulting him, although it did not always follow his advice.

Most importantly, Kellogg urged the Department of State to use the opportunity provided by World War II to grab control of whaling diplomacy from Norway and the United Kingdom. He feared, rightly, that the British and Norwegians would be more concerned with harvesting whales in the aftermath of the war than with conserving them. Only American leadership, he concluded, could give science its proper place relative to the whalers, who seemed to have too much say in London and Oslo. Kellogg, then, was one of the most active advocates of a strong IWC and, indeed, one of the people most disappointed by its failures. His last meeting of the commission came in 1964 at Sandefjord, home to the Norwegian whaling fleet. At that meeting, the whaling countries fended off powerful scientific arguments that whaling needed to be curtailed before the industry destroyed itself, and Kellogg came home embittered by the experience. It was not the happy ending for which some might wish, but it is emblematic of the difficulties of pushing conservation through diplomacy.

United Kingdom, in the fall of 1946 the United States engineered the writing of the International Convention for the Regulation of Whaling. By 1949 enough nations were on board to create the International Whaling Commission (IWC), which, for all of its flaws, is one of the oldest international bodies with a mandate for conservation. The IWC was a step forward in that it established rules for annual meetings to update whaling regulations, it relied explicitly upon the advice of scientists, and it tightened the restrictions on whalers.

That the IWC failed to conserve whales is more a reflection of the limits imposed on it in 1946 than a reflection of the personal failings of its members. Once again, the drafters chose not to have any mechanisms to enforce conservation regulations. Kellogg had strongly advocated trade sanctions against whaling nations that did not join the IWC, but U.S. diplomats decided that trade policy and conservation issues should not be intertwined. The convention created new problems by giving members the right to object to any amendment to the original regulations and thereby exempt themselves from it. In later years, these two facets would be the target of vehement criticism among environmentalists, but the Department of State insisted on them on the reasonable theory that whaling nations would not join any organization that threatened their sovereignty. In other words, a conservation organization could have clout or members, but not both.

What a whaling commission could have was symbolic value and persuasive powers. In fact, it is clear that those two objectives were high on the list of the U.S. scientists and diplomats who drew up plans for the commission and subsequently defended it during its darkest moments. If nations, including the United States, were unwilling to surrender their sovereignty, they were still willing to listen to other nations' arguments. In fact, scientists counted on their ability to present rational, irrefutable arguments to recalcitrant commission members as the only viable means to build the necessary consensus. Even after it became apparent that persuasion was not going to stop Soviet cheating, Panamanian indifference to inspection, or U.S. efforts to restore Japanese whaling, U.S. and British diplomats supported the IWC as an important symbol that the nations of the world could cooperate in regulating the high seas—there was no need for South American nations to resort to such unsporting institutions as the 200-mile territorial limit in the name of conservation.

The IWC became the scene of some bruising political battles in the 1970s and 1980s, when the United States led a coalition of countries fighting for a moratorium on commercial whaling. By 1972, only three nations had any significant commercial whaling operations: Japan, the Soviet Union, and Norway, and Norway's industry was a mere shadow of its former self. As the surging environmental movement bore the greatest responsibility for pushing the moratorium, it was easy for the United States to support a measure that would hurt only its Cold War opponent and a major economic rival that seemed intent on destroying the U.S. auto industry. After several years of trying to push a moratorium through the IWC, only to see the whaling countries suggest that they would leave the commission rather than accept a moratorium, it became clear that the United States would have to use its own economic power to make any headway. Using the 1971 Pelly Amendment and the 1979 Packwood-Magnuson Amendment, Congress gave the president the authority to place unilateral sanctions on fishing rights of countries that continued to hunt whales in the face of IWC regulations. It is debatable how much impact these sanctions had, but they were at least marginally important in leading to the 1982 decision by the IWC to ban commercial whaling.

While the whaling commission might be the best known example of multilateral environmental diplomacy, it was certainly not the only postwar example of several nations convening to resolve their differences. The 1946 Northwest Atlantic Fisheries agreement was the first of several multinational treaties to regulate pelagic fisheries. Beginning in 1959 there was a series of treaties to regulate and protect the resources of Antarctica, including minerals and marine life. And there have been occasional isolated conventions, such as the 1987 agreement among five northern nations to protect polar bears. In each case, these treaties have brought together a set of countries with a mutual interest in a specific, local resource. Given a reasonably small number of countries with focused interests, the United States has been able to lead consistently.

GLOBAL CONVENTIONS

Beginning in the 1950s, thanks largely to United Nations activism and pressure from countries emerging from decolonization, the nations of the world began to gather in huge conferences to discuss truly global issues. One of the first of these grand global conferences was the 1958 meeting of the UN Conference on the Law of the Sea (UNCLOS), and over the next forty years it would be followed by several major attempts to unite the scores of nations of the world on key issues of diplomacy. In these discussions, the United States gradually found itself losing influence and often choosing not to lead. As environmentalism gathered steam in the 1970s, it served as a force to criticize the consumerism of the United States and its role in the Cold War, which helped push the U.S. government away from a leadership role. In addition, the United States found that its sheer power, and ties to former colonial powers, made it a target of developing nations more often than their leader.

The law of the sea negotiations started out with a focus on navigation, although marine resources were never far below the surface of the agenda. In fact, while pollution and fisheries disputes were important postwar motivators for the UN to call the conference, the aforementioned claim by Ecuador, Peru, and Chile in 1952 to a 200-mile band of territorial waters was one of the most important driving forces. The 200-mile limit was also one of the most controversial issues, as the conferees failed to reach an agreement on territorial waters at either the 1958 meeting or UNCLOS II in 1960. Only with the third meeting, which began in 1972 and ran off and on for ten years, did delegates accept the idea of the 200-mile zone.

The resource issues, which at first seemed fairly straightforward, became increasingly difficult to solve. In 1958, one of the four conventions signed addressed fishing and conservation in territorial waters. But that same conference, and the second one in 1960, failed to come to terms for fishing beyond territorial seas, in part because they failed to agree on a definition of those seas. Even after 1993, when the Law of the Sea Convention went into effect, fishing nations could not agree on regulating the seas beyond the new 200-mile economic zones. While treaties covering some regions and some species are open for signature, nothing has been completed, despite intense pressure from environmentalists to ban such practices as long-line fishing and drift-netting. The surprising incident of 1995, when Canadian warships fired on Spanish fishing vessels just outside of Canada's 200-mile zone, suggests that some sort of law is needed to cover these contested fisheries. And yet, as of 2001, only twenty-nine nations, including the United States, had ratified the supplementary agreement managing straddling and highly migratory fish stocks.

The most controversial point had nothing to do with swimming marine resources, but rather with those that have been lying on the ocean floor for millennia—mineral nodules. In the 1960s companies exploring the seabed discovered areas covered with rocks full of manganese, nickel, copper, and other valuable and reasonably scarce minerals. At UNCLOS III in 1982, governments split dramatically over how companies should get access to these minerals. Developing nations, often referred to as the Group of 77, argued that the minerals were the common property of mankind; therefore, an international agency should control the nodule fields, and companies that wished to exploit them would have to transfer technology to poorer countries and pay hefty fees. The United States and other developed nations countered that resources on the high seas had always been free for the taking by anyone with the capital and fortitude to take the necessary risks.

At UNCLOS III, the conferees adopted language closer to the Group of 77 nations' desires, and the Reagan administration refused to sign the convention solely because of the deep seabed articles. After a further twelve years of negotiations, the United States finally found a Deep Seabed agreement to its liking, in part because zealots on both sides were coming to the conclusion that mining there might never be economically feasible. Not only did the United States ratify the convention in 1994, but by then 159 states had at least signed, meaning that just about every national government in the world offered some form of support for the Law of the Sea Convention. When one considers that the UN has forty-two landlocked members, the signature count is especially impressive.

By the 1970s the huge meetings to discuss some global issue had become common, and in fact it is now hard to imagine a year without some grand conference sponsored by the UN. The factors that made such conferences more feasible, such as improvements in air travel, applied of course to environmental conferences, which were themselves furthered by both the strong wave of environmentalism sweeping around the world and the growing sense that some resources were simply the common heritage of humanity and therefore within the purview of all nations, not just a privileged few. Not only did new conventions and conferences come together, but membership rose dramatically in some old organizations, such as the IWC, which grew from fewer than twenty members to more than fifty in a few years. Not surprisingly, then, the 1970s witnessed a slew of conferences to deal with global issues, such as trade in endangered species, wetlands protection, and the general condition of the human environment.

None drew more attention than the 1972 United Nations Conference on the Human Environment (UNCHE) in Stockholm, Sweden. The UN had sponsored large meetings on resource conservation and protection in 1949 and 1968, but they had been limited in their scope. In 1969 the UN accepted Sweden's proposal to host a global conference on the human environment, broadly defined. When delegates from 114 countries and 500 nongovernmental organizations (NGOs) met in 1972, they ensured that the environment would have a prominent place on the diplomatic agenda for decades to come.

As one might expect, UNCHE had both its share of conflicts and cooperation. The first conflict came from the decision of the organizers to invite West Germany but not East Germany, which triggered a boycott from the Soviet bloc. Of course, that conflict contributed to the easing of negotiations by removing most Cold War tensions at the conference. Likewise, developing nations split from their industrialized compatriots in assessing the nature of the threat—was it pollution and the diminution of natural resources, or did economic imbalance lead to the other problems? Again, this disagreement led to some conciliation, as the Western nations agreed in principle that equitable distribution of wealth would lead to a healthier human environment, and both sides agreed that development agencies had to do a better job of considering the environmental impact of their decisions.

In the end, the Stockholm meeting had three practical consequences. First, NGOs gained their status as leaders in environmental diplomacy. Second, the delegates created the UN Environment Programme (UNEP) to serve as a global agency for environmental protection. Third, they produced 109 recommendations for action at local, national, and international levels.

With Stockholm as the impetus, in 1973 the United States took one of its last bold leadership steps by sponsoring the Convention on International Trade in Endangered Species (CITES). In many ways, it was one final example of exporting conservation strategies, as the U.S. Congress had recently passed a tough new endangered species act that served as an ideological template. The goal of CITES was to halt the commercial exploitation of endangered species, with the hope therefore of pulling them back from the brink of extinction. Nations that joined CITES promised not to allow importation of species declared endangered by any other member of the convention. In addition, CITES had a means for scientists to list species as endangered if the home government failed to do so. Threatened species could be put on a "gray list," which allowed only limited trade. At present, about 5,000 animals and 25,000 plants are listed as protected under the convention. Finally, and most critically, CITES actually included provisions to sanction nations that failed to halt trade in endangered species. The United Arab Emirates, Thailand, and Italy have all been punished by CITES, and El Salvador and Equatorial Guinea joined the convention because of sanctions pressure. In all, 154 states are parties to CITES, with the United States holding the distinction of being the first nation to ratify it in 1974.

Despite that rare display of teeth and tusk, CITES still has the problem of any environmental convention. If it enforces the rules strictly, it runs the risk of losing members, who will then be legally free to trade for all of the endangered species parts that they desire. Those who administer such conventions must decide if they would rather bend over backward in the hope of persuading rogue states to abide by the rules eventually, or punish them and hope that global public opinion and political pressure will deter them from leaving the convention. CITES's own evidence suggests that most of its members do not abide by its rules, nor do they wish to be shown the door, which suggests that it can do more than just turning a blind eye to infractions in the hope that nations will slowly develop a willingness to abide by these rules.

One of the holes in CITES was that it said nothing about habitat preservation, a subject covered in a few other treaties. The 1971 Ramsar Agreement required parties to protect at least one wetland of special significance. The convention does provide signatories with the right to revoke protection in case of national emergency, but only if the government provides sufficient compensation in the form of further protection of other sites. While 125 nations had signed on to Ramsar by 2001, they were only slowly getting around to protecting the wetlands in question. In a manner reminiscent of the 1940 Convention on Nature Protection, the wealthy nations that could afford to protect wetlands had already done a great deal of work, whether the United States with its vast system of National Wildlife Refuges or Great Britain with its impressive chain of preserves owned by the Royal Society for the Protection of Birds. Even so, it took the United States until 1987 to ratify the convention, and it has designated fewer hectares as Ramsar sites than some smaller, poorer countries, such as Tanzania.

In contrast to Ramsar's narrow focus on wetlands, in 1972 the United Nations Educational, Scientific, and Cultural Organization (UNESCO) sponsored an agreement to preserve sites of special cultural and natural value, the Convention Concerning the Protection of World Cultural and Natural Heritage. The notion of a treaty to protect sites of cultural value dates back to at least the 1950s, but it was a U.S. idea in 1965 to combine cultural and natural sites into a single convention, and the United States was the first nation to ratify the convention in 1973. By 2001, 164 nations had become parties, making it one of the most inclusive pieces of environmental diplomacy. Member states have access to a small pool of money, about $3.5 million annually, to help them plan for listing and protecting sites, but they join mainly for reasons of public opinion and prestige, and 122 nations had listed nearly 700 sites at the beginning of the twenty-first century. The United States is one of the few countries that listed more natural sites than cultural, with eleven of its eighteen being national parks.

In an attempt to follow up on CITES, Ramsar, and the World Heritage conventions, in 1979 the UN opened for signature the Convention on Migratory Species. The negotiators began with a premise that U.S. conservationists had acted upon at the turn of the twentieth century, that migratory animals inherently needed international cooperation for their protection. Parties agree to protect habitat for endangered and threatened species, pass laws to protect them from hunting, and study them to learn more about means of protecting them. Seventy-four nations ratified the agreement, mostly from Europe and Africa. The United States, like Russia and China, did not sign, but U.S. wildlife officials cooperate with policies from the Convention on Migratory Species. This cooperation suggests a recurrent problem, that the U.S. government is especially reluctant to accede to a convention that might override its own laws.

As if exhausted from the spate of treaties in the early 1970s, the world did not create another major piece of environmental diplomacy until the middle of the 1980s, when it tackled the problem of ozone-depleting chemicals. Ozone, a collection of three oxygen atoms, serves as a shield in the upper atmosphere against ultraviolet radiation from the sun. As such, it makes life on earth possible. In the 1970s, scientists theorized that ozone would break apart when it came into contact with chlorofluorocarbons (CFCs), a family of chemicals widely used in Styrofoam, refrigerants, and aerosol cans. CFCs had been invented in the 1930s, and they seemed like the ideal chemical—inert, nontoxic, cheap, and useful in a variety of ways. But by the 1980s, a move was afoot to ban them based on theoretical concerns.

In a move that surprised many people, the usually antiregulatory Reagan administration vigorously supported efforts to ban CFCs. In part, this position depended on the strong position of U.S. industry to benefit from a ban on CFCs, and perhaps in part it grew from the president's own brush with skin cancer. The first step came in 1985, when delegates from twenty nations met in Vienna and signed the Convention for the Protection of the Ozone Layer, which did no more than commit the signatories to unspecified actions to protect the ozone layer. In addition, they agreed that the UN Environment Programme would monitor the ozone layer and conduct research on it. In short, the signatories could agree on nothing more specific than the theory that the ozone layer was probably in trouble. They did, however, agree to a U.S. proposal to meet two years later to create a binding set of rules.

The discussions evolved from multilateral to global in 1987, as delegates from sixty states convened in Montreal. Evidence that humans were somehow eroding the ozone layer was still sparse, as the famed ozone hole over the Antarctic had just recently become known, and its causes were absolutely uncertain. Still, there can be no doubt that the ozone hole had caught the attention of the U.S. public, although the delegates themselves seemed largely unmoved by it—they were driven still by the scientific theories. Over objections from industry in Japan, western Europe, and, to a lesser extent, the United States, the delegates formally named CFCs as the culprits. Through the Montreal Protocol on Substances that Deplete the Ozone Layer, they agreed to cut production of these chemicals in half by 1999.

In retrospect the Montreal Protocol was at once one of the most amazing pieces of environmental diplomacy and obviously flawed. Working largely on complex scientific theory rather than compelling data, diplomats from around the world agreed that a seemingly benign chemical had disastrous potential and therefore had to be curbed dramatically. At the same time, critics pointed out that developing nations, such as India, China, and Brazil, needed CFCs to raise their standards of living, but the convention said nothing about transferring technology to them. Finally, many Europeans condemned the convention as too strict, while many U.S. environmentalists and industrialists worried that it would be unenforceable.

To address this range of concerns, delegates from eighty-one countries met in Helsinki in 1989. With further research showing that the ozone problem was not just theory, they agreed to ban all CFC production by 2000. In addition, they drew up schemes to facilitate technology transfer, and they tightened up the rules. The next year in London they finalized all of the details of these agreements, and in 1992, President George H. W. Bush announced that the United States would eliminate CFC production by 1995.

The U.S. position on the ozone layer makes especially puzzling its general lack of leadership in the 1990s. On the twentieth anniversary of the Stockholm meeting, the nations of the world met at the Earth Summit in Rio de Janeiro. Known formally as the UN Conference on Environment and Development, the Earth Summit was supposed to provide leaders a chance to assess and build upon the accomplishments of the 1972 meeting. One of the accomplishments of the meeting was the production of a massive document, known as Agenda 21, as a follow-up to the 1972 recommendations for action. In addition to the thousands of activists who attended on their own, 170 nations sent delegations, many led by their head of state, but President Bush publicly vacillated about attending. Rather than taking an opportunity for leadership, Bush was concerned that he might find himself boxed into an uncomfortable position. In the end, he paid a brief visit, but he was unable either to rally other nations to his positions or even tame the dissent within the U.S. delegation.

On two important issues the United States found itself out of step with the majority of the world's governments. First, and perhaps most controversially, the conferees agreed to the Convention on Biological Diversity (CBD). The UN Environment Programme had been working on this convention for four years, goaded by alarming reports of the extinction of hosts of species, many of which had never been scientifically catalogued. The final convention required signatory nations to take appropriate steps to preserve their own biodiversity, and it established a fund for helping poorer countries do just that. Bush noted that the United States already did more than any other country on both points. The real point of disagreement came with the convention's provisions on biotechnology and intellectual property. In a debate reminiscent of the discussions about minerals on the deep seabed, U.S. officials argued that American companies had far more to lose than gain because the protections for their patents were insufficient. Despite great pressure at home, abroad, and within the U.S. delegation, Bush refused to sign the CBD. A year later, after consulting with both business and environmental leaders on an interpretive statement, President William Jefferson Clinton signed the convention just days before it was closed to signatures. While 186 governments signed the CBD, the United States is one of only seven—including such pariahs as Afghanistan and Yugoslavia—who have not ratified it.

The other major agreement to come out of the Earth Summit was the Framework Convention on Climate Change. As concern about the ozone layer was heating up, scientists began to fear that the Earth itself was heating up because of human economic activity. In particular, they were coming to the conclusion that industrial emission of so-called greenhouse gasses, such as carbon dioxide, was resulting in a slow but steady warming of the earth's temperature. By 1989 the UN had endorsed the idea of a convention to curb global warming, and the Rio meeting provided an opportunity to sign an agreement that had been finalized the month before. As usual, there was a split between the developing world and industrialized nations over who should pay for the technological advances necessary to address global warming. In addition, the United States split from its industrialized partners by opposing any hard targets for emissions levels. Without U.S. willingness to commit to anything specific, the convention was necessarily vague. Signatory nations agreed that humans were causing climate change, that more research was necessary, and that they would meet five years later to set specific targets.

In 1997 they convened again at Kyoto, Japan, to update the climate change accord. Each nation received targets for reduced emissions of greenhouse gasses, with the U.S. target set at a 7 percent reduction on 1990 levels by 2012. The

Kyoto Protocol takes effect when at least fifty-five nations, which in aggregate produce 55 percent of the world's greenhouse gas emissions, ratify it, but as of 2001 only thirty-seven nations had in fact completed the ratification process. While the United States is one of eighty-four states to have signed the protocol, the Clinton administration did nothing to move it forward in the Senate. Once again the split between the developing and industrialized worlds presented an insurmountable obstacle. Under Kyoto, nations such as China and India have to make no firm commitments to reduce greenhouse gas emissions. Leaders of those nations argue that they deserve the opportunity to pursue economic growth as the West did before. But many opponents of the protocol in the United States say that they will not accept any agreement that does not commit every nation— and especially the two most populous—to some restrictions. In the fall of 2000, diplomats met at The Hague to iron out differences in the protocol, and they came very close to a deal that would have placated concerns of the United States and some of its allies, notably Canada, Australia, and Japan, by offering credits for the carbon absorption action of forests. European environmentalists took the lead in killing this compromise; within months the new U.S. president, George W. Bush, announced that the United States would no longer work within the Kyoto framework, which his aides described as "dead." Efforts to implement the Kyoto Protocol continued to go forward, but it seemed unlikely that greenhouse gas emissions could be curbed without the enthusiastic support of the United States.

The United States has by no means dropped from its active role in environmental diplomacy, even when various administrations are not strongly committed to environmentalism, and it still uses its power to cajole other countries into such conventions. The administration of the younger Bush surprised many people in the spring of 2001 by signing on to a convention to ban the use of persistent organic pollutants, such as DDT and PCBs. These chemicals have been outlawed in the United States for many years, but U.S. companies still exported them. Instead of focusing on lost export revenue, the administration noted accurately that the convention was necessary to stop these chemicals from winding up in the wind and water currents that bring them to the United States. Likewise, in twelve embassies around the world, the Department of State has recently established centers to promote regional environmental cooperation, which will in turn further the work of the department's Office of Oceans and International Environmental and Scientific Affairs. And yet the action of the Clinton and George W. Bush administrations toward the Kyoto Protocol makes clear several points: the United States, because of the sheer size of its economy and the vast cultural influence of its society, is still the most powerful force in environmental diplomacy; it is also now the power most likely to break up potentially stringent conventions; and unless the United States and the two future behemoths, China and India, can bridge their differences there will be little progress on environmental diplomacy. No global agreement on the use of resources can move forward if the prime consumers of resources fail to cooperate.

BIBLIOGRAPHY

Bailey, Thomas. "The North Pacific Sealing Convention of 1911." *Pacific Historical Review* 4 (1935): 1–14.

Benedick, Richard Elliot. *Ozone Diplomacy: New Directions in Safeguarding the Planet.* Enlarged ed. Cambridge, Mass., 1998. A fascinating firsthand account by a U.S. diplomat of international efforts to protect the ozone layer.

Campbell, Charles Jr. "The Anglo-American Crisis in the Bering Sea, 1890–1891." *Mississippi Valley Historical Review* 66 (1961): 395–410.

———. "The Bering Sea Settlements of 1892." *Pacific Historical Review* 32 (1963): 347–368.

Carroll, John E. *Environmental Diplomacy: An Examination and A Prospective of Canadian–U.S. Transboundary Environmental Relations.* Ann Arbor, Mich., 1983. Examines post-1945 issues in transborder pollution and shared resource use from a natural resources perspective.

Chacko, Chirakaikaran Joseph. *The International Joint Commission Between the United States of America and the Dominion of Canada.* New York, 1968. The best single study of the International Joint Commission.

Dorsey, Kurk. "Scientists, Citizens, and Statesmen: U.S.–Canadian Wildlife Protection Treaties in the Progressive Era." *Diplomatic History* 19 (1995): 407–430.

———. *The Dawn of Conservation Diplomacy: U.S.–Canadian Wildlife Protection Treaties in* the *Progressive Era*. Seattle, 1998. Analyzes early treaties to protect birds, seals, and fish in North America.

French, Hilary F. *Partnership for the Planet: An Environmental Agenda for the United Nations*. Washington, D.C., 1995. One of the leading members of the NGO community presents an agenda for future environmental diplomacy.

Hollick, Ann L. *U.S. Foreign Policy and the Law of the Sea*. Princeton, N.J., 1981.

Innis, Harold A. *The Cod Fisheries: The History of an International Economy*. Rev. ed. Toronto, 1978. A classic work in the field that examines the regulation and use of oceanic fisheries.

Levering, Ralph B., and Miriam L. Levering. *Citizen Action for Global Change: The Neptune Group and Law of the Sea*. Syracuse, N.Y., 1999. Demonstrates the roles of private citizens in shaping UNCLOS III.

Lytle, Mark. "An Environmental Approach to American Diplomatic History." *Diplomatic History* 20 (1996): 279–300. The first work that any historian interested in environmental diplomacy should read.

McNeill, J. R. *Something New Under the Sun: An Environmental History of the Twentieth-Century World*. New York, 2000. An ambitious synthesis and analysis of modern global environmentalism.

Roos, John F. *Restoring Fraser River Salmon: A History of the International Pacific Salmon Fisheries Commission, 1937–1985*. Vancouver, 1991.

Sand, Peter H., ed. *The Effectiveness of International Environmental Agreements: A Survey of Existing Legal Instruments*. Cambridge, 1992.

Susskind, Lawrence E. *Environmental Diplomacy: Negotiating More Effective Global Agreements*. New York, 1994.

Tolba, Mostafa K. *Global Environmental Diplomacy: Negotiating Environmental Agreements for the World, 1973–1992*. Cambridge, Mass., 1998. One of the UN's leading environmental diplomats draws lessons from twenty years of work.

Tønnessen, J. N., and A. O. Johnsen. *The History of Modern Whaling*. Translated by R. I. Christophersen. Berkeley, Calif., 1982. The best single volume on whaling, the whaling commission, and the whaling industry.

Tucker, Richard P. *Insatiable Appetite: The United States and the Ecological Degradation of the Tropical World*. Berkeley, Calif., 2000. Shows the environmental impact of the U.S. informal empire.

Wirth, John D. *Smelter Smoke in North America: The Politics of Transborder Pollution*. Lawrence, Kans., 2000. The most valuable interpretation of the Trail Smelter Case and subsequent U.S.–Mexican pollution problems.

Young, Oran R., George J. Demko, and Kilaparti Ramakrishna, eds. *Global Environmental Change and International Governance*. Hanover, N.H., 1996. A number of political scientists analyze the new trends in environmental diplomacy and their impacts on sovereignty.

See also ARBITRATION, MEDIATION, AND CONCILIATION; GLOBALIZATION; SCIENCE AND TECHNOLOGY; TREATIES.

EXCEPTIONALISM

Trevor B. McCrisken

"American exceptionalism" is a term used to describe the belief that the United States is an extraordinary nation with a special role to play in human history; a nation that is not only unique but also superior. Alexis de Tocqueville was the first to use the term "exceptional" to describe the United States and the American people in his classic work *Democracy in America* (1835–1840), but the idea of America as an exceptional entity can be traced back to the earliest colonial times. Jack P. Greene's analysis of a wealth of contemporary materials has established that by "the beginning of the nineteenth century the idea of America as an exceptional entity had long been an integral component in the identification of America." Many scholars of the belief in American exceptionalism argue that it forms one of the core elements of American national identity and American nationalism. Deborah Madsen, for example, contends that exceptionalism is "one of the most important concepts underlying modern theories of American cultural identity." It is a central part of the American belief system or what Benedict Anderson calls its "imagined community."

The ways in which U.S. foreign policy is made and conducted are influenced by the underlying assumptions that Americans hold about themselves and the rest of the world. Like most nations, the United States has a distinctive pattern of policymaking that is determined by unique aspects of its national culture. Each country's historical and cultural heritage, its montage of national beliefs and experience—its national identity—has an influence, whether consciously or not, upon the way it practices politics. U.S. foreign policy is driven by a variety of causal factors including strategic, economic, political, and bureaucratic interests; international and domestic pressures; the personalities and agendas of policymakers; and the actions of other nations. However, the belief in exceptionalism, since it is a core element of American national identity, has an important underlying influence on foreign policy activity. This belief is one of the main ideas that, according to Michael Hunt, has "performed for generations of Americans that essential function of giving order to their vision of the world and defining their place in it." Although such views are not "codified in formal, systemic terms," Hunt shows that the evidence for their existence and influence can be found in the "private musings" of policymakers and, more importantly, "the public rhetoric by which they have justified their actions and communicated their opinions to one another and to the nation." The belief in American exceptionalism provides an essential element of the cultural and intellectual framework for the making and conduct of U.S. foreign policy.

Two main strands of exceptionalist thought have influenced U.S. foreign policy. One is that of the United States as an exemplar nation, as reflected in ideas such as the "city upon a hill," nonentangling alliances, "anti-imperialism," "isolationism," and "Fortress America." The other, often more dominant strand is that of the missionary nation, as represented by the ideas of "manifest destiny," "imperialism," "internationalism," "leader of the free world," "modernization theory," and the "new world order." Both strands have been present throughout the history of U.S. foreign relations.

WHAT IS EXCEPTIONALISM?

The focus here is on the belief in American exceptionalism and its influence on U.S. foreign policy rather than directly addressing the question of whether U.S. foreign policy itself can be measured as exceptional. Indeed, Joseph Lepgold and Timothy McKeown have found little empirical evidence for claims that American foreign policy behavior is exceptional. Faults and blemishes riddle American history as much as that of any other nation. In foreign policy, the United States has a far from untarnished record. The colonization and expansion of the new nation were accompanied by the displacement or destruction of the indigenous population. Times of war have been plentiful, with the United States imposing its will on peoples in countries as distant as the Philippines and Vietnam, ordering the internment of large numbers of its own citizens, and committing atrocities like any other warfaring nation. Yet despite the abundance of evidence indicating that the United States is just as fallible as any other nation, there has remained throughout American history a strong belief that the United States is an exceptional nation, not only unique but also superior among nations. As Daniel Bell (1989) has argued, in the United States "there has always been a strong belief in American exceptionalism. From the start, Americans have believed that destiny has marked their country as different from others—that the United States is, in Lincoln's marvelous phrase, 'an almost chosen nation.'"

Lepgold and McKeown observe that American leaders make "unusual internal justifications" for their actions abroad, using "idiosyncratic symbols and metaphors . . . based on national self-image and values." It is the belief in American exceptionalism that most commonly provides these symbols and metaphors. Throughout American history, exceptionalist belief has framed the discourse of foreign policymaking by providing the underlying assumptions and terms of reference for foreign policy debate and conduct. Scholars disagree, however, over whether exceptionalism amounts to an ideology as such. Michael Hunt argues that the belief in "national greatness" is a central element of the ideology behind U.S. foreign policy. Alternatively, Siobhan McEvoy-Levy contends that exceptionalism amounts to a "para-ideology" because its influence underwrites much of U.S. foreign policy but it does not have the coherence of a traditional ideology. John Dumbrell argues that American democratic liberalism is the ideology underpinning U.S. foreign policy but a belief in American exceptionalism is a central element of that ideology. It was Richard Hofstadter who observed, "It has been our fate as a nation not to have ideologies but to be one." The idea of "America" as a bastion of democracy, liberty, equality, individualism, and constitutionalism has given meaning and identity to millions of Americans throughout U.S. history (see Huntington, chapter 2). American nationalism, according to Hans Kohn, is not built on the usual elements of nationhood such as shared language, culture, common descent, or historical territory, but on "an idea which singled out the new nation among the nations of the earth." This idea was a "universal message" that American values and principles would benefit the whole of humankind. John Fousek agrees that this belief in the exceptionalism of the United States is a "core theme of American nationalism" that has been expressed most commonly in the "long-standing tradition of thought about American chosenness, mission, and destiny." Anders Stephanson has also shown how a "destinarian discourse" accompanied nineteenth-century American expansion and how it continued to shape the way Americans understood their place in the world during the twentieth century. The belief in American exceptionalism has been central to the formation of American national identity, and thus can be seen to have provided a significant part of the cultural and intellectual framework within which foreign policy has been made.

THE BELIEF IN AMERICAN EXCEPTIONALISM

Exceptionalism is a fluid and adaptive idea that can be interpreted in different ways. Therefore it is necessary not only to identify its major assumptions but also to consider its two main strands—the exemplary and the missionary—and the outcomes these different views have for foreign policy. Three main elements of exceptionalist belief have remained relatively consistent throughout American history.

First and foremost is the belief that the United States is a special nation with a special role to play in human history. Throughout American history there have been repeated claims that the United States is the promised land and its citizens are the chosen people, divinely ordained to lead the world to betterment. This notion goes back to the very beginnings of colonization. The New World was regarded as a virgin land upon which its new inhabitants could attempt to perfect society through social, political, and religious experiment. Americans have been charged by God with the task of reforming themselves and the world—they are a redeemer nation. The United States is thus guided by the invisible hand of God, and American actions are the result of divine will. At the same time, though, the chosen people are exposed to temptation and corruption, most often from abroad or from subversives within. Americans are thus being constantly tested and must undergo continual self-inspection. When they do seem to fail or commit wrongdoing, it is because the forces of evil are working against them. But even in such circumstances, Americans maintain their purity because their intentions are good and they will strive on with their national experiment.

The second main element of exceptionalist belief is the New World's separateness and difference from the Old World of Europe. In Europe, Americans believed, self-interested monarchies exploited the majority of their own people, then sought imperial expansion abroad to increase their treasures, boost their reputations, and increase their power relative to other monarchies. The political systems were invariably corrupt, and pandered to the needs and desires of the traditional elites, leaving little or no means for commoners to improve their lot in life. In contrast, the New World was committed to freedom, morality, and the betterment of humankind.

The third main element of exceptionalism is the belief that the United States, unlike other great nations, is not destined to rise and fall. Americans will escape the "laws of history" which eventually cause the decay and downfall of all great nations and empires. Americans believe their nation is the leader of progress in the world. Practically everything that the United States does as a nation is regarded as pushing forward the boundaries of human achievement, be it in politics, industry, technology, sports, the arts, even warfare. Certainly there are some mistakes made, but they are few, they are learned from, and they are improved upon at the next attempt. No matter how many setbacks they may face along the way, Americans will continue forward resolutely, striving for progress toward forming an ever more perfect union. Americans think of themselves as exceptional, then, not necessarily in what they are but in what they could be. For this reason the sense of exceptionalism can never die, no matter how unexceptional the nation may appear in reality. Exceptionalism persists because of what it promises just as much as, if not more than, what it delivers. It is tied to what it means to be an American: to have faith in the values and principles that caused the nation to be founded and to continue to exist.

Advocates of both the exemplary and the missionary strands of exceptionalist belief tend to share each of these assumptions. Where they differ is in how they believe these assumptions should translate into American actions with regard to the rest of the world. All exceptionalists believe very strongly in the basic benevolence of their actions toward other nations. National motives are not perceived as being driven solely by the desire for material gain but also by a dedication to principles of liberty and freedom for all humankind. A corollary of this belief is that it is the duty of the United States to help the rest of the world follow the example of the chosen people.

Followers of the exemplary strand of American exceptionalism have mostly advocated that the United States remain somewhat aloof from the world's troubles and lead by example. Americans should strive to perfect their own society as much as possible without interfering in the affairs of others. To intervene abroad, the exemplarists argue, not only would probably harm the other nation but also most likely would undermine the American experiment at home. Far better, then, that the United States should have peaceful trade relations abroad but concentrate on building a model society for others to copy rather than forcing the benefits of American life on others.

Adherents to the missionary strand of American exceptionalism who advocate U.S. expansion or intervention in the affairs of other nations nevertheless believe that, unlike other nations, the United States is incapable of seeking dominion over other peoples in its self-interest. The American government will project its power abroad not to subjugate other nations but to help them become like the United States, to become free and democratic. These Americans seem to believe that inside every foreigner there is the potential, even the desire, to be an American. To be an American, after all, is not a birthright but the willingness to believe in a certain set of political and social principles and values. The missionary strand of American exceptionalism suggests that all the people of the world want to be like Americans, whether they realize it or not. This assumption has led Americans to find it very difficult to understand that other peoples may place different values on things and have different perceptions from Americans of how the world should be. In fact, both forms of exceptionalism hold, rather paradoxically, that the unique American political values and principles are actually universal in their nature. The United States is regarded as the embodiment of universal values based on the rights of all humankind—freedom, equality, and justice for all. It is the exceptional champion of these rights, but they are shared by all humans, whether they are Americans or not.

Certainly not all Americans believe wholeheartedly in all these aspects of American exceptionalism. Many Americans are all too aware that major problems exist within their society, many of which they may never adequately solve. They accept that in an increasingly interdependent world the United States cannot claim dominion in international affairs and that when they do intervene abroad, Americans very often undermine the very principles they claim to be defending. Scholars also disagree over the importance of the belief in American exceptionalism. The majority of the academic works on the history of U.S. foreign relations neglect or discount the influence of exceptionalist beliefs. Nevertheless, a growing body of scholarship does recognize that the belief in American exceptionalism has been a persistent and major underlying influence on U.S. foreign policy. These works recognize that despite the inherent contradictions and frequent circularity of exceptionalist thought, the "recurring rhetoric" of the belief in American exceptionalism reveals it to be what Michael Kammen has called "a cultural reality and potent force." The belief in American exceptionalism should not be dismissed as "mere rhetoric," but acknowledged as an important and influential idea that contributes to the framework of discourse in which "policymakers deal with specific issues and in which the attentive public understands those issues." This is not to say that the belief in exceptionalism is the root cause of all foreign policy. Although the following analysis reveals the prevalence of the belief in foreign policy discourse, it should be remembered that at every turn policy was shaped and driven by more tangible determinants such as the preservation of national security, the demand for overseas markets, or, indeed, the personal ambitions of policymakers. As Anders Stephanson makes clear in his study of manifest destiny, the destinarian discourse he identifies did not "cause" policy as such. It was, however, "of signal importance in the way the United States came to understand itself in the world and still does." The same is true about the broader idea of American exceptionalism—it is not "a mere rationalization" but often appears "in the guise of common sense."

THE ROOTS OF EXCEPTIONALISM

The idea of America as an exceptional entity dates back to colonial times. Its roots can be found in the thought of Puritan settlers who regarded the North American continent as a promised land where a new Canaan could be built as a model for the rest of the world. The earliest expression of this belief that continues to live on in American public memory comes from John Winthrop, a Puritan leader and first governor of the Massachusetts Bay colony. Winthrop delivered a lay sermon aboard the *Arbella,* during its passage to New England in 1630, in which he declared that his fellow settlers "must Consider that wee shall be as a Citty upon a Hill, the eies of all people are upon us." Winthrop's words were circulated in manuscript form and have since become one of the main formative texts of American self-identity and meaning. Inherent in this notion of the city on a hill is the belief that the American colonists, and those who have followed them, were uniquely blessed by God to pursue His work on Earth and to establish a society that would provide this beacon for the betterment of all humankind.

American exceptionalism, however, has not only religious but also secular roots. The American Revolution and the formative years of the new Republic reinforced the idea that the United States was a chosen nation which would be an experiment in human society. In his influential revolutionary pamphlet *Common Sense* (1776), Thomas Paine argued that it was America's separateness and difference from the Old World that demanded its independence. Paine saw America as a special land where humankind could "begin the world over again" by establishing a political society built on new, progressive ideas. The framers of the Constitution built on this idea in 1787. Theirs was to be an ambitious political experiment. The United States would be a society based on a republican system of government ensuring the preservation of certain individual rights. Although they were relatively pessimistic about its chances, the framers' greatest hope was that the constitutional framework they had created would allow the United States to develop over time into the most perfect republican society in the world. The geographic isolation of the American continent from Europe seemed to offer hope that the United States could protect itself from falling prey to the degenerative nature of the Old World. As Thomas Jefferson observed in his First Inaugural Address (March 1801), the United States was "kindly separated by nature and a wide ocean from the exterminating havoc of one quarter of the globe; too high-minded to endure the degradations of others." Jefferson and others did not suggest that Americans would be immune from temptation, but they did indicate that, with eternal vigilance, the United States could be prevented from succumbing to the same vices that had destroyed other great nations.

Providential and republican ideology thus combined to firmly entrench the idea of exceptionalism at the center of American national identity. In these early forms it was initially the exemplar strand of exceptionalism that clearly dominated. The United States would provide a model of freedom, liberty, and democracy from which the rest of the world could learn. It would be an example, a beacon of light—a city on a hill. In early U.S. foreign policy, the notion of the United States as a separate, aloof nation was also dominant, but would come to be challenged by a growing missionary spirit as the Republic became stronger and more successful.

THE INFLUENCE OF EXCEPTIONALIST BELIEFS ON FOREIGN AFFAIRS

In the earliest years of the Republic, both George Washington and Thomas Jefferson called upon Americans to actively seek to preserve their nation's unique position of aloofness from the world's ills. In his Farewell Address of 1796, Washington warned against "permanent alliances," while Jefferson, in his First Inaugural Address (March 1801), advised that Americans should avoid "entangling alliances." Such pronouncements laid the foundations for a foreign policy characterized by high levels of unilateralism and so-called isolationism. Jefferson nevertheless presided over the first major expansion of the United States with the Louisiana Purchase (1803) and contributed to the notion that a republic needed to grow in order to remain healthy with his view of the United States as an "empire for liberty."

President James Monroe further emphasized the difference between American and European intentions in foreign affairs on 2 December 1823, in what became known as the Monroe Doctrine. Monroe declared the Western Hemisphere closed to European colonization, warned against European interference in the affairs of the Americas, and signaled the intention of the United States to be the region's dominant power. Although the Monroe Doctrine was based largely on strategic interest, it was couched in terms consistent with the belief in exceptionalism. Monroe stressed that the United States held nothing but goodwill toward the world's nations and emphasized that the U.S. policy of noninterference in European affairs marked it apart from the imperialistic nations of the Old World. As Monroe's Secretary of State John Quincy Adams had stated famously on 4 July 1821, the United States "goes not abroad, in search of monsters to destroy." Adams was expressing another crucial element of the conviction that the United States would avoid repeating the faults of the Old World. The United States is deemed exceptional because it is believed to be incapable of seeking dominion over others in its own self-interest. It would, then, avoid the temptations that had caused all great nations to seek expansion of their power by conquering and subjugating other peoples. If the United States did intervene abroad, it would be for the good of others, in the name of higher principles. As Adams insisted, America's "glory is not dominion, but liberty."

This belief in the basic benevolence of all U.S. actions abroad was further emphasized by President James K. Polk in his reassertion of the Monroe Doctrine on 2 December 1845. He emphasized that the United States had taken upon itself the responsibility not only for its own freedom and security but also for that of all the nations in the Western Hemisphere. According to Polk, the United States did not pursue wars of conquest, but it would do whatever necessary to defend the independence of the Americas. It would not tolerate the interference of a self-interested imperial power in its region yet, paradoxically, it considered its own interference in a neighbor's affairs as being to the benefit of the neighbor. Such a policy was, of course, the declaration of an ambitious state seeking hemispheric dominance. But subsumed within the doctrine was an assumption that American intervention would not amount to self-interested foreign interference. According to the tradition of exceptionalism, the United States is incapable of doing ill to others, and therefore the nature of its interference in the Americas would be inherently more benign than that of any other foreign power. Polk stretched the credibility of such claims with the war against Mexico in 1846. In his public rhetoric, he justified his ambitions for the acquisition of new land and the provocative nature of his actions toward Mexico by couching the conflict in terms that were consistent with his pronouncements on the exceptional nature of U.S. foreign relations, and cast the United States as the innocent party. Indeed, a new phrase had entered the

American vocabulary that helped explain westward expansion as an integral part of American exceptionalism.

MANIFEST DESTINY

The war with Mexico and the annexations of Mexican territory that followed were believed by most Americans to be the result of their "manifest destiny." The term is generally attributed to John L. O'Sullivan, a Democratic newspaper editor from New York. O'Sullivan's conception of manifest destiny came to national attention through an editorial in the *New York Morning News* on 27 December 1845, which claimed the right of the United States to Oregon territory disputed by the British: "And that claim is by the right of our manifest destiny to overspread and to possess the whole of the continent which Providence has given us for the development of the great experiment of Liberty and federated self-government entrusted to us."

In his classic book *Manifest Destiny: A Study of Nationalist Expansion in American History* (1935), Albert K. Weinberg defines manifest destiny as being "in essence the doctrine that one nation has a preeminent social worth, a distinctively lofty mission, and consequently, unique rights in the application of moral principles." He relates how the idea soon became "a firmly established article of the national creed." The idea of manifest destiny is one of the clearest expressions of the belief in the exceptional nature of the United States. Territorial expansion was justified by Americans because they believed theirs was a special nation chosen by Providence to spread its virtues far and wide. As Weinberg has shown, nineteenth-century Americans laid claim to new land using a variety of justifications subsumed under the idea of manifest destiny. Americans believed they had a natural right to expand, and that territorial propinquity determined that they must spread across adjacent lands in North America. American expansion was also thought to be divinely blessed because it would cause the extension of democracy and freedom. Americans argued further that they should expand because they would use the land in ways more beneficial to and desirable for the progress of humankind than could its often sparsely distributed existing inhabitants.

The Mexican War saw a further element of manifest destiny emerge that became a central aspect of the belief in the exceptional nature of American interaction with other nations. Most Americans found moral vindication for the war in what Weinberg characterizes as "the conception of a religious duty to regenerate the unfortunate people of the enemy country by bringing them into the life-giving shrine of American democracy." The Mexican War seemed to confirm the belief among Americans that if the United States did involve itself in the affairs of other peoples, it was not in order to subjugate them but to help them realize their right to the same liberties and freedoms for which Americans had fought in the War of Independence. Countless Mexicans and Native Americans may have perceived events rather differently, but that was of little concern to the exceptional vanguards of civilization and progress.

By the mid-nineteenth century, then, with westward expansion justified by manifest destiny, the missionary strand of exceptionalism was becoming the dominant form. At the end of the nineteenth century, with historian Frederick Jackson Turner having declared the frontier closed, Americans undertook an overseas intervention which is generally regarded as the event that signaled the arrival of the United States as a world power. The highly popular Spanish-American War of 1898 was supposedly fought to secure basic rights of freedom for the oppressed peoples in Cuba and other Spanish colonies. Yet the war gave way to a conflict in the Philippines that left blood on American hands and ignited a nationwide debate over whether the United States was living up to its principles as an exceptional nation or whether it would assume an empire in the tradition of the Old World powers.

THE IMPERIALISM DEBATE AND EXCEPTIONALISM

The Spanish-American War was described by Secretary of State John Hay as "a splendid little war; begun with the highest motives, carried on with magnificent intelligence and spirit, favored by that Fortune which loves the brave." When the war began, little thought was given, at least publicly, to the possibility of an American empire. Yet no sooner had American forces begun to win victories over the Spanish than calls for annexations became widespread. The Treaty of Paris, which officially ended the war on 10 December 1898, recognized eventual Cuban independence, but provided for

EXPRESSIONS OF EXCEPTIONALISM

"Wee must Consider that wee shall be as a Citty upon a Hill, the eies of all people are upon us."

— *John Winthrop, "A Modell of Christian Charity" (1630)* —

"It will be worthy of a free, enlightened, and at no great distant period a great nation to give to mankind the magnanimous and too novel example of a people always guided by an exalted justice and benevolence."

— *George Washington, Farewell Address, 17 September 1796* —

"America . . . goes not abroad, in search of monsters to destroy. She is the well-wisher to the freedom and independence of all."

— *Secretary of State John Quincy Adams, Fourth of July Address, 1821* —

"And that claim [to Oregon] is by the right of our manifest destiny to overspread and to possess the whole of the continent which Providence has given us for the development of the great experiment of Liberty and federated self-government entrusted to us."

— *John L. O'Sullivan, New York Morning News, 27 December 1845* —

"Destiny has laid upon our country the responsibility of the free world's leadership."

— *Dwight D. Eisenhower, First Inaugural Address, 20 January 1953* —

"Let every nation know, whether it wishes us well or ill, that we shall pay any price, bear any burden, meet any hardship, support any friend, oppose any foe to assure the survival and success of liberty. . . . [T]he energy, the faith, the devotion which we bring to this endeavor will light our country and all who serve it—and the glow from that fire can truly light the world."

— *John F. Kennedy, Inaugural Address, 20 January 1961* —

"Our [foreign] policy is designed to serve mankind."

— *Jimmy Carter, commencement address at University of Notre Dame, 22 May 1977* —

"Americans resort to force only when we must. We have never been aggressors. We have always struggled to defend freedom and democracy. We have no territorial ambitions. We occupy no territories."

— *Ronald Reagan, State of the Union Address, 25 January 1984* —

"The fact is America remains the indispensable nation. America, and only America, can make a difference between war and peace, between freedom and repression, between hope and fear [in the world]."

— *Bill Clinton, address at George Washington University, 5 August 1996* —

---

the cession to the United States of Spain's other colonies in the Philippines, Puerto Rico, and Guam. What ensued was a protracted and bloody struggle for control of the Philippines that caused many Americans, known as the "anti-imperialists," to openly question the annexation policy.

The great debate over American overseas expansion saw the two main strands of exceptionalist belief come into direct conflict with one another. Americans on both sides of the imperialism debate utilized arguments based on their beliefs about the exceptional nature of the United States. They did so even when they recognized what they regarded as legitimate economic, strategic, political, racial, or constitutional reasons for or against the annexation of overseas territories.

The commercial and strategic advantages of annexation provided the rationale for most expansionists. Yet many expansionists also expressed their conviction that annexation was a morally acceptable policy because it was the duty of the United States, as God's emissary, to extend freedom and democracy whenever possible. It was their divine destiny that called the Americans to free Cuba, the Philippines, Puerto Rico, and Guam from the grip of Old World imperialism. They believed it was the special duty of the United States to help those people overcome oppression and guide them toward the light of the principles of liberty and freedom. The expansionists frequently argued that America was not simply imposing its own brand of Old World imperialism. Rather, they argued, it was adopting these childlike nations so they could be nurtured to maturity and statehood. In time, once they were ready, these nations could choose for themselves whether to be independent or join the Union. The imperialists, drawing upon the tradition of manifest destiny, were strong believers in and advocates of the missionary strand of American exceptionalism.

The anti-imperialists, on the other hand, had a different view of the special American role in the world that reflected the exemplar strand of exceptionalism. They were more concerned that, having ousted the Spanish, the United States should leave the liberated states to determine their own destinies, in keeping with the American dedication to the idea that governments derive their power from the consent of the governed. The anti-imperialists emphasized the aspects of exceptionalism that regard the United States as being above the meddling immorality of Old World imperialists. They argued that the United States is special because it does not involve itself in the affairs of others, particularly not a nation on the far side of the Pacific Ocean that could hardly be considered within the U.S. geographic sphere of influence. As Charles Eliot Norton made clear, he and his fellow anti-imperialists believed that the transformation of the United States into an imperial power "sounded the close of the America exceptionally blessed among the nations." The anti-imperialists aimed to preserve the exceptionalist nature of the U.S. by preventing Americans from seeking dominion over other peoples in the way that other world powers did. As well as moral arguments, they also gave political, economic, constitutional, diplomatic, racial, and historical reasons for their opposition to annexations. But although their individual opposition varied, the essence of their protest was that they feared the United States was acting in a manner inconsistent with the principles laid down by the Founders. Thus both imperialists and anti-imperialists believed they were arguing for conduct consistent with the idea that the United States was an exceptional nation with a special role to play in human history. They both agreed that the U.S. was different from—indeed, better than—other nations; where they disagreed was on the precise nature of that exceptionalism.

THE BEGINNING OF THE TWENTIETH CENTURY

The anti-imperialists failed to raise widespread public opposition to the McKinley administration's annexation policy. They could not convince the American public that the policy was contrary to American principles, and consequently the Philippine insurrection was defeated, and Puerto Rico, Guam, and the Philippines were annexed. Despite their inability to prevent the annexations and the suppression of the Philippine insurrection, the anti-imperialists were a useful check against the annexationist fever and contributed to the return to the more usual American sentiment of anticolonialism. While the anti-imperialist movement quickly faded after the failed presidential candidacy of William Jennings Bryan in 1900, so did the desire for American imperialism. While European powers were partitioning China, the United States called for an open door trade policy and the protection of China's territorial and political independence.

That the American desire for overseas possessions had subsided appeared to be confirmed on 6 December 1904 by one of expansion's greatest advocates. President Theodore Roosevelt reaffirmed the belief that Americans did not seek imperial dominion over other nations. In a speech adding a further corollary to the Monroe Doctrine, he proclaimed: "It is not true that the United States feels any land hunger or entertains any projects as regards the other nations of the Western Hemisphere save such that are for their welfare." Roosevelt made clear that he believed the United States had nothing but benign intentions with regard to foreign relations. However, he did stress that the United States felt an obligation to help protect the freedom of peoples in the Americas not only, as Monroe had declared, in the face of foreign aggression but also if their citizens faced internal threats to their freedom.

In his speech, Roosevelt effectively pulled together the two main strands of exceptionalist belief. As a rule, he argued, the United States should stay out of the affairs of other nations and concentrate on forging a more perfect union in the spirit of the Founders, thus providing an ever more appropriate example for the rest of the world to follow. However, when extreme circumstances demanded it, the United States, as the chosen nation, had the "manifest duty" to protect the rights that it promoted if their survival was threatened abroad. Roosevelt's reasoning would help define foreign policy discourse for many years to come, with the tension between these two elements of exceptionalism often at the center of debate.

WOODROW WILSON AND EXCEPTIONALISM

In many ways, Woodrow Wilson personified the belief in American exceptionalism. As Robert E. Osgood argues: "Wilson's national altruism . . . was an integral part of his temperament and his philosophy of life, inseparable from his personality." Wilson's idealism was firmly grounded in the belief that the United States was a nation set apart by its values and principles from the rest of the world. He believed strongly that the "force of America is the force of moral principle" and that the "idea of America is to serve humanity." Long before he became president, Wilson wrote of his conviction that the United States had a "plain destiny [to] serve [rather than] subdue the world." Later, as president, he would contend that this destiny to serve was the only possible motivation for American actions in the world. Wilson held that "morality not expediency" must be the guiding principle of all American policy. He applied this principle to the use of American military force. As Frederick Calhoun argues, Wilson "showed no aversion to fighting if the end justified the means." As Wilson stated, he believed that while other nations used force "for the oppression of mankind and their own aggrandizement," the United States would use force only "for the elevation of the spirit of the human race."

Wilson declared that "the United States will never again seek one additional foot of territory by conquest." Nevertheless, he frequently used military intervention in efforts to help other peoples become, in his opinion, more democratic and orderly. Wilson sent American troops into Mexico twice, to Haiti, the Dominican Republic, and Cuba, as well as maintaining the military "protection" of Nicaragua. He also intervened militarily twice in the Russian civil war. Wilson best expressed his attitude toward such interventions in 1914: "They say the Mexicans are not fitted for self-government and to this I reply that, when properly directed, there is no people not fitted for self-government." Wilson was a clear advocate of the missionary strand of American exceptionalism.

When Wilson finally made the decision to enter World War I in April 1917, he justified his action in highly idealistic terms that enabled the American people to come to regard the war as a crusade. Most famously, the determination to "make the world safe for democracy" was proclaimed by President Wilson as he asked Congress for a declaration of war against Germany. The United States, in keeping with its traditions, was joining the hostilities according to Wilson with nothing but the most benign intentions and a sense of a higher purpose. Portraying involvement in the conflict as a just cause in terms consistent with the belief in American exceptionalism was a direct and deliberate appeal to the public and a way to help silence opposition. It was also the only way that Wilson could assuage his own doubts about American involvement in the war. The rhetoric that accompanied intervention made it clear that the United States, in keeping with its strongest principles, was taking a stand against autocratic tyranny, much as it had against the British in the American Revolution and against the Spanish over Cuba. Wilson argued that a peaceful and harmonious postwar international order based on the principle of universal freedom and democracy, as enshrined in the U.S. Constitution, could not be established while autocratic imperialism sought dominance in Europe. Although legitimate political, economic, and strategic justifications for intervention existed, American involvement in World War I was thus justified and conducted in terms consistent with the missionary strand of the belief in American exceptionalism.

ISOLATIONISM AND WORLD WAR II

The tradition of nonentanglement with the affairs of Europe and other countries found a new name in the interwar years: isolationism. The U.S. Senate rejected President Wilson's vision of an international organization, the League of Nations, committed to maintaining world peace through arbitration of conflict and mutual respect of the independence and territorial integrity of all member states. Isolationists believed the United States should not be under obligation to any other nation. As Jefferson, Washington, and others had observed, the United States was uniquely blessed with geographic isolation from the degeneracy of the Old World. With friendly, unthreatening neighbors at its northern and southern borders and vast oceans to the east and west, the United States had little to fear from foreign attack. Why should it jeopardize this exceptional degree of peace and security by involving itself with the affairs of others? Wilson's successor, President Warren G. Harding, made clear in his Inaugural Address (March 1921) that "Confident of our ability to work out our own destiny, and jealously guarding our right to do so, we seek no part in directing the destinies of the Old World. We do not mean to be entangled."

Harding and others did not believe that the United States should have no contact whatsoever with the outside world, but that it should remain aloof from the petty squabbles and adversarial alliances common in Europe while maintaining its traditional interests within its own hemisphere. It would seek to return to the role of having nothing but peaceful relations with others and to present an exemplary nation to which the rest of the world could aspire. The isolationists used language and arguments that were consistent with the exemplar strand of the belief in American exceptionalism.

The two strands of exceptionalism, however, again came into conflict during the interwar period. A major public debate took place between the isolationists and the "internationalists" who believed the United States had a duty to intervene in world affairs. When Britain and France declared war on Germany in September 1939, President Franklin Delano Roosevelt, as expected, declared U.S. neutrality. The isolationist impulse found enough popular approval to cause the Roosevelt administration to seek ways of assisting Britain and France short of intervening directly in the war. But this final popular attachment to isolationism was shattered by the surprise Japanese attack on the U.S. naval base at Pearl Harbor, Hawaii, and other American bases in the Pacific on 7 December 1941. The reality of a devastating military strike on American territory silenced isolationist claims. The threat posed by Germany and Japan was obvious enough to enable the public to base their support for joining the war on political and strategic reasoning, at least after Pearl Harbor. Yet Roosevelt still felt the need to employ exceptionalist rhetoric to justify American intervention. In his fireside chat to the nation following the Japanese attack, he assured the American people that "When we resort to force, as now we must, we are determined that this force shall be directed toward ultimate good as well as against immediate evil. We Americans are not destroyers—we are builders."

In January 1942, Roosevelt declared that American victory in the war would be a "victory for freedom." He made clear that a central U.S. war objective was to establish and secure "freedom of speech, freedom of religion, freedom from want, and freedom from fear everywhere in the world." The "Four Freedoms" rooted the war effort in one of the central ideas of American political culture. The contrast between freedom and fascism was a central metaphor in American public discourse and official rhetoric throughout the war. Even before the United States entered the war, the Atlantic Charter (August 1941) had indicated that Roosevelt believed the United States must assume global responsibilities after Germany and Japan were defeated. To win the war would not be enough. An allied victory must lead to lasting peace and security in the world based upon universal values and principles traditionally espoused by Americans. To lead such a future was an American responsibility and duty that would not only promote U.S. interests but also those of all humankind. Roosevelt acknowledged that American power in itself brought responsibility, but he also invoked the providential idea that it was God's will. In his final inaugural address (20 January 1945), he claimed that God "has given to our country a faith which has become the hope of all peoples in an anguished world."

No matter how convincing the strategic or other tangible reasons for U.S. intervention in World War II, Roosevelt, like presidents before him, couched his justifications in terms consistent with the belief in the exceptional nature of the United States. That he did so when American security was so clearly threatened is substantial evidence that exceptionalism frames the discourse of U.S. foreign policymaking.

THE LEADER OF THE FREE WORLD

The allied victory in World War II seemed to confirm beyond doubt for Americans that the United

States was an exceptional nation with a special role to play in human history. Even before the United States entered the war, Henry Luce, the influential publisher of *Life* magazine, wrote an essay (17 February 1941) in which he declared that the twentieth century should be considered "the American Century." Luce argued that the United States must "accept wholeheartedly our duty and our opportunity as the most powerful and vital nation in the world and in consequence to exert upon the world the full impact of our influence . . . [with] . . . a passionate devotion to great American ideals." By 1945, Luce's vision seemed correct. The United States not only stood victorious but also was the strongest nation in the world militarily and economically. But rather than retreat to the role of exemplar, it remained engaged in world affairs in the postwar years to a greater extent than ever before.

The United States pursued a foreign policy of activist internationalism after World War II as it replaced one global enemy with another. Soviet communism and its containment soon became the focus of U.S. foreign policy as more than forty years of Cold War began. Although strategic, economic and political interests were its central determinants, U.S. Cold War foreign policy and the broad public consensus that supported it were underpinned by an ideology of what John Fousek identifies as "American nationalist globalism" that was rooted in the missionary strand of the belief in American exceptionalism. Anders Stephanson agrees that the "operative framework" of Cold War policy was "the story of American exceptionalism, with its missionary implications."

President Harry S. Truman has been described as "a staunch exponent of American exceptionalism" who frequently referred to the United States as "the greatest nation that the sun ever shone upon." For Truman, the victory in World War II demonstrated American greatness, but it also placed on the United States the responsibility of ensuring peace and freedom in the postwar world. Successive presidents and other public officials and opinion leaders persistently portrayed the Cold War in stark, Manichean terms as a battle between good and evil. The United States was "the leader of the free world" that must prevail and save humanity from the "evils" of communism. Truman provided the guiding principles for American Cold War policy during an address to a joint session of the Congress on 12 March 1947 which became famous for containing the so-called Truman Doctrine. It was the duty of the United States, he contended, to do whatever was necessary to protect the rights of free, democratic nations around the world. In keeping with its traditions, the president claimed, America did not seek dominion over those nations in exchange for their freedom. Truman assured the Congress that "I believe that we must assist free peoples to work out their own destinies in their own way." The task facing the United States was a critical one, he declared, if the values and principles that it held so dear were to survive the challenge of communism and truly enable the world to be led out of darkness: "The free peoples of the world look to us for support in maintaining their freedoms. If we falter in our leadership, we may endanger the peace of the world—and we shall surely endanger the welfare of our own Nation."

Following World War II, President Truman believed that merely to provide an example for the rest of the world to follow would no longer be enough. He was arguing that the United States, as the chosen nation, must take up the gauntlet and defend the rights of free peoples everywhere against what Americans regarded as totalitarian aggression and subversion. The Cold War ethos was, then, firmly grounded in the missionary strand of American exceptionalism. The Truman Doctrine helped define the policy of containment toward the Soviet Union and its allies that was employed by successive U.S. administrations during the cold war. Each of Truman's successors also utilized the language and ideas of American exceptionalism to reinforce the nature of the battle with communism.

Yet it was not only in presidential public rhetoric that the Cold War was defined and discussed in terms of ideas about American destiny, duty and exceptionalism. For example, George Kennan, the original architect of the containment policy, ended his influential article "The Sources of Soviet Conduct" in the journal *Foreign Affairs* (July 1947) by arguing: "The issue of Soviet-American relations is in essence a test of the overall worth of the United States as a nation among nations. To avoid destruction the United States need only measure up to its own best traditions and prove itself worthy of preservation as a great nation." He claimed that the "thoughtful observer" would not object to the Cold War but would "rather experience a certain gratitude to a Providence which, by providing the American people with this implacable challenge, has made their entire security as a nation dependent on their pulling themselves together and accepting the responsibilities of moral and political leadership that history plainly intended them to bear." Kennan, who was often critical of moralism in foreign policy, had nonetheless used the traditional language of exceptionalism to advocate his strategy for containing Soviet communism.

During the Cold War, as Michael Hunt has observed, the private communications of policymakers and even secret national security documents were frequently "couched in the stark and sweeping terms usually reserved for crusades." For example, the authors of the secret National Security Council Paper Number 68 (NSC 68), the document that defined the course of U.S. Cold War policy in 1950, made clear that "Our position as the center of power in the free world places a heavy responsibility upon the United States for leadership." They described the Cold War as "a basic conflict between the idea of freedom under a government of laws, and the idea of slavery under the grim oligarchy of the Kremlin." It was "imperative" that the forces of "freedom" prevail, so the United States must, therefore, build up its political, economic, and military strength. This document was designed only for the eyes of other policymakers yet it was built around the idea of free world leadership that, as Fousek argues, "became the controlling metaphor in U.S. foreign policy discourse throughout the postwar period."

Many Cold War policies reflected exceptionalist assumptions about the American role in the world. The Marshall Plan (1947) for the economic reconstruction of postwar Western Europe was designed to revive European economies using not only American money but also practices and principles. The United States, in the tradition of the redeemer nation, was fulfilling its responsibility of leadership through a program that not only provided benefits for itself but also for the peoples of war-torn Europe. Similarly, modernization theory provided the rationale for much U.S. Cold War policy toward the developing world, particularly during the Kennedy administration. Modernization theorists believed that all societies pass through sequential stages of progress from "traditional" to "modern" and that the West, and in particular the United States, was the "common endpoint" to which all peoples must irresistibly move. Significantly, these influential social scientists also argued that the United States could help underdeveloped countries along the way from being stagnant, traditional societies to active, modern ones—a transition which would not only bring advantages to the peoples of those societies but also to the United States. What made this theory so appealing, according to Michael Latham, was that it gave an "objective" justification for U.S. intervention in other nation's affairs; it provided a useful weapon in the Cold War struggle with the Soviet Union; and it also fit with American values and traditions, in particular the notion that the United States is an exceptional nation with a mission and duty to be the engine of human progress. As Latham observes "modernization reinforced the connections between strategic concerns and assumptions about America's role as a moral, benevolent world leader." Modernization theory shaped the formation, influenced the major practices, and informed the public presentations of so-called "nation building" programs such as the Alliance for Progress with Latin America, the Peace Corps, and the Strategic Hamlet Program in Vietnam. Each program was designed to exemplify the altruistic, benevolent impulses of the United States while also being advocated as an objective, scientifically proven method for aiding developing nations. In the early 1960s, Latham contends, the strength and influence of modernization as an ideology ensured the "continuing power of the widespread belief that America was both called to and capable of remaking the rest of the world."

Not all Americans, however, accepted uncritically the tenets of the Cold War consensus. African Americans in particular focused on the apparent contradiction of the U.S. demanding freedom and democracy throughout the world when such rights were still widely denied to large numbers of its own citizens at home. The civil rights movement used claims of America's leadership of the free world to argue that racial equality must also be achieved in the United States. Such demands contributed to the many advancements made in race relations during the 1950s and 1960s. On the whole, though, raising objections to the Cold War consensus was difficult, even dangerous, particularly during the earlier years of the Cold War, not least because foreign policy dissent was frequently equated with "fundamental disloyalty to the nation and its values."

By the late 1960s, however, much of the Cold War consensus had begun to break down and large numbers of Americans were questioning the direction of U.S. foreign policy, particularly toward Vietnam. The intervention in Vietnam had been conceived in terms consistent with the belief that the United States was the leader of the free world with a duty to contain communism and protect "free peoples" from aggression. But the war's conduct and the resultant defeat of American objectives would raise serious doubts about both the Cold War consensus and the exceptional nature of the United States.

VIETNAM AND THE END OF AMERICAN EXCEPTIONALISM?

In 1975, following the fall of Saigon, the sociologist Daniel Bell declared "The End of American Exceptionalism." He argued that the "American Century . . . foundered on the shoals of Vietnam." Bell concluded: "Today, the belief in American exceptionalism has vanished with the end of empire, the weakening of power, the loss of faith in the nation's future." The chastening experience of Vietnam had made Americans realize that "We are a nation like all other nations."

Americans invariably refer to the Vietnam War as a tragedy or a national trauma. Vietnam divided opinion in the country as no other event had since the Civil War. It contributed to the breakdown in the Cold War foreign policy consensus. It diverted resources from domestic reform programs and caused high levels of inflation and national debt. It created an atmosphere of distrust and even hostility between the public and the government. The United States had failed to achieve its objectives in Vietnam. For the first time in the nation's history, the United States had lost a war. Americans could not help but feel that all the lives and resources expended in Vietnam had been wasted. The United States was supposed to be an exceptional nation, above the corrupt immorality of the rest of the world. Yet in Vietnam its leaders had conducted a war whose legitimacy was questionable and whose objectives were often unclear and increasingly unattainable. The nation's leaders were accused of employing inhumane forms of warfare and of persistently lying to the American people about how the war was progressing and what was being done to bring about a victory. This sense that the American people could no longer trust their leaders was further compounded by the events and revelations surrounding the Watergate affair. The United States seemed to have shown itself to be just as fallible and unexceptional as any other nation in history. The experience of Vietnam raised serious doubts among Americans about the traditional belief that the United States is an exceptional nation.

Yet there was evidence to suggest that the idea of the United States as an exceptional nation would survive the defeat in Vietnam. As in previous times of domestic disagreement over foreign policy content and direction, advocates on both sides of the Vietnam issue utilized the rhetoric of exceptionalism in their arguments. President Johnson and others used the language of exceptionalism to justify American intervention. Meanwhile, the opposition of many of the war's protesters stemmed from a belief that the United States was conducting itself in ways that were inconsistent with the values and principles upon which the nation was founded. That did not necessarily mean that those opponents rejected such values. On the contrary, many believed they must oppose the war in order for those values to be reaffirmed. Like the anti-imperialists of 1898, those who opposed the Vietnam War often did so in terms that were consistent with the belief in American exceptionalism. Although the belief in exceptionalism was certainly shaken by the events surrounding Vietnam, the continued use of its rhetoric during the war indicated that the belief would survive this latest "trauma" or "time of trial" in American history.

EXCEPTIONALISM AND THE LEGACY OF VIETNAM

The experience of the Vietnam War, the Watergate scandal, and the other "traumas" of the 1960s and early 1970s caused many Americans to doubt or even cease to believe that their nation's actions were consistent with the values and principles upon which their society was supposed to function. Following Vietnam, Americans suffered what was labeled a "crisis of confidence" concerning the future of their nation and its purpose in the world. But the belief in American exceptionalism was not destroyed by the experiences of Vietnam and Watergate. Indeed, each post-Vietnam president consistently attempted to bolster American self-confidence and revive the perceived moral legitimacy of U.S. foreign policy, usually by rhetorically justifying actions in terms consistent with the belief in American exceptionalism.

Jimmy Carter's self-proclaimed objective was to restore the "moral compass" to the making of U.S. foreign policy. He attempted to follow a foreign policy rooted in what he perceived as the values and principles upon which the United States was founded. Carter attempted to conduct a foreign policy consistent with the belief in American exceptionalism, particularly through his human rights policy. But the record of Carter's administration shows that moral principles, even in the application of the human rights policy, were usually superseded by strategic, economic, and political interests. Despite repeated appeals to exceptionalist rhetoric, Carter failed to revive American self-confidence and, particularly during his last year in office, following the 1979 Soviet invasion of Afghanistan and the seizing of American hostages in Iran, he was widely criticized for contributing to the sense that the United States was in decline.

Carter's successor, Ronald Reagan, was the greatest advocate of the belief in American exceptionalism during the post-Vietnam era. Reagan imbued his public pronouncements with exceptionalist symbolism and imagery, describing the United States as "a land of hope, a light unto nations, a shining city on a hill." He was a true believer in the exceptional nature of his country. He sought to overcome the crisis of confidence in the United States by largely denying that any problems existed. Reagan insisted that the United States was the greatest nation on earth and that so long as Americans maintained that belief, they would be able to overcome any crises they faced. In foreign policy, he took a tough rhetorical stance against the Soviet Union, which in stark exceptionalist terms he condemned as the "evil empire." He also conducted a massive arms buildup, and demonstrated a willingness to employ force, all in an attempt to overcome the perception of weakness that had characterized Carter's presidency.

Reagan succeeded in bolstering American self-confidence, but his claims that the United States had renewed its strength and overcome the limits imposed by Vietnam were largely illusory. Despite standing tall rhetorically, the president was still reluctant to employ the full power of the United States to back up his strong words. For all the posturing of his foreign policy rhetoric, the Reagan administration employed U.S. military force only twice, and then in extremely low-risk, limited operations against Grenada (1983) and Libya (1986). The only other major deployment of armed forces was as part of the ill-fated peace-keeping operation in Lebanon (1982–1984). Otherwise the administration was prepared to use force only by proxy in Nicaragua, El Salvador, and Afghanistan. Ronald Reagan was far from the overtly activist foreign policy president that his image would suggest. He did couch all his foreign policy in terms of the missionary strand of American exceptionalism but, despite his insistence that all his actions were taken in keeping with the values and principles on which the United States was founded, policies such as the covert war in Nicaragua and his exchange of arms for hostages with Iran indicated that the reality of Reagan's foreign policy did not live up to the claims of his exceptionalist rhetoric.

George H. W. Bush admitted to having a problem with what he called the "vision thing," but, like his predecessors, utilized the language of American exceptionalism in his foreign policy. Following the end of the Cold War (1989–1990), Bush advocated a "new world order" based on global cooperation and the rule of law rather than force. The new world order was Bush's answer to the uncertainties of the post-Cold War world. It was a vision of how the world's nations could strive collectively to achieve, and then maintain, international stability. Significantly, though, Bush maintained that world order was possible only with the leadership, guidance, and protection of the United States—it would continue its tradition as a redeemer nation. For all his talk of universalism, Bush's new world order was distinctly an American idea which assumed that traditional American values and principles had universal applicability. Bush's vision also ensured freedom of action for the United States. The United States would not be subservient to the collective will of the United Nations, but would define and follow its own priorities, preferably with—but if necessary, without—the support of the international community. The new world order was in fact a clear expression of exceptionalist thinking.

Bill Clinton, too, couched his foreign policy in terms of American exceptionalism. He repeatedly identified the United States as "the world's only indispensable nation." Clinton made "democratic enlargement" one of the cornerstones of his foreign policy. The United States would actively support and promote the spread of democracy and free market economies throughout the world. This policy, like so many before it, was underpinned by the idea that unique American values, principles and practices had universal applications.

THE VIETNAM SYNDROME AND AMERICAN EXCEPTIONALISM

Throughout the post-Vietnam era, both the main strands of exceptionalist belief have been influential on the discourse and content of U.S. foreign policy. Indeed, the tension between these two strands has defined many of the debates over the post-Vietnam direction of foreign affairs, particularly with regard to foreign interventions and the use of force. The United States has remained highly engaged in international affairs, but with added pressure that its conduct be exemplary and consistent with its traditional values and principles. Policymakers and public alike have sought to avoid "another Vietnam" by ensuring that foreign policy actions are conducted in keeping with the perceived lessons of that conflict. The defeat of U.S. objectives by a technologically inferior enemy in Vietnam indicated that there were limits to American power. The nature and extent of these limits, however, continues to be a major source of debate, and has come to dominate discussions over foreign policy in each post-Vietnam administration. The term "Vietnam syndrome" became widely used to describe the collective lessons and legacies of the war, particularly in the political-military realm. Although there is no nationwide consensus on the lessons of the Vietnam War, a pattern has developed in policymaking that has remained relatively consistent across post-Vietnam administrations, especially in the threat and use of force. The Vietnam syndrome, in its political-military sense, amounts to a set of criteria that should be met if the United States is to commit troops to combat. These criteria must be satisfied if public support for military intervention is to be sustained. Presidents feel the need to maintain public support for their foreign policy largely because this grants it the moral legitimacy that became so lacking in Vietnam. To avoid another Vietnam, policymakers have therefore followed the central criteria of the Vietnam syndrome: that the United States should not employ force in an international conflict unless just cause can be demonstrated, the objectives are compelling and attainable, and sufficient force is employed to assure a swift victory with a minimum of casualties.

These conditions for the use of force form the content of the Vietnam syndrome and have become increasingly institutionalized with each successive administration. They have been codified in the Weinberger Doctrine, proposed by Reagan's Secretary of Defense Caspar Weinberger in November 1984, and the Powell Doctrine espoused by Colin Powell, the chair of the Joint Chiefs of Staff in the administration of George H. W. Bush and secretary of state under George W. Bush. Even though, as Powell himself has argued, administration officials do not formally go down a list checking off the specific conditions of the Vietnam syndrome, it is clear from public and archival accounts of the decision-making process that deliberate steps are taken to ensure these conditions are met before use of force is authorized. The planning and conduct of all major uses of force since the Vietnam War have been influenced directly by the Vietnam syndrome. Even the Gulf War, which George H. W. Bush claimed "kicked the Vietnam syndrome once and for all," demonstrates how strongly the syndrome's influence persists. The planning and conduct of the Gulf War, with its emphasis on an air war and in particular the decision not to pursue the war to Baghdad once the objective of liberating Kuwait had been achieved, was carefully designed to comply with all of the Vietnam syndrome's central tenets: use force only as a last resort in the pursuit of what can be demonstrated as a just cause with compelling objectives that can be achieved swiftly using maximum force with minimal casualties. Far from "kicking the Vietnam syndrome," the Gulf War helped to institutionalize it.

The Vietnam syndrome actually has the effect of reinforcing and perpetuating crucial elements of the belief in American exceptionalism. It is designed specifically to ensure that the United States does not commit itself to another conflict like the Vietnam War. A central purpose of the syndrome is to avoid situations in which the United States could suffer another military defeat. By following policy based on the Vietnam syndrome, U.S. policymakers can be reasonably assured of achieving victory, and thus reinforcing the exceptionalist belief that the United States is a superior nation which always succeeds in its objectives. The Vietnam syndrome also prevents the United States from undertaking military commitments involving long-term occupations of hostile foreign territory. This requirement perpetuates the exceptionalist notion that the United States does not seek the conquest and subjugation of foreign nations. Finally, and most significantly, if it follows the Vietnam syndrome, the United States will use force only in situations where Americans can perceive a just cause. Whenever a just cause is conceived by American policymakers, no matter whether its roots are economic, strategic, political, or otherwise, it will be couched in terms of American exceptionalism. By following what is perceived as a just cause, any administration will perpetuate the belief that the United States pursues only policy that is consistent with its exceptional values and principles. In this sense, the belief in exceptionalism is self-perpetuating and the Vietnam syndrome does nothing to change that situation; in fact, it reinforces it.

The Vietnam syndrome acts as a constraint on American action in world affairs. It places limits on the strength, resolve, and capabilities of a nation which Americans regard as all-powerful and superior to other nations. In this sense the power of the Vietnam syndrome in the making of American foreign policy suggests that the United States is no longer an exceptional nation but is just as limited in its actions as any other country. Yet, paradoxically, the Vietnam syndrome actually acts as a guarantor of the continued acceptance of the belief in American exceptionalism. If the Vietnam syndrome is followed, then the United States can continue to be at least perceived as an exceptional nation because it will always win its wars, it will remain committed to its tradition of not conquering foreign land for territorial expansion, and it will resort to force only in the pursuit of just causes. The nature of the Vietnam syndrome is a clear example, then, of how the belief in American exceptionalism continues to frame the discourse of U.S. foreign policy.

CONCLUSION

Americans are not unique in their belief that theirs is an exceptional nation. Many, if not all, countries have shared such national vanity at some time or another in their histories. The French *mission civilisatrice,* the British Empire, and the Third Reich, for example, were all accompanied by their own versions of exceptionalism. Americans are clearly not alone in holding exceptionalist beliefs. Neither are they unique in pursuing foreign policies that are informed by those cultural beliefs. In all countries policymaking is based to a certain extent on assumptions formed from unique elements of national culture.

The fact that other nations have their own forms of exceptionalism, however, does not diminish the effects that the belief in American exceptionalism has on the making of U.S. policy. As the United States remains arguably the most powerful nation in the world, it is important to recognize the consequences that the belief in American exceptionalism has on U.S. foreign policy. Political, economic, and strategic interests are the major determinants of U.S. foreign policy. But no matter what the root reasons for a foreign policy decision are, that policy is usually couched in terms consistent with American exceptionalism. Use of this rhetoric assures substantial public support for policy and has proved very effective throughout U.S. history.

This fact begs the question of whether the use of exceptionalist rhetoric is simply a manipulative tool designed to win public approval for policy. Do American policymakers formulate their desired policy, then cloak it in terms they believe will assure the greatest possible public and congressional support? Certainly officials within most U.S. administrations have acknowledged that couching policy in terms of exceptionalism would have positive effects on public opinion, but to suggest this is the only reason for such language being employed would be to ignore other evidence. Nowhere in the public or archive record, including declassified accounts of National Security Council meetings, is it even implied that once a particular course has been chosen, it will then be packaged in exceptionalist terms. In fact, exceptionalist language is not used only in public explanations of policy; it is also used by policymakers themselves in policymaking sessions behind closed doors. Presidents and their foreign policy advisers frequently use arguments couched in exceptionalist language during private meetings and in personal memoranda. They do so even when perfectly good practical arguments for policy options exist, and they often couch even strategic, economic, or political justifications in exceptionalist terms. It appears to be automatic for American public officials to conceive their policies in terms that represent some notion of the exceptional nature of the United States. They do so not simply because it will be politically advantageous but also because those terms form a natural part of the language they use to understand the world around them. American exceptionalism exists deep within the American belief system, and many of its assumptions are shared by the public and officials alike. It therefore provides the framework for much of the discussion of foreign policy, its presentation by officials, and its realization.

Throughout U.S. history the tension between the exemplary and missionary strands of American exceptionalism have been among the defining characteristics of foreign policy. They have survived challenges to their continued acceptance, such as the imperialist debate of the 1890s and the defeat in Vietnam. They form a core element of American national identity, and will continue to provide the cultural and intellectual framework for the making of U.S. foreign policy. Foreign observers in particular often regard with contempt or confusion the use of exceptionalist rhetoric by U.S. policymakers. But if we are to truly understand the ways in which U.S. foreign policy is conducted, it is essential that we take seriously the intellectual and cultural framework in which it is made.

BIBLIOGRAPHY

Anderson, Benedict. *Imagined Communities: Reflections on the Origin and Spread of Nationalism.* Rev. ed. London, 1991.

Baritz, Loren. *Backfire: A History of How American Culture Led Us into Vietnam and Made Us Fight the Way We Did.* New York, 1985.

Bell, Daniel. "The End of American Exceptionalism." *The Public Interest* (fall 1975). Reprinted in his *The Winding Passage: Essays and Sociological Journeys 1960–1980.* Cambridge, Mass., 1980.

——. "'American Exceptionalism' Revisited: The Role of Civil Society." *The Public Interest* (spring 1989): 38–56.

Brands, H. W. *What America Owes the World: The Struggle for the Soul of Foreign Policy.* Cambridge, 1998.

Calhoun, Frederick S. *Power and Principle: Armed Intervention in Wilsonian Foreign Policy.* Kent, Ohio, 1986.

Dallek, Robert. *The American Style of Foreign Policy: Cultural Politics and Foreign Affairs.* New York, 1983.

Dumbrell, John. *The Making of U.S. Foreign Policy.* Manchester, U.K., and New York, 1990.

Fousek, John. *To Lead the Free World: American Nationalism and the Cultural Roots of the Cold War.* Chapel Hill, N.C., 2000.

Greene, Jack P. *The Intellectual Construction of America: Exceptionalism and Identity from 1492 to 1800.* Chapel Hill, N.C., 1993.

Hofstadter, Richard "Manifest Destiny and the Philippines." In Daniel Aaron, ed. *America in Crisis: Fourteen Crucial Episodes in American History.* New York, 1952.

Hunt, Michael H. *Ideology and U.S. Foreign Policy.* New Haven, Conn., 1987.

Huntington, Samuel P. *American Politics: The Promise of Disharmony.* Cambridge, Mass., 1981.

Kammen, Michael. "The Problem of American Exceptionalism: A Reconsideration." *American Quarterly* 45, no. 1 (March 1993): 1–43.

Kohn, Hans. *American Nationalism: An Interpretive Essay.* New York, 1957.

Latham, Michael E. *Modernization as Ideology: American Social Science and "Nation-Building" in the Kennedy Era.* Chapel Hill, N.C., 2000.

Lepgold, Joseph, and Timothy McKeown. "Is American Foreign Policy Exceptional?: An Empirical Analysis." *Political Science Quarterly* 110, no. 3 (fall 1995): 369–384.

Lipset, Seymour Martin. *American Exceptionalism: A Double-Edged Sword.* New York, 1996.

Luce, Henry. "The American Century." *Life* (17 February 1941).

McCrisken, Trevor B. *American Exceptionalism and the Legacy of Vietnam: U.S. Foreign Policy Since 1974.* Basingstoke, U.K., and New York, 2002.

McEvoy-Levy, Siobhán. *American Exceptionalism and U.S. Foreign Policy: Public Diplomacy at the End of the Cold War.* Basingstoke, U.K., and New York, 2001.

Madsen, Deborah L. *American Exceptionalism.* Edinburgh, 1998.

Merk, Frederick. *Manifest Destiny and Mission in American History: A Reinterpretation.* Cambridge, Mass., 1963.

Osgood, Robert Endicott. *Ideals and Self-Interest in America's Foreign Relations: The Great Transformation of the Twentieth Century.* Chicago, 1953.

Ryan, David. *U.S. Foreign Policy in World History.* London and New York, 2000.

Schlesinger, Arthur M., Jr. *The Cycles of American History.* Boston, 1986.

Shafer, Byron E., ed. *Is America Different?: A New Look at American Exceptionalism.* Oxford, 1991.

Smith, Anthony D. *Myths and Memories of the Nation.* Oxford, 1999.

Stephanson, Anders. *Manifest Destiny: American Expansion and the Empire of Right.* New York, 1995.

Tuveson, Ernest Lee. *Redeemer Nation: The Idea of America's Millennial Role.* Chicago, 1968.

Tyrrell, Ian. "American Exceptionalism in an Age of International History." *American Historical Review* 96, no. 4 (October 1991): 1031–1055; Michael McGerr, "The Price of the 'New Transnational History,'" pp. 1056–1067; and a response from Tyrrell, pp. 1068–1072.

Weinberg, Albert K. *Manifest Destiny: A Study of Nationalist Expansionism in American History.* Baltimore, 1935, and Chicago, 1963.

Whitcomb, Roger S. *The American Approach to Foreign Affairs: An Uncertain Tradition.* Westport, Conn., 1998.

See also Anti-Imperialism; Colonialism and Neocolonialism; Continental Expansion; Development Doctrine and Modernization Theory; Ideology; Imperialism; Internationalism; Intervention and Nonintervention; Isolationism; Nationalism; Public Opinion; Realism and Idealism; The Vietnam War.

EXTRATERRITORIALITY

Jules Davids and Jonathan M. Nielson

A vital function of American diplomacy is the protection of persons, property, and trade interests of U.S. citizens, both native-born and naturalized, in foreign countries. Such protection is commonly referred to as "extraterritoriality." However, extraterritoriality was also applied within the United States in regions claimed by or ceded to sovereign Indian nations. For example, beginning in the 1830s in Indian Territory (Oklahoma), Indians charged with offenses on white land and whites charged with offenses on Indian land within the territory were compelled to stand trial in white courts in Missouri. Extraterritoriality embodies a regime of protections, immunities, and exemptions, claimed on behalf of citizens of one nation living abroad, from the legal system and territorial jurisdiction of the state in which they are resident. Such immunities may be limited, that is, they are restricted to a specific territory or region. Or they may be unlimited or nonspecific, that is, global in their application. Guaranteeing such protection, especially in Islamic and Asian countries, resulted in the eventual development of a system of extraterritoriality which the United States established through negotiation or unilateral imposition in fifteen nations: Algeria (Algiers), Borneo, China, Egypt, Iran (Persia), Japan, Korea, Libya (Tripoli), Madagascar, Morocco, Samoa, Tanzania (Zanzibar/Muscat), Thailand (Siam), Tunisia (Tunis), and Turkey (Ottoman Porte).

In establishing such a regime of diplomatic relationships, the United States drew upon established theoretical principles and historical antecedents. The principle and practice of extraterritoriality is fundamentally a state's de jure claim of sovereignty and a de facto expression of its diplomacy and foreign policy. Most authorities would accept the broad view that sovereignty is a system of order and relationships among states that is based on a "mutual recognition of one another's right to exercise exclusive political authority within its territorial limits." Whereas sovereignty involves a state's claim of jurisdiction over citizens within its borders, extraterritoriality extends those claims beyond them.

ORIGINS OF EXTRATERRITORIALITY

While the practice and claims of extraterritoriality originated in antiquity, most notably in Egypt, Greece, and Rome, it was during the Middle Ages that its modern principles were established. As early as the twelfth century, Italian cities such as Genoa, Venice, and Pisa secured protection for their merchants in Egypt, Constantinople, and the Barbary States of North Africa. In northern Europe, the Hanseatic League obtained jurisdictional rights for its merchants within its trading region. During the next three centuries, Turkey granted so-called capitulary rights to Great Britain, the Netherlands, Italy, Denmark, Germany, Russia, Spain, Portugal, and the United States.

The problem of guaranteeing such protection, especially in the Islamic and Asian countries, was responsible for the eventual development of a system of extraterritoriality. Although differences in cultures, religions, and legal systems between Western Christian countries and those of Africa, the Near East, and Asia motivated Western countries to secure legal and economic exemptions for their nationals, the roots of extraterritoriality can be traced to ancient times. During antiquity, legal rights and obligations in Egypt, Greece, and Rome were deemed an integral part of membership in the community and could never be extended to aliens—the "strangers within the gates." However, merchants and traders traveling to distant lands were often permitted to reside and to establish trade factories, to manage their own affairs, to build temples, and to live according to their own customs, ceremonies, and rites.

By the end of the eighteenth century, a significant change had occurred in the concept of extraterritoriality. Before the Treaties of Westphalia (1648), which ended the Thirty Years' War and established the basis for the modern European system of nation-states, the notion of territorial sovereignty had not taken definite and concrete form. Sovereignty was generally viewed as personal rather than territorial, and it was related to the theory of the personalization of laws: that a foreigner carried his own law wherever he went. It was the ruler's duty to protect those who swore personal allegiance to him. Such allegiance was usually rendered by military service, and, in the case of Asian nations, by the payment of tribute as well. Following the Treaties of Westphalia, however, the concept of territorial sovereignty collided with the notions of personal sovereignty and the personality of laws, especially when the national right of territorial jurisdiction became a basic tenet of Western international law.

The recognition of territorial sovereignty in the West had a profound impact on the Ottoman Empire and in the Orient, where the principle that law was personal rather than territorial persisted for a long period of time. It affected, in particular, the relationships between Christian Europe and the Islamic and Asian countries, which were viewed as outside the pale of "civilization." Since these states were considered beyond the sphere of international law, it was held that European subjects and citizens had to be protected from the barbarities of "uncivilized" peoples, at least until the latter conformed to the standards of law and justice that Europeans considered just and equitable. Europeans chafed at the idea of being subservient to the laws of "inferior" civilizations. Such subservience, they felt, did violence to their dignity, pride, and concepts of justice. On their part, Muslims and Chinese held foreigners in disdain because they believed in the superiority of their own virtues and civilization.

From the earliest times, foreign ambassadors, government officials, and diplomatic representatives were granted a special status and exemption from local jurisdiction. This privilege later became known as the right of "exterritoriality." Diplomatic immunities were acknowledged in Western countries and in most non-Western states as well. Extraterritoriality was distinguished from exterritoriality in that it applied not simply to foreign diplomats and government officials, but to foreign nationals residing abroad. The special rights and immunities involved were specifically defined in treaties, and were not reciprocal. Although initially the bestowal of extraterritorial rights did not connote any loss of territorial sovereignty, but instead symbolized the beneficence of the grantor state, such was not the case following the Treaties of Westphalia. The imposition of extraterritoriality clearly came to represent the superiority of Western Christian countries over inferior, backward, and "uncivilized" peoples. In this sense, modern extraterritoriality served not only as a protective shield but also as an instrument to further penetration and imperialistic expansion.

MOROCCO

Before the Declaration of Independence, colonial Americans who engaged in trade in the Mediterranean and with the Barbary States were dependent upon the British for protection from Barbary piracy. France had led the way in securing definite rights or protection not only for foreigners but also for natives in the employ of foreigners. The first treaty granting these privileges was concluded between Morocco and France in May 1767; other nations soon gained similar rights through a most-favored-nation clause. When the United States declared its independence in 1776, England withdrew its admiralty passes. To prevent the plundering of American ships, a committee of the Continental Congress immediately urged the negotiation of a treaty with France to obtain a royal pledge to protect and defend American vessels as effectively as England had previously done. Although Louis XVI promised in the Treaty of Amity and Commerce between the United States and France, signed on 6 February 1778, to interpose with the Barbary States "for the benefit, convenience, and safety" of his American ally, this agreement proved to be of little value.

After the American Revolution, the U.S. Congress took the initiative to establish direct contacts to secure the protection of American ships and seamen in the Mediterranean area. In May 1784, Thomas Jefferson, John Adams, and Benjamin Franklin were commissioned to negotiate treaties with the Barbary States. When an American ship, the *Betsey*, was seized by Moroccan pirates and taken to the port of Tangier, the commissioners authorized Thomas Barclay, the U.S. consul general at Paris, to go to Morocco and act as their agent to conclude a treaty with Morocco. Barclay's mission was successful. In

1786 he signed an agreement with Sultan Sidi Mohammed, which was ratified by Congress on 18 July 1787. This treaty, which established the basis for American extraterritorial rights in Morocco, was modified and renewed in 1836 and again in 1886, and remained in effect until 1956. The United States soon negotiated treaties with the dey of Algiers in 1795, with the sultan of Tripoli in 1796, and with the dey of Tunis in 1797; it did not relinquish these treaty rights until 1912, when Libya became a colony of Italy. But neither the treaty with Morocco nor those concluded with the Barbary States provided protection to American commerce. Tripoli declared war on the United States in 1801, and hostilities ensued with the Barbary pirates until 1816, when new treaties were imposed upon Algiers, Tripoli, and Tunisia. Following the War of 1812, the United States was no longer harassed by piracy in the Mediterranean.

In the Islamic countries, the protectorate system created serious difficulty. Under bilateral treaties, European consuls obtained both almost complete jurisdiction over the persons and properties of their own nationals, and the right to offer this protection to anyone they employed. These persons were not subject to local law and were exempt from all personal or direct taxation or forced levies. The system lent itself to abuses, since many local citizens gladly paid large sums of money to secure these exemptions.

Foreign consuls found the selling of protection an excellent way to augment their incomes. As early as 1859, the Moroccan government demanded more careful regulation of the protectorate system. Complaints were also voiced against the unwarranted interference by consuls in the local courts. Efforts to remedy the situation were made in 1877, when the sultan sought to limit and control the extent of foreign protectorate claims, and to obtain the return to Moroccan jurisdiction of Moroccan subjects who, after naturalization in a foreign country, had returned to live in Morocco. But the discussions with the diplomatic corps brought no agreement, and the United States, while expressing its willingness to remedy the abuses, insisted that naturalized citizens were equal to native-born citizens, and therefore not subject to Moroccan jurisdiction if they returned to that country.

At the Conference of Madrid in 1880, protectorates were the main item on the agenda. Britain favored conceding to Moroccan demands, whereas France urged that no abridgment be made on the right of protection. The conference adopted the French point of view, and the Convention of Madrid not only validated the protectorate system but also, by clarifying, defining, and legalizing the situation, strengthened it by converting the former bilateral treaties and simple consular agreements into an international convention. After the Madrid Convention an orgy of protection selling began, and the protection problem became linked to political penetration.

During the latter decades of the nineteenth century, imperial rivalries steadily exerted a profound impact on extraterritoriality. As European powers pressed to partition Africa and carve out their colonial empires, the danger of the dismemberment of Morocco became increasingly ominous. In 1871 the sultan of Morocco, fearful that his country might be partitioned by European countries, offered to place his entire nation under an American protectorate. Although refusing to accept the offer, the State Department proffered its friendly offices to prevent such an act. To forestall dismemberment or the establishment of hegemony in a region by any one power, and at the same time ensure the maintenance of treaty rights and extraterritoriality, the United States espoused the creation of international settlements, such as that in Shanghai, which had been set up in the 1850s, and the Open Door policy.

Political and economic competition among the European powers intensified efforts to maintain and broaden extraterritorial rights. In Morocco particularly, a decisive shift occurred from concern with persons and property to an interest in economic exploitation and trade. The Moroccan crisis that almost triggered conflict between France and Germany, and was a prelude to World War I, was occasioned by Germany's desire to prevent French economic control of that country. The intervention of President Theodore Roosevelt in this dispute led to the Algeciras Conference in 1906. While the Act of Algeciras effected a compromise that guaranteed equality of economic opportunity and the Open Door, France and Spain secured privileged positions with the Moroccan police force.

The interests of France, Spain, and Britain converged on Tangier, which overlooks the Strait of Gibraltar. England and Germany strongly favored internationalization of Tangier, but France resisted this proposal, insisting on French and Spanish preponderance. Following the Act of Algeciras, France swiftly took steps to establish a protectorate over Morocco. Germany attempted to counter this move by dispatching a gunboat, the *Panther*, to Agadir to "protect German interests." This action, in 1911, precipitated a second Moroccan crisis. But again a compromise was reached. In a Franco-German accord, concluded in November 1911, Germany conceded France a free hand in Morocco in exchange for a sizable slice of the French Congo. After firmly establishing its position in Morocco, and working out arrangements with Germany and Spain, France agreed to cooperate in the creation of an international regime for Tangier, modeled on the International Settlement of Shanghai. A statute was finally approved by most of the Algeciras powers by November 1914.

The American extraterritorial treaties with Morocco were very similar to those with other Islamic states. However, abrogation of American extraterritorial jurisdiction in Morocco was a complicated matter. France established a protectorate in Morocco in 1912, designating special zones for Spain and an "international zone" in Tangier. After the protectorate was established, France began pressing the United States to renounce its extraterritorial rights.

Following the establishment of the French protectorate in Morocco, many countries surrendered their capitulatory rights. With the signing of the Tangier Statute in 1923, the protectorate system was eliminated. England was the last of the signatory powers to formally renounce its right of protection and all capitulatory rights, in a 1937 accord with France. But the United States refused to accept the Tangier Statute or the modification in 1928 that officially established the basis for the internationalization of the city. Since Americans had few political or economic interests in Tangier, Washington decided it would be more advantageous to remain outside the international settlement, thus retaining both its diplomatic status and its extraterritorial rights.

Some vestiges of extraterritoriality persisted after World War II. For example, American extraterritorial rights were not ended in Morocco until 1956, when Moroccan independence was attained; the final economic integration of Tangier was secured only in October 1960. When the United States finally gave up its extraterritorial jurisdiction in Morocco, one issue was its desire to support Arab nationalism without antagonizing France. Moreover, it was sensitive to the danger that the Soviet Union could exploit Moroccan irritation with American extraterritorial claims. Finally, the United States wanted to preserve its military bases in the region and increase the number of American troops.

TURKEY

Meanwhile, prompted by developing interests and problems of missionaries and trade in the Ottoman Empire, the U.S. government initiated direct contacts with Turkey. Efforts to arrange a treaty of amity and commerce were initiated in 1799, but a Turkish-American agreement that extended capitulation privileges to the United States was not concluded until 1830. Article IV of that treaty stipulated that "citizens of America, quietly pursuing their commerce, and not being charged or convicted of any crime or offense shall not be molested; and even when they have committed some offense, they shall not be arrested and put in prison, by the local authorities, but they shall be tried by their minister or consul, and punished according to their offense."

Although the treaty recognized that American plaintiffs and defendants in civil cases would be subject to Turkish law, this was not enforced. Indeed, while the United States relinquished some narrow judicial authority to Turkey with respect to land and real estate transactions in 1874, it continued to claim broad extraterritorial rights, in large measure because it considered the Turkish legal system to be unjust. As the State Department put it, "The intercourse of the Christian world with the Mohammedan world is not founded upon the principle of the law of nations," because "International Law, as professed by the civilized ideas subsisting between them [is] based upon a common origin, and an almost identical religious faith." With the outbreak of World War I, Turkey was the first country to take advantage of the conflict by declaring its intention to rid itself of the capitulatory regime. In September 1914 the Turks, asserting that the capitulatory rights were "in complete opposition to the juridical rules of the century and to the principle of national sovereignty," proclaimed that Turkey's relations with all states would be based on the "general principles of international law" after Turkey abrogated the capitulatory agreements, effective 1 October 1914. The United States promptly denied Turkey's right to abolish the capitulations unilaterally, claiming that such action could be taken only by agreement among all the nations concerned. Nevertheless, Turkey made it clear that it considered the capitulations dead.

Turkey experienced dramatic social, political, and legal changes in the early twentieth century. Kemal Ataturk's nationalist revival and secularization of Turkey helped transform the legal system by granting non-Muslims more equal legal status with Muslims. With these reforms, extraterritoriality did not seem necessary to protect the legal rights of Americans in Turkey. Therefore, the United States was willing to renounce extraterritoriality, Ambassador Joseph Grew informed Turkish foreign minister Tevfik Aras in 1931.

CHINA

Although the Ottoman Empire was the first to enact a capitulatory system that established the basis for extraterritorial privileges, it was in China that the extraterritoriality system was developed most extensively. The origin of extraterritoriality in China has been traced to the T'ang dynasty (618–907). As early as the ninth century, the Chinese allowed Arabs to reside and trade along the coast of Chekiang province and to govern themselves under their own headman. When the Portuguese arrived in Macao in 1557, the emperor permitted them to live according to their own customs and laws. In the first treaty with Russia in 1689, China agreed that each nation would be responsible for its own subjects.

However, though China treated all barbarians equally, permitting them to enjoy the blessings of Chinese civilization and granting to all the privilege of trade, barbarians were required to accept China's conditions of trade. The Chinese exempted foreigners from their law in part because they believed that foreigners lacked the capacity to understand the complex rules of Chinese society; in part because such exemption freed the Chinese from the difficulty of trying to govern aliens who had strange customs, language, and traditions; and in part because the Chinese felt the barbarians should be given a chance to observe their civilized way of life and, by so doing, eventually become assimilated. The Chinese always insisted upon complete control over foreign residence, and Westerners ultimately secured the acknowledgment and extension of extraterritorial rights only by the threat or use of force.

In China, the tribute system established the basis of relationships with barbarians. Foreigners who wanted to trade with China were compelled to abide by the rules and regulations set forth by the emperor. Until the first Anglo-Chinese (Opium) War (1839–1842), Western merchants accepted China's institutional framework and adapted to Chinese requirements of trade. This meant adhering to the Canton system, which confined all foreign trade to the Canton area—the "factory" section of the city and at Whampoa and Macao—and its supervision by the Co-Hong, a Chinese merchants' guild. The Canton system in effect preserved a tribute-and-trade nexus that coincided with the traditional Chinese way of dealing with barbarians.

The Opium War shattered this institutional arrangement. It was replaced by the Western "treaty system," built on treaties signed by China with England, the United States, France, and Russia. The British-dictated Treaty of Nanking (1842) led to the collapse of the Co-Hong system; the opening to trade of the ports of Canton, Amoy, Foochow, Ningpo, and Shanghai; and the altering of relations with China. The treaty system pivoted on two significant stipulations: a most-favored-nation clause, which automatically extended concessions granted by China to one nation to other treaty powers, and the right of extraterritorial jurisdiction.

Before the Opium War, the British and other Europeans had willingly acknowledged, for the most part, China's jurisdiction in both civil and criminal matters. But a gap steadily widened between the British and Chinese on the interpretation and procedures of the law, on matters of responsibility, on evidence, and on punishment. On occasion, the British resisted compliance, particularly by refusing to surrender their nationals who were accused in homicide cases. Westerners were also alarmed by the Chinese practice of torturing prisoners and by the corruption of Chinese magistrates and judicial authorities. Americans, however, readily submitted to China's laws and jurisdiction to avoid interference with trade.

The position of the United States changed drastically after the signing of the Treaty of Nanking, and the supplementary Bogue Convention (1843), which gave British consuls limited jurisdiction to deal with crimes committed by British nationals. Although England first took the initiative in asserting jurisdiction over British subjects in China nearly a decade before the Chinese formally agreed to the principle of extraterritoriality, no direct steps were taken to establish a court of justice, with criminal and admiralty jurisdiction, at Canton. Because this measure was opposed by the Chinese and lacked approval of Parliament and the public, England hesitated to take any action. As a result, the imposition of an extraterritoriality system in China was effected mainly by the United States.

Caleb Cushing, who was appointed the first official American envoy to China in 1843, was responsible for obtaining China's full recognition of the principle of extraterritoriality. Cushing argued that jurisprudence of Western Christendom alone guaranteed equitable treatment of foreigners. "This fact," he boldly claimed, was "the result of evidence of the superior civilization and respect for individual rights consequent thereon, which prevail in Christendom." Cushing insisted that the United States demand extraterritorial rights in China for American citizens, not as a concession on China's part, but as a principle of established international law.

Cushing's major achievement was the negotiation of the Treaty of Wanghia, signed on 3 July 1844, which granted the United States the right not only to determine punishment of American offenders but also to exercise absolute extraterritorial jurisdiction in both civil and criminal cases. Article XXI of the treaty stipulated: "Subjects of China who may be guilty of any criminal acts towards citizens of the United States, shall be arrested and punished by the Chinese authorities according to the laws of China: and citizens of the United States, who may commit any crime in China, shall be subject to be tried and punished only by the Consul, or other public functionary of the United States, thereto authorized according to the laws of the United States." From the mid-nineteenth century to World War II, American diplomacy in China was occupied with problems relating to the administration of judicial affairs, shipping regulations, piracy, and claims. Other matters that explicitly concerned extraterritorial rights dealt with the buying and leasing of land; crimes against American persons and property; ensuring the guarantee of fair trials, whether in Chinese courts or consular courts; the safety of travel inland; and the rights to trade, to worship freely, and to propagate the faith. At the same time, extraterritoriality became a cloak for the development of successful foreign commercial enterprises and a means to secure control over much of China's foreign trade. It also offered a protective shield to Christian missionary activities, buttressed the creation of international settlements, and stimulated the use of foreign gunboats. By the twentieth century, the protection of Americans and other foreign nationals was provided not only by gunboats but also by the presence of foreign troops.

Between 1842 and 1942 the principal symbol and exercise of foreign power in China were the treaty ports, small territorial enclaves or enclosures where foreign governments established extraterritorial jurisdictions throughout much of coastal and eastern China. In them were located foreign consulates, local offices of foreign businesses and commercial concerns, concessions, and settlements. Here also were separate courts, police with foreign officers and staff, and often small military and security forces.

Treaty ports, usually on the coast or along navigable waterways, were open to foreign commerce and contained a Chinese maritime customs office administered by foreigners. In many instances these ports had a de jure foreign district. Direct commercial activities, residence, and property rights were restricted to designated treaty ports and other specified cities open to foreign trade.

Settlements and concessions were municipalities separate from the surrounding Chinese cities. Both foreigners and Chinese were allowed to lease or own property and to live in the settlement area. Foreign nationals dominated the municipal councils of these settlements until the late 1920s. Settlements were generally considered Chinese soil governed by foreigners. Concessions were de jure colonies of the nation leasing the property. Most were organized with a municipal council that had ultimate administrative and political authority over the concession. The law of a concession, which was leased foreign soil, could exclude Chinese and nationals of other countries excluded from entry, residence, and property ownership.

Setting up the machinery and administrative apparatus of the extraterritoriality system produced many problems. For example, down to 1906, few American consuls in China had adequate knowledge or competence to handle legal disputes. Many consuls were attached to American mercantile firms; their meager consular fees and dependence on commercial houses seriously affected judicial administration. Bias for one's own nationals could not be eliminated. Moreover, the complexity of laws and procedures, and the difficulties of appeal, as well as of securing witnesses or producing evidence for trials of foreigners who had committed offenses in the interior, made the handling of cases onerous. The creation of a mixed court at Shanghai in 1864 sought to remedy these judicial problems; a Chinese magistrate presided and a foreign consular "assessor" sat with him as a co-judge. Although the removal of consular appointments from politics and the establishment of the U.S. court at Shanghai in 1906 helped to improve the situation, the abuses of extraterritoriality persisted.

In the 1840s, the Chinese were not aware of the implications of extraterritoriality or of other concessions granted to foreigners. Nor were they disturbed by consular jurisdiction, since it did not directly affect China's political structure. But as foreign control over the Chinese economy steadily increased, these expectations rapidly disappeared. First applied to about 350 foreigners in five treaty ports, the extraterritoriality system by the beginning of the twentieth century was extended to about ninety treaty ports and some twenty-five ports of call for steamships, and embraced approximately a third of a million foreign residents.

For more than a half-century after the Opium War, China was racked by insurrections, economic dislocations, and the spread of European and Japanese imperialism. Compelled to accept the West's goods and ideas, China by the turn of the twentieth century reached the depths of humiliation with its defeat in the first Sino-Japanese War, the crushing of the Boxer Rebellion, and the signing of the Boxer Protocol in 1901. The latter provided for a huge indemnity and the permanent quartering of foreign troops in the capital as legation guards.

Nationalism and reform movements, however, steadily gained momentum. As they did so, the "unequal treaties" and extraterritoriality in China increasingly became targets of attack. To counter the agitation, the Western powers and Japan signed a series of treaties in 1902 and 1903. The agreements indicated the willingness of these powers to help China in its efforts to effect judicial reform so that extraterritoriality could, in time, be ended. In the treaty of 1903, the United States conferred upon China more jurisdiction over domestic affairs, including mineral rights, coinage, and the regulation of trademarks, patents, and copyrights. Article XV conditioned the renunciation of extraterritorial rights on the "Westernization" of Chinese law: "The government of China having expressed a strong desire to reform its judicial system and to bring it into accord with that of Western nations, the United States agrees to give every assistance to such reform and will also be prepared to relinquish extra-territorial rights when satisfied that the state of Chinese laws, the arrangements for their administration, and other considerations warrant it in doing so."

When China entered World War I on the Allied side in 1917, steps were immediately taken to cancel the extraterritorial privileges of Germany and Austria. At the Paris Peace Conference, the Chinese delegation set forth a program that called for the return of all foreign concessions, settlements, and leased territories; the gradual abolition of extraterritoriality; and complete tariff autonomy. But to their dismay and anger, Woodrow Wilson endorsed Japan's claims to Shantung, which had been obtained in 1914 by the expulsion of the Germans. Delegates at the Paris Conference refused to reconsider the Shantung question or China's arguments on the abolition of extraterritoriality. As a result, the Chinese declined to sign the Treaty of Versailles.

After World War I, extraterritoriality was viewed as a key symbol of foreign domination. At the Washington Conference in 1921–1922, the Chinese delegation again made a strong bid for recognition of its full sovereignty. But the United States, Britain, France, and Japan balked at agreeing to treaty revisions. Although the Nine-Power Treaty (1922) confirmed China's independence and its territorial and administrative integrity, the agreement upheld the existing privileges of the signatory powers in the country. China secured only the promise of a study on the question of extraterritoriality, and real tariff autonomy was postponed indefinitely.

Although the Western powers and Japan resisted the relinquishment of extraterritorial rights in China, stressing that significant treaty revisions had to await China's progress in legislation and adoption of adequate judicial reforms, the extraterritoriality system deteriorated during the interwar years. Meanwhile, the Bolshevik Revolution made itself felt in China, spurring the growth of nationalism and radicalism in the country. Affirming its desire to deal with China on the basis of equality, the Soviet Union renounced extraterritoriality, and in May 1924 a Sino-Soviet agreement officially relinquished Russia's privileges.

Although the Washington Conference adopted a resolution that provided for the establishment of a fact-finding commission to investigate extraterritoriality in China, the chaotic conditions in the country and a squabble between France and China over Boxer indemnity payments delayed the convening of the Commission on Extraterritoriality until January 1926. After almost a year of investigation and the assembling of a mass of detailed information on China's judicial system and practices of extraterritoriality, the members unanimously concluded that until more effective judicial reforms were carried out, the abolition of extraterritoriality was unwarranted.

In the meantime, the Nationalist revolution coalesced under Chiang Kai-shek's leadership, and by 1928 defeated the northern government. Pledged to end the extraterritoriality system, the Kuomintang (Nationalists) adopted a provisional constitution in October and immediately took steps to establish a new basis of relations with foreign powers. At the end of the year, China reached agreements with Belgium, Denmark, Italy, Portugal, and Spain that provided for tariff autonomy; accepted, in principle, the ending of extraterritoriality; and promised that rights would be relinquished when other states had done so.

In May 1929 the Kuomintang government announced that it intended to promulgate civil, criminal, and commercial laws to replace the extraterritoriality system. Three months later, it issued regulations that ended the provincial and local handling of diplomatic matters and prescribed new procedures for dealing with aliens. But the Nationalists did not unilaterally abrogate extraterritoriality. They expressed the hope, instead, that the system could be abolished by mutual consent by 1 January 1930. Since the United States and Britain insisted upon a gradual relinquishment of extraterritorial rights—and only if China gave evidence of improvements in its judicial system that ensured "effective enforcement of jurisprudence"—the Kuomintang declared its dissatisfaction with this response. On 28 December 1929, the Western powers were informed that beginning 1 January 1930, "all foreign nationals in the territory of China who are now enjoying extraterritorial privileges shall abide by the laws, ordinances, and regulations duly promulgated by the Central and Local Government of China." This mandate was qualified two days later, when China stated its intent was merely to abolish extraterritoriality in principle. With the understanding that 1 January would be regarded simply as the date from which the process of gradual abolition would be said to have commenced, Washington, London, and Tokyo agreed to further negotiations "within a reasonable time."

For almost a year and a half, the United States and Britain attempted to work out an acceptable agreement with China. By June 1931 the points in dispute were resolved, but London, Washington, and Tokyo left final agreement in abeyance, pending an examination of the treaty terms. When the Japanese invaded Manchuria on 8 September 1931, the treaties, not yet ratified, were suspended indefinitely. Efforts to resume negotiations and to arrive at final agreements on the abolition of extraterritorial rights were made in the mid-1930s, but the outbreak of the second Sino-Japanese War in July 1937 once again halted the discussions.

The issue of extraterritoriality was not further considered until World War II. After Japan's bombing of Pearl Harbor in December 1941 and America's entry into the conflict, the State Department decided that it would be advantageous to end extraterritoriality. On 11 January 1943, China simultaneously concluded with the United States at Washington, and with Britain at Chunking, the Treaty for the Relinquishment of Extraterritorial Rights in China and the Regulation of Related Matters. By these treaties, together with exchanges of notes, the United States and England surrendered not only their extraterritoriality rights but also their unilateral privileges in China that had previously been acquired by the "unequal treaties." American and British nationals would now be subject to the jurisdiction of the government of the Republic of China, in accordance with the principles of international law and practice. The long-standing grievances relating to extraterritoriality, concessions, settlements, legation quarters, and the right to station foreign warships in Chinese waters and foreign troops on Chinese soil were thus ended.

JAPAN

The United States also strengthened the basis for extraterritorial rights in Japan. This was accomplished by Townsend Harris, a New York businessman and merchant who was appointed the first American consul at Shimoda, Japan, in 1855. Three years later, in July 1858, he concluded a treaty of amity and commerce that greatly extended the privileges secured by Commodore Matthew C. Perry in 1854. Perry's treaty, which opened Japan, contained no extraterritorial provisions, but Harris persuaded the Japanese to grant Americans jurisdiction in both civil and criminal matters.

Although critical of the inefficiency of Japanese judicial administration, the Western powers were negligent—as they had been in China and elsewhere—in improving the system of extraterritoriality. Gross interference occurred in the enforcement of Japanese laws, especially with regard to quarantine regulations, drawn up in 1873, and the control and regulation of the opium trade. The British minister, Sir Harry Parkes, adamantly insisted that British subjects could be tried and punished only for violation of British laws. He declared that the Japanese government could not enact laws applicable to British nationals. The United States and the Netherlands opposed this position, claiming that there was no danger in recognizing all Japanese laws as long as the power to try and punish foreigners remained in the consular courts. England subsequently modified its policy.

During the 1880s the Japanese government raised the matter of treaty revision. A concerted attempt was made to secure tariff autonomy and the repudiation of extraterritorial privileges. These efforts provoked vigorous opposition, especially from England. Despite this resistance, Japanese leaders took steps to obtain full judicial autonomy by completing the codification of their laws. At the same time, they pressed for an immediate end to consular jurisdiction over matters relating to police administration, partnerships between Japanese and foreigners, and customs affairs. In January 1882 a preparatory conference for treaty revision, attended by the ministers of twelve treaty powers, was convened at Tokyo. Japan proposed the abolition of extraterritorial jurisdiction in five years and the employment of foreign judges in Japanese courts during the transition period. In return, the Western powers were offered an extension of foreign rights to residence and land tenure within treaty ports and the opening of the country to all foreigners. By 1885 a general agreement was reached that the treaties should be revised. On 1 May 1886, the official conference of the treaty powers opened at Tokyo, and after many lengthy sessions a draft jurisdictional convention was approved.

Although the prospects for treaty revision looked bright, they were quashed by the strong popular opposition to Westernization and the proposals advanced by Japan's leaders. Agitation was especially directed against the system of mixed courts and the promise to submit the constitution of the courts and the codified laws to the Western powers for their approval. Unable to reach a general agreement, the Japanese attempted to abolish extraterritoriality and to obtain tariff autonomy by bilateral treaties. The United States was first approached, and in February 1889 the American minister, Richard D. Hubbard, concluded a treaty with Japan that included the abolition of consular courts in five years. His successor, John Franklin Swift, opposed the treaty's adoption, and Secretary of State James G. Blaine withheld it from the Senate. Meanwhile, Japan signed new treaties, practically the same as that with America, with Germany and Russia.

In 1890 the British agreed to treaty revision, on condition that Japanese jurisdiction over foreigners would be postponed for five years and that the newly codified Japanese laws would be in actual and satisfactory operation for one year before the expiration of that period. In July 1894 the compromise Anglo-Japanese Treaty of Commerce and Navigation was signed. The agreement specified that foreigners would be treated on an equal footing with Japanese in regard to travel, residence, and trade. Consular jurisdiction and foreign settlements were abolished. The implementation of the treaty was made contingent upon the satisfactory operation of Japan's newly codified laws, and provision was made for its termination at the end of twelve years.

The United States thus was not the first power to relinquish extraterritorial rights in Japan. Further delays were caused by Washington's objection to a clause in the Anglo-Japanese treaty that provided for the reciprocal rights of entrance, travel, residence, and property ownership. However, after Japan agreed to include a clause for mutual exemption of laws relating to laborers and labor immigration, a new treaty was signed in November 1894. Early in 1895 the American-Japanese treaty was ratified by both nations. Japan fulfilled all of the conditions that had been specified within the prescribed period of time, and in 1899 extraterritorial jurisdiction in the Japanese Empire was abolished.

The ending of extraterritoriality in Japan coincided with Japan's victory in the Sino-Japanese War (1894–1895) and its emergence as a major world power. However, the retreat of the Western powers in Japan did not immediately have an impact on other countries.

PANAMA

Extraterritorial jurisdiction continues to exist in the Panama Canal Zone, where, on the basis of the Hay-Bunau-Varilla Treaty of 1903, the United States exercises "all the rights, power and authority within the zone" that it "would possess if it were the sovereign of the territory . . . to the entire exclusion of the exercise by the [Panama] Republic of any such sovereign rights, power or authority." Although in 1965 President Lyndon B. Johnson indicated a willingness to negotiate a new treaty, and a Joint Statement of Principles in 1974 affirmed this desire, it was not until 1978 that President James Earl Carter's administration was able to persuade the Senate to ratify treaties recognizing Panama's sovereignty and jurisdiction in the Canal Zone by the year 2000.

TWENTY-FIRST CENTURY EXTRATERRITORIALITY

For the most part, the extraterritoriality system that prevailed in the nineteenth century, and was maintained, especially in China, down to World War II, is now a relic of the past. However, military status-of-forces agreements negotiated after World War II with Japan, Korea, Taiwan, and the Philippines, among others, embody in a new form extraterritorial jurisdiction affecting American military personnel abroad. However, the abandonment of regional or national extraterritoriality by the United States did not mean the abrogation of all extraterritorial claims. Beginning in 1945, U.S. courts commenced redefining the scope of their sovereign jurisdiction over the activities of American corporations doing business abroad.

In three significant cases the United States broadened the definition of sovereignty and proprietary economic hegemony. Authority for such claims was the Sherman Antitrust Act of 1890. However, in its first substantive ruling involving application of the Sherman Act to overseas commercial disputes, the Supreme Court issued a narrow opinion restricting extraterritorial rights. In *American Banana Company* v. *United Fruit Company* (13 U.S. 347), the Court asserted in essence that extraterritoriality was appropriate only on the high seas or in countries where unjust laws prevailed. Subsequently, it declined to assert the jurisdiction of U.S. courts in Costa Rica and stated that the Sherman Act did not apply outside of American sovereign (that is, territorial) jurisdiction. Indeed, in a similar case, *Underhill* v. *Hernandez* (168 U.S. 250), the Court ruled that "Every sovereign State is bound to respect the independence of every other sovereign State, and the courts of one country will not sit in judgment on the acts of the government of another done within its own country."

Since World War II, the Supreme Court has abandoned this narrow interpretation of sovereignty. In a series of rulings—*United States* v. *Aluminum Company of America* (148 U.S.2d 416), *Timberlane Lumber Company* v. *Bank of America Nt&SA* (549 F.2d 597), and *Mannington Mills, Inc.* v. *Congoleum Corp.* (595 F.2d 1287)—the Court has evolved complex tests for ascertaining what constitutes an "act of state," and has come to justify claims of extraterritorial jurisdiction to address the growing economic interdependence of the global economy. It would appear that the United States gradually has broadened the nineteenth-century definition of exclusive territorial sovereignty, now clearly transcended by twenty-first-century developments. It has been replaced by new legal conceptions of sovereignty and by the principles of universal rights that are imperative in international relations, especially in developing countries that once were colonies. There appears to be a growing legal sensitivity to the global impacts of activities by states beyond narrowly territorial considerations that will challenge them to creatively define what were once condoned as "extraterritorial rights."

Finally, it is appropriate to note the application of extraterritoriality in matters of ocean travel, airspace, and international terrorists. Whereas private vessels are subject to local laws, rights of extraterritoriality extend to state-owned vessels in foreign territorial waterways and ports, where they are customarily exempt from local jurisdiction. Likewise, the advent of national "territorial airspace" has given rise to extraterritorial claims, although such claims have found little consensus for an international regime beyond limited bilateral agreements.

In response to terrorist attacks on U.S. embassies and their personnel, in 1999, Congress passed, and President Bill Clinton signed into law, legislation making terrorism abroad a crime punishable as if the attack occurred in the United States (and thus was subject to U.S. laws). In accordance with normal diplomatic practice, the United States retains jurisdiction over its diplomatic officials abroad. It also claims jurisdiction over U.S. military personnel on American military bases abroad. The United States has also criminalized some activities engaged in by Americans abroad. For example, the Foreign Corrupt Practices Act prohibits American companies from paying bribes to foreign officials. However, this legislation is very different from the past practice of extraterritorial jurisdiction over Americans abroad, because it covers American companies. It is, in a sense, a hybrid of regional and global extraterritoriality.

Many states have enacted "blocking statutes" that prevent their citizens and companies from complying with American extraterritorial laws and court rulings. They include Australia, Canada, Denmark, Finland, France, Italy, Japan, Mexico, New Zealand, Norway, Sweden, Switzerland, and the United Kingdom. The European Union and the Organization of American States have also lodged formal protests against American extraterritorial claims.

Clearly, then, the concept of extraterritoriality historically has been an evolving expression of state sovereignty, which, one suspects, will continue to transform to meet the needs of an ever-changing international system.

BIBLIOGRAPHY

Abbey, Phillip R. *Treaty Ports and Extraterritoriality in China* (www.geocities.com/vienna/5048/treatyol.html). Offers a detailed discussion of treaty ports, concessions, and legations.

Anderson, David L. "Anson Burlingame: American Architect of the Cooperative Policy in China, 1861–1871." *Diplomatic History* 1, no. 13 (1977). Explores the formative stages of American policy and its contrasts with European practices.

Bevans, Charles I. *Treaties and Other International Agreements of the United States of America, 1776–1949*. 13 vols. Washington, D.C., 1968–1976.

Bland, Randall Walton. *The Black Robe and the Bald Eagle: The Supreme Court and the Foreign Policy of the United States, 1789–1953*. San Francisco, 1996. Provides authoritative discussion of the Court's role overseas in shaping American diplomacy and foreign policy.

Burley, Anne-Marie. "Law Among Liberal States: Liberal Internationalism and the Act of State Doctrine." *Columbia Law Review* 92, no. 8 (December 1992). Offers useful discussion of sovereignty and interstate relations.

Chan, K. C. "The Abrogation of British Extraterritoriality in China, 1942–43: A Study of Anglo-American Relations." *Modern Asian Studies* 1, no. 2 (1977). Explores Allied discussions with the Nationalist government for a new relationship with China.

Clyde, Paul H. "Attitudes and Policies of George F. Seward, American Minister at Peking, 1876–1880: Some Phases of the Cooperative Policy." *Pacific Historical Review* 2, no. 4 (1933). Contains Seward's views on extraterritoriality and other matters.

Congressional Quarterly Press. *A Collection of Treaties and Alliances Presented to the United States*. Washington, D.C., 2000. Provides one of the best sources for these diplomatic instruments and specific treaty provisions regarding extraterritorial rights.

Davids, Jules, ed. *American Diplomatic and Public Papers: The United States and China. Serial I. The Treaty System and the Taiping Rebellion, 1842–1860*. 21 vols. Wilmington, Del., 1973. Volumes 8–11 contain documents on consular regulations, judicial affairs, and major cases and problems relating to extraterritoriality in China.

Fishel, Wesley R. *The End of Extraterritoriality in China*. Berkeley and Los Angeles, 1952. An excellent, well-balanced account of the abolition of extraterritoriality in China.

"From Personalism to Territoriality: State Authority and Foreign Policy in Medieval and Modern Europe." Paper presented at the International Studies Association Conference, 16–20 April 1966. Offers substantive analysis of extraterritoriality, its early European practice, and the nature of the American regimes in China, Turkey, and Morocco.

Grayton, Jeffrey T. "From Here to Extraterritoriality: The United States Beyond Borders." Paper presented at the International Studies Association Conference, Toronto, Canada, March 1997. Offers substantive analysis of extraterritoriality; its early European practice, and the nature of the American regimes in China, Turkey, and Morocco.

Griffin, Joseph P., ed. *Perspectives on the Extraterritorial Application of U.S. Antitrust and Other Laws*. Chicago, 1979.

Hackworth, Green Haywood. *Digest of International Law*. 8 vols. Washington, D.C., 1940–1944. These volumes, published by the State Department, include the original texts of diplomatic documents on extraterritoriality.

Hall, Luella J. *The United States and Morocco, 1776–1956*. Metuchen, N.J., 1971. Explores the American involvement in Morocco.

Hinckley, Frank E. *American Consular Jurisdiction in the Orient*. Washington, D.C., 1906. An old work but still useful as a survey of American consular jurisdiction in Turkey and East Asia.

Jones, Francis Clifford. *Extraterritoriality in Japan and the Diplomatic Relations Resulting in Its Abolition, 1853–1899.* New York, 1970. Jones's thesis, originally published in 1931, this is the best detailed study of the extraterritoriality system in Japan.

Keeton, George W. *The Development of Extraterritoriality in China.* 2 vols. London and New York, 1928. Comprehensively surveys extraterritoriality in China from a historical and legal point of view.

Krasner, Stephen. "Sovereignty: An International Perspective." *Comparative Political Studies* 21, no. 1 (April 1988). Offers interesting discussion of the changing nature of sovereignty.

Lacey, John R., ed. *Act of State and Extraterritorial Reach: Problems of Law and Policy.* Chicago, 1983.

Land, Dieter, and Gary Born, eds. *The Extraterritorial Application of National Laws.* New York, 1987.

Liu, Shuh Shun. *Extraterritoriality: Its Rise and Decline.* New York, 1969; originally published 1925. Viewing extraterritoriality from the perspective of the Chinese, Liu traces its origins and development, the problems of consular jurisdiction, and the reasons for its decline in China.

Lowe, A. V., ed. *Extraterritorial Jurisdiction: An Annotated Collection of Legal Materials.* Cambridge, Mass., 1983. An indispensable guide to these sources.

Malloy, William M. *Treaties, Conventions, International Acts, Protocols, and Agreements Between the United States of America and Other Powers, 1776–1932.* 4 vols. Washington, D.C., 1910–1938. One of the best sources for these diplomatic instruments and specific treaty provisions regarding extraterritorial rights.

Mooney, Eugene F. *Foreign Seizures: Sabbatino and the Act of State Doctrine.* Lexington, Ky., 1967.

Rosenthal, Douglas E., and William M. Knighton. *National Laws and International Commerce: The Problem of Extraterritoriality.* London and Boston, 1982.

Stuart, Graham H. *The International City of Tangier.* 2d ed. Stanford, Calif., 1955. Explores the background to the creation of the international city of Tangier and its problems from the standpoints of geography, history, and diplomacy.

Susa, Nasim. *The Capitulatory Regime of Turkey: Its History, Origin, and Nature.* Baltimore, 1933. Emphasizes custom and usage as the major reason for the granting of capitulary rights to foreigners by the Islamic states.

Thomson, Janice E. *Mercenaries, Pirates, and Sovereigns: State-Building and Extraterritorial Violence in Early Modern Europe.* Princeton, N.J., 1994. Provides interesting discussion of the complex relationship among these interests.

Townsend, James B. *Extraterritorial Antitrust: The Sherman Act and U.S. Business Abroad.* Boulder, Colo., 1980.

Trask, Roger R. *The United States Response to Turkish Nationalism and Reform, 1914–1939.* Minneapolis, Minn., 1971. Offers insights into the normalization of Turkish-American relations.

Treat, Payson J. *Diplomatic Relations between the United States and Japan, 1853–1895.* 2 vols. Stanford, Calif., and London, 1932. Based primarily on archival sources, this study thoroughly surveys American-Japanese relations and includes extensive material on Japan's efforts to secure treaty revision and the abolition of extraterritoriality.

Wendt, Alexander. "Anarchy Is What States Make of It: The Social Construction of Power Politics." *International Organization* 46, no. 2 (spring 1992). Explores modern concepts of power in international context.

Zimmerman, James Michael. *Extraterritorial Employment Standards of the United States: The Regulation of the Overseas Workplace.* New York, 1992. Offers essential discussion, legal precedent, and case law.

See also AMBASSADORS, EXECUTIVE AGENTS, AND SPECIAL REPRESENTATIVES; INTERNATIONAL LAW; PROTECTION OF AMERICAN CITIZENS ABROAD.

FOREIGN AID

Katherine A. S. Sibley

The United States government first recognized the usefulness of foreign aid as a tool of diplomacy in World War II. Such a program, policymakers believed, would fulfill three goals: it would furnish humanitarian assistance to needy peoples, it would promote liberal capitalist models of development in other countries, and it would enhance national security. The U.S. commitment to foreign aid since has amounted to well over $1 trillion in current dollars—not counting hundreds of billions more donated through the International Monetary Fund, World Bank, and other multilateral agencies. Always a controversial program, foreign assistance drew its broadest support in the early Cold War era. At that time, the effort to undermine communism permeated all other aid considerations, including the plight of the poor, the expansion of democracy abroad, and U.S. economic goals that might be served by foreign assistance, such as stimulating private investment and opening up markets to American products. All of these objectives, however, generated wide support from members of Congress, ranging from those whose chief focus was U.S. security to those who were most interested in developing the Third World.

In the Vietnam era, however, the consensus of support began to unravel. Like the war itself, foreign aid programs were variously attacked as imperialistic, paternalistic, harmful, wasteful, or just plain useless. (Indeed, these imperialistic attributes of aid had contributed to the United States's own birth—without the assistance of the empires of France and Spain, the nascent republic would hardly have survived.) Although American foreign aid has changed its emphasis frequently since the Vietnam era in response to such criticisms, the flow has never stopped and has continued to generate calumny from all sides of the political spectrum. Notwithstanding these attacks, foreign aid has undoubtedly racked up some solid achievements. Third World residents have experienced great advances in their standard of living since the 1960s. The eradication of smallpox, the halving of poverty, the doubling of literacy from 35 to 70 percent, and the sharp rise in life expectancy from forty-one to sixty-three years, are evidence of this. Unfortunately, such improvements have not headed off a broadening economic gap between the rich and poor nations. For instance, Africa's average annual income in adjusted dollars in the 1990s was about the same as it had been in the 1960s, approximately a dollar a day. There, too, the AIDS epidemic has proved as devastating as smallpox. The great ambitions of President John F. Kennedy for foreign aid (see sidebar) were not met in the 1960s "decade of development," nor have they been realized since.

During the Cold War era, bilateral assistance (on a government-to-government level, including that channeled via nongovernmental organizations) broke down in unadjusted dollars to $139 billion in military and economic assistance to the Middle East and South Asia, $70 billion to East Asia, $48 billion to Europe, $29 billion to Latin America, and $23 billion to Africa. In the 1990s, both the demise of the Soviet Union, whose influence U.S. foreign aid was long designed to check, as well as the spectacular economic growth of such former aid recipients as South Korea, led the United States to adopt new targets. Indeed, as Secretary of State Madeleine Albright declared in 1999, "traditional notions of 'foreign aid' have become virtually obsolete." The 1997 State Department strategic plan outlined the following goals for foreign aid: creating "institutions that support democracy, free enterprise, the rule of law and a strengthened civil society"; providing humanitarian aid; and "protecting the United States from such specific global threats as unchecked population growth, disease, the loss of biodiversity, global warming, and narcotics trafficking." At the turn of the twenty-first century,

U.S. funds were defending peace in Kosovo, East Timor, and the Middle East, dismantling Soviet nuclear weapons, disarming drug dealers in Central America, democratizing Nigeria, and developing the armies of America's erstwhile enemies, the former socialist countries. Yet, as Albright herself acknowledged in 2000, the programs continued to support very traditional aims, such as "promoting U.S. exports, spurring overseas development and helping other countries to achieve viable market economies"—in other words, expanding the adoption of liberal capitalist norms of development. While recipient countries have certainly changed, the United States continued to spend about the same amount as it had at the end of the Cold War, utilizing Cold War foreign aid instruments like the Foreign Assistance Act and the Agency for International Development. According to the State Department, in 2000 the United States spent $16.5 billion on foreign operations, ranging from the Peace Corps ($244 million) to the foreign Military Training Program ($4.8 billion).

THE ORIGINS OF FOREIGN AID

Prior to World War II, U.S. government-to-government assistance and loans were extremely rare and limited to emergency situations. The impulse to spend money to spread goodwill and influence abroad was not absent, of course: in the nineteenth century, private individuals supported such causes as Greek independence in the 1820s and victims of the Irish famine in the 1840s; later, major corporations set up international philanthropic arms like the Rockefeller Foundation. During and after World War I, the U.S. government became directly involved in disaster relief, assisting German-occupied Belgium and sending $20 million to Russian famine victims in 1921. Subsequently, enormous U.S. lending helped rebuild Germany and other countries, alongside the efforts of American religious organizations like the American Friends Service Committee and the Young Men's Christian Association. The U.S. loans stopped, however, in the Great Depression and were never repaid. Campaigning in 1932, Franklin D. Roosevelt promised that the United States would sanction no more such foreign investments.

But military aid continued to flow throughout the interwar years to pro-U.S. regimes in neighboring countries, including Cuba, Mexico, and Nicaragua. During World War II, moreover, the State Department's Coordinator for Inter-American Affairs, Nelson Rockefeller, set up the Institute of Inter-American Affairs, which furnished food and sanitation assistance as a counterweight to Nazi influence in Latin America. In the late 1930s, President Roosevelt developed a Western Hemisphere Defense Program to further U.S. influence in the region with greater trade and cultural ties, as well as military aid. Like the subsequent $50 billion lend-lease program for Europe and Asia, which included the first major U.S. effort to export arms outside Latin America, these initiatives were all defense measures. They were supplemented by other programs, such as the $6.1 billion that the United States contributed to the Government and Relief in Occupied Areas program from 1943 to 1951, as well as the $2.6 billion it furnished the United Nations Relief and Rehabilitation Administration from 1943 to 1947. In the immediate aftermath of the war, the United States also sent military surplus items to France, Britain, Nationalist China, and the Philippines, where it maintained bases following independence in 1946. Such assistance remained ad hoc, since Congress as yet resisted an expansion of U.S. military aid. "We should not be sending military missions all over the world to teach people how to fight in American ways," said the Republican senator Robert Taft of Ohio.

Also during World War II, the Bretton Woods Conference led to the creation of the International Monetary Fund (IMF) and the International Bank for Reconstruction and Development (the World Bank), two key instruments of economic relief and reconstruction that were aimed at ending the kinds of economic nationalism that many felt had led to the Great Depression and the war. The IMF established the dollar as the international currency, facilitated international trade, and made loans to governments to fix trade imbalances; the World Bank ensured that foreign investment in developing areas would be less risky by extending loans for reconstruction and development projects, and promoting investment and international trade. The United States dominated both organizations, in 1945 holding one-third of the votes in each and supplying one-third of the financing of the bank, or $3 billion. At century's end, the United States still supplied one-fifth of all IMF funds, and these institutions and their policies continued to generate controversy. In September 2000, at World Bank–IMF meetings in Prague, the debts owed by Third World governments sparked riots as thousands of protesters, dissatisfied with the agencies' debt relief policies and the pace of economic globalization, threw Molotov cocktails and rocks at police and at such bastions of global capitalism as a McDonald's restaurant, cutting short the meetings.

THE COLD WAR FOREIGN AID PROGRAM, 1947–1953

The postwar commitment of the United States to foreign aid stemmed from its vast aid role in World War II but also involved a number of new considerations. Initially, American foreign aid programs in the early Cold War demonstrated the nation's assumption of the economic and political role previously played by Great Britain, as exemplified by the Truman Doctrine and its support to such former British clients as Greece and Turkey. The United States also used foreign aid to promote free-market standards for development, including the integration of West European economies and the curtailing of economic protectionism, through such instruments as the Marshall Plan. These programs, and especially the Marshall Plan, would greatly benefit the U.S. economy by generating orders at home. Finally, and most importantly, these efforts were designed to prevent the spread of international communism. By early 1946, U.S. policymakers were becoming increasingly convinced that the Soviet Union had embarked upon a path toward world domination. The following year, the State Department official George F. Kennan called for "long-term, patient but firm and vigilant containment of Russian expansive tendencies," and the United States adopted containment as its doctrine for dealing with the Soviet Union.

It was Soviet pressure in the Mediterranean that led the United States to announce the Truman Doctrine in March 1947, thereby launching its Cold War foreign aid program in earnest. Extending an unprecedented peacetime aid amount of $650 million, the doctrine proclaimed that "it must be the policy of the U.S. to support free peoples who are resisting attempted subjugation by armed minorities or by outside pressures." It was the first time that the United States had put cold cash as well as warm bodies, in the form of technical advisers, behind the containment policy. In a joint session of Congress, Truman declared that totalitarian regimes "spread and grow in the evil soil of poverty and strife," and thus, U.S. help—the only help available, he declared—was necessary to stop the spread of communism.

Less than three months later, the United States proposed the Marshall Plan, or European Recovery Program, in response to the postwar economic crisis in western Europe that many U.S. officials felt would only make it easier for communist parties to take hold there. Secretary of State George C. Marshall, outlining the aid plan in an address at Harvard University on 5 June 1947, stated that the United States "should do whatever it is able to do to assist in the return of normal economic health to the world, without which there can be no political stability and no assured peace." If not for American aid, the Truman administration contended, no parliamentary regime in western Europe would survive and U.S. security would therefore be threatened. The Marshall Plan provided a $12 billion package to sixteen countries in western Europe that not only rebuilt the economies of its recipients but also instituted liberal economic practices such as lower tariffs and instruments to coordinate economic policies.

U.S. officials envisioned that foreign aid, by establishing beneficiaries' internal political stability, promoting their general economic development, and building military strength, was the best way to counteract Soviet expansion. As the program grew during the Cold War, aid recipients fell into two categories: forward defense countries bordering the communist bloc as well as those located in other strategic areas like South Asia and the Middle East, and the less strategically placed countries. In the forward defense countries, but also in sensitive areas like Latin America, aid was often designed to support existing, pro-American governments, through arms and personnel as well as through economic aid to mitigate internal discontent. It was hoped that aid would prevent these countries from falling into the Soviet orbit, which as a result often put the United States on the side of reactionary domestic forces, as was the case in Vietnam, Iran, and Cuba.

Economic assistance programs faced resistance in a tight-fisted Republican postwar Congress, but Cold War threats helped squelch such recalcitrance. Foreign aid quickly expanded to include the economic stabilization of non-European areas, as well as a new emphasis on military assistance. For example, the United States gave limited aid to such nations as South Korea, the Philippines, and Iran. Its biggest expenditure outside of Europe was the $2.5 billion in military and economic aid to the Nationalists in China, aid that continued even after Chiang Kai-shek's government had proved itself utterly beyond help. Then, at his inauguration in January 1949, Truman put forward a pioneering foreign aid proposal that included (1) support for the United Nations; (2) U.S. programs for world economic recovery; (3) support for "freedom-loving countries against aggression"; and 4) "a bold new program for making the benefits of our scientific advances and industrial progress available for the improvement and growth of undeveloped areas." In the wake of China's "fall" to communism, and the Soviet atomic blast, the military threat of Soviet expansion appeared grave, and Truman's third point, to assist "freedom-loving countries," was quickly put into effect. In October 1949, two months after the United States had officially joined NATO, the Truman administration created a Military Assistance Program under the auspices of the Mutual Defense Assistance Act, with a budget of $1.3 billion. Expenditures continued to rise, and in its first three years, as Chester Pach has noted, the program extended $8 billion in military aid to western Europe, largely with the aim of enhancing "the psychological attitudes and morale of our allies." Despite controversies that have dogged military assistance ever since—for instance, that it was an unwieldy program with "no organized, careful thought about what it was that we were trying to do," as Secretary of State Dean Acheson aptly put it—the program continued to grow. U.S. officials reckoned that if military aid were not continued in ever larger amounts, demoralization would set in, weakening western Europe's military position still further.

Point Four, which the inaugural address is best remembered for, was the basis for the Agency for International Development (AID), a $35 million program that provided technical assistance to the Third World. The Point Four program, according to a State Department official, sought "to strengthen and generalize peace . . . by counteracting the economic conditions that predispose to social and political instability and to war." Europe, now recovering with Marshall Plan aid, would no longer be the major recipient of American economic assistance. Despite Europe's continuing importance, as Acheson told Congress in 1950, "economic development of underdeveloped areas" had become a national concern, since "our military and economic security is vitally dependent on the economic security of other peoples." The process of decolonization had made these countries a key battleground in the Cold War, with both Russia and America vying for influence over the newly formed nation-states of Asia and Africa. (Another undeveloped area, Latin America, received less attention in the 1950s.) The UN and the World Bank also shifted their focus from reconstruction of war-torn Europe to the problems of the Third World at this time. The Third World's stash of raw materials further heightened its importance. In 1952 the President's Materials Policy Commission recommended that the United States look to the countries of Africa, the Middle East, southern and southeastern Asia, and Latin America for imports of minerals and tied aid programs to this end in the 1950s.

Truman's initiatives were incorporated into the Mutual Security Act (MSA) of 1951, which succeeded the Marshall Plan and offered a new program of economic and, especially, military aid both for Europe and the developing world. In its first year, for example, the act extended to Europe a combined military and economic package of $1.02 billion; in 1952, as the Korean War ground on, it included $202 million in military support to Formosa (Taiwan) and Indochina. In the wake of National Security Council document NSC 68 of 1950, which had called for large-scale military aid along with an enormous defense buildup, security-related assistance would become a hallmark of the Eisenhower era (1953–1961). Thus, while military assistance had been a little more than a third of the $28 billion in aid that the United States had extended during the Marshall Plan era (1949–1952), during the succeeding eight years, it was almost 50 percent of a larger, $43 billion total. Meanwhile, technical assistance under Point Four went to such countries as Liberia, Ethiopia, Eritrea (where the United States had a large surveillance post), Libya, Egypt, Saudi Arabia, Lebanon, Iraq, Israel, and Iran. Latin America was largely left out of Point Four until the end of the 1950s, although certain countries in which the United States countered perceived communist threats received significant security assistance.

THE EISENHOWER ADMINISTRATION AND EXPANSION OF FOREIGN AID

Senator Tom Connally, chairman of the Senate Foreign Relations Committee, demonstrated the popular sentiment toward foreign aid when he declared in 1951, "We can't go on supporting countries all over the world with handouts just because we like them—or any other reason." Indeed, many members of Congress in this era were reluctant to vote public funds for development purposes, because they believed that such funds should not replace private investment. Beginning with the Marshall Plan, aid had been traditionally aimed at stimulating private investment through trade liberalization and by making improvements in the global economic climate. In fact, in his first State of the Union message, President Dwight D. Eisenhower unabashedly proclaimed that the explicit purpose of American foreign policy was the encouragement of a hospitable environment for private American investment capital abroad. He called for trade, not aid. Such hard-headed motives did not preclude a significant expansion of U.S. economic aid in the Eisenhower administration, however, as confirmed by a significant augmentation of U.S. Export-Import Bank loans and an increase in soft loans in 1954. Cold War pressures as well as the lobbying efforts of individual countries helped further this trend, and the Mutual Security Act of 1954, the first single piece of legislation to embrace the entire foreign assistance program, became the instrument for this new policy. The United States also launched the Agricultural Trade Development and Assistance Act in 1954, commonly called the Food for Peace program, which was still thriving a half century later. This program initially authorized $350 million in food surplus shipments, payable in local currency. Known as Public Law 480, it was the product of some heavy lobbying by Senator Hubert Humphrey, a Democrat who hailed from the farm-filled state of Minnesota. Designed to "increase the consumption of United States agricultural commodities in foreign countries, to improve the foreign relations of the United States and for other purposes," Public Law 480 would authorize $3 billion in sales by 1956 and become an important element in the foreign aid program, while helping to lower U.S. food surpluses. The foodstuffs served as a development subsidy, enabling recipient countries to sell them on the domestic market and then use the proceeds for development projects. Unfortunately, food aid significantly damaged Third World producers, including many Indian farmers, pushing India close to famine in the 1950s and 1960s.

In addition to providing food, foreign aid was also an important weapon of anticommunist intervention during the mid-1950s. After the United States brought down Iran's nationalist, anti-American prime minister, Mohammad Mossadegh, in 1953, replacing him with Shah Mohammad Reza Pahlavi, it gave that country $85 million in foreign aid, and the shah's army was soon among the best-equipped in the Middle East. Eisenhower and Secretary of State John Foster Dulles also used foreign aid to gain friendship and allies in Latin America. In 1954, the United States intervened in Guatemala to overturn the regime of Jacobo Arbenz Guzmán and assist in the military coup of Carlos Castillo Armas. Guzmán, according to U.S. Ambassador John Peurifoy, "talked like a communist, he thought like a communist, and he acted like a communist, and if he is not one, he will do until one comes along." American aid to Guatemala, which had amounted to just $600,000 over the preceding ten years, rose to $130 million in the six years following Castillo Armas's coup. One of Guatemalan aid's most vigorous supporters was Vice President Richard Nixon, who touted construction of the country's Inter-American Highway as promoting everything from trade to security. Guatemala thus became a "testing ground" in the Eisenhower administration's newly expanded foreign aid program.

At the same time, however, U.S. officials grew increasingly uncomfortable with another Latin American client, Cuban leader Fulgencio Batista, who used American military aid meant for "hemispheric defense" against his own people in the late 1950s. Washington welcomed his departure and, initially, the ascendance of Fidel Castro. Soon, however, American military aid, training, and scuba suits would be furnished to the Cuban foes of the Soviet-leaning Castro, though to little effect. In 1957, the State Department's International Cooperation Administration set up a Development Loan Fund chiefly to assist India, which faced a serious foreign exchange crisis. This program represented the first significant use of subsidized (or soft) loans, which by the end of the decade would become the most important tool employed in U.S. foreign aid programs, replacing development assistance. By 1961, the World Bank had also set up a soft loan agency, the International Development Association. U.S. and World Bank lending to India helped the government build fertilizer plants, power plants, highways, railroad locomotives, and airplanes. In the process, however, it strengthened India's national economic planning apparatus, as Shyam Kamath noted in a 1994 article, and "facilitated the growth of the public sector at the expense of the private sector." Thus, though the United States professed that its aid and technical assistance was aimed at creating a better environment for investment and a more liberal economy, as the Indian example shows it often assisted instead in the entrenchment of heavy-handed central planning agencies in the Third World.

As the loans to India demonstrated, the less-developed countries continued to be a vital battleground for U.S.-Soviet competition. In January 1957, in response to the deepening of relations between Egyptian leader Gamal Abdul Nasser and Soviet premier Nikita Khrushchev, the Eisenhower Doctrine pledged U.S. support to any nation in the Middle East that wanted help "resisting armed attack from any country controlled by international communism," and Congress approved a $200 million economic and military aid program for the defense of this region. Then, as 1960 ushered in the "development decade" (see sidebar), Washington finally recognized its largely neglected neighbors at the Conference of the Organization of American States in Bogotá, pledging $500 million for the Inter-American Fund for Social Development. This fund included a bank to furnish improved sanitation, housing, and technical training, in order to enable "the individual citizen of Latin America to live a better life and to provide him the fullest opportunity to improve his status." At the Punta del Este Conference the following year, the Kennedy administration would launch the Alliance for Progress. This program, funded largely by the United States, had as its goal the modernization of Latin America through reform of its political and economic structures, and the injection of capital and technical assistance.

THE PEAK OF PRESTIGE: FOREIGN AID UNDER KENNEDY

Upon entering office in 1961, President John F. Kennedy very much hoped to burnish the image of American foreign assistance, which had been skewered in such recent books as Eugene Burdick and William J. Lederer's best-selling *The Ugly American* (1958), a novel about an ignorant, insular set of foreign service officers-at-large in Southeast Asia, hopelessly losing the battle to communism owing to their maladroit application of foreign aid. Kennedy saw the Peace Corps as one way to revamp this impression of America abroad. The notion of volunteers living alongside those they sought to help was a far cry from *The Ugly American*'s out of touch bureaucrats and was particularly appealing in an era that came to represent the "high-water mark of idealism concerning what overseas aid could achieve," as Paul Mosley wrote. Kennedy established the agency by executive order less than six weeks after he took office.

While *The Ugly American* no doubt had a salubrious influence on him, perhaps the president should have paid closer attention to a far more chilling and penetrating critique of American foreign intervention in this era, Graham Greene's *The Quiet American* (1955). In this novel, an arrogant, clean-cut young American character, Alden Pyle, idealistically destroys innocent lives in order to save the Vietnamese from communism, eerily foreshadowing the U.S. role in that country that Kennedy helped propel in the early 1960s, in part through foreign aid.

In September 1961, Congress enacted the Foreign Assistance Act (FAA), still the governing charter for U.S. foreign aid. Like the MSA earlier, the FAA attempted to systematize all existing foreign aid programs and included a Development Loan Fund, which would assist with large projects, as well as a Development Grant Fund for technical development. In addition, the FAA provided a "supporting assistance" program (later called the Economic Support Fund) to promote economic and political stability and launched a program to protect American business abroad, the antecedent of the Overseas Private Investment Corporation.

Later that fall, the Agency for International Development (USAID) opened for business, coordinating U.S. assistance programs under the aegis of the State Department. As this flurry of activity shows, Kennedy was a great promoter of foreign aid, which he envisioned as part of his goal to "pay any price, bear any burden" to assist the free world. The fundamental task of our foreign aid program in the 1960s, he said idealistically, "is not negatively to fight Communism . . . it is to make a historical demonstration that in the twentieth century, as in the nineteenth . . . economic growth and political democracy can develop hand in hand." As Michael Hunt notes skeptically, Kennedy and other foreign aid advocates were convinced that "thanks to American wisdom and generosity and to the marvels of social engineering, the peoples of these new nations would accomplish in years what it had taken the advanced countries decades to achieve."

Despite Kennedy's words, fighting communism remained a priority. By its very dynamic, as he recognized, the modernization process that was necessary for economic growth could also

JOHN F. KENNEDY'S SPECIAL MESSAGE TO THE CONGRESS ON FOREIGN AID

"Is a foreign aid program really necessary? Why should we not lay down this burden which our nation has now carried for some fifteen years? The answer is that there is no escaping our obligations: our moral obligations as a wise leader and good neighbor in the interdependent community of free nations—our economic obligations as the wealthiest people in a world of largely poor people . . . and our political obligations as the single largest counter to the adversaries of freedom.

"To fail to meet those obligations now would be disastrous. . . . For widespread poverty and chaos lead to a collapse of existing political and social structures which would inevitably invite the advance of totalitarianism into every weak and unstable area. Thus our own security would be endangered and our prosperity imperiled. . . .

"The whole southern half of the world—Latin America, Africa, the Middle East, and Asia—are caught up in the adventures of asserting their independence and modernizing their old ways of life. . . .

"[T]hese new nations need help for a special reason. Without exception they are under communist pressure. . . . But the fundamental task of our foreign aid program in the 1960s is not negatively to fight communism: Its fundamental task is to help make a historical demonstration that . . . economic growth and political democracy can develop hand in hand. . . .

"The 1960s can be—and must be—the crucial 'Decade of Development'—the period when many less-developed nations make the transition into self-sustained growth—the period in which an enlarged community of free, stable, and self-reliant nations can reduce world tensions and insecurity. . . .

"We must say to the less-developed nations, if they are willing to undertake necessary internal reform and self-help . . . that we then intend during this coming decade of development to achieve a decisive turn-around in the fate of the less-developed world, looking toward the ultimate day when . . . foreign aid will no longer be needed."

— *From* Public Papers of the Presidents of the United States: John F. Kennedy, 1 January to 31 December 1961 *(Washington, D.C., 1964): 203–206* —

unleash unpredictable forces, including mass unrest. This was just the sort of milieu that communists might exploit through sponsorship of internal insurrection, "the so-called war of liberation," as Kennedy put it in a June 1961 speech. An American military response alone would be ineffective in combating such uprisings; aid, too, was necessary, as it would "help prevent the social injustice and economic chaos upon which subversion and revolt feed." Foreign assistance *and* American counterinsurgency expertise, it was believed, would steer countries through these difficult transitions without their resorting to revolutionary, communist regimes.

As USAID administrator Fowler Hamilton put it plainly to Congress in budget hearings in 1962, "The communists are active. The total commitments they are putting out now run on the order of $1.2 billion to $1.3 billion a year." Fortunately, "the free world" was more than holding its own, supplying the Third World with $8 billion in both aid and private investment. "I think that we have the resources and the good sense to prevail," said Fowler, mindful of his budgetary ambitions.

Yet Representative Marguerite Stitt Church of Illinois raised one of foreign aid's most vexing questions during Fowler's testimony. While agreeing with the importance of defending "the cause of human freedom, as exemplified by the ideals of this country," she also worried that the emphasis still placed on major huge projects "would not reach the lives of the 'little people' whom we must touch." A similar plea was made at the time by the foreign aid analyst John D. Montgomery in *The Politics of Foreign Aid*, who argued that the United States was too willing to overlook the undesirable aspects of certain recipient regimes, giving the United States the reputation of being "divorced . . . from the social progress" of the people in these countries.

As such observations revealed, even in the heyday of foreign aid the program faced sharp criticism. Representative J. L. Pilcher asserted that despite over $1 billion already spent in Vietnam, leader Ngo Dinh Diem's lack of popular support would mean that the country would be "in the hands of the communists" within twenty-four hours of the departure of U.S. troops—not such an inaccurate prediction, as it turned out. "Where is all our economic aid going to help stop communism in that country?" he wondered. It was an unanswerable question, and the spending continued.

Indeed, U.S. representatives in the newly decolonizing countries quickly learned that aid would get them improved access to government officials, and by 1963, there were twenty-nine aid programs operating in Africa. Some members of Congress, however, remained dubious about the expansion of foreign aid, and, for that reason, Kennedy asked a prominent detractor of foreign assistance, General Lucius Clay, to look into the matter—the confident Kennedy certain that even the critic Clay would be convinced of the program's value once he looked into it. However, Clay's committee's findings showed that "these new countries value their independence and do not want to acquire a new master in place of the old one . . . there is a feeling that we are trying to do too much for too many too soon . . . and that no end of foreign aid is either in sight or in mind." Clay's verdict as to the indeterminate nature of this program was certainly borne out. And despite Kennedy's fervent conviction of the effectiveness of foreign aid, programs like the Peace Corps and the Alliance for Progress were hard-pressed to meet the social and economic challenges they confronted in the Third World.

Kennedy's idealism, too, could not alter the fact that throughout the 1960s, foreign aid programs were conceived with increasingly close attention to U.S. security interests. Foreign assistance remained largely focused on keeping the Third World from turning to communism, and included support to strengthen resistance to internal communist movements as well as to meet the external Soviet threat. Funds for infrastructural improvements and education were a favorite vehicle for these objectives. Secretary of Defense Robert McNamara, demonstrating the close link Washington envisioned between aid and U.S. predominance in the Cold War, declared in 1964 that "the foreign aid program . . . and the military assistance program [have] now become the most critical element[s] of our overall national security effort." Making the connection even more precise, President Lyndon B. Johnson added that the foreign aid program was "the best weapon we have to ensure that our own men in uniform need not go into combat."

Actually, foreign aid went right into war alongside the soldiers in Vietnam, as part and parcel of the large U.S. pacification program in the southern half of that country. Vietnam drew the fervent involvement of USAID, which, as Nicholas Eberstadt has pointed out, made that country the donor for nearly half of its development grants by 1966. Much of this went to fund the ill-fated strategic hamlet program and other disastrous measures, which, while feeding the dislocated South Vietnamese, gutted their economic foundations and thus worked exactly against the traditional objectives of foreign aid. But at the same time, the United States also showed its sensitivity to indigenous economic conditions by hosting the Tidewater conference in Easton, Maryland, where representatives of seventeen nations mobilized in 1968 in response to the threat of famine in India. Their work led to the "green revolution," a movement that brought innovations to agricultural cultivation in the Third World to produce more staple foods and prevent famine.

FOREIGN AID IN CRISIS: THE VIETNAM EFFECT AND "NEW DIRECTIONS"

Despite such successes, disillusionment arising from the deepening commitment in Southeast Asia led many Americans across the political spectrum to disparage foreign aid, and for the first time such criticisms were heard at the highest levels of the U.S. government. For much of the post–World War II period, the policymaking establishment held foreign assistance as sacrosanct in American politics and diplomacy and often oversold its virtues to a skeptical public and Congress. Democratic and Republican administrations outbid each other in extending aid programs; liberal and conservative members of Congress joined in bipartisan voting on aid appropriations, even as individual members grumbled; and labor, management, religious, and educational groups all voiced approval of foreign aid. Yet the interventionist consensus articulated in the Truman Doctrine and Point Four, and widely supported for two decades, foundered in Vietnam. Arguments that for twenty years had given the greatest urgency and immediacy to the cause of foreign aid—including the threat of communism, the need for continued access to vital raw materials, the economic benefits to be gained through increased trade, and the political dividends to be reaped in terms of peace and democracy—lost much of their force, at least temporarily. At the deepest point in U.S. involvement in the Third World, many Americans began to question the rationale for any involvement.

Thus, by 1970, Washington had dropped its commitment in Africa to ten countries, and in 1971 and 1972 the Senate refused to fund foreign assistance at all, although a year-end catchall resolution covered the budgets. Antiwar legislators joined members of Congress who opposed government waste in tightening the reins on USAID, as the agency became subject to heightened congressional oversight that gave legislators veto power over even the smallest items. Despite considerable public and congressional debate over the objectives and techniques of foreign aid programs—particularly from conservatives in both parties who objected to what Representative Otto Passman called "the greatest give-away in history"—Congress decided to keep foreign aid in the 1970s, although revising its aims significantly.

Meanwhile, Third World nations were also becoming increasingly critical of the existing system of aid distribution. Rejecting reform proposals of the foreign aid establishment such as those contained in the Rockefeller Report (1969), which urged the United States to widen its use of private investment, skills, and other initiatives, these nonaligned nations proposed a new international economic order, which Jeremy Brecher and Tim Costello note called for "the regulation of global market forces in the interest of the development process" through a program of subsidies and other supports for exports. Critics of the proposal like Nicholas Eberstadt, however, claimed that it was simply an attempt to "disassembl[e] the liberal international economic order . . . augmenting instead the capacity of states and the authority of their leaders to plan their local economies" at Western expense.

In the self-critical angst that characterized the late Vietnam era, the United States was only too willing to shed its old shibboleths about capitalism's virtues. Under the U.S. Foreign Assistance Act of 1973 and the Mutual Development and Cooperation Act, also passed that year, the liberal capitalist model for Third World progress and its associated large-scale development projects came under withering criticism. The mantra of the 1973 reforms, known as "New Directions," became the goal of meeting "basic human needs." USAID focused on programs that assisted in the provision of food, medicine, and housing, especially in rural areas, rather than more grandiose infrastructure projects. The act's categories of assistance grants and development loans were replaced with "functional categories aimed at specific problems such as agriculture, family planning, and education," an organizational structure that has largely remained. The new program in some ways resembled the technical assistance efforts of the early 1950s, but in keeping with the move away from liberal capitalist tenets, the U.S. effort emphasized instead top-down government "development planning" as the best tool to foster Third World growth. Unfortunately, this was often "planning without facts"—especially when Texas-style cattle raising proved untenable in sub-Saharan Africa. The World Bank, meanwhile, participated in a $2.4 billion investment in African agriculture in the 1970s, largely for vast state farms and irrigation programs, with dismal results. In a 1994 article, James Bovard attributed these failures to inappropriate technology as well as "soil unsuitability." By the 1980s, food output in Africa had fallen 20 percent from twenty years earlier. Governments' zeal for complex technologies in place of simple and workable changes, coupled with widespread political corruption, was largely responsible for the disasters in Africa.

In the 1970s, the United States increasingly turned to the World Bank and similar agencies as a favored instrument for dispensing aid, a process called multilateralization. Ostensibly, multilateral aid diluted the pressure that bilateral aid placed on recipient countries, although these agencies' funds came with their own chafing leash. During Robert McNamara's tenure at the bank (1970–1981), its lending rate increased thirteen times, from $883 million to $12 billion. This aid was not always helpful to the people of the Third World. In his article, Bovard quotes a former executive director of the International Monetary Fund, who charged that such "unseemly" lending only ratcheted up Third World politicians' control over their own people, assisting the repressive collectivization programs of such leaders as Julius Nyerere of Tanzania in the early 1970s and the brutal social engineering of the Vietnamese government later in that decade.

THE CARTER AND REAGAN ADMINISTRATIONS: FROM HUMAN RIGHTS TO MARKET REFORMS

When President Jimmy Carter entered office in 1977, he made human rights an important priority in U.S. foreign policy, and this focus led him to cut back on aid to such brutal regimes as that of Ethiopia's Mengistu Haile-Mariam. Military aid, however, continued to the Somalian enemies of the now Soviet-backed Mengistu; by 1980, 75 percent of total African aid was going to the Horn of Africa, reflecting Cold War priorities. Carter's human rights campaign helped reform oppressive governments in Brazil and Argentina, but elsewhere, such as in El Salvador, South Korea, and China, Carter's message was more inconsistently applied, with security interests outweighing human rights concerns. Most egregious, perhaps, was his approach to Iran, where Carter, despite strong congressional criticism, sold the shah of Iran sophisticated AWACS radar systems. American support for the shah helped lead to the revolution of Ayatollah Khomeini. At the same time, Carter administration officials sought to deflect criticisms that USAID was a U.S. foreign policy "tool," and they removed it from the State Department, placing it under the new International Development Cooperation Agency (IDCA). USAID remained closely connected with the State Department, however, and foreign aid continued to serve America's state interests. (The IDCA was closed down in 1998.) Carter also continued a practice begun in the wake of the 1973 Yom Kippur War of extending heavy aid to the Middle East, especially Israel and Egypt, following the 1978 Camp David peace accords between those two nations. In 2001 Egypt and Israel remained the largest recipients of U.S. foreign aid.

When Ronald Reagan entered office, his rhetoric harked back to the Eisenhower administration in its emphasis on traditional liberal capitalist models of development that would stimulate private investment, an outlook that over the following decade slowly took hold in the foreign policy establishment, replacing the 1970s New Directions ethos. By the 1990s, this model was manifest in the foreign aid establishment's support for globalization, essentially a process that promotes the opening of national borders and the internationalization of economic and social ties through capitalist models of free trade and investment. However, in the 1980s, USAID administrator M. Peter McPherson could still insist that overpopulation, not underinvestment, corruption, and mismanagement, was the "primary obstacle" to Third World development. Indeed, the United States continued to fund hopelessly crooked regimes in order to keep them from linking up with the Soviet Union, like that of Mobuto Sese Seko in Zaire (now the Democratic Republic of the Congo). As an exasperated USAID official noted later, Washington's $2 billion investment in Zaire "served no purpose."

During the Reagan administration military aid once again became a high priority, with more than 40 percent of U.S. bilateral aid being distributed in the form of loans for military training and equipment between 1981 and 1986. Outside of Israel and Egypt, a good deal of this aid went to Central America's anti-leftist regimes, including the government of El Salvador. Another key shift in foreign aid in the Reagan era was the new importance placed on Africa. Owing in part to the efforts of a growing number of African-American members of Congress, as well as the increasingly influential nongovernmental organizations, Congress created the Development Fund for Africa, which, as Carol Lancaster notes could not be "raided" by other programs. By the early 1990s, the U.S. African effort had more than recovered from the cutbacks of the early 1970s. USAID had programs in forty-three African countries, with thirty field missions.

While the United States certainly changed priorities in its economic aid programs in the wake of Vietnam, Congress was ready to gut military programs in this era. In 1976, President Gerald Ford tried to stem congressional zeal for cutting military assistance, as exemplified in the Foreign Assistance Act of 1974, which called for such aid to be "reduced and terminated as rapidly as feasibly consistent with the security of the United States." Ford compromised by cutting such assistance in the 1977 budget. However, Congress then passed the International Security Assistant and Arms Export Control Act of 1976, which made legislators the final arbiter of arms transfers and deployment of military advisers abroad.

The 1980s, however, also saw a growing debt crisis in the Third World, as many countries defaulted on their foreign obligations. In Africa, debt grew from $55 billion to $160 billion between 1980 and 1990, and servicing the debt proved a crippling task for many governments. The International Monetary Fund and other multilateral agencies, reflecting the growing ethos of "neo-liberalism" in this era, emphasized the importance of markets and market-based reforms to get nations out of debt. Continued aid was made contingent upon policy reforms designed to bring stabilization, such as cutbacks on borrowing and currency devaluation. Gambia, for instance, devalued by 90 percent. In Nigeria, the

World Bank made loans conditional on the ending of subsidies and large-scale irrigation schemes and the furthering of market reforms. In many countries, however, these changes often proved as difficult and culturally dissonant as cattle raising had in the 1970s. As Nguyuru Lipumba noted in a 1988 article, in countries like Tanzania, "streamlining public enterprises and letting them operate as commercial enterprises . . . without central government interference is considered a second-best policy."

THE POST–COLD WAR WORLD

With the fall of the Soviet Union in 1991, U.S. foreign aid programs faced a deep crisis. Senators like Patrick Leahy proclaimed that American aid had lost its purpose and vision and that its connection to foreign policy goals was tenuous at best. This transitional period has provided an opportunity for business groups, among others, to call for a more traditional use of aid: to provide markets for U.S. exports, a sentiment that also led to the 1992 signing of the North American Free Trade Agreement (NAFTA) between the United States, Canada, and Mexico. The NAFTA negotiations were a direct result of Mexico having moved away from more traditional patterns of Third World development, including import substitution and high tariffs, toward a more open market in the 1980s. Such economic openness was touted by foreign aid officials as the best means to improve the plight of the Third World.

The post–Cold War reassessment of aid also brought sharp budget cuts, and by 1997 USAID had lost twenty-four foreign missions and one-third of its staff from a peak in the early 1990s. While traditional in-country development did not disappear, the new emphasis on globalization helped create an agenda of transnational issues, or problems that affect a community of nations, often in a specific region. In 1993, the Clinton administration established the Task Force to Reform AID and the International Affairs Budget, which offered a number of broad-based initiatives reflecting the new transnational perspective on foreign aid such as preventing the spread of disease, environmental destruction, and drug trafficking, and addressing concerns such as child survival, migration, population growth, and the promotion of democracy. The task force's Wharton Report became part of the administration's Peace, Prosperity, and Democracy Act proposal, which called for making foreign assistance more amenable to "emerging international realities"—thus challenging the more narrowly construed national security premises of the venerable Foreign Assistance Act of 1961. This effort did not succeed. Senate Foreign Relations Committee Chairman Jesse Helms decided in 1994 that cuts to foreign aid were more important than an ambitious retooling: "We must stop this stupid business of giving away the taxpayers' money willy-nilly." However, some revamping was unavoidable; the world *had* changed. To assist the former socialist states, in 1994 Congress enacted the Freedom Support Act and the Support for East European Democracies Act. USAID accordingly set up its Center for Democracy and Governance and an Office of Transition Initiatives. Sixteen Eastern European and former Soviet Union countries were targeted for assistance ranging from election financing to media advice. As a result of such initiatives, in 1996 the United States was giving aid to more countries (130) than it did in 1985. Still, traditional priorities did not disappear; while more countries were now getting development aid, it was a small total compared to the security aid that went to the two nations of Israel and Egypt.

The 1990s were also a decade of close reexamination of foreign aid in the international giving arena. The United Nations Development Program issued a study in 1996 that noted that in the 1980s, 100 countries, or 1.6 billion people, had experienced economic decline—despite enormous amounts of global aid. Most of these countries had lower average incomes in 1990 than in 1980, and almost half had smaller incomes than in 1970. The few who seemed to be holding their own were civil servants, whose salaries totaled 20 percent of Zambia's GNP, for instance.

Foreign aid's role in forestalling crises looked dubious too. Much U.S. aid, for example, had gone to so-called "collapsed states," meaning states that have fallen apart due to mismanagement, corruption, civil war, or oppressive leadership, including Somalia, Liberia, Zaire, Rwanda, Sierra Leone, and Sudan. And where states survived, it became difficult to argue that such aid did not have distorting effects on local economies. In 1995, for example, such funds accounted for 46 percent of Lesotho's government expenditures; 77 percent of Ghana's, 97 percent of Malawi's, and an unbelievable 101.4 percent of Madagascar's. In the 1990s, recognition of this fact and its contribution to corrupt practices led the United States to cut off bilateral aid to fifty countries. Washington later replaced some of this aid with assistance designated for humanitarian purposes. The AIDS epidemic in Africa, which by 2001 had created 11 million orphans, was a major impetus behind this new agenda.

In 2000, Congress allocated $715 million to child survival programs that promote maternal and child health and provide vaccines, oral rehydration therapy, and education. Nongovernmental organizations (NGOs) like the Global Alliance for Vaccines and Immunization, backed by corporate constituents including the International Federation of Pharmaceutical Manufacturers Associations, have played a leading role in administering these programs. In 1995, in fact, NGOs registered with USAID spent $4.2 billion on overseas programs, and fourteen of them raised more than $100 million in cash and kind, including government food and freight assistance. These ranged from the giant CARE, with a total of $460 million, to Project Hope with $120 million. The NGO projects were often both simple and innovative. Project HOPE, for instance, used USAID funds to work with tea plantations in Malawi to provide health care for women and children.

Another priority was the promotion of democratic politics in the so-called Second World of former socialist countries. In Serbia, U.S. aid supported resistance movements like Otpor, whose activism helped bring about the ouster of the dictator Slobodan Milosevic. Aid administrators were also tying their works to new transnational priorities. The Clinton administration's Climate Change Initiative, for example, assisted forty-four countries in lowering greenhouse gas emissions. In addition, growing sensitivity to local economies prompted the United States to begin to send farmers along with food supplies in the Food for Peace Program. More than five thousand were sent abroad in the 1990s. Perhaps the largest priority as far as spending was concerned were peacekeeping efforts. These included the well-established programs in the Middle East as well as newer initiatives in the Balkans and in Northern Ireland.

The USAID Development Assistance request from Congress for 2001 illustrated the new global priorities, with $234 million for economic growth, $12 million for human capacity development, $92 million to support democratic participation, $225.7 million for the environment, and $385 million for population programs and protecting human health. The increase in spending on child survival, which rose from $650 million to $724 million between 1998 and 2000, was notable, as was the rise in the International Fund for Ireland (that is, Northern Ireland), which rose from $2.4 billion to $2.7 billion, and the Assistance to Independent States, which rose from $770 million to $836 million. The new emphasis on such programs as child health, which overshadowed development aid, highlighted a continuing debate among the foreign aid establishment as to the relative merits of relief initiatives versus developmental ones.

U.S. economic assistance in the early twenty-first century came through many channels. For example, the Development Assistance program was a mammoth account that included such programs as the Narcotics Control Program of the Department of State, the Development Fund for Africa, Economic Support Funds, Support for East European Democracy, Food for Peace, the InterAmerican Foundation, and the Peace Corps. In addition, many U.S. cabinet agencies, like the Departments of Transportation and Commerce, also provided their own aid and technical assistance programs in such countries as Egypt, Kazakhstan, Russia, South Africa, and Ukraine.

GLOBALIZATION'S IMPACT ON FOREIGN AID

Many of the new priorities reflected a growing recognition of the ongoing process of globalization, which has flourished since the breakdown of rigid trading blocs in the former communist world, as well as the embrace of free trade by Third World nations such as Mexico and South Korea. As noted, it has also brought new attention to transnational issues such as environmental destruction, infectious disease, and terrorism. Globalization has certainly greatly accelerated international communication and trade. It has, for instance, allowed U.S. exports to Central America to double since 1992 to almost $10 billion annually. The process has won a wide following in U.S. foreign aid circles; in 1989 a study conducted by USAID pointed to a seven-point annual growth rate difference between the most and least open economies. In 2000, the World Trade Organization (WTO), an international body that promotes free trade and supports developing countries with technical assistance training, published a paper by Dan Ben-David and L. Alan Winters that argues that poor countries engaged in free trade are able to lift their living standards. The authors cite the experience of South Korea, whose economy jumped 700 percent since the 1960s. In a similar study of eighty countries over four decades, the World Bank agreed that economic openness is linked to higher living standards and growth. The rise of globalization has thus been used by foreign aid administrators to make the case for liberal capitalist models of development, and has undermined the 1970s ethic of direct government-to-government economic transfers to the Third World. As a result, while USAID did not abandon its development projects, it began to tailor them more closely to market results. Yet the U.S. support for just such policies, as exemplified in its leading role in the agencies that promote globalization such as the World Bank, International Monetary Fund, and World Trade Organization, has opened it to criticism that it is forcing them onto Third World nations who would prefer a different path to development.

The 1999 World Trade Organization summit in Seattle, Washington, vividly revealed the wide opposition to globalization, drawing a huge force of protesters from both poor countries and wealthy ones. Many of the protesters would agree with the arguments of Jeremy Brecher and Tim Costello, who have asserted that the WTO "work[s] hand-in-hand with the IMF and the World Bank to impose the Corporate Agenda on developing countries." This corporate agenda, they write, seeks "to reduce all barriers to downward leveling of environmental, labor, and social costs" The American Friends Service Committee went so far as to claim that globalization "has undermined basic rights, cultural and community integrity, the environment, and equity . . . [and] caused economic insecurity." Critics point out that it has also lessened the importance of nations that once could use their resources or strategic locations as bargaining chips for aid, and has helped to create global disasters like the banking crisis in Asia in 1997–1998. Moreover, while some Third World nations like Mexico and Chile were enjoying rebounding economic success from globalization, many were being left behind.

Despite the critics, the process continued apace; in 1998, U.S. exports to the Third World reached $295 billion, showing the increasing importance of these markets to the global economy. Meanwhile, foreign investment in developing nations rose from $70 billion to $118 billion in just two years, 1996–1998. But some globalization supporters have pointed out that Americans and other Westerners could help still further by fully embracing the process themselves and allowing larger quantities of the most impoverished nations' goods to land on their shores. In a 1994 article J. Michael Finger pointed to the stark fact that developed countries' protectionism "reduces developing countries' national income by roughly twice the amount provided by official development assistance."

FOREIGN AID'S CRITICS

Attacks on globalization and its supporters in the foreign aid establishment, interestingly, resembled earlier excoriations of the imperialistic taint of foreign aid programs. In a 1987 study, Michael Hunt contended that "development was the younger sibling of containment" and "drew its inspiration from the old American vision of appropriate or legitimate processes of social change and an abiding sense of superiority over the dark-skinned peoples of the Third World." Writing in 1978, Ian J. Bickerton noted that "foreign aid has enabled former colonial powers, such as the United Kingdom and France, to maintain their historic political, economic, and cultural ties with former colonies . . . it is precisely this network of Atlantic-European domination and imperialism that forms the basis of the current aid programs." This assessment was echoed by the World Trade Organization protesters in Seattle, who accused the United States and other Western countries of perpetuating a mechanism of worldwide economic imperialism—née globalism. In the view of globalization's critics, this process is just another way for rich countries like the United States, with only a fraction of the world's population, area, and natural resources, to manipulate the global money market, to control much of the world's trade, and to reserve most of the world's raw materials for its own use.

In many ways, of course, foreign aid does continue the relationship that began under an earlier, imperialist past, particularly for colonial powers like Britain, France, and Belgium. Yet many other countries, such as the Scandinavian nations and Canada, who lack an imperialist history, have also become foreign aid donors, as Olav Stokke noted in a 1996 article. An overemphasis on the imperialism of foreign aid overlooks the importance of their "humane internationalism," which he termed "an acceptance of the principle that citizens of industrial nations have moral obligations" to the outside world.

Beyond the crimes of imperialism, foreign aid has also been vilified for aiding and abetting despotic regimes that have done little for their people. Scholars such as Hunt, Thomas G. Paterson, Richard H. Immerman and many others have criticized the United States's historic penchant for supporting right-wing military dictatorships in Latin America, Southeast Asia, and the Middle East in order to inhibit the forces of "international communism." Analysts like Nicholas Eberstadt, Doug Bandow, Peter Boone and others agree that aid keeps oppressive political elites in control, but they have focused their critiques more broadly on the overall ineffectiveness of this aid in meeting its stated aims. In several African countries, governments have been so corrupt and countries so wracked by civil war that foreign aid has served only to line the pockets of dictators. While such funds have certainly helped mitigate illiteracy and disease in much of the world, their record of lifting countries out of poverty is more mixed. Many countries have been aid recipients for as many as three decades, including Chile, Egypt, India, Sudan, Turkey, and the former Yugoslavia.

Besides being often ineffective, in some cases aid has been actually damaging. Relief worker Michael Maren, a veteran of the massive Operation Restore Hope campaign in Somalia during the early 1990s, recalled that "the relief program was probably killing as many people as it was saving, and the net result was that Somali soldiers were supplementing their income by selling food," even as rebel forces were using it to further their warfare on Ethiopia. In another ironic example, the U.S.-supported World Bank gave $16 million to Sudan to fight hunger while Sudan's government was starving its own people. Foreign aid, then, has been attacked by critics for imperialistically exploiting the Third World for Western interests, distorting economies, hurting local farmers and peasants, and consolidating the grip of local elites at the expense of the average Third World resident.

Nicholas Eberstadt argues that a chief reason for the inefficacy of U.S. aid is because it has not supported policies that are congruent with American values, including "the defense of liberty" and "the promotion of justice." Instead, the United States has too often relied on a "materialistic" policy limited to financial aid to oppressive regimes, overlooking the plight of those who continue to live under them. Yet Carol Lancaster, a former deputy administrator of USAID who readily admits the failure of aid in many African countries, contended in a 2000 article that foreign aid nevertheless has been "an extremely useful tool of U.S. diplomacy." She points to progress in lowering the rate of poverty worldwide, from 28 percent in the late 1980s to 24 percent a decade later, and to the trend of rising living standards in Europe, Asia, the Middle East, and Latin America. By the end of the twentieth century, these trends had yet to affect much of Africa. Further, she argues that a new policy of foreign aid, one that emphasizes humanitarian relief, democracy, human rights, and development—the latter to be limited to the poorest countries—is precisely the mechanism to further an American "diplomacy of values." Such aid will bring "soft power" to the United States, enhancing "the credibility and trust that the U.S. can command in the world."

This continued emphasis on values recalls the spirit of the 1985 Live Aid concert, orchestrated by rock star Bob Geldof in response to a devastating famine in Ethiopia. This and subsequent events helped create among their numerous participants a "constituency of compassion"—and a conviction that famine was a concern that the world community should respond to. At the time, however, critics dismissed this as so much sentimentalism and called for "development experts" to tackle the problem instead.

In the post–Cold War world both America's money and its position as the world's only superpower have made its global economic influence more significant than ever, especially in remaining areas of tension such as the Middle East and the former Yugoslavia. Peacemaking in such areas has emerged as perhaps the leading foreign policy problem facing the United States, and foreign aid remains the vehicle for most of the money that goes to these areas. In the Balkans, for instance, a promise of $500 million in U.S. aid helped end the war in Bosnia. The Israeli-Arab conflict has proved more intractable, though this seems unlikely to stem the flow of U.S. aid. Of the $3.5 billion in Foreign Military Financing (FMF) grants proposed in the 2001 budget to buy defense products and services, Israel was to receive just under $2 billion and Egypt $1.3 billion. In addition to this military aid, the State Department's Economic Support Fund also listed a $2.3 billion allocation for Israel and Egypt, with $840 million for the former and $695 million for the latter. Despite such hefty grants, Israel requested several billions more for advanced weapons systems not covered by the requested amounts.

Some critics have questioned how consistent these expenditures are with American values or with U.S. interests. As the Center for Defense Information's Rachel Stohl writes, "Selling weapons to these countries can perpetuate autocratic rule.... United States programs should not contribute to the prolonging of these 'un-American' practices." Leon Hadar of the CATO Institute, moreover, argues that the United States should drop its heavy commitment to Middle East peacekeeping, making room for regional powers such as Egypt, Jordan, and Saudi Arabia to get involved instead.

In addition to providing aid to Israel and Egypt, the FMF funds have been used for detonating mines, fighting narcotics traffic, helping to dismantle nuclear weapons in Russia, and integrating Hungary, Poland, and the Czech Republic within NATO. FMF aid, indeed, was part of a sizable U.S. foreign military assistance program that amounted to $17.4 billion in 2000, including both State and Defense Department programs. The International Military Education and Training Program (IMET), for instance, provided military training in the United States for personnel from thirty countries. While the Pentagon asserted that the $50 million program inculcated its students with American values and human rights principles, one of its member institutions, the School of the Americas in Fort Benning, Georgia, came under attack beginning in the 1980s for its connection with military adventurism in Latin America. Nineteen of the twenty-six members of the El Salvadoran military implicated in the murder of six Jesuit priests in that country in 1989 were alumni of Fort Benning. Adverse attention led the school to change its name in late 1999 to the Center for Inter-American Security Cooperation.

Far larger than IMET is the Pentagon's Foreign Military Sales Program, which racked up $12.1 billion in government-subsidized sales abroad in 2000 on such items as the M1A2 tank and the F-16 aircraft. A similar but much smaller effort is the Excess Defense Articles program, which exports military surplus through sales or grants to such countries as Israel, Egypt, Turkey, Poland, and Greece. Under the Foreign Assistance Act, the U.S. president also has "drawdown authority" to use defense monies for foreign emergencies as he sees fit. In 2000, President Bill Clinton put $80 million toward such causes as peacekeeping in Sierra Leone and a program to promote democracy in Iraq.

CONCLUSION

While U.S. economic and military aid continued to grow modestly at the turn of the century, it comprised a far smaller percentage of total global assistance than was the case in the early Cold War. In the late 1940s, during the height of the Marshall Plan, the United States provided 60 percent of the globe's foreign aid; by 1993, its portion had dropped to 16 percent. But the United States has not been alone in decreasing its foreign contributions. In the 1990s, international development assistance declined by one-third in real terms, dropping from $61 billion to $52 billion between 1992 and 1998. Development assistance fell to an average of 0.24 percent of GDP in advanced countries by 1998. The most generous country was Norway, which gave away nearly 1 percent of its GNP; the United States, by contrast, donated only 0.1 percent, the smallest of all members of the Development Assistance Committee of the Organization for Economic Cooperation and Development. However, the United States did furnish the second-highest dollar figure in 1998, $8.8 billion; Japan topped the list with $10.6 billion.

Owing to such expenditures, by the mid-1990s Third World governments owed almost $2 trillion to Western loan agencies and governments. The African debt alone surpassed $230 billion. Beginning in 1996, the IMF and World Bank launched the Heavily Indebted Poor Countries Initiative (HIPC), an attempt to provide significant debt relief (up to 80 percent) based on a program of economic restructuring in the debtor nations. However, when few countries proved able to sustain the restructuring requirements, the funding institutions announced HIPC II in 1998, a bolder initiative that targeted $100 billion in debt reduction. By April 2001, $20 billion in debt had been cancelled for twenty-two countries, eighteen of which were in Africa. Over time the reductions were to bring associated total relief of $34 billion to these countries. When combined with other existing debt relief programs, reductions would amount to $55 billion, about a two-thirds reduction. The millennial year also saw the launching of the international Jubilee 2000 coalition to lobby for further debt relief, using the biblical terminology of a jubilee year, based on ancient Israel's practice of forgiving debts on a fifty-year cycle. To the great enthusiasm of a crowd gathered for a Jubilee 2000 meeting in December of that year, British Chancellor Gordon Brown announced that Britain would cancel or "hold in trust" the debt payments of forty-one countries.

Debt-relief efforts were certainly expected to provide a break for poor nations. However, the fact remained that in 2000 the average person in the richest twenty countries earned thirty-seven times more annually than the typical resident of the poorest twenty nations, double the gap since 1960. Foreign aid, which USAID claims has been responsible for a great deal of the progress in lessening poverty, disease, and illiteracy, indeed may have stopped that gulf from being even wider. The reasons for a continuing gap defy easy explanation, and in general are tied both to rising growth rates in the First World, including a great expansion in private capital, as well as the continuing political, social, and economic problems of the developing world.

With the end of the Cold War's communist threat and a widening perception that foreign aid monies have been ineffective, wasted, or turned to corrupt purposes, America's foreign aid program underwent increasingly close scrutiny. As noted, humanitarian relief and child rescue emerged as the most notable new priorities in the 1990s, supplanting the development paradigm and its oft-discredited large-scale projects. Moreover, a new ideological purpose arose to replace the old Cold War consensus. Upon entering office in January 2001, President George W. Bush cut off U.S. funding to all foreign NGOs with family planning programs that provide abortion or abortion counseling, restoring a policy that his father, George H. W. Bush, and Ronald Reagan also employed, dating back to 1984. At the same time, the longtime critic of foreign aid Jesse Helms called for channeling foreign aid funding directly to religious charities and NGOs, separate from the efforts of USAID's "cold, heartless bureaucrats," as he put it.

American economic and military aid programs, for all their shifting priorities, contested results, and popular distaste, have long outlived the span that their early adherents predicted, and at the turn of the twenty-first century it appeared likely that foreign aid would continue. One may hope that in the next half century, either owing to aid, investment, political reform, or some other set of factors, the developing world will have come much closer to reaching the results predicted by John F. Kennedy for the 1960s "decade of development."

BIBLIOGRAPHY

Baldwin, David. *Economic Development and American Foreign Policy, 1943–1962.* Chicago, 1966. A valuable discussion of the political aspects of American policies of economic development.

Bandow, Doug. "Foreign Aid: Help or Hindrance." Cato Policy Analysis No. 273, 25 April 1997. A strong critique of U.S. foreign aid policies.

Ben-David, Dan, and L. Alan Winters, "Trade, Income Disparity and Poverty." World Trade Organization Special Study No. 5. 1999.

Bill, James A. *The Eagle and the Lion: The Tragedy of Iranian-American Relations.* New Haven, Conn., 1988. A critical look at a controversial relationship.

Boone, Peter, and Jean-Paul Faguet. "Multilateral Aid, Politics and Poverty: Past Failures and Future Challenges." In Richard Grant and Jan Nijman, eds. *The Global Crisis in Foreign Aid.* Syracuse, N.Y., 1998.

Bovard, James. "The World Bank and the Impoverishment of Nations." In Doug Bandow, ed. *Perpetuating Poverty: The World Bank, the IMF, and the Developing World.* Washington, D.C., 1994.

Brecher, Jeremy, and Tim Costello. *Global Village or Global Pillage: Economic Reconstruction from the Bottom Up.* Boston, 1994. The authors strongly critique globalization and argue for greater assistance to the Third World.

Eberstadt, Nicholas. *Foreign Aid and American Purpose.* Washington, D.C., 1988. A powerfully argued critique of foreign aid that suggests American values are missing from the foreign aid calculus.

Edkins, Jenny. *Whose Hunger? Concepts of Famine, Practices of Aid.* Minneapolis, 2000. A study of responses to famine, heavily influenced by postmodern theoretical approaches.

Feis, Herbert. *Foreign Aid and Foreign Policy.* New York, 1964. A strong defense of foreign aid reflecting the ethos of the early 1960s.

Finger, J. Michael. "The High Cost of Trade Protectionism to the Third World." In Doug Bandow, ed. *Perpetuating Poverty: The World Bank, the IMF, and the Developing World.* Washington, D.C., 1994.

Hancock, Graham. *Lords of Poverty: The Power, Prestige, and Corruption of the International Aid Business.* New York, 1989. A highly critical analysis of international aid agencies and their results.

Hogan, Michael. *The Marshall Plan: America, Britain, and the Reconstruction of Western Europe, 1947–1952.* New York, 1987. Still the most comprehensive overview of the program.

Hunt, Michael. *Ideology and U.S. Foreign Policy.* New Haven, Conn., 1987. A well-researched critique of the ideological roots of U.S. diplomacy.

Kamath, Shyam J. "Foreign Aid and India's Leviathan State." In Doug Bandow, ed. *Perpetuating Poverty: The World Bank, the IMF, and the Developing World.* Washington, D.C., 1994.

LaFeber, Walter. *The American Age: United States Foreign Policy at Home and Abroad Since 1750.* New York, 1989. A useful and highly readable survey.

Lancaster, Carol. *Aid for Africa: So Much to Do, So Little Done.* Chicago, 1999. A highly useful, comprehensible, and even-handed survey.

———. "Redesigning Foreign Aid." *Foreign Affairs* 79 (September-October 2000): 74–88.

Landes, David. *The Wealth and Poverty of Nations: Why Some Are So Rich and Some So Poor.* New York, 1998. An innovative study of deep-rooted causes of poverty and wealth.

Lipumba, Nguyuru. "Policy Reforms for Economic Development in Tanzania." In Stephen K. Commins, ed. *Africa's Development Challenges and the World Bank: Hard Questions, Costly Choices.* Boulder, Colo., 1988.

Montgomery, John D. *The Politics of Foreign Aid: American Experience in Southeast Asia.* New York, 1962. A supportive analysis of foreign aid, based on the author's study of the American program in Vietnam.

Mosley, Paul. *Foreign Aid: Its Defense and Reform.* Lexington, Ky., 1987. An optimistic analysis of foreign aid.

Nijman, Jan. "United States Foreign Aid: Crisis? What Crisis?" In Richard Grant and Jan Nijman, eds. *The Global Crisis in Foreign Aid.* Syracuse, 1998.

Pach, Chester J., Jr. "Military Assistance and American Foreign Policy: The Role of Congress." In Michael Barnhart, ed. *Congress and United States Foreign Policy.* Albany, N.Y., 1987. An important study of congressional attempts and effectiveness in influencing foreign military aid.

———. *Arming the Free World: The Origins of the United States Military Assistance Program, 1945–1950.* Chapel Hill, N.C., 1991. Excellent study of the formative years of this program.

Smillie, Ian, and Henny Helmich, eds. *Stakeholders: Government-NGO Partnerships for International Development.* London, 1999.

Stohl, Rachel. "Middle East Remains Attractive Market for U.S. Arms." In Center for Defense Information *Weekly Defense Monitor* 4, no. 7 (17 February 2000).

Stokke, Olav. "Foreign Aid: What Now?" In Olav Stokke, ed. *Foreign Aid Towards the Year 2000: Experiences and Challenges.* London, 1996.

Streeter, Stephen M. *Managing the Counterrevolution: The United States and Guatemala, 1954–1961.* Athens, Ohio, 2000. Argues that the Eisenhower administration intervened in Guatemala to protect U.S. interests against Third World nationalism more than in response to a communist threat.

United Nations Development Programme. *Human Development Report 1996.* New York, 1996.

U.S. Department of State, Agency for International Development. *U.S. Overseas Loans and Grants and Assistance from International Organizations.* Washington, D.C., 1990.

U.S. House of Representatives, 87th Congress, 2d session. *Foreign Assistance Act of 1962, Hearings Before the Committee on Foreign Affairs, on a Draft Bill to Amend Further the Foreign Assistance Act of 1961, as Amended, and for other Purposes.* Washington, D.C., 1962.

See also CONTAINMENT; ECONOMIC POLICY AND THEORY; GLOBALIZATION; INTERNATIONAL MONETARY FUND AND WORLD BANK; TARIFF POLICY.

FREEDOM OF THE SEAS

Armin Rappaport and William Earl Weeks

Freedom of the seas is one of the original and most important principles in the history of American foreign policy. American statesmen have, in essence, defined it as the right of all peoples to travel unmolested in international waters in both war and peace. Historically, it has been one of the chief means by which the United States has influenced international affairs; the vigorous assertion of the principle of freedom of the seas has been a major cause of four armed conflicts: the Quasi-War with France in 1798, the Barbary Wars, the War of 1812, and World War I.

ORIGINS OF THE CONCEPT OF FREEDOM OF THE SEAS

The concept of freedom of the seas predates the American nation, arising in the European world amid the heightened rivalries of the European state system in the fifteenth and sixteenth centuries. It was on the principle of freedom of the seas that King Francis I of France disputed the exclusive right in certain seas that the pope had granted to Spain and Portugal in the fifteenth century. Later, Queen Elizabeth I of England proclaimed: "The use of the sea and air is common to all; neither can any title to the ocean belong to any people or private man." Perhaps the most notable assertion of the principle of freedom of the seas was the book *Mare Liberum* (1609) by Dutch jurist Hugo Grotius. Grotius defined the seas as being, like the air, limitless and therefore common to all people. Despite Grotius's efforts, European mercantilist powers in the seventeenth and eighteenth centuries generally sought to control as much of the world's oceans as they could.

From the beginning of the American nation, U.S. political leaders championed the view that the seas ought to be free in war as well as in peace. As John Adams said in 1783:

The United States of America have propagated far and wide in Europe the ideas of the liberty of navigation and commerce. The powers of Europe, however, cannot agree as yet, in adopting them to their full extent.... For my own part, I think nature wiser than all the courts and estates of the world, and, therefore, I wish all her seas and rivers upon the whole globe free.

Benjamin Franklin was of the same mind. In 1782 he said, "In general, I would only observe that commerce, consisting in a mutual exchange of the necessaries of life, the more free and unrestrained it is the more it flourishes and the happier are all the nations concerned in it." The American assertion of the principle of freedom of the seas thus became closely connected to the principle of freedom of commerce. Applied in wartime, these principles translated into the right of citizens of neutral states to carry on their normal trading pursuits without interference by the belligerents, unless that trade was in a narrowly defined list of war goods destined for a belligerent. Throughout its history, with two exceptions—the Civil War and World War I—the United States has been the principal proponent and defender of that view.

The American position on freedom of the seas was first expressed on 18 July 1776, when John Adams presented to the Continental Congress the report of a committee of which he was chairman and whose other members were Benjamin Franklin, John Dickinson, Benjamin Harrison, and Robert Morris. The committee had been appointed some five weeks earlier and had been charged with preparing a "plan of treaties to be entered into with foreign states and kingdoms." Its report proposed a model set of articles concerning neutral commerce in wartime to be included in treaties of amity and commerce with other powers. On 17 September of the same year, Congress adopted the committee's proposals, which thereupon became the first official American statement on the freedom of the seas.

The proposal contained four articles: first, should one of the signatories be at war and the other neutral, the citizens of the neutral could trade with the enemies of the belligerent in all items except contraband of war, the latter being limited to arms, munitions of war, and horses (food and naval stores were specifically excluded); second, citizens of the neutral could trade with the enemies of the belligerent in noncontraband not only from enemy ports to neutral ports but also between ports of an enemy; third, enemy noncontraband found in neutral ships was not liable to confiscation by the belligerent ("free ships make free goods"); and fourth, neutral goods, whether contraband or noncontraband, found in enemy vessels were liable to confiscation.

These principles, known collectively as the Treaty Plan of 1776, and clearly favorable to neutrals, were not invented by Adams and his colleagues. For more than a century they had been a part of the international maritime scene and had been practiced by neutrals and belligerents during the great dynastic wars of the seventeenth and eighteenth centuries, albeit with occasional modifications. They had also been incorporated in several treaties between European powers, most notably France and Great Britain in 1655, 1686, and 1713.

It is not surprising that Adams's committee proposed, and the Congress accepted, the maritime principles of 1776. For one thing, they were a natural and logical concomitant of the Declaration of Independence. It seemed only reasonable that the "unalienable right to life, liberty, and the pursuit of happiness" should extend to the high seas. More important, the principles were consistent with the visions that the Founders had for the new republic's future. As Adams noted, the country was to "be as little as possible entangled in the politics and controversies of European nations." It would take no part in Europe's wars. Rather, American merchants would be the great neutral carriers of the needs of the belligerents, and for that role they would need the protection of the maritime principles of 1776. Should the United States find itself a belligerent at some future time, a liberal interpretation of the rights of neutrals would still be useful and important. The Founders never expected that the American navy would be large and powerful enough to protect American shipping in wartime—neutral vessels would have to be depended upon to handle American commerce, and for that they would need the cover of the principles of 1776.

American diplomats succeeded in incorporating the cherished maritime articles into the first bilateral treaty signed by the new republic. In 1778 the Franco-American Treaty of Amity and Commerce contained almost without change the language and the substance of the Treaty Plan. But that was only the beginning of the nearly universal acceptance of the American position. Three more agreements—with the Netherlands in 1782, with Sweden in 1783, and with Prussia in 1785—also included the maritime articles of 1776.

Meanwhile, in 1780 the Russian empress, Catherine the Great, had announced that her country's neutral commerce in the war then raging between England and its former colonies would be governed by four principles. Three of them—free ships make free goods, freedom of neutrals to trade between ports of a belligerent, and contraband limited to arms and munitions—came directly from the Treaty Plan of 1776. The fourth—that a port be considered legally blockaded only if there were a sufficient number of vessels at its mouth to make entry dangerous—had not been dealt with by Adams's committee in 1776. It was, however, included in a new treaty plan adopted by the United States in 1784. At Russia's invitation, seven other nations adhered to Catherine's principles. Thus, of the great powers only Great Britain refused to be bound by the liberal maritime principles. Hard though they tried, the American commissioners negotiating the peace that ended the war between mother country and colonies could not get the principles incorporated into the final treaty. English statesmen, envisioning their country more often belligerent than neutral—and big-navy belligerent, at that—rejected the American overtures. The treaty said nothing about the rights of neutrals.

AFFIRMING FREEDOM OF THE SEAS IN THE EARLY NATIONAL PERIOD

A challenge to the principle of freedom of the seas arose soon after the conclusion of the revolutionary war. In 1784 American commercial shipping in the Mediterranean, lacking the protection of the British navy, came under attack from the North African kingdoms along what was known as the Barbary Coast. In 1794, Congress, tired of paying tribute to the Barbary pirates and urged on by New England merchants devastated by ship seizures, passed the Naval Act of 1794, reestablishing the U.S. Navy and authorizing the construction of six frigates to defend American interests in the Mediterranean. President Thomas Jefferson, without seeking congressional approval, dispatched several naval campaigns against the North African kingdoms culminating in the conquest of Tripoli in 1805. In 1815 a U.S. naval squadron bombarded Algiers into agreeing to end its attacks on American shipping. Thus was the principle of freedom of the seas successfully asserted by force.

The wars of the French revolutionary and Napoleonic eras posed an even greater challenge to the principle of freedom of the seas. When war erupted between France and Great Britain in 1793, the United States at once declared neutrality and soon became the chief neutral supplier of belligerent needs. France was legally bound by the terms of the Treaty of 1778 to treat American commerce according to the principles of 1776. Britain, having entered into no agreement with the United States on neutral and belligerent rights, was free to halt, by all means possible, trade between France and America. Unwilling to fight the war at so serious a disadvantage, French warships soon violated the provisions of the 1778 treaty and treated American commerce as the British did. When England and the United States signed a convention in 1794 (Jay's Treaty) that specifically included naval stores on the contraband list and stated that enemy goods were not protected by the neutral flag, France was furious that American diplomats had not forced Britain to accept the principles of 1776. The result was an intensification of French depredations upon American neutral commerce that led in 1798 to an undeclared Franco-American maritime war. Known as the Quasi-War, it lasted until 1800.

France and England made peace in 1802, but war broke out again in the following year. This second phase of the great struggle was marked by intense efforts by each belligerent to prevent neutrals from trading with its enemy. As the chief neutral suppliers and carriers, American citizens suffered severe restrictions on their trade. In 1812 the United States went to war, in part to defend its citizens' neutral rights.

It was true, of course, that the war was fought only against Britain, but not because France's conduct was less reprehensible. Congress, in fact, gave serious consideration to declaring war against both nations. In the end, however, a war against two enemies was unthinkable and Britain was chosen over France for the very good reason that its navy, not France's, dominated the seas and committed the largest number of violations of American neutrality. The point to remember is that the nation risked its lives, its treasure, even its continued existence, in order to defend the rights of its citizens to travel and trade unmolested on the high seas in wartime.

President James Madison, when touching upon maritime reasons for requesting hostilities, referred specifically only to "mock blockades" and to "violations of our coasts" as evidence of Britain's perfidious conduct. More generally, he spoke of Britain "laying waste our neutral trade" and plundering "our commerce . . . in every sea." He surely had in mind three British practices, all contrary to the principles of 1776. One was the interdiction of American trade between ports of the enemy, which England justified on the basis of the Rule of the War of 1756. That rule, established during the French and Indian War of 1754–1763, declared that a trade closed in peacetime could not be opened in wartime. In conformity with mercantilist doctrine, France, as well as every other European nation, prohibited foreigners from engaging in the trade between ports. In wartime, however, when the superior British navy made it unsafe for French vessels to carry the traffic, it was thrown open to non-French bottoms. Thus, the rule deprived American merchants of a lucrative trade. When they sought to evade it by touching at a neutral port (most often in the United States) en route between the two enemy ports, the British were not fooled. Their cruisers picked up the American vessels and their prize courts condemned them on the grounds that the ultimate destination was, in fact, an enemy port and that the voyage between the two enemy ports was "a continuous voyage only ostensibly broken at a neutral port." The two other British practices were the inclusion of naval stores and foodstuffs on the contraband list and the confiscation of enemy goods found in neutral ships.

Now a belligerent, the United States made every effort "to pay the strictest regard to the rights of neutral powers." Naval commanders were instructed "to give them [neutrals] as little molestation or interruption as will consist with the right of ascertaining their neutral character," and the orders were carried out. Neutral rights were respected. Insofar as the war was fought in defense of American neutral rights it proved futile, for the treaty ending the war made no mention of the subject.

Between the end of the war with Britain and the opening of the Civil War, the United States continued to push for the acceptance of the principles of 1776 and the provision on blockade in the Treaty Plan of 1784. To some observers it seemed anomalous that the United States, on the threshold of becoming a significant naval power, should continue to support liberal maritime principles. A clue to the riddle was provided by Secretary of State Henry Clay, who noted in 1828 that the United States did not expect to become involved in maritime wars because its "prosperity is so evidently connected with the preservation of peace." And, he implied, even if the country should become involved in a war—and as a big-navy belligerent—it would value "the general cause of humanity and civilization [which] will be promoted by the adoption of these maritime principles [above] pecuniary interest." Thus, between 1824 and 1850 the United States concluded treaties with ten Latin American republics and one with Prussia incorporating the liberal maritime principles. Efforts to commit Great Britain to the principles remained unsuccessful.

The War with Mexico (1846–1848) provided the United States with the occasion to practice what it preached. Its policy toward neutrals was governed by the instruction of the secretary of the navy to commanding officers of U.S. naval forces in the Pacific, issued on 24 December 1846: "The President has desired to subject neutral commerce to the least possible inconvenience or obstruction compatible with the exercise of the belligerent right necessary to the success of our military operations." One year later, explaining the U.S. position to the newly appointed commander in the Pacific, the secretary wrote: "No present advantage . . . should induce us to depart from that liberal interpretation of the laws of nations which we have always contended for as protecting the interests of neutrals against the violent claims of belligerents." Indeed, in the matter of blockade, contraband, and enemy goods on neutral ships, the United States adhered strictly to the principles of 1776 and 1784.

Six years after the end of the Mexican conflict, the Crimean War broke out and the United States again found itself a neutral—but with two important differences from the period of 1793 to 1812. This time Great Britain and France were on the same side, fighting Russia, and they made clear their intention to pursue a liberal course toward neutral commerce insofar as neutral goods on enemy ships and enemy goods on neutral ships were concerned. In both instances the goods, except for contraband, were to be free from seizure. Russia adopted the same principles and incorporated them in a convention signed with the United States in July 1854.

Encouraged by the action of the three belligerents, especially by that of Great Britain, and recognizing that for Britain and France the policies on neutral rights covered the duration of the war only, the U.S. government sought to incorporate the rules in a multilateral treaty and make them a principle of international law. Secretary of State William L. Marcy, in instructions sent to the American ministers in Paris, London, and St. Petersburg in 1854, enclosed a draft treaty, noting: "The United States are desirous to unite with other powers in a declaration that . . . [the rules] be observed by each hereafter, as a rule of international law." In his annual message to Congress in December of the same year, President Franklin Pierce voiced the same hope.

The three belligerents did, in fact, "unite with other powers in a declaration" on maritime law at the peace conference that met in Paris in the winter and spring of 1856. Four principles constituted the Declaration of Paris, signed on 16 April 1856 by representatives of Austria, France, Great Britain, Prussia, Russia, Sardinia, and Turkey: first, privateering is, and remains, abolished; second, the neutral flag covers enemy goods, except for contraband; third, neutral goods, except for contraband, are not liable to capture under the enemy flag; and fourth, blockades, in order to be binding, must be effective.

The Declaration of Paris proved highly gratifying to the United States. The liberal view on neutral rights that it had so vigorously championed for more than half a century had at last been written, if only in part, into international law. Particularly welcome was the end of British opposition. Still, the United States found itself in the curious situation of refusing to become a party to the declaration. The reason lay in the article on privateering. As Secretary of State Marcy pointed out in a lengthy note to the French minister in Washington, the strong-navy powers could afford to renounce privateering because they could effectively prey upon enemy commerce with their public armed vessels; small-navy states, like the United States, lacking an adequate number of warships, had to rely upon private armed vessels to destroy the enemy's goods. Only if the words "and that the private property of the subjects or citizens of a belligerent on the high seas shall be exempted from seizure by public armed vessels of the other belligerent, except it be contraband" were added to the first article would the United States sign the declaration.

That principle—the complete immunity of (noncontraband) private property—had been advanced by the United States for many years. It was a logical extension of the liberal position on neutral rights. First suggested by Benjamin Franklin in 1780 and again in 1782 for inclusion in the peace treaty ending the War of Independence, it was included in the Treaty Plan of 1784 and incorporated into the Treaty of Amity and Commerce of 1785 with Prussia.

The signatories of the declaration did not summarily reject the American amendment. They deferred action pending a careful examination of the problem and the opportunity to consult among themselves. By March 1857, when President James Buchanan assumed office, no action had been taken and the new secretary of state, Lewis Cass, told the American ministers to suspend negotiations on the subject until the president had time to study "the questions involved." The president, preoccupied with problems closer to home, never did get around to the matter; thus, the United States lost the opportunity to incorporate into a multilateral treaty its historic and traditional position. Because the four principles of the declaration were considered indivisible by the signatories, the United States could not adhere to numbers two, three, and four while rejecting the first.

REVERSING COURSE IN THE CIVIL WAR

Viewed from a different perspective, the failure of the United States to become a party to the Declaration of Paris proved advantageous, for in the Civil War, which broke out in 1861, the United States remained free of any international legal commitments regarding neutral rights vis-à-vis the major naval powers of the time. For the first time in its history, the United States was the preponderant belligerent naval power, and that freedom would permit it to pursue any course at sea calculated to increase the chances of victory. As a matter of fact, the United States did expand its belligerent rights during the war and did constrict those rights of neutrals that it had championed since the earliest days of the Republic.

Early in the war, Secretary of State William H. Seward informed the principal neutral powers that American policy toward their commerce would be governed by the second, third, and fourth articles of the Declaration of Paris. And the United States did, during the course of the war, respect the principles of "free ships make free goods" and the freedom from seizure of neutral goods (not contraband) in enemy ships. On blockade, however, the United States strayed far from its traditional position. It is true that Seward insisted that a blockade not maintained by an adequate force need not be respected and that every effort was made to station a sufficient number of vessels at the blockaded ports to prevent entry and exit. It is true, too, that the British government accepted the existence of an effective (and, hence, a legal) blockade and respected it. But it is also true that in an effort to make the blockade more effective, the United States indulged in some highly questionable practices that the British had used when a belligerent in the French revolutionary and Napoleonic wars (1793–1815) and against which the United States had protested vigorously. One, called the long-range blockade, was accomplished by "flying squadrons" of swift warships that patrolled the sea-lanes and intercepted neutral vessels far from a blockaded port, seizing them if there were grounds for believing their destination to be a blockaded port. Another was to place neutral ports (in Britain, the Bahamas, Mexico, and the West Indies) under surveillance and capture vessels as they left the protection of territorial waters, presumably for a port under blockade. In addition, Union warships took as prizes on the high seas neutral vessels coming from and going to neutral ports, on the ground that the ship and its cargo were ultimately destined for a blockaded port. American prize courts upheld the seizures, considering the voyage between the neutral port of origin and the blockaded port as one continuous, albeit broken, voyage. The doctrine was also applied to contraband. It was strange to find the United States applying the doctrine of continuous voyage, which had been so objectionable when practiced by the British in the wars against France.

In the matter of contraband, the United States did not publish an official list; but the secretary of the Treasury, in a circular sent to collectors of customs at several Southern ports where the blockade had been lifted, enumerated articles considered contraband and therefore banned from the ports. Among them were arms, munitions, and war supplies, as was to be expected. But the list also included naval stores and a host of other items, such as ardent spirits, corn, bullion, printing presses, coal, iron, lead, copper, tin, brass, telegraphic instruments, wire, and marine engines—and those were not to be expected. They flew in the face of the historic American resistance to an expanded contraband list.

Why the United States turned its back on history and tradition, and exchanged the role of champion of the rights of neutrals for that of defender of the rights of belligerents, can be explained only in terms of a sacrifice of principle for expediency. Winning the war was the overriding factor in determining the nation's policy. Nothing else mattered.

EXPANDING THE FREEDOM OF THE SEAS: 1865–1914

From the end of the Civil War to the opening of World War I in 1914, the United States did not concern itself greatly with the freedom of the seas. It was a neutral in three wars during the period (Franco-Prussian, Boer, Russo-Japanese), but none of them presented any serious problems on the seas. The United States was a belligerent once during this period (against Spain), but that conflict was too brief to raise any serious maritime issues. There was, however, one significant development in American policy toward neutral commerce during the Spanish-American War—the division of the contraband list into absolute and conditional contraband. The former included articles primarily and ordinarily used for military purposes and destined for an enemy country; the latter included articles that might be used for purposes of war or peace, according to circumstances, and would be subject to seizure only if actually and specifically consigned to the military or naval forces of an enemy. In the latter category, foodstuffs and coal were the most important items. This division became a permanent feature of American policy when it was incorporated into the United States Naval War Code, adopted in June 1900.

If there was one preoccupation of American diplomacy concerning neutral and belligerent rights and duties, it was the effort to secure international acceptance of the principle of the immunity of private property at sea. The adoption of such a broad principle, long sought by American diplomats, would have applied to all private property, both neutral and belligerent, replacing the more specific provisions covering neutrals, such as "free ships make free goods." It was the subject of negotiation with the North German Confederation in 1870, and was incorporated into a treaty of amity and commerce with Italy in 1871. In December 1898, President William McKinley asked Congress for authority "to correspond with the governments of the principal maritime powers with a view of incorporating into the permanent law of civilized nations the principle of the exemption of all private property at sea, not contraband of war, from capture or destruction by belligerent powers." Five years later his successor, Theodore Roosevelt, reiterated the plea. In the instructions prepared for the U.S. delegation to the First Hague Conference in 1899, the chief item was on immunity of private property at sea; the instructions for the delegates to the Second Hague Conference in 1907 included a congressional resolution of 1904 supporting the same principle. All these efforts proved in vain, however. The United States did not succeed in gaining international acceptance of the doctrine.

The United States did, nonetheless, have the satisfaction of seeing many of its other principles adopted at an international congress that met in London during the winter of 1908–1909, convened at the call of Great Britain. The ten maritime powers represented (Germany, England, Austria-Hungary, the United States, Spain, France, Italy, Japan, the Netherlands, Russia) agreed on a code of prize law that would be administered by an international prize court hearing appeals from national prize courts set up by belligerents. In seventy-one articles contained in ten chapters, precise and detailed rules were established governing blockade, contraband, non-neutral service, treatment of prizes, determination of a vessel's character, convoy, transfers to a neutral flag, and visit and search of vessels. Taken together, the rules that made up the Declaration of London were favorable to neutrals, which may account for the fact that the British House of Lords refused to ratify them (after the House of Commons had given its approval). Thus, they were not binding on any of the other signatories.

WORLD WAR I: A CRITICAL TURNING POINT

The United States sought, at the outbreak of war in August 1914, to have the warring nations accept the Declaration of London as the guide in their treatment of neutrals. Germany was willing, but England was not. As the preponderant navy belligerent, England was not willing to surrender the advantage to be derived from the lack of legal restrictions.

The plight of the neutrals, particularly the United States—the one most heavily involved in the carrying trade—was cruel indeed. As in the titanic struggle between France and England from 1793 to 1815, the only rule followed by the belligerents was expediency. No holds were barred, no measure was neglected that might contribute to the defeat of the enemy. Each contestant used to the utmost the weapon it knew best. German submarines stalked the seas, but mainly the waters surrounding the British Isles, sinking every vessel it could catch—enemy or neutral—carrying supplies to Britain. The British surface navy roamed the oceans enforcing measures designed to halt all traffic to Germany. Those measures were numerous and comprehensive, and reflected the cumulative experience of a nation for which the sea had been a lifeline for three centuries. The contraband list was extended to include the widest variety of articles and the distinction between absolute and conditional categories, which Britain had adopted at the same time as the United States, was gradually blurred until it disappeared altogether.

The blockade of Germany was not effective, in that ships were not stationed at German ports to prevent entry and exit but were, rather, placed in the North Sea and The Downs, a roadstead in the English Channel, from which the traffic to the Continent was more easily controlled. It must be pointed out that the two belligerents were under no legal obligation to treat American commerce according to American wishes. There was no body of international maritime law binding the warring countries (the Declaration of London not being in force and not having been signed by the United States), nor were they bound by any bilateral treaties with the United States concerning the treatment of neutrals. Visit and search were not conducted at the point of interception on the high seas; neutral vessels were taken into British or other Allied ports for a detailed and careful examination of cargo and papers. Neutral mails were opened and inspected for contraband and for clues as to destination of cargo. The principle of "free ships make free goods" gave way to the practice of detaining all goods on neutral vessels of enemy origin or ownership. Neutral firms that dealt with the enemy were put on a blacklist and forbidden to trade with the Allies, while neutral vessels that did not conform to certain conditions laid down by the British were subjected to "bunker control" and denied coal, oil, and other refueling supplies. Finally, the doctrine of continuous voyage, hitherto applied to absolute contraband only, and where the second leg of the broken voyage was by sea, was applied to conditional contraband, and where the second leg was over a contiguous land frontier.

The United States, caught between the two belligerents, protested both the violations of its neutral rights and the destruction of the doctrine of the freedom of the seas. The protests to Germany were sharper, more insistent, and more demanding than those to England, although the policies of both were equally oppressive and damaging. The reason for such discrimination was stated by President Woodrow Wilson when he compared the British to thieves and the Germans to murderers. The former, he said, seized property, a matter that could be adjudicated at the end of the war, while the latter took lives, which were lost forever. There was, of course, another cause for the partiality to the British: Americans were entangled, emotionally and economically, with the British, which made a rupture of relations with them unthinkable. The United States finally went to war against Germany in 1917 to uphold its rights as a neutral and to defend the principle of the freedom of the seas, not only for itself but for other nations as well (the "challenge is to all mankind," said the president). The move might be viewed as the fulfillment of the task set out by Secretary of State Robert Lansing in a note sent to the British government in October 1915 that described the nation as "championing the integrity of neutrals . . . [which] the United States unhesitatingly assumes."

The deep concern the United States exhibited for its neutral rights, as well as for the rights of others, between 1914 and 1917 vanished the moment the country joined the Allied cause. Indeed, as a belligerent the United States outdid its allies in trampling upon neutral rights. The justification of a harsh policy toward neutrals lay in the necessity for winning the war and defeating the enemy of mankind's freedom—on the seas as elsewhere. The neutrals were not impressed by America's beneficence; they were shocked. As one Danish newspaper noted, "It was as a spokesman of the *freedom of the seas* and the *rights of neutral countries* that America came into conflict with Germany, and finally went to war. It would be a strange debut for her to start by committing exactly the same kind of outrage which Mr. Wilson pretended to fight against in the interest of the neutrals." As a matter of fact, the belligerent policy of the United States need not have been so unexpected. It was heralded in a remark made by Secretary Lansing in 1915. He noted: "It was of the highest importance that we should not become a belligerent with our hands tied too tightly by what we had written. We would presumably wish to adopt some of the policies and practices which the British had adopted, though certainly not all of them, for our object would be the same as theirs . . . to break the power of Germany."

Almost every practice against which the United States protested as a neutral it pursued as a belligerent—the blacklist, bunker control, sweeping contraband list, postal censorship, and broadest interpretation of the doctrine of continuous voyage—rather as it had done during the Civil War. In fairness, it must be noted, however, that certain British practices were not adopted by belligerent America. The United States did not join Britain in the blockade or in the routing of neutral vessels into ports to facilitate searching them.

As World War I came to an end, the American view of the freedom of the seas underwent a considerable change. It came about as a consequence of Woodrow Wilson's dream of a new postwar international order. In that order the concept of freedom of the seas would not be used solely to describe the problem of the rights of neutrals to trade in wartime; it would have a much broader meaning. As stated by the president in a message to the Senate on 22 January 1917, it would mean the right of every nation to have free access to "the open paths of the world's commerce." And, he went on to say, "The paths of the sea must alike in law and in fact be free. The freedom of the seas is the sine qua non of peace, equality, and co-operation." One year later, on 8 January 1918, Wilson further elaborated his concept of freedom of the seas in his Fourteen Points. The second of them called for "absolute freedom of navigation upon the seas, outside territorial waters, alike in peace and in war, except as the seas may be closed in whole or in part by international action for the enforcement of international covenants." It should be noted that by the last qualifying phrase, Wilson indicated that restrictions on freedom of the seas could be effected only by the League of Nations, the new international organization for maintaining the peace, when acting to chastise a peace-breaking nation.

Unfortunately, certain nations were not prepared to accept so broad and bold a definition of freedom of the seas. Britain, particularly, balked at its being incorporated into the peace treaty. The British could not afford to leave so vital an element of their national security in any hands other than their own. "This point we cannot accept under any conditions," said Prime Minister David Lloyd George. "It means that the power of blockade goes; Germany has been broken almost as much by the blockade as by military methods; if this power is to be handed over to the League of Nations and Great Britain were fighting for her life, no League of Nations could prevent her from defending herself." France and Italy took much the same view. Said the French premier Georges Clemenceau, "War would not be war if there was freedom of the seas."

For his part, Wilson would not "consent to take part in the negotiation of a peace which did not include freedom of the seas [and] . . . unless Lloyd George would make some reasonable concessions on his attitude upon the freedom of the seas, all hope of Anglo-Saxon unity would be at an end." To avoid such a breakdown among the Allies, which would give Germany so great an advantage, the British finally accepted the point as a basis for discussion at the conference, but on the understanding that they "reserve to themselves complete freedom on this subject when they enter the Peace Conference." The point was never seriously discussed at the conference, and the treaty ending the war made no mention of it. Thus, Wilson's effort to redefine the principle came to naught.

Between the two world wars the freedom of the seas did not figure prominently in international affairs. After the breakdown of the Geneva Naval Conference in 1927, Senator William E. Borah of Idaho called for a conference of the great powers to codify the rights of neutrals and belligerents on the high seas in wartime, but nothing came of it. It was clear that the United States and Britain would not agree—the former supporting the liberal view of neutral rights and the latter championing a broad interpretation of the rights of belligerents. In 1929 Senator Arthur Capper of Kansas introduced a resolution in the Senate that would have revived in some measure the Wilsonian dream of the United States joining other nations in denying the freedom of the seas to an aggressor. Appreciating the fact that America could not participate in the League of Nations' enforcement machinery by virtue of nonmembership, he proposed that should the League of Nations declare a nation to be a violator of the peace, the United States would withhold from that country "arms, munitions, implements of war, or other articles for use in war." Thus, there would be no danger of the United States clashing with League of Nations states in the protection of its neutral rights. Sentiment in America, however, was not ready for a policy of taking sides in an international struggle. A similar effort in 1933 by the U.S. representative at the Geneva Disarmament Conference failed for the same reason.

FREEDOM OF THE SEAS IN THE AMERICAN CENTURY

The outbreak of World War II in 1939 found the United States, for the first time in its history, a neutral unconcerned with the defense of its rights at sea. It had, by drastic legislation enacted between 1935 and 1939, voluntarily withdrawn from the business of supplying the needs of the belligerents. It had also curtailed the travel of Americans on belligerent passenger vessels and had circumscribed trade with neutrals by keeping American ships out of certain areas, designated as combat zones, adjacent to neutral ports. It had, in short, surrendered its traditional insistence that the rights of neutrals be respected.

Before long, however, the country abandoned the role of passive and withdrawn neutral and became virtually a co-belligerent, supplying the Allied powers with the sinews of war. The restrictive legislation was repealed in November 1941 and a vast flow of American goods in American ships started moving across the Atlantic. Now the term "freedom of the seas" was once more on the lips of American statesmen as German submarines, operating in wolf packs, attacked the Anglo-American maritime lifeline. President Franklin D. Roosevelt said in May 1941:

> All freedom—meaning freedom to live and not freedom to conquer and subjugate other peoples—depends on the freedom of the seas—for our own shipping, for the commerce of our sister Republics, for the right of all nations to use the highways of world trade, and for our own safety. . . . As President of a united, determined people, I say solemnly: we reassert the ancient American doctrine of the freedom of the seas.

He had already, in September 1940, labeled submarine warfare as defiance of the "historic American policy" for which, "generation after generation, America has battled . . . that no nation has the right to make the broad oceans of the world . . . unsafe for the commerce of others." And in August 1941, when Roosevelt and Prime Minister Winston Churchill drew up the Atlantic Charter, a blueprint for the postwar world, the seventh of eight principles was the hope that "such a peace should enable all men to traverse the high seas and oceans without hindrance." Thus, the two leaders reiterated the broad concept of the freedom of the seas first proposed by Woodrow Wilson.

Like the Treaty of Versailles, which ended World War I, the several treaties negotiated after World War II made no mention of the freedom of the seas; and as the Covenant of the League of Nations had ignored the principle, so did the Charter of the United Nations. Thus, the hope of Franklin Roosevelt suffered the same fate as did the dream of Woodrow Wilson. The unrestricted right of all people to enjoy the freedom of the seas is still not guaranteed by international agreement. Indeed, since the end of World War II the United States has on three occasions taken actions that tended to limit the use of the seas by other nations. The first time was in June 1950, at the outbreak of the Korean War. President Harry S. Truman ordered the Seventh Fleet to patrol the Formosa Strait to prevent the Chinese communists from attacking Formosa and to keep the forces of Chiang Kai-shek from mounting an assault on the mainland. The Soviet Union promptly labeled the action a blockade, which the United States as promptly denied. As evidence to support its contention, America pointed to the fact that commercial traffic in the strait was unimpeded and untouched. The interdiction applied only to naval forces.

The second occasion came in October 1962, when President John F. Kennedy, upon learning that the Soviet Union had built missile sites in Cuba and had supplied Cuban premier Fidel Castro with missiles, proclaimed his intention "to interdict . . . delivery of offensive weapons and associated material to Cuba." He called the policy a "strict quarantine," yet it had all the markings of a blockade. Vessels were to be stopped, visited, and searched within certain prescribed zones and along certain routes. The Soviets considered it a blockade and protested on the ground that a blockade could be instituted only in wartime. To escape that anomaly, American lawyers called it a "pacific blockade," which international law permits as a means for one nation to seek redress, short of war, from another. The legal difficulty surrounding the use of that term was that in a pacific blockade only the blockaded nation's ships could be stopped and seized—not those of a third party. In this instance Soviet ships were the object of search and seizure. Whatever the terminology, it was clear that the United States had used naval forces to interfere with shipping on the high seas, albeit for the lofty motive of self-defense.

The third example of postwar American practice centered on President Richard M. Nixon's mining of North Vietnamese ports in May 1972. Again there was confusion as to the legal status of the act. Nixon denied the Soviet allegation that it was a blockade. The *New York Times* called it a "semi-blockade." The difficulty was compounded by the fact that the action took place not on the high seas but within the "internal and claimed territorial waters of North Vietnam," to use the words of the Department of State's legal officer. And, indeed, there was no interference with freedom of navigation beyond North Vietnam's territorial waters. Judged by the classic nineteenth-century definition of blockade, the act could not be called a blockade. But by the mid-twentieth century, many of the traditional and historic concepts that made up the doctrine of the freedom of the seas were being altered to suit new conditions of international relations.

One major change concerned the extent of territorial waters. For centuries, the territorial waters of a state were calculated at three miles (a cannon's range). At a conference held in 1930 at The Hague for the codification of international law of the sea, the three-mile limit was adopted officially and the marginal sea was declared to belong to the state. At the same time, several nations, wishing to exploit, without competition from other nations, extensive fishing beds and mineral resources in the subsoil, made claims to a more extended area—up to two hundred miles. The United States made no such claims, but in 1945 President Truman announced the creation of "conservation zones in those areas of the high seas contiguous to the coasts of the United States" for the development of fishing. Similarly, the continental shelf in the same contiguous areas was to be exploited for its natural resources. No specific limits were put on the contiguous areas, but it was known that the government favored an extension of the territorial waters from three to twelve miles and the creation of an economic zone of two hundred miles.

THE UNITED NATIONS LAW OF THE SEA TREATY

To settle the problem, conferences were held at Geneva in 1958 and 1960 and at Caracas in 1974,

LAW OF THE SEA TREATY: DEFINITIONS

"Innocent passage" means the right of warships, merchant ships, and fishing vessels to pass without warning the territorial waters of a state in a manner that is not—in the words of the Law of the Sea Treaty (part II, article 19/2)—"prejudicial to the peace, good order, or security of the coastal State." Beginning in the 1970s the United States vigorously resisted efforts to require warships, nuclear-powered vessels, or vessels carrying environmental hazards to give notification prior to passing through the territorial waters of a sovereign state.

"Right of transit passage" refers to the principle articulated in the Law of the Sea Treaty (part III, article 38) guaranteeing all vessels and aircraft the right to pass through or over straits less than twenty-four miles wide at their narrowest point, that is to say, straits in which the twelve-mile territorial sea claim may have territorialized waters that formerly were international. Such straits include Gibraltar, Hormuz in the Persian Gulf, and Malacca in the South Pacific.

"Archipelagic sea-lanes passage" applies the principle of right of transit passage to archipelagoes, most importantly Indonesia and the Philippines. It guarantees unmolested passage for ships and aircraft through and over archipelagic waters, defined as the area encompassed by the drawing of baselines around the outermost islands of an archipelago. Archipelagic sea-lane passage is guaranteed in part IV of the Law of the Sea Treaty.

but no agreement was reached. At Caracas the United States pushed the twelve- and two-hundred-mile limits, providing freedom of navigation and of scientific research in the economic zone was assured for all nations—"a balance between coastal states' rights and duties within the economic zone"—but some nations appeared hesitant about diluting their sovereignty in the zone.

Finally, in 1982 a comprehensive United Nations Law of the Sea Treaty agreement was reached that established the twelve-mile limit for territorial waters and the two-hundred-mile "exclusive economic zone" that the United States had pushed for. The historic pact deemed the world's oceans the "common heritage of mankind" and represented a dramatic shift away from Grotius's notion that the seas were free owing to their boundlessness. Now the seas were understood to be a zone of interdependence in which all nations (including landlocked ones) had a stake. Although the Law of the Sea Treaty substantially affirmed American notions about the freedom of the seas, the administrations of Ronald Reagan and George H. W. Bush refused to sign it because of restrictions it placed on private enterprise regarding deep seabed mining. In July 1994 the Clinton administration, after negotiations leading to the modification of the deep seabed mining provisions, signed the pact; the Senate, however, perceiving that the treaty still hindered the U.S. freedom of action on the high seas, refused to provide the two-thirds majority needed to ratify it. As of 2001 the United States was not a signatory to the treaty, which went into effect on 16 November 1994 after ratification by sixty nations.

DEFENDING FREEDOM OF THE SEAS INTO THE TWENTY-FIRST CENTURY

The expansion of territorial waters and exclusive economic zones by many nations since World War II encouraged some states to restrict in various ways free passage on the high seas, a phenomenon known as "creeping sovereignty." To resist what American diplomats termed the "excessive maritime claims" of certain states, the United States instituted in 1979 a freedom of navigation policy designed to assert its historic commitment to a broad definition of freedom of the seas. This policy aimed to meet encroachments on the right of passage either by sea or air by a three-pronged strategy of diplomatic protest, operational assertion, and bilateral or multilateral negotiation. The operational assertion part of the policy resulted in several high profile incidents including challenging in 1986 Libya's claim that the Gulf of Sidra was a historic inland sea subject to its complete control and the 1988 bumping of U.S. warships by Soviet naval vessels while exercising the right of "innocent passage" inside the twelve-mile territorial limit in the Black Sea. In 1989 the latter incident resulted in a joint statement signed by Secretary of State James A. Baker and Soviet foreign minister Eduard Schevardnadze affirming the right of American warships to conduct innocent passage through Soviet territorial seas.

For more than two hundred years, from the very beginning of the Republic, the tendency of American policy has been to enlarge rather than to restrict the rights of nations on the seas—that is, except in certain periods when the country was at war and the national interest dictated the extension of American rights at the expense of other nations. The determination and consistency with which the principle of freedom of the seas has been asserted is testimony to its central importance in the history of American foreign policy. It represents the effort to extend American notions of international law and universal human rights to the oceans of the world. It constitutes a massive de facto extension of American sovereignty to the watery borders of all nations. And throughout the nation's history and into the foreseeable future it has been and will be job of the U.S. Navy to enforce the principle of freedom of the seas.

BIBLIOGRAPHY

Amacher, Ryan C., and Richard James Sweeney, eds. *The Law of the Sea: U.S. Interests and Alternatives.* Washington, D.C., 1976.

Borgese, Elisabeth Mann. *The Drama of the Oceans.* New York, 1975.

Charney, Jonathan I. "Law of the Sea: Breaking the Deadlock." *Foreign Affairs* 55 (1977).

Digest of United States Practice in International Law. 8 vols. Washington, D.C., 1973–1980. Contains documents and narrative describing United States policy.

Gidel, Gilbert. *Le Droit international public de la mer.* 3 vols. Châteauroux, France, 1932–1934. A monumental and exhaustive account of the law of the sea.

Hagan, Kenneth J. *This People's Navy: The Making of American Sea Power.* New York, 1991.

Howarth, Stephen. *To Shining Sea: A History of the United States Navy, 1775–1991.* New York, 1991.

Hyde, Charles C. *International Law Chiefly as Interpreted and Applied by the United States.* 2 vols. Boston, 1922. A classic and standard account that deals with a wide range of matters pertaining to the freedom of the seas.

Jessup, Philip C. *Neutrality, Its History, Economics, and Law.* 4 vols. New York, 1935–1936. An excellent account dealing with the practices of all the major maritime nations from the eighteenth century to the end of World War I.

Jia, Bing Bing. *The Regime of Straits in International Law.* New York, 1998. Gives detailed analysis of the new procedures governing passage through international straits.

Long, David F. *Gold Braid and Foreign Relations: Diplomatic Activities of U.S. Naval Officers, 1798–1883.* Annapolis, Md., 1988.

Moore, John Bassett, ed. *A Digest of International Law.* 8 vols. Washington, D.C., 1906. A comprehensive account that fully covers maritime matters and deals with all phases of international law as practiced by the United States. The *Digest* is not a narrative but a collection of documents and cases interspersed with comment; the work has been carried forward chronologically by Green Hackworth, 8 vols. (Washington, D.C., 1940–1944), and Marjorie Whiteman, 15 vols. (Washington, D.C., 1963–1973).

Roach, J. Ashley, and Robert W. Smith. *United States Responses to Excessive Maritime Claims.* 2d ed. The Hague, 1996. Provides a heavily documented analysis of the freedom of navigation policy.

Rothwell, Donald R., and Sam Bateman, eds. *Navigational Rights and Freedoms and the New Law of the Sea.* The Hague, 2000. Discusses the various aspects of the Law of the Sea Treaty.

Savage, Carlton. *Policy of the United States Towards Maritime Commerce in War.* 2 vols. Washington, D.C., 1934–1936. A narrative with documents that covers the period from 1776 to 1918, giving a clear and concise account.

Swing, Jon T. "Who Will Own the Oceans." *Foreign Affairs* 54 (1976).

Van Dyke, John M., et al, eds. *Freedom for the Seas in the 21st Century: Ocean Governance and Environmental Harmony.* Washington, D.C., 1993. Assesses the implications of the Law of the Sea Treaty on traditional notions of freedom of the seas.

Whipple, A. B. C. *To the Shores of Tripoli: The Birth of the U.S. Navy and Marines.* New York, 1991.

See also BLOCKADES; CIVIL WAR DIPLOMACY; THE CONTINENTAL SYSTEM; EMBARGOES AND SANCTIONS; INTERNATIONAL LAW; NEUTRALITY.

GENDER

Laura McEnaney

Although historians have been studying gender for several decades, the study of gender in American foreign policy is a relatively new phenomenon. Indeed, the proliferation of scholarship on this topic in the 1990s suggests that gender has become a permanent and theoretically significant category of analysis for the historian of American foreign relations. It is important to note, however, that this approach has generated lively debate among many historians. In journals and on-line forums and at conferences, scholars at the beginning of the twenty-first century continued to argue about the degree to which gender has affected the creation, conduct, and outcomes of international diplomacy.

WOMEN AND GENDER: DIFFERENT APPROACHES

Many people understandably but mistakenly equate the study of gender with the study of women when, in fact, these are fairly different enterprises. Historians who study women (many but not all of them women) look at women's activities and contributions in various economic, political, cultural, and spatial contexts. Practitioners of women's history see all women as historical actors: they look at an individual woman or women together in social movements, at notable and elite women or anonymous, "ordinary" women, at women in the kitchen or women in the streets. Since the 1970s (and even earlier), women's historians have argued that historical narratives have largely ignored women's experiences, yielding an incomplete, or even misleading, portrait of the American past. Through critical analysis of traditional primary sources—and by uncovering sources that historians previously did not think worthy of study—women's history seeks to expand and complicate our histories of industrialization, electoral politics, and warfare, to name only a few topics. Historians of women insist that their scholarship should not merely add a new set of female characters to the plot line of American history, but rather that the whole story needs to be tested, reconsidered, and revised.

The study of gender is an outgrowth of women's history, which is why people tend to view the study of gender and women as the same thing. The scholarly interest in gender emerged as practitioners of women's history, informed by scholarship in anthropology, psychology, and literary criticism, began to ask critical questions of their own methodologies. Shifting the focus from women to gender, historians of gender explore how males and females (sex) become men and women (gender). That is, to study gender is to examine how a society assigns social meanings to the different biological characteristics of males and females. Historians who study gender see it as a cultural construct—something that human beings create and that changes over time. The differences between men and women, they argue, are rooted in society, not in nature, and as such can be historicized. Moreover, gender scholars point out, if women's lives have been shaped profoundly by gender prescriptions, then so, too, have men's. Cultural ideals and practices of masculinity and femininity have been created together, often in opposition to one another; therefore, both men and women have gender histories that must be analyzed in tandem. Indeed, gender studies is relational in that research into the history of gender ideals and practices is always linked to investigations about the operation of the economy, the construction of racial ideologies, the development of political institutions, and other phenomena typically studied by historians.

So what does it mean to do women's history in comparison to gender history? Actually, most historians in this field do a little bit of both. Still, whereas a women's historian would focus on, for example, women's labor force participation during World War II, a gender historian would examine how gender ideologies shaped the organization of labor on the battlefield and the home front, and how the war remapped the meanings of masculinity, femininity, and labor. Put another way, women's historians foreground women as historical actors, while gender historians foreground ideological systems as agents of history. Certainly, those who do women's history engage the question of how gender norms shape women's experiences and struggles, but they tend to focus on women, as such, more than they examine historical ideological shifts in the meanings of masculine and feminine. At the same time, gender historians do not ignore women altogether; rather they interrogate the very meaning of the term "woman," highlighting historical changes in the construction of masculinity and femininity, manhood and womanhood. Again, many historians do some combination of both, combing the documents for clues about how men and women have both shaped and been shaped by gendered beliefs, practices, and institutions.

The theories and methodologies of gender history have been adapted to many fields, but the integration of gender into the study of American foreign relations has been slow and uneven. Part of the reason for this is that the "high" politics of diplomacy seem far removed from the politics of everyday life that have long been the concern of gender and women's history. Until the late twentieth century, both diplomatic and women's historians were themselves inattentive to the connections between their fields and thus very few conversations took place across the disciplinary divide. Scholarly work in various disciplines since the 1980s, however, has revealed important links between American diplomacy and American culture, and the most recent scholarship reflects a more self-conscious attempt by historians to identify a dynamic interrelationship between the creation of foreign policy and the construction of gender.

FINDING WOMEN IN FOREIGN POLICY

The integration of these two seemingly disparate literatures—gender studies and diplomatic history—is ongoing, and it is important to note that this subfield is still "under construction." Nevertheless, it is possible to describe and analyze the myriad approaches historians have used thus far.

One of the first ways historians have made gender visible in foreign policy is by spotlighting the presence and contributions of the anomalous women who have shaped American foreign policy. This approach reveals how women like Senator Margaret Chase Smith, Eleanor Dulles (the younger sister of John Foster and Allen), and first lady Eleanor Roosevelt have influenced foreign policy in a variety of roles—as elected officials, lobbyists, mid-level bureaucrats, and even first ladies. More recently, women such as Jeane Kirkpatrick, Madeleine Albright, and Condoleeza Rice have risen to the highest levels of statecraft. President Ronald Reagan appointed Kirkpatrick in 1980 to be the U.S. representative to the United Nations. Kirkpatrick's staunch anticommunism and advocacy of a reinvigorated national defense fit comfortably in the Reagan administration, and she became a widely known spokesperson for Reagan's foreign policy positions. President Bill Clinton, too, selected a woman to represent U.S. interests at the UN. Albright served several years at the UN until Clinton appointed her secretary of state in 1996. Secretary Albright was the first woman to serve in that role, and in 2001, President George W. Bush made Rice the first woman assistant to the president for national security affairs.

Tracking these "firsts" and the careers of other notable but lesser known women in the diplomatic corps marks an important contribution to the literature simply because it makes women visible. Biographical information on how these women worked their way through institutions controlled by men can yield important insights about the role of feminism in paving the way for their entry, and about the challenges involved in managing a career in a field still populated with very few women. This approach also encourages scholars to not simply acknowledge women such as Kirkpatrick or Albright but to evaluate their contributions and legacies. Many critical questions have emerged from this literature about the weight of women's influence in foreign policymaking (Albright, for example, enjoyed much more access to policy inner circles than did Kirkpatrick), about whether female policymakers' contributions reflect "a woman's view," and whether American women can effect more change if they operate inside or outside of policy circles.

Still, this quasi-biographical approach to gender and foreign policy has some significant limitations. It tends to focus on elite women, so it is narrow by definition. As a result, we lose something of the story of how the nonelite majority of

American women have shaped foreign policy through different means. Further, its "notable women" orientation just adds women to the story, leaving untapped the methods, questions, and theories that define diplomacy and the discipline of diplomatic history itself. Finally, this approach also supports (probably unintentionally) the misguided notion that truly exceptional women, with enough resources and pluck, can enter the inner circle of statesmen, and that the vast majority of women cannot, because of either native inability or subjugation by a male power structure. Neither of these notions can be supported historically, nor are they the intended arguments of writers, but the impressions remain. Many more important biographies and studies of such women need to be done, but they can contribute only modestly to the knowledge about gender and American foreign relations.

Beyond this approach lies another, broader in scope, more inclusive of nonelite women, and more sensitive to the array of historical forces that have shaped women's inclusion or exclusion from foreign affairs. In this approach, women are written into the history of foreign relations as missionaries—emissaries of Americanism. These more prosperous white women (teachers, reformers, and members of faith communities) become part of the larger narrative about the energetic expansion of the United States in the late nineteenth century, and here they can be cast as both villains and victims. Historians have documented the ways in which women missionaries exported "civilization" to nonwhite populations through "uplift" programs that valorized whiteness, Christianity, and conventional gender and family ideologies. Some newer work has complicated this story further, suggesting that women such as turn-of-the century female travelers abroad and the women photojournalists who documented the violence of the Spanish American War participated in missionary types of civilizing projects, even if not formally engaged in missionary work themselves. At the same time, however, all of these works acknowledge that nineteenth- and early-twentieth-century gender systems prevented women's participation in diplomacy (and domestic electoral politics), relegating women to a separate sphere of foreign affairs. Excluded from formal policymaking, these women were still political actors; they promoted the tenets of American foreign policy through the means available to women of their status. Like their sister reformers who worked in immigrant communities in American cities, female missionaries practiced their "social housekeeping" on a global stage. In this approach, then, women become visible in the dramas of foreign policymaking as collaborators in exile, historical actors who support the worldviews and expansionist agendas of male foreign policymakers but only from a position of exclusion.

Like women missionaries, women in peace movements tried to participate in foreign policymaking from the outskirts. Historians have found in peace histories of the nineteenth and twentieth centuries a meaningful paper trail of women's participation in important national and international debates about U.S. foreign policy. In examining the theories, strategies, and tactics of organized women's peace movements, it becomes difficult to capture the whole of their contributions to policymaking. Historians hold different views about the degree to which peace movements generally have influenced decision makers' choices about interventions and arms buildups. Moreover, historians of women's pacifism have tended to focus less on the policy impact side of the story and more on the social movement story—that is, how it was that women in different eras were able to muster the ideological and material resources to create and sustain movements that addressed foreign policy issues long considered to be "men's business."

It is difficult to generalize about the politics of women's peace movements, because female pacifism has both enshrined conventional gender roles and advanced the ideas of feminism. One safe generalization might be that women in peace movements have capitalized on their outsider perspective; their very exclusion from the "man's world" of diplomacy enabled them to criticize—more perceptively, they argued—the overseas adventurism of the United States. Many female peace activists, whether mothers or not, claimed a maternal identity as the basis of this outsider critique of American diplomacy. Although there was no national, independent women's peace movement before 1914, there were individual women and small peace groups that lobbied in various locales. In these activities we can see a nascent feminist peace consciousness developing over the course of the nineteenth century, and much of this activism sprung from female reformers' maternalist sensibilities. These women, largely middle class, white, and Protestant, argued that U.S. expansion overseas should not extend what they charged were male values of conquest and acquisition, but rather should reflect women's purity, virtue, and maternal morality. By the late nineteenth century, many nationally organized women's groups, such as the Women's Christian Temperance Union (WCTU), had fully incorporated a peace plank into their reform agendas. In fact, the WCTU created a Department of Peace and Arbitration in 1887, which enabled them to link more systematically their crusade against alcohol (a critique of male violence in the family) with a campaign for peace (a critique of male violence overseas).

Over the course of the twentieth century, through both world wars and after, female pacifists continued to claim the mantle of motherhood as an entry into foreign policy politics. Like their nineteenth-century predecessors, these later activists nurtured the notion of a maternalist citizenship, a concept that included not only the demand for the vote, but a full voice in governmental affairs, electoral politics, and any other arena in which foreign policy was made. During the years of World War I, for example, we see the emergence of what Harriet Hyman Alonso calls the "suffrage-pacifists," women who saw peace issues as inextricably linked with women's suffrage. The formation of the Woman's Peace Party in 1915 reflected this fusion of peace and women's rights; its platform called for arms limitation, international jurisprudence and peacekeeping, an end to the war in Europe, and the right to vote for women. Representation from numerous women's clubs at the founding meeting, including the WCTU, the General Federation of Women's Clubs, the Women's Trade Union League, and the Women's National Committee of the Socialist Party, reveals the breadth of interest in suffrage-peace politics. Social reformer and Woman's Peace Party leader Jane Addams encouraged women already active in local matters to pay attention to international affairs—to link local with global. Addams and others noted that peace activism was a natural extension of women's nurturance of family and community, and the Peace Party's appeal to "the mother half of humanity" reflected their maternalist orientation.

Years later, well after women won the right to vote, motherhood continued to be an important identity and organizing base for women's peace groups. In 1961, Women Strike for Peace, an organization of "concerned housewives," called on President John F. Kennedy to "end the arms race—not the human race." They, too, claimed the experiences and insights of motherhood as a foundation for activism. As caretakers of the nation's children, they argued, all women had a responsibility to lobby for peace. Taking a multitude of positions on issues from the nuclear test ban treaty of 1963 to U.S. intervention in Vietnam, members of Women Strike for Peace went further than mere criticism of U.S. policies: they argued passionately that the moral, maternal citizenship they embodied promised a new path to more harmonious local, national, and international relationships.

This ideological fusion of motherhood with peace made women's entrance into national debates about global affairs more hospitable than it might have been had they argued for participation based on more feminist principles of justice and equality. But as historians have aptly pointed out, women's pacifism was a politics of feminism as well as maternalism. Indeed, women active in peace movements saw a connection between militarist diplomacy and male supremacy, and they infused their critique of American foreign policy with a critique of male domination. Maternalist peace activism enabled women to understand not only their exclusion from the military state, but also their cultural and economic disenfranchisement in American society as women and mothers. They identified a link between military violence abroad and domestic violence at home. They argued that the violence of war devalued and destroyed women's values and women's work, since it was women—as mothers—who created and sustained life. The war machine was male owned and operated, they claimed, and an American foreign policy based on military intervention was the logical culmination of men's domination in the workplace, politics, and the family. In this sense, many women activists (especially those in the second wave of the feminist movement) went further than mere condemnation of their exclusion from policymaking bureaucracies—they denounced the whole system itself. These ideological currents could be seen in both nineteenth- and twentieth-century peace movements, and it is significant that women's participation in peace movements often grew out of and coexisted with activism in abolitionist, suffrage, and other feminist causes.

Although the focus on women missionaries and pacifists has been instrumental in writing women into the history of American foreign policy, this approach, too, has its problems. It can often assume an essentialized femininity (the idea that women are all the same) across all racial, class, and regional boundaries. At the same time, it can posit a theory of female difference—that women are a special class of human being, uniquely nurturant, maternal, and peaceful. As historians have suggested, this seemingly powerful vision of women can lead to their exclusion from politics and policymaking, based on the assumption that women would be unfit or somehow corrupted by the rough and tumble world of diplomacy.

More importantly, ideas about women's inherent pacifism are not true. As many studies have demonstrated, women have been an integral part of military engagements as auxiliary military forces, production workers, and home front volunteers. In fact, women themselves have invoked a maternalist ideology to endorse as well as oppose military preparedness and war. And, of course, American foreign policymakers have often depended on the rhetoric of maternalism and family to whip up popular support for their decisions. At different historical moments, American women have strenuously affirmed and participated in a whole range of military mobilizations.

Taken together, these histories reveal women's varied levels of engagement with American diplomacy. They underscore the fact that "women were there" in the making of foreign policy: there were a few in policymaking circles, more in missionary work, and even more in peace movements. Yet finding them has not made it easy to generalize about the meanings of their presence, for women were positioned differently in relation to the state that made foreign policy decisions, and they viewed and acted on those decisions in different ways. Perhaps the most important outcome of writing these women into diplomatic history is that now scholars must widen their lens as they seek to understand how foreign policy has been made and implemented by varieties of historical actors in varied political contexts.

SEEING GENDER IN FOREIGN POLICY

If finding women in foreign policy has broadened the study of American foreign relations, then locating gender has stretched the discipline even further. In the most basic sense, applying a gender analysis to the study of American foreign policy is an attempt to see things differently, or to see new things entirely. Like other tools of analysis, gender offers another angle, another peek into the complicated world of policymaking. Diplomatic historians who use gender analysis are no different than their colleagues in the field; they, too, seek answers to longstanding questions about the emergence of colonialism, the development of tariff and trade policies, the rise of anti-imperialist movements, the origins of the Cold War, and the like. The use of a gender analysis does not preclude the use of any of the customary methodologies of the historian; gender merely adds to the historian's toolbox.

As explained earlier, the emergence of gender studies has made it possible for historians not only to find women but to see both women and men as gendered actors. Indeed, the research on women and femininity as historical subjects has inspired new investigation into the histories of men and masculinity. This has opened a rich vein of scholarship that does not take men's participation in foreign affairs for granted; rather, it interrogates how masculine values and worldviews have shaped diplomacy, enabling students of foreign policy to see anew how normative ideas about manhood inform policymakers' decision making in both domestic and international contexts.

But a gender analysis shows us more than masculinity in action; it offers a critical tool for understanding power in all of its guises. Seeing gender enables historians to scrutinize the organization of power in any arena, from the most public to the most intimate. Gender ideologies can represent relationships of power as innate, fixed, or biologically rooted, but gender history can make transparent the human agency behind those "natural" relationships. Gender analysis can also reveal how ideologies of masculinity and femininity are embedded in language and social structures; the language of warfare, for example, depends on gendered ideas of strength and weakness, protector and protected, which, in turn, shape how an institution like the military utilizes men and women to carry out American foreign policy. A gender analysis can be powerful precisely because it interrogates power itself; it raises fundamental questions about how particular groups have achieved dominance by naturalizing power relations that are, in fact, humanly constituted.

Cold War history offers an illustrative, although by no means exclusive, case of how gender analysis can affect the study of American foreign policy. It was in this field where scholars first began to commingle the study of politics, culture, and gender to expand traditional narratives of diplomatic history. The Cold War's rich imagery of nuclear apocalypse and hyperbolic talk of

GENDER: VOICES FROM THE DOCUMENTS

"The harsh fact of the matter is that there is also an increasingly large number of young Americans who are neglecting their bodies—whose physical fitness is not what it should be—who are getting soft. And such softness on the part of individual citizens can help to strip and destroy the vitality of a nation. . . . Thus in a very real and immediate sense, our growing softness, our increasing lack of physical fitness, is a menace to our security."

— *John F. Kennedy on men's physical fitness and national strength, 1960* —

"The new stronghold of national security is in our homes. . . . For the first time, the personal defense of our homes is . . . being rated *as co-equal in importance* with our military defense."

— *Katherine Howard, Federal Civil Defense Administration Women's Affairs Division, on family responsibility and Cold War national security, 1954* —

"This group of women came together to protest in the name of Womanhood against the cruelty and waste of war, and to give united help toward translating the mother-instinct of life-saving into social terms of the common good."

— *Women's International League for Peace and Freedom statement, 1919* —

"Exactly as each man, while doing first his duty to his wife and the children within his home, must yet, if he hopes to amount to much, strive mightily in the world outside his home, so our nation, while first of all seeing to its own domestic well-being, must not shrink from playing its part among the great nations without."

— *President Theodore Roosevelt on men's domestic and international responsibilities, 1901* —

"What does all this mean for every one of us? It means opportunity for all the glorious young manhood of the republic—the most virile, ambitious, impatient, militant manhood the world has ever seen."

— *Senator Albert J. Beveridge on the annexation of the Philippines in 1900* —

patriotism and subversion first caught the attention of historians of culture and social history, who sought to explain the relationship between the social-cultural politics of the postwar home front and the diplomatic politics of the Cold War. This work tended to locate gender and national security themes in popular culture (film, mass-circulation magazines) and in the burgeoning social scientific "expert" literature translated for public consumption. Scholars have traced how messages about muscular masculinity and dangerously aggressive femininity made their way into the films, novels, advice columns, and even comic book literature of the era. According to this research, new opportunities for women's independence unleashed by World War II (as witnessed by women's rising participation in the postwar wage labor force) generated new fears about the stability of gender roles and family practices. Female independence, often portrayed in popular culture in highly sexualized ways, was likened to the lethal potency of a mushroom cloud. Social science experts and popular advice literature advocated family stability—and female domesticity, in particular—as antidotes to the past disruptions of World War II and the future uncertainties of the nuclear age. This scholarship revealed intriguing symbolic linkages between the generalized anxiety about atomic energy and the popular apprehension about the slow but steady transformations in gender roles and family life.

In a similar vein, historians have pondered how containment doctrine, a policy hatched in high-level diplomatic circles, became a language and practice in the popular realm. Historians of the family and sexuality, for example, have explored how anticommunism and national security policies became manifest in everyday life. The ambient fear of nuclear annihilation, paired with concerns about the resilience of the nuclear family, spurred campaigns to "contain" the social forces that might prove disruptive to gender and family traditionalism. In fact, scholars have argued, postwar America's red scare was as much an attempt to root out nontraditional gender roles and sexual practices as it was an effort to secure America's foreign policy dominance. The preoccupation with national security abroad was bolstered by a security effort at home that enshrined "family values." According to popular cold warriors, with Joseph McCarthy being merely one of a chorus of voices, only heterosexual nuclear families with breadwinner fathers, stay-at-home mothers, and children could anchor a patriotic domestic security endeavor. Anything outside of that configuration was suspect, probably subversive, a potential menace to national security.

This gender conservatism underpinning the red scare was more than simply a cultural mood. Historians have shown it had concrete policy manifestations as well. Despite the changing gender and sexual practices of the wartime and postwar years, McCarthy-era intolerance led to the criminalization of homosexuality, resulting in the federal government's purge of gays and lesbians in government service. Advocates of the purge argued that homosexuals were "sex perverts" whose tastes and habits imperiled national security. Like communists, gays and lesbians could avoid detection and spread their propaganda under the radar screen. Homosexuals were dangerous as well because they were gender outlaws: mannish women who could not be domesticated and weak-willed, "sissified" men who could not stand firm and tall against communist aggression, at home and abroad. The theme of the "homosexual menace" pervaded postwar political culture, reaching from the very top echelons of the federal government to the most local bureaucracies and organizations. Using the screening and firing mechanisms of President Harry Truman's loyalty-security program, anticommunist officials were able to either screen out or discharge thousands of gay and lesbian citizens from government service. This episode illustrates how policymakers, opinion leaders, and ordinary folk imagined gender and sexual dangers as foreign policy or national security dangers. Without a gender analysis, these symbolic and material linkages would be difficult to see.

This early scholarship on the gendered meanings of Cold War culture and the national security state was highly suggestive, urging historians to think about connections not yet made and pointing out directions for future study. This work took the traditional approach of historians—document analysis—and pushed it into new directions, borrowing from postmodern approaches that take discourse (written and spoken language, images, and symbols) analysis seriously. Historians saw in this Cold War discourse rich and varied gender meanings that could broaden our understanding of how language constructed the national security environment in which policymakers formulated their momentous decisions. In the broadest sense, the work on gender, culture, and foreign policy provocatively suggests that the relationship between text and context is more than incidental—that text actually constructs the historical context, it does not merely reflect it. This work has also performed an invaluable service to both diplomatic and social history, because it has successfully linked these heretofore separate historical literatures. The fusion of this previously bifurcated historiography of the postwar era has yielded a more complex understanding of the Cold War as a creature with both domestic and diplomatic dimensions.

Still, the first historians to do this work tended to look for a gender–foreign policy connection primarily in popular culture, leaving unanalyzed the gender content of the more traditional documents (letters, memos, telegrams, agency reports, treaties) found in presidential and security agency archives. In fact, there was arguably a kind of gendering of the sources themselves, whereby scholars who wanted to find gender in diplomacy tended to look at popular discourses (gendered feminine) rather than at the records of diplomacy (gendered masculine). This left the impression, as Amy Kaplan (1994) has argued, that gender "enters diplomatic history only through the aegis of culture." More recent scholarship on gender and Cold War foreign policy has built on these earlier approaches, and historians continue to fine-tune and adapt the methodologies of literary and cultural studies to traditional historical analysis of diplomacy. Much of the newer work on gender and foreign policy now analyzes gender in sources that few postwar Americans would have laid eyes on. Cold War historians excavate the classified archival materials of presidents, defense bureaucracies, military leaders, intelligence agencies, and nongovernmental actors engaged in diplomacy at various levels. Their analysis of these institutional documents produced in relatively remote political environments is no different than the cultural historian's analysis of documents produced for mass consumption. Like Cold War films or science fiction literature, traditional diplomatic documents are cultural artifacts that can reveal something about the operation of gender in the Cold War era.

An examination of particular moments in Cold War history from the Truman, Eisenhower, and Kennedy administrations may help readers see how this work is done. Diplomatic historians have long debated questions about the emergence of chilly relations between the United States and the Soviet Union in the aftermath of World War II. Volumes have been written about how the two superpowers sought military, economic, and territorial advantages as they tried to construct a postwar world hospitable to their own interests. Many scholars have focused on the development of the doctrine of containment, foreshadowed by the 1947 Truman Doctrine (which pledged the United States to fight communism in Greece and Turkey), and then articulated more thoroughly by George Kennan, the State Department analyst who penned the now famous "long telegram" in early 1946, followed by the "Sources of Soviet Conduct" article in July 1947. Historians have scrutinized Kennan's policy recommendations and rhetorical flourishes for decades, but until the late 1990s, no historian had done a close textual analysis that incorporated gender analysis. In fact, the question of how gender has shaped the political assumptions, worldviews, and policies of cold warriors has yet to be asked in a systematic way for the whole of the Cold War. Nevertheless, new studies have yielded some compelling findings on particular episodes in Cold War history.

Using the insights of gender studies, historian Frank Costigliola found that George Kennan's writings were rife with gendered metaphors that represented the Cold War as an emotional, sexually charged struggle between a man and woman. Kennan's favorite analogies to describe the changing postwar relationship between the United States and the Soviet Union depended heavily on gender, family, and sexual ideologies and imagery. For example, Kennan likened the relationship between Soviet citizens and their government to a wife who becomes gradually disillusioned with her husband and seeks a divorce from him. Russian people, in general, were gendered feminine, Kennan's way of conveying his firm view that the Soviet citizenry was beholden to their cruel and despotic government, gendered as a hypermasculine authority figure. In his telegram, Kennan went so far as to portray the Soviet government as a rapist who tried to exert "unceasing pressure" with "penetration" into Western society. These gendered metaphors and tropes are not just casual talk; they are the stuff of politics, according to Costigliola and others. Kennan's writings shaped the political environment in which policymakers thought about and negotiated with the Soviets; the invocation of highly gendered and sexualized motifs, Costigliola notes in "'Unceasing Pressure for Penetration'" (1997), "created an emotionalized context" that made the exaggerations of a Soviet threat seem "rational and credible," thus closing off deeper deliberation about the reality and dimensions of that threat. Other scholars, too, have delved into diplomatic sources to see how policymakers relied on gender to understand diplomatic relations between states. Historian Michelle Mart examined the gendered discourses of U.S. relations with Israel in the Truman and Eisenhower years. In this case, gender helps explain how Israeli Jews became worthy of a close relationship with the United States from 1948 through the 1950s, that is, only after they had proclaimed statehood and strenuously resisted subsequent Arab attacks. An analysis of the diplomatic exchanges between the United States and Israel reveals that the manly pursuits of statehood and warfare transformed Israeli Jews, in the eyes of the U.S. policymakers, from marginal global players to muscular fighters, sex symbols, and triumphant underdogs. Jewish "tough guys" had proven their mettle in the battle for statehood, and the reward for their virile and vigorous struggle was a dependable, long-term alliance with the United States. Gender defined the parameters of that alliance, for a tough-minded masculine orientation was considered by U.S. policymakers an important indicator of a country's fitness for a close political and military alliance with a global superpower.

A study of U.S. relations with India in the same time period reveals how the very gendered perceptions that enabled diplomatic partnership with the Israelis disqualified India as a serious player in Cold War politics. According to a study by Andrew Rotter, America's postwar relationship with India was structured, in part, by the gendered perception that India's desire to remain a neutral player in the standoff between the United States and the Soviet Union was a signal of its passivity and cowardice. American policymakers, frustrated with India's desire for neutrality, portrayed India itself and Indian diplomats as feminine, meaning in this case, weak-willed, irrational, naive about world affairs, and ultimately undependable. Cold War gender ideologies that valorized masculine rationality and decisiveness as a counterpoint to feminine emotionality and passivity thus shaped policymakers' views that India was acting like a frightened woman who could not be relied upon to sustain a long-term diplomatic alliance in Asia.

Moving forward from the Cold War diplomacy of the Truman and Eisenhower administrations into the early 1960s, scholarly work has uncovered the centrality of gender to the policy assumptions and decision making of the Kennedy administration. John F. Kennedy's cultivation of youth, energetic patriotism, and moral courage has been discussed widely. As historian Robert D. Dean argues, scholars and media observers of the Kennedy presidency have often cited President Kennedy's preoccupation with "toughness" as an issue of personal style or habit, not a matter of gender politics. In fact, Kennedy's foreign policy interests and energies were a reflection of his views that American manhood was threatened by indulgent consumption at home and communist insurgency abroad, both of which required the diplomatic muscle flexing of tough-minded cold warriors. Kennedy's physical fitness programs would strengthen youth at home, while his new Peace Corps would dispatch an energetic corps of youth to all ends of the globe to fight the Cold War with American ideology and first-world technology. Meanwhile, his counterinsurgency measures, embodied by the elite Green Berets, would counter Soviet aggression by discouraging any potential—and quashing any real—Soviet-sponsored indigenous uprisings. In essence, Dean claims, Kennedy's policies were a projection of his perception that American men had grown soft and idle in the postwar period, and that the antidote to this crisis of masculinity was an infusion of bellicose and brawny political leadership at home and abroad.

We can reach further back in time, to the nineteenth century, to apprehend gender meanings in American foreign policy. Kristin L. Hoganson's 1998 study about the operation of gender in the Spanish-American War, for example, nudges historians to confront difficult questions about the causal role of gender in American foreign policy decisions. Like the scholarship on gender and the Cold War, her study is premised on the notion "that the conduct of foreign policy does not occur in a vacuum, that political decision makers are shaped by their surrounding cultures," and that "inherited ideas about gender" are a part of that culture and thus shape profoundly the views of foreign policymakers. In the case of the Spanish-American War, Hoganson states that gender ideals "played an exceptionally powerful and traceable role" in the decision to go to war. Advocates of intervention in Cuba and the Philippines believed that international aggression would fortify American nationalism and manhood at the same time. They drew on nineteenth-century ideas about "manly" character and citizenship, arguing that a war for territorial and economic expansion would energize and rehabilitate American manhood, which, they claimed, had grown soft without the challenges of frontier expansion, agricultural production, and warrior experience. Layered upon these concerns was another: women's growing political activism and their insistence on the right to vote. An imperial war, according to interventionists, would certify gender traditionalism (man as protector, women as the protected) and restore the manly (and womanly) virtues and character that were the basis of American democracy.

Interestingly, we see a striking repetition of gender themes between the foreign policy environments of the late nineteenth century and the Cold War era: a perceived crisis of masculinity (notably, associated with consumption in both centuries), an emergent anxiety about women's independence, and a confidence that a virile and robust American diplomatic posture abroad could go far to solve the twin problems of gender disorder at home and global threats abroad. In both periods of expansionist impulse, concerns about masculinity and femininity merged with concerns about affairs of state. Whatever the century or whatever the case study, then, late-twentieth-century scholarship made big and insistent claims that gender ideologies were a fundamental part of foreign policy formulation. In all of the examples cited, it appears that gender shaped the identities of foreign policymakers themselves before they arrived in Washington, and that it continued to shape their assumptions, anxieties, aspirations, and actions once they were fully ensconced in diplomatic circles.

GENDER AND THE HISTORIOGRAPHY OF AMERICAN FOREIGN POLICY

Historians who study gender will find all of the above themes familiar, but scholars who have not yet tangled with gender analysis in their studies of foreign policy might find the approaches dubious and the conclusions unconvincing. Indeed, since gender topics first appeared in the pages of diplomatic history journals, historians have debated the merits of gender analysis at conferences, in on-line forums, in journals, and in their own monographs. One of the reasons for this debate is that some of the gender-themed studies of American foreign relations gained momentum in fields outside of diplomatic history and, indeed, outside of the history discipline itself, in the more literary-focused arena of cultural studies. Skeptics of the gender approach have wondered aloud what diplomatic historians can learn from stories about sexual metaphors, "tough Jews," feminized Indians, and the gender tropes of imperial expansion and war. They have accused gender historians of paying too much attention to issues of representation at the cost of asking hard questions about causation. Some have argued that gender scholars have borrowed too heavily from other disciplines and have introduced questionable theories, methodologies, and insights into the field.

These criticisms are important and worth some elaboration. In fact, a great deal of the work on gender is indebted to postmodernist and cultural studies approaches, which cross disciplinary boundaries, take language seriously, and insist that historians interrogate not only the construction of reality in primary documents but the social construction of their own historical narratives. Cultural studies approaches differ, of course, but all involve close scrutiny of the unarticulated assumptions that underlay the legitimation, expression, and resistance of power. As Costigliola observes in "The Nuclear Family" (1997), "gender norms acted as silent organizers" of power in the diplomatic and political realms. Perhaps, then, what has made gender analysis controversial in diplomatic history is the fact that those who recognized these silences in their documents have also exposed some of the methodological silences of their discipline as well. Turning their critical eye from primary to secondary sources, gender scholars have provocatively suggested that gender norms might have also tacitly shaped the historiography of American foreign relations, thus calling into question some of the disciplinary "truths" of diplomatic history. Drawing on the insights of postmodernism, these scholars have argued that the historiography itself is a social construction, and that narratives about foreign policy (or any historical phenomena) are human creations, subject to the inherited biases and assumptions of time and place.

Such challenges to the discipline and its historiography have evoked spirited criticism of postmodernism, gender analysis, and critical theory in general. Some historians claim that postmodernist gender approaches are jargon-filled intellectual exercises that have done little to enlighten the key debates in the field. More than a few have said that investigations of language and representation have taken diplomatic history too far afield from its traditional units of study (the nation-state, for example) and its tried and true methodology of document analysis and synthesis. In particular, critics have challenged the postmodernist claim that historical evidence does not benignly reveal a "real" world or a central "truth," and that the evidence itself is a selective representation that can suppress multiple truths and heterogeneous realities. They maintain that such critical approaches, of which gender analysis is an elemental part, have spilled too much ink probing language and ideology rather than apprehending the real reasons for foreign policy decisions and outcomes.

While critics have argued that the new work on gender has better explained the connections between gender, culture, and diplomacy, rather than causation, those whose scholarship has been integral to this historiographical turn maintain that clear causation is hard to identify for any scholar, working on any problem, in any era. In fact, most gender scholars would agree that gender analysis does not explain reductively a single cause for a particular action, and that sometimes, gender meanings are not the most salient or significant aspects of a historical puzzle. Rather, they would argue, gender analysis abets the historian's effort to get closer to a reasonable and reliable set of explanations about a particular historical problem. Historians who seriously engage gender do not shy away from questions about causation, but they tend to approach overarching causal explanations with caution. The precise effect of George Kennan's "long telegram" on policymaking, for example, is impossible to discern, but it seems clear that his writings simplified what should have been a complex debate about Soviet intentions, and that his highly gendered, emotional musings naturalized—and thus rationalized—a set of diplomatic maneuvers that positioned the Soviets as unreliable allies and credible threats. In the case of the

Spanish-American War, the societal panic about masculinity in decline reveals how gender "pushed" and "provoked" warfare as an antidote to the changes in nineteenth-century family and gender relations. And in the case of President Kennedy's foreign policy programs, the gender experiences of Kennedy and his elite policy cohort, along with the gender ideologies and anxieties of the postwar era, motivated the president to respond to his Cold War environment as an Ivy League tough guy who could martial the resources to assure American hegemony.

These debates about gender and causation will, no doubt, continue, but in some ways they may miss the point. No historian has endowed gender with monocausal superpowers; in fact, many scholars of gender point out that the causal relationship between gender and foreign policy needs to be teased out even further. And although asking the "how" and "why" questions continues to be a staple of the discipline, perhaps historians need to reexamine this preoccupation with causation. The studies of Kennan and Kennedy are instructive here. As Costigliola's "'Unceasing Pressure for Penetration'" has made clear, the questions about gender's causal effects in foreign policy formulation "arise from the premise that there must be single, clear, unequivocal causes for policies and actions," a premise that historians have repeatedly tested and found wanting. Even vocal critics of the gender approach have acknowledged that no single theory or explanatory framework can possibly explain the complexities of American foreign policymaking. As Dean has aptly stated, "gender must be understood not as an independent *cause* of policy decisions, but as part of the very fabric of reasoning employed by officeholders." And so, too, it should be for historians—that gender become one part of the fabric of our historical analysis, not a separate, unrelated path of inquiry.

Together, women's history and gender studies have enabled historians to conceive of foreign policy more broadly, inviting more actors, methods, and theories into the endeavor. A gender analysis offers one way to recast and expand the debates about the history of diplomacy. Its newness, relative to other approaches, has generated both excitement and skepticism, and as new work is published, historians will have new opportunities to debates its impact and merits.

BIBLIOGRAPHY

Alonso, Harriet Hyman. *Peace as a Women's Issue: A History of the U.S. Movement for World Peace and Women's Rights*. Syracuse, N.Y., 1993.

Cohn, Carol. "Sex and Death in the Rational World of Defense Intellectuals." *Signs* 12 (winter 1987): 687–718. A gender analysis of nuclear strategy debates.

Cooke, Miriam, and Angela Woollacott, eds. *Gendering War Talk*. Princeton, N.J., 1993. An interdisciplinary collection on gender and war.

Costigliola, Frank. "'Unceasing Pressure for Penetration': Gender, Pathology, and Emotion in George Kennan's Formation of the Cold War." *Journal of American History* 83 (March 1997): 1309–1339.

———. "The Nuclear Family: Tropes of Gender and Pathology in the Western Alliance." *Diplomatic History* 21 (spring 1997): 163–183.

Crapol, Edward P. *Women and American Foreign Policy: Lobbyists, Critics, and Insiders*. Wilmington, Del., 1992.

"Culture, Gender, and Foreign Policy: A Symposium." *Diplomatic History* 18 (winter 1994): 47–70. A collection of articles and commentaries on the application of gender analysis to diplomatic history.

Dean, Robert D. "Masculinity as Ideology: John F. Kennedy and the Domestic Politics of Foreign Policy." *Diplomatic History* 22 (winter 1998): 29–62.

D'Emilio, John. "Bonds of Oppression: Gay Life in the 1950s." In his *Sexual Politics, Sexual Communities*. Chicago, 1983. Discusses links between anticommunism and containment of sexuality.

Enloe, Cynthia. *Does Khaki Become You? The Militarisation of Women's Lives*. London, 1983. One of the earliest works to theorize about women, war, and international relations.

———. *Bananas, Beaches, and Bases: Making Feminist Sense of International Politics*. Berkeley, Calif., 1989. A useful primer on gender and foreign relations.

Goedde, Petra. "From Villains to Victims: Fraternization and the Feminization of Germany, 1945–1947." *Diplomatic History* 23 (winter 1999): 1–20.

Harris, Adrienne, and Ynestra King, eds. *Rocking the Ship of State: Toward a Feminist Peace Politics*. Boulder, Colo., 1989. An introduction to issues of women, gender, and peace activism.

Higonnet, Margaret Randolph, Jane Jenson, Sonya Michel, and Margaret Collins Weitz. *Behind the Lines: Gender and the Two World Wars.* New Haven, Conn., 1987.

Hoganson, Kristin L. *Fighting for American Manhood: How Gender Politics Provoked the Spanish-American and Philippine-American Wars.* New Haven, Conn., 1998.

Hunter, Jane. *The Gospel of Gentility: American Women Missionaries in Turn-of-the-Century China.* New Haven, Conn., 1984.

Jeffords, Susan. *The Remasculinization of America: Gender and the Vietnam War.* Bloomington, Ind., 1989.

Jeffreys-Jones, Rhodri. *Changing Differences: Women and the Shaping of American Foreign Policy, 1917–1994.* New Brunswick, N.J., 1995.

Kaplan, Amy. "Domesticating Foreign Policy." *Diplomatic History* 18 (winter 1994): 97–105.

Mart, Michelle. "Tough Guys and American Cold War Policy: Images of Israel, 1948–1960." *Diplomatic History* 20 (summer 1996): 357–380.

May, Elaine Tyler. *Homeward Bound: American Families in the Cold War Era.* New York, 1988. An analysis of gender, family, and Cold War culture.

McEnaney, Laura. *Civil Defense Begins at Home: Militarization Meets Everyday Life in the Fifties.* Princeton, N.J., 2000. Includes lengthy analysis of women, gender, nuclear preparedness, and the national security state.

Meyer, Leisa. *Creating G.I. Jane: Sexuality and Power in the Women's Army Corps During World War II.* New York, 1996. A discussion of gender, sexuality, and military mobilization.

Papachristou, Judith. "American Women and Foreign Policy, 1898–1905: Exploring Gender in Diplomatic History." *Diplomatic History* 14 (fall 1990): 493–509.

Rosenberg, Emily S. "Gender." *Journal of American History* 77 (June 1990): 116–124. An overview of historiographical approaches on women, gender, and foreign policy.

———. "Revisiting Dollar Diplomacy: Narratives of Money and Manliness." *Diplomatic History* 22 (spring 1998): 155–176. A useful discussion of gender, critical theory, and diplomatic history.

———. "Consuming Women: Images of Americanization in the 'American Century.'" *Diplomatic History* 23 (summer 1999): 479–497.

Rotter, Andrew J. "Gender Relations, Foreign Relations: The United States and South Asia, 1947–1964." *Journal of American History* 81 (September 1994): 518–542.

Smith, Geoffrey S. "National Security and Personal Isolation: Sex, Gender, and Disease in the Cold-War United States." *International History Review* 14 (May 1992): 307–337.

Swerdlow, Amy. *Women Strike for Peace: Traditional Motherhood and Radical Politics in the 1960s.* Chicago, 1993.

Tickner, J. Ann. *Gender in International Relations: Feminist Perspectives on Achieving Global Security.* New York, 1992.

Wexler, Laura. *Tender Violence: Domestic Visions in an Age of U.S. Imperialism.* Chapel Hill, N.C., 2000. A study of female photojournalists and the gendered representations of war and foreign relations.

See also COLD WAR EVOLUTION AND INTERPRETATIONS; PACIFISM; PEACE MOVEMENTS.

GLOBALIZATION

Thomas W. Zeiler

Globalization became a buzzword following the end of the Cold War, but the phenomenon has long been a factor in the foreign relations of the United States and has deep roots in history. To the extent that it meant the expansion of trade and investments, it can be defined as economic expansion, as in the transition from territorial expansion in the nineteenth century to the increasing internationalization of markets in the twentieth century. In the aftermath of World War II, economic internationalism, or the suggestion of growing interdependence of nations and the development of international institutions, seemed to capture the essence of what more recently has been termed globalization. But such usages are too limited; they do not adequately define a phenomenon that shaped American diplomacy and its constituent elements of economics and culture.

DEFINITION AND CONCEPTUALIZATION

"Globalization" is a fairly new term. Professor Theodore Levitt, a marketing professor at the Harvard Business School, apparently first employed it in a 1983 article in the *Harvard Business Review*. It is arguable, however, that the basic concept dates to the first humans. Defined broadly, globalization is the process of integrating nations and peoples—politically, economically, and culturally—into a larger community. In this broad sense, it is little different from internationalization. Yet globalization is more than this incremental process that over the centuries has brought people and nations closer together as technological innovation dissolved barriers of time and distance, and enhanced flows of information promoted greater awareness and understanding.

The focus, as the term suggests, is not on nations but on the entire globe. Consequently, a more sophisticated definition might emphasize that contemporary globalization is a complex, controversial, and synergistic process in which improvements in technology (especially in communications and transportation) combine with the deregulation of markets and open borders to bring about vastly expanded flows of people, money, goods, services, and information. This process integrates people, businesses, nongovernmental organizations, and nations into larger networks. Globalization promotes convergence, harmonization, efficiency, growth, and, perhaps, democratization and homogenization.

Globalization also has a dark side. It produces economic and social dislocations and arouses public concerns over job security; the distribution of economic gains; and the impact of volatility on families, communities, and nations. Many also worry about a growing concentration of economic power; harm to the environment; danger to public health and safety; the disintegration of indigenous cultures; and the loss of sovereignty, accountability, and transparency in government. These, too, are issues that have been topics of concern to American diplomats and foreign policymakers throughout the twentieth century.

There are two principal drivers to globalization: technological innovation and changing ideas about how to organize and regulate economic activity. Rapidly changing technologies for transportation and communications continue to dissolve the barriers of time, distance, and ignorance that once complicated long-range relationships. In the twentieth century some of the most important technological innovations that changed diplomacy were the jet plane, satellite communications, fiber-optic cables, and the Internet. Ideas also shape globalization, particularly the widespread belief that free trade, private enterprise, and competitive markets promote efficiency and economic growth. Another set of ideas also influences the globalization process: the belief among international lawyers that harmonization of standards, rules, and legal systems is the most appropriate way to resolve business conflicts. The impact of technology and ideas are the building blocks of globalization, and have shaped U.S. power, policy, and diplomatic conduct.

The globalization process has other independent drivers. In the history of the modern world, a rising population in less-developed areas frequently has triggered emigration to areas of economic opportunity, and this in turn has frequently produced a stream of remittances to family members who remained behind. Famine and malnourishment, as well as the need for energy and industrial raw materials to support advanced economies, also affect the globalization process, promoting greater flows of materials, food, and goods, and thus enhancing the interdependence of people and economies. Also, two World Wars, a Cold War, and the Great Depression disrupted in significant ways the ongoing globalization process through much of the twentieth century. Finally, leadership is an important element of all human activity. Had the United States, as the world's leading economic and military power in the twentieth century, not committed its public policy to promoting an open, and nondiscriminatory, international economic system, it is quite possible that the globalization process would have taken a different course—perhaps one that gave priority to regional blocs.

In explaining the emergence of globalization, it is almost trite to observe that the underlying forces of technology and economics have transformed the traditional nation-state system and compressed once-formidable barriers of time and space. But post–Cold War globalization did just that, although the process had roots in the late-nineteenth-century growth of American power. The concept, therefore, requires scholars of foreign relations to leap outside of the normal parameters of the nation-state and political-military affairs and take into account such elements as the flows of goods, services, and money; the increasing international mobility of people (and especially business professionals and skilled workers); the emergence and growth of large corporations that view the world as a single market in which they allocate resources, shift production, and market goods; the expansion of financial, legal, insurance, and information services; and the interconnections of cultures, customs, political processes, and ideas.

Mindful that the concept addresses historical transformations, scholars in political science, economics, linguistics, anthropology, geography, law, art, and film studies help to define the term. Political scientists, economists, and business historians have accurately identified techno-economic globalization as the precursor of other forms of globalization, such as transnational cultural exchanges. That is, the open and expanding market, in a synergistic relationship with technology (including scientific developments), has given rise to concomitant political, institutional, social, intellectual, and diplomatic changes. Economics and technology exert an enduring impact on international relationships, seemingly proceeding on their own separate tracks but not immune from events.

This calls into question the interpretation of economic determinists, for globalization complicates while it also complements Marxism, corporatism, and the like. To be sure, the power of markets associated with money, goods, services, and information facilitates international relationships, but it does so in diverse ways. Wealth is only one of the critical factors propelling the global economy. When viewed from a perspective of globalization, Marxism overemphasizes capitalism's contradictions of overproduction and underconsumption, diverting attention from the impact of economic and business concerns on diplomacy. Corporatists tend to discount the influence of strategic, humanitarian, and idealist considerations in government circles and within the private sector as well, while world systems theorists draw on an international lineup of states rather than global, private-oriented networks.

Traditional approaches to diplomatic history, including post-revisionism, also ignore the globalization construct in that they relegate economics and technology to a second tier in their levels of analysis. Globalization requires attention to nongovernmental actors, including religious and philanthropic organizations, consumer and environmental groups, workers, and unions, along with those active in business and finance. By including these groups, globalization lends an appreciation to the variety of concerns in U.S. foreign relations, from national security to advancing national ideals to humanitarian concerns.

Globalization is also not event or crisis driven, which are common foci for diplomatic historians. Instead, it explores the factors that are significant to diplomacy in the long run. For instance, the dispute between Guatemala and the United Fruit Company that led to the ouster of the government of Jacobo Arbenz Guzmán in

1954 is considered a crisis point in Cold War diplomacy. But just as important is discussion of the efforts of Carl Lindner, owner of United Fruit's successor, Chiquita Brands. He opened Western European markets to exports of Central American bananas by using the power of the purse to reward American politicians of both parties, thus placing his agenda at the cutting edge of U.S. trade diplomacy toward the European Common Market. Diplomatic history can account for such actions, which are often hidden by more traditional approaches, by placing the Guatemala episode and other flash points in the context of the globalized expansion of business and culture.

With its application to the many strands of the historiography of U.S. foreign relations, it is clear that globalization promotes new ways of explaining American diplomacy. And because globalization is a historical phenomenon, scholars and commentators can draw on it as an interpretive device to examine change and continuity across the world at various times. Technology and economics have long colluded with each other, beginning at least with the Industrial Revolution. Yet conquests, trade, slavery, and religious expansion, across the world as it was then known, have occurred farther back than that. The spread of Islam, the Crusades, the Roman Empire, and continuous agricultural revolution all represented the inexorable push of the market and technology that lay at the foundation of globalization. Economic globalization undergirded strife, growth, and interchange within and beyond local boundaries throughout history, but the globalizing economy, through the penetrating impact of technology, has also changed culture and politics. Globalization is of a synthetic quality in that it addresses the factors that comprise American diplomatic history; it helps group priorities in foreign relations and explain them in a coherent way.

FIRST ERA OF MODERN GLOBALIZATION: TO 1914

The current brand of globalization in American diplomacy can be traced back to the post–Civil War era, when internationalization and Americanization emerged in U.S. ideology and expressions of power. From this period to World War I, globalization came under the rubric of Anglo-American control of the transatlantic economy. From about 1850 to 1914 an international economy existed, managed by Great Britain, resting on free trade and open capital markets and reliant on colonies and developing areas as resource bases and on consumers in advanced nations. It was in the midst of this first international industrial economy that the United States rode to world power on the strength of its economic muscle and competed with Europeans, spurred on by production and technological inventions.

This period did not experience the revolutionary form of globalization that characterized the post–Cold War years, with their highly synchronized and integrated worldwide communications, transportation, and politics. In the earlier era, less production was attributed to foreign operations. Those affected by globalization were mostly of the elite, rather than the masses, in the early twentieth century. In the pre–World War I period, it was clear which nation controlled production, marketing, culture, and the like, while the multitrillion-dollar world market of the 1990s and beyond had no natural owners. The velocity of globalization in the pre-1914 years was immensely slower than at the end of twentieth century, as were the volume and the scope. The years before World War I did not witness the fundamental transformation in the global economy that started in the last century's final two decades.

Evident in the earlier era, however, were improvements in technology and a greater volume of world economic connections that indicated the influence of globalization on American power, diplomacy, and the economy. However, remarkable changes wrought by new business networks were not fully understood by diplomats back then. Some policymakers noted the importance of new technology and economic relationships; the presidents of these times, for instance, became more aware of global economic concerns. That was particularly true of William McKinley, known for the protectionist tariff with his name but actually a far-sighted globalizer. But they could not possibly foresee all of their applications. Movement toward globalization occurred, nascent and incomplete and interrupted by events of the twentieth century though it was. Thus, it is fair to argue that globalization offered, and offers, a new paradigm in which to view not only diplomatic history, but world history as a whole.

By the twentieth century, the United States had begun to replace Britain's colonial and transAtlantic systems of free trade and government-run transportation and communication networks. The new form of organization was a structured but open economic system of private enterprise and business-friendly public support for access to foreign markets, inventions, immigration, and adherence to international law. Private enterprise could export and produce abroad, the fruits of America's leadership in technology and intellectual property. People and ideas could move easily, facilitating the outward diffusion of America's political ideals and cultural values. America practiced an informal imperialism—in which investment and trade accompanied missionaries and, on occasion, the military—that gradually superseded British industrial and agricultural power.

The early era of globalization, before World War I, was greased by the technological leaps of transportation improvements like the steamship, and by marvels like the Suez and Panama Canals, which sped European and American commerce around the globe. Transatlantic cables, then direct telegraph links to Latin America and connections through British cable to Asia, allowed American investors and merchants to communicate faster abroad, thus expanding their markets. The great expositions of the age—in Chicago in 1893, Omaha in 1898, Buffalo in 1901, and St. Louis in 1904, as well as later gatherings in West Coast cities—publicized American achievements and the promise of empire based on progress in technology. Global connections shrunk the world itself.

Globalization was also driven by the emergence of America in the international economy. Capital exports, the plethora of inventions with American trademarks that were sold overseas, and a greater presence in financial markets boosted U.S. power. For instance, one of the most successful exporters was a capital goods firm, the Baldwin Locomotive Works of Philadelphia, whose engines came to symbolize power, speed, and the march of civilization. In 1900 Baldwin exported an average of one engine a day, shipping locomotives to South America, Africa, Asia, Australia and Europe. Exports soared after its engines gained recognition for their speed and for hauling weight up steep grades. At the turn of the twentieth century, Baldwin locomotives climbed Pikes Peak, hauled the Trans-Siberian Express, roamed the Argentine pampas, and whistled past the Egyptian pyramids. In the British Empire, American firms won contracts for building railroad bridges in Uganda and supplying rails for the construction of Cecil Rhodes's Cape to Cairo Railway, a project intended to develop British trade in Africa. Elsewhere, in the world's breadbaskets, Argentine, Australian, and Russian farmers used U.S. machinery to gather grain. Here were the companies that engaged in the international economy, as well as the privately run globalized market that was outside the realm of states.

Such economic connections promoted cultural ones as well. Thus, early signs of globalization in cultural exchanges were evident in sports (the Olympic Games), marriage, tourism, entertainment (Buffalo Bill's Wild West Show), the temperance movement, missionary work, and philanthropy. Regarding the latter, American-led internationalization in the years before World War I involved magnates like Andrew Carnegie and John D. Rockefeller, who turned to global philanthropy to counteract the label of "robber baron" and to advance their social concerns. Carnegie bequeathed millions to build public libraries in the United States and throughout the British dominions. For his part, Rockefeller established a huge foundation with a global mission to promote the well-being of mankind throughout the world. The oil baron personally contributed some $530 million to foundations and his son added another $537 million, which went for medical and scientific research, public health, education, and international exchange programs. The Foundation combated yellow fever and tropical African diseases. In China it established Peking Union Medical College to spread knowledge of medicine and sanitation, conduct research, and support the medical activities of Western missionaries. In addition, Carnegie's associate Henry Phipps in 1908 donated enough money so that Washington, D.C., could host the sixth International Congress on Tuberculosis, a disease that had killed thousands across the world. His contemporary, Darius Ogden Mills, funded an expedition to Chile in 1912 that measured over three hundred of the brightest stars in one-quarter of the sky surrounding the South Pole.

Besides the globalization of science and medicine, the fortunes of Americans were also spent on human rights causes. Jacob Schiff, the famous head of the banking firm Kuhn, Loeb and Company, turned his attention in 1906 to funding the American Jewish Committee, an organization dedicated to alleviating the persecution of Jewry at home and abroad. A host of banking, mining, and export firms, moreover, poured money into relief projects before World War I. For example, the New York Merchants Association raised $8,000 to help the victims of the Valparaiso earthquake of 1906, Guggenheim Sons, W. R. Grace and Company, and others more than matched this amount. In sum, the rich in America transferred some of their wealth to the international stage, in the process moving outside the realm of nations to influence the world economy. This is the essence of globalization.

DISRUPTED GLOBALIZATION: 1914–1939

The period from the end of World War I to 1950 also experienced some elements of globalization as new technology joined expansion in finance, trade, investment, and culture throughout the world. Yet in a major sense this was an era of deglobalization: first, the international economic system malfunctioned or broke down; then, during the Cold War, the world divided along ideological fissures.

World War I accelerated the expansion of U.S. business overseas. American firms were especially successful in replacing dominant British firms in Western Hemisphere and Asian markets. In addition, war requirements created a soaring U.S. demand for raw materials, especially copper, iron, and other key mineral products. Soon American firms, with the help of their government, began scouring the world for essential raw materials. Rubber companies acquired plantations in Sumatra, sugar producers expanded operations in Cuba, and meat packers enlarged their operations in South America. Paper companies opened pulp and papers mills in Canada, while mining companies purchased nitrate, iron, and copper mines in Chile. Oil companies explored China, the Dutch Indies, and other remote regions and invested heavily in unstable Mexico. War needs drove much of this overseas expansion, but American business leaders were not oblivious to long-term opportunities.

President Woodrow Wilson left an enduring mark on U.S. foreign relations, especially in providing American leadership for the postwar economic and financial system. But if he was the father of internationalism, then he also presided over the disruption of globalization. The defeat of the Treaty of Versailles demonstrated the variations in thinking about globalization. Prevailing sentiment was not prepared to abandon nationalism even as the expansive course of global commerce and investment and America's role in the world maintained their momentum. Americans would not fully adopt Wilsonian ideals until after the Cold War. In addition, globalization took a backseat to revolution. Mexico's new constitution under the Carranza government of Venustiano Carranza provided for restrictions on foreign ownership of land and subsoil resources. This meant that American investors would be limited to oil reserves; at the broader level, the clash was between nationalism and international legalism, with the former winning out. In Russia, the Bolshevik government survived a shaky start, including a civil war in which Americans participated, to create a decidedly anti-capitalist regime. At first the Soviet Union promoted globalization of the masses but not capital, lashing out at the imperialist nature of capitalist globalization. Moscow then retreated to building a socialist state under Communist Party control at home. Thus, the world started to split ideologically and politically even as Wilson's vision reached its expressive high point.

Yet many bankers and administration officials still sought outward, long-term solutions to promote peace and prosperity. Because Europe had bought three-fifths of American exports before the war, freer trade was a national interest after World War I. More generally, policymakers embraced internationalism. Understanding that the Great War had caused an explosion in U.S. exports and imports, that suffering farmers could be aided by overseas expansion, and that America held a key role in global finance, Republican administrations of the 1920s did not separate the international from the domestic. They pushed for globalism, albeit a less political brand than Wilson's. Global disarmament indicated one side of Republican engagement in the world. This effort energized citizens, diplomats, and businessmen into even more cooperative, internationalist endeavors during this era than before the war.

Cultural internationalism grew stronger as nations created numerous associations designed to facilitate global ties. An International Office of Museums, and International Congress on Popular Arts, and an International Society for Contemporary Music fostered linkages and understanding. In the United States, political scientists began studying the causes of war and universities offered new courses in various national histories and languages, all a reflection of the need to understand the global context in which America operated. Americans organized hundreds of scholarly discussion groups, such as the Institute of Pacific Relations, a multinational association of journalists, academics, and businessmen based in New York City. The new Guggenheim Foundation funded artistic projects and scholarly research, focusing on Latin American intellectuals. The

Institute of International Education funded and directed foreign students to universities throughout the United States. Asians were the main beneficiaries, but increasingly, Latin American and European youth traveled to America to study. In this globalized ethos, Americans believed in peace and prosperity wrought by international contact. The influence of such private activity on foreign policy was extensive, demonstrating that globalization continued to some degree. Disarmament was one arena, regional stabilization and multilateralism another, and arbitration yet another.

Business made global connections in the 1920s. Air transport and travel became a reality under the machinations of Pan American World Airways under the leadership of Juan Trippe. American trade and investment multiplied. Along with the spread of radio, cinema was not only an American phenomenon but a global one as well; people around the world listened and watched the new media and thus developed some common cultural markers. Hollywood stars such as Douglas Fairbanks and Mary Pickford were known worldwide, for example.

Nonetheless, the onset of the Great Depression and World War II dealt a setback to further globalization. The globalizers of the 1920s—the Republican presidents and bureaucrats, the business and banking establishments—were ultimately limited by their own ideology and by the powerful concentration of forces that elevated the domestic economy over the international order. The effort at privatizing decisions and policy ultimately grounded itself on the Smoot-Hawley Tariff and imperial trade preferences of the 1930s, which reserved British Empire markets for member states and excluded or discriminated against outsiders such as America. And politics could not be taken out of the economy; businessmen could not be trusted with, nor were they capable of, running the global system of trade and finance. The Republican governments promoted the ideology of technoglobalization but often refused to take responsibility through policies of running the world economy. They were unwilling to make the tough moves that involved political haggling at home—on matters like reducing war debts and tariffs, for instance—that were requisites to continuing their brand of internationalism. This proved especially so when economic times spiraled from prosperity to misfortune during the Great Depression.

Paradoxically, however, as governments turned away from efforts to harmonize and integrate the international economy to cope with domestic distresses, advances in technology continued to erode the barriers of time, distance, and ignorance that separated nations and people. Some of the most significant improvements in air travel and mass communications, particularly the movies and short-wave radio, took place during the 1930s. At a time when dire economic circumstances compelled most government leaders to think local, a few leaders in government and business dared to speak up for closer international economic cooperation. Thus, Thomas J. Watson, Jr., the head of International Business Machines (IBM) and the International Chamber of Commerce, mimicked Secretary of State Cordell Hull in proclaiming that freer international economic relations meant world peace, and that if goods did not cross borders, he feared that armies would.

A WORLD DIVIDED: 1940–1950

World War II further threatened Anglo-American-style globalization. The Axis powers—a loose coalition of Germany, Italy, and Japan—resorted to military force to overthrow the post-Versailles world order and to establish closed, regional systems dominated from Berlin, Rome, and Tokyo. The conflict afforded the United States a second chance to provide leadership and to promote its vision of a peaceful, prosperous, and united world. The Roosevelt administration pressed plans for international rules and institutions that would structure the post–World War II global economic and political system. In joining technology with national security, the war forged an enduring partnership among business, government, and science. Afterward, the new military-industrial complex would sustain America as an economic and military superpower, develop endless frontiers for scientific discovery, and speed the globalization process.

In effect, scientists and their laboratories, with government funding and direction, contributed in a major way to the success of the war effort, and in the process they developed many new products that had commercial applications which would transform the postwar world. Atomic energy, for instance, had many peaceful applications, particularly as a source of electrical power. The mass production of penicillin transformed the treatment of disease. Also, radar provided the basis for microwave cooking. The first computers appeared during World War II to assist the military with code breaking and long-distance ballistics calculations. ENIAC, one of the first, was a huge machine, occupying 1,800 square feet and using 18,000 bulky vacuum tubes. Not until the development of transistors and the microchips that resulted from them could cheap and reliable computing power be loaded into desktop and portable units. The transistor, which was developed in 1947 and 1948, grew out of wartime research on silicon and germanium at Bell Telephone Laboratories in New Jersey. The transistor led directly to the technology of the personal computer, which itself spawned the globalized information age in the last third of the twentieth century.

No industry benefited more from wartime cooperation and federal contracts than aviation. At the outbreak of war the Boeing Company of Seattle, renowned for its seaplanes and engineering skills, had fewer than two thousand employees and was on the verge of bankruptcy. From this inauspicious beginning the company flourished on the strength of its bombers (the B-17 Flying Fortress and the B-29 Superfortress). Employment rose to nearly forty-five thousand. At the end of the war Boeing, on the strength of its experience and reputation in military aircraft production, turned its attention to the civilian market, using the B-29 as the basis of the luxurious 377 Stratocruiser that Pan American used on Atlantic routes. It contained a spiral staircase and a downstairs bar, but was soon superseded by the four-engine 707 passenger jet, launched in 1954. The latter also had roots in military work to develop a jet tanker and from wind tunnel experiments with jet engines during World War II. Thus, with government assistance, American companies like Boeing, Douglas, and Lockheed would come to dominate the rapidly expanding world market for civilian aviation.

Growth was also in order for consumer goods, which were also foundations for later globalization. Robert W. Woodruff, who had taken over the Coca-Cola Company in 1923, aimed to make his beverage an ordinary, everyday item for Americans and people around the world. He built on his foreign operations, particularly in Europe, during World War II by having Coke accompany the military overseas. Soldiers not only identified with Woodruff's product during and after the war but heroes requested it—as did an American pilot who crashed in Scotland and asked, upon regaining consciousness, for a Coke. The beverage was so pervasive that the Nazis and Japanese denounced it as a disease of American society. By war's end the company ran sixty-three bottling plants across the globe, on every continent. Its net profits in 1948 soared to $35.6 million, elevating it to near-universal acceptance as the world's beverage of choice.

The Cold War dashed the hopes of internationalists who would have facilitated the globalization of the world economy, but still strides were made toward the technoglobal system, induced particularly by governments working through the United Nations. In these instances, officials instilled international law and arbitration processes in the international economy, yet another foundation of globalization. For instance, the International Civil Aviation Organization (ICAO) pushed for global rules to govern the dynamic medium of air transport and travel. The objective was to establish international law, as well as promote order, safety, and efficient development in aviation, although ICAO authority remained limited by national desires to control lucrative commercial air traffic. The ICAO, established on a permanent basis in April 1947, provided the framework for the vast expansion of commercial airspace after World War II. By the late 1960s its 116 member nations connected markets around the world more closely by integrating various technical aspects of airplane transport, such as air navigation codes, as well as by devising a mechanism to resolve civil disputes, promote simpler procedures at borders, and boost Third World development in civil aviation—all enhancing globalization through air transport.

The protracted Cold War struggle that divided the world into two spheres of influence—one led from Washington, the other from Moscow—prompted national security considerations, rather than invisible market forces, to define international relationships. Governments continued to regulate trade and financial exchanges, despite efforts to lower barriers and promote commerce. But America's technological advantage, adaptable production processes, and access to resources, so decisive in the struggle against Axis aggressors, helped win the conflict. Also, a new generation of U.S. political and corporate leaders, familiar with mistakes made at the end of World War I when the United States shunned overseas responsibilities, chose to accept this second opportunity to guide the world. Furthermore, as it turned out, these internationalists were also better salesmen than Soviet leader Joseph Stalin and his heirs, who presided over a decrepit, controlled Soviet economy unable to satisfy basic consumer wants. Aware that a troubled world had an insatiable appetite for American values, goods, and services, U.S. leaders exploited their comparative advantage in communications and marketing to advance the American dream of democracy, mass consumption, and individual enterprise. In the long Cold War, the formula of guns, butter, and liberal ideals eventually proved a winner that spread American values on a global basis. Without America's Marshall Plan, support for Japan, and containment of the Soviet Union, the history of the Cold War might have turned out quite differently, and likewise for the course of globalization. Had the USSR won the Cold War, Soviet-directed expansion would have been far different—far more capricious, authoritarian, and state-managed—than the American-led alternative based on the rule of law, democratic elections, open markets, and the relentless energy of technology and entrepreneurship. Thus, the era of globalization that began near century's end evolved, ironically, from the deglobalized structure of the Cold War.

GLOBALIZATION UNDERCURRENTS: 1951–1972

The indicators of globalization were present throughout the superpower struggle. Prosperity and peace brought greater individual mobility. Before World War I an average of 1.5 million people arrived annually at U.S. shores, with about half that many departing. Travel lagged until after World War II and then revived. Two million people arrived in 1956, 10 million in 1970. Immigration, which fell to a low of 24,000 in 1943 and stagnated during the Depression and World War II, revived slowly after the war, reaching 327,000 in 1957. The largest numbers of immigrants—many of them war refugees—continued to come from Europe, and at this time particularly from Germany. Air travel also took off. Before the 1940s the typical traveler from abroad came by sea; after World War II the traveler arrived by air. On domestic routes the number of revenue passengers rose rapidly from 6.6 million passengers in 1945 to 48.7 million in 1957 and 153.4 million in 1970. On international routes the rise was equally dramatic: from 476,000 in 1945 to 4.5 million in 1957 and 16.3 million in 1970.

Despite Cold War crises and the further regionalization of the world economy, highlighted by the launching of the European Common Market in 1957 (which lured massive American investment), a revolution in critical technologies—including transatlantic telephone service, satellite communications, computers, and jet travel—accelerated the globalization process and ushered in a new era of rapid intercontinental travel, instantaneous communications, and economic interdependence. America's humbling experience in Vietnam, dollar woes, and the rise of oil exporting nations in the 1970s did not dampen globalization. Americans still enjoyed the benefits of unprecedented prosperity spurred by technology and economic expansion overseas. They bought new homes equipped with the latest labor-saving appliances, vacationed and studied abroad, and followed breaking news and sporting events abroad on new color television sets receiving signals transmitted via space satellites. Despite domestic political turmoil, technoglobalization continued to press forward, gradually transforming the world of separate nations.

Marshall McLuhan, a Canadian who analyzed the impact of mass media on society, made the metaphor of the "global village" famous in 1962 as a reference to the new electronic interdependence that had recreated the world. At the time, McLuhan was concerned largely with how noninteractive communications like radio and television were homogenizing the world: everyone watched the same sporting events, news, and soap operas. He identified a significant trend. The late 1950s was a period of enormous change as technical developments in aviation, transportation, and communications brought cost reductions and improved service. People, goods, and capital began to move across borders, creating interactive bonds among people and between nations. These flows integrated markets, harmonized tastes, and homogenized cultures.

Some of the most significant advances involved air transportation for people and freight. In 1957, Boeing, having gambled 25 percent of its net worth on development of a long-range passenger jet, launched the 707-120, designed as both a tanker for the air force and a civilian jet. Equipped with long-range Pratt and Whitney J-57 engines, it halved flying time across the Atlantic and opened the era of cheap air travel. The number of passengers departing internationally on scheduled airliners rose 340 percent (from 4.3 million to 18.9 million) from 1957 to 1973 as airlines introduced tourist-class fares. A round-trip flight, New York to London, fell to $487. The

THE FAB FOUR AS GLOBAL PHENOMS

Defying the label Americanization, the Beatles epitomized globalization. They emerged in the new era of rapid travel and electronic communications, influenced by black rock 'n' roll brought to Liverpool by American sailors and spurred by their initial fan base from nightclubs in Hamburg, West Germany. Beatlemania seized England in 1962, grew in popularity in Australia, and emerged on the Continent. "I Want to Hold Your Hand" broke the Beatles into the lucrative U.S. market in January 1964, the first song by a British artist to top the American charts. The hit spread to the non-English-speaking world. The Fab Four then debuted in the United States on the Ed Sullivan Show, playing to a television audience of 73 million people, about 60 percent of total U.S. viewers. Mass global hysteria set in. Between 1963 and 1968, they sold $154 million worth of records and became the first band to sell out sports stadiums worldwide. In 1965 the queen honored them for their contribution to the British foreign trade balance. Two years later, they took part in the first live global satellite broadcast, representing Britain on "Our World," a special originating in eighteen countries on five continents. Wit, cleverness, and aggressive marketing catapulted the Beatles to fame, but they also tapped into the growing cohesion of youth worldwide that attested to the cultural and economic pressures of globalization. Timing the release of their 1967 album *Sgt. Pepper's Lonely Hearts Club Band,* for maximum exposure, they caused a mini-explosion within the Beatles craze itself, as youth across the planet apparently bought the record and played it in unison. It was a moment of unified pop culture. The Beatles flowed across borders, commercially and culturally, exploiting communications technology and open markets—elements of the globalization process.

arrival of the wide-bodied Boeing 747 in 1969 further expanded capacity and drove down costs. Originally designed as a cargo carrier, it could accommodate two containers side by side that could be transferred to trucks; soon, high-value goods were moving swiftly by jet freighter. It also offered lower operating costs at a time when fuel prices were rising.

Thus, by the early 1970s improvements in air transport made it possible for business to source suppliers and serve markets globally. From 1957 to 1973 the number of revenue ton miles for air cargo on scheduled international flights rose 866 percent from 128.2 billion tons in 1957 to 1.2 trillion ton in 1973. It would be a decade before the full impact of these improvements worked their way through the marketplace. Air service continued to expand rapidly and airfares fell. Charter service grew rapidly on the transatlantic route and fares on scheduled airliners fell below $200 (New York to London) by 1970. Millions of college students read Arthur Frommer's best-seller, *Europe on $5 a Day* (first published in 1957), put on their backpacks, and set out to see Europe and learn about "foreign affairs." Meanwhile, improved engine design and weight reduction led to longer-range planes. In 1976 Boeing launched the 747 SP, which had the capacity to carry 233 passengers nonstop with full payload between New York and Tokyo. By 1989 Boeing was producing the 747-400; it could carry 412 passengers for up to twenty hours at subsonic speeds.

Along with the arrival of reliable, efficient jet freight in the late 1960s, other important cost-saving developments occurred in maritime shipping, including containerization. In the 1950s longshoremen could typically handle from ten to fifteen tons of cargo per hour. The use of truck-trailer, standard-size containers, brought productivity up to from six hundred to seven hundred tons per hour. This meant faster ship turnaround, better coordination, and lower transportation costs. Beginning in April 1956, when the trucking executive Malcolm McLean first moved loaded trailers between two U.S. port cities on an old World War II tanker, containerization took off. Grace and Matson lines adopted it in 1960 and the rush to containerization peaked in 1969, during the Vietnam War. In addition, the international shipping industry developed specially designed ships for automobiles (the first auto carriers could handle from one thousand to two thousand cars) and LNG (liquified natural gas) tankers after the 1973 war in the Middle East..

Improvements in communications also boosted the globalization process. Until the mid-1950s individuals could not communicate quickly and easily across the Atlantic and the Pacific Oceans. In 1927 commercial telephone service using high-frequency radio opened between New York and London. But this interactive advance was not designed for mass communications. Radio telephones were noisy, unreliable, and costly—forty-five dollars for the first three minutes. September 1956 brought the most significant improvement in communications in over a century when American Telephone and Telegraph opened the first transatlantic telephone cable (TAT-1) by using microwave amplification techniques. The number of transatlantic telephone calls soared—climbing slowly from 10,000 in 1927 to 250,000 in 1957, and then jumping to 4.3 million in 1961. Soon large corporations such as Ford began using the telephone cable to exchange information and coordinate their overseas operations from their U.S. headquarters. While telephone cables improved business communications among metropolitan centers, large areas of the world could not take advantage of telephone communications. Starting in the 1980s, satellite communications ended this isolation and made the emerging global village truly interactive.

The arrival of jet planes and transoceanic telephones facilitated business expansion, but so did American scientific leadership. World War II and the early Cold War saw many technological advances, and U.S. firms moved quickly to commercialize products from military research. Between 1945 and 1965 the number of patents granted in America more than doubled, rising from 25,695 to 62,857. Five times as many patents went to U.S. firms as to foreign corporations. As late as 1967 the United States accounted for 69 percent of research and development in major countries. A good illustration was the transformation of IBM, which took its domination into the global marketplace.

The Cold War generated momentum for globalization in other ways, too. National Science Foundation, National Space and Aeronautics Administration, and Defense Department contracts spurred basic research throughout the 1960s, and space research particularly spun off growth in intelligence gathering, electronics and engineering, and weaponry. Laboratories hired thousands of corporate engineers to work on missile and aerospace projects, and clusters of companies and laboratories sprouted up near major academic institutions. The space program's budget steadily increased to $1.2 billion by 1962, and steps were taken to orbit a man around the earth (via the Mercury Project from 1959 to 1962), and eventually to send him to the moon (through the Apollo Project in 1969). These were the precursors to the space shuttle and satellite communications of the 1980s and beyond, which fueled the globalization of information.

DECENTRALIZATION ACCELERATES: 1973–1989

From the mid-1970s onward the process of world political and economic decentralization, so essential to globalization, picked up momentum. The technological transformations allowed American and other multinational firms to escape national regulations, and also helped free ordinary people from the boundaries of the nation-state. In addition, the rise of the OPEC (Organization of Petroleum Exporting Countries) oil cartel shifted global economic power away from the West. Free exchange rates, unfixed from the gold-dollar standard, gave great flexibility to international investors. American businesses would weather the energy crises and the final phase of the Cold War in different ways. With U.S. tariff barriers continuing to fall and foreign competition surging into the American market, high-cost domestic industries such as steel, autos, and machine tools lost market share to new entrants from abroad. But many big- and medium-sized firms did well in a changing, competitive environment. Firms with leading-edge technologies took advantage of market-opening opportunities to expand abroad. In the era of jet travel and networked business communications, the battle for market share was increasingly fought on a global playing field, involving all of the world's major high-income markets—Japan, Europe, and North America. Companies and nations converged as global markets for standardized consumer products appeared; transnational companies now sold the same reliable, low-priced goods in Brazil as they did in Biafra.

Even as the economic changes occurred, however, and despite the re-ignition of Cold War tensions during the late Carter and early Reagan administrations, ideological shifts occurred that reflected the emerging age of globalization. One was a new international outlook encouraged by better communications, transportation, open borders, deregulation, and the revival of nineteenth-century, laissez-faire liberalism. Business leaders began to think globally and to develop global networks that could exert influence over national political leaders through money and ideas. During the energy crisis of 1973, America's corporate elite reached out to foreign business leaders. Led by Chase Manhattan's David Rockefeller, they formed the multinational Trilateral Commission in 1973, with members from business, politics, law, and academia in America, Western Europe, and Japan. The idea was to facilitate cooperation among resource-rich nations, but outside of government supervision. Similarly, European business leaders began to meet in Davos, Switzerland, in 1982 to develop a common international strategy for European business. This network expanded in the 1980s to include world business and political leaders. In those years it launched the annual World Economic Forum, held every January and bringing together the world's movers and shakers to network, deal, and discuss public policy issues. Similarly in America during the Carter and Reagan years, business lobbying expanded from initial efforts to contain unions to the pursuit of an active agenda of deregulating markets, cutting taxes, and promoting free trade.

The deregulatory business agenda reflected another important paradigm shift that encouraged globalization. The Washington consensus had stressed an active and expansive role for the federal government, but in the 1970s economic thought turned toward a less-regulated marketplace. Under the influence of academic economists Murray Weidenbaum and Milton Friedman, a neoclassical attack on Keynesian interventionism was launched during the Reagan years. It emphasized entrepreneurship, reliance on the Federal Reserve System and monetary policy to manage the economy, tax relief, labor-market competition, deregulation, fluctuating exchange rates, and free trade in goods. In time, this consensus came to include free trade in money, or capital account convertibility.

President Ronald Reagan can be credited with fostering the second era of techno-economic globalization by expounding on the possibilities for freedom, political and economic, under U.S. leadership. He was the first president to push openly for free trade and privatization of government services, and one of the first to appreciate how new technologies of communication were transforming the marketplace and weakening the authority of totalitarian regimes. As he left office the technoglobal revolution was accelerating, bringing major changes to economics and politics, and to culture and society as well. His successors wrestled with the implications of globalization at home and abroad. They initiated new integrative bodies that restructured the global economy, such as the North American Free Trade Agreement (NAFTA) and the World Trade Organization (WTO), institutions that emphasized a rules-based economic system and liberalization of international commerce and that further integrated business processes worldwide. The freer exchanges of goods, capital, and culture inherent in globalization arose from the Cold War's ashes and took America into a new era in which transnational contacts rivaled state power.

AMERICAN-LED GLOBALIZATION: 1990–2001

The Clinton administration perceived that globalization had the potential to harmonize behavior, customs, and politics and usher in prosperity, development, and democracy. As the world's only superpower, the United States would lead the way toward openness, free access, and political stability. Also, President William Jefferson Clinton's enthusiasm for globalization was not shared by all Americans; many wondered if globalization was both inevitable and desirable. As the new millennium began, the business community seemed united in support of globalization, but among ordinary people there were concerns about jobs, food safety, harm to the environment, sovereignty, cultural homogenization, and the like. Americans were as unsure about the costs and benefits of this second era of globalization as they had been during the first one before World War I.

The Clinton administration veered from postwar history and adopted the universalist, integrative, and democratic posture of globalization. Economics replaced security on the U.S. policy agenda; globalization was the focus. The administration tied free markets to democracy. After the Mexican peso crisis of 1994, the president placed economic diplomacy at the center of foreign policy, supporting the consolidation of market democracy throughout the world, an ideology that put him in stride with global business but at odds with many in his own party who were tied to the traditional big government, worker-protection liberalism of the past.

The outpouring of analyses of globalization grew during the mid-1990s. Scholars, journalists, and politicians focused on the concept and process, but above all, on its influence. The widespread use of the Internet (304 million people in 2000) brought the issue into homes throughout the world. When added to the Clinton administration's oftentimes single-minded purpose of expanding American trade and investments overseas, the establishment of NAFTA and the WTO, and the soaring rebound of the U.S. economy from a recession early in the 1990s, globalization had a certain cachet among Americans of all political stripes and economic status.

Americans were not the only ones anxious over globalization. In western Europe and many developing countries, globalization was a dirty word, associated in the public mind with American sneakers, blue jeans, burgers, and videos. The French were most skeptical. In one poll, 65 percent said globalization increased the gap between rich and poor; 56 percent thought it threatened national identity. The French Ministry of Culture sought to rally Europeans and to restrict access for Hollywood films and American television programs.

Around the world, defenders of traditional values sought to block the spread of American-style pop culture, but globalization proved a worthy foe. Iranian religious fundamentalists raided homes to confiscate videos and satellite dishes, and in neighboring Afghanistan the Taliban closed movie theaters, burned films, and denied schooling to women. Try as they might, the fundamentalists could not eradicate this powerfully projected alien culture. Their efforts merely benefited smugglers and the flow of contraband. Many discreetly hid satellite dishes to access Western television. The failure of Islamic fundamentalists to stamp out Western influences, like the inability of state-controlled societies in Eastern Europe to block the appeal of Western democracy and consumerism, demonstrated the power of mass communications in the era of satellites and videocassettes. It also underscored the global appeal of American values to the young, the well-educated, and the affluent, an amorphous yet tangible element of U.S. power in the world.

Yet the argument that globalization led to American cultural dominance ignored the appeal of the competition. At the time anti-globalization demonstrators were protesting in Seattle against the WTO in December 1999, children throughout America were gripped by the Japanese fad game Pokemon. Film industries in India and Hong Kong presented competition to Hollywood, and MTV discovered the need to vary its formula in the world's various regional markets—providing, for example, Chinese music in China and Hindi pop in India. True cultural globalization, not just Americanization, was in effect.

Among the world's cosmopolitan elite—business leaders, government officials, academics, and media types—the requirements of globalization produced a convergence. English became the predominant language of commerce and transnational communications, and business and government leaders wore Western business suits, flew in the same airplanes, stayed in the same hotels, read the same newspapers (the *Wall Street Journal* and the *Financial Times*), and communicated with cellular phones and e-mail. The acceptance of American-style globalization reflected the success of U.S. business, the need to play by the rules of the world's largest open market, U.S. leadership in technological innovation and the information revolution, and the attraction of America's universal values. It also reflected the victories over fascism, militarism, and communism during the twentieth century that allowed the Anglo-American powers to establish the United Nations system, design the institutions of international economic and financial collaboration, and press for acceptance of common standards and the rule of law that were so crucial to globalization.

The post–Cold War era of economic globalization, however, also represented a synergistic dimension in which changes in technology, business strategy, and government policies combined to produce effects far more profound than the sum of incremental steps. The changes hinged on the integration of capital markets, the growing irrelevance of national borders, and the technological leveraging of knowledge and talent worldwide. As the Internet was empowering ordinary people with information, governance of the global system became more segmented in functional supranational institutions run by specialized elites. The International Monetary Fund (IMF), the World Bank, the WTO, and the Bank for International Settlements set the rules and handed out sanctions.

Integration and mobility were keys. Production, capital flows, and workers were increasingly integrated into a global marketplace dictated by transnational corporations. In 1970 there were 7,000 transnational corporations; in 2000 the numbers were some 63,000 parents and 690,000 foreign affiliates as well as a large number of inter-firm arrangements. Gross product affiliated with the production of transnationals increased faster than global GDP and global exports. The foreign affiliates of transnational corporations employed six million persons and had foreign sales of $2 trillion. Their reach in every aspect of the world economy—from production to distribution—grew exponentially. In the last half of the twentieth century, international trade accelerated. The world economy grew sixfold in that time, climbing from $6.7 trillion in constant prices to $41.6 trillion in 1998, while global exports of goods rose seventeenfold, from $311 billion to $5.4 trillion. Much of the growth occurred among units of transnational corporations and involved services, which represented one-fifth of total world trade at the end of the century. From 1970 to 2000, the volume of foreign direct investment rose almost fifteenfold; in the latter year it was twice that of 1990. By then, dozens of nations had enacted special laws to attract foreign capital.

Financial globalization, reflecting the integration of equity and bond markets, was another powerful factor driving world economic integration and growth. As in late-nineteenth-century Britain, the upper and middle classes increasingly invested their savings overseas. The assets of U.S.-based international and global mutual funds climbed from $16 billion in 1986 to $321 billion in late 1996. Forty-four million American households held mutual funds, compared to 4.6 million in 1980. Moreover, the velocity of foreign exchange transactions spiraled. In 1973 average daily turnover in foreign exchange markets was $15 billion compared to $60 billion in 1983, $880 billion in 1993; and an estimated $1.5 trillion in 1998. Moreover, in a world of electronically integrated financial markets, money flowed into and out of countries in response to changing market conditions. In 1996 foreign investors put $100 billion into Asia; the next year they withdrew $100 billion.

Technology abetted globalization. World production of technology multiplied six times between 1975 and 1986; international trade in technology soared nine times. Improvements in communications and transportation abetted the process. In 1956, eighty-nine telephone conversations took place simultaneously through the transatlantic telephone cable. By the end of the millennium, about one million conversations occurred simultaneously by satellite and fiber optics. Add in e-mail and faxes and the ease, speed, and volume of communications have been magnified. Between 1955 and 1998, ship tonnage rose sixfold; the unit cost of carrying freight by sea fell 70 percent between 1920 and 1990. The volume of air freight soared from 730 million to 99 billion ton-kilometers. As with shipping, costs fell sharply. Between 1930 and 1990 the average revenue per mile for air transportation dropped from 68 cents to 11 cents (in constant dollars).

Cheaper airfares also enhanced individual mobility. Between 1950 and 1998 international tourist arrivals rose twenty-five-fold—from 25 million to 635 million. By 2000, two million people crossed a border somewhere in the world every single day. Some of them were political refugees; others simply seeking economic opportunities. At the end of the twentieth century, some 150 million people lived outside the country of their birth. This amounted to 2.5 percent of the world's population, or one in every forty people. Many of them remitted earnings to families and relatives in native countries. From 1970 to 1998, the number of immigrants living in America tripled from 9.6 million to 26.3 million. It is estimated that immigrants from Central America remitted $8 billion a year to their home countries during the last years of the twentieth century. Many of the foreign students who entered the United States for graduate education remain, contributing to the brain drain from developing lands but augmenting the supply of highly trained professionals in America. In 1990 one-third of Silicon Valley's scientists and engineers were foreign born.

Many of the less educated who remained in their homelands, moving from countryside to city, have joined the global economy. Labor became part of a global assembly line; transnationals working for the Nike Company and other multinational firms assembled products from components manufactured in factories throughout the world, while management, administration, and research and development were done at the headquarters. Service jobs in law firms, insurance, and data entry focused on electronic production, which meant that jobs flowed in and out of countries at great speed. Globalization had, simply, changed the world and its business, including the projection of national power and diplomacy.

Along with the globalization of brands like Nike, McDonald's, Coca-Cola, and Marlboro, the process also benefited sports teams. Michael Jordan's star qualities, as well as the global reach of satellite television, established a worldwide following for the Chicago Bulls. Soccer's Manchester United and baseball's New York Yankees also appealed to extensive audiences. An influx of eastern European players strengthened the international appeal of the National Hockey League. The National Basketball Association's open-door policy to talent attracted forty-five foreign players from twenty-nine countries, and as a result the NBA broadcast in 210 countries and forty-two languages. Major League Baseball, which began opening its season in foreign locations, inaugurated the 2001 season with 854 players, 25 percent of them born outside the United States. As a result of Ichiro Suzuki's success with the Seattle Mariners, the team's home games were televised live in Japan. Thousands of Japanese baseball fans even flew to Seattle to attend home games of a club owned by Nintendo president Hiroshi Yamauchi.

Along with rapid growth and increasing integration of markets, however, the age of globalization produced greater volatility. The Mexican peso crisis of 1994 and the Asian economic crisis of 1997–1998 underscored the vulnerability of the market-driven globalization system and how quickly strife could spread in a world linked by high-velocity communication, financial, and transportation networks. The Asian economic crisis also showed globalization's impact in the political arena. It aroused concerns about the merits of Western-style, free-market globalization to an extent that street protests, stimulated by the economic downturn, forced Indonesia's dictator of thirty-two years from power while politicians jockeyed for control in Thailand, the Philippines, South Korea, and Malaysia.

Over the preceding decade Wall Street, Washington, and international financial institutions had encouraged emerging economies to deregulate capital markets and open to foreign banks and financial institutions, but countries in Latin America and Asia paid for the deregulatory bonanza. By opening their markets, they made themselves susceptible to pressures from abroad and the international economy, and also lost independence over their fiscal policies. Abrupt changes in one country, region, or the world economy reverberated throughout these poorer nations, causing crises. Yet the bankers and U.S. financial officials blamed the catastrophic consequences on crony capitalism, the lack of transparency and inadequate disclosure of financial data, the absence of independent regulatory authorities, and the inadequacy of accounting standards. They stressed the benefits of liberalization under the process of globalization.

Opposition to the pro-globalization agenda emerged among a disparate alliance of activists concerned about the environment, labor standards, and national sovereignty. In 1992 the first Bush administration had refused to accept the entire Rio de Janeiro Treaty that protected biodiversity of plant and animal species. An argument also erupted over the existence of global warming, which many scientists and environmental groups blamed on the emission of carbon-based gases into the atmosphere. A total of 150 nations, including the United States, signed the Kyoto accord of 1997 that pledged to reduce such global emissions to 5.2 percent below the 1990 level. America would cut its release of carbon-based gases by 7 percent. But President Bill Clinton faced staunch opposition from powerful business interests such as the Business Roundtable, the Chamber of Commerce, and the National Association of Manufacturers who thought the agreement flawed. The Senate voted 95 to 0 to oppose the protocol if developing countries like China and India were not also required to cut their emissions. As a result, the administration never sent the agreement to Capitol Hill for ratification. The debate over global warming continued into the 2000 election when Democratic candidate Al Gore insisted that America join the Kyoto pact nations and GOP candidate George W. Bush countered that additional studies were needed to better understand the problem. It was clear that, just as with the economy, globalization of environmental concerns might require international intervention. Environmental concerns indicated that there was not a consensus on globalization.

Many people, especially in the labor and environmental movements and within academia, shunned this new globalization system, and argued that globalization undermined stability and prosperity and was leading to the disintegration of national economies and cultures. According to this view, workers had become pawns in transnational corporate agendas, the environment had been deregulated by the free-market rules of the WTO, and financial markets had been so decontrolled that the joint efforts of a handful of individuals could destabilize entire nations (as in Indonesia in 1997). The anti-globalization protesters took to the streets to voice their objections. The WTO ministerial meetings convened in Seattle in December 1999 to plan a new set of world trade negotiations called the Millennium Round, but huge demonstrations shut down the meetings. Seattle turned out not to be an isolated event; there were later demonstrations at gatherings sponsored by the United Nations, the IMF and World Bank, and Davo's World Economic Forum.

There were also optimists who saw the free market and meteoric advances in technology as a great boon or as an irreversible phenomenon that could not be halted. They announced that the world had entered a period of unity (unlike the divisive forty-five-year Cold War) that rewarded flexibility, high technology, and individualism.

Public opinion polls showed Americans divided on such issues as globalization and free trade. In general, those in the middle class and below voiced protectionist sentiments or questioned the fairness of NAFTA and the WTO. Among those warning of the perils of globalization were Pope John Paul II, UN Secretary General Kofi Annan, and former South African president Nelson Mandela.

As the twenty-first century opened, the globalization revolution continued to roll forward. While the global spread of information, the integration of markets, and the erasure of borders had the potential to promote global peace, prosperity, and the convergence of basic values, there was a dark dimension often ignored by corporate boosters. For one, globalization benefited organized criminals as well as corporations. The turnover of the criminal economy was estimated at about $1 trillion annually. Narcotics accounted for about half, but a trade in people was also lucrative. Gangs moved from four to five million people annually and earned some $7 billion in profits. In the health area, globalization presented a number of challenges. Public health officials worried that increased human mobility enhanced opportunities for microbes. The risks ranged from trade in illegal products and contaminated foodstuffs, divergent safety standards, indiscriminate spread of medical technologies and experimentation, and the sale of prescription drugs without approval of national authorities. With some two million people crossing borders daily, industrialized nations faced threats from emerging infectious diseases, exposure to dangerous substances, and violence such as chemical and bioterrorist attack. Furthermore, the spread of information on the Internet empowered individual terrorists like the Unabomber to exact their own revenge on global society.

Globalization was a phenomenon of the twentieth century, although it was often hidden from view. Its effects on diplomacy were enormous. In the age of instantaneous communication, rapid transport, and volatile markets, it was apparent that complexities of international relationships had moved far beyond the expertise of professional diplomats and foreign ministries. Diplomats and governments no longer served as gatekeepers. In the networked world, individuals, nongovernmental organizations, and officials communicated rapidly and regularly. But while technological innovation and information had networked millions of individuals into a system without central control, it is worth emphasizing that governments helped fund the networking revolution. The U.S. government had supported basic research in high-speed computers, telecommunications, networking, and aviation, all essential to the interconnected world of globalization. Moreover, Washington's commitment to market opening, deregulation, and liberalization of trade and finance provided the policy impetus that led to a variety of international agreements and arrangements promoting an open world order. Thus have diplomacy and techno-economic globalization been linked since the post–Civil War era.

BIBLIOGRAPHY

Aaronson, Susan Ariel. *Taking Trade to the Streets: The Lost History of Public Efforts to Shape Globalization*. Ann Arbor, Mich., 2001.

Adler, William M. *Mollie's Job: A Story of Life and Work on the Global Assembly Line*. New York, 2000. By one of the growing number of critics from the labor side.

Anderson, Sarah, and John Kavanagh. *Field Guide to the Global Economy*. New York, 1999.

Barber, Benjamin R. *Jihad vs. MacWorld: How Globalism and Tribalism Are Reshaping the World*. New York, 1996. A classic account of the cultural debate over globalization.

Bauman, Zygmunt. *Globalization: The Human Consequences*. New York, 1998. Covers the dark side of globalization.

Beck, Ulrich. *What Is Globalization?* Cambridge, U.K., and Malden, Mass., 2000.

Boli, John, and George M. Thomas. *Constructing World Culture: International Nongovernmental Organizations Since 1875*. Stanford, Calif., 1999. Explains one of the institutional elements of globalization.

Center for Strategic and International Studies. *Reinventing Diplomacy in the Information Age: A Report of the CSIS Advisory Panel on Diplomacy in the Information Age*. Washington, D.C., October 9, 1998. Discusses how globalization has changed diplomacy.

Chandler, Alfred D., Jr., and James W. Cortada, eds. *A Nation Transformed by Information: How Information Has Shaped the United States from Colonial Times to the Present*. New York, 2000.

Dragsback Schmidt, Johannes, and Jacques Hersh, eds. *Globalization and Social Change*. London, New York, 2000.

Eckes, Alfred E., Jr., "Backlash Against Globalization?" *Global Economic Quarterly* 1 (June 2000): 117–122.

Everard, Jerry. *Virtual States: The Internet and the Boundaries of the Nation State*. London and New York, 2000.

Fraser, Jane, and Jeremy Oppenheim. "What's New About Globalization?" *The McKinsey Quarterly* 2 (1997): 168–179. Accessible and informative account of the velocity and scope of late-twentieth-century globalization compared to other eras.

Friedman, Thomas. *The Lexus and the Olive Tree*. New York, 1999. A spritely, optimistic analysis.

Giddens, Anthony. *Runaway World: How Globalization Is Reshaping Our Lives*. New York, 2000.

Gray, John. *False Dawn: The Delusions of Global Capitalism*. New York, 1998. A leading British conservative intellectual criticizes globalization.

Greider, William. *One World, Ready or Not: The Manic Logic of Global Capitalism*. New York, 1997. Anecdotal but in-depth criticism of the business globalization process by a leading progressive.

Held, David, et al. *Global Transformations: Politics, Economics, and Culture*. Cambridge, 1999.

Holton, Robert J. *Globalization and the Nation-State*. London, 1998. For the role of the state and politics.

Jameson, Fredrick, and Masao Miyashi, eds. *The Cultures of Globalization*. Durham, N.C., 1998. Excellent starting point for understanding the cultural aspects.

LaFeber, Walter. *Michael Jordan and the New Global Capitalism*. New York, 1999. A leading diplomatic history revisionist analyzes globalization through the career of a famous sports star.

Lechner, Frank J., and John Boli, eds. *The Globalization Reader*. Malden, Mass., 2000. Extensive coverage of all aspects of the phenomenon.

Levitt, Theodore. "The Globalization of Markets." *Harvard Business Review* 61 (May–June 1983): 1–11. The article in which the term "globalization" was coined.

Luttwak, Edward. *Turbo-Capitalism: Winners and Losers in the Global Economy*. New York, 1999.

Micklethwait, John, and Adrian Wooldridge. *A Future Perfect: The Challenge and the Hidden Promise of Globalization*. New York, 2000.

Mittelman, James H. *The Globalization Syndrome: Transformation and Resistance*. Princeton, N.J., 2000.

Oloka-Onyango, J., and Deepika Udagama. *The Realization of Economic, Social, and Cultural Rights: Globalization and Its Impact on the Full Enjoyment of Human Rights*. New York, 2000. A useful United Nations–based summary, including globalization's noneconomic impact.

O'Rourke, Kevin H., and Jeffrey G. Williamson. *Globalization and History: The Evolution of a Nineteenth-Century Atlantic Economy*. Cambridge, Mass., 1999. One of a handful of historical treatments.

Prakash, Aseem, and Jeffrey A. Hart, ed. *Responding to Globalization*. London, New York, 2000.

Rodrik, Dani. *Has Globalization Gone Too Far?* Washington, D.C., 1997. Articulate and thought-provoking early warning about the negative effects of globalization.

Rupert, Mark. *Ideologies of Globalization: Contending Visions of a New World Order*. London and New York, 2000.

Sassen, Saskia. *Globalization and Its Discontents: Essays on the New Mobility of People and Money*. New York, 1998.

Soros, George. *The Open Society: Reforming of Global Capitalism*. New York, 2000. Warnings of impending collapse from a giant of global finance capital.

Tomlinson, John. *Globalization and Culture*. Chicago, 1999. Highly theoretical treatment of the complex interaction of culture in international society.

Wallach, Lori, and Michell Sforza. *The WTO: Five Years of Reasons to Resist Corporate Globalization*. New York, 2000. Criticism of the globalization phenomenon from Wallach, one of the protest organizers.

Went, Robert. *Globalization: Neoliberal Challenge, Radical Responses*. London, 2000. Concise but balanced assessment.

Zachary, G. Pascal. *The Global Me: New Cosmopolitans and the Competitive Edge—Picking Globalism's Winners and Losers*. New York, 2000.

Zeiler, Thomas W., and Alfred E. Eckes, Jr. *Globalization and the American Century: A New Historical Paradigm*. New York, 2002. First history that addresses the synergistic relationship of globalization and U.S. diplomacy since the late nineteenth century.

See also COLD WAR TERMINATION; CULTURAL IMPERIALISM; CULTURAL RELATIONS AND POLICIES; ECONOMIC POLICY AND THEORY; INTERNATIONALISM; POST–COLD WAR POLICY.

HUMANITARIAN INTERVENTION AND RELIEF

Darlene Rivas

The phrase "humanitarian intervention and relief" reflects recent usage. Yet the types of activities that it incorporates have a long history. At times, natural disasters such as floods, hurricanes, or human-compounded disasters such as famine or war, have caused great human suffering and material damage, resulting in efforts to provide relief in the form of basic necessities such as food, clothing, and shelter. Despite the view that Americans have shown exceptional generosity, the practice of caring for the victims of disasters is as old as human communities and is widespread among cultures. The scale of the human response to human suffering has changed, however, largely because of the development of institutionalized structures to provide relief, and Americans have been at the forefront of such development. In the modern era, the idea that states or peoples should respond to victims of calamities in other states has grown dramatically. Especially since World War II, nongovernmental and intergovernmental organizations for humanitarian assistance have multiplied and become institutionalized.

Debates about humanitarian assistance abroad have increasingly focused on whether states have a right and even a duty to alleviate distress, and whether the acceptable means include forcible intervention to end suffering and protect human rights. Intervention implies interfering in a situation in order to change an outcome. It may or may not indicate the use of force in achieving its objectives, although in the recent past that has been a key issue in its definition. Humanitarian relief and intervention implies short-term rather than long-term action. In the period after World War II, however, what began as efforts to prevent imminent harm increasingly took on the character of efforts to promote social and economic development or provide longer-term protection of civilians during intractable civil conflicts. Nation building, efforts to promote economic and social development, and peacekeeping seemed to follow efforts at humanitarian intervention and relief, with the distinction between these efforts becoming increasingly blurred.

Both humanitarianism and self-interest have inspired actions by individual Americans and the U.S. government to provide assistance and relief to people of other nations. The idea that individuals, nations, or governments intervene purely to promote the well-being of other humans is contested. Some believe that the essence of being human is to be humane, to act out of compassion, kindness, and sympathy so as to aid fellow humans in distress or danger. Others, however, believe that people act only out of self-interest. Indeed, some biologists conduct research to understand what they deem as the aberrant behavior of individuals who sacrifice their personal interests for the good of others. Considerations of whether humans behave solely on the basis of survival mechanisms largely ignore moral and ethical studies, religious or otherwise. The most common position avoids extremes, holding that humans often act out of humanitarian impulses, but that these are neither purely altruistic nor purely selfish.

The question of how states or governments respond used to be less murky. National self-interest, including the promotion of the well-being of the state's citizens and its survival, has been the raison d'être for the state. Yet with economic, demographic, and technological change in the twentieth century, some observers suggest that the erosion of borders has created an international community in which old conceptions of national interest are inappropriate. The interrelationships of a global community, and increasingly common values as evidenced by the development of international law in support of human rights, seem to warrant international responses to human distress wherever it may be found.

EARLY HISTORY OF AMERICAN FOREIGN RELIEF

The United States and the other nations born of the Enlightenment laid claim to the notion that nations could be based on ideals as well as interests. Religious beliefs also contributed to American conceptions of their role in the world. In addition to developing a vision of a city on a hill, a model community as exemplar to the world, the Puritans and other Christian groups emphasized the importance of doing good, which was interpreted in light of the biblical injunction to love thy neighbor. In the nineteenth century, millennial hopes of hastening the Kingdom of God also inspired some Americans to work for an ideal society that elevated or protected human rights. To many Americans the expansion of liberty through the spread of American-style institutions promised to free humanity everywhere from political oppression, and in the twentieth century, to free them from poverty.

A commitment to public good in the colonial and early national eras resulted in providing relief for the poor or those injured by disasters, which was usually conducted by those closest to the victims, members of one's religious organization, or local communities, but at times by colonial or state governments. There was some stigma attached to poor relief, but victims of fires or floods received greater public sympathy. Emergency relief escaped the stigma associated with poor relief, because victims of disasters were viewed as suffering only temporary misfortune. Such victims escaped questions as to whether they were morally unfit or somehow deserved their fate. Indeed, in times of emergency Americans quickly proved adept at organizing; they created private agencies to alleviate human suffering, since generally that was not seen as the responsibility of the state. Most assistance went to local communities. Early in the Republic's history, however, there were both public and private efforts to help victims of disaster abroad.

In 1812 a Venezuelan earthquake resulted in as many as ten thousand deaths. Concern about the extent of devastation, sympathy with the republican cause in Latin America, and hopes for commercial ties should Venezuela win its independence from Spain resulted in an appropriation of $50,000 from Congress for the purchase of food to avert famine. This type of federal appropriation was rare in early American history. Fires in Canada in 1816 and 1825 spurred private donations in Boston and New York, primarily raised by merchants and churches. Certainly, much human suffering occurred during this period, and when reports from merchants or consuls or other Americans stirred sympathy, Americans sent aid to, for example, survivors of French floods or to victims of famine and disease in the Cape Verde Islands.

Americans often responded to international crises because of cultural and political affinity. The prospects for republican government in Latin America and in Europe sometimes led to calls for intervention, but Congress resisted the impulse to do so. George Washington's pleas to remain neutral and avoid entangling alliances deeply impacted American views of their role in the world, particularly after the War of 1812. In 1821 Greeks rose against Turkey. Some Americans saw themselves as heirs to the freedom represented by ancient Greece. The portrayal of Muslim Turks as barbarous and the Christian Greeks as noble and civilized fed American prejudices. Support for the Greek cause provoked interest by groups as diverse as women's organizations and university students in a spate of fund-raising, and even in talk of government support. In 1824 Congress debated a resolution in support of Greek independence. It failed, however, and the government refused to allocate funds for either the Greek cause or Greek relief. Some Americans volunteered to fight, but they were few in number. Money already raised was used to purchase limited amounts of arms. In 1827 and 1828, however, the most significant support was in the form of relief assistance to the victims of violence. Individuals, churches, and other organizations like the Ladies Greek Committee of New York raised funds, purchased clothes, foodstuffs, and other supplies, and shipped them to Greece. Around $100,000 worth of goods was sent during the spring of 1827 and another $59,000 the next year. Samuel Gridley Howe, a Boston doctor and later an ardent reformer, helped coordinate the delivery of the relief aid. Americans, largely missionaries and diplomats, supervised the distribution of clothes and food, which were designated for civilians. As would future deliverers of relief aid, Howe soon engaged in efforts to provide more lasting assistance. Granted government lands for the purpose, he organized an agricultural colony that eventually included fifty families.

The next instance of large-scale relief led to an ardent debate in Congress over the constitutionality of congressional appropriations for foreign assistance. Senator John J. Crittenden of Kentucky proposed that the United States provide $500,000 for famine relief for Scotland and Ireland in 1847. Some proponents of relief argued that doing nothing was unconscionable, even if providing help violated the constitution. Some suggested pointedly that the United States was willing to coerce Mexico to "sell" land but was unwilling to alleviate human suffering in Ireland. Opponents argued that the measure was unconstitutional, and their argument won. On the other hand, naval vessels helped in delivering assistance raised through voluntary donations. Relief assistance came largely as a result of humanitarian and religious appeals whose effectiveness was increased by anti-English sentiment. The hope that feeding starving Irish would keep them in Ireland and away from American shores motivated some contributions. According to Merle Curti in *American Philanthropy Abroad: A History* (1963), some Americans contributed as a way to relieve personal and national guilt for participation in the Mexican-American War. Americans sent aid, but they did not distribute it. This was left to British government officials, the Catholic Church, and the Central Relief Committee of the Dublin Society of Friends (Quakers).

In the nineteenth century, opposition to relief led on occasion to criticism of the political and economic systems that created the conditions leading to famine, as in the case of Ireland and later Russia. Relief assistance, however, did not come with expectations or requirements for change. Except for isolated instances of technical missions, and more often in the case of missionary efforts, there was little attempt to reorder other societies in the nineteenth century.

Instances of relief efforts grew along with the nation, almost all of it on a voluntary basis. Famine was the most common disaster that brought forth American resources, although concern for victims of war or political violence also stimulated American relief efforts. Missionaries and diplomats often brought word of the need for assistance in places like Crete, Persia, China, and Turkey. Areas like Africa that had been colonized by other nations were hardly ever at the forefront of American concern. While the U.S. government rarely appropriated funds for the relief of disasters in other countries, there were occasional episodes in which American military forces provided limited assistance. For example, if a U.S. naval vessel was nearby, crew members sometimes assisted local populations in disaster, as in St. Thomas, Virgin Islands, in 1825; Nicaragua in 1852; Peru in 1873; and Chios, Greece, in 1881.

THE CIVIL WAR AND THE ORIGINS OF THE AMERICAN RED CROSS

In the latter half of the nineteenth century, international law and various institutions addressed the issue of humanitarian relief to those involved in war. In Europe, a movement emerged to improve treatment of the wounded in the wake of the Crimean and Austro-Italian wars. Swiss philanthropist Henry Dunant inspired the founding of the Red Cross after witnessing the hardships faced by the wounded and medical personnel at the Battle of Solferino. Within the space of two years, support for his idea led to the Geneva Convention of 1864, which elaborated the principle that both the injured and medical personnel should be treated as neutrals during war. Later Geneva conventions and protocols extended these provisions to war at sea, then to prisoners of war, and later to protection of civilians in enemy and occupied territories, with an emphasis on the needs of refugees and displaced persons. But although it had a tradition of neutrality, the United States was slow to join this international movement because of America's tradition of avoiding noncommercial treaties.

When these international developments began, the United States was in the midst of a destructive Civil War. In America's early wars, care of wounded soldiers was provided by family members and limited numbers of military medical personnel. Local communities, religious groups, and women's groups sometimes organized relief efforts to get supplies and medical care to their loved ones.

The Civil War, with wider consequences than previous calamities requiring American assistance, witnessed even greater voluntary mobilization. Women of high social prestige in both Union and Confederacy established organizations like the Women's Central Association of Relief in New York to help provide clothing and other supplies. The growing movement for an expanded role for women in nursing during war as well as desperate need led other women to volunteer for a more direct role in the relief of suffering. This voluntary relief movement had lasting importance, since women tapped into popular conceptions of gender roles, arguing more and more successfully that women brought uniquely feminine compassion to assist the wounded. Professional standards for nursing, a gendered profession, would expand in the late nineteenth and early twentieth centuries. Ladies' Soldiers Aid Societies provided food and other services at camps behind the front lines.

The mobilization of relief during the Civil War set new precedents in organization. In addition to local efforts, the United States Sanitary Commission, a voluntary yet government-approved organization, was established with the aim of coordinating the activities of the local groups. The Sanitary Commission organized the collection and delivery of supplies and appealed for funds, raising $5 million by the end of the war.

The Civil War also provided experience in dealing with refugees. Inspired to action first by the needs of "contrabands"—slaves fleeing the ravages of war who went behind Union lines—sympathetic individuals founded voluntary organizations called freedmen's aid societies to provide food and clothing to contraband camps. Soon, Congress entered into relief and refugee efforts, creating the Bureau of Refugees, Freedmen, and Abandoned Lands, established in March 1865 to provide relief assistance to southerners, black and white. The Freedman's Bureau, as it evolved, also came to provide rehabilitation or reconstruction, making efforts not only to feed and clothe refugees but also to provide freedmen with education and assistance in negotiating job contracts and in leasing or purchasing land. The issue of the constitutional right of the federal government to engage in these kinds of activities led to fierce struggles over the Freedman's Bureau and contributed to its eventual demise. The pattern of dealing with emergency needs to relieve human suffering, followed by attempts to create conditions in which the victims of disaster could build or rebuild institutions and sustainable economic activity, would be repeated in the twentieth century.

Civil War experiences raised hopes for U.S. approval of the Geneva Convention of 1864. Although the United States did not participate officially in the 1864 conference, Charles S. Bowles, a member of the Sanitary Commission, attended the convention as an American observer and reported on the commission's experience. Congress was reluctant to support an international treaty that seemed to undermine the American principle of nonentanglement with other nations. Secretary of State William Seward refused to consider the treaty, arguing that it was political and would violate the principle of U.S. neutrality. Henry W. Bellows, who had headed the Sanitary Commission, Bowles, and other members of the commission created the American Association for the Relief of Misery on the Battlefield in 1866, lobbying futilely for Congress to ratify the Geneva Convention. Seward and, later, Secretary of State Hamilton Fish continued to reject U.S. participation in the treaty.

Another veteran of Civil War relief efforts was ultimately more successful in convincing American statesmen to support the Geneva Convention. In 1870 Clara Barton, who had gained pubic attention during the Civil War for her relief activities, met members of the International Committee of the Red Cross in Geneva. Inspired, she worked with the national organizations of the Red Cross during the Franco-Prussian War and later during the Russo-Turkish War of 1877. She tirelessly argued for a Red Cross in the United States, and wrote a pamphlet, *The Red Cross of the Geneva Convention: What It Is* (1878). In it she emphasized not only the potential for Red Cross activities in war, but the role it could play in peacetime in the United States to provide relief in the wake of disasters and emergencies. Recent devastating fires in Chicago and Boston as well as floods, industrial accidents, outbreaks of disease, and other emergencies required organized action and Americans in growing numbers supported the Red Cross largely because of its potential to help at home. Barton also petitioned Presidents Rutherford B. Hayes, James A. Garfield, and Chester A. Arthur to promote the ratification of the Geneva treaty. Barton's success came all at once. She finally succeeded in establishing an American Red Cross (ARC) in 1881 and in 1882, with the support of Secretary of State James G. Blaine, the United States Congress ratified the Geneva treaty.

In its early years the ARC was mostly involved in disaster relief at home rather than relief to victims of war, but its future role in world affairs would be extensive. Although a latecomer to the League of the Red Cross, the name of the federation to which national organizations belong, the ARC had some impact on the international movement. Henry Dunant had suggested the Red Cross should also assist in disaster relief, and the International Committee of the Red Cross considered such activities as a part of their role. The adoption by the ARC in 1884 of an explicit article calling for relief of suffering in times of peace was known as the American Amendment.

HUMANITARIAN RELIEF AND INTERVENTION IN THE AGE OF IMPERIALISM

United States approval of the Geneva Convention occurred in the context of increasing engagement in international political affairs. Motivated by a search for markets for increasing industrial and agricultural production, a desire to enhance security and expand influence, and a sense of national importance and confidence in its political values and institutions, the United States flexed its power and asserted its role as a force for human improvement. A global economy was increasingly connected through enhanced transportation and communication technology. People, goods, and information flowed rapidly among areas of the world that were far apart. While the reporting of world events had long influenced public sentiment in favor of relieving human suffering, the expansion of diplomatic, commercial, missionary, and recreational connections spawned wider interest in distant wars and disasters. Competition for circulation and low journalistic standards prompted sensationalized accounts of human distress. Large efforts focused on Russian famine relief in 1892, when Americans offered $1 million in goods and services. A former missionary to India, Louis Klopsch, the editor of the *Christian Herald,* supported the Russian famine effort and relief for victims of the Indian famines of 1897 and 1900. The *Christian Herald,* like other newspapers, published lurid accounts of the effects of starvation and guilt-inducing appeals for relief funds.

Although in the 1890s the ARC primarily engaged in domestic disaster relief, it cooperated with three major relief efforts abroad. The first was in response to the famine in Russia in 1892. The second was a relief mission in 1895–1897 to Armenians in Turkey. Again, the media played an important role in galvanizing American opinion to intervene. In the first instance, Russian crop failures from drought brought sympathetic outpourings of grain and other food supplies from the Midwest. Various groups participated in the effort, and the American Red Cross coordinated the shipments. An estimated 700,000 people were saved in one month from starvation.

Not long after this effort, news came from American missionaries and diplomatic personnel of the persecution of Armenian Christians in Turkey, allegedly by Kurds with the tacit approval of Ottoman officials. Americans were outraged by the reports. Pleas for assistance came from the American Board of Foreign Missions and the Armenian Relief Committee. After hope for European intervention dimmed, the ARC—led by Clara Barton—undertook a relief mission to Turkey. Barton convinced Turkish officials that the ARC would play a neutral role, assisting all victims of the ethnic and religious conflict. Under the protection of the Turkish government, the ARC team traveled into the zones where conflict had occurred, appalled at the loss of life, hunger, malnutrition, and disease they witnessed. The relief efforts included distribution of food and medicine, but American relief assistance also involved efforts to help restore economic activity through aid in reopening shops to gifts of seeds and tools to reestablish agriculture. These activities ceased after several months because of a lack of funds and reports of further carnage.

However, the attempt to provide humanitarian relief set a precedent for action within a country where the state was implicated in violence against minorities or insurgents. There had been hopes of a more official intervention. But a congressional resolution to intervene and to support the establishment of an independent Armenia never got out of committee, although Congress did pass a joint resolution that called on the president to support European powers in pressuring the Turkish government to end the carnage. Humanitarian relief had widespread support; humanitarian intervention did not.

The United States was about to emerge as an imperial power, complete with subject colonies. Yet this development originated with humanitarian concern for the victims of a repressive government and violence spawned by a Cuban struggle for independence from Spain in the 1890s. As Cuban rebels waged guerrilla war, both insurgents and Spanish officials engaged in acts of cruelty and excessive violence. Governor General Valeriano Weyler y Nicolau initiated the infamous *reconcentrado* policy, in which civilians were moved into concentration camps to isolate the rebels from the civilian population. Spanish atrocities were easy to believe for Americans, many of whom harbored anti-Spanish and anti-Catholic bias. Moreover, the initial refusal of Spanish officials to undertake reforms frustrated first Grover Cleveland's and then William McKinley's administration to seek a diplomatic solution.

The American press, including the competing *New York Journal* of William Randolph Hearst and *New York World* of Joseph Pulitzer, reported sensational accounts of Spanish abuses. Then came the sinking of the USS *Maine* in Havana harbor in 1898, which was widely viewed as a Spanish act. Still, McKinley resisted forcible intervention. He did, however, call upon the public for relief funds, to be forwarded to a Central Cuban Relief Committee that included the ARC, the New York Chamber of Commerce, and the *Christian Herald*. Fund-raising ran into some difficulty because some Americans thought forceful action to end Spanish rule, rather than relief or charity, was necessary. The Red Cross in Havana coordinated the distribution of food, clothing, and medicine. A turning point in American support for intervention came after Senator Redfield Proctor traveled to the Cuban reconcentration camps, accompanied by an entourage that included Barton. Appalled by the miserable conditions in the camps, including inadequate food, sanitation, and health care, Red Cross personnel provided relief supplies and set up health facilities for the internees. Back in Congress, Proctor outlined to his colleagues the appalling conditions facing civilians in the camps. McKinley's efforts at diplomacy increasingly turned on ultimatums, which the Spanish refused to accept. In April 1898 McKinley and Congress opted for war.

Humanitarian reasons motivated many Americans to support war with Spain. The desire to end the needless hunger and deaths of innocents seemed a just cause, even a Christian duty. Furthermore, proponents of American intervention could refer to the Teller Amendment—which proclaimed that the United States had no intention of annexing Cuba—as evidence of U.S. selflessness. Some, though, were caught up in an emotional frenzy of nationalism, seeking national prestige and power through "unselfish" intervention. U.S. intervention in the Cuban war for independence had economic and political reasons as well, namely to end the destruction of American property in Cuba and to bolster the political standing of the Republican Party. At the end of the war, moreover, U.S. imperialists, like their European counterparts, justified annexation of territory by citing a duty to uplift and civilize other peoples for their ultimate good. Violent means to that end, especially in the Philippines, shook Americans who believed the United States acted out of altruism, not selfishness.

With the outbreak of the Spanish-American War, the largest international relief activity in the nation's history to that point began. Much of the relief activity was coordinated by the ARC, which faced its biggest undertaking to that point.

McKinley declared the ARC the sole representative of the International Committee of the Red Cross under the Geneva Convention, and it followed a pattern that would recur in future wars. In wartime, the national Red Cross organization served the state. Competition between the Army Medical Corps and the Red Cross limited the activities of the Red Cross in some ways, and much of its work involved helping the military at home; after the war, however, the ARC also aided the victims, both military and civilian, in Cuba. Around six thousand tons of food and clothing, valued at $500,000, were distributed by the ARC in Cuba, and further assistance was provided in Puerto Rico.

THE PROGRESSIVE ERA

The Spanish-American War set off alarms that the United States was ill-prepared to fight in war. The "splendid little war," as it was called by John Hay, U.S. ambassador to Britain, was actually a lesson in poor management and planning, with soldiers suffering disease exacerbated by inadequate sanitation and poor food. Progressive-era efforts at the rationalization and organization of modern society extended to the military, but they also affected relief efforts of the kind conducted primarily by the ARC. Increasingly, the ARC faced charges of inept management, and foes targeted the personal leadership of its founder. In 1900 the ARC was incorporated by Congress and in 1905 it underwent reorganization and reincorporation. The ARC was subjected to a national audit by the War Department and officials of the government were placed on its Central Committee. In a sense the ARC, recognized under the provisions of the Geneva treaty, was now a quasi-governmental institution. While still funded by private donations, it was now akin to other Red Cross organizations in other nations in its relationship to the state. Still, the organization remained small and had difficulty in raising funds, especially on a consistent basis.

Before World War I natural disasters rather than wars were the focus of the international activity of the ARC and other, more spontaneous (ad hoc), organizations. The most significant assistance went to Asia and Italy, with lesser amounts going in response to crises such as an earthquake in Costa Rica, a fire in Istanbul, a typhoon in Samoa, and a cholera outbreak in Tripoli's Jewish community. Occupations by U.S. armed forces in the Caribbean region led to military relief efforts during disasters, but given the larger consequences of occupation, the assistance did little to endear the United States to local populations. Limited assistance was provided for civilian victims of war in the Balkans and in Mexico. Famines in Japan and China drew sympathy. Missionaries and commercial interests there drew attention to the plight of the starving after crop failures in Japan and flooding in China. While many voluntary organizations participated, Theodore Roosevelt designated the ARC as the official relief agent to deal with the crisis in Japan. Over $245,000 worth of money, food, and supplies was sent to Japan, where the Japanese Red Cross oversaw the receipt and distribution of relief assistance. The large foreign presence in China was the context for an international effort composed of diplomats, businessmen, missionaries, and some Chinese, who created the Central China Famine Relief Committee. In addition to providing foodstuffs, the committee promoted public works and distributed seed. Much of the U.S. aid was funneled through the ARC, which participated in the relief effort.

The deep American economic and missionary involvement in China and concerns about the poverty and vulnerability of the local population led to efforts to move beyond temporary relief measures. American observers noted that repeated flooding along the heavily populated rivers of northern China resulted in frequent famine. Dismayed that relief efforts were required again and again, and confident that American engineering could find a solution to the underlying problems, the ARC initiated flood control schemes, a major departure from its customary practice. The Chinese government paid for American engineers retained by the Red Cross to study the problem and propose a solution. In 1914 they completed a proposal for a flood control project in the Huai River basin, with a cost estimated at $30 million. The ARC agreed with the Chinese government to assist in rallying U.S. bankers to the cause, but the eruption of World War I sidetracked their efforts. The Red Cross had spent over $1 million in China before World War I and would again provide relief. However, despite later Chinese requests that the Red Cross again join in supporting the Huai River project, the ARC determined that it was outside the scope of its activities.

Another departure from early Red Cross practice occurred in Italy. In 1908 southern Italy suffered a destructive earthquake and tidal wave near Messina. The resulting campaign to raise contributions to the Red Cross disaster fund was wildly successful. Americans provided over $1 million. Some relief money went directly to Italian relief agencies, but in contrast to the experience in Japan, charges of abuses of funds and unwise expenditures led to a decision by ARC officials to direct relief efforts themselves. American missionaries and religious organizations also participated in relief efforts. Once again, the Red Cross experimented in this period with assistance that went beyond the scope of immediate relief of hunger or sickness. Because so many Italians were left homeless, Congress appropriated funds for the construction of housing for the displaced. The ARC combined its resources with this federal funding and, along with U.S. naval personnel and Italians, participated in an early experiment in prefabricated home construction using partially constructed cottages shipped from the United States.

Before World War I the ARC primarily involved itself in disaster relief, but there were exceptions. The Mexican Revolution spawned intense human suffering and widespread displacement. In response, churches, the ARC, and spontaneously organized local groups provided sporadic relief. Much of the relief efforts were concentrated along the U.S.–Mexican border and conducted by local organizations, including local chapters of the Red Cross. The ARC expended only $125,000, a minuscule sum given the extent of the humanitarian crisis. A special appeal by President Woodrow Wilson brought in only $69,000. Civil breakdown in Mexico, along with physical destruction of transportation, fears of anti-American sentiment, and uncertainty of political protection from competing political factions led the Red Cross to undertake just a few projects. The lack of empathy generated by the Mexican Revolution, compared to the response to the Italian earthquake, may be explained in part by the contrast in American attitudes toward victims of natural disaster and victims of political and social violence. Frustration over economic losses from the revolution, indifference or outright hostility resulting from racism, fears of political radicalism, uncertainty about how the seemingly intractable conflict would be resolved, and reflexive disdain for Mexican disorder may have hardened Americans to the plight of the suffering.

The Mexican Revolution posed a special dilemma for humanitarian relief efforts because the United States occasionally intervened in the conflict. The ARC was presumably neutral, but matters were confused by its recognition by the government and the fact that at this time the president of the United States was also the president of the ARC. In this era legal problems arose because the Mexican revolution was a civil conflict. The judge advocate general of the army ruled that the Geneva provisions for Red Cross neutrality during war did not apply, because the belligerents in this conflict had no legal status. Practically, the American Red Cross could operate only insofar as warring factions agreed to give it protection.

WORLD WAR I

World War I transformed humanitarian relief. The magnitude of the conflict, the extent of civilian suffering, particularly in occupied areas, and the destruction and consequences after the end of hostilities accelerated the rationalization of humanitarian relief. Organizations, both temporary and permanent, embraced the challenge of alleviating human suffering, creating new precedents for international cooperation. Among the new organizations was one that would have a long legacy in foreign assistance, the American Friends Service Committee (AFSC), an association of Quakers. Spontaneous organizations such as the American Committee for Armenian and Syrian Relief, the American Jewish Relief Committee, Christian Science Relief, and the Smith College Relief Unit sprang up. Established organizations like the Rockefeller Foundation, which set up a War Relief Commission, and the YMCA and the Salvation Army participated. In all, 130 U.S. agencies involved themselves in war relief. The ARC, the oldest and most organized relief group in 1914, had less than 150 chapters and twenty thousand members. The agency had a new national headquarters in Washington, D.C., signifying its arrival as part of the American establishment. When World War I began in Europe, the ARC offered war relief only to sick and wounded combatants. It sent medical and hospital supplies, and at first even established hospital units. Soon it was obvious that civilians were in dire straits, particularly in occupied nations like Belgium. Under the leadership of Henry P. Davison, chair of the War Council of the ARC, the organization engaged in intensive fund-raising and publicity. The ARC raised $400 million during the war and immediate postwar for relief. Membership grew from 250,000 in early 1917 to 21 million at the start of 1919.

An individual whose reputation took on heroic proportions emerged as the most important figure in the history of American humanitarian assistance and relief, with the singular exception of Barton. Herbert C. Hoover, Quaker, Stanford-trained engineer, and millionaire had spent his early career in international mining endeavors, primarily in Australia and China. His first experience at providing relief came in Tientsin, when he and his wife, Lou, helped distribute food and supplies to anti-Boxer Chinese. Appalled by the devastating effects of German occupation, American diplomats called for relief for Belgium. They asked Hoover, who was in Europe, to head what became the American Commission for Relief in Belgium (CRB) and was later transformed into an international undertaking. The primary goals of the CRB were to provide food to prevent starvation and, by its neutral presence, to offer protection to the population. It was the start of almost a decade of American relief efforts in Europe.

Efforts to provide relief required close cooperation with the belligerents. The image of starving Belgians swayed British officials to reject the seemingly callous position of those like Winston Churchill, who believed that feeding Belgians helped Germany and impeded Britain's war goals. Conflicts with the belligerents emerged, yet Hoover cajoled and manipulated German and British officials throughout the war to keep the relief program going.

Hoover attempted to distribute relief assistance in ways that kept the Belgian economy functioning. Although some food was handed out freely, Hoover purchased wheat (mostly from the United States) and sold it at fixed prices to millers, who then sold flour at fixed prices to bakers, and so on to consumers. Belgian town leaders also helped distribute food in an equitable manner. While Hoover favored voluntary efforts, he sought public funds since the CRB required more resources than the organization could raise through private donations. Voluntary contributions totaled $52 million to the CRB. But the organization spent about $1 billion between November 1914 and August 1919. Much of it was Belgian money in banks outside of Belgium, British and French government funds, and U.S. government loans, which came after 1917.

The CRB also coordinated relief in northern France after 1915, and made some effort to provide relief in other parts of Europe. Suffering in Poland and Serbia in particular gained American attention. The CRB cooperated in a limited way with the Rockefeller Foundation to extend relief to Poland, but Britain opposed Polish relief. Talk of starving Poles bolstered public support for the war. Despite U.S. diplomatic pressure on Britain to permit food for Poland and on Germany to stop requisitioning Polish food, both countries remained intransigent and little was accomplished, except for some food shipments for children. These relief attempts, however, spurred later support for Polish independence, in part by promoting the organization of Polish American lobbies, which along with Polish constituents in other countries rallied to press for Polish interests. Also, while President Wilson was already moving toward support for Polish independence, the failure of relief to Poland helped stimulate sympathy and thus domestic political support for an independent Poland. Efforts to provide relief to Serbia won more support from Britain than the United States. Hoover thought Serbian relief too complicated and he resented British efforts to tie Polish relief to relief in the Balkans.

When the United States entered the war, Belgian relief was turned over to the Comité Hispanico-Hollandais, with figureheads at the helm in the persons of the king of Spain and the queen of Holland. Hoover still ran the show, but now he did so from Washington. The CBR ended its activities in 1919. According to auditors, its overhead costs came to only about one-half of one percent. Some 2.5 million tons of food at a value of $300 million fed nine million people in France and Belgium. As David Burner concludes in his biography *Herbert Hoover: A Public Life* (1979), these projects "constituted a superb accomplishment, technically, morally, and practically."

ARMISTICE AND REHABILITATION

When America entered the war, Hoover headed to Washington, D.C., as U.S. food administrator; he was a volunteer receiving no salary. His goal was to rationalize the production and distribution of food for the war effort. When the war ended in November 1918, Hoover transformed the Food Administration into the American Relief Administration (ARA) to help Europe recover from the devastating aftermath of the war. On 24 February 1919 Congress appropriated $100 million for the ARA. Undamaged by war, the United States provided the bulk of relief assistance, including food, medical supplies, other goods, and credits to Europe after World War I. Concerned for efficiency and for U.S. public relations, Hoover insisted that Americans, rather than the Allies, supervise the relief efforts.

Hoover and other Americans were motivated by humanitarianism and other factors. Food surpluses in pork, wheat, and other commodities, fostered by the Food Administration's efforts to stimulate production to support the war effort, now served to feed Europe. Hoover was criticized for being motivated more by concern for the American economy than by genuine humanitarian feeling. Hoover claimed food was not political, but it occasionally was. He ensured the flow of food to nurture new countries in eastern Europe, but to discourage Bolshevism in Hungary, Hoover temporarily withheld food aid from Bela Kun, leader of the communist revolution there. Certainly, Hoover believed that food and other supplies would help provide greater order and stability. Food promoted peacemaking in that sense, and if at the same time it reduced the appeal of Bolshevism, all the better. On the other hand, Hoover opposed an Allied invasion of Soviet Russia.

After the armistice the Allies held back humanitarian relief to the defeated powers until Germany signed the peace terms. When they did, Hoover tried to get food to Germany partly to use up the American surplus but largely out of his desire to feed hungry people. The AFSC helped coordinate relief assistance to Germany. In some ways it served as a buffer between the ARA, which had helped Belgium and was seen as anti-German, and the German American community. It was expected that the German Americans would offer substantial support for German relief, especially since they had contributed proportionately less after the war than Hungarian, Polish, and South Slavic Americans.

Hoover assisted the German relief effort by providing $5 million in ARA funds. The ARC became deeply involved in providing civilian relief once the war ended. The Inter-Allied Relief Commission recommended that the ARC focus on civilian relief in eastern Europe. Surplus army food, equipment, and supplies were handed over to the Red Cross following congressional approval. It was not until 1923 that the American Red Cross brought the last of its foreign civilian relief workers home. Once again, while relief was intended to respond to an emergency, occasional attempts were made to have a lasting impact on the societies where relief was provided. For example, in central and eastern Europe the Red Cross helped communities develop health centers that were designed to promote child welfare.

In late 1919 the publicly funded ARA endowed private organizations for specific tasks, essentially privatizing the relief effort. One such organization was the Children's Relief Bureau, later renamed the American Relief Administration Children's Fund. Although it continued to provide important feeding and health services to Europe's children, it also was the vehicle by which the ARA became a private relief agency under Hoover's leadership. Although Hoover had objected to U.S. intervention against the Bolsheviks, he used the ARA to provide support for the anti-Soviet White Russian forces. The ARC also offered relief to the anti-Soviet forces.

In 1921 Hoover, now secretary of commerce, responded to word of a devastating Russian famine in the Volga region. American assistance for famine relief included the work of the ARA, the Volga Relief Society, the Southern Baptist Convention, the American Friends Service Committee, the Laura Spelman Rockefeller Memorial Fund, and others. Despite concern in the United States that the assistance would succor the Bolshevik regime, Hoover was successful in rallying new congressional appropriations for the ARA. Agricultural interests supported such funding because of eagerness for subsidies, but the measure passed largely because of a widespread understanding that regardless of anti-Bolshevik feeling, this famine threatened large-scale suffering. Soviet authorities, at first suspicious, cooperated with Hoover, and American relief assistance prevented the loss of millions of lives.

Domestic American support for the relief effort was high when the war ended, but Americans soon turned inward, disillusioned by the results of war in Europe, consumed by developments at home, and eager to return to their regular peacetime pursuits. Despite pleas by ARC officials that relief work counteracted the threat of Bolshevism, Americans were less willing than during the war to support relief efforts either through volunteer activities or financial contributions. Despite the decline in giving, it still exceeded prewar levels. In 1919 and 1920, $35 million was spent in the United States and $75 million was spent for overseas relief. By the end of 1922, $15 million in additional funds went to foreign relief.

Total U.S. relief efforts in the armistice and rehabilitation period were approximately $1.255 billion. Much of it came from the ARA, the European Relief Council, and other U.S. agencies (including loans and congressional appropriations); about 10 percent came from the Red Cross.

In an unprecedented effort, a cooperative fund-raising campaign called United War Work raised $200 million for seven relief organizations. Despite extensive American generosity, loans required repayment and would later spark European resentment against the United States.

While many relief organizations had ceased operations by the early 1920s, some, like the AFSC, became permanent. The American Red Cross grew dramatically. Increasingly, the ARC was operated by paid professionals rather than volunteers. The monthly payroll grew from less than $12,000 per month in 1914 to $1 million in 1919. As support for foreign relief fell, ARC officials determined to expand domestic operations. Increasingly, the ARC engaged in activities designed to promote health and well-being on a permanent basis rather than concentrating on responding to emergencies. While this shift focused largely on the domestic front during the interwar period, it set precedents for an expanded understanding of the role of relief agencies that was later applied abroad.

THE INTERWAR PERIOD

In the 1920s public interest in international affairs declined, partly out of weariness with Europe and disillusionment with international diplomacy. However, Americans still responded to disasters abroad such as famines and earthquakes. A Japanese earthquake in 1923 led to a large outpouring of relief assistance, which the navy helped deliver.

The 1930s saw a renewal of international conflict, and while Americans strongly supported neutrality, they contributed to relief efforts in China and Spain and for persecuted Jews. Economic hardship during the Depression, however, reduced the success of fund-raising. In 1938 the ARC tried to raise $1 million for China relief. It was unsuccessful. The Committee for Impartial Civilian Relief in Spain failed to reach its goal of $300,000. But while Americans sought to stay out of war, the conflicts in China and Spain provoked partiality toward one side or another.

European Jews suffered increasingly from harsh anti-Semitic policies as the decade wore on. Jewish Americans had long participated in relief efforts, and in 1914 the Joint Distribution Committee (JDC), a multinational organization, had been formed to provide relief to Jews persecuted in Europe. Much more than a relief agency, its leaders sought to combat anti-Semitism and promote a Jewish homeland in Palestine. The JDC did not just assist Jews. For example, it assisted in famine relief in Russia without regard to religion. The JDC and other Jewish organizations such as the American Palestine Appeal grew in the 1920s, although they differed over the goal of Zionism, which was the creation of a Jewish homeland in Palestine. The JDC and other groups provided relief assistance in the 1930s for Jews in Europe and migrants to Palestine and elsewhere.

The Japanese war in China led to a great outpouring of sympathy for the plight of the Chinese. Chinese Americans raised relief funds, as did the American Red Cross, churches, missionaries, and business leaders. Seven agencies working together established United China Relief, buoyed by such prominent supporters as *Time* publisher Henry Luce, who had long promoted Chinese cultural affinity with the United States; Pearl Buck; Paul G. Hoffman; David O. Selznick; Thomas Lamont; and John D. Rockefeller III. The honorary chairman was Eleanor Roosevelt. Despite its success, United China Relief was criticized for its high administrative costs. Still, funds sent to China provided basic necessities and supported Chinese Industrial Cooperatives that employed Chinese refugees and produced a variety of goods, including some for the military resistance to Japanese. The immensity of Chinese suffering continued as China fought Japan and faced civil conflict.

The Spanish Civil War represented the type of civil conflict in which even neutral groups like the ARC had been reluctant to operate. To provide relief assistance, specialized organizations such as the Spanish Child Welfare Association and the Committee for Impartial Relief of Spain joined with the ARC and long-established religious relief groups, including the Mennonite Central Relief Committee, the Brethren Board of Christian Education, and the American Friends Service Committee, all from religious peace traditions. The most active group was the American Friends Service Committee, which coordinated relief and fed hundreds of thousands of hungry people, especially children. Shortages of supplies led to the practice of weighing children and keeping records to determine who most desperately needed food. While a desperate compassion motivated this practice, it was also consonant with the growing rationalization of relief efforts. The ideological nature of the conflict led to tension both within the AFSC and between the relief effort and Americans at home who chose sides. The U.S. government, despite neutrality legislation, provided agricultural surpluses through the U.S. Federal Surplus Commodities Corporation, which was given authority by Congress to offer wheat to the Red Cross in 1938.

After the outbreak of war in 1939, organizing and fund-raising activity for relief purposes expanded. The Neutrality Act of 1939 required voluntary agencies engaged in relief to register with the State Department and keep it apprised of their activities. The law did not apply to areas outside of Europe, like China, the Soviet Union, or Finland, but only to belligerent nations. It also exempted the ARC. From 1939 to 1941, when the United States entered the war, almost $50 million was raised for the relief of civilians and refugees by registered voluntary agencies. Congress appropriated $50 million for the ARC, which continued to receive donated funds. The Department of Commerce reported $174.4 million in goods and funds sent abroad, which included relief sent to areas not covered by the neutrality legislation.

WORLD WAR II

During World War II the U.S. government extended its role in relief and rehabilitation assistance. It also asserted control over the many voluntary agencies that were a hallmark of the American experience in humanitarian relief. The neutrality legislation of 1939 required detailed information from organizations involved in activities with states at war. Philanthropic organizations engaging in foreign activities, including relief organizations, had to be licensed by the State Department. The department refused to allow relief assistance for refugees in Axis-occupied countries. This limitation, of course, continued after the United States entered the war. Despite the efforts of Herbert Hoover, who organized the Committee on Food for the Small Democracies to undertake relief along the lines of the CRB in World War I, President Franklin D. Roosevelt refused to allow relief to German-occupied countries on the grounds that this would help Germany.

Public criticism of frivolous and unscrupulous fund-raising and of high overhead by some agencies gave credence to the U.S. effort to oversee the voluntary agencies, but the primary goal of the State Department was to assure that they operated in the service of larger policy goals. During the war the government sought to keep the relief agencies' operations efficient and to avoid overlap with the ARC, with which it preferred to work. In the spring of 1941, Roosevelt named Joseph E. Davies to head the new Committee on War Relief Agencies, later the Relief Control Board (RCB). Through consolidation, the number of licensed voluntary agencies was reduced from 300 at the end of 1941 to 67 by war's end. The agencies were organized into country groups. After the war the Relief Control Board became the Advisory Committee on Voluntary Foreign Aid, which did not require licensing, although it did decide which private groups would get government funds. In addition, during the war a private group known as the Council of Voluntary Agencies worked with the RCB. Although voluntary groups continued to raise funds from the American public, they relied heavily on government resources. From 1939 through 1954 government funding to voluntary groups totaled $54 million for Russia, $38 million for Great Britain, $36 million for Palestine, $35 million for China, and $30 million for Greece.

During World War II the ARC made a sharp distinction between civilian war relief and services for American armed forces. While the ARC provided supervisory and coordinating functions for relief to civilians, it generally did not send personnel to direct civilian war relief during World War II, except for some milk distribution to children in North Africa and limited efforts in Italy. Instead, civilian war relief delivery became the province of the state through the armed forces, the Office of Foreign Relief and Rehabilitation (OFRR), the United Nations High Commissioner for Refugees (UNHCR), and the United Nations Relief and Rehabilitation Administration (UNRRA). The Red Cross spent as much as half of its funds on returning servicemen and women and their dependents. The government's extensive role in relief and rehabilitation contrasted sharply with its practice in World War I.

Another departure from World War I regarded measures for providing relief to prisoners of war, the latest addition to the Geneva Convention role for the Red Cross. The combatants in World War II were, except for the Soviet Union and Japan, signatories to the 1929 Geneva Convention Relative to the Treatment of Prisoners of War. The convention established the principle that national relief societies could work among prisoners of war to assure humane treatment, with the assumption that the International Red Cross would direct such activities. German authorities allowed the Red Cross to send packages according to the rules, but the Japanese government had never ratified the Geneva Convention and did not permit International Red Cross inspection of its prisoner of war camps or give safe conduct to neutral relief ships. During World War II, attempts by relief organizations to provide relief to prisoners of war set enduring precedents. The State Department gave the ARC authority to coordinate all relief supplies to American soldiers held by enemy powers. In addition to government financing and cooperation from the navy and army, the ARC spent over $6 million providing relief to prisoners of war with weekly food packages to American prisoners of war and monthly packages to many Allied prisoners of war. Other supplies, including clothing, toiletries, and medicine, were sent as well. The International Committee of the Red Cross also carried out inspections to make sure camp authorities complied with the terms of the Geneva Convention. Standards were uneven in the various camps and over time, but given the hardships of the war, it was clear that the Geneva Convention and the activities of the Red Cross ensured humane treatment for prisoners of war of nations signatory to the agreement. Unfortunately, since the Soviet Union had not signed the Geneva Convention, its prisoners of war were badly treated by the Germans, and prisoners of Soviet forces also faced harsh conditions and brutal treatment.

Most prisoner of war relief supplies went to prisoners in Europe. Some International Red Cross officials were permitted to inspect Japanese prisoner of war camps in some parts of the Philippines and Japan, but inspectors were not permitted in most camps in Asia. Japanese officials permitted limited delivery of relief supplies, but not on a regular basis, and some relief supplies sat in Vladivostok until the end of the war, when they were finally distributed to liberated prisoners.

German concentration camps were filled with civilians (including political prisoners) and did not come under the purview of the Geneva Convention. Whether detention or extermination camps, internees faced intolerable conditions, and the International Red Cross was not permitted to inspect them. Millions died in such camps, including Jewish victims of the Final Solution, the Nazi campaign to eliminate European Jews.

RECONSTRUCTION

The United States cooperated with other nations to provide relief in World War II, but as in the previous world war, the leadership and resources came largely from the United States. In 1942 President Roosevelt placed the OFRR under the direction of Herbert H. Lehman, and when it merged into the UNRRA he made sure Lehman headed the new multinational agency. Despite Herbert Hoover's protests that the UNRRA would allow too much Allied influence on American relief, Roosevelt saw to it that the UNRRA would largely be directed by the United States. The UNRRA provided relief assistance to refugees and communities devastated by the effects of war.

By 1946 President Harry Truman was worried that some UNRRA funds were going to communists, so he stopped providing U.S. contributions. The United States continued to provide relief and rehabilitation assistance, particularly in occupied Germany and Japan, with the U.S. Army administering much of it until 1947. Concern for reconstruction as well as relief guided U.S. policy. The United States oversaw the creation of the International Bank for Reconstruction and Development at the end of the war; it offered loans so that governments could purchase needed supplies. The Marshall Plan, or the Economic Recovery Program (ERP), initiated in 1947, represented a commitment by the United States government to foster the long-term rehabilitation of Europe and its dependencies through massive foreign aid, including grants and loans. While initiated out of concern for continued suffering and fear of communist inroads among discontented populations in Europe, the ERP signaled an end to emergency relief efforts and the transition to foreign aid for development.

The ARC also stepped up its activities with the war's end, playing a particularly valuable role in dealing with refugees and displaced persons, including prisoners of war and internees of concentration camps. Voluntary agencies, some representing church groups, labor organizations, and colleges and universities, offered relief services as wartime control measures were lifted. The government welcomed such groups, which extended the resource base for operations and demonstrated overwhelming generosity and concern by Americans moved by extensive suffering. Some groups focused on non-European regions such as China, but most American attention and resources went to Europe.

THE COLD WAR

As the Cold War began, an institutional framework to respond to humanitarian emergencies came into existence. The United States played a primary role in the development of the major institutions of the international relief and rehabilitation network—including the United Nations International Children's Emergency Fund (UNICEF), the Food and Agriculture Organization (FAO), and the World Health Organization (WHO)—and contributed significantly to the funding of such organizations. Although the United States could not completely control the directions of these institutions, the State Department carefully oversaw U.S. relations with these intergovernmental organizations, and their growth did not displace unilateral efforts. Voluntary organizations, increasingly institutionalized, frequently served the larger purposes of American foreign policy as well as their own relief goals.

The functions and priorities of U.S. government agencies, intergovernmental organizations, and nongovernmental organizations shifted from emergency relief to economic and social development. Rising aspirations for political and economic independence in European colonies sparked greater U.S. attention to these underdeveloped areas, later known as the Third World. Fear of Soviet communist expansion into those areas generated efforts to promote economic development in order to undercut communist appeal. Increasingly, foreign aid became a permanent practice. The academic community produced development studies that emphasized the need to link political, economic, and social development and which suggested that the United States could assist nations to develop. Organizations involved in foreign assistance proliferated and moved from a focus on emergency relief as a response to disaster to attempts to solve underlying conditions of poverty that often led to crises. During the immediate postwar era, much relief was sent to Europe; afterward it went increasingly to the Third World. While some voluntary agencies resented government efforts to use them in the service of American foreign policy, others reveled in the role. As the government expanded its involvement in foreign relief, federal grants became easy money in comparison to the tremendous effort required to raise private funds.

An organization that reflects many of these trends is the Cooperative for Assistance and Relief Everywhere (CARE). In 1945, twenty-two American organizations collaborated to found what was originally called the Cooperative for American Remittances in Europe. At first a parcel service, the organization shipped "CARE packages" of Army surplus food to friends or relatives of Americans in Europe. Soon, specially prepared packages of purchased items were being sent to strangers in Europe, and then to Asia and the developing world. CARE packages captured the imagination of the American public, and celebrities like Ingrid Bergman helped spread the organization's appeal. CARE eventually stopped sending the famous packages and, like other such organizations, expanded from relief during emergencies into other areas including health care and development advice and assistance. CARE relied heavily on government grants as well as private donations.

During the Cold War, much CARE activity was focused on areas of strategic significance to the United States, such as the Phillippines in 1949, Korea in 1951, and Vietnam in 1966. In the early 1950s, relief assistance was targeted to areas of political concern including Korea (through UN auspices, during the Korean War), Yugoslavia (to encourage its break with the Soviet Union), and India (which was offered food loans, not grants). In 1954 Congress passed the Agricultural Trade Development and Assistance Act (Public Law 480), later known as Food for Peace. Under Title I of this legislation food surpluses, owned by the U.S. government, were sold at reduced rates to foreign nations and could be sold in the open market. This use of the market was intended to deter charges that the United States was dumping its surplus and to alleviate concerns about fostering dependence on relief assistance. Title II provided for U.S. food surplus to be used as grants for humanitarian assistance. Most of this food surplus was distributed through the auspices of the nongovernmental groups, especially CARE and Catholic Relief Services. In practice, both Title I and Title II food aid usually went to allies or friendly governments.

In the early 1960s the Kennedy administration reconsidered food assistance, hoping that the rationalizing of food needs and distribution would combat world hunger and malnutrition. Food assistance remained political, although the new emphasis on economic development meant that food aid went to development programs as well as for emergency assistance. The United Nations, increasingly conscious of the significance of food, created the World Food Programme (WFP) in 1963. Reflecting the new emphasis on development, only 25 percent of WFP funds were targeted for emergency relief. U.S. organizations like CARE continued to work with the American government through the Agency for International Development (AID), which was charged with coordinating both relief and economic development assistance, with the priority on development. The world's reliance on U.S. food to handle world crises led President Lyndon B. Johnson to call for greater multilateral cooperation to handle famines like those faced by India in the mid-1960s. Indeed, world agriculture was changing, with nations like Canada also being well-endowed with agricultural surpluses. However, in the early 1970s a world food crisis emerged as the U.S. agricultural surplus dwindled and bad harvests in the Soviet Union and elsewhere taxed world food supplies. The wealthier food-importing nations purchased at higher prices, leaving the poorer nations unable to afford what remained. Food assistance reflected U.S. strategic priorities. Food shipments to Southeast Asia made up half the commodities under the Agricultural Trade Development and Assistance Act in 1974, leaving less available for the Sahel region in western Africa, wracked by famine caused by an extended drought.

Increasingly, a network of organizations responded quickly to humanitarian crises. Although relief organizations extended their functions to focus on development, most retained their capacity for responding to disasters. Despite the more permanent character of a large number of institutions like CARE, Save the Children, American Near East Refugee Aid, Catholic Relief Services, World Vision, and Lutheran World Relief, ad hoc responses to natural disasters sometimes led to the creation of short-term organizations or committees to handle a crisis, often but not always by coordinating through other, more permanent, relief agencies like the American Red Cross. Such emergencies as flooding in Bangladesh, an earthquake in India, a hurricane in Central America, and famine in Ethiopia led to outpourings of voluntary private assistance as well as government aid. Refugees from civil conflicts, such as the thousands of Southeast Asians who fled Vietnam and Cambodia in the 1970s and 1980s, generated similar outpourings of assistance, with the added complication that relief organizations had to work with suspicious governments. In such cases, while intergovernmental organizations sought to help, the nongovernmental organizations were often able to maneuver more successfully to provide relief. While critics complained of overlapping and duplication of effort, inefficient fund-raising, inadequate or unfair distribution of food, cultural insensitivity and racism, excessive emphasis on institutional self-preservation, impersonal and unfeeling treatment of the suffering, corruption and mismanagement, poor analysis by media and relief organizations, inattention to underlying causes of crises, and a host of other flaws in the network, international relief was largely effective in reducing immediate suffering and resolving emergencies.

The phrase "repeat disasters" came into use as certain areas faced recurring crises. For example, in the early 1970s famine in western Africa resulted in hundreds of thousands of deaths. Some of the same regions faced an even worse crisis in the 1980s. Such events heightened calls for means to prevent or mitigate disasters. In the 1960s and 1970s foreign aid came under increasing criticism, and some of those criticisms were applied to relief assistance. Food aid often undermined self-reliance, injuring indigenous agriculture by reducing incentives to produce and tempting governments to rely on free or inexpensive foreign food to the detriment of their own farmers. Critics pointed out that food relief, not just food aid, could have this effect, citing as an example the response to a 1976 Guatemalan earthquake. An abundant Guatemalan harvest spoiled as people stood in line for free food. Short-term relief of disaster rarely faced such criticisms, but short-term relief efforts continued to face charges that they failed to address underlying political, social, and economic conditions that lead to continued distress. Efforts to reduce the effects of dependence and to foster dignity resulted in renewed emphasis on developing indigenous organizations for relief, particularly in areas subject to recurring crises. International assistance increasingly operated in cooperation with such local organizations, some private, many governmental.

Much of the criticism of foreign aid was linked to the political uses to which it was sometimes put. Clearly, all disasters did not receive the same response. When Nicaragua suffered a devastating earthquake in 1972, President Richard M. Nixon provided aid to the dictatorial pro-U.S. regime. When Hurricane Fifi devastated Honduras in 1974, the regime of General Oswaldo López was out of U.S. favor because he supported labor and land reforms and had nationalized the timber industry. Fifi left 8,000 dead and as many as 300,000 Hondurans homeless, yet U.S. assistance was not forthcoming. López slowed the pace of reform and eventually resigned.

HUMANITARIAN INTERVENTION DURING THE COLD WAR

Humanitarian assistance had long implied the potential of forceful intervention. International responsibility for the protection of human rights and alleviation of human suffering led to the development of international institutions, including the multinational United Nations. The development of international law, from the Geneva conventions to the response to the Holocaust at Nuremberg and the UN Declaration of Universal Rights increasingly reflected the idea that the international community could hold individuals and nations responsible for violations of human rights. Still, what this meant in practice was not clear, and the United Nations was based on respect for national sovereignty. So despite some precedents for humanitarian intervention, the notion that states could intervene in other nations' affairs to protect human rights was not pursued with great vigor until after the Cold War had ended.

Still, Cold War competition led to numerous interventions by the United States and the Soviet Union. Since the Cold War was not only a strategic contest but also an ideological one, each side felt compelled to proclaim the moral basis for their actions, resulting in dubious claims that such interventions as that of the Soviet Union in Hungary in 1956 and Czechoslovakia in 1968, and that of the United States in the Dominican Republic in 1965 and Grenada in 1983, were for humanitarian purposes.

Each side could argue that their political and economic system served humanity's interests, while the other side's represented oppression and the violation of human rights. In such a contest, the definition of "humanitarian intervention" could apply to any superpower attempts to influence a nation to choose sides. By the late 1960s and the 1970s, backlash against this idea spread as some Americans grew frustrated with the nation's foreign policy as a whole, but in particular toward its policy in Southeast Asia. The Vietnam intervention, ostensibly to uphold freedom in the face of communist aggression, alienated Americans as they realized the vast physical, ecological, and human destruction it was causing and as they grew to doubt not necessarily the ability of the United States to defeat the enemy, but its capability to build a nation. By 1979 and 1980, when Vietnam intervened in Cambodia to end the murderous holocaust initiated by Pol Pot and the

Khmer Rouge, Americans supported relief efforts for the tens of thousands of Cambodian refugees. On the other hand, they did not support U.S. intervention. The relief efforts were carried out almost entirely by nongovernmental relief agencies, such as Oxfam, a British relief agency, Catholic Relief Services, and the AFSC.

Although there was a revival of support for intervention in the name of humanitarianism during the presidency of Ronald Reagan from 1981 to 1989, it was highly contested. For example, Congress placed curbs on the ability of the Reagan administration to assist the contras in Nicaragua against the leftist Sandinistas, despite administration claims that the Sandinistas were violating the human rights of Miskito Indians. In fact, during the 1980s Reagan faced constant criticism from voluntary humanitarian organizations regarding the administration's policy toward El Salvador. They charged his administration with failing to intervene on behalf of victims of that nation's civil war, choosing instead to support the government despite its failure to curb abuses by the military and right-wing death squads.

THE POST–COLD WAR ERA

The end of the Cold War brought tremendous changes. Triumphalists hailed the victory of democracy over communism, claiming it heralded a new age of freedom. New ideas circulated regarding approaches to humanitarian relief and intervention, many of them reflecting a new optimism, even hubris, about the ability of humans, in the form of the international community, to reduce human conflict and suffering. Perhaps the approaching millennium influenced such trends. In 1989 the United Nations General Assembly declared the 1990s the International Decade for Natural Disaster Reduction. The goal of reducing vulnerability to destruction was not new, witness Red Cross flood control planning in China in the early twentieth century. Meteorological advances after World War II led to progress in predicting some natural disasters. Satellite imaging later increased information on creeping desertification, the process by which land grew increasingly arid and unsupportive of vegetation.

There was also awareness of the human role in magnifying the effects of natural disaster, both because of political crises and human pressures on the environment. Environmental degradation in the form of deforestation and desertification were the result of human decisions. Poor urban populations settled on tree-denuded hillsides, for example, vulnerable to the impact of flooding and mudslides from hurricanes. Growing confidence in the ability to reduce the impact of disasters emerged from a sense that there was a confluence of helpful technology with greater understanding of the human sources of disaster. In *Anatomy of Disaster Relief: The International Network in Action* (1987), Randolph Kent wrote, "In the final analysis disasters are about vulnerability, and vulnerability—whatever the disaster agent—is created by mankind." Absent was a sense of fatalism or talk of "acts of God." If humans created problems, humans could solve them. In 2001, the USAID/OFDA (Office of Foreign Disaster Assistance) website declared cheerily "Where There's A Will, There's A Way." "Prevention, reduction, preparedness" were the focus of USAID/OFDA, resulting in such programs as the Central American Mitigation Initiative (CAMI). After Hurricane Mitch hit Central America in 1998, President William Jefferson Clinton promised $11 million to establish CAMI to assess vulnerability and suggest plans to reduce it.

As the disaster relief network sought ways to prevent future disaster by relying on science, engineering, and organization, there were also increasing calls for building democracy. Humanitarianism was no longer narrowly defined as a compassionate response to human suffering but included the responsibility to protect human rights. Human rights were defined to include universal rights to basic material goods like food, clothing, and shelter and to political freedom as well. If these rights were denied, the human community had an obligation to intervene to preserve and protect them, whether this violated the sovereignty of nations or not. Whether or not the United States should undertake such interventions alone or multilaterally was another question hotly debated, but the idea of a responsibility to police other nations grew as the twenty-first century began.

Proponents of humanitarian intervention sometimes sought to support and enhance the leadership role of the United States. They might prefer that the United States intervene multilaterally, but believed it should lead its allies and international community. To others, the end of the Cold War paved the way for intergovernmental institutions to grow in effectiveness, unhampered by competition between superpowers. They believed in the idea of a global community.

In the 1990s the United States, in conjunc-

HUMANITARIANISM AND SENSATIONALISM

In the 1990s scholars and pundits spoke of the "media effect" or the "CNN effect" because of their sense that the American public responded to foreign crises based on visual images. Concerned with the consequences of the immediacy of information, critics worried that the U.S. government, under public pressure, would make decisions based on emotional responses and inadequate analysis. Thus, television images of precision bombing in Iraq led to American confidence in the humaneness of contemporary war, while images of emaciated, starving Somali children and the brutal indifference of other Somalis resulted in cries for intervention.

Critics of the media complained that journalists often misunderstood the crises about which they reported, relying on relief or aid workers for information, or even intentionally manipulating opinion to foster public pressure on politicians on behalf of the journalists' pet causes. Americans were accustomed to seeing images of starving children on television as relief and development organizations sought to raise funds by evoking compassion. Save the Children pioneered in television and print advertisements of pitiful, blank-eyed children to help raise funds for its efforts. World Vision filmed and aired documentaries of its activities, often showing actress Sally Struthers caring for unclothed and hungry children while appealing for assistance. Critics charged that such images bolster stereotypical perspectives of other peoples, and imply helplessness and victimization rather than resourcefulness and dignity.

Sensationalized accounts of human suffering, however, have long been used to enhance giving. In the early days of the American republic, broadsides, newspapers, and sermons offered dramatic descriptions to promote fund-raising. In 1832 initial reports of hunger in the Cape Verde Islands stirred little sympathy until dramatic accounts of misery (including a comparison to Dante's Hell) spurred citizens from Portland to Philadelphia to Richmond to raise generous funds. In the 1890s sensationalist press accounts stirred support for intervention in the Cuban struggle for independence against Spain. Less well-known are similar stories of starving Russians, with reports of desperate peasants eating hair, leather, grass, leaves, and even each other. This type of reporting was powerful. Indeed, Clara Barton found it helpful to assure skeptical Turkish authorities that she did not have any journalists with her. The power of words and images to evoke compassion has long been problematic.

tion with the United Nations or the Organization of American States (OAS), engaged in humanitarian interventions in Iraq, Somalia, Haiti, and the former Yugoslavia. The United States and the UN did not intervene to stop all human rights disasters—the most notable examples, including Sudan and Rwanda, being in Africa. (The French conducted a limited intervention in Rwanda, and the international relief network provided humanitarian relief.) Noninterventionists complained that humanitarian explanations for intervention masked ulterior motives or that U.S. policies had served to create the very crises they were now addressing. From a very different perspective, others suggested that the U.S. national interest was not at stake and deplored the possibility that the lives of Americans and innocents might be lost while "doing good." Some opponents argued that the United States should set its own house in order, spending its resources and energies at home on behalf of American workers or to combat American poverty. Some feared a tremendous drain on American resources in areas of intractable conflict.

In 1991 the United States intervened with allies in Operation Desert Storm to force Iraqi dictator Saddam Hussein out of Kuwait. While the Bush administration portrayed the intervention in humanitarian terms, important strategic interests were at stake. The claim of humanitarianism was weakened because although President George Bush had urged the Iraqi Kurd and Shi'ite minorities to rise up against Saddam, the United States stood by while the dictator repressed them. However, the Bush administration initiated a relief effort, Operation Provide Comfort. Along with the United Nations, the United States set up refugee communities along the northern border of Iraq in a predominantly Kurdish region. A security zone was established and a no-fly zone instituted for protection. Because the Kurds could be isolated geographically, it was easier to intervene at a low cost in lives (although not in military resources) than in the later Bosnia and Kosovo crises.

Despite its strategic purposes, the Persian Gulf War had the flavor of a humanitarian intervention because although Hussein continued to defy Western attempts to weaken his regime, his military power and potential to wage destructive war was limited as UN inspectors discovered and oversaw the destruction of chemical, biological, and nuclear weapons capabilities. On the other hand, a new humanitarian crisis emerged as the Iraqi people suffered from an embargo to force Hussein's compliance. The embargo reduced stocks of food and medicine as well as stifling the flow of oil. Measures to increase the flow of basic items were restored after harsh criticism of this policy.

The United States had occupied Haiti in the early twentieth century. Resulting mostly from strategic and economic concerns, the early occupation was also a result of an American sense that the United States could make Haiti reform its political institutions to provide greater democracy. Reforms also included efforts to improve the health and well-being of Haitians. Near the end of the twentieth century, the United States intervened again. A political crisis in Haiti resulted when in 1991 a military faction toppled the elected regime of President Jean-Bertrand Aristide. For three years a military regime ruled Haiti, with as many as five thousand dying in the political violence that ensued. Meanwhile, Haitians left the country in boats, creating a refugee crisis. The OAS and the UN's efforts at mediation failed. The UN, attempting to monitor human rights in Haiti, was expelled in mid-1994. Pressure mounted for a military intervention to restore Aristide to power. President Clinton favored a multilateral response, and along with the United Nations prepared a multinational force (MNF) to enter Haiti. With the MNF on the way and in the midst of talks with former President Jimmy Carter, the military government of General Raoul Cedras agreed to permit the MNF to land and oversee a peaceful governmental transition. Troops numbering twenty-one thousand landed in Haiti. Initially hailed as a successful humanitarian intervention, disillusion grew as the Haitian political situation deteriorated. Troops remained in Haiti, although their mission was redefined to peacekeeping in 1995 and then peace building in 2000, after the last of the U.S. troops departed.

In the early 1990s scenes from Somalia, located on the horn of Africa and wracked by civil war, stirred Americans. In addition to images of skeletal, desperate people, they also witnessed the abuse of the weak at the hands of the strong as the private armies of competing warlords stole food sent through humanitarian auspices. Guilt may also have moved Americans. During the Cold War the United States had been a patron of dictator Siad Barre after he left the Soviet orbit in 1977. U.S. economic and military assistance had distorted the Somalian economy. With the end of the Cold War, aid to Somalia dried up and Barre lost out in an emerging civil war. American and international humanitarian organizations sought to provide relief to civilians caught up in this turmoil, but they found themselves in danger and the relief supplies at the mercy of competing warlords. UN secretary general Boutros Boutros-Ghali of Egypt complained that Westerners, including the United States, were paying more attention to the Bosnian crisis than the Somalian one.

President George H. W. Bush decided to take action in Somalia. His advisers suggested that the case of Somalia was quite different from Bosnia, where they opposed intervention. While each was in some sense torn by a civil war, it seemed that intervention in Somalia would save hundreds of thousands of lives by halting starvation. In addition, it seemed that while political efforts to promote mediation would be required, the whole process could be done quickly. This was important, because in the post-Vietnam era the United States had developed criteria for intervention that called for an "exit strategy" to avoid open-ended commitment. Another factor that may have stirred Bush was the desire to expand the post–Cold War mission of the American military in response to some domestic pressures to downsize and others to maintain a strong military. Humanitarian intervention might satisfy both sets of critics. Operation Restore Hope was thus initiated in December 1992, when Bush sent in 23,150 U.S. troops. Americans celebrated as Operation Restore Hope met its early goals by organizing and protecting the distribution of relief supplies and fostering mediation between rival clans. Although the United States had intervened militarily with the blessing of the UN secretary general, the United Nations oversaw much of the relief effort.

Unfortunately, the U.S. presence in Somalia soon became an irritant to Somalians. President Clinton reduced U.S. forces, but left a small contingent as part of a larger UN peacekeeping force.

General Mohamed Farah Aidid, with whom the Americans had cooperated to conduct relief operations, began to harass the UN troops. After twenty-four Pakistani troops were killed by Aidid's forces, the U.S. forces sought to capture or kill Aidid. Hostilities between the United States and Somalians grew as U.S. forces were increasingly viewed as an imperial, invading power. After eighteen U.S. Army Rangers were killed and dragged through the streets of Mogadishu, Clinton made plans to bring all U.S. forces home, leaving the United Nations with the responsibility to oversee peacekeeping in Somalia. In retrospect, observers agreed more on intervention in Somalia than in Haiti. The general consensus was that the widespread starvation had been averted by the time of the killing of U.S. forces, and that the intervention failed when the political goal turned toward capturing Aidid. Earlier recognition of the consequences of growing anti-Americanism might have led to a complete withdrawal of U.S. troops. What troubled critics of humanitarian intervention was what they saw as the unrealistic goal of nation building. Competing perspectives over whether it was more moral to respond only to an immediate emergency or also to address the underlying conditions that led to the emergency seemed irreconcilable.

In 1991 and 1992 Yugoslavia dissolved into civil war. The demise of the Communist Party's monopoly on power in 1989 had paved the way for the rise of nationalist political leaders who sought greater autonomy or even independence for their regions. Croatia and Slovenia declared independence in 1991. In turn, Serbia and Montenegro under the leadership of Serbian president Slobodan Milosevic created a new Federal Republic of Yugoslavia and initiated policies to intimidate non-Serbian ethnic groups in Croatia and Bosnia. With assistance from Milosevic, the Serb minority in Croatia fought the Croat ethnic majority, and the Serb minority in Bosnia battled the Croat and Muslim majority. Croatia won its independence. In Bosnia, the civil war dragged on, although it declared independence in April 1992. The international community watched these developments in horror, because one of the characteristics of this civil war, practiced by all sides on at least some level, was what came to be called ethnic cleansing. Villages or entire regions were violently swept clean of Serbs, or Croats, or Muslims by opposition forces who hoped to gain control of an area for their own ethnic group. The shooting of unarmed women and children shocked observers, as did reports of mass rapes of Muslim women by Serbs. Despite comparisons by some to the Nazi holocaust and talk of genocide, however, both Americans and Europeans reacted in uncertain fashion.

The question of intervention to prevent human suffering, to prevent holocaust, was debated in multiple arenas: in Europe, in the United States, in the United Nations. Using force for humanitarian purposes provoked ambivalent responses. Moreover, historical precedents for intervention in civil war were not promising. The specter of Vietnam loomed in the United States, as did the more recent fiasco in Lebanon in 1983. There were political consequences and emotional anguish when American service personnel lost their lives in what many Americans viewed as hopeless endeavors. Therefore, the United States thus at first portrayed the problem as a European one and encouraged European solutions. Europeans had similar concerns, and in addition Germany faced constitutional limits on its ability to use force except in self-defense or in defense of allies. The international community understood the complexity of ethnic animosities in the former Yugoslavia and the intransigence of such conflicts to political solution. Stopping the carnage seemed undeniably important, yet assigning resources to what promised to be an indefinite, long-term commitment seemed unwise. Most of the military options in which the Europeans and United States were willing to engage involved air strikes that, while punitive, seemed unlikely to promote a long-term cessation of ethnic violence. As chairman of the U.S. Joint Chiefs of Staff, Colin Powell, opposing intervention, pointed out that the only effective way to end violence was to send in ground troops, which all sides were reluctant to do.

President Bill Clinton wavered indecisively from indications of possible forceful action to declarations that the United States could not fix Balkan problems. In February 1994 Clinton gave Serbs surrounding Sarajevo an ultimatum to abandon their siege. At the last minute the Serbs complied, although only after several Serbian planes had been shot down by U.S. jets acting under NATO auspices. Attempts to mediate the conflict were finally successful, resulting in the 1995 Dayton Peace Accords. The settlement partitioned Bosnia between Muslim and Croats on the one hand and Serbs on the other. This political solution seemed the only way to prevent continued violence, yet it worried many observers because old animosities continued to simmer. The diplomatic solution, achieved through threat of force, was seen as an example of successful humanitarian intervention. But the violence was not over, and international attention soon turned to Kosovo, a predominantly ethnic Albanian area of Yugoslavia.

In the name of the Serbian minority in Kosovo, Milosevic encouraged the repression of Kosovar Albanians, often through the offices of the Serbian police in Kosovo. In response, the Kosovo Liberation Army retaliated with bombings and attacks on Serbian police and government officials. In 1988 UN resolutions denounced the abuse of civilians by the police, established an embargo against Yugoslavia, and warned that the international community would consider "additional measures to maintain or restore peace and stability in the region."

Representatives of the United States, the European Community, and the Russian Federation comediated peace talks. In mid-March 1999 the talks broke down, and on 20 March, Serbia launched an offensive in Kosovo, burning homes, killing ethnic Albanians, and driving them into the mountains and into neighboring Albania and Macedonia. With U.S. approval, NATO began forceful humanitarian intervention in the form of air strikes on 24 March, which Russia condemned. NATO targeted sites in Belgrade such as the Yugoslav and Serbian interior ministries, Milosevic's Serbian Socialist Party headquarters and his home, and Serbian state television. But air strikes also killed civilians, including sixty-four Kosovars in a convoy and eighty-seven Kosovar Albanians in an air attack on Korisa. In addition, three U.S. airmen were captured by Serbia and several pilots were killed. An international incident occurred when NATO planes hit the Chinese Embassy in Belgrade, killing three. Russia continued to criticize the bombings and suggested to China that the bombing of its embassy was deliberate.

Meanwhile, relief to refugees in Bosnia, Albania, and Macedonia was undertaken primarily by organizations of the United Nations such as UNHCR that oversaw the needs of refugees in Bosnia, Albania, and Macedonia. Some refugees gained temporary or even permanent entry into the United States. As more and more reports of ethnic cleansing seemed verifiable, the UN war crimes tribunal indicted Milosevic and four other Serbians for crimes against humanity.

This was no disaster relief operation. In Kosovo providing relief from suffering meant intervention to stop mass killings. While traditional relief aid was offered by UN agencies, the International Red Cross, and nongovernmental organizations, an additional goal of the operation was the protection of civilians, not only Kosovar Albanians but also Serbs who faced vengeful reprisals. Getting in, restoring "normal" life, and getting out was not a viable option. As in Somalia, it was clear that humanitarian intervention had to be followed by peacekeeping, which in UN practice had come to mean efforts to maintain ceasefires while remaining neutral between warring parties. British, French, and U.S. troops were chosen for the purpose. In 2001, forty thousand NATO troops remained in Kosovo and in Macedonia, where ethnic tensions threatened to create a new humanitarian emergency.

Rwanda gained international attention in the spring and summer of 1994. Presidents Juvenal Habyarimana of Rwanda and Cyprien Ntaryamira of Burundi were killed when their plane was shot down, an incident followed by terrible slaughter in a competition for power fueled by ethnic rivalry between rival Hutus and Tutsis. The Rwanda Patriotic Front moved through the countryside, murdering civilians, mostly Tutsis, as they went. UN forces in the country left, having no mandate to intervene. Some human rights organizations called for international action to stop the massacres, which resulted in over half a million dead. French forces created a safe zone in southern Rwanda, but that was the extent of international intervention. As over 800,000 Rwandan refugees fled to neighboring Zaire, American and other relief organizations swung into high gear, offering typical relief assistance. Cholera swept through refugee camps and shortages of supplies plagued the relief effort. Some criticized the relief community for failing to do more, expressing confusion over the roles and responsibilities of the relief community. Should the relief network do something to stop the genocide, to relieve suffering under dangerous conditions, to use its cumulative voice in the international community to explain the political sources of the violence? The decision by the United States not to intervene disappointed even some critics of intervention, who could agree with interventionists on stopping genocide. Charges of racism and inconsistency in American foreign policy were made.

CONCLUSION

There is no question that forceful humanitarian intervention violates state sovereignty. Debates on international law and philosophy focus on this problem. Do human rights inhere only in states, which reflect particular cultures, or are there universal rights that supersede the laws of states? Statists argue that human rights can only be guaranteed by the state, not by an international community. International law is between states, not individuals. If a state violates a people's rights or restricts their liberty, it is up to the people to make the necessary changes. Liberty, by its very nature, cannot be won by outsiders. Supporters of intervention argue that states which fail to protect citizens' rights forfeit their international rights. They point to the weakness of many oppressed peoples, who have no recourse to advance their own liberty without assistance. Moreover, some proponents of humanitarian intervention argue that not only does the international community have a right to intervene, but a duty to do so. The history of genocide in the twentieth century, from the massacres of Armenians to Jews to Cambodians, has impacted both interventionists and noninterventionists, with even many of the latter supporting intervention in the case of massacre or genocide. The problem is more complex when it is asked what rights so violate international norms that states should intervene. What if a state engages in torture or kills its opponents? Is one such death enough for intervention or thousands or more? If parts of the population are denied basic needs or rights like free speech and the right to organize, should other states intervene? Most interventionists argue for proportionality, the idea that the response of the international community should be proportional to the nature of the violations. This includes calculations of the damage to property and loss of life that will occur when force is applied as well as the extent of the violations.

While there has been much discussion on these points in recent years, the underlying tension between these positions has a long history. Statesmen like George Washington and John Quincy Adams warned of the dangers of intervention and advocated a position akin to the Puritans, that the republic of liberty should stand as a beacon, living by its example rather than seeking to mold other peoples. As the United States emerged as a world power in the late nineteenth and early twentieth centuries, such a limited view became increasingly unpopular—but, ironically, largely because of a similar underlying premise, that the United States should use its power to advance human progress. In the late twentieth century, U.S. policy reflected ambivalence and competing perspectives. Confidence in American values and institutions and the seeming convergence of liberal values in the world seemed reason enough to assert American power to protect human rights. On the other hand, historical experience seemed to suggest that nation building was a complicated task and that well-intentioned intervention could lead to unhappy consequences. Another factor at century's end was that in many ways the United States not only led, but followed, as international nongovernmental human rights organizations and intergovernmental organizations like the United Nations also set agendas. In the 1990s Pope John Paul II and UN Secretary General Boutros Boutros-Ghali both pressed for humanitarian intervention in certain cases as not merely a right, but a duty.

Humanitarian assistance (as opposed to intervention) is designed to relieve suffering and prevent imminent loss of life that results from natural or human-made disasters. Despite growing dissatisfaction with the limited scope of humanitarian relief, its short-term duration, and its inability to promote fundamental structural changes in societies, relief efforts will continue so long as humans respond as humans. The American-led international relief network reflects historic continuities. Despite institutionalization and pressures toward self-preservation and bureaucratization, U.S. nongovernmental institutions for humanitarian relief reflect diverse segments of American society, experience wide success at raising funds, and offer compassionate service to ameliorate human distress in crisis situations.

BIBLIOGRAPHY

Bolling, Landrum R. *Private Foreign Aid: U.S. Philanthropy for Relief and Development.* Boulder, Colo., 1982.

Bremmer, Robert H. *American Philanthropy.* 2d ed. Chicago, 1988.

Burner, David. *Herbert Hoover: A Public Life.* New York, 1979.

Curti, Merle. *American Philanthropy Abroad: A History.* New Brunswick, N.J., 1963. The most comprehensive survey of the history of American international relief efforts.

Curti, Merle, and Kendall Birr. *Prelude to Point Four: American Technical Missions Overseas, 1838–1938.* Madison, Wisc., 1954.

De Waal, Alexander. *Famine Crimes: Politics and the Disaster Relief Industry in Africa.* Bloomington, Ind., 1997.

Dulles, Foster Rhea. *The American Red Cross: A History.* New York, 1950. A detailed survey of the early history of the American Red Cross.

Field, James A. *America and the Mediterranean World, 1776–1882.* Princeton, N.J., 1969.

Garrett, Stephen A. *Doing Good and Doing Well: An Examination of Humanitarian Intervention.* Westport, Conn., 1999. Discusses philosophical and legal arguments for humanitarian intervention.

Gorman, Robert F. *Historical Dictionary of Refugee and Disaster Relief Organizations.* International Organizations Series, no. 7. Metuchen, N.J., 1994.

Hoover, Herbert. *An American Epic.* 4 vols. Chicago, 1959–1964. Hoover's own account of his relief activities.

Kent, Randolph C. *The Anatomy of Disaster Relief: The International Network in Action.* New York, 1987. An analysis of the network of organizations that responds to disasters, including nongovernmental organizations, governments, and intergovernmental organizations. Kent favors the development of an international relief system that is more effectively coordinated.

Kuperman, Alan J. *The Limits of Humanitarian Intervention: Genocide in Rwanda.* Washington, D.C., 2001.

Minear, Larry, and Thomas G. Weiss. *Mercy Under Fire: War and the Global Humanitarian Community.* Boulder, Colo, 1995.

Nash, George H. *The Life of Herbert Hoover.* 2 vols. New York, 1983, 1988.

Nichols, J. Bruce. *The Uneasy Alliance: Religion, Refugee Work, and U.S. Foreign Policy.* New York, 1988.

O'Hanlon, Michael. *Saving Lives With Force: Military Criteria for Humanitarian Intervention.* Washington, D.C., 1997. A 1990s argument for selective use of force in humanitarian intervention with conditions for its application.

Osgood, Robert. *Ideals and Self-Interest in America's Foreign Relations.* Chicago, 1953.

Rosenberg, Emily S. *Spreading the American Dream: American Economic and Cultural Expansion, 1890–1945.* New York, 1982. Humanitarian intervention and relief are not the focus of this book, but it is one of the few examples of diplomatic history monographs that incorporate this aspect of American foreign relations.

Ross, Ishbel. *Angel of the Battlefield: The Life of Clara Barton.* New York, 1956.

Rotberg, Robert I., and Thomas G. Weiss, eds. *From Massacres to Genocide: The Media, Public Policy, and Humanitarian Crises.* Washington, D.C., 1996.

Shawcross, William. *The Quality of Mercy: Cambodia, Holocaust, and Modern Conscience.* New York, 1984. A reflective discussion of the response to disasters, based largely on an eyewitness to the international response to the mass slaughter in Cambodia from 1979 into the early 1980s.

Technical Assistance Information Clearing House. *U.S. Non-Profit Organizations in Development Assistance Abroad.* New York, 1956–. Published in varying years by the American Council of Voluntary Agencies.

Tesón, Fernando R. *Humanitarian Intervention: An Inquiry into Law and Morality.* Dobbs Ferry, N.Y., 1988. A philosophical defense of humanitarian intervention, with a discussion of the evolution of international law.

Wallerstein, Mitchel B. *Food for War—Food for Peace: United States Food Aid in a Global Context.* Cambridge, Mass., 1980.

Weiss, Thomas G., and Larry Minear, eds. *Humanitarianism across Borders: Sustaining Civilians in Times of War.* Boulder, Colo., 1993.

Weissman, Benjamin M. *Herbert Hoover and Famine Relief to Soviet Russia, 1921–1923.* Stanford, Calif., 1974.

Wilson, Joan Hoff. *Herbert Hoover: Forgotten Progressive.* Boston, 1975.

Winters, Paul A, ed. *Interventionism.* San Diego, Calif., 1995. A textbook providing an overview of arguments on interventionism, this book reflects much of the debate on humanitarian intervention in the 1990s.

See also FOREIGN AID; HUMAN RIGHTS; INTERNATIONAL LAW; PHILANTHROPY.

HUMAN RIGHTS

T. Christopher Jespersen

Since its inception as an independent nation, the United States has claimed a special relationship with the issue of human rights. When Thomas Jefferson wrote the Declaration of Independence, he captured—as well as spoke to—the yearnings of the colonists along the eastern seaboard of North America to break free from tyrannical rule across the Atlantic Ocean. Theirs was a collective action, of a people striving to achieve the right to determine their own form of government, but Jefferson's rhetoric struck a balance between those collective aspirations and the rights of individuals. It is worth noting that his most famous words on the subject of individual rights—"We hold these truths to be self-evident, that all men are created equal, that they are endowed by their Creator with certain unalienable Rights, that among these are Life, Liberty, and the Pursuit of Happiness"—are preceded by the collective right of "one people to dissolve the political bands which have connected them with another." Since 1776, Jefferson's sentiments as both an expression of collective as well as individual human rights have continued to draw the attention of peoples around the globe. Although Jefferson was primarily concerned with focusing on the specific grievances and complaints the colonists had against the British king George III, his language gave expression to larger sentiments, coming partly from the Enlightenment philosophy that had recently swept the Western world. As a result, his words seemed transcendent in thought, though they were not necessarily so in their application.

Indeed, there was one major problem with what Jefferson wrote. The nature of his insistence on the collective right of peoples to determine their own form of government, not to mention the right to pursue happiness as individuals, when juxtaposed with his ownership of slaves and his subsequent refusal to disavow the practice by releasing them, draws attention to the danger of assessing the United States' stand on human rights by national rhetoric alone. Or as David D. Newsom expressed it more recently, "United States diplomacy in the human rights field suffers inevitably from the contradictions between promise and fulfillment." Ever since 1776, America's diplomatic policymakers have spoken to the issue of human rights in both the collective and individual manifestations, and no one more eloquently than Thomas Jefferson. But as Newsom warned, the actual implementation of policies designed to address those concerns have not always lived up to their high-sounding intentions.

A major surprise occurred 225 years after Jefferson wrote the Declaration of Independence, when the United States failed to retain its seat on the United Nations Human Rights Commission. Coming in fourth in the voting in May 2001, behind France, Austria, and Sweden, the United States missed out because only three spots were available. Representatives from forty-three countries had pledged to Secretary of State Colin Powell prior to the vote that they would cast their ballots for the United States, more than enough for the United States to keep its place. But when the results were tabulated, it became clear that fourteen of them had not done as promised, leaving the United States off the commission for the first time since its creation in 1947.

At first glance, the removal of the United States, while Sudan, Libya, and China kept their seats because of the geographical division of placings, seemed almost Orwellian. That the land of Thomas Jefferson, Woodrow Wilson, Eleanor Roosevelt, and James Earl Carter, to name only four of the nation's most ardent and eloquent proponents of human rights, was excluded from the panel, while on it sat clear violators of their own people's rights like Sudan, where slavery still exists and where religious persecution and civil war have raged for decades, Libya, where dictator Muammar Qaddafi has ruled for decades through brutality against his own people and whose support of terrorism has been documented on a number of occasions, and China, where the government massacred protestors at Tiananmen Square in 1989 and where the persecution of groups like Falun Gong continued a decade later despite international pressure, appeared to make a mockery of the whole notion of a commission dedicated to monitoring and improving human rights conditions around the world.

In the aftermath of the vote that removed the United States, columnists and political pundits in Washington called the act outrageous, and cartoonists had a field day with images of Libya, Sudan, and China setting the human rights agenda. The consensus seemed to be that the United States had been wronged and that the nation's absence from the commission ridiculed the entire notion of promoting human rights. But the long history of America's relationship with human rights displays a series of domestic and international contradictions between the policies pursued and the rhetoric espoused by administration after administration. Considered in total, these contradictions raise serious questions about the nation's commitment to the very idea of human rights. In short, Newsom is right: the gap between ideal and practice has been substantial, and upon closer scrutiny, the American record on human rights has been far more ambiguous, less consistent, and marked by more blemishes than jingoistic boosters of national honor would like to admit.

INITIAL CONTRADICTIONS

For the first century of its existence the United States, despite the language of the Declaration of Independence, did not advocate policies to effect human rights changes in other countries. Until 1865 the country faced a serious problem: no matter how eloquent Jefferson's pronunciation that all men are created equal, slavery remained a contentious domestic matter, indicating quite clearly that some men were not as equal as others. Slaves were considered property, not individuals, and the Supreme Court endorsed this idea with the Dred Scott decision in 1857. A resolution came only through a bloody, four-year civil war. Notwithstanding a northern victory and aggressive efforts by Radical Republicans in Congress to reform the South in the late 1860s and 1870s, the states of the South moved shortly after those years to impose a system of economic and political control over African Americans through sharecropping and Jim Crow segregation. The pattern of the southern states' actions received national ratification when the Supreme Court yet again provided its imprimatur for racist practices. This time the Court's *Plessy* v. *Ferguson* ruling in 1896 allowed for separate and decidedly unequal (despite pretenses) facilities for blacks and whites.

Meanwhile, Asian immigrants trying to enter the United States on the West Coast received a vastly different reception than the Europeans entering the nation through Ellis Island over three thousand miles to the east. Conditions on San Francisco Bay's Angel Island, where they were held pending review of their status, were deplorable, and more and more Chinese were barred from entering the United States after 1882. Finally, in the West, Indian tribes were forced off their lands to accommodate an onrush of white settlers to the region.

In short, human rights did not constitute a force in American diplomacy prior to 1913. The nation's struggle with slavery, the mistreatment of Asian immigrants, the efforts to relocate, if not eradicate, Indians, and the national proscription on women participating in the political process meant that the nation had far too many serious problems of its own to address. In addition, the nation had not reached the level of international prominence it would later achieve. The entrance of Woodrow Wilson into the White House, coupled with the outbreak of World War I, changed all that.

WOODROW WILSON

When the European nations went to war in August 1914, President Wilson saw the conflict as a sign that the old international system created by the Europeans had failed. Now was the time for new leadership. Wilson sought to create mechanisms for ensuring peace and stability, and one of his concerns was for the peoples of other nations. Wilson wanted to reconfigure the old diplomacy and replace it with an open system, one based on cooperation and communication. An ardent and eloquent advocate for liberalism, Wilson believed that democracy should prevail as the system of political governance around the world. In speaking to this issue time and again, he advocated the collective human rights of peoples to determine their own fates. More specifically, he pledged himself to the rights of eastern European peoples to choose their own form of government as the Austro-Hungarian Empire collapsed at the end of the war.

Wilson's call to liberalism came at a moment in world history when the United States rose from a regional power to a global one. American economic prowess provided the equipment and munitions France and Great Britain needed to fight the Central Powers from 1914 until the American entrance into the war in 1917. When they could no longer pay cash for the goods, the United States provided loans. In short, Woodrow Wilson possessed the economic and military clout to back up his calls for recognizing the collective rights of certain peoples.

The president's international commitment in this area, however, was not matched by any personal dedication to ensure that African Americans be allowed to participate in the domestic political process, nor did his push for self-determination extend to the victims of European colonialism in Africa, India, or East Asia. Like his predecessor from Virginia, Thomas Jefferson, Wilson was both eloquent and passionate on the theoretical rights of peoples, and he had problems reconciling his rhetoric with his practices. In addition to offering a hearty endorsement of D. W. Griffith's virulently racist film *Birth of a Nation* (1915), for example, Wilson pursued a domestic program shortly after coming into office that segregated the federal service, one of the few places where African Americans could enjoy some semblance of equal employment opportunities.

Regionally, Wilson acted with what had become customary American arrogance when he dispatched marines to Haiti in 1915, denying Haitians the right to determine their own political system. Indeed, Wilson intervened with military force more times in Central America and the Caribbean than any other president. He also spurned the inclusion of a racial equality clause at the Versailles Conference in 1919 when the matter was raised by the Japanese delegation. Better for the Japanese to be given territory in China against Chinese wishes than have any language referring to racial equality make its way into the final text.

Despite his actions toward nonwhites inside and outside the United States, Wilson managed to articulate the notion of peoples freely determining their own government, an idea that continues to draw the attention of repressed peoples around the world. Unfortunately, Wilson was thinking solely of those peoples in eastern Europe who had lived under the Austro-Hungarian Empire. In part, he was worried about how to contain the spread of communism coming out of the Soviet Union after the Bolshevik Revolution of 1917, and one way he hoped to achieve that goal was through the creation of a series of small states in the region, a sanitary cordon to thwart the movement of communism westward.

Wilson's rhetorical proclamations notwithstanding, the United States found it difficult to implement diplomatic policies that adhered to his commitments regarding democracy and collective rights. If anything, starting in the 1920s the United States began a consistent policy of supporting right-wing dictatorships around the world. As the historian David F. Schmitz has astutely noted in his study of U.S. support for these types of leaders, "promoting human rights and democracy demands a toleration of instability and change in regions considered crucial to American business or defense, often leaving no clear choice between conscience and self-interest and making strong, stable right-wing dictators attractive to policymakers." Thus, the ability of Italian dictator Benito Mussolini to bring stability and order to his nation during the 1920s meant more to American policymakers than his fascist inclinations. All three Republican presidents during the decade agreed that "order and stability had to be the primary considerations," stated Schmitz.

FRANKLIN D. ROOSEVELT AND THE ATLANTIC CHARTER

When President Franklin D. Roosevelt issued the Atlantic Charter in August 1941 in conjunction with British prime minister Winston Churchill, the two leaders followed in Wilson's footsteps by renouncing any intentions for territorial acquisition and by proclaiming the right of all peoples to determine their own form of government. This did not mean that the British prime minister had suddenly experienced a change of heart and was now prepared to recognize the independence of all His Majesty's colonies. Churchill understood the provisions differently from Roosevelt, and the president did not have a problem with that, although he did ultimately wish to see an end to European colonial holdings. The context to this announcement, of course, was World War II, which had begun in September 1939, and which was not going well from the Allied perspective at the time of the Atlantic Charter. Germany had defeated

France, invaded the Balkans, and was aggressively pushing back Soviet troops along the Eastern front. Great Britain stood alone in the West, since the United States had yet to enter the war. Roosevelt and Churchill wanted to cast the struggle in moral terms, with the one side committed to freedom and collective rights in clear contrast to the despotism of the fascist nations.

Domestically, Roosevelt acquiesced to political pressure by issuing the executive order that allowed Japanese Americans along the West Coast to be rounded up and placed into camps in the interior. In all, 110,000 Japanese Americans were moved and the Supreme Court, which ruled the infringement on their civil rights to be perfectly legal in *Hirabayashi* (1943) and *Korematsu* (1944), once again acquiesced in the denial of individual liberties.

Although he did not take up the interventionist approach in Latin America with the same degree of alacrity as Wilson, neither did President Roosevelt press on the issue of human rights. He ignored the actions of the brutal dictator Rafael Trujillo in the Dominican Republic. He reached agreements with fascist leaders in Spain (General Francisco Franco), Vichy North Africa (Admiral Jean Darlan), and Italy (Pietro Badoglio from 1943) in an effort to win the war. Human rights were not expressly a part of the fight against fascism in Asia and Europe, but they were very much a part of the basic differentiation between the two sides.

Their different ideas about fundamental human rights became glaringly obvious at the end of the war as Allied troops made their way into the concentration camps set up by Germany to oversee the extermination of the entire Jewish population in Europe. Scenes of mass graves, crematoriums, and emaciated survivors testified to the Nazi determination to commit genocide.

THE UN DECLARATION OF HUMAN RIGHTS AND PRESIDENT HARRY TRUMAN

With the defeat of Germany, Italy, and Japan, the United States stood militarily triumphant and economically prosperous in 1945. Whereas the rest of the world's powers had suffered from the fighting, the United States possessed a combination of military, economic, and political power that, when combined with strong moral leadership, meant that its pronouncements on human rights could, if provided with sufficient backing, carry real weight.

In the place of Wilson's failed League of Nations came the United Nations, and prominent amongst its considerations was the issue of human rights. In 1948 the United Nations issued its Declaration of Human Rights, which listed, among others, the right to life, liberty, security of person, nationality, recognition before the law as a person, and freedom of movement, including leaving one's country of residence. People had the right to marry, own property, think freely in conscience and religious beliefs, have an opinion and express it freely, assemble peacefully, and take part in the functioning of government—thirty articles in all. It stated that people shall have the right to a free education, at least at the elementary level; people shall have the right to work; they shall have the right to "rest and leisure," and the right to "a standard of living adequate for the health and well-being" of the individual and family, "including food, clothing, housing and medical care and necessary social services." Playing a crucial role in the adoption of the Declaration of Human Rights was Eleanor Roosevelt.

President Harry S. Truman offered his strong support for the UN's human rights work. At the same time that he spoke out in favor of protecting human rights worldwide, the president experienced political disappointment domestically. He failed in his effort to secure passage of a federal antilynching law. In many parts of the South, white citizens took matters into their own hands when it came to offering justice to African Americans who had either committed crimes or were simply thought to have committed them. Many times a mob hunted down the alleged perpetrator and executed a swift form of punishment, which usually involved hanging without the benefit of the legal proceedings. That this practice still existed in postwar America, and that certain senators refused to allow the passage of federal legislation outlawing it, spoke all too chillingly to the failure of the United States to practice what it espoused in the field of human rights.

Truman pressed ahead just the same. At a ceremony for laying the United Nations building's cornerstone on 24 October 1949, he spoke of the link between individual human rights and security: "The member nations have learned from bitter experience that regard for human rights is indispensable to political, economic, and social progress. They have learned that disregard of human rights is the beginning of tyranny and, too often, the beginning of war." Truman indicated that the success of the UN would be "measured by the extent to which the rights of individual human beings [were] realized," and he also included "economic and social progress" in the equation for determining success in realizing those goals.

The next year at Gonzaga University, Truman brought his message of individual human rights into the domestic sphere, speaking of the need to prevent "discrimination in our country because of religion, color, or national origin," all three of which were basic tenets of the UN Declaration of Human Rights. Truman then indicated that "the same moral principles that underlie our national life govern our relations with all other nations and peoples in the world." Domestically, the president backed up his talk with action. He appointed a presidential Committee on Civil Rights to investigate the domestic situation; asked Congress in February 1948 to pass legislation to address the recommendations made by the committee; barred discrimination in federal employment that July; and moved to end discrimination in the armed forces, though the last of those would not be accomplished until the Korean War.

Much of what Truman did in the area of civil rights was politically motivated, to be sure, but Truman also worried about the ability of the Soviet Union to exploit America's racial problems internationally. His administration decided to support, through a legal brief, the effort to overturn the Supreme Court–sanctioned discrimination against African Americans as set forth in the *Plessy* v. *Ferguson* decision. The president and many of his staff recognized the problems created internationally by the country's hypocritical position: publicly advocating human rights for peoples worldwide, while systematically denying those very same rights at home to some of the nation's citizens because of their skin color.

BROWN V. BOARD OF EDUCATION AND THE EISENHOWER ADMINISTRATION

Unlike Truman, Dwight D. Eisenhower possessed, at most, a tepid commitment to human rights, and his noticeable lack of enthusiasm evidenced itself in a number of telling ways. First, Eisenhower supported the involvement of the Central Intelligence Agency in overthrowing or attempting to overthrow governments in Iran (1953), Guatemala (1954), and Cuba (1960, though it was President Kennedy who ultimately authorized the ill-fated Bay of Pigs mission in April 1961).

Indeed, in the case of Guatemala, the CIA abetted the overthrow of the democratically elected leader, Jacobo Arbenz Guzman, ostensibly because his government was riddled with communists and constituted a threat to regional stability, although questions of land reform and their impact on U.S. business interests clearly played a role.

Eisenhower occasionally echoed Wilson's commitment to see peoples around the world determine their own form of government, but he did so primarily as part of a broader anticommunist effort. Secretary of State John Foster Dulles was particularly strident in his anticommunism, but his rhetorical calls for Eastern European freedom ran into problems in 1956 when Hungarians sought to control their own destiny and withdraw from the Warsaw Pact. The Soviet Union, under the leadership of Nikita Khrushchev, found such actions unacceptable. In November, Soviet troops arrived in Budapest to quash the revolution. Shortly after the brutal outcome to the episode was apparent, President Eisenhower used the occasion of Human Rights Day on 10 December 1956 to express the nation's "deepest sympathy" for "the courageous, liberty-loving people of Hungary." But that was all; nothing more was done.

The real problem for the administration came in the form of the civil rights movement domestically and the growing attention it received outside the United States. The Supreme Court reversed *Plessy* in its historic decision in *Brown* v. *Board of Education of Topeka, Kansas* in May 1954, a ruling followed in 1955 by the Montgomery bus boycott in Alabama, and then by the refusal of Arkansas governor Orville Faubus to allow the integration of Little Rock's Central High School in the fall of 1957. A clearly distressed Eisenhower was compelled to call in the National Guard to enforce the court's decision and to protect from mob violence the African American students who were scheduled to attend the high school.

The embarrassment over strident domestic opposition to integration and to the equal participation by African Americans in the nation's social and political systems hurt the nation's image abroad. At the 1958 World's Fair in Brussels, as Michael L. Krenn has insightfully noted, the Eisenhower administration ran into trouble with the American exhibit. One State Department memo observed that continuing racial discrimination, along the lines of what had happened in Little Rock the previous year, "clearly result[ed] to some extent in the weakening of our moral position as the champion of freedom and democracy." Wanting to assert the nation's moral superiority vis-à-vis the Soviet Union, but having to concede that there were continuing domestic problems over integration, the State Department sent an exhibit to Brussels, "Unfinished Business," that acknowledged some of the problems still faced by African Americans. Although popular with audiences that visited the American pavilion, "Unfinished Business" closed for "renovations," which was a euphemism for deleting the sections that dealt with segregation and thus raised the ire of southern politicians back home. Senator Herman Talmadge, for example, a Democrat from Georgia, declared that segregation "was an issue for the individual states of America and 'cannot by any stretch of the imagination be said to be one of legitimate concern to the citizens of other countries.'" Of course, that has traditionally been the argument of all governments accused of violating their citizens' human rights, whether it be the United States in the 1950s; the apartheid government in South Africa in the 1960s, 1970s, and 1980s; China after Tiananmen Square; or the Taliban government in Afghanistan early in the twenty-first century.

THE KENNEDY, JOHNSON, NIXON, AND FORD PRESIDENCIES

David P. Forsythe has argued that not much with respect to human rights happened during the 1960s, largely because the Kennedy administration was cut short by assassination and the Johnson administration became preoccupied with Vietnam. Yet however brief his time in the White House, President John F. Kennedy recognized the problem created by opposition to civil rights at home for the nation's international standing. Speaking before the United Nations in 1963, nearly fifteen years after the UN Declaration of Human Rights, Kennedy remarked, "The United States of America is opposed to discrimination and persecution on grounds of race and religion anywhere in the world, including our own nation. We are working to right the wrongs." Indeed, Kennedy, who argued that the competition with the Soviet Union was moving from Europe to the countries of the Third World, where mostly darker-skinned peoples lived, understood the need to address prejudice at home in order to appeal effectively to those peoples abroad. For his part, Lyndon B. Johnson ushered through two of the most important pieces of civil rights legislation in American history: the Civil Rights Act of 1964 and the Voting Rights Act of 1965. Johnson brought the power of the federal government to bear so as to ensure that the states could not continue discriminating against African Americans. The United States was finally beginning to act in the domestic sphere in accordance with its proclamations internationally.

Human rights lost ground as a matter of importance in the nation's diplomacy under President Richard M. Nixon and his national security adviser (and, later, secretary of state), Henry Kissinger. The two emphasized geographical, political, and strategic considerations. Human rights, whether individual or collective, were of little concern to them. In his rush to embrace Communist China in a geostrategic partnership against the Soviet Union, for example, Kissinger basically cast aside the collective rights of the Taiwanese, who had been America's ally in the Pacific against communist aggression since 1949. Kissinger's disdain for human rights came through clearly at other times, too. From the administration's support for the military overthrow of the democratically elected socialist Salvador Allende in Chile in 1973 to the secret bombing of Cambodia from 1969 to 1973, the Nixon White House valued anticommunism, the exercise of power, and promoting stability over human rights.

Richard Nixon resigned in August 1974 and his successor, Gerald Ford, did not exhibit any greater concern for human rights. Later, Ford would claim credit for supporting human rights by virtue of his signing the Helsinki Accord, also known as the final text from the Conference on Security and Cooperation in Europe, which was signed by thirty-three nations in Helsinki, Finland, in 1975. At the time, however, the Ford administration thought of the agreement as more of a strategic pact than as one that brought a new human rights emphasis to U.S. diplomacy. It was the western European nations that insisted on the insertion of Breadbasket Three, which asserted that "the participating States will respect human rights and fundamental freedoms, including freedom of thought, conscience, religion or belief, for all without distinction as to race, sex, language or religion." Since the Soviet Union also signed the agreement, this language later became useful in criticizing Soviet practices in Eastern Europe.

CONGRESSIONAL ACTIVISM

A backlash arose from the lies about the Vietnam War told to Congress by Presidents Johnson and

Nixon, and from Nixon's blatant usurpations of power, leading to the rise of what became known as the imperial presidency. In the 1970s representatives and senators took matters into their own hands and asserted themselves more aggressively into the nation's diplomatic processes, including the area of human rights. One of the most prominent in this respect was a Democratic representative from Minnesota, Donald Fraser. Beginning with hearings in 1973 before his subcommittee of International Relations Committee, Fraser repeatedly raised the issue of human rights and made it a matter of legitimate diplomatic discussion. Human rights would no longer be an afterthought.

More than simply discussing the issue, moreover, Congress decided to act. In 1974, it strengthened law relating to trade and human rights when it passed the Trade Assistance Act; section 504 specifically dealt with human rights, indicating that aid should be linked to human rights considerations. In 1978 that language was changed to make mandatory the link between assistance and human rights considerations. Also in 1974, Congress passed the Jackson-Vanik Amendment to the Trade Act. Named after Democratic Senator Henry Jackson from Washington and Democratic Representative Charles Vanik from Ohio, the amendment insisted that for other nations to receive most-favored-nation status for trade purposes, they had to be certified as allowing their citizens the right to emigrate. The amendment targeted the Soviet Union for its refusal to allow Jews to leave for Israel. In 1976 Congress created the position of coordinator of human rights in the Department of State. As a result, the State Department reports on human rights conditions in countries receiving U.S. aid, totaling eighty-two in 1977. Twenty-three years later, and no longer focusing solely on aid recipients, the State Department published reports on 195 countries through its Bureau of Democracy, Human Rights, and Labor. In short, congressional action during the 1970s brought human rights into the nation's diplomatic considerations to an unprecedented degree.

PRESIDENT JAMES EARL CARTER

In this human-rights-friendly environment, Jimmy Carter was elected president in 1976. Carter has justly received much attention for emphasizing human rights as part of his administration's diplomacy; he did not, however, invent the issue. Gaddis Smith has, along with other writers, shown that, in Smith's words, "Carter joined the crusade and made it his own." The principle impetus came from Congress, to the point that even such a strong supporter of human rights as Carter found himself arguing that Congress took human rights considerations too far. Still, Carter was more committed to promoting human rights than any other president into the early twenty-first century, in both words and action. As he wrote in his memoirs, "Our country has been strongest and most effective when morality and a commitment to freedom and democracy have been most clearly emphasized in our foreign policy."

Having grown up in the rural segregated South, Carter linked the issue of civil rights for African Americans with the promotion of human rights abroad and cited President Truman, of all the recent presidents, as "the strongest and most effective advocate of human rights on an international scale." He acknowledged problems with the nation's past conduct, admitting that "much of the time we failed to exhibit as an American characteristic the idealism of Jefferson or Wilson," but he rejected the accepted wisdom that the nation had to choose between realism and morality: "To me, the demonstration of American idealism was a practical and realistic approach to foreign affairs, and moral principles were the best foundation for the exertion of American power and influence." His secretary of state, Cyrus Vance, concurred fully in the need to promote human rights; even National Security Adviser Zbigniew Brzezinski, himself more in tune with the geopolitical and strategic mind-set of Henry Kissinger than were Carter or Vance, conceded in his memoirs that "a major emphasis on human rights as a component of U.S. foreign policy would advance America's global interests by demonstrating to the emerging nations of the Third World the reality of our democratic system, in sharp contrast to the political system and practices of our adversaries."

Carter understood the inconsistency in the nation's past talk about human rights when considered alongside its efforts to deny rights to some of its own citizens. In his memoirs, he acknowledged that "I know perhaps as well as anyone that our own ideals in the area of human rights have not always been attained in the United States, but the American people have an abiding commitment to the full realization of these ideals." The problem for Carter was that despite his efforts to ensure that the nation's commitment to human rights was total and unconditional, he like his predecessors (and successors) had to deal with the international situation as it was, not as he wanted it to be. Thus, while he criticized certain governments, including the Soviet Union and the military regime in Argentina, for violating their people's basic human rights, he laid himself open to charges of inconsistency, if not hypocrisy, by ignoring violations in strategically vital allies like Iran, the Philippines, and South Korea.

Still, Carter made human rights a public commitment for his administration, in contrast to many of his predecessors. Speaking before the United Nations on 17 March 1977, he told the delegates, "The basic thrust of human affairs points toward a more universal demand for fundamental human rights. The United States has a historical birthright to be associated with this process." Secretary of State Vance spoke on 30 April 1977 at the University of Georgia School of Law on the integrity of the person, the fulfillment of basic needs, and classical civil and political liberties that required protection. Vance raised certain questions that needed to be asked when investigating human rights in other nations: What were the specifics of the human rights situation under examination? What were the prospects for effective action to bring about change? What were the historical and other perspectives needed to evaluate the situation reasonably? He also offered a slightly tempered sense of what could be expected: "We must always keep in mind the limits of our power and of our wisdom. A sure formula for defeat of our goals would be a rigid, hubristic attempt to impose our values on others."

President Carter followed on 22 May 1977 with a commencement speech at the University of Notre Dame, where he outlined his administration's premises for the nation's diplomacy. The first item that he mentioned was human rights: "We have reaffirmed America's commitment to human rights as a fundamental tenet of our foreign policy," he stated.

Carter followed these words with deeds. First, on 1 June 1977 he signed the American Convention on Human Rights, an agreement that was reached between the United States and the other nations of the Western Hemisphere seven and one-half years before on 22 November 1969 but not officially endorsed by either Presidents Nixon or Ford. Second, although it was Congress that mandated so many of the changes that led to greater attention being paid to human rights during the 1970s, it was Jimmy Carter who appointed an assistant secretary of state for human rights effective August 1977. His choice for the post was Patricia M. Derian, an aggressive advocate for civil rights albeit lacking diplomatic experience. That, however, did not cause her to back down from confrontations with seasoned diplomats, She repeatedly clashed with more traditionally minded State Department personnel, like Assistant Secretary Richard Holbrooke on East Asian issues or Ambassador Terence Todman on Latin American matters. Derian did not shape every position the administration took, but she gave concrete evidence of a newfound commitment to human rights, however short lived it ultimately turned out to be.

As international events unfolded in 1978 and 1979, Carter began to focus his energies on more traditional considerations in the nation's diplomacy. First came the war between Somalia and Ethiopia in the horn of Africa, which National Security Adviser Brzezinski viewed as a Soviet proxy war for control over yet another vital region. Further difficulties arose with the collapse of traditional right-wing allies in Nicaragua (Anastasio Somoza in 1979) and Iran (Shah Mohammed Reza Pahlavi in 1979). Andrew Young's resignation as ambassador to the United Nations in August 1979 effectively ended Carter's push on human rights in that international organization. And things only got worse. In Iran, students stormed the American embassy in Tehran in November 1979 and took Americans hostage. A month later the Soviet Union invaded Afghanistan. Concern over human rights quickly fell into the background, and nowhere did that become clearer than in South Korea. When President Park Chung Hee was assassinated in October 1979 and succeeded by a military regime led by Chun Doo Hwan in December, and when that government decided to suppress brutally an uprising in the southern city of Kwangju in the spring of 1980, Carter said nothing, despite his earlier criticisms of Park's record on human rights. Administration officials feared that South Korea could become another Iran. In short, even a president as rhetorically committed to promoting human rights as Jimmy Carter found himself overwhelmed by strategic considerations that weighed in on the side of protecting stability.

PRESIDENTS RONALD REAGAN AND GEORGE H. W. BUSH

Congress and President Jimmy Carter made enough of human rights as a central tenet of American diplomacy so that subsequent chief executives could not ignore the issue entirely, regardless of how little attention they really wanted to give the matter. The Reagan administration, for example, took Kissinger's emphasis on geographical, strategic, and political considerations, combined that with its own brand of politically conservative, fervent anticommunism, and added the requisite dose of human rights rhetoric in castigating the Soviet Union, all the while supporting right-wing dictators throughout the world. The spokesperson for the administration on this topic was the ambassador to the United Nations, Jeane Kirkpatrick. In a 1979 article she had criticized the Carter administration for failing to discern the difference between authoritarian (good) and totalitarian (bad) regimes around the world. The former were to be embraced as friends and allies, because of their ability eventually to change and their present inflexibility when it came to communism. The latter regimes not only would not change, they were communist. Matters of human rights abuses by authoritarian leaders were far less important in her schematic than their willingness to tow the anticommunist line. This was the theoretical framework the administration wanted to employ in its support of right-wing dictators.

The Reagan administration, therefore, offered its full support for repressive governments in places like El Salvador and Guatemala. In both countries the administration lied and covered up numerous atrocities and human rights abuses by the military, all in the name of supporting anticommunism. But from President Reagan's perspective, his predecessor's policies had fared no better. In a 1981 interview with Walter Cronkite, Reagan said with respect to the Carter administration's contradictory behavior on human rights, "We took countries that were pro-Western, that were maybe authoritarian in government, but not totalitarian . . . [that] did not meet all of our principles of what constitutes human rights, and we punished them at the same time that we were claiming detente with countries where there are no human rights." Secretary of State George P. Shultz assessed the situation similarly. He pointed to the differences between the East and West on moral principles, principles from which their basic policies arose. He argued that human rights could not be used to spurn other nations. That was a cop-out, he insisted, stating that although it made certain Americans feel better about themselves in their righteous indignation, it did not promote the kind of real change that improved human rights. On the contrary, according to Kirkpatrick and Shultz, U.S. pressure on Iran, Nicaragua, and South Vietnam in the 1970s to conform to certain human rights practices brought about these regimes' downfalls, which decidedly worsened the day-to-day circumstances faced by the millions of peoples in those countries.

The practical test for the Reagan administration position came in South Africa, where the administration took to the idea of working with the apartheid regime in the hope of bringing about affirmative changes in race relations there. Assistant Secretary for African Affairs Chester Crocker coined the term "constructive engagement" when discussing the administration's policy toward the white minority government. The idea was to reassure the South African leaders of American support in their time of transition to democracy. That was the option preferred by the administration; the other was to isolate South Africa through sanctions in an effort to force the situation. Congress, as it had during the 1970s, took a more activist position and in 1986 passed the Comprehensive Anti-Apartheid Act, which imposed economic sanctions on South Africa until significant changes were made, in direct opposition to the Reagan administration's constructive engagement policy.

Elsewhere, the Reagan administration appeared to have better luck, though not because of its dedication to constructive engagement or democratic principles. In the Philippines, longtime dictator Ferdinand Marcos stepped aside and allowed the election of Corazon Aquino in 1986, but the principal impetus for change came from the Filipinos. Reagan hesitated at key moments until the matter was all but decided.

The Bush administration made much the same argument on constructive engagement with respect to China in 1989, even after the government had cracked down on the Tiananmen Square protestors, using the People's Liberation Army to crush them on 3 June. Bush secretly sent two high-ranking advisers—National Security Adviser Brent Scowcroft and Deputy Secretary of State Lawrence Eagleburger—to Beijing on 30 June to assure the Chinese leadership that his administration still intended to promote Sino-American relations once the furor over Tiananmen died down. The president sent the two to China again in December, the same month that the administration announced the release of $300 million in business contracts between American corporations and the Chinese government that had been suspended in the wake of Tiananmen. The administration was intent on downplaying human rights violations.

EXTRADITION, NATIONAL LEADERS, AND HUMAN RIGHTS

On 16 October 1998 Spanish magistrate Baltasar Garzón issued an extradition order for former Chilean dictator Augusto Pinochet, who was in Great Britain for medical treatment at the time. Although the British government eventually permitted Pinochet to return to Chile in March 2000 because of his supposed poor health, Britain's highest court, the Law Lords, had ruled on 24 March 1999 that the charges against Pinochet were so serious—including the murder and torture of Chileans—that they overrode defense counsel's argument that Pinochet was immune from prosecution under Britain's State Immunity Act of 1978. In short, Pinochet could be held legally accountable for his actions while head of state.

In 1999, Henry Kissinger published the third volume of his memoirs, in which he explained the reasons why the Nixon and Ford administrations supported Salvador Allende's overthrow in 1973 and then endorsed the regime under General Pinochet that followed. First, he asserted that the dangers posed by communist expansion in the Western Hemisphere were real, citing Fidel Castro in Cuba and leftist guerrilla activities elsewhere. Second, Kissinger argued that Allende was determined to destroy the democratic institutions in Chile and replace them with a communist dictatorship. Kissinger's defense thus turned on denying involvement in Allende's overthrow and recalling the Cold War context to justify supporting Pinochet.

The Pinochet ruling in Britain gave some officials reason for pause: the United States has held other nations and their leaders accountable for violating human rights, but eventually American leaders may be placed under the same microscope. There is something very chilling, and quite healthy and appropriate, about the prospect of some deliberative body being able to sit in judgment of actions taken by the United States. The notion that American leaders will be held accountable for violating human rights is certainly dim, but such accountability would bring equity to the way in which human rights violations are handled around the world.

On 20 December 1989 the United States invaded Panama. The official reasons floated for the invasion ranged from harassment by Panamanian Defense Forces of American military officials (and their wives), to Panamanian leader Manuel Noriega's involvement with drug trafficking, to human rights violations. The drug connection was well-known in the early 1980s, but Noriega then cleaned up his act to the point where he received a letter from the Drug Enforcement Agency in 1986 that thanked him for his cooperation in stopping the drug trade. The last of the reasons given was a sheer fabrication, since the Bush administration was more than willing to ignore much more serious human rights violations in China and Iraq or, closer to home, in El Salvador and Guatemala.

THE CLINTON YEARS

Since 1989 the United States has faced a number of humanitarian crises, including ones involving the gross violation, either individually or collectively, of human rights. In 1994, for example, some in the Hutu majority in Rwanda orchestrated massive killings of Tutsis beginning in April. The brutal massacres clearly violated the UN's Declaration of Human Rights, but governments around the world refused to intervene to stop the killing. The administration of William Jefferson Clinton purposely avoided using the word genocide because to have uttered it publicly might have obligated the United States to take action under the UN Convention on the Prevention and Punishment of the Crime of Genocide, approved in December 1948 but not signed by the United States until 4 November 1988. Instead, the administration used phrases like "acts of genocide." When questioned as to the difference between genocide and acts of genocide, Christine Shelley, a State Department spokesperson, responded that "clearly not all of the killings that have taken place in Rwanda are killings to which you might apply that label." When pressed as to how many "acts of genocide" were needed to constitute "genocide," Shelly answered, "That's just not a question that I'm in a position to answer." In other words, better to avoid the issue through linguistic parsing than acknowledge what was truly happening and doing something about it. President Clinton apologized for America's inaction while visiting Rwanda in 1998, but that was years after 800,000 people had been massacred.

The proliferation of independence movements in the wake of the Soviet Union's collapse apparently arose in partial response to Woodrow Wilson's call at the end of the First World War to support such efforts. To their surprise, however, those groups seeking U.S. assistance in their attempts to form independent governments ran into traditional American worries about instability possibly ensuing. In 1999, to cite one example, the leaders of Kosovo traveled to Rambouillet, France, to discuss its status within Yugoslavia. Meeting with American secretary of state Madeleine Albright, they found the United States much less keen than they had hoped regarding their desire to separate from Serbia and what remained of the Yugoslav republic. From the American perspective, supporting independence for Kosovo would set a dangerous precedent: What of the Kurds in Iraq and Turkey, the Tibetans in western China, and the Taiwanese? If those peoples also publicly asserted their desire for independent states, the consequences could possibly involve the United States in a major war, especially in the case of Taiwan. Hence, the Clinton administration remained exceedingly cautious about supporting the collective human rights of the Kosovars, despite their obvious suffering at the hands of the Serbian authorities led by Slobodan Milosevic.

AMERICA'S RECORD AT HOME

In 2001, Francis Fukuyama wrote about the debate between "rights" and "interests" and what difference it makes to speak of "human rights" as opposed to "human interests." More specifically, he delved into why certain groups assert claims to rights when what they are really discussing are interests. In a sense, this is merely a broadening of what Jefferson began when he wrote of the "right" to "life, liberty, and the pursuit of happiness." The United Nations declaration is about "universal human rights," not human interests, and after incisively noting the distinction between the two, Fukuyama concluded that the reason for the proliferating assertions of "rights" in the half century after the UN's declaration had to do with how "rights trump interests because they are invested with greater moral significance." The problem with injecting human rights issues into the nation's diplomacy, he insisted, was that they set up a basic premise for the nation's diplomacy that could never really be fulfilled: "A country that makes human rights a significant element of its foreign policy tends toward ineffectual moralizing at best, and unconstrained violence in pursuit of moral aims at worst." Jimmy Carter seemed to have discovered that the hard way.

On another level, Americans still fail to understand how arrogant some of their national pronouncements on human rights seem to peoples in other countries. While condemning human rights infractions elsewhere, Americans blithely go about ignoring or rationalizing their own society's violations. To cite one example, polls generally show that a vast majority of Americans consider the death penalty a domestic matter, and popular support for allowing states to execute prisoners convicted of certain crimes remains high, although revelations in the late 1990s and early 2000s demonstrated the inconsistent, indeed arbitrary, way in which the death penalty is frequently applied, not to mention the fact that a good number of death-row inmates had recently been proven innocent through DNA testing. The governor of Illinois went so far as to suspend all executions pending a review of the state's legal system regarding capital cases. Nongovernmental organizations that monitor human rights abuses around the world, including Amnesty International and Human Rights Watch, regularly cite the use of the death penalty as a violation of human rights, and the United States receives special mention since some of its states also allow for individuals under the age of eighteen to receive the death penalty for certain crimes. That puts the United States in the same league as Iran, Nigeria, Pakistan, Saudi Arabia, and Yemen, nations not normally listed as standing at the forefront of the world's human rights protectors. And it gets even worse. In 2001, 52 percent of all death-row inmates were African American or Latino, far in excess of their percentage of the general population, which in 2000 stood at 24.8 percent, suggesting a disparity based on racial and ethnic prejudice. Yet the Supreme Court has ruled that statistical findings of uneven sentencing across racial lines regarding capital cases do not constitute sufficient evidence of racial bias. An intent to discriminate must be proven in each case, the court ruled, a nearly impossible burden for defendants appealing their convictions. The United States signed the UN Covenant on Civil and Political Rights but by 2001 had not ratified it, largely because of objections to the covenant's prohibition against using the death penalty on individuals under the age of eighteen.

PRESIDENT GEORGE W. BUSH

That the United States failed to retain its seat on the UN Commission on Human Rights, on second thought, begins to look less and less outrageous when the long history of the nation's own violations is considered. Compounding those problems is resentment at the fact that the United States is the only truly global power. The administration of George W. Bush has not done much to allay concerns or ease tensions. Its unilateral decision to reject the Kyoto Agreement on curbing global warming, its resolve to withdraw from the Antiballistic Missile Treaty with Russia in order to pursue a National Missile Defense plan, and the refusal to send Secretary of State Colin Powell to the UN Council on Racism in Durban, South Africa (and then the withdrawal of the delegation) all seemed to mark even more examples of American arrogance.

The Bush administration argued that it sent only a low-level delegation to Durban to protest the language already proposed by Arab delegates calling Israeli's treatment of Palestinians as racist; the president also objected to discussing reparations for past acts of slavery. Whatever the reasons, the Bush administration should have weighed the importance of the nation's past leadership in the field of human rights against its displeasure over particular language in draft texts prior to the start of the conference. David D. Newsom was right to call attention to the disparity between the ideals articulated by the likes of Thomas Jefferson, Woodrow Wilson, or Eleanor Roosevelt and the reality of the actions pursued or not by the United States. But Jimmy Carter was right when he argued that the nation could not shirk its duty to promote human rights just because of its own imperfections.

BIBLIOGRAPHY

Brzezinski, Zbigniew. *Power and Principle: Memoirs of the National Security Adviser, 1977–1981.* New York, 1983.

Carter, Jimmy. *Keeping Faith: Memoirs of a President.* New York, 1982. The most vocal president on human rights in the nation's history discusses his reasons for making it so important to his administration's diplomacy.

Chomsky, Noam. *Deterring Democracy.* New York, 1991. Essential for understanding the duplicitous language employed by policymakers to rationalize actions.

Forsythe, David P. *Human Rights and U.S. Foreign Policy: Congress Reconsidered.* Gainesville, Fla., 1988. A very good discussion of Congress's assertiveness after 1973.

———. "Human Rights in U.S. Foreign Policy: Retrospect and Prospect." *Political Science Quarterly* 105 (autumn 1990): 435–454. One of his many excellent writings on the topic, this one being especially useful as a summary.

Fukuyama, Francis. "Natural Rights and Human History." *The National Interest* 64 (summer 2001): 19–30.

Kirkpatrick, Jeane. "Dictatorships and Double Standards." *Commentary* 68 (November 1979): 34–45. The classic criticism of the Carter administration's policies.

Kluger, Richard. *Simple Justice: The History of Brown v. Board of Education and Black America's Struggle for Equality.* New York, 1977.

Krenn, Michael L. "'Unfinished Business': Segregation and U.S. Diplomacy at the 1958 World's Fair." *Diplomatic History* 20 (fall 1996): 591–612.

Lapham, Lewis. "The American Rome: On the Theory of Virtuous Empire." *Harper's Magazine* (August 2001). A biting analysis of the hypocrisy in American diplomacy and human rights.

Mower, A. Glenn, Jr. *The United States, the United Nations, and Human Rights: The Eleanor Roosevelt and Jimmy Carter Eras.* Westport, Conn., 1979.

———. *Human Rights and American Foreign Policy: The Carter and Reagan Experiences.* New York, 1987.

Newsom, David D., ed. *The Diplomacy of Human Rights.* Lanham, Md., 1986. Good collection of articles that covers a wide range of topics relating to the subject.

Schmitz, David F. *Thank God They're on Our Side: The United States and Right-Wing Dictatorships, 1921–1965.* Chapel Hill, N.C., 1999. A chilling reminder of how stability has usually trumped human rights in, among other things, considering what governments to support.

Smith, Gaddis. *Morality, Reason, and Power: American Diplomacy in the Carter Years.* New York, 1986. A helpful and succinct overview of the Carter administration, including its emphasis on human rights.

Smith, Tony. *America's Mission: The United States and the Worldwide Struggle for Democracy in the Twentieth Century.* Princeton, N.J., 1994. A ringing and eloquent endorsement of the benefits provided by America's efforts to promote democracy, but best if read in conjunction with Schmitz.

Vance, Cyrus R. *Hard Choices: Critical Years in America's Foreign Policy.* New York, 1983.

Vincent, R. J., ed. *Foreign Policy and Human Rights: Issues and Responses.* Cambridge, 1986.

See also FOREIGN AID; HUMANITARIAN INTERVENTION AND RELIEF; MOST-FAVORED-NATION PRINCIPLE; RECOGNITION.

IDEOLOGY

Jennifer W. See

In the last few decades of the twentieth century diplomatic historians increasingly turned their attention to the study of ideology. Previously scholars had largely ignored ideology, choosing instead to focus upon economic or political interests in their explanations. More and more, however, historians found explanations centered on economic imperatives and geopolitical calculations insufficient, even anemic, and many began drawing on new approaches borrowed from other disciplines. The work of the anthropologist Clifford Geertz, in particular, has proven influential among historians and social scientists, offering a powerful tool for understanding the content of ideology and for uncovering its role in policymaking. Geertz's conception of ideology as part of the context within which social interactions unfold has played a significant role in the renewed interest in how ideology influences foreign policy. A rich literature has developed around this subject.

Nevertheless, scholars of American foreign policy still disagree sharply over the importance of ideology in the policymaking process and precisely how it determines outcomes. Even those who emphasize the primacy of ideology in shaping policy concede it is an elusive concept. In particular, at the level of specific policy decisions—and foreign relations historians in the United States have tended overwhelmingly to focus their attention on policymaking—ideology has a way of disappearing. Moreover, little consensus exists over theoretical issues such as definition.

Nowhere has the debate been more intense than among scholars of the Cold War. This dynamic in part results from the intense attention that diplomatic historians have devoted to the superpower conflict—a quick glance through a half dozen back issues of the journal *Diplomatic History* makes clear just how overrepresented the post-1945 period has been. But the nature of the Soviet-American rivalry has also forced scholars to confront the issue of ideology, because both superpowers used strongly ideological rhetoric during the period. Did policymakers during the Cold War believe the ideological claims they made about the world in their public statements, and shape policies accordingly? Or did ideology represent an instrument of politics used to win over their publics and serve as a kind of ex post facto justification for decisions reached on other grounds? Despite the lack of consensus, the intense and ongoing debate over the Cold War highlights both the challenges and the importance of examining ideology.

WHAT IS IDEOLOGY?

According to *Webster's Tenth New Collegiate Dictionary*, "ideology" is "visionary theorizing." Alternatively, it is "a systematic body of concepts especially about human life or culture," or "a manner or the content of thinking characteristic of an individual, group, or culture." Malcolm Hamilton, in his article "The Elements of the Concept of Ideology," offers a more scholarly formulation, writing that ideology is "a system of collectively held normative and reputedly factual ideas and beliefs and attitudes advocating and/or justifying a particular pattern of political and/or economic relationships, arrangements, and conduct." The historian Michael Hunt, meanwhile, views ideology in more specific terms as performing a particular function: it is "an interrelated set of convictions or assumptions that reduces the complexities of a particular slice of reality to easily comprehensible terms and suggests appropriate ways of dealing with that reality." These are just a few examples of scholars' many efforts to define ideology.

Expanding upon these three examples, however, we may construct a meaningful definition. It might read as follows: Ideology is a shared belief system that may serve at once to motivate and to justify. It generally asserts normative values and includes causative beliefs. How do things happen? What does it all mean? An ideology may be utopian and progressive or protective of the status quo. It offers a way in which to order the world, defining enemies and allies, dangers and opportunities, us and them. Ideologies are formal, structured, and involve their own particular logic, often appearing in the guise of science or objective knowledge. Ideology is implicated in collective action, as criticism, goad, explanation, or promise. It is represented in symbols and beliefs held by a community and is publicly expressed. Ideology is at once philosophy, science, religion, and imagination.

ANTECEDENTS

The concept of ideology is generally considered to date from the early nineteenth century, when French theorists, the idéologues, sought through a science of ideas to discover truth and dissolve illusion. For the idéologues, ideology represented a neutral, scientific term. It soon, however, took on a more negative and even pejorative connotation. (The contemporary term "ideologue" derives from this history.) The nineteenth-century reaction against the French Revolution, which for conservatives represented Enlightenment rationalism taken to dangerous extremes, struck the first blow to ideology's reputation. But it was the work of a nineteenth-century revolutionary that truly sundered ideology from its rationalist beginnings.

For Karl Marx ideology had more to do with illusion than truth. In his best-known works, such as *Capital,* the German philosopher and revolutionary provides surprisingly little explanation of either the role or the nature of ideology. Yet Marx has had a lasting influence on the understanding of ideology. Marxist theory finds the determinants of social reality in material factors and especially in economic structures. Marx argued that human society was passing through a series of historical periods or stages. A different form of economic organization—feudalism, capitalism, and eventually communism—each with its own dominant class defined the various stages. And this is where ideology comes in: For Marx ideology served the interests of the dominant class, whether kings or merchants. Ideology acted as a camera obscura, to use one of his many metaphors for the concept, providing individuals with a distorted view of reality. The view through the camera obscura concealed the realities of class conflict that define social relationships. It created the alienation of workers in capitalist society and slowed the inexorable revolutionary progress toward the end of history, the communist utopia. Only Marxist theory, which offered a true vision of history, was free from ideological distortion.

Marx's views proved enduring. Although subsequent theorists further developed his ideas the outlines of his view remained largely unchanged, and ideology continued well into the twentieth century to be understood as an instrument to justify power. Lenin represents perhaps the most significant and influential of Marx's successors. To Marxist theory Lenin added a revolutionary caste of intellectuals who could provide an ideology for the working class. These revolutionary intellectuals exposed the economic and social realities obscured by the ideology of the dominant class, thereby intervening in the progress of history. In Leninist theory revolution became not just inevitable but also intentional. Ideology took on a more conspiratorial aspect, since now it could be created and manipulated. The revolution of 1917 in Russia, engineered in part by Lenin's Bolsheviks, seemed to attest to the connection between ideology and revolutionary upheaval.

Marxist ideas, however, came under challenge in the early decades of the century by sociologists such as Karl Mannheim and Max Weber, who sought a more objective understanding of the term. Mannheim, for one, understood ideology as a worldview, or *Weltanschauung,* shared by a particular social group. For Mannheim, Marxism represented just one example of an ideology. But common usage still largely followed the dictates of Marxist theory: ideology was distorting and irrational, an instrument of power. Max Lerner, writing in the 1930s, declared that ideas were weapons. Most Americans shared this view, and influenced by the events of 1917 and the experience of World War II, identified ideology with totalitarianism. The particulars of Marxist-Leninism and the excesses of Nazi Germany linked ideology with the enemies of American ideals. It was something others—like Hitler or Stalin—had. Students of totalitarianism such as Hannah Arendt reinforced these views. In her influential *The Origins of Totalitarianism* (1951), Arendt wrote that totalitarian states had introduced into international affairs a new and dangerous dynamic. To these states she attributed a neglect of national interests, a contempt for utilitarian motives, and an unwavering faith in an ideological fictitious world. Terror and ideology became inseparable in her interpretation. Yet at the same time, amidst the explicitly ideological rhetoric of the Cold War, many American observers remained curiously blind to the importance of ideology in American society.

The work of realist writers such as George F. Kennan and Hans Morgenthau, however, challenged the notion that American foreign policy remained devoid of ideology. The "realists," as they called themselves to emphasize their critique of idealism in international affairs, became especially prominent in the early 1950s. For these writers ideology acted as a cover for the "real" interests that drove foreign policy. In Morgenthau's 1948 *Politics Among Nations,* the struggle for power that defined international politics wore an ideological disguise. This disguise might prove impenetrable to even the policymaker himself. For realists like Morgenthau ideology holds the danger of distraction and delusion while at the same time serving as justification and cover. Whereas in Marxist theory ideology provided a camera obscura image of class interests, for these writers state interests represented the "reality" that ideology distorted. The idea of ideology as obscuring power politics and "real" interests appeared in Kennan's writing explicitly tied to American foreign policy. In *American Diplomacy,* Kennan described American foreign policy in the twentieth century as woven with "the red skein" of legalistic moralism. Kennan argued that legalistic-moralistic tendencies had long marred American diplomacy and called on policymakers to remove their ideological blinders and pursue a policy based upon calculations of interest. Kennan never explicitly labeled this moralistic-legalistic "approach" as ideology. Yet the analogy remained clear.

Beginning in the 1960s revisionist historians and New Left critics such as William Appleman Williams further developed the idea of ideology as at once driving and distorting American policy. But for Williams the problem with American foreign policy lay not in its moralism. Rather, drawing on the Marxist link between ideology and political economy, Williams in his 1959 *The Tragedy of American Diplomacy* discovered the "open door." He defined open door ideology as a belief that American prosperity and security depended upon an informal empire of markets around the globe. Market capitalism underlay this ideology, of course, and Williams argued that it had served only to lead American policymakers astray. In his revised 1972 edition of *Tragedy,* he wrote that Vietnam offered a clear example. Williams described the war in Vietnam as a disaster born of efforts to extend the reach of America's informal empire abroad. It represented one more incident in a history of "blustering and self-righteous crusades." In the context of Vietnam, the realists and the New Left agreed on this point, if little else: American ideology served to obscure and distort American interests, drawing the United States into an endless, and hopeless, crusade against communism. Ideology thus stood reaffirmed as a corrosive blight rather than a creative force. Williams's take on ideology and foreign policy proved influential among historians and shaped scholarship during the 1960s and 1970s. The Marxist connection between political economy and ideology along with the conception of ideology as distortion remained alive and well.

But in the field of anthropology, Clifford Geertz was turning away from these ideas. No longer should ideology carry the negative baggage of distortion and concealment traditionally loaded upon it, he argued. Beginning in the 1970s Geertz began to separate it from the role of maintaining power relationships. Instead the anthropologist redefined ideology as an integrated and coherent system of symbols, values, and beliefs. Although still at times the province of a dominant class or group and able to act in the context of power, ideology takes on a broader meaning in Geertz's interpretation. Rather than obscuring social relationships, ideology both formulates and communicates social reality. Geertz's understanding of ideology depended upon his conception of culture, which offers a context within which events can be "thickly" described and which is embodied in public symbols. Within the context of culture, ideology provides a necessary symbol system to make sense of the world, especially significant in times of crisis or rapid change. And here is a crucial distinction between Geertz's understanding of ideology and Mannheim's *Weltanschauung:* For Geertz, ideology is publicly expressed and can be found in the rituals and symbols of a society, not just in the heads of individuals. Thus for the student of culture ideology offers an entrée into the ways in which societies understand their collective experiences, daily realities, and identities. Through the lens of ideology one can read the truth of a culture and society.

Subsequently, Michael Hunt extended the insights of Clifford Geertz to the study of American foreign policy. And for many in the field, Hunt's book proved a revelation. In *U.S. Ideology and Foreign Policy,* Hunt argues that three main ideas constitute American ideology: the promise of national greatness, a hierarchy of race, and a fear of social revolution. American ideology entwined the fate of liberty at home and abroad with a sense of mission and a belief in America as an agent of progress. The efforts of Woodrow Wilson in 1918 to secure acceptance of his Fourteen Points provide a case in point. In Hunt's view Wilson sought a leading international role for the United States, promoting liberty abroad and ensuring Anglo-Saxon cultural supremacy. Like the critics of the 1960s and 1970s, Hunt finds that ideology had largely led Americans astray. Significantly, however, it was the details of the ideology Americans had adopted rather than ideology in itself that had caused all the trouble. By changing the symbols and language of American foreign policy, Hunt offers the possibility of altering its substance.

Other scholars working across disciplinary lines of sociology, political science, and history have similarly turned their attention to the close study and interpretation of ideology and culture. Drawing on the work of French theorists such as Michel Foucault and Jacques Derrida, they examine the language used by policymakers and analyze the meanings, or "genealogies," of the very words that compose policy. By placing language at the center of social reality, the "linguistic turn" reaffirms ideology's importance. For postmodernists, language constitutes reality; that is, we cannot understand the world around us outside of the words that we use to describe it. For these theorists language serves to replicate and reinforce power relationships much in the way that ideology had in Marxist theory. Postmodernist scholars of the Cold War have explored the meaning of national security and the images of contagion and disease that were often used in the context of Cold War foreign policy. Others, like David Campbell, have examined closely the ways in which foreign policy and the language used to describe it reinforce identity and serve to define a state. In *Writing Security,* Campbell argues that the United States represents an imagined community par excellence, which relies on the language and metaphors of its foreign policy to affirm its existence. For these scholars, the ideas and the language are the reality of foreign policy.

HOW DOES IDEOLOGY CAUSE POLICY?

The renewed interest in ideology and the demand by scholars like Geertz that social scientists and historians must take it seriously has prompted a crucial question: How does ideology cause foreign policy? In Geertz's work this question was intentionally evaded. In his view ideology could not be a cause of action. Ideology is a part of culture and as such acts as the context of, and provides the language and symbols for, social action. Postmodernist theorists have proven similarly uninterested in traditional questions about the causes of the phenomena they study. But for historians, the question of causes, of how things happen, is central to their project. Critics of Hunt's work have raised just this question. How, for example, did the American belief in a hierarchy of race influence particular decisions? Neither have political scientists proved willing to abandon the question of causes. Although theorists of foreign policy increasingly accept that ideas and ideology, not just interests, matter in foreign policy, for many political scientists and historians, ideology needs a "causal mechanism"—a way to act on policy—in order to be useful in explaining events.

This remains a sharply contested issue. Some scholars have focused on institutions and groups of policymakers, arguing that over time these take on a shared culture and world view that influences policy. Others have taken a biographical approach, searching through personal papers in an effort to uncover the beliefs and cultural heritage of individual policymakers. The work of the theorist Walter Carlsnaes suggests one answer to the problem of causation. Like Geertz, Carlsnaes views ideology as a contextual variable in decision making. In *Ideology and Foreign Policy,* Carlsnaes argues that ideology does not cause foreign policy; the decisions of statesmen do. Yet those decisions are made in a particular context, in which ideology is significant. Policymakers react to a particular situation and draw on ideological and cultural resources to make their decisions. While ideology does not intervene in international politics directly, it thus remains a significant determinant of policy by influencing the participants.

This formulation suggests an important pair of insights: Foreign policy cannot be understood in terms of ideology alone, but neither can ideology be ignored. Policymakers struggle for power and respond to threats and opportunities just as realists like Morgenthau have long held. But ideology provides a context—open to analysis in the way of Geertz—that serves to condition those responses and shape the particulars of decision making. The sociologist Max Weber, in his 1913 essay "The Social Psychology of the World's Religions," aptly envisioned ideas as determining the track along which action is pushed by the dynamic of interest. Ideas and interest are separate yet entwined. Interests come out of the context in which policymakers operate and are revealed in the language and the form of their decisions. In this way ideology, despite not serving as a direct cause of policy, remains a significant part of foreign policy.

IDEOLOGY AND AMERICAN FOREIGN POLICY

Four themes in particular form the frame for American foreign policy during its first hundred years: independence, territorial expansion, belief in a national destiny, and commerce. Throughout, ideological visions combined with a hunger for land and territory, a healthy respect for European power, commercial interests, and fears for American security. From the vantage point of the present, American foreign policy during the eighteenth and nineteenth centuries appears relatively inactive and isolationist. Compared with the global reach of American foreign policy during the Cold War and after, the Monroe Doctrine, for example, seems a small thing. Yet the experiences of the early republic contributed lasting pieces to the ideological perspective from which Americans came to view the world in the twentieth century and beyond.

The history of American foreign policy begins with the assertion of independence. One historian, Bradford Perkins, has characterized the American Revolution as "an act of isolation." Although the colonial relationship with Britain was soon severed by the Treaty of Paris (1783), the theme of independence reoccurred throughout the foreign policy of the early Republic. Americans envisioned a New World free from what they saw as the corrupting influences of the old. John Quincy Adams, for one, articulated a "Doctrine of Two Spheres," dividing the Old World and the new. And George Washington famously warned in his Farewell Address in 1796 against "entangling alliances" with Europe.

Perhaps the most significant expression of new world separatism came in the Monroe Doctrine of December 1823. The Monroe Doctrine had two main elements. First, President James Monroe asserted that the Americas were "not to be considered as subjects for future colonization by any European powers." Although the United States did not propose to challenge existing colonial territories, it pledged to resist any further extension of European power into the Western Hemisphere. The second aspect of the Monroe Doctrine asserted U.S. opposition to European intervention in New World conflicts. The president declared that his government would view any European effort to intervene in Latin American affairs as "the manifestation of an unfriendly disposition toward the United States." Monroe set up his country as the protector of the New World, though he had little power as yet to back up his claims. The Monroe Doctrine was nonetheless of lasting significance: As Bradford Perkins has written, the 1823 statement amounted to a "diplomatic declaration of independence."

The great powers of Europe, especially Britain, France, and Spain, did not acquiesce all at once to this division of the world. Following the war for independence from the British empire, the United States spent the early years of the nineteenth century in the Quasi-War with France after refusing to join Napoleon's war against Britain. Then, after an embargo on both British and French trade failed, the republic found itself again at war with Britain. The United States fought the War of 1812 to protect neutral trading rights, but most contemporaries viewed it as a second war for independence. The Treaty of Ghent (1814), which ended the war, changed little, but it did ratify American independence from Britain. Although Europeans generally denied the legitimacy of the Monroe Doctrine, characterizing it as a statement of ambition rather than reality, none of the great powers openly challenged it, allowing Americans to believe themselves successful. Throughout the nineteenth century European preoccupations such as the Crimean War (1854–1856) left Americans largely to their own devices, encouraging the illusion of isolation from European conflicts and a belief in a true separation of the Old World from the new.

A second theme of early foreign policy was a belief in American destiny. Few among the early generation of Americans questioned that their new nation was meant for greatness. In part this belief came from the Puritan heritage. The United States represented a "city on a hill" that God had chosen for a special destiny and mission in the world. This mission was understood over time in different ways, but the survival of America's republican government remained central. Early Americans believed that republican government was fragile, easily corrupted into tyranny from above or anarchy from below. After all, the republican experiments of the past had ended in failure. Moreover, the French Revolution raised significant questions for Americans about whether republican government could succeed elsewhere in the world. The excesses of the French Revolution, in particular the Terror (1793–1794) and the eventual rise of Napoleon as emperor (1804), reinforced a sense of exceptionalism and superiority in the American mind. This sense of superiority also had a racial aspect. American destiny was an Anglo-Saxon destiny. As Hunt explains, belief in racial hierarchy was part and parcel of American ideology.

The mixture of mission and race played out in a third theme of early foreign policy: expansion. For nineteenth-century Americans geography was destiny. To the west lay an empty continent, and expansion was nothing less than inevitable. For Americans at the time the same divine providence that had guided the founding seemed to sanction a right to expansion. In the 1840s the writer John O'Sullivan gave name to this impulse: manifest destiny. O'Sullivan believed in the inevitability of American greatness and the necessity of the American example for the world. Americans must "carry the glad tidings of peace and good will where myriads now endure an existence scarcely more enviable than that of the beast of the field," he wrote. The United States had a mission "to overspread the continent allotted by Providence for the free development of our yearly multiplying millions." The new nation would make "manifest" the virtues of freedom and Anglo-Saxon civilization. As the historian Anders Stephanson explains, manifest destiny served as a legitimizing myth of empire. Manifest destiny helped reconcile the national mythology of exceptionalism and virtue with ambition and acquisitiveness. Americans thus understood their territorial expansion in a particularly American way, drawing on ideas deeply embedded in their cultural heritage and self-identity.

And the United States quickly overspread the continent. Thomas Jefferson's Louisiana Purchase (1803) marked the first major expansion, extending the boundaries of the United States to the Mississippi River. Subsequently, John Quincy Adams became a key architect of American expansion, negotiating the 1819 Transcontinental Treaty with Spain, which extended American claims all the way to the Pacific. These claims did not go entirely unchallenged, as the British sought to retain their foothold in the Pacific Northwest and Mexico claimed significant portions of the Southwest. Moreover the issue of slavery complicated considerably the process of admitting new states into the union. And of course the continent was not empty: The Cherokee and Iroquois among others tried desperately to keep their ancestral lands. But with a combination of war and treaty the United States managed to secure hold over much of the continent by mid-century. Racial attitudes of superiority helped rationalize the bloody and dangerous work of subduing the native populations, as did the ideology of destiny and divine mission. At the same time, race paradoxically limited American expansion to the south. During the Mexican-American War (1846–1848), President James K. Polk turned away from conquering the whole of Mexico, believing that Latin Americans were not ready for republican government. This belief in Latin American inferiority proved lasting, though ambivalence toward spreading democracy did not.

The final ingredient of early foreign policy was commerce. Revisionist historians such as William Appleman Williams argue that the search for markets has driven American foreign policy from the beginning. Commerce and efforts to protect American trade in particular have always been an element of foreign policy. Americans have long shown a tendency to assert universalistic claims and champion neutral rights that serve American interests. The rebellion against Britain was in part over trading privileges. Even more so was the War of 1812. There were territorial issues and domestic political positions at stake in the War of 1812, but maritime rights were central to the American grievance with Britain. The United States opposed the British efforts to blockade France by decree, known as a "paper blockade," and demanded that Britain recognize the principle of "free ships free goods." Goods transported by neutral American shipping should be immune from seizure by British naval forces and American seamen free from impressment into the British navy, argued the Madison administration. The War of 1812 did not resolve these issues, though the principles of free trade and neutral shipping won some protection under international law in subsequent decades.

At the end of the nineteenth century, Secretary of State John Hay passed the Open Door Notes to the other great powers. Hay hoped to establish the principle of free trade and open markets. The subject was the China trade, but the principle involved transcended the particulars. Much as the Monroe Doctrine expressed a long-held belief in the separation of the Old and New Worlds, the open door notes signified the importance of trade and commerce to American policymakers. Williams has argued that the open door represents the keystone of American foreign policy. Americans have throughout their history sought to secure global markets, an open door, for American goods. To Williams and other revisionist scholars, the impetus of the open door has made for an inherently expansionist U.S. policy that has in effect created an informal empire under the guise of asserting neutral rights. Revisionists exaggerate, perhaps, the dominance, the power of the open door, but trade and commerce nonetheless have remained central elements of the story.

Until the end of the nineteenth century American ideology had little influence beyond its borders. The mythology of the founding and the other tenets of American identity served to reinforce unity at home. Most Americans perceived the United States as a nation apart and clung to isolationist attitudes. But growing American power and widening commercial and political interests meant a turn to a more activist foreign policy beginning in the early years of the twentieth century. The first president of the new century, Theodore Roosevelt, proved an able champion of American power, sending his new navy around the world. Roosevelt also involved himself in Old World diplomacy, winning a Nobel Peace Prize for his role in negotiating an end to the Russo-Japanese War (1904–1905). Events in the Old World soon ensured that Roosevelt's successors would see little alternative but to continue the project of asserting American power.

World War I (1914–1918) and the 1917 Bolshevik Revolution in Russia stand together as the defining events of the twentieth century. World War I brought to an end the Habsburg and Turkish empires, opening the question of nationalism and self-determination in eastern and central Europe. The Bolshevik Revolution, meanwhile, introduced a new ideology to the world: Marxist-Leninism. The conflicts created by the combination of declining empires, unleashed nationalisms, and new ideologies proved lasting, shaping events for the rest of the century. President Woodrow Wilson, who served from 1912 to 1920, proved a pivotal figure who redefined American traditions to meet the new circumstances of the twentieth century. The growing power of nationalism, the ideological challenge of Marxist-Leninism, and the revolutions set loose by retreating empires: to these challenges Wilson brought a distinctly American response.

Wilson has remained a controversial figure. Scholars have variously seen him as a starry-eyed idealist and as a wise statesman who pursued a kind of enlightened realism. An idealist Wilson certainly was. The president believed in the perfectibility of man and his institutions and that extending democracy could make for a more peaceful world. He sought to channel nationalism into democratic direction and find an alternative to the political arrangements of the past, in particular the secret treaties and multinational empires he believed had brought about the Great War. He hoped the orderly legal arrangements of the League of Nations would prevent conflict while at the same time protect traditional American interests in free trade and neutrality.

With a liberal's fear of radicalism Wilson intervened in the Mexican revolution (1910–1915) to "teach Mexicans to elect good men." With equal distaste for conservatism he saw little reason to regret the breakup of the multinational Habsburg empire in central and eastern Europe. And with a traditional American ambivalence toward social change he sought to turn back revolution in Russia, fearing the challenge to property rights Marxist-Leninism seemed to represent and the instability the revolution threatened. The president believed in democracy. But he also saw spreading democracy abroad as a way to ensure the American way of life at home. In this he abandoned his predecessors' pessimism about the possibilities for republican government elsewhere. The United States should not only serve as an example, but also actively promote liberal values abroad. In Wilson, moralism, ideology, and interest entwined in an activist, universalist liberalism. That Wilson's vision ran aground against the radicalism of revolution, the impossibility of intervention on behalf of self-determination, and the institutionalized rivalries of the European great powers in no way lessened its lasting influence.

Yet despite the universalist implications of the Wilsonian vision, the United States in the interwar period limited its involvement in world affairs, refusing to join the League of Nations. This is not to say that the U.S. withdrew entirely from the world during the 1920s and 1930s. It participated in naval conferences with the other great powers and tangled with Japan in the Pacific, but not with the kind of far-reaching universalist claims and hopes of 1918. For all the importance Wilsonian ideology seemed posed to have in shaping American foreign policy in the aftermath of World War I, it was rivaled by isolationism. Prosperity at home took precedence over idealism abroad, particularly after the onset of the Great Depression in 1929.

But this aloofness from the world could not last. The 1933 Nazi seizure of power in Germany meant little to most Americans at the time, but its effects soon rippled throughout the international system. After the invasion of Poland in 1939 the United States was not entirely uninvolved in World War II but proved able to avoid direct intervention. Instead President Franklin D. Roosevelt made his country an arsenal for democracy against Germany and its allies. After Japanese pilots bombarded Pearl Harbor on 7 December 1941, however, events again drew the United States into a pivotal role in world affairs, and it faced the challenge of reconciling its traditions and self-image with the ways of the world.

Although Wilsonianism was held responsible by the 1940s for the failed peace settlement of Versailles, it still exerted a powerful hold on the American imagination. The bipartisan support for the United Nations, the new collective security organization proposed in 1945, and Roosevelt's wartime rhetoric testified to the continued power of Wilsonian ideals. But against these hopes the post–World War II peace felt fragile, in part as a result of the new vulnerability that technology imposed and Pearl Harbor symbolized. The lessons of history hard learned at Munich and Versailles combined with old beliefs in American mission and exceptionalism as policymakers of the 1940s wrestled with the dilemmas of the postwar world. It soon became clear, even as World War II was coming to a close, that chief among these dilemmas was the reality of Soviet power. Within two years of the end of the war, a unique kind of conflict, soon dubbed the Cold War, was on. America's new vulnerability had an agent, Soviet communism, and a panacea, the strategy of containment.

THE COLD WAR

Traditional scholarship on the Cold War assigned a central but sharply circumscribed role to ideology. The writers of the 1950s drew on the official rationales that the Truman administration had used to explain the nature of the Cold War and the necessity for the American Cold War policy of containment. This literature portrayed the Soviets as bent on expansion, driven by a combination of traditional interests and Marxist-Leninist ideology. The United States in response acted prudently and pragmatically to defend its interests against this obvious security threat. This view did not go unchallenged. Although initially an advocate of containing the Soviet Union, George Kennan soon joined another realist critic, Walter Lippmann, and turned against his creation. Kennan argued that the Truman Doctrine overcommitted the United States by defining American interests in ideological and expansive terms. For Kennan and Lippmann both, ideology influenced not only Soviet but also American policymakers. Beginning in the 1960s revisionist scholars turned traditional scholarship on its head, arguing that American, not Soviet, policy was ideological, and that the Soviet actions in the immediate postwar period were motivated by legitimate security needs.

In reaction to the sharp disjunction between revisionist and traditional scholarship, historians working in the 1970s and 1980s set aside ideology altogether and redefined the Cold War as a traditional conflict of interests between two great powers. This conflict came as the inevitable outgrowth of World War II and particularly the power vacuum in central Europe resulting from the destruction of Germany. Louis Halle in *The Cold War as History* famously describes the two superpowers as scorpions in a bottle. They could not help but come into conflict. Writing very much in this tradition, Melvyn Leffler argues in his award-winning account of the Truman administration, *A Preponderance of Power*, that American policymakers were driven by national security considerations and sought to increase American power in the postwar world. In *A Preponderance of Power*, ideology has little to do with American policy. Instead, American policymakers acted out of fear for American security. Truman and his advisers were prudent in reacting to the possibility of Soviet aggression, yet they were foolish to seek so exaggerated a security for the United States. Although the wisdom of American policymakers and the question of Soviet intentions remained a subject of scholarly disagreement, ideology seemed to fall out of the picture. For a time, there the debate rested.

But in the 1990s newly available archival sources from the Soviet side of the conflict reopened the question of the relationship between ideology and the Cold War. Writing in 1997, John Lewis Gaddis declared in *We Now Know* that the new Cold War history must of necessity concern itself with ideology. Similarly, Martin Malia in *The Soviet Tragedy*, an account of Soviet foreign policy, places ideology at the center of the conflict between East and West and argues that the 1917 Bolshevik Revolution virtually guaranteed the Cold War that followed. The Russian scholars Vladislav Zubok and Constantine Pleshakov also emphasize ideology in their interpretation of Cold War Soviet foreign policy, though in their account Marxist-Leninism and self-interest combined to shape Stalin's decision making.

American ideology has received less attention, but the arguments of this new scholarship implied a role for American ideology as well. Two scholars in particular, Odd Arne Westad and Anders Stephanson, emphasize the importance of American ideology during the Cold War. As Westad states in his 2000 Bernath Lecture, "It was to a great extent American ideas and their influence that made the Soviet-American conflict into a *Cold War*." Meanwhile, Stephanson finds in Cold War documents a particularly American language of politics built around the opposition between "freedom" and "slavery." The kind of ideological absolutism embodied in Patrick Henry's famous "Give me liberty or give me death" lived on in America's conceptions of the Cold War world. Ideology thus seemed to have returned to a central place in the analysis of the Cold War.

Amidst this rediscovery of ideology, however, Marc Trachtenberg, in an important 1999 book, *A Constructed Peace*, argues precisely the opposite: the Cold War in fact had little to do with ideology at all. In Trachtenberg's view the central problem of the postwar world was power, specifically German power. Soviet and American leaders in the postwar period understood this reality, and far from being influenced by ideology pursued their interests with cool calculation. This is not to say that the superpowers did not distrust one another, or that there were not very real conflicts of interest between them. But the conflicts were precisely that: of interest, not of ideology. Trachtenberg argues that the Cold War began as a result of Soviet actions in Iran in April 1946, actions that American policymakers perceived as signaling expansive intentions. In response the United States tightened its hold on western Germany, and the Cold War rivalry ensued. The crucial question of the Cold War continued to be the problem of Germany, although much of the actual conflict took place on the periphery. Once the superpowers reached a settlement on Germany, which Trachtenberg argues occurred in 1963, the Cold War was for all intents and purposes over.

The gap between those who write in terms of national security and those who emphasize ideology remains wide. The relationship between ideology and national security is often portrayed as an either-or proposition: either ideology or national interest motivates policymaking. Ideology tends to be associated with irrational or particularly aggressive actions. And in fact the literature has tended to portray the more aggressive side of the Cold War rivalry as the more ideological. For traditionalists this meant the Soviet leadership acted according to the tenets of Marxist-Leninism, while for revisionists it was American policy that had fallen victim to the siren song of ideology. In this respect the literature treats ideology as a kind of pathology of policymaking. Moreover, national security is often treated as a given, a kind of objective truth that exists unchanging across time and space. By this logic leaders on all sides of the Cold War conflict understood the risks and opportunities they faced in much the same way. Each calculated his (and they were all men) options and reactions carefully and rationally and shared similar goals of ensuring territorial security and increasing state power. Calculations complete, policymakers reached into the same toolbox for the means to achieve their goals. Perhaps they did.

But as Tony Smith asserts in his study of twentieth-century American foreign policy, *America's Mission*, "security definitions arise out of particular domestically engendered perceptions of foreign affairs." Ideology acts to define the boundaries of legitimate action and to define what is dangerous and what is not. It is thus complicit in the process of creating interests and defining national security, because ideology provides the context within which policy decisions are made. As a result we must take seriously historical experience, the language policymakers use, and the very different tools on which they rely to pursue their ends. Foreign policy decisions are rarely made in a vacuum, and domestic political debates influence the process. During the Cold War, and particularly in the United States, ideological context conditioned foreign policy outcomes. Ideology defined the issues at stake.

For Americans the issue at stake became the survival of freedom, and Soviet communism became the primary threat. This view did not come all at once. Although suspicious of Soviet intentions, to be sure, Truman and especially his secretary of state James Byrnes remained open to efforts at accommodation and compromise with the Soviet Union throughout 1945 and the early months of 1946. Meanwhile, officials like Secretary of the Navy James Forrestal and George Kennan, chargé d'affaires in Moscow, were raising the alarm, prompting debate within the administration over how to deal with the Soviets in the postwar world. In February 1946, Kennan telegraphed some eight thousand words from his post at the embassy in Moscow. His Long Telegram offered one of the first interpretations of Soviet policy. Similar views were already floating around the corridors of Washington policymaking bureaucracies, but Kennan, as he would do several more times in the early Cold War, put American attitudes into articulate form.

Kennan described the Soviet Union as committed "fanatically" to the belief that there could be "no permanent modus vivendi" between East and West. In Kennan's view the Kremlin's perspective resulted from a combination of Marxist-Leninist ideology and a traditional and instinctive insecurity. Marxist-Leninist ideology and the closed society that limited contact with the outside world had a hypnotic effect on Soviet officials, leaving them unlikely and unable to question their assumptions about the West. Kennan argued that Soviet policy could not be changed by talk; it was "highly sensitive to the logic of force." He warned that much depended upon the "health and vigor" of American society and urged his colleagues in Washington to have the "courage and self-confidence" to protect American traditions. "World communism is like a malignant parasite. . . . This is point at which domestic and foreign policies meet."

The Long Telegram echoed earlier traditions of exceptionalism and mission, which likely in part explains its appeal to official Washington. Kennan's analysis made the rounds (it appears in the personal papers of nearly every major figure in the Truman administration), and most agreed with its analysis. The Soviet Union represented a clear threat to American values and to freedom at home and abroad. The Kremlin sought to expand communist influence throughout the world, and it would not be deterred by negotiation. The American way of life increasingly appeared under siege to many of these officials. Soviet actions in eastern Europe, particularly in Bulgaria, Hungary, and Poland, as well as the April crisis in Iran, seemed only to confirm these fears. So too did the emergence of strong communist parties in France and Italy. At the same time, however, the crisis in Iran proved resolvable by diplomacy when Iran made a protest to the United Nations. Even better, the apparent Soviet acceptance of the UN's decisions in the case suggested that the new organization was not doomed as many had feared. Moreover, in July 1946 the Paris Peace Conference began and by the end of the summer successfully concluded peace treaties with the Axis powers, though a German peace treaty and particularly the problem of reparations remained on the table. Despite the alarmist language of many administration officials in their private memos and growing public suspicion of Soviet intentions, the possibility of postwar settlement was not yet foreclosed.

But the limited diplomatic successes of the Council of Foreign Ministers and the Paris Peace Conference could not erase the growing fears of the threat Marxist-Leninism posed to American society and interests. A September 1946 report prepared by White House staffers Clark Clifford and George Elsey reveals that the perspective expressed by Kennan's Long Telegram was taking hold throughout the administration. The Clifford-Elsey report expressed the opinion of its authors to be sure, but the two officials drew on documents prepared by all of the major policymaking institutions, and their views were thus informed by the combined wisdom of the Departments of State, War, Navy, and Commerce. The report placed the U.S.–Soviet relationship at the center of American foreign policy. It expressed no ambiguity about Soviet intentions: "Soviet leaders appear to be conducting their nation on a course of aggrandizement designed to lead to eventual world domination by the U.S.S.R." This aim could not be turned aside by conventional diplomacy, and the authors borrowed Kennan's interpretation that the Kremlin leadership believed in the impossibility of peaceful coexistence between Marxist-Leninism and capitalism. Like Kennan, Clifford and Elsey took Soviet rhetoric and ideology seriously. The pronouncements of Kremlin leaders such as Stalin and Vyacheslav Molotov represented the reality of Soviet policy. The United States must prepare itself for total war, the authors declared. Economic aid programs and an information policy (propaganda, like ideology, was something the other side had) articulating the benefits of American society and the goals of U.S. policy should not be neglected. But the United States should never lose sight of Soviet preparations for eventual war with the "capitalistic powers," preparations that represented a direct threat to American security. By autumn 1946 the language and content of the Clifford-Elsey report was emblematic of the emerging consensus held by official Washington.

The fate of Secretary of Commerce Henry Wallace signaled perhaps more than anything else the hardening of this new perspective. Wallace had long argued for negotiations with the Soviets, and in September 1946 he expressed his views publicly in a speech at Madison Square Garden. Wallace argued that the United States should work to allay Russian suspicions and distrust and recognize Soviet security needs in eastern Europe as legitimate. In retrospect there seems to be little in Wallace's speech that is particularly radical. But his apparent support for a Soviet sphere of influence in eastern Europe set off a firestorm of controversy. The tone of the speech created a dissonant echo amidst the increasingly hard-line atmosphere of official Washington. An embarrassed President Truman, who had upon cursory reading endorsed Wallace's address, demanded the secretary's resignation. Arguments that the United States should attempt to resolve the diplomatic disputes that separated the superpowers and that the Soviets acted in eastern Europe out of legitimate security concerns slipped increasingly to the margins of mainstream opinion. Consensus about ideological conflict in the postwar world, the expansive tendencies of Soviet Union, and the necessity for a policy of containment was taking hold, and American policy evolved to match these views.

By the end of 1946 American officials increasingly turned away from negotiating with the Soviets. When Secretary of State James Byrnes returned from a December conference of foreign ministers meeting in Moscow, where he had attempted to conclude agreements on eastern Europe and international control of atomic energy, he faced sharp criticism. To American observers Stalin showed every sign of emulating Hitler in his efforts to expand Soviet power, his allegiance to ideology, and his willingness to break agreements. Both policymakers and the informed public drew on the analogy of the Munich Conference (1938), at which British Prime Minister Neville Chamberlain bargained away territory in Czechoslovakia in the hope that he could achieve peace for all time.

Chamberlain failed. And the lesson Americans learned was that dictators could not be trusted, appeasement only fed greater ambition, and negotiations suggested weakness. It is striking how powerful in fact this analogy became and how often officials referred to it during the postwar period. The decision largely to renounce negotiation and the tools of traditional diplomacy held an appeal linked to the American heritage of exceptionalism and aloofness from the messiness and compromise of European politics. The failed diplomacy of 1939 fit neatly into the existing preconceptions and predisposition of American diplomacy. And the "lessons" of history seemed to lend legitimacy to the desire to contain Stalin's Soviet Union and wait for it to fall victim to its own "internal contradictions."

But containment meant more than a policy of waiting. Beginning in spring 1947 the United States turned ideas into action. In late February the British government notified the Department of State that the British would be forced for financial reasons to withdraw its support from Greece. In the midst of a civil war, Greece had become a site of a great power contest, lying as it did in a strategic corner of the Mediterranean. Anxious to prevent Soviet influence from taking hold in Greece, the Truman administration resolved to take action. The decision resulted from a combination of ideological and strategic interests: Greek geography rendered it significant from a strategic perspective. But American policymakers also feared the spread of communism into Greece and believed that from Greece the contagion would almost certainly spread to Italy and France. Greece offered a test.

It was a test that Harry Truman met with a commitment to defend freedom throughout the world. In a speech before both Houses of Congress on 12 March 1947, Truman asked Congress to fund economic and military aid to Greece and to neighboring Turkey. The president emphasized that the United States had a responsibility to protect freedom worldwide, declaring that "the free peoples of the world look to us for support in maintaining their freedoms." Continued peace depended upon American leadership. Truman drew a close connection between poverty and totalitarianism and argued that the United States must provide economic and political support for freedom. The United States should stand on the side of self-determination—by intervention, if necessary. "I believe we must assist free peoples to work out their own destinies in their own way," the president told Congress. Implicit in Truman's statement, of course, was the belief that most of the world's peoples would choose a way of life compatible, if not identical, with that of the United States. A *New York Times* article declared that "the epoch of isolation and occasional intervention" was over. An "epoch of American responsibility" was just beginning. The American impulse to withdraw from the world, suggested by the decision to "contain" the Soviet Union, stood alongside the Wilsonian mission to spread democracy. The tension between these two impulses determined the nature of America's Cold War policies.

In part the ideological content of Truman's speech represented a tool of politics. Truman required congressional support to put his policy into action, and the administration needed to head off any perception that the U.S. decision to intervene in Greece represented an effort to shore up the British empire. Yet the ideological content went deeper than public rhetoric, since these were terms that had appeared in confidential government documents such as the Clifford-Elsey report throughout the preceding months. Officials within the administration thought in these terms themselves, and thus public rhetoric matched private perceptions. Subsequently, with the announcement of the Marshall Plan in June 1947, the United States added economic aid to Europe to its arsenal against the Soviet Union. Secretary of State George C. Marshall declared that the policy was not aimed at any particular country but instead against "hunger, poverty, desperation, and chaos." But to most observers, the goal was clear. A rebuilt western Europe tied to the United States by a flow of dollars and trade would offer a significant barrier to Soviet expansion. The parasite of communism preyed upon societies weakened by poverty and unstable institutions. The Marshall Plan offered an answer.

The following month in an article published in *Foreign Affairs*, George Kennan summarized the new consensus for the educated public. The Soviet Union holds within it the "seeds of its own destruction," he declared. Despite Kennan's claims to objectivity, his analysis of "The Sources of Soviet Conduct," as the article was entitled, revealed as much about the ideological content of American conduct as it explained about the Soviet Union. Kennan declared that "the political personality of Soviet power as we know it today is the product of ideology and circumstances." Marxist-Leninism provided the ideology, which together with geography, a history of invasion, and Stalin's personal paranoia resulted in dangerous and expansive tendencies. Kennan argued that Soviet ideology taught that the outside world was hostile and not to be trusted. Capitalism and socialism could not long coexist. Moreover, in Kennan's interpretation, the Soviet Union pictured itself as a center of socialist enlightenment adrift in a dark and misguided world. The logic of history was on its side and in the long run, revolution was inevitable. Here was a rival city on a hill.

To Kennan the challenge that Soviet communism posed to the United States offered a test of faith and an opportunity for reaffirmation. In the closing paragraph of the article he wrote that the Soviet challenge offered "a test of the overall worth of the United States as a nation among nations." Kennan believed that American virtue and strength at home translated into power to meet the Soviet threat abroad. By maintaining its free society the United States could best counter the appeal and the promise that Marxist-Leninism offered. The United States stood as a model of freedom for the world, an alternative to totalitarianism, and a shining example in a hostile world. He wrote that the United States should "offer gratitude to providence," which had chosen the United States for the great task of resisting the spread of Soviet communist oppression and protecting freedom at home and abroad. For history had "plainly intended" that the United States bear the burdens of moral and political leadership. The city on a hill must become the leader of the free world. Failing to arrest the spread of communism would lead to destruction and the end of freedom everywhere. Although Kennan came to be identified as the father of containment, he came to question the implications of his creation, criticizing American foreign policy as overly ideological in 1951 in *American Diplomacy*. Ironically, he failed to realize the degree to which his own worldview was shot through with "the red skein" of ideology.

Realist scholars like Marc Trachtenberg are correct to emphasize that American policymakers reacted to the perceived dangers and opportunities of particular situations. In this respect external conditions drove America's Cold War foreign policy. The problem of Germany, the occupation of Japan, and the future of Europe represented real dilemmas for policymakers. And the global political and economic instability of the immediate postwar period posed a potential danger to American security and prosperity. But American policymakers' interpretations of these threats and opportunities was influenced by American concerns about freedom, independence, exceptionalism, and democracy. For them the source of both economic and political instability came from the Soviet Union and in particular the nature of the Soviet state. Truman and his key advisers defined the Soviet Union in explicitly ideological terms. The threat was not the power of the Soviet state (in fact, most administration officials considered the Soviets the weaker of the two superpowers) so much as the appeal of Marxist-Leninist ideology and the promise of revolution that it held.

Contrast this with the perspective of the British Foreign Office, which in the early months of the postwar period retained its nineteenth-century concern with maintaining a balance among the main European powers and protecting their imperial holdings. For British policymakers, at least initially, the threat to postwar peace came from an unequal division of the spoils and an extension of Soviet power. This distinction between the worldviews of the Foreign Office in London and the Department of State in Washington highlights the role of ideology in providing the context for policy decision making. For realists ideology is an instrument of policy; it serves to rationalize and justify decisions already made. Yet as Stephanson explains in "Liberty or Death," "an instrumental view of ideology as rhetorical means to strategic ends misses the question." Why did policymakers choose the particular language they did and how did they come to "inhabit" it? While the power vacuums and risks of the postwar world may have provided the occasion for a more activist foreign policy, American ideology determined the form American intervention in the world would take, defined the nature of American national interests, and informed the decisions that issued from Washington. Ideological suspicion of communism reinforced distrust of Soviet intentions. Americans viewed all dictators as the same, and all compromise as appeasement. At the same time, these fears warred with traditional American ambivalence toward European affairs and intervention abroad. American Cold War policy grew out of these contradictions. Containment drew from the ideological foundations of liberalism, anticommunism, and American mission.

The superpower conflict soon stalemated in Europe. By the 1960s Soviet and American positions had hardened, and little change seemed likely. Moreover, the ideological rivalry seemed to ease, such that some commentators such as Walter Lippmann began to believe by the early 1960s that the Cold War might be ending. Yet despite signs of a willingness to coexist in Europe and to open the way to a more "normal" diplomatic relationship through arms control and the like, the Soviet-American rivalry continued unabated in the Third World. Throughout the postwar period instability and conflict infected the old colonial areas of Southeast Asia, the Middle East, Africa, and Latin America as the imperial powers retreated. Rapid social and economic change hit the newly created postcolonial states, and they became ripe for outside intervention. Here was a crucial arena of the Cold War conflict.

At times at the invitation of local elites and at times of their own decision, the two superpowers intervened throughout the Third World, playing a violent and risky game of dominoes. And like Wilson in Mexico, American policymakers throughout the postwar period attempted to curb the radicalism of social change and to intervene on behalf of self-determination. Under the Cold War imperative of containing the spread of communism, they argued that the United States was spreading democracy abroad and acting on the side of right. Often, however, the United States supported very undemocratic regimes, such as those of Anastasio Somoza in Nicaragua and Carlos Castillo Armas in Guatemala. The effort to contain communism more often than not contradicted the lingering Wilsonian heritage. A deep ambivalence toward social change and revolution conflicted with the goal of spreading democracy abroad, particularly in societies long subject to colonial control. Thus, for every Alliance for Progress, the Kennedy administration's economic development program for Latin America, there was a Somoza in Nicaragua or a Ngo Dinh Diem in South Vietnam.

Nowhere did the contradictions among American ideals and the demands of American interests explode so spectacularly as Vietnam. And like the scholarly debate over the Cold War, the literature on Vietnam is rich with disagreement. Two studies of the Johnson administration illustrate this disjunction clearly. Lloyd Gardner in *Pay Any Price* emphasizes what he sees as the powerful hold that liberal ideals had over President Johnson. For Gardner, Johnson's intervention in Vietnam resulted from a deeply held belief in liberalism and an effort to promote American ideals abroad. A student of Williams, Gardner similarly finds tragedy amidst the ruins of American policy. Johnson's efforts to transplant liberalism and promote economic development amidst social revolution in Vietnam could not but end in failure.

Fredrik Logevall, by contrast, finds that liberal ideology mattered relatively little in Johnson's decision making. The president, Logevall argues in *Choosing War,* certainly had a vision for the future of Vietnam, a future shaped along liberal principles. But the driving force in his decision making was not that vision but rather his fears for his domestic political as well as his personal credibility. In Logevall's account the president and his advisers were gloomy realists on Vietnam in the key months following the 1964 election. Many of them were pessimistic about the prospects for success in the war, and many privately questioned whether the outcome really mattered to U.S. security. Thus Johnson's liberal rhetoric and economic development programs provided the window dressing for what was in reality a cynical and self-serving use of American power.

CONCLUSION

The disparity between these two accounts highlights the complexity of ideology and the continued disagreement among scholars over its role in the policy process. Moreover, the experience of the United States in the Third World reveals clearly how difficult it is to understand the role of ideology and how ambiguous that role can be. How, for example, do we reconcile American ideology of liberalism with the support of dictators such as Somoza? Must we see ideology as little more than a cynical tool of justification? Or did American officials truly believe in the rhetoric they used? If they believed it, did it drive their decision making? The answer to these questions seems to be an unsatisfying "sometimes." But that in itself is significant. "Sometimes" means that as scholars we must approach the empirical evidence with an open mind, willing to find ideology as a primary cause of decision making or as mostly irrelevant to the policy process. It seems reasonable to conclude that some periods of American history proved more ideological than others, and that some administrations were more influenced by it than others. Moreover, while ideology may always lurk in the background, it may be pushed aside by other considerations in the evolution of particular decisions.

In the context of the Cold War, an open-mindedness toward ideology seems especially important. The Cold War was not only a classic political power struggle, but neither was it a purely ideological conflict. The Cold War rivalry arose over the traditional problems of creating a stable postwar settlement and in particular finding a solution for the instability of central Europe. But the Cold War was also a rivalry between two states that each embraced a universalist ideology (Marxist-Leninism and liberal democracy, respectively), each made certain predictions about the future, and each held certain causative assumptions about the world. American foreign policy during the Cold War thus entwined ideology and interest. A close study of the period shows us the importance of ideology in foreign policy. To ignore ideology in the context of the Cold War is, in some respects, to miss the point.

At the same time, however, renewed scholarly interest in ideology and the continuing debate over its significance has revealed the difficulties the concept entails. For foreign relations historians, causality is a central concern. They want to zero in on why appeasement failed in the 1930s, or how the Cold War began, or why exactly the United States intervened in Vietnam. Finding the role of ideology in the context of these questions is quite a task. Little wonder that many have dismissed ideology altogether, and that even those who have embraced it have often done so with misgivings and qualifications. Yet despite these complexities, we should not too quickly consign ideology to the scholarly rubbish heap. As Geertz has pointed out, events unfold within the bounds of culture, which is open to interpretation. Thus, an awareness of the ideological context of particular decisions adds a layer of complexity and richness to our analysis. It allows us to understand why some policy options appeared more appealing than others, and why some received no attention at all.

Consider for a moment one final example. During the 1962 Cuban missile crisis, some among John F. Kennedy's advisers argued that the president should authorize a surprise attack on Cuba in an effort to destroy the Soviet missiles. It would have been a dangerous move. Moreover, it is likely that practical considerations would have prevented the plan from progressing beyond the conference table. Yet in rejecting the idea, Kennedy cited none of these reasons. Instead the president referred to the Japanese attack on Pearl Harbor. At the time Franklin Roosevelt had called it a day that would live in infamy. For Kennedy, a surprise attack on Cuba did not fit his image of the United States, and this policy option was quickly ruled out. To be sure, ideology did not determine the outcome of the missile crisis. But an examination of the ideological context of the decision offers us a greater degree of understanding of the Kennedy White House.

BIBLIOGRAPHY

Arendt, Hannah. *The Origins of Totalitarianism.* New ed. New York, 1973.

Campbell, David. *Writing Security: United States Foreign Policy and the Politics of Identity.* Rev. ed. Minneapolis, Minn., 1998. An analysis of American foreign policy from a postmodernist perspective.

Carlsnaes, Walter. *Ideology and Foreign Policy: Problems of Comparative Conceptualization.* Oxford and New York, 1987.

Gaddis, John Lewis. *We Now Know: Rethinking Cold War History.* Oxford and New York, 1997.

Gardner, Lloyd C. *Safe For Democracy: The Anglo-American Response to Revolution, 1913–1923.* New York, 1987.

———. *Pay Any Price: Lyndon Johnson and the Wars for Vietnam.* Chicago, 1995.

Geertz, Clifford. "Ideology as a Cultural System." In David E. Apter, ed. *Ideology and Discontent.* New York, 1964. See also "Thick Description: Toward an Interpretive Theory of Culture." In Clifford Geertz, *The Interpretation of Cultures.* New York, 1973. Of Geertz's many writings, these two essays offer the clearest explanation of his views on ideology.

Halle, Louis J. *The Cold War as History.* New ed. New York, 1991.

Hamilton, Malcolm B. "The Elements of the Concept of Ideology." *Political Studies* 35 (1987): 18–38. A useful analysis on the question of definition.

Hunt, Michael. *Ideology and U.S. Foreign Policy.* New Haven, Conn., 1987. An excellent starting place on the subject from a historical perspective. For an explanation by the same author of the complexities of ideology as a category of analysis, see "Ideology," in Michael J. Hogan and Thomas G. Paterson, eds. *Explaining the History of American Foreign Relations.* New York, 1991.

Kennan, George F. *American Diplomacy.* Expanded ed. Chicago, 1984. The classic realist critique of American foreign policy.

Larraín, Jorge. *Marxism and Ideology.* London and Atlantic Highlands, N.J., 1983.

Leffler, Melvyn. *A Preponderance of Power: National Security, the Truman Administration, and the Cold War.* Stanford, Calif., 1992. Highlights the role of national security calculations in early Cold War policymaking.

Logevall, Fredrik. *Choosing War: The Lost Chance for Peace and the Escalation of War in Vietnam.* Berkeley, Calif., 1999.

Lukacs, John. *The End of the Twentieth Century and the End of the Modern Age.* New York, 1993.

Malia, Martin. *The Soviet Tragedy: A History of Socialism in Russia, 1917–1991.* New York, 1994.

McCoy, Drew R. *The Elusive Republic: Political Economy in Jeffersonian America.* Chapel Hill, N.C., 1980. An analysis of the role of republican ideology in early America.

McDougall, Walter A. *Promised Land, Crusader State: The American Encounter with the World Since 1776.* New York, 1997.

McLellan, David S. *Ideology.* Minneapolis, Minn., 1986. A straightforward introduction to the subject.

Morgenthau, Hans. *Politics Among Nations: The Struggle for Power and Peace.* 5th ed. New York, 1973. See especially chapters 7–8.

Mullins, Willard A. "On the Concept of Ideology in Political Science." *American Political Science Review* 66 (1972): 498–510. A helpful if somewhat dated survey.

Perkins, Bradford. *The Cambridge History of American Foreign Relations: The Creation of a Republican Empire, 1776–1865.* Vol. 1. Cambridge and New York, 1993.

Smith, Tony. *America's Mission: The United States and the Worldwide Struggle for Democracy in the Twentieth Century.* Princeton, N.J., 1994. Ideology, and particularly Wilsonian ideology, is central in this account of American foreign policy. For a contrasting view that examines American intervention in the Third World, see David F. Schmitz. *Thank God They're On Our Side: The United States and Right-Wing Dictatorships, 1921–1965.* Chapel Hill, N.C., 1999.

Stephanson, Anders. *Manifest Destiny: American Expansionism and the Empire of Right.* New York, 1995. A short but thoughtful look at how an ideology of destiny has shaped American foreign policy. An interpretation of American ideology during the Cold War by the same author is "Liberty or Death: The Cold War as U.S. Ideology." In Odd Arne Westad, ed. *Reviewing the Cold War: Approaches, Interpretation, Theory.* Portland, Ore., 2000.

Trachtenberg, Marc. *A Constructed Peace: The Making of the European Settlement, 1945–1963.* Princeton, N.J., 1999. A history of the Cold War written from a realist perspective.

Weber, Max. "The Social Psychology of the World Religions." In H. H. Gerth and C. Wright Mills, eds. *From Max Weber: Essays in Sociology.* New York, 1948.

Westad, Odd Arne. "Bernath Lecture: The New International History of the Cold War." *Diplomatic History* 24 (2000): 551–565.

Williams, William Appleman. *The Tragedy of American Diplomacy.* 2d ed. New York, 1972. The classic revisionist work on American foreign policy.

Zubok, Vladislav, and Constantine Pleshakov. *Inside the Kremlin's Cold War: From Stalin to Khrushchev.* Cambridge, Mass., 1996.

See also OPEN DOOR INTERPRETATION; REALISM AND IDEALISM; REVISIONISM.

IMMIGRATION

Roger Daniels

Immigration and immigration policy have been an integral part of the American polity since the early years of the American Republic. Until late in the nineteenth century it had been the aim of American policy, and thus its diplomacy, to facilitate the entrance of free immigrants. From the 1880s until World War II—an era of immigration restriction of increasing severity—the diplomacy of immigration was chiefly concerned with the consequences of keeping some people out and, after 1924, when Congress made the diplomatic establishment partially responsible for immigration selection and its control, with keeping some prospective immigrants out. Since 1945, after only seemingly minor changes in policy during World War II, and partly due to the shift in American foreign policy from quasi-isolation to a quest for global leadership and hegemony, immigration policy has become less and less restrictive. Cold War imperatives plus a growing tendency toward more egalitarian attitudes about ethnic and racial minorities contributed to a change in immigration policy.

Many foreigners clearly understood that there were certain ironies in these long-term changes. No one was more aware of this than the Chinese leader Deng Xiaoping. Visiting Washington in 1979 during a time when the United States was urging the Soviet Union to allow more Jews to emigrate, the Chinese leader, according to Jimmy Carter's memoirs, told the American president: "If you want me to release ten million Chinese to come to the United States I'd be glad to do that." Obviously, Deng was "pulling Carter's chain," but it is not clear from the text whether the Georgian realized that. Immigration was part of the raison d'être of the early Republic. One of the complaints in Thomas Jefferson's Declaration of Independence was that George III had "endeavoured to prevent the population of these States; for that purpose obstructing the Laws for Naturalization of Foreigners; refusing to pass others to encourage their migrations hither, and raising the conditions of new Appropriations of Lands." The Constitution, while not mentioning immigration directly, did instruct Congress "to establish an uniform Rule of Naturalization" (Article 1, Section 8) and provided that naturalized persons might hold any office under the Constitution save only President and Vice President. (Article 2, Section 1). The only other reference to migration referred obliquely to the African slave trade, providing that "the Migration or Importation of such Persons as any of the States now existing shall think proper to admit, shall not be prohibited by the Congress prior to the Year one thousand eight hundred and eight" (Article 1, Section 9).

In 1790 Congress passed the first naturalization act, limiting those eligible to "free white persons." This put the new nation on a collision course with Great Britain, which, although it had naturalization statutes of its own, often refused to recognize the switch of allegiance of its subjects. The question of the impressment of seamen was one of the issues that troubled Anglo-American relations from 1787, when the first of many American protests against impressment was made, until the end of the War of 1812. Foreign Secretary George Canning put the British case nicely when he declared that when British seamen "are employed in the private service of foreigners, they enter into engagements inconsistent with the duty of subjects. In such cases, the species of redress which the practice of all times has . . . sanctioned is that of taking those subjects at sea out of the service of such foreign individuals." Impressment, of course, became one of the issues that led to the War of 1812. After that the British recognized, in practice, the right of naturalization, but one of the ongoing tasks of American diplomatic officials has been trying to ensure that naturalized American citizens are recognized as such when they visit their former native lands. This has been particularly a problem for men of military age during time of war.

While barring the African slave trade at the earliest possible moment in 1808, immigration "policy" in the new nation universally welcomed free immigrants. American leaders understood that immigration was necessary to fill up their largely empty and expanding country and would have endorsed the nineteenth-century Argentine statesman Juan Bautista Alberdi's maxim that "to govern is to populate." Even Millard Fillmore, while running for president on the nativist American Party ticket in 1856, found it necessary to insist that he had "no hostility to foreigners" and "would open wide the gates and invite the oppressed of every land to our happy country, excluding only the pauper and the criminal." Actually the gates were open, and Fillmore's suggestion of restriction on economic grounds would not become law until 1882. As long as American immigration policy welcomed all free immigrants there were no policy issues for American diplomats to negotiate. Immigration first became a special subject for diplomatic negotiation during the long run-up to the Chinese Exclusion Act of 1882.

A few Chinese had come to the United States—chiefly to East Coast ports—in the late eighteenth century in connection with the China trade. After American missionaries were established in China, some Chinese, mostly young men, came to the eastern United States for education without raising any stir. But relatively large-scale Chinese immigration, mostly to California beginning with the gold rush of 1849, produced an anti-Chinese movement. Before this movement became a national concern, Secretary of State William H. Seward appointed a former Massachusetts congressman, Anson Burlingame, as minister to China in 1861. He was the first to reside in Beijing. A radical former free-soiler and antislavery orator, Burlingame supported Chinese desires for equal treatment by the Western powers. While still in Beijing, he resigned his post in late 1867 and accepted a commission as China's first official envoy to the West. With an entourage that included two Chinese co-envoys and a large staff, he traveled to Britain, France, Germany, Russia, and the United States seeking modification of China's unequal status. He was successful only in Washington. There he negotiated in 1868 what became known as the Burlingame Treaty—actually articles added to the Treaty of Tientsin (1858). The 1868 agreement, China's first equal treaty, was ratified without controversy and contained the first immigration clause in any American treaty:

> The United States and the Emperor of China cordially recognize the inherent and inalienable right of man to change his home and allegiance and also the mutual advantage of free migration and emigration . . . for the purposes of curiosity, of trade, or as permanent residents . . . but nothing contained herein shall be held to confer naturalization upon the citizens of the United States in China, nor upon the subjects of China in the United States.

The United States would never again recognize a universal "right to immigrate," and by 1870 the anti-Chinese movement was becoming national. Spurred by economic distress in California and a few instances of Chinese being used as strikebreakers in Massachusetts, New Jersey, and Pennsylvania, anti-Chinese forces stemming largely from the labor movement made increasingly powerful demands for an end to Chinese immigration, usually blending their economic arguments with naked racism. That summer Congress was legislating the changes in the existing naturalization statute impelled by the end of slavery and the Fourteenth Amendment. Republican Senator Charles Sumner and a few other radicals wanted to make the new naturalization statute color blind, but the majority did not wish to extend that fundamental right to Chinese. The new statute amended the eligibility from "free white persons" to "white persons and to aliens of African nativity and persons of African descent."

In 1876 Congress created a joint congressional committee to investigate Chinese immigration. It took testimony in the Palace Hotel in San Francisco just before and after that year's presidential election. By that time both national party platforms had anti-Chinese planks. The Republican version was somewhat tentative, declaring it "the immediate duty of Congress to investigate the effects of the immigration and importation of Mongolians." The out-of-power Democrats denounced "the policy which tolerates the revival of the coolie-trade in Mongolian women held for immoral purposes, and Mongolian men to perform servile labor." The majority report of the joint congressional committee claimed that the Pacific Coast had to become "either American or Mongolian," insisting that there was "not sufficient brain capacity in the Chinese race to furnish motive power for self-government" and that "there is no Aryan or European race which is not far superior to the Chinese." The committee report urged the president to get the Burlingame Treaty modified and Congress to legislate against

"Asiatic immigration." The report was presented to Congress while it was settling the election of 1876, so no immediate action was taken. After much debate the next Congress passed the so-called Fifteen Passenger bill, which barred any vessel from bringing in more than fifteen Chinese immigrants. The sticking point for many was the existing Burlingame Treaty: some wanted to override it completely while others wanted to wait until the treaty was revised. The bill also instructed the president to notify the Chinese that portions of the treaty were abrogated, which passage of the bill would have accomplished.

Rutherford B. Hayes responded with a reasoned veto message that accepted the desirability of stemming Chinese immigration. He argued that the Chinese manifested "all the traits of race, religion, manners, and customs, habitations, mode of life, segregation here, and the keeping up of the ties of their original home . . . [which] stamp them as strangers and sojourners, and not as incorporated elements of our national life." But, he insisted, there was no emergency to justify unilateral abrogation of the treaty, which could have disastrous consequences for American merchants and missionaries in China. He promised that there would be a renegotiation of the treaty.

A somewhat protracted diplomatic renegotiation was completed by the end of 1880, and the new treaty was ratified and proclaimed in October 1881. It unilaterally gave the United States the right to "regulate, limit, or suspend" the "coming or residence" of Chinese laborers, but it allowed Chinese subjects "proceeding to the United States as teachers, students, merchants, or from curiosity, together with their body and household servants, and Chinese laborers now in the United States to go and come of their own free will and accord."

In the spring of 1882, Congress passed a bill suspending the immigration of Chinese laborers for twenty years. President Chester A. Arthur vetoed it, arguing that while a permanent bar to Chinese labor might be eventually justified, prudence dictated a shorter initial term. Congress responded by repassing the bill but with a ten-year suspension, and Arthur signed it into law in May 1882. The law prohibited the entry of Chinese laborers—defined as "both skilled and unskilled laborers and Chinese employed in mining"—after 4 August 1882. It also provided that any Chinese who was in the country on 17 November 1880—the effective date of the Sino-American treaty—or had come between that date and 4 August 1882 had the right to leave and return. The law, as opposed to the treaty, did not spell out who was entitled to enter, although it did specify that diplomats and other officials of the Chinese government doing government business, along with their body and household servants, were admissible. Fines for bringing Chinese in illegally could run as high as $1,000 per individual, and vessels landing Chinese illegally were liable to seizure and condemnation.

Thus, what is commonly called the Chinese Exclusion Act—its proper title is "To Execute Certain Treaty Stipulations Relating to Chinese"—became law. The typical textbook treatment is a sentence or two, sometimes relating it to other discriminatory treatment. Its real significance goes much deeper than that. Viewed from the perspective of the early twenty-first century, the Exclusion Act is clearly a pivot on which subsequent American immigration policy turned, the hinge on which the poet Emma Lazarus's "Golden Door" began to swing toward a closed position. It initiated what can be called an era of steadily increasing restrictions on immigration of all kinds that would last for sixty-one years. It was also the first time that immigration policy per se became a focal point of a bilateral diplomatic relationship between the United States and another nation.

During the exclusion era—1882–1943—the problematic enforcement of changing immigration statutes and regulations for Chinese created future diplomatic problems, brought the principle of family reunification into American immigration policy, shaped the culture of immigration enforcement in the United States, and established a precedent for negotiations about American immigration policies. Various changes, generally of a more restrictive character, were added to the Chinese exclusion laws and regulations between 1882 and 1902, when a modified law extended them "until otherwise provided by law." These changes exacerbated relations and triggered repeated negotiations between the two nations.

The most significant of these negotiations occurred in the aftermath of the Geary Act of 1892, which not only extended exclusion for ten years but also required that all Chinese in the United States get a residence certificate (a kind of internal passport) within a year or be deported. The statute also reversed the usual presumption of innocence and provided that "any Chinese person or person of Chinese descent" was deemed to be in the country illegally unless he or she could demonstrate otherwise. This set off a mass civil disobedience campaign orchestrated by Chinese-

American community organizations. They urged Chinese Americans not to register and hired a trio of leading constitutional lawyers to challenge the statute. Their suit, *Fong Yue Ting* v. *United States* (1893), was expedited to the Supreme Court, which quickly ruled, five to three, against Fong and two other litigants. Justice Horace Gray, writing for the majority, held that Chinese, like other resident aliens, were entitled "to the safeguards of the Constitution, and to the protection of the laws, in regard to their rights of persons and of property, and to their civil and criminal responsibility," but insisted that the Constitution could not shield them if Congress decided that "their removal is necessary or expedient for the public interest."

At the time of the Court's ruling only some 13,000 Chinese had registered; perhaps 90,000 had not and were presumably liable to immediate deportation. But both cabinet officers responsible for enforcement—Treasury Secretary John G. Carlisle and Attorney General Richard Olney—instructed their subordinates not to enforce the law. Carlisle estimated that mass deportations would cost at least $7.3 million and noted that his annual enforcement budget was $25,000. Secretary of State Walter Q. Gresham confidentially informed the Chinese minister, Yung Yu, that Congress would soon amend the law so that Chinese could register even though the deadline had passed. In November 1893, Congress extended the deadline by six months, and in that time about 93,000 additional Chinese registered and received the disputed certificates.

While relations between China and the United States were complicated by actions of the federal government toward immigrants, those between Italy and the United States deteriorated because of discrimination by lesser governmental bodies. There was widespread violence directed against Italian Americans, but one outbreak in particular had the most serious international consequences. On 15 October 1890 the police superintendent in New Orleans was murdered by a group of men using sawed-off shotguns; before he died he whispered that the Italians had done it. He had been investigating so-called Mafia influence among the city's large Italian-American population. New Orleans authorities quickly arrested almost 250 local Italian Americans and eventually indicted nineteen of them, including one fourteen-year-old boy, for the murder. Nine were brought to trial. On 13 March 1891 the jury found six not guilty and could not agree on three others. All nine were returned to jail for trial on another charge. The day after the verdict, a notice signed by sixty-one prominent local residents was placed in the morning newspaper inviting "all good citizens" to a 10 A.M. mass meeting "to remedy the failure of justice." A mob of perhaps 5,000 persons assembled, and, led by three members of the local bar, went first to the arsenal where many were issued firearms and then to the parish prison, where they shot and killed eight incarcerated Italians and removed three others and lynched them. Three or four of the victims were Italian citizens and the others were naturalized American citizens. None of the mob was ever punished.

Local public opinion hailed the result, as did much of the nation's press. The *New York Times* wrote that the victims were "sneaking and cowardly Sicilians, the descendants of bandits and assassins" but insisted in the same editorial that the lynching "was not incited by any prejudice against Italians." The Italian government protested, demanding punishment for the lynchers, protection for the Italian Americans of New Orleans, and an indemnity. President Benjamin Harrison himself, acting during an illness of Secretary of State James G. Blaine, directed the American minister in Rome to explain "the embarrassing gap in federalism—that in such cases the state alone has jurisdiction," while rejecting all the demands. There was nothing new about this. Similar responses had been made by the federal government in a number of previous instances, most notably in 1851 when Spaniards had been killed in New Orleans; in 1885 after the Rock Springs, Wyoming, massacre of twenty-eight Chinese miners; and in a whole host of other outrages, mostly against Chinese in the Far West. In all of these cases the president eventually called upon Congress to make an ex gratia payment. Congress, after debate, did so, and the matters were ended. For the Rock Springs affair, for example, the payment was nearly $150,000.

The lynching of Italians in New Orleans took a somewhat different course to the same essential result. Exasperated by the initial stonewalling, the Italian government recalled its minister in Washington but did not break relations. There was foolish talk of war in the press—all agreed that the Italian navy was superior to the American—and naval preparedness advocates used the speculation to their advantage. Eventually good relations were restored, but Harrison settled the matter without the traditional reference to Congress. In his December 1892 message to Congress Harrison reported the payment of

$24,330.90 (125,000 francs) to the Italian government, a little over $6,000 per person. The money was taken from the general appropriation for diplomatic expenses. Congress was furious—or pretended to be—because of executive usurpation of its prerogatives and reduced the fund for diplomatic contingencies by $20,000.

A more complex and potentially more serious situation developed from the mistreatment of Japanese in the United States—more serious because of the growing hostility between the United States and Japan over conflicting plans for Pacific expansion and more complex because both local and national discrimination was involved and because major tensions about Japanese immigrants continued for more than two decades. Long before diplomatic tensions over Japanese immigration to western states and the Territory of Hawaii surfaced, Tokyo had shown concern about possible mistreatment of its immigrants in America. As early as the 1890s internal Japanese diplomatic correspondence shows that there were fears in Tokyo that emigrant Japanese workers in the United States, who in many places were filling niches once occupied by Chinese workers, would eventually evoke the same kinds of official treatment—exclusion—that Chinese workers had experienced. This, Japanese officials were convinced, would negatively affect Japan's ambitions to achieve great-power status. The greatest fear—Tokyo's worst nightmare about this subject—was that someday there would be a "Japanese Exclusion Act." This fear—and eventually resentment at the result, which was in effect exclusion—so pervaded Japanese culture that for decades Japanese texts continued to refer to the U.S. Immigration Act of 1924 as the "Japanese Exclusion Act."

Anti-Japanese activity had flared in race-sensitive California as early as 1892, when there were fewer than 5,000 Japanese persons in the entire country. In 1905 the state's leading newspaper, the *San Francisco Chronicle,* began what can be called an anti-Japanese immigrant crusade—a crusade that the rival publisher William Randolph Hearst soon made his own. In the same year San Francisco labor leaders organized the Japanese and Korean Exclusion League, the California legislature passed a resolution calling on Congress to "limit and diminish Japanese immigration," and two California congressmen introduced the first bills calling for exclusion of Japanese into Congress.

Although these events all took place beneath the radar of national press consciousness, they did not escape the notice of the man in the White House. In May 1905, Theodore Roosevelt fumed in a (private) letter about the "foolish offensiveness" of the [mostly Republican] "idiots" of the California legislature, while indicating sympathy for the notion of exclusion of Japanese and muttering about their being "a serious problem in Hawaii." Two months later he instructed the U.S. Minister to Japan, Lloyd C. Griscom, to inform Tokyo that "the American Government and . . . people" had no sympathy with the agitation and that while "I am President" Japanese would be treated like "other civilized peoples." In his prolix annual message of December 1905, Roosevelt insisted that there should be no discrimination "against any man" who wished to immigrate and be a good citizen, and he specifically included Japanese in a short list of examples of acceptable ethnic groups. In the next paragraph, Roosevelt, who had signed the 1902 extension of Chinese exclusion without hesitation, made it clear that Chinese laborers, "skilled and unskilled," were not acceptable.

Almost a year later, on 11 October 1906, the San Francisco Board of Education ordered all Japanese and Korean pupils to attend the long established "Oriental" school in Chinatown. The announcement attracted little attention in the San Francisco press and seems to have been ignored outside California until nine days later, when garbled reports of what had happened were printed in Tokyo newspapers claiming that all Japanese pupils had been excluded from the public schools. Roosevelt reacted quickly. He wrote his high-ranking Harvard classmate Baron Kentaro Kaneko that he would take action; he also met with and gave similar assurances to the Japanese minister, Viscount Siuzo Aoki, and dispatched a cabinet member and former California congressman, Secretary of Commerce and Labor Victor H. Metcalf, to San Francisco to investigate the matter. In his December 1906 annual message the president formally recommended legislation "providing for the naturalization of Japanese who come here intending to become American citizens." Roosevelt made no serious effort to get such legislation introduced, let alone passed, and just two months later Secretary of State Elihu Root, in reacting to a Japanese proposal that acceptance of exclusion be traded for naturalization, informed American negotiators that "no statute could be passed or treaty ratified" that granted naturalization.

Secretary Metcalf's report was made public on 18 December 1906 and showed that rather than the hundreds or thousands of Japanese pupils discussed in the press there were only ninety-five Japanese students in the entire San Francisco school system, twenty-five of them native-born American citizens. He did find that twenty-seven of the aliens were teenagers enrolled in inappropriate grades because of language problems; the most extreme example was two nineteen-year-olds in the fourth grade. Metcalf's report recommended that age-grade limits be enforced, something that was acceptable to the Japanese community. Otherwise Metcalf found the segregation order unjust and against the public interest. But since the Supreme Court's decision in *Plessy v. Ferguson* (1896) had affirmed the legality of racial segregation in the United States, the federal government had no power over a state's right to practice it. California politicians of all parties, undoubtedly representing the will of their constituents, adamantly refused to mitigate their discrimination in any way, and, in the session of the legislature that began in January 1907, proposed enacting more anti-Japanese legislation. Roosevelt and Root set to work to ameliorate the situation, and, in something over a year, worked out a solution that is known as the Gentlemen's Agreement, the substance of which is contained in six notes exchanged between the two governments in late 1907 and early 1908. It is instructive to note that Root actually instituted an action in the northern federal district court of California to prohibit segregation of alien Japanese schoolchildren, who enjoyed most-favored-nation rights under the existing commercial treaty with Japan, but could do nothing for the pupils who were American citizens.

In the event, no suit was necessary. Roosevelt summoned members of the school board to Washington, jawboned them in the White House, and got them to rescind their order in February 1907. (The only Japanese pupils actually segregated in California were in a few rural districts around Sacramento. Although that segregation continued, no fuss was made about it, so the Japanese government, which was concerned with "face" rather than principle, never complained.) Then Congress passed an amendment, drafted in the State Department, to a pending immigration bill, which enabled the president to bar by executive order persons with passports issued for any country other than the United States from entering the country. Japan, in turn, agreed to mark any passports issued to laborers, skilled or unskilled, who had not previously established American residence, as not valid for the United States. But the eventual agreement allowed Japan to issue passports valid for the United States to "laborers who have already been in America and to the parents, wives and children of laborers already resident there." Thus the principle of family reunification, which would become a hallmark of American immigration policy, was first introduced as a part of the process of restricting Asian immigration.

The Gentlemen's Agreement is an excellent example of the "unintended consequences" that have characterized much of the legal side of American immigration history. The diplomats and politicians involved assumed that with labor immigration at an end the Japanese American population would decline and the problems that its presence created in a white-dominated racist society would gradually fade away. They did not realize that through the family reunification provisions of the agreement tens of thousands of Japanese men would bring wives to California. Many if not most of these were "picture brides," women married by proxy in Japan to men who in most instances they would not see until they came to America. Most of these newly married couples soon had children who were American citizens by virtue of being born on American soil, which meant that the American Japanese population grew steadily. Eventually the anti-Japanese forces in the United States campaigned without success for a constitutional amendment that would repeal the "birthright citizenship" clause of the Fourteenth Amendment and make the children of "aliens ineligible to citizenship" similarly ineligible. (In the 1970s nativist forces in the United States revived such demands but with a different target: they proposed making the American-born children of illegal immigrants ineligible for automatic citizenship.) When the Gentlemen's Agreement went into effect there were probably some 60,000 Japanese persons in the continental United States, the vast majority of them aliens. By 1940 there were more than 125,000, more than two-thirds of them native-born American citizens. Many white Californians and other concerned westerners who had been assured that the Gentlemen's Agreement was tantamount to exclusion came to believe that they had been betrayed by the uncaring politicians back east.

But even before the demographic consequences of the Gentlemen's Agreement became clear, a second crisis arose over Japanese immigrants. This one erupted in 1913 and focused on land rather than on people. Although most Japanese immigrants had come to California as laborers, many soon were able to become agricultural proprietors. As early as 1909 bills had been introduced into the California legislature barring the sale of agricultural land to Japanese, but Republican governors then and in 1911—the California legislature met only every other year—cooperated with Republican presidents in Washington and "sat upon the lid," as Governor Hiram W. Johnson put it. But in 1913, with Johnson still governor and Democrat Woodrow Wilson in the White House, the lid was off. Although Washington was again taken unawares by the crisis, Tokyo had been expecting it. Its consul general in San Francisco had warned in November 1912 that "the fear-laden anti-Japanese emotion of the people [of California] is a sleeping lion." By the time Wilson took office on 4 March 1913, bills restricting Japanese and other alien landholding had made considerable progress in the California legislature. The Japanese ambassador, Sutemi Chinda, called on the president during Wilson's second day in office: his dispatch to Tokyo quoted Wilson as saying "that the constitution did not allow the federal government to intervene in matters relating to the rights of the individual states." After much debate and publicity, in mid-April the California legislature passed legislation forbidding the ownership of agricultural land by "aliens ineligible to citizenship." This, of course, pointed the bill at Japanese, although it also affected other Asians. Californians argued that the discrimination—if such it was—was caused by federal rather than state law.

Even before Governor Johnson signed the bill, angry anti-American demonstrations erupted in Tokyo: the California legislature had again helped to create an international crisis. The Wilson administration, while trying to adhere to traditional states' rights doctrines, nevertheless felt that it had to at least seem to be taking action. Wilson sent Secretary of State William Jennings Bryan on a cross-country train trip to Sacramento to meet with Governor Johnson and the legislature and urged that the bill not be enacted before Bryan arrived. In the event, Bryan's trip was anticlimactic. Unlike Roosevelt and Root, Wilson and Bryan had nothing to offer the Californians in return for moderation. Bryan returned to Washington, and Johnson signed the Alien Land Act into law: eventually ten other western states passed similar measures.

The California law, which was strengthened in 1920, was relatively ineffective. Japanese farmers and the white entrepreneurs with whom they dealt evaded the law in a number of ways, most of which had been foreseen by Johnson and his advisers. The two major methods were placing land in the name of citizen children or leasing rather than purchasing the land. For a few relatively large-scale operators adoption of a corporate form was also effective. When the California legislature passed an amendment to the land act barring "aliens ineligible to citizenship" from exercising guardianship over their citizen children, the federal courts ruled that such a statute violated the constitutional rights of those children to have their natural parents as guardians.

These disputes, of course, helped to poison relations between Japan and the United States, which were already problematic on other grounds. During the Versailles treaty negotiations and in early sessions of the League of Nations, Japan tried to get questions of immigration and racial equality discussed but the imperialist powers successfully stifled every attempt. (Of course Japan did not have clean hands in such matters, but that is another story.) The final and most traumatic act in the conflicts between the Pacific powers over immigration came in 1924 and involved federal rather than state discrimination.

By the 1920s the American people and the Congress were ready for a general and massive curtailment of immigration. Prior to that time statutory immigration restriction based on race or national origin had been directed only at Asians. The Immigration Act of 1917—best known for imposing a literacy test on some immigrants—had created a "barred zone" expressed in degrees of latitude and longitude, which halted the immigration of most Asians not previously excluded or limited. The first statute to limit most immigration, the Quota Act of 1921, placed numerical limits on European immigration while leaving immigration from the Western Hemisphere largely alone; it did not directly impact Japanese immigration, which was still governed by the Gentlemen's Agreement of 1907–1908. Under the 1921 act Japan got a small quota, and Tokyo could not and did not complain that the law was discriminatory. Had Japan been treated as European nations were in the 1924 statute, it would have received the minimum quota of 100, but the version of the more generally restrictive 1924 law that passed the House contained overt discrimination against Japanese by forbidding the immigration of "aliens ineligible to citizenship." In an ill-starred attempt to preserve the Gentlemen's Agreement, Secretary of State Charles Evans Hughes suggested verbally that

>
>
> ## THE IMMIGRATION ACT OF 1965
>
> The Immigration Act of 1965 changed the face of America and is one of three laws passed that year—the others being the Voting Rights Act and the establishment of Medicare and Medicaid—which collectively represent the high-water mark of twentieth-century American liberalism. Yet the immigration statute was not always so perceived. At the signing ceremony on Liberty Island, with Ellis Island in the background, President Lyndon Johnson minimized the act's importance: "The bill that we sign today is not a revolutionary bill. It does not affect the lives of millions. It will not reshape the structure of our daily lives, or add importantly to our wealth and power."
>
> The law, in fact, changed the focus of immigration to the United States, greatly increasing the share going to Asia and the Western Hemisphere, and, through its heightened emphasis on family migration, led to a massive increase in the volume of immigration. Johnson was not dissimulating in his assessment. He was repeating what his advisers in the State and Justice departments had told him. They had focused on righting what they saw to be past mistakes of American immigration policy, and Johnson, following them, stressed the wrong done to those "from southern or eastern Europe." Members of both departments had testified before Congress that few persons from the Third World would enter under its provisions, and it is highly doubtful that the law would have been recommended or enacted had anyone understood what the results would be. Political scientists later developed the concept of unintended consequences. As Stephen M. Gillion points out in *"That's Not What We Meant to Do"* (2000), the 1965 Immigration Act is one of the prime examples of this phenomenon.

Japanese Ambassador Masanao Hanihara write him a letter explaining the Gentlemen's Agreement, whereupon the American would transmit the letter to the Senate in an attempt to get the offending phrase removed. The note, which was not in itself either threatening or blustering, did contain the phrase "grave consequences" in referring to what might happen if the law were enacted with the offending phrase. Henry Cabot Lodge and other senators insisted that the phrase was a "veiled threat" against the United States and stampeded the Senate into accepting the House language. In *The Presidency of Calvin Coolidge* (1998), the historian Robert H. Ferrell presented evidence suggesting that Hughes and others in the State Department either drafted or helped to draft the original note, something that all those concerned categorically denied at the time and later.

How grave were the actual consequences? No one can say. Japan and the United States might well have engaged in what became a "war without mercy" even if no Japanese immigrant had ever come to America. But some authorities, such as George F. Kennan, have argued that the "long and unhappy story" of U.S.–Japanese relations were negatively affected by the fact that "we would repeatedly irritate and offend the sensitive Japanese by our immigration policies and the treatment of people of Japanese lineage."

The 1924 act, which established a pattern of immigration restriction that prevailed until 1965, also established a "consular control system" by providing that aliens subject to immigration control could not be admitted to the United States without a valid visa issued by an American consular officer abroad. Visas were first required as a wartime measure in a 1918 act and were continued in peacetime by a 1921 act, but they were primarily an identification device. The 1924 act for the first time made the visa a major factor in immigration control. Although the State Department often claimed that Congress had tied the government's hands, the fact of the matter is that since 1924 much actual restriction of immigration has been based on the judgment of the individual federal officials administering it. That responsibility has been shared between the State Department and the Immigration and Naturalization Service (INS), then in the Department of Labor but switched to the Department of Justice in 1940. The diplomatic control is exercised by granting or failing to grant visas; the INS control is exercised largely at the borders, although since 1925 some INS personnel have been attached to some American embassies abroad as technical advisers. (The number of foreign countries with INS personnel has fluctuated. At the outset of the twenty-first century they were operating in thirty-eight countries. In Canada and a few other places, mostly in the Western Hemisphere, it has become possible to clear U.S. immigration and customs while still on foreign soil.)

The American foreign service—which was white, Christian (overwhelmingly Protestant), and elitist—had long exercised a largely negative influence on American immigration policy. Consular reports had provided much ammunition for the immigration restriction movement since the late nineteenth century. The tenure of Wilbur J. Carr as, in effect, head of the consular service from 1909 to 1937, placed a determined and convinced anti-Semitic nativist in a position to shape the formulation of both immigration and refugee policy. We now know that Carr, a skilled and manipulative bureaucrat, regularly fed anti-immigrant excerpts from unpublished consular reports to restrictionists such as Representative Albert Johnson, chief author of the 1924 immigration act. One Carr memo to him described Polish and Russian Jews as "filthy, Un-American and often dangerous in their habits." Many American consuls shared these views. Richard C. Beer, for example, a career officer serving in Budapest in 1922–1923, complained that the law forced him to give visas to Hungarians, Gypsies, and Jews who were all barbarians and gave his office an odor that "no zoo in the world can equal." Other consular officials, who might not have held such views, took their cues from their chief and the whole tone of the foreign service. During what was left of the "prosperity decade" after 1924 the INS and the State Department were pretty much on the same nativist page, although some INS officials resented their loss of control.

Although there were no statutory limits on immigration from independent nations of the Western Hemisphere until 1965, President Herbert Hoover administratively limited Mexican and other Latin American immigration by use of the highly subjective "likely to become a public charge" clause that had been on the statute books since 1882. The clause had originally been designed to keep out persons who for reasons of physical or mental disability were patently unable to support themselves. From the Hoover administration on, the clause has been interpreted at times to bar persons who were able-bodied but poor. The prospective immigrant could be stopped at the border or at an immigrant receiving station by INS personnel or could have a visa denied by someone in the diplomatic service in the country of origin.

The onset of the Great Depression temporarily reduced immigration pressures—during two years in the early 1930s more immigrants left the United States than entered it—but an entirely different situation developed after the Nazi seizure of power in Germany. The unprecedented situation of large numbers of refugees and would-be refugees stemming from a western European power had not been foreseen by the drafters of American immigration legislation. The United States had an immigration policy but not a refugee policy. Congress had previously been favorable to political and religious refugees. Restrictive immigration acts dating from the nineteenth century barred persons with criminal records but always specifically excluded those convicted of political offenses. As late as 1917, in the part of a statute imposing a not very strenuous literacy test as a criterion for admission, Congress specifically exempted any person seeking admission "to avoid religious persecution."

By 1933, however, under the stresses of the Great Depression and after going through what John Higham has aptly termed the "tribal twenties," Congress was in no mood to ease immigration restrictions. And although some of the later apologists for the lack of an effective American refugee policy before the onset of the Holocaust put all or most of the onus on Congress, the administration of Franklin D. Roosevelt must share that blame. There was nothing even resembling a new deal for immigration policy. To be sure, New Dealers at the top of Frances Perkins's Department of Labor, which continued to administer the INS until 1940, were much more sympathetic to immigrant concerns than the labor movement bureaucrats who had previously run the department. But the anti-immigrant culture of the INS continued. Moreover, the State Department's personnel and policies about immigration and many other matters were little affected by the New Deal. The administrative regulation of immigration was tightened during the early years of the Depression by both sets of government agents: the consular officials abroad and the INS at the borders.

Jews and others seeking visas in the 1930s quickly learned that some American consuls were better than others. George S. Messersmith, consul general in Berlin in the early 1930s and minister to Austria before the *Anschluss,* at a time when the German quota was undersubscribed, gained a positive rating from Jewish individuals and organizations. Even more proactive for refugees was Messersmith's successor in Berlin, Raymond

Geist, who on occasion actually went to concentration camps to arrange the release of Jews with American visas. Although there is no thorough study of the work of American consular officials in Europe during the period between 1933 and Pearl Harbor, it is clear that men like Messersmith and Geist were exceptions and that the majority of consuls were indifferent if not hostile to Jews desiring American visas. The signals consuls received from Carr and other officials in the State Department certainly encouraged them to interpret the law as narrowly as possible.

For example, when Herbert Lehman, Franklin Roosevelt's successor as governor of New York, wrote the president on two occasions in 1935 and 1936 about the difficulties German Jews were having in getting visas from American consulates, Roosevelt assured him, in responses drafted by the State Department, that consular officials were carrying out their duties "in a considerate and humane manner." Irrefutable evidence exists in a number of places to demonstrate that, to the contrary, many officials of the Department of State at home and abroad consistently made it difficult and in many cases impossible for fully eligible refugees to obtain visas. One example will have to stand as surrogate for hundreds of demonstrable cases of consular misfeasance and malfeasance. Hebrew Union College (HUC) in Cincinnati, the oldest Jewish seminary in America, had a Refugee Scholars Project that between 1935 and 1942 brought eleven such scholars to its campus. The 1924 immigration act specifically exempted from quota restriction professors and ministers of any religion as well as their wives and minor children. There should have been no difficulties on the American end in bringing the chosen scholars to Cincinnati. But in almost every case the State Department and especially Avra M. Warren, head of the visa division, raised difficulties, some of which seem to have been invented. In some instances the college, often helped by the intervention of influential individuals, managed to overcome them. In two instances, however, the college was unsuccessful.

The men involved were Arthur Spanier and Albert Lewkowitz. Spanier had been the Hebraica librarian at the Prussian State Library, and after the Nazis dismissed him, a teacher at the Hochschule für die Wissenschaft des Judentums. After *Kristallnacht* in November 1938, Spanier was sent to a concentration camp. The guaranteed offer of an appointment was enough to get him released from the camp but not enough to get him an American visa. The president of Hebrew Union College had to go to Washington even to discover why this was the case. Warren explained that the rejection was because Spanier's principal occupation was as a librarian and because after 1934 the Nazis had demoted the *Hochschule* (a general term for a place of higher education) to a *Lehranstalt* (educational institute), and an administrative regulation of the State Department not found in the statute held that a nonquota visa could not be given to a scholar coming to a high status institute in the United States from one of lower status abroad. Lewkowitz, a teacher of philosophy at the Breslau Jewish Theological Seminary, did get an American visa in Germany. Both men were able to get to the Netherlands and were there when the Germans invaded. The German bombing of Rotterdam destroyed Lewkowitz's papers, and American consular officials there insisted that he get new documents from Germany, an obviously impossible requirement. Visaless, both men were sent to the Bergen-Belsen concentration camp. Lewkowitz was one of the few concentration camp inmates exchanged, and he reached Palestine in 1944. Spanier was murdered in Bergen-Belsen. If highly qualified scholars with impressive institutional sponsorship had difficulties, one can imagine what it was like for less well-placed individuals.

Apart from creating difficulties for refugees seeking visas, the State Department consistently downplayed international attempts to solve or ameliorate the refugee situation. For example, in 1936 brain trusters Felix Frankfurter and Raymond Moley urged Roosevelt to send a delegation that included such prominent persons as Rabbi Stephen S. Wise to a 1936 League of Nations conference on refugees. The president instead took the advice of the State Department and sent only a minor diplomatic functionary as an observer. It was then politic for him to accept the State Department's insistence that "the status of all aliens is covered by law and there is no latitude left to the Executive to discuss questions concerning the legal status of aliens." When Roosevelt wanted to do something to he could almost always find a way. Immediately after the *Anschluss,* he directed that the Austrian quota numbers be used to expand the German quota, and shortly after *Kristallnacht,* he quietly directed the INS that any political or religious refugees in the United States on six-month visitor's visas could have such visas extended or rolled over every six months. Perhaps 15,000 persons were thus enabled to stay in the United States. On more public occasions however, such as the infamous early 1939 voyage of the German liner *Saint Louis,* loaded with nearly a thousand refugees whose Cuban visas had been canceled, he again took State Department advice and turned a deaf ear to appeals for American visas while the vessel hove to just off Miami Beach. The *Saint Louis* returned its passengers to Europe, where many of them perished in the Holocaust.

After the Nazis overran France, Roosevelt showed what a determined president could do. In the summer of 1940 he instructed his Advisory Committee on Refugees to make lists of eminent refugees and told the State Department to issue visas for them. An agent named Varian Fry, operating out of Marseilles and with the cooperation of American vice consuls, managed to get more than a thousand eminent refugees into Spain and on to the United States. Those rescued by these means included Heinrich Mann, Marc Chagall, and Wanda Landowska. But at the same time, Roosevelt appointed his friend Breckinridge Long as assistant secretary of state. A confirmed nativist and anti-Semite, Long was in charge of the visa section and thus oversaw refugee policy. The president eventually became aware of the biases in the State Department, and when he decided in mid-1944 to bring in a "token shipment" of nearly a thousand refugees from American-run camps in Europe, he put Interior Secretary Harold L. Ickes in charge. Vice President Walter Mondale's acute 1979 observation that before and during the war the nations of the West "failed the test of civilization" is a sound assessment of American policy.

Two other wartime developments should be noted. First, the State Department became involved in American agricultural policy in connection with the wartime Bracero program, which brought temporary Mexican workers to the United States for work in agriculture and on railroads. The Mexican government was, with good reason, apprehensive about the treatment they might receive, so the State Department was in part responsible for the United States living up to its agreement. Second, the State Department was responsible for the wartime exchanges of diplomats and other enemy nationals with the Axis powers. It was also concerned with the treatment of American civilians in enemy hands, particularly Japan, and because of that justified concern persistently argued for humane treatment for both the few thousand interned Japanese nationals in INS custody and the 120,000 Japanese Americans, both citizen and alien, who were in the custody of the War Relocation Authority.

The war years also witnessed a historic if seemingly minor reversal of American immigration policy with the 1943 repeal of the Chinese Exclusion Act. Few episodes show the connection between immigration and foreign policy so explicitly. President Roosevelt sent a special message to Congress urging the action. Speaking as commander in chief, he regarded the legislation "as important in the cause of winning the war and of establishing a secure peace." Since China was a U.S. ally and its resistance depended in part on "the spirit of her people and her faith in her allies," the president argued for a show of support:

> We owe it to the Chinese to strengthen that faith. One step in this direction is to wipe from the statute books those anachronisms in our laws which forbid the immigration of Chinese people into this country and which bar Chinese residents from American citizenship. Nations, like individuals, make mistakes. We must be big enough to acknowledge our mistakes of the past and correct them.

In addition, Roosevelt argued that repeal would silence Japanese propaganda and that the small number of Chinese who would enter would cause neither unemployment nor job competition. The president admitted that "While the law would give the Chinese a preferred status over certain other Oriental people, their great contribution to the cause of decency and freedom entitles them to such preference. . . . Passage will be an earnest of our purpose to apply the policy of the good neighbor to our relations with other peoples."

The repeal of Chinese exclusion was thus sold as a kind of good-behavior prize not for Chinese Americans, thousands of whom were then serving in the U.S. armed forces, but for the Chinese people. Nevertheless, Roosevelt's hint about future policy was right on the mark. Within three years Congress would pass similar special legislation granting naturalization rights and quotas to Filipinos and "natives of India," and in 1952 it would enact legislation ending racial discrimination in naturalization policy. By that time the emphasis was on winning "hearts and minds" in the Cold War.

THE COLD WAR AND BEYOND

Even before the Cold War came to dominate almost every facet of American policies toward the rest of the world, attitudes about immigration and immigration policies were beginning to change, as were the policies themselves. The increasing prevalence of an internationalist ideology, membership in the United Nations, and a growing guilt about and horror at the Holocaust all combined to impel the United States to do something about the European refugee crisis symbolized by the millions of displaced persons there. After some crucial months of inaction, Harry Truman issued a presidential directive just before Christmas 1945 that got some refugees into the United States. One important and often overlooked aspect of this directive enabled voluntary agencies, largely religious, to sponsor refugees, which virtually negated the application of the "likely to become a public charge" clause in such cases. Previously, sponsorship of most refugees without significant assets had to be assumed by American relatives. But it was only after passage and implementation of the Displaced Persons Acts of 1948 and 1950 that the United States could be said to have a refugee policy, one that the increasingly more diverse personnel of the State Department helped to carry out. That legislation brought more than 400,000 European refugees into the United States and expanded the use of voluntary agencies—later called VOLAGS (Voluntary Agencies Responsible for Refugees)—such as the Catholic and Lutheran welfare organizations and the Hebrew Immigrant Aid Association. In addition, U.S. sponsorship of the United Nations Relief and Rehabilitation Administration and membership in its successors, the International Refugee Organization and the United Nations High Commission for Refugees, contributed to changed attitudes about and policies toward refugees even though general immigration policy remained tied to the quota principle introduced in 1921–1924, which lasted until 1965.

Even the notorious McCarran-Walter Immigration Act of 1952—a quintessential piece of Cold War legislation that passed over Truman's veto and seemed merely to continue the restrictive policies begun in 1921 and 1924—contained liberalizing provisions that were more significant than most of its advocates and opponents realized. Chief of these was the total elimination of a color bar in naturalization. While some of the impetus for this came from liberals on racial issues, the push from those impelled by Cold War imperatives was probably more important. State Department representatives and others testified how difficult it was to become the leader of what they liked to term the "free world" when American immigration and naturalization policies blatantly discriminated against the majority of the world's peoples. In addition, a growing understanding that an important diplomatic objective was to win the hearts and minds of peoples and not just the consent of governments made diplomats more aware of the significance of immigrants and immigration. For example, when Dalip Singh Saund, the first Asian-born member of Congress, was elected in 1956, the State Department and the United States Information Agency sponsored him and his wife on a tour of his native India.

Although the word "refugee" does not appear in the 1952 immigration act, an obscure section of it gave the attorney general discretionary parole power to admit aliens "for emergency reasons or for reasons in the public interest." This was the method that Roosevelt had used in 1944, without congressional authorization, to bring in nearly a thousand refugees. This allowed the executive branch to respond quickly to emergency situations such as the Hungarian revolt of 1956 and the Cuban revolution of 1959. Between the displaced persons acts of the Truman administration and the inauguration of Ronald Reagan in 1981 about 2.25 million refugees were admitted, with about 750,000 Cubans and 400,000 refugees from America's misbegotten wars in Southeast Asia the largest increments. Since during that period some 10.4 million legal immigrants entered the United States, refugees accounted for some 20 percent of the total.

Although most textbook accounts trace the transformation of post–World War II immigration and immigration policy to the act signed by Lyndon Johnson in the shadow of the Statue of Liberty in 1965, that is a gross exaggeration. The reality can be better glimpsed by considering the numerical incidence of immigration to colonial America and the United States over time. No official enumeration of immigration took place before 1819, but most authorities agree that perhaps a million European and African immigrants came before then. Between 1819 and the enactment of the 1924 immigration act some 36 million immigrants arrived. Between 1925 and 1945—with immigration inhibited first by the new restrictive law and then much more effectively by the Great Depression and World War II—nearly 2.5 million came, an average of fewer than 125,000 annually. In the decade before World War I more than a million came each year. Well into the post–World War II era, many authorities felt that as a major factor in American history immigration was a thing of the past, but as

LEGAL IMMIGRATION TO THE U.S. BY DECADE, 1951–1998	
Decade	Number
1951–1960	2,515,479
1961–1970	3,321,677
1971–1980	4,493,314
1981–1990	7,338,062
1991–1998	7,605,068
	(eight years only)

the table indicates, based on INS data, this was a serious misperception.

With the self deconstruction of the Soviet Union at the end of the 1980s, domestic policy began to reassume paramount importance in American policy, including immigration policy. Input from the Department of State assumed less significance in immigration matters than during the Cold War era, although the increased volume of immigration greatly taxed and often overtaxed American embassies and consulates. For example, the State Department was given the responsibility of administering the lottery provisions of the Immigration Reform and Control Act (IRCA) of 1986 and its successors. The department announced on 10 May 2001 that for the 2002 lottery its Consular Center in Williamsburg, Kentucky, had managed to sift 10 million qualified entries while rejecting an additional 3 million applicants for not following directions and notified 90,000 potential winners chosen at random what they had to do to gain admission to the United States as resident aliens. Each overseas applicant would have to pass an interview examination for eligibility at an American consulate; those applying from within the United States would apply through the INS. Only a maximum of 50,000 of the 90,000 could actually win and gain admittance to the United States along with certain of their qualified dependents. All paper work would have to be completed by 30 September 2002. Anyone who did not have a visa by then lost the presumed advantage of winning. Applications for the 2003 lottery were scheduled to take place during the following month, October 2002.

The major functions of IRCA were the so-called "amnesty," which legalized some 2.7 million immigrants illegally in the United States, the majority of whom were from Mexico, and the promise of effective control measures to "gain control of our borders" by more effective interdiction of illegal border crosses and intensified deportation of remaining resident illegals. This created great fears in many nations of the circum-Caribbean, particularly the Dominican Republic and El Salvador, whose economies were greatly dependent on immigrant remittances, that large numbers of their citizens would be excluded and their remittances ended. These fears were chimerical; borders remained porous. But, in the meantime, to cite just one example, President José Napoleón Duarte wrote President Reagan in early 1987 requesting that Salvadorans in the United States illegally be given "extended voluntary departure" (EVD) status, an aspect of the attorney general's parole power enabling illegal immigrants to remain. While EVD was usually granted on humanitarian grounds, Duarte stressed the economic loss if immigrant remittances ceased. Assistant Secretary of State Elliot Abrams, who had opposed EVD on humanitarian grounds, now supported it, but the negative views of the Department of Justice and the congressional leadership prevailed. Forms of EVD or its equivalent were put into place during the Clinton presidency for Salvadorans and Nicaraguans by both the administration and Congress.

The State Department also had to deal with increasing complaints from foreign countries about the execution of its citizens by the criminal justice systems of American states, most of which had been practicing capital punishment with increased enthusiasm at a time when many nations had abolished it. Since it is a legal action, the United States cannot even consider paying compensation of any kind.

The more than 25 million post-1950 immigrants, as is well known, have changed the face of America. As late as the 1950s, immigrants from Europe, who had contributed the lion's share of nineteenth- and early-twentieth century immigrants, still were a bare majority of all immigrants. By the 1980s, thanks largely to the liberal 1965 immigration act and the Refugee Act of 1980, the European share was down to about 10 percent, and immigrants from Latin America and Asia predominated. Although anti-immigrant attitudes again came to the fore in 1980s—sparked in part by Ronald Reagan's warnings about being overrun by "feet people"—and some scholars saw "a turn against immigration" and predicted effective legislative restriction of immigration, those feelings were not turned into an effective legislative consensus. At the beginning of the twenty-first century, immigration continued at a very high rate, and screening and facilitating that influx continued to be an important aspect of the work of American diplomacy.

BIBLIOGRAPHY

Breitman, Richard, and Alan M. Kraut. *American Refugee Policy and European Jewry, 1933–1945*. Bloomington, Ind., 1987. A good account of nativist sentiment and activity in the State Department.

Corbett, P. Scott. *Quiet Passages: The Exchange of Civilians Between the United States and Japan During the Second World War*. Kent, Ohio, 1987. Tells the story of the State Department's Special Division.

Daniels, Roger. *Coming to America: A History of Immigration and Ethnicity in American Life*. New York, 1990. Surveys immigration and naturalization policy.

———. *The Politics of Prejudice: The Anti-Japanese Movement in California and the Struggle for Japanese Exclusion*. 2d ed. Berkeley, Calif., 1991.

Dinnerstein, Leonard. *America and the Survivors of the Holocaust*. New York, 1982. Fundamental to an understanding of the postwar shift in American policy toward refugees.

Fry, Varian. *Surrender on Demand*. New York, 1945. Fry, whose papers are at Columbia University, tells his story.

Gillion, Steven M. *"That's Not What We Meant to Do": Reform and Its Unintended Consequences in Twentieth-Century America*. New York, 2000. A series of case studies, including one on the 1965 immigration act.

Higham, John. *Strangers in the Land: Patterns of American Nativism, 1860–1925*. New Brunswick, N.J., 1955. The classic work on American nativism.

Karlin, J. Alexander. "The Indemnification of Aliens Injured by Mob Violence." *Southwestern Social Science Quarterly* 25 (1945): 235–246. Treats indemnification for victims of violence.

Loewenstein, Sharon. *Token Refuge: The Story of the Jewish Refugee Shelter at Oswego, 1944–1946*. Bloomington, Ind., 1986. Describes the first mass shipment of refugees.

Meyer, Michael A. "The Refugee Scholars Project of the Hebrew Union College." In Bertram Wallace Korn, ed. *A Bicentennial Festschrift for Jacob Rader Marcus*. New York, 1976. Most instructive about difficulties to refugee admission created by the State Department.

Mitchell, Christopher, ed. *Western Hemisphere Immigration and U.S. Foreign Policy*. University Park, Pa., 1992. A collection of essays largely by political scientists.

Peffer, George Anthony. *If They Don't Bring Their Women Here: Chinese Female Immigration Before Exclusion*. Urbana, Ill., 1999.

Reimers, David M. *Still the Golden Door: The Third World Comes to America*. 2d ed. New York, 1992.

———. *Unwelcome Strangers: American Identity and the Turn Against Immigration*. New York, 1998. Along with *Still the Golden Door*, this book is part of the cutting edge of late-twentieth-century immigration history.

Sandmeyer, Elmer Clarence. *The Anti-Chinese Movement in California*. 2d ed. Urbana, Ill., 1991.

Schulzinger, Robert D. *The Making of the Diplomatic Mind: The Training, Outlook, and Style of United States Foreign Service Officers, 1908–1931*. Middletown, Conn., 1975. Although many works on the foreign service ignore its immigration functions, this work is a happy exception.

Schwartz, Donald. "Breckinridge Long." In John A. Garraty and Mark C. Carnes, eds. *American National Biography*. New York, 2000. This sketch makes the subject's prejudices explicit.

Smith, David A. "From the Mississippi to the Mediterranean: The 1891 New Orleans Lynching and Its Effects on United States Diplomacy and the American Navy." *Southern Historian* 19 (1998): 60–85.

Wilson, Theodore A. "Wilbur J. Carr." In John A. Garraty and Mark C. Carnes, eds. *American National Biography*. New York, 2000. This laudatory sketch of Wilbur J. Carr ignores Carr's prejudices and his role in immigration policy.

See also ASYLUM; DEPARTMENT OF STATE; REFUGEE POLICIES.

IMPERIALISM

David Healy

Imperialism, in its most precise traditional usage, means the forcible extension of governmental control over foreign areas not designated for incorporation as integral parts of the nation. The term is commonly used to mean any significant degree of national influence, public or private, over other societies; but to some it refers principally to foreign economic exploitation with or without other actions. In all usages, however, the essential element is that one society must in some way impose itself upon another in a continuing unequal relationship. Thus, American expansionism dated from the beginning of the national experience, while its evolution into true imperialism occurred only in the later nineteenth century.

CONTINENTAL EXPANSION

The expansion of the United States from 1803 to 1853 into contiguous areas such as Louisiana, Florida, Texas, the Oregon territories, and the Mexican cession is not best described as imperialism, although it contained related elements. This expansion involved lightly populated areas in which the influx of settlement from the older portions of the nation soon constituted the great bulk of the inhabitants. The Northwest Ordinance of 1787, a profoundly anti-imperialist measure, had early defined the process by which such areas could be divided into prospective states and ultimately brought into the union as equal members. The resulting expansion represented the continuous extension of a single society over vast neighboring areas, rather than the takeover of one society by another.

The North American continent was not unoccupied; indigenous Indian tribes were found in every part of it, while the areas taken from Mexico contained many scattered settlements, particularly in California and around Santa Fe. Neither the people nor the government of the United States showed much interest in such pre-existing societies; the aim of the United States was to brush them aside and replace them with the society and culture of the incoming majority. This was particularly true in regard to the Indians; rather than take over Indian society, the whites virtually destroyed it. The process was tragic for its victims, and Americans' constant assertions that they were peopling an empty continent contained the seeds of hypocrisy. There were nevertheless important differences between the movement of such a settlement frontier and the establishment of a true empire. For example, while the United States acquired half of Mexico's national territory between 1845 and 1848, the transfer entailed less than 2 percent of the Mexican population. Broadly speaking, the Mexican War was fought to gain territory, not a captive people, and the land thus gained would be populated largely from the existing United States. For purposes of comparison, the activities of the British in India, where they ruled a teeming alien society, and the British in Australia, where they settled a continent and built a self-governing nation, were so dissimilar that the use of a single term to describe both cases does more to obscure than enlighten. Prior to the Civil War, American expansion came closer to the Australian example, though dispossessing a more numerous indigenous people, and the end result cannot be accurately classified as imperialism.

There were, of course, common features in the earlier expansion and later imperialism of the United States. Chief among these were a strong sense of national mission and special destiny, a general confidence in the unique superiority of American institutions, a belief in the inequality of races and peoples, and the very habit of expansion itself. The expansionism of "manifest destiny" could lead toward true imperialism, as in the abortive movement to annex all of Mexico during the Mexican War. If westward expansion was not the same as imperialism, it furnished some of the materials out of which the latter could grow.

POST–CIVIL WAR PERIOD

The purchase of Alaska in 1867 ended the period when new territory was assumed to be on the path to eventual statehood. By that time the nation's policymakers were already debating a new and more truly imperialist form of expansion. Schemes to acquire Cuba, by purchase or otherwise, had been current from 1848 onward, while in 1870 the Ulysses S. Grant administration negotiated the annexation of the Dominican Republic, only to see the Senate reject the instrumental treaty. Critics of this latter scheme were quick to point out the break with tradition implicit in the quest for territory already compactly settled by an alien society. Such a society could be assimilated into the nation proper only with great difficulty and over a long period, or more probably it could not be assimilated at all. Thus, the United States had to choose between incorporating an unassimilated people into its federal system, thereby endangering its integrity, or ruling them as colonial subjects in violation of the right to self-government supposedly inherent in the American political system. Foreshadowed by the earlier opposition to the all-Mexico movement of the late 1840s, the Senate debate over the annexation of the Dominican Republic developed the main lines of the controversy over imperialist expansion and marked the maturing of an active anti-imperialism in the United States.

For a generation after 1870, projects for further expansion attracted little support in the United States, and most people assumed that imperialism had become a dead issue. A number of developments, however, prepared the nation for imperial ventures at the end of the century. Chief were the rapid industrialization and soaring productivity of the national economy, which made the United States the leading industrial power by 1900. Increasingly conscious of their numbers, wealth, and strength, and proud of their unique institutions and sprawling territory, Americans began to aspire to a place for their country among the world's great powers. The severe economic depression of the 1890s added material aims to the drive for prestige, as the nation's business leaders and political spokesmen hoped for economic salvation in increased exports of American manufactures. By the mid-1890s, a new mood had brought a reappraisal of America's world position.

While largely internal forces first prompted the nation's leaders to look outward, the global sweep of European imperialism was reaching its high point, providing both the model and the final impetus for the new activism. Initially, Americans reacted to European imperialism as a threat to be repelled, fearing its penetration into the Western Hemisphere. Still mindful of France's incursion into Mexico in the 1860s, Americans were startled by a French project in 1879 to build a ship canal across the Isthmus of Panama. Later they also came to see Great Britain as a potential interloper, inspiring Secretary of State Richard Olney to a famous warning against such penetration during the Venezuelan crisis of 1895. Fears of European encroachment undoubtedly added urgency to the drive for Hawaiian annexation after 1894 and figured in discussions of Caribbean expansion later in the decade. One result of such fears was advocacy of a sort of preemptive imperialism, a conviction that the United States should seize desirable areas before a rival power got them.

In addition, the constant example of the European powers in time led many in the United States to take a more positive view of imperialism. Thirsting for national prestige, they saw that colonies were highly valued status symbols in Europe and that colonial empires had already swallowed up most of the non-Western world. Furthermore, if Europeans claimed to spread civilization to unenlightened peoples, did not the United States have a more compelling mission to implant its own superior institutions? Finally, the theorists of the Old World had proclaimed that colonial empires could provide strategic bases, captive markets, raw materials, and investment opportunities—in short, could alleviate the persistent distresses from which the American economy suffered.

By 1895 a small but growing number of American politicians, publicists, naval officers, and businessmen supported a modest expansionist program. This generally included the annexation of Hawaii, the acquisition of one or more base areas in the West Indies, and the construction of an isthmian canal across Central America to facilitate naval and mercantile movement between the eastern United States and the Pacific Ocean. Some also aspired to the peaceable annexation of Canada, while others wished to challenge

British political and economic leadership in South America. But virtually all limited their ambitions to the Western Hemisphere, and most to areas traditionally within the sphere of American interests. While this program fell short of a full-fledged scheme of empire, it gave a specific direction to expansionist currents and reinforced the appeal of the imperialist idea.

Many Americans continued to be suspicious of imperialism, but others found that it was increasingly easy to identify imperialism with many aspects of the American tradition. Territorial expansion, a strong sense of national mission, and a dynamic economic growth had been dominant themes in American history. The belief in the inequality of man, which imperialism demanded, offered few problems at a time when the South was even then perfecting a system of segregation and disfranchisement of blacks, the West was in the final stages of suppressing the Indians, and the East fulminated against the inferiority of the new immigrants from southern and eastern Europe. Currently popular theories of social Darwinism held that the various races of man progressed at differing rates according to their place on the evolutionary scale, or failed to progress and fell victim to "natural selection." No one believed more devoutly in progress than Americans, and the presumed duty of carrying progress to backward lands was popularly called "the white man's burden." This combined belief in progress and human inequality, along with boundless self-confidence and a hope of gain, constituted the principal attitudes that underlay imperialism.

Whether the imperialist appeal was chiefly economic, psychological, nationalist, or idealistic has long been the subject of contention. In fact, it was all of these, and perhaps more. The most fundamental explanation of the global imperialism of the nineteenth century was that the Western world, containing a relatively small minority of the world's people, had achieved a virtual monopoly of effective power. The development of the nation-state enabled the effective mobilization of a society's resources, and coincided with the growth of modern science and industrialization. The latter developments created societies of unprecedented wealth and armed them with weapons of unparalleled destructiveness, while the steamship, the railroad, the telegraph, and the oceanic cable greatly diminished the distances that separated the Western peoples from the rest of the world.

The disparity of power between "modern" and preindustrial societies reached its maximum in the nineteenth century, and it was this disparity that was, quite directly, the driving force behind the breakneck colonialism of the period. Conscious of their strength and brought into close contact with weaker peoples, Europeans quickly developed a sense of superiority and discovered desirable goals to seek in vulnerable foreign places. The process soon created its own mystique, which could be shared by almost any member-state in the Western world. While American imperialism had special national characteristics—as did that of England, France, Germany, and other nations—during the 1890s, American imperialism was not essentially different from the parent European variety. Its American disciples believed otherwise, having as firm a faith in their own uniqueness as their European rivals.

THE ERA OF GLOBAL IMPERIALISM

Although this new thinking rapidly gained ground during the 1890s, it took the shock of tangible events to bridge the gap between ideas and action. After a revolution in Hawaii, which American officials actively abetted, the proposed annexation of Hawaii in 1893 reawakened the debate over colonial expansion but was blocked by the transfer of the presidency from Benjamin Harrison to Grover Cleveland. It was rather the revolt that began in Cuba in 1895 that ultimately mobilized the emotions and ideas of the new expansionism. In 1898 the United States was drawn into a struggle between Cuba and Spain that had brought mass suffering and wholesale destruction to its very borders. An aggressive national pride, emotional partisanship in favor of the Cubans, and tangible damage to American trade and property—all worked to arouse the public and the press, while the dramatic destruction of the battleship *Maine* acted as a spark to these combustibles. Originally regarded by most Americans as a crusade to free Cuba, the Spanish-American War quickly took on an expansionist thrust. The retention of Puerto Rico, Spain's other Caribbean colony, was soon regarded as a necessary war reparation. Strategically the key to the Pacific, Hawaii was annexed during the war by a joint resolution of Congress. Even the cries to free Cuba gave way to protests that the Cubans needed a period of tutelage before essaying complete self-government.

It was the Philippine Islands, however, that most forcefully brought the imperialist issue to a head. Large, populous, alien, and distant, they neither fell within the traditional geographical scope of American expansionism nor seemed even remotely assimilable to the American federal system. In the United States there had been little thought of acquiring the Philippines before the Spanish-American War, but once war came, the U.S. armed forces attacked them because they represented valuable enemy territory that was highly vulnerable. The initial American victories quickly led to a national conviction that the United States now controlled the islands and was responsible for determining their destiny. Expansionists were quick to argue that the nation should not turn the Filipinos back to Spanish misrule, while to let them drift would invite an Anglo-German struggle for their control. On the other hand, American rule could bring enlightenment to the islands, and their proximity to China might aid American penetration of what was assumed to be one of the great world markets of the future.

Expansionism carried the day, and the peace treaty with Spain provided for American possession of Puerto Rico, the Philippines, and Guam. Hawaii had already been separately annexed, and Cuba was subjected to a three-year military occupation followed by a theoretically sovereign independence in 1902. In fact, however, Cuba became a self-governing protectorate of the United States, with the latter nation retaining important governmental controls and the right of military intervention at its discretion, under the terms of the Platt Amendment of 1901. In the Philippines, meanwhile, an armed independence movement revolted against American rule in 1899, and the ensuing three-year Filipino-American War introduced the Americans to the frustrations and mutual atrocities characteristic of antiguerrilla warfare. The public had expected the Filipinos to greet the advent of American rule with cheers and were disillusioned to meet with hostility instead. Critics questioned the utility of the new colony and the morality of subduing it by force. While U.S. forces finally succeeded in crushing all resistance, anti-imperialists made the most of the contradictions inherent in spreading enlightenment at the point of a bayonet. Colonial empire quickly lost its glamour in the United States, while less formal techniques of expansion gained easier acceptance from the relative success of the Cuban protectorate program. In the twentieth century, American imperialism would be characterized by the extension of influence or control rather than by the outright annexation of territory.

THE ADVENT OF INFORMAL EMPIRE

After 1900 the American public lost interest in its new colonies, but the United States continued to expand its power in essentially imperialist ways. This was true principally in the Caribbean region, where the creation of formal and informal protectorates characterized American foreign policy in the period after the Spanish-American War. The war had spurred interest in the building of an isthmian canal, which was to be built as a national project; and following Panama's secession from Colombia in 1903, the project became a reality. The great strategic importance of the Panama Canal, thereafter joined with the considerable American stake in Cuba and its direct sovereignty over Puerto Rico, drew the nation further into Caribbean affairs.

Still fearful of European intervention and solicitous of the growing American economic interest in the area, policymakers in Washington viewed the chronic political instability of the Caribbean and Central American nations as an invitation to foreign penetration and an obstacle to local development. The Roosevelt Corollary to the Monroe Doctrine, enunciated by President Theodore Roosevelt in 1904, claimed for the United States an "international police power," which entailed a general right to intervene and keep order in the Western Hemisphere. Not only Roosevelt but his successors, William Howard Taft and Woodrow Wilson, steadily expanded American hegemony in the Caribbean. By World War I, Cuba, Panama, the Dominican Republic, Haiti, and Nicaragua were in some kind of protectorate status, while Puerto Rico remained an outright colony. Actual military interventions occurred in Cuba (1906–1909), Haiti (1915–1934), the Dominican Republic (1916–1924), Nicaragua (1912, 1927–1933), and Panama (intermittently and on a lesser scale).

Besides the use of special treaty relationships and military force, the United States attempted to maintain a "monopoly of lending," under which Caribbean governments would borrow money only in the United States; it also established customs receiverships in several countries, which effectively placed their government revenues under control of the United States. Meanwhile, private enterprise had permeated the region with

>
>
> ## THE ROOSEVELT COROLLARY
>
> "It is not true that the United States feels any land hunger or entertains any projects as regards the other nations of the Western Hemisphere save as are for their welfare. All this country desires is to see the neighboring countries stable, orderly, and prosperous. Any country whose people conduct themselves well can count upon our hearty friendship. If a nation shows that it knows how to act with reasonable efficiency and decency in social and political matters, if it keeps order and pays its obligations, it need fear no interference from the United States. Chronic wrongdoing, or an impotence which results in a general loosening of the ties of civilized society, may in America, as elsewhere, ultimately require intervention by some civilized nation, and in the Western Hemisphere the adherence of the United States to the Monroe Doctrine may force the United States, however reluctantly, in flagrant cases of such wrongdoing or impotence, to the exercise of an international police power. . . .
>
> "Our interests and those of our southern neighbors are in reality identical. They have great natural riches, and if within their borders the reign of law and justice obtains, prosperity is sure to come to them."
>
> — *From President Theodore Roosevelt's annual message to Congress, 6 December 1904* —

American investment and business activity, while the one-crop economies of the Caribbean nations made them heavily dependent upon the American market. Thus, the nominally sovereign states of the Caribbean area were subject to American controls, both formal and informal, which made their real status essentially colonial.

After 1898, the United States was also active in the Far East, but its impact was weaker there than in the Caribbean. Faced with a huge and populous China, and competing with most of the other major world powers, American policymakers could not aspire to regional dominance or military solutions. The "dollar diplomacy" of the William Howard Taft administration (1909–1913) attempted to foster American investment in China and to create international financial arrangements, which would impose a Caribbean-style "monopoly of lending" upon the government of China. This attempt to mobilize American economic strength as a diplomatic tool accomplished little in the Far East, however, on account of both the difficulties of the situation itself and the limited interest of the nation's business and financial leaders. The earlier Open Door policy of 1899–1900, therefore, remained the principal basis of policy. It represented little more than an attempt to obtain a general agreement to preserve the existing treaty system of shared control in China, and thus equality of economic opportunity in China for the United States. The policy was not very effective, and the Chinese market never came near to meeting the inflated expectations of the West. In general, the limited objectives and relative ineffectiveness of American activities in the Far East fell well short of real imperialism in this period, although the United States was long a party to the treaty system by which the Western powers jointly had imposed a limited protectorate upon China.

ISOLATIONISM AND THE WORLD WARS

American participation in World War I led to a revulsion against overseas commitments, which reached its peak in the Senate rejection of the Treaty of Versailles (1919) and the new League of Nations. Rising domestic criticism in the 1920s brought about the liquidation of the military government in the Dominican Republic and moderate relaxation of American political controls elsewhere in the Caribbean. At the same time, however, the U.S. government and business community cooperated in pushing American exports and foreign loans, leading some later historians to envision an "open door imperialism" based on American economic influence abroad. An alternate view was that the United States did indeed seek such economic influence, but that most Americans then thought it possible to separate the political and economic aspects of international relations in a manner considered unrealistic by later generations.

The Great Depression of the 1930s brought an even greater emphasis on the economic side of foreign policy and a corresponding decline in interest in other aspects. The Good Neighbor policy of Franklin D. Roosevelt brought the dismantling of Caribbean military interventions and political protectorates, at the same time that Latin America was tied more closely to the American economy by means of reciprocal trade agreements. The Philippine Islands were set on the path to independence in 1934, while the Neutrality Acts of 1935–1938 were designed to minimize economic ties to belligerents in foreign wars. The Monroe Doctrine took on a new theoretical formulation as an association of hemispheric equals for collective security, and the isolationist majority in the United States eschewed any national interest in the world's affairs outside the Western Hemisphere. American imperialism was declared to be dead, never to arise again.

At the end of the 1930s there was a rapid reversal of thinking largely caused by the early victories of Nazi Germany during the new European war, and particularly by the shock created by the fall of France in 1940. Americans quickly became internationalists, the new consensus being that the world's democracies must stand together to check the crimes of "gangster nations" like Germany, Italy, and Japan. It now appeared that peace was indivisible and that the United States must be concerned with events in every corner of the globe. With the Japanese attack on Pearl Harbor late in 1941, the United States went to war in both Europe and Asia. During World War II, the United States fought as a member of a coalition that included Great Britain, the Soviet Union, Nationalist China, and many lesser members—a circumstance that drew the United States even further into global affairs. Mobilizing enormous fighting power and productivity, Americans found themselves at the close of the struggle with their armed forces deployed in Europe, Asia, North Africa, the Middle East, Australasia, and Latin America.

THE COLD WAR AND ITS AFTERMATH

World War II humbled or drastically weakened every great power except the United States and the Soviet Union, both of which emerged with greatly enhanced power and prestige. In a world full of power vacuums, this dangerously simplified bipolar balance contributed to a growing rivalry between the two superpowers, as did the strong but mutually contradictory ideas of mission that each possessed. Initially competing for hegemony in Europe, this postwar rivalry soon became global in scope, and American military and political commitments proliferated. At the same time, the preeminent economic position of the United States at the end of World War II much enhanced its influence abroad and gave it great weight in shaping the economic structure of the noncommunist world. Thus, American influence over other societies reached a new high and took many different forms. In the Caribbean, the United States supported anticommunist military ventures in Guatemala (1954) and Cuba (1961), and in 1965, out of fear that a leftist government would come to power, intervened in the Dominican Republic. In East Asia, South Korea, Taiwan, and, later, South Vietnam and Cambodia became heavily dependent upon U.S. military aid. Japan grew into an economic giant but retained close ties to the United States. Other initiatives in the Middle East, Africa, and elsewhere made American activities truly global.

In the economic sphere, the United States overwhelmingly became the chief investor, source of credit, and supplier of new technologies. From the 1940s to the 1960s, the American dollar was the yardstick of international currency exchanges, while an American-sponsored drive toward freer world trade facilitated American exports of goods and money. The purchase of foreign subsidiaries and the development of multinational corporations gave American business enterprise increased influence abroad, while many foreign nations found their principal export markets in the United States.

The political and economic impact of the United States was accompanied by significant social effects. American-style mass consumption spread its appeal everywhere, as the elite of half the globe rushed to emulate the lifestyles of New York and California. American tourists, motion pictures, and television programs went everywhere, while students flocked to American universities from all over the world. Even an economically advanced country like Japan assimilated American models of dress and amusement, and readily accepted bondage to the automobile.

Some viewed the international vogue of American lifestyles and consumer products as cultural imperialism, or a thinly veiled form of economic exploitation. Others deplored the subversion of native cultures and the consequent destabilization of traditional societies by the tide of westernization. Many twenty-first-century scholars, however, are skeptical of the idea of a one-sided cultural aggression, citing the eagerness with which Eastern Europeans and others sought Western fashions, films, and popular music even when their governments attempted to shut these things out. In this view, developments in the Western world have set off an irresistible global cultural change, in which cross-fertilization complicates any notion of a simple one-way influence. Terms such as "modernization" and "globalization" are used to suggest a generalized force beyond the control of any one society. It was nevertheless the United States that led the way in the process.

In any case, the worldwide distribution of U.S. military bases, security agreements, investments, multinational corporations, foreign-aid programs, and open and undercover political activities gave rise to the charge that American imperialism had not only revived but had expanded over enormous areas. Some critics described an "open door empire" in which American foreign policy sought to impose everywhere the conditions necessary for the penetration of American exports and enterprise, while keeping underdeveloped nations in a state of perpetual economic colonialism. From this point of view, the term "imperialism" applied to virtually every overseas activity of the United States.

Given the undeniably great impact of the United States in the postwar world, the issue was not whether there had been an American influence on other societies but whether that influence was best described as imperialism. Since the United States annexed no territory during the period in question, the most obvious form of imperialism does not apply; there was no formal empire. There were, however, attempts at neo-imperial control of other states. In 1965 the Dominican Republic experienced a U.S. military intervention that imposed a new president, who was retained in power for many years by the active use of American influence and machinations of the Central Intelligence Agency. The Ronald Reagan administration (1981–1989) supported civil wars in El Salvador and Nicaragua in an attempt to bolster right-wing regimes against leftist opponents. Other cases could be cited, but blanket assertions of imperialism went too far. It was doubtful terminology to apply that label to the postwar American record in Europe. It is true that the United States threw its influence into an effort to erect a liberal-capitalist system in Western Europe, just as the Soviet Union worked for Marxist-Leninist states in Eastern Europe. Given a virtual power vacuum in one of the world's vital centers, no less was to be expected of either superpower. It is also true that the Marshall Plan and companion policies were designed not only to aid European economic recovery but to boost European purchases of American exports. Yet the end result was not merely exploitive, for it helped to recreate in Western Europe one of the great industrial centers of the world, which soon offered stiff competition to the United States itself. Like Japan, West Germany pressed American manufacturers hard in their own markets and often bested them in markets abroad. In time, many European states became effective competitors. To call this performance economic imperialism is both misleading and intellectually counterproductive.

The U.S. military intervention in Southeast Asia during the 1960s ended in the following decade in humiliating failure and a national reappraisal of the American role abroad. For a time, the shadow of Vietnam inhibited further overseas adventures, but the global network of American commitments and interests continued largely intact. Foreign involvements reappeared with the previously mentioned Reagan administration's activities in Central America, as well as its military deployments in Grenada (1983) and Lebanon (1984), but on a limited scale.

The end of the Cold War in 1989 and the subsequent breakup of the Soviet Union changed the global situation fundamentally, leaving the United States as the only superpower. The Cold War justification for foreign military interventions thereby disappeared, but new reasons for such ventures multiplied. In varying scales of magnitude, U.S. armed forces were deployed in Panama (1989), Somalia (1992), Haiti (1994), Bosnia (1995), and Kosovo (1999), the latter including a bombing campaign against Serbia. By far the largest overseas operation was the Gulf War of 1991 against Iraq, which involved more than 500,000 U.S. troops to protect the industrial world's oil supply, but motives for the other interventions varied widely. In Somalia, for example, where no visible U.S. interests were at stake, the goal was to remove the obstacles to feeding a starving population, and in Bosnia and Kosovo it was to prevent the outbreak of regional war and prevent mass genocide. Some saw the United States as world policeman, others as global bully, but none could deny the reality of the nation's power and influence virtually everywhere on the globe.

As the world's strongest and wealthiest nation for the last half century, the United States was responsible for its full share of neo-imperialist hegemony. At times, however, it acted abroad in conjunction with less powerful nations that lacked the American capacity to project force quickly to crisis areas. The North Atlantic Treaty Organization and the Gulf War both saw U.S. military power enlisted in the service of a broad coalition of nations and interests. Operating within a highly competitive global economy, U.S. economic power was great but hardly hegemonic, while its cultural influences were eagerly received in large parts of the world even if deeply resented in others. No single definition can contain the enormous variety of American activities, motives, and effects on the world; certainly the term "imperialism" cannot.

BIBLIOGRAPHY

Gienow-Hecht, Jessica C. E. "Shame on US? Academics, Cultural Transfer, and the Cold War—A Critical Review." *Diplomatic History* 24 (summer 2000). Traces the evolving debate about U.S. cultural expansion since 1945.

Healy, David. *U.S. Expansionism: The Imperialist Urge in the 1890s.* Madison, Wis., 1970. A multi-causal approach that shows the convergence of numerous and dissimilar forces in the movement for overseas empire.

Hollander, Paul. *Anti-Americanism: Critiques at Home and Abroad, 1965–1990.* New York, 1992. A stimulating look at the views of the naysayers, domestic and foreign.

LaFeber, Walter. *The New Empire: An Interpretation of American Expansion, 1860–1898.* Ithaca, N.Y., 1963. Depicts American overseas expansion as creating a commercial empire in order to serve a drive for export markets.

Lundestad, Geir. *The American "Empire" and Other Studies of U.S. Foreign Policy in a Comparative Prospect.* New York, 1990. Explores the ambiguities of American power abroad.

May, Ernest R. *Imperial Democracy: The Emergence of America as a Great Power.* New York, 1961. Sees the expansionism of 1898 in terms of an eruption of public opinion that swept the nation's leaders before it.

Rosenberg, Emily S. *Spreading the American Dream: American Economic and Cultural Expansion, 1890–1945.* New York, 1982. A useful broad-gauge approach.

Thornton, A. P. *Doctrines of Imperialism.* New York, 1965. A short but good conceptual study of imperialism.

Trask, David. *The War with Spain in 1898.* New York and London, 1981. The best work on that conflict.

Weinberg, Albert K. *Manifest Destiny: A Study of Nationalist Expansionism in American History.* Baltimore, 1935. Still a standard work on the ideology of continental expansion.

Williams, William Appleman. *The Tragedy of American Diplomacy.* Cleveland, Ohio, 1959. An influential book that helped launch a revisionist movement in American diplomatic history and popularize an "Open Door School," which held that the economic goals of capitalism were central to the formation of U.S. foreign policy.

See also ANTI-IMPERIALISM; COLONIALISM AND NEOCOLONIALISM; CONTINENTAL EXPANSION; DOLLAR DIPLOMACY; ECONOMIC POLICY AND THEORY; INTERVENTION AND NONINTERVENTION; ISOLATIONISM; MANDATES AND TRUSTEESHIPS; OPEN DOOR POLICY; PROTECTORATES AND SPHERES OF INFLUENCE.

Intelligence and Counterintelligence

John Prados

Observers over the years have provided many definitions for the term "intelligence." Many of these definitions are burdensome, or technical, or drawn directly from the term of art. Intelligence is simply information, gathered however necessary and arranged in such fashion as to be of use to those who require it. In foreign policy (and national defense) intelligence guides the hands of policymakers and helps them conduct relations wisely. (However, there are aspects of intelligence that can be obstacles to wise policy.) Foreign policy without intelligence can succeed, but at greater cost and difficulty than well-informed initiatives. In American foreign policy, at least since the end of World War II, there has been a conscious effort to harness intelligence in service of national goals.

THE INTELLIGENCE CYCLE

Careful selection, integration, and analysis distinguish intelligence from other information. In the United Sates, where practitioners have made a greater effort than in most other nations to develop a conscious theory of intelligence, the terms "intelligence cycle" and "intelligence process" now denote the procedure by which information is brought to the support of policymakers. Because in the theory the word "process" is also used as a verb—to mean the act of taking information and converting it into useful intelligence—this essay will use the term "intelligence cycle."

The intelligence cycle consists of a number of sequential stages, beginning with realization of what is unknown or uncertain. Officials can ask to find out about those subjects, or intelligence officers themselves may point out a gap in information, actions that lead to an order to collect data on that topic, known as an "intelligence requirement." Some kinds of information can come only from particular sources, so the capability to gather data from a particular source may be limited, or indeed there may be several ways to get at a piece of knowledge. This means that how to meet an intelligence requirement is a matter of choice, another stage of the cycle. The act of choosing how to gather given intelligence is known as "collection tasking." What many people think of as the totality of intelligence—the act of actually securing the data—is a stage of the cycle called "collection."

In principle, in developing any kind of fact-based knowledge, collection must necessarily be by source, while appreciation is by subject. Many facts from a variety of sources may bear on a given subject. Different sources might be a photograph, a radio intercept, a newspaper article, a report from a spy, a diplomatic exchange, a scholarly paper, a radio broadcast, or the like. A given source may supply information on more than one subject, and subjects can be as diverse as a nation's military power, its economic position, or the health of a leader. Therefore, an act of transformation must occur in the cycle; this is termed "processing." The American conception is that "raw" information data is processed to become "finished intelligence." Occasionally, raw dispatches are given to policymakers, but most often they benefit from the skills of professionals who analyze the data to compile finished intelligence reports. This analysis is a further stage of the intelligence cycle, and the act of printing or otherwise creating the finished report, called "production," is another. Of course, the report is useless unless it actually reaches the policymaker who needs it; circulation of finished intelligence constitutes a stage of the cycle called "dissemination." Users of the data can then supply feedback on what they liked or did not like, or what they still want to know or find out, thereby completing the cycle by generating new intelligence requirements. Obviously, this is an oversimplified account of a series of repeated and interrelated steps that may impact on each other as well as on the finished intelligence report, but it does supply a basic picture of how intelligence is derived.

To make this picture more concrete, consider the Cuban missile crisis of 1962. In that event of Cold War history, the United States was gravely concerned over Russian military aid to Cuba. President John F. Kennedy publicly warned the Soviet Union not to supply Cuba with certain types of weapons. That created a collection requirement for U.S. intelligence to verify that the specified categories of weapons were not in Cuba. Russian cargoes arrived in Cuba by ship, and the United States had a number of spies in Cuba, as well as reports from Cuban refugees arriving in the United States. In addition, the United States had access to diplomatic and intelligence reporting from allied nations, primarily the United Kingdom and France. U.S. intelligence also had its own diplomatic and intelligence reporting from Eastern European countries and direct from the Soviet Union. These sources enabled U.S. intelligence to see that Soviet shipments were arriving in Cuba in great numbers.

The Central Intelligence Agency, one of the primary entities in the American effort, responded with a program of aircraft reconnaissance over Cuba, using U-2 spy planes to photograph suspicious targets. One U-2 flight brought back pictures that caused the CIA director to suspect the Russians of deploying weapons (antiaircraft missiles) in such fashion as to deny a reconnaissance capability over Cuba, an action he believed was intended to enable the quiet placing of Soviet offensive weapons (the kind Kennedy had warned against) in Cuba. A few weeks later, several refugee and agent reports indicated a possibility that offensive missiles were being deployed at certain locations in Cuba. Previous intelligence reports by the CIA and the U.S. intelligence community, called national intelligence estimates (NIEs), had found no offensive weapons in Cuba, but additional U-2 flights were eventually scheduled, and one of them checked the suspect areas identified by agents. That flight discovered Soviet missiles on 14 October 1962, leading President Kennedy to decide on a quarantine (blockade) of Cuba and other diplomatic actions. Maritime intelligence subsequently kept close track of the progress of Soviet ships steaming toward Cuba, aerial intelligence monitored the cargoes aboard the ships and the progress of the missile sites in Cuba, and intelligence reports thereafter kept Kennedy closely informed.

A WORLD OF SECRETS

Almost every kind of information can be relevant to intelligence, as becomes evident by reviewing the variety of intelligence outputs. Diplomacy requires information on the private opinions, negotiating positions, and political factors impinging upon actors with whom foreign relations are being conducted. This political intelligence may need to be supplemented by economic intelligence, which covers such areas as resources, national economic organization and strength, labor skills, industrial processes, long-term growth trends, foreign trade, balance of payments, and other information. Military intelligence is of key import and ranges beyond simple counting of numbers of men, ships, and planes. Naval and air intelligence may consider necessary information different from that needed by ground force experts. All will want material on foreign forces, but also predictions on how those forces may change in the future, and on the quality and flexibility of their support systems, weapons technology, trained manpower, planning processes, and the like. Filling in those blanks, in turn, requires more recourse to economic intelligence, as well as scientific and technical intelligence. The latter attempts to judge the capabilities of weapons by reference to data regarding scientific achievement, industrial base, research and development programs, general levels of technological sophistication, and other information.

Judgments in any of the particular intelligence fields may be influenced by additional kinds of information. These include biographical intelligence on the individuals who may be key actors in policies or programs in which intelligence may be interested. In addition, there is basic intelligence, which is a compendium of social, demographic, geographic, economic, and other data about societies of interest to the analyst.

There is also intelligence that is primarily about the adversary's own intelligence organizations and activities. A foreign nation, even a friendly country, may be of interest for the intelligence operations it conducts, the results achieved with a given style of organization, the threat it poses, some opportunity offered, some specific activity parallel to or interfering with friendly activities, or for many other reasons. In addition, separate intelligence requirements, collection, and analysis may be conducted for the precise purpose of carrying out an operation against a foreign intelligence service, most commonly in espionage or in attempts to recruit an agent.

The above represents a wide panoply of information that can be relevant, truly a world of secrets. The concept that so much raw information is required is a relatively recent development. In the United States, with arguably the most sophisticated approach to intelligence, the practice of closely meshing and piecing together huge arrays of information of many different kinds to derive knowledge on a single discrete question dates from only about World War II (1939–1945). At that time, benefiting from British (and other) experience, and building on a foundation of code breaking, the United States fashioned methods that relied upon several pillars of intelligence, representing different kinds of collection techniques. In the Cold War period and after, those techniques were successively improved and integrated, in a process that continues today. In contrast, prior to World War II, intelligence reporting remained episodic, focused on a single (or a few) sources, and did not explicitly aim at information for policymakers, except where given reports seemed to demand it.

A good example of crosscutting influences and the impact of different kinds of intelligence reporting is the history of U.S. intelligence on Soviet nuclear missile programs. In the period immediately after World War II, scientific, economic, and biographical data, along with intelligence sharing with British allies, enabled the United States to discover that the Soviet Union was pursuing creation of an atomic bomb. Predictions by U.S. military intelligence and the nascent CIA were not accurate on when the Soviets would acquire nuclear weapons, in part due to Soviet espionage, which reduced the technical uncertainties associated with the Soviet program. On the other hand, U.S. scientific intelligence in the form of atomic test monitoring aircraft provided instant knowledge that a nuclear test had been carried out in August 1949.

Predicting the rate at which the Soviets might manufacture nuclear weapons; their ability to deliver such weapons against the United States, either by bomber aircraft or by ballistic missiles; and the attendant production rates for those weapons became priority issues for U.S. intelligence. These concerns drove intelligence tasking and even technological research and development programs (especially those for the U-2 and SR-71 aircraft and the CORONA/Discoverer KH-4 photographic reconnaissance satellite) through the 1950s and even into the 1960s. The CIA sought to recruit agents for information in these same areas, and defectors leaving Russia, along with German scientists returning from working in Russia, were interrogated for their knowledge. Estimates of Soviet factory floor space, fissile materials availability, and other items were compiled from the intelligence and used to predict the size of the Soviet bomb and the delivery vehicle inventory.

In intelligence estimates between 1955 and 1960, the CIA successively overestimated Soviet bomber and missile forces. These estimates led to decisions by President Dwight D. Eisenhower to build up U.S. bomber and missile forces to very high levels, in fact levels that arguably led Soviet leaders in the 1960s to create land- and submarine-based missile forces far greater than required for basic security. Meanwhile, Eisenhower's confidence in his intelligence also led him to offer, at the Geneva Summit of 1955, an "Open Skies" plan for mutual verification of nuclear forces and confidence building, which Soviet leader Nikita S. Khrushchev rejected. In a negative impact of intelligence, in 1960 another Eisenhower-Khrushchev summit scheduled for Paris was aborted as a consequence of the shooting down of an American U-2 spy plane over the Soviet Union on 1 May 1960.

The planes and satellites provided U.S. intelligence with unprecedented information-gathering abilities. They served as platforms for high-resolution cameras to take pictures or for sensitive radio and electronic recording equipment to monitor radio communications or electronic emissions of all kinds. Even though Eisenhower prohibited further overflights of the Soviet Union after the U-2 was shot down, satellite capabilities soon replaced and outshone those of the aircraft. In this period, as John F. Kennedy took office as president in January 1961, the United States also enjoyed excellent data from a Russian agent, Colonel Oleg Penkovsky, an officer of the Soviet military intelligence with access to much highly secret information of interest to the CIA.

During the 1960s the arms race between U.S. and Russian missile forces continued to be the focus of the secret world of intelligence. This arms race was punctuated by the Cuban missile crisis of 1962. It was not until after the crisis that the Russians had a dependable ballistic missile capable of mass deployment in a protected mode. The Soviet Union began to build these missiles at an increasing rate. President Kennedy, who had discovered that the gap in missile strength actually favored the United States, relied upon this intelligence in canceling further U.S. production, capping the land-based missile forces at 1,052.

The Soviets continued to deploy until they reached the figure of 1,512 in the early 1970s.

Predicting how quickly the Russians would increase their missile force, at what level they might curtail deployment, and whether they would also field novel technologies such as ballistic missile defenses or multiple independently targetable warheads became the key intelligence issues of the 1960s. The CIA and other agencies, even with the considerable intelligence gathered by their machine spies, underestimated the numbers of Soviet missiles in the long term (that is, beyond those under construction, which could be directly observed by reconnaissance satellites). On the other hand, the intelligence estimates did much better on predicting when the Russians would acquire new technologies. However, the estimates seem to have been less influential in the major weapons decisions made by the administration of President Lyndon B. Johnson, who initiated multiple warhead programs for both land-based (Minuteman III) and sea-based (Poseidon) missiles, as well as development of an advanced manned strategic aircraft (eventually the B-1 bomber).

Growth in Soviet strategic forces moved the United States to seek arms control negotiations with the Soviet Union. The Johnson administration concluded a nonproliferation treaty and other agreements prohibiting nuclear weapons on the seabed or in outer space. Johnson also attempted to open talks on strategic nuclear weapons, but the effort was canceled in August 1968, when the Soviets invaded Czechoslovakia. The administration of Richard M. Nixon followed up and actually began Strategic Arms Limitation Talks (SALT) in mid-1969, culminating in the SALT I agreement, signed on 26 May 1972. The course of those negotiations was influenced by diplomatic intelligence the United States picked up from Russian officials—in particular a technical collection program codenamed "Gamma Guppy," in which the United States intercepted radiotelephone conversations among Russian leaders, as well as information gleaned directly from Russian negotiators. The intelligence estimates also gave the Nixon administration confidence that its negotiations covered relevant issues and that it had a handle on what Soviet strength would be under various possible outcomes. After the SALT I agreement, intelligence verified compliance, tracked technological developments, and assisted follow-up negotiations for SALT II and the two Strategic Arms Reduction Treaties (START I and START II), plus the Intermediate Range Nuclear Forces (INF) Treaty. Various intelligence disputes occurred in the 1970s and 1980s that affected these negotiations and U.S.–Soviet bilateral relations, but the essential point is that many types of intelligence reporting were relevant and that the intelligence had crosscutting influence.

TYPES OF INTELLIGENCE REPORTING

In the U.S. system there are various documents that reflect intelligence appreciations, each with different standing. With knowledge of the generic type of an analysis, the observer can better understand the importance of intelligence.

National Intelligence Estimates The national intelligence estimates (NIEs) represent the highest category of intelligence document (or "product"). The director of central intelligence (DCI), the official who heads the entire American intelligence community, is responsible for the NIEs. He is advised in this by the National Foreign Intelligence Board, a committee on which sits the head of each U.S. agency in this field. The NIEs are drafted by a subordinate unit on the basis of "contributions" from the member agencies. Since 1973 the drafts have been written by area specialists known as national intelligence officers, who collectively constitute the National Intelligence Council. Before 1973 the drafters were generalists in an office subordinate to the Board of National Estimates. Some DCIs (including all since 1973) have had the council/board within their own office; a few earlier intelligence leaders subordinated the board to the CIA's Directorate for Intelligence. Either way, the director has always had the power to require that specific language (and therefore particular substantive judgments) be included in an NIE. There is also a procedure whereby agencies belonging to the National Foreign Intelligence Board can take exception to a conclusion in the NIE, usually expressed as a footnote to the main text. (At times these dissents have appeared as footnotes or as appendices to a paper or have been written in the main text, depending on the preferences of the director, but the colloquialism for a dissent in an NIE remains to "take a footnote.") A change in intelligence appreciations that occurs after an NIE has been issued is reflected in a paper known as a "memorandum to holders" of the NIE. A more important change can require a fresh estimate. Presidents, national security advisers, and top officials have varied in the amount of attention they pay to NIEs. Dwight D. Eisenhower and Lyndon Johnson accorded them great importance; Ronald Reagan and George H. W. Bush paid little heed; others have been somewhere in the middle. Perhaps the main significance of NIEs has been political—these documents represent the considered opinion of the U.S. intelligence community; their substance can be expected to leak if presidents take actions contrary to them, embarrassing the senior policymakers. The NIEs also have a more formal role in weapons system acquisition decisions and military budget planning that should not be ignored.

Special National Intelligence Estimates Like the NIEs, special national intelligence estimates (SNIEs) are created by the interagency process of drafting and review. Their scope and content differ, however. The NIEs tend to be long-term studies of large subjects, for example, the NIE 11/3-8 series, which were five-year predictions for the evolution of Soviet nuclear forces. The SNIE is an analysis of the near-term impact of a specific course of action. For example, in July 1965, when the United States intervened in South Vietnam with massive ground forces, SNIE 10-9-65 analyzed foreign reactions to the new deployment. Similarly, in July 1961, when the United States considered military intervention in Laos, SNIE 58-2-61 predicted probable reactions to this and several other possible courses of action. The national estimates tend to be produced following set schedules, and the SNIEs most often at the request of the president or other senior officials. Partly for this reason the SNIEs can garner more attention than the NIEs.

President's Daily Brief President Harry S. Truman was the first chief executive to demand daily intelligence on key subjects. Since then every president has gotten this kind of reporting, though the form has varied. For Eisenhower, the reports went to his staff secretary, Colonel (later General) Andrew J. Goodpaster, who created summaries he related to the president. John F. Kennedy and Lyndon B. Johnson were provided a president's intelligence checklist, and the president's daily brief (PDB) nomenclature was in use by 1968. During the Clinton administration a vice president's supplement has been added to reflect that official's special concerns. The PDB is an example of "current," as opposed to estimative (predictive), intelligence. Because it reflects immediate events and concerns, the PDB tends to get the most attention. For example, Lieutenant General Brent Scowcroft, national security adviser to President George H. W. Bush, related that Bush devoured the PDBs but had little time for the NIEs.

Other Current Intelligence Publications In the United States, intelligence has long supported the government with daily, weekly, or other periodic reports containing the latest data. These range from daily briefings for directors (the CIA takes care of the DCI; the Defense Intelligence Agency, of the secretary of defense; and the Bureau of Intelligence and Research, of the State Department), to newspaper equivalents to digests of communications intercepts or photo imagery. The *Central Intelligence Bulletin,* published since the 1950s, and the *National Intelligence Daily,* started in the 1970s, are classic examples of the genre. At the turn of the millennium, excluding the PDB, intelligence published about ten different dailies containing current intelligence items and at least as many weeklies or monthlies, including such titles as *Terrorism Review, Narcotics Monitor, Organized Crime Report, Illicit Finance Review, Proliferation Digest,* and *Arms Trade Report.* Burgeoning U.S. interest in global trade is reflected in the daily (five times a week) started under the Clinton administration, *Economic Executives' Intelligence Brief.* In general, the current intelligence field is characterized by increasing specialization, which follows from explosive growth in interagency centers focused on single issues or sets of issues.

A further initiative of the 1990s, a product of the computer age, is a distributed information network connecting intelligence analysts and policymakers. Originally called Intelink, this system gives users immediate access to current data on subjects of interest. The system also permits officials to rise above the simple database and contact analysts directly for the most current knowledge. This kind of distributed network has the potential to change the way current intelligence is disseminated, modifying the intelligence cycle by reducing the importance of publication of reports as part of intelligence production.

One more type of intelligence product from specialized intelligence agencies or staffs also bears mention. The National Security Agency produces a paper, *The SIGINT Digest,* which describes daily developments, the knowledge of which is derived from signals intelligence. Similarly, the National Imagery and Mapping Agency produces *World Imagery Report,* which serves the same function, although it is produced in the format of a television news broadcast. In terms of format, the television news approach for delivery of intelligence information has gained in popularity in recent years, and the Defense Intelligence Agency and Central Intelligence Agency both now create some film-type reports.

Warning Intelligence A significant type of intelligence, usually ignored because of its similarity to current intelligence, is data intended to warn policymakers of sudden major developments, such as the outbreak of wars, military coups, or comparable crises. The director of central intelligence employs a national intelligence officer (NIO) for warning who is specifically responsible for this function. The NIO is backed by an interagency committee of second-tier officials from the intelligence community that meets weekly. Both the committee as a group and the NIO have the authority to issue warning memoranda that activate crisis management efforts by the U.S. government. The warning committee also maintains a checklist of potential hot spots and troublesome situations anticipated in the next half-year or so. The committee reports twice a month on the countries and issues carried on the list. An example of warning occurred in the Gulf War of 1990–1991, when the Iraqi invasion of Kuwait on 2 August 1990 included a military buildup along the Kuwaiti border that caught the attention of the NIO and led him to issue a warning memorandum some hours before the invasion began.

Basic Intelligence Much analytical work builds upon data maintained and updated on a constant basis. Economic statistics; biographies of foreign leaders and officials, not to say adversary intelligence officers; and information on nations' populations, political parties, transportation infrastructures, and the like are all necessary from time to time. The intelligence agencies all utilize research libraries and have units that produce such basic intelligence. At the CIA the Office of Support Services (formerly the Central Reference Service) performs this task. Its best-known publication is called *The World Factbook,* though it also produces monthly statistical collections and biographical registers.

PILLARS OF INTELLIGENCE

With outputs of so many different kinds, it is clear that information requirements must necessarily be massive. Intelligence has long since ceased to be a game of spy versus spy and has become a field in which almost every imaginable source is plumbed for its contribution to the whole. Alongside the secret agents are ranged what former CIA director Richard Helms called in a 1967 speech the "machine spies." The raw information is massaged by analysts and value is added to it by careful comparison, review, and fitting together what are, in effect, jigsaw puzzles. Intelligence authorities are loath to discuss these "sources and methods," but the outlines of the process are readily apparent and an understanding of this process is important to according intelligence its correct place in American foreign policy.

Until the early nineteenth century, spies remained virtually the only source of intelligence, while intelligence organizations were most notable by their absence. Both organizations and technical means of intelligence collection began to enter the field about the time of the American Civil War. Scientific inventions drove these changes as the twentieth century opened, World War I demonstrated a continuing need for intelligence, and World War II provided a huge impetus for all kinds of intelligence collection methods. The coherent theory of intelligence discussed in this essay also began to come into focus with World War II. The sophistication of all techniques has improved constantly since then, and the Cold War served to spotlight evolving methods. Intelligence is now characterized by a synergistic dynamic in which information requirements drive technological improvements, while scientific talent solves collection problems, thus making new information important and creating fresh requirements.

Agents Spying has been characterized as "the second oldest profession," in the sense that its attempts to divine an adversary's intentions and capabilities are recorded throughout history. Agents remained important even in the era of the machine spy, for some kinds of information cannot be gathered by technical collection means. In the post–Cold War era, with an intelligence focus dominated by terrorism, drug trafficking, international criminal activity, and concerns regarding the proliferation of weapons of mass destruction, much of the key thinking and decision making of adversaries took place in a manner more accessible to the spy than to the machine. As cost became a factor as well, it was evident that in many cases spies were cheaper than machines, even with the extensive networks of the CIA and other agencies for the care and feeding of spies. At the beginning of the twenty-first century, spies were the province of the CIA's Directorate of Operations and the Defense Human Intelligence Service of the Defense Intelligence Agency. There were continuing conflicts, to some degree inherent in the nature of this kind of activity, between employment of spies to gather intelligence and their role in covert action, political action, or other fields. In addition, there were difficulties from a human rights perspective, because individuals recruited as agents frequently had checkered pasts. Only in the 1990s did the United States establish standards for personal character in individuals recruited as agents, and these were sometimes honored more in the breach than in the observance. Spies remained a necessary evil.

Individuals to be recruited were often identified by a third party and sometimes solicited by them as well. All aspects of the agent's relationship with intelligence were handled by a case officer, a CIA (or other agency) person who was not himself or herself the spy. The case officer typically reported to the CIA station in the country in which the espionage took place, though in exceptional cases a relationship might have run directly to headquarters. Material from agents was rewritten by "reports officers" before being circulated to analysts who used it to compile finished intelligence of the kinds noted already. Some policymakers, for example national security adviser Zbigniew Brzezinski during the Carter administration, insisted upon being shown the raw agent reports.

Attachés   The diplomatic service assigns individuals to posts in foreign capitals as commercial, economic, and cultural attachés. These posts are often used by the CIA and other agencies to provide a cover occupation for intelligence officers overseas. More important, the military services openly send officers to foreign countries as attachés. These officers provide a channel of communication between the U.S. military and foreign services, provide occasional diplomatic assistance, and more or less openly gather intelligence. The practice of sending military attachés in general dates from the late eighteenth century and was adopted as a standard by Napoleonic France (1799–1815). In the United States, the army colonel Emory Upton conducted a two-year research visit to Europe and Asia in the 1870s and demonstrated the value of military officers gathering information abroad.

The U.S. Navy also conducted such roving visits beginning in 1870. Naval attachés (the Marine Corps shares in naval attaché assignments) have been permanently stationed in foreign nations since 1882, army attachés since 1889, and air force attachés (first as part of the Army Air Corps) since the 1930s. The Defense Intelligence Agency (DIA) administers the attaché program, using officers seconded from all the armed services. Reports go to DIA, where they are used in publications and circulated to other intelligence agencies. Attachés can provide considerable amounts of information, even from closed societies. For example, in 1954 an air attaché in Moscow furnished the initial intelligence on a Soviet heavy jet bomber. Similarly, U.S. naval attachés in Japan before World War II reported on Japanese technological improvements, including early data on oxygen-powered torpedoes, the highly capable Zero fighter, the large-caliber guns of the Yamato-class superbattleships, and other matters. Military attachés in Czechoslovakia (now the Czech Republic) during that same period sent home valuable material on Soviet military doctrine and organization.

Combat Intelligence   Often ignored, combat intelligence is acquired by military forces in the course of their activities, and not only in wartime. A wide variety of intelligence can be encompassed by this category, which includes things learned by scout patrols sent out by ground forces, data from interrogation of prisoners (and defectors), lucky finds by forces in the field, and observations made during normal operations. Information from defectors proved a fruitful source during the Cold War, and would merit its own category except that interrogation of prisoners—the same function—fits more naturally into this category.

A few examples illustrate this category nicely. Union armies in the Civil War made a lucky find in September 1862 when a copy of General Robert E. Lee's orders to his Army of Northern Virginia was discovered wrapped around some cigars shortly before the Battle of Antietam. In World War II, German prisoners taken before the Battle of the Bulge (December 1944) revealed details of preparations for an attack that were not taken seriously, leading to surprise of U.S. troops along the front. Beginning in March 1978, in the course of normal operations, the submarine USS *Batfish* detected and followed a Soviet Yankee-class ballistic missile submarine for some seventy-seven days, thereby gaining key information about the practices and habits of these Soviet strategic forces. In 1983 information from the Russian intelligence officer and defector Oleg Gordievsky proved critical in interpreting a series of Soviet moves indicating they believed nuclear war might be at hand. The case of the war scare of 1983 also shows directly how this kind of intelligence can be reflected in analytical reports, since Gordievsky's information was incorporated in a special NIE done in early 1984.

Scientific Intelligence Scientific intelligence is gleaned from study of technical or scientific documents (often research papers) produced by the intelligence target, or from direct examination of equipment or machinery captured from an enemy in wartime or somehow acquired during peace. Scientific intelligence reached a takeoff point during World War II when the effort to gather information in this fashion first became systematic. Notable examples from that period include British successes in countering radio navigation systems used by German bombers in the Battle of Britain (1940), and in deceiving the Germans as to the accuracy of their rockets and ramjets (V-weapons) launched against Great Britain in 1944–1945. A U.S. example is the capture and analysis of the Japanese Zero fighter aircraft, results of which were incorporated into the design of a countering aircraft, the Grumman F6F Hellcat. A Cold War example is how the United States learned of Soviet aircraft design techniques from examining a MiG-25 supersonic aircraft whose pilot flew it to Japan to defect in 1977.

Electronic Intelligence Related to scientific intelligence in that it is also analyzed by scientists, electronic intelligence, too, received a great boost in World War II. It involves the reception and recording of electronic emissions, usually from radars, or of the telemetry transmissions from guided missiles, ships, or aircraft undergoing testing. Scientists are able to deduce from this information the radio frequency bands and other characteristics of radars, or a variety of information about systems being tested. Submarines, surface ships, aircraft, and space satellites have all been used to gather electronic intelligence. From the 1940s until at least the 1980s the United States maintained a vigorous program of flights by aircraft equipped to collect electronic intelligence along the periphery of the Soviet Union, China, and other communist countries. These flights, known in the trade as "ferret" operations, numbered over 20,000 and account for the vast majority of the planes shot down in the course of Cold War spy flights. In August 1964 the American destroyers involved in the Gulf of Tonkin incident in the Vietnam War were on an electronic intelligence mission. The same was true of the ship *Liberty*, attacked by the Israeli air force during the Six-Day War (June 1967), and the ship *Pueblo*, captured by North Korea in January 1968. Similarly, a U.S. Navy EP-3E reconnaissance plane off the southern Chinese coast became involved in an incident on 1 April 2001, when a jet fighter of the People's Republic of China subjected the American plane to such intense harassment that the two craft collided. The Chinese aircraft was lost, and the American plane had to make a forced landing in China, where the crew was held in custody for eleven days, until the United States made a formal statement that could be taken as an apology. In general, gathering electronic intelligence has been among the most dangerous kind of intelligence missions, and has provoked serious diplomatic repercussions as well. On the other hand, electronic intelligence can be quite useful. An example can be taken from 1978, when telemetry data from Russian missile tests indicated that a certain Russian ICBM was being tested with more reentry vehicles than it was credited with by diplomats negotiating the SALT II treaty. In this case the result was to negotiate new definitions for the treaty on how to count missiles for inclusion in the categories allowed by the treaty.

Communications Intelligence Communications intelligence is a large subject that includes secret writing, codes and ciphers, transmission and interception, and decryption. All these are aspects of the process of gaining access to, and then knowledge of the contents of, the private communications of a target, whether an individual or a state. This type of intelligence has probably existed as long as there have been spies, given the advantages of knowing what a spy was reporting. Government messages have long been sent in code, and breaking those codes offers knowledge of the inner thoughts of the opponent. In modern usage, messages are most often sent by radio, cable, teletype, E-mail, or other forms of electronic transmission. These communications are subject to interception, and this source of intelligence is considered among the best (and most sensitive, from a security standpoint). The general label of "communications intelligence" used here encompasses all aspects of contriving to intercept messages, analysis of the transmissions, decryption and decoding of the contents, and translation and making the results available to friendly intelligence analysts. In the United States each of the armed services has a component dedicated to communications intelligence, and all feed material to an umbrella civilian unit, the National Security Agency (NSA). With increasing technical sophistication the personnel requirements for collection of radio transmissions have decreased—the armed services alone employed roughly 120,000 people for this purpose in the 1960s, but the number went down to about half of that by 2000. The NSA employs approximately 20,000 people. With much of the burden of collection switched to satellites, ground stations have been abandoned in Pakistan (1969), Ethiopia (around 1975), Subic Bay in the Philippines (1985), and Berlin (about 1995). In 2000 there were still ground stations in Turkey, Japan, South Korea, and, by means of liaison relationship, in China. Diplomacy and foreign aid required to maintain communications intelligence ground stations have been a complicating factor in U.S. foreign policy.

Special collection operations are sometimes conducted by the CIA or other agencies for the benefit of the NSA. Best known of these are the tunnels built in Vienna (1949) and Berlin (1945–1955), and under the Russian embassy in Washington, D.C. (1985–?), for the purpose of placing listening devices and taps on telephone or teleprinter cables. Diplomatic fallout adverse to the United States occurred when these operations were revealed. In almost every case the target became aware of the special collection activity before its public revelation, and used that knowledge to feed false information to U.S. intelligence. Another special activity involved the use of submarines to secretly place taps on telephone cables underwater in the Russian Far East.

Communications intelligence works like a huge vacuum cleaner, and for all of its difficulties has proved a highly valuable intelligence source. Communications provided key information on the structure and activities of Soviet armed forces; important insights into negotiating aims of Soviet-American arms control talks from the 1970s to the 1990s; data on Chinese involvement in the Korean War; vital information on North Vietnamese commands and on the Ho Chi Minh Trail during the Vietnam War; material on Soviet maneuvers in various international crises; knowledge of the activities of drug cartels and others using telephone communications from the 1980s on; and much else. Communications intelligence played a huge role in World War II, a significant role in World War I, and evolved continuously from the moment when Morse code telegraphy began in the 1850s.

Photographic Intelligence Images taken with a camera have been an intelligence source since World War I. Observation from above ground level increases the scope of this intelligence, and aerial observation has been in use since a French officer used a balloon to watch the Austro-German enemy at the Battle of Fleurus in 1794. In the American Civil War balloons were used in this manner, and the first recorded instance of aerial photography dates from that time. The airplane was an important scout in World War I, with cameras soon added, and purpose-built cameras and aerial photography reached a stage of advanced development in World War II. During the Cold War the U.S. Air Force used specialized reconnaissance squadrons for overhead photography. In the mid-1950s the CIA joined the effort, first with high-altitude photo planes (the U-2 and SR-71) and then space satellites (CORONA, or KH-4, with follow-ons, currently up to KH-12). Sophisticated films, cameras, computer-driven digital readout techniques, and database-linked photo interpretation techniques have made overhead reconnaissance a premier intelligence source. The National Reconnaissance Office, formed in 1960 but whose existence was admitted only in 1992, controls the production and operation of satellite systems (aircraft reconnaissance systems known today remain under the auspices of the air force). Interpretation of imagery and circulation of intelligence reports based on photographic intelligence is the province of the National Imagery and Mapping Agency, formed in 1995 from components merged from the CIA and the Pentagon.

Some photography other than overhead reconnaissance is also important to intelligence. Submarines have taken pictures through their periscopes of coastal targets ranging from invasion beaches to adversaries' naval bases. Casual pictures taken by private citizens ("Aunt Minnie photographs") may show objects of intelligence interest. In addition, a quite critical contribution through photography is made by the miniature cameras that secret agents use to surreptitiously photograph documents, and the microdot and other photographic methods used to assist the communication of secrets from agent to handlers. These aspects of photography, and related research and development to create the cameras, are the responsibility of the CIA's directorates of administration, science and technology, and operations.

Domestic Collection Intelligence services acquire some information directly from Americans or from foreign citizens who are not agents or spies in any traditional sense. An individual traveling to a foreign country might be asked about impressions gained during the visit. Journalists, missionaries, and others residing abroad have frequently been a source for well-grounded local information. Academics expert in a certain field can provide information or perspectives of which agency personnel are unaware. Businesspeople may have valuable contacts and knowledge. At times, such as the period of the communist Union of Soviet Socialist Republics, this kind of collection from individuals was such a significant source that the CIA made efforts in advance to ask persons traveling to that country to be alert for information on specific matters. This technique remains useful in closed societies. At one time the CIA maintained the Domestic Contact Service to gather this information. The function still exists, although the work of that office has been subdivided elsewhere within the agency.

Open Source Information Evaluations of sources of intelligence consistently find that perhaps 80 to 90 percent of information necessary to intelligence can be obtained from sources that are completely public. The term "open sources" has become current for this category of material, which includes newspapers, magazines, technical journals, scientific papers, books, video programs, information that appears on the Internet, and similar items. Since the mid-1990s there has been a more explicit effort to improve the collection and use of open source material. For a short time the CIA contemplated a major directorate for open sources, but eventually settled on the Office for Open Source Collection, which today is located within the Directorate for Science and Technology. Open source information is highly desirable in that its collection involves no political or diplomatic obstacles, often includes material that already has been analyzed to some extent, and is relatively inexpensive compared to data gathered from technical collection sources. A significant drawback lies in the fact that intelligence officers and the policymakers who rely upon them often attribute greater credibility, almost automatically, to information that is "born secret," simply because it is secret.

Liaison with Friendly Intelligence Services Foreign intelligence services with which the United States is allied or maintains private relations are significant sources of information. The best known of these relationships is that with the British, forged during World War II and regularly renewed since. Similar relationships exist with Canada, Australia, New Zealand, Japan, France, Germany, Italy, Turkey, Greece, Israel, and other nations. Some relationships are multilateral and general in nature, similar to military alliances. Others pertain to specific subjects. Some relations exist even with former enemies, such as between the United States and Russia on organized crime. Sharing of intelligence information varies with the degree of trust—for example, the United States shares a wide range of information with Great Britain, but much less with France. The use of the CIA as an intermediary, such as between Israel and the Palestinian Authority from 1998 to 2001, can also have diplomatic aspects. The question of liaison relationships is also complicated by efforts of the partners to spy on one another. United States–Israeli intelligence cooperation soured after 1985, when naval intelligence analyst Jonathan J. Pollard was revealed as an Israeli agent. More recently, French–U.S. relations have been complicated by allegations that the nations engaged in industrial spying against one another, a situation that led to the recall of a CIA station chief in Paris in February 1995. Interests in preserving intelligence relationships may factor in diplomatic initiatives in many instances.

Counterintelligence The work of uncovering foreign spies in one's own country or intelligence services is termed counterintelligence or counterespionage. This work predates creation of the Office of Strategic Services in World War II, having been a major focus of U.S. naval intelligence even during the prewar years. From its inception the CIA had a counterintelligence staff within the Directorate of Operations; in recent years this has risen to the status of a center combining both CIA and FBI resources and headed by an FBI official. Counterintelligence can be a double-edged sword. The knowledge and access to secret information of counterintelligence units made them a favorite target for the Soviet secret service during the Cold War, as epitomized by the Russian recruitment of British counterintelligence chief Harold ("Kim") Philby, who, after years of suspicion, fled to Russia in early 1963.

The existence and duration of counterintelligence investigations can also have a negative impact on an intelligence organization. During the 1960s, when James J. Angleton headed the CIA's counterintelligence staff, inquiries aimed at suspected (but innocent) agency officers came close to paralyzing the CIA's foreign intelligence effort against the Soviet Union. Some observers argue that the reaction to the excesses of the 1960s was to dismantle much of the counterintelligence effort, leading to a permissive climate in which espionage flourished—thus "the year of the spy" in 1985, during which half a dozen major spies for Russia or China were uncovered, and the cases of Aldrich Ames (1994) and Robert Hanssen (2001), each of whom succeeded in spying for Russia for at least a decade without being caught.

Counterintelligence failures like these invariably lead to more stringent security regulations and regular monitoring and reinvestigation of veteran intelligence officers. In the United States there are demands for the broad use of polygraph (lie detector) tests, whose utility and accuracy are disputed. The net effect of heightened security, aside from catching spies, is that at some level the work of everyone engaged in intelligence becomes more difficult due to the compartmentalization, degree of precaution, and breadth of disclosure to security officials. In turn, this makes personnel retention a problem. In addition, stringent counterintelligence regimes inhibit the recruitment of spies in the adversary's camp because of the fear that the agents are enemy personnel deliberately attempting to mislead the side recruiting them. Consequently there is a trade-off between efficiency of intelligence work (with danger of espionage as a result) and tight security (with the consequence of lowered morale and performance from intelligence officers). The United States has not yet been able to solve this equation and has vacillated between extremely permissive and tight regimes.

Leaks of information owing to espionage damage the credibility of intelligence, with both policymakers and the public; relations with cooperating intelligence services (which fear information they share may end up in the hands of enemies); and the cohesion of the intelligence community. Counterintelligence is necessary but poses a continuing dilemma.

EVOLUTION OF U.S. INTELLIGENCE

A factor in American history since the revolutionary war, the intelligence community that uses the methods here discussed and produces the kinds of data enumerated is necessarily the product of a long evolution. At the time of the Revolution, there was no such thing as the "community" of today; there was not even an organization in the conventional sense. Spying was largely a freelance business. Paul Revere's ride in April 1775 alerting colonists to a British foray from Boston—a classic example of warning intelligence—was a personal initiative. For the most part, generals ran spies directly as part of their scout services. This was the relationship between British General Henry Clinton and his agent Major John André, as well as that of George Washington with spies John Honeyman and Joshua Merserau, and scouts like Knowlton's Rangers (Nathan Hale, possibly the best known revolutionary war spy, was a volunteer from that unit.) This approach continued through the Civil War, which saw the beginnings of a distinct intelligence mission. In 1861–1862 General George S. McClellan relied upon Allan Pinkerton's organization, the Pinkerton National Detective Agency, for both intelligence and counterespionage work. Many of the Pinkerton reports exaggerated Confederate strength, and McClellan's successors terminated the Pinkerton connection, but spying nevertheless became much more systematic. No formal arrangements for spying existed on the Confederate side, but there, too, agents were often used. Scholars of the period have identified more than 4,200 persons who functioned as spies, informants, guides, scouts, and so on. President Abraham Lincoln's assassin, John Wilkes Booth, certainly a Confederate sympathizer, may have been a southern agent as well.

After the Civil War the U.S. military began to collect information on foreign militaries more systematically. In 1866 the Assistant Secretary of the Navy Gustavus Fox went to Russia on an official information-gathering mission. In 1882 the Office of Naval Intelligence became the first official U.S. intelligence agency. The army created an information office in 1885 that became the Military Intelligence Division in 1918. World War I stimulated growth of both units, as well as the

Cipher Bureau within the State Department on 17 June 1917. The latter contained a code-breaking unit that achieved notoriety (revealed in the 1930s) for unraveling Japanese instructions to their diplomats at the Washington Naval Conference of 1921–1922, an early illustration of the utility of intelligence. The code-breaking unit was abolished in 1929, but State continued to play a coordinating role among U.S. agencies in the field right through World War II.

The need for coordination grew when President Franklin D. Roosevelt ordered the Federal Bureau of Investigation, previously entirely involved in crime solving, to carry out counterespionage activities in Latin America. Roosevelt also created a propaganda organization with quasi-intelligence functions, the Office of Coordination of Information, in 1941. This soon evolved into a true intelligence organization, the Office of Strategic Services (OSS), with propaganda left to the Office of War Information. The OSS developed both analytical and operational sides, greatly benefiting from the pillars of intelligence developed during the war. When the OSS was abolished in 1945, its espionage (and counterespionage) elements went to the War Department, while its analytical unit was absorbed by the State Department, eventually becoming the Bureau of Intelligence and Research that exists today. The other former OSS elements, meanwhile, had a difficult time within the War Department, where OSS counterespionage was seen to be in competition with the army's Counterintelligence Corps, and its espionage nets as having little to contribute.

A far cry from the dreams of former OSS chief General William J. Donovan for a peacetime permanent intelligence service, the postwar situation resulted from decisions by President Harry S. Truman, who was concerned primarily with ending the ravages of war, and not especially fond of Donovan or his ideas. With a growing Cold War in 1946 and later, Truman worried more about intelligence. He approved formation of the National Intelligence Authority in January 1946, under which the former clandestine units from OSS were gathered with the Central Intelligence Group. This order also created the post of director of central intelligence. But the National Intelligence Authority proved to be moribund, and the Central Intelligence Group, of very limited utility, was stymied by the departments of government in competition with it. In 1947, as part of the National Security Act (Public Law 80-253), which also established the Department of Defense and National Security Council, the Central Intelligence Agency became the legally authorized U.S. foreign intelligence organization. As Truman described his intentions to an aide several years later, he had wanted a unit to take the intelligence flowing to him from "200 different sources" and boil it down to make presentations—exactly the kind of activity at the heart of the intelligence cycle described at the outset of this narrative. Functions of the National Intelligence Authority were taken over by the National Security Council (NSC) while the CIA absorbed the Central Intelligence Group.

For several years the CIA grew slowly and gradually acquired missions. Covert operations and political action were added to the agency's basic analytical and espionage functions with the formation of the Office of Policy Coordination by NSC directive in 1948. A 1949 review by a panel of outside consultants found flaws in CIA operations and led to covert action and espionage both being merged in the Directorate of Operations (called the Directorate of Plans until 1973). Agency work interpreting photography led to formation of the National Photographic Interpretation Center in 1953, which the CIA ran on behalf of the entire intelligence community until the 1995 creation of the National Imagery and Mapping Agency. The need for development of machine spies obliged the director of central intelligence to conduct certain research programs, such as U-2, SR-71, and CORONA development, directly out of his own office, but this became formalized in 1962 with creation of the Directorate of Science and Technology (called Directorate of Research until 1964). The Directorate of Administration is responsible for support, security, data processing, recruitment, printing, finance, logistics, training, and other functions.

Air Force General Hoyt S. Vandenberg, who played a key role in the elaboration of the original legislation creating the CIA, left intelligence shortly before the actual creation of the agency. President Truman continued to appoint military officers as his directors of central intelligence, with Admiral Roscoe Hillenkoetter presiding over the CIA's first few years but damaged by a controversy regarding whether the CIA had been surprised by the outbreak of the Korean War or by Chinese intervention in that conflict. Walter Bedell Smith, an army general, instituted important reforms, including strengthening CIA analytical capabilities with the Directorate of Intelligence and the Board of National Estimates.

It was Smith who began the practice of assembling the interagency National Intelligence Estimates. Under President Dwight D. Eisenhower, DCI Allen W. Dulles emphasized covert operations and began the U-2 and other scientific development programs. Dulles served on into the administration of President John F. Kennedy, but the CIA's spectacular failure at the Bay of Pigs invasion of Cuba, a covert operations disaster in April 1961, effectively bankrupted his leadership, and he left the CIA that fall.

During the 1950s the U.S. intelligence community as a whole assumed the basic shape it still retained at the beginning of the twenty-first century. Code-breaking branches of the army and navy had contributed greatly to the outcome of World War II, and each of the services had retained its unit subsequently; the air force and marines added their own radio intelligence branches as well. In search of better coordination, the joint Armed Forces Security Agency was created in 1949 but, beset by interservice rivalries, never achieved its intended effect. President Truman replaced this unit with the National Security Agency in 1952. President Eisenhower, concerned with the multiplication of satellite intelligence mechanisms, and with infighting over programs between the CIA and the air force, created the National Reconnaissance Office (NRO) in 1960 (although its existence remained a secret until 1992). President Kennedy, upset with the tendency of the armed services intelligence branches to promote views favoring their parent services, set up the Defense Intelligence Agency (DIA) in 1961. Armed forces intelligence regenerated over time, and the services always remained crucial in the NSA- and NRO-led activities. Not until 1995, when President William J. Clinton approved formation of the National Imagery and Mapping Agency, a merging of offices from the Pentagon, CIA, NRO, and the services, was any new national-level intelligence agency added to the community. All these units are agencies of the Department of Defense. These agencies also operate in some of the most highly technical—and expensive—areas of intelligence work. The result is that the secretary of defense controls the vast majority (85–95 percent) of the intelligence budget even while the director of central intelligence carries the official mantle of leadership in the community.

Beginning with John A. McCone, director of central intelligence from November 1961 to April 1964, DCIs have made a more intense effort to lead the community, often through procedures for coordinating among the various agencies, multi-year budget studies, or setting requirements for intelligence collection. These efforts have met with very limited success. The Pentagon's control of a large proportion of appropriated funds has been a key obstacle but not the only one. In the case of the FBI and the State Department's Bureau of Intelligence and Research, and certain other entities, small elements of large government departments participate in the intelligence community but are responsible to cabinet officials over whom the DCI has no authority. The actual degree to which a director of central intelligence can lead the intelligence community is a recurrent issue in American policy.

McCone and his successors, notably Richard Helms (1966–1973) and Williams E. Colby (1973–1975), faced the major task of integrating the new intelligence technologies into the old framework. Satellites, sophisticated electronic emissions receivers and recording devices, underwater receivers, airborne interception mechanisms, computer data handling and image interpretation, and many other innovations transformed the intelligence business during the 1960s and 1970s. In particular, the sheer volume of information collected that was deemed to have intelligence value grew astronomically. Finished intelligence reports that used all the new information were a great improvement over earlier products, as exemplified by the way the missile gap dispute was resolved through the advent of satellite photography. But management of the new mechanisms, scientific research and development for intelligence purposes, funding these expensive systems, and finding ways to use the information without compromising the security of intelligence collection all posed problems for community leaders. These issues recur as new generations of intelligence technology reach the hands of operators.

The opposite side of the same coin is the need for old-fashioned spies, "human intelligence." The machines gather vast amounts of information whose importance is difficult to gauge. The inside information given by agents is often a key to interpretation. This issue became salient during the 1970s, and virtually every policy review of intelligence since then has upheld the need for more human intelligence sources. In response to the felt need, the CIA redoubled efforts to recruit agents. During the Cold War the agency enjoyed considerable success; in the Vietnam War and against China spying proved more difficult. On terrorism and drug trafficking, key intelligence questions of the 1990s and the twenty-first century, the need for spies was still acute. At the same time evolving human rights and moral standards make unacceptable the recruitment of agents whose character would have been ignored in an earlier age. There will be continuing tension between different aspects of agency interest in human intelligence.

A thorny issue that has also recurred for U.S. policymakers is the degree to which intelligence does, or should, directly impact on U.S. foreign policy. The ideal concept has been that intelligence speaks truth to power; that is, secret information to policymakers informs decisions that are made on the basis of this private knowledge. In theory, the information is disinterested and devoid of private agendas; in practice this is often not the case, even for simple intelligence analysis. One reason alone justifies the existence of the CIA, despite the many objections made about it: this organization provides presidents and their top officials with a source of information independent of the government departments responsible for actions. Military intelligence traditionally takes the most dire view of the threat, thus justifying large defense budgets and weapons purchases to counter that threat. In war, military intelligence reports most optimistically on the results of operations. In the Vietnam War, the Gulf War, and the Kosovo War (1999), military intelligence estimates of the effectiveness of bombing in every case had to be revised downward after they were made. During the Vietnam War, there were notorious controversies between the military, both air force and DIA, and the CIA over the degree of success obtained in bombing North Vietnam. For its part, State Department intelligence sees possibilities for negotiation where none may exist. Here, too, the CIA can play a cautionary role.

However, the pure archetype of intelligence theory is difficult to achieve in fact. Directors of central intelligence can be, and have been, asked for their opinions on policy subjects. The mere act of a president putting his DCI on the spot by asking an opinion takes the CIA (and the intelligence community more broadly) out of the role of neutral arbiter and inserts it into the policy process as an interested player. Declassified records of the National Security Council, which are currently available for a period spanning the 1940s through the 1970s, show DCIs Allen Dulles, John A. McCone, Richard Helms, William Colby, and George H. W. Bush all commenting on policy, not merely intelligence matters. When more documents covering these and later periods become available, they will undoubtedly demonstrate the same pattern for other DCIs. It is the president's prerogative to solicit advice from anyone, not excepting intelligence officials, but this adds to the difficulty of preserving separation between intelligence and policy roles.

Another facet of the problem of preserving a separation in roles arises from the DCI's responsibility to protect intelligence sources and methods. That statutory responsibility may conflict with policy in ways we are not aware of today. Desire to protect an intelligence source may lead a director to furnish disguised or watered-down information that presents less than a full picture. Conversely, full disclosure may result in compromise of sources. For example, it has been reported that during the Carter administration, a leak from an NSC staffer led the Soviet Union to arrest aircraft designer Adolf Tolkachev, who had been one of the CIA's most valuable sources. Directors of central intelligence must be aware of the dangers that lie at the nexus of policy and intelligence.

A further aspect to the policy-intelligence conundrum is that the CIA, and the intelligence community more broadly, do have certain policy interests. In particular, these arise when intelligence engages in covert operations. Political action in western Europe during the Truman administration; paramilitary operations in the Far East, South Asia, and Latin America during the Eisenhower administration; and paramilitary actions in Nicaragua, Angola, Cambodia, Mozambique, and Afghanistan during the Reagan administration all represented real U.S. foreign policy initiatives in which the CIA was a principal player. To say that agency advice to a president can be divorced from policy interests in such cases is wishful thinking. It is also nugatory to argue that such covert operations are small items that can safely be ignored within the confines of a larger global policy. The Kennedy administration's failure with the CIA invasion of Cuba at the Bay of Pigs in 1961 had major impact on Kennedy's predispositions in many policy areas. The Iran-Contra affair during the Reagan administration triggered a near-constitutional crisis in the United States. Another Reagan-era covert operation, the CIA paramilitary action in Afghanistan, encouraged the development of, and provided weapons and training to, fundamentalist Islamic guerrillas who transformed themselves into anti-U.S. terrorists in the years after the war. As of 2001, Islamic terror was construed to be one of the top national security threats to the United States. Programmatic interests in supportive capabilities, such as military special forces, intelligence satellites and booster rockets, information and propaganda resources, and so on, are clearly also areas where intelligence has an actual policy stake. In short, the separation of intelligence from policy has always been imperfect and waxes and wanes depending on the president, his policy proclivities, and the constellation of senior officials surrounding the chief executive.

INTELLIGENCE ISSUES IN FOREIGN AND NATIONAL SECURITY POLICY

Intelligence can have great value in foreign policy and national security, but good intelligence is difficult to come by. Among the leading foreign policy dilemmas posed by intelligence is the need to frame relations with nations as affected by certain aspects of the spy business. The desire to maintain ground bases for certain technical collection means, or for covert operations, may drive decisions on economic and military assistance. General bilateral relations can be affected by nations' spying against one another, particularly when major agents are caught and revealed or ships and aircraft crash or are captured. A desire to recruit agents may dictate waiver of human rights concerns that should be upheld, with the consequent danger of difficulties should such relationships surface. The desire to preserve a stream of intelligence sharing may be threatened by friendly nations spying on one another, or by fears of secret information leaking to third countries. In addition, bilateral relations can be directly affected by intelligence covert operations, while the general image of the United States in the world can be influenced by impressions of how ready the United States may be to resort to covert operations.

In theory, intelligence represents a disinterested purveyor of unbiased information to the president and other leaders. This ideal remains an ideal because presidents are people—they ask for help and advice, recommendations on anything from policy to politics. Directors of central intelligence can be pulled into the policy fray even if they would prefer to avoid it. In addition, the notion that intelligence does not have any real policy interests of its own is flawed, for directors of central intelligence may also be drawn into policy issues due to their responsibility to protect sources and methods. The policy versus intelligence question remains a live issue in America.

Finally, there are issues that may require policy decisions that are directly intelligence matters. Most obvious is the budget—how much should the nation pay for intelligence, and are the data worth the outlays? Related budgetary issues include the distribution of funds among technical collectors, agents, development programs, analysts, support functions, and the rest. Information issues include the emphasis to be placed upon current reporting versus that devoted to long-range prediction. Also vital is the packaging of intelligence—what kinds of reports of what types are the most useful? An information issue that persists is the relative emphasis to be given to secret, as opposed to open source, information. Then there is the technical issue of the tension between the need for high-security counterintelligence and the desire for the most efficient intelligence community. At the apex is the community role of the director of central intelligence—how much leadership can or should the director exercise, and can or should Department of Defense and other players in the intelligence field be brought under the director's authority?

These are not the only recurring issues regarding intelligence and American foreign policy, but they are among the most salient. Each of the issues is relevant to structuring intelligence to best support American policy. All of the issues can confidently be expected to arise in the future, whatever their status may be in the present context. For this reason alone, they should be carefully considered.

BIBLIOGRAPHY

Andrew, Christopher. *For the President's Eyes Only: Secret Intelligence and the American Presidency from Washington to Bush.* New York, 1995.

Bamford, James. *Body of Secrets: Anatomy of the Ultra-Secret National Security Agency from the Cold War Through the Dawn of a New Century.* New York, 2001.

Brugioni, Dino A. *Eyeball to Eyeball: The Inside Story of the Cuban Missile Crisis.* New York, 1991.

Gates, Robert M. *From the Shadows: The Ultimate Insider's Story of Five Presidents and How They Won the Cold War.* New York, 1996.

Kent, Sherman. *Strategic Intelligence for American World Policy.* Princeton, N.J., 1949.

Peebles, Curtis. *The Corona Project: America's First Spy Satellites.* Annapolis, Md., 1997.

Prados, John. *The Soviet Estimate: U.S. Intelligence Analysis and Soviet Strategic Forces.* Princeton, N.J., 1986.

———. *President's Secret Wars: CIA and Pentagon Covert Operations from World War II Through the Persian Gulf War.* Chicago, 1996.

Richelson, Jeffrey T. *The U.S. Intelligence Community.* 4th ed. Boulder, Colo., 1999.

See also COLD WAR EVOLUTION AND INTERPRETATIONS; COLD WARRIORS; COVERT OPERATIONS; DECISION MAKING; PRESIDENTIAL POWER; PROPAGANDA; TERRORISM AND COUNTERTERRORISM.

INTERNATIONALISM

Warren F. Kuehl and Gary B. Ostrower

Internationalism in American foreign policy has had different meanings for nearly every generation of citizens and diplomats. It has been associated with all forms of external contact with the world, the relationships becoming more extensive and political with the passage of time. As a foreign policy, it has usually been viewed as the antithesis of isolationism, and in that sense it has involved political commitments or "entanglements" through multinational treaties as well as membership in international organizations. In a broader context, it has also encompassed official and unofficial nonpolitical activities—economic, social, cultural, and scientific—usually evidenced through affiliation with specialized international societies or agencies. Some internationalists have thought in terms of a universal community, a broad brotherhood of people with common concerns, needs, and aspirations that exists as a reality beyond the confines of nation-states. In recent times, internationalism has taken on a new meaning under a doctrine of responsibility, with the United States assuming the burden of "policeman of the world," both unilaterally and multilaterally.

THE EARLY YEARS

Long before isolationism became an established policy in the nineteenth century, citizens of the American colonies recognized that they could not live apart from the rest of the world. They existed within an imperial system that involved them in numerous crises and four world wars (Queen Anne's War, King William's War, King George's War, and the French and Indian War), mostly related to trade and territories. Early Americans understood that international law applied to them as they redefined their relationships toward their neighbors and their mother country. William Penn reflected the cosmopolitan atmosphere when he drafted his *Essay Towards the Present and Future Peace of Europe* (1693), in which he called for a congress of states to promote stability. Evidence of a broad perspective also appeared in a colonial union, the New England Confederation of 1643, and in the suggestion for joint action embodied in the Albany Plan of 1754. Joseph Galloway's proposal for an Anglo-American council in 1774 also expressed a cosmopolitan outlook. Such experiences, as well as an awareness of the Iroquois League of the Five Nations, may explain why revolutionary leaders like Benjamin Franklin and Thomas Paine spoke favorably of an international organization. Certainly, the Articles of Confederation and the Constitution of 1789 revealed a general awareness that sovereign states could combine to promote their interests.

Events during and after the Revolution related to the treaty of alliance with France, as well as difficulties arising over the neutrality policy pursued during the French revolutionary wars and the Napoleonic wars, encouraged another perspective. A desire for separateness and unilateral freedom of action merged with national pride and a sense of continental safety to foster the policy of isolation. Although the United States maintained diplomatic relations and economic contacts abroad, it sought to restrict these as narrowly as possible in order to retain its independence. The Department of State continually rejected proposals for joint cooperation, a policy made explicit in the Monroe Doctrine's emphasis on unilateral action. Not until 1863 did an American delegate attend an international conference. Even so, Secretary of State William H. Seward reflected prevailing views by refusing to sign an 1864 multilateral treaty related to the Red Cross. The United States did not subscribe to such a convention until 1882. Thereafter, cooperation on economic and social matters seemed acceptable, but political issues, especially those involving Europe, were generally avoided until the end of the century.

THE BEGINNINGS OF ORGANIZED INTERNATIONALISM

Although most citizens accepted the principle of isolationism, scattered voices throughout the nineteenth century called for a more cooperative stance toward the world. As early as the 1830s the American Peace Society, under the direction of William Ladd, sponsored essay contests concerning international organization, and in 1840 Ladd utilized many of the ideas in drafting his well-known *Essay on a Congress of Nations*. His proposal for both a political body and a judicial agency gained considerable public notice through petition and educational campaigns during the ensuing years. After Ladd's death in 1841, Elihu Burritt, a reformer known as "The Learned Blacksmith," presented the congress of nations program to European pacifists with such regularity that they referred to it as the "American idea."

The Civil War in America (1861–1865) and conflicts in Europe (1854–1856, 1870–1871) undermined the peace movement, but a developing interest in the law of nations kept alive the concept of global cooperation during the last third of the century. Several societies emerged to promote the codification of international rules of behavior and to encourage the settlement of disputes through arbitration by a third party. These were not new ideas, but leading citizens in many nations around the turn of the twentieth century seized upon the arbitration concept to guarantee a warless world.

This activity contributed substantially to the evolution of thought concerning an international organization. As countries signed arbitration accords, men—and a few women—began to think beyond such limited agreements. Agencies would be needed to implement the treaties; laws would have to be codified. As John Westlake, an English law professor, observed, "When we assert that there is such a thing as International Law, we assert that there is a society of States; when we recognize that there is a society of States, we recognize that there is International Law."

The arbitration settlement in 1871–1872 of the Alabama Claims, an Anglo-American dispute over damages caused by Confederate cruisers, led to the signing of many other arbitration agreements during the next four decades. Most were disputes involving monetary and boundary claims and questions arising under treaty clauses; this discouraged pacifists, who hoped to see accords calling for all controversies to be arbitrated. They rallied to promote their goal, gaining public endorsement in the 1890s. The Lake Mohonk (New York) Conference on International Arbitration, which began in 1895 and met annually through 1916, united American civic, business, religious, and educational leaders in a quest to institutionalize arbitration. Proponents recognized that the Senate would not subscribe to unlimited agreements, so they agreed that matters involving national honor and vital interests be exempted. Their support resulted in the Olney-Pauncefote Treaty with Great Britain in 1897, which called for the arbitration of monetary and territorial differences. As expected, the Senate exempted disputes affecting national interest and honor, and then insisted that the Senate have authority to exempt from arbitration any dispute submitted for settlement. Even these safeguards did not satisfy the extreme isolationists. After adding yet other reservations, the Senate refused to ratify the treaty.

These developments had a lasting impact upon American internationalist thought. First, arbitration accords encouraged the exploration of cooperative methods of resolving disputes and breached barriers that had kept statesmen from previously examining such subjects. Second, these experiences warned internationalists that they must be cautious about proposals for a union of nations. It was quite clear by the time that the United States fought Spain in 1898 that Washington would not assume obligations that would weaken its sovereignty or jeopardize interests deemed vital to its welfare. Finally, the advances in arbitration influenced discussions at the first genuine international assembly of nations, the Hague Conference of 1899.

ARBITRATION AND LEGALISM

U.S. delegates at The Hague supported a convention to create the Permanent Court of Arbitration. Because the Court was little more than a list of names of persons who could be called upon to hear issues, because the convention exempted matters of national honor or interest, and because the submission of disputes was optional for governments, isolationists in the Senate put up little serious resistance. The convention proved popular, especially after the American delegates added a proviso that ratification would not mean abandoning traditional policies of nonentanglement or policies like those found in the Monroe Doctrine.

The convention fertilized the young internationalist movement. By 1900 a number of persons had presented plans that would move the world beyond courts of arbitration. Most of these called for a world federation that vaguely reflected the American political experience. Benjamin F. Trueblood, secretary of the American Peace Society, advanced the idea in *The Federation of the World* (1899), in articles, and in lectures. The interdependence of men and nations, he argued, would lead inevitably to "a complete political union of the world, a great international world state, built up somewhat on the pattern of our union of States, with supreme legislative, judicial and executive functions touching those interests which the nations have in common." Trueblood quickly cautioned that he envisioned no powerful agency. The union would operate primarily in a legislative and judicial capacity, without a formal executive, and it would possess no authority to compel its members to maintain peace. Between 1899 and 1914 a wide variety of proposals appeared, with a few internationalists devoting exceptional thought and time to the subject. Their suggestions unquestionably influenced the twentieth-century movement toward international organization, and their writings reflected a number of basic assumptions. First, they believed that an inexorable evolutionary process was at work. That process included the arbitration treaties, the willingness of governments to cooperate at The Hague in 1899, and the budding interest of governments in a court of justice. Secretary of State Elihu Root in 1907 enunciated this viewpoint when he declared that the importance of The Hague meeting of 1899 was that it made a follow-up meeting possible. Out of this he foresaw law, order, and peace. Said Root, "The world has entered upon an orderly process through which, step-by-step, in successive conferences, each taking the work of its predecessor as its point of departure, there may be continual progress toward making the practice of civilized nations conform to their peaceful professions."

Raymond Bridgman, a Boston journalist, echoed Root in a volume of essays, *World Organization* (1905). He saw continued meetings as the foundation stone for an international body. It could begin with a legislature modeled after the U.S. Congress, and then be followed by a court and an executive agency. New York attorney Hayne Davis also reflected this philosophy in articles published between 1903 and 1912. A "United Nations" would emerge, said Davis in what appears to have been the first use of that term. Just as the United States had been forced to develop a more perfect government after the Revolution and the Confederation period, so would the world be compelled to build a better system to keep the peace.

This evolutionary concept appeared in nearly all of the internationalist proposals. Each began by calling for further development of the arbitral network through a series of treaties that would bind nations together. Then states could explore other ways to promote their common needs. Events seemed to confirm such logic. Between 1903 and 1914 governments concluded more than 162 arbitration accords, and in 1907 the Second Hague Conference convened. The State Department kept step by negotiating a series of treaties in 1904 and 1905 that respected the Senate's concern for American rights, honor, and interests. Nevertheless, senators inserted into each agreement a clause giving the Senate the right to veto arbitration of a dispute. President Theodore Roosevelt reacted sharply. He considered the Senate action to be a violation of the constitutional authority of the chief executive and refused to exchange ratifications. In 1908, however, he relented, authorizing Root to negotiate other agreements that reflected the Senate's wishes.

In 1910, President William Howard Taft decided to go further and seek agreements to arbitrate all disputes. Two such treaties in 1911 inevitably ran afoul of the Senate, which nullified his efforts and restricted the process in such a way that Taft abandoned his quest. In short, even before Woodrow Wilson became president, internationalists understood that the Senate would likely object to any meaningful proposal for American participation in a world organization.

This may explain why Wilson's secretary of state, William Jennings Bryan, took a less controversial course by signing conciliation accords with many governments. Unlike arbitration agreements, these did not bind the signatories to the decisions of a third party. Bryan also introduced the "cooling-off" principle, whereby political leaders promised they would not resort to force while a case was pending. This concept was widely adopted after 1914.

Internationalists soon moved beyond their advocacy for an arbitration system and presented an even more important proposal. The world, they argued, needed a genuine court of justice. They viewed arbitration as limited because it contained no fixed principles that could be universally applied. With established laws and impartial judges, nations could submit disputes to a reliable and fair tribunal. With the U.S. Supreme Court as their (usually) unstated example, internationalists believed that an international system incorporating universally accepted rules (laws) might prompt governments to allow the court to hear even cases involving honor and independence.

The United States officially supported the goal of a court of justice at the Second Hague Conference, but the delegates had been unable to agree on a method of selecting judges. International lawyers and advocates of the evolutionary hypothesis continued to work for some type of judicial agency. The American Society of International Law, established in 1906, and the American Society for Judicial Settlement of International Disputes along with the Carnegie Endowment for International Peace, both formed in 1910, concentrated on this objective. Resolutions of peace congresses and other internationalist organizations reflected a popular desire for a judicial tribunal. President Taft's secretary of state, former corporate lawyer Philander C. Knox, proposed in 1909 that a maritime prize court discussed at the Second Hague Conference be reconstituted as an international court of justice. The proposal went nowhere. The fears of nationalists continued to be more influential than the hopes of the internationalists.

Nevertheless, proposals concerning an international court of justice inevitably revived interest in the old scheme of a periodic congress. Evolutionists viewed it as a vital next step. Even more significantly, advocates of an international court saw it as an important development because, they argued, some agency had to establish the rules (the international law) that would guide the judges. The First Hague Conference had stimulated demands for additional meetings, and the congress theme became increasingly popular after 1900. Bridgman began a successful petition campaign to obtain the endorsement of the Massachusetts legislature, while the American Peace Society embarked upon an extensive propaganda campaign to reach religious and civic bodies. One writer breathlessly called the periodic congress idea "the demand of the hour."

Such agitation prompted action that had a direct bearing upon calls for the Second Hague Conference. In 1904, representatives of the Interparliamentary Union, an association of legislators from congresses within nations, met at St. Louis, where they resolved to support the convening of a second Hague Conference. Under the leadership of U.S. Representative Richard Bartholdt of Missouri, they persuaded President Roosevelt to join them in calling on foreign chancelleries to support the plan. The 1907 conference was the fruit of their labors.

Bartholdt had launched this project along with peace advocate Hayne Davis, and the two men proposed that "a regular Congress of Nations be created, to meet at stated periods, to discuss international questions and make recommendations to the governments." By April 1906 the nearly two hundred congressmen who had joined the Interparliamentary Union agreed to endorse Bartholdt and Davis's aims. The periodic congress proposal gained acceptance at The Hague in 1907 in the form of a resolution calling for further meetings. Internationalists hoped that a third session might convene in 1914 or 1915. The outbreak of war, however, frustrated their aims.

As the periodic congress idea gained in popularity, some planners began to focus on specifics, exploring, for instance, how an evolving organization would operate and the powers that it must have. Perhaps unsurprisingly, most of these planners thought in terms of a federation modeled after that of the United States, with legislative, judicial, and executive agencies. Such a structure would allow nations to divide their sovereignty. They would allocate certain responsibilities to the central body while retaining control over those affairs most important to themselves, an arrangement that many internationalists hoped, or perhaps assumed, would mollify nationalistic members of the Senate. Hamilton Holt, managing editor of *The Independent* magazine, popularized this theme, with help from other prominent internationalists like Andrew Carnegie. The steel magnate repeatedly called for a "league of peace," a proposal that may well have inspired Theodore Roosevelt to float his own version of a league of peace in 1910.

The most ambitious undertaking in the years from 1910 to 1912 was what Holt and his co-activist, Oscar Crosby, called a World-Federation League. Its intricacy may have owed much to Crosby's background as an inventor and engineer. He and Holt had been energized by Roosevelt's brand of skeptical idealism. They called for the creation of a U.S. commission authorized to draft for Congress "articles of Federation" for the "maintenance of peace, through the establishment of a court that could decide any dispute between nations." This was revolutionary enough, but what especially distinguished their proposal was that the court would have the ability to enforce its judgments by calling for the use of military force by members of the federation. The Holt-Crosby emphasis on legal procedures backed up by military force would become more common—and more controversial—during the next decade.

Although Congress failed to address their proposal, in 1910 it did unanimously pass a resolution sponsored by Representative William S. Bennet of New York. Perhaps the fact that the resolution passed unanimously signifies that it had little real importance, for it actually committed the United States to nothing that nationalists viewed as threatening the concept of sovereignty. What the resolution did do, however, was to call for a commission to explore the possibility of both arms reduction and the creation of an international naval force (composed of existing navies) that could police the oceans. In a sense, this may have been less radical than it appears. Former President Theodore Roosevelt had recently incorporated the policing idea into what historians call the Roosevelt Corollary of the Monroe Doctrine as well as his league of peace proposal. Although his motives were no less nationalist than internationalist, he more or less legitimized the concept sufficiently to elicit congressional approval of Bennet's 1910 resolution.

President Taft, however, never acted. Despite pressure from pacifists and federationists, Taft—who would later contribute a great deal to the movement for a league of nations—kept his own counsel. Yet it is worth noting that Taft, whom historians generally view as much more conservative than either his predecessor or his successor, reflected the progressive emphasis on settling international disputes peacefully. Taft was the most legalistic president of the twentieth century, even more so than Woodrow Wilson. His commitment to the so-called conciliation treaties, along with his dedication to international law, provided additional foundation work for the flowering of internationalism later in the century.

ORGANIZATION FOR WORLD GOVERNMENT

A few internationalists of the pre-1914 period went beyond federal principles to advocate a world government. Sixty years later, this kind of thinking would fuel a backlash against internationalism. Not so before World War I, when the idea was too novel to inspire great fear. Journalist Raymond Bridgman called for an internationalist agency that would coin money, regulate trade, control patents and copyrights, and (again reflecting a powerful current in turn-of-the-century progressivism) even supervise global monopolies. He and his followers also favored the establishment of an international executive with considerable authority, including the authority to use force to maintain peace. Roosevelt incorporated this latter idea in his Nobel Peace Prize address; Holt occasionally flirted with the idea; and Bartholdt's suggestions to the Interparliamentary Union in 1905, no less than the Bennet resolution of 1910, embodied this principle. Andrew Carnegie, too, endorsed the need for an international police force, as did Lucia Ames Mead, a prominent Boston reformer and peace advocate. Publisher Edwin Ginn favored an army to maintain order, and Cyrus Street, an eccentric realtor from San Francisco, presented some extreme views along this vein. He published a small journal, called *The United Nations,* in which he noted the need for a government "with power to make, judge, and execute laws; and to provide for the final disposal of all their armies and navies." He meant by this that a United Nations would have the sole authority "to *enforce peace* and prevent war from *ever* occurring again" (italics in original). After 1919, of course, this would hardly seem so eccentric.

Representative James L. Slayden of Texas added another feature when he introduced House Joint Resolution 72 in April 1913. It called for all Western Hemisphere nations to unite in "the mutual guaranty of their sovereignty and territorial integrity." Although the resolution never got out of committee, it again points to the degree to which traditional isolationism—or, more accurately, the unilateralism expressed by such things as the Roosevelt Corollary—was subject to challenge.

In truth, such suggestions represented a minority opinion among those who favored the creation of an international organization prior to 1914. The plans for periodic congresses (inspired by the Congress System that emerged from the Vienna Conference of 1815), for a federal approach to order that clearly limited a single organization's powers, and for a court of justice appealed to many more Americans. Even the court idea, however, was complicated by competing legal visions. American delegates had proposed the formation of a court of justice at the Second Hague Peace Conference in 1907. The court concept, however, stood in conflict with the arbitration ideal that emerged from both the First and Second Hague Conferences. The formation of a Permanent Court of Arbitration appealed powerfully to some internationalists, but it contradicted the hopes of those, like legal scholar James Brown Scott, who hoped to see a court more committed to "adjudication" and less to arbitration. The differences between these concepts was not always clear, even among internationalists, but the former was usually viewed as more useful in legal disputes among nations, while the latter would presumably handle more "political" matters that involved the necessity for compromise.

While such debates monopolized the attention of lawyers, other internationalists gravitated toward more modest proposals. Historian George L. Beer advocated an English-speaking union, while Ellery C. Stowell, who taught law at Columbia University, believed that a general alignment of states along geographical lines would provide the basis of order. Stowell was among the first to use the term "internationalism," a concept that he viewed as binding America and its allies along both political and economic lines.

Cultural and racial considerations, too, came into play. The new Rhodes Scholarship program appealed to Americans—many of them imperialists like Theodore Roosevelt—who believed that the United States indeed should share the white man's burden. Internationalism and imperialism would part company in the United States after World War I, but there was yet no consensus about this in the prewar period, as the turn-of-the-century debate over the U.S. role in the Philippines had shown.

One thing, however, was becoming increasingly clear. The development of turbine-engine ocean liners and the telegraph had already compressed both time and space in ways that would profoundly influence the growth of internationalist thought. Since the end of the Civil War, Americans had participated in a growing number of meetings on an ever-widening variety of topics. "Functionalism," modern writers call this theme, as if to emphasize that cooperation regarding such functions has powered the growth of internationalism generally. Subjects as varied as communications, health and sanitation, weights and measures, patents, copyrights, currency, and agriculture provided the basis for international conferences. And not just conferences. The late nineteenth and early twentieth centuries became an age of organizations such as the General Postal Union, founded in 1875, followed by a telegraphic union, a health organization, and many others. These bodies redefined the very context in which isolationism could survive and internationalism would thrive. Not only public officials, but private citizens, served as delegates to these organizations and attended these conferences. Such contacts engendered a growing awareness of global interdependence as the United States developed industrially and thrust outward economically and territorially.

The result was the development among some internationalists of a genuine sense of global community, promoting what is commonly called cultural internationalism at the beginning of the twenty-first century. Unlike the more typical internationalists who took the Darwinian system of sovereign states for granted and sought to tame interstate competition through legal restrictions and, occasionally, military cooperation to enforce the peace, the cultural internationalists approached their task in a very different frame of mind. They saw the process of unity advancing not through a political process involving institutions and agencies created by the nation-state, but through the relationships of people more or less transcending the state. They were precursors of those who, a century later, would describe the world as a global village, and they viewed international society as much more organic than the political and legal internationalists who emphasized individual rights rather than the rights of societies (whether national or international). If the political and legal internationalists tended to approach their task via the rule of law and military enforcement, the cultural internationalists more often appealed to common interests and a sense of common humanity.

WORLD WAR I

The First World War began in Europe in 1914, engulfing the United States nearly three years later. This was the war that Americans of a progressive generation had sought to avoid, isolationists by ignoring Europe, internationalists by erecting the machinery that might prevent a small dispute from becoming a larger conflict. At first, internationalists despaired. In 1915, however, the military carnage in Europe energized Americans who argued not that international cooperation was impossible, but that it had not been sufficiently tried. In short, they resolved to work harder, to construct peacekeeping machinery that might work much more effectively than the failed pre-1914 arbitration and conciliation treaties.

Although arbitration and conciliation had been discredited, few internationalists gave up on the quintessentially American faith in law. Led by former president Taft, many Americans joined what soon became the most important internationalist organization of the wartime years, the League to Enforce Peace. Such a league, argued its founders, would incorporate a judicial court to provide the basis for international stability. Formed in the spring of 1915, it aimed to prevent war, not to win a war once war broke out or to use force as a threat to prevent states from violating the peace in the first place. This point is important, because the League to Enforce Peace really had little inclination to enforce anything. Its program reflected the prewar faith in procedural machinery that could be used to resolve differences before they erupted in war. It would compel nations to submit their disputes to various agencies in order to guarantee that peaceful disputes did not turn violent. Sanctions, both economic and military, theoretically existed to compel a state (or states, as long as they were members of the organization) to resolve differences peacefully. Presumably, sanctions would be applied whenever a party to a dispute refused to follow prescribed procedures. But theory and practice were never reconciled, for the League to Enforce Peace recommended no use of force in the event that states rejected its recommendations or decisions. As one of its leaders, Harvard president A. Lawrence Lowell, put it, no international organization could be effective once war erupted; it had to succeed in preventing war, not ending war.

Other internationalists agreed. Few would endorse the potential use of force by any international organization. The World's Court League, second only to the League to Enforce Peace as an internationalist organization with substantial national influence, called for a judicially centered body with no power to compel the submission of controversies or to uphold decisions. No power meant no effectiveness, but the noise of war ironically shrouded this reality in the context of World War I. The emphasis on judicial authority without enforcement provisions spoke to the aspirations of most Americans, who believed that it really made no sense to fight a war to prevent a war. Pacifists, of course, applauded such an approach. So did many lawyers who either neglected the need for enforcement to compel people (or states) to obey the law, or who were so enamored of the logic and sanctity of law that they ignored the fundamentally anarchic nature of the international system.

WILSON'S LEAGUE OF NATIONS

Despite the limitations of these plans, both organizations—the League to Enforce Peace and the World's Court League—campaigned vigorously to promote not only their projects but the more general idea of a league. Even the critics of international organization did not doubt that a vast majority of citizens found the league idea attractive by 1919. President Wilson incorporated it into the famous Fourteen Points address, his most important speech regarding war aims. At the Paris Peace Conference, he then insisted that the final peace treaty contain the League of Nations proposal. Nevertheless, Wilson had done little to clarify his thinking about a league during the war. He consciously and consistently rejected suggestions to spell out a peace plan before the summer of 1918. Only after the British presented their own plan and the fortunes of war turned decisively in favor of the Allies did the American president encourage more detailed thinking about the subject.

In part because he believed the British plan, authored mainly by Lord Phillimore, to be toothless, he increasingly emphasized the importance of both economic and military sanctions to compel states to maintain the peace. This approach not only differed from that of the British but substantially deviated from that of the League to Enforce Peace. Wilson not only became increasingly sympathetic to sanctions, but veered away from the League to Enforce Peace plan in a number of other ways. These included his insistence on a guarantee of territorial integrity, his emphasis on disarmament, and his stress on the binding and compulsory nature of arbitration. Oddly, the president, who had written some serious history, ignored the main lines of prewar American internationalist thought. By calling for an organization with considerable authority that emphasized elements of power politics rather than legal principles, he virtually guaranteed that his plan would encounter stiff opposition at home.

Americans bided their time while Wilson in Paris, together with a handful of colleagues from the larger states, hammered out the League of Nations Covenant behind closed doors. French skepticism about a league and British fear of too strong a league gave way before Wilson's influence. Moreover, the president's willingness to compromise on territorial, imperial, and financial issues was contingent on European willingness to approve his version of the Covenant. At the heart of that Covenant were four articles that, Wilson had come to believe, would make war a thing of the past. Article 10 guaranteed the territorial and political independence of every member state. Article 11 mandated that any threat to the peace was of concern to every member of the organization and authorized the league to take "any action that may be deemed wise and effectual to safeguard the peace of nations." Article 15 established procedures to settle matters that could not be arbitrated or settled in court, and Article 16 provided the machinery for economic and military sanctions. For a nation schooled in isolationism and quite unprepared for the kind of commitments that Wilson had championed in Paris, the change in course was quite radical. Wilson gambled that the fear of another world war would persuade Americans to embrace his proposals. Nonetheless, by failing to prepare the public for such a radical change, and by ignoring the crassly political crosscurrents that the treaty fight unleashed, the president found himself on the defensive during the remainder of his term.

The story of the treaty fight of 1919–1920 has been recounted many times. Conventional interpretations emphasize the clash between isolationism and internationalism, and between the Democratic president and his chief Republican opponent, Senate Foreign Relations Committee chairman Henry Cabot Lodge. Isolationism, of course, was an extension of nationalism, and the next two years would witness a real clash between internationalism and nationalism. Even former president Theodore Roosevelt would repudiate his internationalist leanings by damning the league as pro-German. "We are not internationalists," he said as he denounced the league, "we are American nationalists." His own hatred of Wilson was reflected in his indictment of the league. Substituting internationalism for nationalism meant, he argued, the rejection of patriotism. "The professional pacifist and the professional internationalist are equally undesirable citizens," said the still-popular ex-president.

This kind of demagoguery took its toll. Even though historians agree that most Americans favored a league of some kind, the public grew increasingly wary of a league that contained the kind of advance commitments regarding force embodied in Articles 10 and 16. To many Americans, fighting a war to prevent a war just did not make much sense, as the prewar internationalists in the World's Court League had claimed. Perhaps Wilson really believed that the threat of using force against an aggressor state that violated the League of Nations Covenant would suffice to guarantee the peace. The American public was less sure. The result was that the Senate debated not membership itself, but the kind of league the United States might join. The slim Republican majority in the Senate, and even some Democrats, sought to whittle away the obligations of membership. Wilson remained uncompromising. The president's supporters, therefore, failed to mobilize the two-thirds Senate majority needed to ratify the Treaty of Versailles. Sadly for Wilson, the first twenty-six articles of that treaty constituted the League Covenant.

INTERWAR ISOLATIONISM AND INTERNATIONALISM

The refusal of the Senate to ratify the Treaty of Versailles, followed by the victory in the 1920 presidential election of Warren G. Harding, who had rejected the league, claiming to favor a mythical "association of nations," meant that the United States never joined the League of Nations. Neither would the Senate ratify a treaty to join the country to the Permanent Court of International Justice, organized in 1921 as an affiliated agency of the league. Did this in fact represent a repudiation of internationalism? Scholars are not of one mind. Almost surely the voting public in 1920 would have approved a somewhat scaled-down League of Nations that lacked the automatic territorial guarantee embodied in Article 10. And although the Harding administration refused even to answer mail from the League Secretariat in Geneva, there are few indicators that the public approved the administration's rigid rejection of international cooperation. Indeed, by 1923 the State Department had begun to soften its anti-league policy by accepting invitations to league-sponsored meetings and sending unofficial observers ("something between a guest and a spy," quipped one league proponent) to Geneva on a regular basis.

Another piece of evidence that many Americans remained sympathetic to internationalism was the Harding administration's disarmament and foreign policy. State Department support for hosting the Washington Naval Conference—held from November 1921 to February 1922—stemmed at least in part from the fear that, with the League of Nations a going concern, America might find itself more isolated than was desirable. Certainly many isolationists favored the naval limitation treaty that emerged from the conference, but the treaty garnered overwhelming support among internationalists, both of the idealist variety and those who would later be called realists, like Secretary of State Charles Evans Hughes and future Secretary of State Henry L. Stimson. The other agreements signed at Washington also spoke to the belief among internationalists that U.S. strategic and economic interests made isolationism obsolete. The Four-Power Pact guaranteeing the status quo in the western Pacific may not have contained enforcement provisions, but it did obligate the signatories to consult in the event of a threat to the peace. Internationalists likewise supported the Nine-Power Pact guaranteeing the "open door" and the status quo in China.

In short, the Harding administration forged a web of relationships that did not support overt intervention abroad but did contradict the fundamental basis of isolationism. These relationships were further supported by an economic policy that increasingly reflected the corporate side of American life. The post–Civil War Industrial Revolution tied American prosperity to a healthy global economy. The policymakers who promoted U.S. loans to China and Latin America were internationalists, not isolationists, as were their banker and industrialist friends. They may have differed among themselves over such issues as imperialism and even military intervention, but few still doubted that America needed to be involved in the global economy of the twentieth century. Some of these policymakers were themselves financiers and industrialists, like oil magnate Charles G. Dawes, who served as vice president during the Coolidge Administration (1925–1929), and banker Norman Davis, who served both Wilson and Franklin D. Roosevelt in various foreign policy posts. Their prominence gave substance to the belief that international cooperation had become an article of faith in post–World War I Washington.

No wonder, therefore, that even President Harding favored U.S. membership on the World Court, officially the Permanent Court of International Justice. The Advisory Committee of Jurists who met at The Hague in 1920 and drafted the court's statute included the influential Elihu Root, a Republican Wall Street lawyer who had served Theodore Roosevelt as secretary first in the War Department and then in the State Department. Root typified many of the Republican internationalists during the 1920s. He had misgivings about President Wilson's brand of enforcement internationalism, preferring the prewar legal approach that emphasized the importance of judicial processes and the codification of international law. His prestige, along with that of future World Court judges like Charles Evans Hughes and the legal scholar John Bassett Moore, helped to legitimize the court for most Americans. The unimaginative Calvin Coolidge, who succeeded Harding in the White House and has often (and too simplistically) been described as an isolationist, also called for membership on the court. So did every subsequent president and secretary of state during the interwar period. Enough isolationist opponents of the court remained in and out of Congress, however, to prevent ratification of court membership until after World War II. When the most important Senate vote on membership occurred in 1935, these isolationists capitalized on the insecurities generated by the Great Depression and the fear of an aggressive Germany and Japan to block ratification by a two-thirds vote. Americans favored international cooperation, but not to the extent of risking war. This may not have been full-blown internationalism, but neither was it isolationism.

It is important to remember that support for World Court membership during the interwar period did not always translate into support for league membership. Nevertheless, many internationalists continued their Wilsonian campaign into the early 1930s, believing (perhaps correctly) that the new organization could not succeed without U.S. participation. As with so much else regarding foreign policy between the wars, the results were mixed.

Pro-league spokesmen lobbied with some success for support in the political platforms of the two major parties, and they publicized the league's work in order to generate renewed interest. Hamilton Holt, former Supreme Court justice John H. Clarke, and Theodore Roosevelt's former attorney general, George W. Wickersham, founded in 1922 the most focused supportive organization, the League of Nations Non-Partisan Association, later renamed the League of Nations Association. Women's and religious organizations, such as Jane Addams's Women's International League for Peace and Freedom, strongly endorsed the league, while pacifist groups and legal bodies supported World Court membership. The World Peace Foundation, the Carnegie Endowment for International Peace, and the American Society of International Law led the pro-Court parade.

Internationalist educational activity complemented these efforts. The establishment of organizations like the Foreign Policy Association, with its many local chapters, publicized international affairs generally and cooperative international activity in and out of Geneva specifically. The Carnegie Endowment helped to sponsor international clubs in high schools, while a number of colleges and universities instituted major programs in international relations. A few, like Harvard, Princeton, and Johns Hopkins, founded graduate institutes to produce specialists who might find their way into the State Department or into teaching positions at other institutions.

Other organizations, too, warrant mention, including some that encouraged cultural internationalism. Of special importance was the establishment in 1919 of the Institute of International Education. The IIE promoted educational exchanges abroad for both students and teachers and, after World War II, administered the Fulbright scholarship program. It shared an assumption common among interwar internationalists: that familiarity with foreign cultures would promote understanding and therefore peace.

A few internationalist enthusiasts, such as the journalist Clarence Streit, who founded one of the more popular internationalist organizations, Federal Union, favored a plan to organize the world's democracies into a world federation to ensure peace. Streit's movement eventually included more than a quarter of a million Americans in local chapters and represented the most popular prointernationalist response before Pearl Harbor. Other internationalist organizations, like the Council on Foreign Relations, which first appeared in 1921, headed in a more traditional, or "realist," direction. Founded by former cabinet members Elihu Root and Henry L. Stimson, the council capped its membership at about 550 prestigious individuals from government, business, journalism, and university life who met with domestic and foreign officials, hosted seminars on wide-ranging issues concerning foreign policy, and published the prestigious journal *Foreign Affairs*. The council's influence was much greater than its actual membership would suggest. The degree to which it closed its doors to the general public led many isolationists, both then and later, to see it as the center of an internationalist conspiracy to involve the United States in foreign entanglements or wars. Unlike Streit's organization, it remained committed to a very traditional model of state sovereignty, albeit one that rejected the assumptions undergirding American isolationism.

When by 1923 it was clear that the United States would not join the League of Nations, internationalists turned their attention to increasing American cooperation with the league and its agencies short of membership. But they also sought to influence American attitudes toward the outside world by creating a sense of collective "responsibility"—the word would soon achieve almost religious meaning—to support Covenant principles that advanced peace.

The first program succeeded reasonably well. By the mid-1920s the United States regularly participated in league commissions dealing with nonpolitical matters, notably health, social, and economic problems. It also cooperated in the disarmament area, though without much success. International cooperation, of course, was not pursued exclusively through the league or league-related agencies. Some Americans continued to work for pre-league internationalist objectives such as arbitration of interstate disputes and legal, not political, means to resolve problems. The arbitration ideal, discredited by World War I, bounced back among Americans with short memories and received additional support by the league itself with the establishment in 1927 of the Arbitration and Security Commission. Partly through the commission's efforts, Washington would eventually negotiate twenty-seven arbitration treaties between 1928 and 1931, though these treaties, as earlier, usually excepted consideration of such important interests as the Monroe Doctrine.

Efforts to further strengthen international law as a bulwark against disorder led the Carnegie Endowment for International Peace in 1923 to establish and fund the Academy of International Law at The Hague. The Carnegie Endowment also funded efforts to continue the codification of international law, particularly in the Western Hemisphere. James Brown Scott, who founded and led the American Society of International Law, spearheaded this work. To the disappointment of Scott and his colleagues, little of it captured the public imagination as it had before World War I. At best, the limited agreements that resulted from these efforts allowed the United States to balance its economic interests and its legal ideals.

Those economic interests carried the U.S. government in both directions during the interwar period, sometimes at the same time. Internationalists applauded the involvement of Washington in forging the loan programs embodied in the Dawes Plan (1924) and Young Plan (1929) to stabilize the European economy. They were silenced, however, by the economic nationalism expressed in 1930 when President Herbert Hoover signed the protectionist Smoot-Hawley Act. Nor did the Democrats who joined the Roosevelt administration offer consistent support to the economic internationalists. When Franklin Roosevelt's secretary of state, Cordell Hull, an orthodox Wilsonian, attended the London Economic Conference of 1933 to forge a global solution to the economic crisis, the president undermined his efforts by siding with economic nationalists who opposed Hull. Yet the following year, Roosevelt gave his blessing to Hull's internationalist program for reciprocal tariff agreements to lower rates.

MANCHURIA AND COLLECTIVE SECURITY

It was shortly before Franklin Roosevelt became president that Japan set in motion a series of challenges to the existing international order that eventually led to American involvement in World War II. These were the kind of affronts to the post–World War I treaties that the League of Nations had been created to prevent. For good or ill, American officials had shunned league consideration of such political controversies until the Manchurian crisis of 1931–1932. Secretary of State Henry L. Stimson, a staunch internationalist who believed powerfully in the sanctity of treaties, sent a delegate to the league council debates in October 1931 to consider Japan's violation of the Nine-Power Pact of 1922. Stimson's anger at Tokyo almost triggered a fundamental shift in Republican Party policy toward Geneva. The secretary, a proponent of what would soon be called collective security, gave serious consideration to embargoing American trade to Japan should the league invoke the sanctions authorized by the Covenant's Article 16. President Herbert Hoover demurred, however. He feared that economic sanctions would inevitably lead to military sanctions, which in his mind meant war. As a result, Stimson's initiatives, while heartening the battered internationalist movement at home, ultimately led nowhere.

Nor was the next president, Franklin D. Roosevelt, able to repair things. He had been a strong supporter of league membership when he ran for vice president in 1920. In 1932, however, he reversed his position, fearing that he might alienate isolationist progressives from the Midwest and West whose support he needed for the presidential nomination. Domestic political considerations overrode his internationalist instincts.

Nevertheless, by the time he became president in 1933, cooperation with Geneva concerning nonpolitical subjects had become so routine as to be hardly newsworthy. Internationalists had established extensive ties at Geneva. American citizens held league administrative posts and promoted both official and unofficial contact between Washington and Geneva. Arthur Sweetser, a Boston journalist who served in the league's Information Section, became the focus of such contacts. He worked closely with the Harvard law professor Manley Hudson, who established a study and research center at Geneva. Hudson even sought gifts from Americans to underwrite league programs, and those he obtained included a Rockefeller Foundation grant of $2 million to establish a library at the league's headquarters.

Until the late 1930s, however, little of this kind of activity made much difference. Even Roosevelt, privately sympathetic to international cooperation, remained publicly wary of proleague enthusiasts who advocated outright membership or even just political cooperation with Geneva. Nevertheless, amid the indifference or even hostility of many depression-scarred Americans concerning international cooperation, a few well-known internationalists kept the faith. The historian James T. Shotwell became the leading advocate of the idea that the United States must reject doing business as usual with governments that broke treaties or defied the League Covenant. If this could not be done through league membership, then states should morally condemn violations of international law through such treaties as the Kellogg-Briand Pact (Pact of Paris) of 1928, which renounced war as an instrument of policy. Similar was internationalist support for Secretary Stimson's 1932 nonrecognition doctrine, enunciated to deprive Japan of legal sanction for its occupation of Manchuria. Internationalists also applauded Roosevelt's support for the Neutrality Act of 1935 because it permitted the United States to establish economic sanctions parallel to potential league sanctions against an aggressor by prohibiting American trade in war-related materials. But like so much other activity during the Great Depression, these measures were not unambiguously internationalist. Isolationists, too, generally supported them—indeed, it was Senator Gerald Nye, an isolationist, who initially proposed neutrality legislation—because neutrality posed so little risk to the United States. The result was a foreign policy that veered erratically between internationalism and isolationism, leading critics to claim, with some justification, that the Roosevelt administration had no foreign policy at all.

WAR IN EUROPE AND THE UNITED NATIONS

This ambiguity dissipated after the European phase of World War II began in September 1939, ushering in what eventually became the most internationalist phase of American foreign policy. Between 1939 and the attack on Pearl Harbor, the country was sharply divided between internationalist advocates of aid to America's European allies and isolationists who feared such aid would lead to an unwanted and unnecessary American involvement in the war. The internationalists were themselves divided between outright interventionists and those who, led by William Allen White and his Committee to Defend America by Aiding the Allies, argued that sending military equipment and loans would make American participation in the war against Adolf Hitler unnecessary. All these internationalists called for the repeal or modification of neutrality legislation and other laws that hindered the free flow of materials to governments fighting the Axis Powers. By late 1941, Washington had lifted most restrictions against sending aid to Great Britain. Rejecting the charge of inconsistency, these same internationalists applauded the imposition of economic sanctions against Japan regarding oil and scrap iron.

The European war in 1939 and the attack on Pearl Harbor in 1941 seemed to confirm what internationalists had been saying for years about the need for an effective collective security organization. They also reinforced the argument in favor of American membership. Isolation, charged the internationalists, had not only failed but made world wars more rather than less likely. Even months before Pearl Harbor, 87 percent of Americans claimed they favored some kind of postwar organization. To most Americans, Hitler had made internationalism not only respectable but necessary.

The president of the League of Nations Association, James T. Shotwell, and his executive director, Clark M. Eichelberger, founded the somewhat pompously named Commission to Study the Organization of Peace, which cooperated with the State Department in formulating U.S. proposals for what eventually became the United Nations. (The League of Nations Association changed its name to the American Association for the United Nations in 1943.) Next in importance to the commission was the Federal Council of Churches to Study the Basis of a Just and Durable Peace, led by collective-security advocate and future secretary of state John Foster Dulles. Altogether, thirty-six private internationalist organizations joined this effort to create the UN, threatening to make the task chaotic.

The task of coordinating the planning for the UN fell mainly on an obscure State Department economist, Leo Pasvolsky, who headed the department's Division of Special Research (which had, at various times, other bland titles). No one worked more tirelessly or anonymously than he. At a time when American planning for the UN was hampered by rivalries between State Department officers, between Republicans and Democrats, and between congressional leaders and State Department officials, Pasvolsky managed to keep the project afloat. And because American officials had done much more planning than their counterparts in other countries, the final charter would reflect American thinking to a great extent.

The UN Charter was drafted primarily at three conferences: Dumbarton Oaks (August–October 1944), Yalta (February 1945), and the special UN conference at San Francisco (April to June 1945). Although the president had raised the issue of a postwar organization with the USSR's Joseph Stalin and Britain's Winston Churchill at various wartime conferences, the details—including the critical questions relating to membership and great power authority—were postponed until the latter stages of the war. A small group of officials, not the internationalist movement generally, resolved these matters, agreeing with Stalin's insistence that each of the great powers possess a permanent veto in the UN's Security Council. They also agreed that the Security Council, and not the larger General Assembly, would control the UN's enforcement machinery.

This time the president and his advisers, in contrast to President Wilson, did their political homework. They employed a broad spectrum of American internationalists to prepare the way for ratification of the UN Charter. Preceding the vote the administration launched the most ambitious campaign to support a foreign policy objective of the entire twentieth century. It included parades, parties, lectures, and radio and school programs. UN supporters turned isolationism into a dirty word. Everyone, it seemed, had become an internationalist, which masked the real differences within the movement. Even many Republicans who had opposed League of Nations membership a quarter of a century earlier now promoted UN membership. Less than a month after the San Francisco Conference, the Senate ratified the UN Charter by 89 to 2.

The charter reflected much of the structure and many of the operational features of the League Covenant, including a basic reliance upon power politics and a response to crises only after a breach of the peace. Like Woodrow Wilson, Franklin Roosevelt believed that an alliance of nations, functioning through an organization, could best maintain stability (though Wilson thought more in terms of universality, Roosevelt more in terms of great power cooperation). The United Nations Charter called for states to sacrifice very little sovereignty. Even former American isolationists could call themselves internationalists, knowing that American interests were protected by the permanent veto.

UN SKEPTICS

Nevertheless, the nation had indeed shifted decisively toward a more internationalist position. Washington quickly and quietly joined UN-related agencies like the new International Court of Justice (which replaced the older Permanent Court of International Justice) and the International Labor Organization. (The United States had actually joined that organization in 1935, but only because ILO proponents emphasized its separation from the League of Nations itself.) Membership in both came with some of the usual nationalist protections, such as the Connally Amendment preventing the International Court from hearing cases that Congress considered within the "domestic jurisdiction" of the United States.

Not all Americans accepted the United Nations unquestioningly. A vocal isolationist remnant, led by Senator Robert Taft, challenged the new internationalist faith and its emphasis on sanctions and entanglement. A small but visible group of internationalists, too, raised concerns about the UN. They complained not that the UN had too much power, but that it had too little. Where isolationists and nationalists feared that the new organization would compromise American sovereignty, the internationalist critics mainly argued that the UN left its members with too much sovereignty. Many called for a world federation, more or less inspired by Clarence Streit's *Union Now* (1939). UN proponents may have stolen much of Streit's thunder, but his movement continued to promote the federation ideal, which emphasized the primacy of people rather than states. This became evident in 1958, when Grenville Clark and Louis B. Sohn published the most famous treatise on the subject of federalism, *World Peace Through World Law*. They proposed that the UN General Assembly become the foundation of the new system, with delegates elected by subject populations and not selected by sovereign governments. Law, not national interest, would be the driving force behind the federation, therefore ensuring the likelihood of permanent peace.

Considered utopian by most academic writers, this brand of internationalism never achieved real popularity. A diverse coalition of groups called Americans United for World Organization sought to mobilize support for this kind of federalism even before the end of the war, but internal disputes eventually rendered it impotent. In 1947 it merged with a few other federalist groups to form its better-known successor, United World Federalists. This organization, too, failed to dent the pro-UN consensus. In part, its timing was wrong. Federalism necessitated international cooperation, exactly the opposite of what occurred after 1947 as the Cold War became the dominant international reality. Ideological differences and military alliances rendered the federalists irrelevant.

COLD WAR

Ironically, the American love affair with the UN would mask some real changes to the organization. Not only did the Cold War make the federalists irrelevant, it stripped the Security Council of authority at the very moment that it most needed support. With the Soviet Union increasingly using its permanent veto to block enforcement action by the UN's American-led majority, the UN could not live up to its promise. Only in Korea during 1950, and then solely because a Soviet boycott of the Security Council left the USSR unable to exercise its veto, did the UN come close to addressing its original purpose. As a rule, the veto shifted the

UN to the periphery of world politics. Americans increasingly came to associate collective security not with the UN but with the North Atlantic Treaty Organization, formed in 1949. But NATO was much closer to being a traditional military alliance than a universal collective security organization. As long as the UN would be hampered by the Soviet veto—which meant that so long as the UN would not serve as a convenient instrument of American foreign policy—Cold War internationalists like Dean Acheson, secretary of state from 1949 to 1953, would hold it in disdain.

The Great Depression, World War II, nuclear weapons, and the Cold War had discredited isolationism. But internationalists may have celebrated their victory too casually. If nearly everyone had become an internationalist, then the term was in danger of losing its meaning, which is exactly what happened during the next forty years. Indeed, many outspoken nationalists proclaimed themselves internationalists, promoting the projection of U.S. power throughout the world through the new system of alliances. Yes, they admitted, the world had shrunk. Economic interdependence and advances in communications and weaponry—including intercontinental bombers and missiles—made cooperation expedient. But it was anticommunism, not technology, that served as the glue holding their foreign policy worldview together, and anticommunism, as the McCarthy era proved, was often associated with xenophobia and unilateralism.

INTERNATIONALIST INCONSISTENCY

What did all this mean? Confusion, at least. Scholarly terms reflected the confusion: internationalism, interventionism, globalism, multilateralism, transnationalism, hegemonism. But some things are clear, including that for many members of the post–World War II generation of internationalists, U.S. involvement abroad, utilizing UN agencies or other institutions, lacked a commitment to equality that the pre–World War II internationalists had promoted. Prewar internationalists generally viewed internationalism as a way to create a warless world and a more just international society. Post–World War II internationalists proved more willing to ignore both. Justice played second fiddle to the national interest. Especially after 1970, as Third World countries became the UN majority, Washington rejected what it viewed as radical proposals to share the resources of the industrialized North with the developing and needy South. From 1972, when the State Department rejected Third World demands for a new international economic order, to 2000, when the Clinton administration ignored proposals to forgive the debts of sub-Saharan African nations, issues of economic justice have been greeted unsympathetically by official Washington.

Americans after World War II also proved more willing to entertain—and occasionally even promote—the use of military force, as they did in Korea and Vietnam, but also in less risky areas such as the Dominican Republic (1965), Grenada (1983), Panama (1989), the Persian Gulf (1991), and the former Yugoslavia (1999). Motives varied, ranging from anticommunism to regional hegemony to humanitarianism. So did the degree of international cooperation. In Korea, Cold War internationalists fought under a UN flag; during the Gulf War, under less formal UN authorization; in Yugoslavia, under NATO command. But in Latin America there was barely a pretense of cooperation. In fact, the Organization of American States formally condemned the U.S. intervention in Grenada.

The inconsistency concerning collective military activity also characterized the record of the United States in areas even more traditionally viewed as internationalist, such as support for international law and arms negotiations. Ever since the Hague Conferences, internationalist lawyers had promoted the creation of an international court to reduce the anarchy inherent in a system of sovereign states. They believed that the codification of international law would promote stability and peace, and that an international court would serve as a capstone of the legal system. Their dreams were partially fulfilled when, after both world wars, the victorious nations established international courts. But the court ideal never attained its promise, partly because of American policy. During the interwar period, Congress refused to ratify the statute of the Permanent Court of International Justice. Nearly forty years after World War II, American support for its successor, the International Court of Justice, would be dramatically reversed when the Reagan administration in 1984 rejected the court's authority in a celebrated case brought against the United States by Nicaragua. To accentuate the retreat from internationalism, Washington then formally repudiated the court's compulsory jurisdiction in all cases involving U.S. interests unless specifically mandated by treaty. Nevertheless, inconsistency triumphed here, too, as the United States joined with other countries at the end of the century to create the International Criminal Court with authority to try defendants charged with genocide and other violations of the law of war.

Arms negotiations offered another version of the same story. The development of atomic weapons by the United States and the Soviet Union during and after World War II dramatized the need for arms reduction and limitation. Internationalists helped to negotiate and ratify a number of agreements, most notably the Nuclear Test Ban Treaty of 1963, the bilateral accords negotiated with the Soviet Union during the 1970s, 1980s, and early 1990s (SALT I, the 1972 ABM Treaty, the 1987 International Nuclear Forces Treaty, and the 1991 Strategic Arms Reduction Treaty, known as START). In 1997 the Clinton administration, with some support from Republican nationalists, persuaded the Senate to ratify a comprehensive chemical weapons ban. But other treaties, including SALT II, signed by the Carter administration in 1979, the Comprehensive Nuclear Test Ban Treaty of 1996, and a 1997 treaty prohibiting the use of land mines, failed to win Senate approval, the latter two supported by more than one hundred governments. Indeed, in 2001 the administration of George W. Bush not only ended efforts to have the Senate ratify the Comprehensive Nuclear Test Ban Treaty of 1996, but to terminate the 1972 ABM Treaty despite strong objections from America's European allies.

The theme of inconsistency also applied to the subject of international economic cooperation. During the late stages of World War II, the United States had initiated efforts to create international financial institutions that would economically stabilize the postwar world and prevent another Great Depression. The most important such institutions emerging from the war were the World Bank, to provide bank-sponsored development loans, and the International Monetary Fund, to grant government loans to stabilize currencies.

The last half of the twentieth century also witnessed tariff reduction, long applauded by internationalists. The General Agreement on Trade and Tariffs dates back to 1947; the agreement involved numerous conferences held over decades. GATT addressed the hopes of Wilsonians, who continued to argue that economic nationalism was a powerful cause of war. But here, too, internationalists met increasing resistance at home. Labor unions, fearful of losing jobs to low-wage workers abroad, joined forces with (generally) small businesses fearing foreign competition, nationalists, environmentalists, and neo-isolationists to pass measures like the 1988 Omnibus Trade and Competitiveness Act undermining the free-trade aims of internationally oriented businesses and banks. For the most part, the legislative record from 1962 to 2001 favored the free traders. The North American Free Trade Agreement of 1993, membership for the United States and its trading partners (most controversially, China) in the World Trade Organization (GATT's successor), and the Clinton and George W. Bush administrations' support for the Free Trade for the Americas Treaty (not yet finalized in 2001) exemplify this trend.

Inconsistency also characterized international cooperation regarding the environment. Internationalists successfully promoted modest environmental reform, such as the creation of a UN Environment Program that emerged out of the 113-member UN Stockholm Conference of 1972, and two agreements (Vienna in 1985 and Montreal in 1987) limiting the release of ozone into the atmosphere. However, the Senate refused to ratify the Law of the Sea Treaty negotiated between 1972 and 1982, the 1992 Convention on Biological Diversity negotiated at Rio de Janeiro, and the 1997 Kyoto Accords limiting carbon dioxide emissions negotiated at the UN Conference on Climate Change. Indeed, by the early twenty-first century, American environmentalists were themselves aligning in opposition to internationalism, fearing that looser environmental standards abroad would undermine environmental protections at home.

RETREAT

There is a larger issue here: the last third of the twentieth century witnessed a general deterioration of support for internationalism. The causes were many. They have included the upsurge of nationalism that accompanied the appearance of the evangelical religious right; disillusionment concerning foreign entanglements stemming from the American defeat in Vietnam; the decline of the industrial economy resulting from foreign competition in low-wage countries; the failure of the UN in highly publicized peacekeeping ventures (most importantly, Somalia and Bosnia during the early and mid-1990s); the increase in international terrorism; and the rise of anti-American policies at the UN (seen in programs like the New International Economic Order of 1972 and the New World Information and Communications Order of 1978). A former president of the Carnegie Endowment for International Peace described the late twentieth century as "the twilight of internationalism."

He may have exaggerated the reaction against internationalism, but he was onto something important. Since 1994, the United States has sharply curtailed its support for UN peacekeeping missions. Facing criticism of U.S. peacekeeping activity in both Somalia and Bosnia, President William Jefferson Clinton sharply scaled down American support (including both military and financial support) for these missions. Some 74,000 peacekeeping troops from seventy-six countries served in 1994; by 2000 this number had shrunk to less than 20,000. Presidential Decision Directive 25, the most important State Department policy paper concerning peacekeeping since the Congo crisis of 1960, placed stringent criteria on peacekeeping, reversing calls for more U.S. involvement uttered just two years earlier by Bill Clinton as he campaigned for the presidency.

Nor was the disillusionment with internationalism confined to peacekeeping. After the 1970s it spread to the UN generally. During the mid-1980s, President Ronald Reagan began to withhold American dues to the UN, a process encouraged by Congress when it passed the 1983 Kassenbaum Amendment unilaterally cutting the American share of UN assessments. The growth of conservative nationalism during the 1990s intensified anti-UN sentiment, especially after the Republicans gained control of Congress in 1995. Dues and peacekeeping assessments went unpaid, threatening America with the loss of its vote. Congressional critics of the UN more or less blackmailed the Secretariat not only into bureaucratic reform (which was overdue), but into further reducing the percentage of revenues paid by the United States. Tellingly, few internationalist voices inside or outside Washington expressed strong objections.

Other important developments during the last third of the century also reflected the decline of internationalism. In 1977 the United States withdrew from the ILO for what turned into a three-year absence. A similar story was repeated at the International Atomic Energy Agency between 1981 and 1983. Washington withdrew from the UN Educational, Scientific, and Cultural Organization (UNESCO) in 1984 and from the UN Industrial Development Organization in 1995. American officials may have rightly deplored the politicization of these agencies. Nevertheless, Washington's decisions to withdraw altogether symbolized the priority that Congress and the White House increasingly gave to national rather than international interests.

American internationalism, of course, ranges far beyond the subject of the UN. Regional organizations, most importantly the Organization of American States (OAS), which rests on three treaties ratified in 1947 and 1948, have also been a part of this story, but without the centrality or the visibility of the League of Nations or the UN. Indeed, Article 51 of the UN Charter sought to make room for regional collective defense, a matter that was central to some of the negotiations regarding the UN Charter during World War II. Moreover, American obligations under the OAS charter regarding nonintervention have occasionally clashed with U.S. Cold War objectives, a clash that led some Western Hemispheric countries to seek recourse at the UN. This was especially the case regarding crises in Guatemala (1954), Cuba (1962), and Grenada (1983). During each episode U.S. officials gave short shrift to UN and OAS objections regarding American intervention.

Washington also gave little heed to OAS demands to highlight the principle of collective economic security, which many in Washington viewed as a regional variation of the New International Economic Order. Although U.S. policymakers have never been sympathetic to resource transfers from rich nations to poor (with the possible exception of technology transfers), some of the Latin American demands for wealth sharing contributed to Washington's willingness to negotiate the free trade agreements of the 1990s. This was an area in which internationalist sentiment coincided with what every presidential administration from Reagan to George W. Bush has viewed as U.S. economic interests.

CULTURAL INTERNATIONALISM

With the end of the Cold War, the subject of cultural internationalism returned to prominence as it had after World War I. Disillusionment with political internationalism has not yet affected the health of the Fulbright scholarship program, begun after World War II to promote among Americans knowledge of other cultures and to attract foreign scholars to the United States. Cultural, athletic, and scientific exchanges thrived during the last third of the twentieth century. The degree to which Americans have taken up soccer, long considered a foreign sport, is a small sign of this, as is the internationalization of baseball, with American players in Japan and a great many Latin American players along with a growing number of Japanese players in the Major Leagues.

A similar story can be told about other sports, as with the internationalization of rock and roll and American films. More moviegoers saw *Schindler's List* (1993) and *Titanic* (1997) outside of the United States than inside. Michael Jordan T-shirts are worn by Asian teenagers who never saw a basketball game. The Internet, for good or ill, has connected people in different countries in ways that seemed unimaginable in 1990. This may not be exactly what the founders of the Carnegie Endowment for International Peace had in mind when they formed their organization in 1910. Neither is it likely to be what President George H. W. Bush meant when he called for a new world order in 1990. Nevertheless, it addresses the vitality of cultural internationalism even when disillusionment, pessimism, and cynicism have crippled the movement politically.

In short, the history of American internationalism has been the history of complexity and inconsistency. This remains as true at the beginning of the twenty-first century as it was one hundred years earlier.

BIBLIOGRAPHY

Alder, Selig. *The Isolationist Impulse: Its Twentieth Century Reaction.* New York, 1957. Covers internationalism while addressing isolationism.

Bartlett, Ruhl J. *The League to Enforce Peace.* Chapel Hill, N.C., 1944. Excellent on developments between 1914 and 1919.

Brinkley, Douglas, and Townsend Hoopes. *FDR and the Creation of the U.N.* New Haven, Conn., 1997. Updates Robert Divine's well-known study.

Curti, Merle. *Peace or War: The American Struggle, 1636–1936.* New York, 1936. A classic intellectual history.

Davis, Calvin D. *The United States and the First Hague Peace Conference.* Ithaca, N.Y., 1962. Describes the politics leading to the conference.

———. *The United States and the Second Hague Peace Conference: American Diplomacy and International Organization, 1899–1914.* Durham, N.C., 1975. Describes the politics leading to the conference.

Divine, Robert A. *Second Chance: The Triumph of Internationalism in America During World War II.* New York, 1967. Somewhat dated but still very useful in tracing the United States's role in writing the UN Charter.

Dunne, Michael. *The United States and the World Court, 1920–1935.* New York, 1988. The very best work on the legal issue. Dunne also wrote a number of fine articles about American diplomacy and internationalism that appeared in the British journal *International Affairs* during the 1990s.

Gill, George. *The League of Nations from 1929 to 1946.* Garden City, N.Y., 1997. A companion volume to Ostrower's work on the 1920s.

Herman, Sondra R. *Eleven Against War: Studies in American Internationalist Thought, 1898–1921.* Stanford, Calif., 1969. Develops the position of the "community-minded" internationalists.

Hilderbrand, Robert C. *Dumbarton Oaks: The Origins of the United Nations and the Search for Postwar Security.* Chapel Hill, N.C., 1990. Views the UN as a combination of Wilsonian idealism and Franklin Roosevelt's "Four Policeman" realism.

Hoffman, Stanley. "The Crisis of Liberal Internationalism." *Foreign Policy* 98 (Spring 1995). Indispensable in understanding end-of-the-century internationalism.

Hughes, Thomas L. "The Twilight of Internationalism." *Foreign Policy* 61 (winter 1985–1986): 25–48. Traces the reasons for the resurgence of nationalism.

Iriye, Akira. *Cultural Internationalism and World Order.* Baltimore, 1997. Provides an excellent overview of the nonpolitical side of internationalism from the perspective of a committed internationalist.

Johnson, Robert David, ed. *On Cultural Ground: Essays in International History.* Chicago, 1994. Contains essays that redefine the subject of internationalist thinking.

Josephson, Harold. *James T. Shotwell and the Rise of Internationalism in America.* Rutherford, N.J., 1975. Offers insight into the most active proponent of an organized world.

Knock, Thomas J. *To End All Wars: Woodrow Wilson and the Quest for a New World Order.* New York, 1992. A rousing and exceptionally insightful defense of Wilson as liberal idealist.

Kuehl, Warren F. *Hamilton Holt: Journalist, Internationalist, Educator.* Gainesville, Fla., 1960. The standard biography of a key internationalist.

———. *Seeking World Order: The United States and International Organization to 1920.* Nashville, Tenn., 1969. Provides the fullest account of early support for cooperation.

Kuehl, Warren F., and Lynne K. Dunne. *Keeping the Covenant: American Internationalists and the League of Nations, 1920–1939.* Kent, Ohio, 1997. Provides an overview of pro-league sentiment by individuals and organized groups.

Marchand, C. Roland. *The American Peace Movement and Social Reform, 1898–1918.* Princeton, N.J., 1972. Sees internationalism emerging from the progressive movement generally.

Michalak, Stanley J. "The UN and the League." In Leon Gordenker, ed. *The United Nations in International Politics.* Princeton, N.J., 1971. Skillfully compares U.S. policy toward the League of Nations and the UN.

Ninkovich, Frank A. *The Diplomacy of Ideas: U.S. Foreign Policy and Cultural Relations, 1938–1950.* New York, 1981. Offers insight into the American shift from isolationism to Cold War interventionism.

———. *The Wilsonian Century: U.S. Foreign Policy Since 1900.* Chicago, 1999. Provides a less idealistic view of Wilson than is traditional, comparing Wilson's "crisis internationalism" to the more benign variety.

Nordholt, Jan Willem Schulte. *Woodrow Wilson: A Life for World Peace.* Berkeley, Calif., 1991. A very insightful and underrated biography that explores the nature of internationalism.

Ostrower, Gary B. *Collective Insecurity: The United States and the League of Nations During the Early Thirties.* Lewisburg, Pa., 1979. Provides an in-depth view of American policy during the Manchurian crisis.

———. "The United States and the League of Nations, 1919–1939." In Zara S. Steiner, ed. *The League of Nations in Retrospect.* Berlin, New York, 1983. A concise overview of the U.S.–League of Nations story.

———. *The League of Nations: From 1919 to 1929.* Garden City, N.Y., 1996. Offers a general history of the league including its nonpolitical work.

———. *The United Nations and the United States: From 1940 to 1998.* New York, 1998. Emphasizing the inconsistency of American policy, this is the best single survey of the U.S.–UN relationship.

Patterson, David S. *Toward a Warless World: The Travail of the American Peace Movement, 1887–1914.* Bloomington, Ind., 1976. Competently explores the internationalist perspective of peace workers.

Righter, Rosemary. *Utopia Lost: The United Nations and World Order.* New York, 1995. A superb study critical of U.S. policy at the UN.

Widenor, William C. *Henry Cabot Lodge and the Search for an American Foreign Policy.* Berkeley, Calif., 1980. One of the best examinations of the isolationist-internationalist debates after World War I, viewing Lodge as motivated by principle, not political advantage.

Wittner, Lawrence S. *Rebels Against War: The American Peace Movement, 1941–60.* New York, 1969. Contains the fullest presentation of post-1945 popular attitudes.

See also ARBITRATION, MEDIATION, AND CONCILIATION; COLLECTIVE SECURITY; CULTURAL RELATIONS AND POLICIES; EMBARGOES AND SANCTIONS; GLOBALIZATION; IMPERIALISM; INTERNATIONAL LAW; INTERNATIONAL ORGANIZATION; ISOLATIONISM; WILSONIANISM.

INTERNATIONAL LAW

Christopher C. Joyner

International law is the body of customs, principles, and rules recognized as effectively binding legal obligations by sovereign states and other international actors. International law stems from three main sources: treaties and international conventions, customs and customary usage, and the generally accepted principles of law and equity. Judicial decisions rendered by international tribunals and domestic courts are important elements of the lawmaking process of the international community. Resolutions of international organizations, the United Nations in particular, may also affect the growth of the so-called customary international law that is synonymous with general principles of international law. The present system of international legal rules is based on the premise of state sovereignty. It is within the discretion of each state to participate in the negotiation of, or to sign or ratify, any international treaty. Likewise, each member state of an international agency such as the United Nations is free to ratify any convention adopted by that agency.

American history confirms that the functions of international law and U.S. foreign policy are inextricably intertwined. The rules of modern international law are in great part products of negotiations in which U.S. diplomats played important roles, and U.S. foreign policy is in great part dependent on the rules of international law for its operation. The willingness of the U.S. government to employ international law as an instrument of foreign policy arises from the historical experience that shapes the political attitudes of the American people. Its vast size and abundant natural resources allowed the United States to grow into an economic power that rivaled its European peers. The United States was permitted to develop internally, in large measure without external distractions. Throughout the first half of the twentieth century, save for the interruption of World War I, the United States remained mainly on the sidelines, contributing little to expanding or modernizing the rules of international intercourse. After World War II, however, the United States emerged as a global superpower. Coincident with this newfound responsibility, and with the onset of Cold War rivalry with the Soviet Union, the United States asserted greater prominence in shaping the direction of international law—a role that became more salient over time.

To appreciate how international legal rules function in the making and performance of U.S. foreign policy, it must be understood that both tangible and intangible factors impose constraints on policymakers. The essence of these constraints lies within the nature of the international system.

CONSTRAINTS ON U.S. FOREIGN POLICY

The international system imposes structural constraints on the ability of American decision makers to create legal rules favorable to U.S. national interests. The enduring feature of the international system is its decentralization. There are no central institutions to legislate standards or to ensure their enforcement. Nor does a common political culture exist in which to anchor an agreed-upon body of norms for governing the behavior of states. The upshot for U.S. foreign policy is a highly competitive international system in which there is constant expectation of violence and conflict and little expectation that either international law or appeals to normative principles will significantly influence the resolution of contentious issues.

A decentralized international system does not mean that U.S. foreign policy operates in a legal vacuum or under conditions of global anarchy. While there is no world government, and universally enforceable laws and common values are lacking, rules affecting the conduct of U.S. foreign policy do matter, and such rules lend greater predictability and more certainty to international transactions. These legal rules indicate the limits of permissible behavior, the norms for interstate conduct, and the ways and means of settling disputes. To the extent that the U.S. government subscribes to these legal rules, it becomes obligated to perform certain duties to those ends. That is, the United States as a sovereign, independent state is affected by legal principles contained in fundamental legal constructs. For its foreign policy to function the United States must be diplomatically recognized by other governments. In its foreign affairs, the government must accept and exercise certain rights and duties under international law, which are motivated by pragmatism and reciprocity. These rights and duties ensure that governments can deal with one another in a systematic, orderly fashion. The United States has the rights, inter alia, to recognize other states and to secure its national territorial integrity, sovereignty, and independence, by forcible self-defense if necessary. The United States also has corresponding obligations, key among which are not to intervene militarily into the affairs of other states, not to pollute the air, water, or land such that it causes transboundary harm, and to abide by international agreements made with other states or international actors. Although constrained by the world system, the United States is able to perform critical legal functions that ensure its survival as a legal entity in interstate relations.

A second structural constraint flows from the fact that the world system is a self-help system. The United States, like all governments, ultimately relies upon itself to accomplish foreign policy objectives. To do otherwise risks being manipulated by other governments. Similarly, the self-help principle impresses upon U.S. officials the need to bring policy goals and national resources into balance. International law strives to facilitate that. The pursuit of excessive goals, without adequate resources to attain them, can enervate a government and diminish its ability to respond effectively to future challenges. For the United States the tragedy of the Vietnam War remains a constant reminder of that truth.

A third structural constraint rests in the hierarchical character of the international system. The equality of states implicit in the legal principle of sovereignty is a political fiction. The notion of sovereignty dates back to the Treaty of Westphalia in 1648 and the origins of modern states. As a political construct, the sovereignty principle affirms that no legal authority exists above the state except that which the government voluntarily accepts. The reality of twenty-first-century international relations is markedly different. Sovereignty remains more a matter of degree than an absolute condition. States are inherently unequal, and the resources they use to exercise power in their international dealings are distributed unequally around the world. As the lone superpower state in the early twenty-first century, the United States has access to more resources, possesses greater capabilities, and can exercise greater power than any other state. In this context international law defines permissible ways and means that the U.S. government may employ those resources and capabilities in its foreign relations.

Despite systemic constraints, an international society does exist. International legal rules do affect the structure of that society—its institutions, actors, and procedures for transnational activity; the assumptions on which the society was founded; the status, rights, responsibilities, and obligations of states within this society; and the various relations between those states. Through its foreign policy the United States maintains, establishes, changes, and terminates relationships with other international actors—all through international legal means. Although international law may be primitive, the United States employs it to formalize, regulate, and regularize interstate relationships. For the United States most of the time, its foreign policy is constructed in a way that preserves international order, so that government policymakers might pursue the best perceived course for U.S. national interests, both foreign and domestic. Such international order depends on a framework of agreed presumptions, customs, commitments, expectations, and sanctions that all states, including the United States, accept to regulate international society. International law furnishes the rules for relations between states, sets standards for the conduct of governments within this international system, and facilitates establishment of multilateral institutions toward these ends. In these regards the United States has become the chief state architect and purveyor of international legal rules in the twenty-first century.

LAW AND U.S. FOREIGN POLICY APPROACHES

Public attitudes in the United States toward the utility of international law have shifted with its government's perceptions of how the United States best fits into the world scene. At the same time, government officials do not agree to international legal rules in a political void—domestic political considerations and national interests figure prominently, and often preeminently, in negotiating legal instruments. Historically, the propensity of U.S. government officials for creating legal rules was caught in the tension between two opposing policy approaches—isolationism and internationalism. Up until 1940 these approaches were more or less cyclical throughout American history. Since then the East-West ideological rivalry of the Cold War, escalating international economic interdependence, and ever-increasing technological globalization have combined to render the internationalist approach politically, commercially, and legally imperative for the United States.

Isolationism reflects the belief that the United States should avoid getting involved in the political affairs of other states. This rejection of foreign political involvement was not meant to imply that the United States should ignore the rest of the world. Indeed, diplomatic and commercial contacts were critical for the United States as it developed throughout the nineteenth and early twentieth centuries. In these respects, international legal rules and multilateral instruments assumed cardinal importance in rendering American foreign policy practical and effective. Instead, from the isolationist perspective, American national interests are best served by withdrawing from the rest of the world, or at least remaining detached from events elsewhere. In this regard, international legal rules play only a minimal role. Less international involvement abroad results in less interest in world affairs and fosters the perception that the United States has little need to be bound by international law.

Isolationism draws its inspiration from George Washington's Farewell Address of 1796, in which he admonished Americans to "steer clear of permanent alliance with any portion of the foreign world." This tendency to avoid foreign involvement was fueled by the fact that, save for the War of 1812, the United States was never physically endangered by foreign military attack, and a sense of physical security from the threat of foreign intervention prevailed. Later, the horrors of the Civil War fostered a less militaristic attitude within the American political culture. When combined, these attitudes contributed to the isolationist impulse and a relative indifference to international legal concerns. Among the major isolationist foreign policy decisions that heavily impacted on principles of international law are the Monroe Doctrine (1823), the refusal to join the League of Nations (by the U.S. Senate's rejection of the Treaty of Versailles in 1919), the neutrality laws of the 1930s, and the legacy of the Vietnam syndrome, that is, the reluctance to commit American troops abroad.

The internationalist perspective sees the protection and promotion of U.S. national interests through pursuit of a legally based, activist, global foreign policy. Internationalists argue that the United States cannot escape the world. Events in other places inevitably encroach upon U.S. interests, and policy rooted in the retreat from global involvement is self-defeating. Thus, the United States has a stake in the general nature of the international system, and its government must be willing to become actively involved in world affairs on a regular basis. To bolster this contention, internationalists point to the Great Depression of the 1930s, the rise of Hitler in Europe, the outbreak of World War II, and the expansion of communism in the war's aftermath. Hence, the United States must be involved in world affairs. To this end, international law provides proven conduits for integrating U.S. national interests into constructive foreign policy opportunities. American national interests are best served by remaining active internationally and by negotiating legal rules that promote foreign policy goals as they foster international order. Evidence that internationalism best serves U.S. national interests is seen in the preeminent place of the United States since 1945 in establishing the United Nations, the North Atlantic Treaty Organization (NATO), and many other international organizations; in promoting the Marshall Plan and the Helsinki Human Rights Agreement; in U.S. involvement in armed conflicts in Korea, Vietnam, the Persian Gulf, Bosnia, and Kosovo; and in vigorous support of a massive expansion of U.S. international trade relations. In all of these areas, the ways in which the United States employed international legal rules proved critical for implementing its foreign policy in ways acceptable to international society.

The war in Vietnam frayed American confidence about internationalism in general and the containment doctrine in particular. The tremendous human, financial, and political costs traumatized the American people, gave rise to a domestic antiwar movement, and undermined the faith of Americans in their government. More than 58,000 American lives were lost, and four million Vietnamese on both sides were killed or injured. Over eleven years the war cost the United States approximately $150 billion to fight and lose. Consequently, since 1975 American attitudes have been ambivalent toward activist internationalism. On the one hand, the realization persists that as the world's only superpower, the United States retains a special responsibility for maintaining international peace and security. But, on the other hand, the American people are profoundly reluctant to support long-term commitments of American blood and treasure abroad to defend other states, especially those with little strategic value to the United States. American government officials therefore are wary about sending U.S. forces abroad and have done so only in selected cases. They are fully aware that a high political price can be incurred for American soldiers coming home in body bags—namely, defeat in the next general election.

Isolationism and internationalism have both shaped the course of American foreign policy and determined the relative degree of importance that international law has assumed in policy formulation. Both approaches are joined in the conviction that international law should be used to serve and protect the institutions and ideals of the American experience. The approaches differ, however, on how to achieve these national ambitions. Isolationism aims to insulate the American experience from the corruption of foreign influences and protect U.S. sovereignty from burdensome international commitments. The isolationist approach attributes little utility to international law, except insofar as it segregates the United States from extraterritorial commitments and facilitates the government's foreign relations to secure needed resources and sustain trade relations. Conversely, internationalism works to attain U.S. policy goals by promoting a more stable global environment for the United States, which opens the door to foreign opportunities to fulfill American political, economic, and legal interests. To these internationalist ends, international law assumes a more fundamental, more comprehensive place in U.S. foreign policy. International legal rules become channels for closer, more regularized international contact as well as regulatory standards that encourage such cooperation. Regardless of the approach taken, consideration of and regard for international legal rules remain important in the process and formulation of American foreign policy.

AMERICAN POLITICAL CULTURE

American political culture determines how individual policymakers regard the place and authority of international law in U.S. foreign policy. Political culture, which embraces fundamental attitudes and practices of American society, draws from two main sources. One is historical experience. Americans are products of their past. The second is the national belief system, that is, the ideas and ideologies held by the American people. The relevance and status of international law in the making of U.S. foreign policy derive from the American people's self-image, their norms and values, and the ways in which American political culture influences their perceptions of international relations. This national outlook, which might be called the American ideology, inculcates an American style in world affairs and helps to explain why and how international legal rules are integrated into U.S. foreign policy actions.

Understanding the sets of beliefs that comprise the American ideology is critical for appreciating why, where, and how much legal considerations figure into the process and patterns of American foreign policymaking. This national ideology emanates from four sets of core American self-perceptions and values, namely, the predispositions toward exceptionalism, legalism, liberalism, and pragmatism. When evaluating how these elements of American political culture affect policymakers, one must remember that each element influences personal attitudes, though in various ways and to differing degrees. A person's attitudes toward some international event can invite struggle over the priority between these elements and engender conflicted feelings over which policy appears most appropriate for U.S. interests. Similarly, a person's strength of convictions toward these elements can change over time, relative to perceptions, circumstances, and particular events.

EXCEPTIONALISM

A principal set of core elements in the American ideology that affects feelings about international law's role in U.S. foreign policy originates from a sense of exceptionalism, often expressed as self-virtuosity. That is, Americans seem to be self-confident to the degree that they and their political culture are admired and thought special by the rest of the world. To early Americans the New

World was a gift from God, which settlers transformed out of wilderness into the most prosperous and advanced society in history. Traditional perceptions of history reinforce this conclusion: Americans conquered native, "uncivilized" peoples, survived a brutal civil war, moved westward and secured the continent, established a country founded on private, free-enterprise capitalism and democratic principles, rescued Europe from the evils of nazism in World War II, and saved the world from communist domination in the four decades thereafter. In the American mind, these profound accomplishments make the United States the envy of the world and correspondingly reinforce the sense of being uniquely special. Americans thus are prone to view the United States as having evolved into an exceptional country that is not merely different from, but actually superior to, all other states.

Exceptionalists admit that the United States has a certain moral responsibility for the fate of people living in other countries. As such, they advocate international activism and interventionism in a wide variety of global situations. They do not concede to any clear, universally accepted international code of foreign policy behavior. Their chief belief is that the United States should advance principally American values in its foreign policy.

Belief in American exceptionalism has sometimes bred U.S. unilateralism in foreign affairs. That is, integral to Americans' belief that their country's experience has produced the best social and political order in history is the predilection of the United States to act alone in addressing foreign concerns. This go-it-alone tendency in U.S. foreign policy represents the rejection of a balance-of-power approach for promoting national security in international relations. Given the geography and natural assets of the United States, national security was once largely assumed, making efforts at multilateral collaboration unnecessary. After World War II, the rise of the United States to superpower status exaggerated its self-perceived virtuosity in world affairs, which generated more acts of unilateralism in its foreign relations and international law attitudes.

Another facet of American self-virtuosity arises in the tendency to engage in messianism abroad. American foreign policy sometimes takes up crusadelike causes for ends that are perceived as just and noble. U.S. policymakers conclude that they must bring the benefits of American ideals and institutions to other, less fortunate, peoples. Such feelings blend the traits of the American self-image of political, moral, and ideological superiority to produce within the American political culture a tendency to engage in messianic campaigns. There emerges a missionary-like compulsion in U.S. foreign policy ambitions to recreate the world in the American image, to establish models of governance grounded in American values and democratic institutions, by force if necessary. Such attitudes can foster a sense of paternalism. More ominously, they breed resentment from other societies who see the United States as attempting to impose its cultural values and political lifestyle upon them. In the extreme, such a doctrine of internationalized manifest destiny can become the political rationalization for unlawful U.S. intervention. Witness, during the second half of the twentieth century, U.S. involvement in Iran (1953), Guatemala (1954), Cuba (1961), the Dominican Republic (1965), Chile (1973), Nicaragua (1981–1984), Grenada (1983), Panama (1989), and Serbia (Kosovo) (2000).

The clearest historical statement of American unilateralism remains the Monroe Doctrine in 1823. This declaration by President James Monroe came in reaction to U.S. concern over the possibility of European interference into affairs of newly independent Latin American countries. The doctrine proclaimed that the United States would not tolerate European intervention into the Western Hemisphere, and, in return, the United States pledged not to interfere in European affairs. The Roosevelt Corollary, articulated by President Theodore Roosevelt in his annual message to Congress on 6 December 1904, expanded the scope of the doctrine by making the United States the self-appointed policeman of the Western Hemisphere, thereby providing a unilateral justification for increased intervention into the affairs of Latin American countries.

Important to realize is that neither the Monroe Doctrine nor its Roosevelt Corollary drew validity from any U.S. legislative pronouncement, nor from any international treaty instrument. Nor was the reach of jurisdiction or application of either doctrine ever precisely defined by specific law or fiat. Indeed, both doctrines were applied historically on an ad hoc basis, in circumstances defined only by perceptions of U.S. policymakers, to explain the rationale for interventionist actions. From 1850 to 1935, both doctrines were held out as pillars of U.S. foreign policy and were invoked periodically to justify unilateral interventions taken in the name of defending the Americas from European intrusions. For example, in the first three decades of the twentieth century, the United States intervened militarily on some sixty occasions in several small Caribbean and Central American states. In all these cases, little diplomatic consideration or formal concern was expressed by the U.S. government about the international legal implications of these interventions or the critical attitudes of other states.

Although largely repudiated with the rise of Pan Americanism during the administration of President Franklin Roosevelt during the 1930s, the legacy of the Monroe Doctrine persisted in modern times. Involvement of the Central Intelligence Agency in overthrowing the Arbenz government in Guatemala in 1954 and the Allende government in Chile in 1973, U.S. complicity in the 1961 Bay of Pigs invasion and in blockading Cuba during the missile crisis in 1962, the 1965 invasion of the Dominican Republic, the 1983 invasion of Grenada, and the 1989 invasion of Panama attest to the continued influence of U.S. unilateralist behavior in the Western Hemisphere.

LEGALISM

Legalism—the tendency to profess legal grounds for U.S. foreign policies—is a second core belief underpinning the American ideology. The inclination to embrace legalism springs from rejection of the balance-of-power approach as the means for preserving U.S. national security and from the liberal assumptions that people are rational human beings who loathe war and prefer the peaceful settlement of disputes. In modern times U.S. foreign policy clearly contributed to the creation of a global system of institutions and legal rules that allow states to settle their disputes without resource to use of force. This legalism perspective is well embodied in active U.S. participation in international rule-making and in the multitude of contemporary international institutions that the United States has joined and in great part has been responsible for establishing. Paramount among these is the United Nations, which was envisaged through the political initiative of the United States at Dumbarton Oaks in 1944 and San Francisco in 1945. The United States was also the main architect for designing and negotiating the International Bank for Reconstruction and Development (the World Bank) and the International Monetary Fund to reconstruct the post–World War II international economic order. From 1987 to 1994 the United States assumed the leading role in negotiating the World Trade Organization, which effectively rewrote the 1947 General Agreement on Tariffs and Trade in an effort to provide legal rules, inclusive of mandatory dispute settlement, for international commercial transactions. At the end of the twentieth century the United States assumed an intensely active internationalist role as it participated in more than one thousand intergovernmental organizations, most of which were conceived through U.S. political initiatives and were sustained with substantial U.S. financial support. In this regard it is critical to appreciate that nearly all of these international organizations were empowered to negotiate and create new legal rules, both for internal administration and as international regulations. As a global superpower with worldwide interests, the United States remained intimately involved in that norm-creating process through these global institutions.

For the United States, the rule-making facet of legalism rests in the critical legal principle of a government pledging its willingness to abide by international agreements to which it has voluntarily committed itself. This legal principle, known as *pacta sunt servanda* and drawn from the domestic practice of contract law, asserts that treaties made in good faith between governments are binding. While no meaningful police or judicial mechanisms are available to enforce international agreements, state practice clearly indicates that all governments, including the United States, overwhelmingly abide by their treaty obligations for two fundamental reasons: first, it is in their national interests to do so; second, abrogation of treaty commitments absent legitimate justification deprives a government of its political and legal credibility with the rest of the international community. The United States, like all states, honors its treaty obligations principally because those rules benefit American foreign policy interests. To spotlight this point, in 2001 the United States was party to more than five thousand international agreements, of which more than five hundred were prominent multilateral conventions. If treaty-based legal rules were nugatory for U.S. foreign policy, why pursue the painstaking political effort to negotiate, ratify, and consolidate such an impressive array of international instruments into legally binding obligations? The answer is plain: international legal agreements are not worthless. These rule-making documents well serve U.S. national interests, and upholding their obligations provides the United States with greater constructive opportunities and legal latitude in its relations with other states.

Legalism places heavy burdens on U.S. foreign policy, especially when considerations are given to the use of military force internationally. By rejecting the power-politics approach, policymakers cannot assert national security self-interests as the only justification for engaging in armed conflict abroad. Instead, U.S. foreign policy actions may be dressed in legal principles to explain the bases for those decisions. Several examples demonstrate this pronounced tendency to justify the grounds for military action in legal terms, including resort to using the United Nations as an umbrella of legitimacy to prosecute the Korean War in 1950 and the Gulf War in 1991, citing a request by the Organization of Eastern Caribbean States as partial legal justification for the 1983 invasion of Grenada, and use of NATO to sanction the lawfulness of U.S. action in Bosnia in 1994–1995 and in Kosovo in 2000.

The American resort to legalism contains a proclivity toward moralism. Moralistic assertions may be used to explain how international legal rules and institutions are integrated into U.S. foreign policy outcomes. This American sense of morality in its international relations rests on two presumptions. First, the belief persists that the conduct of states can be judged by moral standards. Second, there is the assumption that American morality supplies the universal standard for making those judgments. By definition, American foreign policy actions are presumed morally right and legally justifiable. Thus, when flawed policy initiatives occur, they are not attributed to "American" values that guide the policy action. Rather, such fallacies are rationalized as resulting from leadership deficiencies, information failures, bureaucratic miscommunications, or organizational lapses.

Americans often justify political goals and foreign policy actions in moral terms and evaluate outcomes of events through a prism of moralistic values. This occurs when the government seeks to explain to the American public why foreign assistance for some state might be necessary. Numerous examples of such cases can be found during the Cold War, as the United States often asserted moral principles to justify aid to prodemocratic governments aimed at suppressing communist insurgencies in Greece in 1947, Lebanon in 1958, the Dominican Republic in 1965, El Salvador in 1981–1984, and Grenada in 1983. One might also add the decision to send military and food aid during the widespread famine in Somalia in late 1992. U.S. participation in massive refugee relief efforts similarly rests on pillars of moral values, well illustrated in the tragedies that gripped Bosnia (1992–1994), Burundi (1993), Rwanda (1994), and Kosovo (2000).

Idealism, or the vision that advocates that international peace is desirable and possible, also remains salient as a theme in American legalism. American idealists believe that violence and conflict represent human failures that can be overcome through education. Idealists find clear, accepted moral values in international agreements such as the United Nations Charter and the Universal Declaration of Human Rights. They are closely aware of moral claims by other governments and tend to advocate greater access for peoples in other countries to civil rights and liberties, health care, housing, and education. Idealists emphasize the importance of applying the principle of self-determination in U.S. foreign policy to peoples abroad and are more likely to advocate multilateral than unilateral action in world affairs. The integration of idealism with legalism's proclivity for establishing institutional structures served as the catalyst for the United States—through President Woodrow Wilson—to assume the leading role in establishing the League of Nations in 1919 and for supporting the United Nations in 1945. Idealism also fostered the rapid promotion and acceptability of human rights law in U.S. foreign policy programs and treaty commitments.

U.S. foreign policy at times assumes an approach of idealistic legalism to seek means of attaining international peace and cooperation. Such ambitions are seen in the nation's leadership in several disarmament conferences throughout the twentieth century, among them the Hague Peace Conferences of 1899 and 1907, Washington Naval Conference of 1922, Geneva Conference of 1922, London Conferences of 1930 and 1935, and Kellogg-Briand Pact of 1928, in which sixty-two contracting parties, including the United States, renounced the use of war as an instrument of national policy.

Idealism furnishes the bedrock of international humanitarian law, which governs the use of armed force and the treatment of individuals during armed conflict. International humanitarian law is designed to reduce and limit suffering of individuals in war. It thus extends the principles and protections of human rights to the rules governing armed conflict. In substantial part, such international humanitarian law is the product of U.S. foreign policy. In 1907, the Second Hague Peace Conference adopted Hague Convention IV, Respecting the Laws and Customs of War on Land, which remains the core legal statement on the law of land warfare. These regulations originated in the code of principles set out in 1863 by Francis Leiber, a U.S. physician during the American Civil War, to provide Union troops with rules of conduct on the battlefield. In reacting to the horrors of World War I, the United States in 1929 played a pivotal part in drafting two Geneva conventions that codified protections for prisoners of war and ameliorated conditions of sick and wounded soldiers in the field. The experiences of World War II reaffirmed the need to broaden the 1929 accords, and in 1949 in Geneva four major conventions were adopted that codified more comprehensibly legal rules for the protection of victims of war. Although drafted under the aegis of the International Committee of the Red Cross, the United States assumed the lead role in revising and developing these agreements, which dealt with the wounded and sick in the field and at sea, treatment of prisoners of war, and the protection of civilians. The four Geneva conventions of 1949 represent the most important codification of international humanitarian law protecting armed forces and civilian victims of armed conflict. As such they have been ratified by virtually every state in the world.

Idealism also underpins modern international criminal law, the main goal of which is to make accountable persons accused of committing atrocities and gross violations of human rights law. International criminal law descends substantially from American jurisprudential values and U.S. foreign policy initiatives. The trials in 1945 by the International Military Tribunal at Nuremberg, which prosecuted twenty-two German Nazi officials for committing acts of genocide, crimes against humanity, war crimes, and crimes against the peace during World War II, were innovations of and productions by American lawyers. So, too, were the Tokyo War Crimes Trials during 1947–1948 that prosecuted Japanese war leaders and industrialists. In reaction to "ethnic cleansing" in Bosnia during 1992–1993, the United States diplomatically steered the UN Security Council into the May 1993 establishment of the International Criminal Tribunal for the Former Yugoslavia (the Hague Tribunal). With U.S. diplomatic and financial support, this court emerged as a credible institution for investigating, prosecuting, and punishing persons accused of committing genocide, crimes against humanity, and war crimes against persons in the former Yugoslavia (mainly Bosnia). By 2001 the Hague Tribunal had publicly indicted one hundred persons for alleged atrocities, and nineteen had been convicted. Among those in custody and being tried was Slobodan Milosevic, former president of the Republic of Yugoslavia. In 1994 the United States again acted through the UN Security Council to create a special tribunal to try and prosecute persons accused of committing similar offenses in Rwanda. By 2001 the International Criminal Tribunal for Rwanda had indicted at least fifty-five persons, had fifty-one cases in progress, and found eight individuals guilty, including former Prime Minister Jean Kambanda, the first head of state ever convicted of such crimes. The United States also actively participated in the 1998 Rome negotiations that produced the Convention for the International Criminal Court. Ironically, while this instrument was the product of considerable American jurisprudential influence, the U.S. government continued to have strong reservations about the convention text. In particular, American objections centered on the fact that no provision existed for the United States to veto in the Security Council a particular case coming before the court and the possibility that U.S. troops abroad might be made subject to the court's jurisdiction on trumped-up charges.

Idealistic traits in U.S. foreign policy have generated support within the American public for humanitarian military intervention in situations where gross human rights atrocities or flagrant acts of genocide are perpetrated. Led by the Clinton administration, from 24 March to 10 June 1999, NATO conducted an air campaign against the Federal Republic of Yugoslavia. NATO aircraft flew more than 38,000 combat sorties against targets in Kosovo, Serbia, and Montenegro. Geostrategic and Realpolitik concerns clearly motivated the United States to act, especially the belief that ethnic conflict within Kosovo could destabilize the Balkans and inflame tensions between Greece and Turkey. Criticism was leveled at the Clinton administration for sketchy legal rationales proffered to justify NATO's military attacks, which caused severe collateral damage and civilian deaths. Nevertheless, strong evidence suggests that Serbian forces were undertaking a wide range of human rights and humanitarian law violations throughout Kosovo under the guise of "ethnic cleansing." An estimated six to ten thousand Kosovar Albanians were victims of mass murder, and more than 250,000 Kosovars were displaced and forced to flee to Albania, Macedonia, and Montenegro. The Clinton administration contended that a cardinal objective of NATO in its military action was to deter Belgrade from launching an all-out offensive against its own civilians. In this sense, the NATO bombing campaign took on the character of a humanitarian intervention, motivated by both moral and idealistic concerns. Strictly speaking, the lawfulness of U.S.–NATO action remains suspect because it was taken neither in self-defense to a military attack by Serbia nor legitimized by the approval of the UN Security Council. Still, it is reasonable to infer that the U.S.–NATO action may have saved thousands of Kosovar Albanian lives and might be considered an act of anticipatory humanitarian intervention.

LIBERALISM

A third critical ingredient in American ideology is a belief in the political and economic values associated with liberalism. Dominant as an American political philosophy, liberalism stipulates that the rights of the individual supersede rights of the government, and as such, the individual must be protected by law. Such notions, which are enshrined in the Declaration of Independence and the Constitution's Bill of Rights, proclaim the Lockean notions of protection of individual liberty, private property, and the rule of law.

Belief in principles of liberalism imbues Americans with antagonism toward authoritarian governments that suppress the civil and political rights of their citizens. This can be seen in Woodrow Wilson's principle of self-determination (1919); Jimmy Carter's human rights policy (1976–1980); the Clinton administration's efforts to restore democracy in Haiti and to use military force if necessary to overthrow the military junta (1994); and the anticommunist impulse, especially during the 1950s and 1960s, toward the Soviet Union and Eastern Europe, when communist governments were viewed as enslaving their populations under the control of a police state. Americans believe in individual rights and democratic principles, and the U.S. government often seeks to translate those beliefs into policies abroad.

During the 1990s these beliefs gave rise to the democratic peace theory, a notion of democratic idealism. Liberals argue that democratic states are less likely to wage war against each other, the fundamental proposition in the democratic peace theory. Democracies are more law-abiding and pacific because democratic norms and culture inhibit the leadership from taking actions that might precipitate war. Democratic leaders must listen to multiple voices that tend to restrain decision makers, and citizens of democracies share a certain kinship toward one other. All of these factors work together, the thinking goes, to diminish the possibilities of war. Promoting democracy fosters peace, political stability, and greater cooperation and collaboration in solving problems. Integrating this notion into its foreign policy, the Clinton administration successfully used economic and political incentives to promote democracy in Russia as well as states in Latin America, Eastern Europe, and Asia. By the beginning of the twenty-first century more states than ever before were nominally democracies.

Since revelations of the Holocaust in 1945, the protection of human rights has emerged as a major concern of international law. World attention to human rights has intensified because of television coverage of the horrors of gross violations, increasing efforts of nongovernmental organizations to promote concern for human rights abroad, and growing awareness that human rights violations are a major source of international instability. For the United States, the contemporary realm of human rights law flows directly from both the government's evolving experience in protecting the civil rights and liberties of its citizens and the goal of extending those protections to peoples everywhere. Many human rights norms are modeled after rights, liberties, and protections incorporated into U.S. constitutional law, American jurisprudence, and the national welfare system instituted during the mid-1930s under the administration of Franklin D. Roosevelt. Not surprisingly, the American people tend to support foreign policies that champion and enforce such human rights standards. To codify such standards, U.S. foreign policy has strived to create global human rights law through the adoption of prominent international legal agreements, to which most states have become lawfully obligated. As a consequence, the United States has assumed a leading role in promoting the negotiation and promulgation of human rights instruments. Yet a paradox persists here for U.S. foreign policy and international human rights law. On the one hand, the United States, more than any other government, is responsible for initiating, engineering, and bringing into force most of these agreements. On the other hand, the political concerns of some U.S. government officials that these treaties might be used to interfere into domestic affairs have prompted partisan isolationist impulses that continue to preclude a number of them from being ratified into U.S. law. Even so, the United States can take credit for substantially contributing to the codification of global human rights law and became a contracting party to several core instruments: the 1948 Genocide Convention (132 contracting parties); the 1966 Convention on the Elimination of All Forms of Racial Discrimination (157 contracting parties); the 1966 International Covenant on Civil and Political Rights (147 contracting parties); and the 1984 Convention against Torture and Other Cruel, Inhuman, or Degrading Treatment or Punishment (124 contracting parties). Although actively participating in negotiations leading to their promulgation, at the turn of the century the United States remained outside legal obligations associated with a number of other important human rights treaties, including the 1951 Convention Relating to the Status of Refugees (137 contracting parties); the 1966 Covenant on Economic, Social, and Cultural Rights (147 contracting parties); the 1973 Convention on the Prevention and Punishment of the Crime of Apartheid (101 contracting parties); the 1979 Convention on the Elimination of All Forms of Discrimination Against Women (168 contracting parties); and the 1989 Convention on the Rights of the Child (191 contracting parties). Each of these treaties includes specific human rights protections that have generated ideological preferences in the U.S. Senate for isolationism, exceptionalism, and pragmatism—considerations that supersede that of codifying idealism and moralism into legal obligations binding American policy.

Even though democracy and respect for human rights have prominent stature as American political values, the application of such norms to U.S. foreign policy remains inconsistent. Throughout the Cold War years, a state's human rights record had little to do with whether it received foreign aid from the United States, which sought to aid anticommunist governments even if they were oppressive to their own people. Witness, for example, U.S. support for the Somoza regime in Nicaragua, the shah in Iran, the Marcos government in the Philippines, and the white minority government in South Africa even during the Carter administration, the strongest proponent of a U.S. foreign policy grounded in human rights considerations.

There likewise persists among Americans a strong aversion to military intervention into another state's affairs even to install a democratic regime or to protect principles of human rights. Americans appear quick to champion human rights rhetorically, but they abhor taking action to implement or guarantee them for peoples in other states. This penchant is a legacy of the Vietnam War and the manifest disinclination to send troops abroad. American policymakers usually rule out U.S. military intervention undertaken to protect the human rights of peoples elsewhere because of the high political costs that casualties would produce at home for the administration. This so-called Vietnam syndrome explains in large part the readiness of the Clinton administration to quit Somalia abruptly in 1993 and its unwillingness to send U.S. troops to suppress gross genocidal atrocities being perpetrated in Bosnia during 1991–1994, Rwanda in 1994, and Sierra Leone in 1999. In the same vein, the Clinton administration downplayed human rights abuses in the People's Republic of China in favor of consistently supporting renewal of its most-favored-nation trade status, as well as in supporting the admission of China into the World Trade Organization. Clearly the strategic implications for the United States of a secure economic relationship with China overrode moralistic concerns that advocate stronger protection for human rights for its population.

As instilled in the American political culture, liberalism also assumes an economic dimension. This aspect takes the form of laissez-faire capitalism, which, like liberal democracy, concentrates on the free will of the individual. Key values earmarking the U.S. brand of capitalism turn on the profit motive, private property, and the free market as a means of guaranteeing rewards for persons who earn their way. Sustained U.S. commitment to capitalism during the Cold War years worked to define socialism under the former Soviet Union and its communist satellites as dysfunctional and menacing to the world economy. Pursuit of capitalism by the United States also coalesced with American economic and political supremacy after World War II to facilitate its ability to assert the leading role in constructing the postwar world economic order. Critical was the U.S. capacity for proposing and legally assembling core international treaties and institutions, which have continued to regulate international economic relations. Put tersely, the American conviction in the liberal values of capitalism bolsters the U.S. emphasis on international trade and commerce and generates pronounced impacts for the role that international law must perform in U.S. foreign policy.

LEGAL RULES FOR U.S. POLICY

The past informs the future. For American foreign policy in the twenty-first century, this realization is critical for assessing what role international legal rules play in making and carrying out U.S. policy objectives abroad. The future of U.S. foreign policy still turns on the costs and advantages of three persistent conflicting impulses: the choices between isolationism and internationalism, realism and idealism, and intervention and nonintervention. International legal issues and concerns lie at the heart of each debate, and American policymakers bear the burden of reconciling these divergent viewpoints in rapidly changing global circumstances. The challenges for American foreign policy are daunting, particularly given the economic, political, and military superpower roles in which the United States is cast. The threats to U.S. security are no less menacing, among them: the proliferation of weapons of mass destruction; the degradation of the planet's environment through natural resource depletion; increased global warming, ozone depletion, and transnational pollution; pervasive poverty and overpopulation; terrorist violence; the rise of intrastate ethnic wars that produce genocidal atrocities and massive violations of human rights; accelerating forces of interdependence and globalization that make economic, technological, and electronic penetration of national borders increasingly facile; and the massive expansion in international commerce, which makes all states increasingly dependent on (and vulnerable to) others for needed goods and services.

The United States, despite its preponderant military, cultural, and economic power, cannot manage, much less mitigate, these global threats alone. Remedies lie in producing multilateral cooperation, collaboration, and commitment of mutual political wills among governments. The policy means for attaining these remedies come through active American diplomacy that strives to elaborate international legal strategies and agreements for meeting those ends. The conclusion is clear: international law is far from being an idealist pipe dream. International legal means are in fact realistic policy instruments that the United States must increasingly exercise if multilateral agreements are to be secured on common solutions and approaches for dealing with common global problems. In a world of intensifying interdependence and globalization, the United States needs international law to protect its fundamental national interests. Similarly, American foreign policy must be formulated in such a way that the United States accepts the norm of state responsibility to uphold its international legal obligations. To do otherwise is to ignore the lessons of U.S. diplomatic history and, more perturbing, to render the world an even more politically, economically, and ecologically complicated place in which to live.

The United States emerged as the world's economic superpower during the last half of the twentieth century. It did so by realizing that international trade with other states and foreign multinational corporations would be essential to its continued economic well-being and prosperity and by negotiating bilateral treaties of friendship, navigation, and commerce with nearly every state in the international community. In addition, the national economies of states devastated by World War II, especially those of Europe, had to be rebuilt. To this end the United States assumed the lead role as early as 1944 in proposing and negotiating the Bretton Woods agreement, which established a new monetary order and created the International Monetary Fund and the International Bank for Reconstruction and Development (the World Bank) to advance and regulate the world economy. In late 1947 the United States successfully promoted negotiation of the General Agreement on Tariffs and Trade (GATT), which became effective on 1 January 1948. Initially signed by twenty-three countries accounting for four-fifths of world trade, this multilateral trade agreement prescribed fundamental principles to guide international commercial transactions among most states: free, nondiscriminatory trade; unconditional use of the most-favored-nation clause; reciprocity and mutual advantage in trade relations; reduction of tariffs; and elimination of protective barriers. These principles became the cornerstones of U.S. trade goals in the postwar economic order, and by 1993 the GATT had attracted 130 states as contracting parties.

From 1947 to 1993 the United States played the pivotal role in the GATT's multilateral trade conference negotiations (called "rounds"). The 1986–1994 Uruguay Round produced the most ambitious trade liberalization policies yet, and led to creation of the World Trade Organization (WTO), an institution proposed and strongly supported by the United States in its foreign economic policy. On 1 January 1995 the GATT was replaced by the WTO. Charged with monitoring and regulating international commerce, in 2001 the WTO had 142 members, accounting for 90 percent of world trade. The organization serves as a forum for administering trade agreements, conducting negotiations, and settling trade disputes; it also has the power to enforce provisions of the GATT and to assess trade penalties against countries that violate the accord. WTO rules, which cover commerce in goods, trade in services, intellectual property rights, dispute settlement, and trade policy reviews, consist of sixty agreements that run thirty thousand pages in length. While critics might grumble about diminished sovereignty, U.S. foreign policy clearly benefits from the WTO's legal guarantees of nondiscriminatory free trade and the mandatory legal process created for settlement of disputes between member states. From 1995 through 2001 the United States brought fifty-seven complaints to the WTO and had to answer forty-nine complaints by other countries. In cases actually decided by the WTO litigation process, the United States prevailed sixteen times and lost sixteen times. In twenty-seven cases, disputes were resolved to U.S. satisfaction without litigation. Critical to appreciate is that the U.S. government complied with WTO juridical processes and its arbitral panels' rulings, irrespective of the outcome. In these dispute situations, U.S. foreign policy allocates greater import to the rule of law than to pragmatic self-interest or belief in the virtues of America's economic might.

The GATT and the WTO strengthen and make more stable the international trading system that has fostered unprecedented global economic growth since the 1950s. More than any other government, the United States has been the architect of that system. While the lawfulness of its foreign trade policy might be tested at times through multilateral institutions, the United States is willing to accept that price to preserve economic order and support for the liberal principles of international commerce. To this end, U.S. foreign policymakers cede preference to the long-term benefits of international legalism and liberalism over the costs that would be incurred by national exceptionalism and isolationism.

The regional dimension of U.S. economic policy exists in the North American Free Trade Agreement (NAFTA), which entered into force for the United States, Canada, and Mexico on 1 January 1994. The agreement, which exceeds two thousand pages, established schedules for reducing tariff and nontariff barriers in nearly all of twenty thousand product categories. NAFTA also expanded foreign investment opportunities and other financial transactions among the three states. While many uncertainties persist over the economic impacts of NAFTA, one obvious reality is the much freer flow of goods, services, and investments among the three member countries. Once again, U.S. foreign policy operates through agreed-upon international legal conduits to attain liberal economic goals of freer, nondiscriminatory trade relations with its neighbors. In a world of accelerating globalism and economic interdependence, the creation, implementation, and respect for international economic law becomes increasingly necessary for the United States.

U.S. foreign policy sometimes uses economic instruments as sanctions against other states. Throughout the Cold War, strategic embargoes were levied against trade with communist bloc countries in Eastern Europe as well as the Soviet Union, China, Vietnam, North Korea, and Cambodia. With the end of the Cold War the United States continued to apply its own legislative sanctions against certain states, namely, Cuba, Iran, Iraq, and Libya, and cooperated with the UN Security Council in imposing economic sanctions against a number of other governments. The U.S. economic embargo of Cuba reflected a policy steeped in liberal, ideologically messianic ambitions to install democracy in that country. At the same time, the sanctions stood as a symbol of U.S. unilateralism, driven by forces of self-virtuosity. A number of measures, including the 1996 Helms-Burton Act, applied sanctions against Cuba and foreign companies doing business with the Castro government. These sanctions represented the effort by the United States to link trade relations to the nature of the Cuban government in order to pressure the Cuban people to overthrow Castro in favor of democracy. But this policy was condemned by the UN General Assembly, Organization of American States, Canada, and several European governments. While the goal of turning Cuba into a democracy may have seemed admirable, the means used appeared counterproductive.

PRAGMATISM

The fourth core belief set in the American national ideology is pragmatism, that is, resort to an applied practical approach to foreign policy decisions. It stems from the realization that Americans built a country out of the wilderness, created their own government institutions, and achieved more economic and ideological success than any other people in modern history. American pragmatism thus resembles an engineering approach to foreign policy problem solving. U.S. involvement is often viewed as working to make things politically stable and morally right. The assumption is that right answers do exist for world problems, and the U.S. response contains those right answers. Complications arise in international relations when other governments do not perceive these problems in the same way as the United States. As a consequence, the preferred American approach in seeking solutions for law-related foreign policy issues is to deconstruct the problem, much as an engineer would use a blueprint to break tasks down into sub-problems. A mechanical solution is then devised for each legal component of a problem, while all the time keeping in mind the political implications. It bears mentioning that in this process one runs the risk of losing sight of the problem's larger legal context in order to protect perceived political interests inherent in each sub-problem. When this occurs, the result can be the substitution of means for ends and the tendency to improvise solutions that are unlikely to lead to resolution of the greater problem.

Resort to pragmatism means that legal situations are dealt with on an individual basis, as opposed to long-term planning. Pragmatist policymakers tend to evaluate policies based on whether they solve the problem, rather than on what is legally permissible, ethically required, or even morally acceptable. In this regard, reliance on pragmatism invites U.S. decision makers to assert a strong realist approach in foreign policy. The theory of realism involves application of power politics to international relations. Realists are generally skeptical about human nature and are willing to accept that governments will inevitably act aggressively in their foreign policy. Hence, governments must pursue and protect their national interests, including use of force if deemed necessary. Realists advocate the prudent management of economic and military power. In sum, for U.S. foreign policy realists, the main objectives that the government should advance in its international relations are its military security and economic prosperity, that is, its national interests. Legal considerations are pushed aside, save insofar as they contribute to securing military security and economic objectives. Hence, when such realist tendencies occur, the likelihood arises that foreign policy decisions might compromise or circumvent international legal rules for the sake of obtaining perceived direct political gains. To attain greater short-term benefits for U.S. national interests, a strictly pragmatic approach might conclude that international legal commitments should be short-circuited or overridden. Unilateralist political ambitions are given higher value than multilateral legal obligations.

Resort to pragmatic foreign policies by the United States frequently occurs in situations involving the use of force abroad, which often produce fundamental conflicts with legalism, especially in terms of moral constraints and idealistic principles. When that occurs, historical experience suggests that pragmatism usually prevails. This can be seen in the American attitude toward policies of intervention abroad and government rationales devised to politically support those actions. To put this into legal perspective, international law holds that military intervention by one state into the territory of another state is flatly prohibited, except under four special circumstances: (1) if there is a treaty agreement permitting such intervention between the two states; (2) if the intervention comes at the genuine invitation of the legitimate government of a state; (3) if the intervention is undertaken as part of a collective security action involving an international organization; and, more controversially, (4) if the intervention is done for humanitarian purposes. Throughout most of its history, the United States chose not to rely on these legal justifications to substantiate the legitimacy of its intervention actions abroad.

Historically, the legal logic used by the United States to support foreign intervention is couched in the articulation of presidential doctrines. These policy proclamations, which significantly shape U.S. legal attitudes toward the permissibility of international intervention, are greatly influenced by pragmatic motivations but increasingly assume ideological traits irrespective of relevant legal considerations. The Monroe Doctrine and its Roosevelt Corollary were historically the most widely applied of these doctrines. The Cold War markedly affected U.S. policy attitudes and resurrected American willingness to engage in military intervention abroad. Consequently, during the last half of the twentieth century the U.S. perception of aggression (that is, legally impermissible intervention) became framed in terms of evaluating and containing radical communist regimes throughout the Third World generally and the Western Hemisphere in particular. U.S. policymakers believed radical influence upon the domestic politics or governmental structure of a state produced regional instability and therefore plowed fertile ground for that country to become a victim of communist aggression. Concerns about the threat of communist expansion worldwide resurrected and reactivated the fundamental policy motive contained in the Monroe Doctrine—intervention for self-defense—and fostered its application through a number of post–World War II policy doctrines.

The first doctrine of the post–World War II era, the Truman Doctrine, was asserted in 1947 and committed the United States to a global policy aimed at stopping the spread of communism. The Truman Doctrine was designed specifically to send $400 million to help Greece and Turkey put down communist insurgencies that threatened those governments' stability. The lawfulness of this aid was not at issue, nor did the United States intervene militarily. The scope of U.S. anticommunist assistance was expanded in January 1957 when President Dwight D. Eisenhower formally asked Congress to authorize the use of armed force to assist any country that requested help against communist aggression. In March 1957, Congress ratified the Eisenhower Doctrine, which became the legal rationale for U.S. intervention into the Middle East, where radical nationalism had sharpened in the aftermath of the Suez crisis of 1956. The Eisenhower Doctrine assumed Realpolitik policy objectives and affirmed U.S. determination to become the leading power in the region. The U.S. government invoked the Eisenhower Doctrine only twice, and in neither case was it in response to external aggression. In April 1957, Washington dispatched emergency aid to Jordan, which was threatened by an abortive coup. In January 1958, U.S. marines landed in Lebanon to support the Chamoun government, which was in the midst of a civil war. Importantly, in both cases, U.S. assistance had been formally invited by the legitimate government in power, making the action lawful notwithstanding the obvious Realpolitik ramifications.

The administration of President Lyndon B. Johnson produced a new intervention doctrine for U.S. foreign policy. The Johnson Doctrine derived from the episode in April 1965 when the United States sent 21,000 troops into the Dominican Republic to restore civil order on the pretext of preventing a "second Cuba" from emerging in the hemisphere. The principal legal rationale for the action was self-defense (more accurately, exaggerated national security concerns) against the perceived threat of communism being established in the Dominican Republic. Shortly thereafter, this doctrine was applied globally to shore up justification for U.S. military assistance to the government of South Vietnam in the face of the communist aggression of North Vietnam and China.

The Vietnam War imbroglio produced a new doctrine for U.S. foreign policy toward regions threatened by communist aggression. By the late 1960s, the enormous costs of the conflict in lives and dollars, coupled with the eruption of strong domestic antiwar sentiment, demonstrated to the Nixon administration the need to shift the American approach to military assistance. The new policy, articulated in 1969, aimed to transfer immediate self-defense responsibilities to the South Vietnamese indigenous forces. While the United States would continue to bear responsibility for deterring nuclear and conventional war, the burden for deterring localized conflicts would shift to the countries involved. This so-called Nixon Doctrine was later broadened to encompass the entire globe. As with other American doctrines, considerations of international law were largely omitted from the policy calculus. The change in military assistance policy was not done in response to international criticisms of U.S. military intervention into Vietnam or the widely reported American violations of the laws of war. Rather it was done to counter domestic public discontent and to produce more opportunity for an early withdrawal of U.S. forces from Southeast Asia. These were actions motivated by pragmatism and Realpolitik, not for reasons of legalism or moral commitment.

The administration of President Jimmy Carter revived the expansion of U.S. military commitment to the Middle East. On 29 December 1979 the Soviet Union invaded and seized control of Afghanistan. The Carter administration reacted by withdrawing the SALT II Treaty from Senate consideration, increasing aid to Pakistan, cutting off grain sales to the Soviet Union, and calling for a boycott of the 1980 summer Olympic Games in Moscow. More provocative was the president's proclamation in January 1980 that warned the Soviets to halt their expansion into the Middle East. In effect, Carter declared that the Soviet invasion of Afghanistan threatened the Persian

Gulf and Indian Ocean oil supply pipelines and asserted that the United States would act alone if necessary to protect Middle East oil from Soviet takeover. Thus, the Carter Doctrine identified the continued flow of oil from the Persian Gulf as a paramount strategic interest of the United States, to be defended with U.S. military force if necessary. In so doing, it broke with the Nixon Doctrine, which called for partnership in preference to the unilateral approach in the Truman, Eisenhower, and Johnson doctrines. The United States in this case responded to an unlawful act of foreign intervention by asserting the strategic necessity—as opposed to the predicate of lawfulness—of military assistance to a victim state. Again, pre-eminence was given to motivations of American exceptionalism and pragmatism over normative elements found in policies of legalism, liberalism, and moralism.

Finally, during the 1980s, President Ronald Reagan articulated his own policy dictum to reinforce the central theme of halting the spread of communism. The Reagan administration expanded military and economic assistance to friendly Third World governments battling leftist insurgencies and actively supported guerrilla movements and other opposition forces in countries with leftist governments. This policy, which became known as the Reagan Doctrine, was applied with particular zeal in Latin America. Central to these efforts was supplying military and economic aid to the government of El Salvador in its civil war against the Farabundo Marti National Liberation Front and in organizing, funding, and training the contras, a guerrilla force of 15,000 who sought to overthrow the Marxist Sandinista government in neighboring Nicaragua. Support for such "freedom fighters" was also extended to Angola, Afghanistan, and Cambodia to assist those irregular forces in their struggles against totalitarian leftist regimes. In these ways the Reagan Doctrine can be viewed as a natural corollary of the Nixon Doctrine, albeit one whose permissibility under international law is seriously in question. Such assistance to rebel insurgents is generally viewed as unlawful intervention into the internal affairs of another state and is prohibited under international legal rules, irrespective of the ideological character of the ruling government.

Other U.S. policies highlight the salience of pragmatism over legalism. For example, even though the Reagan administration was adamant about not dealing with terrorists, in 1985 it agreed to sell weapons to Iran in the hope that this might persuade Islamic fundamentalists holding hostages in Lebanon to release them. Interestingly, the monies from the arms sales went to support of the contras in their war against the Nicaraguan Sandinistas. Similarly, the invasion of Grenada in 1983 (on the pretext of rescuing one thousand American medical students on the island) and the bombing of Libya in 1986 (on the pretext of acting in self-defense against Libya for its bombing of a West Berlin discotheque) further eroded the respect for law by the Reagan administration in its foreign policy. Although praised by Congress and the American pubic, these actions were widely condemned by the international community for their shaky legal underpinnings. Propelled by ideological concerns, U.S. foreign policy was characterized by American pragmatism, self-virtuosity, and unilateralism exercised at the expense of the legal, moral, and liberal considerations that embody the fundamental legal principle of noninterference in the internal affairs of other states. Throughout the Cold War years, presidential doctrines articulated policies in which international legal considerations were conspicuously omitted, as unilateralist ideology assumed paramount importance.

Since the end of the Cold War, pragmatism in U.S. foreign policy has remained ascendant over legal and moral considerations when issues of using armed force are involved. Even so moral, liberal, and legal considerations have been integrated more and more to explain and justify U.S. rationales for using armed force abroad. There has evolved the need to advocate normative arguments for American actions to foster greater international acceptance of the lawfulness of that policy.

For President George H. W. Bush, the invasion of Panama and the Gulf War were principal U.S. actions involving use of force. In December 1989, U.S. armed forces intervened militarily into Panama in Operation Just Cause. The Bush administration provided three pragmatic reasons, grounded in nationalist considerations, to justify the action: to keep the Panama Canal open; on grounds of self-defense, to protect the lives of U.S. citizens living there; and to apprehend the self-proclaimed "maximum leader," General Manuel Noriega, so that he could be put on trial for alleged violations of U.S. narcotics laws. One liberal objective was given in support of the action: to restore democracy in Panama. None of these directly relate to international law, and, in fact, a joint communiqué of reservations and understandings appended to the Panama Canal Treaties of 1977 flatly renounces any right of the United States to intrude into the internal affairs of Panama. The legal rule of nonintervention into Panama was overridden for perceived pragmatic short-term objectives of U.S. policy interests, to protect the canal and to seize Noriega.

The Gulf War of 1991 was the first major military conflict involving U.S. intervention after the Cold War. Importantly, it came not as a unilateral U.S. response to Iraq's aggressive conquest of Kuwait in August 1990. Rather, American military action was taken as part of a collective responsibility, formally approved in seventeen resolutions by the UN Security Council in order to force Saddam Hussein's forces to quit their unlawful occupation of the Persian Gulf sheikdom. Sponsored by the United States, Security Council Resolution 678, adopted on 29 November 1990, asserted that unless Iraq unconditionally withdrew from Kuwait and released all foreigners by 15 January 1991, UN member states would be allowed to "use all necessary means to restore the international peace and security in the area." On 16 January, UN efforts to deal with Iraq culminated in a U.S.-led coalition of twenty-eight countries instigating an intense air attack against Iraq. On 23 February a massive ground assault was launched to eject Iraqi troops forcibly from Kuwait. Four days later the war ended.

While American motivations for prosecuting the war against Iraq were more strategic than moral—that is, to maintain secure access to oil resources in the Persian Gulf, to prevent Iraq from controlling nearly one-half of the world's known oil reserves, and to preclude Iraq from building up a military machine that included weapons of mass destruction—a strong case can be made for the lawfulness of its action. The United States might have acted unilaterally to oust Saddam Hussein, but it did not. Resort to the Security Council (and obtaining its concurrence) was essential for substantiating the legitimacy of the U.S. use of force. In this instance U.S. military intervention was implemented legitimately through multilateralism (through an international coalition) and attained the aims of moralism (to reverse aggression) as well as liberalism (to install greater respect for democracy and human rights) and legalism (to proceed through universally accepted UN procedures for dealing with aggressor states).

At the time, many analysts even agreed that the Gulf War served well the prospects for a "new world order." In the succeeding years, such an order did not come to pass, as violence between states became supplanted by the rise of violence between ethnic and tribal groups within states. To appreciate the tragedy of this point, one only has to think of the civil wars in Somalia (1992–1993), Burundi (1993), Rwanda (1994), Bosnia (1992–1995), Sierra Leone (1999–2000), Serbia-Kosovo (1999), and the Congo (2000–2001) that killed or displaced more than five million people over a decade.

Pragmatism affects U.S. foreign policy in several ways. It alleviates the requirement that American decision makers only make policy that is grounded in strict legal principles or ideological tenets. Policy is not wedded to philosophical or moral stricture. It can be decided with greater flexibility, based mainly on political perceptions as opposed to rigid normative considerations. Further, U.S. foreign policy tends to be reactive rather than proactive. In its international dealings the United States reacts to certain events as they occur rather than anticipating that they will occur. In this sense pragmatism contributes to the American tendency to prefer short-term national goals over long-term international solutions—an approach that invites inconsistency in foreign policy actions. Pragmatism can also blind policymakers to the more idealistic sides of liberalism, especially with regard to respect for human rights. One only has to recall that the United States has supported a number of governments that had egregious human rights records in the treatment of their own citizens, to wit, Anastasio Somoza in Nicaragua, Rafael Trujillo in the Dominican Republic, Fulgencio Batista in Cuba, the shah in Iran, Duarte in El Salvador, Ferdinand Marcos in the Philippines, and the minority white government in South Africa.

One can similarly conclude that when vital interests are perceived to be at stake, U.S. officials sometimes bend legal rules to justify their policies rather than conform their actions strictly to the letter of the law. In 1998 the Clinton administration fired cruise missiles against Iraq in retaliation for Saddam Hussein's refusal to permit UN inspections of suspected chemical and biological weapons facilities. More missiles were fired in 1998 against Sudan and Afghanistan in response to those governments' alleged complicity in the bombings of the U.S. embassies in Kenya and Tanzania. American claims that their actions were motivated by lawful considerations of self-defense are suspect, and the evidence of these governments' complicity is not well founded. More likely, these attacks were acts of military reprisal against those states, acts that are impermissible under the rules of modern international law.

On certain national security issues, international law provides the preferred practical recourse in U.S. foreign policy. Two critical areas of intense U.S. involvement stand out: the threat of transnational terrorism and the preclusive strategy of arms control. Regarding international terrorism, such violence has become a regular event in modern times, with Americans and their property frequent targets. Between 1981 and 2000 the number of terrorist attacks worldwide remained relatively consistent, with 9,170 incidents, including 422 attacks in 2000. While domestic terrorism—such as the bombs that seriously damaged the World Trade Center in 1993 and destroyed the Alfred P. Murrah federal building in Oklahoma City in 1995—is a matter for American civil authorities, concern over transnational terrorism has escalated in U.S. foreign policy priorities. These worries not only pertain to conventional problems such as bombing and kidnapping but also to the possibility that terrorists might use chemical, biological, or nuclear weapons against a city in the United States.

Accordingly, the United States has assumed the leading role in establishing specific prohibitions against such violent acts through the negotiation of special international legal agreements. Chiefly toward this end, American negotiators, beginning in 1970, have proposed international legal instruments that stipulate not only the unlawful nature of terrorist acts but also the fundamental requirement for governments to prosecute persons who perpetrate such acts, or at least extradite accused offenders to those states who will. Outstanding among U.S.-inspired agreements to outlaw and prosecute criminal acts of transnational terrorism are the following instruments: the 1963 Tokyo Convention on Offenses and Certain Other Acts Committed on Board Aircraft (171 contracting states); the 1970 Hague Convention for the Suppression of Unlawful Seizure of Aircraft (173 contracting states); the 1971 Montreal Convention for the Suppression of Unlawful Acts Against the Safety of Civil Aviation (174 contracting states); the 1973 Convention on the Prevention and Punishment of Crimes Against Internationally Protected Persons, including Diplomatic Agents (107 contracting states); the 1979 International Convention Against the Taking of Hostages (75 contracting states); the 1980 Convention on the Physical Protection of Nuclear Materials (69 contracting states); the 1988 Convention for the Suppression of Unlawful Acts Against the Safety of Maritime Navigation (53 contracting states) and its protocol to suppress unlawful acts against the safety of fixed platforms on the continental shelf (49 contracting states); and the 1991 Convention on the Marking of Plastic Explosives for the Purpose of Detection (67 contracting states). Importantly, though, the United States by 2001 had yet to become a contracting party to the 1998 International Convention for the Suppression of Terrorist Bombings (24 contracting states) or the 1999 Convention for the Suppression of the Financing of Terrorism (3 contracting states). Through these legal means, U.S. foreign policy sought to integrate the moral aspiration of protecting innocent people with a pragmatic approach that provides diplomatically available international channels for political cooperation and legal prosecution of persons accused of such offenses.

To regulate the use of force and weapons systems in interstate relations, U.S. foreign policy has assumed a highly pragmatic approach. The end goal of policy might appear idealistic (to promote international peace and national security through disarmament), but the means taken are clearly more realistic in their intent and application (to negotiate instruments for arms control guided by President Reagan's maxim of "trust but verify"). The United States has thus employed diplomacy to create legal rules so as to promote greater order and stability in interstate relations, thereby contributing to its own national security. Nowhere is this strategy more apparent than in efforts to control the use and spread of weapons of mass destruction globally and, more particularly, in its bilateral relationship with the former Soviet Union, now Russia. To assist in curbing proliferation of various weapons, the United States was instrumental in drafting, negotiating, and promoting numerous international agreements.

Through negotiation of international legal instruments, the U.S. government has put limitations on the types and power of weapons permissible in national arsenals. What makes the U.S.-led negotiation of these agreements even more impressive is that many states have become legally obligated to most of them, simply because they realize these limitations best serve their national interests. The United States is party and legally obligated to all of the following: The 1963 Limited Test Ban Treaty, which bans tests in the atmosphere, outer space, and under water (124 contracting parties); the 1968 Nonproliferation Treaty, which prohibits selling, giving, or receiving nuclear weapons (189 contracting states); the 1971 Seabed Arms Control Treaty, which bans placement of nuclear weapons in or under the deep seabed (99 contracting states); the 1972 Biological and Toxin Weapons Convention, which bans the production and possession of biological weapons (143 contracting states); the 1972 Strategic Arms Limitation Talks Treaty (SALT I), which limits the number and types of U.S. and Soviet nuclear weapons; the 1972 Anti-Ballistic Missile Treaty, the pact between the United States and Soviet Union that sets limits on antiballistic missile testing and deployment; the 1976 Environmental Modification Convention, which bans modification of the environment as a form of warfare (66 contracting states); the 1979 SALT II Treaty, which limits the number and types of U.S. and Soviet strategic weapons; the 1987 Intermediate-Range Nuclear Forces (INF) Agreement, which eliminates all U.S. and Soviet missiles with ranges between 500 and 5,500 kilometers; the 1987 Missile Technology Control Regime, which limits transfer of missiles or missile technology (25 contracting states); the 1991 Strategic Arms Limitation Talks agreement (START I), which reduces strategic nuclear forces between the United States and the Soviet Union, Belarus, Kazakhstan, Russia, and the Ukraine; the 1992 Chemical Weapons Convention, which bans possession of chemical weapons after the year 2005 (143 contracting states); and the 1993 START II agreement that reduces U.S. and Russian strategic nuclear forces.

Notable exceptions cloud U.S. practice and highlight the force of pragmatic realism over multilateral legalism. The U.S. Senate in 1999 rejected the Comprehensive Nuclear Test Ban Treaty (77 contracting states), largely for reasons of partisan politics and to ensure that the ability to test nuclear weapons would be available to the United States so as to maintain nuclear parity with other states. Nor has the United States contracted to the Convention on the Prohibition of Anti-Personnel Mines (117 contracting states), because of the deterrent value of landmines for protecting U.S. troops in South Korea. Unilateral exceptionalism, ostensibly on pragmatic security grounds, reemerged in the presidency of George W. Bush. The Bush administration indicated that it would withdraw from the 1972 Anti-Ballistic Missile Treaty with Russia so that the United States may go forward with testing and deployment of a space-based missile system to protect America from an attack by a "rogue state" armed with nuclear missiles. Moreover, the Bush administration announced in 2001 that the United States opposed a UN treaty to limit the international sale of small arms, because the accord would constrain the legitimate weapons trade and infringe on the right of American citizens to bear arms. The fact that the United States is the leading exporter of such weapons, selling $1.2 billion of the estimated $6 billion worldwide total, seems a more pragmatic explanation of that policy decision.

Such international legal agreements demonstrate the American recourse to legalism, but they are steeped in motives of pragmatism and realism. A treaty in and of itself cannot prevent the use of any weapon by any party, no more than domestic laws can prevent a person from using a handgun to rob a bank or commit murder. Still, multilateral agreements articulate rules and norms that states are expected to follow in their conduct. If all contracting parties adhered to all these legal rules all of the time, the possibility of these weapons being used would be considerably reduced, and the prospects for obtaining international peace and security would be greatly enhanced. Once again, the motivations for U.S. foreign policy emerge as a national blend of realistic pragmatism and idealistic legalism, the success of which ultimately rests in the political will of the involved governments.

The blend of pragmatism with recourse to multilateral legalism is also well illustrated in issues concerning conservation of natural resources and protection of the biosphere. As the greatest industrial superpower in history, the United States consumes 35 percent of the world's energy resources and emits nearly 25 percent of the world's carbon dioxide. American economic consumption at home generates serious environmental repercussions abroad. Since 1960 the U.S. government, along with other states and international organizations, has grown more attuned to how burgeoning industrial output affects its own air, water, and land area, as well as how international legal agreements might best be fashioned to minimize the corrosive impacts of industrialization on the earth's environment beyond the limits of national jurisdiction. To these ends more than five hundred multilateral agreements have been concluded on conservation and protection of the biosphere, many done with vigorous U.S. participation in UN-sponsored conferences. The obligatory presumption underpinning these instruments is that governments and individuals must use the biosphere responsibly, on the theory that it belongs to no one individually and to everyone collectively. These views are crystallized in multilateral agreements negotiated as legal regimes to govern national activities in global common areas, that is, in those spaces such as the oceans, Antarctica, and the atmosphere. Importantly, the United States is formally obligated to most of these legal regimes.

The legal status of the world's oceans has been a legal concern for four hundred years, though more recent attention has focused on how best to use them without causing pollution, resource depletion, or harm to living creatures. The first global effort to codify the oceans' legal status came in 1958 with the promulgation of the four 1958 Geneva Conventions on the Law of the Sea. The United States assumed the pivotal role in drafting these agreements. When advances in technology overwhelmed the relevance of these instruments, the United Nations in 1973 convened a complex, protracted series of negotiations to recodify ocean law. Again, the United States assumed the central role in these negotiations, which in 1982 produced the UN Convention on the Law of the Sea. This framework convention seeks to regulate issues of offshore territorial jurisdiction, ownership of the continental shelf region, exploration and exploitation of living and nonliving resources in the ocean and on the deep seabed, as well as protection of the marine environment. The convention defines coastal zones, establishes an International Seabed Authority to regulate mining on the ocean floor beyond the limits of national jurisdiction, and provides for sharing revenues derived from such operations.

For modern ocean law, the 1982 convention rules the waves for most nations. Yet the United States has remained resistant to becoming a party to this agreement, principally because of the deep seabed issue. The United States possesses the most advanced seabed mining technology and would contribute the most dues to the authority's operations, which would likely most benefit developing countries. On these grounds some U.S. senators argued vigorously during the 1980s against the treaty, although since the treaty entered into force in 1994, those objections have largely waned. In this respect the U.S. role in the modern law of the sea inculcates an ideological struggle in the American mind between the benefits of international legalism versus unilateral exceptionalism, as well as the virtues of economic liberalism versus international socialism. The irony is that, over the course of nearly a decade, the United States contributed more legal wherewithal and technical insights to the negotiation of this convention than any other government. In the end, the fundamental issue came down to that of sovereign self-interest versus international common interest, and in this case, sovereign self-interest appears to have won out.

Nevertheless, U.S. foreign policy was essential for forging many other treaties that contributed to more orderly use of ocean space. Among these were the 1946 International Convention for the Regulation of Whaling; the 1969 International Convention on Civil Liability for Oil Pollution Damage; the 1973 International Convention for the Prevention of Pollution from Ships, with its protocol of 1978 (MARPOL 73/78) and six annexes; the 1972 Convention on the Prevention of Marine Pollution by Dumping of Wastes and Other Matter, with its 1996 protocol; the 1966 Load Line Convention; the 1974 Safety of Life at Sea Convention; and the 1972 International Convention on the International Regulations for Preventing Collisions at Sea. In addition, the United States figured mightily in the negotiation of two other major ocean conservation documents, the 1993 UN Food and Agriculture Organization Agreement to Promote Compliance with International Conservation and Management Measures by Fishing Vessels on the High Seas; and the 1995 Agreement for the Conservation and Management of Straddling Fish Stocks and Highly Migratory Fish Stocks.

In the case of Antarctica, the United States remains key as the contributor to forming new rules for administering the legal regime there. The Treaty on Antarctica was largely an American inspiration and culminated on 1 December 1959 from a special negotiating conference of twelve states in Washington, D.C. The United States also emerged as the critical influence in producing three other agreements that comprise the modern Antarctic Treaty System. These are the 1972 Convention on the Conservation of Antarctic Seals, which protects Antarctic seals from being harvested; the 1980 Convention on the Conservation of Antarctic Marine Living Resources, designed to conserve krill, fish, birds, and other marine life in the Southern Ocean; and the 1991 Protocol to the Antarctic Treaty on the Protection of the Antarctic Environment, which establishes the norms, rules, and procedures that Antarctic Treaty contracting parties must apply to their activities in the region. Each instrument was negotiated and entered into force with full U.S. concurrence, because protection of the environment and conservation of

Antarctic resources are perceived as best serving long-term U.S. national interests. In this regard, elements of pragmatism stand out in U.S. policy. But what also stands out is the important proclivity toward multilateral legalism that is idealistically intended to secure environmental protection and resource conservation in the region. For U.S. interests to be best protected, other governments concerned with Antarctic matters must be likewise legally bound. Only multilateral agreements, as opposed to exceptionalist, unilateral initiatives, can suitably attain that purpose.

A quartet of instruments comprises the regime for regulating the protection of the atmosphere by eliminating or stabilizing anthropogenic emissions of substances that threaten its environment. The first of these, the 1985 Vienna Convention for the Protection of the Ozone Layer, was instigated and promoted mainly by the United States. This treaty aims to protect human health and the environment against the adverse effects of modification of the ozone layer. Its 1987 Montreal Protocol, which entered into force with strong support from the U.S. government, was negotiated to institute precautionary measures to control global emissions of substances that deplete the ozone layer. The UN Framework Convention on Climate Change, a product of the 1992 Earth Summit at Rio de Janeiro, seeks to regulate the level of greenhouse gases contaminating the atmosphere in order to avoid creating climate changes that impede economic development worldwide. Its companion instrument, the 1997 Kyoto Protocol, was negotiated as a means to implement the framework global warming convention. Even though U.S. industry is responsible for producing 25 percent of the world's greenhouse gas emissions, the administration of George W. Bush indicated in 2001 that it would not participate further in negotiations on the Kyoto Protocol, mainly because the economic price paid by U.S. industry was considered unfairly too high, especially given that India and China were not participating and developing countries were exempt from the protocol's restrictive terms.

By 2001 the United States had not accepted the 1992 Convention on Biological Diversity, which aims to conserve and promote sustainable use of biodiversity resources. Although 180 other states had ratified this accord, the United States rejected it on grounds that it encourages "equitable sharing of benefits" arising out of the use of genetic resources and "appropriate" transfer of technology, while taking into account rights over such resources. The legal logic here supposes that, as the largest developer of biotechnology industries, the United States stands to lose most from these obligations. These costs are seen as not worth the price of legal agreement. Nor had the United States contracted to the 1989 Basel Convention on the Control of Transboundary Movements of Hazardous Wastes and Their Disposal, ostensibly because critical terms in the agreement were left vague and open to interpretation. Rejection of the Basel Convention more likely came because U.S. industry is the world's largest exporter and importer of precious-metal wastes and scrap and would be severely affected by the accord's legal restrictions.

An attitude of exceptionalism for the world's largest consumer and greatest polluter cannot produce benefits for the planet's environment. To correct this, the United States has contracted to three important agreements: the 1973 Convention on International Trade in Endangered Species of Wild Fauna and Flora (CITES), which seeks to protect certain species from overexploitation by a system of import-export permits; the 1979 Geneva Convention on Long-Range Transboundary Air Pollution, which aims to limit the discharge of air pollutants, especially sulfur dioxide, that cause distant damage in other states; and the 1992 UN Convention to Combat Desertification, which strives to halt spreading desert lands.

CONCLUSION

U.S. foreign relations depend on legal order, operate within a legal framework, and require legal principles and concepts that influence policy and limit choices. To be sure, the United States derives benefits from international legal rules and agreements with other states. Legal rules keep international society functional, contribute to economic order and political stability, and provide a basis for common ventures and mutual intercourse. Given that international law serves to limit the actions of all governments, it therefore enhances the security and independence of the United States in its dealings with other states. International legal rules establish common standards where they are deemed by states to be desirable and make more predictable what behavior to expect from states in their relations with each other. That is no less true for the United States in this age of globalization and increasing interdependence.

But international law also limits the freedom of the United States to act in its foreign affairs. The

United States is obligated to certain restraints, irrespective of what its government might like to do when the time comes to act. Political arrangements legitimized by formal agreements are more difficult to unravel or modify. The predictability of state behavior established by international law means that the United States is not free to be disorderly or promote changes on its own whim. To foster the security and independence of its own territory and limit the conduct of other governments, the United States must accept corresponding limitations on its own behavior. To secure the confidence accrued from law, the United States must consent to being restricted in its ability to frustrate the expectations of other states. U.S. foreign policy therefore evolves in tandem with how international legal rules are regarded. Each successive administration builds its foreign policy on the legal framework constructed by its predecessors. Since World War II, U.S. foreign policy has moved slowly but perceptibly away from pragmatic, nationalist principles toward a more legalist, international doctrine. With the end of the Cold War, this tendency has accelerated. In the early twenty-first century, U.S. foreign policy was moving toward more universal values, bound by increasing legal commitments in formal multilateral agreements.

For American foreign policy, international law is most effective in regulating the rapidly expanding range of functional relations between the United States and other international actors. Such functional interstate relations are considered to be "low politics" (trade, communications, rules of diplomacy) and are motivated by a combination of idealism, moralism, and pragmatism. National security issues, however, retain their critical importance as pragmatic considerations, though increasingly the tendency has been to negotiate arms control agreements whenever possible, as opposed to seeking a straightforward balance of power amongst military adversaries. For the United States the restraint of legal rules appears least effective when applied to "high politics," meaning its national security relations between sovereign states. Under these circumstances, realism and pragmatism are prone to fostering American unilateralism in foreign dealings. Yet the wide range of arms control agreements, environmental regulations, and rules for war negotiated through U.S. leadership suggests that recourse to international legal solutions to deal with "high politics" issues retains great sway for U.S. foreign policy as well.

The American experience demonstrates that international law best serves those who make it work over the long term. As the body of rules for the international relations game, international law provides the formal ways and means for communicating to U.S. policymakers the perceived international consensus on policy questions and legal issues. Thus, the United States employs international law in its foreign policy and contributes to its creation. This explains why, with few exceptions, the United States formally recognizes and agrees to respect fundamental rules and principles intended to guide its foreign policy behavior. For the preeminent actor in international relations at the dawn of the twenty-first century, it cannot be otherwise.

BIBLIOGRAPHY

Ambrose, Stephen E. *Rise to Globalism: American Foreign Policy Since 1938.* 8th ed. New York, 1997. Among the best treatments of U.S. diplomacy during the Cold War years and since.

Arend, Anthony C., and Robert J. Beck. *International Law and the Use of Force: Beyond the U.N. Charter.* London, 1993.

Bailey, Thomas A. *A Diplomatic History of the American People.* 10th ed. New York, 1980. The best-written history of U.S. diplomacy.

Barkun, Michael. *Law Without Sanctions.* New Haven, Conn., 1968.

Brierly, James. *The Law of Nations.* 6th ed. Oxford, 1976.

Brownlie, Ian. *Principles of International Law.* 4th ed. Oxford, 1990.

Cingranelli, David Louis. *Ethics, American Foreign Policy, and the Third World.* New York, 1993.

Cohen, Stephen D. *The Making of United States International Economic Policy.* 5th ed. Westport, Conn. 2000. Definitive study of U.S. policymaking for trade agreements.

Devine, Donald J. *The Political Culture of the United States: The Influence of Member Values on Regime Maintenance.* Boston, 1972. Insights on political culture's impact on policymaking.

Falk, Richard A. *Law in an Emerging Village: A Post Westphalian Perspective.* Ardsley, N.Y., 1998.

Ferrell, Robert H. *American Diplomacy: The Twentieth Century.* New York. 1988.

Forsythe, David P., ed. *The United States and Human Rights: Looking Inward and Outward.* Lincoln, Neb., 2000.

Gaddis, John Lewis. *The United States and the End of the Cold War: Implications, Reconsiderations, and Provocations.* New York, 1992. Useful reflections on the future of U.S. foreign policy.

Goldstein, Judith, and Robert O. Keohane, eds. *Ideas and Foreign Policy: Beliefs, Institutions, and Political Change.* London and Ithaca, N.Y., 1993.

Gruber, Lloyd. *Ruling the World: Power Politics and the Rise of Supranational Institutions.* Princeton, N.J., 2000.

Hermann, Margaret G., and Charles W. Kegley, Jr. "Rethinking Democracy and International Peace." *International Studies Quarterly* 39 (1995): 511–533.

———. "Democracies and Intervention." *Journal of Peace Research* 38 (2001): 237–245.

Hoffmann, Stanley. "International Law and the Control of Force." In Karl Deutsch and Stanley Hoffmann, eds. *The Relevance of International Law.* Garden City, N.Y., 1971.

Hsiung, James C. *Anarchy and Order: The Interplay of Politics and Law in International Relations.* Boulder, Colo., 1997.

Jentleson, Bruce W. *American Foreign Policy: The Dynamics of Choice in the 21st Century.* New York, 2000.

Jentleson, Bruce W., ed. *Perspectives on American Foreign Policy: Reading and Cases.* New York, 2000.

Joyner, Christopher C. "The United States Action in Grenada: Reflections on the Lawfulness of Invasion." *American Journal of International Law* 78 (1984): 131–144. Succinct treatment of intervention as U.S. policy.

———. "The United States and the Genocide Convention." *Indian Journal of International Law* 27 (1987): 441–482. Scrutiny of U.S. interests and legal concerns in the genocide treaty.

———. "International Law." In Peter Schraeder, ed. *Intervention into the 1990s.* 2d ed. Boulder, Colo., 1992.

———. "The United States and the New Law of the Sea." *Ocean Development and International Law* 27 (1996): 41–58. Examines U.S. criticisms of the 1982 ocean law convention.

———. "International Law and the Conduct of Foreign Policy." In Shirley Scott and Anthony Bergin, eds. *International Law and Australian Security.* Canberra, Australia, 1997.

———. "The Reality and Relevance of International Law in the Twenty-First Century." In Charles W. Kegley, Jr., and Eugene Wittkopf, eds. *The Global Agenda: Issues and Perspectives.* New York, 2001.

Joyner, Christopher C., and Anthony Clark Arend. "Anticipatory Humanitarian Intervention: An Emerging Legal Norm?" *Journal of Legal Studies* 10 (2000): 27–60. Examines international law and U.S. policy in Kosovo.

Joyner, Christopher C., and Michael Grimaldi. "The United States and Nicaragua: Reflections on the Lawfulness of Contemporary Intervention." *Virginia Journal of International Law* 25 (1985): 621-689. A useful critique of the lawfulness of U.S. policy toward Nicaragua.

Joyner, Christopher C., and Christopher Posteraro. "The United States and the International Criminal Court: Rethinking the Struggle between National Interests and International Justice." *Criminal Law Forum* 10 (1999): 359–385. Why the U.S. opposes the ICC.

Kegley, Charles W. "The Bush Administration and the Future of American Foreign Policy: Pragmaticism or Procrastination?" *Presidential Studies Quarterly* 19 (1989): 717–731.

———. *How Nations Make Peace.* New York, 1999.

Kegley, Charles W., and Gregory A. Raymond. *Exorcizing the Ghost of Westphalia: Building World Order in the New Millennium.* Upper Saddle River, N.J., 2002.

Kegley, Charles W., and Eugene Wittkopf. *American Foreign Policy: Pattern and Process.* 5th ed. New York, 1996. One of the best texts on U.S. foreign policy.

———. *World Politics.* 8th ed. Boston, 2001. Leading academic text on international relations.

Mansfield, Edward, and Jack Snyder. "Democratization and War." *Foreign Affairs* 74 (1995): 79–97.

Melanson, Richard A. *American Foreign Policy Since the Vietnam War: The Search for Consensus from Nixon to Clinton.* Armonk, N.Y., 2001.

Moore, Rebecca R. "Globalization and the Future of U.S. Human Rights Policy." *Washington Quarterly* 21 (1998):193–212.

Newsome, David C. *The Public Discussion of Foreign Policy.* Bloomington, Ind., 1996. Thoughtful treatment of public opinion and U.S. foreign policy.

Pangle, Thomas L., and Peter J. Ahrensdorf. *Justice Among Nations: On the Moral Basis of Power and Peace.* Lawrence, Kan., 1999.

Perkins, Dexter. *Hands Off: A History of the Monroe Doctrine.* Boston, 1941. The authoritative history of the Monroe Doctrine.

———. *The American Approach to Foreign Policy.* Cambridge, Mass., 1962. A historian's history of U.S. foreign policymaking.

Russett, Bruce. *Grasping the Democratic Peace: Principles for a Post–Cold War World.* Princeton, N.J., 1993. Excellent assessment of democratic peace theory.

Schlesinger, Arthur. "Foreign Policy and the American Character." *Foreign Affairs* 62 (1983): 1–16.

Slomanson, William R. *Fundamental Perspectives on International Law.* Belmont, Calif., 2000. Leading text on international law.

Spanier, John, and Steven W. Hook. *American Foreign Policy Since World War II.* 14th ed. Washington, D.C., 2000. Very useful historical account of U.S. foreign affairs since 1945.

Spero, Joan Edelman, and Jeffrey A. Hart. *The Politics of International Economic Relations.* 5th ed. New York, 1996. Authoritative text of international political economy.

Stoessinger, John G. *Crusaders and Pragmatists: Movers of Modern American Foreign Policy.* 2d ed. New York, 1985.

Wittkopf, Eugene R., and Christopher M. Jones, eds. *The Future of American Foreign Policy.* 3d ed. New York, 1999. Provocative essays on challenges for U.S. policy abroad.

See also DOCTRINES; ENVIRONMENTAL DIPLOMACY; EXCEPTIONALISM; HUMAN RIGHTS; HUMANITARIAN INTERVENTION AND RELIEF; INTERNATIONALISM; INTERNATIONAL MONETARY FUND AND WORLD BANK; INTERNATIONAL ORGANIZATION; INTERVENTION AND NONINTERVENTION; ISOLATIONISM; THE NATIONAL INTEREST; REALISM AND IDEALISM.

INTERNATIONAL MONETARY FUND AND WORLD BANK

Francis J. Gavin

If the success of institutions were judged by the breadth and passion of their critics, then both the International Monetary Fund (IMF) and the International Bank for Reconstruction and Development (World Bank) would count among the most effective multilateral organizations in the world. Beginning in the late 1990s it became an annual ritual for tens of thousands of anti-globalization protesters to descend upon Washington, D.C., in late September to disrupt their annual meetings. But the left has had no monopoly on criticism of the IMF and World Bank. Republican U.S. congressmen and free-market economists have long derided both entities as misguided and even corrupt. Furthermore, these protests were nothing new: both the left and the right in the United States vehemently objected to the Bretton Woods agreements that created the IMF and World Bank near the end of World War II.

Do the arguments made against the Bretton Woods institutions, both now and in the past, have any merit? And why do these multilateral institutions, created for the noble goals of preventing international monetary turmoil and alleviating global poverty, incite such heated responses, both in the United States and abroad? Finally, are the IMF and World Bank simply tools of American foreign policy, as is often claimed? At first glance these criticisms are puzzling, especially since protesters have vastly overestimated the power and effect these institutions have had on the world economy. The second half of the twentieth century witnessed tremendous changes in all parts of the domestic and global economy, including in those areas that are the responsibility of the two Bretton Woods institutions: international monetary relations and economic development. But a strong case could be made that other forces—the Cold War, macroeconomic reform, technology, the massive increase in capital and trade flows—were far more crucial to unleashing and sustaining these changes than either the IMF or the World Bank.

In fact, in order to understand the influence and development of these organizations during their first few decades, it is more useful to talk about a "Bretton Woods system" rather than dissecting the specific institutional histories of the IMF and World Bank. The agencies themselves were both anemic and ineffective during their early years. For example, the World Bank was established in order to aid postwar European reconstruction but was quickly supplanted when the United States established the European Recovery Plan and the Marshall Plan. Only later did it embrace the mission of funding development, infrastructure, and anti-poverty programs in the underdeveloped countries of the world. The IMF was similarly pushed to the side during its early years, as bilateral negotiations, currency blocs (like those for sterling and the franc), or Marshall Plan institutions such as the European Payments Union drove postwar international monetary relations.

Still, while the IMF and World Bank were moribund for some time, and are not particularly influential in the early twenty-first century, the Bretton Woods agreements did set down certain "rules of the game" that, if not always enforced by the IMF and World Bank, certainly have animated much of the spirit of international economic activity since World War II. Furthermore, in spite of their weaknesses, it is important to remember that at the time of their inception, the idea of creating such multilateral economic institutions was truly revolutionary. The logic behind these organizations and their mission emerged from a powerful if sometimes flawed causal and historical logic. After the economic collapse of the 1930s and destructive war of the 1940s, the conventional wisdom held that unfettered capitalism was unstable, prone to crisis, and unfair in its international distribution of wealth. Just as the U.S. federal government intervened in the domestic economy through the New Deal to eliminate the extremes of market capitalism while maintaining the benefits, so too were the newly formed global organizations formed to regulate, but not stifle, the global economy.

Depression and war had ushered in a profound shift in the relationship between governments, national economies, and the global economic order by the time representatives of forty-four nations met at Bretton Woods, New Hampshire, in July 1944. Before World War I, international monetary relations were not considered the province of national governments. Rarely did any entity intervene in foreign exchange markets, and when one did, it was nongovernmental banks such as the House of Morgan or the still private Bank of England. There were several attempts at monetary cooperation and collaboration among international private bankers during the late nineteenth century, but it was sporadic. And while the idea of providing aid to rebuild the devastated, war-torn economies had been considered after World War I, the notion of a permanent international bank to guide global efforts to increase living standards and eliminate global poverty was truly remarkable.

One criticism is, however, quite justified. Both the World Bank and especially the IMF have often been tools for U.S. foreign policy and foreign economic goals. Part of this has to do with the nature of constituent power within these organizations. Unlike the United Nations, where each state has an equal vote, representation within the Bretton Woods institutions is established by the size of the financial contribution. Since the United States is by far the largest contributor, it has the principal voice in determining the policies and procedures of both institutions. Furthermore, the United States is able to pressure many of the other large contributors, like Japan, Germany, Saudi Arabia, and Kuwait, into following their policy preferences.

In fact, it is fair to say that America has dominated both of these institutions since their founding. To give just a few examples: in the 1940s, it was the United States bypassing these institutions through the Marshall Plan and regional aid schemes. In the 1950s and 1960s, the United States used the IMF to bail out sterling, the currency of its close ally Great Britain, and the World Bank to promote its modernization schemes. During the 1990s the relationship between the IMF and the Clinton administration's Treasury Department was downright incestuous, as both institutions forged the now controversial "Washington consensus" in its aid and economic reform packages. Rarely has either Bretton Woods institution pursued policies at odds with U.S. foreign policy goals.

THE IMF BRETTON WOODS MONETARY SYSTEM

The Bretton Woods conference of 1944 produced the most ambitious and far-reaching international economic agreement between sovereign states in history. By far the most important aspect of these arrangements were the articles that created the International Monetary Fund and established the rules for global monetary relations. American and British financial officials, led by John Maynard Keynes and Harry Dexter White, hoped to establish a system that would maintain stable, fixed exchange rates, allow national currencies to be converted into an asset over which they had no issuing control (gold), and to provide an effective mechanism to adjust exchange rates in the hopefully rare event that a "fundamental" balance-of-payments disequilibrium emerged. In the event of nonfundamental deficits that normally arose in international transactions, the deficit country would pay with a reserve asset (gold or a key currency convertible into gold), or seek short-term financing from the International Monetary Fund, which would supply the currency needed. The IMF was also assigned the task of overseeing and enforcing these arrangements.

This IMF-guided system was much different from any previous international monetary system. It was not like a traditional gold standard, where the domestic money supply, and hence the domestic price level, was directly determined by the national gold stock. Under the gold standard, a balance-of-payments deficit would be paid for through the export of gold, resulting in a decrease in the domestic money base and a deflation of prices. The decreased purchasing power would lower that country's imports, and the increased international demand for that country's lower-priced goods would increase exports, naturally correcting the balance-of-payments deficit. Conversely, an influx of gold, by increasing the domestic monetary base and domestic prices, had the opposite effect of boosting imports and discouraging exports, thereby eliminating a payments surplus. According to standard market theory, any balance-of-payments disequilibrium would be adjusted more or less automatically, eliminating the need for government interference. But the cost of making payments balance could be very high, and included deflation that caused widespread unemployment in deficit countries. In reality this system worked much better when capital flows from London, and to a lesser extent Paris, kept the system functioning smoothly.

The founders of the IMF explicitly rejected the gold standard as a model for future international monetary relations. White and especially Keynes believed that the interwar experience had demonstrated that a balance-of-payments adjustment process that relied on deflating the economy of a deficit country was draconian in an age when national governments promised full employment and a wide array of social spending. Decreasing the monetary base in a deficit country would lead to a fall in national income, unleashing unemployment and necessitating large cuts in government spending. To avoid such a politically unacceptable system, the Bretton Woods IMF regime allowed nations to import and export gold without penalty (that is, without having to change their domestic monetary base). If and when balance-of-payments deficits arose between countries, they would be corrected through short-term IMF financing and small, IMF-approved changes in the exchange rate. This points to an interesting fact about the Bretton Woods conference and agreement. Although Bretton Woods was hailed as the hallmark of international cooperation, in reality it provided national economic and political authorities an unprecedented amount of immunity from the international pressures of the global market. To a large degree, this was the policy preference of both the United States and Great Britain. Macroeconomic decisions were the sole province of national governments, which were quick to sacrifice measures that would bring about balance-of-payments equilibrium in order to achieve important domestic goals.

Because U.S. economic foreign policymakers worried that the existing gold stock was too small to sustain the growing demand for international liquidity, the Bretton Woods IMF regime was set up to be a two-tiered system in which certain key currencies—those convertible into gold, such as the dollar and (it was hoped) sterling—could be used in lieu of gold to settle international transactions. It was hoped that this would conserve the use of gold and dramatically increase the amount of liquidity available to finance international transactions. This meant that much of the world's reserve requirements would be supplied through the balance-of-payments deficits of the key currency economies. Why did the Bretton Woods planners allow such a thing? Keynes recognized that Great Britain would face postwar deficits, and he wanted a system that did not penalize sterling. Ironically the British economist also feared American surpluses and wanted to guarantee that the United States fulfilled international liquidity needs.

But it was unclear how large these deficits had to be to fulfill international reserve needs. If the key currency economies had no deficit, or too small a deficit, then the world would have to rely on gold alone to finance trade. Without key currency deficits, liquidity would dry up and international transactions disappear. But if the key currency country ran balance-of-payments deficits that were too large, the resulting inflation would test the value of the key currency and set off a large-scale conversion of the currency into gold. This would remove valuable liquidity from the system and set off a fierce competition for gold, with deflationary effects on the international economy. Capital controls, trade restrictions, and currency blocs might ensue. This made the meaning of British, and to a greater extent, American balance-of-payments deficits somewhat ambiguous. The system was designed to make deficits necessary, but it was never clear how large or how small a deficit was needed to supply liquidity without undermining confidence in the value of the dollar.

What were the larger motives of the founders of the IMF plan? U.S. and British foreign and economic policy goals were often at cross-purposes by 1944. It has often been noted how remarkable it was that Keynes and White, despite the vastly different economic priorities of the countries they represented, were able to come up with such an extraordinary compromise. Indeed, Keynes's original proposal envisioned a "currency union" in which countries would have had to pay a penalty on their surplus payment balances. Additionally debtor nations would have unrestricted and virtually unlimited access to the resources of the clearing fund without having to seek international approval or make domestic adjustments to correct payments disequilibria. Keynes's original plan had an enormous inflationary bias, and would have allowed Great Britain to tap the immense resources of the United States without having to go through the arduous and embarrassing process of asking for direct aid.

The IMF Bretton Woods system has often been portrayed as an attempt to move away from the vicious economic competition of the late nineteenth and early twentieth centuries. American policymakers were motivated, it has been suggested, "by a humanitarian desire to prevent the kind of financial stresses and economic dislocations that might lead to future wars." The noted policy analyst Judy Shelton summed up the conventional wisdom when she argued in 1994 that "Keynes and White were convinced that international economic cooperation would provide a new foundation of hope for a world all too prone to violence. 'If we can continue,' Keynes observed, 'this nightmare will be over. The brotherhood of man will have become more than a phrase.'"

Keynes's own writings call this interpretation into doubt. Not only would his blueprint protect Great Britain's planned full-employment policies from balance of payments pressures, it would also present a convenient and politically painless way to get money out of the United States in the guise of international banking and monetary reform:

> It would also be a mistake to invite of our own motion, direct financial assistance after the war from the United States to ourselves. Whether as a gift or a loan without interest or a gratuitous redistribution of gold reserves. The U.S. will consider that we have had our whack in the shape of lend lease and a generous settlement of consideration. . . . We in particular, in a distressed & ruined continent, will not bear the guise of the most suitable claimant for a dole . . . On the contrary. If we are to attract the interest and enthusiasm of the Americans, *we must come with an ambitious plan of an international complexion, suitable to serve the interests of others sides ourselves*. . . . It is not with our problems of ways and means that idealistic and internationally minded Americans will be particularly concerned.

While the Americans rejected the currency union plan as too radical, the British came up with a substitute in the scarce-currency clause for the IMF, which permitted extensive capital controls and trade discrimination against major surplus countries. Roy F. Harrod, a U.S. Treasury official and Keynes protégé, even suggested that the scarce currency not be discussed in public, for fear that the U.S. Congress might figure out its true implications. Keynes agreed, stating, "the monetary fund, in particular, has the great advantage that to the average Congressman it is extremely boring." But the heated debates in Congress over the IMF demonstrated that some Americans had a better understanding of the scarce-currency clause than Keynes assumed.

The controversial scarce-currency clause was eventually included as Article 7 in the IMF Bretton Woods agreement, but the Truman administration interpreted its provisions very narrowly. This angered many British policymakers, who in later years blamed many of Britain's economic woes on the Americans' narrow interpretation of the clause. During deliberations over whether or not to devalue sterling in 1949, the UK president of the Board of Trade bitterly lamented the American position:

> In particular, United States policy in the Fund has been directed . . . to making the "scarce currency" clause a dead letter. We thought originally that this clause might give some real protection against a dollar shortage; indeed, Lord Keynes's conviction that this was so was one of the main factors which led His Majesty's Government and Parliament to accept the Loan Agreement. Once the clause comes into operation, it gives wide freedom for discriminatory exchange and trade controls against the scarce currency; and then there is real pressure on the country concerned to play its full part in putting the scarcity right, e.g., by drastic action such as we want the United States to take to stimulate imports.

In the end, the British had little to complain about. By the late 1940s the Truman administration's foreign policy goal of promoting European reconstruction and eventual integration led the United States to permit extensive dollar discrimination while furnishing billions of dollars of aid through the Marshall Plan. Furthermore, to the surprise of many, the United States ran consistently large balance-of-payments deficits throughout the postwar period. The problem was not, as Keynes and White had feared, too little liquidity. The opposite was the case. By the late 1950s and early 1960s, there was a growing sense that the flood of postwar dollars had become too large, and that measures had to be taken to choke off the persistent American balance-of-payments deficit.

A ROUGH START FOR BRETTON WOODS AND THE IMF

The Bretton Woods blueprint for exchange-rate stability, hard convertibility, and international cooperation through the International Monetary Fund proved untenable from the start. In 1947, buoyed by an enormous stabilization loan given by the United States after the cessation of lend-lease, Great Britain attempted to make sterling convertible into gold and dollars, as stipulated by the Bretton Woods agreement. This first real test of the agreement proved a dismal failure. There was an immediate run on the pound, and within months Britain used the entire proceeds of the loan. Current account convertibility of sterling was suspended, and no other major currency would attempt anything approaching hard convertibility until the end of 1958. The failed attempt to make sterling fully convertible was a major reason the United States decided to circumvent both the IMF and World Bank to provide direct aid to Great Britain and western Europe through the Marshall Plan. The sterling crisis also persuaded the Truman and Eisenhower administrations to accept widespread trade discrimination and monetary controls aimed at the dollar and dollar goods, in clear violation of the terms of the IMF's rules and regulations. Some of the monetary restrictions were lifted in 1958, but much of the trade discrimination against American goods continued for decades.

The pretense of IMF-monitored exchange-rate stability was abandoned in 1949, when Great Britain undertook a massive devaluation of sterling in order to make its exports more competitive and to write down wartime debts. Great Britain did not seek the approval of the IMF or any of its major non-Commonwealth trading partners. It did secretly consult with a small, high-level group of Truman administration officials led by Secretary of State Dean Acheson. The 1949 devaluation outraged officials from the IMF and the international community and threatened to undo the tentative movement toward European economic integration and the dismantling of worldwide trade and currency controls. The lesson learned by other nations was that there was no punishment for a unilateral devaluation if national interests warranted it. If one of the countries that helped design the IMF and the Bretton Woods system flouted its rules, how could other nations be expected to tow the line? The IMF was powerless to stop any transgression against its charter.

Perhaps the most shocking fact was that the International Monetary Fund, which was supposed to be both the source of liquidity for temporary payments imbalances and the enforcer of Keynes and White's international monetary rules, was almost entirely excluded from Great Britain's decision (which was made in close consultation with the Truman administration). In actuality, the IMF was emasculated in the 1940s and 1950s, with little authority or voice in international economics. Desperately needed liquidity was supplied to the world by direct American aid, through programs like the Marshall Plan, Point Four, and the Military Assistance Program. In fact, signatories of the Marshall Plan were strictly forbidden from using the IMF to correct payments imbalances. The Marshall Plan actually created a separate monetary system for western Europe, the European Payments Union, which had its own rules that flouted both the spirit and the letter of IMF regulations. The EPU allowed only extremely limited intra-European convertibility and permitted discrimination against dollar transactions. It was only much later that the IMF became a player in world monetary relations, a period that began when the United States used the IMF as a vehicle to make an enormous loan for Great Britain after the Suez crisis in 1956–1957.

"Disequilibrium" characterized the postwar IMF monetary system throughout the so-called Bretton Woods period. During the early postwar period, there were large payments imbalances between the devastated economies of western Europe and the United States. Large European deficits were to be expected, but they were made worse by the fact that currency par values were often established in an arbitrary manner. Although the IMF was supposed to approve initial par values and any subsequent changes, in actuality each country could pretty much establish whatever rate it wished. If exchange rates had "floated" on foreign exchange markets after the war, they might have found a sustainable rate that would have closed the payments gap with the United States more quickly and efficiently. But after rates were set, changes came in dramatic and disruptive devaluations, the direction of which was always known in advance. Extensive trade and capital controls that discriminated against dollar goods were established instead. In order to fill the large payments gap, the United States provided enormous amounts of aid (in fact, initially Marshall Plan disbursements by the United States were determined by the payments deficit of individual European countries). The adjustment process during the postwar period was not automatic but had to be managed by governmental policy and controls. This made the Bretton Woods period different from the gold standard and the free exchange-rate period in one important respect: because the adjustment process could only be accomplished by government intervention and policy, the system was highly politicized.

THE FLAWS OF THE IMF BRETTON WOODS SYSTEM

Why did the Nixon administration finally pull the plug on the IMF Bretton Woods system on 15 August 1971, after two decades of monetary chaos and instability? In fact the decision was to a large degree inevitable. In its final form the Bretton Woods Monetary Agreement that created the IMF was unworkable because it lacked a mechanism to adjust persistent payments imbalances between countries. Exchange-rate stability could only be maintained by providing ever-increasing amounts of "liquidity," a process that created enormous political difficulties and ultimately undermined confidence in the IMF system.

Why were the fixed exchange rates unstable? The IMF plan, unlike a pure gold standard, affirmed the primacy of domestic economic goals, which included the maintenance of full-employment economies over strict balance-of-payments concerns. But exchange-rate stability can only be sustained when there is comparable price stability between countries, a near impossibility. If prices change markedly because of inflation or deflation in a given domestic economy, then currency exchange rates must shift accordingly or else their initial par rates will quickly be rendered obsolete. When exchange rates are not changed to reflect price shifts, balance-of-payments deficits and surpluses quickly emerge. Such a situation would be especially problematic if the initial par values were already out of line, which was often the case under the IMF Bretton Woods system, because nations were given wide discretion to establish their own rates.

The ensuing balance-of-payments disequilibria were a constant source of monetary instability in the IMF Bretton Woods system. For example, if Great Britain's domestic economic goals produced a yearly inflation rate of 6 percent, and the United States pursued policies that resulted in 4 percent inflation, then the exchange rate would have to be adjusted if balance-of-payments disequilibrium was to be avoided. But this obviously contradicted the IMF's goal of exchange-rate stability, and without market-determined rates there was no easy mechanism to adjust the exchange rate without creating havoc. Deflating the domestic economy to bring the balance-of-payments into balance was not politically realistic or desirable after World War II. Furthermore, the IMF system actually rewarded speculators, who knew the direction of any revaluation and could simply put pressure on a vulnerable currency until a nation exhausted its reserves or its will defending the old exchange rate. Speculators made a fortune forcing the devaluation of sterling in 1949 and 1967. The only option to avoid damaging devaluations was capital and trade controls. Every major country, including the United States, had to install capital controls in one form or another during the early years of the IMF Bretton Woods system in order to maintain their exchange rate, despite the fact they were forbidden (except in extreme cases) by the IMF.

A second flaw, less well recognized but equally serious, was the method of providing "liquidity" in the IMF Bretton Woods system. Liquidity is simply another word used to describe reserve assets that are transferred from debtor to surplus countries to cover their payments gap. In order to offset a negative payments balance and maintain a fixed exchange rate, governments had to supply some universally accepted asset over which they had no issuing control to cover. Until 1914 this asset was, at least in theory, gold. Because the IMF Bretton Woods planners believed that there was not enough gold to supply world liquidity (reserve) needs, key currencies, such as the dollar and sterling, should be used to supplement or replace gold to settle international transactions.

The failure to make sterling fully convertible in 1947 meant that the dollar alone would serve the reserve asset, or "liquidity," function. As a result the dollar was demanded by foreign nations both as a reserve asset and to finance much of the world's trade. These factors, in conjunction with the economic recovery of Europe, helped produce a sizable American balance-of-payments deficit. But it was not like the payments deficit of any other nation. Some of these excess dollars were actually desired by the rest of the world, not to purchase American goods and services but for reserve and international settlement purposes. In other words, the dollar's unique role in world trade and reserve creation meant that a certain level of American balance-of-payments deficit was desirable and in fact necessary for the international economy. But how much of a payments deficit was needed to supply global liquidity was difficult, if not impossible, to determine. Initially most foreign central banks preferred to hold dollars because they earned interest and had lower transaction costs than gold. But as American dollar liabilities—created by the yearly payments deficits—increased, confidence in the gold convertibility of the dollar fell. After convertibility was established by the major economies of western Europe at the end of 1958, central banks began to buy increasing amounts of gold from the United States with their excess dollars.

This brought up a larger question: how stable and cooperative could the IMF Bretton Woods system be if it only worked when the world's largest economy, the United States, ran yearly balance-of-payments deficits? Much has been made of the advantages and disadvantages this system conferred on the American economy. When foreign central banks held dollars for reserve and transaction purposes, it enabled American consumers to receive foreign goods and services without having to give anything other than a promise to pay in return. It was like automatic credit, or, if the reserves built up indefinitely, like getting things for almost nothing. This arrangement, which is the benefit of seigniorage, could be maintained as long as the dollar was "as good as gold," when holding dollars in the form of short-term interest-bearing securities was probably preferable to buying gold, which earned no interest income and had high transaction costs. The danger came when overseas holders of dollars worried that the dollar was not as good as gold or for noneconomic reasons preferred holding gold to dollars. This sentiment emerged in the late 1950s and 1960s.

Under the IMF Bretton Woods system, overseas central bankers could turn in their excess dollars for gold at any time. But at some point the ratio of dollar liabilities to American gold would increase to a level that might cause a loss of foreign confidence in the dollar and a run to the U.S. Treasury gold window. American policymakers saw this as a threat to the economic well-being and foreign policy of the United States. The loss of American gold was also seen as a threat to the world economy, because it was believed that a worldwide preference for gold over dollars would decrease the amount of liquidity needed to finance and balance ever-expanding world trade. A mass conversion to gold would force the United States to suspend convertibility, which would wipe out the dollar's value as a reserve and transaction currency. It was feared that competition between central banks for scarce gold could subject the international economy to paralyzing deflation. Another fear was that the resulting collapse of liquidity would freeze world trade and investment, restoring the disastrous conditions that paralyzed the world during the 1930s and created depression and world war.

The IMF Bretton Woods monetary system did have certain disadvantages for the United States. The fact that overseas central bankers held dollars in their reserves meant that the United States could be pressured for political reasons by the countries within the IMF Bretton Woods system. While the United States accrued benefits from the system, its pledge to convert dollars into gold made it vulnerable in ways other countries were not, especially as the ratio of gold to dollars decreased over time. To some extent Great Britain ran a similar gold-exchange standard before 1914 with a very low gold to sterling ratio, but international monetary relations were far less politicized before World War I. If France held a large supply of dollars as reserves and wanted to express dissatisfaction with some aspect of American foreign or economic policy, it could convert those dollars into gold. Converting dollars into gold gave surplus countries an important source of political leverage. It was this scenario that caused President John F. Kennedy to exclaim that "the two things which scared him most were nuclear weapons and the payments deficit."

The IMF Bretton Woods system trapped reserve countries in another way. If a nonreserve country ran a persistent balance-of-payments deficit, it had the option of devaluing its currency to improve the terms of trade of its exports. The dollar was priced in terms of gold, so if it was devalued, other currencies could simply shift the value of their currencies so that no real devaluation could take place. The only true devaluation option that the United States had was to suspend the convertibility of the dollar into gold. The rest of the world would be left with a choice. Overseas central bankers could support the exchange rate of the dollar by using their own reserves to maintain their exchange rates with the dollar. Or they could "float" their currencies in all the foreign-exchange markets to determine their true value. Suspending dollar-gold convertibility was an option few American policymakers wanted to consider during the 1950s and 1960s. For their part, most European surplus countries dreaded either option.

Why was there such a fear—both in the United States and abroad—of abandoning the IMF Bretton Woods fixed exchange rates and moving to a market-determined, free-floating exchange-rate regime? It is hard to underestimate the powerful influence of the received wisdom concerning the history of monetary relations between the wars. In the postwar period it was a widely held belief that the economic collapse of the 1930s was caused by a failure of international monetary cooperation. In the minds of most postwar economists and policymakers, capital flight, which had its roots in free-market speculation, had ruined the gold exchange standard, which destroyed international liquidity and froze international trade and financial transactions. The collapse of the rules of the game unleashed a vicious competition whereby countries pursued beggar-thy-neighbor policies of competitive devaluations and trade restrictions. To most, the culprit behind the international economic collapse was a free market out of control, fueled by pernicious speculators who had no concern for the larger implications of their greed-driven actions. This economic collapse unleashed autarky and eventually war. A market-driven international monetary system was no longer compatible with stability and international cooperation. Any situation that remotely looked like a repeat of the 1930s was to be avoided at all costs. IMF planners and Western policymakers determined that in the postwar world the market had to be tamed and national interest replaced with international cooperation that would be fostered by enlightened rules and institutions. Strangely, few seemed to understand how chaotic and inefficient the IMF Bretton Woods system eventually became. Massive American aid and constant intervention tended to obscure the system's failings. The intellectual framework that produced the IMF Bretton Woods blueprint, though deeply flawed, had a profound impact on the postwar planners in most Western countries, including the United States, and thrived well into the 1970s.

More than anything else, policymakers in America and western Europe were afraid of the unknown. While the system was inefficient and prone to crisis, monetary relations, no matter how strained, were far better than during the interwar period. Furthermore, Western monetary relations were interwoven into a complex fabric that included key political and military relationships, including U.S. troop commitments to West Germany and Japan. No one knew what would happen to this fabric if the IMF Bretton Woods system collapsed, and few were anxious to find out.

What eventually destroyed the original IMF Bretton Woods system was that it did not have an effective, consistent process to adjust payments imbalances between countries. In order to preserve or restore a balance in international payments, payments imbalances between a country and the rest of the world must be brought into equilibrium through an adjustment process. The adjustment process can take many different forms, depending upon the rules of the international monetary system in question. There are two monetary systems where the adjustment mechanism is automatic, at least in theory: a gold standard and a system of free exchange rates. The nineteenth-century gold standard eliminated payments deficits and surpluses automatically through changes in a country's aggregate demand brought about by importing or exporting gold. The present system of free exchange rates eliminates prospective payments imbalances through market-driven shifts in exchange rates. In both systems, payments imbalances are brought into equilibrium through processes that are largely automatic and independent of any governmental interference. The adjustment process in gold standard and free exchange rate regimes tends to be less politicized.

But this is not how payments imbalances were adjusted in the IMF Bretton Woods system. Instead, domestic economies were protected from demand fluctuations produced by gold or other reserve movements, and the system of fixed exchange rates prevented the market from determining the equilibrium price for a nation's currency. Since there were inevitably great differences among national monetary policies, some method was needed to adjust for the changes in the relative value of currencies produced by differential rates of inflation and savings. But exchange-rate variations were difficult because they unsettled foreign exchange markets, and it was impossible to get countries to agree to shifts because they feared the adverse effects on their terms of trade. Countries were equally reluctant to sacrifice full employment and social policy goals for balance-of-payments purposes. This left no effective means to close balance-of-payments gaps automatically. As the economist Robert Stern stated in 1973, "Since the functioning of the pegged rate system may appear to avoid rather than expedite adjustment, it might be more fitting to characterize this system . . . as the 'international disequilibrium system.'"

Consider the lengths to which the Kennedy and Johnson administrations went to settle America's balance-of-payments deficits in the early 1960s. After the Eisenhower administration went into a near panic over the loss of gold in the days immediately before and after the 1960 presidential election (Eisenhower even proposed using the more abundant uranium in place of gold to settle

America's payments deficit), the new Democratic administration made solving the problem one of its key foreign policy goals. A whole series of complicated formal and informal arrangements ensued—some through the IMF, others bilaterally, and still others with the so-called Group of Ten, or industrialized nations. But none of these American policies dealt with the crucial issue of creating a more effective adjustment mechanism.

The liquidity issue was much discussed both within and outside of the IMF during the late 1950s, 1960s, and 1970s. Liquidity, which was merely a euphemism for reserves, was the vehicle for financing balance-of-payments deficits in the Bretton Woods system. The greater and more persistent the imbalances, the more reserves, or liquidity, are needed to make the system work. In a system of fixed exchange rates that does not have an automatic adjustment mechanism, differential inflation and savings rates will quickly produce large imbalances between countries. Government leaders, unwilling to adjust exchange rates or alter domestic priorities for balance-of-payments purposes, clamored for more liquidity to finance balance-of-payments deficits. But it was rarely pointed out that this liquidity would be unnecessary if there was an efficient, effective, and automatic process for adjusting imbalances.

During the late 1950s and 1960s, when both policymakers and academics recognized that the international monetary system was flawed, hardly a proposal for reform was produced that did not emphasize the need for more liquidity. Suggestions ranged from increasing the country subscriptions to the IMF to inventing a whole new form of liquidity. The most dramatic American proposal came during the summer of 1965, when the Johnson administration's secretary of the treasury, Henry Fowler, called for a "new Bretton Woods conference" to create new liquidity. When the major western European nations eased capital controls and allowed for convertibility of their currencies into dollars, trade and capital flows increased dramatically. This made liquidity a more important issue: larger trade and capital flows increased the payments imbalances that inevitably arose in a fixed exchange-rate regime. More reserve assets were needed by national foreign exchange authorities to defend their exchange rate in the face of increasingly large and sophisticated currency markets. If controls were to be avoided (and they were not), countries would have to cooperate to manage disequilibrium. This would require agreements and institutional arrangements, such as the IMF, the General Agreement to Borrow, the swap arrangements, the Group of Ten, and the gold pool. But in the end, all of these reforms and ad hoc measures were merely Band-Aids to cover the deep structural flaws within the IMF Bretton Woods monetary system.

THE IMF AFTER THE COLLAPSE OF BRETTON WOODS

Despite the strenuous efforts of U.S. foreign policymakers, the IMF Bretton Woods system suffered a slow, painful death in the 1960s and early 1970s. Institutionally the IMF was at the center of many of the attempts to keep the system on life support. The organization's deposits, and ability to loan, were increased substantially in the 1960s. The IMF was also at the center of a series of proposals to reform and recast international monetary relations. The most interesting was the American proposal to supplant the dollar's reserve and liquidity role with an instrument called "Special Drawing Rights," or SDRs. The idea for the SDRs emerged from a 1963 G-10 study on the need for additional liquidity and was formally proposed by the United States in the summer of 1965. The French were vehemently against the SDR, or any instrument that increased the IMF's power, since they believed the organization was a vehicle for American hegemony. Tough and at times acrimonious negotiations finally produced an agreement that was signed in Rio de Janeiro in September 1967. The SDRs were hailed as a major accomplishment, a needed supplement to the IMF Bretton Woods system, but in fact they were never widely used.

Ironically the greatest beneficiary of the monetary disorder of the 1960s and 1970s might have been the IMF. Irrelevant during the late 1940s and 1950s, the organization became the focal point of efforts to fix a broken international monetary system. Increased capital and trade flows brought more balance of payments volatility, and the IMF was called upon repeatedly to bail countries out of foreign exchange crises. The British requested billions to stave off monetary crises in 1961, 1964, and 1966. None of this aid helped, as sterling was finally devalued in 1967, although unlike the 1949 devaluation, the IMF played a key role. Even the French were forced to ask the IMF for help to defend their currency after their currency collapsed in the wake of the May

> ### CAPITAL MOBILITY
>
> It is not widely recognized that the worldwide explosion of capital flows came only after the IMF–Bretton Woods system of fixed exchange rates and dollar-gold convertibility collapsed in the early 1970s. By the late 1970s, many developed countries began to abandon the array of capital controls that had been necessary to maintain strict par values. Exchange-rate flexibility combined with deregulation of the financial markets, improved technology, and the development of innovative financial hedge instruments to protect against exchange-rate risks to encourage a massive increase in cross-border capital movements. Even more significantly, the direction of these flows changed, as more capital began to move to the developing economies around the world, particularly in East Asia and Latin America.
>
> Has this revolution in capital mobility been a good thing for the world? Previously poor East Asian economies have become economic dynamos in record time, most of the former Soviet empire has joined the world trading system, and Europe has begun a once-unthinkable experiment of a single currency. Never in history has there been such breathtaking change in international monetary relations in so short a period of time.
>
> There is no doubting the benefits that the international financial revolution has brought to the world. But there have also been troubling crises that deserve attention: the volatility of the dollar's exchange rate in the 1980s, the developing-country debt crisis that burdened Latin America and threatened the solvency of major Western banks, and the bumpy road to the European Monetary Union. But most monetary and financial crises are not simply the product of unfair speculation or herd behavior. There is almost always a real-world culprit, whether it is loose monetary policies, fiscal largesse, or insufficient supervision of domestic financial institutions. Fortunately, as the link between these macroeconomic and regulatory problems and monetary chaos are better understood, there should be far fewer destabilizing crises in the future.

1968 Paris street protests. The IMF also served as a convenient vehicle for U.S. foreign policy goals when direct aid was not politically feasible, especially in the case of the bailout of sterling.

The IMF's power and influence as an organization increased even more after the collapse of the global monetary rules it was assigned to oversee. Nixon ended dollar-gold convertibility at Camp David on 15 August 1971 without consulting the IMF. But every American attempt to restructure the system during the ensuing sixteen months did so with the IMF as the centerpiece organization. Any attempt to maintain the Bretton Woods fixed exchange rate system collapsed, however, after February 1973, when the United States and the world abandoned the short-lived Smithsonian agreement. The world returned to market-determined free exchange rates, the very system the IMF was established to prevent.

Economic malaise, in the form of international recession and a fourfold increase in oil prices, combined with exchange-rate volatility to spread balance-of-payments chaos worldwide. After Camp David the IMF's role, and even its customers, changed dramatically. After abandoning fixed exchange rates the large industrialized countries like Japan and the countries of western Europe were less concerned about balance-of-payments difficulties. Market-determined changes in cross exchange rates replaced the ineffective adjustment mechanism of the old IMF Bretton Woods system. Nor did these large countries need the liquidity provided by the IMF, unless they wanted to defend their exchange rates against the overwhelming forces of the market. But the countries of the developing world could not as easily ignore dramatic changes in their exchange rates, and the oil price surge left many unable to close their balance-of-payments gaps without outside help.

Thus in the 1970s the IMF acquired a new client—the developing world. The fund also had new subscribers—the states of the Middle East that had grown rich with profits from their oil. Countries like Kuwait and Saudi Arabia had vast amounts of money, some of which went to increased subscriptions to international organizations like the IMF, and most of which was "recycled" through American banks and invested in the underdeveloped world. This massive recycling was both a response to and the reason for the Third World debt crisis of the late 1970s and 1980s. The IMF increasingly found itself providing balance-of-payments financing to poorer countries hit hard by the energy price spikes of the 1970s and the debt crisis of the 1980s.

One of the most controversial aspects of the IMF's post–Bretton Woods lending program has been its requirement that funded countries undergo what is called "structural adjustment." Since IMF funding is meant to fill a balance-of-payments deficit, stabilize the foreign exchange rate, and avoid devaluation, the institution demands fundamental macroeconomic and institutional reforms to remove the causes of the payments imbalance. Stabilizing a currency and halting massive capital flows usually require policies that deflate the domestic economy, such as raising interest rates and slashing the size of the state's budget. Many critics contend that these measures hurt the weakest members of the affected society. The first programs cut are usually in much-needed social welfare, health care, and educational programs that help the poor. Higher interest rates deflate the economy and lead to increased unemployment. Furthermore, the poor do not have the option of transferring their assets and capital abroad, as the wealthy often do during currency crises in the underdeveloped world.

The harshness of the IMF's structural adjustment program—and U.S. policymakers' role in promoting these controversial plans—came into greater focus in the late twentieth century. Largely at the behest of the Clinton administration's Treasury Department, the massive IMF bailout of Mexico in 1995 required an economic reform plan that led to large layoffs and sharp downward pressure on workers' wages. Similar complaints have been voiced in East Asia, where Indonesia's efforts to calm a currency crisis through "structural readjustment" led to political turmoil, domestic unrest, and economic collapse. The IMF's reputation has been further damaged by the widespread misuse of its funds in Russia. Things got so bad that the IMF was publicly criticized by Joseph Stiglitz, the chief economist of its sister organization, the World Bank. Worse, the IMF was seen as a handmaiden for America's foreign policy goal of privatizing, reforming, and opening overseas markets. The sharp criticism forced the IMF to reassess all of its lending procedures and requirements, including its structural adjustment programs.

THE WORLD BANK AND ITS OFFSHOOTS

The World Bank, though far less influential than the IMF, has certainly been no less controversial since its opening in 1946. The bank has actually gone through fundamental changes since accepting its original agenda to promote the postwar recovery of Europe and Japan—its first loan was for $250 million to France in 1947. As it has added to its mandate, it spawned several new organizations to the original International Bank of Reconstruction and Development (IBRD).

In 1956 the bank established the International Finance Corporation (IFC) to provide subsidized loans and guarantees to poor, underdeveloped countries. The IFC provides long-term financing at near-market rates. The IFC provides $4 to $5 billion in new loans annually. The International Development Association (IDA) is perhaps the most controversial additional arm of the World Bank. The IDA was created in 1960 to provide money to countries too poor to borrow from the World Bank's primary institution, the International Bank of Reconstruction and Development. IDA loans carry no interest rate, are very long term (thirty-five to fifty years), a small yearly fee (.75 percent), and a ten-year grace period. The United States has been the largest contributor to the IDA, providing more than $20 billion between 1960 and 2000. The International Center for Settlement of Investment Disputes (ICSID) was established in 1966 to promote increased private investment to the underdeveloped world. Similarly, the Multilateral Investment Guarantee Agency (MIGA) was created in 1988 to reduce the risk faced by private global investors in poor countries. In addition to providing advice, MIGA insures and guarantees up to 90 percent of a project's investment.

The bank gets its money from country contributions and its investments in financial markets. The membership has increased from the original 44 nations that met at Bretton Woods to 183 in 2001. The United States is by far the largest contributor, providing over $50 billion since 1944. Although its total share has decreased, the United States still provides more than 17 percent of total funds. Several bodies govern the bank, including a board of governors (with a member from each country), a twenty-five-member executive directorate (with the five largest donors—the United States, Japan, Germany, France, and Great Britain holding permanent seats), and a president, who is by tradition an American.

EXECUTIVE PERSONALITY AND THE WORLD BANK

Far more than the IMF, the World Bank's direction and policies have been established by the personality of the executive director. The director's authority came largely as the result of a power struggle in the bank's early years between the first president, Eugene Meyer, a seventy-year-old investment banker selected by the Truman administration, and the bank's management and executive board. This dispute over power sharing led to Meyer's resignation after only six months. The high-profile "wise man" John J. McCloy was brought in to succeed him and to place the tottering bank on a better footing. McCloy's first act was to get the bank's executive board to relinquish its activist position and allow the president to dictate the organization's policies and directions. Though McCloy only stayed two and a half years, he began the tradition of powerful American World Bank presidents who drove the multilateral organization's agenda.

The World Bank's original mission was to provide reconstruction loans to war-torn Europe and Japan. These loans were intended for basic infrastructure projects such as roads, bridges, electrical plants, and the like. But the bank's lending policies were very conservative at first, and the recipients both demanded more funds and resisted the conditions attached to financing. The European Recovery Program, or Marshall Plan, soon eclipsed the World Bank. This U.S.-financed program provided far more money and attached fewer strings. During its first four years the World Bank provided only $500 million to western Europe, a figure dwarfed by the Marshall Plan and even by private American investment.

The World Bank's conservative lending policies continued under the long-term leadership of Eugene Black (1949–1962). While Black, a former president of Chase Manhattan Bank, enjoyed a solid reputation in the financial world, he was wary of moving too quickly away from the bank's original mandate. But by the late 1950s and 1960s the World Bank decided to escape its international irrelevance by reinventing itself. Western Europe and Japan were well on their way to a robust economic recovery that the World Bank had little to do with. The key event was the creation of the International Development Association in 1960. The IDA was established to make subsidized loans to poor countries that were credit risks and could not afford private commercial loans.

In order to borrow from the IDA a country must meet four criteria. It must be very poor (less than $800 per capita GNP in 2001). It must have sufficient political and economic stability to warrant financing over the long term. The country must have extremely difficult balance-of-payments problems, with little opportunity to earn the needed foreign exchange. Finally, its national policies must reflect a real commitment to development. These goals and policies reflected a new passion within the U.S. academic and foreign policy community for using foreign aid to promote "modernization" in the so-called Third World.

The IDA did not start out well. In fact a whole series of regional institutions were developed in order to fill the perceived void created by the World Bank's stingy loan practices. In 1958 the European Development Bank was created, largely for the benefit of francophone Africa. The European Investment Bank was established to finance infrastructure projects within the European Economic Community. In 1958 the Inter-American Development Bank was set up in Washington, D.C., to spur growth in Latin America. The African Development Bank was created in 1964, and the very successful Asian Development Bank began operations in 1966. If imitation is the sincerest form of flattery, then the World Bank was successful indeed. But the proliferation of regional banks also signaled the failure of the Bretton Woods institution to fully embrace the enormous global development challenges that arose in the 1960s.

The World Bank began its real transformation under the controversial leadership of Robert S. McNamara (1968–1981). McNamara took over the bank after his resignation (or firing—he was never sure which) as President Lyndon B. Johnson's secretary of defense in 1968. McNamara became the father of a much-contested lending concept called "sustainable development." He dramatically increased the bank's lending portfolio, and by the time he left in 1981, lending had increased more than tenfold, from almost $900 million to $12 billion. McNamara succeeded in finally making the World Bank relevant to the global economy, particularly in the underdeveloped world. But he also left a legacy of continuing controversy that has fueled passionate anti–World Bank rhetoric from both the extreme left and right.

By the time McNamara had decided to leave the bank, there had been a sharp shift in orthodoxy within both the economics profession and policymaking community toward development aid. The election of Margaret Thatcher in England and Ronald Reagan in the United States signaled a move away from Keynesian demand management toward a more laissez-faire philosophy. This was bound to affect the bank. In fact, just as the last years of Jimmy Carter's presidency witnessed a defense buildup and a spate of economic deregulation that foreshadowed the Reagan years, so too did the final period of the McNamara presidency bring a sea shift in World Bank policies. By the end of the 1970s there was a growing dissatisfaction with the results and perceived lack of accountability in World Bank lending. This led the bank to institute its own "structural adjustment" policies in the hope of encouraging macroeconomic reform among countries receiving funding.

McNamara's successor, A. W. Claussen (1981–1986), faced mounting challenges: hostility from the new U.S. administration, a poorly performing portfolio, and increasing fears of a full-blown debt crisis in the developing world. Over time, Claussen replaced McNamara's more progressive staff members with neoclassical economists like Anne Krueger. Claussen maintained a far more low-key style that served the bank well during this period of transition. Claussen's successors Barber Conable (1986–1991) and Lewis Preston (1991–1995) did not fare as well. The World Bank was forced to suspend its lending to its largest (and in many ways most successful) client, the People's Republic of China, after the June 1989 Tiananmen Square massacre. This set a precedent of sorts for the bank, as it had scrupulously tried to stay out of "borrower politics." The Preston presidency faced growing questions about the bank's effectiveness, detailed below, which continued to plague Preston's successor, James Wolfensohn, who took over after Preston's untimely death in 1995.

WORLD BANK CRITICS ON THE RIGHT AND LEFT

The World Bank and its lending practices have come under increasing scrutiny. The critique from the right contends that the World Bank has shifted from being a "lender of last resort" to an international welfare organization. In doing so the World Bank has become, according to critics, bloated, incompetent, and even corrupt. Worse, the bank's lending policies often reward macroeconomic inefficiency in the underdeveloped world, allowing inefficient kleptocracies to avoid the types of fundamental reforms that would in the long run end poverty in their countries. These critics like to compare the fantastic growth in East Asia to the deplorable economic conditions of Africa. In 1950 the regions were alike—South Korea had a lower per capita GDP than Nigeria. But by pursuing macroeconomic reforms, high savings, investing in education and basic social services, and opening their economies to the global trading order, the "Pacific Tigers" have been able to lift themselves out of poverty and into wealth with very little help from the World Bank. Many countries in Africa, however, have relied primarily on multilateral assistance from organizations like the World Bank while avoiding fundamental macroeconomic reforms, with deplorable but predictable results.

Conservatives point out that the World Bank has lent more than $350 billion over a half-century, mostly to the underdeveloped world, with little to show for it. One study argued that of the sixty-six countries that received funding from the bank from 1975 to 2000, well over half were no better off than before, and twenty were actually worse off. The study pointed out that Niger received $637 million between 1965 and 1995, yet its per capita GNP had fallen, in real terms, more than 50 percent during that time. In the same period Singapore, which received one-seventh as much World Bank aid, had seen its per capita GNP increase by more than 6 percent a year.

The left has been no less harsh in its criticisms of the World Bank. They claim that World Bank loans privilege large infrastructure projects like building dams and electric plants over projects that would benefit the poor, such as education and basic health care. Worse, these projects often have wreaked havoc on the local environment. Forests, rivers, and fisheries have been devastated by World Bank–financed projects. Some projects even have led to the forced resettlement of indigenous communities. One estimate holds that more than two and a half million people have been displaced by projects made possible through World Bank loans.

Environmentalist and anti-globalization groups point to specific failed projects. The Sardar Sarovar dam on the Narmada River in India was expected to displace almost a quarter of a million people into squalid resettlement sites. The Polonoroeste Frontier Development scheme has led to large-scale deforestation in the Brazilian rain forest. In Thailand, the Pak Mun dam has destroyed the fisheries of the Mun River, impoverishing thousands who had made their living fishing and forever altering the diet of the region.

In response to these accusations, the World Bank has attempted reforms, appointing its own inspection panel in 1993. But critics point out that the bank needs to be more responsive to outside forces and criticisms. The World Bank has never rejected a single project since 1944. The bank staff is very highly paid—the average compensation of a World Bank employee in 1994 was $134,000. The bank can't even properly manage the construction of its own headquarters: the 1993–1994 project came in almost $100 million over budget. Perhaps most damning, the bank's lax lending standards have led to a rapidly deteriorating loan portfolio.

CONCLUSION

The future of both Bretton Woods institutions remains uncertain. Both the IMF and World Bank escaped the efforts of the Republican U.S. Congress in the mid-1990s to sharply curtail and even eliminate both organizations. These agencies have been less successful in answering the charges from the left, as the IMF retains its demand for "structural adjustments" and the World Bank still favors funding for large, project-driven funding. While both the IMF and the World Bank have instituted some reforms, they have been unable to appease the concerns of outraged environmentalists, labor unionists, and nationalists and advocates of indigenous peoples in the developing world.

Still, as this essay has suggested, these two organizations are really the misguided target for the legitimate concerns people of all ideological stripes have had about the rapid pace of globalization in the past half century. It is likely this globalization would have occurred whether or not there had been a Bretton Woods conference, and it is all but certain it will continue in the future regardless of the policies pursued by the IMF and World Bank. While it is true that they have often been too driven by U.S. foreign policy concerns, in the end the influence of both institutions has been widely overstated. And despite their mistakes during the past half century, they have rarely been given credit for many of the little things they do well. For example, both institutions perform economic surveillance over most of the world's economy, a valuable task that no other international or private organization could perform with such skill. Both agencies also serve as a store of expert knowledge and wisdom for countries throughout the world that lack trained specialists. While neither the IMF nor the World Bank has met the lofty goals of their founders or wielded the nefarious influence charged by their critics, they have and should continue to play a small but important role in promoting prosperity and economic stability worldwide.

BIBLIOGRAPHY

Argy, Victor. *The Postwar International Money Crisis: An Analysis.* London, 1981.

Aronson, Jonathan David. *Money and Power: Banks and the World Monetary System.* London and Beverly Hills, Calif., 1977.

Block, Fred L. *The Origins of International Economic Disorder: A Study of United States International Monetary Policy from World War II to the Present.* Berkeley, Calif., 1977.

Bordo, Michael D., and Barry Eichengreen, eds. *A Retrospective on the Bretton Woods System: Lessons for International Monetary Reform.* Chicago, 1993.

Brown, Brendan. *The Flight of International Capital: A Contemporary History.* London and New York, 1987.

Caincross, Alec, and Barry Eichengreen. *Sterling in Decline: The Devaluations of 1931, 1949, and 1967.* Oxford, 1983.

Calleo, David P. *The Imperious Economy.* Cambridge, Mass., 1982.

Cassis, Youssef. *Finance and Financiers in European History, 1880–1960.* Cambridge and New York, 1992.

Cohen, Benjamin J. *Organizing the World's Money: The Political Economy of International Monetary Relations.* New York, 1977.

Cooper, Richard N. *The International Monetary System: Essays in World Economics.* Cambridge, Mass., 1987.

Corden, W. M. *Inflation, Exchange Rates and the World Economy: Lectures on International Monetary Economics.* 3d ed. Chicago, 1986.

De Grauwe, Paul. *International Money: Post-War Trends and Theories.* Oxford and New York, 1989.

De Vries, Margaret Garritsen. *The International Monetary Fund 1966–1971: The System Under Stress.* Vols. 1–2. Washington, D.C., 1976.

———. *Balance of Payments Adjustment 1945 to 1986: The IMF Experience.* Washington, D.C., 1987.

Dormael, Armand van. *Bretton Woods: Birth of a Monetary System.* New York, 1978.

Eckes, Alfred E. *A Search for Solvency: Bretton Woods and the International Monetary System, 1941–1971.* Austin, Tex., 1975.

Eichengreen, Barry. *Golden Fetters: The Gold Standard and the Great Depression, 1919–1939.* New York, 1992.

———. *International Monetary Arrangements for the 21st Century.* Washington, D.C., 1994.

Fischer, Stanley. "Stability and Exchange Rate Systems in a Monetarist Model of the Balance of Payments." In Robert Z. Aliber, ed. *The Political Economy of Monetary Reform.* London and Montclair, N.J., 1977.

Friedman, Milton. "The Case for Flexible Exchange Rates." In his *Essays in Positive Economics.* Chicago, 1953.

———. *Money Mischief: Episodes in Monetary History.* New York, 1992.

Friedman, Milton, and Anna Jacobson Schwartz. *A Monetary History of the United States: 1867–1960.* Princeton, N.J., 1963.

Gallarotti, Giulio. *The Anatomy of an International Monetary Regime: The Classical Gold Standard, 1880–1914.* New York, 1995.

Gardner, Richard N. *Sterling-Dollar Diplomacy: The Origins and the Prospects of Our International Economic Order.* New ed. New York, 1980.

Gavin, Francis J. "The Legends of Bretton Woods." *Orbis* (spring 1996).

Gilbert, Martin. *Quest for World Monetary Order: The Gold-Dollar System and Its Aftermath.* New York, 1980.

Gilpin, Robert. *The Political Economy of International Relations.* Princeton, N.J., 1987.

Gowa, Joanne. *Closing the Gold Window: Domestic Politics and the End of Bretton Woods.* Ithaca, N.Y., 1983.

Hogan, Michael. *The Marshall Plan: America, Britain, and the Reconstruction of Western Europe, 1947–1952.* Cambridge and New York, 1987.

Horsefield, J. Keith, ed. *The International Monetary Fund, 1945–1965: Twenty Years of International Monetary Cooperation.* Washington, D.C. 1969.

Ikenberry, John G. "A World Economy Restored: Expert Consensus and the Anglo-American Postwar Settlement." *International Organizations* 46 (winter 1992).

James, Harold. *International Monetary Cooperation Since Bretton Woods.* New York, 1996.

Johnson, H. G. "Theoretical Problems of the International Monetary System." In Richard N. Cooper, ed. *International Finance.* Baltimore, 1969.

Kaplan, Jacob J., and Günter Schleiminger. *The European Payments Union: Financial Diplomacy in the 1950s.* Oxford and New York, 1989.

Kapur, Devesh, John P. Lewis, and Richard Webb. *The World Bank: Its First Half Century.* Washington, D.C., 1997.

Kelly, Janet. "International Monetary Systems and National Security." In Klaus Knorr and Frank N. Trager, eds. *Economic Issues and National Security.* Lawrence, Kans., 1977.

Kenen, Peter B., Francesco Papadia, and Fabrizio Saccomanni, eds. *The International Monetary System.* Cambridge and New York, 1994.

Keohane, Robert O. *After Hegemony: Cooperation and Discord in the World Political Economy.* Princeton, N.J., 1984.

Keynes, John M. *The Collected Writings of John Maynard Keynes.* Vol. 25. Edited by Donald Moggridge. London and New York, 1980.

Kindleberger, Charles. *A Financial History of Western Europe.* 2d ed. Oxford and New York, 1993.

Kirshner, Jonathan. *Currency and Coercion: The Political Economy of International Monetary Power.* Princeton, N.J., 1995.

Kunz, Diane. *Butter and Guns: America's Cold War Economic Diplomacy.* New York, 1997.

Maier, Charles. "The Two Postwar Eras and the Conditions for Stability in Twentieth-Century Western Europe." *American Historical Review* 86 (April 1981).

Mason, Edward, and Robert E. Asher. *The World Bank Since Bretton Woods.* Washington, D.C., 1973.

Meier, Gerald M. *The Problems of a World Monetary Order.* 2d ed. Oxford and New York, 1982.

Milward, Alan S. *The Reconstruction of Western Europe, 1945–1951.* London and Berkeley, Calif., 1984.

Newton, Scott. "The Sterling Crisis of 1947 and the British Response to the Marshall Plan." *Economic History Review* 37 (August 1984).

———. "The 1949 Sterling Crisis and British Policy Toward European Integration." *Review of International Studies* 11 (July 1985).

Odell, John S. *U.S. International Monetary Policy: Markets, Power, and Ideas as Sources of Change.* Princeton, N.J., 1982.

Pollard, Robert A. *Economic Security and the Origins of the Cold War, 1945–1950.* New York, 1985.

Rueff, Jacques. *Balance of Payments: Proposals for Resolving the Most Pressing World Economic Problem of Our Time.* New York, 1967.

Salda, Anne C. M. *Historical Dictionary of the World Bank.* Lanham, Md., 1997.

Shelton, Judy. *Money Meltdown: Restoring Order to the Global Currency System.* New York, 1994.

Solomon, Robert. *The International Monetary System, 1945–1976: An Insider's View.* New York, 1977.

Stern, Robert M. *The Balance of Payments: Theory and Economic Policy.* Chicago, 1973.

Strange, Susan. *Sterling and British Policy: A Political Study of an International Currency in Decline.* New York, 1971.

———. *International Economic Relations of the Western World: 1959–1971.* Vol. 2. London and New York, 1976.

Temin, Peter. *Lessons from the Great Depression.* Cambridge, Mass., 1989.

Tew, Brian. *The Evolution of the International Monetary System, 1945–1988.* 4th ed. London, 1988.

Triffin, Robert. *Gold and the Dollar Crisis.* New Haven, Conn., 1960.

Wee, Herman van der. *Prosperity and Upheaval: The World Economy During 1945–80.* New York, 1985.

See also BALANCE OF POWER; ECONOMIC POLICY AND THEORY; FOREIGN AID; INTERNATIONAL ORGANIZATION; POST–COLD WAR POLICY.

INTERNATIONAL ORGANIZATION

Inis L. Claude, Jr., and Klaus Larres

International organizations (IOs) serve as crucial forces of coordination and cooperation on many political, economic, social, military and cultural issues. Aside from the traditional domination of international politics by established or recently codified nation-states, IOs are important participants of the international system. The growth of transnational IOs was greatly facilitated by the rise of an increasing number of tenuous networks of nation-states in political, economic, and financial affairs in early modern Europe. They began to proliferate in the course of the nineteenth century. As will be seen, the United States first participated in the development of IOs in a relatively minor way in the first two decades after the Civil War and in a more important way when American statesmen attended the Hague conferences of 1899 and 1907. For much of the twentieth century the United States remained a leading proponent of the formation and development of IOs. Washington was even instrumental in the creation of two of the most important IOs ever: the League of Nations founded in 1919 after World War I and the United Nations established in 1945 at the end of World War II.

The breakdown of the international system in the 1910s and late 1930s and the global bloodshed, devastation, and unsurpassed misery brought about by two world wars convinced the international community, led by the United States and Britain, of the urgency for the establishment of a new universal and cooperative order. In the course of World War II traditional American political isolationism was marginalized to a considerable degree. Beginning with the Atlantic Charter of 1941 and continuing with the 1944 Dumbarton Oaks and Bretton Woods conferences, the establishment of the United Nations in 1945 and the formation of many other international political and economic institutions, the pillars for a new multilateral order were created. The Cold War soon added another dimension to this, which led to the shelving of the dream of a new cooperative world order for more than four decades: the politics and culture of bipolar containment. Genuine multilateralism was sidelined during much of the second half of the twentieth century. Instead international institutions, in particular the General Assembly of the United Nations, were frequently exploited as a mere talking shop and a forum for ventilating hostile rhetoric.

From the mid-1970s, however, a cautious revival of multilateralism, in the form of the Helsinki process inaugurated in 1975, may even have contributed to hastening the end of the Cold War in 1989–1991. The dangers of an ever-increasing nuclear arms race, as well as economic and financial globalization and, paradoxically, the simultaneous development of a politically and culturally ever more fragmented world, once again gave IOs a crucial role as a forum for consultation, mediation, and arbitration. In the late twentieth and early twenty-first centuries not only globalization and fragmentation but also the influence of more sophisticated means of transportation and communication and the increasingly transnational character of military, political, and environmental conflicts posed entirely new challenges. Despite recurrent bouts of political isolationism, the United States—like most other countries—recognized the impossibility of addressing contemporary problems merely on a nation-state basis. After the end of the East-West conflict and the gradual realignment of eastern and western Europe, this led to the formation of a host of new international organizations and institutions. Yet in the post–Cold War era the policies of the United States toward international organizations remained ambiguous; a widespread revival of both isolationism and unilateralism could be observed. However, the unprecedented terrorist attack on the World Trade Center and the Pentagon on 11 September 2001 had a fundamental impact on American political strategy. In the immediate wake of the attack no one could say whether it would result in the abandonment of unilateralism, but many policy analysts believed that it might well lead to a much greater American reengagement with international organizations to fight global terrorism.

Intellectually the development of IOs was rooted in Immanuel Kant's eighteenth-century insight that only the "pacific federation" of liberal democratic, interdependent, and lawful republics could overcome the inherent anarchy of the international system, as described by Thomas Hobbes, and therefore the permanent danger of the outbreak of war. While Hobbes believed that a strong authoritarian state and the balance of power among the world's greatest powers could rectify this situation and provide lasting international security, Kant was not convinced. He was in favor of the establishment of peace-creating confederations and thus, in effect, of bringing about the interdependence of nation-states. Over time these insights developed into the contemporary conviction that interdependent democratic states will hardly ever embark on military action against one another. Democracy and cooperative multilateralism within (but also outside) international organizations were thus seen as the best vehicles for the creation of a more stable and peaceful world.

WHAT ARE INTERNATIONAL ORGANIZATIONS?

In general international organizations are based on multilateral treaties between at least two sovereign nation-states. The formation of an initially fairly loose bond among the participants is generally fortified by the development of more or less stringent institutional structures and organs to pursue certain more or less clearly defined common aims in the international arena. IOs can either have a global or a regional character, with the latter in general displaying a more centralized structure due to the limited number of regional state actors available. While many IOs are single-issue organizations, others focus their attention on a multitude of issues. IOs can either be open to new members or consist of a closed system. On occasion IOs are established for a certain duration as specified in their respective charters, but more often than not no time restriction is applied.

In some of the older literature IOs tend to be subdivided into political and apolitical organizations, the former referring to military and political alliances to further the power of their member states and the latter referring to organizations dealing with mere administrative and technical issues. However, in the last few decades of the twentieth century many of the allegedly technical and "apolitical" suborganizations of the United Nations (for example, the Atomic Energy Commission and the World Health Organization), as well as such wide-ranging entities as the International Olympic Committee, the International Monetary Fund, and even many large multinational corporations, developed into highly politicized organizations with a multitude of political aims. The differentiation between political and technical IOs is therefore unhelpful. It makes much more sense to differentiate between international governmental organizations (IGOs) like the United Nations, NATO, the IMF, and the World Bank, to name some of the best-known ones, and international nongovernmental organizations (INGOs) like Amnesty International and the International Red Cross. Although estimates differ profoundly, at the turn of the twenty-first century at least five hundred IGOs and eleven thousand INGOs were in existence. They were organized in the Union of International Organizations (founded 1907), which is based in Brussels and publishes the annual *Yearbook of International Organizations*.

While INGOs help to clarify international rules and regulations that enable at least two societal actors (parties, issue groups, unions, associations, international businesses, and corporations) to cooperate in the coordination of certain specified transnational and cross-border issues, IGOs, with which this essay is mostly concerned, are based on the cooperation of nation-states. An IGO is usually based on a multilateral treaty of two or more sovereign nation-states for the pursuit of certain common aims in the international arena. It is helpful to differentiate between supranational or semi-supranational IGOs, like the European Union, or looser confederations of states and nonsupranational IGOs, like the United Nations and NATO. While the former limit the sovereignty of the participating nations to a lesser or greater degree, the latter normally do not infringe on the sovereignty of their member states; they therefore tend to have only a limited degree of influence over their members. Despite the equality of recognized nation-states in international law, in fact a hierarchy of power and influence exists even within nonsupranational IGOs. The UN Security Council, dominated by its five permanent members, as well as the IMF, the

World Bank, and many other IOs, are all dominated by the established great powers, not least on account of their political and military influence and capabilities as well as their financial and economic clout. With the exception of China and Russia, the influential powers of the early twenty-first century all come from the ranks of the West.

There are some institutionalized meetings and conferences that can easily be mistaken as IGOs. Among these are the increasingly controversial G7/G8 meetings of developed nations and the meetings of the World Trade Organization as well as summit meetings between heads of states and, for example, the Conference on Security and Cooperation in Europe (CSCE), which played such an important role in overcoming the Cold War. In fact they are not IGOs; instead these loose organizational structures are only very temporary alliances of a hybrid nature. But they are increasingly important and, in addition to the IGOs and INGOs, must be characterized as a third—albeit no less ambiguous and still largely unexplored—actor in international diplomacy.

DEVELOPMENT OF IOS AND THE ROLE OF THE UNITED STATES

International organizations began to appear during the nineteenth century in the predominantly European state system. A considerable number of separate and limited-purpose agencies had accumulated by the outbreak of World War I. The organization-creating tendency of this period was stimulated primarily by the interdependencies engendered by the Industrial Revolution. New forms of production and new methods of transport and communication created problems and opportunities that necessitated more elaborate and systematic responses than those traditionally associated with bilateral diplomacy. International organization was an outgrowth of the multilateral consultation that came into vogue. It was a short step, and sometimes an almost imperceptible one, from convening a meeting of the several or many states whose interests were involved in a given problem and whose cooperation was essential to solving it, to establishing permanent machinery for collecting information, preparing studies and proposals, arranging recurrent consultations, and administering schemes agreed upon by the participating states.

The nineteenth-century concern with the challenge of developing rational multilateral responses to the changes wrought by steam and electricity in the economic and social spheres did not exclude concern with either the perennial or the newly developing problems of the "higher" sphere of international relations: war and peace, politics and security, law and order. Indeed it was clear that changes in the former spheres contributed to difficulties in the latter, and it was hoped that organized collaboration in the first might contribute to improvement in the second. Awareness of the increasing complexity of international politics, anxiety about the problems of preventing and limiting war, concern about the orderly balancing of stability and change, and hope for the strengthening of international law combined to inspire the ideal of applying international organization to the politico-legal realm.

The effort to do this at the end of the Napoleonic wars had yielded meager results, but the idea of giving firm institutional shape to the Concert of Europe persisted and was supplemented during the nineteenth century by the ideal of developing judicial means for the resolution of international disputes. It remained for the Hague Conferences of 1899 and 1907 to stimulate the hope, and for World War I to demonstrate the necessity, of extending the concept of international organization into the "higher" sphere of international relations. The League of Nations embodied that extension, represented an effort to provide a central focus for the varied organizational activities that had emerged in the preceding century, and accelerated the growth of the organizing process among states. The collapse of the League and the outbreak of World War II gave rise to the establishment of the United Nations and a network of affiliated organizations. It also gave impetus to the institution-building disposition of statesmen, not least on the European continent, that has produced scores of agencies of almost every conceivable size and concern. If the nineteenth century was the period of the beginning of the movement toward international organization, the twentieth century has been the era of its multiplication. In the post–Cold War world the landscape is dotted with international agencies: global and regional, single-purpose and multipurpose, technical and political, regulatory and promotional, consultative and operational, modest and ambitious. And the habit of creating new ones and maintaining old ones remains well established among statesmen. By any test of quantity and variety, international organization has become a major phenomenon in international politics.

The beginning of the trend toward international organization in the nineteenth century and the proliferation of that trend in the next substantially involved the United States. The well-known isolationist tradition of the United States and the fact that it rejected membership in the League of Nations but joined the United Nations at its creation should not be taken as evidence that America is a latecomer to international organization. On the contrary, American participation in the nineteenth-century organizing process was at least as active as might reasonably have been expected given the country's geographic remoteness from the European center of the movement and its modest standing among the powers. American initiative contributed to the formation of such multilateral agencies as the Universal Postal Union (1874) and, within the Western Hemisphere, the Pan American Union (1890). Although the determination of the dates of establishment of international organizations and of adherence by particular states is by no means an exact science, one can take it as approximately correct that by 1900 the United States was a member of ten international bodies, and that by the outbreak of World War I it participated in twenty-seven, as against twenty-eight for Great Britain and thirty-six for France.

This record would seem to substantiate Henry Reiff's assertion that "The United States ... is a veteran, if not an inveterate, joiner of unions or leagues of nations," despite its failure to affiliate with the League of Nations and the Permanent Court of International Justice. America's record of interest and involvement in international organization made it less surprising that President Woodrow Wilson took the lead in creating the League of Nations than that the United States refrained from joining it. The American rejection of the league, historically considered, was an aberration rather than a continuation of settled policy regarding international organization. Moreover, it did not presage a drastically altered policy. Although the United States never accepted membership, it gradually developed cooperative relationships with the league in many areas of activity and ultimately assumed a formal role in several of its component parts. In the final analysis the United States became a more active and more useful participant in the operation of the league than many of the states that were officially listed as members. In addition, between the world wars the United States continued to join organizations outside the league family to such an extent that by 1940 it held a greater number of organizational memberships than did Britain and France, the leading powers in the league. Following World War II the United States became the world's unchallenged leader in promoting and supporting the development of international organizations of every sort.

AMERICAN AMBIGUITY TOWARD IOS

The attitude of the United States toward international organization, however, has been very ambivalent. Presumably the United States has gone along with, and has sometimes displayed enthusiasm for, the organizing process for essentially the same reasons that have moved other states: it has recognized the practical necessity, in its own interest, of developing and participating in systematic arrangements for dealing with the complex problems of the modern world. It has also shared the ideal of creating a global mechanism better adapted to promoting and maintaining peace and human welfare. Even when it has been skeptical of the utility or importance of particular multilateral institutions, the United States, like most other states, has generally inclined to the view that it can ill afford to be unrepresented in their functioning or to give the appearance of being indifferent to the ideals they purport to serve.

America's limited and informal engagement in the operation of the League of Nations illustrated the first of these points. The United States could bring itself neither to join nor to abstain entirely from the League. Its enthusiastic adherence to the United Nations in 1945 can be interpreted as in part a symbolic act of repentance and reversal, a conscious repudiation of the American abandonment of the League. Moreover, already during World War II, American statesman had been very active in planning for the postwar world. Even though idealistic and quite unrealistic plans predominated—such as Franklin Roosevelt's strong advocacy of a "one world" system including something approaching a world government, the abolition of the balance-of-power concept and of geographical spheres of influence, and Secretary of State Cordell Hull's enthusiasm for uninhibited global free trade—this still compared favorably to the passivity of Britain, the nation that had hitherto dominated the international system. While the British hesitated to embark on any postwar planning exercises for fear of undermining the war effort, Washington began planning for the postwar world before the country had even become a belligerent power. After Pearl Harbor, and once Hitler had declared war on the United States, it was unlikely that a return to the political isolationism of the interwar years would occur despite the continuation of a strong isolationist strand in American thinking.

Thus, America's joining the United Nations with New York as the new organization's headquarters and San Francisco as the venue for the ceremonial signing of the UN Charter was much more than a mere symbolic denial of indifference to the high ideals enunciated in the charter. It was, more positively, a declaration of resolve to accept a position of leadership in world affairs, an affirmation of the intention to play a role that this country had never before assumed in international relations. In this sense American ratification of the UN Charter was a unique act, a dramatization of an event of peculiar significance: the decision of the United States to transform its approach to world affairs. The country's subsequent role in the distribution of Marshall Plan aid to western Europe and, above all, its adherence to the North Atlantic Treaty Organization in April 1949, reaffirmed the same point and even strengthened it. After all, NATO membership carried more concrete obligations and more definite alliance commitments than did membership in the United Nations. Article 5 of the NATO treaty pledged all member states to regard an attack on a member state as an attack on itself. Although during the ratification process the U.S. Senate insisted that the last decision of how the United States would react to any such emergency had to be left to Congress, article 5 imposed a firm obligation of some form of assistance on NATO member states.

In most cases decisions by the United States to take part in international agencies can be assumed to be motivated in much the same way and can be assigned essentially the same meaning as such decisions by other states. Neither in the case of the United States nor in other instances does it make sense to regard acceptance or support of international organizations as in itself a demonstration of virtue comparable with the virtue sometimes attributed to the individual because he goes to church and pays his tithe. International agencies are not embodiments of a sacred cause but, rather, instruments of the purposes of their members, susceptible of use to promote both noble and ignoble causes. States join them for mixed reasons, and the mere act of affiliation typically provides no solid information about the constructiveness, willingness to cooperate, or the peacefulness of the intentions of the state concerned.

America's inhibitions and reservations concerning international organization are a blend of the typical and the peculiar. Despite the vogue of creating new international organizations since the 1990s and the strong trend toward economic and financial globalization, it is clear that all states maintain some measure of reluctance to become too encompassed, circumscribed, and absorbed by international bodies. It is perhaps unfair to accuse them of harboring the illogical desire to have their cake and eat it too, for in the relations between organization and sovereignty, just as in the relations between national society and individualism, the real question is not which to choose but how much of each to include in the package. In either the domestic or the international case, however, the perennial tension between control and autonomy remains, and it becomes especially acute when circumstances require reconsideration of the necessary and proper balance between them. The fact that states need and want international organizations does not eliminate their desire to retain as much as possible of the autonomy that the traditionally decentralized international system affords them. The tension between the desire for effective and useful international organization and the urge to continue to enjoy and exploit the freewheeling possibilities of a simpler era profoundly affects the behavior of states in creating, joining, and operating multilateral agencies. In the Western world both NATO and in particular the European Union are prime examples of this.

SOVEREIGNTY AND AUTONOMY

Although sovereignty may figure as an abstract concept with definable meaning in legal and political scholarship, in the real world of states and peoples it is a symbol and slogan no less powerful for its having indistinct and highly variable meaning. "Sovereigntyism" as a subjective phenomenon is a more important factor in international relations than sovereignty as an objective fact. Concern about sovereignty has pervaded America's policy with respect to international institutions from the earliest days to the present. While it has rarely prevented the joining of organizations, it has always affected American contributions to their design and the style of participation in their functioning. The fear that organizational involvements might cut more deeply into national autonomy than originally intended or agreed has never been far beneath the surface of American politics.

American "sovereigntyism" was originally linked with isolationism, which was based upon the fact that the new state was substantially isolated from the European cockpit of world affairs; it was distant, separate, and different. Moreover, it was weak and vulnerable to exploitation in any intimate association with European powers. Fixation on sovereignty reflected the conviction that prudence required the fledgling state to go its own way, capitalizing upon its peculiar situation to maintain political distance between itself and the leading states of the day. Isolationist doctrine related to political and military embroilments, not to economic and commercial ties, and for that reason it did not significantly inhibit American participation in the public international unions that began to emerge in the nineteenth century.

It was when international organization turned political, with the formation of the League of Nations, that jealous regard for sovereignty, nurtured in the era of isolationism, came to the fore as an impediment to American involvement. President Wilson's leading contribution to the formulation of the covenant made the league largely an American enterprise, but it was nevertheless profoundly un-American in certain fundamental respects. The league promised or threatened to involve the United States deeply and systematically in the political and security problems of a world that was still fundamentally Europe-centered. The covenant prescribed commitments that seemed to restrict America's freedom to keep its distance, to stand aside. By this time the United States had lost its isolation and the cogency of much of the rationale for isolationism had faded. However, Americans continued to value the freedom to decide, unilaterally and ad hoc, whether, when, and how to become involved in the quarrels of other states. The right to be unpredictable constituted a major part of the substance of the American idea of sovereignty, and membership in the league was regarded as involving the drastic curtailment of that right.

Wilson lost his battle for American affiliation with the league not to nineteenth-century isolationists who believed that their country was safely encapsulated by the huge continent it had ruthlessly conquered and now inhabited without challenge but to proponents of the idea that the United States should continue its recently espoused auxiliary role in world affairs, the central feature of which was untrammeled discretion concerning engagement and disengagement. Wilson's successor, Warren G. Harding, expressed this idea succinctly: "If our people are ever to decide upon war they will choose to decide according to our own national conscience at the time and in the constitutional manner without advance commitment, or the advice and consent of any other power." When the league actually dealt with political and military crises, the United States was sometimes willing and eager to take an active role, but it was never willing to accept an obligation to do so.

Sovereignty, interpreted as the retention of a free hand, continues to have a major impact upon American policy regarding international organization. World War II convinced most Americans that the advance and well-understood commitment of the United States to throw its weight onto the scales was essential to the preservation of world peace, and the United States made the shift from the policy of the free hand to the policy of commitment that it had rejected when Wilson proposed it. Nevertheless the urge to keep options open has not been displaced by recognition of the value of clear and credible commitments. The strength of that urge was demonstrated in American insistence upon having the power to veto substantive decisions in the UN Security Council. It could also be observed in the careful hedging of obligations under the various bilateral and multilateral security treaties concluded during the Cold War. The United States has wanted to put the world on notice as to its future strategy while retaining the possibility of deciding its policy ad hoc. It has wanted to enjoy the benefits of being committed without paying the price of losing the national freedom to choose its course of action.

THE ROLE OF DOMESTIC JURISDICTION

The American conception of sovereignty has traditionally included another element: the right to national privacy, the capacity to fend off external intrusions into domestic affairs. This concern was rooted in the original American sense of separateness and differentiation from Europe. The New World had broken off from the Old World, and maintaining the sharpness of the break was deemed essential to retaining the valued newness of the qualities of American political society. The isolationist tradition combined cautions against being drawn into European affairs and against Europe's poking into American affairs.

The latter concern is typically expressed with reference to international organization by the concept of domestic jurisdiction. Participation in multilateral agencies necessarily involves exposure as well as commitment; nothing can be done with the collaboration of, or for the benefit of, a member state without something being done to that state. American enthusiasm for international organization has always been qualified by fear of expanding the national vulnerability to external interference, a concern that was manifested in the drafting of both the League Covenant and the UN Charter by vigorous insistence upon provisions protecting domestic jurisdiction. The campaign that defeated American affiliation with the league concentrated as heavily upon what might be done to this country by and through the organization as upon what the United States might be required to do on behalf of the league. Similarly, misgivings about the United Nations and the specialized agencies have often expressed the belief that the United States has been, or the fear that it might be, improperly penetrated by foreign influences flowing through those institutional channels.

This concern for sovereignty, translated as domestic jurisdiction, is shared by all states. It has received peculiar emphasis in American policy for reasons that go beyond the attitudes that were initially associated with an isolated position and an isolationist doctrine. It seems probable that, perhaps until very recently, the United States never shared the keen need for international organization to serve its particular interests—as distinguished from its broader interest in a stable and peaceful world—that most other states have felt. As a big country, a continental state, the United States appeared not to require the relief of difficulties posed by cramped territorial area that many other states have been compelled to seek through international organizations. It did not fully share the need of European states, now matched by states on other continents with numerous national divisions, for mechanisms of coordination to facilitate interchange across state boundaries. In this respect the American situation was analogous to that of a great rural landowner, in contrast with that of residents in congested urban areas.

Throughout the twentieth century the United States perceived itself as a powerful, wealthy, and highly developed state, not dependent upon others for protection or for economic and technical assistance. This feeling of independence and omnipotence even increased at the end of the Cold War. Given these characteristics it is perhaps understandable that the United States tended to conceive of participation in international agencies as a matter more of giving than of receiving, and that it insisted upon limiting both what it gave and what it received. The United States could afford to resist having undesired things done to it by international organizations because it had little stake in having essential things done for it by those bodies. With regard to the impact of multilateral programs and activities upon and within national societies, the United States accepted the biblical proposition that it was more blessed to give than to receive. America, more than most other states, could plausibly consider its engagement in organized international activities as predominantly a means of contributing to the general welfare of the global body politic rather than as a means of acquiring particular benefits for itself. Perhaps for this reason Americans appeared especially prone to believe that international organizations were, or should be, expressions of collective idealism and altruism. The sudden awareness of the exposure of the hitherto invulnerable American continent to international terrorism, however, changed this attitude dramatically at the beginning of the twenty-first century.

Another set of difficulties and inhibitions that affected American participation in international organization in the twentieth century might be said to derive from the reverse of the attitude toward national sovereignty discussed above. International organizations inevitably cut into the sovereignty of participating states in the sense that they require them to accept commitments—thereby restricting in some measure their freedom to decide what they will and will not do—and in the sense that states' domestic exposure to external impacts is enhanced, thereby diminishing their sense of national privacy. Yet the development of so-called international rogue states like Iraq and North Korea in the 1990s, and in particular the increasing vulnerability of the United States to international terrorism, led to a much greater sense of the inevitability of American involvement with the rest of the world. A wide spectrum of U.S. policymakers began to embrace the idea that even the territory of such a vast and powerful and geographically protected country like the United States could not do without the support of the international community to safeguard its physical security.

DEMOCRATIC CONSTITUTIONALISM VERSUS INTERNATIONAL COMMITMENTS

One should not conclude that the relationship between national sovereignty and international organization is in all respects a competitive one. International agencies are not engaged in a zero-sum game with states, a situation in which the weakening of the latter is the condition of the strengthening of the former. On the contrary, effective international organization requires the participation of broadly competent states—states that are able as well as willing to meet their obligations, that are capable of formulating responsible positions and reaching meaningful decisions, and that can manage their resources, people, and territories to the degree required for dependable cooperation in multilateral activities. States deficient in these respects are frequently pressed by involvement in international organization to remedy their deficiencies, and the agencies of the United Nations system have attempted to give attention to building up the capabilities of particularly deficient member states to increasing, rather than diminishing, the meaningfulness and effectiveness of their sovereignty.

America's engagement in international organizations has always been handicapped by limited possession of the kind of national sovereignty essential for effective and reliable participation. Its collaboration in multilateral enterprises has been restrained by reluctance to bend to pressure for strengthening the national capabilities in question. When Americans worry about the implications of membership in international bodies, they are at least as likely to exhibit concern about the enlargement as about the diminution of the sovereign competence of the U.S. government.

The essence of the matter is that the United States is a political society dedicated to the ideal of constitutional democracy, a state whose central government is designed to operate within a framework of limitations derived from the principles of democracy and constitutionalism. Democracy implies that government must be responsive to the majority will more than, and in case of conflict, instead of, the exigencies of the international situation, the rules or decisions or pressures of the organs of international agencies, or the obligations prescribed either by general international law or by treaties. The problem posed by the tension between international commitment to order and domestic commitment to democracy is a real one for the United States; and the more the country becomes involved in multilateral agencies and activities the more intense it becomes.

Unfortunately for international organizations, the democratic principle is not exhausted by the proposition that national commitment requires popular consent. Consent theory implies the right of a nation to change its mind and the obligation of a government to accept the implications of the withdrawal of popular consent. The international legal sanctity of national commitments is challenged by the democratic legitimacy of popularly inspired decisions to violate or repudiate such commitments. The government of the United States came face to face with this problem in the 1960s and 1970s, when the popular consensus that had supported the acceptance of commitments in the two preceding decades began to dissolve. So long as the United States undertakes to combine international responsibility with domestic democracy, its leaders will confront serious dilemmas, and uncertainty will prevail in international organizations as to what can be expected from the United States. Democracy coexists uncomfortably with international law and organization.

Constitutionalism, no less than democracy, creates difficulties for the United States as a participant in international agencies. The president's responsibility for the conduct of American foreign relations, including the management of American participation in international organizations, is not fully matched by his legal authority or his political power to exercise this responsibility. He must compete and cooperate with the Congress, which shares in the control of foreign policy. The division of powers associated with American federalism limits the capacity of the federal government to accept and carry out obligations, or to engage in cooperative arrangements, under the auspices of international bodies. The national commitments to preserve a significant degree of autonomy for the private sector of the economy, to maintain the freedom of a press that zealously guards the right to self-definition of its responsibility, and to respect individual rights enshrined in a written constitution and interpreted by an independent judiciary, establish further limitations upon the capacity of those who speak and act officially for the United States to engage the country fully and reliably in the work of international organizations.

To say that the United States is a constitutional democracy is to say that the body politic has not conferred upon its central government the full powers, usually associated with the concept of sovereignty, that may be required for loyal and effective performance in foreign relations, including the country's effective performance in international organizations. To say that the American public is dedicated to the preservation of the system of constitutional democracy is to emphasize its reluctance to enlarge, or to countenance the enlargement of, governmental capacities relevant to involvement in multilateral enterprises, capacities to make and carry out commitments, to act decisively, and to exercise the degree of control over a variety of internal matters that may be entailed by acceptance of international schemes of regulation or cooperation.

There is a constitutional doctrine, derived from the Supreme Court opinion in *Missouri v. Holland* (1920), supporting the view that the valid acceptance of international obligations carries with it the enhancement of federal powers to the extent required for meeting those obligations. Moreover, early enthusiasm for membership in the United Nations was reflected in a widespread tendency to acquiesce in a broad interpretation of executive authority to act as might be required for effective collaboration with the organization. This acquiescence proved to be short-lived. In the 1950s the Bricker amendment campaign argued—at least according to President Eisenhower—in favor of curtailing presidential power and empowering Congress with the obligation to ratify all treaties negotiated by the executive. Yet the campaign revealed the high regard for the U.S. Constitution. The doctrine of *Missouri v. Holland* was more generally feared as a threat to the integrity of the American constitutional system than valued as a promise of the adaptability of that system to the requirements of the age of international organization. The formal constitutional renunciation of the doctrine was obviated by assurances that it would not be exploited. Less than two decades later there emerged a political mood dominated by insistence that the competence of the president to commit the country in international affairs should be significantly reduced. In 1973, in view of the lost war in Vietnam and the Watergate crisis, this led a Democratic Congress to pass the War Powers Act, which compelled the president to consult with Congress about sending American troops into combat abroad and required him to withdraw these troops within sixty days unless Congress gave its approval for a longer mission abroad.

Generally, however, it appeared that Americans were more concerned about preventing involvement in international organization from impinging upon the distribution of authority within their political system than about preventing the peculiarities of their domestic arrangements from handicapping the nation's performance in international organization. The dominance of this concern had a great deal to do with American rejection of the League of Nations. Acceptance of the United Nations clearly has not eliminated this element from the American attitude toward involvement in world affairs.

Nineteenth-century isolationist doctrine, with its emphasis upon aloofness from European political entanglements and intrigues, expressed not only a pragmatic judgment concerning the best way for the United States to survive in a dangerous world but also a moral aspiration, an ideal of national virtue defined as innocent abstention from the evils of power politics. This heritage of moral distaste for international politics colored early American thinking about international organization to promote world peace and order. Nineteenth-century Americans, ranging from spokesmen for the various peace societies that sprang up after 1815 to leaders in government, tended to conceive organization for peace in essentially apolitical terms, emphasizing legal formulas and arbitral or judicial settlement of disputes. World courts figured more prominently than diplomatic forums or international armies in favored formulations, and the ground was prepared for the perennial popularity of the "rule of law" in American internationalist thought. In particular the vision of the future did not include the involvement of the United States in the international political arena or the burdening of the United States with weighty political responsibilities. It certainly did not refer to the obligation to participate in military sanctions against disturbers of the peace. America was not to be contaminated by being dragged into power politics; rather, the world was to be purified by being persuaded to rise above politics, to the realm of law. Global salvation was to be achieved by formula and gadget, not by American commitment to share in the hard, dangerous, and dirty work of an organized political system.

The scheme, set forth during World War I by the League to Enforce Peace and by similar organizations in Europe, then formulated in the League of Nations Covenant under the leadership of President Wilson, was not in accord with this American vision. Calling for an essentially political approach to world order supported ultimately by national obligation to engage in military sanctions, it violated the basic tenets of the traditional American creed. It offered a painful, not a painless, solution to the problem of order. The American peace movement had hoped for the appointment of a judge; it was confronted by the demand that the United States serve as a policeman. The league promised not reliance upon predictable legal process but involvement in the uncertainties of political and military activity. True, the new machinery included the World Court, and there was massive American support throughout the life of the league for membership in that body. The movement to join the court was ultimately frustrated, however, by the fear of involvement in the political league through adherence to its judicial annex. The American legalistic tradition demanded acceptance of a court, but it did not permit acceptance of that particular court.

IOS IN THE COLD WAR AND THE POST–COLD WAR WORLD

During the Cold War the role of the United States in creating, supporting, and operating the United Nations reflected the official abandonment of preoccupation with legal system-building and of aversion to engagement in the political and military aspects of international affairs. Nevertheless the Cold War record contains numerous indications of the survival of these sentiments. The mood engendered by the Vietnam War was characterized by the revival of the tendency to conceive national virtue in terms of innocence rather than of responsibility. Fighting for peace, the central motif of the twentieth-century ideal of collective security, tended to be regarded not as paradoxical but as inconsistent at best and hypocritical at worst. Self-critical Americans are inclined to interpret the performance of the United States in the early years of the United Nations as a record of shameful manipulation and abuse of the organization, not of constructive leadership and loyal support.

The image of the responsible defender of international order was overshadowed by the image of the irresponsible adventurer and imperialist. In the eyes of self-pitying Americans, the national image was that of an overloaded and insufficiently appreciated bearer of international burdens. Those who put the matter as the abdication of a discredited tyrant and those who put it as the retirement of a weary servant were advocating the same thing: the diminution of the American role in world affairs. The appeal of this prescription was strengthened by the rise to dominance in the United Nations of political forces and factions that the United States could neither lead nor control; America's opportunity to exercise leadership declined as much as its inclination to do so.

Traditional American misgivings about involvement in international political organization was thus confirmed. Discounting the excesses of guilt and self-pity, it must nevertheless be concluded that participation in the United Nations entailed the disappointment of national hopes, the frustration of national efforts, and the dirtying of national hands. It required that the luxury of pure adherence to principle be sacrificed in favor of the more ambiguous and less satisfying morality of responsibility. The glamour of sharing in the formulation of a grand design gave way to the never-finished work of international housekeeping and the never-solved problem of managing the affairs of an almost unmanageable international system. It was not surprising that the United States failed to find this work inspiring or pleasant.

From the late 1960s to the 1980s—strongly influenced by the disastrous involvement in Vietnam, the country's subsequent severe economic problems, and, due to East-West détente, the diminishing Soviet threat—the shift from isolationism to international engagement that occurred during World War II was temporarily reversed. Instead attention was focused once more upon the dangers of overcommitment and the advantages of unilateralism. The pursuit of the national right to make foreign policy decisions unfettered by promises to, or participation by, other states was vigorously asserted by the Nixon, Carter, and Reagan administrations. But widespread talk of "American decline" and the loss of will to preserve the standing of the United States as one of two superpowers proved premature. Instead the crisis situation brought about by the end of the Cold War and the subsequent Gulf War of 1990–1991 to liberate Kuwait from the

Iraqi invasion saw impressive American leadership and the country's constructive reengagement with IOs like NATO, the European Union, and the United Nations. Above all, leading U.S. involvement in the "two-plus-four" negotiations (the two German states and the United States, Soviet Union, Britain, and France) for bringing about German unification within the NATO, European Union, and United Nations framework, along with constructive American engagement with the Conference on Security and Cooperation in Europe, did much to achieve a relatively peaceful and stable transition to the post–Cold War era.

After the end of the Cold War and the collapse and disappearance of the Soviet Union in December 1991, with the United States remaining the only global superpower and by far the most powerful nation on earth, once again American suspicion of restrictive international commitments and American preference for unilateral activities increased dramatically. The symbolic significance of American membership in the United Nations and its many suborganizations was drastically reduced. Washington's reluctance to pay its full dues to the United Nations was indicative of the United States's ambiguous position toward its involvement and responsibilities in international affairs. While the American superpower was unwilling to pay its dues to the United Nations, the UN itself was in debt to some poor countries such as Bangladesh, owing it $15 million. Between 1994 and 1999 the United States built up a bill of $2.3 billion, arguing that it was asked to pay too much to the United Nations. By late 2001 Washington still owed a substantial amount to the world organization; it was committed to pay the outstanding amount of $582 million in 2001 and the remainder of $244 million in 2002. In 1999 and 2000, after passage of the Helms-Biden act, the United States paid some of the $1 billion it had promised to contribute belatedly to the UN coffers. In return the United States had asked for and obtained various UN reforms and the elimination of the rest of the American debt and a reduction of its future annual dues. (Instead of 25 percent, the United States would now finance only 22 percent of the UN's regular budget; it would also reduce its contributions for UN peacekeeping missions from 31 to 27 percent of the overall costs.) While the Senate accepted this, the repayment of the remaining debt was controversial among Republican leaders in the House of Representatives who wished to impose further conditions and asked for greater UN reforms. The attitude of the House of Representatives was partially also a reaction to the fact that the United States was voted off the UN Human Rights Commission in May 2001 by some UN members (including some of America's European allies) who were running out of patience with Washington's less than constructive role in the human rights body and the administration's general lack of support for the United Nations.

Washington's manifold policy of suspicion toward the United Nations, Franklin Roosevelt's harbinger of hope, must serve as just one example for the claim that an increasing concentration on domestic affairs and a neglect of American involvement in IOs was indeed the dominant feature of American policy in the 1990s. The few years of renewed international activism at the end of the Cold War—President George H. W. Bush's somewhat rash announcement of a "new world order" in 1990 and the occasional brief burst of peacemaking activities that characterized the foreign policy of the Clinton administration after 1993—must be regarded as exceptions rather than the rule. Senate majority leader and 1996 Republican presidential candidate Robert Dole's assessment in the mid-1990s reflected the deep and widespread American unease about IOs. Dole believed that frequently IOs either "reflect a consensus that opposes American interests or do not reflect American principles and ideas."

Yet as G. John Ikenberry wrote in 1996, while the bipolar order of the Cold War years came to an end in 1989–1991, the dense economic and political "web of multilateralist institutions" and thus the "world order created in the 1940s is still with us." Despite a tendency to focus on the domestic enjoyment of the prosperity and rising share values of the multiplying "dot com" companies of the Clinton years, the United States was unable and indeed unwilling to abdicate its global leadership. In fact globalization demanded the opposite, and the administration made sure that the United States would continue to dominate the World Bank and the increasingly important International Monetary Fund. The efforts the Clinton administration made for the full implementation and expansion of the North American Free Trade Agreement (NAFTA) and for enabling China to become a member of the World Trade Organization, allowing it to enjoy most-favored-nation status, are further examples that indicate that the Clinton administration had no intention to revert to economic isolationism.

The same applied to the political sphere. The Clinton administration was careful to denounce any talk of a new isolationism in the post–Cold War world, including alleged American disinterest in Europe in favor of a Pacific-first policy. In fact, despite the administration's ambiguous if not outright negative attitude to the United Nations and the many petty trade wars with the European Union, the post–Cold War world at times saw a vigorous and often constructive reengagement of the United States in many parts of the world. However, this became frequently mixed with a strong dose of American unilateralism. Clinton called this "assertive multilateralism." For example, despite much international pressure, for largely domestic reasons the Clinton administration insisted on preventing a UN treaty controlling the trade in small arms. The administration's ambiguity toward the United Nations had disastrous consequences in the East Timor crisis of 1999–2000, when the lack of U.S. support induced a withdrawal of UN troops, which in turn led to the wholesale slaughter of many East Timorese people in the Indonesian civil war. Clinton's unsuccessful and unilateral bombing raids on buildings in Sudan and elsewhere in response to terrorist attacks on American diplomatic and military targets abroad also turned out to be ill-advised; they may well have contributed to inflaming even more hatred of the United States in the Islamic world.

Still, American peacemaking efforts in cooperation with IOs during the Clinton era often added a constructive element to the frequently chaotic and very violent developments in such embattled regions as the Middle East and the Balkans. It is unlikely that the successful NATO pursuit of the 1999 Kosovo war and the ousting and subsequent handover of Serbian president Slobodan Milosevic to the International War Crimes Tribunal in The Hague in 2001 would have been achieved without strong American involvement. The Clinton administration's attempts to act as a neutral arbiter in the "Troubles" in Northern Ireland and in the reconciliation between South and North Korea were also relatively successful. This explained the regret voiced in many parts of the world of Clinton's departure in January 2001. Paradoxically, despite Clinton's contempt for the United Nations and his many other unilateral activities, the president's reputation as an international peacemaker far surpassed his embattled and scandal-ridden standing within the United States. Yet his years in office may well be primarily remembered for his administration's ability to maintain and increase America's prosperity and the achievement of a substantial budget surplus rather than for a far-sighted foreign policy.

After the drama of the presidential election of 2000, which was only narrowly decided by the Supreme Court in December, it was not Vice President Al Gore but Texas governor George W. Bush who moved into the White House. The new president immediately surrounded himself with many right-wing and unilateralist if not isolationist advisers. Many of these people were very experienced policymakers who had already served under Bush's father in the early 1990s and even under Presidents Ford and Reagan in the 1970s and 1980s. Yet his administration did not appear to consist of a vigorous modernizing team prepared to tackle the international problems of globalization and fragmentation. In a 1999 article in *Foreign Affairs*, Condoleezza Rice, who became Bush's national security adviser in January 2001, tellingly talked at length about the importance of the pursuit of America's "national interest" but rather less about American international involvement and engagement in IOs. She wrote that a Republican administration would "proceed from the firm ground of the national interest, not from the interest of an illusory international community." Indeed, the Bush administration treated the United Nations with even greater disdain and suspicion than Clinton had done. During its first eight months in office the new administration walked out of five international treaties (and withdrew from the conference on racism in protest at anti-Israel passages in the draft communiqué in South Africa in early September 2001). Among the treaties the United States opposed were the Kyoto Protocol on climate change supported by much of the rest of the world and a treaty for the enforcement of the important Biological and Toxin Weapons Convention of 1972. The administration also withheld support from the establishment of the World Court to be based in The Hague. Although Washington agreed with the principle of establishing such a court, it did not wish any of its nationals ever to appear before it. The Bush administration also threatened to abandon several other contractual pillars of the postwar world, notably the 1972 Anti-Ballistic Missile (ABM) Treaty concluded between Nixon and Leonid Brezhnev to contain the nuclear arms race.

Above all, Bush's insistence on implementing a national missile defense (NMD) to protect the United States (and perhaps its NATO allies) from nuclear attacks from rogue states like North Korea and Iraq caused great unease in the Western world. Not even Britain, traditionally America's closest ally, was able to show much enthusiasm for a missile plan that had not been tested successfully and would cost billions of dollars and resembled Reagan's ill-fated Strategic Defense Initiative ("Star Wars"), a plan that had not been tested successfully and would cost billions of dollars. America's allies reasoned that not least for financial reasons the implementation of Bush's missile shield scheme would in all likelihood prevent the United States from giving equal attention to the development of other defensive and military schemes that deserved greater priority. Moreover, the Bush administration showed scant regard for international institutions like NATO by making clear that the missile shield decision had already been made. While America's allies would be consulted and informed and would hopefully participate in the project, any allied advice to abandon the project would not be heeded. Unilateralism was triumphing. Multilateralism and constructive open-minded engagement with IOs had been abandoned for good.

Or so it seemed. Then, in September 2001, the terrorist attacks on the World Trade Center and the Pentagon occurred. This was not only a severe shock to the American people, who for so long had felt secure on a continent that was geographically very distant from most of the world's battlegrounds, it also shook the Bush administration to its core. Alexis de Tocqueville's statement in his famous *Democracy in America* (1835) that the United States was a nation without neighbors, securely enveloped in a huge continent and thus separate from the problems of the rest of the world, became out of date within a matter of hours. Despite its superpower status, and probably even because of it, it was recognized that America was no longer invulnerable. The *Economist* wrote presciently that the United States and the entire world realized that America was "not merely vulnerable to terrorism, but more vulnerable than others. It is the most open and technologically dependent country in the world, and its power attracts the hatred of enemies of freedom everywhere. The attacks have shattered the illusions of post-cold war peace and replaced them with an uncertain world of 'asymmetric threats.'"

The value of American reengagement with IOs was recognized in many quarters almost immediately. Suddenly the United States was not merely the provider of benefits to the international community but could also greatly benefit itself from a close cooperative engagement with IOs. Within a matter of days the Security Council of the United Nations had unanimously condemned the attack in the strongest terms and pledged its support to the American intention to embark on a prolonged war against international terrorism. The European Union and many other IOs followed suit. NATO went even further. For the first time in its history the North Atlantic Alliance invoked article 5 of its charter, which obliged each member to take "such action as it deems necessary, including the use of armed force" if a member state was attacked from abroad. The terrorist attacks in New York and Washington were interpreted as a military attack on a NATO member state, which obliged all NATO members to come to the common defense of NATO territory. This was unprecedented; above all, it demonstrated the value of IOs to the hitherto unilateral Bush administration.

While it was unlikely that the Bush administration would not resort to unilateralist activities in the fight against international terrorism, it was equally improbable that even a state as powerful as the United States could win this fight by itself. Engagement with international organizations like NATO and the United Nations and cooperative multilateralism appeared to be decisive. Thus the occasional bouts of American neo-isolationism that could frequently be observed in the 1990s were thought by many to be largely a thing of the past. This, however, would also depend on whether or not the unity of NATO and its member states could be upheld for a prolonged period of time. Quite understandably, both the American people and the Bush administration were sufficiently enraged by the appalling attacks that cost the lives of more than six thousand people and caused damage in excess of $30 billion to "go it alone" if Western and indeed international unity could not be preserved. While the danger existed that the attacks might have the opposite effect and induce America to withdraw from international engagement altogether, this is unlikely; after all even an entirely isolationist America would continue to be exposed to the threats posed by international terrorism. Multilateralist engagement with international organizations and acting in concert with its allies appeared to be the best chance of reestablishing a degree of national and international security. However, it was thought abroad, at least, that this could well take the form of the controversial American "assertive multilateralism" that the world had to put up with during the Clinton years.

Still, after 11 September it appeared that unilateralism and isolationism were no longer regarded as viable political concepts. In view of the Bush administration's active engagement with the international community to fight the "war against international terrorism," the *Financial Times* concluded that multilateralism was "no longer a dirty word." Similarly, British Prime Minister Tony Blair expressed the belief that the answer to the unprecedented challenge confronting the world was "not isolationism but the world coming together with America as a community." It was generally recognized that the world had to look beyond bombing Afghanistan, the country that hosted the terrorist network responsible for planning the attacks, and other military options. An American correspondent put it succinctly in a letter to the *International Herald Tribune* in early October 2001: "The Bush administration's unilateralism has been revealed as hollow. Rather than infringe our sovereignty, international institutions enhance our ability to perform the functions of national government, including the ability to fight international crime."

BIBLIOGRAPHY

Abi-Saab, Georges, ed. *The Concept of International Organization*. Paris, 1981.

Armstrong, David. *The Rise of International Organization: A Short History*. London, 1982.

Archer, Clive. *International Organizations*. 2d ed. London and New York, 1992.

Baratta, Joseph P., comp. *The United Nations System*. Oxford and New Brunswick, N.J., 1995.

Bennett, A. Leroy. *Historical Dictionary of the United Nations*. Lanham, Md., 1995.

———. *International Organizations: Principles and Issues*. 6th ed. Englewood Cliffs, N.J., 1995.

Boutros-Ghali, Boutros. *Unvanquished: A U.S.–U.N. Saga*. London and New York, 1999.

Clark, Ian. *Globalization and Fragmentation: International Relations in the Twentieth Century* New York, 1997.

Claude, Inis L., Jr. *Swords into Plowshares: The Problems and Progress of International Organizations*. 4th ed. New York, 1971.

Claude, Inis L., Jr., ed. *States and the Global System: Politics, Law, and Organization*. Basingstoke, U.K., and New York, 1988.

Diehl, Paul F., ed. *The Politics of Global Governance: International Organizations in an Interdependent World*. London and Boulder, Colo., 1997.

Feld, Werner J., and Robert S. Jordon. *International Institutions: A Comparative Approach*. 3d ed. Westport, Conn., 1994.

Finkelstein, Lawrence S., ed. *Politics in the United Nations System*. Durham, N.C., 1988.

Franck, Thomas M. *Nation Against Nation: What Happened to the UN Dream and What the U.S. Can Do About It*. New York, 1985.

Haas, Ernst B. *Beyond the Nation State: Functionalism and International Organization*. Stanford, Calif., 1964.

Iriye, Akira. "A Century of NGOs." *Diplomatic History* 23, no. 3 (summer 1999): 421–435.

Jacobson, Harold K. *Networks of Interdependence: International Organizations and the Global Political System*. 2d ed. New York, 1984.

Karns, Margaret P., and Karen A. Mingst, eds. *The United States and Multilateral Institutions: Patterns of Changing Instrumentality and Influence*. Boston, 1990.

Krasner, Stephen D. *International Regimes*. London and Ithaca, N.Y., 1983.

Kratochwil, Friedrich, and Edward D. Mansfield, eds. *International Organization: A Reader*. New York, 1994.

Luck, Edward C. *Mixed Messages: American Politics and International Organizations, 1919–1999*. Washington, D.C., 1999.

Maynes, Charles William, and Richard S. Williamson, eds. *U.S. Foreign Policy and the United Nations System*. New York, 1996.

Moore, John Allphin, Jr., and Jerry Pubantz. *To Create a New World? American Presidents and the United Nations*. New York, 1999.

Osma'nczyk, Edmund Jan. *Encyclopedia of the United Nations and International Agreements*. 2d ed. New York, 1990.

Ostrower, Gary B. *The United Nations and the United States*. New York, 1998.

Parsons, Anthony. *From Cold War to Hot Peace: UN Interventions, 1946–1994*. London and New York, 1995.

Taylor, Paul. *International Organization in the Modern World: The Regional and Global Process*. London and New York, 1993.

Taylor, Paul, and A. J. R. Groom, eds. *International Institutions at Work*. London and New York, 1988.

Union of International Associations. *Yearbook of International Organizations*. Brussels. Annual.

Weiss, Thomas G., and Leon Gordenker, eds. *NGOs, the UN, and Global Governance*. London and Boulder, Colo., 1996. A brief but useful compilation of essays on the role of NGOs.

Wells, Robert N., ed. *Peace by Pieces: United Nations Agencies and Their Roles*. Metuchen, N.J., 1991.

Williams, Douglas. *The Specialized Agencies and the United Nations: The System in Crisis*. New York, 1987.

See also COLLECTIVE SECURITY; INTERNATIONAL MONETARY FUND AND WORLD BANK; NORTH ATLANTIC TREATY ORGANIZATION; SUMMIT CONFERENCES.

INTERVENTION AND NONINTERVENTION

Doris A. Graber

Analysis of the intervention and nonintervention theories and practices of the United States requires examination of four distinct facets of the issue. They are the theory underlying the use of intervention in international relations, the policy doctrines proclaimed by the United States regarding intervention, the international law regarding the legality of intervention, and the actual practice of intervention adopted by the United States.

THE THEORY

The theory of intervention is based on the concept of state sovereignty, which was incorporated into the 1648 Treaty of Westphalia that ended the Thirty Years' War to prevent rulers from meddling in the affairs of their neighbors at the risk of provoking wars. Sovereignty of a state means that it is entitled to exercise absolute control over its territory and people and can choose to govern its realm as it chooses. In a world of sovereign states, where no overarching governmental unit exists, nobody has the right to interfere with the state's activities unless the interference has been explicitly authorized by the state. In other words, by virtue of its sovereignty, every state, no matter how small and weak or large and powerful, has the legal right to be free from intervention by other states.

The problem with this theory is that it is based on an unrealistic assumption: namely, that all states are completely independent actors who are not affected by what other states do and whose activities do not affect other states. Nonintervention is an impossibility for political units sharing the same world, particularly when they exist in close physical proximity. National borders, which demarcate the state's sphere of control, have become increasingly porous, especially in the modern age of surveillance satellites and the Internet. The fact that international law acknowledges that states have the right of self-defense to protect their sovereignty has always been an implicit acknowledgment that intrusions on state sovereignty should be expected.

THE POLICY DOCTRINES

Throughout modern history, the principle of nonintervention, tempered by the right of self-defense, has been cherished, especially by small and weak nations that lacked the strength to resist intrusions by stronger rivals. The United States, which started its political life as a small and weak nation, was no exception. Its vocal support of the principles of nonintervention—the nonintervention doctrine—has served three major purposes throughout the years, aside from its use as a guideline for policy. First, it was meant to deter European interventions directed against the United States and its neighbors. President George Washington, in his Farewell Address to the nation, repeated a mantra common to the Founders. The United States would not intervene in Europe's affairs in return for reciprocity by European powers. Accordingly, it would object to interventions by other powers because it considered nonintervention as the normal rule to be applied by the world community.

Second, the doctrine was intended to inform the American people that pressures on their government for a policy of intervention were likely to be rejected on principle, even when Americans were eager to help European colonies in Latin America to become independent states. Expectations were that repeated proclamations of the nonintervention policy would deter interventions that the country could ill afford to undertake.

Third, once the principle had become venerable and established as right and moral conduct, it became useful as a psychological tool of politics. Many undesirable international activities could be readily condemned by labeling them as "intervention." Desired interventions could be excused by denying that they constituted interventions. Alternatively, the United States could claim that a particular intervention was within the scope of interventions permitted under the hallowed nonintervention doctrine. Putting policies within a framework of "moral" and "immoral" actions is particularly important for a democratic country where political leaders depend on the support of elected government officials and public opinion. It is easier to secure support when policies can be defended as moral principles, rather than as complex bargaining schemes or maneuvers in political power games.

All three purposes appeared to be particularly well served during the early years of the nation. It is therefore not surprising that American presidents, starting with George Washington, almost routinely advocated nonintervention. During the decades when the country was most vulnerable to foreign intervention and ill-equipped to intervene individually or collectively in faraway Europe, the doctrine was credited with keeping European powers from intervening in the affairs of the United States as a reward for American nonintervention in Europe's liberation struggles. The doctrine permitted American leaders to refuse most requests for political as well as humanitarian interventions. The successes claimed for the doctrine strengthened faith in its value.

At first, the doctrine was generally expressed in absolute terms to give it the strongest possible impact. This formulation was never viewed as a renunciation of the presumably inalienable right of every country to use intervention to protect its vital interests. Rather, the doctrine was avowed for its practical usefulness for American policy needs. That the nonintervention doctrine involved legal considerations under international law was not stressed until 1842, when Secretary of State Daniel Webster alluded to its grounding in the legal doctrine of sovereign rights.

Because the absolute formulation of the doctrine was literally interpreted by many people, it grew embarrassing when the United States engaged in numerous interventions in the Western Hemisphere. Therefore, American statesmen reformulated the doctrine so that it would specify the exceptional conditions under which intervention would be permitted. The ebb and flow of efforts to spell out the limits of nonintervention, without abandoning the nonintervention doctrine as a general principle, constitute the major aspects of doctrinal developments over the ensuing decades.

President James Buchanan's inaugural address in 1857 is an early example of reformulation. He declared it to be the nation's policy never to interfere in the domestic concerns of other nations "unless this shall be imperatively required by the great law of self-preservation." He did not specify the occasions when the law of self-preservation might apply and the ways in which such occasions could be identified. Buchanan also contended that the nonintervention doctrine did not preclude the duty of preventive intervention. When, as happened in Mexico in 1859, a Western Hemisphere country was afflicted by internal unrest that spilled over its borders, it was the duty of the United States to intervene to stop the unrest and thereby prevent intervention by other powers. Congress did not accept this argument at that time. But when the argument was revived and amplified during the closing decades of the nineteenth century, it became an accepted clarification of the scope of the nonintervention doctrine.

Officially, a number of major clarifications were labeled corollaries to the Monroe Doctrine, which had become an icon for the nonintervention principle. Linking interventionist policies to this icon served to maintain the aura that the nonintervention doctrine remained absolute. For example, the Olney Corollary of 1895 asserted the right of the United States to intervene in any conflict between an American and non-American power that endangered the security of the United States. Under the Roosevelt Corollary of 1904, the United States claimed an even broader right and duty to act as policeman of the Western Hemisphere. If any nation in the hemisphere permitted conditions on its territory that might invite intervention by another country, then it was incumbent on the United States to intervene to remedy these conditions and forestall intervention by others. The United States must assume this obligation because the Monroe Doctrine prevented other powers from exercising their right of intervention in troubled Western Hemisphere countries.

Many American political leaders were dissatisfied with the doctrinal and practical consequences of the Roosevelt Corollary. In an attempt to adhere more closely to the spirit of nonintervention, President William Howard Taft sought to control internal political affairs in other nations through economic, rather than military, pressures. Since the nonintervention doctrine did not prohibit intervention for the protection of nationals, his administration encouraged American business interests to settle in potentially unstable neighboring countries. Presumably, they would help the country to stabilize its economy and prevent political turmoil. If the presence of American businesses failed to prevent unrest, the United States could then send protective missions as part of its right to protect its citizens abroad. In this manner it could control the politics of unstable countries without violating restraints commanded by the nonintervention doctrine.

During the presidency of Woodrow Wilson, the nonintervention doctrine received yet another interpretation. Wilson's claim that the United States must discourage dictatorships or unconstitutional governments in Latin America by refusing to recognize them was accompanied by strong professions that such interventions accorded with the principles embodied in the established doctrine of nonintervention. Destruction of unpopular governments, Wilson argued, freed foreign nations from undue restraints on their sovereign right to opt for democratic rulers. Rather than serving as a tool for coercing these nations into unwanted action, intervention thus became a tool to enable their people to exercise their will. While Wilson expanded the scope of the right of intervention on one hand, he also laid the groundwork for subsequent contractions of the right. His stress on the sovereign rights of states to determine their own fates, regardless of size, led to a series of international agreements that proclaimed the nonintervention principle as a prescription of international law except for individual or collective self-defense. Such agreements became part of the Covenant of the League of Nations (1918) and later the United Nations Charter (1945).

Nations of the Western Hemisphere went even further than the rest of the international community. Through a series of agreements and declarations springing from successive inter-American conferences in the 1930s, Western Hemisphere countries, including the United States, adopted a principle of absolute nonintervention by individual countries within the Western Hemisphere. Individual countries retained the right to protect the personal security of their citizens. Beyond that, only collective intervention by the combined forces of Western Hemisphere countries would remain lawful.

The United States was willing to bind itself to such absolute declarations of nonintervention because it believed that the collective intervention arrangements made in the Western Hemisphere and on the broader international scene provided a viable alternative to intervention by individual countries. At the same time, a series of presidential declarations emphasized more strongly than had been done in the early years that nonintervention pledges did not mean an abandonment of the right of self-defense when there was no effective collective action. Whenever possible, the United States also tried to conclude mutual defense and economic assistance treaties to provide a legal basis for coming to the aid of selected countries when counterintervention was needed to resist a communist takeover.

In addition, the United States explicitly asserted a right of counterintervention against illegal interventions by other powers. Protection from intervention was a privilege earned by deserving countries; it was not an absolute right. Secretary of State Cordell Hull, during the administration of President Franklin D. Roosevelt, declared that the nonintervention principle applied only to nations that respected the rights of others. The United States, as a powerful member of the community of nations, had a right and duty to intervene in order to prevent or stop illegal interventions directed against countries that lacked the power or will to resist such interventions.

The dangers that would give rise to interventions were identified explicitly but broadly in the 1930s and 1940s. During that period, American political leaders believed that the efforts of the Axis powers to expand their control over Europe and Asia endangered peace and warranted intervention. American leaders sought—sometimes successfully and sometimes unsuccessfully—to have these concerns incorporated into multinational declarations to indicate that nonintervention pledges did not apply to power plays by the Axis powers. The idea that mutual nonintervention pledges by the United States and the Axis powers might be a better way to protect the United States was rejected by the administration of Franklin D. Roosevelt.

Following the defeat of the Axis powers in World War II, communism was viewed as the main danger to the national integrity and security of the United States and the world. In the Truman Doctrine, proclaimed in 1947, the United States declared broadly that either unilateral or collective intervention was justified to protect any country in the world from falling under communist rule. The peace and security of the United States and the world were at stake. The Eisenhower Doctrine, proclaimed in 1957, pinpointed some of the areas where intervention might be expected. Specifically, the political integrity of Middle Eastern nations was declared to be vital to world peace and American interests. If nations in the Middle East were threatened by overt armed aggression by communist forces, the United States would come to their aid if they requested help.

The 1970s saw a retrenchment in overt interventions against communist expansion. Accordingly, it seemed appropriate once more to redefine the scope of the nonintervention doctrine to conform to the prevailing official interpretation of the limits set by the policy. The Nixon Doctrine of 1970 expressed the principle that the United States did not consider it an obligation to protect other countries against communist intervention unless it had determined, in specific cases, that American security interests were involved. Even then, intervention was not the sole duty of the United States but was an obligation shared by all countries opposed to the overthrow of noncommunist governments by communist contenders. President Jimmy Carter deemed the Soviet Union's invasion of Afghanistan in 1979 a major threat to the West's oil lifeline. He responded in 1980 with the Carter Doctrine, declaring with unusual specificity that attempts by any foreign power to gain control over the Persian Gulf region would be considered a threat to the vital interests of the United States. It would be repelled, using military force if necessary. Five years later, in 1985, President Ronald Reagan once more pledged support for a policy of unilateral armed intervention in Third World countries if this became necessary to overthrow Marxist-Leninist regimes. The policy was to be applied selectively anywhere in the world where people were fighting against communism. In practice, it was implemented mostly in Central America.

The Truman, Eisenhower, Nixon, and Reagan doctrines did not pinpoint the conditions that might trigger a specific intervention. However, high-level military leaders often laid out the policy in somewhat more detail. For instance, General Colin Powell, who was chairman of the Joint Chiefs of Staff during the administration of George H. W. Bush (1989–1993), declared that military interventions should be undertaken only when a number of conditions were met. Most importantly, the political objectives of the intervention had to be clearly defined and the gains and risks and likely outcomes had to be adequately assessed. Based on these assessments, it should be clear that the objectives of the intervention could be reached through military means at a defensible cost. Finally, nonviolent alternative policies, if suitable, had been tried first and failed.

Many observers argued that the various and sundry doctrines and statements by military leaders should not be viewed as blueprints for action. Rather, like the previously proclaimed nonintervention principles, they were tailored primarily for psychological impact. They were intended to discourage intervention-minded leaders and to give moral support to nations fearing communist attacks. It was hoped that policy pronouncements would obviate the need for remedial action. If action became necessary, the pronouncements could be characterized as prior warnings that legitimized subsequent actions.

Thus, the nonintervention doctrine has ebbed and flowed in its more than 200-year history. It has gone from an absolute expression, tempered by the implicit exception that interventions for vital purposes were permissible, to an emphasis on a broad range of exceptions to the doctrine, which left it little more than an empty shell. Then it was reformulated in absolute terms, tempered by statements of exceptions stressing that collective or unilateral intervention would still be used by the United States to protect vital security interests. But the absolutism abated again in the wake of major international threats posed by upheavals in Europe and Asia and evidence that collective interventions were difficult to orchestrate.

By the early twenty-first century, the policy implications of the doctrine were that the United States, like all sovereign states, claimed the right to protect its security by all means within its power—including intervention—whenever its leaders believed that this security was seriously endangered. Despite American capacity to intervene freely in the politics of most small nations, however, intervention would be used sparingly, primarily when conditions existed that potentially threatened the security of the United States and its allies and when all other means to resolve the problems failed. The pledges of nonintervention made in the twentieth century indicated the areas where intervention was most likely to occur and the conditions most likely to provoke it. They served as a rough guide to the government in its choice of policy options.

INTERNATIONAL LAW

Definition and General Rules As defined by international lawyers, intervention is unsolicited interference by one state in the affairs of another; nonintervention is the avoidance of such interference. Intervention may be directed against a single state or factions within it, or it may involve interference with the interactions among a group of states. It may take the form of military action or economic or political pressures. These pressures force states to act in a manner prescribed or foreordained by the intervening state. Alternatively, the intervening state may use its own agents to carry out the policies that it desires. States yield because they fear military coercion or nonmilitary punitive actions or because they cannot stop the intervening state's agents or activities.

Although the elements of intervention can be readily outlined, they are hard to identify in specific political situations. Most relations among states contain elements of coercion whenever interacting parties feel constrained to make some concessions to each others' wishes. It is difficult to determine at what point pressure becomes coercive enough to be considered an intervention because consent was unwilling and therefore deemed void. For instance, when a country desperately needs economic aid from the United States or international agencies whose policies the U.S. controls, is it intervention to make aid contingent on privatizing that country's banking system? Normal intercourse among states merges almost imperceptibly into interventionist practices. In a community of nations that is comprised of states of varying powers and degrees of interdependence, nations lacking in economic and political resources are most likely to experience interventionist pressures. The world community has not yet agreed on the borderline between the right of the stronger power to insist on its terms, and the right of the weaker power to conduct its affairs free from coercion. At the other end of the spectrum of coercion, it has at times been difficult to determine when interventions become outright warfare.

A second problem arises from the interdependence of nations in the community of nations, which makes the complete independence envisaged by the concept of sovereignty a legal fiction, rather than a viable reality. In a community of interdependent nations, the domestic or foreign policies of state A frequently have a direct effect on the affairs of state B. When the United States closes its borders to Mexican farm laborers hired for seasonal work in the United States, the Mexican economy suffers. There is disagreement about whether intervention has taken place when the actions of A—and even inactions—seriously affect B but have not been primarily designed to affect B. If, as many international lawyers contend, intent to intervene is essential to establish the fact of intervention, the difficulty of proving intent seriously impedes accurate findings. For instance, the United States stopped the exportation of scrap metal to Japan prior to World War II, giving U.S. national defense needs as the reason. Japan claimed that the measure was intended to force a change in its military policies. It was difficult to prove at the time which claim was correct.

A third problem is tied to the question of responsibility of a state for the actions of its nationals. Citizens of country A, enraged about the treatment of religious minorities, revolutionaries, or foreign business establishments in country B, may openly or covertly interfere in the politics of country B to change policies that they think are offensive. It remains unsettled whether and under what circumstances their government becomes implicated by their activities. For example, Americans who were outraged by the racial policies of a South African government controlled by whites who were an ethnic minority pressured various American enterprises in the 1980s and 1990s to withdraw their investments from South Africa unless racial policies were changed. The withdrawals caused major economic dislocations and contributed to the ultimate fall of the minority government.

The problem of accurate identification of interventionist actions was of minor significance in the eighteenth and nineteenth centuries, because most interventions by the major European powers in the affairs of weak states were then deemed permissible self-defense actions under international law. In fact, rulers in Europe considered intervention a moral duty to uphold their common culture and to protect the political status quo. When the status quo was threatened by the French Revolution, the major European powers pledged support of interventions that would uphold the existing balance of power and maintain established governments.

Numerous interventions took place for these causes. For example, Prussia, Austria, and Russia intervened in Spain, Naples, and Piedmont in 1820 to suppress revolution against the established governments. Similarly, from 1827 to 1832, during the Greek war of independence, Britain, France, and Russia repeatedly intervened in the internal affairs of Greece and Turkey to maintain the balance of power in the Middle East. Other interventions were designed to protect religious groups and minorities, especially when they had ties to the intervening country. Despite high regard for the principle of state sovereignty, international law and practice in the nineteenth century sanctioned a broad right of intervention to protect the interests of nations strong enough to exercise this right to maintain the political status quo.

In the twentieth century, international developments changed the concept of unquestioned legality of all interventions, raising the problem of defining the nature of legal and illegal interventions. The decline of autocratic monarchies and the rise of democratically controlled nations in the wake of the French Revolution had weakened the idea of a community of nations jointly responsible for preserving the existing political landscape. Democratic and autocratic governments had little in common except the reciprocal fear that one was determined to destroy the other. They did not share the sense of kinship and personal moral obligation that had united the crowned heads of Europe. Nor did they agree about the most advantageous policies for Europe and the aims worthy of individual or collective intervention.

Fearing each other, European states wanted to make sure that they would be able to conduct their affairs unhindered by other nations. They therefore looked to the theory of state sovereignty and to claims of an inherent freedom of self-determination as foundations for legal restraints that would protect them from unbridled interventionism by other members of the international community. Gradually, the efforts of small nations, supported by larger countries opposed to interventions to sustain absolute governments in Europe, undermined the concept of an unlimited right of intervention. The notion of a duty of intervention to prevent politically harmful changes was replaced by the concept of a duty of nonintervention subject only to a small number of exceptions.

By the middle of the twentieth century, changing legal philosophies, buttressed by a number of specific resolutions and multilateral treaties, including the Montevideo Convention on the Rights and Duties of States (1933) and the United Nations Charter (1945), had made it a general rule of international law that states may not interfere in matters customarily deemed to be the exclusive purview of another state. A state's internal affairs and its relations with third parties are inviolable. Article 2, paragraph 7 of the UN Charter states that "Nothing contained in the present Charter shall authorize the United Nations to intervene in matters which are essentially within the domestic jurisdiction of any state."

While nonintervention is the general rule, it is still limited by a right of intervention in cases where the current or imminent actions of one state endanger vital concerns of another state or of the community of nations. The clamor of small states for a total prohibition of all interventions has never been heeded. Accordingly, Article 2, paragraph 7 of the charter also provides that the nonintervention principle "shall not prejudice the application of enforcement measures under Chapter VII." Under Chapter VII, states retain the right of coercive action, including the use of military force, to protect international peace and security.

In fact, there has been a partial swing back to the notion that intervention may be a duty to assure the right of people everywhere to be governed democratically and to be protected from violations of their basic rights as human beings. The Universal Declaration of Human Rights, adopted by the United Nations General Assembly in 1948, laid out the scope of these rights. They include bans on genocide and war crimes. The declaration urges member nations to secure "universal and effective recognition and observance" of these rights. Subsequently, the 1951 Convention on the Prevention and Punishment of the Crime of Genocide spelled out in detail that actions such as killing members of national, ethnic, racial, or religious groups, or harming them bodily or mentally, or preventing them from having children, constitutes genocide. The Nuremberg Tribunal, set up to try German war criminals after World War II, established the principle that political leaders and their minions are personally responsible for atrocities they commit as part of their official duties. In the 1990s, international criminal tribunals were set up to try individuals accused of crimes against humanity in Rwanda and the former Yugoslavia. The activities of these tribunals demonstrate that individual responsibility for crimes against humanity can be enforced to some degree under existing international laws. The 1998 Rome Statute for creating an International Criminal Court, which was signed by 120 countries within two years of its adoption, is further evidence that the world community concurs that human rights should be protected under international law.

In 1999, United Nations Secretary-General Kofi Annan urged UN members to devise and pursue more effective policies to stop egregious human rights violations. He acknowledged that some nations might oppose humanitarian interventions as violations of state sovereignty. He countered this contention by arguing that the moral duty of the world community to stop human rights violations trumped an offending state's rights to sovereignty. In line with such widespread sentiments, which nonetheless lack the force of law, the United States has been criticized by political leaders at home and abroad for neglecting its "duty" to prevent or stop genocide, irrespective of its own interests. The issue arose in the Balkans, in Uganda, and in Indonesia when civil strife led to "ethnic cleansing" policies because ruling factions in these states or regions committed atrocities designed to kill or otherwise eliminate undesired minorities from their lands.

Application Problems The general rule that states may intervene in the affairs of other states to protect their own vital interests has been difficult to apply because there is no agreement on the definition of "vital interests." Are the interests that may be protected limited to matters of military security, or do they include major economic and social stakes? Must the danger be imminent or is there a right of preventive intervention? Is it a vital right to protect the property of one's citizens from physical harm in states where effective government has collapsed? Who determines that vital interests are endangered and that intervention is needed to protect them? What is an equitable balance between the safeguarding of vital interests of the intervening state and those of the state subject to intervention? If a state violates the human or political rights of individuals within its borders, or if its actions endanger international peace, do members of the international community have the duty to interfere to enforce the norms of the international community? May they intervene on behalf of established governments under attack by revolutionary forces within their own borders? The answers to these questions remain highly controversial.

These problems are further clouded by vociferous statements of political activists who invoke moral and ethical norms. They claim that interventions on behalf of "good" causes, as they define them, are legal and a moral duty, while interventions for "bad" causes are illegal, unethical, and immoral. Good causes range from aiding persecuted individuals to the duty to provide peoples with good governments to the obligation to stop civil wars or bring about the victory of the allegedly more virtuous side.

A second area of controversy concerns the means of intervention. There is substantial consensus that illegal intervention has occurred when a state dispatches armed forces to the territory of another. The Covenant of the League of Nations (1918), the Kellogg-Briand Pact (1928), and the United Nations Charter (1945) are examples of international agreements outlawing such armed interventions. There is far less agreement about the legality of the vast array of nonmilitary pressures by which states can affect the affairs of other states. These include economic pressures, such as an offer or withdrawal of loans, trade, or aid, including military supplies; political pressures, such as granting recognition to an acceptable government to bolster its power, and withholding of recognition from an unacceptable government in hopes of toppling it; and psychological pressures, such as expressing support for one side in a revolution, denouncing the policies of another state, or excluding it from international meetings. There is a good deal of disagreement about which of such economic, political, and psychological pressures are legitimate exercises of a state's right to conduct its affairs with others as it pleases or undue interferences in the affairs of another state.

A third area of dispute involves the validity of consent to intervention. Many legal experts contend that intervention is legal if it is carried out pursuant to treaty rights or in response to an invitation by an incumbent government. Others dispute the legality of such interventions because treaties granting the right to intervention and requests for intervention frequently spring from duress or are initiated by unrepresentative governments eager to keep themselves in power. Whether these factors invalidate the consent expressed in the treaty or invitation is a controversial legal question. For example, when Colombia refused the request of President Theodore Roosevelt's administration to allow the United States to build a canal in Panama, then a part of Colombia, an uprising leading to Panama's independence was engineered with U.S. support. The pro-independence forces then requested U.S. aid in resisting Colombia's efforts to prevent the secession. The United States complied, ignoring Colombia's objections that the rebels lacked legitimacy and the right to request foreign aid. Once independent, Panama granted the United States the canal rights that its parent state had refused.

A related problem involves the right of collective intervention. For example, member states of the United Nations have agreed in principle to collective interventions. Is this tantamount to automatic approval of interventions by the United Nations in a member country that has violated UN rules and demands? Can a nonmember of the United Nations validly argue that collective intervention directed against it is illegal because it has not given prior consent? For example, could Iraq contend that the UN coalition cobbled together by the Bush administration in 1990–1991 amounted to illegal intervention when Iraq claimed that its incursions into neighboring Kuwait were legitimate because part of the region legally belonged to Iraq? Moreover, Iraq claimed that the government of Kuwait was ruling the country against the objections of the Kuwaiti population.

The official position of the United States on legality and illegality of interventions has generally leaned toward a fairly broad construction of the right of intervention. Presidents and secretaries of state have argued since the end of World War I that international law permits states to retain the right to determine which of their national interests may be protected through intervention and the occasions when intervention is required. Likewise, the United States contends that states retain the right to intervene individually when collective intervention machinery fails to operate efficiently. At the same time, the United States has narrowed the scope of American interests defined as vital enough to justify protection through intervention. Examples of circumstances claimed as justifying intervention include the establishment of Soviet missile sites in Cuba in 1962 and aid to the corrupt but noncommunist government of Vietnam in the 1960s when communist forces attempted to wrest power from the regime of President Ngo Dinh Diem.

The determination of what constitutes legal intervention has been further complicated by the fact that it is deemed derogatory to charge a government with the practice of intervention. For many of the world's governments and people, interventions are policies pursued by international bullies and oppressors, while nonintervention is the hallmark of virtuous nations. These evaluative connotations tempt intervening governments to avoid the label of "intervention" even when their actions are lawful. Instead, they use deceptive names, such as "interposition" or "police action." Similarly, they may misrepresent illegal interventions as legal activities by using deceptive names or spurious legal justifications. The countries that are the targets of interventions may give the false taint of illegality to them by attaching the intervention label to them. Such misuses of political terms make it difficult to ascertain prevailing views within the community of nations on the precise nature of intervention and the criteria by which one can judge whether intervention has occurred and is legal or illegal.

THE PRACTICE OF INTERVENTION

If one were to draw a curve charting the number of American interventions over a 200-year span, it would begin at a fairly low point, reach a peak roughly at the center, then move sharply downward and rebound after World War II. The curve would show several lesser fluctuations during the years of ascent and descent. The major rationale for this ebb and flow of interventionism is the change in perceptions about the security of U.S. hegemony in the Western Hemisphere.

The United States has intervened in the affairs of other nations, or seriously considered intervening, primarily to prevent or foil anticipated attempts by powers on other continents to gain a foothold in the Western Hemisphere from which they might mount an attack on the United States. It has also intervened to maintain power balances among nations in Europe and Asia so that no single nation or combination of nations might become strong enough in these regions to launch an assault on the Western Hemisphere from abroad. Occasionally, the United States has also intervened to establish American strategic and economic bases abroad in order to protect its vital connecting routes to other parts of the world.

When challenges to hegemony were deemed minor, or when interventions were urged for goals not clearly involving the protection of hegemonic interests, the United States has generally shunned intervention. A major exception has been the policy of intervening on behalf of U.S. citizens abroad whenever their lives and property were threatened by political events in a weak foreign country. American statesmen have generally viewed the protective aspects of such actions as paramount and the interventionist aspects as strictly subordinate. Protective interventions, if limited to safeguard Americans, were ordinarily not counted in the record of interventions, at least not by American officials. Of course, the target country often viewed the matter differently.

Humanitarian interventions are another exception. They are viewed primarily as attempts to help suffering human beings whose lives are endangered, rather than as attempts to challenge or interfere with the political situation in the states where these individuals happen to live. In fact, the United States has resisted protecting people from violation of many of their economic and social rights stipulated in human rights conventions, claiming that such interventions would constitute illegal interference.

The argument that infringements of state sovereignty to achieve humanitarian goals are nonpolitical becomes more difficult to sustain when humanitarian crises are precipitated by political events, as was true in the 1990s for starvation relief in Somalia or rescue of Muslims in Bosnia and Kosovo from annihilation. States where humanitarian interventions are taking place generally condemn them. They consider all actions taken by a foreign power on their soil against their expressed wishes as intervention, regardless of the motivation for the action. This is why intervening states, including the United States, often supplement the humanitarian argument by claiming that the action is also undertaken because their vital interests are at stake or because extreme human suffering brings instability that endangers international peace.

While protection of the security of the United States has been the major reason for considering interventions as policy options, additional concerns have influenced specific policy decisions. Foremost, particularly in the early years of the country, was the question of capability to intervene effectively. Intervention usually requires substantial military, economic, and political resources. When the United States lacked such resources or was already using them to their fullest extent, it could not spare them for interventions.

The balance between political gains and political disadvantages derived from the intervention is also important. Intervention by one state may spur counterintervention by another. It may alienate the government and people of the state against which it is undertaken. It may antagonize other members of the community of nations. The chances that it will accomplish the objectives for which it was undertaken may be slim. All these factors are weighed in determining whether a particular intervention is advisable.

Policies of intervention, like other foreign policies, also tend to become entangled with events on the domestic political scene. Political competition for the allocation of human and material resources for various goals may lead to strong opposition to spending resources for a particular intervention. In the years before the Civil War, many interventions were appraised within the context of the proslavery-antislavery dispute. Later, the intervention policy became entangled in the debate over the merits of imperialist expansion. Differences in the appraisal of individual situations also are important. Political leaders often disagreed about whether hegemonic interests were really involved in a particular situation and whether intervention was likely to produce the anticipated results. Considering the high economic and political stakes involved in most decisions to intervene or to abstain, heated debates have been the rule. Political partisanship has also played a part in opposing or supporting particular interventions even though the policy of intervention and nonintervention has never carried a party label. Periods of plentiful and of scarce interventions have been unrelated to the partisan orientation of the government.

Public opinion within the United States has also had a discernible impact on foreign policy choices. When the public mood leaned toward isolationism and concentration on domestic problems, interventions were chosen less frequently than when the public mood was expansionist or imbued with the idea that the United States, as a world power, must involve itself fully with external affairs. Such swings in public opinion have been common, often based on reactions to the success or failure of the most recent foreign policies and on the country's economic strength.

The history of U.S. intervention and nonintervention policies can be divided into four periods. The first, in which the stress on nonintervention was greatest, encompasses roughly the first century of the nation's existence. Then followed an interlude of unabashed interventionism during the closing decades of the nineteenth century and the beginning of the twentieth century. This period ended with the Great Depression years of the 1930s. Third, there were the frustrating decades leading up to World War II, followed by the Cold War era of confrontation between communist and noncommunist power blocs. Hopes for meeting dangers to the national interest through collective interventions turned to dust in the Cold War era. Despite a desire to abandon unilateral interventions, the United States felt compelled to intervene repeatedly to safeguard its national security when American leaders deemed it endangered by the policies of authoritarian governments in various parts of the world. Finally, the end of the Cold War and collapse of the Soviet Union ushered in a new era. Humanitarian interventions in ethnic conflicts and interventions to aid countries in creating democratic governments became fairly common interventionist activities, usually after prolonged and heated verbal battles in the halls of government.

The First Century During the first century of the nation's history, numerous interventions were undertaken to consolidate control over the American mainland and adjacent regions. Territories held by European countries or in danger of being taken over by a European country were acquired or kept from passing under the control of a European rival or changing hands from a weaker to a stronger European ruler. Several major interventions to acquire Spanish Florida and minor meddling in Texas and California are examples. However, while the country was still weak compared to strong European powers, and during the turmoil of the Civil War and Reconstruction, interventions were undertaken only if the outcome seemed highly promising and few dire consequences appeared in the offing. For instance, intervention to acquire Canada was ruled out because of fear that it might bring war with Britain. Diplomatic activities to acquire Cuba were kept short of intervention lest they embroil the country in war with Spain and its allies. Likewise, intervention to annex the Dominican Republic was scotched by Congress.

Intervention was also considered repeatedly during this period in order to keep European powers from intervening in the affairs of independent Western Hemisphere states. But few of these plans bore fruit. Internal weakness kept the United States from pursuing its policies through intervention on a number of occasions when, at a later period, it would have intervened. For example, the United States did not stop interventions by France in Mexico and Haiti to collect debts, nor did it halt incursions by Britain into Guatemala, Nicaragua, and Argentina. Verbal protests were made repeatedly. The United States objected to France's intervention in Mexico to support a monarchy, to Spain's intervention in Peru and annexation of the Dominican Republic, and to Britain's acquisition of parts of Honduras.

The United States also attempted to strengthen American influence in areas threatened by European intervention by expressing a strong interest in the fate of these regions. But the United States could do little more. Powerful influences in Congress and among the public opposed preventive interventions that various presidents had suggested to restore public order in Mexico and the Caribbean area or to overturn military dictatorships and thereby forestall corrective measures by European powers. The United States even kept largely aloof from the efforts of European colonies in the Western Hemisphere to free themselves from control by their mother countries.

Interventions by the United States in revolutions outside the Western Hemisphere were also kept to a minimum, although many revolutions were taking place in Europe to replace absolute monarchies with democratic governments. Two centuries later, the support of democratic factions and countries against absolute governments of a different sort would be deemed sound reason for intervention by the United States, but that time had not yet arrived.

The United States did intervene in China, Japan, and Korea to coerce them to grant trade privileges to American merchants, beginning with a government trade mission in 1844 headed by Commissioner Caleb Cushing. At the time, such missions were the usual practice when foreign nations wanted to trade with Asian countries. The eagerness of the United States to have its citizens participate in the spoils of trade in the Far East was explained as much by strategic as by economic considerations. American leaders feared that the European powers would divide the Far East, particularly China, into spheres of influence from which other powers would be excluded. Land bases in China would give them control over the shipping lanes of the Pacific Ocean. The United States, unless it supported retention of control by the weak Asiatic powers or secured spheres of interest of its own, would be deprived of Pacific outposts to protect its access routes to Asia. The United States therefore pursued a two-pronged policy in the area: it protested against increased domination by European powers, and it intervened to acquire trade privileges for itself and to lay the foundations for ultimate acquisition of a number of naval bases in the Pacific.

The Imperial Period The heady philosophy of the interventionist phase of American foreign policy is epitomized by Secretary of State Richard Olney's claim in 1895 that the United States had become master of the American continent "practically invulnerable as against any or all other powers." Consequently, "its fiat is law upon the subjects to which it confines its interposition." Within the next decade the United States would satisfy all its remaining territorial ambitions, largely through interventions and war with Spain. Puerto Rico, the Philippines, and Guam came under its control, as well as Hawaii and Samoa. Nonetheless, even during this period, reluctance to intervene did not disappear entirely. For instance, President Grover Cleveland's administration resisted pleas for intervention in Cuba although intermittent civil strife on the island was deemed hazardous to American security.

From the standpoint of intervention policy, the most crucial territorial acquisition during this period was the Panama Canal Zone. It was acquired through interventionist policies that assured that the Panama region would break away successfully from Colombia and would grant ample concessions to the United States for construction and protection of an isthmian canal. The United States regarded the canal as a lifeline permitting its naval units to shuttle rapidly between the East and West coasts to guard against dangers emanating from Europe or Asia. To protect this vital route, the United States appointed itself policeman of the Western Hemisphere who must and did intervene frequently to restore political order in the small countries near the canal. American political leaders assumed that political unrest automatically spelled danger to the canal area, warranting intervention. No specific proof was required in a particular situation that an attack on the canal was imminent. In a number of Caribbean countries, the United States even secured treaty rights of automatic intervention in case of unrest. The most famous advance authorization for intervention was the Platt Amendment to the Cuban constitution, which was in force for more than thirty years.

In areas farther from the canal, interventions were undertaken with more restraint. During this period, Mexico was a source of great concern to American policymakers because of constant internal turmoil, a succession of brutal dictatorial governments, and serious attacks on American citizens and their property in Mexico. The United States used a number of pressures, particularly economic sanctions and arms embargoes, to control turmoil in Mexico, but refrained from full-scale military intervention despite domestic pressures.

During the interventionist period the United States protested more strongly than ever before against European incursions into the affairs of the hemisphere. Boundary difficulties between Venezuela and Britain in the 1880s provide a good example. The United States intervened in the dispute, contending that it had a general right to interpose in any conflict in which the political or territorial integrity of an American state was threatened by a non-American power. It claimed that it could insist on arbitration and the enforcement of the arbitration award, even if one of the parties opposed the award.

By nonrecognition of an undesirable government, the United States also intervened repeatedly, although not consistently, to overthrow authoritarian regimes, particularly military dictatorships that had come to power in Latin America. Regimes that had ascended through unconstitutional means and represented authoritarian philosophies were deemed potential sources of instability. They might produce internal unrest, encouraging foreign intervention that would threaten the hegemonic interests of the United States. It was hoped that nonrecognition would make it so difficult for the unrecognized government to conduct its political and economic affairs that it would be weakened and overthrown by democratic forces. While potential danger to the security of the Western Hemisphere usually was the motivating force for nonrecognition, at times the policy was used on purely ideological grounds. Several instances occurred during the Woodrow Wilson administration because President Wilson was loathe to recognize governments that had come to power by force or ruled undemocratically.

Major challenges to the international balance of power continued in Asia during this period. European nations and Japan were establishing spheres of interest at the expense of China. More assiduously than before, the United States aimed to prevent this by means of an Open Door policy for China. This involved securing pledges by European nations and Japan to refrain from closing any part of China to access by other powers. The United States protested whenever other powers violated the policy, which it regarded as a guarantee of China's territorial integrity and independence. When protests failed, the United States did not usually attempt stronger pressures for fear that they might lead to war.

The United States did intervene in the Russo-Japanese War (1904–1905) to prevent Russia and Japan from encroaching on China's sovereignty. Later it refused to recognize damaging concessions extorted by Japan from China in the vain hope that this would produce a policy change on Japan's part. The United States also continued to engage in intervention designed to strengthen China economically and politically and to assure an American presence in the area to checkmate European power plays.

The peak of interventionism, if one judges by the frequency of interventions and the number of countries involved, was reached during the first two decades of the twentieth century. Besides numerous interventions in the Western Hemisphere and Asia, this phase included U.S. intervention in World War I on behalf of the anti-German coalition. Ultimately, intervention led to full-scale American participation in the war.

In the postwar years, the number of interventions declined. The weakness of European powers after World War I was one major factor. They no longer presented a real threat to the hegemony of the United States in the Western Hemisphere. No European power was strong enough to assume control over Europe or the tottering Chinese empire. Another major factor was the realization that many goals that the United States had tried to accomplish in the course of interventions in the Western Hemisphere could not be achieved through intervention. For instance, it had been impossible to lay the groundwork for politically stable, economically sound, and democratically governed states in the Caribbean area, despite lengthy U.S. military interventions. Attempts to establish economic influence abroad and to use it for political purposes (known as dollar diplomacy) had also largely failed.

Lastly, interventions had aroused a great deal of opposition from other countries, particularly the nations of the Western Hemisphere, and from groups within the United States. The policy was attacked on legal, moral, and practical grounds as improper coercion of the weak by the strong for the selfish aims of the strong. Behind such charges lay a changing climate of world opinion that placed greater emphasis on the sovereign rights of small nations and condemned coercive diplomacy, particularly the use of military force, to achieve national objectives.

The Collective Security Phase The dominant feature of American intervention and nonintervention policies after the end of the openly interventionist years was the desire to make interventions—particularly those involving the use of military force—collective enterprises of the world community or regional groupings. Dangers to the vital interests of the international community that would justify protection through intervention were to be carefully defined in advance. The United States hoped that they would encompass all the circumstances that had hitherto tempted it into individual interventions. In addition, the United States expected to influence the policies of other countries through conditions attached to its economic and military aid policies. It did not consider such conditions interventionist. Rather, they were deemed the right of the donor to dictate the terms of a grant.

Unfortunately, the goals set for conditional aid policies were rarely achieved. The stipulated conditions often proved impossible to implement or failed to produce the desired results because of unstable internal conditions in the recipient nations. Fraud and corruption were major problems worldwide. In many cases, the conditions attached to the aid were flouted. Occasionally, the prospective recipient refused the aid because the conditions were deemed interventionist, destabilizing, or insulting.

The goals set for collective interventions fared somewhat better, but also fell short on many occasions. Prolonged negotiations over many years made it possible to organize a moderately effective collective intervention system in the Western Hemisphere. Spurred on by the United States and its supporters, the system was activated repeatedly to curb Axis and communist influence in Latin America. Strong objections by countries such as pro-Axis Argentina and Chile and pro-communist Cuba, Guatemala, and their supporters were overruled. But efforts to use the system failed frequently when the goal was to control major political problems endemic to Western Hemisphere countries.

On the wider international level, the League of Nations Covenant, and the United Nations Charter and interpretive resolutions thereafter, also contained provisions for collective intervention to protect the vital interests of members of the community of nations. But agreement could rarely be reached on the kinds of menaces to which this machinery should respond. Nations could not even agree during international gatherings or when faced with specific situations on what sets of circumstances should be considered threats to world peace.

The weaknesses of the collective intervention machinery encouraged the United States to continue to determine unilaterally whether its security was menaced by particular international developments. When protective interventions seemed necessary, it would then try to initiate collective action. If this failed, or if the collective machinery could not be put into operation quickly and decisively enough to halt the danger, the United States claimed and continued to exercise a right of unilateral intervention.

Two major dangers, similar in nature, roused the United States to a large number of verbal, economic, political, and military interventions during this and the preceding period. The first was the attempt of right-wing authoritarian regimes in Europe, and later in the Far East as well, to destroy the balance of power in Europe and Asia and to establish their own hegemony. The United States first intervened in World War II in Europe and Asia by verbal attacks and warnings directed against the dictators. It tried to engender and support policies by neutral powers that would be harmful to the dictators' aims, and it gave economic and military aid to the dictators' enemies. Along with other countries in the Western Hemisphere, it interfered with the rights of belligerent powers to conduct hostilities on the high seas surrounding the Americas in a band 300 to 1,000 miles wide. To protect the hemisphere from Axis footholds, the territorial status of European possessions in the Americas was declared frozen in 1940. Inter-American machinery was established to administer the possessions of subjugated European countries. All of these verbal, political, and economic interventions failed to halt Axis advances. The United States then entered the war in 1941 in response to Axis war declarations and attacks on U.S. territories.

The victory of the Allied powers in World War II ended the menace to American security created by rightist totalitarian imperialism in Europe and Japanese empire building in Asia. New challenges to hemispheric safety soon arose from attempts by the Soviet Union and other communist powers to spread their ideology and political and even territorial control over a widening circle of countries in Europe, Asia, and other parts of the world. American leaders believed that the United States had a legal right to intervene to halt communist advances because its own survival as a democratic country was deemed at stake. Every addition to the communist coalition diminished the potential of the United States to defend itself successfully against communist subversion and military aggression.

Interventions by the United States to halt or prevent the spread of communist control throughout the world explain most of its far-flung operations during the latter four-fifths of the twentieth century. In almost every case in which the United States had identified a situation as potential or actual communist intervention, it tried to work through collective action. These efforts failed frequently because other countries disagreed that communist intervention was imminent or because they feared the consequences of the spread of communism less. Moreover, struggles by national liberation movements to free their countries from foreign control or domestic tyranny and corruption had often become so entwined with insurgency by procommunist forces that it was hard to fight communism without destroying liberation and reform movements. When the United States intervened unilaterally, claiming to act in the name of collectively approved principles to maintain established governments in power, its reputation as a champion of popular, honest government often suffered serious damage at home and abroad.

The United States intervened to prevent the ascendancy of communist governments in Eastern Europe by means of a policy of nonrecognition and economic pressures. It tried to checkmate Soviet influence in places like Iran, Turkey, and Greece. It aided anticommunist nations in the Middle East, particularly the new state of Israel, as well as pro-Western Jordan and Lebanon in their struggles against covert and overt attacks by Soviet-supported Arab nations. The United States sent aid and rescue missions to assist anticommunist forces in the Congo and, to a lesser extent, Angola. It used a number of interventionist tactics to bring about black majority rule in Rhodesia (now Zimbabwe), South Africa, and Namibia, in hopes of preventing racial warfare in southern Africa that might provide a cover for further expansion of Soviet influence in the area. It also used such tactics to keep Soviet influence in the Mediterranean and the Persian Gulf at bay.

To strengthen noncommunist governments faced with strong domestic opposition from communist parties, and to support governments fighting against communist insurgents, the United States intervened in widely scattered parts of the globe, such as Central and Western Europe, the Far East, and Latin America. In the Far East, intervention was used to prevent the expansion of communist control over much of Southeast Asia, particularly South Vietnam, Laos, Cambodia, and Thailand, and over South Korea. In Korea, the United States intervened unilaterally in 1950 until a United Nations force could take over. The bulk of military power that was made available to the United Nations for collective intervention had to be furnished by the United States because other powers gave only verbal support. The Korean intervention and other interventions undertaken to stop the advances of communism made it clear that gains won on the battlefield could not be maintained without permanently stationing noncommunist military forces in areas coveted by communist powers.

The most protracted and costly intervention to halt the advance of communist-controlled forces occurred in Vietnam. There the United States and a number of its allies attempted to support noncommunist governments against attacks by procommunist forces eager to reunite North Vietnam and South Vietnam under a communist government. The fierce controversy over the legality and wisdom of the Vietnam intervention led to serious political cleavages within the United States and within the international community. Opponents of the intervention claimed that the situation involved a domestic struggle between procommunist and anticommunist Vietnamese that did not seriously involve U.S. security interests. Proponents disagreed and their views prevailed. The United States finally withdrew its military forces from Vietnam in 1973. Economic and military aid to the South Vietnamese government was discontinued in 1975. By that time, communist forces had assumed full control of the country and further resistance to the spread of communism in Southeast Asia appeared hopeless.

In many instances, it is easy to refute charges of illegal interventionism by the United States because American policymakers based their actions on treaty rights providing for joint defense against communist attacks or on requests for help by anticommunist governments in various nations. But, as indicated earlier, the moral and even legal validity of these arrangements is often challenged when the agreements were concluded under circumstances that made it practically impossible for one party to decline or when the moral authority of the government to agree to intervention is questionable. A more solid, legal defense for anticommunist interventions is the claim to a right of counterintervention. The United States acted in most instances in response to proved, presumed, or anticipated interventions by communist forces that were intervening around the world to guide politics to their advantage. It can be argued that, akin to the right of self-defense, there exists a right of preventive or curative counterintervention.

While it may seem at first glance that the United States missed no opportunity to intervene against the spread of communism, this was not the case. Many possibilities for intervention were bypassed because the threat of advancing communist influence was comparatively limited, because the costs of intervention, including likely counterinterventions, seemed too high, or because the United States realized that it could not muster sufficient strength in faraway places to engage in effective intervention.

A situation involving all three of these contingencies occurred on mainland China. The United States had initially given some aid to the forces of General Chiang Kai-shek to assist him in wresting control of North China from the communist forces in that country. When it became clear that only massive military involvement would save the Chinese mainland from communist control, U.S. policymakers in the period following World War II, in a highly contested policy judgment, decided against such a major commitment. But limited aid to Chiang Kai-shek, who had retreated to the island of Formosa, continued. Similarly, despite explicit declarations and implicit threats, interventions on behalf of noncommunist factions in Eastern European countries to help them shed communist control never materialized. Insurgents in East Germany in 1953, Poland and Hungary in 1956, and Czechoslovakia in 1968 received no official help.

Nor did the United States intervene in most instances when left- or right-wing dictatorships came to power in Latin America in the period after World War II, or when governments expropriated the assets of large American businesses without adequate compensation. For example, it failed to intervene in Bolivia in 1952 when a coup d'état supported by Argentina's pro-fascist Juan Perón regime put a radical regime into power. It nationalized the tin mines that supplied tin to the United States and failed to compensate U.S. business interests for losses suffered through expropriations. Major exceptions to this hands-off policy occurred generally only in areas close to the American mainland and the access routes to the Panama Canal. For instance, the United States intervened to topple a left-wing anti-American government in Guatemala in 1954 by aiding exile forces attempting military invasion of their homeland.

The United States also helped to plan and execute an invasion by anti-Castro Cuban refugees in 1961 who wanted to overthrow the communist government of Premier Fidel Castro in Cuba. The attack failed and the tactics of the United States were widely condemned as illegal. Few such charges were made a year later when the United States intervened in Cuban-Soviet relations by demanding removal of Soviet missiles stationed in Cuba. In the Cuban missile crisis, most Latin American states and most noncommunist members of the world community concurred that the security of the United States was sufficiently endangered by Soviet missiles ninety miles from its territory to justify intervention. Subsequently, the inter-American community acted jointly to exclude Cuba from the inter-American system and to embargo the shipment of arms and other goods to Cuba. This fell short of the collective break in diplomatic relations favored by the United States in response to Cuba's publicized plans to subvert other Latin American governments, if necessary by guerrilla violence and civil war. Venezuela, Colombia, and Bolivia had been singled out as primary targets. When the dominance of the United States over hemispheric relations declined in the 1970s, restrictions against Cuba were lifted one by one.

Another major intervention against a Latin American government was the attempt to forestall a leftist takeover in the Dominican Republic. More than 30,000 U.S. troops were dispatched in 1965 to stop fighting between forces that President Lyndon Johnson deemed procommunist and anticommunist. Ultimately, a right-wing regime prevailed. Although the United States managed to involve the inter-American collective intervention machinery, participation by the Organization of American States did little to erase the bitterness within the United States, Latin America, and other parts of the globe about the initial failure of the United States to abide by its pledge to abstain from unilateral military intervention. Many observers doubted that the Dominican situation had presented a sufficiently serious threat to the security of the United States to warrant major preventive measures.

After costly, often fruitless interventions had soured American policymakers on benefits to be reaped from intervention, a renewed retreat from overt interventionism began in 1969. It was hastened by a policy of détente and bargaining between the United States, the Soviet Union, and mainland China that helped to reduce the climate of mutual fear that had spawned interventions earlier. The ascent of communist-controlled or communist-influenced governments was no longer deemed an ipso facto threat to the security of the noncommunist world. The United States reduced its interventions and military commitments in Asia. It tried to lessen occasions for intervention in the Middle East by pacifying the area and resuming more normal relations with countries that had drawn their support from the Soviet Union. It also took a more aloof stance toward the tumultuous politics of Latin America. Moreover, to avoid the onus of charges of interventionism, a number of interventions were conducted as covert enterprises. The activities of the Central Intelligence Agency, which contributed to the overthrow of the Marxist government of President Salvador Allende Gossens in Chile in 1973, are examples of the types of actions that were undertaken covertly to weaken governments and policies deemed hostile and dangerous to the United States.

However, increased reluctance to engage in interventions and decreased concern about the dangers posed by the ascendancy of Marxist governments in various parts of the world should not be construed as a complete retreat from the use of collective or unilateral intervention to protect the security of the United States from damage caused by attempts to spread communism. For instance, the United States invaded Grenada, a Caribbean island, in 1983 on the grounds that the Fidel Castro's communist government in nearby Cuba had designs on the island.

Overall, the more restrained approach to anticommunist interventionism was gradually counterbalanced by increased interventionism on behalf of humanitarian and civil rights causes. President Jimmy Carter, following policies reminiscent of the Woodrow Wilson presidency, proclaimed in 1977 that the United States would intervene on behalf of persecuted peoples anywhere in the world where states were denying human or civil rights to their citizens on account of race, religion, or political persuasion. Numerous such interventions took place. However, they were neither prompt nor consistent. In a haphazard pattern, influenced by a multiplicity of political and logistical factors, humanitarian interventions were carried out promptly or sluggishly in some situations but forgone in others involving equal or greater human catastrophes.

The Post–Cold War Decades During the Cold War era, most interventions could be defended as counterinterventions that were needed to implement the policy of containment designed to stop the spread of communism. Following the collapse of communism in the Soviet Union in 1991, different rationales came to the fore. The new potential dangers to U.S. interests came primarily from an epidemic of violent internal conflicts and human rights violations in formerly communist nations and in developing countries throughout the globe. To justify intervention under these circumstances, U.S. presidents used three major rationales. Most commonly, presidents contended that these upheavals endangered world peace and security in general and hence the security of the United States. This argument served two purposes. It was useful in justifying collective interventions under the United Nations Charter and it weakened complaints by domestic critics in the United States, especially in the Senate, who denied that the country's national security was imperiled and therefore charged that the United States had no business undertaking these foreign interventions.

The second major rationale was the evolving consensus that humanitarian interventions are a moral duty as well as a requirement in the wake of the various human rights declarations. However, this argument has never been considered strong enough to silence influential critics of intervention. Hence, it is usually accompanied by claims that the human rights violations, besides endangering vulnerable populations, also constitute a threat to peace.

The final major rationale—also usually buttressed by individual or collective self-defense arguments—is the claim that the United States is a world power that must protect the world from major misbehavior by members of the international community. The argument was clearly articulated by President Bill Clinton in his Farewell Address to the nation in 2001. He declared that "America cannot and must not disengage itself from the world. If we want the world to embody our shared values, then we must assume shared responsibility." Clinton's plea resembles to a surprising extent the claims made by President Theodore Roosevelt a century earlier. The Roosevelt Corollary that pictured the United States as the world's policeman was never accepted by the rest of the international community. Its modern version is likely to be equally unpopular, especially among small nations that are the most likely targets of intervention.

The argument that international peace and security are endangered by political unrest in a foreign country was used by Clinton's predecessor, President George H. W. Bush, to displace General Manuel Noriega, who headed the government of Panama in 1990 when the country was in turmoil and there were rampant violations of the human rights of Noriega's enemies. Economic sanctions, such as freezing Panamanian assets in the United States and revoking Panama's most-favored-nation trade status, had failed to drive the general from office. As in so many other interventions, the brunt of the suffering produced by these economic sanctions was borne by the poorest segments of the population while the leaders of the country continued to prosper and lead lives of luxury.

On 17 December 1989, President Bush ordered Operation Just Cause to replace Noriega by military force. American troops landed on 20 December. The officially stated "just causes" for the intervention were protection of American lives and property in Panama at a time of internal political unrest, restoration of democracy, the security of the Panama Canal, and brutalities and illegal drug trafficking ascribed to Noriega and his cronies. It remains a matter of controversy whether these were the actual motives or merely cover-ups for more mundane political objectives of the Bush administration. Among other reasons, President Bush, like many of his predecessors and like his successor, President Clinton, may have felt that the "leader of the free world" could not risk his international image by allowing a tin-pot dictator in a tiny country to defy his demands.

The argument that internal domestic conditions in a small country threatened world peace seemed spurious to devotees of nonintervention in the United States and abroad. Accordingly, the Panama intervention led to charges of unlawful intervention by the United States. On 29 December 1989, the UN General Assembly condemned the intervention by a vote of 75 to 20 and demanded that the United States remove its troops from Panama. Likewise, the Organization of American States condemned the intervention unanimously, even though many members detested Noriega and his actions. In defense of its actions, the United States cited the self-defense provisions of the UN and OAS charters, without specifying in what way Panama constituted a major threat to U.S. security. U.S. representatives also argued that the survival of democratic nations was at stake and that all available peaceful means of displacing Noriega had been tried and failed. There was no solid proof for these claims or for the claim that American citizens or the Panama Canal were in imminent danger of suffering major harm. However, public opinion polls by the CBS television network indicated that most Panamanians approved of the intervention and were happy that it had led to the removal of Noriega from government power and from the country.

PRESIDENT CLINTON'S FAREWELL ADDRESS, 19 JANUARY 2001

"Because the world is more connected every day in every way, America's security and prosperity require us to continue to lead in the world. At this remarkable moment in history, more people live in freedom than ever before. Our alliances are stronger than ever. People all around the world look to America to be a force for peace and prosperity, freedom and security. The global economy is giving more of our own people and millions around the world the chance to work and live and raise their families with dignity. But the forces of integration that have created these good opportunities also make us more subject to global forces of destruction, to terrorism, organized crime and narcotics trafficking, the spread of deadly weapons and disease, the degradation of the global environment. The expansion of trade hasn't fully closed the gap between those of us who live on the cutting edge of the global economy and the billions around the world who live on the knife's edge of survival. This global gap requires more than compassion. It requires action. Global poverty is a powder keg that could be ignited by our indifference.

"In his first inaugural address, Thomas Jefferson warned of entangling alliances. But in our times, America cannot and must not disentangle itself from the world. If we want the world to embody our shared values, then we must assume a shared responsibility. If the wars of the twentieth century, especially the recent ones in Kosovo and Bosnia, have taught us anything, it is that we achieve our aims by defending our values and leading the forces of freedom and peace. We must embrace boldly and resolutely that duty to lead, to stand with our allies in word and deed, and to put a human face on the global economy so that expanded trade benefits all peoples in all nations, lifting lives and hopes all across the world."

A less political, and initially less controversial, intervention took place in Somalia in 1992. It began as a purely humanitarian venture to provide starvation relief and stop human rights abuses in that African country. No strategic, economic, or drug trafficking issues were involved, and Somalian leaders had not seized territory illegally. However, the country was in the throes of a civil war without an effective government in place. Proponents of the intervention argued therefore that it made no sense for foreign powers to ask anyone's permission to enter the country. The United Nations, with strong member support, had approved the mission after it had become impossible for relief agencies to function in the war-torn country. The United States then dispatched 37,000 troops to Somalia to keep food relief supplies out of the reach of the feuding warlords and distribute it to the starving population. The initial plans called for completing the mission within five months.

But, as often happens in unstable areas, the various UN forces involved in the mission, including the American contingents, soon became embroiled in the civil war, changing the nature of the venture in unforeseen and unplanned ways. It had become obvious that effective delivery of aid to the people required bringing about at least some semblance of political order. In the wake of political efforts to pacify the country—which turned out to be futile—Somali soldiers attacked the relief teams, inflicting heavy casualties. Eighteen U.S. soldiers were among the dead. After some hesitation, President Clinton withdrew U.S. forces in October 1993, in the wake of the killings. Pictures of the corpse of an American soldier dragged along the streets of Somalia's capital city had outraged the American public and led to angry recriminations in Congress about the wisdom of undertaking the mission.

The Somalia intervention, besides souring the U.S. government's taste for humanitarian interventions, gave rise to the belief that ample television coverage of human disasters throughout the world can arouse the anger and compassion of the American public. In turn, the public may then pressure the national government to intervene to stop human suffering. This putative phenomenon was dubbed "the CNN effect." As evidence that such an effect had spawned the initial intervention in Somalia, scholars pointed out that graphic pictures and reports about atrocities, starvation, and devastation in Somalia had been widely aired on CNN television. Pressure groups, so it was alleged, had then forced the government, against its better judgment, to airlift relief supplies and later send U.S. troops to Somalia. Other scholars denied this sequence of events and contended that relief plans for Somalia antedated the CNN publicity by more than a year. They claimed that government officials, including members of Congress who had visited Somalia, had inspired the action.

It is impossible to prove that the pressure by government officials would have been sufficient to lead to the decision to intervene—and to withdraw when the bodies of dead soldiers were shown—if the decision had not been supported by media-induced public pressure. Hence, media buffs continue to believe that the CNN effect exists. They argue that graphic coverage of human suffering is an important determinant of whether or not a particular disaster will generate U.S. intervention. In general, public-opinion polls show that the American public supports purely humanitarian interventions by a substantial margin, especially if there are no American casualties. The same holds true when the public becomes convinced that the intervention seeks to subdue an aggressor eager to attack the United States, injure its vital interests, or damage its citizens. The public is far less supportive of interventions that seem designed to change another country's politics when there appears to be no immediate threat to vital U.S. interests.

Many interventions that involve important humanitarian concerns serve multiple purposes, of course. For example, the intervention in Haiti in 1994 combined humanitarian and democracy-building objectives with an exceptionally strong emphasis on restoring democracy to a country where a democratic election had been aborted. Because of Haiti's proximity to the U.S. mainland, large refugee flows into Florida were quite likely. Rumors suggested that more than 300,000 Haitians were eager to leave their country, most of them heading for the United States. Similarly, the 1989–1990 Panama intervention, besides stopping humanitarian outrages and supporting democracy in Panama, became a cog in U.S. efforts to stop the inflow of dangerous recreational drugs into the United States.

The policy of intervention to support democratic governments was originally part of the policy of containment of communism. If a country had a strong democratic government, presumably it would not succumb to an authoritarian ideology. After the Cold War ended, supporting or even creating democracies was viewed as an aid to international peace on the dubious assumption that democratic countries rarely go to war with other democratically governed states. Hence, the United States could argue that its intervention in Haiti was justified under the UN Charter to maintain world peace. The claim was bolstered by the fact that the United Nations had officially sanctioned the intervention.

As if to underline the importance of sponsoring the growth of democratic institutions worldwide, the U.S. State Department created a Bureau of Democracy, Human Rights, and Labor Affairs during the Clinton years. The bureau's mission was defined as promotion of democracy throughout the world and formulation of human rights policies, including those relating to labor issues. In addition, the Clinton administration, like several of its predecessors, used the granting or withholding of economic resources as a weapon in the fight to democratize the nations of the world.

It has always been easier to claim concerns about the security of the United States as reasons for intervention when the location of the trouble is close to America's shores. This is the U.S. "sphere of influence," designated as its prime concern and fief since the days of the Monroe Doctrine. Reluctance to become entangled in conflicts outside of the Western Hemisphere, especially when international organizations are available with authority to handle such situations, explains why the United States initially tried to avoid intervention in the civil strife in Bosnia that entailed major human rights violations. But the combined pull of a number of motives—humanitarian concerns, the importance of U.S. support for NATO involvement in the Balkan situation, and the desire to maintain U.S. influence in European affairs—finally persuaded the Clinton administration in 1995 to join its NATO partners in air strikes to try to end ground fighting in Bosnia.

Overall, when U.S. policymakers weigh the options in situations where intervention is under consideration in the post–Cold War world, several factors seem to weigh especially heavily in favor of becoming involved. They are the location of the trouble spot, the relative size and power of the country in question, the degree of defiance of U.S. requests displayed by the local rulers, and the chances of a successful outcome. Given these criteria, Western Hemisphere locations, especially if they are close to the United States, are most likely to elicit intervention, provided the country is small and headed by an arrogant, democracy-defying ruler, and provided the United States is ready and willing to commit sufficient resources to carry the intervention through to a successful conclusion.

Other important factors are the magnitude and viciousness of human rights violations, the effectiveness of mass media in depicting them to large audiences, the impact of unrest on American citizens in the country in question, and the likelihood that an exodus of refugees will seek asylum in the United States or allied nations. While absence of most of these conditions explains why the United States abstained from intervention in numerous major human rights tragedies in the post–Cold War era, U.S. policies have not been entirely consistent. The complex international and domestic environment that surrounds foreign policy decisions has always made it impossible to predict specific political actions with certainty.

A number of the interventions mentioned thus far are examples of cooperation between the United Nations and the United States. When interventions have been undertaken under UN auspices, the organization has repeatedly encouraged one nation to take charge of a collective intervention enterprise. For example, it entrusted the United States with major responsibilities for the conduct of UN interventions in the Persian Gulf War, in Somalia, and in Haiti. In such cases, the leading country is expected to take control of the operation and to foot most of its expenses. Other UN members contribute personnel and material resources.

The Gulf War of 1991 is the best example of the United States working effectively with the United Nations to implement a policy that seemed in its own as well as in the collective interest. When Saddam Hussein invaded Kuwait in 1990, destabilizing the balance of power in the Middle East and threatening the uninterrupted flow of oil, the UN Security Council condemned the aggression and imposed economic sanctions. When these measures failed to persuade Hussein to withdraw his troops, President George H. W. Bush threatened U.S. military intervention. The U.S. position was legitimized and strengthened by a Security Council resolution that authorized "all necessary means," including the use of military force, to get Saddam out of Kuwait. Operation Desert Storm, which was launched in 1991 with full control by the U.S. military, thus became a UN operation supported by a coalition of twenty-seven nations. The drawback to the collaborative arrangement was that U.S. freedom of action in the military operations and the peace settlement that followed the brief span of hostilities was limited by political pressures to include coalition members in decision making and make concessions to their wishes.

Initially, the U.S. foreign policy establishment was bullish about the usefulness of interventions conducted within the UN framework. But the euphoria about collective action was short-lived. Disillusionment set in during subsequent crises in Somalia and Bosnia when disagreements between U.S. and UN policymakers hampered the United States in structuring and executing the missions. It was difficult, for example, to make threats of military intervention credible when the United States could not act without first securing UN approval.

Problems incurred in orchestrating interventions in the Balkans with the help of members of both the United Nations and the North Atlantic Treaty Association (NATO) were blamed for delaying subsequent U.S. intervention until after massive killing and ethnic cleansing had already occurred. Similarly, the failure of the Somalia intervention allegedly scotched all plans for intervention in the Rwanda genocides, which were the next major humanitarian crisis in Africa. Observers of U.S. diplomacy therefore believe that Americans have little patience with policies, especially when they involve military force, when these policies do not produce quick successes. Failed policies become a barrier to future action in the same vein. Like most generalizations, this is only partly true. The slogan "No More Vietnams" after the failed Vietnam War presumably precluded future military interventions but only for a while.

Still, in light of these policies of self-restraint whenever obstacles occur, it seems unlikely that the United States will make ample use of its proclaimed duty to act as the world's chief law enforcement power. This is especially true because the experiences of the Bush and Clinton administrations with a number of interventions have made it clear that interventions carry high personnel costs. Airpower alone, even if massively deployed, will not generally displace violent governments or end brutal civil wars. But fighting on the ground risks large numbers of casualties. Such losses are both humanly and politically extraordinarily painful. Many members of Congress are very unwilling to become mired in interventions and resist them with all of the means at their disposal. Their opposition, often via claims that the 1973 War Powers Act has been violated, is a potent political deterrent to interventions, especially when they seem problematic for other reasons as well. High on the list of deterrents is the difficulty of coordinating multinational ventures that involve widely diverse nations and public- as well as private-sector organizations.

Opponents of policies involving military intervention often recommend economic sanctions as an alternative to constrain international troublemakers. Unfortunately, the occasions when such policies have worked are few. The breakdown of apartheid policies in South Africa is often cited as a most conspicuous success. However, even in that situation, it remains controversial what the precise influence of economic sanctions was, compared to other factors in the breakdown of apartheid. Unfortunately, failures of even prolonged sanctions are easier to demonstrate, such as the defiance of sanctions by Fidel Castro's Cuba and by the despotic rulers of Haiti, Panama, Somalia, and Bosnia, where interventions followed failed sanctions. Another galling example of the impotence of sanctions was the political survival and prospering of Iraq's Saddam Hussein in the face of massive sanctions imposed by the international community and maintained for more than a decade.

DOCTRINE VERSUS PRACTICE

How does this record of numerous American interventions over two hundred years of national history square with the claim that the United States has always upheld the principle of nonintervention? How does it accord with the frequent declarations that nonintervention is the official policy of the United States? The answers require putting intervention policies into the perspective of available options, and also discussing the role that political doctrines play in the conduct of foreign affairs.

Countries, like individuals, rarely act with total consistency. Champions of peace do go to war; a preference for free trade may yield to protectionism when circumstances make protectionism highly advantageous. One generally characterizes a country's policies by prevailing trends within the policy and within the international community. As discussed, in the case of American intervention policies, the large numbers of interventions are matched by an even larger number of occasions when the United States eschewed intervention, although it was a viable and potentially beneficial policy alternative. This was particularly true during the first century of the nation's existence when it first proclaimed that nonintervention would be its preferred policy. Whether it will again become true in the twenty-first century remains an open question in the wake of many disappointing results of intervention policies, the high costs of such ventures, and competing domestic claims on available national resources. One thing is clear however: choices of intervention and nonintervention in particular situations will always be controversial. Proponents will claim that they are necessary and legal while opponents will argue the reverse.

Throughout American history, whenever intervention was the preferred policy choice, it has always been pictured as a last, undesired option. Nonintervention has been hailed even when the country's practices were clearly interventions. One may call this hypocrisy and denounce it. Or one may recognize that the belief in a country's right to freedom and independence from outside interference runs strong. After all, that was the legacy left to Americans in 1796 when President George Washington warned that "History and experience prove that foreign influence is one of the most baneful foes of republican government." Therefore, "it must be unwise for us to implicate ourselves . . . in the ordinary vicissitudes of [other nations'] . . . politics."

BIBLIOGRAPHY

Brown, Michael E., ed. *The International Dimensions of Internal Conflict.* Cambridge, Mass., 1996. Claims that deadly internal conflicts threaten dozens of countries and major regions around the world.

Brune, Lester H. *The United States and Post-Cold War Interventions: Bush and Clinton in Somalia, Haiti and Bosnia, 1992–1998.* Claremont, Calif., 1998. Presents fairly detailed chronologies of events in these three interventions.

Bull, Hedley, ed. *Intervention in World Politics.* Oxford and New York, 1984. Based on a series of 1983 lectures at Oxford University about sovereignty and international relations and law.

Chayes, Antonia Handler, and Abram Chayes. *Planning for Intervention: International Cooperation in Conflict Management.* The Hague and Boston, 1999. Offers a new strategy for the world community's handling of intervention into internal state conflicts.

Chopra, Jarat, and Thomas G. Weiss. "Sovereignty Is No Longer Sacrosanct: Codifying Humanitarian Intervention." *Ethics and International Affairs* 6 (1992).

Clarke, Walter, and Jeffrey Herbst, eds. *Learning from Somalia: The Lessons of Armed Humanitarian Intervention.* Boulder, Colo., 1997. Deals with peacemaking problems, such as rebuilding the economy, and with the relationship between the military and nongovernmental organizations.

Franck, Thomas. "The Emerging Right to Democratic Governance." *American Journal of International Law* 86 (1992). Discusses an international trend toward considering democracy a legal right that entails international legal obligations.

Freedman, Lawrence, ed. *Strategic Coercion: Concepts and Cases.* Oxford and New York, 1998. Argues for a reappraisal of the role of strategic coercion by drawing on the experiences of countries other than the United States.

Freedman, Lawrence, and Efraim Karsh. *The Gulf Conflict 1990–1991: Diplomacy and War in the New World Order.* Princeton, N.J., 1993.

Frenderschub, Helmut. "Between Universalism and Collective Security: Authorisation for the Use of Force by the UN Security Council." *European Journal of International Law* 5 (1994).

Gilboa, Eytan. "The Panama Invasion Revisited: Lessons for the Use of Force in the Post Cold War Era." *Political Science Quarterly* 110 (1995–1996).

Goodpaster, Andrew J. *When Diplomacy Is Not Enough: Managing Multinational Interventions.* New York, 1996. Analyzes the difficult problems encountered when interventions involve multiple governmental and nongovernmental organizations.

Haass, Richard N. *Intervention: The Use of American Military Force in the Post–Cold War World.* Washington, D.C., 1994. Discusses U.S. intervention in Haiti, Bosnia, and Iraq and nonintervention in genocide activities in Central Africa.

Hippel, Karin von. *Democracy by Force: U.S. Military Intervention in the Post–Cold War World.* Cambridge and New York, 2000. Focuses on U.S. interventions that were followed by nation-building efforts in Panama, Somalia, Haiti, and Bosnia.

Hoffman, Stanley. "The Politics and Ethics of Military Intervention." *Survival* 37 (winter 1995–1996).

Joes, Anthony James, ed. *Saving Democracies: U.S. Intervention in Threatened Democratic States.* Westport, Conn., 1999. Covers multiple interventions over much of the twentieth century.

Kanter, Arnold, and Linton F. Brooks, eds. *U.S. Intervention Policy for the Post–Cold War World: New Challenges and New Responses.* New York, 1994.

Lepgold, Joseph, and Thomas G. Weiss, eds. *Collective Conflict Management and Changing World Politics.* Albany, N.Y., 1998. Examines the prospects for collective management of international conflict in the post–Cold War.

Livingston, Steven, and Todd Eachus. "Humanitarian Crisis and U.S. Foreign Policy: Somalia and the CNN Effect Reconsidered." *Political Communication* 12 (1995): 413–429.

Mansfield, Edward D., and Jack Snyder. "Democratization and the Danger of War." *International Security* 20 (summer 1995).

Maynes, Charles William. "Relearning Intervention." *Foreign Policy* (spring 1995).

Moore, John Norton. *Law and the Grenada Mission.* Charlottesville, Va., and Washington, D.C., 1984.

Murphy, Sean D. *Humanitarian Intervention: The United Nations in an Evolving World Order.* Philadelphia, 1996. Analyzes the law as it applies to humanitarian interventions, especially when the United Nations becomes involved.

Pasic, Amir, and Thomas G. Weiss. "The Politics of Rescue: Yugoslavia's Wars and the Humanitarian Impulse." *Ethics and International Affairs* 11 (1997).

Robinson, William I. *Promoting Polyarchy: Globalization, U.S. Intervention, and Hegemony.* Cambridge and New York, 1996. Provides a view of intervention policies from a less conventional perspective.

Sassen, Saskia. *Losing Control?: Sovereignty in an Age of Globalization.* New York, 1996.

Weiss, Thomas G. *Military-Civilian Interactions: Intervening in Humanitarian Crises.* Lanham, Md., 1999.

Zartman, I. William, ed. *Collapsed States: The Disintegration and Restoration of Legitimate Authority.* Boulder, Colo., 1995. Case studies of problems in African states.

See also BLOCKADES; COLLECTIVE SECURITY; CONTAINMENT; COVERT OPERATIONS; DOCTRINES; ECONOMIC POLICY AND THEORY; EMBARGOES AND SANCTIONS; HUMAN RIGHTS; HUMANITARIAN INTERVENTION AND RELIEF; IMPERIALISM; INTERNATIONAL LAW; THE NATIONAL INTEREST; OIL; PROTECTION OF AMERICAN CITIZENS ABROAD; RECOGNITION; REVOLUTION; THE VIETNAM WAR.

ISOLATIONISM

Manfred Jonas

The term "isolationism" has been used—most often in derogation—to designate the attitudes and policies of those Americans who have urged the continued adherence in the twentieth century to what they conceived to have been the key element of American foreign policy in the nineteenth century, that is, the avoidance of political and military commitments to or alliances with foreign powers, particularly those of Europe. It was most nearly applicable to American policy between the two world wars, especially after 1935, when the U.S. Congress attempted to insulate the country from an increasingly dangerous world situation through the enactment of so-called neutrality laws. Since World War II, efforts to limit or reduce the vastly increased American commitments abroad have sometimes been called neo-isolationism.

The term itself is of relatively recent origin. Its first known application to the foreign policies of the United States was by Edward Price Bell, the London correspondent of the *Chicago Daily News*. In an article entitled "America and Peace" (*Nineteenth Century*, November 1922), Bell was critical of what he called the essentially negative attitude of the United States toward international cooperation, but noted that the country was nevertheless in the process of moving gradually "from isolation into partnership." Pointing out that the United States had, despite strong misgivings, ultimately declared war on Germany in 1917, he concluded: "Her isolationism, such as it was, discovered that the strain of a formidable advance against freedom was more than it could bear."

The word "isolationist" was listed for the first time in the 1901 edition of the *Oxford English Dictionary*, although without any indication as to when or where it had been used in its political sense. Standard American dictionaries did not incorporate the word until 1922, and the 1933 supplement to the *Oxford English Dictionary* cites no political use of it before 21 April 1921, when it appeared in the *Glasgow Herald*. Mitford M. Matthews, in *A Dictionary of Americanisms on Historical Principles* (Chicago, 1951), makes a logical but erroneous inference from the listing in the 1901 edition of the *Oxford English Dictionary* (it remains unchanged in the current edition) and traces "isolationist" in a political sense to an article in the *Philadelphia Press* of 25 March 1899. This article, however, uses the word in a medical sense in connection with a smallpox epidemic in Laredo, Texas.

THE SCHOLARLY LITERATURE

The scholarly literature on isolationism began in 1924 with J. Fred Rippy and Angie Debo's essay "The Historical Background of the American Policy of Isolation" (*Smith College Studies in History* 9). The term was not prominently used, however, until 1935, when Albert K. Weinberg offered a provocative interpretation of it in *Manifest Destiny*. World War II and its immediate aftermath, when the United States for the first time actively sought to assume the mantle of a major power, provided the major impetus for its serious study.

American policy during the interwar years, which frequently was described as isolationist, came then to be regarded as an anomalous one that required explanation and analysis. Isolation, it was argued, had generally been imposed on major powers only against their will, as in the case of France after the Franco-Prussian War (1870–1871) or of Great Britain in the 1890s. Although the speech by George Eulas Foster in the Canadian House of Commons on 16 January 1896 led to a flurry of oratory concerning Britain's "splendid isolation," it was clear that the term had been used ironically more often than not and that British policy had been designed to help the empire emerge from that apparently undesirable state. Voluntary isolation had been sought only by some smaller nations, such as Switzerland, as a way to avoid falling victim to more powerful neighbors, and by culturally threatened ones, such as China and Japan, as a defense against Western incursions.

The United States was the only major Western industrialized nation that had apparently displayed a positive interest in some form of isolation, and that phenomenon attracted the attention of scholars in the late 1940s, and with increasing frequency in the two decades that followed. Ray Allen Billington sought to give isolationism a geographic base in his "The Origins of Middle Western Isolationism" (*Political Science Quarterly,* March 1945); Henry Nash Smith examined its relationship to "the myth of the garden" (*Virgin Land,* 1950); Samuel Lubell exposed what he took to be its "ethnic and emotional roots" (*The Future of American Politics,* 1952); and Wayne S. Cole explained it as an expression of the "needs, desires, and value systems" of American agricultural society (*Senator Gerald P. Nye and American Foreign Policy,* 1962).

Extended analyses of isolationism were also published by Robert E. Osgood, who defined it as a form of "passive egoism" in his *Ideals and Self-Interest in American Foreign Relations* (1953); by Selig Adler, who stressed economic self-sufficiency, the illusion of security, and ethnic prejudices as causative factors (*The Isolationist Impulse,* 1957); by Arthur A. Ekirch, Jr., who explained isolationism as a policy designed to assure de facto independence after the American Revolution had been won (*Ideas, Ideals, and American Diplomacy,* 1966); and by Manfred Jonas, whose *Isolationism in America, 1935–1941* (1966) analyzed the assumptions underlying the isolationist position prior to World War II and suggested that these indicated a survival of unilateralism bolstered by a fear of war. John Milton Cooper, Jr., sought to define isolationism as "a political position with programmatic and ideological dimensions" somewhat akin to a political movement (*The Vanity of Power,* 1969), and a host of other scholars—historians, political scientists, sociologists, and even psychologists—have investigated the subject from the perspective of their respective disciplines.

THE MYTH OF THE FOUNDERS

While controversy continues about the precise meaning of the term "isolationism" and about the relative importance of various factors that might explain the phenomenon, some areas of agreement emerged from the research. It became clear, for example, that isolationists of whatever stripe always regarded themselves as traditionalists with respect to American foreign policy and regularly invoked the Founders, particularly George Washington and Thomas Jefferson, in support of their position.

Washington was the father of the first American neutrality act (1794), which incorporated both the principle of his Proclamation of Neutrality (1793)—that the United States should pursue "a conduct friendly and impartial towards the Belligerent Powers"—and the subsequently developed Rules Governing Belligerents. The neutral stance of the United States was noteworthy primarily because of its obvious incompatibility with the French alliance that had been concluded despite strong misgivings in 1778. Since France chose not to invoke the alliance in the 1790s, American neutrality remained unchallenged, and could thus develop into a tradition that was reasserted, at least initially, with respect to every major international conflict up to World War II.

In his Farewell Address in 1796, Washington supplied the rationale for this policy and urged its continuance. He pointed out that "Europe has a set of primary interests which to us have none or a very remote relation," and advised his countrymen "to steer clear of permanent Alliances" and involvement "by artificial ties in the ordinary vicissitudes of her politics and the ordinary combinations and collisions of her friendships and enmities." Less than five years later, Jefferson put substantially the same advice into even more enduring phraseology in his first inaugural address, where he insisted that American policy should continue to be based on the principle of "peace, commerce and honest friendship with all nations, entangling alliances with none."

Neither Washington nor Jefferson, however, regarded themselves as advocates of a policy of isolation and, indeed, that word had not yet migrated to the English language from the French at the time they expressed their views. Both men actually sought to increase American contacts with the outside world. Washington vigorously espoused the expansion of foreign trade and promoted a series of commercial agreements on the model of the one negotiated with Prussia in 1785. Jefferson, although he would, in moments of great frustration, have preferred the United States "to practise neither commerce nor navigation, but to stand, with respect to Europe, precisely on the footing of China," clearly recognized after he had become president the necessity of fostering commerce and other forms of international intercourse. Indeed, he sent the U.S. marines to the shores of Tripoli to protect American commerce and acquired the whole Louisiana Territory from France in order to keep the mouth of the Mississippi open to the new nation's trade. Both presidents welcomed continued immigration and, Jefferson in particular, the influx of European ideas and culture.

The two did not even categorically rule out alliances. Washington indicated in his Farewell Address that the new nation might "safely trust to temporary alliances for extraordinary emergencies." Jefferson advised President James Monroe in 1823 to accept Foreign Secretary George Canning's invitation to joint action with Great Britain against the threat posed to Latin America by the Holy Alliance. While reasserting that the "first and fundamental maxim [of the United States] should be never to entangle ourselves in the broils of Europe" and the second maxim, "never to suffer Europe to meddle with cis-Atlantic affairs," Jefferson nevertheless concluded that "the war in which the present proposition might engage us, should that be its consequence, is not her war, but ours," and that if "we can effect a division in the body of the European powers, and draw over to our side its most powerful member, surely we should do it."

The basic aim of both Washington and Jefferson was to safeguard the independence of a new and weak nation by avoiding, whenever possible, involvement in the military and political affairs of the major powers while at the same time expanding trade and commerce as a means of fostering national development. But both men were fully aware that economic and political matters could not be separated as neatly as their phraseology suggested, and neither can be regarded in any meaningful way as an isolationist. Together with many of the other Founders, they merely followed the logic of the American Revolution and its consequences.

Thomas Paine had pointed out in *Common Sense* (1776) that one of the advantages of breaking the connection with Great Britain lay in the possibility of assuming a position of neutrality with respect to a Europe "too thickly planted with Kingdoms to be long at peace" and thus promoting and protecting trade with all nations even in wartime. John Adams urged the Continental Congress to enter only into treaties of commerce and "to lay it down, as a first principle and a maxim never to be forgotten, to maintain an entire neutrality in all future European wars." Were the fledgling United States to do otherwise, Adams feared, "we should be little better than puppets, danced on the wires of the cabinets of Europe." The Congress that he addressed had earlier established a committee to draft a declaration of independence and, at the very same time, one to devise a model treaty for regulating relations with foreign nations. The model treaty, Adams declared, was to be only commercial and have neither political nor military clauses. Such a treaty proved impossible to conclude, however, and foreign aid was needed if independence were to become a reality. Less than six months after adopting the Declaration of Independence, therefore, Congress dispatched John Jay to Spain, Benjamin Franklin to France, and John Adams himself to Holland to seek both money and full-fledged alliances. Isolating the United States from the rest of the world was the last thing they had in mind.

The United States was involved almost from the beginning in the first world crisis after independence was achieved: the quarter century of wars spawned by the French Revolution. That was due in part to the fact that the new nation could not be indifferent to the outcome of these wars, and that Jefferson and the Republicans generally favored the cause of France, while Washington, Hamilton, and the Federalists favored Great Britain. Washington's Neutrality Proclamation of 1793 was not intended primarily to insulate the United States against foreign conflicts, but was rather an anti-French measure for evading America's obligations under the Treaty of Amity and Commerce of 1778 and thereby helping the British cause. Both Jefferson and James Madison denounced it on that account, particularly after the Washington administration negotiated a new treaty, this one with Great Britain, shortly thereafter. Alexander J. Dallas, the future secretary of the Treasury who would have been much happier to have the French alliance continue, in 1795 denounced the treaty that John Jay had negotiated in London as a scheme for "wantonly involving ourselves in the political intrigues and squabbles of the European nations."

After Napoleon came to power in France, Jefferson played a role in the ongoing struggles by buying Louisiana from the financially strapped emperor and by a series of manipulative trade measures including the Embargo Act of 1807 and the Nonintercourse Act of the following year. Over the protests of staunchly Federalist New England, the United States even went to war in 1812 with Great Britain and attempted to conquer Canada, thereby becoming in effect an ally of Napoleon. The *Boston Gazette* promptly lamented the shedding of American "blood for Bonaparte" and, after the French occupied Moscow, Czar Alexander I offered his services as mediator in the conflict between his British ally and the United States.

The nation was thus, in its early years, neither isolated nor isolationist. It consistently recognized its involvement with the world but sought to pursue its international interests unilaterally without making long-term commitments or entering formal alliances. Secretary of State John Quincy Adams correctly assured the assembled multitude on 4 July 1821 that the United States "does not go forth in search of monsters to destroy" because "by once enlisting under banners other than her own" it would become party to "all the wars of interest and intrigue, of individual avarice, envy and ambition." But Adams had already served as minister to the Netherlands, Prussia, Russia, and Great Britain and had been one of America's negotiators of the Treaty of Ghent ending the War of 1812. As secretary of state, he was to conclude formal treaties with Spain and Great Britain and to protect the newly independent states of Latin America with the Monroe Doctrine.

AMERICA'S FOREIGN POLICY IN THE NINETEENTH CENTURY

The unilateralist foreign policy that Adams pursued—the actual legacy of the Founders—proved serviceable and was followed with reasonable consistency until the end of the nineteenth century. It was a policy peculiar to the United States not in its motivation but only in the circumstances that allowed it to work. Americans had deliberately shaken off their major tie with Europe during the Revolution and understandably had little interest in replacing it with other ties. Moreover, in 1776 Americans had acted partly out of a sense of uniqueness and of superiority to the Old World and its institutions, and they regarded it as essential to the success of the mission of the United States that its policies remain uncontaminated and free from foreign influence. The development of the traditional American foreign policy was thus coeval with the first flowering of an assertive American nationalism.

The freedom of action that the United States sought for itself during the nineteenth century is, however, the ideal of all nation-states. Alliances, however desirable or even necessary under certain circumstances, inevitably circumscribe that freedom, and the avoidance of alliances and the maintenance of neutrality in the quarrels of others are, therefore, a universally appealing policy.

For most nations, however, the policy is also self-defeating and dangerous, since it is often incompatible with the continuance and further development of commercial and cultural ties, largely rules out assistance from others when that may be necessary, and invites attack by stronger neighbors. For the United States in the early nineteenth century, as a country of little economic and no military importance, without strong neighbors, protected by wide expanses of ocean and the polar ice cap, and favored by a world balance of power that tended in most instances to safeguard its interest, the policy was not only appealing, however, but also practicable. Unallied and uncommitted, threatened neither by invasion nor loss of territory, and possessed of a vast, rich, and sparsely developed hinterland, the United States was able to act independently and at its own discretion in those cases in which events elsewhere in the world seemed to affect the nation's interests.

Over the course of the century, the United States was able to expand its trade and commercial relations to an extraordinary degree, absorbed European immigrants in unparalleled numbers, and engaged freely in the process of cultural exchange. Moreover, it quite consistently displayed strong interest in political and military matters outside its borders.

It encouraged the revolutions in Spain's American colonies and sought to protect their newly won independence with the Monroe Doctrine. It followed the Greek Revolution and the European revolutions of 1830 and 1848 with sympathetic interest, and treated at least one of their leaders, the Hungarian Lajos Kossuth, to a hero's welcome. It vied with the British for control of the Oregon Territory in the 1840s and tried to buy Cuba in the 1850s. It went to war with Mexico in order to acquire not only Texas but California as well, and was instrumental in bringing Japan, a truly isolated country, into contact with the world at large. At the close of the Civil War, it helped effect the withdrawal of French troops from Mexico and acquired Alaska, its first noncontiguous territory, from Russia.

At the same time, the United States consistently sought to avoid "entanglements" by either acting alone or, when that proved impossible, refraining from action. Not only did it take part in the Napoleonic Wars without entering into an alliance with France, it never made certain the support of the British fleet by formal treaty even though that fleet was essential to the effectiveness of the Monroe Doctrine. Despite some strong sentiments to the contrary, the United States consistently refused to commit itself to active support of the European revolutionaries, and limited its treaty making during the entire nineteenth century to the settlement of specific disputes concerning boundaries, immigration, and fishing and sealing rights. The only treaty to carry even the suggestion of joint action with another power, the Clayton-Bulwer Treaty of 1850 with Great Britain, which limited action by the United States with regard to the building of a trans-isthmian canal, has been called by the historian Thomas A. Bailey "the most persistently unpopular pact ever concluded by the United States."

By the middle of the nineteenth century, America's traditional policy had become so firmly established that it was above serious challenge. In rejecting, on 11 May 1863, an invitation to join with France, Great Britain, and Austria in an attempt to persuade Czar Alexander II to modify his designs on Poland, Secretary of State William H. Seward cited Washington's Farewell Address as the basis for his action, and applauded the hitherto successful resistance to "seductions from what, superficially viewed, seemed a course of isolation and indifference." It was the first known official use of the term "isolation" in connection with the traditional American policy, and it was used, of course, only to be rejected as inapplicable. "Our policy of nonintervention, straight, absolute, and peculiar as it may seem to other nations," concluded Seward, "has . . . become a traditional one, which could not be abandoned without the most urgent occasion, amounting to manifest necessity."

TRYING THE ROLE OF WORLD POWER

As long as this policy was regarded as natural and obvious, it provided no basis for factional disputes and required, therefore, neither ideological nor programmatic definition nor a specific label. Isolationism emerged as a distinctive and definable political position only when the foreign policy consensus derived from the teachings of Washington and Jefferson began to break down, a development that found its basis in the conditions of the late nineteenth century but full expression only in the period of World War I.

By the end of the nineteenth century, virtually all of the circumstances that had made the traditional policy of the United States possible had either been greatly modified or disappeared altogether. With rapid industrialization and the opening of vast new lands to agriculture, the United States had become a serious factor in the world economy and was converting itself from an importer into an exporter of capital. The need for the protection of trade and investments, as well as the chauvinistic search for the sinews and symbols of power that infected all Western nations in these years, led the United States to follow the teachings of Alfred Thayer Mahan, who in his lectures at the newly established Naval War College—subsequently published as *The Influence of Sea Power on History, 1660–1783* (1890)—argued that great countries were built by great navies. Even as the United States thus embarked on the road to military power, advances in technology and communications continued to shrink the oceans and thereby to move the country from the periphery of power to a place closer to the center. And the nineteenth-century balance of power, which, for all the abuse that had been heaped on it by American statesmen, had served the nation well, was upset by the simultaneous rise to international prominence of two ambitious newcomers, Germany and Japan.

The United States responded to these changes with a more active foreign policy and greater international involvement. In 1884 it joined the International Red Cross and participated in the Berlin Conference that was intended to solve the problems in the Congo. Three years later, it hosted the first international conference of its own, the Washington Conference on Samoa, and in 1889 the first Pan-American Conference. These expanded international contacts soon led to further involvement. The Venezuela Crisis of 1895 was followed by the War with Spain, the acquisition of Hawaii, Puerto Rico, and the Philippines, and the enunciation of the Open Door policy designed to assure equal international access to the markets of China. The United States sent delegates to the First International Peace Conference at The Hague in 1899, and the following year contributed 5,000 troops to an international expeditionary force that put down the Boxer Rebellion in China.

The pace of America's involvement with the world quickened during the presidency of Theodore Roosevelt, who hugely enjoyed asserting America's growing power. In 1902, after Great Britain, Germany, and Italy had blockaded Venezuela and brought its dictator, Cipriano Castro, to his knees, he facilitated an arbitration of the dispute that protected America's long-standing interests in Latin America. In 1903 he encouraged rebellion in Colombia, promptly recognized the new country of Panama that emerged, and acquired territory from it on which to build a trans-isthmian canal. In 1904 his corollary to the Monroe Doctrine arrogated to the United States the exercise of an international police power in the Caribbean, and for the next twenty years U.S. marines landed periodically in Cuba, the Dominican Republic, Nicaragua, Haiti, and, on occasion, even Mexico. In 1905 he mediated the peace treaty between Russia and Japan that was concluded at a conference in Portsmouth, New Hampshire. For his efforts he became the first of three Americans who were to win the Nobel Peace Prize before 1920.

All of this activism in international affairs was deemed to be compatible with the foreign policy of the Founders, and the traditional American consensus therefore remained largely intact. Even the anti-imperialists at the turn of the century, while opposing the acquisition of colonies on the grounds that this would fundamentally change the character of the American Republic, made surprisingly little of the fact that it would inevitably lead to involvement in the great power rivalries against which President Washington had warned, and that the Open Door policy would have the same effect if attempts were made to enforce it. When the Senate ratified the Algeciras Agreement of 1906, an international compact dealing with the future of Morocco, and the Hague Convention of 1908 that established the rights of neutrals and of noncombatants—both clearly "entangling" in nature—it simply added the proviso that agreeing to them was "without purpose to depart from the traditional American foreign policy."

Less than three months before the outbreak of World War I, Woodrow Wilson, who still insisted that "we need not and we should not form alliances with any nation in the world," reasserted the traditional policy: "Those who are right, those who study their consciences in determining their policies, those who hold their honor higher than their advantages, do not need alliances." Consequently, the onset of hostilities in Europe produced the traditional American response: a declaration of neutrality and a reassertion of the policy of friendship with all and entanglements with none, which, as an editorial in the magazine *World's Work* put it, "was made for us by wise men a hundred years ago."

INTERVENTIONISM AND ISOLATIONISM

World War I nevertheless proved to be the first clear indicator that the United States, would, by virtue of its new power position, find it difficult, and perhaps also undesirable, to remain "unentangled." Since the conflict pitted many ideological friends and major trading partners of the United States against a group of European autocracies—most particularly after the March Revolution of 1917 in Russia—it proved extraordinarily difficult, even for the president himself, to heed Wilson's admonition to be "impartial in thought as well as in action." The wartime increase in trade flowed naturally into previously developed channels, and loans and credits largely followed the route of established business connections, thus not only favoring one set of belligerents and arousing the ire of the other but giving the United States a tangible stake in the outcome of the war.

Even aside from such specific considerations, the possibility that nations with political systems and economic aims different from those of the United States might dominate the world after the war could be ignored only with difficulty. For all of his original devotion to neutrality, Wilson himself was moved to his desire for a negotiated "peace without victory" at least in part because he found one of the other alternatives—the victory of the Central Powers—to be wholly incompatible with American interests. "The world," he was to say in his declaration of war, "must be made safe for democracy."

The situation of the United States during World War I brought respectability for the first time to the proposition that, given its changed world position, the United States might best protect its interests by more active cooperation with other nations, even through commitments and alliances not in keeping with the traditional policy. Wilson's espousal of such ideas led him to propose a League of Nations, which required full-fledged American participation in a system of collective security. Others with similar views joined together in June 1915 to found the League to Enforce Peace, an American counterpart to the Netherlands-based Organisation Centrale pour une Paix Durable. Among the leaders of the new organization were former president William Howard Taft, President A. Lawrence Lowell of Harvard, and Hamilton Holt, the influential editor of the *Independent*.

This initial articulation of an approach to foreign policy that differed from the traditional one chiefly in its espousal of collective action as a necessary element in the defense of the national interest produced, in its turn, the defensive position generally called isolationism. In the context of the time, it amounted to an assertion, implicit or explicit, that changed world conditions had not made a departure from traditional policies either necessary or desirable and that entanglement in what continued to be regarded as the affairs of other nations was more dangerous to the United States than any conceivable result of continued noninvolvement. Among the early isolationists, in this sense, were Secretary of State William Jennings Bryan, Senators William E. Borah of Idaho and George W. Norris of Nebraska, and the pacifist-intellectual Randolph S. Bourne. On a popular level, such sentiments found support in the Hearst press beginning in early 1917.

Although the occasion for this development of an isolationist position was the debate over American entry into World War I, the actual declaration of war did not prove to be the really divisive issue. If the United States entered the war on its own volition and in defense of its own interests, such a step did not necessarily violate traditional policy, particularly not if it fought, as it did, not in formal alliance with other nations, but simply as an "associated power." Accordingly, a number of confirmed isolationists in the Senate voted for war. Among these were not only Democrats like Charles S. Thomas of Colorado and Thomas P. Gore of Oklahoma, who might be considered to have put partisanship ahead of conviction, but also Republicans Joseph I. France of Maryland, Hiram Johnson of California, and Borah.

Wilson soon realized, however, that any serious effort to make the world safe for democracy required that the United States enter into de facto alliance with the European powers, under whatever label, so that he himself would be able to exert the leadership necessary to the attainment of that objective. In his Fourteen Points address of 18 January 1918 he in effect supplied all of the Allies with a set of war aims that included the removal of economic barriers among nations, the adjustment of competing colonial claims, the freedom of the seas, and a "general association of nations" to secure "mutual guarantees of political independence and territorial integrity to great and small states alike." Less than a year later, he went to Paris in an effort to have these objectives, especially the establishment of a League of Nations, incorporated in the Treaty of Versailles that ended the war.

America's entry into the League of Nations would have been an obvious violation of the traditional policy. The league was clearly an alliance, an open-ended commitment of the very sort against which the Founders had warned. Wilson in fact promoted U.S. participation in the international organization as "an entirely new course of action" made necessary by the fact that the isolation of the United States was at an end, "not because we chose to go into the politics of the world, but because by the sheer genius of this people and the growth of our power we have become a determining factor in the history of mankind and after you have become a determining factor you cannot remain isolated, whether you want to or not."

The isolationists would have none of that. They generally agreed with the contention that isolation was no longer a realistic aim, if indeed it had ever been one, but took sharp issue with the proposed policy reversal. "We may set aside all this empty talk about isolation," Henry Cabot Lodge of Massachusetts, the chairman of the Senate's Committee on Foreign Relations, told his colleagues in 1919. "Nobody expects to isolate the United States or make it a hermit Nation, which is sheer absurdity." At the same time, however, he warned against the injury the United States would do itself by "meddling in all the differences which may arise among any portion or fragment of humankind" and urged continued adherence to "the policy of Washington and Hamilton, of Jefferson and Monroe, under which we have risen to our present greatness and prosperity." The Senate debate over ratification of the Treaty of Versailles sharpened and clarified the isolationist position. It turned entirely on the question of America's so-called meddling, and set the course of American foreign policy for the next two decades.

THE TRIUMPH OF ISOLATIONISM

The rejection of the Treaty of Versailles by the Senate and the overwhelming popular ratification of that action in the election of 1920 can be regarded as a triumph of American isolationism. It was not, as has sometimes been argued, a return to an earlier policy. The world had changed too much to allow that. But it was a reassertion of that policy in the face of the first fundamental challenge it had ever faced. The isolationism of the 1920s was real, despite the continuing commercial expansion of the United States and despite the greater influence on world affairs that the country enjoyed. The traditional policy, which the isolationists thought they were preserving, had always, after all, emphasized trade and commerce even while shrinking from political commitments, and American influence and the desire for it had traditionally been a component of the "mission" of the United States.

Nevertheless, the American position during the 1920s was in some ways an ambiguous one. The experience of World War I had greatly increased the role of the United States as an economic, political, and even military factor in world affairs, and made some degree of coordination with other nations all the more crucial. At the same time, the war had served as an object lesson on the danger of international commitments. The success of the Bolshevik Revolution in Russia was only the most threatening of the postwar events that persuaded most Americans that their intervention had clearly failed to make the world safe for democracy. It thus appeared to demonstrate the wisdom of the contention that meddling in the affairs of others was useless and self-defeating. The reflexive logic that this intervention had almost led to a total abandonment of the policy of the Founders only served as a further warning.

On the basis of such perceptions, the United States set out on an isolationist course that could best be described as one of cooperation without commitment. The United States, for the first time in its history, sharply curtailed immigration. It took the lead in negotiations on naval disarmament that would make war less likely and took pains to clarify the purely hortatory character of the Open Door policy. The Four-Power Treaty of 1921 changed any commitments the United States might once have assumed with respect to the openness or territorial integrity of China into a commitment, proposed by Senator Lodge, "to communicate . . . fully and frankly in order to arrive at an understanding as to the most efficient measures to be taken, jointly or separately, to meet the exigencies of the particular situation." Even then, the Senate ratified the treaty only after adding a further disclaimer: "The United States understands that under the statement in the preamble or under the terms of this treaty there is no

---

THE SWANSON RESOLUTION (1926)

Resolved (two thirds of the Senate present concurring), That the Senate advise and consent to the adherence on the part of the United States to . . . the Permanent Court of International Justice . . . subject to the following reservations and understandings, which are hereby made a part and condition of this resolution, namely:

1. That such adherence shall not be taken to involve any legal relation on the part of the United States to the League of Nations or the assumption of any obligations by the United States under the Treaty of Versailles. . . .

4. That the United States may at any time withdraw its adherence to the said protocol and that the statute for the Permanent Court of International Justice adjoined to the protocol shall not be amended without the consent of the United States.

5. That the court shall not . . . without the consent of the United States, entertain any request for an advisory opinion touching any dispute or question in which the United States has or claims an interest. . . .

Resolved further, That adherence to the said protocol and statute hereby approved shall not be so construed as to require the United States to depart from its traditional policy of not intruding upon, interfering with, or entangling itself in the political questions of policy or internal administration of any foreign state; nor shall adherence to the said protocol and statute be construed to imply a relinquishment by the United States of its traditional attitude towards purely American questions.

— *From Congressional Record 67 (1926): 2306* —

commitment to armed force, no alliance, no obligation to join in any defense."

During these years the most heralded diplomatic achievement by the United States, the Kellogg-Briand Pact (1928), was in its origins simply a way of gracefully denying France the security guarantees it had sought to obtain. Although generally regarded at the time as a positive contribution to the maintenance of world peace and order, it formally committed the United States to no action of any kind and was strongly supported by many of the most prominent isolationists, including the new chairman of the Senate Foreign Relations Committee, Senator Borah.

By the beginning of the 1930s, the United States was retreating from military intervention in Latin America by adopting the so-called Good Neighbor Policy, and Secretary of State Henry L. Stimson reacted to the Japanese conquest of Manchuria with a unilateral action that threatened nothing more serious than nonrecognition. President Herbert Hoover restated the isolationist consensus in 1931. Although recognizing a greater interdependence among nations in the modern world, Hoover nonetheless distinguished between the path of the United States and that of other nations. "We should cooperate with the rest of the world," he told his cabinet, "we should do so as long as that cooperation remains in the field of moral pressures. . . . But that is the limit." There were few dissenters.

ISOLATIONISM AT HIGH TIDE

During the remainder of the 1930s, America's isolationism was most clearly defined and most ardently defended, and it reigned triumphant until fatally undermined by the very world events that had helped to promote it. The isolationism of the 1930s emanated clearly from a world situation in which the totalitarian states—most notably Germany, Japan, and Italy—challenged the status quo and with it the power position and security of the United States. Traditional American foreign policy had always rested on the assumption that the United States was safe from attack and that American trade and ideas would continue to find acceptance regardless of developments elsewhere. As that assurance diminished, it seemed more important than ever before to try and seal off the United States from threats from abroad, especially the threat of war. It was not until the end of the decade that most Americans faced up to the question then raised rhetorically by the formerly isolationist *Progressive* of Madison, Wisconsin: "If Hitler defeats England and the British fleet is destroyed, what becomes of our splendid isolation, with Hitler on the Atlantic side and Japan and Russia on the Pacific side?"

Until that time, the Great Depression provided a new and for a time persuasive rationale for the isolationist position. Confronted by urgent domestic problems, the immediate impulse of the United States was to turn inward and to regard events outside its borders as distractions tending to impede the solution of problems at home. Even President Franklin D. Roosevelt, who, as a disciple of Woodrow Wilson was anything but an isolationist, spurned international cooperation to alleviate the crisis in favor of unilateral American action and, in effect, torpedoed the London Economic Conference in 1933.

The depression also deflated confidence in the strength of the United States and in its ability to influence events elsewhere. Faced with evidence that much was wrong at home, many Americans abandoned the traditional belief that their institutions should serve as a model for the rest of the world. Others reasoned that the economic crisis had so sapped the nation's strength that it would be futile to intervene in international affairs. Both lines of thought led to essentially isolationist conclusions. Finally, the depression increased popular distrust of bankers and businessmen and thus the willingness to sacrifice even trade and commerce, if necessary, to maintain political and military noninvolvement. Because the reputation of the American businessman reached its nadir in the 1930s, the attempt was made to resolve the increasingly apparent dichotomy between "commerce and honest friendship with all nations" and "entangling alliances with none" not by increasing American political involvement but by circumscribing the then suspect commercial contacts.

The high-water mark of American isolationism was therefore reached in the years from 1934 to 1937, in the depth of the Great Depression. Beginning with the Johnson Act, which in 1934 prohibited loans to countries in default on previous debts—only Finland could qualify for a loan under that provision—Congress took a series of actions designed to prohibit activities of the sort that were presumed to have involved the United States in World War I. The Senate established a committee headed by the isolationist Gerald P. Nye of North Dakota to investigate the American munitions industry and its ties to European arms makers. In 1935, 1936, and 1937, by means of so-called neutrality acts, the United States banned loans and the export of arms and ammunition to countries at war, prohibited Americans from traveling on belligerent vessels, forbade the arming of American merchant ships trading with countries at war, and prohibited the sale on credit of war materials other than arms and ammunitions as well as transportation of such materials on U.S. vessels. A substantial majority of the members of Congress believed that such measures could insulate the country against increasingly threatening world events.

The rationale behind these acts provides us with the clearest expression of isolationist assumptions. Their purpose was simply to make possible in the twentieth century the stance first adopted by the United States in 1794. Although the recognition that legislation was necessary to achieve this implied an acknowledgment that the world had changed since the eighteenth century, it also suggested that the United States might accommodate itself to these changes and maintain its traditional position of neutrality by simply taking certain relatively minor precautions. This assumption required a continuing belief that the vital interests of the United States were not substantially affected by events elsewhere; that Europe still had a set of interests "which to us have none or a very remote relation"; and that the country had become involved in other international quarrels, particularly in World War I, for reasons having little to do with genuine national interest.

The last of these beliefs was given powerful support not only by the conclusions of the Nye Committee that the greed of America's "merchants of death" had led the nation into war in 1917, but also by the work of so-called revisionist historians who, at least since the appearance of Harry Elmer Barnes's *The Genesis of the World War* (1926), had been hammering away at the theme that the entry of the United States into the world war had been brought about, contrary to the true interests of the United States, by direct and indirect Allied pressure and by the machinations of bankers, brokers, and businessmen who had unwisely tied American prosperity to the cause of Great Britain and France. In the mid-1930s, Charles A. Beard and Charles C. Tansill were the most prominent of the historians who repeated this theme and alleged the existence of a "deadly parallel" to the situation twenty years before. Walter Millis repeated these arguments in his best-selling *Road to War* (1935).

The neutrality legislation of the 1930s clearly reflected the isolationist contention that the United States went to war in 1917, and might do so again, not because its interests were threatened, but merely because its activities, particularly those relating to trade, produced incidents that blurred judgment and inflamed passions. By prohibiting loans and the trade in arms, by keeping Americans off belligerent vessels, and by insisting that title to all war material had passed to the purchaser and that such material be carried only in non-American ships, the United States expected to avoid such incidents and thereby involvement in war.

ISOLATIONISM IN RETREAT

The isolationist's beliefs, however, no longer reflected the realities of the world situation. The United States had acquired a far greater stake in the international power balance and exerted far more influence on it than the isolationists were prepared to admit. Neutrality legislation did not reduce this influence but simply redirected it, not necessarily into desirable channels.

In general, the American policy gave aid and comfort to would-be aggressors since it offered tacit assurance that this country would not actively oppose their actions as long as they did not directly threaten the United States. More specifically, the neutrality legislation in effect aided the Fascist dictators—Italy's Benito Mussolini when applied to the Italo-Ethiopian War and Spain's Francisco Franco when applied to the Spanish Civil War. The legislation also tended, at least in the first of these cases, to undercut possible peacekeeping actions by the League of Nations.

Since even most isolationists agreed that the victories of the Italian and Spanish fascists were less desirable from the American viewpoint than were other possible outcomes, the wisdom of a policy that contributed to such a result came increasingly to be questioned. "In the long run," the Socialist Party leader Norman Thomas, a staunch isolationist and an original proponent of neutrality legislation, told President Roosevelt in December 1936, "it is not peace for the world, even for America which will be served by applying to the Spanish rebellion a general principle which should be asserted more rigorously than is yet the case in Congressional legislation concerning neutrality in international law." As a socialist who supported the elected government of Spain and abhorred Franco, Thomas was caught in a dilemma that could not be resolved in isolationist terms.

The two events that destroyed the rationale for American isolationism altogether were the fall of France in June 1940 and the attack on Pearl Harbor in December of the following year. The defeat of France by a seemingly invincible Germany created a profound sense of insecurity in the United States. It raised fears not only of an Axis victory but also of a direct attack on this country in the event, now deemed possible, that the British fleet would either be destroyed or captured. The founding of the Committee to Defend America by Aiding the Allies, the first influential interventionist organization, was a direct result of this fear, and the success of that organization produced the establishment of the America First Committee, the last stronghold of the embattled and soon outnumbered isolationists.

The attack on Pearl Harbor, in its turn, graphically demonstrated the vulnerability of American territory to foreign aggressors. Under these circumstances cooperation and even alliance with others to forestall further danger seemed dictated by prudence and common sense. "In my own mind," one of the most outspoken and influential of the congressional isolationists, Senator Arthur H. Vandenberg of Michigan, confided in his diary some time after the event, "my convictions regarding international cooperation and collective security for peace took firm form on the afternoon of the Pearl Harbor attack. That day ended isolationism for any realist."

THE END OF AMERICA'S ISOLATIONISM

Vandenberg was essentially right. Both the traditional American foreign policy, based on the precepts of Washington and Jefferson, and isolationism, regarded by its proponents as an adaptation of that policy to the conditions of the twentieth century, had rested on the assumption that Europe's interests were sufficiently different from those of the United States and that the United States was sufficiently safe from attack to make political or military involvement with Europe unnecessary. If unnecessary, such involvement was undesirable by definition, since it could only limit the country's freedom of action and thereby its sovereignty without bringing any compensating benefits. Although these assumptions had been challenged by world events since the end of the nineteenth century, they had never before been clearly disproved. When the assumptions were disproved, the isolationist structure was no longer a viable one, and the United States moved rapidly not only into tacit alliance with Great Britain and into war as a formal ally of the anti-Axis powers but also very consciously into a commitment to collective security.

Even before World War II had ended, the world economy and the political structure of the new league of nations, the United Nations, would be laid out under American leadership at international conferences at the Bretton Woods resort in New Hampshire and the Dumbarton Oaks estate in Washington, D.C. The United States not only joined the United Nations without serious opposition, but also symbolized its change of course by welcoming that organization's headquarters to New York City.

What had been destroyed, of course, had only been the practicality of the isolationist position. Its emotional appeal remained largely intact, as it had in nations for whom isolationism had never been a realistic position. Isolationist rhetoric, therefore, continued to be used by some opponents of American postwar policies. In the debate over military aid to Europe, which began late in 1950, Joseph P. Kennedy, the isolationist former ambassador to Great Britain, spoke of "unwise commitments" in Berlin and Korea and scoffed at the idea that the United States had any interest in or responsibility for the defense of Western Europe. Herbert Hoover argued that the Americas were still "surrounded by a great moat," and referred once again to "the eternal malign forces of Europe" with which this country should have as little as possible to do. Senator Robert A. Taft of Ohio, a leading prewar isolationist, minimized the danger that this country faced from the Soviet Union in terms virtually identical to those in which he had discussed the threat emanating from Nazi Germany.

Although some observers promptly labeled this outburst "the new isolationism," it bore little practical relation to true isolationism. Hoover, in fact, strongly favored an American commitment to the defense of a "Western Hemisphere Gibraltar," the outlying bastions of which were the British Isles, Japan, Taiwan, the Philippines, and, possibly, Australia and New Zealand. Taft recognized that an effective international organization would give the best assurance of world peace and, therefore, of American peace, and stated flatly that "nobody is an isolationist today." The whole discussion centered largely on the extent of American military and economic aid to other nations, and not on the necessity for such assistance. It turned on the question of how the cooperation among allies of the United States might best be secured, not how American alliances could be terminated most rapidly.

Isolationism was simply no longer viable in a world in which neutrality for the United States was impossible, if for no other reason than that the Soviet Union regarded the United States as its primary foe; in which the United States could clearly not be indifferent to wars in Europe or Asia that affected the world power balance; and in which the development of nuclear weapons and intercontinental missiles had eliminated the margin of safety that geography had once provided. In short, isolationism was made practically impossible when the United States emerged as the dominant world power in an unstable world. Just as "splendid isolation" had emotional appeal but dangerous practical implications for Great Britain at the close of the nineteenth century, so isolation in any form posed a threat to the position of the United States in the postwar world.

For a brief period, even the traces of the isolationist strain in American foreign policy seemed to disappear. The United States embraced its world leadership role at a time when it was, by a considerable margin, the strongest power on earth. It thus could expect to control whatever alliances it entered and saw no necessary conflict between such alliances and the traditional insistence on unilateral action. The refusal of the Soviet Union to recognize a Pax Americana did not shatter that expectation, but initially strengthened the belief that America's security required cooperation with and commitments to likeminded nations. In the Cold War that resulted, the United States laid claim, without having to consult anyone, to the leadership of what it chose to define as the free world. That leadership produced the Marshall Plan, a massive program to rebuild war-devastated Western Europe, in 1948 and, in 1949, the North Atlantic Treaty Organization, a permanent formal, military alliance—its first in 171 years—with Canada and a group of ten Western European nations. It was manifested again the following year, when the United States was able to use the UN to muster an international force to serve under American command in Korea. A powerful United States controlling its allies fully met the test of unilateralism.

ISOLATIONISM RECONFIGURED?

Over time, however, American control of the UN and of its allies declined even as its worldwide commitments multiplied. As a result, U.S. foreign policy became both less effective and more costly, and domestic criticism of it increased. The Vietnam War, in particular, spawned critics who argued that there were limits to America's power and that, in consequence, the United States should withdraw from some of its more exposed positions and reduce its international commitments. These critics were often referred to as "neo-isolationists" and sometimes even applied that label to themselves. A leading scholar of American foreign policy, Robert W. Tucker, applauded their position in his book *A New Isolationism: Threat or Promise?* (New York, 1972).

Yet major spokesmen for this point of view, such as Senators Wayne Morse of Oregon, Ernest Gruening of Alaska, J. William Fulbright of Arkansas, George McGovern of South Dakota, and Eugene McCarthy of Minnesota, or George F. Kennan, who as a foreign service officer had been the first to advocate "containment" of the Soviet Union, were not isolationists in any meaningful sense. All favored increasing the role of the United Nations, the maintenance of key alliances, and new attempts to reach agreements with the Soviet Union and the People's Republic of China. None suggested, even remotely, that the cure for current problems might be found in a return to the foreign policies of the 1920s or 1930s.

The Vietnam War, to be sure, had a traumatic effect on both American policymakers and the American public. It caused President Lyndon Johnson to withdraw as a candidate for reelection, assured the defeat of his vice-president, Hubert Humphrey, in the 1968 election, and produced major reassessments of American military and strategic policies. But the lessons that were drawn from the failure in Vietnam did not seriously question America's international commitments. They concentrated instead on the clearer and perhaps more limited definition of American goals, the avoidance, where possible, of no-win situations, and, above all, the avoidance of American casualties in future conflicts.

The internationalist consensus thus remained largely intact, and all subsequent presidents vigorously exercised their presumed prerogative of world leadership. Richard Nixon traveled to China in 1972 to definitively change that nation's relationship to the Soviet Union as well as to the United States. President Jimmy Carter tried policies based on the ideas of the Trilateral Commission, a private group of American, Western European, and Japanese businessmen, and in 1979 negotiated a peace treaty between Egypt and Israel at Camp David in Maryland.

Ronald Reagan outdid even Woodrow Wilson in what Frank Ninkovich has defined as crisis internationalism (*The Wilsonian Century,* Chicago and London, 1999). "Our mission is to nourish and defend freedom and democracy" runs the so-called Reagan Doctrine he enunciated in his State of the Union message in 1985. "We must stand by all of our democratic allies. And we must not break faith with those who are risking their lives—on every continent . . .—to defy Soviet-supported aggression." Reagan's successor, George H. W. Bush, launched the Gulf War against Iraq in 1991 and brought a number of European and Middle Eastern allies into it. President Clinton, throughout the 1990s, played a direct role in conflicts throughout the world, from Ireland to Israel to Yugoslavia and even beyond.

Throughout these years, isolationism has, to be sure, remained in the area of public discourse. But it has remained there largely as a bogeyman. All presidents since Nixon have defended their policies by labeling their opponents isolationists, and they continue to do so. On 8 December 2000, President Clinton traveled to Kearney, Nebraska, for a foreign policy speech in which he warned his listeners against "isolationist sentiment," and at his confirmation hearing on 17 January 2001, incoming Secretary of State Colin L. Powell found it necessary to assure the Senate that under his guidance the United States would not become "an island of isolationism."

Political commentators continued to treat such allegations with great seriousness. The American Enterprise Institute as recently as 1996 found good cause to publish Joshua Muravchik's *The Imperative of American Leadership: A Challenge to Neo-Isolationism,* and publications on both sides of the question abound. Yet isolationism is no longer a serious prescription for American policy. With the possible exceptions of the pseudo-populist industrialist Ross Perot, an independent candidate for president in 1992, and Patrick Buchanan, a disgruntled Republican who ran on the Reform Party ticket in 2000, no responsible leader has proposed withdrawal from NATO or the UN or urged the United States to go it alone in a world still considered dangerous, even after the end of the Cold War and the relative triumph of both democracy and free-market capitalism. Ironically, even Buchanan's *A Republic Not An Empire* (Washington, D.C., 1999) contains a section entitled "The Myth of American Isolationism."

The persistence of isolationism as a talking point half a century after its effective demise led some scholars, particularly in the field of security policy, to redefine the term, sometimes in quite sophisticated ways. Eric Nordlinger's *Isolationism Reconfigured* (Princeton, N.J., 1995), for example, sees isolationism essentially as the unilateralist component of the traditional American foreign policy that is wary of entangling alliances and, therefore, as a permanent counterweight to the traditional policy's internationalist component that has carried the day since World War II. In somewhat similar fashion, Frank Ninkovich has defined isolationism as the "normal internationalism" he attributes to the Founders. The Wilsonian counterpart to that which has dominated U.S. foreign policy for the past half century he calls "crisis internationalism."

Either redefinition does away with the need to explain isolationism or to account for its appearance, especially in the 1920s. For that reason, both lend themselves to the development of ingenious and highly persuasive analyses with substantial postmodernist appeal. They do so, however, by dealing scarcely, if at all, with the objective reality of that isolationism that was an important phase in the development of American foreign policy. That phase has now been superseded, and reentry into it seems no longer possible, even if a nostalgic longing for it survives.

Born of the universal aspiration for unrestricted national sovereignty and the peculiar relation of the United States to the rest of the world in the nineteenth century, isolationism was staunchly defended and raised to the level of dogma when world events in the twentieth century threatened America's traditional foreign policy consensus. In a shrinking world with an increasingly global economy and ever more deadly weapons that can be delivered anywhere, however, it is an untenable position for a country that has gone to great expense to develop and maintain a fully global military reach, dominates virtually every international institution or agency to which it belongs, and labors ceaselessly to remain the center of global finance and of world trade.

BIBLIOGRAPHY

Adler, Selig. *The Isolationist Impulse: Its Twentieth Century Reaction.* London and New York,

1957. The classic early work that regards economic self-sufficiency and the illusion of security, as well as some ethnic prejudices, as the causes of isolationism.

Clemens, Diane Shaver. *From Isolationism to Internationalism: The Case Study of American Occupation Planning for Post-War Germany, 1945–1946.* An exceptionally detailed examination of the definitive turning point.

Cole, Wayne S. *America First: The Battle Against Intervention, 1940–1941.* Madison, Wis., 1953. Still the only full-scale study of an isolationist organization.

———. *Roosevelt and the Isolationists, 1935–1945.* Lincoln, Neb., 1983. The isolationists' heyday and how they were outflanked by FDR.

Cooper, John Milton, Jr. *The Vanity of Power: American Isolationism and the First World War, 1914–1917.* Westport, Conn., 1969. Defines isolationism as a political position with ideological dimensions.

Doenecke, Justus D. *Not to the Swift: The Old Isolationists and the Cold War.* Lewisburg, Pa., 1979. Traces the varied responses of the old isolationist to the new world created by World War II.

———. *Storm on the Horizon: The Challenge to American Intervention, 1939–1941.* Lanham, Md., and Oxford, 2000. The most complete analysis of anti-interventionist assumptions and arguments prior to Pearl Harbor.

Fensterwald, Bernard, Jr. "The Anatomy of American 'Isolationism' and Expansionism." *Journal of Conflict Resolution* 2 (1958). An interesting though unprovable psychological explanation for the persistence of American isolationism.

Foster, H. Schuyler. *Activism Replaces Isolationism: U.S. Public Attitudes, 1840–1975.* Washington, D.C., 1983. The public opinion studies conducted by the State Department.

Graebner, Norman A. *The New Isolationism: A Study in Politics and Foreign Policy Since 1950.* New York, 1956. A "realist" view of America's postwar role.

Guinsburg, Thomas N. *The Pursuit of Isolationism in the United States from Versailles to Pearl Harbor.* New York, 1982. A full-scale study of the most clearly isolationist period in U.S. history.

Jonas, Manfred. *Isolationism in America, 1935–1941.* Ithaca, N.Y., 1966, and Chicago, 1990. Analyzes the arguments and actions of the isolationists up to Pearl Harbor and concludes that their common denominator was unilateralism strengthened by the fear of war.

Kull, Steven. *Misreading the Public: The Myth of a New Isolationism.* Washington, D.C., 1999. Defends those looking to limit America's commitments against the charge of isolationism.

McDougall, Walter A. *Promised Land, Crusader State.* Boston, 1997. Divides U.S. diplomatic history into "Old Testament" and "New Testament" phases and argues that foreign policy debates revolve around the differences between the two.

Muravchik, Joshua. *The Imperative of American Leadership: A Challenge to Neo-Isolationism.* Washington, D.C., 1996. Argues that the United States must remain the fully committed leader of the free world.

Ninkovich, Frank. *The Wilsonian Century: U.S. Foreign Policy Since 1900.* Chicago and London, 1999. A brief analytical survey that does away with isolationism by defining American policy as a tug of war between the "normal" internationalism of the Founders and the "crisis" internationalism of Woodrow Wilson.

Nordlinger, Eric A. *Isolationism Reconfigured: American Foreign Policy for a New Century.* Princeton, N.J., 1995. Argues that isolationism is simply the unilateralist component of the traditional and relatively constant American foreign policy.

Osgood, Robert E. *Ideals and Self-Interest in American Foreign Relations: The Great Transformation of the Twentieth Century.* Chicago, 1953. A classic.

Powaski, Ronald E. *Toward an Entangling Alliance: American Isolationism, Internationalism and Europe, 1901–1950.* New York, 1991. A straightforward account of how the "isolated" United States came in time to create the North Atlantic Treaty.

Rieselbach, Leroy N. *The Roots of Isolationism: Congressional Voting and Presidential Leadership in Foreign Policy.* Indianapolis, 1966. The most ambitious behavioral analysis of congressional isolationism.

Rossina, Daniela, ed. *From Theodore Roosevelt to FDR: Internationalism and Isolationism in American Foreign Policy.* Staffordshire, England, 1995. A collection of essays most of which offer a European view of the United States.

Russett, Bruce M. "Demography, Salience, and Isolationist Behavior." *Public Opinion Quarterly* 24 (1960). Offers the most serious challenge to ethnic and geographical explanations for isolationism.

Smith, Glenn H. *Langer of North Dakota: A Study in Isolationism, 1940–1959.* New York, 1979. One of the few biographies of a leading isolationist senator.

Tucker, Robert W. *A New Isolationism: Threat or Promise?* New York, 1972.

Weinberg, Albert K. "The Historical Meaning of the American Doctrine of Isolationism." *American Political Science Review* 34 (1940). The classic brief statement of what traditional American foreign policy was and what it was not.

Williams, William A. "The Legend of Isolationism in the 1920s." *Science and Society* 18 (1954). Argues that the absence of genuine economic isolationism demonstrates the mythical nature of the entire concept.

See also ALLIANCES, COALITIONS, AND ENTENTES; INTERNATIONALISM; INTERVENTION AND NONINTERVENTION; NEUTRALITY; WILSONIANISM.

Judiciary Power and Practice

Terrence R. Guay

The words "foreign policy" and "foreign affairs" do not appear in the U.S. Constitution, and there is nothing in the document to suggest that the three branches of government should treat this policy area any differently than others. Yet with a few notable exceptions, the judiciary branch has played a limited role in foreign policy. The courts have preferred to refrain from influencing foreign policy, often regarding disputes between the executive and legislative branches in this area to be political, rather than legal, questions. Indeed, Article 3, Section 2 states that "judicial Power shall extend to all Cases, in Law and Equity, arising under this Constitution, the Laws of the United States, and Treaties made, or which shall be made, under their Authority." This judicial deference is controversial, particularly among those who feel that foreign policy has no special claim to be treated differently than other policy areas.

JUDICIAL REVIEW AND POLITICAL QUESTIONS

The judiciary's traditional refusal to be drawn into foreign policy matters has its origins in the Constitution, which established responsibility for exercising foreign policy with the executive and the legislature. The president as commander in chief is responsible for conducting war, but Congress is empowered to declare war and raise and maintain military forces. The president may negotiate treaties, but the Senate must ratify them. Congress appropriates funds for the president to use for international diplomacy. While Article 3, Section 2 of the Constitution extends judicial power to cases related to treaties, ambassadors, and the admiralty, and to controversies to which the United States is a party, there is no explicit constitutional role or responsibility for the judiciary in foreign affairs.

The lack of an enumerated constitutional power for the judiciary has not kept foreign policy questions out of the courts. The case of *Marbury v. Madison* (1803) established the Supreme Court's power of judicial review. This power has come to mean that the Court can determine whether legislative and executive branch actions are permitted within the powers outlined for these branches in the Constitution. Although the case details of *Marbury* were clearly domestic in nature, judicial review is applicable to all policy areas, including foreign policy.

Despite this power, the Supreme Court has often refused to review cases related to foreign affairs on the grounds that they are "political questions," which are solvable only by the political branches of government, Congress and the president. The Court first adopted this stance in *Foster & Elam v. Neilson* (1829), which involved an international dispute over title to part of the Louisiana Territory. In those cases it has heard, the Court generally has upheld exercise of the power in question—a power usually delegated by Congress to the president during a foreign affairs crisis.

Judicial abstention in questions involving foreign affairs is controversial. On the one hand, the Constitution provides no expressed powers for the judiciary in foreign affairs. The general foreign affairs powers distributed to the legislative and executive branches are clearly enumerated, although the specifics are vague and contradictory. Given the emotional nature of war, the absence of tools for the judiciary to apply its own foreign policy preferences, and its reliance on the executive to carry out a decision, deference is the only responsible approach for the courts to take. On the other hand is the argument that deference on political questions is an abdication of the judiciary's constitutional responsibilities. Article 3, Section 2 seems to bestow responsibility on the judiciary to review all cases under the laws and treaties of the United States. There is no exclusion for foreign policy, and treaties certainly are elements of foreign affairs. There is little in the Constitution to suggest that the framers regarded foreign affairs as privileged and beyond the safeguards established by the separation of powers. Yet at various times the Court has ruled the following to be political questions: matters of sovereignty of either the United States or another country; boundaries and territorial authority; the determination of U.S. neutrality; the existence of peace and war; the length of a military occupation; the recognition of the independence or belligerency of a foreign state or government; the acknowledgment of diplomatic immunity; the status of aliens; and the validity or breach of a treaty. The doctrine of political questions, then, must be seen as a product of judicial self-restraint.

The other side of the self-restraint coin is a willingness to let stand legislation that increases the authority of the other two branches, especially the executive, to shape foreign affairs. The courts often have used the "necessary and proper" clause of the Constitution (Article 1, Section 8) to permit congressional actions. Sometimes known as the "elastic clause," the necessary and proper clause has been interpreted broadly by the courts, beginning with *McCulloch v. Maryland* (1819), to give considerable discretion to the ways that the federal government, and in particular Congress, utilizes its expressed powers. In *Missouri v. Holland* (1920), the Supreme Court ruled that the necessary and proper clause could justify the supremacy of international treaties. Upset that lower courts had ruled a congressional act to protect migratory birds from hunters unconstitutional as a violation of state sovereignty, the federal government negotiated a treaty with Canada to protect the birds. Following Senate ratification of the treaty, Congress passed another law prohibiting hunting of the birds, using compliance with the U.S.–Canada treaty as its justification. In affirming the constitutionality of the second law under the necessary and proper clause, the Court opened itself to the criticism that the excuse to implement legislation to comply with international treaties circumvented constitutional restrictions on federal government power, thereby expanding federal authority.

Judicial deference is controversial on other grounds. In *Harisiades v. Shaughnessy* (1952), the Supreme Court heard an appeal brought by an alien being deported because of his membership in the Communist Party earlier in his life. The opinion of the Court was that policy toward aliens is a component of foreign relations, and that such matters "are so exclusively entrusted to the political branches of government as to be largely immune from judicial inquiry or interference." The decision was contentious because it did not appear that the Court had considered how restraint in reviewing political questions related to national security and foreign policy conflicts with other constitutional values and civil liberties.

Another justification for deference is that courts are not equipped with the expertise to rule on complicated foreign policy issues or treaties based on international law. It may be more expedient for domestic judges to rely upon the views of the executive branch. However, even in foreign policy cases, attorneys provide the necessary information in their roles as advocates. While deference may be the norm in cases with a foreign policy dimension, the judiciary has weighed in with important opinions at critical times in the country's history. Many of these moments occurred while the country was at war.

WAR AND THE COURTS

While it is generally accepted that the Constitution grants war powers to the federal government, and the courts have never seriously questioned this, the source and division of war powers has been much disputed. Reasons for judicial acceptance of federal war powers include: that the power to declare war carries with it the power to conduct war (*McCulloch v. Maryland*); that the power to wage war derives from a country's sovereignty and is not dependent on the enumerated powers of the Constitution (*United States v. Curtiss-Wright Export Corporations*, 1936); and that the power to wage war comes from the expressed powers as well as the necessary and proper clause. With such acceptance of the federal government's central role in war (and foreign policy generally), the Supreme Court has been reluctant to place any limits on the powers Congress or the president devise to conduct it. The courts have declared some statutes created during wartime unconstitutional, but in nearly every case it has been done on grounds that the law abused a power other than war power, and the decision has been rendered only after combat has ceased.

It is perhaps surprising that Congress has declared war on only five occasions: the War of 1812; the Mexican War; the Spanish-American War, World War I, and World War II. When U.S.

> ★★★★
>
> ## UNITED STATES V. CURTISS-WRIGHT EXPORT CORPORATION
>
> The majority opinion in this Supreme Court case, 299 U.S. 304 (1936), upheld an embargo on arms destined for Paraguay and Bolivia, two nations at war. Justice George Sutherland's majority opinion included the following statements:
>
>> It will contribute to the elucidation of the question if we first consider the differences between the powers of the federal government in respect of foreign or external affairs and those in respect of domestic or internal affairs. That there are differences between them, and that these differences are fundamental, may not be doubted. The two classes of powers are different, both in respect of their origin and their nature. The broad statement that the federal government can exercise no powers except those specifically enumerated in the Constitution, and such implied powers as are necessary and proper to carry into effect the enumerated powers, is categorically true only in respect of our internal affairs. . . .
>>
>> It results that the investment of the federal government with the powers of external sovereignty did not depend upon the affirmative grants of the Constitution. The powers to declare and wage war, to conclude peace, to make treaties, to maintain diplomatic relations with other sovereignties, if they had never been mentioned in the Constitution, would have vested in the federal government as necessary concomitants of nationality. . . .
>>
>> Not only, as we have shown, is the federal power over external affairs in origin and essential character different from that over internal affairs, but participation in the exercise of the power is significantly limited. In this vast external realm, with its important, complicated, delicate and manifold problems, the President alone has the power to speak or listen as a representative of the nation. . . .
>>
>> It is important to bear in mind that we are here dealing not alone with an authority vested in the President by an exertion of legislative power, but with such an authority plus the very delicate, plenary and exclusive power of the President as the sole organ of the federal government in the field of international relations.

involvement in other international conflicts was challenged in the courts, the judiciary has ruled that declaration is not required. For example, in *Bas* v. *Tingy* (1800), the Supreme Court held that Congress need not declare full-scale war and could engage in a limited naval conflict with France. During the latter half of the twentieth century the United States engaged in numerous military conflicts without declaring war, the most controversial being the Vietnam War. Lower courts ruled that the absence of a formal declaration of war in Vietnam raised political questions not resolvable in the courts. The Supreme Court refused all appeals to review the lower court rulings, although not all its denials were unanimously agreed (for example, *Mora* v. *McNamara*, 1967).

The courts have also rebuffed state challenges to federal government war-related actions. In 1990 the Supreme Court upheld a law in which Congress eliminated the requirement that governors consent before their states' National Guard units are called up for deployment (*Perpich* v. *Department of Defense*, 1990). Specifically, Minnesota objected to National Guard units being sent to Honduras for joint exercises with that country's military. The issue was between states' control over the National Guard under the Constitution's militia clauses and congressional authority to provide trained forces. The unanimous decision in *Perpich* further strengthened the power of the federal government in military affairs.

While there has been little disagreement on the federal government's authority to go to war, the appropriate roles of Congress and the president have sparked considerable debate. Article 2, Section 2 of the Constitution begins: "The President shall be Commander in Chief of the Army and Navy of the United States, and of the Militia of the several States, when called into the actual Service of the United States." This sentence has been the source of controversy between the three branches of government. Of particular concern are the circumstances under which the president can authorize the use of force abroad and how and whether Congress should be involved in making such decisions. The role of the judiciary in such matters seems crucial, but the courts have been unwilling participants in these debates.

While such abandonment of judicial review is questionable, there are a series of historical precedents to support the courts' approach. In 1795, Congress authorized the president to call out the militia of any state to quell resistance to the law. The Court sanctioned the president's discretion to determine when an emergency existed and subsequent calling of state militia. Several New England states challenged that law during the War of 1812, but the Supreme Court upheld the delegation of congressional authority as a limited power in *Martin* v. *Mott* (1827). In subsequent decades the Court and Congress regarded the president's war power as primarily military in nature. The Supreme Court has never opposed the president's authority as commander in chief to deploy forces abroad. However, during most of the nineteenth century Congress provided the initiative in foreign policy. When presidents in peacetime sought expansionist policies that threatened war, Congress stopped them.

Supreme Court decisions during the Civil War played a central role in shaping the courts' approach to war powers. Congress was in recess when hostilities broke out, so President Abraham Lincoln declared a blockade of Confederate ports, issued a proclamation increasing the size of the army and navy, ordered new naval ships, and requested funds from the Treasury to cover military expenditures. When Congress returned it adopted a resolution that approved the president's actions. However, owners of vessels seized during the blockade and sold as prizes brought suit, arguing that no war had been declared between the North and the South. The Supreme Court ruled in the *Prize Cases* (1863) that President Lincoln's actions in the early weeks of the war were constitutional, because the threat to the nation justified the broadest range of authority in the commander in chief.

Despite a narrow 5–4 ruling, the *Prize Cases* bolstered the powers of the presidency and shaped the tendency of the judiciary to abstain from rulings that would curb war powers. The Supreme Court's decisions, which interpreted broadly the powers of the president as commander in chief, marked the beginning of expansionary presidential actions during war. The national emergency of civil war required that the executive be able to exercise powers that might not be permitted during peacetime. Thus, Lincoln's decisions to declare the existence of a rebellion, call out state militia to suppress it, blockade southern ports, increase the size of the army and navy, and spend federal money on the war effort were not rebuked by the courts. Even the Emancipation Proclamation was issued under Lincoln's authority as commander in chief. Only Lincoln's suspension of habeas corpus in certain parts of the country earned a censure from the Supreme Court.

The world wars of the twentieth century provided opportunities for Presidents Woodrow Wilson and Franklin Roosevelt to push the constitutional envelope. As the United States entered World War I in 1917, President Wilson sought and obtained from Congress broad delegations of power to prepare for war and to mobilize the country. He used these powers to manage the country's economy, creating war management and production boards (coordinated by the Council of National Defense) to coordinate production and supply. His actions included taking over mines and factories, fixing prices, taking over the transportation and communications networks, and managing the production and distribution of food. Because the president had obtained prior congressional approval for these actions, there were no legal challenges to Wilson's authority during the war.

In a novel interpretation of the economic turmoil of the 1930s, President Roosevelt equated the challenge of the Great Depression to war. He sought wide executive-branch powers to address the economic crisis, but the Supreme Court was reluctant to sanction such authority during peacetime. However, once the United States entered World War II, Roosevelt was on more solid footing. Congress again delegated vast federal powers to the president to help win the war, and Roosevelt created many new administrative agencies to aid in the effort. There were very few objections on constitutional grounds, largely because the three branches assumed that the use of war powers by Lincoln and Wilson applied to the current conflict. The Supreme Court never upheld challenges to the authority of wartime agencies or to the authority of the 101 government corporations created by Roosevelt to engage in production, insurance, transportation, banking, housing, and other lines of business designed to aid the war effort. The Court also upheld the power of the president to apply sanctions to individuals, labor unions, and industries that refused to comply with wartime guidelines. Even the case of the removal and relocation of Japanese Americans was considered by the Supreme Court, which ruled that, because Congress had ratified Roosevelt's executive order as an emergency war measure, this joint action was permitted.

The assertion of broad emergency powers by Presidents Wilson and Roosevelt obfuscated the constitutional separation between Congress's authority to declare war and the president's power to wage it. As long as Congress delegated authority to the president and appropriated funds (through its "power of the purse") to support such powers, the judiciary would interpret this as congressional sanction of the president's decision. The courts would not challenge this "fusion" of the two branches' warmaking powers.

The onset of the Cold War did not result in a curb in executive war powers. In 1950, President Harry Truman decided to commit U.S. forces to help South Korea without a declaration of war from Congress. He based the authority for his actions on the United Nations Security Council vote to condemn North Korea's invasion and urge member countries to assist South Korea. However, the Supreme Court ruled that President Truman went too far when he ordered the secretary of commerce to seize and operate most of the country's steel mills to prevent a nationwide strike of steelworkers. The president justified his actions by arguing that the strike would interrupt military production and cripple the war effort in Korea and by claiming authority as commander in chief. In *Youngstown Sheet and Tube Company* v. *Sawyer* (1952), also known as the Steel Seizure Case, the Court agreed that the president had overstepped constitutional bounds, but it did not rule out the possibility that such seizures might be legal if done with the consent of Congress. Nonetheless, the Steel Seizure Case is significant as the strongest rebuke by the Court of unilateral presidential national security authority. The country was at war when Truman acted, and Congress had not expressly denied him the authority to act. It was extraordinary for the Court to find that the president lacked authority under those circumstances.

Thus, the Cold War environment did little to curb the gradual expansion of presidential authority during war. In 1955, Congress authorized President Dwight D. Eisenhower to use force if necessary to defend Taiwan if China attacked the island. In 1962, President John F. Kennedy obtained a joint congressional resolution authorizing him to use force if necessary to prevent the spread of communism in the Western Hemisphere. Two years later, Congress passed the Gulf of Tonkin Resolution, which empowered President Lyndon B. Johnson to take all necessary steps, including the use of armed force, to assist in the defense of members of the Southeast Asia Collective Defense Treaty. President Johnson relied on this resolution to wage the war in Vietnam instead of asking Congress to declare war on North Vietnam. Federal courts were asked repeatedly during the late 1960s and early 1970s to rule on the constitutionality of the war. The Supreme Court declined to hear such cases on the view that war was a political question. Although opponents of the war contended that U.S. involvement was unconstitutional because Congress had never declared war, the legislative body continued to appropriate funds for defense, thus implying support for Johnson's, and then Richard Nixon's, policies in Southeast Asia.

THE WAR POWERS RESOLUTION

While the commander in chief role of the president has stirred little debate in those instances when the United States was attacked by another country, the president's authority to send forces into hostile situations abroad without a declaration of war or congressional authorization has generated much controversy. The tension reached a head during the latter years of the Vietnam War. Beginning in 1969, President Richard Nixon authorized secret bombing raids on neutral Cambodia without informing Congress. The following year he ordered U.S. forces on "search and destroy" missions in that country. In 1972 he directed the mining of North Vietnamese ports, which risked collisions with Russian and Chinese vessels, and one year later ordered the carpet-bombing of Hanoi. The president neither sought nor obtained explicit congressional approval for any of these policies, and he negotiated the 1973 Paris treaty ending the Vietnam War without congressional participation. Nixon defended his actions by arguing that the constitutional distinction between Congress's war power and the president's commander in chief role had become blurred.

For Congress, this was the last straw. The perception that presidents had assumed more authority to commit forces than the Constitution's framers had intended led Congress in 1973 to pass the War Powers Resolution (also known as the War Powers Act) over President Nixon's veto. The main purpose of the resolution was to assure that both the executive and legislative branches participate in decisions that might get the United States involved in war. Congress wanted to circumscribe the president's authority to use armed forces abroad without a declaration of war or other congressional authorization, yet provide enough flexibility to permit the president to respond to attack or other emergencies. Specifically, the War Powers Resolution requires the president to provide written notification to Congress of the introduction of U.S. armed forces into hostilities within forty-eight hours of such action. The president must explain the reasons forces were inserted in a hostile situation, the executive's authority for doing so, and the scope and duration of the military action. In addition, the president is required to terminate the use of military forces after sixty days unless Congress has declared war, extended the period by law, or cannot meet the sixty-day deadline as a result of an armed attack on the United States. The sixty days can be extended for thirty days by the president if the safety of armed forces would be jeopardized by immediate removal. The president is also required to remove forces at any time if Congress so demands by concurrent resolutions (known as a legislative veto). In essence, most members of Congress supported the notion that the president, as commander in chief, is empowered by the Constitution to lead U.S. forces once the decision to wage war is made or an attack on the United States has commenced. What Congress sought with the War Powers Resolution was participation in the decision to commit armed forces at the beginning of hostilities.

Predictably, Nixon and all subsequent presidents contended that the War Powers Resolution was unconstitutional. In virtually every commitment of U.S. troops since 1973, including the Iran hostage rescue attempt (1980), military exercises in Honduras (1983), the participation of U.S. marines in a multinational force in Lebanon (1982–1983), invasion of Grenada (1983), bombing of Libya (1986), invasion of Panama (1989), humanitarian mission to Somalia (1992–1994), and bombing of Kosovo (1999), members of Congress complained that the president had not fully complied with the War Powers Resolution.

Critics of the resolution argue that Congress has always held the power to forbid or terminate military action by statute or refusal of appropriations, and that without the clear will to act the resolution is ineffective. The sixty-day termination requirement is a major reason why presidents do not report force deployments to Congress, thereby undermining the objective of the resolution. The imposition of a deadline, some critics contend, would signal a divided country to the enemy, which might then seek to prolong the conflict to at least sixty days, thereby forcing the president to either seek a congressional declaration of war or withdraw U.S. forces. Alternatively, the resolution could be seen as a blank check to commit troops anywhere and for any purpose, subject only to the time limitations, thereby defeating the intended goal of restricting the president's war-making ability. A more fundamental problem is defining presidential consultation of Congress.

Does the War Powers Resolution require the president to seek congressional opinion prior to making a decision to commit armed forces, or simply to notify Congress after a decision to deploy troops has been made but before their actual introduction to the area of hostility? Such wide differences in interpretation of the War Powers Resolution would suggest a clear role for the judiciary.

Surprisingly, the courts have not ruled on the constitutionality of the War Powers Resolution. The first legal challenge to noncompliance with the resolution, *Crockett v. Reagan* (1982), was filed by eleven members of Congress who contended that President Ronald Reagan's decision to send military advisers to El Salvador must be reported to Congress. A district court ruled that Congress, not the court, must resolve the question of whether U.S. forces in El Salvador were involved in a hostile or potentially hostile situation. The Supreme Court declined consideration of a later appeal. In *Lowry v. Reagan* (1987), the courts refused to decide whether President Reagan had failed to comply with the War Powers Resolution when he dispatched naval forces to the Persian Gulf. A suit was brought by 110 members of Congress, arguing that sending forces close to the Iran-Iraq war zone required congressional approval. The district court held that it was a political dispute to be dismissed "as a prudential matter under the political question doctrine."

An important question in the post–Cold War world is whether the War Powers Resolution applies to U.S. participation in United Nations military actions. During the 1990s the United Nations sent multinational forces to trouble spots around the world, usually for peacekeeping and humanitarian purposes. However, after Iraq invaded Kuwait in August 1990, the United Nations contemplated and approved military force against Iraq. The United States took a leading role in this effort. Between August and December 1990, President George H. W. Bush deployed 350,000 troops to the Persian Gulf in response to Iraq's invasion of Kuwait. Although the president sent reports to Congress describing the buildup, he did not seek the legislative body's approval. Forty-five Democratic members of Congress sought a judicial order enjoining the president from offensive military operations in connection with Operation Desert Shield unless he consulted with and obtained an authorization from Congress. However, a federal district court denied the injunction, holding that the controversy was not ripe for judicial resolution because a majority of Congress had not sought relief and the executive branch had not shown sufficient commitment to a definitive course of action (*Dellums v. Bush,* 1990). On the same day, another federal judge issued a decision in *Ange v. Bush* (1990), holding that the courts could not decide whether President Bush needed congressional permission to go to war because it was a political question.

Bush claimed that he did not need a congressional declaration of war to use military force against Iraq. However, to bolster political support for the commencement of hostilities with Iraq, and to obtain legislative legitimacy for the participation of U.S. troops in a multinational coalition, the president requested a congressional resolution supporting the implementation of the UN Security Council resolution authorizing member states to use "all necessary means" to restore peace to the region. The Senate (in a 52–47 vote) and House (302–131) passed the Authorization for Use of Military Force Against Iraq Resolution, stating that it was intended to constitute authorization within the meaning of the War Powers Resolution. Bush's action during the Gulf War was not unique. The deployment of U.S. troops to Somalia, the former Yugoslavia, and Haiti by Presidents Bush and William Jefferson Clinton did not fully comply with the War Powers Resolution either.

The main point here is that the courts have provided no guidance in how to interpret the War Powers Resolution, or in whether the resolution is constitutional at all. Only *Immigration and Naturalization Service v. Chadha* (1983), which ruled unconstitutional a one-house legislative veto, has implications for the legality of the concurrent resolutions section of the War Powers Resolution. This is because a concurrent resolution is adopted by both legislative chambers but is not presented to the president for signature or veto. The larger question of the appropriate amount of congressional participation in presidential decisions to commit U.S. troops abroad, a question that the War Powers Resolution tried to address, remained unanswered by the judiciary.

THE COURTS AND FOREIGN POLICY

While war can be viewed as a specific component of foreign relations, foreign relations in general suffer from the same constitutional ambiguities as war. In addition to the president's commander in chief powers, the Constitution grants the president the power to make treaties and to receive and appoint ambassadors. Together, these grants of power are the source of the president's authority to conduct foreign policy. The Constitution's framers did not want the president to be as powerful as European monarchs in international matters, so Congress was given a voice too. While the president is free to negotiate treaties, they must be ratified by two-thirds of the Senate. Congress's only other constitutional authorizations over foreign policy derive from the powers mentioned earlier: the power to declare war, raise a military, and appropriate funds.

The judiciary has provided little guidance in more clearly demarcating executive and legislative branch powers in foreign policy, often invoking the political question doctrine. The result is that Court rulings either supported the actions of the political branches or refused to judge them. *Baker v. Carr* (1962) is the principle case outlining the Supreme Court's position on political questions. Although *Baker v. Carr* concerned the malapportionment of election districts in Tennessee, the Court's comments on political questions apply to domestic and foreign policy issues. Writing for the majority, Justice William Brennan outlined the circumstances under which a case involved a political question and the obligation of federal courts to abstain from ruling. Among other instances, Justice Brennan opined that judicial abstention would be appropriate whenever a case raised foreign policy questions that "uniquely demand single-voiced statement of the Government's views." Despite this attempt at clarification, *Baker v. Carr* continued to confuse constitutional scholars and lower courts because the guidelines set forth by Justice Brennan did little to clarify the definition of political questions, the circumstances under which an issue is nonjusticiable, or the approach the courts should take when confronted by cases that appear political and nonjusticiable.

For several reasons, then—an explicit constitutional role for Congress confined to treaties, the exclusion of individual states from traditional foreign policy, and judicial deference to the political branches in such matters—the president and executive branch have been the principle beneficiaries of Court rulings in foreign policy matters. *United States v. Curtiss-Wright Export Corporation* (1936) was a landmark case that confirmed the president's lead role in foreign affairs. In this case, Congress approved a joint resolution authorizing President Roosevelt to embargo arms shipments to Paraguay and Bolivia, if doing so might contribute to ending the war. After Roosevelt declared an embargo in effect, *Curtiss-Wright* was subsequently convicted of selling weapons to Bolivia in violation of the embargo. The company challenged the constitutionality of the resolution, arguing that it was an improper delegation of congressional power to the president.

Given that the Court had already struck down major New Deal programs, there was some expectation that it would do the same with respect to arms embargoes. However, in his 7–1 majority opinion, Justice George Sutherland presented an original and controversial defense of presidential authority in foreign affairs. Sutherland argued that independence from Britain fused the thirteen original colonies into a sovereign nation. He also distinguished between internal (domestic policy) and external (foreign policy) powers of the federal government. Internal powers, he argued, lay with the individual states and are conferred upon the federal government by the Constitution. External powers, however, derive the sovereignty that all countries enjoy, and sovereignty was passed from Britain to the union of states upon independence. Since the powers of the United States to conduct its foreign relations do not derive from, nor are enumerated in, the Constitution, it is impossible to identify or infer them from constitutional language. As a result, the Court's view was that delegation of power to the president in foreign affairs was not to be judged by the same standards as delegation of power over domestic matters. Consequently, the "president alone has the power to speak as a representative of the nation."

Sutherland's opinion is open to criticism from several angles. If the federal government derives powers from sources other than the Constitution, neither the Constitution nor the courts provide guidance in the distribution of such powers between the branches. The implication that foreign affairs powers of the federal government are extra-constitutional goes beyond previous Court opinions that, less controversially, found foreign affairs powers to be vested in the federal government by the Constitution. Further, the notion that the federal government was to have major powers outside the Constitution is not insinuated in the document itself, the records of the Constitutional Convention, the *Federalist Papers,* or contemporary debates. Sutherland's opinion is grounded in sovereignty, but it is also possible to interpret the Declaration of Independence as creating thirteen sovereign states, and many did conduct their own foreign relations until the Articles of Confederation. Sutherland's reliance on political philosophy and international law, rather than constitutional interpretation, as a basis for foreign policy powers is also controversial. Finally, drawing a clear distinction between foreign and domestic policy is becoming increasingly difficult to do, and an approach that derives different sources of power for each is bound to generate legal challenges. Sutherland's position holds up best if one takes the view that the Constitution is a document whose principle objective is to distribute power between the states and federal government, and among the branches of the federal government. Despite the criticisms, *Curtiss-Wright* is a landmark case in the broadening of federal and, in particular, presidential authority in foreign affairs.

Presidents have found additional means to increase their foreign policy powers. One is to use executive agreements, since they do not require Senate ratification but have been held by the Court to have the same legal status as treaties (*United States* v. *Pink,* 1942). Executive agreements are of two forms: those authorized by Congress and those made on presidential initiative. Authorized executive agreements have provided authority for presidents to negotiate the lowering of tariff barriers and trade agreements. The Lend-Lease Act (1941) granted President Roosevelt the power to enter into executive agreements that would provide war material to "any country deemed vital to the defense of the United States." Numerous executive agreements have been negotiated regarding the stationing of U.S. military forces in other countries. Executive agreements made on presidential initiative have often been obtained during international conflict, including the ending of the Spanish-American War and the deployment of troops during China's Boxer Rebellion. The Supreme Court, in *United States* v. *Belmont* (1937), upheld Roosevelt's use of an executive agreement to formalize his decision to recognize the Soviet Union, noting that it had the effect of a treaty and overruled conflicting state laws. Roosevelt used executive agreements extensively in the years leading up to World War II and to negotiate agreements at the Cairo, Tehran, and Yalta conferences. President Lyndon Johnson made many secret agreements with Asian countries during the 1960s, and President Jimmy Carter used executive agreements that constituted the financial arrangement necessary to free American hostages in Iran. In *Dames & Moore v. Regan* (1981), the Supreme Court ruled that Presidents Carter and Reagan had acted consistently with emergency powers granted by statute to use executive agreements to suspend the financial claims of Americans against Iran, in return for the safe release of the hostages seized during the 1979 Iranian revolution.

While the treaty approval process is described in the Constitution and has raised few problems, the relationship between treaties, domestic laws, and the Constitution is less clear. One area of confusion was whether treaties were superior to national legislation. In *Foster & Elam v. Neilson* (1829), Chief Justice John Marshall distinguished between a self-executing treaty and a non-self-executing treaty. The former requires no legislation to put it into effect, while the latter does not take effect until implemented through legislation approved by the Congress and president. The superiority of a treaty or statute is determined by whichever is most recent. However, in the case of a non-self-executing treaty, congressional acts take precedence (Head Money Cases, 1884). In *Missouri v. Holland* (1920), the Court's ruling illustrated how treaties could increase the power of the federal government vis-à-vis the states. The Court upheld the national law protecting migratory birds on the grounds that it was necessary to carry the provisions of this non-self-executing treaty into effect.

The Court has also considered the termination of treaties. It has held that termination requires an act of Congress. If international obligations are violated as a result of the termination, the matter will need to be renegotiated with the international parties. However, the Court has also ruled that treaties may be terminated by agreement between the contracting parties, by treaty provisions, by congressional repeal, by the president, and by the president and Senate acting jointly. When President Carter decided to officially recognize the government of the People's Republic of China, he unilaterally terminated a mutual defense treaty between the United States and Taiwan. The Supreme Court refused to hear a case brought by Senator Barry Goldwater and nineteen other senators (*Goldwater v. Carter,* 1979) asking the Court to require the president to first obtain congressional authorization.

It is clear that, for two centuries, the courts have played an important role in resolving foreign policy disputes between the executive and legislative branches. But this is only one of the two principle divisions of power established by the Constitution. The other principle is dividing power between the states and federal government. Along this division, too, the courts have been required to resolve disputes over foreign policy powers.

FEDERALISM AND FOREIGN POLICY

It is widely believed that the Constitution's framers sought to place control of the new country's foreign relations in the hands of the federal government rather than the states. To ensure that the country spoke with one voice in international matters, the Constitution granted the federal courts power to hear all cases between a state or its citizens and a foreign state or its citizens, and all cases involving ambassadors, public ministers, or consuls. To the framers of the Constitution, foreign policy was first and foremost the arena for waging war and making treaties. However, they also understood that the federal government must have power over some economic issues like setting tariffs and duties and issuing currency, all of which affect international trade and investment. Article 1, Section 10 of the Constitution lists the activities that states are prohibited from doing, most of which are related to foreign policy. However, the Tenth Amendment reserves powers not delegated to the federal government, or prohibited by the Constitution to the states, to the states or to the people.

The ambiguity of this notion of "dual federalism" has been a source of confusion from the start. The role of states in foreign policy was one of the first controversies addressed by the Court in the years following the writing of the Constitution. In *Penhallow v. Doane* (1795) and *Ware v. Hylton* (1796), the Supreme Court denied to the states any role in foreign policy matters, ruling that treaty-making power was not affected by the doctrine of dual federalism. It helped to minimize disputes in this area because, for most of the country's history, it was easy to distinguish between domestic and foreign matters. In the later years of the twentieth century, however, the lines blurred. This was particularly true in international economic matters. States and cities routinely sent trade missions abroad to help local firms export and to encourage foreign companies to invest locally. Local government forays into foreign policy accelerated in the 1980s. Many localities enacted boycott legislation to pressure South Africa to end apartheid. Others passed resolutions criticizing nuclear weapons, supporting a freeze in the arms race, and banning nuclear testing. Some formed linkages with Nicaragua and, along with grassroots organizations, provided more humanitarian aid to the Nicaraguan people than all the military aid Congress authorized for the contras, the anticommunist forces supported by the Reagan administration. Still others welcomed Guatemalan and Salvadoran refugees, established "sister city" relationships with communities in other countries (including the Soviet Union), and passed ordinances phasing out ozone-depleting chemicals.

Opponents of local government involvement in foreign policy proposed three arguments. The first was that U.S. foreign policy is most effective when the country speaks with one voice. The second was that foreign affairs, like all public policies, should be shaped democratically by all who would be affected. It would be unfair for some states and cities to make decisions that affect the entire country. The third proposition was that only the federal government has the expertise to make foreign policy. The president, through the National Security Council, Central Intelligence Agency, Departments of State and Defense, and other executive branch organizations, has far more resources and information (much of it secret or sensitive) than governors and mayors. These arguments were countered by the fact that U.S. foreign policy is rarely of one voice. Members of Congress, different departments within the executive branch, multinational corporations, and special interest groups have all expressed views at odds with the president or State Department. In addition, local government foreign policies may be viewed as an extension of the democratic process, since local governments concerned about an international issue can develop policies specific to their citizens' needs, as well as accountability, since there is no national security apparatus for local officials to hide behind. Finally, while the federal government may have access to more information in traditional foreign policy areas (like war and security), local governments are perhaps more knowledgeable in economic policy and have more tools at their disposal (such as tax and other incentives to attract foreign direct investment).

There have been few cases challenging local government foreign policies, and the Constitution helps to explain why. Under the Articles of Confederation, the states engaged in trade wars, pursued their own military campaigns, and carried out independent diplomacy. The Constitution's framers sought to correct this. First, it is broadly understood that the framers sought to place foreign policy firmly at the national level. Second, the Constitution clearly prohibits states from some foreign activities, including making treaties or engaging in war. Third, Article 6 of the Constitution provides that laws and treaties of the United States are "the supreme law of the land" and prevail (or preempt) state law. Fourth, states may not levy taxes or duties on imports or exports, or enact regulations that unduly inhibit interstate or foreign commerce. Consequently, until the late twentieth century there were relatively few foreign policies enacted by local government, and only a handful that posed a serious threat to the ability of the United States to speak with one voice in international relations.

An alternative reading of the Constitution suggests that the framers could have taken all foreign policy activities away from state and local governments but chose not to do so. Instead, they enumerated a small number of limitations on state power. In those instances when local government has become involved in foreign policy, the executive and legislative branches usually have done little to discourage such activity. During the Reagan administration, conservatives in the Justice Department were reluctant to file suit against municipal foreign policies because of their support for the principle of states' rights. Thus, local government foreign policies bring two constitutional principles, states' rights and a national-level foreign policy, into conflict.

Many of the local government activities of the 1980s and 1990s do not fall neatly into constitutional categories (like war, treaties, and duties). For example, the Comprehensive Anti-Apartheid Act of 1986 made it clear that state and local divestment and antiapartheid legislation could remain in effect. In such cases, the judiciary resorted to other interpretations. In *Zschernig* v. *Miller* (1968), the Supreme Court ruled against Oregon. That state's government had enacted a law requiring reciprocal treatment of property inherited by a resident alien in Oregon and in the alien's home country. The Court announced that it would now strike down any municipal foreign policies having more than "some incidental or indirect effect" on U.S. foreign relations. The fact that such an effect could vary in importance over time creates an opening for the judiciary to increase its influence in foreign policy matters.

One increasingly popular type of nontraditional foreign policy of local governments is economic sanctions. In 1996, Massachusetts passed a law that made it more difficult for companies with investments in Burma (Myanmar) to receive state procurement contracts. This "selective purchasing" law applied to U.S. and foreign companies and was challenged at two levels. The European Union and several Asian countries asked the World Trade Organization (WTO) to determine whether the "Burma law" violated international trade rules. They felt that the law was yet another example of U.S. "extraterritoriality," that is, applying laws originating within the United States on parties operating beyond the country's borders. However, the claimants agreed to let the U.S. courts decide on the case before pressing for a WTO ruling. A group of companies formed the National Foreign Trade Council (NFTC) and challenged the law within the federal court system in 1998 in *National Foreign Trade Council v. Baker*. The NFTC's argument rested on three points. The first was that the Constitution gives only the federal government the right to make foreign policy. The second was that the Massachusetts law violated the Constitution's commerce clause, which gives Congress exclusive powers over interstate commerce. The third was that a federal law prohibiting new investment by U.S. companies in Burma, but passed a few months after the Massachusetts law, preempted the state law.

Massachusetts supported its position with several arguments. First, the Constitution explicitly lists the activities in which states may not engage, but economic sanctions is not one of them. Second, because the Massachusetts law did not establish direct contact between the state and Burma, it was not a foreign policy question. Third, important state interests embodied in the First (freedom of speech) and Tenth Amendments to the Constitution permitted the law. Finally, since the foreign affairs doctrine is vague, the courts should leave to the legislative branch the issue of whether to invalidate the Massachusetts Burma law.

The fuzzy area of the constitutionality of state actions in the international realm was underlined by the ways in which federal courts ruled as this case made its way through the judicial system. A federal judge ruled that the Massachusetts law "unconstitutionally impinges on the federal government's exclusive authority to regulate foreign affairs," since the objective of the legislation was to change Myanmar's domestic politics (specifically, to force the military junta to recognize the results of a 1990 election). The appeals court's 1999 ruling was much more sweeping, as it found the Burma law unconstitutional on all three grounds presented by the NFTC. The Supreme Court agreed to hear the case (*Crosby v. National Foreign Trade Council*, 2000) and ruled against Massachusetts—but for yet a different reason. The Clinton administration avoided taking sides in this dispute, but revealed its support for the NFTC during the Supreme Court hearing. In a unanimous ruling, the Supreme Court concluded that the federal statute banning investment in Burma (enacted shortly after the Massachusetts law) preempted the Massachusetts law on procurement. In other words, the law passed by Congress prevented states from having their own sanctions laws aimed at Burma. The Court has taken a similar approach in other cases, whereby it has nullified a state or local foreign policy because it contradicted a specific federal statute, treaty, executive agreement, or constitutional clause.

Unfortunately, the narrow ruling in the Massachusetts case left the door open for other state and local government actions in the foreign policy area. For example, it was not clear whether a state sanctions law is constitutional when no national law exists aimed at the same country. Nor did the ruling prohibit other measures, such as divestment by state pension funds of stock held in firms doing business in undesirable places. Most importantly, this case presented the courts with the opportunity to clearly demarcate the limits of states' actions in the foreign realm, but the Supreme Court was unwilling to make such a bold statement.

The conflicting constitutional principles that thus arose were difficult to resolve. One solution to controversies of this type was for the courts to treat local government involvement in foreign policy in the same way that they usually treat disputes over war powers. By holding that these are political questions, the courts could leave it to the legislative and executive branches to create laws permitting or barring various activities. For example, if Congress did not want states like Massachusetts enacting selective purchasing laws, it could pass a law prohibiting them from doing so. In this line of thinking, the courts should uphold all local government foreign policies, unless such activities are specifically barred by national legislation or the Constitution.

CONCLUSION

The constitutional law expert Louis Henkin summarized the judiciary's role in foreign affairs nicely when he wrote:

Overall, the contribution of the courts to foreign policy and their impact on foreign relations are significant but not large. The Supreme Court in particular intervenes only infrequently and its foreign affairs cases are few and haphazard. The Court does not build and refine steadily case by case, it develops no expertise or experts; the Justices have no matured or clear philosophies; the precedents are flimsy and often reflect the spirit of another day. But though the courts have only a supporting part, it is indispensable and inevitable, and if their competence and equipment for making foreign policy are uncertain, they can be improved by stronger, continuing guidance by Congress and, perhaps, by the President.

In examining the power and practice of the judiciary in foreign affairs, one is struck by the potential power of this branch but the rare use of it in practice. In general, the judiciary has tended to regard foreign affairs as fundamentally different from other areas of power. In so doing, it has been more willing (either through actual rulings or the dismissal of cases as political questions) to permit the federal power under consideration, and to give the president the benefit of the doubt in disputes over executive and legislative branch authority. The blurring of the domestic and international, the increasing activism of state and local governments in foreign affairs, and the form and timing of U.S. military intervention abroad will be major factors in coming years that will determine whether the judiciary's restraint in foreign affairs continues.

BIBLIOGRAPHY

Biskupic, Joan, and Elder Witt. *The Supreme Court and the Powers of the American Government.* Washington, D.C., 1997.

Bradley, Curtis A. "The Treaty Power and American Federalism." *Michigan Law Review* 97 (Nov. 1998): 390–461.

Dycus, Stephen, Arthur L. Berney, William C. Banks, and Peter Raven-Hansen. *National Security Law.* Boston, 1997.

Franck, Thomas M. "Courts and Foreign Policy." *Foreign Policy* 83 (summer 1991): 66–86.

Gibson, Martha Liebler. "Managing Conflict: The Role of the Legislative Veto in American Foreign Policy." *Polity* 26 (spring 1994): 441–472.

Grimmett, Richard F. *The War Powers Resolution: Twenty-Two Years of Experience.* Washington, D.C., 1996.

Guay, Terrence R. "Local Government and Global Politics: The Implications of Massachusetts' 'Burma Law.'" *Political Science Quarterly* 115 (fall 2000): 353–376.

Henkin, Louis. *Foreign Affairs and the United States Constitution.* 2d ed. Oxford and New York, 1996.

Henkin, Louis, Michael J. Glennon, and William D. Rogers, eds. *Foreign Affairs and the U.S. Constitution.* Ardsley-on-Hudson, N.Y., 1990.

Hicks, Bruce D. "Dueling Decisions: Contrasting Constitutional Vision of the United States President's Foreign Policy Role." *Policy Studies Journal* 24 (summer 1996): 245–258.

Koh, Harold H. "Why the President (Almost) Always Wins in Foreign Affairs." *Yale Law Journal* 97 (1988): 1255–1342.

Rossiter, Clinton Lawrence, and Richard P. Longaker. *The Supreme Court and the Commander in Chief.* Expanded ed. Ithaca, N.Y., 1976.

Schmahmann, David, and James Finch. "The Unconstitutionality of State and Local Enactments in the United States Restricting Business Ties with Burma." *Vanderbilt Journal of Transnational Law* 30 (March 1997): 175–207.

Shuman, Howard E., and Walter R. Thomas, eds. *The Constitution and National Security: A Bicentennial View.* Washington, D.C., 1990.

Shuman, Michael H. "Dateline Main Street: Courts v. Local Foreign Policies." *Foreign Policy* 86 (spring 1992): 158–177.

See also CONGRESSIONAL POWER; INTERNATIONAL LAW; PRESIDENTIAL POWER.

LOANS AND DEBT RESOLUTION

Richard W. Van Alstyne and Joseph M. Siracusa

Problems arising from unpaid debts owed by foreign governments to private bankers and, later, to international agencies, troubled American policymakers during the twentieth century. Initial concerns arose regarding the political motives of European governments who sought to employ their military forces to enforce repayment of financial debts incurred by South American and Central American countries. When its World War I allies stopped paying on wartime loans during the 1920s and 1930s, U.S. officials were faced with a series of unpleasant choices. To avoid this problem during World War II, President Franklin D. Roosevelt established the lend-lease program that provided economic and military aid to America's allies yet left no substantial postwar debt.

During the Cold War years, the United States employed foreign aid packages that consisted largely of grants with occasional loans to aid its allies. Initially, the new International Monetary Fund and the World Bank provided developing countries with economic assistance; later, in the 1970s, commercial agents—individual banks and consortiums—extended loans to the same clients. This subsequent surge of credit resulted in greatly increasing Third World debt and, after 1981, increasing concern with possible defaults and debt rescheduling.

CARIBBEAN PROTECTORATES

In the early twentieth century, debt repayment emerged as a significant U.S. foreign policy issue when dictatorships in several Caribbean republics—regimes that had managed to live on loans granted by European banking and speculative interests—demonstrated an incapacity or plain unwillingness to pay that brought threats of armed intervention from European powers. The classic instance was that of Venezuela, whose reckless behavior had aroused the anger and contempt of the great powers, including the United States. In 1902 the British and German governments, joined nominally by Italy, blockaded Venezuela and seized the country's customs, the revenues from which would then be utilized toward redemption of the debts. This method, which proved effective but also aroused American susceptibilities over the Monroe Doctrine (1823), soon brought from the administration of Theodore Roosevelt (1901–1909) an important policy shift, namely, that the United States would henceforth be responsible for the behavior of the Latin American republics toward Europe. In due course, then, the United States assumed fiscal supervision over several Caribbean countries.

The principal recipients of American "protection" were Cuba, Panama, the Dominican Republic, Nicaragua, and Haiti. The special relations of the United States to these republics were embodied in treaties, no two of which were exactly alike. To only one such state—the Republic of Panama—did the United States actually promise "protection," in the declaration that "the United States guarantees and will maintain the independence of the Republic of Panama." Other treaties, such as those with Cuba and Haiti, contained engagements on the part of the "protected" states not to impair their independence or cede any of their territory to a third party; and the same two treaties permitted intervention by the United States for the maintenance of independence or of orderly government. Since careless public finance was likely to lead to foreign intervention and possible loss of independence, a number of the treaties—those with Cuba, Haiti, and the Dominican Republic—contained restrictions upon, or gave the United States supervision over, financial policy.

American investments existed in all the countries of this Caribbean semicircle of protectorates. These no doubt benefited from the increased stability and financial responsibility induced by governmental policy. In the Dominican Republic, Haiti, and Nicaragua that policy resulted in a transfer of the ownership of government obligations from European to American bankers. Yet in none of the five republics save Cuba were American financial interests especially large or important. The dominant motive was clearly political and strategic rather than economic. The acquisition of the Canal Zone and the building of the Panama Canal made the isthmian area a crucial concern in the American defense system.

CUBA AND THE PLATT AMENDMENT (1901)

The end of the war with Spain in 1898 left Cuba occupied by the armed forces of the United States but with the future status of the island not clearly defined. Spain had relinquished sovereignty over Cuba, and the United States had renounced any thought of annexing it. But that renunciation did not absolve the United States, in its own eyes, from responsibility for Cuba's future. President William McKinley remarked in his annual message of 5 December 1899 that the United States had assumed "a grave responsibility for the future good government of Cuba." The island, he continued, "must needs be bound to us by ties of singular intimacy and strength of its enduring welfare is to be assured."

What those ties were to be was defined by Elihu Root, McKinley's secretary of war. General Leonard Wood, America's military governor of Cuba, convoked a constitutional convention, which sat in Havana from November 1900 to February 1901. It completed a constitution for independent Cuba but failed to carry out a directive of the governor to provide for relations between the Cuban government and the government of the United States. Secretary Root outlined his concept of what those relations should be in a set of proposals that were introduced in the U.S. Senate by Senator Orville H. Platt of Connecticut and were known henceforth as the Platt Amendment. This was actually an amendment to the Army Appropriation Bill of 2 March 1901; the amendment authorized the president to terminate the military occupation of Cuba as soon as a Cuban government was established under a constitution that provided, among other things, that Cuba should never permit any "foreign power" to gain a foothold in its territory or contract any debt beyond the capacity of its ordinary revenues to pay; and that Cuba should consent that the United States might intervene in its affairs for the preservation of Cuba's independence.

The new Cuban government was inaugurated on 20 May 1902. The Platt Amendment took its place as an annex to the Cuban constitution and was embodied in the permanent treaty of 1903 between Cuba and the United States. It remained in force until 1934, when all of the treaty except the naval base article was abrogated. Under that article the United States enjoyed the use of Guantánamo Bay, on the south coast near Santiago, as a naval station. Under Article 3 the United States exercised the right of intervention from time to time, notably in 1906–1909, following a breakdown of the Cuban government, but more frequently in subsequent years.

THE ROOSEVELT COROLLARY OF THE MONROE DOCTRINE

Secretary Root spoke of the Platt Amendment as supplying a basis in international law for intervention by the United States under the Monroe Doctrine to protect the independence of Cuba. But with how much justice or logic could the United States enforce the Monroe Doctrine against European intervention in turbulent Western Hemisphere republics if it took no responsibility for the behavior of such republics or for the fulfillment of their obligations to Europe? The Platt Amendment, by restricting the debt-contracting power of Cuba and permitting the United States to intervene for the preservation of orderly government, hinted that the Monroe Doctrine involved certain policing responsibilities for the United States. That idea, though previously suggested from time to time, was now for the first time written into law. Need for such a principle was emphasized by events in Venezuela in 1902–1903.

In 1901, when the German and British governments were contemplating the use of force to collect debts from the Venezuelan dictator, Cipriano Castro, Theodore Roosevelt (then vice president) wrote to a German friend: "If any South American country misbehaves toward any European country spank it." In his first annual message as president a few months later he declared that the Monroe Doctrine gave no guarantee to any state in the Americas against punishment for misconduct, provided that punishment did not take the form of acquisition of territory. When, however, in the winter of 1902–1903, Germany and Great Britain actually undertook to bring Castro to terms by a "pacific blockade," anti-German sentiment flared up in the United States, and Roosevelt became alarmed over the possibility that such a situation might produce a serious quarrel between the United States and some European power. The Venezuelan crisis was settled when Castro agreed to submit the question of his debts to arbitration, but no one knew when Venezuela or one of its neighbors might present a new invitation to coercion. It seemed to Roosevelt desirable to find a formula by which all excuses for European intervention in the New World might be removed.

The formula was announced by Roosevelt in 1904, first in May in a letter to Secretary Root, then, in almost identical language, in his annual message of 6 December 1904. As stated in the annual message:

> Any country whose people conduct themselves well can count upon our hearty friendship. If a nation shows that it knows how to act with reasonable efficiency and decency in social and political matters, if it keeps order and pays its obligations, it need fear no interference from the United States. Chronic wrongdoing, or an impotence which results in a general loosening of the ties of civilized society, may in America, as elsewhere, ultimately require intervention of some civilized nation, and in the Western Hemisphere, the adherence of the United States to the Monroe Doctrine may force the United States, however reluctantly, in flagrant cases of such wrongdoing or impotence, to the exercise of an international police power.

THE DOMINICAN RECEIVERSHIP

The Roosevelt Corollary of the Monroe Doctrine—so called because it was assumed to follow as a necessary consequence of the doctrine—was to serve, whether expressly mentioned or not, as the theoretical basis for the subsequent establishment of protectorates in the Caribbean. The United States now assumed the role of international policeman—kindly to the law-abiding but apt to lay a stern hand upon little nations that fell into disorder or defaulted on their obligations, since disorder or default, if allowed to continue, might invite intervention from outside the hemisphere. The first application of the new doctrine was in the Dominican Republic.

The government of the Dominican Republic, or Santo Domingo, after that state won its independence from Haiti in 1844, had been a dictatorship generously tempered by revolution. Revolutions were costly, and by 1904 the Dominican debt had grown to a figure—some $32 million—which the national revenues, as administered by native collectors of taxes and customs, were incapable of servicing. The foreign debt was widely distributed. Portions of it were held in France, Belgium, Italy, and Germany. The largest single creditor, representing both American and British capital, was the U.S.-based San Domingo Improvement Company. From time to time, the Dominican government pledged the customs duties at various ports as security for its debts, and the pledges sometimes conflicted. Intervention by the United States on the company's behalf resulted, in 1903 and 1904, in the San Domingo Improvement Company being placed in charge of the collection of customs at Puerto Plata and Monte Cristi on the north coast. This action brought protests from the European creditors, who claimed that those same revenues had previously been pledged to them. An international scramble for control of the Dominican customhouses threatened, with the possible development of a situation resembling the one in Venezuela that had alarmed Roosevelt a scant two years earlier.

It was under these circumstances that Roosevelt formulated his famous corollary, which was without doubt intended as a forecast of coming events. With the encouragement of Thomas C. Dawson, U.S. minister to the Dominican Republic, President Morales invited the United States to take charge of the nation's customhouses and administer the collection of import duties for the purpose of satisfying the creditors of the republic and providing its government with revenue. An executive agreement to this effect was signed on 20 January 1905, but this attempt of Roosevelt to bypass the Senate excited so much criticism that Dawson was instructed to put the agreement into the form of a treaty, subject to ratification in the constitutional manner. The treaty was duly signed and its approval urged upon the Senate by President Roosevelt with reasoning based, like his corollary message, upon the Monroe Doctrine.

Democratic opposition prevented action upon the treaty, but the president, with characteristic determination, put the essence of the arrangement into effect by a new executive agreement, referred to as a modus vivendi, signed 1 April 1905. The Dominican government agreed to appoint as receiver of customs a citizen of the United States nominated by the U.S. president. As in the proposed treaty, 45 percent of the receipts were to be turned over to the Dominican government; the remainder, less costs of collection, was to be deposited in a New York bank, to be apportioned among the creditors of the republic if the Senate approved the treaty, or returned to the Dominican government if the treaty was finally rejected.

The modus vivendi remained operative for more than two years. During that period the creditors of the Dominican government agreed to a downward adjustment of the debt from over $30 million to $17 million. A new $20 million bond issue was floated in the United States, and the proceeds were applied to the paying off of the adjusted debt and to the execution of needful public works on the island. In February 1907 a new treaty was signed, which the Senate promptly approved through the switch of a few Democratic votes to its support. The treaty, proclaimed 25 July 1907, perpetuated the arrangement under the modus vivendi, with minor modifications. A general receiver of Dominican customs, named by the president of the United States, was to have full control of the collection of customs duties until the $20 million bond issue was liquidated.

The Dominican receivership, under the modus vivendi and the subsequent treaty, produced results. For some four years after the conclusion of the treaty, the republic experienced the unaccustomed blessings of financial solvency and political stability. Then began a new series of revolutionary disturbances that led to a more drastic form of intervention by the United States.

DOLLAR DIPLOMACY IN NICARAGUA

The next Caribbean country to receive the "protection" of the United States was Nicaragua. Intervention in Nicaragua, initiated under President William H. Taft and Secretary of State Philander C. Knox in 1912, was a prominent example of the so-called dollar diplomacy usually associated with that administration. Dollar diplomacy had a dual character. On one side, it was the use of diplomacy to advance and protect American business abroad; on the other side, it was the use of dollars abroad to promote the needs of American diplomacy. In the first sense, it was practiced by many an administration before Taft and since. The employment of American dollars to advance the political and strategic aims of diplomacy was a less familiar technique.

There was a hint of it in the Platt Amendment. It was plainly seen in the refunding of the debt and the instituting of the receivership in the Dominican Republic under Theodore Roosevelt. Invoking, as Roosevelt had done, the Monroe Doctrine as their justification, Taft and Knox made a similar arrangement with Nicaragua and sought unsuccessfully to do the same with Honduras and Guatemala.

The setting up of the Nicaraguan customs receivership came at the conclusion of some years of turmoil in Central America, largely the work of the Nicaraguan dictator, José Santos Zelaya. Having lent support to the ousting of Zelaya, Taft and Knox were anxious to bring peace and order to Central America by applying in Nicaragua the same remedy that had some success in the Dominican Republic. They found a cooperative leader in Nicaragua in the person of Adolfo Díaz, who succeeded Zelaya as president in 1911. A businessman who despised militarism and craved order and good government, Díaz was willing to compromise his country's independence by granting to the United States broad powers of intervention. In 1912, when he was faced with insurrection, the United States, at his request, sent 2,000 U.S. marines to Nicaragua, suppressed the rebellion, deported its leaders, and left a legation guard of one hundred marines that—until 1925—"stabilized" the Nicaraguan government under Díaz and his successors.

Secretary Knox's attempt, with the aid of Díaz, to set up a customs receivership in Nicaragua by treaty was blocked in the U.S. Senate, but a receivership was established nevertheless by agreement between Nicaragua, certain American banks, and the State Department. A mixed claims commission reduced claims against Nicaragua from $13.75 million to a mere $1.75 million. Another mixed commission was given limited control over Nicaragua's spending policy. The policy of Taft and Knox was continued by their successors, President Woodrow Wilson and his first secretary of state, William Jennings Bryan. To meet Nicaragua's urgent need for funds and at the same time to provide for the future canal needs of the United States, the Bryan-Chamorro Treaty, signed 5 August 1914 and approved nearly two years later, provided for a payment of $3 million to Nicaragua in return for the grant of certain concessions to the United States. These included the perpetual and exclusive right to construct a canal through Nicaragua and the right for ninety-nine years to establish naval bases at either end of the route, in the Corn Islands in the Caribbean and on the Gulf of Fonseca on the Pacific.

The United States also succeeded, not by treaty but by informal agreement with Nicaragua and the bankers, in reducing and simplifying the Nicaraguan debt and in setting up a customs receivership that would see to it that a suitable portion of the national revenue was applied on the debt. Application of the Roosevelt Corollary, implemented by dollar diplomacy and the landing of a few marines, had made Nicaragua secure against any violation of the Monroe Doctrine.

WILSONIAN INTERVENTION

It is ironic that the treaty that consummated the success of dollar diplomacy in Nicaragua bore the name of William Jennings Bryan, for Bryan, out of office, had been a severe critic of dollar diplomacy. Other inconsistencies were to follow. The anti-imperialist Wilson administration (1913–1921), with first Bryan and later Robert Lansing as secretary of state, although promoting independence for the Philippines and self-government for Puerto Rico, imposed upon Haiti a protectorate treaty of unprecedented severity and set up a regime of pure force in the Dominican Republic.

There is perhaps less of a contradiction than at first appears between the new administration's policy in the Philippines and Puerto Rico and its policy toward the independent republics of the Caribbean. The Philippines and Puerto Rico, under American tutelage, had been learning the lessons of democracy and conducting orderly elections in which ballots, not bullets, determined the outcome. Perhaps a few years of American tutelage would suffice to complete the political education of the natives of Haiti and the Dominican Republic, who hitherto had found the bullet a more congenial instrument than the ballot. At the very beginning of his administration, Wilson made it clear that he would frown upon revolutions in the neighboring republics. "I am going to teach the South American republics to elect good men," he remarked with optimism to a British visitor.

Such remarks foreshadowed a new turn in American interventionist policy in which the promotion of democracy would take its place as an objective beside the preservation of the Monroe Doctrine and the protection of the economic and strategic interests of the United States. Unfortunately, although the new measures were effective in restoring order and preventing revolutions by force, they did little or nothing toward providing a substitute for revolutions in the form of free and fair elections.

HAITI

The republic of Haiti, unlike the Dominican Republic, its companion on the island of Hispaniola, had maintained its independence continuously since the time of Toussaint Louverture in the late eighteenth century. It had also been more successful than its neighbors in meeting the interest payments on its rather large foreign debt; but in the prevalence of corrupt tyranny complicated by frequent revolution, it surpassed the Dominican Republic. In the early twentieth century, corruption grew more flagrant and revolution more frequent, and bankruptcy, default, and the menace of European intervention loomed on the horizon.

Under these circumstances the United States began urging upon Haitian presidents measures designed to bring some order out of the chaos into which the country had fallen and to guard against European intervention. Bryan asked for the United States the right to appoint a customs receiver, as in Santo Domingo, and a financial adviser. He asked for the right to supervise Haitian elections and for a nonalienation pledge regarding Môle St. Nicolas, a potential naval base at the northwest corner of the island. Negotiations along these lines proceeded, but so kaleidoscopic were the changes in Haitian administrations that no results had been achieved by July 1915, when President Guillaume Sam, following the cold-blooded massacre of 170 political prisoners in the government jail, was pulled by an angry mob from his sanctuary in the French legation, thrown into the street, and assassinated. On the same afternoon (28 July), the USS *Washington*, flagship of Rear Admiral Caperton, dropped anchor in Port-au-Prince harbor, and before nightfall the U.S. marines occupied the town.

Exasperated at the long reign of anarchy in Haiti and at the failure of treaty negotiations, Washington was resolved to use the new crisis to enforce its demands upon the Haitian government. By taking control of the customhouses and impounding the revenue, and by the threat of continued military government if its wishes were not obeyed, the United States was able to dictate the choice of a president as successor to Guillaume Sam and to prevail upon the new president and the National Assembly to accept a treaty embodying all the American demands.

The Treaty of 1915 with Haiti went further in establishing U.S. control and supervision than the Platt Amendment treaty with Cuba or the Dominican treaty of 1907 combined. It provided that the top officials should be appointed by the president of Haiti upon nomination by the president of the United States. Moreover, all Haitian governmental debts were to be classified, arranged, and serviced from funds collected by the general receiver, and Haiti was not to increase its debt without the consent of the United States, nor do anything to alienate any of its territory or impair its independence. The treaty was to remain in force for ten years, but a clause permitting its extension for another ten-year period upon either party's showing sufficient cause was invoked by the United States in 1917, thus prolonging to 1936 the prospective life of the treaty.

THE NAVY GOVERNS THE DOMINICAN REPUBLIC

Until 1911, the customs receivership of 1905 and 1907 in the Dominican Republic worked admirably. Under the presidency of Ramón Cáceres (1906–1911), stable government and orderly finance had been the rule: constitutional reforms had been adopted, and surplus revenues had been applied to port improvements, highway and railroad construction, and education. Such a novel employment of the powers and resources of government was displeasing to many Dominican politicians, and on 19 November 1911, Cáceres fell victim to an assassin's bullet. At once the republic reverted to its seemingly normal condition of factional turmoil and civil war, and the necessities incident to the conducting and suppressing of revolutions resulted in the contraction of a large floating debt, contrary to the spirit, if not the letter, of the 1907 treaty with the United States.

Thus, the Wilson administration found in the Dominican Republic a situation as difficult as that in Haiti. Under a plan drafted by Wilson himself and accepted by the Dominican leaders, the United States supervised the 1914 elections. From the new leadership, the United States demanded a treaty providing for the appointment of a financial adviser with control over disbursements, for the extension of the authority of the general receiver to cover internal revenue as well as customs, and for the organization of a constabulary. These demands were rejected as violative of Dominican sovereignty, and in the spring of 1916 the situation went from bad to worse when the Dominican secretary of war, Desiderio Arias, launched a new revolution and seized the capital. On 15 May, U.S. marines landed in Santo Domingo and the country was soon placed under military government. This arrangement lasted six years.

ECONOMIC FOREIGN POLICY DURING THE INTERWAR PERIOD

A consequence of World War I, the significance of which was little recognized save the wartime flow of gold across the Atlantic, was the sudden transformation of the United States from a debtor to a creditor nation. Like other new countries, the United States hitherto had been consistently a borrower. Its canals, railroads, and industry had been built in large measure with capital borrowed in Europe, which it had been enabled to service by an excess of exports over imports. By the end of the century, the United States was also lending or investing money abroad, but in 1914 it was still on balance a debtor, owing Europe from $4.5 to $5 billion against $2.5 billion invested abroad, chiefly in Canada, Mexico, and Cuba.

Early in the war, large quantities of U.S. securities held abroad were sold in New York in order to finance purchases of American war materials by the Allied governments. By the fall of 1915, those governments found it necessary to float a bond issue of $500 million in the United States through the agency of J. P. Morgan and Company, and such borrowings continued until the United States entered the war (1917). The role of lender was then assumed by the U.S. government, which advanced to friendly governments more than $7 billion before the armistice of 11 November 1918, and $3.75 billion in subsequent months. Without counting interest, therefore, the U.S. government at the close of World War I was a creditor to its wartime associates to the extent of $10.35 billion. Although the war impoverished Europe, it brought great wealth to the United States and thereby created a large fund of surplus capital ready to seek investment abroad. By 1928 private investments in foreign lands totaled between $11.5 and $13.5 billion. Acceptance of the new creditor role should have entailed changes in policy, especially tariff policy, which American statesmanship proved incapable of making.

WORLD WAR I FOREIGN DEBT COMMISSION RATES

Country	Principal	Rate of Interest	Percentage of Cancellation
Austria	$ 24,614,885	—	70.5
Belgium	417,780,000	1.8	53.5
Czechoslovakia	115,000,000	3.3	25.7
Estonia	13,830,000	3.3	19.5
Finland	9,000,000	3.3	19.3
France	4,025,000,000	1.6	52.8
Great Britain	4,600,000,000	3.3	19.7
Greece	32,467,000	0.3	67.3
Hungary	1,939,000	3.3	19.6
Italy	2,042,000,000	0.4	75.4
Latvia	5,775,000	3.3	19.3
Lithuania	6,030,000	3.3	20.1
Poland	178,560,000	3.3	19.5
Romania	44,590,000	3.3	25.1
Yugoslavia	62,850,000	1.0	69.7
Total	$11,579,435,885		

SETTLING THE WAR DEBTS

The $10 billion advanced by the United States to friendly governments during and immediately after the war had unquestionably been regarded as loans by both lender and receivers. In the U.S. Congress, a few voices were raised in support of the thesis that the advances should be viewed simply as part of America's contribution to the war, as a means of enabling others to do what, for the moment, the United States could not do with its own army and navy. There were warnings, too, of the ill will that might result from an American effort to collect the debts from governments that the war left close to bankruptcy. But such pleas and warnings went almost unnoticed, and President Wilson and his advisers rebuffed all proposals for cancellation of the debts or for discussing them at the Paris Peace Conference.

In June 1921, President Warren G. Harding proposed that Congress empower the secretary of the Treasury to negotiate with the debtor governments adjustments of the war debts as to terms, interest rates, and dates of maturity. Congress responded by an act (9 February 1922) creating the World War Foreign Debt Commission, with the secretary of the Treasury as chairman and authorizing it to negotiate settlements on terms defined by the act. No portion of any debt might be canceled; the interest rate must not be less than 4.5 percent, nor the date of maturity later than 1947. The commission found no debtor government willing to settle on these difficult terms. The procedure it adopted, therefore, was to make with each debtor the best terms possible (taking into account in the later settlements "capacity to pay") and then to ask Congress in each case to approve the departure from the formula originally prescribed.

In this way, between May 1923 and May 1926, the World War Foreign Debt Commission negotiated settlements with thirteen governments. Settlements with Austria and Greece were later made by the Treasury Department. With the exception of Austria, which received special treatment, all the settlements provided for initial payments over sixty-two years. No part of the principal was canceled in practice, and the rates of interest were so adjusted downward that varying portions of the debts were actually forgiven. Comparing the total amounts to be paid under the settlements with the amounts that would have been paid at the interest rate of 4.5 percent originally prescribed by Congress, one finds effective cancellations ranging from 19.3 percent for Finland and 19.7 percent for Great Britain to 52.8 percent for

France and 75.4 percent for Italy. The amounts of the principal funded, the rates of interest to be paid, and the portions of the debts that were in effect canceled can be seen in the table.

THE REPARATIONS PROBLEM

Throughout the debt-settlement negotiations, the European debtor governments argued that payments on the debts should be dependent upon the collection of reparations from Germany. The United States refused consistently to recognize any relation between the two transactions. In American eyes, the Allied governments that had borrowed from the United States—had "hired the money," as President Calvin Coolidge put it—were under obligation to repay their borrowings regardless of what they might be able to collect from Germany. In actual fact, however, it was obvious that the ability of the Allied governments to pay their debts would be affected by their success or failure in collecting reparations, and it is for this reason the United States took a sympathetic attitude toward efforts to solve the reparations problem.

The peace conference had left to the Reparations Commission the determination of the amount to be paid by Germany. In May 1921 the commission set the figure at 132 billion marks, or approximately $33 billion. Germany accepted the figure under threat of occupation of additional German territory. Annual payments of a minimum of 2 billion marks were to begin at once, with later payments to be adjusted in the light of estimates of capacity to pay and evaluation of payments in kind already made.

Within just fifteen months of the settlement, Germany was in default on the required payments, whether willfully or through inability to meet the schedules. Over British objection (backed by that of the American observer), the Reparations Commission authorized occupation of the great German industrial area of the Ruhr Valley. French and Belgian armies carried out the mandate in January 1923 and held the Ruhr until September 1924. Germany met the occupation with passive resistance, and its economy suffered a prolonged and disastrous inflation. Reparations payments stopped entirely.

In the meantime, Secretary of State Charles Evans Hughes had proposed that a committee of experts study Germany's capacity to pay and devise a plan to facilitate payments. Late in 1923, all the governments concerned agreed to the suggestion, and the Reparations Commission appointed two committees to study different aspects of the problem. One of the committees was headed by the Chicago banker Charles G. Dawes. The Dawes Plan, which went into effect on 1 September 1924, was admittedly a temporary expedient, providing a rising scale of reparations payments over a period in which it was hoped the German economic and monetary system could be restored to a healthy condition. Germany received an international loan of $200 million. It agreed to make reparations payments beginning at 1 billion gold marks the first year, rising to 2.5 billion in the fifth year and thereafter. Payments would be made in German currency to an agent general for reparations. Thereupon Germany's responsibility would cease. The problem of converting the marks into foreign currencies would be the responsibility of the Inter-Allied Transfer Committee. No attempt was made to reassess the total or to set a date for the termination of payments.

During the prosperous years 1924 to 1928 the Dawes Plan worked satisfactorily, and by the latter year, the time appeared ripe for an attempt at a final settlement. A new committee headed by another American, the New York financier Owen D. Young, proposed the Young Plan, which was agreed to by Germany and its creditors in January 1930. By the new arrangement, which was intended to make a final disposition of the reparations problem, Germany agreed to make thirty-seven annual payments averaging a little over $500 million, followed by twenty-two annual payments averaging slightly under $400 million. By the end of the fifty-nine years, Germany would have paid altogether about $9 billion of principal and $17 billion of interest—a drastic reduction from the $33 billion of principal at first demanded by the Reparations Commission. Furthermore, the Young Plan clearly recognized the relationship between reparations and war debts through a concurrent agreement (not participated in by the United States) that any scaling down of the debts would bring about a corresponding reduction in reparations. The annuities to be distributed under the plan were so proportioned as to cover the war debt payments to be made by the recipients. As long as Germany continued to pay the Young Plan annuities, the debtor governments would have the wherewithal to satisfy their creditors, of whom the chief was the United States. If general prosperity had continued, the plan would have been workable.

MAKING THE CONNECTION

None of the presidents from Wilson to Franklin D. Roosevelt or the high officials under them evinced any economic enlightenment on the subject. Herbert Hoover stuck to his rigid belief in the sanctity of contracts, and in October 1930 his secretary of state, Henry L. Stimson, rejected the idea of a connection between the Allied war debts and German reparations. But by this time the Great Depression had entered its serious stage, and voices were being raised at home and abroad for a drastic reduction of the debts just as German reparations had been twice reduced. Senator Alben W. Barkley of Kentucky returned from a trip to Europe to announce publicly that the American tariff was a handicap—that there was no possibility that Britain could continue to pay, that "in every circle with which I came in contact, official and unofficial, there was a profound feeling bordering on despair and even bitterness." Europeans could not understand "our demand that they pay us what they owed us and buy the goods we send them while at the same time denying them the ability to do either by preventing them from selling anything to us." Barkley's reference was to the new Smoot-Hawley Act (June 1930), the effect of which was to reduce foreign trade to a trickle. President Hoover had brushed aside warnings of the evil consequences of the bill. Senator Reed Smoot, the principal author, had been a member of the World War Foreign Debt Funding Commission, but to his mind no "good American" would advocate cancellation of the debts or oppose his tariff bill.

The basic economic consequence of the war was to advance the United States to a position of supremacy. Despite the difficulties surrounding the war debt settlements, dollar loans poured from private American banks and investment syndicates on a vast scale, accelerating after 1924 but coming to an almost complete stop in 1930. European governments, municipalities, and private corporations sought and received these loans, paying high interest rates (in dollars) and meeting their war debt installments from the proceeds of these loans. Germany was a leading recipient of American loans and was thus able to pay reparations to the Allies, who in turn were able to pay their American creditors. The source of these extraordinary loans was the profits of American industry in the sale of its products both at home and abroad, and in the abundance of speculative capital-seeking outlets. An open door—or rather, open doors—appeared as if by magic to dazzle the American investor. Latin America, Australasia, Africa, and East Asia obtained dollar loans. The lending process was a continuation of the Open Door policy pursued in China: an attempt by means of loans to capture the world's markets, but without serious consideration as to how these loans were to be repaid. Actually interest was being paid out of principal, not out of returns on the investment. As secretary of commerce under Coolidge, Herbert Hoover encouraged loans of this type, particularly to South American countries. Criticism, scrutiny, and hints to the naive individual investor to exercise caution were alien to Hoover's peculiar laissez-faire cast of mind.

When the bubble burst in 1930, total U.S. private long-term foreign investments stood at $15.17 billion, triple the figure in 1919. Germany still routinely made payments on its reparations account, and at least some of the Allied governments were forwarding their installments to Washington. But the principal of the war debts (including the postwar loans) carried on the books of the U.S. Treasury stood at $11.64 billion, which was $120 million more than the total shown at the time the thirteen governments signed the settlement agreements. Supposing that all thirteen had continued to pay principal and interest through the entire sixty-two-year period, the grand total would have exceeded $22 billion. Meanwhile, the fascist dictatorship under Benito Mussolini had installed itself in Italy; and in Germany, the Nazis, now on the high road to power in that country, had promised to repudiate all further reparations payments. Bolshevik Russia had long ago repudiated czarist Russia's war debts.

By June 1931, Germany, the greatest of the world's debtors, was near collapse; and while continuing to maintain that debts and reparations were unconnected, Hoover, after assuring himself of sufficient congressional support, proposed a year's moratorium on all intergovernmental debts. Hoover was at last ready to admit that debt redemption on the part of any country depended upon its capacity to pay, although probably as a political gesture, he again declared his disapproval of cancellation. Hoover's opponent, Franklin D. Roosevelt, declined to take a position but did not miss his opportunity to ridicule the Republicans for their absurd policy "of demanding payment and at the same time making payment impossible."

Meanwhile, the Lausanne Agreement (1932) between Germany and its creditors put an end, for

HITLER REPUDIATES THE VERSAILLES TREATY AND REPARATIONS

In a speech to the Reichstag on 17 May 1933, Adolf Hitler denounced the Treaty of Versailles because, in part, it had imposed such large reparations payments as to leave Germany in economic shambles.

"All the problems which are causing such unrest today lie in the deficiencies of the Treaty of Peace which did not succeed in solving in a clear and reasonable way the questions of the most decisive importance for the future. Neither national nor economic—to say nothing of legal—problems and demands of the nations were settled by this treaty in such a way as to stand the criticism of reason in the future. It is therefore natural that the idea of revision is not only one of the constant accompaniments of the effects of this treaty, but that it was actually foreseen as necessary by the authors of the Treaty and therefore given a legal foundation in the Treaty itself. . . .

"It is not wise to deprive a people of the economic resources necessary for its existence without taking into consideration the fact that the population dependent on them are bound to the soil and will have to be fed. The idea that the economic extermination of a nation of sixty-five millions would be of service to other nations is absurd. Any people inclined to follow such a line of thought would, under the law of cause and effect, soon experience that the doom which they were preparing for another nation would swiftly overtake them. The very idea of reparations and the way in which they were enforced will become a classic example in the history of the nations of how seriously international welfare can be damaged by hasty and unconsidered action.

"As a matter of fact, the policy of reparations could only be financed by German exports. To the same extent as Germany, for the sake of reparations, was regarded in the light of an international exporting concern, the export of the creditor nations was bound to suffer. The economic benefit accruing from the reparation payments could therefore never make good the damage which the system of reparations inflicted upon the individual economic systems.

"The attempt to prevent such a development by compensating for a limitation of German exports by the grant of credits, in order to render payments possible, was no less short-sighted and mistaken in the end. For the conversion of political debts into private obligations led to an interest service which was bound to have the same results. The worst feature, however, was that the development of internal economic life was artificially hindered and ruined. The struggle to gain the world markets by constant underselling led to excessive rationalization measures in the economic field.

"The millions of German unemployed are the final result of this development. If it was desired, however, to restrict reparation obligations to deliveries in kind, this must naturally cause equally serious damage to the internal production of the nations receiving them. For deliveries in kind to the amount involved are unthinkable without most seriously endangering the production of the individual nations.

"The Treaty of Versailles is to blame for having inaugurated a period in which financial calculations appear to destroy economic reason.

"Germany has faithfully fulfilled the obligations imposed upon her, in spite of their intrinsic lack of reason and the obviously suicidal consequences of this fulfillment.

"The international economic crisis is the indisputable proof of the correctness of this statement."

— *From Norman H. Baynes, ed.*
The Speeches of Adolf Hitler,
April 1922–August 1939. Vol. 2.
New York, 1969 —

---

all practical purposes, to reparations payments. Then Belgium, followed by France, defaulted. Britain and Italy managed to make partial payments through December 1932. It was at this time that Finland became conspicuous. "Sturdy little Finland" earned a high mark with the American public for meeting its semiannual installment of $166,538 punctually and in full. Britain offered a token payment in 1934 but, on being informed that this would not save it from the stigma of being a defaulter, decided to make no further gesture. Spurred by Senator Hiram Johnson, most vociferous among the diehards, Congress in April 1934 made certain there would be a stigma. It passed the Johnson Debt Default Act, which originally sought to close the door to any foreign government in default on its debts. Although this is what Johnson intended to do in the bill, the act as passed applied only to World War I debts owed to the U.S. Treasury. As Harry Dexter White pointed out to Treasury Secretary Henry Morgenthau, this left open the door to public lending to Latin American states and others that defaulted on private debts only. And the act did not apply to Export-Import Bank loans, though members of Congress frowned on lending the bank's funds to governments in default on their private debt. The Johnson Act had no practical effect; no foreign nation offered to resume payments, and none of those at whom the act was pointed was in the market for further American credits.

LEND-LEASE

The reparations experience had a marked affect on the way in which the United States provided the bulk of its aid to nations fighting the Axis powers in World War II. Under the provisions of the Lend-Lease Act (1941) and in lieu of credits and loans, the United States supplied to more than thirty-eight nations whatever goods were certified by President Franklin D. Roosevelt as "in the interests of national defense."

After reelection in 1940, the president received from Prime Minister Winston Churchill a long letter setting forth Great Britain's financial straits. That nation was scraping the bottom of the barrel to pay for goods already ordered and would need "ten times as much" for the extension of the war. Churchill hoped that Roosevelt would regard his letter "not as an appeal for aid, but as a statement of the minimum action necessary to achieve our common purpose." The problem, as Roosevelt saw it, was how to aid England in the common cause without incurring such a breeder of ill-will as the war debt problem after World War I. After brooding over the matter for days during a Caribbean cruise on the cruiser *Tuscaloosa,* he came up with the ingenious idea of lending goods instead of money. He wanted, as he told a press conference, to get away from that "silly, foolish old dollar sign," and he compared what he proposed to do to lending a garden hose to a neighbor to put out a fire that might otherwise spread to one's own house.

In his "fireside chat" radio broadcast on 29 December 1940, Roosevelt depicted the United States as the "arsenal of democracy," and in his message to Congress a few days later, he made official the proposal that resulted in the Lend-Lease Act of 11 March 1941. The act, the complete negation of traditional neutrality, empowered the president to make available to "the government of any country whose defense the President deems vital to the defense of the United States" any "defense article," any service, or any "defense information." "Defense articles" might be manufactured expressly for the government that was to receive them, or they might be taken from existing stocks in the possession of the United States. Launched on a modest scale, the lend-lease program eventually conveyed goods and services valued at more than $50 billion to the friends and allies of the United States in World War II, and it left in its wake no such exasperating war debt problem as that of the 1920s.

Against the $50 billion of lend-lease aid furnished by the United States, it received approximately $10 billion in so-called reverse lend-lease from its allies. After the war the United States negotiated settlement agreements with most of the recipients. In general, the agreements stipulated that lend-lease materials not used in the war should be returned or paid for, but the settlements were also shaped by the proviso written into the original lend-lease agreements, that final settlement terms should "be such as not to burden commerce but to promote mutually advantageous economic relations . . . and the betterment of worldwide economic relations." Within a decade of the war's end, settlement agreements totaling more than $1.5 billion had been negotiated, on which $477 million had been paid. The Soviet Union, which had received $11 billion, did not settle its account until 1990, in the glow of *glasnost* and the end of the Cold War, eager to qualify for U.S. credits.

UNILATERAL FOREIGN ASSISTANCE: AID, GRANTS, AND LOANS

The first notice of a new American foreign economic policy that recognized aid as an integral part of its overall approach to the world came on 12 March 1947, when President Harry Truman went before Congress to ask for $400 million in military and economic aid for Greece and Turkey. Since 1945 the royal government of Greece had been struggling against communist forces within, aided by heavy infiltration from Greece's three northern neighbors, all satellites of the Soviet Union. Great Britain, which had been aiding both

Greece and Turkey, informed the United States in February 1947 that it was no longer able to do so. Truman promptly accepted the responsibility for the United States. In asking authority and funds to assist Greece and Turkey, he propounded a general principle that came to be called the Truman Doctrine: "I believe that it must be the policy of the United States to support free peoples who are resisting attempted subjugation by armed minorities or by outside pressures."

President Truman's proposal met a general favorable response in America, though some critics thought its scope was too broad. Congress acted after two months of debate. An act of 22 May 1947 authorized the expenditure of $100 million in military aid to Turkey and, for Greece, $300 million to be equally divided between military and economic assistance. The act also empowered the president to send military and civilian experts as advisers to Greece and Turkey. American aid thus begun and continued from year to year proved effective as a means of "containment" in that quarter. But the Truman administration moved quickly to assume broader responsibilities.

To Europe as a whole the danger from communism lay principally in the economic stagnation that had followed the war. Western Europe in the spring of 1947 was facing catastrophe after a severe winter. Food and fuel were in short supply, and foreign exchange would be exhausted by the end of the year. Large communist parties in France and Italy stood ready to profit from the impending economic collapse and human suffering.

The best protection against the spread of communism to western Europe would be economic recovery. On this reasoning, Secretary of State George Marshall, speaking at the Harvard commencement on 5 June 1947, offered American aid to such European nations as would agree to coordinate their efforts for recovery and present the United States with a program and specifications of their needs. Congress established the Economic Cooperation Administration to handle the program in April 1948 and at the end of June appropriated an initial $4 billion for the purpose. Thus was launched the Marshall Plan, or European Recovery Program, which was to continue for three years, cost the United States nearly $13 billion, and contribute to an impressive economic recovery in Europe.

The Marshall Plan was designed to aid in the recovery of nations with advanced economies that had been dislocated by the war. But communism was also a threat among the poverty-stricken masses in countries of Asia, Africa, and Latin America, where the modern economy had made little or no progress. The containment of communism required measures to raise the standard of living in countries such as these. It was with this purpose in mind that Truman, in his Inaugural Address of 20 January 1949, proposed his "Point Four," or Technical Assistance program: "We must embark on a bold new program for making the benefits of our scientific advances and industrial progress available for the improvement and growth of underdeveloped areas." The Point Four program got under way in 1950 with a modest appropriation of $35 million. Authorized expenditures for the next three years nearly totaled $400 million.

To stimulate the flow of private capital that hopefully would supplement government-to-government loans and grants, the legislation creating the Marshall Plan also called for establishing the Investment Guaranty Program. Initially, the agency issued insurance contracts for investments in Europe against the possible inconvertibility of local currency; in 1950 the coverage was extended to loss through expropriation or confiscation. As a result of the Korean War, U.S. foreign aid programs shifted in emphasis in 1951 from economic to military aid, thus increasing the importance of private U.S. overseas investment. In that vein, the Mutual Security Acts of 1951 (amended in 1953) and 1954 expanded the focus to guarantees to certain friendly developing countries. After several mutations, including a stay in the Agency for International Development, the guaranty program in 1969 was reestablished as the Overseas Private Investment Corporation and placed under the jurisdiction of the secretary of state. The program history over three decades appears to have been both a substantial inducement to private investment and, because of the fees charged, a profitable undertaking for the government.

MULTILATERAL FOREIGN LOANS

The Bretton Woods Conference of 1944, also known as the United Nations Monetary and Financial Conference and chaired by Secretary of Treasury Henry Morgenthau, ushered in a new era of international monetary cooperation. Designed to abolish the economic ills believed to be responsible for the Great Depression and World War II, it brought together delegates from most of the Allied nations. From the conference came recommendations to establish a new international monetary system and to make international rules for an exchange-rate system, balance-of-payment adjustments, and supplies of reserve assets. The conference's proposals led forty-five nations to establish the International Monetary Fund (IMF) in 1945 and the International Bank for Reconstruction and Development, or World Bank, in 1946. (Membership in the IMF is a prerequisite to membership in the World Bank. Traditionally, the managing director of the IMF is a European, whereas the president of the World Bank is an American.)

The IMF, the brainchild of Harry Dexter White, had as its chief purpose restoring exchange-rate stability in the countries that had been in the war and then to promote international monetary cooperation and the expansion of world trade. It was to provide short- to medium-term monetary assistance to member states experiencing balance-of-payments deficits and to prescribe methods by which recipient nations would be able to eliminate their deficit positions. The IMF has played a significant role in facilitating the growth of the world economy, but it has not been without its critics, who have argued that it imposes inflexible and onerous conditions on individual nations who are having difficulties in meeting their payments. They have charged that the IMF shows little consideration for differences in types of economies; that some of the stabilization programs offer no hope of permanent adjustment; and that the fund is often more interested in short-term, painful, quick-fix programs that do not address the fundamental problems. The latter complaint is bolstered by an examination of the fund's policies during the Yugoslavia crisis in the later 1980s and its failures in meeting the needs of the Haitian crisis of the 1990s. Additionally, critics have complained that the IMF is biased against socialism and favors the free-market approach. While this charge may be debated, it does appear that strategic and political concerns have led the United States to lobby the IMF for increased leniency in the rescheduling of debts for Latin American countries, especially Mexico.

The World Bank's purpose, after initially emphasizing the reconstruction of Europe after World War II, has been both to lend funds to nations at commercial rates and to provide technical assistance to facilitate economic development in its poorer member countries. Essentially, the World Bank was designed to complement the IMF's short-term focus with longer-term developmental goals. It would provide loans aimed at encouraging the development of new, productive resources in countries facing a deficit—especially those resources for which there were reliable foreign markets. The bank's charter stated that it was to promote foreign investment for development through loan guarantees; it was also to supplement private investment in projects it viewed appropriate when other sources of financing were lacking.

The World Bank obtained funds from four sources: capital subscriptions of its member countries, capital market borrowing, loan repayments, and retained earnings. In terms of its financial practices, the bank has had an excellent performance history in that it has earned a profit every year since 1948. In fiscal year 1991, it earned a net income of nearly $1.2 billion on loans in forty-two currencies of some $90 billion.

Robert S. McNamara, president of the World Bank from 1968 to 1981, shifted its goals from concentrating on infrastructure to the alleviation of poverty—the meeting of basic human needs. His successor, A. W. Clausen, a former president of the Bank of America, changed the World Bank's focus in the early 1980s toward reducing the role of state in the economy and the possibilities of privatizing state-owned enterprises. By the end of the 1980s, the bank had shifted again and now began emphasizing the role of women in development and the idea of sustainable development and the environment.

As with the IMF, the World Bank has generated its share of criticism. There were complaints that the two were not coordinating their activities and in some instances actually weakened the fiscal basis of their debtor states. Also, critics have pointed out the bank's efforts to reduce the role of state in the economy—in the belief that it would produce greater efficiency and better economic performance—often did not address the root problems. But it was the bank's difficulties in dealing with debt crises, beginning in the early 1980s, that have prompted the most complaints.

THE INTERNATIONAL DEBT CRISES

From the end of World War II to the 1973–1974 oil crisis, governments gave and loaned to other governments in various ways, but increasingly through international institutions. Defaults were rare. However, the oil crisis resulted in an increase in oil prices that led to the sudden availability of vast sums of "petrodollars" that banks desired to lend, often unwisely, and developing countries eagerly accepted. For example, the bank-held debt of non–oil developing countries increased from $34.5 billion in 1975 to $98.6 billion in 1982, with U.S. banks holding 36.7 percent of the loans.

With the Polish debt crisis of 1981 and Mexican crisis in 1982, the lending stopped abruptly, and since 1982 capital has flowed back from debtors to creditors, impairing the future of developing nations. In the early stages of the crises, at least nine large U.S. banks would have become insolvent if all of their foreign governmental clients had defaulted on their loans. By 1985 the severity of the crisis had passed for the creditor nations; however, the crisis was not over for developing countries, still confronted with staggering debts, who saw their standards of living decline significantly and found little hope for future relief.

Since the early 1980s, the heavily indebted developing nations have been involved in extensive financial negotiations with their international creditors. In 1992 the IMF was managing arrangements with fifty-six countries, twenty-eight in Africa, but the total number of agreements involved in the extraordinarily complex negotiations was much larger. These multilateral debt rescheduling and adjustment undertakings involved widely disparate parties, often with contradictory objectives, which included international financial institutions (such as the IMF, the World Bank, and the creditor clubs in Paris and London), plus a number of transnational banks and official aid agencies of the major creditor nations. While most Latin American debtor countries had borrowed heavily from private, transnational banks, most of the African countries had loans from official bilateral and multilateral agencies. And the debt problem varied greatly. For some nations it was a question of short-term financial liquidity; for others it was more a matter of basic financial solvency. As a result of these negotiations, a global debt regime evolved with most developing countries undertaking substantial economic reforms, but it was not evident that these reforms, by themselves, would deal with the problems.

In 1982, Mexican credits accounted for 41 percent of the total combined capital of the nine largest U.S. banks, threatening their existence should Mexico default on its repayments. In August, when Mexico did not have the $2 billion needed to meet its repayment schedule, Secretary of the Treasury James Baker's staff arranged for $1 billion from the Commodity Credit Corporation to guarantee purchases of U.S. agricultural surpluses. The second billion came in a complicated package from the Department of Energy for future oil deliveries to the Strategic Petroleum Reserve, for which Mexico ended up paying roughly 30 percent interest. The Reagan administration also provided Brazil with $1.2 billion in additional loans to allow it to meet its repayment schedules. Two other U.S. allies, Turkey and the Philippines, both of which faced defaulting on their loans, benefited from reloan packages worked out with the United States and the IMF. The United States, aiming to rescue American banks from their overexposure, had put forward a number of plans—most notably Baker's plan (1989)—which sought to relend without incurring loan writeoffs.

The 1990s saw a continuation of international financial problems. When Mexico again needed financial assistance in 1994, President William Clinton arranged for loan guarantees amounting to some $25 billion despite considerable congressional resistence. In 1997 and 1998 currency speculators disrupted the financial systems of Thailand, Indonesia, South Korea, Malaysia, the Philippines and Taiwan, and eventually impacted the American economy. With U.S. support, the IMF was able to stabilize the situation.

By the end of the 1990s many people believed that the problems of the huge debt being carried by developing countries was threatening the survivability of the creditor nations. This concern was reflected in the popular protests against the World Trade Organization, the IMF, and the World Bank in Seattle, Washington (November 1999), Washington, D.C. (April 2000), and Prague, Czechoslovakia (September 2000). The protestors argued that the developed nations were draining the developing countries of the natural resources without adequate compensation and incurring an ecological debt. They contended that this debt should be used to pay the financial debts incurred by developing nations and owed to the IMF and World Bank.

CONCLUSION

The impact of the experiences of trying to collect World War I war debts had led to the employment of lend-lease in World War II and to a grant system during the Cold War. The United States no longer wanted its foreign policy mired in the business of debt collection or to have the issue of debts cloud its relations with other nations. In 1953 the Point Four program was placed, with other forms of foreign aid, under the Foreign Operations Administration. The so-called foreign aid appropriated annually and intended for friendly nations included aid for economic development and military assistance—which often was the larger package—in the form of grants. While somewhat diminished, grants of economic aid and military support continued into the post–Cold War decades.

The loans and extension of credits by the IMF and World Bank, as well as American banks, gradually came to play a major role in providing loans to developing nations. Indeed, the amount of these loans had become so large and burdensome in the post–Cold War decades that by the end of the century a movement had developed which asked, with modest success, that the wealthier nations agree to "forgive" substantial portions of these obligations.

BIBLIOGRAPHY

Aggarwal, Vinod K. *Debt Game: Strategic Interaction in International Debt Rescheduling.* New York, 1996.

Biersteker, Thomas J., ed. *Dealing with Debt: International Financial Negotiations and Adjustment Bargaining.* Boulder, Colo., 1993. A most helpful introduction to the basic issues of the post-1980 debt crisis.

Bergmann, Carl. *The History of Reparations.* Boston and New York, 1927. Presents the German side of the reparations question.

Brennglass, Alan C. *The Overseas Private Investment Corporation: A Study in Political Risk.* New York, 1983. Reviews the use of government loan guarantees to private investors from 1948 to 1980s.

Carew, Anthony. *Labour Under the Marshall Plan: The Politics of Productivity and the Marketing of Management Science.* Detroit, Mich., 1987.

Dobson, Alan P. *U.S. Wartime Aid to Britain, 1940–1946.* London and Dover, N.H., 1986.

Dougherty, James J. *The Politics of Wartime Aid: American Economic Assistance to France and French Northwest Africa, 1940–1946.* Westport, Conn., 1978.

Eckes, Alfred E. *A Search for Solvency: Bretton Woods and the International Monetary System, 1941–1947.* Austin, Tex., 1975. Standard account of the Bretton Woods system.

Eichengreen, Barry, and Peter H. Lindert, eds. *The International Debt Crisis in Historical Perspective.* Cambridge, Mass., 1989. Very helpful in relating the various financial and debt crises to U.S. policy.

Feis, Herbert. *The Diplomacy of the Dollar: First Era, 1919–1932.* Baltimore, 1950.

———. *Foreign Aid and Foreign Policy.* New York, 1964. A thorough pragmatic and standard postwar analysis of Allied foreign aid and international politics.

Fossedal, Gregory A. *Our Finest Hour: Will Clayton, the Marshall Plan and the Triumph of Democracy.* Stanford, Calif., 1993.

George, Susan. *The Debt Boomerang: How Third World Debt Harms Us All.* Boulder, Colo., 1992. A critical look at World Bank and IMF policies and the dangers of the huge Third World debt to developed nations.

Healy, David. *Drive to Hegemony: The United States in the Caribbean, 1898–1917.* Madison, Wis., 1963. A revisionist study of the rise of American official dominance of independent states of Central America and Greater Antilles.

Herring, George C. *Aid to Russia, 1941–1946: Strategy, Diplomacy, the Origins of the Cold War.* New York, 1973. The starting point for the study of lend-lease.

Hogan, Michael. *The Marshall Plan: America, Britain, and the Reconstruction of Western Europe, 1947–1952.* New York, 1987.

James, Harold. *The German Slump: Politics and Economics, 1924–1936.* Oxford and New York, 1986.

Johannsson, Haraldur. *From Lend-Lease to Marshall Plan Aid: The Policy Implications of U.S. Assistance, 1941–1951.* Reykjavik, 1997.

Jones, Kenneth P. "Discord and Collaboration: Choosing an Agent General for Reparations." *Diplomatic History* 1 (1977): 118–139.

Kent, Bruce. *The Spoils of War: The Politics, Economics, and Diplomacy of Reparations, 1918–1932.* Oxford and New York, 1989. Argues that creditor governments understood Germany could not pay but prolonged the agony to stave off challenges from below.

Keynes, J. M. *The Economic Consequences of the Peace.* New York, 1920. Argues that the reparations forced upon Germany were more than three times the capacity of that nation to pay.

Leffler, Melvyn P. "The Origins of Republican War Debt Policy." *Journal of American History* 59 (1972): 585–601. Makes the case that

Republican Party leaders decided that debts should be collected for domestic reasons.

Martel, Leon. *Lend-Lease, Loans, and the Coming of the Cold War.* Boulder, Colo., 1979.

Miller, Morris. *Coping Is Not Enough! The International Debt Crisis and the Roles of the World Bank and the International Monetary Fund.* Homewood, Ill., 1986.

Massad, Carlos, ed. *The Debt Problem: Acute and Chronic Aspects.* New York, 1985.

Moulton, Harold G., and Leo Pasvolsky. *War Debts and World Prosperity.* Washington, D.C., 1932. The indispensable study of the subject.

Munro, Dana G. *Intervention and Dollar Diplomacy in the Caribbean, 1900–1921.* Westport, Conn., 1964. Contends that the United States intervened in the Caribbean to promote stability and progress in order to prevent imperialist European nations from intervening and thus threatening American security.

Nelson, Joan M. *Aid, Influence, and Foreign Policy.* New York, 1968. A brief but useful introduction to the rationale behind American foreign aid from the end of World War II to the late 1960s.

O'Leary, Michael K. *The Politics of American Foreign Aid.* New York, 1967. One of the first attempts at a comprehensive analysis of how foreign aid appropriations are made.

Perkins, Dexter. *The Monroe Doctrine, 1867–1907.* Gloucester, Mass., 1937. Classic multicultural examination of the subject.

Pisani, Sallie. *The CIA and the Marshall Plan.* Lawrence, Kans., 1991.

Rhodes, Benjamin D. "Reassessing 'Uncle Shylock': The United States and the French War Debt, 1917–1929." *Journal of American History* 55 (1969): 787–803.

———. "Herbert Hoover and the War Debts, 1919–33." *Prologue* 6 (1974): 130–144. Discusses that settlement of World War I debts revolved around the person of Herbert Hoover.

Schuker, Stephen A. *American "Reparations" to Germany, 1919–33: Implications for the Third World Debt Crisis.* Princeton, N.J., 1988.

Silverman, Dan P. *Reconstructing Europe after the Great War.* Cambridge, Mass., 1982. A persuasive account of events.

Siracusa, Joseph M. *Safe for Democracy: A History of America, 1914–1945.* Claremont, Calif., 1993. A good survey of the interwar period from an American perspective.

Siracusa, Joseph M., ed. *The American Diplomatic Revolution: A Documentary History of the Cold War, 1941–1947.* New York, 1976. Provides a good discussion of the background leading up to the Truman Doctrine and the Marshall Plan.

Trachtenberg, Marc. *Reparation in World Politics: France and European Economic Diplomacy, 1916–1923.* New York, 1980. Argues that French efforts to use reparations claims to shift costs of war and reconstruction to other countries were repeatedly rebuffed by the other major powers.

Van Tuyll, Hubert P. *Feeding the Bear: American Aid to the Soviet Union, 1941–1945.* New York, 1989.

Wertman, Patricia A. *Lend-Lease: An Historical Overview and Repayment Issues.* Washington, D.C., 1985.

Williams, Benjamin H. *Economic Foreign Policy of the United States.* New York, 1929. Perceptive and fair-minded contemporary account.

Wood, Robert E. *From Marshall Plan to Debt Crisis: Foreign Aid and Development Choices in the World Economy.* Berkeley, Calif., 1986.

Yielding, Thomas D. *United States Lend-Lease Policy in Latin America.* Denton, Tex., 1983.

See also DOLLAR DIPLOMACY; ECONOMIC POLICY AND THEORY; FOREIGN AID; INTERNATIONAL MONETARY FUND AND WORLD BANK; INTERVENTION AND NONINTERVENTION; OPEN DOOR POLICY; REPARATIONS; WILSONIAN MISSIONARY DIPLOMACY.

MANDATES AND TRUSTEESHIPS

Edward M. Bennett

Mandates and trusteeships have played an important role in the evolution of U.S. diplomacy and perceptions of the foreign policy process. After World War I, the mandate system was introduced at the insistence of President Woodrow Wilson, who believed that indigenous populations in the areas held under colonial rule should be brought either to independence or under benevolent tutorship of the powers holding sway over them. This was part of Wilson's dream to replace the monarchies with democratic republics. Very few new nations actually evolved from the mandate system, and it remained for the trusteeship council emergent from the United Nations structure after World War II to carry on what Wilson began. The mandate name was abandoned in favor of trusteeships in order not to have the stigma of the moribund League of Nations to carry in its baggage. By the end of the 1990s, the membership of the UN reached 187 nations due largely to the work of the trusteeship council's bringing them to nationhood.

LEAGUE OF NATIONS MANDATES

President Woodrow Wilson presented the text of the Covenant of the League of Nations to the Paris Peace Conference on 14 February 1919. He explained to his colleagues that they would find incorporated in the document an old principle intended for more universal use and development—the reference was to mandates for former colonies. In this fashion the mandate system became a part of the new world that Wilson imagined would emerge from the deliberations in Paris. Mandates developed historically from the practice of great power supervision of areas subservient to the controlling power usually adjacent to that power's territory; acceptance of British, French, and American conceptions of the rule of law and colonial freedom and self-government; Edmund Burke's suggestion of the trusteeship principle in administering British colonies in the interest of the inhabitants, taken to heart and subsequently expanded by Parliament after the American Revolution; and the Concert of Europe concept, in which Prince Metternich of Austria attempted to create a conservative coalition to preserve stability and prevent revolutionary changes in Europe at the end of the Napoleonic wars, and its application to former Turkish and French holdings in Africa and the Near East. While the principle may have been old, Wilson's perception of it was new because he wished to universalize it.

Although the British and French delegations at Paris did not oppose the mandate system, they were not in the forefront of those demanding it. Nor were they particularly eager to accept Wilson's freewheeling interpretation of the general mandate system as applying to any and all former enemy colonies. The Japanese and Italian representatives were even less enthusiastic about mandates that might restrict their control of former German colonies. They preferred a division of territory. The Americans were insistent that former enemy colonies would not be treated as spoils of war. In a meeting of the Council of Ten on 28 January 1919, the mandatory principle was discussed. Vittorio Orlando of Italy asked how the former colonies should be divided, what provisions should be made for government, and what should be said about independence. Baron Shinken Makino of Japan asked whether mandates had been accepted, and Georges Clemenceau of France responded that the question was to be taken up later. Wilson would not permit the subject to be buried, so the British prime minister, David Lloyd George, presented a proposal for defining mandates on 30 January 1919, suggesting a division into three types—ultimately defined as A, B, and C mandates. Without citing specific locations, it is sufficient to observe that most of Africa, part of the Middle East, and most of the Pacific island groups were considered to be in one of the categories: A—mandates quickly able to be prepared for independence; B—mandates needing tutelage for some time before being considered for independence; and C—mandates that probably would never be ready for independence.

Wilson's associates at Paris hoped for U.S. participation in the postwar enforcement of the Versailles settlement and did not feel they could strongly oppose him on the mandate issue. Many members of the conference sincerely believed that the mandate system might work, but that it had to draw on existing experience in the colonies and should not promise too much to peoples who could not in the foreseeable future be prepared for nationhood and full citizenship rights. Wilson agreed that in some cases this would be true, but he was less restrictive in the number of former colonies he would place in this category than were some of his colleagues.

There was a tendency at the peace conference to identify someone else's mandates as ready to be placed in the category reasonably close to independence with minimum preparation rather than one's own. Lloyd George, for example, saw most of the colonies being assigned to Great Britain and British Commonwealth nations as more suitable for either direct annexation or deferral. South-West Africa (Namibia), he argued, should be annexed to South Africa because it was not likely to proceed to independence; and South Africa would be better able to care for the people of South-West Africa under South African laws and tax structure. Papua might better be classed as an area that would never be self-governing, and therefore should be permanently assigned to Australia. He could visualize French mandates in northern Africa being prepared for independence. Clemenceau, however, was more inclined to see British mandates as nearing preparation for independence. In effect, then, the mandate system would only be as good as the determination of the powers in the league to carry it out.

Woodrow Wilson was the master planner for the mandate system, but the man responsible for laying out the detailed plans of the process was General Jan Christian Smuts of South Africa. The process began with Wilson's Fourteen Points, drawn up by the journalists Walter Lippmann and Frank Cobb under the general supervision of Colonel Edward House. They read through the president's statements of war aims and compacted them into the program that Wilson set forth in an address to Congress on 8 January 1918. Point 5 called for "A free, open-minded, and absolutely impartial adjustment of all colonial claims, based upon a strict observance of the principle that in determining all such questions of sovereignty the interests of the populations concerned must have equal weight with the equitable claims of the government whose title is to be determined." It was made clear in the Council of Ten discussions at Paris, partly because of British fears concerning the Irish and Indian independence claims, that colonial questions would be restricted to colonies belonging to Germany or coming into being as a result of the war. In practical terms this meant that mandates applied only to the German African and Far Eastern holdings and the non-Turkish parts of the former Ottoman Empire.

Secret treaties signed before or during the war had divided these territories among the victorious powers except the United States, which was not a party to them. Wilson went to Paris determined to set aside these treaties and for that purpose had formulated Point 1 of the Fourteen Points, which called for "open covenants of peace, openly arrived at, after which there shall be no private international understandings of any kind but diplomacy shall proceed always frankly and in the public view."

General Smuts set to work to carry out the mandates charge embodied, at Wilson's insistence, in Article 22 of the League Covenant. The article made it clear that certain of the Turkish territories were ready for nationhood almost immediately, that central African peoples needed mandatory powers that would guarantee their human rights and political and moral tutelage, and that the open door to trade would apply in all mandates. It also determined that South-West Africa and certain of the Pacific islands, because of the sparseness of population, isolation, size, and other circumstances, could best be administered under the laws of the mandatory and as integral portions of its territory, with safeguards for the well-being of the inhabitants supervised by the Mandates Commission. The Permanent Mandates Commission, the later official title of the commission, was to receive annual reports from mandatory powers and complaints relative to the treatment of inhabitants. The reports and complaints were to be sent to the League Council for deliberation.

Wilson met his first defeat on the mandate issue when his allies refused to consider turning mandates over to the administration of small neutral nations. The distribution followed the pattern of the secret treaties, with some other powers added to the list. Motives concerning the possession of mandates were mixed. Some Japanese saw mandates as preludes to annexation or as convenient means to establish secure military and market areas, while others saw them as symbolic of great power status and the promise of a stronger position in the future whether the system worked or not. The open door to trade and the defense of colonial peoples, plus democratization of the world, were the primary American objectives. British, French, and Belgian motives shaded to a greater or lesser degree along the lines of Japanese thinking. "Little England" advocates, who supported reduction in the size of the British Empire and a refocusing on trade expansion, were relieved to see the lessening of colonial responsibilities, while the imperial advocates were alarmed but convinced that the empire could hold together and peace could be secured while the United States participated in the peacekeeping system. France and Belgium were pleased to see the diminution of German power and could live with mandates if that were the result.

Japan proved a special case because it had emerged as a great power at a time when the main symbol of such status—empire—was on the decline. Japanese ambitions in China were set in the old imperial structure. During the war Japan secured a position as a major force in colonial exploitation of China as a result of the Twenty-one Demands presented to China, only to encounter demands for surrender of these privileges at the end of the war. Lloyd George and Clemenceau sided with Japan. This, combined with Japan's threat not to join the League of Nations, forced Wilson to accept the assignment of German rights in Shantung to the Japanese—but with a pledge to return the province to full Chinese sovereignty with only the former German economic privileges remaining to them; Japan was also given the right to establish a settlement at Tsingtao (Qingdao). Thus, Wilson's hopes for an anticolonial postwar structure were already on shaky ground.

Some scholars have argued that the Allies were not sincere in adopting the mandate process and intended to use it as a subterfuge for expanding colonial control. While in some instances this proved to be true, generally the mandates were administered in the interest of the people concerned and a large percentage of the Class A mandates were moved into independence. Most of these were in the former Ottoman Empire, such as Trans-Jordan, Syria, Palestine, and Lebanon. Wilson's charge to the peace conference in the plenary session of 14 February 1919 was only partially observed; but his expectations on mandates were more fulfilled than in most other areas of the Fourteen Points. Wilson told the conference members that they were "done with annexation of helpless peoples," and henceforth nations would consider it their responsibility to protect and promote the interests of people under their tutelage before their own interests. It would remain for the United Nations, not the League of Nations, to carry out this promise.

Often overlooked in judging Wilson's objectives are the underlying premise and promise that he undertook to deliver as a result of American participation in the war—making the world safe for democracy. Success meant the elimination of the monarchical and colonial systems. Wilson envisioned the states that were to emerge from the mandate system as democratic republics.

UNITED NATIONS TRUSTEESHIPS

The United States entered the era following World War II with the same idea and again faced opposition from its allies. President Franklin D. Roosevelt attempted in the Atlantic Charter to reestablish the framework for bringing the colonial peoples of the world to free government. The ramifications of this were not lost on British Prime Minister Winston Churchill, who at one point, in a fit of pique, told Roosevelt that he did not become his majesty's first minister in order to preside over the disintegration of the British Empire. Soviet Premier Josef Stalin, on the other hand, was ready with his own interpretation of what free government meant; it included only the right to be a communist state, insofar as the Soviet Union had the military power to ensure such determination of national sovereignty.

President Roosevelt, as a follower of President Wilson's view of dependent peoples, spoke frequently to the issue of independent states in his foreign policy pronouncements of the 1930s. He attempted to promote a new relationship away from the orientation of his predecessors in his Good Neighbor policy in Latin America. His focus was on the preservation and expansion of democracy, and, in the vein of Wilson's Fourteen Points, he set forth war aims in the Atlantic Charter and his Four Freedoms speech. In the former, he persuaded his allies to agree to the principle of self-determination, and in the latter, he attempted to promote freedom of speech, religion, and from fear and want, which he related to his Atlantic Charter objectives. He irritated Churchill by his inclination to encourage the Indians by trying to contact Gandhi while the Indian leader was incarcerated and tried to establish rapport with such leaders in the Middle East as King Saud of Arabia. Also, he tried to convince the French and British to withdraw from their colonial holdings in the Far East.

The concept of trusteeship appeared first in discussions of the Big Three at Yalta in 1945 but was also discussed in general form in the Department of State during the war. It was agreed at Yalta that trusts would be set up under United Nations auspices, with decisions being made on the general procedure by the five powers having permanent seats on the Security Council. (Trusts were substituted for mandates in order not to have any carryover from the moribund League of Nations and because they were to have a broader definition.) Trusteeships would apply only to territories still under mandate in 1939, areas detached from the defeated enemies, or territories voluntarily placed under the system, with the specific geographic areas to be determined later.

John Foster Dulles represented the United States on the Fourth Committee at the twenty-seventh plenary meeting of the United Nations in 1945, which was charged with developing the trusteeship system. Dulles followed Wilson in his challenge to the colonial system, proclaiming that the committee was determined to assume the responsibility for boldly addressing the whole colonial problem, which involved hundreds of millions of people, not just the 15 million who might come under trusteeship. He presented a clarion call for the destruction of colonialism. The anticolonial thrust initiated by Dulles in the name of the committee became a part of the United Nations trusteeship system and continued over the next fifty-five years, implementing Wilson's dreams beyond his expectations and with results not imagined in his time. According to Alger Hiss, the State Department official who in 1948 would be accused of being part of a communist spy ring, there is considerable irony in the wholehearted support for the trusteeship system outlined by the United States at San Francisco. Hiss recalled that Churchill was skeptical of the operation and that Secretary of State Edward R. Stettinius turned to Hiss and told him to explain it to Churchill. Hiss off the top of his head set forth the structure of the trusteeship system, and Churchill put his okay on it. Thus, Dulles adopted as gospel a plan put forth by Hiss, whom he later treated as a pariah. There emerged such a myriad of states in Africa, the Near East, and Asia, with differing national objectives and systems, as to boggle the minds of those who originated the mandate system and its objectives.

Chapter 4 of the report of the United Nations Preparatory Commission ordered the Fourth Committee to deal with trusteeships in the interest of the trust peoples. Accordingly, the committee outlined the rules and procedures, including creation of the Trusteeship Council. While this looked very good to the creators of the trust system, reservations appeared immediately, including objections from U.S. Army and Navy spokesmen, who urged outright annexation of the strategic Pacific islands taken from the Japanese. The president and the Department of State proposed a compromise based on the anticolonial position in Articles 82 and 83 of the charter. As primary sponsor of the trusteeships, the United States could scarcely reserve certain areas for annexation. Article 76 sets forth the provisions and restrictions applying to trustee powers and includes procedures leading to independence, representative government, and economic development. It was overridden at the San Francisco conference establishing the United Nations, however, by insertion of articles 82 and 83 of the charter. These articles provide that areas within trust territories might be set aside as "strategic areas" under the direct control of the trustee, which is answerable to the Security Council, where the veto power applies, instead of to the General Assembly, where it does not apply. In this fashion Micronesia—comprising the Marshall, Caroline, and Mariana islands, but not the Gilbert, Nauru, and Ocean islands administered by Australia and the United Kingdom—became the strategic area of the Pacific under U.S. supervision.

CONCLUSION

The trust principle seems to work more effectively for the objectives established in the Charter of the United Nations than did the mandate system under the League of Nations, because the Trusteeship Council is composed of those determined to carry it through and because it is under constant public scrutiny. Regular and voluminous

MICRONESIA: THE ROAD TO SELF-GOVERNANCE

By the mid-1970s, the complex process of negotiating the eventual end of the U.S.-supervised Trust Territory of the Pacific Islands was well underway. The UN Trusteeship Council report in the July 1974 issue of the *UN Monthly Chronicle* noted the council's concern as discussions between the United States and the Micronesian congress continued to be oriented toward the choice of free association for six districts represented in the congress. The district comprising the northern Marianas engaged in separate negotiations concerning commonwealth status under United States sovereignty. Reported discussions between representatives of the Marshall Islands and the United States also disturbed the council, which wondered how they would affect the inhabitants of the Carolines. Micronesia's landmass was only about 700 square miles, comprising more than 2,000 islands in the three major archipelagoes and spanning some 3 million square miles of ocean. The northern Marianas's apparent movement toward becoming the first territory acquired by the United States since the purchase of the Virgin Islands in 1917 was considered by the Trusteeship Council to be a literal violation of the trust arrangement intended to keep Micronesia together as an integral unit.

Members of the Trusteeship Council insisted that the United States should not proceed with incorporation of the area unless satisfactory arrangements were made with the Micronesian congress. The congress agreed to separate discussions, and a commonwealth agreement was signed on Saipan in February 1975, climaxing two years of formal negotiations; it was then to go to the sixteen-member Marianas district legislature for approval. In June 1975 the agreement was submitted to a United Nations–administered plebiscite, which was overseen by a committee of the Trusteeship Council. The council reported that it was properly conducted and that the results, which favored joining the northern Mariana Islands to the United States by commonwealth status, represented the will of the people. The islands were to be self-governing, and when all steps were carried out to accomplish this, the Trusteeship Agreement would be terminated for the entire Trust Territory as well as for the northern Marianas.

In 1979 four districts (Kosrae, Pohnpei, Truk, and Yap, in the Carolines) established themselves as the new Federated States of Micronesia (FSM), while two other districts formed republics, the Marshall Islands (1979) and Palau (1981). In 1986 the United States declared that the Trust Territory was terminated, and though the Soviet Union blocked UN Security Council approval of this measure, it was approved by the UN Trusteeship Council. In 1994 Palau became, like the FSM and Marshall Islands, a self-governing sovereign state with the United States responsible for its defense.

---

reports from the Trusteeship Council had dwindled to pamphlet size by 1972. By 1975 the last two trust territories, Papua New Guinea and Micronesia, were determining their course toward independence or other disposition. In all, eleven trusteeships had originally been assigned to the council. The other nine had been Nauru, Ruanda-Urundi, French Cameroons, French Togoland, Italian Somaliland, Western Samoa, British Cameroons, British Togoland, and Tanganyika. From the trusteeships or released territories, ten nations had emerged in 1947, several in the 1950s, fourteen in 1960, and others later. Very often the result has not been satisfying, for the virulent nationalism exhibited by the new states has mirrored the worst traits of their older counterparts. Many celebrated nationhood by immediately sinking into anarchy or by trying to annex neighbors in wars of "liberation."

If success for the mandates and trusteeships is measured in terms of achieving independence, the trusteeship system obviously has been more successful. If it is measured in terms of achieving economic, political, and cultural development before nationhood, perhaps the more cautious approach of the mandate system has provided better results. In any case, the net result was that colonialism of the old order, with direct control of territory and people, and with no pretense of self-government, was dead by the end of 1975.

The objective of creating a nation-state system of democratic republics operating on a constitutional structure with governments of, by, and for the people—Woodrow Wilson's dream—is far from achievement. The most orderly and stable transitions came in the states that emerged from territories formerly under British control, where the population was generally educated for self-rule. Trust territories where there was literally no preparation for self-rule and independence emerged with bloody struggles for power and unstable systems of government. In a considerable measure this result arose from the failure of mandate and trusteeship powers to take seriously their charge to use all deliberate speed to prepare the populations for independence. All too often, however, the period of preparation was too short; and in some instances the viability of the states created might be questioned in terms of their ability to become economically self-sufficient. For better or for worse, the states now exist, and the next problem for them is to learn some degree of tolerance for one another and to curb the excesses of nationalism thus far exhibited.

BIBLIOGRAPHY

Hall, H. Duncan. *Mandates, Dependencies and Trusteeships.* London and Washington, D.C., 1948. The most comprehensive study of the background, origins, and development of the mandate system.

Leibowitz, Arnold H. *A Comprehensive Analysis of United States Territorial Relations.* Dordrecht, Netherlands, 1989. An overview of U.S. policy and results in the U.S. dependencies.

Mezerik, A. G., ed. *Colonialism and the United Nations.* New York, 1964. An academic study of the trust system in the general context of international relations or international organization.

Nevin, David. *The American Touch in Micronesia.* New York, 1977. Provides a perspective on the U.S. influence in the region.

Pomeroy, Earl S. *Pacific Outpost: American Strategy in Guam and Micronesia.* Stanford, Calif., 1951. An excellent account of the American concern for strategic position in the Pacific region; it treats the single exception to the general trust system.

Roff, Sue Rabbitt. *Overreaching in Paradise: United States Policy in Palau Since 1945.* Juneau, Alaska, 1991.

Russell, Ruth B., and Jeanne E. Muther. *A History of the United Nations Charter: The Role of the United States, 1940–1945.* Washington, D.C., 1958. Useful in tracing the background of the trusteeship principle.

Stuart, Peter C. *Isles of Empire: The United States and Its Overseas Possessions.* Lanham, Md., 1999. This is the most comprehensive analysis to date of U.S. policy relating to the trust territories and other dependencies.

Temperley, H. W. V. *A History of the Peace Conference of Paris.* 6 vols. London, 1920–1924. Provides considerable insight on the discussions and development of the mandate question.

United Nations Department of Public Information. *Everyman's United Nations.* 8th ed. New York, 1968. Provides extensive information on the development and implementation of the trusteeship system.

United States Department of State. *The Foreign Relations of the United States: The Paris Peace Conference.* 13 vols. Washington, D.C., 1942–1945. Gives the best information on Woodrow Wilson's perspective on mandates.

Upthegrove, Campbell L. *Empire by Mandate: A History of the Relations of Great Britain with the Permanent Mandates Commission of the League of Nations.* New York, 1954. The most comprehensive work tracing the British adjustment to the mandate concept and the British government's dealings with the Mandates Commission.

See also ANTI-IMPERIALISM; COLONIALISM AND NEOCOLONIALISM; IMPERIALISM; PROTECTORATES AND SPHERES OF INFLUENCE; SELF-DETERMINATION; WILSONIANISM.

MILITARISM

William Kamman

Near the turn of the twentieth century, Secretary of War Elihu Root told a Chicago audience: "We are a peaceful, not a military people, but we are made of fighting fiber and whenever fighting is by hard necessity the business of the hour we always do it as becomes the children of great, warlike races." Theodore Roosevelt's admonition, "Speak softly and carry a big stick," says it more succinctly, and the great seal of the United States with an eagle clutching both an olive branch and thirteen arrows expresses the idea symbolically. The history of the United States offers many examples of the nation at peace and war, speaking softly while carrying a big stick. But does one characteristic dominate?

Although the nation's rise to imperial size and world power during the twentieth century may suggest military influence, historians do not agree among themselves. Samuel Flagg Bemis, a distinguished diplomatic historian, described manifest destiny as a popular conviction that the nation would expand peacefully and by republican example; it was not, in his view, predicated on militarism. During the expansionist period (excepting the Civil War), the army and navy were small and there was no conscription. Dexter Perkins, another distinguished historian of the same generation, would agree with this interpretation. The United States completed its continental domain, he said, with less violence than usually accompanies such expansion. Perkins believed that Americans have only reluctantly recognized the role of power in international affairs and that they desire a reduction of armaments compatible with national security. Undoubtedly influenced by Cold War events, particularly intervention in Vietnam, many writers have challenged such interpretations. Dissenters such as J. William Fulbright, chairman of the Senate Committee on Foreign Relations, saw a trend toward militarism in foreign policy arising after 1945, when extreme emphasis on defense and anticommunism led to a national security state with huge military budgets, increased executive power, and greater commitments abroad. Others maintain that militarism emerged at the beginning of the twentieth century, when—according to historian Gabriel Kolko—Presidents William McKinley, Theodore Roosevelt, and Woodrow Wilson "scaled the objectives of American foreign policy to the capacity of American power to extend into the world." Still others discern imperialism broadly defined as a goal of American policy from the very beginning and suggest that recent military events are the logical culmination of trends over two centuries.

Militarism, like its frequent handmaiden, imperialism, is an avowedly distasteful phenomenon to Americans. The term can be broadly or narrowly defined and may be tailored to circumstances. Noah Webster defines militarism as predominance of the military class or prevalence of their ideals; the spirit that exalts military virtues and ideals; the policy of aggressive military preparedness. In his history of militarism, Alfred Vagts distinguished between militarism and the military way, the latter referring to the legitimate use of men and matériel to prepare for and fight a war decided on by the civilian powers of a state. Militarism does not necessarily seek war and therefore is not the opposite of pacifism; in its spirit, ideals, and values it pairs more precisely with civilianism.

Although most nations offer examples of militarism, the attitude is most often associated in the American mind with Prussia and Wilhelmian Germany. Expressions of militarism and policies reflecting it were clearly discernible in the Germany of that time. The writings of the historian Heinrich von Treitschke and of General Friedrich von Bernhardi seemed representative of a general view that war was natural and right; and Otto von Bismarck, called to lead the Prussian king's struggle for army reform without parliamentary interference, emphasized power at the expense of liberalism, once telling the parliamentary budget commission that iron and blood, not speeches and majority decisions, settled the great questions of the day. For a time the Prussian nobility regarded the army as their almost exclusive opportunity for power and rank and sought to discourage the rise of bourgeois elements in the officer corps. Loyalty was to their noble class for the maintenance of its privileges. With his swashbuckling manner, Kaiser Wilhelm II epitomized German militarism for Americans, and the 1914 invasion of Belgium—despite a treaty guaranteeing that nation's neutrality ("just a scrap of paper" and "necessity knows no law" said Berlin)—represented the immorality of German militarism and its refusal to accept any constraints.

THE EIGHTEENTH CENTURY

In the American experience, some of the traditional marks of militarism are lacking. There has been no aristocratic class, except perhaps in the antebellum South, which regarded military values highly and the army as a career preferable to business and civilian professions. There have been few challenges to civilian dominance over the military and little disagreement during most of American history about a small standing army. In the United States, any militarism must exist alongside democratic, liberal, civilian traditions and sometimes even have their support. Generally, this support has not been lacking when achievement of foreign policy goals (continental expansion, defense of the Monroe Doctrine, neutral rights, preservation of the European or world balance of power) has seemed to require military power. With that support the evidence of militarism in the United States increases as the nation accepts greater foreign policy commitments.

Late eighteenth- and nineteenth-century American history shows few signs of militarism. Americans were not militaristic because there was no rationale for it. Yet these were not years of unbroken peace, for, as Root said, Americans were willing to fight when need was apparent. American fortune allowed war preparations after the crisis developed and permitted rapid demobilization when it was past, or as historian Daniel J. Boorstin, referring to the American Revolution and later American wars, said, "the end of the war and the end of the army were substantially . . . the same." Strong pressures for militarism in the United States came mainly after a long development of antimilitaristic sentiment.

American military efforts in the Revolution and the successful preservation of independence brought no changes in colonial antipathy (learned from the English cousins) to standing armies. A standing army was, for the revolutionary generation, dangerous to liberty and a tool for establishing intolerable despotisms. Americans believed that those who had arms and were disciplined in their use would dominate and that a standing army was inconsistent with free government. As noted by Bernard Bailyn in *The Ideological Origins of the American Revolution,* such thoughts reflected the influence of earlier English writers and was dogma that prevailed with little dispute throughout nineteenth- and into twentieth-century American history. For colonists the British army might provide needed defense, but it should do so with few demands on colonial life or pocketbook. After 1763, when England kept several thousand troops in America, there was distrust in the colonies; on the eve of the Revolution, the Continental Congress memorialized the king with their grievances about the standing army in their midst and the commander in chief's assertion of authority over civil governments in America. In the Declaration of Independence, the Founders repeated these charges. Many Americans were convinced that the army was not needed and colonial wars of past years—referred to by the names of the British monarchs—were of little interest to them. This attitude reflects the isolation of the colonies and illustrates its effect on military thinking. Thomas Paine emphasized it when he urged separation from Britain. Britain fought for its own interests, he said, not for any attachment to Americans: "She did not protect us from our enemies on our account; but from her enemies on her own account." Independence would demonstrate America's isolation and lessen the need for a large professional military establishment.

More important in colonial experience was the armed citizen, the embattled farmer who was ready at a minute's notice to defend family and community. Most of the able free male inhabitants of an English settlement were armed because dispersed settlement made it necessary. They were accustomed to the rigors of hard life and were familiar with firearms. Although most of them served in the militia, the drills and reviews offered little instruction; the men were little inclined to military training or subordination. These plain citizens with arms were the military men; their presence made civilian control over the army a reality well before adoption of a constitution in which that principle was firmly embedded. During the Revolution many of these armed men served in the Continental army, the militia, or in some irregular capacity. They have been variously described as ragged, dirty, sickly, and ill-disciplined, unused to service, impatient of command, and destitute of resources.

One foreign observer, however, believed the whole nation had much natural talent for war and military life. All descriptions were apt for the citizen soldiers for whom General George Washington sometimes despaired, but with favorable geography and foreign aid, without which success would have been difficult, they won. The victory amid political and economic confusion did not emphasize the military prowess of the Continental army or of the militiamen, and fortunately, too, for the civilian tradition, the man who commanded those victorious arms did not have the seeming messianic impulse of Napoleon, Charles de Gaulle, or Douglas MacArthur.

Washington reinforced civilian dominance at the time the nation was formed and precedents were set. He understood that the Revolution needed the support of public opinion as well as successful military efforts; he emphasized to his civilian soldiers their own interests (not those of some king) in the conflict; and he remained subordinate to Congress. At the end of the war, when soldiers were grumbling about back pay and unkept promises of future reward, Washington counseled patience and obedience. It was a time when politicians were scheming with discontented officers and there was imminent danger of military interference in political matters, but Washington's position prevailed. In June 1783, most of the army disbanded and the following December the Virginia planter-turned-general resigned his commission and went home. Never again in American history would the army be so close to open defiance of civilian authority. The disbanded troops met general public opposition to their demands for further pay; many received little or nothing. Civilian suspicion of military men was also revealed in public reaction to the Society of Cincinnati, a social and charitable organization of officers with membership passing through primogeniture. Opposition focused on the aristocratic trappings and possible military pressure on government. It was a natural civilian and democratic reaction from the likes of Thomas Jefferson, John Adams, and John Jay.

THE NINETEENTH CENTURY

The colonial heritage, experience in the Revolution, and constitutional constraints influenced the military policy of the new nation. The Constitution firmly established civilian dominance, although it did not prohibit a standing army. The president was commander in chief of the armed forces of the United States, including state militiamen called into the nation's service; Congress had the power to provide and support an army and navy but no appropriations for the army would be for more than two years; and Congress had the power to declare war. Under Congress's suspicious eye, the army remained small throughout the nineteenth century, except for bulges during the century's four major wars. Liberal sentiment—a heritage of the Enlightenment as accepted by Americans and passed on through the Declaration of Independence—emphasized tolerance, progress, and the individual; these traits allowed only restricted acceptance of military development, especially in the absence of any great threat and as American expansion moved apace with little opposition. Alexander Hamilton might call for substantial military preparations in 1797–1798 and support creation of a U.S. military academy (a proposal attacked as aristocratic and militaristic but nonetheless implemented in 1802), Secretary of War John C. Calhoun might in 1820 make a well-reasoned plea for the standing army against economy cuts, or Henry Clay might argue for greater defense in the face of an alleged European threat during the Latin American revolutions—but they failed to alter substantially the American mood for a small army. Diplomatic efforts of John Adams preserving peace in the late 1790s, or of Thomas Jefferson and John Quincy Adams extending the nation's boundaries, or unilateral pronouncements such as the no-transfer resolution and the Monroe Doctrine all seemed to provide at little expense what Americans wanted.

When diplomacy faltered, the United States did turn to war. Some of these wars were aggressive, fought by a young, nationalistic, and expansionist people. In the case of the Mexican War, there was heavy opposition to the conflict, marked notably by Henry David Thoreau's call for civil disobedience, more a challenge to the extension of slavery than to the war itself. There were many other armed conflicts in nineteenth-century American history than students may remember, if they ignore the numerous army engagements with the Indians—estimated between 1,200 and

1,500—lasting until 1898. These conflicts with Native Americans have posed serious and complicated questions for interpreters of U.S. history. Wars and diplomatic negotiations with England, France, Spain, and Mexico established the country's continental boundaries by mid-nineteenth century, but relations with the native inhabitants of these lands remained ambiguous and problematic into the latter part of the century. These relations were clashes of culture besmirched with greed, maladministration, and corruption and based on force to overcome resistance. Reconciling the territorial desires of the country and its people with respect for Indian lands was in the end impossible. While some leaders of the new nation might want to advance the nation's perceived well-being without sacrificing its honor in treating with indigenous people, it was never, as the historian Francis Paul Prucha notes in his *Sword of the Republic* (1969), the intent of the U.S. government to halt the westward movement for all time.

There was bound to be conflict, and despite their hostility toward standing armies, the country's leaders established an army, although small, to resolve problems caused by the movement of Americans into frontier lands. U.S. policy was established by treaties and laws and generally administered by civilian agents at first from the War Department and later the Department of the Interior. The regular army, frequently supplemented by militia troops, was available to provide force when deemed necessary. Many officers and their men had contempt for Native Americans, and there was excessive violence in handling Indian affairs, including extensive bloody wars to remove tribes from their homes as in Florida (1835–1842, a result of government policy on removal) or in actions of militiamen, as in the Chivington massacre in Colorado (1864). Robert Wooster in *The Military and United States Indian Policy, 1865–1903* (1988) remarks that a view of Indians as subhumans obstructing civilization's advance allowed officers to avoid moral misgivings in the face of brutal actions. Yet some officers such as General William Tecumseh Sherman, who supported strong action against Indians and did not view them as equals, understood their resistance.

The westward advance—imperialism under the name of manifest destiny, with army support—provides evidence of militarism, but there was little or no glorification of martial virtues or the martial spirit except as Hollywood might in later years portray it. Despite the army's role, there was a strong civilian influence on what was done. Sometimes when the army removed white invaders from Indian land or controlled trade with Indians there were complaints of military tyranny. Early legislation provided that persons apprehended for violating Indian territory would be subject to civil, not military, courts, and there were cases of civil actions brought against officers for performing such duties. There was also the belief among some army personnel that civilians frequently caused Indian problems, hoping to encourage military action. While fighting was an important part of the army's assignment in the West, it had a multipurpose role well beyond the use of force. Michael L. Tate in *The Frontier Army in the Settlement of the West* (1999) describes the army's major accomplishments in civilian-oriented tasks, including exploration and mapping, road and bridge building, agricultural experimentation, meteorological service, and a variety of services for persons going to and returning from the West.

Slavery provided the moral setting for the greatest threat to the Union and the most severe test of the civilian-military relationship in the nineteenth century. The occasion was a civil rather than a foreign war, and for that reason the internal threat seemed more imminent and restrictions on civil liberties more justified. President Abraham Lincoln was not happy about some measures taken nor the exuberance of some officers in carrying out regulations, but he thought preservation of the Union required adequate measures, even including suspending the writ of habeas corpus, detaining thousands of persons for disloyalty, sending hundreds of provost marshals into the country to oversee conscription and internal security, and using military officers and men in political campaigns to ensure election of administration supporters. Few people today would question Lincoln's motives, although his means are debatable. Yet national elections were not canceled (Lincoln defeated a general he had earlier removed from command), and the restrictions were not permanent although military governments were established in the South, some occupation troops remaining until 1877. Noteworthy, too, is the civilian control of the restrictive militaristic policies—a condition, according to some historians, not dissimilar to the civilian aspect of present-day militarism. In foreign relations, the Civil War demonstrated the nation's relative immunity to foreign dangers even at a time of great internal peril—what better argument to challenge calls for greater military preparedness after the war? Also significant was Lincoln's broad interpretation of presidential powers during wartime, a legacy enlarged by future chief executives whose actions have fed much of the debate on militarism and imperialism in recent American history.

When the guns fell silent after Appomattox, more than a million men went home and the fleet of almost 700 ships declined to fewer than 200, many unseaworthy. Public attitude was the usual postwar aversion to things military, although the war had its heroes and the people elected General Ulysses S. Grant president as earlier they had chosen George Washington, Andrew Jackson, William Henry Harrison, and Zachary Taylor. Also, as after earlier wars, veterans' organizations developed to promote patriotism and economic self-interest and preserve wartime camaraderie. The Military Order of the Loyal Legion of the United States, as the Aztec Club after the Mexican War, was modeled on the Society of the Cincinnati and had little impact. The Grand Army of the Republic was of greater importance. Its influence was probably more effective on veterans' benefits and patriotic observance than its sometimes divided opinions on foreign and military policies. As the historian May Dearing has noted, the GAR was so busy with patriotic exercises, textbooks with a loyal Northern bias, and military instruction in schools (denounced by writers, peace groups, and some labor unions as militaristic) that it had little time for "jingoistic fulminations against other countries." Nonetheless, the patriotic exuberance may have encouraged public sentiment for war in 1898, and when war came the GAR leadership supported it and the territorial expansion that followed.

Still, old dogmas of civilian dominance over the military and a small army and navy prevailed, but there were changes affecting the economy and foreign policy that would alter the traditional civilian-military relationship over the next decades. In the thirty-five years following the war, the nation's population more than doubled; by the end of the century, American manufacturers had made the United States the world's industrial giant; American exports during the latter half of the 1890s exceeded a billion dollars annually. Few people could doubt America's claim to the status of a world power: there remained only the emulation of European imperialism to give formal recognition of that fact, and that came with the Spanish-American War of 1898. Whether America's fin de siècle imperialism was a great aberration, part of a search for markets, a continuation of earlier expansionism, an expression of manifest destiny, or simply a duplication of European practices, U.S. policy would not be the same again, and in the formulation of that foreign policy there were unmistakable signs of militaristic thinking.

As early as the 1840s, General Dennis Hart Mahan, father of the naval officer and historian Alfred Thayer Mahan, had urged creation of a more effective regular army to carry America's influence to the world. Mahan believed that the United States was probably the least military of the civilized nations, "though not behind the foremost as a warlike one." "To be warlike," he went on, "does not render a nation formidable to its neighbors. They may dread to attack it, but have no apprehensions from its offensive demonstrations." The Mexican War had demonstrated the military potential of the United States, and, however slow Americans were in profiting from the lesson, the rest of the world recognized it. General Mahan's vision of military glory went far beyond defense of the nation to an extension of its power outside the continent. Despite Mahan's vision and the arguments of such generals as Emory Upton, who deplored civilian control over strictly military matters and overdependence on armed citizenry in war, there was little change in American opinion.

While the navy experienced the same reluctance to abandon traditional military policies and became embroiled in politics and spoils, it was free of some of the public's extreme suspicion of a standing army and benefited immensely from that apostle of navalism and imperialism, Alfred Thayer Mahan, and two of his sometimes overlooked contemporaries, Rear Admiral Stephen B. Luce, founder of the Naval War College where Mahan expounded his ideas, and Benjamin Harrison's secretary of the navy, Benjamin F. Tracy, advocate of a battleship fleet. The naval building program also spawned lobbyists and vested interests in the industries providing the new matériel and equipment. Wanting to avoid overdependence on foreign suppliers, Congress in 1886 required navy shipbuilders to use only matériel of domestic manufacture. The following year the Bethlehem Iron Company agreed to supply the first American-made armor plate and in 1888 began production of the first steel propeller shafts for U.S. warships.

Like his father, Alfred T. Mahan had a vision of America's world position—a vision, perceived through study of British naval history, not confined to defensive preparations. The younger Mahan's message emphasized sea power as a source of national greatness: the building of a battleship fleet to protect U.S. interests, if not to reach distant countries at least to keep clear the main approaches to America. The sea is a highway, he said, and ships providing access to the world's wealth and traveling on that highway must have secure ports and must, as far as possible, have "the protection of their country throughout the voyage." The United States with safe frontiers and plentiful internal resources might live off itself indefinitely in "our little corner" but, suggested Mahan with a tone more of warning than speculation, "should that little corner be invaded by a new commercial route through the Isthmus, the United States in her turn might have the rude awakening of those who have abandoned their share in the common birthright of all people, the sea. The canal—a great commercial path—would bring the great nations of Europe closer to our shores than ever before and it will not be so easy as heretofore to stand aloof from international complications." He saw in Americans an instinct for commerce, preferably in their own ships, a possibility for colonies, and a need to control an isthmian canal. For him, war was sometimes necessary just as the policeman's work was necessary; through such organized force the world progressed.

As many Americans accepted Mahan's strategic proposals to give a historical validity to their imperialist, militarist policies, so many also adopted Charles Darwin's theory of biological development to lend scientific support for survival of the fittest in international relations. In his study of social Darwinism, the historian Richard Hofstadter remarked that although Americans did not have to wait for Darwin to justify racism, militarism, or imperialism—all present in American history before 1859—Darwinism was a convenient handle to explain their beliefs in Anglo-Saxon superiority, meaning pacific and belligerent expansion.

Few people typify the spirit of Mahan in the milieu of Darwinism as well as Theodore Roosevelt, a strong exponent of the "large policy" designed to make the United States a world power and possessor of colonies to provide bases and encourage trade. As a Rough Rider, public official, or historian, Roosevelt admired strength, pursued power, was sometimes a demagogue, sometimes chauvinistic, his ardent nationalism easily becoming militaristic. Roosevelt's call for a strenuous life revealed much that could be ominously dangerous: "We do not admire the man of timid peace. We admire the man who embodies victorious effort; the man who never wrongs his neighbor, who is prompt to help a friend, but who has those virile qualities necessary to win in the stern strife of actual life." He did not want to avoid war simply to save lives or money; the cause was what mattered. "If we," he said, "are to be a great people, we must strive in good faith to play a great part in the world. . . . The timid man, the lazy man, the man who distrusts his country, the over-civilized man, who has lost the great fighting, masterful virtues, the ignorant man of dull mind, whose soul is incapable of feeling the mighty lift that thrills 'stern men with empires in their brains'"—thus he characterized people unwilling to undertake the duties of empire by supporting an adequate army and navy. He urged Americans to read the *Congressional Record* to identify those opposed to appropriations for new ships, or the purchase of armor, or other military preparations. These men, Roosevelt declared, worked to bring disaster on the country; they had no share in the glory of Manila; "they did ill for the national honor." He feared the nation would become a weak giant like China. That tragedy could be avoided through a life of strenuous endeavor. Every man, woman, and child had duties: the man, to do man's work; the woman, to be homemaker and "fearless mother of many healthy children"; and the child, to be taught not to shirk difficulties. Roosevelt had little patience for the timidity of those who opposed empire or their canting about liberty and consent of the governed "in order to excuse themselves for their unwillingness to play the part of men." Not many Americans had Roosevelt's eloquence or his platform, but many shared his sentiments.

THE TWENTIETH CENTURY

Nationalism, an effort to exert greater influence beyond the country's borders, and a willingness to threaten or use force, while not new in United States foreign policy, seemed more apparent as the country moved into the twentieth century. Several episodes of American foreign and military policy highlight this trend.

Deficiencies of the U.S. Army in the Spanish war necessitated a revamping of the military organization. Using European precedents, Secretary of War Elihu Root proposed several changes, including creation of the Army War College and a general staff. Much opposition came from entrenched interests in the army and the state militias, but through compromise Root's proposals passed. America's participation in World War I was more effective because of these changes. For some people development of the general staff raised a specter of militarism. Walter Millis, a student of militarism, writing in 1958 commented on Root's contribution and mused that without it American participation in the Great War might not have occurred. "But Root, like all large figures," Millis said, "was only a reflection of his times. There were many other architects of the great disaster of militarism which was to supervene in 1914–18."

The new navy was begun under the administrations of James A. Garfield and Chester A. Arthur. In 1883, Congress approved four steel vessels, and the building program continued through subsequent administrations, especially the Mahan-influenced presidency of Theodore Roosevelt, when emphasis was on battleship construction. A major turn came after war broke out in Europe. Since Roosevelt's presidency, American naval policy had called for a navy second only to Great Britain. In 1915 policy proclaimed a navy second to none. The naval appropriations act of 1916 had no precedent for its naval construction plans. A strong opponent, House majority leader Claude Kitchin, argued futilely that approval would make the United States "the greatest military-naval Nation the world has ever seen." The act reveals an interesting dichotomy, showing the uneasy American attitude toward military measures by combining large appropriations for warships with a renunciation of armed aggression, and an endorsement, in principle, of disarmament. Wilson's support for a strong navy shows his realization of the interaction of military power and diplomacy. The navy would allow the United States to meet existing challenges and to perform the international tasks it expected after the war.

In Latin American policy and in implementation of the Monroe Doctrine, Americans showed a new assertiveness resulting, particularly in the twentieth century, in frequent military interventions, intervention to remain a standard response to political instability until the 1930s. In 1896, Secretary of State Richard Olney and President Grover Cleveland confronted the British with "the United States is practically sovereign on this continent, and its fiat is law upon the subjects to which it confines its interposition." A few years later, Theodore Roosevelt, fearful of European intervention (perhaps a German naval base in the debt-ridden Dominican Republic), accepted for the United States the role of international policeman in the Caribbean. From the Roosevelt Corollary, the Platt Amendment with Cuba, the responsibilities of dollar diplomacy, and the 1903 canal treaty with Panama, whose independence Roosevelt assured by timely naval maneuvers, there emerged a Caribbean foreign policy often characterized by the big stick. American troops and tutelage countered political and economic chaos. Clashes were bound to occur: in 1912, U.S. forces in the Caribbean for the first time went into battle to suppress revolutionaries, this time in Nicaragua. In ensuing years, the Dominican Republic, Haiti, Mexico, and Nicaragua experienced extensive interventions, often with violence and with a full-scale guerrilla war in Nicaragua in the 1920s and early 1930s. Guerrilla opposition was not new to Americans, who had faced it in the Philippines after the Spanish-American War.

If broad interpretation of the Monroe Doctrine in areas near the Panama Canal and if growing interests in Far Eastern affairs born of the Open Door and the search for that vast Asian market cast the United States in a role of greater involvement calling for more reliance on military solutions, this was not accompanied by surrender of traditional attitudes toward military matters. Compromises were always necessary: even entering the war in 1917 was put in the perspective of fighting German militarism, of fighting a war to end war. While most Americans might applaud a combative nationalism that had Roosevelt proclaiming, "Perdicaris alive or Raisuli dead"—when Raisuli, a Moroccan bandit, abducted an alleged American citizen near Tangier—or while pacifist Jane Addams might lose much of her popularity during World War I and have her speeches considered dangerous, or while Eugene Debs might be sent to jail in 1918 for a speech condemning war, these and similar events were more a result of the exuberant patriotism of the times than a widespread tendency toward militarism. In the postwar years there is substantial evidence that Americans wished to return to policies less likely to involve force. Much of the opposition to the League of Nations came from those who thought Article X of the Covenant deprived Congress of a free hand in deciding on war. These men did not want to guarantee the "territorial integrity and existing political independence of all members of the League," for that might lead to a war not in America's interest. The disarmament conferences and the Kellogg-Briand Pact to outlaw war as an instrument of national policy did not usher in a long era of peace, but they were symptomatic of peaceful desire. Weary of the Nicaraguan imbroglio, President Herbert Hoover and Secretary of State Henry L. Stimson concluded that marine interventions were too costly and should end. Revelations of war profiteering, exposés of the armament industry, and the revisionist historical literature on U.S. entry into the Great War brought disillusionment and a determination that it should not happen again. Presidential power in foreign policy was suspect, the neutrality laws of the 1930s tried to close all loopholes that might lead to war, and there were restraints on presidential flexibility in foreign policy. One proposal, the Ludlow Resolution (1935–1938), even indicated distrust of Congress on the matter of war by urging that declarations of war should be by national referendum. These questions became more pressing as world crises multiplied. During the debate on American foreign policy in the late 1930s and early 1940s, each side proclaimed its approach as the true road to peace while the opponent's was sure to involve the United States in war.

THE INTERWAR PERIOD

Among isolationists in the interwar period there was fear of militarism. The historian Charles A. Beard felt the military interests seeking a larger navy would, if left to themselves, "extend America's 'strategic frontiers' to the moon." If Americans rejected the policy encouraged by Alfred Thayer Mahan, Theodore Roosevelt, John Hay, and Henry Cabot Lodge, and if by plan, will, and effort they provided "a high standard of life and security for the American people," using to the fullest the national resources, technical arts, and managerial skills in the United States, there would be no need for large military forces. Defense policy should be based on "security of life for the American people in their present geographical home"; the army and navy should not be huckstering and drumming agencies for profit seekers, promoters, and speculators or defenders of every dollar invested abroad. Guided by such a clarification of policy, Beard said, military authorities could make calculations adapted to clearly defined ends; until then they "will demand every gun and ship they can get." Beard saw military leaders committing themselves to a policy of trade promotion and defense all over the world. Sometimes, he believed, they took dangerous chances and then tried to convince the people that national interest or points of honor were at stake. As long as naval strategists demanded more ships, men, and financial support, by using "the kind of propaganda they have been employing," they were more a danger to American security than a guarantee of it.

Senators also frequently spoke out on these issues. Robert A. Taft also urged restraint on interventionist policies because he opposed war. He did not trust President Roosevelt; he thought there was little the United States could do about democracy abroad; and he felt war would expand the power of the federal government to the detriment of democracy at home. Not all isolationists would agree with this reasoning, especially since German and Japanese aims appeared more aggressive. Senator George Norris came to believe by the late 1930s that despite the dangers of militarism the United States must rearm.

The American Legion, an organization of veterans that emerged in the interwar period, also advocated programs of preparedness. The legion supported the idea of a naval disarmament conference in Washington in 1921–1922 but did not want to sacrifice an adequate navy for maintaining the position of the United States as a world power; nor did the legion want its support of the Kellogg-Briand Pact (1928) outlawing war as an instrument of national policy to imply any support for reduction in the nation's military establishment. Whether the American Legion has influenced public opinion or merely reflected it is uncertain. In the great foreign policy debate before Pearl Harbor, the organization had its own divisions on internationalism and isolationism; and, as for many Americans, the legion's general anticommunist stance gave way before the realities of World War II, returned with the Cold War, and adjusted to détente and the post–Cold War years. The size and organization of the American Legion have made it a more powerful lobby than its first antecedent, the Society of the Cincinnati; but it has also had public suspicion and criticism, reflecting perhaps the American civilian's distrust of military influence.

The first four decades of the twentieth century witnessed no marked trend toward militarism in the United States. But more than ever before in the nation's history, Americans were having to come to terms with world power, having to think about international relationships that had been far from their minds in earlier times. Many Americans believed that the old truths of civil-military relations were still valid, although they realized that some concessions were necessary for adequate defense in a world not free of war. The big question then and still today centers on how much is adequate. In the interwar years, the army was seldom above 200,000 men and most often below 150,000; there was rejection of conscription until 1940 and much debate on the advisability of compulsory Reserve Officers Training Corps in colleges. The navy also suffered postwar neglect, and many officers regretted naval weakness in the Pacific, where they considered Japan the enemy. A change came with Franklin D. Roosevelt's support of naval expansion and more jobs in the shipbuilding industry.

WORLD WAR II

A majority of Americans came to accept Roosevelt's policy of gradually increasing both aid to the Allies and military preparation at home. When war erupted most people were still unaware that the free security from which they had unknowingly benefited for so long was gone forever. Many Americans believed that when the war was over national life would return to the prewar style. As Samuel A. Stouffer and others note in their sociopsychological study *The American Soldier* (1949), there was little feeling of personal commitment to war after the early sense of national peril had disappeared. The war was simply a detour that must be taken before one could return to the main, or civilian, road. At war's end the soldier had no desire to reform the United States or the world; he was interested in himself and his family. Cessation of hostilities brought not-surprising demands for rapid release of fathers, sons, and husbands; by 1946 the number of men on active duty had fallen from over 12 million to little more than 3 million, which was reduced by half the following year. In his plans for the postwar world, Roosevelt had sensed the public mood and anticipated a small armed force. At Tehran, when Stalin suggested that Roosevelt's idea of four policemen to preserve world peace might require sending U.S. troops to Europe, Roosevelt envisaged the United States providing ships and planes while Britain and the Soviet Union provided the land armies. And at Yalta the president doubted if U.S support for future peace would include "maintenance of an appreciable American force in Europe." Clearly, the United States accepted an international role and would not make the mistake of rejecting membership in the new world organization, but Americans expected to fit their participation into a familiar mold requiring only limited military effort. This paralleled Wilson's first hopes in 1917 that the American contribution to the war would come mainly from the navy and industrial production, and Roosevelt's hopes in 1940 and 1941 that nonbelligerency would prevent defeat of Germany's enemies while keeping the United States out of war. These hopes were lost in events.

Although most Americans during and immediately after the war thought mainly of returning to peacetime pursuits with little or no consideration of America's role in the world and what that role might require, there were military leaders pondering the country's future and how to protect its interests. Even shortly before the Pearl Harbor attack, as noted by Michael S. Sherry in his *Preparing for the Next War*, General George Marshall was thinking about peace after the imminent war and the war to follow it. Despite this slight beginning, postwar planning did not become serious for more than a year, and even then the planners had to deal with many uncertainties including vaguely expressed plans from political leaders and lack of cooperation inherent in the rivalries among the army, navy, and virtually autonomous army air force. All aspired to a preeminent place in defending national interests perhaps challenged by Soviet expansion, a concern of the Joint Chiefs of Staff since 1942. Planning proposals that emerged included universal military training, unification of the services, and an independent and large air force, but unanimity was lacking except on the essential ability for rapid mobilization. A proposal for universal military training eventually received President Harry Truman's support but never passed Congress. The country relied on the draft until 1973 with a brief hiatus in 1947–1948. The National Security Act of 1947 provided for coordination of the armed services and an independent air force. Although the war ended without planning consensus, hurried efforts in the latter half of 1945 brought recommendations advocating a policy of deterrence and preventive war. Sherry points out that such recommendations contrasted with earlier practice—going from a passive to an active defense. There followed military budgets lower than those of wartime but higher than prewar levels and continued large research-and-development funding, allowing soldiers and scientists to remain partners. All of this, Sherry believes, created an ideology of preparedness and Cold War mentality permitting militarist influence to permeate American society.

THE COLD WAR AND AFTER

With the destruction of western Europe and the decline of Great Britain as a balancer of European power, the door to American retreat in the face of any new totalitarian threat closed. The challenge seemed to come from the Soviet Union, and this challenge as perceived by Americans has largely determined American foreign and military policies since 1945. Wartime cooperation with the Soviet Union had always been a marriage of convenience, although some hoped the social, economic, and political differences could be smoothed over to allow a peaceful working relationship after the war. Disagreements over Poland and Germany soon revealed the incompatibility of American and Soviet postwar goals. By 1947 the Truman administration was convinced that the world was polarized between the United States and the Soviet Union, and to protect itself the United States must preserve the balance of power against Soviet expansion. Truman came forth in broad rhetoric to tell the American people that the United States would support "free peoples who are resisting attempted subjugation by armed minorities or by outside pressures." Not long after, the diplomat George F. Kennan in his "X" article in *Foreign Affairs* provided an analysis of Russian behavior and prescribed a response in the form of "a long-term patient but firm and vigilant containment of Russian expansive tendencies." On these appraisals the U.S. government based its foreign and military policies and over the years perhaps went far beyond what Truman and Kennan had intended. In his *Memoirs,* Kennan regretted his failure to make clear that he was not talking about "containment by military means of a military threat" and his failure to "distinguish between various geographic areas." Later reference to containment to explain American involvement in Vietnam disturbed Kennan. Certain areas of the world were more important to the United States, he said, and the world situation had changed since 1947; there was no longer only one center of communist power.

Although the major change in American defense policy came with the Korean War (1950–1953), even before that conflict there was much of the temper of the war years. Despite rapid demobilization of U.S. forces after World War II, they were still larger than during any peacetime in American history; the military budget was many times the 1940 level; President Truman was pushing for universal military training; and the United States was heavily armed, with a monopoly on the atomic bomb.

Nonetheless, Truman was reluctant to raise defense spending above $15 billion, much to the concern of military leaders and Secretary of Defense James Forrestal. On the eve of the Korean War, a committee of State and Defense Department officials described in a plan (NSC 68) the potentially rapid economic and military growth of the Soviet Union and emphasized the need for strength if there were to be any successful negotiations with the Soviet Union or any agreement on arms regulation. According to Paul Hammond, it was a program calling Americans to rise to the occasion by giving more effort and resources to prevent further deterioration of the strategic situation of the United States. The Korean War provided the impetus for the administration and public to accept the call: the national security budget shortly went above $40 billion and the number of military personnel on active duty more than doubled.

Events occurring and attitudes established during the five years after the end of World War II set a pattern for response to subsequent challenges to American foreign and military policies. Supporters argued that reliance on well-prepared armed forces supplied with the latest weaponry and stationed around the globe was a deterrent to war, while critics perceived it as an example of militarism little related to the defense needs of the United States and, as in Vietnam, sometimes disastrous.

Many conditions acceptable for achieving victory during World War II have been denounced as militarism in the postwar era. Believing that the war was essential for the achievement of legitimate national goals, most Americans accepted industrial mobilization, strong and sometimes secretive executive leadership, large armed forces, large military budgets, and the use of whatever weapons were available. From the beginning of the Cold War, however, there have been many dissenters who doubt any international danger and question the military

>
>
> ## NSC 68
>
> One of the important Cold War documents that rationalized the military buildup to meet the communist challenge was NSC 68, principally authored by Paul H. Nitze, director of the State Department's Policy Planning Staff, sent to the president in April 1950, and referred to the National Security Council for comment. Influenced by the Berlin blockade, the communist victory in China, and the Soviet testing of an atomic weapon, the authors of NSC 68 composed a ringing, frightening call to rearm. Whether the strategies outlined in NSC 68 were proper and prudent for winning the Cold War or were excessive, too expensive, and a misinterpretation of Soviet intent, they are part of the general debate on the Cold War and the extent of militarism in American policy and life.
>
> NSC 68 states that "the Soviet Union, unlike previous aspirants to hegemony, is animated by a new fanatic faith, antithetical to our own, and seeks to impose its absolute authority over the rest of the world." If there is "any substantial further extension of the area under domination of the Kremlin [it] would raise the possibility that no coalition adequate to confront the Kremlin with greater strength could be assembled." The authors described the military power of the Soviet Union and expressed belief that if a major war occurred in 1950 the Soviet Union would be capable of attacking selected targets in the United States with atomic bombs. To meet the Soviet threat the United States must possess superior overall power including military strength to guarantee national security and to conduct a policy of containment. The country should also produce and stockpile thermonuclear weapons. The rapid buildup would be costly but, "Budgetary considerations will need to be subordinated to the stark fact that our very independence as a nation may be at stake."

and foreign policies designed to counter communist aggression.

Probably the most cited example of militarism in American life is the military-industrial complex—an alliance between the military establishment and the companies supplying weapons and matériel used by the armed forces. The relationship was not new during World War II, but huge postwar defense budgets and the great dependence of some companies on government orders brought lobbying activities to new heights and saw substantial increases in the number of former military men on corporation payrolls. Add to this intellectual, political, labor, and geographic interests in various research projects or companies whose operations represented thousands of jobs, and there emerges a vast constituency to influence defense decisions. Defense spending for research and development also has had great impact on the nation's universities. The historian Stuart W. Leslie has described how large contracts from the military have influenced academic scientific research and maintained or established new laboratories under university management. The science and engineering departments did the research, consulted, and trained the graduates for work that was in demand by the defense establishment with the result, as Leslie says, that the military was establishing the scientific priorities.

In his Farewell Address of 1961, President Dwight D. Eisenhower warned against unwarranted influence from the industrial-military complex. Many critics of the complex disagree with much of American foreign and defense policy since 1945 and fail to see any challenge requiring a large military response. The sociologist C. Wright Mills saw a greater penetration of military men in the corporate economy, which seemingly had become a permanent war economy, while Gabriel Kolko argues that the military establishment is only an instrument of civilian business leaders who seek strategic and economic objectives. Many of the critics reveal the old animosity toward munitions makers who peddle their wares that soon become obsolete and necessitate a new round of even more sophisticated and destructive weapons. Modern weapons are many times greater than needed to destroy an enemy, but the nation's security is less than ever before. Failure to achieve international control over weapons, for which some critics blame America's lack of suitable initiative when it had a monopoly of the atomic bomb, continued the wasteful arms race and increased chances for their use—an unthinkable event, or so it seemed until Herman Kahn's *Thinking About the Unthinkable* (1969).

Opponents of postwar policies frequently centered their attacks on the president and his almost exclusive direction of foreign policy and his broad use of powers as commander in chief. According to critics, presidents have exaggerated foreign dangers and secretly committed the United States to other countries, entangling the nation in war in violation of the Constitution. Broad use of executive power from Washington's declaration of neutrality, through James K. Polk's occupation of disputed territory, Lincoln's reinforcement of Fort Sumter, Franklin D. Roosevelt's destroyer-base deal, and Ronald Reagan's Iran-Contra deal appears often in American history. The American people and their historians generally praise and admire (at least in historical perspective) the strong, active executive, but the Vietnam War and Watergate revelations caused a reexamination of presidential use of power. Some writers who supported presidential prerogative but became disillusioned in the later years of the Vietnam War have been at pains to distinguish which presidents faced real emergencies and were justified in wielding their authority. The distinction is difficult.

Critics also note Defense Department influence in foreign policy decisions as another example of militarism. During the John F. Kennedy administration, the Joint Chiefs of Staff at first opposed a comprehensive test ban treaty because it might reduce American vigilance and finally gave support only with extensive safeguards. During the Cuban missile crisis, the Joint Chiefs advised an air strike against Cuba, and earlier they had seemed at least tacitly to support American participation in military operations against Fidel Castro. Often cited are the optimistic and frequently misleading military reports of progress in Vietnam, reports that suggested victory was within reach with a little more effort. Acceptance of the idea that only the military people had the facts made effective challenging of Pentagon estimates difficult even for the sometimes skeptical President Kennedy. According to reporter David Halberstam, Kennedy's failure to match his growing inner doubts with his public statements would have made his successor's task extremely difficult even if President Lyndon B. Johnson had been less accepting and admiring of his military advisers.

No one can deny the widespread emphasis on military preparedness, the evident abuse of power by agencies created to improve American defense, the questionable American presence in Southeast Asia, and myriad other examples of militarism in American life. Reluctance to maintain a large standing army has given way before international realities that no longer allow the United States the cheap security described by the historian C. Vann Woodward. There have been attempts to maintain civilian control, and the Korean War is a case in point. The controversy between Harry Truman and General Douglas MacArthur over limiting the conflict to the Korean peninsula ended in victory for the president. While the people might wildly welcome MacArthur home and while they might be bemused by the concept of a limited war, they wanted little of his plan to broaden the war; nor were there many ready to accept MacArthur's belief that military men owe primary allegiance to the country and the Constitution rather than those "who temporarily exercise the authority of the Executive Branch." General MacArthur won a brief, emotional victory—his New York ticker-tape parade bested Charles Lindbergh's almost two-to-one in paper tonnage—but it was General Eisenhower, with his promise to go to Korea to seek an early and honorable end to the war, who won the votes and became the soldier-hero president. His willingness to please the fiscally conservative Robert A. Taft wing of the Republican Party and his search for a strong military policy compatible with a sound, growing economy—a concern not new with Eisenhower—was no surrender to militaristic thinking. In fact, he feared that a prolonged military program might lead to a garrison state, and he wished "to keep our boys at our side instead of on a foreign shore," even though some American troops remained abroad. At times, Secretary of State John Foster Dulles engaged in militaristic rhetoric, but policy remained generally cautious, although "massive retaliation," "going to the brink," and "liberation" were added to the slogans "containment" and "aiding free peoples everywhere"—slogans that undoubtedly affected popular thinking and allowed people to accept policies or actions without serious consideration. Involvement in Vietnam, where these policies and actions merged and gradually escalated, had no willing hand or perceptive mind to limit it until the commitment was very large. It was a self-perpetuating and self-deluding conflict without clear purpose, entangled in personal and national pride. Yet popular sentiment and journalistic and historical accounts of the war reveal a lively antimilitaristic feeling that challenged authority and induced eventual withdrawal.

For some Americans the end of the Vietnam War dispelled fears of militarism. Others suggested only abandonment of American economic expansionist goals as seen in the open door, or open world, policies would reverse conditions feeding militarism. For still others, greater congressional supervision of foreign and defense policies, limiting executive initiative, was needed.

The end of the Cold War and the collapse of the Soviet Union by the early 1990s understandably encouraged greater questioning of America's military and related policies that had been in place for over half a century. For many Americans the certainties posed by the fascist and communist threats were no longer present to bolster long-held assumptions. Ever since 1940 the United States had been preparing in varying degrees for one war or another. Was it not time now to enjoy a peace dividend? The question presumed that the new circumstances were strong arguments for change. There were reductions, but not to the extent that many critics hoped. By 1998 defense spending was 12 percent below the average level from 1976–1990. There was downsizing of military personnel, down to about 1.4 million in 1996. There were base closings, approximately seventy by 1998, but all proposals were strongly fought because of feared effects on local economies. Defense Department plans to cut military reservist positions ran into congressional roadblocks for similar reasons. These changes represented a halting, rather grudging trend. Michael Sherry, writing in the mid-1990s about America's "militarization," a more broadly defined and perhaps vaguer concept than the classic "militarism," believed that the main rationale for militarization disappeared with the Cold War and that America would probably drift away from its militarized past without a clear or formal indication that it was doing so.

While Americans like Sherry might approve the trend but prefer a more deliberate course, others worried that the country was becoming complacent in the face of future dangers. In 1999, Secretary of Defense William Cohen was concerned about a widening gap between America's civilian and military cultures and the possible effect on the well-being of the United States as well as the international community if the American people did not understand and support the military that helped to ensure global stability. The historians Donald Kagan and Frederick W. Kagan, in a study comparing the United States at the beginning of the twenty-first century with England in the 1920s, suggest that as England was unwilling then to prepare properly for defense, the United States seventy-five years later might not be maintaining sufficient armed forces to pursue an active foreign policy aimed at preventing war. The Cold War and its end, they argue, disguised America's continuing interest as a world power in maintaining peace and stability in an increasingly fluid and still dangerous international community.

These views of America's military and diplomatic policies and the dangers they pose for its democratic nature and its security are speculative. Finally, any control of militarism rests with the people and their traditions. Democracy is not always reliable, for a warfare economy has many constituents and overzealous patriotism may lead to uncustomary actions. American tradition is firmly on the civilian side. Americans have not easily accepted the martial virtues emphasizing authority and subordination, and, at least in theory, they have accepted beliefs in freedom and the pursuit of happiness. Nonetheless, civilian supremacy as a basic tenet in America's civil-military tradition is not above challenge in the country's history, even in recent years. The Truman-MacArthur controversy, while often cited as a victory for civilian dominance, was possible because other prominent military leaders supported Truman, and, as noted by the historian Ernest May, Congress and the public sided with one set of military leaders instead of another. The military historian Russell F. Weigley has suggested that the principle of civilian control in civil-military relations may need reexamination. He cites post–Cold War examples involving General Colin L. Powell, who publicly questioned U.S. intervention in Bosnia while the George H. W. Bush administration was debating the use of armed force there and later was critical of president-elect Clinton's campaign proposal on admitting homosexuals to the military. Weigley also notes that General H. Norman Schwarzkopf, after retirement, was critical of aspects of Gulf War diplomacy. These examples followed the Vietnam War era when civil-military relations were strained by various policy constraints not to the liking of the military. Weigley concludes that the traditional civilian dominance may have an uncertain future. Obviously, tradition is not immune to erosion.

The historian Howard K. Beale believed that Theodore Roosevelt's more ominous predilections were restrained by democratic tradition, respect for public opinion, fear of political defeat in elections, concern for the nation's well-being, acceptance of a cautious middle-of-the-road approach to problems, and a sense of the worth and dignity of the individual. These traits continue to have support from an American consensus. When American policy seems to veer too far from democratic traditions, opposition grows, particularly if there is no clear relation between policy and national security and, in the case of Vietnam, if there are continuing demands for men and matériel. Withdrawal from Vietnam did not alter the general trend of American foreign and defense policy, and the militarism that critics saw as part of it remained, but the end of the Cold War brought new, if still somewhat uncertain, directions.

Complicating the outlook may be the evolution of technology allowing development of more sophisticated and precise weaponry. Examples include use of cruise missiles or other "standoff" weapons destroying clearly defined targets without widespread damage and casualties while preserving no-fly zones over Iraq or intervening in Kosovo. Does such conflict, called "virtual war" by Michael Ignatieff in referring to Kosovo, mean that this type of violence becomes more acceptable to people reluctant to go to war? If American servicemen operate their weapons out of harm's way and there are no body bags shown on evening television or if society is not called upon to mobilize, will there be less attention paid to such military action?

Technological innovation in warmaking and attempts to restrict casualty lists as much as possible are not new. One reason expressed for use of the A-bomb was that it might obviate the need for an invasion of the Japanese home islands and the anticipated loss of American lives. What is new is the extensive television coverage since the Vietnam War and its effect on public opinion. American military leaders and politicians may be concerned not only about their own casualties but also about civilian casualties on the other side and appearing too aggressive, thus losing public support. Fighting a virtual war has many complications and unresolved political, military, and moral issues, as Michael Ignatieff describes in his book, and there is no reason to believe that the United States will retain exclusive control of the new weapons. In the face of rapid international political and technological changes, what remains for the United States is to strive to maintain the credibility of its arms in the context of its democratic traditions.

CONCLUSION

Militarism is not a precise term and its definition may depend on one's ideology or point of view, and one's judgment of it may be determined by its extent and form. Classic militarism, epitomized for most Americans by Wilhelmian Germany or pre-Hiroshima Japan, has few examples in the American past, but war and preparation for war influencing the country's society and having its support is increasingly apparent, particularly beginning in the last half of the twentieth century. This is not to say that the country has not engaged in war or military conflicts or that manifestations of militarism have not existed in earlier America. Nonetheless, general antipathy toward the military and a Congress keeping tight reins on military appropriations are readily apparent through the first century and more of U.S. history. In the beginning, the War Department (including naval affairs until 1798) had the secretary of war and one clerk and was considered in those early years, as recorded by Leonard D. White in his administrative history of the period, as a "difficult and unpopular department." A century later, although the size had changed, it was still unpopular with many people, including politicians and labor leaders like Samuel Gompers, who may have been remembering the Pullman Strike when he said, "Standing armies are always used to exercise tyranny over people."

While the early twentieth century may have begun to erode such views, it was World War II and the Cold War that brought significant changes to the country's diplomatic and military policies, symbolized by the great growth of the State and Defense Departments. The secretary of war and his clerk at the beginning of George Washington's administration grew by the beginning of the twenty-first century to about 90,000 civilian and military personnel occupying millions of square feet of office space in the Pentagon and numerous other federal and commercial buildings in the Washington, D.C., area. After World War II, Americans were willing to accept these changes because most of them no longer believed that isolationism was a viable choice for the United States, and many were convinced that there was a new totalitarian threat, similar in their minds to Hitler and Nazism. When events in Poland, Germany, Greece, China, and Korea seemed to confirm their fears, many Americans, perhaps influenced by Munich and the belief that appeasement was futile for stopping aggressors, accepted containment, deterrence, and a buildup of armaments with an ample supply of nuclear weapons. Through these policies the Cold War came to permeate American society.

While militarism, or at least the preparation for war, was clearly evident during the Cold War, its justification, if not all of its aspects, remained a subject of debate. For critics who blamed the Cold War on the United States by failing to recognize the Soviet Union's security interests, Washington's military response was dangerous, wasteful, tragic, with a mindset that continued into the post–Cold War era. For those who believed the Soviet Union posed a real danger to this country and its friends, the preparation for war was correct and need not be regretted. The requirements for the future, with its changing political arrangements and new technologies, remained open for even more concern and debate as evidenced by proposals, which continued into the twenty-first century, for a missile defense shield.

BIBLIOGRAPHY

Coffin, Tristram. *The Armed Society: Militarism in Modern America.* Baltimore, 1964. Recounts the growing military influence.

Donovan, James A. *Militarism, U.S.A.* New York, 1970. Suggests a cut in military manpower and reduction in defense appropriations as the best means for controlling militarism.

Ekirch, Arthur A., Jr. *The Civilian and the Military.* New York, 1956. Notes the importance of antimilitarism in American history but sees the penetration of militarism through the technological implications of modern warfare and perpetual mobilization in the post-1945 world.

Gaddis, John Lewis, and Paul H. Nitze. "NSC 68 and the Soviet Threat Reconsidered." *International Security* 4 (spring 1980): 164–176. Comments on NSC 68, one by a historian of the Cold War and the other by the document's principal author.

Gholz, Eugene. "The Curtiss-Wright Corporation and Cold War-Era Defense Procurement: A Challenge to Military-Industrial Complex Theory." *Journal of Cold War Studies* 2 (winter 2000): 35–75. Questions whether the military-industrial complex protected its industrial components from going bankrupt by an examination of the Curtiss-Wright Corporation.

Hogan, Michael J. *A Cross of Iron: Harry S. Truman and the Origins of the National Security State, 1945–1954.* Cambridge and New York, 1998. Describes how America prepared to fight the Cold War and tried to preserve traditional values and institutions.

Ignatieff, Michael. *Virtual War: Kosovo and Beyond.* New York, 2000. Looks at the NATO action in Kosovo as a virtual war where technology allowed it to be fought with no deaths on the American side and was thus less than fully real to the United States. The author attempts to explain "why nations that have never been more immune from the risks of waging war should remain so unwilling to run them" by his examination of the new technology and the morality governing its use.

Kagan, Donald, and Frederick W. Kagan. *While America Sleeps: Self-Delusion, Military Weakness, and the Threat to Peace Today.* New York, 2000. Fears that the United States at the beginning of the twenty-first century was emulating England in the 1920s in defense policy.

Knoll, Erwin, and Judith Nies McFadden, eds. *American Militarism 1970.* New York, 1969. A dialogue among politicians and intellectuals who bemoan then current trends in military and foreign policies and doubt if they are defending the basic values of American society.

Kolko, Gabriel. *The Roots of American Foreign Policy.* Boston, 1969. Emphasizes that the growing military establishment is a result of political policy not its cause.

Lauterbach, Albert T. "Militarism in the Western World: A Comparative Study." *Journal of the History of Ideas* 5 (1944): 446–478.

Leffler, Melvyn P. *A Preponderance of Power: National Security, the Truman Administration, and the Cold War.* Stanford, Calif., 1992. How the Truman administration coped with legacies of World War II and took steps to contain the Soviet Union but at costs higher than necessary.

Leslie, Stuart W. *The Cold War and American Science: The Military-Industrial-Academic Complex at MIT and Stanford.* New York, 1993. The influence of the Cold War on American scientific research.

May, Ernest R. "The U.S. Government, a Legacy of the Cold War." In Michael J. Hogan, ed. *The End of the Cold War: Its Meaning and Implica-*

tions. Cambridge and New York, 1992. Does not look with regret at the militarization of American government during the Cold War but questions how this government structure will fare in the post–Cold War period.

Millis, Walter. *Arms and Men: A Study of American Military History.* New York, 1958.

———. *American Military Thought.* Indianapolis, Ind., 1966. An anthology.

Mills, C. Wright. *The Power Elite.* New York, 1956. Sees a unity of the power elite based on the coincidence of interests among economic, political, and military organizations.

Perkins, Dexter. *The American Approach to Foreign Policy.* Rev. ed. New York, 1968. Suggests that Americans on the whole have not been imperialistic and have not surrendered their essential liberties and democratic customs to demands of war.

Shaw, Martin. *Post Military Society: Militarism, Demilitarization and War at the End of the Twentieth Century.* Philadelphia, 1991. An examination of the concept of post-military society, bringing not necessarily the end of militarism but the possibility of peace, and, despite contradictions, a period when militarism is less dominant of society.

Sherry, Michael S. *Preparing for the Next War: American Plans for Postwar Defense, 1941–45.* New Haven, Conn., 1977. An examination of military planning to shape post–World War II policies and attitudes.

———. *In the Shadow of War: The United States Since the 1930s.* New Haven, Conn., 1995. A history of militarization, "the process by which war and national security . . . shaped broad areas of national life."

Speier, Hans. "Militarism in the Eighteenth Century." *Social Research: An International Quarterly of Political and Social Science* 3 (1936): 304–336.

Sprout, Harold, and Margaret Sprout. *The Rise of American Naval Power, 1776–1918.* Princeton, N.J., 1969.

Vagts, Alfred. *A History of Militarism, Civilian and Military.* Rev. ed. New York, 1959.

Weigley, Russell F. *Towards an American Army: Military Thought from Washington to Marshall.* New York, 1962.

———. "The American Military and the Principle of Civilian Control from McClellan to Powell." *Journal of Military History* 57, no. 5, special issue (1993): 27–58. Suggests that the principle of civil control of the military in the United States has an uncertain future.

Yarmolinsky, Adam. *The Military Establishment: Its Impact on American Society.* New York, 1971. Describes the influence of the military in nonmilitary areas.

Yergin, Daniel. *Shattered Peace: The Origins of the Cold War and the National Security State.* Boston, 1977. Development of U.S. policy influenced by what the author terms the Riga axioms and the Yalta axioms—one distrustful, the other cooperative.

See also CONTAINMENT; CONTINENTAL EXPANSION; DEPARTMENT OF DEFENSE; IMPERIALISM; INTERVENTION AND NONINTERVENTION; MILITARY-INDUSTRIAL COMPLEX; NATIONALISM; PRESIDENTIAL POWER; PUBLIC OPINION.

THE MILITARY-INDUSTRIAL COMPLEX

James A. Huston

Probably no presidential farewell address since that of George Washington in 1796 has had a greater impact or more lasting quality than that of Dwight Eisenhower in 1961. Washington's is remembered mainly for his warnings against political factions and foreign alliances. Eisenhower's is remembered for his warning against the military-industrial complex. Coming from Eisenhower, who had risen through the military ranks and was assumed to be a "friend of big business," the words surprised listeners but also carried great weight. Apparently the term itself may be attributed to him.

In mid-December 1960, Norman Cousins, editor of the *Saturday Review*, had suggested the idea of a farewell address. Eisenhower turned to one of his special assistants, Malcolm Moos, a young political scientist from Johns Hopkins University, to draft the speech, and worked closely with him in preparing the text. The president's closest economic advisers were not aware of the contents of the speech until they heard it broadcast.

Speaking to the nation on radio and television on the evening of Tuesday, 17 January 1961, Eisenhower said the following about the military-industrial complex:

> Until the latest of our world conflicts, the United States had no armaments industry. American makers of plowshares could, with time and as required, make swords as well. But now we can no longer risk emergency improvisation of national defense; we have been compelled to create a permanent armaments industry of vast proportions. Added to this, three and a half million men and women are directly engaged in the defense establishment. We annually spend on military security more than the net income of all United States corporations.
>
> The conjunction of an immense military establishment and a large arms industry is new in the American experience. The total influence—economic, political, even spiritual—is felt in every city, every State house, every office of the federal government. We recognize the imperative need for this development. Yet we must not fail to comprehend its grave implications. Our toil, resources and livelihood are all involved; so is the very structure of our society.
>
> In the councils of government, we must guard against the acquisition of unwarranted influence, whether sought or unsought, by the military-industrial complex. The potential for the disastrous rise of misplaced power exists and will persist.

At a press conference the next morning, Eisenhower expanded on the military-industrial complex theme. In response to one question he said:

> It is only a citizenry, an alert and informed citizenry, which can keep these abuses from coming about. And . . . some of this misuse of influence and power could come about unwittingly but just by the very nature of the thing, . . . almost every one of your magazines, no matter what they are advertising, has a picture of the Titan missile or the Atlas or solid fuel or other things, there is . . . almost an insidious penetration of our own minds that the only thing this country is engaged in is weaponry and missiles. And, I'll tell you we just can't afford to do that. The reason we have them is to protect the great values in which we believe, and they are far deeper even than our own lives and our own property.

Eisenhower's main concern was that military industries would exert an undue influence on government policy. Munitions makers were likely to encourage warlike policies in the interest of their own profits. Beyond that, Eisenhower saw a danger that individual companies might influence military strategy by their advocacy of their own weapon systems. Further, a great conglomerate of military industrial power might threaten individual liberty.

The main concern of others, like Seymour Melman, an industrial engineer and economist at Columbia University, has been that government policy, concentrating on the development and maintenance of a big military industry, would have an unfortunate impact on the national economy.

Indeed, Eisenhower shared the concern about the economic cost of maintaining large armaments. In an address before the American Society of Newspaper Editors on 16 April 1953, he had called for control and reduction of armaments. He said that if an unchecked armaments race continued, "the best that could be expected" would be:

> a life of perpetual fear and tension; a burden of arms draining the wealth and the labor of all peoples; a wasting of strength that defies the American system or the Soviet system or any system to achieve true abundance and happiness for the people of this earth.
>
> Every gun that is made, every warship launched, every rocket fired signifies, in the final sense, a theft from those who hunger and are not fed, those who are cold and are not clothed.
>
> This world in arms . . . is spending the sweat of its laborers, the genius of its scientists, the hopes of its children.
>
> The cost of one modern heavy bomber is this: a modern brick school in more than thirty cities. It is two electric power plants, each serving a town of sixty thousand population. It is two fine, fully equipped hospitals. It is some fifty miles of concrete highway.
>
> We pay for a single fighter plane with a half million bushels of wheat. We pay for a single destroyer with new homes that could have housed more than eight thousand people. . . .
>
> This is not a way of life at all, in any true sense. Under the cloud of threatening war, it is humanity hanging from a cross of iron.

FORCES BEHIND THE MILITARY-INDUSTRIAL COMPLEX

Historians have not yet devoted much study to the military-industrial complex. It has surfaced as a concept and concern only in very recent times. Moreover, well-developed bodies of theory and data are not readily available. The editors of the *Journal of International Affairs* have aptly summarized the situation:

> Of all the political ideas that gained popular currency in the 1960s, the military-industrial complex is the concept perhaps most gravely deformed by public mastication. The debate of 1968 and 1969 over the influence of the military establishment in the United States proved, with few exceptions, consistently unsatisfying. After all was said, the concept of the military-industrial complex remained muddled and its attendant questions of international and domestic political influence were still unanswered.

Political leaders reflected the confusion of the man in the street, of business leaders, industrial workers, farmers, college students, and activists for conflicting causes. All were caught up in a dilemma—that armaments cause wars, and that arms industries create prosperity. At the same time, nearly everyone agreed that some military forces were needed for national security, and these in turn depended upon some kind of military industry.

Here we can see the great dilemma of U.S. military-industrial policy: Can the security of the United States be better served, can the economy of the nation flourish more, and can the attending evils of arms manufacture be better reduced or avoided by government or by private manufacture of munitions? This was a question to which leaders gave their attention from the early days of the Republic.

The American military-industrial complex may be said to have had its origins with Alexander Hamilton and Eli Whitney. Those two men of genius were in the vanguard of a group of imaginative men who set the course for the national arms policy of the United States. Hamilton emphasized government manufacture of arms, though he recognized the need to develop a private arms industry as well if what he conceived to be the defense requirements of the country were to be met. Whitney was the entrepreneur par excellence who saw opportunities for profit in making arms for the government.

In 1783, Hamilton, a twenty-eight-year-old former lieutenant colonel, presented a report on a military peace establishment to the Continental Congress. In it he called for the establishment of "public manufactories of arms, powder, etc." and proposed the employment of troops in the national armories. This, he maintained, would be far more economical than the importation of arms from Europe. But Hamilton's concern for domestic arms manufacture went beyond the possible economies. He thought independence from foreign arms makers to be essential for national security.

In his celebrated "Report on Manufactures" in 1791, Hamilton offered a program whose central theme was the development of domestic industries for national security. Hamilton would encourage domestic arms production by a protective tariff and by an annual purchase of weapons as an incentive for continuous manufacture. Still, in the long run, Hamilton looked to the desirability of government manufacture of all arms of war. His concern about the private manufacture of weapons was not that the private companies would become too powerful and would exert undue influence on national policy. It was that private companies could not be relied upon to provide the arms necessary for national security.

Eli Whitney of New Haven, Connecticut, desperately in need of capital, turned to the U.S. government with a fantastic proposal to manufacture 10,000 or 15,000 stand of arms at the very moment—when war with France threatened—that the government could not afford to turn down any halfway realistic proposal for making arms. As he followed the debates in Congress on proposed appropriations for arms procurement, Whitney decided that here was the best possible opportunity to get a government contract.

Whitney decided that the only practical way to produce 10,000 satisfactory muskets in the United States, where skilled armorers were few, was to reduce the complex steps of gunmaking to a series of more simple tasks, each of which could be done with less skilled hands, and to design machines that would duplicate some of the armorer's skill. For best results, it would be necessary to make parts precise enough to be interchangeable. This would permit the maximum division of labor and make it possible to accomplish repairs simply by replacing parts.

One of the most important contributions to the development of a domestic arms industry was the act of 1808 for arming the militia. By this time the national armories were making 5,000 to 10,000 muskets a year, but relatively few were being delivered by private makers under contracts of 1798, and, even though they were admitted duty free, almost none were coming in from Europe, where the Napoleonic wars were raging.

The act of 23 April 1808 provided for the appropriation of an annual sum of $200,000 for arms and military equipment for the militia of the United States, by either purchase or manufacture. The purveyor of public supplies, Tench Coxe, advertised in newspapers of the leading cities for bids for contracts to make muskets. Between 30 June and 9 November of that year, Coxe let contracts to nineteen firms for a total of 85,200 muskets. The contracts were for five years, with one-fifth of the total number, in most cases, due each year. However, the time schedules proved to be unrealistic and a number of the manufacturers unreliable.

Unique among the states, Virginia took upon itself the task of manufacturing arms for its militia independent of outside sources. Authorized in 1798, the Virginia Manufactory of Arms, occupying an impressive building along the James River in Richmond, turned out enough weapons between 1802 and 1821 to arm all the county militia—58,400 muskets, 2,100 rifles, 4,200 pistols, and 10,300 swords.

Soon a national arms system based upon two national armories and a group of dependable private firms was fairly well established. Beginning with the funds appropriated for the arming of the militia, the government gradually developed a policy of providing orders for the most promising establishments on a long-term basis. As to the advantages of public versus private manufacture of military arms, there was much to be said on both sides. In the earlier period there was strong sentiment in favor of depending solely on national armories. The national armories were readily available and less expensive, and they established price standards for private contractors. Private manufacturers seemed more likely to improve models, and to experiment with new materials and new methods. Both were needed for the best possible system of arms production.

Recognizing that the military-industrial complex does exist as a powerful, if informal, structure in American military and economic affairs, the following questions arise: How did it get that way? What are its consequences? What can be done about it?

The forces that have driven the development of the military-industrial complex include the following:

1. The national arms policy during the first half of the nineteenth century. The early decision to rely on production both in government facilities and by private firms for providing armaments set the stage. The policy of long-term contracts with private arms manufacturers planted the seeds for a permanent arms industry in peacetime.
2. Industrial expansion during the Civil War. The first industrial mobilization that approached total war created undreamed-of opportunities for profit and showed what might be done in arms production.
3. Industrial mobilization during World War I. This carried the opportunities a step higher, but the effects were only temporary, because no large-scale defense industry persisted

after the war, when the drives for disarmament and isolation amid cries against profiteering by "merchants of death" discouraged such activities.

4. World War II expansion. This was several notches higher than the mobilization for World War I and was when many firms got their start in military production, and then continued after the war under conditions far different from the post–World War I period.
5. Government-sponsored research and development on a large scale. This major development during World War II had important consequences in the years that followed. This has been one of the keys to the growth of the military-industrial complex.
6. Nuclear weapons. This was another legacy of World War II that overshadowed defense policies in the postwar world.
7. The Cold War. The perceived threat of the Soviet Union to security in Europe, and the perception of communism as a worldwide threat led to an armaments race in both nuclear and conventional forces that gave a certain permanence to defense industries. Broad programs of foreign military assistance became a part of this, and added to demand for military production.
8. Korea. The communist attack against South Korea called up further military-industrial efforts and gave credibility to the fears of the Cold War.
9. Vietnam. This conflict maintained the demand for military equipment at a high level over a long period of time.
10. The Gulf War. Just when there were growing demands for cuts in military expenditures to help reduce the national deficit, the crisis in the Persian Gulf served to renew requirements for production.
11. The policy of maintaining a "guns and butter" economy in the buildup for Korea, for Vietnam, for the Gulf War, and for the Cold War in general meant that if the unsettling impact of continuous conversion and reconversion on domestic industries was to be avoided, some measure of a military industry on a more or less permanent basis would have to be maintained.
12. The economic impact of defense industries on local economies, and the supposed stimulus of defense spending on the national economy. This brings pressure from local industrial leaders and from local labor unions and workers in general who are employed in defense plants, from local chambers of commerce and businesses that stand to benefit from providing consumer goods and services to defense workers and their families, and from members of Congress and other political leaders anxious to stimulate employment in their districts.

THE IMPACT OF A PERMANENT MILITARY INDUSTRY

With all these forces at work, what are the consequences spawned from the powerful military-industrial complex? Several unfortunate consequences emerge—an undue influence on military policy and strategy, a tendency to extravagance and waste in defense spending, a negative long-range impact on the economy, and a possible weakening of the country itself.

To what extent do the pressures of manufacturers worried about profits, communities worried about unemployment, and members of Congress and presidents worried about local or general business depression—and ultimately about votes in key states—influence our choice of weapon systems, and thus affect the military considerations in our national strategy? Do we build a new bomber or a new missile or a new aircraft carrier because our strategy requires it, or because some group demands it, and then develop a strategy to include it? There always is the prospect that elements of a powerful military-industrial complex will influence national policy and strategy in the interest of favoring certain weapon systems not simply on the basis of military advantage, but for the benefit of the companies making them, or for the armed service using them, or for the locale where they and subsidiary instruments are made.

Why else would General Dynamics take out a two-page, full-color advertisement in *Smithsonian* magazine to proclaim its F-16 Fighting Falcon "the finest fighter in the world" and to review its achievements in producing the B-24 bomber during World War II and the B-36 afterward? Why would the same company take a two-page, color ad in *National Review* to extol the virtues of its M-1 Abrams tank? Why does McDonnell Douglas present a television commercial to "sell" its F-15 Eagle fighter aircraft?

In the fifty years after the conclusion of World War II, three forces led to the maintenance of a military establishment of unprecedented pro-

TOP TEN DEFENSE CONTRACTORS, 1968

Contractor	Headquarters	DOD Contracts FY 1968 (billions of dollars)	Main Projects
General Dynamics	New York	$ 2.24	F-111 fighter-bomber, Polaris submarine
Lockheed Aircraft	California	1.87	C-141, C-5A transports, Polaris missile
General Electric	New York	1.49	jet engines, electronics
United Aircraft	Connecticut	1.32	jet engines, helicopters
McDonnell Douglas	Missouri	1.10	Phantom F-4, Douglas A-4 bomber
AT&T	New York	.78	Safeguard missile, antisubmarine projects
Boeing	Washington	.76	B-52, helicopters, Minuteman missile
Ling-Temco-Vought	Texas	.76	A-7 fighter, electronics, Lance missile
North American Rockwell	California	.67	avionics, submarine electronics
General Motors	Michigan	.63	gas-turbine aircraft engines, tanks, M-16 rifle

TOP TEN DEFENSE CONTRACTORS, 1999

Contractor	DOD Contracts
Lockheed Martin	$ 12.67 billion
Boeing	11.57
Raytheon	6.40
General Dynamics	4.56
Northrop Grumman	3.19
United Technologies	2.37
Litton Industries	2.10
General Electric	1.71
TRW	1.43
Textron	1.42

portions for the United States over such a length of time: the Cold War with the Soviet Union, involving an arms race throughout most of the period; the Korean War (1950–1953), and the Vietnam War (1964–1975). As the period ended (that is, as the Cold War at last appeared to have come to a close), a fourth situation assured continuation of military-industrial production—the deployment of forces and combat operations in the Persian Gulf region.

Military orders for goods and services went from $27.5 billion in 1964 to about $42.3 billion in 1969. The total defense budget for fiscal year 1969 was $79.788 billion, which amounted to 42.9 percent of the total federal budget, and between 9 and 10 percent of the gross national product (about the same percent as throughout the preceding decade). Defense funds went to every state, to 363 of the 435 congressional districts and to over 5,000 communities. Workers in defense industries and in defense-related production in mining, agriculture, construction, and services comprised over 10 percent of the total labor force. The Defense Department itself employed as many civilians as the populations of New Hampshire, Vermont, and Maine combined.

Despite the lowering of tensions between the United States and the Soviet Union—and between Eastern Europe and western Europe—in 1989 and 1990, the Pentagon in 1990 still was planning to put $100 billion into the improvement of the nuclear arsenal over the next ten years. This was in addition to the continuation of the Strategic Defense Initiative ("Star Wars") research program. The SDI effort began in a television address to the nation by President Ronald Reagan on 23 March 1983. It was a call for a defense system that would protect the United States from enemy nuclear missiles. The specific objectives of the program were not clear. At first it was offered as a more or less total net to protect against all missiles. Then it was suggested as something that would be valuable against missiles from China, North Korea, or other countries. Then it was seen mainly as protection of American missile silos so that the capacity to retaliate against a first strike would be guaranteed. To say the least, it was controversial largely out of conviction on the part of many scientists that it never would work, and on account of the vast expense involved. By 1987 the funding for SDI research and development had reached about $6 billion a year. The Department of Defense in 1990 estimated that the annual outlay would rise to about $12.5 billion in 1997. In September 2000 President Bill Clinton announced that he would not proceed with an order to build the missile defense system. Incoming President George W. Bush announced that he would continue the program. The total cost was estimated at $60 billion.

In any case, "Star Wars" was the epitome of the kind of program best calculated to encourage the military-industrial complex. It involved the expenditure of billions of dollars a year for many years, with no end in sight. Its effects spread into many kinds of activities and into many parts of the country. Much of it was conducted in secrecy. There was no way that it could be criticized for being over budget or behind schedule. Even many scientists who remained skeptical about the possible effectiveness of such a scheme were willing to acquiesce, and even to participate in it, for they saw it as a significant source for research funds when other sources were drying up.

At the end of the 1980s, Department of Defense officials were becoming concerned, not about an expanding military-industrial complex, but about a decline in American industrial capacity for military production. In 1990 the share of the United States in the world machine-tool market was less than half of what it had been in 1980. In the first half of the 1980s, the rate of growth of productivity in the United States was 3.5 percent, compared to nearly 6.5 percent in Japan. Deployment of forces to the Persian Gulf region changed all the impetus for reduction. That exercise in 1990–1991 added an estimated $30 billion to defense expenditures.

An increasingly significant arm of the military-industrial complex was the research community—the universities and private think tanks that lived on defense contracts. About half of all the scientific research being carried on in the United States in fiscal year 1969 was related to the military. Some 195 educational institutions received defense contracts of $10,000 or more during the year. The Massachusetts Institute of Technology, Stanford, and Johns Hopkins were among the nation's top 100 defense contractors.

A MILITARY-INDUSTRIAL COMPLEX INTERNATIONAL

Surely the greatest direct impact of the military-industrial complex on American foreign policy, and the greatest direct impact of American foreign policy on the military-industrial complex, has been in the transfer of arms among nations, programs of military assistance, cooperative production programs, arms sales abroad, and the rise of multinational corporations in arms and related industries.

One of the most serious charges leveled against the military-industrial complex is that it campaigns actively and effectively against arms control and disarmament, and exerts a controlling influence on the shaping of foreign policy. Those who traffic in military procurement have a vested interest in an unstable international environment. According to proponents of this view, the profits and power of the complex would decline catastrophically if real progress were made in limiting strategic nuclear weaponry and conventional weapon systems. For this reason, it is claimed, advocates of huge arms expenditures use all available means of shaping public attitudes and governmental behavior to perpetuate an illusion of great international danger emanating particularly from the communist bloc of nations. Modern "merchants of death" are said to pursue their own interests in complete disregard of humanitarian considerations.

Juan Bosch, former president of the Dominican Republic, writes of what he calls "Pentagonism." No longer do advanced capitalist nations send out their military to conquer and exploit colonies. Foreign warfare or the threat of warfare provides "access to the generous economic resources being mobilized for industrial war production. What is being sought are profits where arms are manufactured, not where they are employed, and these profits are obtained in, and bring money in from, the place where the center of pentagonist power lies." In short, the domestic population is exploited now as colonies were in the past.

But the serious question remains: Do not countries that have no substantial arms industry have a right to obtain arms from outside sources in order to defend themselves? And is it not in the national security interest of the United States to have allies who are well armed and equipped for military action?

The opening rounds of the Cold War took place in the intercontinental crossroads of the Near East. Only there did Russian efforts fail to consolidate a system of "friendly" buffer states along the Soviet borders. Communist guerrillas in Greece had threatened to extend communist influence in the Balkans and to deliver to the Soviets another strategic area for possible domination of the eastern Mediterranean.

What had brought matters to a head so far as American policy was concerned was not a new and sudden communist attack, but the announcement by the British in February 1947 that they no longer would be able to continue the assistance they had been giving to Greece and Turkey. This might have opened the door to communist penetration. Actually, it set the stage for the policy of military aid that came to be known as mutual defense assistance.

Even as the North Atlantic Treaty was being discussed in early 1949, the implication was clear that American matériel assistance to the participating countries would be necessary if the new organization were to have any real effectiveness as a deterrent to aggression. But President Harry Truman waited until the day after he signed the instrument of ratification to follow it up with a formal request for military assistance. Calling for $1.45 billion, this proposal would consolidate in one act the existing programs for Greece and Turkey, Iran, Korea, the Philippines, and the Western Hemisphere, with a new program for North Atlantic Treaty countries. It envisaged three types of assistance: (1) direct transfer of American military equipment; (2) expert guidance in using the equipment and in production of equipment; and (3) dollar aid to increase direct military production in Europe. Ten weeks later Congress approved the program in the Mutual Defense Assistance Act.

In three years of war in Korea, allied forces other than those of the United States and the Republic of Korea never reached as much as 10 percent of the total troop strength. The United States provided half or more of the logistic support for these forces, but this amounted to a relatively insignificant fraction of the total supplies and services furnished by the United States and Korean forces. But the problems of coordination, negotiation, and accounting were as great as if troop contributions had been several times as large.

A truck rebuilding program in Japan grew to a large scale for the Korean War efforts. Civilian automotive experts sent by the Department of the Army began to arrive in Japan in December 1947 to set up the first production lines. The plan was to rebuild motor trucks on a mass production basis. Although Japan was the foremost industrial power of the East, much in American methods of mass production was foreign to many Japanese workers and supervisors. They were not used to the close tolerances and rigid inspections necessary for the complete interchangeability of parts that is the basis for mass production, and many of their work habits and customs seemed quaint when compared with American factory methods. A training program soon overcame most of those obstacles, and completely renovated trucks began to roll off the assembly lines in ever-increasing numbers.

Old trucks brought into the plants first went to the disassembly line, where they were completely broken down to the last nut and bolt. These parts were then sorted, cleaned, and sent to the various shops. Engines, transmissions, carburetors, and other major assemblies were rebuilt in separate plants. Various parts came together on the assembly line after the fashion of Detroit. The new trucks—built of old parts—then went through a tune-up shop, received a new coat of paint, and a thorough final inspection, and then entered the supply system. In 1951 vehicles were coming off some assembly lines at the rate of one every four minutes. Some 30,000 Japanese were working on the project under the supervision of 50 ordnance officers, nearly 300 civilian experts from the Department of the Army, and about 500 enlisted men from the Ordnance Corps. Here, surely, was an indirect boost to the Japanese automobile industry, and perhaps a further thrust toward a "military-industrial complex international."

An aspect of the defense business that was becoming more significant, with a new twist and a different thrust, was the sale of arms and equipment abroad. The provision of military equipment to foreign countries around the world under the mutual defense assistance programs and other programs already has been mentioned, but there was more to it than that. Now there was a studied effort to persuade other governments to buy American military matériel.

As a part of military assistance to other countries, the United States at first emphasized cooperative production programs with certain of those countries. Undoubtedly, the cooperative production programs contributed significantly to European defense. But Europeans saw the whole effort as too much of a one-way street. The United States showed little inclination to accept European designs for cooperative production either in the United States or in other European countries, even when European designs were favored by those countries. According to one view expressed at the time, this situation was the natural result of American technological superiority and Yankee salesmanship. Another suggested that it was due at least in part to pressure by the U.S. government, which had been lobbied by its own defense industries.

Recognizing what was appearing to many to be the growth of an unhealthy situation, Secretary of Defense Robert McNamara suggested a "common market" in armaments within the NATO alliance. This would encourage trade among all the allies on the basis of economy and quality, including better opportunities for European nations to sell to the United States. The impediment to this scheme came not mainly from trade barriers but from government procurement policies. A serious blow to anything approaching the kind of "common market" that McNamara envisaged came in the fall of 1967 with a nationalistic restriction that Congress imposed on the Defense Appropriation Act. In this instance, the members of Congress who offered the restrictive amendment evidently were interested mainly in eliminating foreign competition for shipbuilding industries in their home districts. But the vote in support was so large that it seemed likely that other members might be seeking similar protection for other kinds of goods at a later time.

Another point of some criticism was in U.S. arms sales to developing countries that could ill afford them. In 1972 four nations—the United States (which accounted for one-third of the world's total weapons), the Soviet Union, Britain and France—were responsible for more than 90 percent of all exports of arms to ninety-one developing countries. Total exports of U.S. arms to foreign countries from 1945 to 1972 (whether in grants or in sales) amounted to approximately $60 billion. This was a significant addition to the orders of American defense industries—and a further impetus to expansion and consolidation of the military-industrial complex.

Some critics have suggested that American enthusiasm for the expansion of NATO to include Poland, Hungary, and the Czech Republic was based less on concerns for national security than on the opening of new markets for the American arms industry. William Greider writes in *Fortress America* (1998) that an official of Lockheed Martin was on the ground in those three countries, and in other potential new member countries, even before the expansion agreements had been accepted. He was there to make a sales pitch for his company's fighter planes, air transports, communication satellites, radar, and other matériel. Not that there was any new threat to the security of those countries, but now they would be moving to replace their old Russian-made armaments with more modern and compatible items from the United States. With pressure sales from British and French concerns as well as American, something of an arms race was under way in Latin America and in Asia.

After dropping sharply from an all-time high of $81.5 billion in 1984 (in 1997 prices) to a low of $42.2 billion in 1994, international trade in arms took a sharp upturn. By 1997 it had risen by 26 percent from that low point, and by 23 percent just over the previous year, to $54.6 billion. Three regions—the Middle East, East Asia, and western Europe—accounted for 80 percent of that trade in 1997, but arms sales to South American countries were rising at a rate of 20 percent a year from 1992 to 1997.

During the 1995–1997 period, Saudi Arabia was the leading arms importer, with a total of $31.3 billion. Others in the top ten arms importers were Taiwan, $12.5 billion; Japan, $6.8 billion; Egypt, $5.3 billion; Kuwait, $5 billion; Turkey, $4.9 billion; United Kingdom, $4.5 billion; South Korea, $4.2 billion; United States, $3.8 billion; United Arab Emirates, $3.8 billion. The United States was the main supplier of arms for eight of those countries (all except the Arab emirates, where France was the chief supplier).

The American share of world arms exports grew from 29 percent in 1987 to 58 percent in 1997. During that period, the Russian share of world arms exports declined from 37 percent to 4 percent; the British increased from 8 percent to 12, and the French from 4 percent to 11. In dollar amounts, world arms exports in 1995–1997 totaled $142 billion. The total for the United States during that period was $77.8 billion; for the United Kingdom, $18 billion; for France, $12 billion, and for Russia, $9.2 billion. In 1997 arms exports represented 4.6 percent of the total exports of the United States, 2.3 percent of the exports of the United Kingdom, 2 percent of the exports of France, and 2.6 percent of the exports of Russia.

While arms trade totals of North Korea were not high when compared with totals of other nations, it should be noted that in 1988, 32.3 percent of North Korea's total imports were in armaments, and 29.2 percent of its total exports were in armaments. By 1997 those figures had declined to 2.1 percent and 8.1 percent, respectively. The People's Republic of China's arms exports amounted to $1.1 billion in 1997, 0.6 percent of its total exports, and its arms imports were $142.2 million, 0.4 percent of its total.

A further complication on the international scene is the growth of domestic arms industries into international conglomerates and multinational corporations. When a great military aircraft manufacturer leaps national boundaries and takes in companies or builds plants in many countries, where does its loyalty lie? What control does its home country have over it? If a foreign branch builds planes or tanks or guns for a country that has become an adversary, how can the company be accused of trading with the enemy?

CONTROL OF THE COMPLEX

Granted that the national security of the United States requires a substantial military industry, a question remains: How can the unfortunate consequences of a powerful military-industrial complex—the kind of conglomerate of special economic and military interests against which Eisenhower warned—be alleviated? One measure might be that favored by Woodrow Wilson and the League of Nations, that is, nationalization of the armaments industry.

Jan Christian Smuts, a distinguished South African soldier and statesman who served in the British war cabinet (and who sometimes is regarded with Woodrow Wilson as a cofounder of the League of Nations), in December 1916 circulated his draft of a constitution for a league of nations. Its paragraph 17 stated:

> That all factories for the production of direct weapons of war shall be nationalized and their production shall be subject to the inspection of the officers of the council; and the council shall be furnished periodically with returns of imports and exports of munitions of war into or from the territories of war into or from the territories of its members, and as far as possible into or from other countries.

Why, it can be asked, should a private company such as General Dynamics, most or all of whose business is with the government, be private? It has been shown that defense contractors often show less profit than comparable companies in civilian production, but with little or no risk, why should their profits be as great? Jacques Gansler estimated that in 1967 just four firms held 93 percent of the contracts for satellites, nuclear submarines, missile guidance systems, space boosters, aircraft fire-control systems, inertial navigation systems, jet aircraft engines, helicopters, and fighter, attack, transport, and tanker aircraft. This concentration became even more pronounced over the next twenty years. The number of military contractors and subcontractors of all types fell from 138,000 in 1982 to fewer than 40,000 in 1987.

Government ownership and operation would eliminate the need for any profit at all and reduce the pressures on the government for big defense spending for the benefit of a company. Of course, it would not eliminate this kind of pressure altogether. As we have seen, locales and political leaders apply pressure for defense orders in their areas whether the facility concerned is government or private, and subsidiary industries that benefit from defense production still would urge those expenditures that would benefit them indirectly.

There are those who contend that government industrial facilities would be less efficient and more costly than private concerns. That is not necessarily true. The Springfield and Harpers Ferry armories were effective in producing high-quality rifles at lower cost than private factories; government navy yards have been effective in building ships (sometimes they were more costly because they paid higher wages and granted more paid holidays than private shipyards); the government's Philadelphia clothing factory has been effective; an army depot has been effective and far less costly than private contractors in overhauling tank engines.

In the development of ballistic missiles in the 1950s the army probably did as well in terms of cost and effectiveness at its Huntsville (Alabama) Redstone Arsenal as the air force did with its favored private contractors. In the end, the air force won out in that competition, some allege on account of politics, and thus gave a great boost to the private military industry of southern California.

Wartime still might require the conversion of civilian plants to military production. But that is a different matter. A thriving automobile factory has no real stake in converting to tanks or aircraft, and it would be reconverted to the civilian production when the immediate need had been met. Another approach might be to prohibit the export of armaments. This usually brings the rejoinder, "Well, if we did not sell arms to other countries, someone else would." The answer to that is, "So be it; at least we would not be putting advanced American weaponry into the hands of potential enemies."

A further step toward reducing undue influences of the military-industrial complex might be a more complete separation of government-sponsored research and development from those who have an immediate stake in the production of the items concerned. In any case, control must depend upon effective and sympathetic leadership at the top, in the White House and in the Pentagon.

CONCLUSION

An army that had resisted breech-loading rifles and cannon, automatic rifles, machine guns, motor trucks, and airplanes has now, since World War II, done a complete about-face. Now anything old is likely to be discarded. Certainly, improved weapons and equipment are desirable. But the military-industrial complex has betrayed an almost "Detroit mind-set" in developing new models every year or so. It is difficult to escape the conclusion that the constant quest for novelty is due in part to the activities of researchers and industrialists anxious to maintain the flow of research and development dollars and anxious to keep production lines going. This was a major factor in keeping defense budgets high. When people looked forward to a "peace dividend"—funds that might be available for other purposes—after the pullout from Vietnam, they were disappointed to find that there was little of a peace dividend. All kinds of new weapon systems were waiting to eat it up.

A more serious consequence of a powerful military-industrial complex is the drain that a permanent defense industry on a large scale creates on the national economy. Many people accept the myth that a big defense industry brings prosperity. They point to the economic well-being of a community that is dependent on a local defense industry. They point out that it really was World War II that brought the United States completely out of the Great Depression. There is some truth, of course, to those contentions. Defense industries do provide an economic shot in the arm. But in the long run, and for the country as a whole, defense industries on a big scale can only be a drain on the actual or potential economic well-being and strength.

A healthy partnership between the military establishment and private industry was sought from the early days of the nation. In more recent years, this has been actively cultivated as demands for national security have required a greater industrial base. It has been in the interest of corporate profits and individual careers as well as in the interest of national defense. At times, there have been evidences of costly mismanagement and of collusion, conspiracy, and even fraud. But for the most part the growth of what has come to be known as the military-industrial complex has been benign. Gaining a kind of momentum of its own, it has grown to have unfortunate consequences in spite of itself.

The greatest military rival of the United States in the post–World War II period was the Soviet Union. It devoted a large share of its resources to military production (from 9 to 10 percent of gross national product). By 1990 its economy was in chaos. The greatest economic rival of the United States, Japan, devoted a small share of its resources to defense (less than 1 percent of GNP). Its economy was flourishing at a high level.

Related to the question of prosperity and economic well-being is the broader question of the long-range strength of the nation. Military expenditures, stimulated by the military-industrial complex to unnecessarily high levels over extended periods of time, actually can pose a threat to national security. This was the concern that Eisenhower expressed in his address of 16 April 1953 and in other speeches early in his presidential term. It was a concern that General Douglas MacArthur expressed during the same period: "In final analysis the mounting cost of preparation for war is in many ways as materially destructive as war itself."

The problem is to maintain a balance between overcommitment beyond capabilities of the armed forces and overextension of the military at the expense of the domestic economy. For example, after World War II, Great Britain was facing military commitments beyond its resources and had to call upon the United States to fill the gap. Arnold Toynbee wrote, on the other hand, that the ancient Assyrian Empire fell of its own military weight. And in the Peloponnesian War, the overextension of its military effort in the expedition to Sicily was the undoing of Athens.

In *The Rise and Fall of the Great Powers*, a provocative study published in 1987, Paul Kennedy warns that overextension in military commitments has been a critical factor in the decline of great powers over the past five centuries. He concludes:

> Yet the history of the past five hundred years of international rivalry demonstrates that military "security" alone is never enough. It may, over the shorter term, deter or defeat rival states (and that, for most political leaders and their publics, is perfectly satisfactory). But if, by such victories, the nation over-extends itself geographically and strategically; if, even at a less imperial level, it chooses to devote a large proportion of its total income to "protection," leaving less for "productive investment," it is likely to find its economic output slowing down, with dire implications for its long-term capacity to maintain both its citizens' consumption demands and its international position....
>
> We therefore return to the conundrum which has exercised strategists and economists and political leaders from classical times onward. To be a Great Power—by definition, a state capable of holding its own against any other nation—demands a flourishing economic base.... Yet by going to war, or by devoting a large share of the nation's "manufacturing power" to expenditures upon "unproductive" armaments, one runs the risk of eroding the national economic base, especially vis-a-vis states which are concentrating a greater share of their income upon productive investment for long-term growth.

An irony of modern war is that to preserve victory, the victors must maintain a large military establishment. At the same time, they force a strict limitation of arms on the late enemies. This permits the latter to devote their resources to expand their economies, and then they forge ahead of the victors economically.

But a major development of the last half of the twentieth century was the spread of low-intensity conflict with the support of international trade in arms. As John Keegan put it in *A History of Warfare* (1993):

> The Western-style militarisation of the new independent states of Asia and Africa in the four decades after 1945 was as remarkable a phenomenon as it had been with the non-warrior populations of Europe in the nineteenth century. That it had many of the same doleful effects—overspending on arms, subordination of civilian to military values, superordination of self-chosen military elites and even resort to war—could be expected. It was equally to be expected that most of the hundred or so armies brought into being after decolonisation were of little objective military worth; Western "technology transfers," a euphemism for selfish arms sales by rich Western nations to poor ones that could rarely afford the outlay, did not entail the transfusion of culture which made advanced weapons so deadly in Western hands.

Yet, African rebels and irregulars and government forces came to inflict casualties upon each other in appalling numbers.

BIBLIOGRAPHY

Ambrose, Stephen E. *Eisenhower.* New York, 1984.

Brendon, Piers. *Ike: The Life and Times of Dwight D. Eisenhower.* New York, 1986.

Bush, Vannevar. *Modern Arms and Free Men: A Discussion of the Role of Science in Preserving Democracy.* New York, 1949.

Campbell, Levin H., Jr. *The Industry-Ordnance Team.* New York and London, 1946.

Carey, Omer L., ed. *The Military-Industrial Complex and United States Foreign Policy.* Pullman, Wash., 1969.

Caves, Richard E. *Multinational Enterprise and Economic Analysis.* 2d ed. Cambridge and New York, 1996.

Chinn, George M. *The Machine Gun.* 5 vols. Washington, D.C., 1951–1987. A broad treatment of the development of automatic weapons.

Clark, Victor S. "Manufacturing During the Civil War." *Military Historian and Economist* 3 (April 1918).

Clarkson, Grosvenor B. *Industrial America in the World War: The Strategy Behind the Line, 1917–1918.* Boston, 1923.

Clayton, James L. *The Economic Impact of the Cold War: Sources and Readings.* New York, 1970.

Coates, James, and Michael Kilian. *Heavy Losses: The Dangerous Decline of American Defense.* New York, 1985.

Connery, Robert H. *The Navy and Industrial Mobilization in World War II.* Princeton, N.J., 1951.

Craven, Wesley Frank, and James Lea Cate. *The Army Air Forces in World War II.* Vol. 6, *Men and Planes.* Chicago, 1954. Well-balanced official history.

Crowell, Benedict, and Robert Forrest Wilson. *How America Went to War.* New Haven, Conn., 1921. Detailed coverage of industrial development during World War I.

Danhoff, Clarence H. *Government Contracting and Technological Change.* Washington, D.C., 1968.

Deitchman, Seymour J. *Military Power and the Advance of Technology: General Purpose Military Forces for the 1980s and Beyond.* Boulder, Colo., 1983.

Deyrup, Felicia Johnson. *Arms Makers of the Connecticut Valley: A Regional Study of the Economic Development of the Small Arms Industry, 1798–1870.* Northampton, Mass., 1948. A useful general survey of the early period.

Dickson, Thomas L., Jr. "Military-Industrial Complex." *Military Review* (December 1971): 29–35.

Doremus, Paul N., William W. Keller, Louis W. Pauley, and Simon Reich. *The Myth of the Global Corporation.* Princeton, N.J., 1998.

Duscha, Julius. *Arms, Money and Politics.* New York, 1965.

Eccles, Henry E. *Military Power in a Free Society.* Newport, R.I., 1979. By a former naval officer with a special interest in logistics.

Edwards, David V. *Arms Control in International Politics.* New York, 1969.

Fuller, Claud E. *The Whitney Firearms.* Huntington, W.Va., 1946.

Galbraith, John Kenneth. "How to Control the Military." *Harper's* (June 1969).

Greider, William. *Fortress America: The American Military and the Consequences of Peace.* New York, 1998.

Herzog, Arthur. *The War-Peace Establishment.* New York, 1965.

Huston, James A. *The Sinews of War: Army Logistics, 1775–1953.* Washington, D.C., 1966.

———. *One for All: NATO Strategy and Logistics Through the Formative Period, 1949–1969.* Newark, Del., and London, 1984.

———. *Outposts and Allies: U.S. Army Logistics in the Cold War, 1945–1953.* London, 1988.

———. *Guns and Butter, Powder and Rice: U.S. Army Logistics in the Korean War.* London, 1989.

———. *Logistics of Liberty: American Services of Supply in the Revolutionary War and After.* Newark, Del., 1991.

Kaufman, Richard F. *The War Profiteers.* Indianapolis, 1970.

Keegan, John. *A History of Warfare.* New York, 1993.

Kennedy, Paul. *The Rise and Fall of the Great Powers: Economic Change and Military Conflict from 1500 to 2000.* New York, 1987. An impressive study in which the author holds that the decline of great powers can usually be attributed to an overextension of military power.

Korstinen, Paul A. C. "The Industrial-Military Complex in Historical Perspective: The Inter-War Years." *Journal of American History* (March 1970): 819–839.

Lapp, Ralph Eugene. *The Weapons Culture.* New York, 1968. A critical study by a popular scientist.

Lens, Sidney. *The Military-Industrial Complex.* Philadelphia, 1970.

Melman, Seymour. *Pentagon Capitalism: The Political Economy of War.* New York, 1970.

———. *The Permanent War Economy: American Capitalism in Decline.* New York, 1974.

Millis, Walter. *Arms and Men: A Study in American Military History.* New York, 1956.

Mills, C. Wright. *The Power Elite.* London and New York, 1956.

Mirsky, Jeannette, and Allan Nevins. *The World of Eli Whitney.* New York, 1952. A study by two outstanding historians emphasizing Whitney's industrial development based on Whitney's papers.

Mytelka, Lynn Krieger. *Strategic Partnerships: States, Firms and International Competition.* Rutherford, N.J., 1991.

Olvey, Lee D., James R. Golden, and Robert C. Kelly. *The Economics of National Security.* Wayne, N.J., 1984.

Phillips, J. B. "Special Report: The Military-Industrial Complex." *Congressional Quarterly Weekly Report* (24 May 1968).

Proxmire, William. "The Pentagon vs. Free Enterprise." *Saturday Review* (31 January 1970). A critique by a critical senator from Wisconsin.

———. *Report from Wasteland: America's Military-Industrial Complex.* New York, 1970.

Smith, R. Elberton. *The Army and Economic Mobilization.* Washington, D.C., 1959.

Somers, Herman Miles. "Civil-Military Relations in Mutual Security." *Annals of the American Academy of Political and Social Science* 288 (July 1953): 27–35.

Sutton, John L., and Geoffrey Kemp. "Arms to Developing Countries." *Adelphi Papers* 28 (October 1966).

Thayer, George. *The War Business: The International Trade in Armaments.* New York, 1969.

U.S. Arms Control and Disarmament Agency. *World Military Expenditures and Arms Transfers 1967–1976.* Washington, D.C., 1978.

U.S. Bureau of the Budget. *The United States at War: Development and Administration of the War Program by the Federal Government.* Washington, D.C., 1946.

U.S. Department of State, Bureau of Verification and Compliance. *World Military Expenditures and Arms Transfers 1998.* Washington, D.C., 2000.

Van Creveld, Martin. *Technology and War: From 2000 B.C. to the Present.* London and Washington, D.C., 1989.

See also ARMS CONTROL AND DISARMAMENT; ARMS TRANSFERS AND TRADE; FOREIGN AID; NUCLEAR STRATEGY AND DIPLOMACY.

MOST-FAVORED-NATION PRINCIPLE

Justus D. Doenecke and Michael R. Adamson

From its inception, the United States has incorporated the most-favored-nation (MFN) principle into its trade policy. Until 1923 it adhered to its conditional form and thereafter to unconditional MFN treatment. Only with the passage of the 1934 Reciprocal Trade Agreements Act (RTAA), however, did Congress allow U.S. trade negotiators to use unconditional MFN treatment as an instrument of trade liberalization. That is, the MFN principle does not equate with free or freer trading environments. From 1778 until 1934, U.S. trade policy was explicitly protectionist. In this environment, the adoption by the State Department of unconditional MFN treatment did nothing to advance its program of trade liberalization. MFN treatment is an instrument of trade policy. Its use must be understood within the context of trade policy. In the United States, interest group pressures, the actions of policymakers, and the constraints and opportunities presented by the international political economy shaped policy over time.

MFN treatment means that policy discriminates among nationals and foreigners but treats all foreigners equally. National treatment extends the same privileges to foreigners and nationals alike. Equal treatment in general is known as nondiscrimination. As far as U.S. trade policy is concerned, two types of MFN treatment are relevant. Unconditional MFN treatment is provided gratuitously to nations eligible for MFN status. Under conditional MFN treatment, third parties must bargain and provide equal compensation in order to benefit from MFN status. Linked historically to MFN treatment in practice is the instrument of reciprocity. Reciprocity, or the exchange of trading privileges through bargaining, implies discrimination among trading partners. That is, benefits are not conferred freely.

The following example illustrates the difference between conditional and unconditional MFN treatment. Assume that the United States extends conditional MFN treatment to Germany, then signs a trade deal with Japan that provides for a reduced tariff on the import of Japanese televisions. Under conditional MFN, however, the United States will not allow German television imports at the new rate until German trade negotiators offer equivalent compensation. German trade negotiators may then offer, for instance, to accept imports of U.S. sewing machines at a lower rate. U.S. trade negotiators—since 1962, officials of the Office of the U.S. Trade Representative; before then, State Department officers—may accept the offer, if the increased value of American sewing machine exports to Germany balances the increased value of German television imports into America. If America were to extend unconditional MFN treatment to Germany, however, the latter would receive benefit of the U.S.–Japanese treaty without having to make any concessions.

As this illustration suggests, unconditional MFN treatment may constitute the means by which a multilateral trading regime is created from a series of bilateral agreements, since its use ensures that all eligible countries enjoy the benefits of past and future concessions. This has been the experience internationally during most of the post–World War II period. As discussed below, both the General Agreement on Tariffs and Trade (GATT) and its successor, the World Trade Organization (WTO), incorporated unconditional MFN treatment into their charters.

MFN TREATMENT IN PRACTICE, 1776–1887: CONDITIONAL MFN WITHIN PROTECTIONISM

At the time of the American Revolution, Great Britain and continental Europe adhered to unconditional MFN treatment, which they had done since the seventeenth century. To maintain the political and economic independence of the new American republic, the Founders focused on balancing internal economic development among industry, agriculture, and commerce. Once established, the national government aimed to develop the nation's resources and secure neutral rights internationally. Leaders of the early republic did not seek autarky (that is, national economic self-sufficiency and independence). Indeed, Benjamin Franklin and Thomas Jefferson, for example, leaned toward free trade. However, since they believed that free trade would threaten America's political viability, they sought access to overseas markets for U.S. commodities through both reciprocity and nondiscrimination. Ideally, they wanted the benefits of unconditional MFN treatment. But they were prepared to settle for equality of treatment with foreign nations. Moreover, they recognized that the great powers of Europe were unlikely to reciprocate on trade. Ultimately, they adhered to conditional MFN treatment to preserve the means to bargain for access to overseas markets, but this approach ensured that all trade treaties were bilateral, unique, and discriminatory.

In July 1776 the delegates to the Continental Congress were prepared to allow unrestricted imports into the U.S. market in order to gain diplomatic recognition and break Britain's hold on Atlantic trade. John Adams, assisted by Benjamin Franklin, drafted a model commercial agreement that was approved by the delegates. It instructed trade negotiators to obtain equal national treatment or unconditional MFN treatment to gain access to Europe's markets (and those of its colonies).

America's first trade treaty, the 1778 Franco-American Treaty of Amity and Commerce, secured neither equal national treatment nor unconditional MFN status for American goods. U.S. trade negotiators Benjamin Franklin, Silas Deane, and Arthur Lee settled for a conditional MFN clause (Article II).

Neither side wanted the treaty to benefit Britain; French negotiators feared the consequences of a possible U.S.–British political reconciliation. U.S. negotiators wanted Britain and other European countries to buy access to the U.S. market with reciprocal trading privileges to their home and colonial markets. French officials only offered access to its home market. In 1783, France reverted to unconditional treatment and tried to interpret Article II in this way. U.S. officials balked; they decided to use reciprocity to secure equality of treatment.

During the early national period, U.S. officials had little success in opening overseas markets to American goods. They concluded treaties with Sweden and the Netherlands, but only the latter offered MFN access to both its home and colonial markets. In 1784 U.S. negotiators initiated another round of trade talks, using the 1776 plan as a blueprint. They succeeded only in securing a pact with Prussia in 1785, which secured the conditional MFN treatment granted by France in the 1778 treaty. Officials such as John Jay and Elbridge Gerry became convinced that a strict reciprocity approach would best serve U.S. interests, at least until negotiators gained experience in trade matters and America gained in importance within the international economy.

Crucial aspects of U.S. trade policy hampered the use of either reciprocity or conditional MFN treatment in a manner that benefited American exporters. Treasury Secretary Alexander Hamilton's 1791 Report on Manufactures provided the justification for a protective tariff system to enable America to establish its own manufacturing base as the basis for economic development. After the War of 1812, Congress took up the recommendations of Hamilton and James Madison's Treasury secretary, Albert Gallatin, and adopted the so-called American System sponsored by Senator Henry Clay: a nationalistic industrial policy based on high tariffs and support for domestic manufacturers. Until the Great Depression, many U.S. leaders, especially Whigs and Republicans, remained adamant that protectionism was the key to U.S. economic development, class harmony, and political independence.

Congress also subjected all imports to a uniform (single-schedule) tariff, leaving little room for officials to negotiate preferential bilateral agreements. Until Congress adopted a dual-schedule tariff in the 1909 Payne-Aldrich Act, there was little chance that trade negotiators could wield reciprocity, not to mention MFN treatment, to win concessions from trading partners. This limited policymakers in the executive branch to adjusting the level of tariffs: Democrats tended to lower tariffs to levels adequate to fund the budget, and Whigs and Republicans tended to raise tariffs to protect domestic producers from foreign competition.

Until the late nineteenth century, foreign markets were the concern only of commodity producers in the South and timber and fur exporters in the North. Hence, there was little interest-group pressure to persuade Congress to lower the barriers that protected domestic industries and workers. Diplomacy served the economic and security interests of a developing country with a large domestic market and little disposition to global leadership.

State Department negotiators therefore sought equal access for American goods to the markets of European competitors by offering equal access in return. The administrations of Presidents John Tyler, James Polk, Franklin Pierce, and James Buchanan were especially interested in using reciprocity to pry open overseas markets. However, Congress generally refused to ratify the reciprocal pacts that State Department officials negotiated, fearing that the MFN clauses in earlier treaties might compel the United States to generalize proposed concessions. Opponents also recognized that the State Department paid inadequate attention to negotiating an equivalent exchange of concessions.

With others—Canada, Latin America, and Asia—U.S. trade officials sought special privileges and offered special concessions for raw materials and agricultural goods in the U.S. market. The expansionist Polk, Pierce, and Buchanan administrations were eager to experiment with new approaches. They sought either unilateral MFN treatment or one-sided agreements that assured the United States of MFN treatment. For example, treaties with China in 1844 and Japan in 1854 provided America with MFN access to both markets, but did not extend equality of treatment to the U.S. market for either China or Japan in return.

The United States held contracting parties to conditional MFN treatment even when commercial agreements contained ambiguous language or appeared to contradict each other. As Secretary of State John Jay put it in 1787, it would be inconsistent with "reason and equity," as well as with "the most obvious principles of justice and fair construction," to demand that the United States grant unconditional MFN treatment simply because a treaty—in this case the 1782 treaty with the Netherlands—failed to specify conditional MFN treatment. Just because "France purchases, at a great price, a privilege of the United States," the Netherlands cannot "immediately insist on having the like privileges without [paying] any price at all."

The use of conditional MFN treatment led to disputes with trading partners. For example, the so-called Convention of 1815 with Britain set the stage for a dispute with France over the Louisiana Purchase. The convention extended privileges to British ships in American harbors that French ships did not enjoy. In the absence of a specific MFN clause, France insisted that the United States adhere to the literal interpretation of the MFN clause. France claimed that it had given America an equivalent concession at the time of the Louisiana Purchase. Nonetheless, Secretary of State John Quincy Adams asserted that "the condition, though not expressed in the article, is inherent in the advantage claimed under it." Only when France reduced duties on wines in 1831—acceding to a request from Secretary of State Martin Van Buren—did the United States grant France the commercial privileges it sought.

MFN TREATMENT IN PRACTICE, 1887–1933: CONDITIONAL AND UNCONDITIONAL MFN WITHIN PROTECTIONISM AND EXPORT EXPANSIONISM

Until 1887, the United States was a relatively passive and highly protectionist country within the international economy. U.S. trade policy was nonnegotiable and nondiscriminatory and characterized by high tariffs. By the late nineteenth century, this policy complicated efforts of export-oriented sectors that sought to gain access to foreign markets. From the late 1880s, U.S. administrations identified opportunities that the international economy offered these interest groups and attempted to facilitate the expansion of exports on the basis of reciprocity and conditional MFN treatment. But Congress, dominated by powerful Republican protectionists such as Senators Nelson Aldrich and Reed Smoot, remained opposed to trade liberalization on principle. Before World War I, U.S. administrations from Grover Cleveland to Woodrow Wilson focused on export expansion. This was possible because Britain adhered to free trade even as America and Germany challenged and surpassed it in economic productivity and output. That is, the United States could continue to enjoy the benefits of Britain's free-trade policy without compromising its own protectionist policy. Yet the United States had limited success in gaining access to major overseas markets. Indeed, after World War I, the United States and its trading partners raised barriers to trade, exacerbating the financial and commercial imbalances created by the war. Both reciprocity and MFN treatment—conditional or unconditional—proved to be poor

NELSON W. ALDRICH: ARDENT TRADE PROTECTIONIST

An influential Republican senator from 1881 until 1911, Nelson W. Aldrich (1841–1915) used his position on the Senate Finance Committee—which he chaired from 1899 to 1911—to maintain protection. Elected to the U.S. House of Representatives in 1878, Aldrich was selected in October 1881 to fill the Rhode Island seat vacated by the death of Senator Ambrose Burnside. As a member of the Finance Committee, Aldrich apprenticed under Justin Morrill of Vermont, who chaired the committee for twenty-two years, until 1898. An ardent defender of both the American System and Congress's authority over trade policy, Morrill opposed free trade, reciprocal trade agreements, and unconditional MFN treatment. When he assumed the chair of the Finance Committee, Aldrich remained steadfast to Morrill's views on trade.

Aldrich championed the position held by the Republican Party that economic nationalism promoted class harmony. By excluding competition from imports, so the argument went, a high tariff wall would promote the well-being not only of producers and workers but also of consumers. As Aldrich put it in the *Congressional Record* of 5 August 1909: "If we permit American industries to live by the imposition of protective duties, competition in this country will so affect prices that it will give the American consumer the best possible results." For Aldrich, the tariff was the price that overseas producers had to pay to enter the U.S. market. As such, protectionism placed the burden of generating revenue for the federal government on foreign producers and domestic consumers of imported "luxury" items.

Aldrich had a major hand in writing the McKinley (1890) and Dingley (1897) Acts, which allowed the executive branch to negotiate reciprocal trade treaties. However, he opposed the deals that administrations subsequently negotiated because they lacked equivalent exchanges of concessions. Wedded to the congressional committee system as the institutional basis for policymaking, Aldrich also fought the creation of a commission of experts to study the tariff "scientifically" and make policy recommendations. Committed to protecting the textile industries of his state, Aldrich obstructed the modest efforts of the Taft administration to reduce tariffs and sought to make what became the 1909 Payne-Aldrich Act as conservative a piece of trade legislation as possible.

---

instruments of trade liberalization as long as U.S. markets remained closed to competing goods from overseas.

As administrations and Congresses reaffirmed their commitment to Clay's American System in the immediate post–Civil War period, Europe followed Britain's lead toward trade liberalization. The 1860 Cobden-Chevalier Treaty, also known as the Anglo-French Treaty of 1860, between Britain and France epitomized the free trade–low tariff regime established across much of Europe by treaty and unconditional MFN treatment. The treaty was meant to eliminate all tariffs between Britain and France and induced them to initiate a round of bilateral tariff reduction treaties with other European nations. Almost all commercial treaties involving European nations thereafter included the MFN clause. With the entry of Germany into the European system in the late 1870s, however, Europe began to retreat from liberal trade. In 1878, under Chancellor Otto von Bismarck, Germany raised tariffs on agricultural products and sheltered so-called infant industries. France also retreated, giving up the Cobden-Chevalier Treaty in 1892 with its adoption of the Méline tariff, which raised average rates on dutiable items and implemented a dual minimum-maximum schedule. (The maximum rate constituted the conventional rate. The minimum rate could be extended to trading partners through negotiation.)

In 1887, President Grover Cleveland called for duty-free status on raw materials. He wanted to recast the tariff as an instrument of export expansion. The 1890 McKinley and 1894 Wilson-Gorman Acts supported this approach. Both laws maintained protectionism, but they also sanctioned the pursuit of special reciprocal relationships with Latin American countries through lower duties on selected raw materials. Their aim was to expand U.S. exports to the region at the expense of British and European traders.

By the late 1890s, American exporters faced the probability of losing access to European markets. Some European countries now attached conditions to their MFN clauses. Average European tariff levels remained far below those of the United States—in 1900 European minimum or conventional rates averaged 10 percent while U.S. tariffs on dutiable items averaged 30 percent (and America offered concessions only on noncompetitive goods). But these tariff levels were trending upward. The goal of expanding exports was clearly under threat. The administrations of Presidents William McKinley, Theodore Roosevelt, and William Howard Taft responded by differentiating among trading partners. They maintained the approach of expanding markets in Latin America and protecting the domestic market, but they now used bilateral reciprocity to counter European trade restrictions. Under section 4 of the 1897 Dingley Tariff Act, Congress extended the bilateral reciprocity provisions of the McKinley tariff beyond Latin America to "France, Germany, Belgium, and other European countries."

Because the single-schedule tariff and conditional MFN treatment remained features of U.S. trade policy, the efficacy of using reciprocity to maintain or expand access to European markets was limited. Indeed, U.S trade negotiators could not compete with free-trading Britain for favorable tariff treatment from continental Europe. With U.S. manufacturers able to compete against European producers, European governments showed their displeasure with U.S. trade policy by putting tariff arrangements on a temporary basis and discriminating against U.S. products.

The ambiguity of MFN treatment among trade treaties created the basis for increasing commercial frictions between the United States and its trading partners once the executive branch acquired the capacity to use reciprocity as an instrument for expanding exports. The most notable example was the degradation of U.S. trade relations with Germany, beginning in 1905, which almost exploded into a tariff war but was resolved in 1907.

Beginning in the late 1890s, the German government pointed to numerous trade pacts, including the 1828 U.S.–Prussia Commercial Treaty, as evidence that America accepted unconditional MFN treatment. The Germans were particularly critical of the special commercial benefits the United States accorded Switzerland in 1898, in response to the Swiss government's demand that the United States extend the same concessions granted France earlier in the year. Since an 1850 U.S.–Switzerland trade treaty explicitly provided for unconditional MFN treatment, the United States decided that "both justice and honor" required meeting the Swiss claims. When Germany claimed the same treatment, however, the United States renounced the MFN clauses in the 1850 treaty.

Germany renewed its protests when a 1902 reciprocity treaty with Cuba gave the latter an exclusive rate 20 percent below the rates provided for in the Dingley tariff. Germany argued that Cuba's sovereign status required the United States to grant it commensurate reductions. The administration of President Theodore Roosevelt cheekily advanced the theory that the 1901 Platt Amendment, which forbade Cuba from entering into foreign agreements contrary to U.S. interests, rendered Cuba part of the U.S. political system, akin to a European colony. The incredulous German government threatened to retaliate with tariff revisions that targeted U.S. exports. It did so to induce the U.S. government to adopt unconditional MFN status, as Europe understood it. But powerful Republicans in Congress, including Speaker of the House Joseph Cannon and Senate Finance Committee Chair Nelson Aldrich, refused to budge. A major trade war was averted only when the U.S. and German governments concluded an executive agreement regarding a possible customs agreement. It outlined the terms of an exchange of the German conventional rate on nearly all items in return for U.S. concessions along the lines of the 20 percent cuts provided for in section 4 of the Dingley tariff.

With the introduction of a statutory minimum-maximum tariff schedule in the 1909 Payne-Aldrich tariff, U.S. trade negotiators held that the minimum rates in effect constituted unconditional MFN treatment as Europeans practiced it. Although the executive branch did not renounce conditional MFN treatment, and therefore remained technically free to alter policy, State Department officials were determined to use the minimum-maximum provisions in the act to embed the nondiscrimination principles of the Open Door policy in trade policy. Trade liberalizers in the executive branch adopted this approach to gain access to overseas markets and to attract the support of agricultural and export manufacturing interests as allies in the battle for a more liberal trade policy.

The administrative features of the Payne-Aldrich Act, including its establishment of the

Tariff Board, also enabled trade agreements to be hammered out within the executive branch, independent of Congress and largely free from public scrutiny. Unfortunately for trade liberalizers, the system proved rigid in operation, because Congress successfully resisted lowering U.S. minimum rates to European levels. Conditional MFN also remained in place. The Wilson administration and the Democratic majority in Congress thus abandoned the dual-schedule tariff for unilateral rate reduction and a single schedule in the 1913 Underwood-Simmons Act. Nevertheless, the 1909 Payne-Aldrich Act contemplated and institutionalized ways of dealing with liberalizing trade that would be built upon by the 1934 Reciprocal Trade Agreements Act.

After World War I, Republican Congresses and administrations rejected reciprocity altogether and reestablished protectionism. In this context, Secretary of State Charles Evans Hughes used the equality-of-treatment clause in section 317 of the 1922 Fordney-McCumber Act to put U.S. trade policy on an unconditional MFN footing. But this failed to increase international economic cooperation, since Congress also precluded any liberalization of the tariff in the act.

The third of President Wilson's Fourteen Points included a demand for "equality of trade conditions." He recognized that nations that expected to increase exports needed to open their own markets to imports. This was especially so for America, which, Wilson hoped, would demonstrate international political and economic leadership in the post–World War I era. In addition to reinstating protectionism, the Fordney-McCumber Act addressed the issue of access to overseas markets for U.S. exports. Officials in the State, Treasury, and Commerce departments sought flexible retaliatory authority to counter discrimination. After much wrangling, Congress authorized the president to retaliate unilaterally against foreign discrimination. In addition, it stipulated in section 317 that the Tariff Commission established in 1916 monitor discrimination and make recommendations to the president. The State Department interpreted section 317 to be in harmony with unconditional MFN treatment.

As part of a State Department policy review, William Culbertson, a member of the Tariff Commission, suggested using section 317 to negotiate a series of trade treaties to extend equality of treatment and implement unconditional MFN treatment as broadly as possible. Inclined intellectually to free trade and uninhibited flows of capital, and institutionally sensitive to allowing trade wars to disrupt political relationships, State Department economic advisers Stanley Hornbeck and Wallace McClure agreed that discrimination against U.S. goods should be monitored, but recommended against retaliation unless officials determined it to be absolutely necessary. The policy review elicited strong support for the unconditional MFN approach. State Department officials wanted to avoid the bargaining associated with conditional MFN treatment, and they viewed unconditional MFN treatment as a way of avoiding diplomatic conflict, promoting trade, and improving foreign relations, including the trade negotiation process. They pressed Secretary Hughes to initiate a new round of trade talks based on the unconditional MFN principle. Hughes sold President Warren Harding on the idea. Congress offered no opposition; most members at this time did not engage trade as an issue at the technical level. The administration went forward with the decision on unconditional MFN treatment in February 1923. Hughes announced it in a circular letter to overseas posts in August.

In justifying the decision in a note to the Senate Foreign Relations Committee, Hughes argued that conditional MFN treatment was incapable of winning equality of treatment for U.S. exports, and that what might constitute equivalent compensation was "found to be difficult or impracticable." "Reciprocal commercial arrangements," Hughes averred, "were but temporary makeshifts; they caused constant negotiation and created uncertainty." In his August circular, Hughes explained why a new series of trade pacts had to be concluded: "The enlarged productive capacity of the United States developed during the World War has increased the need for assured equality of treatment in foreign markets."

From 1923 to 1930, the State Department negotiated trade treaties with forty-three countries; twenty-one of them contained unconditional MFN clauses. Nonetheless, in the context of the financial chaos and the payments imbalances created by world war and the postwar Versailles settlement, important markets such as Canada, Britain, France, and Germany increasingly shut their doors to U.S. exports.

U.S. trade negotiators had little to offer any country that accepted unconditional MFN treatment and equal treatment for U.S. exports. The Fordney-McCumber Act raised the average tariff on dutiable items some 38 percent and on all imports to an average of almost 14 percent. This was lower than the average rate of the Dingley tariff. Yet the new tariff granted more protection than its 1897 predecessor, since Congress also instructed the executive branch to adjust duties by up to 50 percent to equalize production costs between home and foreign manufactured products. Moreover, the act redefined dumping to include any product imported at a price below the U.S. cost of production (rather than the producers' own costs). In addition, Congress allowed the president to strip MFN status from any country that discriminated against American products or dumped goods into the U.S. market. The tariff now effectively excluded all competing goods.

The punitive responses and the single-schedule tariff regime reestablished by the Fordney-McCumber Act hamstrung all State Department efforts to negotiate unconditional MFN clauses in trade agreements. Tariffs could be adjusted only to equalize production costs or punish others for uncooperative acts. Equalization applied to all nations regardless of their MFN status. Discrimination applied selectively to nations that lost MFN status for their treatment of U.S. goods. To make matters worse for trade liberalizers, Congress supplemented tariffs with selectively applied quotas: a form of protection totally at odds with the MFN principle.

U.S. trade policy under the Fordney-McCumber Act, together with congressional insistence that allies repay their war loans to the U.S. Treasury, undermined international efforts to stabilize and reconstruct the post–World War I international system. Rather than assume the mantle of global leadership as Britain's economic power waned, the Republican administrations of Warren Harding, Calvin Coolidge, and Herbert Hoover relied on private capital flows to ameliorate the payments imbalances created by war debts and reparations. These flows ultimately proved insufficient to overcome the foreign economic policy of these administrations.

In its ongoing search for a way to liberalize trade that Congress might find politically acceptable, the State Department began thinking in terms of an approach that involved both reciprocal bargaining and unconditional MFN treatment. During the Coolidge administration, economic adviser McClure suggested as much, saying that it might pave the way for bilateral negotiations with important trading partners. McClure, a friend of fellow Tennesseean Representative Cordell Hull, worked closely with the future secretary of state to develop what would become the reciprocal trade agreements program. Both McClure and Hull preferred lowering trade barriers through bargaining rather than unilaterally reducing tariffs, which was the approach employed by the Wilson administration in the Underwood tariff. However, congressional Democrats adhered to the Wilsonian approach until the election of Franklin Roosevelt.

Congress reinforced its commitment to protectionism with its passage of the debilitating Smoot-Hawley Act in 1930. The act produced additional international economic conflict. Trading partners retaliated to protect themselves from the loss of the U.S. market, worsening relations and reinforcing the effects of global depression. The defensive reactions of trading partners, Britain and Canada in particular, demonstrated that the U.S. economy could be injured by foreign reaction. Politicians and officials recognized that trade policy could no longer be treated as an independent domestic issue. Further, when Britain failed to restore its pre-1914 position of international economic leadership following its return to the gold standard in 1925, the idea that international economy stability required American leadership began to gain support in some circles. Above all, the Smoot-Hawley Act demonstrated that the costs of protectionism were too high, prompting a turn toward a more liberal approach in trade policy, one within which all trade instruments, including unconditional MFN treatment, could serve as tools to lower trade barriers.

MFN TREATMENT IN PRACTICE, 1934–1974: UNCONDITIONAL MFN AS ONE INSTRUMENT OF TRADE LIBERALIZATION

The State Department under Cordell Hull moved forward with the trade liberalization program that it had championed since the nineteenth century. The 1934 Reciprocal Trade Agreements Act marked the beginning of a successful U.S. effort to liberalize trade and create a multilateral regime of commercial cooperation. The most important aspects of the RTAA were institutional. Foremost, Congress ceded to the executive branch the power to set and manage the trade agenda. Members of Congress voted to do so partially in response to the fallout from the Smoot-Hawley Act and the persistence and depth of depression. They were also persuaded by executive branch promises to compensate producers that were harmed by subsequent trade deals.

The RTAA formed the basis for the post–World War II multilateral system that employed bilateral reciprocity to negotiate lower trade barriers and enforce fair trade norms, and used unconditional MFN treatment to spread the benefits of reciprocal bargaining. The State Department used the RTAA to promote international trade, rather than just U.S. exports, and its officials recognized that America had to lower its trade barriers. In the run-up to World War II, the State Department granted concessions on an unconditional MFN basis as part of an effort to build an alliance to counter German and Japanese aggression. The RTAA approach—equality of treatment, a negotiable tariff, and executive-branch authority to negotiate agreements that would be binding without congressional ratification—would become the framework for international cooperation under the General Agreement on Tariffs and Trade.

Many State Department officials were liberals in the nineteenth-century tradition. They linked trade discrimination to political conflict. As such, they believed in free trade, to which Britain adhered until 1932. At the same time, they appreciated the power that Congress retained over trade policy. Hull and his advisers therefore chose reciprocity as a way to both lower trade barriers and placate members of Congress who remained wedded to protection. Unconditional MFN treatment would be the tool to maximize the benefit of bilateral treaties.

After keeping trade off the agenda during his first year of office to concentrate on reviving and regulating the U.S. economy, President Franklin D. Roosevelt proposed the RTAA to Congress, selling it as a domestic recovery measure. To placate wary members of Congress, the administration proposed no changes to the 1921 Anti-Dumping Act, retained the countervailing duty provisions in section 338 of the Smoot-Hawley Act, and agreed to subject the act to reauthorization in three years. The RTAA also said nothing about dismantling protection. The State Department took it upon itself to use both reciprocity and unconditional MFN treatment—linked for the first time in U.S. trade policy—as tools of trade liberalization.

In the interests of trade liberalization and international security, State Department officials pressed for few concessions in the series of negotiations that occurred before and during World War II. This was especially the case with Europe. (In Latin America, U.S. officials threatened to refuse to negotiate reciprocal trade and to withhold Export-Import Bank credits and other financial assistance unless governments satisfied their demands to settle debts in default to U.S. bondholders, treat U.S. direct investment in a fair and equitable manner, and adopt political reforms.) Determined to reverse the ill effects of U.S. protectionism, U.S. trade negotiators offered concessions to Belgium, Britain, Switzerland, and others, while tolerating trade barriers, currency depreciation, and other actions that closed overseas markets to U.S. products.

The State Department also decided to extend unconditional MFN treatment to most third-party countries. Under the RTAA, it was unclear which countries should be eligible to receive such treatment. The department moved initially to extend concessions to countries that did not discriminate against U.S. exports. Since all of America's major trading partners continued to discriminate against U.S. products, however, the State Department deemed this approach to be impractical. It concluded that the administration should withhold benefits only when others' discrimination was flagrant. In its view, such a stance would improve relations among nations. It therefore singled out Nazi Germany for retaliatory action. In moving in this direction, the State Department departed from the bilateral approach to reciprocity for which Roosevelt campaigned in 1932 and that Congress intended in the RTAA. (Roosevelt, his "brain trust" advisers, and key cabinet officials such as Treasury Secretary Henry Morgenthau Jr. doubted that the reciprocal trade program could play the role that Hull designed for it in achieving either the security or economic goals of the administration's foreign policy. For Roosevelt, trade, like all matters of foreign economic policy, took a backseat to domestic issues.)

In terms of expanding U.S. trade, the reciprocal trade agreements concluded between 1934 and 1945 achieved limited results. But actual trade expansion was secondary to building international cooperation against the Axis threat. In arguing for extensions of the RTAA in 1937, 1940, 1943, and 1945, State Department officials were explicit about the national security role of the trade program. Moreover, the State Department became convinced that the institutional structure of the RTAA, linking reciprocity and unconditional MFN treatment, should serve as the basis for constructing a post–World War II multilateral trade regime.

Hence, the linkage between reciprocity and unconditional MFN treatment was translated into the norms of the General Agreement on Tariffs and Trade (GATT). In the view of State Department analysts, economic autarky and fascist aggression were bound together as causes of the world war. Thus, political cooperation was possible only if economic cooperation was established. During the war, State Department officials developed a blueprint for the structure of commercial cooperation in the postwar world. The lack of cooperation during the interwar period persuaded them that economic nationalism was the root of instability in the international system and degraded relations among nations. They resolved to make nondiscrimination in trade the basis for economic cooperation, which they believed was essential to an enduring postwar peace. The International Trade Organization (ITO) would monitor commercial relations on the basis of unconditional MFN treatment. But countries would also negotiate bilaterally to both open markets and preserve their recourse to measures to protect domestic producers and social welfare policies, as the RTAA prescribed.

In 1947 the administration of Harry Truman invited countries, including Russia, to Geneva, Switzerland, to negotiate a multilateral trade agreement; twenty-four nations accepted the invitation. Although the Soviet Union opted out of the process, twenty-three countries negotiated bilaterally on a product-by-product basis. The bilateral pacts became the multilateral GATT, since every signatory enjoyed unconditional MFN treatment. The nine countries that felt they could adhere to the demands of the treaty, accounting for 80 percent of world trade, implemented the GATT on 1 January 1948.

The State Department supported a more liberal approach to trade policy than the still-protectionist Congress and the other agencies of the executive branch, most of which were solidly "New Deal" in orientation. But it recognized political reality and retained the "fair" trade elements of the Reciprocal Trade Agreements Act in its negotiations for the International Trade Organization (and the GATT, after Congress rejected the ITO over sovereignty issues). The elements of the New Deal that provided for state responsibility for economic growth and social welfare were not going to be repealed. The United States, Great Britain, and other participants wanted to retain flexibility on domestic economic policy even as they agreed to liberalize international trade. And given their expectations regarding America's position of leadership in the postwar order, U.S. archi-tects of postwar trade policy concluded that it was America's responsibility to offer asymmetrical concessions in order to establish the trade regime in which they were interested. Thus, unconditional MFN treatment became the guiding principle of an emerging liberal regime that retained the safeguards, restrictions, and exemptions of "fair" trade. Parties to the GATT promised to consult each other when conflicts arose and to resolve differences through a dispute settlement procedure. Reciprocity would be used as an instrument of both freer and fairer trade.

The GATT governed international trade until the World Trade Organization was established on 1 January 1995. Beginning with the 1947 session in Geneva, the GATT promoted trade liberalization through a series of negotiating rounds. With the Kennedy Round (May 1964–January 1967), negotiators adopted—with some exceptions—a formula for across-the-board percentage cuts, doing away with bilateral negotiating. For this round and the 1947 Geneva parley, Congress authorized tariff reductions of up to 50 percent of existing rates. Both rounds reduced tariffs some 35 percent. In both rounds, the U.S. promptly provided concessions to its trading partners, even if, like western Europe in 1947 and Japan and many developing countries in 1964–1967, they lagged in reciprocating. From 1947 to 1967, six GATT rounds removed tariffs as a barrier to the U.S. market. In doing so, U.S. policymakers placed a higher priority on stabilizing the American-led anticommunist alliance and promoting the economic reconstruction of its allies than on shielding domestic producers from foreign competition.

MFN TREATMENT IN PRACTICE, 1974–2000: UNCONDITIONAL MFN UNDER SIEGE BUT PRESERVED

The GATT relied on discrimination and retaliation to enforce an open, multilateral trade regime. The coexistence of unconditional MFN treatment and reciprocity in the GATT gave rise to tensions among members, because disparities in liberalization among participants widened over time. Under unconditional MFN treatment, countries that lagged in opening their markets enjoyed the benefits of a free ride on the system. When the United States experienced economic downturn during the 1970s and 1980s, domestic interest groups called for redress from participants who seemed to be unfairly "gaming" the GATT. The United States seemed to be suffering within a system in which its trade negotiators ceded more to their counterparts from increasingly competitive trading partners—Japan in particular—than they received. In response, Congress resumed the activist trade-policy role from which it had retreated in 1934. Members of Congress introduced a plethora of retaliatory bills that had the potential of compromising America's commitment to unconditional MFN treatment within the GATT framework. In most instances, the actions threatened by these so-called fair, or strategic, trade measures constituted interest group efforts to push policy in a nationalistic direction. But the administrations of Presidents Gerald Ford, Jimmy Carter, Ronald Reagan, George H. W. Bush, and Bill Clinton handled them in (often illiberal) ways that kept the United States committed to the GATT.

Transparency in trade relations constituted a key principle of the GATT. Trade barriers were to be converted into tariffs, which then were to be lowered through negotiation. This approach reached its point of diminishing returns with the Kennedy Round. Nontariff barriers, which included such things as countervailing duties, technical barriers, import licensing, voluntary export restraints, and local content rules, were becoming significant obstacles to trade. The United States still adhered to the principle of nondiscrimination, but the GATT commitment to transparency was being lost.

Congress insisted that President Richard Nixon's administration use reciprocity to defend U.S. producers when it authorized the so-called fast track negotiating process for the Tokyo Round (1973–1979). (Under fast track, Congress had to approve or reject a trade treaty. Its members could not amend it.) Most significantly, the Tokyo Round extended the GATT to cover nontariff barriers (NTBs). While tariff negotiations continued on the basis of unconditional MFN treatment, however, NTB bargaining proceeded on a conditional MFN basis. The Tokyo Round in practice did little to reduce these barriers or to equalize access among the American, European, and Japanese markets. U.S. consumers were soon benefiting from a flood of well-made Japanese autos and electronic consumer goods. Besieged U.S. industries, however, petitioned Congress for assistance.

The 1974 Trade Act provided the basis for relief. Section 201 of the act authorized tariffs, quotas, and other remedies to facilitate orderly adjustment to increased competition from abroad. If the U.S. International Trade Commission (ITC) determined that imports were causing "serious injury, or threat thereof" to a petitioning industry, it could order up to five years of relief. As U.S. automakers and the United Auto Workers union discovered in 1980, however, ITC approval of import relief could not be counted upon. In such cases, interested parties appealed again to Congress for help. Congress proved willing to consider measures that violated the GATT to redress sectorial trade imbalances and compensate injured firms and dislocated workers. U.S. administrations used reciprocity to derail such efforts. In the case of the U.S.–Japan auto dispute, for example, the Reagan administration negotiated and secured a voluntary export restraint agreement in May 1981. This strategy kept U.S. trade policy within the GATT framework and thereby preserved the U.S. commitment overall to unconditional MFN treatment.

During the 1980s and 1990s, regional trade agreements posed another threat to the principle of nondiscrimination in U.S. trade policy. After the protracted Tokyo Round, the Reagan administration pursued regional free trade agreements even as it pushed for a new GATT round. The Bush and Clinton administrations did so as well, even after the Uruguay Round commenced in 1986. Advocates insisted that free trade agreements not only were compatible with multilateral trade liberalization, they actually promoted it, since the agreements addressed issues not handled successfully with the GATT framework (such as agriculture, services, investment, intellectual property rights, and various nontariff barriers). Nonetheless, free trade agreements with Israel in 1985 and Canada in 1987, as well as the North American Free Trade Agreement (NAFTA) with Canada and Mexico in 1992, marked a digression in U.S. trade policy from unconditional MFN treatment. At the same time, the Clinton administration remained committed to the successful conclusion of the Uruguay Round, which was completed in 1994. One hundred and eleven countries signed the pact, which established the World Trade Organization as the successor organization to the GATT.

During this period, Congress also linked MFN treatment to human rights. The Jackson-Vanik Amendment to the 1974 Trade Act, championed by Senator Henry Jackson, prohibited granting MFN treatment or Export-Import Bank credits to any "non-market economy country" that restricted emigration. Jackson was primarily concerned about the emigration of Jews from the Soviet Union. To achieve its broader aims of diplomacy, the Nixon administration wanted to extend MFN treatment and access to export credits to the Soviet Union. The Nixon administration was also interested in the emigration of Jews but preferred to accomplish it through quiet diplomacy. Administration officials believed that Jackson's amendment had some value in sending a signal to the Kremlin regarding America's concern for human rights. However, as National Security Adviser Henry Kissinger argued, the administration would likely lose any leverage it had on the emigration issue once the Jackson-Vanik Amendment became law. This proved to be the case. From 1972 to 1974, some 87,000 people emigrated from Russia. For the period 1975–1977, the figure fell to a little more than 44,000.

The Jackson-Vanik Amendment also ensured that human rights became intertwined with the MFN debate on China, particularly after the Tiananmen Square massacre of June 1989. In this case, the Bush and Clinton administrations successfully "de-linked" MFN treatment from human rights. In 1999 the Clinton administration secured congressional approval of "permanent normal trade relations" with China.

From their first commercial agreement in 1979, the United States and the People's Republic of China conducted trade relations on the basis of unconditional MFN treatment. China was not a member of the GATT. MFN treatment for China was subject to annual renewal by the president, per the Jackson-Vanik Amendment, and had to conform to various requirements stipulated by the 1974 Trade Act. Until the Chinese government cracked down on the student demonstrators in Tiananmen Square, the renewal of MFN treatment for China was a pro forma affair. After the massacre, in which more than a thousand protestors and bystanders were killed by soldiers, members of the House and Senate sought to condition MFN status on China's performance on human rights. In 1990, the Bush administration gathered enough Republican support in the Senate to renew unconditional MFN treatment for China. But soon thereafter, members of Congress complicated the issue by demonstrating their willingness to condition MFN status for China not only on human rights but also on a range of strategic, political, and economic issues. To meet the concerns of Congress (and businesses interested in such matters as intellectual property rights and Chinese textile imports), both the Bush and Clinton administrations adopted a policy of "constructive engagement." They used diplomacy to address human rights and other issues. At the same time, they continued to renew MFN status for the purpose of expanding trade and developing investment opportunities for U.S. corporations.

The Clinton administration initially favored linking unconditional MFN treatment to China's human rights record, but President Clinton ultimately proved unwilling to sacrifice the China market. After a protracted battle with human rights groups and members of Congress, the administration succeeding in "de-coupling" human rights from its trade policy on China in 1994. Over the next five years, Clinton administration officials worked to bring China into the newly created World Trade Organization and to put unconditional MFN treatment for China on a permanent basis. This culminated in an agreement of 15 November 1999 to make China a full member of the WTO.

The United States remained committed to unconditional MFN treatment within the WTO framework. However, by the end of the 1990s, further liberalization of trade within the WTO had stalled. Congress revoked fast track bargaining authority from the executive branch after the Uruguay Round, and the Clinton administration did not put a high priority on regaining it. The administration also declined to take a leadership position on the expansion of NAFTA to Latin America, as the Chilean and other governments hoped. With the remarkable expansion of the U.S. economy during the late 1990s, demands by Congress and interest groups for retaliation became less strident. To be sure, trade disputes continued. However, outside of MFN status for China, trade retreated in importance relative to finance as the "high-visibility" foreign economic policy issue.

BIBLIOGRAPHY

Boudreau, Donald G. "Beyond Tiananmen Square: China and the MFN Debate." *World Affairs* 153 (spring 1993): 140–147.

Culbertson, W. S. "Commercial Treaties." In *Encyclopedia of the Social Sciences*. New York, 1934. Puts MFN in broad historical context.

Eckes, Alfred E., Jr. *Opening America's Market: U.S. Trade Policy Since 1776.* Chapel Hill, N.C., 1995. A defense of protectionism in U.S trade policy.

———. "U.S. Trade History." In *U.S. Trade Policy: History, Theory, and the WTO.* Armonk, N.Y., 1999. An excellent overview of more than two hundred years of U.S. trade policy.

Goldstein, Judith. "Ideas, Institutions, and American Trade Policy." *International Organization* 42 (winter 1988): 179–217. Argues that state-based actor behavior is crucial to understanding U.S. trade policy.

Gordon, Wendell C. *International Trade: Goods, People, and Ideas.* New York, 1965. Contains examples of both conditional and unconditional MFN provisions in trade agreements.

Haggard, Stephan. "The Institutional Foundations of Hegemony: Explaining the Reciprocal Trade Agreements Act of 1934." *International Organization* 42 (winter 1988): 91–119. Focuses on the institutional changes in trade policy produced by the RTAA.

Hornbeck, Stanley K. *The Most-Favored-Nation Clause in Commercial Treaties.* Madison, Wis., 1910. A defense of conditional MFN treatment.

Lake, David A. *Power, Protection, and Free Trade: International Sources of U.S. Commercial Strategy, 1887–1939.* Ithaca, N.Y., 1988. Argues that executive branch responses to the constraints and opportunities of the international economic structure shaped policy in conjunction with congressional responses to interest-group pressures.

League of Nations Committee on Experts for Progressive Codification of International Law. "Report on the Most-Favored-Nation Clause." *American Journal of International Law* 20, supplement (1928).

Milner, Helen V., and David B. Yoffie. "Between Free Trade and Protectionism: Strategic Trade Policy and a Theory of Corporate Trade Demands." *International Organization* 43 (spring 1989): 239–272.

Moore, John Bassett. "Most-Favored-Nation Clauses." *Digest of International Law* 5 (1906).

Ratner, Sidney. *The Tariff in American History.* New York, 1972. Provides useful material on the reciprocal trade agreements of the 1930s and the GATT.

Rhodes, Carolyn. "Reciprocity in Trade: The Utility of a Bargaining Strategy." *International Organization* 43 (spring 1989): 273–299. Assesses the use of reciprocity to achieve trade liberalization within the GATT regime.

———. *Reciprocity, U.S. Trade Policy, and the GATT Regime.* Ithaca, N.Y., 1993. Argues that instruments of trade policy, such as reciprocity and unconditional MFN treatment, can be tools of liberalization or protectionism, depending on the overall direction of policy.

Schaefer, Donald D. A. "U.S. Foreign Policies of Presidents Bush and Clinton: The Influence of China's Most Favored Nation Status upon Human Rights Issues." *Social Science Journal* 35 (1998): 407–421.

Viner, Jacob. "The Most-Favored-Nation Clause in American Commercial Treaties." *Journal of Political Economy* 32 (1924). A vigorous argument against the use of conditional MFN treatment in U.S. trade policy by a University of Chicago economics professor and adviser to the Treasury Department during the Roosevelt administration.

Wang, Yangmin. "The Politics of U.S.–China Economic Relations: MFN, Constructive Engagement, and the Trade Issue Proper." *Asian Survey* 33 (May 1993): 441–462.

Wolman, Paul. *Most Favored Nation: The Republican Revisionists and U.S. Tariff Policy, 1987–1912.* Chapel Hill, N.C., 1992.

See also DOLLAR DIPLOMACY; ECONOMIC POLICY AND THEORY; RECIPROCITY; TARIFF POLICY.

MULTINATIONAL CORPORATIONS

Burton I. Kaufman

The influence of multinational corporations on U.S. foreign policy is complex, but, generally speaking, they have not played a major role in the formulation and execution of foreign policy. This may seem a surprising conclusion, because it is now widely recognized that for much of U.S. history, but especially for the period beginning at the end of the nineteenth century and continuing throughout the twentieth century, there has been a strong correlation between U.S. foreign economic policy and U.S. foreign policy. Simply stated, historians and others have shown, rather convincingly, that economic expansion—the search for foreign markets for U.S. surplus agricultural and industrial production—has played a key role in American foreign policy, particularly after President Woodrow Wilson (1913–1921) enunciated his concept of a new world order predicated on classical liberal and capitalist principles.

In writing about the role of multinational corporations on U.S. foreign policy, however, the following points need to be made: (1) the first multinational corporations were not established until the latter part of the nineteenth century; (2) most of the first multinational corporations became "multinational" by reinvesting their foreign profits abroad, not by making investments overseas; (3) large businesses invested abroad where and when their executives thought profits were to be made, not because of foreign policy concerns, and, with some exceptions, because they did not unduly seek to influence the formulation of foreign policy; (4) while there were certainly loud calls for expanding markets overseas, even to the point of permitting businesses to engage in joint combinations otherwise prohibited by the nation's antitrust laws, those business leaders advocating such policies were generally from smaller or midsize businesses and/or represented regional interests; and (5) to the extent that there was collusion or collaboration between public policymakers and business leaders (as in the case of the oil industry), it was just as often government that sought to use the nation's industrial giants to achieve foreign policy objectives rather than the other way around.

Multinational corporations (MNCs) are corporations whose home offices are in one country but have significant fixed investments in other countries. These investments might be in factories or warehouses, transportation or telecommunications, mining or agriculture. Businesses that merely maintain local or regional sales offices abroad are generally not thought of as multinational corporations.

Corporations invest abroad for a variety of reasons. Among them are to open new markets or to hold onto existing ones; to avoid tariffs or other trade restrictions; to tap new sources of raw materials and agricultural production; and to take advantage of cheap foreign labor. Although the history of American MNCs goes back to at least the mid-nineteenth century and a significant number of MNCs had been established by the turn of the twentieth century, their emergence as a key factor in international commerce is really a product of the post–World War II period.

Americans had, of course, been involved in world commerce ever since the founding of the colonies in the seventeenth and eighteenth centuries. Colonial merchants often employed agents abroad (frequently family members) to promote their interests wherever they conducted significant commerce, most notably in London and the West Indies. Following the American Revolution and through much of the nineteenth century, they expanded their stakes abroad by opening branches that sometimes included fixed investments like warehouses. Some Americans even opened small businesses overseas or inherited existing businesses through loan defaults and bankruptcies.

Until the latter part of the nineteenth century, however, American businesses had not made the types of direct investments abroad that would have classified them as multinational corporations. The reasons why were much the same as the reasons why even America's largest business enterprises sold mainly in local and regional markets. The United States lacked the transportation and communication facilities to allow businesses to operate on a national scale. American businesses also lacked the organizational structure and capital to compete nationally or internationally.

By the end of the nineteenth century all that had changed. With the establishment of transcontinental railroads and a network of branch lines that laced much of the nation together and a telegraph and telephone system that made nearly instantaneous communication possible, American business leaders could think in broad national terms. Other developments, including a single national currency and the expansion of capital markets, the mass production of consumer goods like food products and manufactured clothing, and major technological advances such as the manufacture of electrical generators, office equipment, and sewing machines, each requiring a specially trained sales force to sell and service them, made national expansion viable, even inevitable.

The same was true of the international marketplace. A dramatic increase in the speed of steamships plying the oceans between American and world ports, the completion in 1866 of the first transatlantic cable, the need or desire on the part of American business leaders to seek out new markets for increased U.S. industrial and agricultural production, and the need also to have reliable sources of raw materials and native agriculture, such as bananas from Central America, were only some of the supply-side forces driving U.S. economic expansion overseas after the Civil War. On the demand side were the attraction abroad of new U.S. industrial output and the importance of having a trained sales force able to explain and service the highly sophisticated technology that American manufacturers were producing.

EARLY MULTINATIONAL CORPORATIONS

The first American multinational corporation was I. M. Singer and Company (later changed to Singer Manufacturing Company), whose name became synonymous with the sewing machine. Established in 1851, Singer relied at first on independent foreign agents to sell its machines in Europe, even transferring to a French entrepreneur, Charles Callebaut, the rights to its French patent. Having successfully developed its own sales force and branches in the United States, however, and unhappy with the lack of control over these agents, some of whom even sold competing machines, the company decided to rely on its own salaried sales force and branch offices to market its product. By 1879 Singer was selling more machines abroad than at home and had branches in such distant places as India, Australia, South Africa, and New Zealand. In response to Europe's demand for its machines, moreover, it opened its first foreign factory in Glasgow, Scotland, in 1867. In 1883 it built a new modern plant outside Glasgow, where it consolidated the operations of the original factory and two others that had grown alongside it. It also built much smaller plants in Canada and Austria. By the end of the century other American corporations, including Westinghouse, General Electric, Western Electric, Eastman Kodak, and Standard Oil, often following Singer's experience abroad, had also opened plants or refineries in Europe.

Although talk was ripe at the end of the nineteenth and beginning of the twentieth centuries about gaining a larger American presence in the Far East and Latin America, most large American companies invested abroad where market success seemed most promising or where sources of raw materials could easily be developed; this meant primarily Canada, Mexico, and Europe. Canada was both a market for American exports and a source of such raw materials as gold, timber, and oil. As such it was the largest market for American investments, which totaled $618 million by 1914. In second place was Mexico, where Americans invested $587 million, mostly in mining and railroads but also increasingly in oil.

Europe was a primary market for U.S. industrial goods, including heavy industrial machinery, steam pumps, cash registers, electrical generators, reapers, and consumer goods, most of which were superior to European technology. American firms grew abroad largely by reinvesting their overseas earnings. In fact, by the turn of the twentieth century the United States had made such inroads into European markets that Europeans even talked and wrote about an "American invasion" of Europe, not dissimilar from American cries seventy-five years later against a Japanese "invasion" of the United States. By 1914, U.S. direct investment in Europe amounted to $573 million.

Worldwide, Americans invested $2.65 billion. Although this might not seem noteworthy by contemporary standards, it amounted to about 7 percent of the nation's gross national product or about the same percentage of the GNP as for the 1960s. On the eve of World War I, in other words, the United States had entered the still new world of multinational corporations, although that term was still unfamiliar and would remain so to most Americans for another half century.

WORLD WAR I AND ITS AFTERMATH

The outbreak of war in Europe in 1914 offered MNCs both danger and opportunity at the same time. On the one hand the belligerent powers had to be fed and equipped. Furthermore, the war opened to the United States the opportunity to move into markets in Latin America and the Far East hitherto dominated by Europe's two major industrial powers, the United Kingdom and Germany, each of which had to concentrate its attention on winning the war for its side. Furthermore, the opening of the Panama Canal in 1914 afforded new opportunities for increased trade between ports along the East and Gulf coasts of the United States and the west coast of South America and the Far East. In the Mississippi Valley it also kindled plans among the region's business and financial leaders to redirect some of the nation's largely east-west commercial traffic to such Gulf ports as New Orleans, Mobile, and Galveston.

The war turned the United States from a debtor to a creditor nation. Despite tremendous losses as a result of Germany's on-and-off submarine campaign, the United States supplied Britain and its allies with the goods and credits necessary to sustain the war effort before America's own entry into the war in 1917. The United States was even able to make substantial gains in Latin American markets at the expense of the European belligerents, more so, however, in mining and ore processing than in manufacturing.

After the war Washington passed two measures designed to strengthen the nation's position in foreign trade, especially in Latin America. The first of these was the Webb-Pomerene Act (1918), which exempted business combinations from the provisions of the antitrust laws. Congress approved the measure as a way to help small businessmen enter the foreign field by being allowed to form joint selling agencies engaged in business abroad. But the measure had also been pushed by larger business concerns interested in organizing more complex vertical combinations (that is, combinations performing more than one function in the chain of production, extending from the acquisition of raw materials through the manufacturing process and ending with the distribution and sale of the finished product). Although fewer than two hundred associations ever registered under the act, a number of supporters of the measure, including the Department of Commerce, continued to seek ways to strengthen it.

The second measure approved by Congress after the war was the Edge Act (1919), which provided for federal incorporation of long-term investment and short-term banking subsidiaries doing business abroad. Like the Webb-Pomerene Act, the measure was intended to encourage small banking firms to compete successfully against more established British firms and a few American financial institutions like the National City Bank, which had established foreign branches throughout Latin America, more in order to attract accounts at home than to make profits abroad. The Edge Act was also part of the government's program for meeting Europe's capital and banking needs and President Woodrow Wilson's larger program for economic expansion.

Also like the Webb-Pomerene Act, the Edge Act never lived up to its promise. In the two years after its passage only two corporations were established under its provisions. As late as 1956 there were only three Edge corporations. The simple fact was that, despite government encouragement to foreign investment and a brief flurry of activity in the two years immediately following the war's end, too much uncertainty about world economic conditions existed to sustain this level of effort.

EXPANSION: 1925–1930

Not until the mid-1920s, when the international economy seemed to stabilize, particularly in Europe, and the United States' own economy was booming, did U.S. corporations start to make substantial direct foreign investments. Encouraged by President Calvin Coolidge and his fellow Republican Herbert Hoover, first in his capacity as Coolidge's secretary of commerce and then as Coolidge's successor in the White House, the largest U.S. firms began to invest heavily in Europe, both in search of new markets and as a way of protecting themselves against trade barriers. Such investments, usually in the form of foreign subsidiaries, branches, or joint ventures, also fitted well into the multidivisional, decentralized organizational structure begun at General Motors (GM) under the leadership of Alfred Sloan but adopted very quickly by other major industrial concerns.

Yet, as Sloan later wrote, the decision to invest overseas did not come easily, nor was it perceived as inevitable. GM's executives, for example, had to decide whether there was a market abroad for American cars and, if so, which models were likely to fare the best. They also had to determine whether to export entire cars from the United States, build plants to assemble imported parts, or engage in the entire manufacturing process overseas. If the latter, they then had to consider whether to buy existing plants or build their own. Invariably, these decisions involved such other considerations as the taxes and tariffs of host nations, the state of existing facilities and dealerships abroad, and the desire of foreign governments to protect jobs and national industries. In the case of General Motors, the corporation almost bought the French carmaker Citroën but decided against doing so, in large part because of the French government's opposition to an American takeover of what it considered a vital industry. GM did, however, buy the British firm Vauxhall Motors Ltd. and the German carmaker Opel. Even more important, it made a decision at the end of the 1920s to be an international manufacturer seeking markets wherever they existed and to build the industrial infrastructure necessary to penetrate and maintain them.

Although direct foreign investment as a percentage of the GNP remained about the same in the 1920s as it did at the turn of the century (about 7 percent), what made the 1920s different from earlier decades were where and what kinds of investment were being made. Investments in manufacturing, which had lagged behind mining and agriculture, now vaulted ahead of both. As it did so, direct investments in Europe almost doubled, from approximately $700 million in 1920 to about $1.35 billion by 1929; manufacturing and petroleum accounted for most of this increase. Significantly, much of the new investment came from firms that previously had not braved the waters of overseas markets. Businesses like Pet and Carnation Milk had well-established brand names at home on which they hoped to capitalize by joining together under the Webb-Pomerene Act to open new plants and factories in France, Holland, and Germany in the 1920s.

Almost as dramatic as the increase in direct investments in manufacturing abroad were those in petroleum, which increased from $604 million in 1919 to $1.34 billion by 1929. Although this included everything from the exploration of petroleum to its production, refining, and distribution, most of the increase was in exploration and production. Thanks to vast increases in the production of oil in Venezuela, American direct investments in petroleum in South America jumped from $113 million in 1919 to $512 million by 1929.

Even in the Middle East, which remained largely a British preserve, the United States made important inroads. Fearful of an oil shortage after the war and worried that the region might be shut to American interests, the United States pressured the European powers to give a group of American oil companies a 23 percent share of a consortium of British, French, and Dutch oil producers. Among these companies were Standard Oil of New Jersey (now Exxon) and Standard Oil of New York (now Mobil), which later bought out the other American firms. The consortium became the Iraq Petroleum Company (IPC), whose purpose was to explore and develop mineral rights in the former Ottoman Empire.

As a result of developments like these, total American investment in foreign petroleum increased from $604 million in 1919 to $1.34 billion dollars in 1929. By that year petroleum had become the second-largest sector in terms of American direct foreign investment, with mining ($1.23 billion) and agriculture ($986 million) falling to second and third places.

THE GREAT DEPRESSION

The Great Depression of the 1930s, beginning with the crash of the stock market in 1929, affected multinational corporations worldwide. As purchasing power overseas dried up, and as governments sought to protect existing markets by erecting high tariffs and other trade barriers, some U.S. corporations closed or sold factories and other foreign facilities and curtailed or stopped entirely making investments abroad.

At the same time, however, other American businesses sought to leapfrog obstacles to trade and protect existing markets by entering into business arrangements with foreign concerns, such as licensing and market-sharing agreements. With all the major world currencies having gone off the gold standard and become nonconvertible (that is, not convertible into gold or other currencies like the American dollar or the British pound), most multinational corporations simply chose or were forced by host governments, as in the case of Nazi Germany, to reinvest their foreign profits.

In Latin America, American corporations also continued to invest, sometimes with assistance from Washington, in the development of resources, such as copper in Chile and Peru and lead and zinc in Argentina (although overall investments in South American mining dropped dramatically), and in public utilities including railroads. In the Middle East, American oil companies continued to challenge British oil hegemony by investing heavily in production facilities in Saudi Arabia, Kuwait, and Bahrain. Gulf Oil Company negotiated an oil concession from Kuwait. Standard Oil of California (Socal) established the Bahrain Oil Company and received a concession to look for oil in Saudi Arabia. Texas Oil Company (Texaco) acquired a half interest in the Bahrain Oil Company and in the California Arabian Oil Company (now Aramco) organized by Socal to develop its Arabian fields.

These same companies also entered into a number of agreements among themselves and with two British and Dutch companies, Anglo-Iranian Oil (now British Petroleum, or BP) and Royal Dutch Shell, to control the sale of crude oil and finished products to independent refiners and marketers. Of these agreements the most significant were the so-called "Red Line" and "As Is" agreements of 1928, which placed severe restrictions on where, with whom, and under what conditions the signatories could explore for oil and develop oil fields in the Middle East. Between 1928 and 1934 the As Is partners entered into three supplementary agreements to carry out these purposes. So successful were they that by 1939, seven oil corporations, five of which were American, monopolized the oil industry in the Middle East and controlled much of the world's other oil supplies.

More generally, multinational corporations were able to weather the depression of the 1930s reasonably well. Between 1929 and 1940 total direct foreign investment by American firms declined only slightly, dropping from about $7.53 billion in 1929 to $7 billion in 1940. In Europe they increased from $1.34 billion in 1929 to $1.42 billion in 1940, while in South America they stayed the same, at about $1.5 billion for both years. In Europe manufacturing remained dominant, edging up slightly from about $629 million in 1929 to about $639 million in 1940. The most significant increase occurred in the petroleum sector, rising from $239 million in 1929 to $306 million in 1940. In contrast, in South America public utilities jumped from $348 million to $506 million during these same years, while petroleum actually dropped from $512 million to $330 million and mining fell from $528 million to $330 million; by 1940, public utilities had become the leading sector for direct American foreign investment in South America.

WORLD WAR II

As one might expect, U.S. entry into World War II in 1941 disrupted the normal channels of American commerce, discouraging or making impossible direct investments overseas. Between 1940 and 1946 such investments grew only marginally, from $7.0 billion in 1940 to $7.2 billion in 1946. In that year they amounted to only 3.4 percent of the GNP, the lowest percentage in the century. What American investments made abroad during the war were largely in the Western Hemisphere. Although investments in Canada and Latin America grew from $4.9 billion in 1940 to $5.6 billion in 1946, investments in Europe declined from $1.4 billion in 1940 to $1 billion in 1946. In Africa and the Middle East they remained steady at about $200 million for each of these years, while in the rest of the world they declined from $500 million in 1940 to $400 million in 1946.

Most of these investments went to further the war effort. No commodity was more important in this regard than oil, on which the entire machinery of war depended. So urgent was the need for oil, in fact, that the War Department invested $134 million in the construction of a refinery and pipeline in Canada as part of a project (the Canol Project) to open a new oil field in the Canadian Northwest Territories. The project had little commercial utility, and after the war it was abandoned when none of the parties to the project showed any interest in continuing it.

In the Middle East, Secretary of the Interior Harold Ickes, who also served as petroleum administrator for the war and generally distrusted the oil industry, even tried to obtain government ownership of American oil concessions in Saudi Arabia and Bahrain. Opposition from oil interests and doubts even within the administration about a government takeover of private enterprise ultimately doomed Ickes's plans. An

FEDERAL POWER VERSUS THE POWER OF THE MULTINATIONALS: THE OIL DILEMMA

A power with great wealth and influence, the oil industry has often been seen by historians as a sovereign entity capable of dictating the terms and conditions under which oil is produced and sold throughout the world. Although this view is still widely held, it was especially prominent during the energy crisis of the 1970s, when a slew of books was published highly critical of oil's alleged power over the public weal. Inter-industry correspondence and memoranda, first revealed in congressional hearings in the 1970s, seemed to substantiate this view. So did the outcome of an antitrust action that the Department of Justice brought in 1953 against the five major U.S. oil corporations—Standard Oil of New Jersey (Exxon), Gulf, Socony Mobil (Mobil), Standard Oil of California (Socal), and Texaco—and two alleged coconspirators, Royal Dutch Shell and Anglo-Iranian Oil (now British Petroleum), charging them with maintaining monopolistic control of oil from the Middle East. The case was so sharply curtailed before it was settled in 1968 that it left the multinational giants' control of oil from the Middle East largely intact. For this reason it seemed to provide additional support to the argument that the multinational giants dictate federal policy.

There can be little doubt about the historic power of the oil industry to influence—and sometimes dictate—federal policy. If anything, however, the oil cartel case of 1953–1968 reveals that it was the federal government that used the oil corporations for foreign policy purposes rather than the other way around. In perhaps the darkest period of the Cold War, the oil cartel ensured a cheap supply of energy to western Europe and Japan. It also ensured a certain degree of stability in a troubled area of the world and was a way of limiting Soviet influence in the region, a matter of great concern to policymakers in Washington. Through tax policies that allowed the oil companies to offset increased royalties to host nations with decreases in taxes paid to the federal government, the oil companies also provided a useful conduit of financial aid to Arab producing nations without providing a cause of action on the part of the strong pro-Israeli forces on Capitol Hill.

Through the fifteen-year history of the oil cartel case, in fact, officials of the Department of Justice remained at loggerheads with the Department of State about pursuing the case, with antitrust officials in the Justice Department anxious to prosecute the defendants and the State Department opposing prosecution on the basis of national security and the national interest. In the end, the Department of State prevailed.

---

effort, on the other hand, by several American oil companies to gain an ownership stake in the Anglo-Iranian Oil Company led to strong and ultimately successful opposition by the British, who objected to what they regarded as an attempt by Washington to lock them out of oil development in the Mideast, and by the Iranians, who wanted to delay until after the war any decision on its most vital resource.

During the war a number of major multinational corporations engaged in the production of strategic materials, such as oil and synthetic rubber, were accused in congressional hearings and on the floor of Congress of having conspired with the enemy before the war. In particular, the oil and petrochemical industries were charged with exchanging trade secrets in chemicals with the chemical giant I. G. Farben and other German firms deemed instruments of Nazi policy in return for trade secrets in oil refining. Civil and criminal actions were even brought against a number of these companies, the most notable being against Exxon, which in 1929 had signed an agreement with Farben recognizing its "preferred position" in chemicals in return for Farben's recognition of Exxon's "preferred position" in oil and natural gas. The two giant corporations also pledged close cooperation in their respective enterprises.

In 1942 the Justice Department brought a civil antitrust suit against Exxon, charging it with delaying the development of high-quality synthetic rubber because of its agreement with Farben, which prevented easy access to important data by other U.S. rubber companies. Although Exxon blamed the German government and not Farben for withholding the needed data, it entered a plea of "no contest." As part of its plea bargain it also agreed to release all its rubber patents free during the war, with the royalty on these patents to be determined after the war ended.

POSTWAR INVESTMENT: 1945–1955

Despite wartime criticism of the foreign operations of some American firms, including their ties with Nazi firms before the war, and notwithstanding the economic uncertainties that were bound to accompany the war's end, a few of the largest U.S. corporations, often with considerable assets seized or destroyed during the war, began to plan for the postwar period. Among these was General Motors. As early as 1942 the company had set up a postwar planning policy group to estimate the likely shape of the world after the war and to make recommendations on GM's postwar policies abroad.

In 1943 the policy group reported the likelihood that relations between the Western powers and the Soviet Union would deteriorate after the war. It also concluded that, except for Australia, General Motors should not buy plants and factories to make cars in any country that had not had facilities before the conflict. At the same time, though, it stated that after the war the United States would be in a stronger state politically and economically than it had been after World War I and that overseas operations would flourish in much of the world. The bottom line for GM, therefore, was to proceed with caution once the conflict ended but to stick to the policy it had enunciated in the 1920s—seeking out markets wherever they were available and building whatever facilities were needed to improve GM's market share.

Other MNCs, however, adopted more cautious positions. Significant investments were made in Canada and Latin America in the mining of iron, uranium, and other minerals that had been scarce during the war, but of all the major industries, only the oil industry, worried as it had been after World War I about a postwar oil shortage, invested heavily overseas after World War II. Between 1946 and 1954 the value of these investments grew from $1.4 billion to $5.27 billion.

Even then, the type of oil investments before and after the war differed significantly. Previously they had been largely market oriented, their purpose being mainly to eliminate market competition. After the war Exxon, BP, Shell, and Mobil shifted their emphasis from market control to control of supply. The companies found that the infrastructure called for by the Red Line and As Is agreements of 1928, with their elaborate system of local and national cartels and quotas, was inefficient and difficult to maintain; moreover, the Red Line agreement established geographical limits to oil exploration in the Middle East. Much more effective, they concluded, would be control of a few crucial petroleum sources in the Mideast.

The opening of new fields by Gulf, Texaco, and Socal also raised the possibility that the As Is structure might be undermined. Conversely, control of these fields would guarantee the dominance of all the majors for years to come. Therefore, while maintaining their hold over marketing, the companies became much more interested in the supply end of petroleum. Exxon and Mobil withdrew from the Iraq Petroleum Corporation, which would have prohibited them from investing in the Arabian Peninsula without their other IPC partners, and instead bought a 40 percent share of Aramco. Socal and Texaco were glad to have them as partners both for their infusion of capital in what was a still risky venture and for their vast marketing capacity. The multinational oil companies also established a system of long-term supply agreements and expanded the number of interlocking, jointly owned production companies. In effect, the era of formal oil cartels gave way in the postwar era to a system of long-term supply agreements and an expansion in the number of interlocking, jointly owned production companies.

For other industries, however, pent-up consumer demand at home, the scarcity of similar demand in war-ravaged Europe and elsewhere, the lack of convertible foreign currencies, the risks attendant upon overseas investments as illustrated by the experiences of two world wars, restrictions on remittances, and the fact that a new generation of chief executive officers with less of an entrepreneurial spirit and more of a concern with stability and predictability than many of their predecessors, all served to limit foreign investment in the years immediately after World War II. Although investments in manufacturing, for example, grew from $2.4 billion in 1946 to $5.71 billion in 1954, most of this increase was in the reinvestment of profits of existing corporations, either because host governments blocked repatriation of scarce currencies or for tax and other reasons not related directly to growing consumer demand. Investments in other industries such as public utilities

($1.3 billion in 1946 and $1.54 billion in 1954) scarcely grew at all.

In at least one respect, government policy discouraged overseas investment after the war, particularly in manufacturing. As never before, foreign economic policy became tied to foreign policy. As the Cold War hardened in the ten years following the war, Washington imposed severe restrictions on trade and investment within the communist bloc of nations. The Export Control Acts of 1948 and 1949, for example, placed licensing restrictions on trade and technical assistance deemed harmful to national security. During the Korean War (1950–1953) even tighter controls, extending to nonstrategic as well as strategic goods, were imposed on the People's Republic of China (Communist China).

It would be absurd to suggest that, absent these controls, American companies would have made substantial investments within the communist bloc. Nevertheless, the economic boycott of a vast region of the world contributed to the global economic uncertainty that normally inhibits direct foreign investment. According to the British, who were anxious to relax controls on the potentially rich markets of China, it also delayed its own economic recovery, another inhibitor to foreign investors.

That said, in the decade following the war the administrations of both Harry Truman and Dwight Eisenhower looked to the private sector to assist in the recovery of western Europe, both through increased trade and direct foreign investments. In fact, the $13 billion Marshall Plan, which became the engine of European recovery between 1948 and 1952, was predicated on a close working relationship between the public and private sectors. Similarly, Eisenhower intended to bring about world economic recovery through liberalized world commerce and private investment abroad rather than through foreign aid. Over the course of his two administrations (1953–1961), the president modified his policy of "trade not aid" to one of "trade and aid" and changed his focus from western Europe to the Third World, which he felt was most threatened by communist expansion. In particular he was concerned by what he termed a "Soviet economic offensive" in the Middle East, that is, Soviet loans and economic assistance to such countries as Egypt and Syria. But even then he intended that international commerce and direct foreign investments would play a major role in achieving global economic growth and prosperity.

THE INTERNATIONAL MONETARY FUND AND WORLD BANK

As European recovery became increasingly apparent in the early 1950s and as the demand at home for consumer goods began to be satiated, U.S. corporations started to look once more at overseas markets. Problems still remained, such as a shortage of dollars (the so-called "dollar gap") and the lack of convertible foreign currencies needed to pay for essential goods from the United States and to remit foreign profits. But the International Monetary Fund (IMF) and the International Bank for Reconstruction and Development (IBRD, or World Bank) began to make loans intended to spur foreign trade and economic development. Established in 1944 at Bretton Woods, New Hampshire, as part of a new international monetary system based on the dollar, these twin financial institutions had remained largely dormant and ineffective as instruments of a new economic order. The IMF's primary purpose was to stabilize exchange rates, mainly by setting par values and supporting them with short-term balance-of-payments loans. The World Bank was intended to serve as a reconstruction rather than a development bank.

In the years immediately following the end of World War II neither financial institution was able to achieve its objectives. Faced with a staggering imbalance of trade and a severe dollar shortage, the IMF husbanded its resources and acquiesced in the growing number of exchange restrictions that took place as nations sought to protect their exchange values from the pressures of the free market. As for the World Bank, the problems of reconstruction and the degree of international financial instability after the war were far greater than the architects of the Bretton Woods system had anticipated. Unable to meet Europe's reconstruction needs with its own limited resources, much less to promote economic development in the Third World, and seeking to win the confidence of the American investor in order to float its bonds on the American capital markets, the bank followed conservative lending policies. It made a few reconstruction loans, but after the inauguration of the Marshall Plan in 1948, it purposely subordinated its lending activities to the new aid program.

Beginning around 1950, however, the World Bank expanded its long-term lending program from a level of $350 million in 1950 to more than $750 million by 1958. By the fall of 1958 it had invested $3.8 billion in development projects in forty-seven countries, mostly in the Third World. The IMF went through a more protracted transition than the World Bank, largely due to the fundamental disequilibria that existed in the international economy and the fact that the dollar was the only fully convertible currency. Not until the Suez crisis of 1956 did the fund, which had stopped all lending with the inauguration of the Marshall Plan, resume lending. That year it approved a standby credit of $738 million for England to pay for oil imported from the Western Hemisphere. By 1958 the fund had extended short-term loans of $3 billion to thirty-five countries.

In other ways as well, the government sought to spur direct foreign investments. For example, the United States negotiated tax treaties with a number of countries to prevent American businesses overseas from being taxed twice. It made investment guarantees to American firms venturing in western Europe. It increased the lending power of the Export-Import Bank, which had been established in 1934 to make short-term loans to American exporters but which over the years had made a number of long-term loans for development purposes.

THE OIL CARTEL CASE

Near the end of Truman's term in office the Justice Department instituted an antitrust suit against the multinational oil corporations operating in the Middle East. Both Truman and subsequently the Eisenhower administration sharply cut back the suit. The government charged the five major U.S. oil corporations—Exxon, Mobil, Socal, Texaco, and Gulf Oil—along with two alleged coconspirators, Royal Dutch Shell and British Petroleum, with criminal violation of the nation's antitrust laws by having engaged in a worldwide combination to restrain and monopolize U.S. domestic and foreign commerce in crude oil and petroleum products. The suit sought relief through divestiture of the defendants' joint production, refining, pipeline, and marketing operations.

The oil cartel was one of a series of cases that the Justice Department brought against industries after the war believed to have collaborated with enemy powers before the conflict. In the short term, the cases were disruptive to a number of multinational corporations that had made major investments overseas before the war and may even have discouraged them from engaging in international business after the conflict; certainly this was the case with General Electric (GE), which had suffered losses during the war and had to fight a suit accusing it and its subsidiary, International General Electric, of having maintained a cartel in lamps and electric equipment. Eventually GE sold off a major part of its foreign holdings.

By the end of Truman's administration, however, the White House had begun to rethink its foreign antitrust policies. This was most apparent in the oil cartel case. In 1951 Iran nationalized British Petroleum's Iranian holdings. BP responded with a highly successful worldwide embargo of Iranian oil, which led to serious European oil shortages. For reasons of national security having to do with needing the same oil companies against which it had brought a criminal antitrust action to meet these shortages, President Truman had the criminal charges reduced to much less punitive civil actions. He did this over strong objections from Justice Department and Federal Trade Commission officials, who maintained that the agreement constituted a waiver of the antitrust laws as applied to the foreign cartel arrangements of the oil majors.

President Eisenhower believed that enforcement of the antitrust laws should not interfere with programs and policies deemed important or essential to the national interest, such as the promotion of trade and private investment overseas. Accordingly, he later ordered the oil cartel case confined strictly to firms headquartered in the United States and then pressured the Justice Department to grant a newly formed Iranian oil consortium (consisting of BP, Royal Dutch Shell, the five American majors, and a number of smaller independents) a waiver in the exploration and refining of Iranian oil. Since it was nearly impossible to prosecute the very actions it had encouraged and sanctioned on the grounds of national security, the antitrust case was now effectively reduced to just the marketing and price-fixing of oil. Although the case was to drag through the courts until 1968, its final outcome left intact the scaffolding of the cartel arrangements among the oil majors. The decrees obtained were limited to price-fixing and marketing arrangements only.

MULTINATIONAL CORPORATIONS, 1955–1990

By the middle of the 1950s the wave of antitrust suits by the Justice Department against major industries with direct foreign investment had about run its course, although not all cases, such as the oil cartel case, had yet been settled. Furthermore, western Europe had largely recovered from the worst ravages of the war and in 1957 would form what became known as the Common Market. Great Britain, which would not be invited to join the Common Market, was moving toward full convertibility of the British pound. The "dollar gap," which had worsened because of the Korean War and European rearmament, was turning into a "dollar surplus" that would cause its own problems in the 1960s. Thanks largely to American spending in Japan as a result of the conflict in Korea, that country had also begun its long course toward becoming a major industrial power, one that twenty-five years later would make it the envy of much of the rest of the industrial world, including the United States. Following the death of Soviet leader Joseph Stalin in 1953 and the end of the Korean War that same year, there was even a short lull in the Cold War, as Moscow's new leader, Nikita Khrushchev, made new peaceful overtures to the United States that would lead to the Geneva Conference of 1957 between Khrushchev and President Eisenhower and the so-called "spirit of Geneva."

By the middle of the 1950s, in other words, economic growth had reached a point, and the world political situation had stabilized to such a degree, that many of the largest U.S. corporations were looking again to invest abroad. The country's foreign aid programs, which increasingly tied foreign loans and economic assistance to the procurement of American goods and services, also helped stimulate direct foreign investment.

The result was an expansion of MNCs in the middle of the 1950s that has continued largely unabated. Between 1950 and 1965 alone, the leading U.S. corporations increased their manufacturing subsidiaries in Europe nearly fourfold. In Australia, General Motors made significant investments. Even during the war GM had decided to manufacture and sell cars in Australia, where it had earlier purchased plants and established distributorships for its automobiles. In 1948 it still only manufactured and sold 112 vehicles. By 1950 production was up, but only to 20,000 cars. By 1962, however, GM was manufacturing 133,000 automobiles with expansion to a capacity of 175,000 already under way.

As the industrialized world recovered from World War II and as the United States built plants and factories and other facilities abroad, the nation's balance of payments turned into a deficit and gold reserves declined sharply. When he took office President John F. Kennedy responded by curtailing government spending abroad and encouraging American exports. President Lyndon Johnson established a program of voluntary—later made mandatory—restraints on direct foreign investment. Nevertheless the deficit continued to grow, and instead of being hoarded as they had been during the war, dollars in Europe began to be sold in what became known as the Eurodollar market. The selling of American dollars for other currencies and the inability of the United States to regulate the Eurodollar market led in 1971 to President Richard Nixon's decision to float the currency against other world currencies rather than to keep the dollar pegged to a fixed gold price as it had done since the Bretton Woods system of 1944.

While these measures had some immediate impact, in the long term they failed to prevent overseas investments by American firms. There were too many ways, for example, for these corporations to get around voluntary or mandatory controls, such as by downstreaming capital investments to foreign subsidiaries and by borrowing on the Eurodollar market. Furthermore, the opportunities abroad, the uncertain future of the dollar, the attraction of cheap labor in Third World countries, the growing importance of foreign oil and other raw materials, and the perceived need to be close to foreign consumers all encouraged the migration of American capital overseas.

Interestingly, while Washington was trying to limit direct investments in the world's largest industrial nations, it actually sought to promote such investments in the Third World, which through the Vietnam War of the 1960s and early 1970s was viewed as a battleground in the Cold War between the United States and the Soviet Union. In 1969 Congress approved the creation of the Overseas Private Investment Corporation, the mission of which was to encourage private investment in less developed countries. To help build the infrastructure needed to attract private investors, the World Bank increased the number of soft loans (loans with below-market interest rates and generous repayment schedules) it made to less developed countries. Even the IMF got into the soft-loan business despite the fact that this had not been part of its original mission.

As American-owned MNCs continued to expand abroad they met increased foreign resistance and growing competition from foreign rivals. The 1970s were a particularly troublesome decade for many of these enterprises, not so much in terms of competition as in overseas opposition to what many foreign nationals regarded as a form of rapacious American imperialism. Still operating in the poisonous world and domestic climate that was an outgrowth of twenty-five years of Cold War rhetoric and a highly unpopular war in Vietnam, MNCs were maligned as part of an American military-industrial establishment seeking world economic and political hegemony. Nor were these views limited to a radical left-wing fringe. Many respected national and international political officials, political theorists, international business leaders, and academics joined in the chorus against the MNCs. A spate of books appeared in the 1970s highlighting the world power of the multinational corporations and arguing that they had become states unto themselves beyond the control of any single nation.

A particular target, but certainly not the only one, of the critics was the oil industry. Drastic increases in energy prices resulted from huge consumer demand in the United States and the decision of the Organization of Petroleum Exporting Countries (OPEC), which had been formed in 1960, to use oil as a political weapon following renewed war between the Arab states and Israel in 1973. This led to a depletion of oil supplies, and prices for gasoline more than doubled in the United States.

Even respected authorities on the oil industry portrayed the multinational oil firms as a sovereign entity with its own form of government and with sources of revenue and influence that allowed it to dictate pretty much the terms and conditions under which oil would be produced and sold in the world. Although this was an oversimplified version of the power of the oil companies to control the production and price of oil, it resonated with the American public. Secret inter-industry correspondence and memoranda, much of it highly damaging and much of it revealed for the first time in 1974 by the Senate Subcommittee on Multinational Corporations, provided the basis for many of the charges made against the oil industry.

None of the charges made in the 1970s against the oil industry or, more generally, against multinational businesses prevented their further growth. In 1978 Congress passed legislation effectively deregulating most domestic commercial aviation, a process that had already been started by Alfred Kahn, head of the Civil Aeronautics Board. In the 1980s deregulation was expanded to include international aviation. By 1997 the United States had concluded agreements with twenty-four nations, thereby allowing U.S.-owned airlines to enter into operational and strategic alliances with foreign-owned airlines and in some cases even to partially own them. Deregulation of the telecommunications industry, concluding with the 1996 General Agreement on Trade in Services, allowed American Telephone and Telegraph (AT&T) and other American corporations in the telecommunications industry to enter into similar arrangements with their foreign counterparts. Between 1960 and 1965 assets of U.S. banks abroad grew from $3.5 billion to $458 billion. Fast-food chains and retailers like McDonald's, Kentucky Fried Chicken, the Gap, and Nike opened thousands of outlets overseas. So did firms in such industries as chemicals and heavy machinery. As a result, in the 1990s sales abroad of U.S. subsidiaries were, on average, five times larger than all of U.S. exports.

Nor were direct foreign investments limited to American-headquartered firms as they had been for most of the postwar period prior to 1980. Businesses in South Korea, Taiwan, and most of western Europe competed against the United States for foreign markets and, indeed, for the U.S. market as well. As a result, between 1980 and 1995 the total amount of direct foreign investment grew more than six times to approximately $3.2 trillion. Between 1975 and 1992 the number of persons employed by multinational firms also increased from about 40 million to 73 million. In 1977 U.S.-based firms accounted for about 69 percent of the U.S. gross manufacturing output; by 1994 that figure had dropped to 57.6 percent. During these same years foreign-owned subsidiaries in the United States increased their market share of U.S. manufacturing from 3.4 percent to 13.2 percent. As of 1996 western Europe actually accounted for $1.59 trillion (about 50 percent) of the world's foreign direct investment, while North America accounted for $905 billion (about 28 percent). Of the remainder, other developed countries, most notably Japan, accounted for about $402 billion (12.7 percent), while the rest of the world accounted for just $286 billion (or approximately 9 percent).

A GLOBAL ECONOMY: THE 1990S

With the development of a truly global economy by the 1990s, opinion with respect to the multinational corporations in home and host countries varied considerably. American multinationals have often been viewed abroad as purveyors of technology and business efficiencies and as bearers of products meeting an insatiable appetite for American goods. But a more negative image also developed. The growing competitiveness of the new world economy and a heightened emphasis on cost efficiencies, job reductions, retooling, and relocation led to complaints in home and host nations about declining market shares and lost jobs.

The transnational character of the multinationals proved irksome to the growing legion of laid-off workers and lower- and mid-level managers who felt most victimized by the new competition and the search for cheaper labor markets. Government officials sensed a loss of their sovereignty because of the ability of these corporations to move their operations, transactions, and profits upstream or downstream as their self-interests dictated. Transfers of technology were another issue pitting MNCs and host and home governments against one another, as they jockeyed to maintain or gain control of technological breakthroughs for reasons of national security and profits.

By the beginning of the twenty-first century, the fact that more and more of the world economy seemed to be dominated by a relatively few multinational giants also led to the ringing of alarm bells. (Estimates of U.S. multinational corporations in 2001 ranged around three thousand, but the numbers were declining because of a wave of corporate mergers.) Other problems creating tensions between MNCs, host governments, and home governments included jurisdictional disputes, cultural differences, nontariff barriers to trade, international agreements among the multinational corporations, and conflicting political agendas on such matters of principle as the environment, energy, human rights, accessibility to proper medical treatment and high-cost pharmaceuticals, sweatshops, and child labor laws.

CONCLUSION

Public opinion and government policy with respect to MNCs, in other words, conjure up the image of a fault line along the earth's crust, quiet for the moment but with pressures building below that could—will—divide the earth above. Despite the best-educated guesses, however, nobody really knows just when and under what circumstances this will happen or how severe the damage will be. Already odd alliances have been formed among the parties most affected by the growth of MNCs. One of these took place beginning in 1991 when free-trade advocates in the United States found themselves joined by the multinationals but strongly opposed by rank-and-file workers over the approval of the North American Free Trade Agreement (NAFTA), which was ratified in 1992 despite labor's objections. In 1994 the MNCs and free traders won a limited victory with the establishment of the World Trade Organization (WTO), which since its founding has focused much of its attention on breaking down remaining restrictions on the expansion of MNCs worldwide. It has had only moderate success, however, because it lacks judicial authority, something the U.S. negotiators refused to give it because of congressional reservations about granting extensive powers to the new body.

In the late 1980s, free traders in Europe joined with European workers in successfully opposing the proposed merger of Honeywell International and General Electric on antitrust grounds. The United States and the European Union also entered in a trade war. They clashed over European restrictions on imports of American beef and bananas, and the U.S. steel industry accused European firms of dumping steel on American markets. European business and political leaders retaliated with charges that Washington unfairly subsidized U.S. exports and rejected its efforts to resolve trade disputes.

These claims and counterclaims suggest that, in a world becoming smaller each day, with corporate mergers across national boundaries becoming more common and a technological and information revolution unlike any in the past, calls will continue to grow about bringing the aspirations of private enterprise more in line with national needs. How that will happen or whether it is even possible remain unanswered questions. The failure of the United States and Europe to resolve their economic differences and a growing movement toward economic regionalism in East Asia, including mutual currency supports, cooperative exchange systems, and an East Asian free trade area, even suggest a worldwide backlash already under way against economic globalization. At the same time, it is difficult to imagine anything less than a highly integrated world economy or one without the glue of the multinational corporations that helped bring it about in the first place.

BIBLIOGRAPHY

Barnet, Richard J., and Ronald E. Müller. *Global Reach: The Power of the Multinational Corporations.* New York, 1974. This indictment of multinational corporations argues that MNCs constitute a state within a state. Well-researched but not entirely persuasive.

Doremus, Paul N., et al. *The Myth of the Global Corporation.* Princeton, N.J., 1998. Persuasively argues against the widely held view that multinational enterprises are able to act autonomously in international economic matters.

Ferguson, Niall. *The House of Rothschild: The World's Banker, 1849–1999.* New York, 1999. The second of a two-volume history of one of the great international banking houses of the nineteenth and twentieth centuries.

James, Harold. *The End of Globalization: Lessons from the Great Depression.* Cambridge, Mass., 2001. Argues that, while there are parallels between today's situation and the end of the movement toward globalization following the Great Depression, one of the essential developments of the 1930s—economic nationalism tied to two of the major powers of the era, Nazi Germany and the Soviet Union—is not in evidence in the early twenty-first century.

Kanter, Rosabeth Moss. *World Class: Thriving Locally in the Global Economy.* New York, 1995. Points to the difficulty of multinational corporations blending in with the local communities of their host nations.

Kapstein, Ethan B. "Workers and the World Economy." *Foreign Affairs* 75 (May–June 1996): 16–37. Argues that the global economy, with its implicit promise of a better life for the working class, has not lived up to that promise primarily because the institutional structure established after World War II to support economic growth and development has forced many governments to follow stringent fiscal policies at labor's expense.

Kaufman, Burton I. *The Oil Cartel Case: A Documentary Study of Antitrust Activity in the Cold War.* Westport, Conn., 1978. A history in which the author argues that Washington used the oil companies to achieve its foreign policy objectives.

Moran, Theodore H. *Foreign Direct Investment and Development: The New Policy Agenda for Developing Countries and Economies in Transition.* Washington, D.C., 1998. Emphasizes the positive role that foreign direct investment can play in developing countries and those nations moving toward a free market economy.

Nathan, John. *Sony: The Private Life.* New York, 1999. Fascinating history of one of Japan's great success stories after World War II.

Rangan, Subramanian, and Robert Z. Lawrence. *A Prism on Globalization: Corporate Responses to the Dollar.* Washington, D.C., 1999. Argues that multinational corporations have worked to assure currency stability rather than the flexible rates characteristic of the 1980s because that is what their customers prefer.

Rodrick, Dani. *Has Globalization Gone Too Far?* Washington, D.C., 1997. Argues that globalization, including the expansion of the multinationals, may indeed have gone too far and that governments need to be more sensitive to the domestic ramifications resulting from economic globalization.

Sampson, Anthony. *The Sovereign State of ITT.* New York, 1973. Maintains that, through ruthless and sometimes illicit practices, ITT, one of the largest conglomerates of the 1960s and 1970s, became a worldwide business empire that defied control by any sovereign nation.

———. *The Seven Sisters: The Great Oil Companies and the World They Shaped.* New York, 1975. Adopts the argument that multinational corporations have had excessive control over the formulation of American foreign policy, but an important study and a solid history.

Spar, Debora L. "The Spotlight and the Bottom Line." *Foreign Affairs* 77 (March–April, 1998): 7–12. Maintains that, instead of exploiting foreign workers with low wages and unsafe working conditions, multinational manufacturers of consumer goods have actually helped to promote human rights because of the impact of the public spotlight and human rights activism.

Vernon, Raymond. *Sovereignty at Bay.* New York, 1971. Classic study of multinational corporations that traces their growth and the challenge they pose for sovereign nations.

———. *In the Hurricane's Eye: The Troubled Prospects of Multinational Enterprises.* Cambridge, Mass., 1998. Maintains that multinationals are facing increasing efforts by host and home governments to regulate their operations as a result of an increasingly hostile domestic environment.

Wilkins, Mira. *The Emergence of Multinational Enterprise: American Business from the Colonial Era to 1914.* Cambridge, Mass., 1970. The first of a two-volume study; deeply researched and thorough and comprehensive in coverage.

———. *The Maturing of Multinational Enterprise: American Business Abroad from 1914 to 1970.* Cambridge, Mass., 1974. The second volume of Wilkins's classic study and the place to start for any study on the subject.

Wolf, Martin. "Will the Nation-State Survive Globalization?" *Foreign Affairs* 80 (January–February 2001): 178–190. Argues that nation-states will become stronger rather than weaker in the evolving international economy, and that further globalization will not be the destined result of market forces associated with the technological revolution but rather of conscious decision by nation-states to enhance their economic well-being.

See also ECONOMIC THEORY AND POLICY; OIL.

THE MUNICH ANALOGY

Joseph M. Siracusa

At the Munich Conference of 1938, France and England followed a policy of appeasement toward Adolf Hitler, choosing not to challenge him on his takeover of Czechoslovakia in the hope that German aggression toward neighboring states would stop there and that war in Europe could be averted. The failure of this appeasement approach in preventing the outbreak of World War II subsequently made the Munich agreement a metaphor for weakness in foreign policy, and the "lesson" of the Munich Conference has permeated the American political world ever since. The Munich analogy has not only been used consistently in American presidential and governmental rhetoric but has also affected foreign policy decisions at crucial moments in U.S. history. Presidents from Franklin D. Roosevelt to George H. W. Bush, from the 1940s to the 1980s, have used the example of Munich as a warning to the public about the inherent dangers of appeasing aggressors.

THE ROAD TO MUNICH

During the fateful year 1938, the Nazi dictator Adolf Hitler took the first two steps in his *Drang nach Osten,* or drive to the east, by annexing Austria and the predominantly German sections of Czechoslovakia. In order to win Italian support, Hitler had promised to respect Austrian independence and to refrain from interfering in the small republic's internal politics. At heart, though, he had never really abandoned his hope of uniting the land of his birth with his adopted fatherland, a feeling reciprocated by some Austrians. (Indeed, at the end of World War I, Austria asked to be united with Germany, but subsequently this was expressly forbidden in the Treaty of Versailles.) By early 1938 Hitler felt strong enough to cast his promises to the winds.

In February he summoned Kurt von Schuschnigg, the Austrian chancellor, to a conference at Berchtesgaden, the führer's mountain retreat in the Bavarian Alps, and demanded the admission of prominent Austrian Nazis to the cabinet. Schuschnigg complied but called for an immediate plebiscite, which he felt certain would demonstrate popular opposition to union with Germany. The Nazis were apparently of the same opinion, for they at once demanded the resignation of Schuschnigg and a postponement of the plebiscite, threatening invasion by German troops as the alternative. Schuschnigg resigned on 11 March. His successor as chancellor, the Nazi Arthur Seyss-Inquart, immediately called in the Wehrmacht, allegedly to suppress disorders in Austria. On 12 March the German government proclaimed Austria to be a state of the German Reich, and two days later Hitler entered Vienna amid a great show of rejoicing. *Anschluss* was complete. France and Great Britain protested, but since neither had an interest sufficiently vital to go to war to prevent this action, no one raised a hand in resistance.

Hitler next turned to "rescue" what he termed the "tortured and oppressed" Germans of Czechoslovakia, in point of fact the most democratic state of Central Europe. Of Czechoslovakia's 14 million people, about 3.5 million were Germans. These lived for the most part in the Sudeten area that fringed the western end of the republic, facing German territory to the north, west, and south. The Sudeten Germans, comprising just one of numerous ethnic minorities in Czechoslovakia, had shown little dissatisfaction with their government until 1932, when the Nazi movement first gained some strength among them. From then until 1938, the Sudeten Nazis, led by Konrad Henlein, kept up a growing agitation, first for complete cultural and political autonomy within Czechoslovakia and finally for union with Nazi Germany.

The Czechoslovak government made a succession of compromise offers, but these were one by one rejected by Henlein, who consulted Hitler at each step. By September 1938 it was evident that nothing less than cession of the Sudetenland to Germany would satisfy the führer. The Czechoslovak government did not propose to yield to dismemberment without putting up a fight. It had a relatively efficient army and a defensible frontier. It also had defensive alliances with France and Soviet Russia. If it were attacked by Germany, and if its allies fulfilled their solemn obligations, a general European war was certain. This would, in all probability, involve England also.

In an effort to find a peaceful settlement for the Sudeten problem, Prime Minister Neville Chamberlain of Great Britain paid two visits to Hitler, at Berchtesgaden and at Godesberg, on the Rhine a few miles above Cologne. In the first (15 September 1938) Chamberlain ascertained that the führer would take nothing less than surrender of the Sudetenland to Germany. In the second, a week later, he submitted to Hitler a plan for the prompt and peaceful transfer to Germany of the areas of Czechoslovakia with populations more than 50 percent German, the fixing of the new frontier by an international commission, and an international guarantee of the independence of a Czechoslovakia shorn of these important segments of its territory and population. The Prague government agreed to these terms under combined and relentless British and French pressure.

To Chamberlain's consternation, Hitler rejected this proposal as too slow. Instead he demanded the immediate withdrawal of all Czech military and official civilian personnel from areas that he specified, with plebiscites to follow in other areas where the percentage of German population was doubtful. German troops, he warned, would occupy the specified areas on 1 October, whether or not Czechoslovakia accepted his ultimatum.

Czechoslovakia at once rejected this proposal and mobilized its army of 1.5 million men. France followed with partial mobilization, as did Belgium. France and Britain made it clear that they would assist Czechoslovakia if it were attacked, while Italy announced its intention of standing by its Axis partner. The threat of war was real.

AMERICA HAS A STAKE IN APPEASEMENT

At this point (27 September 1938) U.S. President Franklin D. Roosevelt entered the picture. Urging Hitler to lay the controversy before an international conference, he added: "Should you agree to a solution in this peaceful manner I am convinced that hundreds of millions throughout the world would recognize your action as an outstanding historic service to all humanity."

Roosevelt also joined with Chamberlain and French Premier Édouard Daladier in a plea to the Italian dictator Benito Mussolini to persuade Hitler to accept a peaceful settlement that would give him substantially all he asked for. Hitler yielded to the extent of agreeing to meet with Mussolini and the French and British leaders at Munich. There, on 29 September, Hitler and Mussolini and Chamberlain and Daladier agreed on a plan that the Czech government perforce accepted. It differed little from Hitler's ultimatum of a week before, merely allowing slightly more time for Czech withdrawal from the surrendered area. The American contribution to the crisis was confined to a message from Roosevelt reminding all the European powers concerned of their solemn obligation under the Kellogg-Briand Pact (1928) not to go to war with one another. The Soviet Union was not invited. In any case, it was assumed that war had been averted. Prime Minister Chamberlain told the people of England that he had brought back "peace with honour," adding, "I believe it is peace in our time."

Two Czechoslovak diplomats summoned to Munich were held overnight under Gestapo guard and confronted on the morning of 30 September with what the great powers had done. Prague was forced to give in to the pact's terms. Jan Masaryk, son of the founding father of the Czech Republic, warned Britain and France, "If you have sacrificed my nation to preserve the peace of the world, I will be the first to applaud you. But if not, gentlemen, God help your souls!"

The Wehrmacht was to be allowed to take over the German-speaking frontier area of Czechoslovakia during the first ten days of October with all the military installations it contained. What was left of the republic was to be placed under some kind of indeterminate guarantee, never enacted.

The Munich pact was hailed as a triumph of diplomacy over war, and Chamberlain returned home to a hero's welcome. Nevile Henderson, the British ambassador to Berlin at the time of the conference, later wrote that "it was solely thanks to Mr. Chamberlain's courage and pertinacity that a futile and senseless war was averted." He wrote to his prime minister, saying, "Millions of mothers will be blessing your name tonight for having saved their sons from the horrors of war." The *London Times* reported that "No conqueror returning from a victory on a battlefield has come home adorned with nobler laurels." Americans greeted the Munich settlement with profound relief that war had been avoided. Thus, the American government and people at this time obviously favored appeasement with Hitler as the alternative to war.

As Hitler violated his pledges and anti-Semitic outrages multiplied in Germany, Roosevelt publicly voiced disapproval. He recalled the American ambassador after the violent *Kristallnacht* ("night of broken glass" on 9–10 November 1938) in Germany, a wave of anti-Jewish riots and stringent repressive measures that followed the assassination of a German diplomat in Paris by a Jew.

Hitler fully reciprocated American dislike and recalled his ambassador. He viewed the United States as a racial mixture that could not even cope with the economic depression. The United States, with its political weakness and degenerate culture, he told his intimates in 1938, would prove no match for German will. The United States was too impotent to fight and would not go beyond meaningless moral gestures in international affairs. The German military shared his opinion. Using "racial arithmetic," Hitler concluded that the polyglot United States was held together only by the glue of 20 million superior Anglo-Saxons or 60 million of valuable racial stock, therefore Germany, with its larger population of Aryans, was far more powerful. America's neutrality laws in the 1930s merely strengthened his contempt.

The Munich settlement proved to be but the prelude to the complete extinction of Czechoslovakia as an independent nation. Hungary and Poland demanded and received slices of Czech territory where Magyars and Poles were numerous. As a result of the crisis, Hitler annexed to Germany more than 3 million Germans of the Sudeten region. Politically, Hitler's success broke the back of the "Little Entente"(the alliance system of smaller states that sought to preserve the central European status quo as established by the Versailles system), gutted the French alliance system in Eastern Europe, and made the Third Reich easily the dominant power in the continent.

Internal dissension between Czechs and Slovaks in March 1939 afforded Hitler the final pretext for taking control of the destinies of those two ethnic divisions of the former republic. Hitler summoned President Emil Hácha to Berlin and induced him to "place the fate of the Czech people . . . trustingly in the hands of the Führer," who presumably guaranteed "an autonomous development of its national life corresponding to its peculiarities." On 15 March, Bohemia and Moravia became a German protectorate, which was promptly occupied by German troops. The Czech army offered no resistance. The disappearance of Czechoslovakia demonstrated Hitler's readiness to extend his claims beyond "racial" areas and base them on the Reich's needs for *Lebensraum,* or "living area."

Hitler had declared at Munich: "This [Sudetenland] is the last territorial claim which I have to make in Europe." His absorption of Czechoslovakia had given the lie to that declaration, and by April 1939 he was pressing Poland for consent to annexation of the free city of Danzig and a sort of German corridor across the Polish corridor to give Germany freer access to East Prussia. By this time even Chamberlain had lost faith in Hitler's promises. He abruptly abandoned appeasement and, with France, gave guarantees of aid against aggression to Poland and later to Romania and to Greece, the latter threatened by Italy's occupation of Albania. Geography would make it difficult to implement these guarantees effectively, but they at least served notice on the Axis powers that further aggression against their small neighbors would mean war with the great western democracies.

On 1 September, German forces, led by mechanized divisions and supported by overwhelming airpower, invaded Poland. Two days later, making good their pledge, Great Britain and France declared war against Hitler's Germany. World War II had at last begun. Appeasement was finished.

THE MUNICH LEGACY

The very term "Munich" has since become synonymous with a typical example of dishonorable appeasement, that is, a situation when the vital interests of a nation are bartered away in return for minor concessions or none at all. Appeasement, according to this line of argument, may often result from national weakness or, worse, ignorance either from an inability to fight or a fundamental misconception of reality. In the case of Czechoslovakia, interests were literally given away without any concessions being extracted from Germany. This occurred because Great Britain and France were not militarily or economically prepared to fight another war, nor were they psychologically prepared to fight for causes that, although just, did not affect them personally. Prime Minister Chamberlain summarized public opinion to Parliament prior to leaving for the Munich Conference, pointing out "how horrible, fantastic, incredible that we should be digging trenches . . . here because of a quarrel in a far away country, between people of whom we know nothing." Furthermore, Chamberlain was motivated by a belief that by conceding to the demands of a minority people who wished to be reunited with their traditional nation, he would be able to avoid war and achieve "peace with honour."

The Munich agreement soon became the archetype of failure of will in the face of moral confrontation, turning firmness into an essential virtue in the conduct of foreign policy. Statesmen, for fear of being called "Municheers," have since been encouraged to go to the brink of war in the hope that by adopting an inflexible position, the aggressor will be forced to go to retreat. This outlook has been pervasive in the American political world since World War II. As Telford Taylor points out in his seminal work *Munich: The Price of Peace* (p. xvi), "Munich has become a standard weapon in the dialectic of politics," but always in a pejorative sense.

AMERICA'S MUNICH GENERATION

It is impossible to understand American politics and diplomacy since Munich without understanding the intellectual world of those Americans who came to maturity in the interwar period. These were the same politicians, policymakers, and diplomats who had experienced the disillusionment of the Versailles system and the folly of isolationism. They had struggled through the Great Depression, which had reduced half of America's population to penury. They witnessed the rise of communism (with its forced collectivization and purges), fascism, and nazism. They recoiled from the West's abandonment of Czechoslovakia to Hitler in 1938 under the aegis of appeasement and were dragged into the second world war of their lifetime, the death toll this time probably reaching 60 million, including 6 million murdered Jews.

They also perceived a shrinking world in which war and peace were judged indivisible—the hard lesson of Munich, learned on both sides of the Iron Curtain. The analogy shaped a generation of diplomacy. Moreover, modern warfare, with its awful weapons of death and destruction and the equally awful contemplation that they could be delivered anywhere with impunity, caused the majority of Americans to rethink past policies and their role in the world. The usually cautious American public placed its faith in the collective security of the fledgling United Nations. The fact that the UN would not or could not play this promised role produced the moment of truth: Would the United States play the keeper of the balance of power? The answer would prove to be yes, launching what W. W. Rostow once described as the "American Diplomatic Revolution."

In 1938 President Franklin D. Roosevelt had been unwilling to involve America in another war, and so had done little to strengthen British and French resolve at the Munich Conference. When Hitler invaded Czechoslovakia in March 1939, the United States reacted with shock and anger. The U.S. ambassador to Italy later recalled how he had expressed America's dissatisfaction with Germany's actions. He told the Italian minister for foreign affairs that "Hitler's performance had greatly shocked American public opinion and that . . . the brutal methods employed by Hitler in seizing Bohemia and Moravia by armed force had created a profound impression on the United States." Thus, when Hitler finished off Czechoslovakia, the United States lost all hope it had held of appeasement preventing war. The ambassador to France, William C. Bullitt, wrote to the secretary of state describing the feeling there: "The invasion of Czechoslovakia ends definitely all possibility of diplomatic negotiations. . . . There is only regret that Hitler's action has ended the period when it was still possible to hope that constructive diplomatic action might maintain peace." It became clear that war was imminent and that the policy of appeasement had failed.

By the time war came to America, Roosevelt had fully learned the harsh lesson of appeasement. In his Christmas Eve "fireside chat" of 1943, he assured the public that while the allies stuck together "there will be no possibility of an aggressor nation arising to start another world war. . . . For too many years we lived on pious hopes that aggressor and warlike nations would learn and understand and carry out the doctrine of purely voluntary peace. The well-intentioned but ill-fated experiments of former years did not work." From this moment on, American presidents would time and again refer to Munich and the appeasement policies of the 1930s as the prime example of what to avoid in the future.

Munich was also an example of what had to be avoided during an election. During the 1944 presidential campaign, American journalists and politicians alike predicted that Roosevelt would lose many votes because of his presumably conciliatory attitude toward the Soviet Union. The Republican Party actually campaigned against the Roosevelt administration's "appeasement" policies, arguing for a tougher stance against the "communist threat." This trend continued throughout the decade, as shown by a March 1946 poll in which 71 percent of the public disapproved of the administration's policy toward Russia, while 60 percent considered their policies toward the Soviets as "too soft."

THE COLD WAR

After Roosevelt's death in April 1945, the incoming Truman administration was equally concerned with avoiding the experiences of the 1930s. President Harry S. Truman and his advisers believed that in order to avoid the mistakes of the previous decade, they had to resist the "totalitarian" Soviet Union before its appetite and power increased. In the postwar period this attitude emerged when the administration was faced with the issue of whether to share the secret of the atomic bomb with the Soviet Union or retain control for as long as possible. In arguing against sharing any knowledge with the Soviets, Secretary of the Navy James Forrestal stated that "it seems doubtful that we should endeavor to buy their understanding and sympathy. We tried that once with Hitler. There are no returns on appeasement." The Munich analogy was invoked to emphasize the futility of treating as reasonable an immoral and irrational adversary.

Another instance in which the Munich analogy came into play was the debate over the control of the Turkish Straits in August 1946. The Soviet Union proposed a joint system of control and defense by a body composed of Turkey and the other Black Sea powers, instead of Turkey retaining complete control. This proposal was met with alarm by the U.S. State Department, which saw this as an example of what was to become known as the "domino theory." This situation reminded politicians of the tumbling European dominoes of the 1930s. With loss of control in one area of Asia, the Soviet Union might move into other areas, increasing its strength along the way, which would only mean that the United States would have to fight communism later and under less favorable conditions. The Soviet Union could only be checked by employing a policy of containment, the rough intellectual outlines of which had been developed by George F. Kennan during and immediately after the war. As interpreted by Paul H. Nitze, Kennan's successor as director of the State Department's Policy Planning Staff, containment meant essentially a policy that sought to (1) block further expansion of Soviet power, (2) expose the falsities of Soviet pretensions, (3) induce a retraction of the Kremlin's control and influence, and (4) in general, foster the seeds of destruction within the Soviet system so that the Kremlin could be brought to the point of modifying its behavior to conform to generally accepted international standards. A key feature of containment envisaged the United States dealing with the Soviets from the position of strength. "In the concept of 'containment,'" noted Nitze, "the maintenance of a strong military posture is an ultimate guarantee of national security and as an indispensable backdrop to the conduct of the policy of containment." To Nitze, there was no substitute for the maintenance of superior force: "Without superior aggregate military strength, in being ready and mobilizable, a policy of 'containment'—which is in effect a policy of calculated or gradual coercion—is no more than a bluff."

The "lesson" of Munich, therefore, was to encourage firmness at all costs, even the risk of war. "Containing" Joseph Stalin was at the heart of America's Cold War.

THE KOREAN WAR

The best example of the manner in which the Munich analogy came to grip the minds of Truman and his advisers was the decision of the president to intervene in Korea in 1950. This is striking because the U.S. government completely changed its policy toward Korea on the basis of parallels between this situation and that of the 1930s. Prior to North Korea's invasion of South Korea on 25 June 1950, the United States had followed a policy of avoiding military engagement in the Korean Peninsula. This was mainly because American policymakers believed that Korea lay outside the "defense perimeter" of the United States and was relatively unimportant to its national security. Even at the beginning of June, American policy was to avoid sending military forces to Korea. This was the consistent position

> ## AN AMERICAN DIPLOMAT REMEMBERS
>
> George F. Kennan was director of the Policy Planning Staff of the State Department from 1947 to 1949. In his book *Russia and the West Under Lenin and Stalin* (1960), he wrote about the Munich agreement:
>
> "Throughout that summer of 1938, the Nazi buildup against Czechoslovakia proceeded apace; and in September there occurred the celebrated Munich crisis which rocked Europe to its foundations. With the details of this crisis—Chamberlain's meeting with Hitler at Bad Godesberg, his later dramatic flight to Munich, his concession that Hitler should have the Sudeten areas of Czechoslovakia, the Czech capitulation, the fall and flight of the Czech government, the occupation by the Germans of a large part of Bohemia and Moravia, and the reduction of what was left of the Czechoslovak Republic to the condition of a defenseless dependency of Germany—with all this, we are familiar. European history knows no more tragic day than that of Munich. I remember it well; for I was in Prague at the time, and I shall never forget the sight of the people weeping in the streets as the news of what had occurred came in over the loud-speakers.
>
> "The Munich agreement was a tragically misconceived and desperate act of appeasement at the cost of the Czechoslovak state, performed by Chamberlain and the French premier, Daladier, in the vain hope that it would satisfy Hitler's stormy ambition, and thus secure for Europe a peaceful future. We know today that it was unnecessary—unnecessary because the Czech defenses were very strong, and had the Czechs decided to fight they could have put up considerable resistance; even more unnecessary because the German generals, conscious of Germany's relative weakness at that moment, were actually prepared to attempt the removal of Hitler then and there, had he persisted in driving things to the point of war. It was the fact that the Western powers and the Czechoslovak government did yield at the last moment, and that Hitler once again achieved a bloodless triumph, which deprived the generals of any excuse for such a move. One sees again, as so often in the record of history, that it sometimes pays to stand up manfully to one's problems, even when no certain victory is in sight."

of the Joint Chiefs of Staff, one that was twice considered by the National Security Council and twice approved by the president. Furthermore, during his famous National Press Club speech of 12 January 1950, the secretary of state, Dean Acheson, made this position plain.

The North Korean invasion changed policy dramatically. This was primarily because President Truman perceived the invasion as analogous to the aggressive actions of Hitler and Mussolini in the 1930s. Truman stated that when he first heard the news of the North Korean invasion his first thought was of the 1930s. He wrote:

> I remembered how each time that the democracies failed to act, it had encouraged the aggressors to keep going ahead. Communism was acting in Korea just as Hitler, Mussolini and the Japanese had acted ten, fifteen and twenty years earlier. . . . If this was allowed to go unchallenged it would mean a third world war, just as similar incidents had brought on a second world war.

Not only the president equated North Korean actions with those of the Nazis. The *Washington Post, Baltimore Sun, New York Herald Tribune,* and *New York Times* all alluded to the appeasement of the 1930s in their editorials on Korea. In the House of Representatives, Democrat Abraham Ribicoff of Connecticut asked, "What difference is there in the action of North Korea today and the actions which led to the Second World War? Talk about parallels!"

By classifying the Korean invasion as comparable to the aggressive actions of Hitler in the 1930s, Truman and his associates were led to the conclusion that in order to avoid the "appeasement" of the 1930s and Munich, they had to act to protect the lesser power from this aggression. Refusal to repel aggression would be nothing but appeasement. And appeasement, as history allegedly had shown, would ultimately lead to war.

The analogy with Munich would continue to be cited during the Korean War. Truman used it time and again to reassure the public of the continuing need for U.S. troops to be stationed in Korea. In December 1950, the first year of the war, Truman assured the country that "We will continue to take every honorable step we can to avoid general war.... But we will not engage in appeasement.... The world learned from Munich that security cannot be bought by appeasement." Critics who charged that the government was not employing sufficient force to counter the threat in Korea also used the analogy. The specter of Munich overshadowed everything. For example, Republican Senator William F. Knowland criticized the government, stating, "Talk of seating the Reds in the UN is appeasement. Talk of establishing a neutral zone in Korea is appeasement. Waiting around for Mao Zedong to become Tito is appeasement."

In November 1950, Chinese "volunteers" entered the war and the Munich analogy began to take on the form of the argument that failure to wage total war was appeasement itself. General Douglas MacArthur, in charge of the United Nations forces in Korea, used this argument forcefully to criticize his own government as well as that of the British, taunting them with allegations of appeasement. When the British began to consider creating a demilitarized zone south of the Yalu River, the U.S. Joint Chiefs of Staff warned MacArthur that his war objectives might be altered "in the interests of pursuing negotiations with the Chinese." MacArthur denounced this "widely reported British desire to appease the Chinese Communists by giving them a strip of Northern Korea." He once again used the Munich analogy to remind the U.S. government that its credibility would suffer unless it stood firm on this issue. "Indeed, to yield to so immoral a proposition would bankrupt our leadership and influence in Asia and render untenable our position both politically and military." Even more inflammatory was MacArthur's statement following a remark by British Prime Minister Ernest Bevin that the "young" nation, America, needed sage advice, gained by experience, from Britain. MacArthur retorted that he "needed no lessons from the successors of Neville Chamberlain." MacArthur played the Munich analogy for all it was worth, and eventually he discovered the consequences of pushing the analogy too far: in April 1951, after months of sparring, Truman fired him.

THE GENEVA CONFERENCE

The outbreak of the Korean War and the American reaction to it, more than any other single event, crystallized the Cold War mentality that had been more or less in a state of fluidity from 1945 to 1950. As part of this process, American understanding and appreciation of the realities and aspirations of Indochina were transformed. With the North Korean invasion across the Thirty-eighth Parallel, Indochina came to be seen mainly as an aspect of the larger problem of coping with the communist conquest of the Free World by the Soviets and Chinese. Or, as Truman put it: "We were seeing a pattern in Indo-China timed to coincide with the attack in Korea as a challenge to the Western world ... a challenge by the Communists alone, aimed at intensifying the smouldering and anti-foreign feeling among most Asian peoples."

The Cold War paradigm that portrayed the Indochina conflict as but a functional aspect of worldwide communist aggression was passed on intact to the Eisenhower administration. The Korean War, argued President Dwight D. Eisenhower, was "clearly part of the same calculated assault that the aggressor is simultaneously pursuing in Indo-China." And, conversely, the working out of a settlement of the Korean War would presumably have a lasting impact on Indochina as well as on other nations in the region. In this way, then, the American fear of another Munich carried over into the Eisenhower administration.

In 1954 the administration feared that the Geneva Conference called to discuss the future of Korea and the division of Indochina would turn into "another Munich." An armistice had been signed in Korea the previous year, but new concerns had arisen over the eight-year war in Indochina between France and the French Union and the communist-led Viet Minh resistance movement. The conference was arranged by Great Britain, the United States, the Soviet Union, and France and was also attended by countries with an interest in the issue, including the People's Republic of China.

The United States was exceptionally hostile to any negotiation with Beijing. The Americans, especially Secretary of State John Foster Dulles, described the talks as "phoney" and "unpalatable" because they represented the "psychology of appeasement." Dulles was obsessed with the seating arrangements at the conference and even refused to shake hands with Chinese Foreign Minister Chou En-lai. Because Dulles equated Geneva with the Munich Conference he was determined to be firm whatever the outcome.

The United States has been roundly criticized for its behavior at the Geneva Conference. The delegation was so opposed to negotiations before the conference started that they even attempted to sabotage efforts to reach any political settlement. As Richard H. Immerman observed:

> If by these actions it exacted some concessions from the Communists, they were limited and more than offset by the strains they placed on the western alliance. If by resisting compromise and dissociating the United States from the result officials managed to avoid the label "appeaser," they cost America countless hearts and minds, particularly those in the third world. Worst of all, by refusing to sanction the elections, Washington signaled the diplomacy—and international law—were not substitutes for force.

The American attitude was simply that any concession amounted to capitulation, for by this time the American political culture had come to equate all forms of negotiation with appeasement at Munich. The United States finally refused to sign the Geneva agreement, which divided Vietnam along the Seventeenth Parallel and promised elections in 1956 to unify the country under one government. When President Eisenhower returned from the conference, he gave the usual speech at the airport immediately upon his arrival. Although it was raining, Vice President Richard M. Nixon was adamant that Eisenhower should not carry an umbrella, lest the nation and the media be reminded of Neville Chamberlain and his famous umbrella.

THE CUBAN MISSILE CRISIS

The 1960s provided a classic situation in which the Munich analogy was called into play. During the Cuban Missile Crisis, President John F. Kennedy pointedly used the analogy in his speech of 22 October 1962, when he announced that he would implement a quarantine on communist Cuba in response to the discovery that the Soviet Union had been placing offensive weapons there. Explaining his decision, the president reminded the nation that "the 1930s taught us a clear lesson: Aggressive conduct, if allowed to grow unchecked and unchallenged, ultimately leads to war." The transcripts of the Executive Committee of the National Security Council (ExCom) show that the Munich analogy was extensively used in governmental discussions during the crisis. In a meeting with the Joint Chiefs of Staff, at which the president explained that he was leaning toward implementing a blockade rather than more aggressive military action, General Curtis LeMay exclaimed: "This blockade and political action, I see leading into war. I don't see any other solution. It will lead right into war. This is almost as bad as the appeasement at Munich." The president was at a loss for words.

The lessons of Munich had particular meaning for Kennedy. His father, Joseph Kennedy, had been Roosevelt's ambassador to Britain at the time of the Munich Conference, and John Kennedy had been a twenty-one-year-old university student. The elder Kennedy had been a longtime supporter of Britain's policy of appeasement and continued to be throughout the war. John Kennedy, however, formed his own beliefs with the coming of World War II. He disagreed with appeasement so fervently that his honors thesis at Harvard was entitled "Appeasement at Munich." This was published after his graduation under the title *Why England Slept* (1940) and became a bestseller. The book argued that appeasement was a weak policy that the United States should avoid at all costs. One can therefore imagine the effect on Kennedy of being labeled a "Municheer."

This damaging term was also applied to Kennedy's ambassador to the United Nations, Adlai Stevenson, in the wake of the crisis. There had been a confrontation during talks before the crisis on what to do about the Soviet threat. Stevenson had suggested that the president "should consider offering to withdraw from the Guantánamo naval base as part of a plan to demilitarize, neutralize and guarantee the territorial integrity of Cuba . . . [and offer] to remove the Jupiter [missiles in Turkey] in exchange for the Russian missiles from Cuba." Kennedy vehemently disagreed with these proposals, saying that this was not the right time for concessions that could divide the allies and sacrifice their interests.

Stevenson's suggestion met with a strong reaction from other members of ExCom, leading to the subsequent charge that Stevenson had "wanted a Munich." This accusation appeared in a postmortem article by the journalist Joseph Alsop, who attributed the statement to a "non-admiring official." It turned out that President Kennedy was actually the "non-admiring official" whose comments were used to discredit Stevenson. As a result, the article made Stevenson's arguments for trading the Turkish bases seem less rational than they really were. This charge of being a "Municheer" was especially damaging to Stevenson's political reputation. The irony, of course, was that the Jupiter missiles did play a secret role in resolving the crisis.

THE VIETNAM WAR

The Munich analogy was increasingly used by Washington to justify various actions during the Vietnam War. In 1954, when the French were nearing defeat in Vietnam, Eisenhower considered sending additional aid to supplement the economic aid already being supplied. In fact, by this stage, the United States was already funding three-quarters of the cost of the war but had not actually intervened militarily. Eisenhower considered this move and sought British support to use U.S. air and naval power in Indochina. In a letter to Winston Churchill, he used the Munich analogy in order to persuade the British to support American actions: "If I may refer again to history; we failed to halt Hirohito, Mussolini and Hitler by not acting in unity and in time. That marked the beginning of many years of stark tragedy and desperate peril. May it not be that our nations have learned something from that lesson?"

That John F. Kennedy thought and acted upon the same assumptions can hardly be open to question. In his words:

> Viet-Nam represents the cornerstone of the Free World in Southeast Asia, the Keystone of the arch, the finger in the dike. Burma, Thailand, India, Japan, the Philippines and obviously Laos and Cambodia are among those whose security would be threatened if the red tide of Communism overflowed into Viet-Nam.... Moreover, the independence of Free Viet-Nam is crucial to the free world in fields other than military. Her economy is essential to the economy of all of Southeast Asia; and her political liberty is an inspiration to those seeking to obtain or maintain their liberty in all parts of Asia—and indeed the world.

For these reasons, added Kennedy, "the fundamental tenets of this nation's foreign policy . . . depend in considerable measure upon a strong and free Vietnamese nation."

Under Kennedy, the number of U.S. troops in South Vietnam increased steadily, reaching some 14,500 before the end of 1963. Technically, they were engaged only in transportation, training, and advice, but these activities invariably exposed them to combat. Few questioned why they were there.

It was not until the advent of the Johnson administration, however, that the Munich analogy came into its own. President Lyndon B. Johnson and his secretary of state, Dean Rusk, considered Munich to be the most important historical lesson of their time. Remembering Munich, they saw weakness overseas as leading to World War III. Johnson explained, "Everything I knew about history told me that if I got out of Vietnam and let Ho Chi Minh run through the streets of Saigon, then I'd be doing exactly what Chamberlain did in World War II. I'd be giving a big fat reward to aggression." Rusk was equally attuned to the lessons of the 1930s, which he described as the realization that "aggression must be dealt with wherever it occurs and no matter what mask it may wear. . . . The rearmament of the Rhineland was regarded as regrettable but not worth a shooting war. Yet after that came Austria, and after Austria came Czechoslovakia. Then Poland. Then the Second World War."

This belief in the applicability of the Munich analogy to his situation led Johnson to increase troop levels, first to 300,000 and then to 500,000 by 1968. At a National Security Council meeting in July 1965 to discuss an increase in troops, an exchange occurred between Undersecretary of State George Ball, who was opposed to committing more men, and the U.S. ambassador to Vietnam, Henry Cabot Lodge. Lodge rebutted Ball's arguments, explaining that "I feel there is a greater threat to start World War III if we don't go in. Can't we see the similarity to our own indolence at Munich?" No one present at the meeting questioned this statement. Even McGeorge Bundy, the national security adviser who often criticized others for using inaccurate analogies, did not comment. The administration's policymakers were convinced of the appropriateness of the analogy to their own situation in Vietnam, and often reminded one another of this fact. Even former president Eisenhower resorted to the analogy in advising Johnson in 1965. He warned the president not to be convinced by Britain's arguments for negotiation. Prime Minister Harold Wilson, he said, "has not had experience with this kind of problem. We, however, have learned that Munichs win nothing."

Most important, the Johnson administration used the analogy to convince the public that its Southeast Asia policy was appropriate. A government film produced in 1965 entitled *Why Vietnam?* contained flickering images of Neville Chamberlain at Munich throughout the film. Further, when announcing his decision to send combat troops to Vietnam in March 1965, Johnson explained to the public: "Nor would surrender in Vietnam bring peace, because we learned from Hitler at Munich that success only feeds the appetite of aggression. The battle would be renewed . . . bringing with it perhaps even larger and crueler conflict, as we learned from the lessons of history."

In the same year, Johnson argued that defeat in South Vietnam "would encourage those who seek to conquer all free nations within their reach. ... This is the dearest lesson of our time. From Munich until today we have learned that to yield to aggression brings only greater threats." Worse yet, a new wave of McCarthyism might pose rhetorical questions about how Vietnam was lost.

Similarly, Richard M. Nixon's policy of détente with the Soviet Union and China failed appreciably to alter the image of Vietnam as a vital test case and an aspect of a larger problem. "An American defeat in Viet-Nam," declared Nixon on 8 May 1972, in a message to the American people explaining his decision to mine the entrances to North Vietnamese ports, "would encourage this kind of aggression all over the world. ... Small nations, armed by their major allies, could be tempted to attack neighboring nations at will, in the Mid-East, in Europe and other areas."

No change was to be expected in the attitude of Gerald Ford's administration. In his formal and foredoomed request to Congress in early 1975 for continued military aid to South Vietnam (and Cambodia), President Ford reminded his recent colleagues that "U.S. unwillingness to provide adequate assistance to allies fighting for their lives would seriously affect our credibility as an ally." Saigon fell on 30 April. The collapse of South Vietnam together with the defeat of the pro-Western forces in Cambodia and subsequently in Laos marked the end of American influence in the area. For some, it came as no real surprise, for others, there were no words to explain it. The Munich analogy, in time, gave way to the "Vietnam syndrome," which led many Americans to question the wisdom of using military power at all.

REAGAN, BUSH, AND THE GULF WAR

President Ronald Reagan's foreign policy perspective was clearly the product of the past. Reagan's mental pictures of the world had been formed when the Nazi storm was gathering in Europe and Imperial Japan was on the march in China. He viewed the world through 1930s eyes, and he learned his generation's lesson that unwillingness to confront aggression invariably invited war. For him, the very word "appeasement" connoted surrender. President Reagan often invoked the image of Munich in order to belittle the critics of his Nicaraguan policies as "appeasers" of the Sandinistas. His administration had used Nicaraguan rebels, the contras, to pressure and ultimately cause the overthrow of the legitimate Sandinista regime. He was supported in this by the ambassador to the United Nations, Jeane Kirkpatrick, who argued in 1985 that the Munich analogy was appropriate in this case.

Reagan frequently made use of the Munich analogy during his presidency. In a March 1983 address before the Evangelist Society about the threat of Marxist-Leninism, he criticized the "historical reluctance to see totalitarian powers for what they are. ... We saw this phenomenon in the 1930s." He cautioned that "if history teaches us anything, it teaches that simpleminded or wishful thinking about our adversaries is folly." In August 1983 he told the American Legion that "Neville Chamberlain thought of peace as a vague policy in the 1930s, and the result brought us closer to World War II. History teaches us that by being strong and resolute we can keep the peace." Throughout its eight years, the Reagan administration bargained from a position of strength, at great cost to the public purse, to prove its point.

President George H. W. Bush relied heavily upon the Munich analogy in his speeches during the crisis in the Persian Gulf, which ultimately led to the Gulf War of 1990–1991. Munich was the perfect example in this case, and Bush used it to argue that to forget the lessons of appeasement would be to betray the sacrifices made in World War II. In a speech to the Veterans of Foreign Wars, Bush invoked World War II to reinforce his message of intervention. The United States, he said, had to stand "where it always has—against aggression, against those who would use force to replace the rule of law." The Iraqi ruler Saddam Hussein particularly was linked to Hitler, to reinforce the necessity of standing up to dictators. "Half a century ago, the world had the chance to stop a ruthless aggressor and missed it. I pledge to you: We will not make the same mistake again."

Possibly because the Vietnam syndrome had come to overshadow all foreign policy, Bush needed a historical analogy that would convince the American public that this was the fight worth fighting to the end. In doing so, Bush tried to avoid parallels between the Gulf crisis and Vietnam, which carried the stigma of a protracted and unwinnable involvement in a foreign war, by using Munich as the relevant analogy. When Bush announced that he was sending forces to Saudi Arabia, he reminded the country that "a half century ago our nation and the world paid dearly for appeasing an aggressor who should and could have been stopped. We're not about to make that mistake twice."

Bush invoked the Munich analogy to persuade other nations that the world would be even more dangerous if the United States were to refuse to fight, and also used it when he praised the Soviet leader Mikhail Gorbachev for condemning the Iraqi invasion. He said that this demonstrated "that nations which joined to fight aggression in the Second World War can work together to stop the aggressors of today." Consequently, the construction of a narrative in which Munich, not Vietnam, served as the perfect unifying symbol struck just the right chord.

CONCLUSION

Political leaders have used the Munich analogy to justify what they believe is critical foreign intervention and to remind the public of its obligations to defend liberty. They also have used it to divert attention away from thorny "public relations" problems such as the Vietnam War syndrome and even to discredit critics. In fact, the "lesson" of Munich has continued to be relevant even in the present, as each generation ostensibly seeks to avoid the mistakes of its predecessors. Just as the leaders of the 1930s learned much from World War I, post–World War II and Cold War leaders learned much from Munich: the consequences of futile good intentions. And while leaders of the twenty-first century may not fully comprehend the process whereby the Munich agreement became the prologue to the even greater tragedy of World War II, they do seem unlikely to dismiss it from their realm of political discourse. As Donald N. Lammers reminds us in *Explaining Munich*, "Taken one way or another, Munich has become the great 'object lesson' of our age."

BIBLIOGRAPHY

Abel, Elie. *The Missiles of October: The Story of the Cuban Missile Crisis, 1962.* London, 1966.

Beck, Robert J. "Munich's Lessons Reconsidered." *International Security* 14 (1989): 161–191.

Cannon, Lou. *President Reagan: The Role of a Lifetime.* New York, 1991.

Fry, Michael G., ed. *History, the White House, and the Kremlin: Statesmen as Historians.* London, 1991. Depicts historical knowledge as one of the basic intellectual resources used by statesmen habitually if unevenly.

Graebner, Norman A. *Roosevelt and the Search for a European Policy, 1937–1939.* Oxford, 1980. A realist critique of FDR's policies.

Henderson, Nevile. *Failure of a Mission: Berlin, 1937–1939.* London, 1940.

Immerman, Richard H. "The U.S. and the Geneva Conference of 1954: A New Look." *Diplomatic History* 14 (1990): 51–74.

Kennan, George F. *Russia and the West under Lenin and Stalin.* New York, 1962. An important American perspective.

Khong, Yuen Foong. *Analogies at War: Korea, Munich, Dien Bien Phu, and the Vietnam Decisions of 1965.* Princeton, N.J., 1992. The best available introduction to the subject of analogizing history.

Kiewe, Amos. *The Modern Presidency and Crisis Rhetoric.* Westport, Conn., 1994.

Lammers, Donald N. *Explaining Munich: The Search for Motive in British Policy.* Stanford, Calif., 1966. Doubts that a desire to destroy Soviet Russia played a role in British calculations.

May, Ernest R. *"Lessons" of the Past: The Use and Misuse of History in American Foreign Policy.* New York, 1973. Argues that policymakers often use history badly.

May, Ernest R., and Philip Zelikov. *The Kennedy Tapes: Inside the White House during the Cuban Missile Crisis.* Cambridge, Mass., 1997.

Medhurst, Martin J., and H. W. Brands, eds. *Critical Reflections on the Cold War: Linking Rhetoric and History.* College Station, Tex., 2000. Writings by historians and communications scholars on Cold War discourse.

Neustadt, Richard E., and Ernest R. May. *Thinking in Time: The Uses of History for Decision-Makers.* New York, 1986.

Noguères, Henri. *Munich or the Phoney Peace.* Translated from the French by Patrick O'Brien. London, 1963. Critical discussion of the French role at Munich.

Public Papers of President John F. Kennedy, 1962. Washington, D.C., 1964.

Robbins, Keith. *Munich 1938.* London, 1968. Argues that there are no great "lessons" to be learned from Munich.

Rostow, W. W. *The American Diplomatic Revolution.* Oxford, 1946.

Rystad, Göran. *Prisoners of the Past? The Munich Syndrome and Makers of American Foreign Policy in the Cold War Era.* Lund, 1982.

Shepardson, Donald E. "Munich Reconsidered." *Midwest Quarterly* 23 (1981): 78–102.

Siracusa, Joseph M. *Into the Dark House: American Diplomacy and the Ideological Origins of the Cold War.* Claremont, Calif., 1998. Argues that American Cold War politicians, policymakers, and diplomats were greatly influenced by the events of the interwar period.

Small, Melvin, and Otto Feinstein, eds. *Appeasing Fascism.* Lanham, Md., 1991.

Taylor, Andrew J., and John T. Rourke. "Historical Analogies in the Congressional Foreign Policy Process." *Journal of Politics* 57 (1995): 460–468. A useful survey.

Taylor, Telford. *Munich: The Price of Peace.* Garden City, N.Y., 1979. A defense of Chamberlain's appeasement policy.

U.S. Department of State. *Foreign Relations of the United States, 1939.* Washington, D.C., 1956.

Weinberg, Gerhard L. "Munich After 50 Years." *Foreign Affairs* 67 (1988): 165–178.

Wheeler-Bennett, John W. *Munich: Prologue to Tragedy.* London, 1966. Classic treatment of Munich, from a British perspective.

See also ARBITRATION, MEDIATION, AND CONCILIATION; COLD WAR EVOLUTION AND INTERPRETATIONS; COLD WAR ORIGINS; INTERVENTION AND NONINTERVENTION; ISOLATIONISM.

NARCOTICS POLICY

William O. Walker III

Efforts to control the production of and traffic in illicit drugs, commonly referred to as "the war on drugs," seem like a relatively recent phenomenon. The visibility of struggles since the late 1970s against drug organizations, or "cartels," based in the prosperous Colombian cities of Cali and Medellín did much to shape that perception. Narcotraffickers, as major figures in the South American drug business are called, were responsible for the influx of powdered cocaine, crack cocaine, and, increasingly since the late 1980s, heroin into the United States.

Public awareness of drug control as an aspect of U.S. foreign policy likely began with Operation Intercept in August 1969. U.S. officials designed Intercept as an intensive effort to curb the flow of marijuana and other drugs from Mexico into California. Within two years, as narcotics like heroin began entering the United States in unprecedented amounts from various points of origin, President Richard M. Nixon had declared a war on drugs, calling them a serious threat to the security of the nation.

The Colombian, Mexican, and other examples illustrate the fact that campaigns to control drugs have a history of their own, unknown though they may be. The impetus for international drug control, commencing at the beginning of the twentieth century, arose from concern among industrialized nations, most notably the United States, about the havoc that drugs could potentially wreak upon society. Alarmed at the incidence of opium smoking in their new colony in the Philippines, U.S. authorities acted to stamp out the practice among the overseas Chinese population. They discontinued Spain's contract system under which Chinese smokers had purchased opium from licensed dens. Surprisingly elimination of the Spanish system actually increased the availability of smoking opium in the islands and led as well to a greater incidence of usage by the Filipinos themselves.

The motivation behind opium prohibition was simultaneously moralistic and economic. In the eyes of reformers and U.S. officials, good Christians only consumed intoxicants like tobacco and alcohol if they consumed any such substances at all. The smoking of opium betokened spiritual degradation if not personal depravity. Moreover, colonials habituated to opium and opiates were deemed unproductive subjects who potentially could weaken a market economy. Drug usage therefore had no place in the American empire or, for that matter, in any colonial setting.

For nearly a century the United States clung to the idea of control at the source as the only possible path to effective drug control. Whether at international parleys or through bilateral and regional diplomatic efforts, U.S. officials steadfastly pursued this goal. At the same time, as this essay demonstrates, drug control did not, indeed could not, exist in a vacuum isolated from other foreign policy concerns. Ultimately this state of affairs meant that control at the source had to give way to competing, often more important, priorities. During World War II, for instance, drug policy reflected the exigencies of global war by encouraging the production of raw narcotic material should it be necessary for the medical needs of the Allies. Throughout the Cold War, U.S. drug control officials frequently subordinated their traditional objectives to larger security considerations. This practice all too often entailed countenancing involvement with illicit drugs by so-called security assets. In the 1990s, as the Cold War ended, efforts by the United States to promote comprehensive drug control abroad became indistinguishable from the very issues of governance and state stability. This was particularly true in the Andes, most notably in Colombia, and to a lesser extent in Mexico.

THE ORIGINS OF DRUG CONTROL

The United States was not the first imperial power to try to halt the consumption of proscribed substances. Spanish authorities in colonial Peru, for instance, reversed their early tolerance of coca chewing, known as *el coqueo,* as they sought to transform indigenous Inca culture and develop a productive workforce to serve Spain's material and spiritual interests. In the process there arose a debate, which continued well into the twentieth century, over whether to prohibit native cultivation and use of coca. Like coca, opium has a complex past that is intermingled with issues of culture and power. The grafting of opium onto the culture of China roughly coincides with the history of the Qing dynasty. Opium smoking, likely enjoyed first by Chinese in Jakarta, Indonesia, evolved out of the habit of tobacco smoking. By the time of the mid-nineteenth century Opium Wars, when the dynasty showed unmistakable signs of instability, opium addiction permeated Chinese society.

The persistence of *el coqueo* among the indigenous people of Peru and the prevalence of opium cultivation and smoking among the very poor in China coincided around 1900 with a wave of reform, or prohibitionist, sentiments in both countries. The War of the Pacific, in which Chile defeated both Peru and Bolivia, lasted from 1879 to 1883 and briefly devastated Peru. Andean Indians endured especially oppressive conditions in the war's aftermath. The prospect of political change and with it, a wide spectrum of social reforms, revitalized Peru after a revolution in 1895. Inevitably some reformers asked whether traditional Indian reliance on coca had a place in modern Peru. Around the same time in Asia, the Qing dynasty came under intense pressure from Confucian scholars and others to implement broad reforms as foreign powers vied with one another to obtain concessions and create spheres of influence. Destroying the opium business became a basic part of the reform agenda in China. Chang Chih-tung, a powerful scholar-official and advocate of reform, wrote, "The development of education is the best medicine to use for the suppression of opium."

DRUGS IN THE UNITED STATES

The emergence of a drug culture, usually called a subculture, also occurred during an age of reform in the United States. The Progressive Era, as scholars have characterized the U.S. political scene, began around 1890 and persisted until just after 1920. The reform spirit of the time arose out of a felt need for order and stability amid waves of immigration, the promises and challenges of industrial consolidation, and recurring threats of recession. The historian Richard Hofstadter found that the reformers were responding to real conditions that needed to be addressed in a nation undergoing rapid urbanization. Perhaps more important, he also believed that they were engaged in a quest for meaning in their lives and, hence, were desirous of finding something akin to the sense of mission that had earlier inspired the Civil War generation. Social reform naturally became one of the causes they championed.

To be sure, Americans had inveighed against drink throughout their history, especially since the Jacksonian era. The influx of immigrants, many of whom drank as a matter of course, gave the temperance movement a new urgency in the late nineteenth century. Assimilation through acculturation became the standard by which reformers measured the success of their endeavors to transform immigrants into good Americans.

Moral and social reformers did not limit their evangelism to newcomers. They sought to curb, if not stop, excessive drinking among the male citizenry of the republic and tried to restrict, if not eliminate, the practice of prostitution. Ultimately they turned their attention to the use and abuse of opiates. In their striving to make the United States what is now inaccurately termed a "drug-free" nation, reformers created a deviant class within society. Before reformers singled out and stereotyped casual users and addicts as deviants, though, the educated and the well respected were more likely to use narcotics than members of the working class, who typically drank alcohol because of its comparatively low cost. The medical community, for instance, especially seemed to fall prey to opiate abuse. By the early 1900s researchers feared that middle-class women, young people with time on their hands, and hard-working, progressive professionals would succumb to the temptation of drugs.

The concern that educated whites would find drug use an exhilarating experience had some basis in fact. No less a social reformer than Jane Addams wrote in her account of life at Hull House that she and four classmates had experimented with opium while attending Rockford College. The data are not available to establish the extent of drug abuse or addiction during the Progressive Era; estimates range widely between one hundred thousand and one million persons. Usage, of course, often remained a secret known only to the user's doctor or druggist. Despite public impressions that addiction was rapidly increasing, consumption may actually have been in decline in the early 1900s. Consequently the reality of a serious drug problem at that time remains open to question.

Even before the inception of progressivism, some reformers in the United States, baffled by the intractability of addiction, associated the prevalence of drugs in America with a foreign presence. These reformers did not directly charge foreigners with causing America's problem with drugs. What they were alleging was rather more sinister. They contended that foreigners, often Asians, and other purveyors of drugs had managed to unlock the worst instincts of the American populace. That is, many Americans were predisposed to surrender themselves to the drug habit "based as it is," in the words of a Massachusetts physician, "upon a [human] craving no laws can eradicate."

It seems evident, therefore, that reformers in several drug producing or consuming countries around the world had a common objective in the early twentieth century: to save from themselves those people living in a culture of drugs. Drug reformers rarely asked whether their basic assumptions about the drug cultures within their societies were accurate. By failing to so inquire, they consigned those subcultures to the margins of society. The ready identification of involvement with drugs as characteristic of a dangerous culture enabled Washington to promote its style of drug control as a desperately needed international goal. In 1903 the governing Philippine Commission failed in its attempt to return to the Spanish contract system in the Philippines. Charles H. Brent, Episcopal bishop of the Philippines and a leading antidrug crusader, declared the entire opium enterprise from import to sale to consumption an unacceptable "social vice . . . a crime."

A report by the Philippine Opium Committee, set up in 1903 to study opium throughout East Asia, had recommended the creation of a government monopoly in the islands. Deriving revenue from opium, critics charged, would make the United States no different from Great Britain, which was still selling chests of Indian opium to the Chinese. Thus the U.S. Congress passed a law in 1905 mandating for the Philippines the total prohibition by 1 March 1908 of all commerce in opium except for governmental and medical purposes. As the law went into effect the opium business went underground, thereby creating not only an illegal drug subculture but also a chronic law enforcement problem.

The inability of law enforcement personnel in the Philippines to curtail the illicit trade in opium allowed the United States to propose a deceptively simple solution to the emerging global drug problem: control at the source. First at Shanghai in 1909 and thereafter at three meetings held at The Hague beginning in 1911, U.S. officials, notably with the help of Chinese reformers, called upon other major powers to control the production and manufacturing of narcotics. How such controls would come about could not easily be agreed upon. The British, for example, were reluctant to put a premature end to the declining Indian trade, and commercial interests in China did not want to surrender a lucrative source of revenue. Asian opium smokers living outside of China understandably feared the loss of accustomed access to their drug.

The Shanghai meeting constituted the opening skirmish in what some analysts have called a new Hundred Years' War: the campaigns to control drugs in the twentieth century. The U.S. delegation, led by Brent and Dr. Hamilton Wright, who was well known for his work in Asia on communicable diseases, knew that mobilizing an antiopium alliance would be no easy task. The meeting accomplished little more, therefore, than the introduction of the issue of opium control. Great Britain, for its part, continued not unreasonably to doubt China's willingness and ability to prevent the spread of poppy production and opium smoking.

Shanghai did, however, set the stage for additional international meetings and gave Wright and other reformers a basis for insisting that the U.S. Congress pass domestic drug control legislation. Armed with the moral high ground for having put in place a program of strict prohibition in its Asian colony, the United States was determined to accept nothing less than the same from other regional imperial powers, namely the British, the French, and the Dutch. The realities of the economic importance of opium in East and Southeast Asia and the inception of the Great War impeded American plans. Other major nations in attendance at the Hague Opium Conference of 1911–1912 agreed only to take preliminary steps to bring the illicit trade in opium under control.

Meanwhile the United States moved toward passage of its first comprehensive drug control law, the Harrison Act of 1914. During the first week of the Shanghai meeting the U.S. Congress had prohibited the importation of smoking opium. The limited and, for Wright, disappointing outcome of the meeting at Shanghai convinced him to intensify his efforts on behalf of federal regulation. Only when the United States had in place adequate federal antidrug legislation, he reasoned, could America legitimately ask other nations to follow its lead.

Fears based on race and class clinched the case for federal drug control. America's cultural majority perceived heroin, which was usually taken through subcutaneous injection, and cocaine, a drug reportedly favored by African Americans in the South, as substances that decent people shied away from. By definition those who consumed these drugs were exhibiting antisocial, deviant behavior. Since the American public feared the spread of addiction and its attendant dangerous and often criminal behavior, the advocates of federal control had virtually no trouble making their case.

With scant debate Congress passed the Harrison Narcotics Act in December 1914. President Woodrow Wilson soon signed it into law, and it took effect on 1 March 1915. This law, typical of the regulatory legislation of its time, promised to promote cultural homogeneity and social stability through the unlikely though quintessentially progressive device of revenue collection. Despite widespread popular support for prohibition, the Harrison law did not cut off access to narcotics any more than imperial edicts in Qing China had eliminated the practice of opium smoking.

THE TROUBLED 1920S AND 1930S

Ironically the domestic successes of drug reformers adversely affected U.S. efforts to promote a global antidrug strategy of control at the source. Expectations in America about how long it would take to put comprehensive controls into effect did not accord with the reality of the situation abroad. Any delay was unconscionable, in the view of some American observers, because the international drug problem had evidently become a grave one. "[S]muggling of narcotics in the United States," lamented Secretary of the Treasury Andrew W. Mellon in 1921, "is on the increase to such an extent that the customs officers are unable to suppress the traffic to any appreciable extent." The secretary's assertion gave anecdotal credence to unfounded public perceptions about the severity of the drug situation.

The newly created Advisory Committee on Traffic in Opium and Other Dangerous Drugs (OAC) of the League of Nations took charge of supervising the obligations incurred by the states signatory to the Hague conventions. Private individuals and those government officials who favored strict drug control doubted whether member states as well as the league itself possessed the political will to enact strict drug control measures. An impasse between Washington and Geneva developed during the early 1920s and kept the United States from influencing the work of the OAC until early in the 1930s. The Department of State's Division of Far Eastern Affairs, the bureau responsible for implementing drug policy, had initially hoped to find some way of cooperating with the OAC. In that spirit Dr. Rupert Blue, formerly the U.S. assistant surgeon general, attended the fourth session of the OAC in January 1923. He made it clear in his remarks to the OAC that the United States held both producing and manufacturing states responsible for escalating international drug problems. In Blue's estimation the only recourse was to call for strict controls on production and manufacture. Representative Stephen G. Porter, chairman of the powerful House Foreign Affairs Committee, who was as adamant as Blue about what U.S. foreign drug policy should be, wrote Secretary of State Charles Evans Hughes that "an effective remedy [to drug problems] cannot be secured by compromise."

Porter quickly transformed Blue's skepticism about the OAC into outright hostility. In May 1923 at the fifth session of the OAC, Porter refused even to engage in debate about U.S. proposals for immediate, comprehensive controls on manufacturing. In defense of his position, which had caused much consternation at Geneva, he belligerently remarked: "If when I get back to America anybody says 'League of Nations' to me, he ought to say it conveniently near a hospital." Porter's bellicosity was in line with Department of State thinking. Secretary Hughes had made it clear that the nonmedical or nonscientific use of drugs was unacceptable and that global production of narcotics had to be controlled. In so doing, Hughes captured the essence of the dogmatic approach to drug control—control at the source—that the United States has pursued throughout the twentieth century. Hughes once observed: "Unrestricted production leads to uncontrollable consumption, especially when the product enters international channels." This assessment of the roots of the drug problem in America resulted in February 1924 in a walkout, led by Porter, of the U.S. delegation from the second Geneva Opium Conference, which had been convened to discuss the manufacturing of narcotics. Other states in attendance would not accept without reservations an American-initiated proposal to bring a rapid cessation to the drug business.

Compounding matters, and making multilateral action against drugs difficult to achieve, was the willingness to hold foreigners responsible, if not accountable, for whatever problems impaired U.S. antidrug efforts. The substances that most captured the attention of U.S. officials in the 1920s were opiates and, to a much lesser extent, cocaine and marijuana. Opiate traffic, increasingly in the form of heroin instead of smoking opium, primarily originated in East Asia. Heroin, once believed by some in the medical community to be a cure for morphine addiction, had initially reached a wide audience as a medicine for coughs courtesy of the Bayer chemical company of Germany. A manufactured drug, heroin could be synthesized from morphine fairly easily; as a result, officials could not readily pinpoint the precise origin of the heroin found in the illicit trade.

In the early 1920s drug manufacturing was concentrated among European nations, the United States, and Japan. The U.S. Congress had tried to control the export of manufactured drugs in a section of the Narcotic Drugs Import and Export Act of 1922 by requiring exporters of such drugs to possess a proper certificate from the importing country. Congress amended the act in 1924 to prohibit opium importation for the manufacture of heroin. This legislation was meant to serve as a model for other countries but did not prevent the diversion of heroin manufactured outside the United States into illegal international channels.

The reluctance of manufacturing states to accede to controls that would mean a loss of market share turned the attention of the U.S. government to the less economically advanced drug-producing nations. Perhaps surprisingly Washington did not redouble prior efforts to curb opium poppy growth in China. Nor did diplomats serving in the Andes pressure leaders in Peru or Bolivia, where *el coqueo* was an integral part of national culture, to force peasants to stop farming coca. The fall of China after 1915 into a decade of internal strife dominated by regional warlords made efforts to halt poppy growing impossible. Not surprisingly, opium played a vital role in China's economy during the warlord era. As for cocaine, many urban users switched to heroin as a cheaper drug of choice after scarcity and strict enforcement of state laws combined to drive up black-market prices for cocaine. Accordingly U.S. officials encouraged Andean nations to move toward gradual compliance with international agreements relating to coca production. More serious problems lay elsewhere.

It was almost by process of elimination, therefore, that Mexico emerged as the country where U.S. officials hoped to demonstrate that control at the source was possible. Turkey and Persia, as producers of vast quantities of raw opium for both the licit and illicit trade, would also have been suitable candidates for such an effort. Turkey, though, refused to comply with anti-opium agreements until 1932, which rendered diplomatic overtures from Washington useless. Persia, which by 1920 had replaced India in the opium trade with East Asia, depended heavily on opium-based revenue and had a deeply entrenched opium culture of its own, one that transcended class lines. As a result, implementation of international accords by either country was not feasible in the 1920s and early 1930s. Diplomatic efforts to force compliance would almost certainly have failed. Mexico therefore became the proving ground for control at the source.

Mexico's proximity to the United States had rarely served it well. Not only had Mexico lost in war territory that became the states of New Mexico, Arizona, and California, it had also experienced U.S. involvement and intervention in its revolution during the 1910s. On economic and political matters the United States had frequently treated Mexican sovereignty as subordinate to Washington's own national interests. So it would be, commencing in the 1920s, with the issue of drug control.

The United States disdained Mexican sovereignty for several reasons. In the first place many government authorities and private citizens looked upon Mexico's Indian heritage as evidence of an inferior race. To make matters worse in the eyes of their detractors, the people of Mexico were not just inferior; they were unpredictable, an unpardonable trait in the age of progressive reform. In other words, cultural cohesion and political order in Mexico seemed unimaginable to many North Americans. Critics had to look no farther than Pancho Villa's raid on Columbus, New

Mexico, in March 1916 for incontrovertible proof of this societal failing. Villa's men, rumor had it, steeled themselves for the raid by smoking marijuana; Villa himself reputedly neither smoked marijuana nor drank intoxicating beverages.

Marijuana seemed to be in plentiful supply along the vast open border between the two countries. U.S. officials concluded, not for the last time, that Mexican authorities lacked the political will to fight domestically produced drugs. With the creation of a black market for opiates in the United States following the enactment of the Harrison law, Mexico became an important transit country for illicit substances. Citizens of Yuma, Arizona, appealed in 1924 to the Department of State for help in dealing with the "unbridled vice and debauchery" they contended was plaguing the border region.

Moreover, corruption served to undermine Mexico's drug control efforts into the 1920s. In fact the matter was as much a question of the limits of federal authority as one of corruption, but U.S. critics of Mexico emphasized corruption wherever they seemed to find it. The State Department, predisposed to see corruption by Mexican officials who were believed to harbor Bolshevist sympathies, allowed a 1926 treaty with Mexico for the exchange of information about drugs to lapse after only one year of operation. U.S. consular officials in Ciudad Juárez had long doubted Mexico's good faith about drug control. When authorities in Mexico City dispatched a special agent to the Juárez–El Paso region in 1931, U.S. Consul William P. Blocker commented disdainfully, "The Mexican Government has at last decided to clean up the drug traffic on this section of the border."

That attitude and the coercive diplomacy to which it gave rise would often characterize U.S. antidrug diplomacy, particularly in the Americas, from the 1930s through the 1980s; it tended to ignore not only the historical but also the practical reasons limiting the prospects for control at the source. The blinders that U.S. bureaucrats wore as they endeavored to contend with illegal drug trafficking for more than fifty years made it hard for them to understand why their presumably unobjectionable goals were unattainable.

In contrast to their attitude toward Mexico, U.S. officials did not judge Bolivia, Persia, or China to be models worthy of emulation in the pursuit of control at the source. In the case of Bolivia, folk wisdom had maintained long before the modern era that without coca there would be no Bolivia. The movement toward coca prohibition that surfaced from time to time before 1900 in Peru had made few discernible inroads into Bolivia. For U.S. authorities to presume that they could alter the real economic and symbolic value of Bolivian coca was akin to cultural arrogance. Try they did, however, to influence public policy in Bolivia, although not as overtly as in Mexico. Conferees at the first Opium Conference at The Hague had agreed that drug control could never become a reality unless coca and cocaine were included among the substances being controlled. That determination meant that effective coca control must come to Bolivia. U.S. representatives in La Paz suggested to government officials there that cuts in coca production would indicate Bolivia's willingness to work with the international drug control movement. The effort got nowhere.

At Geneva in 1924 the Bolivian delegate, Arturo Pinto Escalier, said that his government found coca chewing to be "a perfectly innocuous activity." More to the point he identified how vital coca was to maintaining the integrity of Bolivian culture. It would, he had previously told the OAC, "be impossible for the Bolivian Government to contemplate restricting the production of coca leaves without seriously interfering with the needs and economic life of the working population, particularly in mining districts, as coca leaves constitute for them a source of energy which cannot be replaced." The United States would have to look elsewhere for control at the source.

The situation in Persia was also instructive for U.S. policy goals. Prior to the second Geneva Opium Conference, Moshar-ol-Molk, Persian minister for foreign affairs, declared that it would be difficult to establish an international anti-opium movement. The foremost obstacle was economic, even for those states fundamentally in agreement with the strict U.S. objectives. It was "impracticable suddenly to place a prohibition on [the opium business] without . . . the substitution of other products for the production of opium, and the adoption of an appropriate decision whereby the domestic consumption of opium could be gradually stopped."

Persia's request for a program of crop substitution did not catch U.S. officials off guard. Elizabeth Washburn Wright, the widow of Dr. Hamilton Wright, had examined firsthand the opium situation there and became an advocate of increased silk production as a replacement for opium. She made the case for economic diversification in informal conversations with the Department of State and in her capacity as an assessor to the Opium Advisory Committee.

A former State Department economic adviser, Arthur C. Millspaugh, who headed the American Financial Mission to Persia from 1922 to 1927, also made the connection between Persia's economic stability and the status of the opium trade. In the course of reorganizing Persia's finances the American mission assumed the task of collecting opium revenues. Millspaugh soon realized that any precipitous change in the opium situation would probably result in economic chaos and political instability. At the urging of the mission Persia indicated its willingness as early as 1923 gradually to reduce dependence on opium, particularly if foreign assistance were forthcoming. No one should underestimate opium's importance, Millspaugh noted, because "irrespective of the revenue which is derived by the Government from it, opium-cultivation in Persia constitutes one of the important agricultural industries, and the only one which makes any substantial contribution to the export trade."

By mid-1926, however, the Persian government, on Millspaugh's advice, had withdrawn an official request for a U.S. loan to help finance the difficult transition from opium to other commodities. U.S. officials had let it be known that they did not want to set a precedent by underwriting such a momentous change. If American banks bailed out Persia's drug-reliant economy, would they do the same for Bolivia or China? What would be the limits of such a potentially open-ended commitment? Also, why would banks invest heavily in an agriculturally based economy like Persia's? Short-term profits were unlikely to flow from the agricultural sectors of the world economy in the 1920s. Nor did the United States, after its withdrawal from the Geneva Opium Conference in 1925, want to be even remotely associated with the work of the league. A league-sponsored commission of inquiry to Persia after the Geneva conference recommended consideration of a crop substitution program. Persia itself, having worked within the confines of Millspaugh's mission since 1922, was increasingly unwilling further to surrender its financial autonomy to foreign control. For the foreseeable future the substitution of other crops for opium remained out of the question in Persia.

As for China, well into the 1920s conditions there were so chaotic that there existed no realistic hope for implementation of controls on opium growing. Even before the death of Yuan Shikai in mid-1916 and the subsequent onset of the warlord period, opium production and consumption was spreading throughout China, as had been the case in the late nineteenth century. British Minister Sir John Jordan, believing that the situation would lead to a desperate quest by the government for a reliable source of revenue, termed a proposal to establish an opium monopoly "a retrograde step." Opium's hold on China precluded the chance for significant reform. To American officials, plans to create a government opium monopoly, which meant adopting and enforcing over time a program of gradual suppression, flew in the face of reason. By the mid-1920s U.S. authorities concluded that gradualism was merely a cover for continuation of the twin vices of opium production and consumption. Making matters worse for proponents of opium control was an apparently successful effort by Japanese nationals to dominate a burgeoning market in North China for illegal morphine.

U.S. appeals to Chinese authorities to control the situation where practicable fell on deaf ears. Having reasserted nominal Republican control of China with the success of the Northern Expedition in 1928, the government of Chiang Kai-shek (Jiang Jieshi) thereafter strove to appease Washington while continuing to profit from the trade. Headquartered in Nanking, Kuomintang leaders managed, simply by announcing a policy of suppression, largely to place the blame on Japan for China's opium troubles, many of which were of its own making. This accomplishment was all the more remarkable because of the Kuomintang's intimate ties to the notorious Green Gang of Shanghai, a secret society that dominated the Chinese underworld and by 1930 controlled a great percentage of the illicit trade in smoking opium in South China. Its most notorious figure, Du Yuesheng, headed the local opium suppression bureau at various times. Few knowledgeable foreigners believed that opium suppression would come anytime soon to Shanghai and, hence, to South China.

Japanese adventurism rendered largely irrelevant the actual steps taken against opium by Nationalist China. Herbert L. May of the New York–based Foreign Policy Association remarked in 1926 that the Japanese "were manufacturing drugs on a large scale and the government [in Tokyo] was closing its eyes to what was going on." Like the regional militarists, or *tuchuns,* of China's warlord era, Japanese civilian and military officials in North China and Manchuria were seeking to profit from the opium and morphine trade. The assassination in June 1928 of Zhang Zuolin helped to expose both Japan's expansionist ambitions in North China and beyond, as well as the role of its Kwantung Army in the opiate business there.

The League of Nations dispatched a Commission of Enquiry to East and Southeast Asia in September 1929 to investigate both opium traffic originating in China and the incidence of opium smoking among resident Chinese outside of China. The commissioners found that local opium cultures created more than a social problem; they created alternative, underground economies that helped to destabilize the political economy of the region. The commission, linking the opium business to the security of nations beyond Asia, predicted further trouble with opium unless China brought production under control. This concern was echoed by delegates and observers attending the Conference for the Suppression of Opium Smoking held at Bangkok in November 1931. The American observer, John Kenneth Caldwell of the Department of State, condemned the smuggling of opiates from East Asia, which he declared was a growing problem for the United States. Nanking's refusal to attend the Bangkok conference underlined the near stranglehold of opium on China.

China's unwillingness to participate at the Bangkok meeting derived in part, though, from the threat to its security posed by the seizure in September of Manchuria by Japan's Kwantung Army. Kuomintang leaders were persuaded that they would need all the resources they could muster, including those purchased by revenues from the opium trade, in order to contain Japan's advance into North China. In that sense the Mukden Incident, which precipitated the taking of Manchuria by Japan, allowed Chiang Kai-shek to continue to use opium revenues for his own political and economic purposes while at the same time blaming Japanese military forces for poisoning China with narcotics.

The United States, though suspicious of the Kuomintang's motives where opium suppression was concerned, increasingly supported China in its dispute with Japan over opium. The adoption of a tougher stand against Japan came with the appointment of Stuart J. Fuller to the position of narcotics chief in the State Department's Division of Far Eastern Affairs. Fuller had served in the 1920s as a consular official in Tanjin where he observed the growth of Japanese involvement with the narcotics trade in North China. Fuller's antinarcotic zeal was matched by that of Harry J. Anslinger, a onetime State Department official who had become commissioner of the Federal Bureau of Narcotics (FBN) with the creation of the bureau in 1930. Importantly, unlike their predecessors they were able to put aside tactical differences with the OAC and turn the League of Nation's efforts against drugs toward the larger American policy goals of drug control at the source and improved interdiction of the illicit narcotics traffic.

Under the obvious fiction of a suppression movement, opium production, consumption, and addiction worsened in Nationalist China. U.S. military attaché Colonel Joseph W. Stillwell succinctly summed up the situation when he observed, "Opium is the chief prop of all power in China, civil and military." U.S. reaction to conditions in China was remarkably muted. Fuller, U.S. ambassador Nelson T. Johnson, and Anslinger evidently believed that Chiang would turn against the traffic as soon as it was in his interest to do so. They therefore began to hold Japan to a stricter measure of accountability than China. Johnson wrote Fuller in March 1934 that the Japanese "have no moral scruples when it comes to opium or the use of the gun or the sword."

Even though Fuller actually did criticize China before the OAC in May 1936, he saved his strongest language for Japan. "Let us face facts," he intoned, "where Japanese influence advances in the Far East, what goes with it? Drug traffic." One year later, as tensions were mounting between China and Japan, he told the OAC that conditions in Japanese-occupied areas of North China were "appalling and beyond description." Yet neither in North China nor in Manchukuo were conditions quite what Fuller and other critics of Japan claimed them to be, either before or immediately after the inception of the Sino-Japanese War in July 1937. The reality of the situation scarcely mattered, however, to critics of Japanese expansion. To some observers the battle against drugs in North China was bigger than a mere defense of security. "Humanity," stated the *South China Morning Post,* "has come to rely heavily upon American aid in the war on drugs."

The characterization of American drug policy as a war on drugs precisely captured the spirit of what Fuller and Anslinger were trying to achieve in the 1930s through participation at OAC meetings and by means of bilateral diplomacy. In assessing the threat posed by drugs the two Americans viewed traffickers and producers of drugs as criminals who, in their most heinous incarnation, were also mortal enemies of the state.

Anslinger later wrote about the use of opium as a weapon of war in occupied China: "The Japanese had coldly calculated its devastating value as forerunner to an advancing army; long before the steel missiles began to fly, opium pellets were sent as a vanguard of the military attack." The inception of general war in Europe in September 1939 served to intensify American efforts to expose Japanese dependence on opiates as a way of maintaining order in their budding empire on the mainland. When the Pacific War spread to include the United States after the bombing of Pearl Harbor, the Federal Bureau of Narcotics chief declared in January 1942: "We in the Treasury Department have been in a war against Japanese narcotics policy for more than ten years. . . . We have experienced Pearl Harbors many times in the past in the nature of dangerous drugs from Japan which were meant to poison the blood of the American people."

In slightly more than a decade narcotics had become inseparable from the security of Washington's closest ally in Asia, China, and were playing a significant role in the development of Japan's foreign policy. It scarcely mattered whether high-level Japanese officials in Tokyo actually countenanced a policy of using drugs as a weapon of war in China at any time in the 1930s; what was important was the perception, especially in Washington, that they were doing so. In sum the drug scene in East Asia in the 1930s announced the opening of an era in which antidrug policy would become an important, if not well known, aspect of the foreign policy of many nations.

Developments in Latin America during the 1930s also offered an indication of how drugs could undermine political stability and civic order and thereby have a deleterious effect upon a nation's security. Shipments of illicit narcotics from Europe to Central America, which presumably were destined for the United States, nearly destabilized the Honduran government in the mid-1930s. While urging Honduras to deal more forcefully with the situation, Fuller and Anslinger were unable to determine the accuracy of reports alleging the involvement of North Americans in the trade.

That U.S. officials endeavored to influence the drug control policies of other countries partly resulted from a decision made by the League of Nations and reflected a tactical departure by Washington from its former hostility toward league-sponsored antinarcotic activities. The 1931 Manufacturing Limitation Convention had urged all countries, at the behest of the United States, to create an independent drug control office. In fact, the league singled out the Federal Bureau of Narcotics as a bureaucratic model that others might profitably adopt. Honduras, however, had neither the will nor the resources to follow the U.S. example.

More than any other country in the 1930s and early 1940s, with the possible exception of China, Mexico tested the limits of U.S. drug foreign policy. Would the United States be able to replicate abroad, whether through persuasion or coercion, its own restrictive approach to drug control? One prominent official in Mexico, Leopoldo Salazar Viniegra, did not believe that U.S. policy was worth emulating, a view essentially shared by domestic critics of Anslinger and the FBN. As a result of his dissent from Washington's supply-side philosophy, Salazar found himself the object of intense public and diplomatic pressures that proved impossible to resist. In August 1939 he was forced from office as head of the Federal Narcotics Service and was immediately replaced by an individual more inclined to follow the lead of the Department of State and the FBN. The change in personnel did not soon lead, however, to a noticeable improvement in the drug situation at the U.S.–Mexican border. That did not occur until World War II, when the two nations experienced limited success in controlling drugs. Even then progress seems to have reflected as much the decline in wartime demand for illicit drugs as a victory for control at the source.

ORIGINS OF THE DRUG-SECURITY NEXUS

The advent of global conflict in the late 1930s presented U.S. policymakers with an opportunity and a challenge. In the first place war in Europe and Asia slowed the world's illicit narcotics traffic, thus allowing Anslinger, Fuller, and George A. Morlock, who succeeded Fuller at the Department of State in 1941 upon Fuller's death, to strengthen U.S. influence over the global drug control movement by moving the operations of the Permanent Central Opium Board and the Drug Supervisory Body to the United States. By the end of the Second World War, U.S. officials were virtually setting the agenda of the Commission on Narcotic Drugs (CND) in the newly created United Nations. The commission essentially accepted U.S. antinarcotics objectives as its own well into the 1970s.

Anslinger and his colleagues did not easily meet the challenge posed by global war, which brought into question his conviction that he and other antidrug officials should be seen as prominent policymakers in Washington. Yet during both the immediate prewar years and the war itself, the Federal Bureau of Narcotics and the narcotics office in the Department of State helped to maintain the security of the West against the Axis powers. On the most basic level, the FBN commissioner was responsible for meeting Allied demands for medicinal drugs. He did so under a directive issued through the War Production Board by working with the Defense Supplies Corporation and the Board of Economic Warfare. So long as the primary opium-producing nations outside of China neither fell to Germany or Japan nor adopted a neutral position in the war, Anslinger's task was fairly straightforward.

In the Americas the FBN learned, however, that Argentina and Chile might be producing opiates for Germany. There existed some fear too that opium from Peru and Mexico could find its way to the Axis. In the case of Argentina, Anslinger threatened unspecified reprisals against one major firm, Hoffmann-LaRoche Inc., if the allegations were proven. In the case of Peru, its role in the Allied war effort was secured by the sale of cocaine for medicinal needs through the lend-lease program. And in what can be interpreted as an important foray into the world of intelligence, the U.S. government may have paid informants as much as $10,000 per year during the war for information about drug production in Mexico.

Moreover, the inexorable spread of Japanese influence into the fertile poppy-growing regions of Burma gave the Japanese government a major source of opium for its medical needs. Anslinger and other U.S. officials did manage to prevent a similar accretion of Japanese power and influence in the Near East in Iran and Turkey by engaging in a preemptive purchase of large quantities of opium from those two willing suppliers. Anslinger would subsequently have the occasion in the early Cold War to reward the Iranian government for its wartime loyalty, if that is an apt description, to the Allied cause by not pressing the young shah on Iran's vast production of illicit opium, much of which found its way onto the black market in Indochina. Such diplomatic largess was repaid following the shah's ascension to the peacock throne in the wake of the coup of 1953 against Mohammad Mossaddeq's regime, when Iran became a reliable ally at the UN's Commission on Narcotic Drugs in the global struggle against drugs.

Providing the Allies with reliable sources of narcotics during the war and overseeing the maintenance of the global antiopium apparatus were not, however, the most important actions Anslinger undertook to guarantee the relevance of his bureau to U.S. global security interests. He avidly interpreted President Franklin D. Roosevelt's vague anticolonial sentiments regarding Southeast Asia as a clarion call to eliminate opium smoking from the former colonial possessions of France, Great Britain, and the Netherlands. Anslinger and officials in the State Department warned that continued opium smoking would render former colonies more susceptible to internal decay and, as a result, to either revolution or foreign subversion.

In the immediate aftermath of the war Anslinger was not so preoccupied with the FBN's role in the national security state that he ignored the opportunity to advance his country's supply-side agenda at the United Nations. Two examples demonstrate his remarkable attention to virtually all drug-related matters and at the same time reveal his apparent inability to learn from past experience about the limits of policies based upon the elusive goal of control at the source.

The end of the war witnessed both a gradual rise in drug use and addiction in the United States and the revival of an active, illicit drug trade from Mexico. Not satisfied with the dilatory response of the Mexican government to diplomatic overtures, Anslinger took Mexico to task in 1947 at the second meeting of the CND for what he saw as unacceptable laxity in its antidrug activity. The public rebuke evidently had the desired effect because officials in Mexico City soon promised to strengthen their antidrug efforts at home and became more actively involved in the work of the CND.

U.S. drug control authorities also feared that prosperity after the war might stimulate the international cocaine trade, which had substantially declined in volume even before the onset of the Great Depression. Hoping to prevent a recurrence they supported sending a mission to Bolivia and Peru, the purpose of which was to evaluate the place of coca in modern Andean society. Wartime developments led U.S. officials to believe that Peru might be willing to consider strictly controlling coca leaf production, but that hope proved premature. The Commission of Inquiry on the Coca Leaf recalled the integral place of coca in the Andes and concluded that only either improved socioeconomic conditions in producing regions or stronger government action, meaning political will, could bring about the desired results. Important for present purposes is that nothing about the commission's findings, however negative in tone, persuaded U.S. officials to question their belief that Andean authorities were more or less favorably disposed toward a U.S.-style coca control program. The basic assumption that control at the source was a matter of time in the Andes would not be seriously challenged until the 1960s and after.

Instances like those involving Mexico and Bolivia and Peru were not unimportant to U.S. officials in the early Cold War, but they do not adequately show the intersection of security policy and drug control activities. It was in Asia that such a nexus was most readily discernible. FBN and State Department officials alleged that communists in China, like the Japanese before them, were prepared to ply their enemies with opium in order to suit their ideological ends. With the coming to power of the Chinese Communist Party in October 1949 and its subsequent exclusion of Western influence from China, Anslinger's allegations about drug-related subversion of the West and Japan from Beijing could not be disproved. But having an adversary that was presumably willing to use narcotics as a weapon of war appeared to support the FBN chief's traditional supply-side strategy. The Chinese communists had learned a vital lesson, however, by observing the actions of imperial Japan as it sought to subjugate China in the late 1930s: a people drugged with opium do not make good subjects.

Communist China's centrality to the issue of drugs and security policy in the early Cold War merits elaboration. Traffic in heroin destined for Western markets resumed as World War II came to an end. Despite indications that the source of opium came partially from those areas of China controlled by the Kuomintang, Anslinger and the State Department were reluctant to blame their Chinese friends for the reappearance of the trade. For some months before the communists seized power and for some years thereafter, policymakers in Washington blamed Mao Zedong's forces for orchestrating the world heroin business. The less Western observers had access to China and its remote opium-growing regions, the stronger the allegations were against the communists. Occasional doubters, whether in London or Washington, were drowned out by the mass of unverifiable information emanating from the FBN and Foggy Bottom. The CND became an important vehicle for disseminating Anslinger's anti-China message.

It is hard not to conclude that a campaign of intentional disinformation was taking place. Available evidence indicates that to an extremely limited extent some communists did seek to exchange opiates for hard currency. There is no reliable indication, however, of a plan on the part of the Chinese Communist Party to demoralize the West with heroin. Instead it seems more likely that the head of the FBN, in making his allegations against the communists, actually was collaborating in the effort to hide covert operations against the Beijing government by Kuomintang forces operating out of the Golden Triangle, the heart of opium production and traffic in Asia. The objectives of U.S. security policy toward China, although in theory separate from drug control policy, had taken precedence over the pursuit of control at the source, which in the early 1950s was seen by some officials in Washington as an obstacle to the containment of communism.

In Thailand the logic of Cold War policy fashioned dubious linkages with unscrupulous leaders like General Phao Sriyanon, whose personal and political fortunes derived from and depended upon the trade in opium. Throughout Indochina numerous participants in the opium trade, whether in the hills or the cities, offered their allegiance to the United States and its allies in Saigon. In return their reliance upon opium as a source of income remained undisturbed and probably increased. The export trade in heroin from Southeast Asia grew rapidly. And in Indochina the appearance of U.S. advisers in the 1950s and combat forces a decade later sparked a resurgence of the regional drug trade. Thus the 1953 UN Opium Conference, which on paper adopted a spectrum of controls on opium, was an exercise in futility where Southeast Asia was concerned. Rising levels of drug usage and addiction in the West by 1960 and after resulted to some extent from a countenancing of the drug trade in the name of national security.

The convergence of narcotics policy and security interests in the early Cold War made drugs available to untold numbers of Americans. Another important long-term legacy of the drug and security policy nexus from the 1950s onward was the willingness of authorities to ignore the drug-related activities of Central Intelligence Agency assets such as the contras in Nicaragua, General Manuel Noriega in Panama, spymaster Vladimiro Montesinos in Peru, and others, until those assets became expendable. A drug policy bureaucracy that set aside its own primary goals in the name of security was virtually abandoning the right to define its own mission. Objectively, illicit drug trafficking constituted a serious foreign policy problem for the United States, not a dire threat to the nation. Yet the historical efforts of Anslinger and others to propagate a supply-side strategy as the only acceptable road to drug control rendered drug policy hostage to other, more important foreign and security policy interests. In this way the linkage between drugs and security was cemented. To perpetuate the influence of the FBN, drug control authorities accepted a subordinate place at the policymaking table.

In the 1960s several important developments marked U.S. drug control policy. As if in testimony to Harry Anslinger's tenure as narcotics commissioner, which came to a close in 1962, nations from around the world signed and ultimately ratified the 1961 Single Convention on Narcotic Drugs, thereby placing under one instrument nearly all international antidrug accords. A consensus, more symbolic than real, had been reached favoring a supply-side approach to drug control. The practical effect for Washington of the convention was to place increasing emphasis upon bilateral relations. In that process frustration became the order of the day: drugs from Southeast Asia continued to reach consumers in the West. Latin America became an even greater source for cocaine, marijuana, and heroin. Demand for drugs by recreational consumers and chronic users seemed to rise exponentially. Organizational changes did little to reduce demand; without Anslinger the FBN, mired in scandal, became in 1968 the Bureau of Narcotics and Dangerous Drugs (BNDD). But the BNDD had no leader with Anslinger's stature to dominate the policymaking process.

Chaos, however, did not necessarily come to characterize U.S. drug policy. The 1960s had begun with an appeal from Mexico to the Eisenhower administration for antidrug help. By 1964 the Agency for International Development (AID) in the State Department had devised a program that previewed the future direction of U.S. antidrug assistance programs. Included in the aid package were funds for both crop eradication and weapons to combat the illicit traffic out of Mexico. Throughout Lyndon Johnson's presidency U.S. authorities tried but were unable to formalize trans-border antidrug operations with Mexico.

In the Andes an Inter-American Consultative Group on Coca Leaf Problems met at Lima in 1964 but achieved little. Bolivia refused even to sign the Single Convention on Narcotic Drugs until 1975, and Peru, although a signatory power, declared that reducing its coca crop could not be considered for perhaps twenty-five years. Complicating the already sensitive relations between Washington and Lima was the creation of a national coca monopoly in 1969.

Notwithstanding these several setbacks in the cause of drug control, the earlier linkage of drugs and security offered a new way to promote drug control. A variant of supply-side tactics, the road to drug control would increasingly emphasize law enforcement as part of a general foreign aid package. U.S. policymakers in the 1960s worried that the "revolution of rising expectations" in the Third World, which encompassed important drug-producing countries, could not easily be controlled. They nevertheless sought to do so by tying together development and security assistance as provided to local law enforcement programs by AID, part of which was intended to be used for narcotics control. It is not clear from available evidence whether the drug control performance of producer states improved, but that outcome is doubtful given the frequent additional funding that Washington made available for drug control in the 1970s and after. Drug control, therefore, had all but disappeared by the late 1960s as an autonomous foreign policy issue. Starting in 1969 the association between drugs and security would grow closer still.

THE LIMITS OF DRUG CONTROL

The more U.S. drug officials equated their activities with security policy, the more diversified became policy objectives. The event that brought about this diversification was Operation Intercept at the Mexican border. In subjecting all traffic at the border to great delays in order to restrict the flow of drugs north from Mexico, the administration of President Richard M. Nixon did two things. First, it made drug interdiction as important as control at the source. Second, and more significant, it served notice that drug production and trafficking threatened U.S. security and was evidence of a lack of political will by the country of origin in the fight against drugs. Since Intercept, U.S. policymakers in the executive branch and Congress have assumed the existence of an adversarial relationship with most producer and trafficking states.

In a major exception to this general rule, Turkey and the United States worked out an arrangement in 1972 that persuaded the Turkish government briefly to halt state-regulated production of opium poppies. Large amounts of Turkish opium had found its way into the heroin trade destined for western Europe and the United States. In severing what was termed the "French Connection," the Nixon administration temporarily muted congressional and public criticism of federal drug policy without disturbing the linkage between drug control and security policy.

Despite the administration's success with Turkey, congressional committees took an increasing interest in the course of U.S. drug policy and strategy. As early as 1971 the House Foreign Affairs Committee expressed concerns about the extent of abuse of Southeast Asian heroin by servicemen returning from Indochina. One committee report, in line with traditional U.S. policy, held that "the problem must be attacked at the source." What differed was the manner of attack that Congress had under consideration: a preemptive buy of the Southeast Asian heroin supply. Officials in the executive branch summarily rejected such a proposal at least twice by mid-decade. Even without knowing the costs of annual preemptive buys, the idea found scant favor in the White House or among drug control officials because it threatened to raise drug control as an issue on its own merits, which might undermine the favored drug-security relationship.

As the assault on executive policymaking prerogatives was being defeated on one front, the drug-security nexus was being reinforced on another. The patience of the United States for the apparent inability of Latin American states to control production and trafficking was wearing thin. In the process, the pre-1969 diplomacy of persuasion inexorably gave way to the politics of pressure and coercion. Following Operation Intercept both the United States and Mexico had endeavored to put the best possible face on a contentious situation by hastily devising what they termed "Operation Cooperation." Soon thereafter authorities in Mexico City initiated La Campaña Permanente, in which Mexican resources and assistance from the Drug Enforcement Administration (DEA), one of the successor agencies to the FBN, were used to curtail opium poppy growth and heroin production.

So far as can be ascertained, Mexico's drug control record in the late 1970s was a relatively good one. But as the United States and Mexico tried to find common ground against drugs, political developments in Washington made that task more difficult. The House Select Committee on Narcotics Abuse and Control came into existence in 1976. Headed by activist congressmen who were dedicated to crop eradication and wanted to militarize the antidrug fight, the committee looked beyond recurring promises and began to assess performance in Latin America's drug control record. Mexico naturally caught the eye of drug control proponents in the United States. It is clear that President Jose López Portillo had in his government officials who were profiting from drug production and trafficking. What López Portillo knew about that situation remains unclear; in any event, by the time Ronald Reagan's presidency began in January 1981 members of Congress and some administration officials, although few then in DEA headquarters, were doubting Mexico's good faith regarding drug control. Ironically Mexicans had their own doubts about the U.S. antidrug commitment because of strict legal prohibitions against the spraying of paraquat on domestic marijuana. The inequality of power in U.S.–Mexican relations made that concern irrelevant in the bilateral relationship.

Mexico, of course, was not the only country subjected to close scrutiny by the United States. Colombia called attention to itself when it considered a plan to legalize and tax the marijuana trade and also after the boom in the cocaine industry became apparent. Peru and Bolivia were heavily criticized in Washington for failure to enforce the coca controls envisioned by the 1961 Single Convention on Narcotic Drugs. Bolivia especially fell out of favor with Washington during and after the year-long hold on power by General Luis García Meza as a result of what has been accurately termed a "cocaine coup." To U.S. authorities Bolivia seemed little more than a nation in thrall to the coca leaf and hence cocaine. Throughout the Andes the so-called kings of cocaine were in the process of constructing a powerful, albeit decentralized narco-empire.

Viewed from the perspective of official Washington it is not surprising that pressure instead of persuasion increasingly characterized U.S. drug policy by the 1980s. The United States consciously set out to transform drug control policies and operations in Latin America at that time. The House Select Committee on Narcotics Abuse and Control, more than any other congressional committee, resolved to hold to account Latin Americans, and the Reagan administration as well, for the integrity of antidrug activities. With no specific mandate except for the presumed interests and fears of an ill-defined public constituency, the committee held hearings, conducted study missions, and released reports about the status of drug control in the Western Hemisphere.

Not only did the committee rally support in Congress during the 1980s for a foreign policy calling for a comprehensive eradication of crops in the Andes and in Mexico, it also demanded a dramatic improvement in the rate of drug interdiction, thereby criticizing the antidrug efforts of the Reagan administration. Committee leaders encouraged militarization of the war on drugs over the vocal opposition of Secretary Caspar Weinberger and the Department of Defense. By the end of the decade, though, it seemed as if selective low-intensity warfare had taken its place, next to control at the source and interdiction, as another basic component of U.S. antidrug strategy. Low-intensity conflict as a fundamental aspect of U.S. strategy would come to the fore after the drug summit held at Cartagena, Colombia, in February 1990, with U.S. assistance to Peru and Colombia increasingly emphasizing law enforcement assistance and military aid against drug production and trafficking. It would continue throughout the 1990s and ultimately metamorphose into Plan Colombia at the turn of the twenty-first century.

Also desirous of pressuring Latin American leaders to do more to control drugs were the three agencies most responsible for drug law enforcement: the DEA, Customs, and the Coast Guard. DEA agents had operated abroad at the invitation of host governments since the agency's creation in 1973. In the strictest sense their mission was to gather information and assist in the training of local antidrug forces, such as the mobile units created in the early 1980s in Bolivia and Peru. Nowhere was the DEA presence more controversial than in Mexico, where in early 1985 the agent Enrique Camarena Salazar and his Mexican pilot were abducted, tortured, and killed. The case remained unsettled to the satisfaction of the DEA for some time, despite the arrest and successful prosecution of many of those allegedly responsible for the crime.

Demonstrating how negatively the Camarena case affected U.S.–Mexican relations was the national-interest certification accorded Mexico in 1988. Several years earlier Congress had passed a law requiring the White House to "certify" whether drug producing and trafficking nations were complying fully with U.S. drug policy objectives. Failure to do so could result in the suspension, and possibly termination, of various kinds of foreign assistance. In 1988, in order to lessen congressional pressure on the administration to name Mexico as a country lacking the political will to attack drugs and to express displeasure with Mexico about the Camarena incident, the White House accorded Mexico less than full certification.

Whether or not that was the case, narcotics foreign policy became highly politicized under Ronald Reagan. Fidel Castro's Cuba and the Sandinista leadership in Nicaragua were charged with sponsoring the transport of drugs, especially cocaine, to the United States. At the same time, the Reagan administration largely ignored drug trafficking by anti-Castro Cubans and the Nicaraguan contras. The administration's readiness to portray the situation so greatly at odds with reality had historical precedent, as we have seen, in Anslinger's allegations about Communist China's involvement with the opiate trade.

Pressure for Latin America to adopt U.S.-style drug control programs can also be seen in the handling of economic development programs funded by the Agency for International Development. So limited was U.S. and international help for crop substitution and alternative development strategies that few farmers in Bolivia or Peru, the countries where this assistance was needed most, could have been expected to turn away from coca for another crop no matter how volatile the market price of coca leaves. The point is not that Bolivians or Peruvians were demanding absolute dollar-for-dollar income replacement; they were not. Rather, coca farmers, as well as processors and small-time traffickers, sought a reliable source of income if they were going to ignore the market forces that made coca an attractive economic choice. As structured in the 1980s and early 1990s, though, the development strategies devised in the United States failed to address the basic concerns of thousands of South Americans participating in the coca-cocaine business.

Indeed, aid programs were closely linked to effective crop destruction and hence were tied as well to presidential certification. The Agency for International Development never had the financial means, let alone the disposition, to address any but the most visible symptoms of this vicious cycle. When viewed in that light President George H. W. Bush's promises at Cartagena about development assistance for the Andes, as one component of the Andean Strategy announced in September 1989, seems somewhat disingenuous. U.S. drug policy toward Latin America was relying on pressure rather than diplomacy and persuasion in two other important respects. On 8 April 1986 President Reagan issued a national security decision directive to the effect that drug production and trafficking constituted a grave threat to the security of the hemisphere. Hence those nations under attack by the drug lords, especially in the Andes, ought to defend themselves individually or in concert. In practice this meant a greater emphasis on control at the source and a relentless effort in source countries to interdict illegal drugs. The United States would provide advice, training, and equipment, although the drug war would be waged first in South America and second in its surrounding international waters.

This strategy largely ignored competing security objectives that tended to compromise antidrug objectives. Panama's Noriega, for example, was arguably the Reagan administration's most vital security asset in Central America despite his well-deserved reputation for double-dealing. Noriega was deemed indispensable to the administration and remained so as long as William Casey headed the CIA. Also, the administration chose to overlook the involvement of several Honduran military officials in the drug trade because Honduras served as a sanctuary for the contras. Such contradictions in security priorities were not lost on those nations, notably Colombia, that were on the front line of the drug war.

U.S. pressure against producer, processing, and transit countries accompanied the militarization of drug strategy. Going far beyond an upgrading of the mission of the Coast Guard, the United States virtually insisted that the battle be taken to source countries. To be sure, aid for military operations came after being requested by Latin American governments. Yet it is worth asking how much of a choice Bolivia had in March of 1986 when Operation Blast Furnace was being proposed. So long as Colombia sought U.S. assistance, it had few viable options other than armed confrontation with the Medellín cartel after the assassination of presidential candidate Luis Carlos Galán in August 1989. The Bush White House viewed the response to the killing as a test of the will of the government of Virgilio Barco Vargas. (Indeed, when Barco's successor, César Gaviria, sought to craft a Colombian response to the violence of the Medellín and Cali cartels, Bob Martinez, head of the Office of National Drug Control Policy, proclaimed that Colombia was on trial before the world.)

Unwillingness abroad to strike directly at illicit production and trafficking would have jeopardized U.S. aid programs. With this implicit threat at the ready, the United States—in early 1987, more than two years before the Galán murder—had fashioned a more extensive antidrug strategy for the Andes, Operation Snowcap. But Snowcap, slow in getting underway, soon ran into difficulty, especially in Peru where the Maoist Sendero Luminoso (Shining Path) controlled coca-growing areas in the Upper Huallaga Valley. Proposals to dispatch U.S. special forces into the Andes were too controversial for Lima to accept openly, but by mid-1991 President Alberto K. Fujimori had agreed to their limited use.

The evolution of a more coercive antidrug strategy in the 1990s inevitably led to greater expectations about Latin American performance in Washington. Controlling drugs moved into the highest rank of foreign policy priorities, at least rhetorically, as the Cold War ended. Yet neither crop eradication nor drug interdiction, despite several spectacular, singular achievements, significantly reduced the flow of drugs in the Americas until after mid-decade.

Policymakers had long argued that an activist drug control strategy abroad would help to control consumption at home. Not until Congress passed the 1988 Anti-Drug Abuse Act would they seriously begin to address the issue of demand, and they did so thereafter largely as an aspect of law enforcement. Demand reduction strategies primarily existed as a by-product of other goals. In effect authorities were betting that widespread craving for popular drugs, notably cocaine, would eventually decline. What they assumed, however, to be a cyclical theory of demand in reality resembled a spiral model, that is, one with absolute usage steadily increasing.

Drug control strategy was also intended to deter newcomers from entering the business at all stages, from production to sale on the street. A tougher approach in the Chapare of Bolivia, in the Upper Huallaga Valley of Peru, or even in the cays of the Caribbean would produce the desired result of lowering drug availability and consumption on the streets of New York, for example. Likewise a strategy that emphasized strict and certain law enforcement might compel lesser players to get out of the game. Had policymakers paid closer attention to what they read in the analyses of Peter Reuter and his colleagues at the Rand Corporation, they would not have been so sanguine about the prospects for success of such a strategy. The risk factor for entrepreneurs entering the drug business was statistically insignificant, whereas the rewards were sufficient to sustain the promise of unaccustomed wealth.

Also anticipated as a result of drug strategy in the 1980s, particularly after Reagan issued his national security directive, was the apprehension of major traffickers. A number of seizures of important figures did take place, especially in Mexico and Gaviria's Colombia, but they did not appreciably affect the structure or functioning of the drug trade out of South America or Mexico, let alone within the United States. (Likewise, the heroin trade out of Southeast Asia scarcely depended upon the continued participation of its two most notorious leaders of the late twentieth century, Lo Hsing-han and Khun Sa, each of whom at one time or another swore off further involvement with opium.)

One outcome of the focus on major traffickers in Latin America would be a reduction in money laundering. The seizure of Noriega and the arrest of top officials of several major banks by the mid-1990s held out the promise of greater success over time, yet that hope was leavened by the realization that the laundering of money remained a serious problem in Panama, a nation whose government owed its very existence to the United States.

Another expected result of the battle against drugs was an increase in the price of drugs so that the economic incentive to consume them would decline. Again, U.S. strategists would do well to heed the analyses prepared at the Rand Corporation. For street prices appreciably to rise, the rate of interdiction would have to be far greater than it has ever been. Even if as much as 30 percent of illegal cocaine is seized, and few experts claim that seizures come close to that figure, the available supply would probably keep prices down and profits for traffickers acceptably high. Not even the vigorous pursuit of the longtime strategy of interdiction presents a serious threat to the major trafficking networks.

As the Cold War waned, policymakers looked to the war on drugs to provide U.S. forces with a contemporary military mission, however limited. After the Department of Defense under Secretary Dick Cheney overcame its reluctance to get involved in the drug war in Latin America and the Caribbean, commitments in the form of advice, training, and limited operations proliferated on a unilateral and bilateral basis. Yet the war remained a low-intensity conflict for both practical political and diplomatic reasons. As a result the drug war was deemed a losing budgetary and doctrinal proposition for the U.S. military and evoked demands for little more than a minimal expenditure of resources. Until the late 1990s it remained unclear what the mission for U.S. forces would be.

The unanticipated consequences of the Reagan-Bush drug war in Latin America were no more salutary. Inter-American relations were strained by the politics of pressure, which would decisively turn to coercion particularly toward Colombia after Ernesto Samper took office as president in 1994. Earlier, palpable tension at the San Antonio drug summit in February 1992, dubbed Cartagena 2, challenged the facade of a common front against drugs. The militarization of antidrug strategy and the process of certification, both of which arguably constituted an implicit denial of the sovereignty of producer, processing, and trafficking nations, placed the United States in the position of dictating a major aspect of regional relations. At the least, certification was demeaning to producer nations in that it assumed a lack of willingness to take action against drugs. The process of certification was something of a throwback to the 1920s and early 1930s in assuming that the drug issue existed apart from other vital issues such as the suppression of radical insurgencies.

It seemed too that defining the drug business as a threat to national security contributed to the realization of that very condition in the Andes. The institutional integrity of Bolivia, Colombia, and Peru was weaker in the early 1990s than before. Perhaps the economic troubles confronting those countries would have undermined national political and social institutions even without the compounding factor of the illicit drug business. Yet pressure from Washington to wage war against drugs in the name of national security made the governing process more difficult.

The Clinton administration continued to prod the three Andean nations as well as Mexico to act more vigorously to attack drug production and trafficking. Nevertheless, during President Bill Clinton's first term in office, the fiery rhetoric of the recent pas was missing. This approach to drug diplomacy reflected the reduced priority the

White House was giving to drug control as a foreign policy objective.

CONTINUING CHALLENGES

Beginning in the mid-1990s there were a number of positive developments in the war on drugs. DEA agents were advising their counterparts around the world; even China and Vietnam turned to the United States for assistance. The defeat of Sendero Luminoso in Peru, combined with a disease that severely damaged the nation's coca crop, drove the drug business out of the Upper Huallaga Valley until late in 2000. The Bolivian government of Hugo Banzer adopted a policy of "zero tolerance" toward coca growing outside of government-approved areas. An uneasy peace existed between growers' unions and the government as alternative development projects failed to provide sufficient income for former coca farmers. Also at the turn of the new century, Iran was cracking down on the opium business; and aid in the form of $43 million in spring 2001 persuaded the Taliban in Afghanistan to go after the heroin trade. Following the terrorist attacks on the United States on 11 September, however, the price for heroin from Afghanistan plummeted. U.S. and international drug control officials believed that the Taliban was dumping large stockpiles of heroin to pay for weapons in the event of conflict as the United States sought to capture or kill the reputed leader of the terrorist network, Osama bin Laden, whose headquarters were located in Afghanistan.

Serious challenges nevertheless remained for U.S. drug control officials, especially in the Caribbean and Mexico. Mexican authorities at all levels remained susceptible to bribery and threats from that nation's major drug organizations even as cartel leaders were arrested and faced the prospect of extradition to the United States to face trial for their activities. During a visit to Washington in late summer 2001 President Vicente Fox pledged to cooperate closely with the administration of George W. Bush on common problems related to drugs. Whether that effort would be enough to lessen the expanding role of the drug business in Mexican politics, particularly at the state level, remained to be seen.

Illicit drugs from Latin America that were not transported to the United States from Mexico often came through Caribbean nations where authorities were unable, and in some instances unwilling, to handle a problem as complex as the one posed by drugs. The result was a greater presence of U.S. law enforcement personnel as advisers. Even Cuba began to share information with Washington about drug trafficking. Nothing happened in either Mexico or the Caribbean to suggest that drug control would soon disappear as a major foreign policy issue in the region.

However serious a challenge drugs posed to governance elsewhere, that threat paled in comparison to drug-related problems in Colombia. By 2002 foreign assistance to Colombia as part of Plan Colombia, a multiyear effort by the government of President Andres Pastrana to wipe out the drug business and defeat his nation's guerrilla insurgencies, made Colombia the third-largest recipient of U.S. foreign aid behind Israel and Egypt. Indications of progress by Bogotá against drugs in the early and mid-1990s proved illusory. Neither the destruction of the Medellín and Cali cartels nor the death or incarceration or extradition to the United States of cartel leaders slowed the traffic in cocaine and crack, heroin, and (to a lesser extent) marijuana out of Colombia. Indeed, antidrug assistance served to embroil the United States more deeply than anticipated in the Colombian crisis. The government in Bogotá controlled barely 60 percent of the national territory. How U.S. aid could affect that perilous situation remained anyone's guess. The leftist insurgency had begun in the mid-1960s and showed little sign of abating, all the more so because rebel forces increasingly relied upon income from drugs to fund their activities. Negotiations between the government and rebels had created a safe zone, dubbed "Narcolandia." Should a settlement eventuate, there was no way of predicting its durability.

What had begun a hundred years earlier as an effort by the United States to promote social reform abroad was closely linked in the twenty-first century with matters of governance and national identity. Foreign lands continued to supply the United States with illicit substances; in so doing they met rather than created a demand for drugs, though U.S. leaders did not publicly admit that reality until the early 1990s. The more that supplier and transit nations accepted U.S. antidrug strategy, and declared drugs to constitute a security threat, the more difficult for them became the process of governing. Attention to demand alone, long advocated by some producer states, could not overcome the multifaceted problems posed by drugs. For better or worse drug control had become an important, sometimes crucial, facet of American foreign policy.

BIBLIOGRAPHY

Bertram, Eva, et al. *Drug War Politics: The Price of Denial.* Berkeley, Calif., 1996. Critical overview of the proscriptive, punitive nature of U.S. domestic and foreign drug policies.

Courtwright, David T. *Forces of Habit: Drugs and the Making of the Modern World.* Cambridge, Mass., 2001. Outstanding assessment of the role of licit and illicit drugs in modern history.

Griffith, Ivelaw Lloyd. *Drugs and Security in the Caribbean: Sovereignty Under Siege.* University Park, Pa., 1997. Survey of the implications of the war on drugs in the Caribbean region.

Kwitny, Jonathan. *The Crimes of Patriots: A True Tale of Dope, Dirty Money, and the CIA.* New York, 1987. A skilled reporter's investigation of the links between illegal drugs and U.S. security interests in the 1970s and 1980s.

Lamour, Catherine, and Michel R. Lamberti. *The International Connection: Opium from Growers to Pushers.* Translated by Peter and Betty Ross. New York, 1974. Important book about the international dimensions of the modern commerce in illegal drugs.

McAllister, William B. *Drug Diplomacy in the Twentieth Century: An International History.* London and New York, 2000. The finest scholarly survey on the subject.

McCoy, Alfred W. *The Politics of Heroin: CIA Complicity in the Global Drug Trade.* Brooklyn, N.Y., 1991. Updated, classic account of the post-1945 nexus of drugs and security policy throughout Asia.

Meyer, Kathryn, and Terry Parssinen. *Webs of Smoke: Smugglers, Warlords, Spies, and the History of the International Drug Trade.* Lanham, Md., 1998.

Morgan, H. Wayne. *Drugs in America: A Social History, 1800–1980.* Syracuse, N.Y., 1981.

Musto, David F. *The American Disease: Origins of Narcotic Control.* Expanded ed. New York, 1987. Best account of the origins and history of illegal drugs in the United States.

Powis, Robert E. *The Money Launderers: Lessons from the Drug Wars, How Billions of Illegal Dollars Are Washed Through Banks and Businesses.* Chicago, 1992.

Riley, Kevin Jack. *Snow Job?: The War Against International Cocaine Trafficking.* New Brunswick, N.J., 1996. Skeptical look at recent U.S. and international efforts to combat cocaine.

Scott, Peter Dale, and Jonathan Marshall. *Cocaine Politics: Drugs, Armies, and the CIA in Central America.* Updated ed. Berkeley, Calif., 1998. Riveting account of the convergence of drugs and U.S. foreign policy in the 1980s.

Stares, Paul B. *Global Habit: The Drug Problem in a Borderless World.* Washington, D.C., 1996. Cautionary account about the limits of drug control.

Taylor, Arnold. *American Diplomacy and the Narcotics Traffic, 1900–1939: A Study in International Humanitarian Reform.* Durham, N.C., 1969. A pathbreaking study of international drug control.

Tokatlian, Juan. *Globalización, Narcotráfico y Violencia: Siete Ensayos sobre Colombia.* Buenos Aires, 2000. An impassioned inquiry into the effect of drugs on Colombia late in the twentieth century.

Walker, William O., III. *Drug Control in the Americas.* Rev. ed. Albuquerque, N.Mex., 1989. Leading account of drug control as an issue in the Western Hemisphere.

———. *Opium and Foreign Policy: The Anglo-American Search for Order in Asia, 1912–1954.* Chapel Hill, N.C., 1991. International history of the drug problem in East Asia.

See also INTERVENTION AND NONINTERVENTION; THE NATIONAL INTEREST; PAN-AMERICANISM.

THE NATIONAL INTEREST

H. W. Brands

No concept in the history of American foreign policy has been more contentious than the "national interest." Both words in the phrase are troublesome. "National" implies something the entire nation can rally around; hence, the phrase often serves as a summons to patriotism. To oppose, or even question, the national interest pushes the opponent or questioner perilously close to sedition or treason. As for "interest," few terms are more elastic. The inhabitants of any country would have to be dull indeed not to be "interested" in much that goes on in the world; the inhabitants of a powerful, ambitious country like the United States can expand interests almost ad infinitum. Complicating the matter further is the fact that definitions do not necessarily the national interest make. What actually *is* the national interest is for history to determine. And even history does not always get it right.

For every country, national interest starts with safety of the national territory; for Americans, the arguing started just past that irreducible minimum. And it started early.

WHAT WASHINGTON AND JEFFERSON (EVENTUALLY) AGREED ON

Quarrels over the national interest commenced with America's birth as an independent nation. Nearly everyone in the Continental Congress, and everyone not a Loyalist, agreed on the advisability of an alliance with France and cheered when that alliance was obtained in 1778. But no sooner had the French held up their end of the bargain—by cornering Cornwallis at Yorktown—than Americans began to squabble about how far beyond victory attachment to France ought to extend. Benjamin Franklin, the senior American commissioner in Paris, counseled continued closeness, both from gratitude for services already rendered and in expectation of additional French aid.

Franklin doubtless was influenced by the adulation he received in Paris (a staged meeting between Franklin and Voltaire set the philosophes swooning), but, personal popularity aside, he believed the infant United States would need French help to avoid being sucked back into Britain's orbit. Franklin's fellow commissioners, John Adams and John Jay, were more inclined to doubt French bona fides and less inclined to fear the attraction of America's late colonial master. (Adams in addition suffered from excruciating envy of Franklin, and his Puritan mores were scandalized by Franklin's liaisons with the ladies of Paris.) As it happened, the tension between the two conceptions of the infant national interest produced a peace treaty that preserved the alliance with France while extracting important concessions from Britain.

Unfortunately, the concessions proved to be more impressive on paper than on the ground—particularly the ground of the Ohio Valley and the Great Lakes. The British refused to evacuate forts in the region and defied the Americans to do anything to oust them. (The rationale for their continued occupation was the failure of the American government to honor pledges regarding debts and Loyalists, but their reason was simply that they could, and that influential groups in Britain defined Britain's national interest as holding what Britain had.) Thomas Jefferson, who had inherited Franklin's Francophilia along with Franklin's diplomatic post in Paris, and who carried this attitude to his position as President George Washington's secretary of state, found the British intransigence insufferable. The group that grew up around Jefferson—the nascent Republican Party—agitated to punish perfidious Albion.

Their cause was complicated by the outbreak of the French Revolution, and the onset of the wars provoked by that pregnant event. For most of a century, the American colonies had been caught in the crossfire between Britain and France; the most recent installment of this modern Hundred Years' War had sprung the colonies free from Britain's grasp. But freedom did not preserve them when the crossfire resumed in 1792. The question that then faced Americans was: With which side did the American national interest lie?

Jefferson and the Republicans answered the question one way—France's way. The Jeffersonians did not necessarily forgive French violations of American neutrality (centering on seizure of American ships), but they felt more threatened by Britain's infractions, which now also included seizure of ships. The more fervent among them would have repaid French help in the war of the American Revolution with American help in this war of the French Revolution; yet even those who stopped short of wanting to honor the alliance to the letter conceived a kinship with the new republic on the Atlantic's eastern shore. In this view (and in a pattern that would persist for two centuries in American politics), the national interest at home and the national interest abroad were intimately entwined. Domestic republicanism dictated support for foreign republicanism.

Alexander Hamilton and the Federalists demonstrated a similarly married definition of the national interests at home and abroad. Hamilton was no great fan of American republicanism, having argued at the Constitutional Convention for a monarchy; not surprisingly, he held no candle for French republicanism. On the contrary, he admired the energetic executive of the British government (which he did his best to imitate as Washington's Treasury secretary and most trusted adviser), and he judged that America's future lay in close ties to Britain's governing and merchandising classes.

The national interest was whipsawed between the Republican and Federalist views for two decades. The Federalists (under Washington) negotiated and ratified the easy-on-Britain Jay's Treaty and (under John Adams) fought an undeclared naval war against France. During this conflict, the Federalists succeeded in outlawing—by the Sedition Act—their opponents' definition of the national interest. The Republicans (under James Madison) fought a formal war against Britain. The Republicans' war—of 1812—was a fiasco for the United States, with the burning of Washington City being but the most egregious example of America's inability to defend itself.

Yet the conflict had the salutary effect of ending the first phase of the debate over the national interest. Americans had learned something from their long ordeal. The Bonapartist turn of events in France cured the Jeffersonians of their revolutionary romanticism, while the Hamiltonians (who lost their champion in the infamous duel with Aaron Burr) were disabused of their Anglophilia by British impressment of American seamen. Both sides settled on the wisdom of staying out of other countries' wars. George Washington had urged eschewing "permanent alliances"; Thomas Jefferson denounced "entangling alliances." Permanent or entangling, alliances seemed unwise, and a strong majority of Americans concurred in keeping clear of them. No definition of the national interest would persist longer or sustain more general acceptance than this idea that other people's quarrels were for other people to settle. God in his wisdom had put an ocean between Europe and America; Americans in their wisdom had crossed it. Most saw no reason to cross back.

EXPANSIONISTS ALL

One reason Americans did not go back east was that they were too busy going farther west. The end of Europe's wars freed Americans to concentrate on what they and their ancestors had been doing since the start of the seventeenth century: claiming new territory and dispossessing the aboriginal inhabitants. Independent America inherited from imperial England the general idea that Indians had no rights worth respecting; Indian lands might be claimed and parceled out, subject only to the ability of the claimants to drive the Indians off. This attitude was not quite universal; a few English and Americans spoke up for the Indians. But between the more common view of Indians as beneath respect, and the ravages of introduced diseases upon the aboriginal populations, Americans expanded west almost as though the Indians were not there.

The Treaty of Paris of 1783 confirmed American title to the lands lying east of the Mississippi. (Confirmed title against European claimants, that is. No Indians sat at the Paris negotiations, and none were asked to approve the treaty.) The Louisiana Purchase of 1803 doubled the American national domain again, pushing the western boundary to the crest of the Rocky Mountains. Diplomatic and extra-diplomatic machinations brought Florida into the American fold.

Nearly all Americans approved this heady expansion. Federalists poked fun at Jefferson, who had to abandon his strict constructionism lest Napoleon change his mind about Louisiana; and General Andrew Jackson incurred criticism for hanging one British trader and shooting another in Florida. But on the whole, more land was conceived to be in the obvious national interest.

There was something else behind the pro-expansionist feeling. Since Puritan times, many Americans believed their country was unique: the site of the terrestrial working-out of the will of God (either the Christian God of the Puritans or the natural God of Jefferson and Madison). The expansion of America, in this view, signified the extension of providential designs, with benefits not merely for America but for humanity at large. Other nations have defined their national interests to include people beyond their borders, but none have done so more vigorously or consistently than the United States.

The identification of the American national interest with the interest of humanity reached an early apex during the 1840s, in the era of "manifest destiny." The annexation of Texas, the conquest of California and New Mexico, and the acquisition of Oregon seemed to most Americans a convenient collaboration between God and the United States. To be sure, the war with Mexico occasioned complaint among northern Whigs, but their complaint had less to do with the extension of American authority than with a fear that the territory acquired in the war would strengthen the institution of southern slavery.

In fact, slavery never sank roots in the trans-Texas southwest. Yet difficulties in organizing governments for the Mexican cession did reopen the slavery debate and led, via "bleeding Kansas" and the Dred Scott decision, to the Civil War. The bitter sectional ordeal took the smugness out of the manifest destinarians and the wind out of the sails of territorial expansion. The generation that came of age with the Compromise of 1850 and remained in power until the Compromise of 1877 had trouble enough holding together the territory America already owned; it had little energy or inclination to acquire more. Secretary of State William Seward got Congress to purchase Alaska in 1867, but only because Russia's sale price made it a bargain the legislators could not refuse (especially when the price included generous kickbacks to the legislators themselves). Ulysses Grant tried to annex Santo Domingo, but the Senate said no.

A DEMOCRATIC EMPIRE?

By the end of Reconstruction, the Industrial Revolution in America was under full steam. And as the country redefined itself—from rural and agricultural to urban and industrial—it similarly redefined its national interest. Or tried to. Many Americans interpreted the shift from agriculture to industry as indicating that territory per se no longer mattered; America's expansionist impulses —which none denied still existed—should look to markets rather than land. Yet others contended that land still counted. They observed the overseas empires of the other great powers and judged that American greatness would be measured by the same material yardstick. Moreover, enough of the spirit of manifest destiny survived the Civil War (the Union victory did wonders for the self-confidence of the winners) to support a sense that American institutions and values could revivify a weary and corrupted world.

After fighting broke out in Cuba in 1895 between Cuban nationalists and Spanish loyalists, Americans sided with the nationalists: first sentimentally, then politically, and finally militarily. The American war party—led by Republicans Theodore Roosevelt and Henry Cabot Lodge and journalists Joseph Pulitzer and William Randolph Hearst—included individuals who dreamed of an American empire akin to the empires of Britain, France, and Germany. But what won William McKinley his war declaration against Spain in April 1898 was a feeling that America had an obligation to prevent atrocities in its own backyard. (It was during the 1890s that the Monroe Doctrine of 1823, asserting American primacy in the Western Hemisphere, achieved the status of an enforceable national interest.) When congressional skeptics of the McKinley administration's motives, led by Henry Teller, attached to the war resolution an amendment forswearing American ownership of Cuba, the amendment sailed through the Senate without debate.

But wars have a way of altering reality, and after American forces captured Manila, the urge to empire took a different tack. McKinley negotiated a treaty with Spain granting Cuba independence but transferring the Philippines to the United States. The president claimed that Providence told him his country had an obligation to uplift and Christianize the Filipinos. (Obviously, it was a Protestant Providence, as most Filipinos were already Christians—but Roman Catholics.)

When McKinley laid the treaty before the Senate for ratification, the country witnessed one of the most distilled debates in American history on the nature of the national interest. The imperialists asserted that annexation of the Philippines would benefit the United States economically (by providing a stepping-stone to the markets of Asia), diplomatically (by anteing America into the imperial sweepstakes that dominated international affairs), and militarily (by providing naval bases and coaling stations for the U.S. fleet). Beyond this, American control of the Philippines would advance the interests of world civilization. "It is elemental," Albert Beveridge told his Senate colleagues. "It is racial. God has not been preparing the English-speaking and Teutonic peoples for a thousand years for nothing but vain and idle self-contemplation and self-admiration. . . . He has made us the master organizers of the world to establish system where chaos reigns. He has given us the spirit of progress to overwhelm the forces of reaction throughout the earth."

The anti-imperialists construed the national interest quite differently. A radical few denied that God had any special plan for America, but others simply held that American exceptionalism worked better by example than by force. Indeed, to ape the European imperialists would undermine all that made America unique and worth emulating. Carl Schurz, a refugee republican from Prussia after the failed revolution of 1848 there, and a Lincoln Republican in the American Civil War, predicted that annexation would embroil the United States in an imperial conflict like those that ate the blood and treasure of the other imperial powers. "The Filipinos fought against Spain for their freedom and independence, and unless they abandon their recently proclaimed purpose for their freedom and independence, they will fight us," Schurz said. The imperial road would lead his adopted country into dire peril. "The character and future of the Republic and the welfare of its people now living and yet to be born are in unprecedented jeopardy."

The imperialists won the battle but lost the war. Even as the Senate (narrowly) accepted McKinley's treaty, Filipino nationalists launched the war of independence Schurz predicted. The American war in the Philippines was the long, dirty antithesis of the short, clean American war in Cuba. Americans committed (and suffered) atrocities like those they had castigated Spain for committing against Cuba; the whole experience soured the American people on empire. By the time U.S. forces finally suppressed the Philippine insurgency, Americans had discovered that their national interest did not include empire. They needed another four decades to divest themselves of the Philippines (Puerto Rico, which did not want to be divested, remained American), but they were never tempted to repeat the imperial experiment.

A SIGH FOR VERSAILLES

Reinforcing Americans' reluctance to engage in entanglements abroad was the suicidal behavior of the European imperialists, who locked themselves in a death struggle starting in 1914. For the first year of the Great War, Americans once again congratulated themselves and their forebears for having left that benighted continent; by consensus the national interest indicated adhering to the advice of Washington and Jefferson about eschewing alliances.

But the twentieth century was not the eighteenth or early nineteenth. American commercial and financial interests had grown tremendously, making the United States more dependent than ever on foreign markets. American merchants demanded the right to trade with the belligerents; American bankers insisted on being able to lend in London and Paris and Berlin. Woodrow Wilson wanted to keep clear of the conflict and tried for a time to rally his compatriots to neutral thinking as well as a neutral policy. But he could not resist the calls for belligerent trade and belligerent loans, and before long the tentacles of capitalism began to draw the United States into the war. Because the British had a better fleet than the Germans, most American trade, and the financing that funded the trade, flowed to Britain and France, making the United States a de facto member of the Allied powers by 1916. Germany recognized the situation, and in early 1917 declared war on American shipping. Wilson responded with a request for a formal war declaration, which Congress granted.

At the time, few in Congress or outside it questioned that the American national interest required defending American vessels and American nationals against German attack. Some, however, did question whether U.S. participation in the war required putting U.S. troops on the ground in Europe. "Good Lord! You're not going to send soldiers over there, are you?" queried a shocked senator of a War Department spokesman.

The War Department did send the troops, which helped break the back of Germany's desperate final offensive.

But what else they accomplished was open to doubt. The British and French knew what *they* were fighting for (although the rest of the world did not until Lenin leaked the secret treaties that spelled out the Allies' imperialistic war aims). The Americans were far less sure of their own purposes, not least because Wilson had waffled all over the landscape of politics and diplomacy. At various times he talked of being too proud to fight, then of achieving peace without victory, then of making the world safe for democracy. His Fourteen Points seemed rather many, with some too vague and others too specific. In any case, the British and French demonstrated at the postwar peace conference that they would have nothing to do with Wilson's airy abstractions. Germany had lost, and Germany would pay—in treasure, territory, colonies, and markets. Wilson could have his precious League of Nations, the proto–world government he hoped would prevent another such war. But he would have to make of it what he could.

Which turned out to be nothing at all. Even more than Wilson, Americans were confused as to why they entered the war. The only national interest that seemed directly threatened was the right to trade with belligerents. But the British violated America's neutral rights as consistently, if less egregiously, than the Germans (who, short on surface ships, had to resort to U-boat torpedoes to enforce a blockade). Was there an American national interest in preventing another European war? On this point, as on any other meaningful topic touching the national interest, the answer turned on the cost. Of course, it would be to America's benefit for Europe to remain at peace, but would the benefit outweigh the cost of an indefinite commitment to enforce the mandates of this new League of Nations? Did Americans wish to play policemen to the world?

The Senate said no in twice rejecting the Treaty of Versailles. Wilson summoned a simple majority for the treaty, but not the two-thirds supermajority ratification required. Under the rules specified by the Constitution, the Senate declared that membership in the League of Nations was not in the American national interest. Whether it really was not in the national interest, time would tell.

WILSON WITHOUT THE PREACHING

And not much time, at that. Calvin Coolidge may not have spoken for all Americans when he proclaimed that the business of America was business, but he spoke for those who counted during the Republican decade after the war. Disillusionment with the war's outcome—millions killed, including 60,000 Americans, to little positive effect observable from across the Atlantic—reinforced the feeling that Washington and Jefferson had been right. Foreign entanglements were a fool's game. There was still American engagement abroad, but it was chiefly the engagement of private, corporate interests, backed at times by federal officials (including the bright new star of the Republicans, Commerce Secretary Herbert Hoover) yet rarely rising to the level of a widely supported national interest.

If anything, the national interest seemed to point in precisely the opposite direction. During the latter half of the 1920s, the authors Harry Elmer Barnes, C. Hartley Grattan, and others attacked American participation in the late war as the work of private interests—chiefly financial and mercantile—parading as the national interest. During the 1930s this attitude enveloped Capitol Hill, where an investigative committee headed by Senator Gerald Nye laid blame for America's feckless involvement in the war at the feet of the "merchants of death." The Nye committee provided ammunition to congressional isolationists, who legislated neutrality for the United States in the event of another war. Yet this was a different neutrality from that which had defined much of the national interest from the 1790s to the 1910s. Where America's historic neutrality had been actively defended, twice by war (in 1812 and 1917), the legislated neutrality of the 1930s would be preserved by abandoning American neutral rights. The Neutrality Act of 1937, for example, forbade the sale of munitions to belligerents (no more "merchants of death"), outlawed loans to belligerents (no more lopsided lending) and barred American travel on belligerent ships (no more *Lusitanias*—or at least no more American deaths on such ships). The neutrality law also allowed the president to insist that trade in goods other than munitions be conducted on a cash-and-carry basis, with the purchasers taking responsibility for the cargoes before they left U.S. shores (no more American ships showing up in the crosshairs of belligerent periscopes).

THE INTELLECTUAL—AND LIGHTNING ROD—OF THE ISOLATIONISTS

Charles A. Beard (1874–1948) was no stranger to controversy. His iconoclastic 1913 *Economic Interpretation of the Constitution* cast doubt on the disinterest of the Founders, and during World War I he quit Columbia University in protest over the firing of a colleague. In the 1920s, he carved a niche as a critic on the left of the policies of the Republican administrations. Franklin Roosevelt initially mollified him somewhat, but Beard was always more comfortable in opposition than in agreement, and he soon discovered grounds for criticizing the Democratic president. In *The Idea of National Interest* and elsewhere, Beard attacked Roosevelt for building more ships and otherwise laying the basis for intervention in Europe and Asia. To Beard, foreign intervention was something that benefited not the American people generally but only the rich and well-connected—the same groups he criticized in *Economic Interpretation*.

Beard's writings abetted the isolationism of the 1930s, yet where much isolationist thinking was more emotional than rational, Beard offered a carefully reasoned theory of nonintervention, based on a challenge to received wisdom regarding foreign markets. Beard acknowledged that nonintervention would require abandoning some foreign markets, and he conceded this would have a negative direct effect on American incomes. But he countered that much, perhaps all, of this loss would be recouped in savings on weapons not required and wars not fought. And even if it were not recouped, there was more to life, and to the national interest, than money. "National interest involves stability and standard of life deliberately adjusted to each other in a long time perspective," he explained.

Beard applauded the neutrality laws but did not think they would hold. "We're blundering into war," he predicted in 1938. When war did come, Beard suspended his attacks on Roosevelt, but he rejected the administration's high rhetoric and its enthusiasm regarding America's partners. "I refuse to take the world-saving business at face value and think that Churchill and Stalin are less concerned with world saving than with saving the British empire and building a new and bigger Russian empire."

For his forthrightness, Beard fell under intellectual obloquy. Erstwhile allies criticized him for failing to condemn Hitler and the Japanese with sufficient vigor. But he did not waver. "History to come will pass judgment on them and me," he said.

Americans might have quibbled over the details of the neutrality laws, but by all evidence they supported the general idea. Twenty years after the fact, American involvement in World War I seemed an exercise in fatuity, the likes of which should be avoided at nearly all cost.

Yet no sooner had they reached this consensus than events began to erode it. In appallingly short order, Italy brutalized Ethiopia, Japan raped China, and Germany severed Czechoslovakia. Many Americans thought it would be impossible to retain the country's self-respect without taking action against the organized violence abroad. Others concluded that if the violence was not stopped now, it would inevitably engulf the United States, as it had in World War I. But still others came to the opposite conclusion: to them, the muggings abroad underscored the necessity of neutrality. If the world insisted on going to hell, let it do so, but do not let it take America down with it.

The outbreak of the second great European war of the twentieth century, in September 1939, polarized American opinion further. A group calling itself America First wanted to widen the Atlantic and Pacific oceans and keep American boys securely at home. Mere discussion of U.S. intervention, the America Firsters said, discouraged Britain and France from doing for themselves what needed to be done. An opposing group, the Committee to Defend America by Aiding the Allies, advocated a forthright policy of supporting those countries opposing Nazi Germany. With luck, such support might stop short of American belligerence, but that ultimate step could not be ruled out—nor should it be, lest Adolf Hitler take heart from American aloofness.

This latest round of the debate over the national interest continued for two years, until the Japanese attack on Pearl Harbor. As even the narrowest definition demanded defending American territory, by transgressing U.S. borders the

Japanese guaranteed American belligerence. Had Hitler not gratuitously declared war on the United States while the waters of Hawaii were still stained with American blood, debate doubtless would have continued regarding whether the national interest required fighting Germany. But in the event, Americans entered both wars—in the Pacific and in Europe—united in defining the national interest as requiring the defeat of the Axis. Woodrow Wilson might have been wrong about some things, but he now seemed right about America's inability to insulate itself from a world at war.

ENTER IDEOLOGY

Defining national interest during war is easy: to defeat the enemy. Things get harder after the war. Wilson discovered this; so did Harry Truman. In each case the trouble was with the Allies, who during war agreed on the primacy of victory but after victory had their own national interests to pursue.

The interests of the Soviet Union after World War II entailed control of its East European neighbors. This was not what the United States had been fighting for, and in denying democracy and self-determination, it constituted an affront to American principles. Whether it constituted a challenge to the American national interest was a separate question. Franklin Roosevelt gave signs of thinking it did not, at least not seriously; Harry Truman, upon succeeding Roosevelt, thought it did.

More precisely, what Truman and his Cold War cabinet considered the challenge to the national interest was the aggressive expansionism they perceived to be inherent in Soviet communist ideology, and which was currently manifested in the Soviet occupation of Eastern Europe. Had Truman and his advisers been convinced the Kremlin had no designs west of the Elbe River, they would have slept more soundly and planned less ambitiously for the future of Western Europe; but instead they chose to interpret trouble in Iran, Greece, and Turkey as leading indicators of trouble farther west. In the March 1947 speech that unveiled the Truman Doctrine, the president described the world as divided between "alternative ways of life," with the communist way attempting to subvert and destroy the democratic way. By Truman's reasoning, the fate of America hung on the fate of Greece and the other countries under threat; it followed that the American national interest required defending Greece and those other countries.

Congress, and apparently the American people, endorsed Truman's definition of the national interest. Truman got the $400 million he requested for Greece and Turkey. Then he got the several billions he requested for aid to Europe. He got the Senate to accept the North Atlantic Treaty, committing the United States to the defense of Western Europe. And although he did not ask for a formal declaration of war, he got the Congress to underwrite his decision to defend South Korea against North Korea when war broke out on that divided peninsula in 1950.

Never in American history had the national interest been redefined so radically and swiftly. Scarcely a decade before, Congress had forsworn the use of force even to defend American ships and citizens against direct attack. Now, the United States was pledged to defend half the world and was actively fighting in a small and intrinsically unimportant country half a world away.

Why the change? Two reasons. First, although World War I had suggested that any major European conflict would eventually embroil the United States, Americans required World War II for the lesson to stick. In the twentieth century, American peacetime connections to Europe—business and financial connections primarily, but also cultural and social connections—were so deep and pervasive that Europe's troubles became America's troubles, and Europe's wars became America's wars. The Cold War commitment to Europe—through the Marshall Plan and the North Atlantic Treaty Organization (NATO), especially—represented an effort to keep America out of war by keeping Europe out of war.

The second reason for the radical redefining of the national interest was simply that Americans *could*. Had the United States been Luxembourg, Americans never would have dreamed of underwriting European reconstruction or defending South Korea. But after 1945 the United States was the richest, most powerful country in the history of the world. Rich people buy insurance policies the poor decline, both because the rich have more to insure and because they can afford the premiums. The ambitious policies undertaken by the Truman administration represented a form of insurance—a way of keeping Americans richer and more powerful than anyone else.

NATIONAL SECURITY, NATIONAL INSECURITY

But as any savvy insurance agent discovers, there is no end to what might be insured. Buying a house? Insure the house, of course, but also ensure the mortgage payments. Taking a vacation? Insure against bad weather.

Likewise for the United States during the Cold War. America's assorted alliance systems—NATO, SEATO (Southeast Asia Treaty Organization), CENTO (Central Treaty Organization), the Rio Pact, ANZUS (the Pacific Security Treaty among Australia, New Zealand, and the United States)—insured not primarily against attacks on the United States but against attacks on countries related, in one way or another, to American security. Pakistan offered electronic listening posts and launchpads for spy planes. Australia pledged troops to the defense of the Middle East, whose oil then meant little to America directly (the United States still exported oil) but meant much to Western Europe. South Vietnam mattered psychologically: if that wobbling domino fell, it would unsettle the neighbors and might ultimately ruin the neighborhood.

This would be bad for American business, which had a bottom-line interest in preserving as much of the world as possible for market penetration. It would also be bad for American morale. Since Plymouth Rock and the "city on the hill" John Winthrop had promised next door at Boston, Americans had always considered themselves the wave of the future. Two communist revolutions in the twentieth century—in Russia and in China—cast serious doubt on this presumption. Additional advances by the communists could only unnerve Americans further.

During the Cold War, the term "national security" often supplanted "national interest" in American political parlance. And security connoted not simply physical security—the ability to fend off foreign attack—but also psychological security. In no other way can the hysteria that gripped the United States during the McCarthy era be explained. Indeed, by most measures the United States was more secure than it had ever been. Its power—military, economic, political—compared to its closest rivals had never been greater. Americans, however, often acted as though they were in greater danger than ever. Red screenwriters and pink professors apparently lurked in every studio and on every campus, ready to deliver America to communist tyranny; accordingly, Congress and the courts mobilized to identify and silence them. Nationalism in Iran and land reform in Guatemala aimed a dagger at America's heart; the Eisenhower administration sent secret warriors to overthrow the offending regimes.

Although much of the danger existed only in American heads (and on the agendas of those elected officials, bureaucrats, arms makers, and others who had profit and career incentives to magnify the communist threat), it was not entirely fabricated. In 1949 the Soviet Union broke the U.S. nuclear monopoly; by the mid-1950s, the Soviet air force possessed hydrogen bombs and long-range bombers; and by the early 1960s, Moscow's strategic rocket forces could deliver the big bombs across oceans and over the pole. For centuries, other countries had lived with the threat of imminent physical attack, but until now the twin moats of the Atlantic and Pacific had protected the United States and allowed Americans the luxury of time in organizing armies when war did come. The nuclear revolution in military technology erased the oceans and collapsed time; with luck, Americans might now get twenty minutes' warning of Soviet attack. By definition, paranoia is unreasonable, but it is not always unexplainable. If the American definition of national security exhibited a certain paranoia during the Cold War—and it did—the country's unaccustomed vulnerability to sudden and potentially annihilating attack was as good an explanation as any.

NO MORE VIETNAMS

Even for rich folks, insurance premiums can be a burden. The insurance Americans purchased for Southeast Asia eventually broke the bank—or at least the willingness of Americans to continue to pay.

In one sense Vietnam was inevitable. By the 1960s the American national interest was being defined so globally that hardly a sparrow could fall anywhere on earth without the U.S. government wanting to know why, to know whether the sparrow had jumped or been pushed, and, if pushed, to know whether the pusher wore scarlet plumage. Somewhere or other, sooner or later, the United States was bound to find itself defending a regime so weak, corrupt, or unpopular—especially since the chief criterion for American support was opposition to communism, rather than the positive embrace of democracy—as to be indefensible at any reasonable cost. The country where this occurred happened to be Vietnam, but it might have been Cuba (actually, it *was* Cuba also, but Fidel Castro worked too fast and cleverly for the Eisenhower and Kennedy administrations) or Iraq (Iraq likewise, but again the revolution succeeded before the United States reacted) or the Philippines (which similarly faced a leftist insurgency but managed to hold on).

Beyond its own problems, South Vietnam revealed something fundamental about the Cold War definition of the American national interest. As the world's only full-service superpower (the Soviet Union possessed a first-rate military but its strength in other areas was vastly overrated, as time revealed), the United States was more or less free to define its national interest however it chose. But having once agreed upon a definition, Americans were constrained to defend that definition lest they lose face with friends and enemies. Credibility counted when American commitments outran American capabilities. By no stretch of anyone's imagination could the United States have defended simultaneously all the regimes it was pledged by the 1960s to defend; its resolve and success anywhere had implications for its prospects everywhere.

That was why Lyndon Johnson and Richard Nixon went to such lengths to prevent the communist conquest of South Vietnam, and why Americans took failure there so hard. They might reasonably have accounted Vietnam simply as someplace where local conditions could not support an incompetent regime; if the American approach to Vietnam had actually (rather than metaphorically) been an insurance policy, Vietnam would have been written off and Americans would have gone about their business.

But Vietnam was not merely business—certainly not to the families and friends of the 60,000 service men and women who lost their lives there. Americans had indulged the illusion they could secure half the planet against revolution. In their post-Vietnam disillusionment, many Americans wondered whether they could secure any of the planet against revolution, or whether they ought to try. "For too many years," explained Jimmy Carter, the first president elected after Vietnam, "we've been willing to adopt the flawed and erroneous principles and tactics of our adversaries, sometimes abandoning our own values for theirs. We've fought fire with fire, never thinking that fire is better quenched with water. This approach failed, with Vietnam being the best example of its intellectual and moral poverty. But through its failure we have now found our way back to our own principles and values."

Carter was certainly speaking for his own administration, but how many other Americans his "we" comprised was problematic. The reflexively anticommunist definition of the American national interest—the definition that had enjoyed consensus support since the early Cold War—had indeed been discredited in Vietnam, but a credible replacement had yet to appear. Nixon's candidate, détente, based on the provocative notion that capitalism and communism—even Chinese communism—could coexist, had spawned an entire school of opposition, called neoconservatism. Carter's human rights–based approach appealed to those appalled by the dirty linen that kept tumbling out of the Cold War hamper, but struck others as naively woolly-minded.

The only thing nearly all Americans could agree on was that the national interest dictated avoiding anything that looked or smelled like another Vietnam. Liberals interpreted this to mean not sending troops to prop up ugly autocracies abroad. Neoconservatives interpreted it to mean not sending troops unless the U.S. government and the American people were willing to follow through to victory. With the blades of the last helicopters from Saigon still whomp-whomping in American ears, the liberal and neoconservative conditions amounted to the same thing.

LONELY AT THE TOP

The neoconservatives helped Ronald Reagan win the White House in 1980, and they strove, shortly thereafter, to forge a new consensus around the old verities of the Cold War. Their man mouthed the right words, calling the Soviet Union an "evil empire" and summoning America to "stand tall" again. He dispatched troops to Grenada to loosen what he called "the tightening grip of the totalitarian left" there, and he added the Reagan Doctrine to the list that had started with Monroe, continued through Truman, and made lesser stops at Eisenhower, Johnson, Nixon, and Carter. In its own way, the Reagan Doctrine was more ambitious than its predecessors, which were essentially negative in concept and formulation (that is, aimed to prevent—respectively—European expansion in the Americas, communist subversion, destabilization of the Middle East, another Cuba, another Vietnam, and a Soviet takeover of the Persian Gulf). The Reagan Doctrine advocated something positive: the replacement by rightists of leftist Third World regimes, notably in Nicaragua, Afghanistan, Angola, and Cambodia. Above and beyond all this, the Reagan administration embarked on a big defense buildup, including the first steps toward what Reagan's partisans respectfully called the Strategic Defense Initiative and others derisively, or merely conveniently, called "Star Wars."

Although the American people cheered Reagan's speeches (which made all but hardened skeptics feel warm and fuzzy), supported his defense buildup (which provided welcome jobs during a nasty first-term recession), and reelected him by a large margin (over a candidate, Walter Mondale, who imprudently promised to raise taxes), they never cottoned to the neoconservative definition of the national interest. In the case of Nicaragua, the Congress explicitly cut off funding for Reagan's covert war against the Sandinista government. (Administration operatives would not take no for an answer and circumvented the congressional ban by the methods that produced the Iran-Contra scandal.)

Americans were much happier at a turn of events that started in Moscow in 1985 and gradually, then rapidly, redefined the politics of Europe. Soviet Premier Mikhail Gorbachev's plan to revitalize Soviet socialism required a respite with the West and led to the first important arms reduction agreements since the start of the Cold War. More important, Gorbachev's reforms required the Soviet client states of Eastern Europe to initiate reforms of their own, which led, in rapid-fire succession during the second half of 1989, to the dismantling of East European communism. By then, the anticommunist momentum was overwhelming, and before dissipating at the end of 1991 it swept aside Gorbachev and the Soviet Union itself.

The end of the Cold War was dazzling—and disorienting. Although the definition of the American national interest had shifted during the four decades since the start of the Cold War, with a particular break at Vietnam, it had always included the Soviet Union as a fundamental reference point. Now that reference point was gone, and Americans struggled to find a new one. Defense of the American homeland remained the sine qua non of the national interest, but nothing and no one offered a credible, or even conceivable, challenge on that count. (Terrorists, the new staple of Tom Clancy and other writers of thrillers, might blow up a building here or there, but such activity fell into the category of crime rather than war.) Defense of the U.S. economy could still arouse the American people: when Saddam Hussein seized the oil of Kuwait and threatened the wells of Saudi Arabia, President George H. W. Bush was able to marshal support behind an effort to protect what his secretary of state, James Baker, summarized in a word: "jobs." But military force was a blunt instrument for economic diplomacy; more appropriate were the North American Free Trade Agreement and the accords that moved China toward membership in the World Trade Organization. Even these noncoercive measures, however, enlisted far from unanimous support. Despite the unprecedented prosperity of the decade after the Cold War, many Americans registered real skepticism of the general phenomenon of globalization.

The hardest question for Americans during the 1990s was whether the American national interest included the defense of human rights overseas. Did the national interest require, or even suggest, dispatching troops to Bosnia to stop the "ethnic cleansing" there? To Somalia to deliver food to starving children and restore order where government had vanished? To Haiti to reinstall a president democratically elected but driven from office? To Rwanda to prevent the massacre of a half million men, women, and children on the wrong side of a murderous tribal conflict? To Serbia to secure self-determination for the Kosovo Albanians?

Beyond the basics of human rights, what about the promotion of democracy? Since the French Revolution, Americans had applauded the installation of governments responsible to the governed; but was this something worth making a fuss, or a fight, over? Should economic aid to the former Soviet republics be conditioned on elections and the rule of law? Should China be pressured to allow dissent and competitive politics?

By the beginning of the twenty-first century, Americans had reached no consensus on these issues. No single definition of the national interest commanded the support of any substantial majority. The concept was still invoked: the administration of George W. Bush entered office in 2001 promising a foreign policy based on the "national interest" (rather, the new Bush men and women implied, than on the squishier standards of the outgoing Clinton administration). But they offered few specifics as to what their definition of the national interest entailed. Perhaps when they did, it would rally their compatriots behind a single, stirring vision. More likely, given the experience of two centuries of American history, it would simply spark more debate.

BIBLIOGRAPHY

Barnes, Harry Elmer. *The Genesis of the World War: An Introduction to the Problem of War Guilt.* New York, 1926, 1929, 1970.

Beard, Charles Austin, and G. H. E. Smith. *The Idea of National Interest: An Analytical Study in American Foreign Policy.* New York, 1934.

Beisner, Robert L. *Twelve Against Empire: The Anti-Imperialists, 1898–1900.* New York, 1968. The debate about the Philippines and empire.

Brands, H. W. *The Devil We Knew: Americans and the Cold War.* New York, 1993. What we thought, why we fought.

———. *What America Owes the World: The Struggle for the Soul of Foreign Policy.* New York, 1998.

———. "The Idea of the National Interest." *Diplomatic History* 23 (1999): 239–261. Reprinted in Michael J. Hogan, ed. *Ambiguous Legacy: U.S. Foreign Relations in the "American Century."* New York, 1999. Concentrates on the twentieth century.

Brands, H. W., ed. *The Use of Force After the Cold War.* College Station, Tex., 2000. For and against.

Cole, Wayne S. *America First: The Battle Against Intervention, 1940–1941.* Madison, Wis., 1953.

Dallek, Robert. *The American Style of Foreign Policy: Cultural Politics and Foreign Affairs.* New York, 1983.

Divine, Robert A. *The Illusion of Neutrality.* New York, 1962. Where the isolationists went wrong.

Ehrman, John. *The Rise of Neoconservatism: Intellectuals and Foreign Affairs, 1945–1994.* New Haven, Conn., 1995.

Gilbert, Felix. *To the Farewell Address: Ideas of Early American Foreign Policy.* Princeton, N.J., 1961. What Hamilton thought and Washington said.

Graebner, Norman A., ed. *Ideas and Diplomacy: Readings in the Intellectual Tradition of American Foreign Policy.* New York, 1964.

Grattan, C. Hartley. *Why We Fought.* New York, 1929.

Haass, Richard N. *The Reluctant Sheriff: The United States After the Cold War.* New York, 1997.

Hunt, Michael H. *Ideology and U.S. Foreign Policy.* New Haven, Conn., 1987.

Jonas, Manfred. *Isolationism in America, 1935–1941.* Ithaca, N.Y., 1966, and Chicago, 1990.

Kaplan, Lawrence S. *Jefferson and France: An Essay on Politics and Political Ideas.* New Haven, Conn., 1967. The roots of Republican foreign policy.

McDougall, Walter A. *Promised Land, Crusader State: The American Encounter with the World Since 1776.* Boston, 1997.

Merk, Frederick, and Louis Bannister Merk. *Manifest Destiny and Mission in American History; A Reinterpretation.* New York, 1963. A response to Albert K. Weinberg's *Manifest Destiny.*

Morgenthau, Hans Joachim. *Politics Among Nations: The Struggle for Power and Peace.* New York, 1948, 6th ed., New York, 1985. The bible of Cold War realism.

Smith, Tony. *America's Mission: The United States and the Worldwide Struggle for Democracy in the Twentieth Century.* Princeton, N.J., 1994.

Weinberg, Albert K. *Manifest Destiny: A Study of Nationalist Expansionism in American History.* Baltimore, 1935. A classic.

Williams, William Appleman. *The Tragedy of American Diplomacy.* Rev. ed. New York, 1962. By the father of Cold War revisionism.

See also ANTI-IMPERIALISM; CONTINENTAL EXPANSION; DOCTRINES; IMPERIALISM; NEUTRALITY; OPEN DOOR INTERPRETATION; PUBLIC OPINION; WILSONIANISM.

NATIONALISM

Lawrence S. Kaplan

Nationalism suffers from confusion both over the meaning of the term and over its role in the modern world. Its antecedents may be found in the fifteenth and sixteenth centuries, with the rise of the nation-state under dynastic rule, but its ideology and vitality are no older than the late eighteenth century, the period of the American and French revolutions. Nationalism represents a political creed in which the people offer their supreme allegiance to a nation-state. It underlies the cohesion of modern societies and legitimizes a nation's assertions of authority over the lives of its inhabitants.

DEFINING "AMERICAN" NATIONALISM

The earliest manifestation of nationalism, as opposed to mere patriotic impulses, was the rejection of an ancien régime and the transfer of sovereignty from monarch to people. There is in this event a note of liberation of the nation from oppression, either internal or external. As Hans Kohn pointed out in 1957, "Nationalism is inconceivable without the ideas of popular sovereignty preceding." In the words of Carlton Hayes, it is a state of mind, "a modern emotional fusion of two very old phenomena; nationality and patriotism." If freedom to realize one's individual potential can be realized only in the nation-state, then nationalism becomes the antithesis of tyranny and oppression.

But this is not necessarily the totality of the nationalist experience. When the nation demands the supreme loyalty of its citizens, the freedom of the individual may be sacrificed to the welfare of the state. In this elevation of the state there is the concomitant denigration of the outsider and the temptation to advance the nation at the expense of other nations. As nationalism evolved in the nineteenth century, it assumed the ugly forms of imperialism, racism, and totalitarianism; it helped to stimulate world wars in the twentieth century.

It is these pejorative qualities that have led some American critics of nationalism to separate the American experience from the nationalism of Europe. Paul Nagel, an intellectual historian at the University of Missouri, refused even to use the term in dealing with American nationality. For him, "'Nationalism' regularly has implied a doctrine or a specific form of consciousness conveying superiority or prestige." Such glorification of country, he felt, should not be part of American loyalties because of the essentially different view of their land and themselves that distinguished Americans from other nationalities. Despite disquieting links between manifest destiny and European imperialism, most American critics find a qualitative difference in American nationalism.

One of the fundaments of nationalism is the sense of folk, of a kinship derived from a common ancestry. Where this bond is lacking or is of secondary importance, a common religion serves as a unifying force. Usually a people united in race or religion also have a clearly defined territory with which they are identified, either in the present or in the past. None of these attributes fits American history. Although England was the primary supplier of settlers, colonial Americans were also fully conscious of their Scottish and German roots at the time of the Revolution. An attenuated Calvinist heritage was as close to common religion as could be found in the eighteenth century, and this was vitiated by the fact that where there were established churches, they were more likely to be Anglican than Calvinist. It was a secularized religious spirit that was found in America. A specific territorial claim evoking national emotions was lacking among a people for whom territorial concerns were equated with an expanding frontier. America was more an idea than a geographical entity.

The "invention of America," as the Mexican historian Edmundo O'Gorman has happily phrased it, marks a major departure from the experience of more organically developed nations. The mythic roots of Italian or Japanese peoples are nourished by a prehistory that tells of special strengths an Aeneas brought to Rome from Troy and special considerations conferred on Japan by virtue of divine descent. It is difficult to locate these qualities in a nation whose beginnings followed the invention of the printing press in western Europe by little more than a generation. The words and deeds of founders could be checked and countered, just as John Smith's tales about Virginia were examined by contemporaries who kept modern records.

Granted that every nation is a mixture of races with synoptic religious values, America is one of the very few nations the distinguishing features of which may be traced directly to the needs of other peoples at a particular period. The courage to embark on an American adventure, as well as the knowledge and skills necessary to discover and settle the New World, stemmed from a Renaissance belief in the capacity of man to achieve a new life. Such a conception was beyond the grasp of the medieval mind. The Reformation's pursuit of individual salvation outside the claims of established religions provided a moral imperative to much of the colonizing experience. Boston became a new Jerusalem when older Zions in Rome, London, and even Geneva had failed. Above all, the potential existence of vast quantities of precious metals in the New World gave a powerful impetus to the discovery and exploitation of American resources. The road to a transformation of life in a secular world, opened by the information of the Crusaders about the Levant and the Orient, led to Europe's colonizing of the Western Hemisphere. American nationalism was touched by all these forces.

The first problem, then, in defining American nationalism is to identify it. An automatic expression of nationalism did not accompany the establishment of the United States. The emotions of the American Revolution were attached to state rather than to nation, and the search for a substitute for a historic memory or a common church or a unifying ruling elite required forty years before it could bind the loyalties of Americans. It was an issue that absorbed the energies of the founders of the new republic and achieved a tentative resolution only after the War of 1812. By that time, the focus of nationalist sentiment was on the special conditions of liberty protected by a new and superior government that had no counterpart elsewhere.

The development of a national identity proceeded throughout the nineteenth century, and continued to be a preoccupation of Americans in the twentieth century. The effort to find suitable symbols to display loyalty was a lengthy process. As late as the Civil War there was more than one design of the national flag. It was not until 1942 that the ritual for its display on buildings or on platforms was completed, and the pledge of allegiance was made obligatory in many schools only a generation earlier. The insertion of "under God" in the pledge of allegiance was a product of the pieties of the post–World War II era. Even the national anthem, "The Star-Spangled Banner," was not so designated until 1931. The insecurity over identification of nationalism is equally apparent in the sensitivity over the meanings of "Americanism" and "un-Americanism."

A second, and overlapping, element in nationalism is the peculiar relationship between state and federal governments. The question had its roots in the making of the Constitution, as did the term "federal" used by its framers. It was a euphemism designed to secure support for a new basic law that implied the supremacy of a strong central government. An open affirmation of this purpose in 1787 would have meant the failure of the Constitutional Convention in a country where primary loyalties still belonged to the states and where the word "federal" suggested a fair sharing of power. The struggle between state and nation, begun with the failure of a genuine federal system under the Confederation, was a persistent theme in American life for three-quarters of a century. Although it was present in the Jeffersonian challenge to Alexander Hamilton in the 1790s and in Federalist disaffection from the Jeffersonian conflict with England in the next decade and a half, its dominance over American life coincided with southern sectionalism, culminating in the Civil War. That conflict ended not only in the triumph of the North but also in the vesting of new mystical powers in the Union and the Constitution. Nationalism after 1865 would always be equated with a nation, "one and indivisible," with the "unum" in "e pluribus unum" superior to the "pluribus."

A third strand in American nationalism, which is also as old as the Republic, is the special destiny of America. The hand of Providence as well as of man is involved. If America is a "new world," its rise must have a divine meaning; and that meaning was always translated into some form of sharing the blessings of liberty with less-favored peoples. The religious quality inherent in the image of a "chosen people" was enhanced by the secular opportunities open to Americans. Vast, empty, rich lands held insecurely by European imperialists seemed manifestly destined for American occupation. Movement into Texas and California was a fulfillment of a destiny not only to occupy the entire continent but also to help the rest of humanity see how that occupation would spread the principles of free speech, free religion, self-government, and boundless economic opportunities that were denied to the Old World. Here was a sense of mission that sharpened in clashes with Britain or with Spain, but it was a mission that was susceptible to foreign influence. The unique character of a civilization serving as a beacon to others, a model to be copied, could be (and was) compromised by the change in status from a small, vulnerable republic to a continental empire with overseas ambitions. The altruism of an earlier time was thoroughly mixed, at the end of the nineteenth century, with prevailing influences of social Darwinism and Anglo-Saxon racism.

Most of the elements making up America's self-image of a divinely favored nation still survive, even though the trauma of a great economic depression in the 1930s, the burdens of world governance in the 1950s, and increasing doubts over social injustice and corruption at home and exploitation abroad have had disillusioning effects upon the meaning of the American mission. Yet with all these doubts, the connection between God's special favor and the American way of life remains part of nationalism. And, for all its flaws, the virtues associated with the record of American nationalism suggest distinctive qualities not found in other national experiences.

CONSTRUCTING AN AMERICAN IDENTITY

The most difficult period to identify in the evolution of nationalism is the time of its inception. The very name of America came comparatively late into the consciousness of the British colonies, and the first awareness of a separate destiny is a matter of continuing speculation. Boyd Shafer found an incipient national loyalty appearing as far back as 1740, during King George's War. Paul Varg of Michigan State University settled on 1759, Britain's annus mirabilis in the war with France. Richard Merritt, a Yale political scientist, employed quantitative techniques to determine that 1770 was the year when key colonial newspapers cited "America" more frequently than "British colonies" in their columns. Although by the middle of the eighteenth century it was obvious that Americans were becoming something more than transplanted Englishmen, many future revolutionaries were quick to proclaim their British affiliations as the mother country triumphed over France in the French and Indian War. There was genuine pride in membership in a great British empire. As late as 1775, the poet Philip Freneau was convinced that Britain could and should "rule our hearts again," if only the rights of the American part of the empire were respected.

After the Revolution had shattered that empire, no automatic transfer of loyalty from London to the Confederation, with its seat in Philadelphia, took place. To a New Englander or a Georgian, Philadelphia was as distant as London. The differences between North and South, tidewater and piedmont, were potentially as deep as differences between Americans and Englishmen. Culture as well as geography distinguished the Bostonian from the Virginian, and the tidewater Virginian from the Scottish frontiersman of the Blue Ridge. Some of the most fundamental characteristics of the American way of life—freedom from arbitrary government and freedom of speech and religion—were Virginian or Pennsylvanian as well as American. The America of 1776 could have remained as much an abstraction as Europe was then and now. The experience of Latin American revolutions a generation later could have been that of the former British colonies.

The vulnerability of a young republic in a world of hostile monarchies provided a major incentive for the cultivation of an American identity. The strength of nationalism was an inspiration to American statesmen aware of the temptations that quarreling American states offered to Europeans awaiting the demise of the American experiment. An anxious neighbor like Spain to the west and south, and an angry neighbor like Britain to the north, looked forward to exploiting the divisions among the former colonies. Even the ally France observed American weakness with complacence, knowing that it would bind Americans to their French patron.

The anticipated failure of the republican regime made success all the more important to the Founders, and this success depended on a strong pride in their achievements. Richard Morris pointed out that an ideology of nationalism could be built on what Europeans regarded as intolerable infirmities: the spectacle of a free people governing themselves under conditions of liberty no other people enjoyed, and managing their affairs in such a way as to be an inspiration to the less fortunate. As Thomas Paine phrased it in his *Crisis,* the United States would be in a position "to make a world happy, to teach mankind the art of being so—to exhibit on the theatre of the universe a character hitherto unknown, and to have, as it were, a new creation intrusted to our hands."

There was an important distinction, however, between pronouncing American superiority on such grounds and building a foundation to support it. Poets, playwrights, and even lexicographers were as sensitive to the importance of building institutions to sustain American achievements as were the diplomats and statesmen. Noah Webster's labors on a dictionary were intended to establish an American language distinct from the English of the mother country. At one and the same time his dictionary would proclaim the differences between the two nations and provide a standard that could be used to deepen those differences in the future. His work was a success, but not quite on the terms he had set. The American language was only partially freed from its inferiority complexes.

Other intellectuals of this period harked back to classical antiquity to assert the American distinctiveness. The American republic was to be accepted, not as a replication of any contemporary European nation but as an improved reincarnation of ancient Greece and Rome. From language to architecture to political imagery, the classical period was invoked. If Rome had its *Aeneid* to glorify its origins, the Connecticut poet Joel Barlow was willing to offer his country *The Columbiad,* which attested to

> A work so vast a second world required,
> By oceans bourn'd, from elder states retired;
> Where, uncontaminated, unconfined,
> Free contemplation might expand the mind,
> To form, fix, prove the well-adjusted plan
> And base and build the commonwealth of man.

Whatever its poetic merits, *The Columbiad* claimed a new world to be even more superior to the Old World than Rome was to its rivals. But, like Rome, the United States was prepared to grant to mankind something better in human relations than it had ever witnessed before.

This language was the stuff of nationalism. It was also braggadocio, inviting the mockery of enemies and condescending friends. If, as Europe observed, America was no Rome, certainly Barlow and Freneau were neither Virgils nor Homers. America's pretensions were fair game for Europeans of all stripes. It was the American abroad whose national sensibilities were most exposed. John Adams, minister to Great Britain under the Confederation, was never more the American than when he was snubbed at the Court of St. James's. Even in France, which came to the aid of the United States in war, Thomas Jefferson, Adams's counterpart at the Bourbon court, was a victim of many of the slights suffered by Adams, although French motives were less hostile.

That America was unlike other nations was not the question. It was the nature of the differences that distressed diplomats in Europe. French enthusiasts of America were frequently as negative as open adversaries were. The idealization of Americans as Rousseau's "noble savages" stirred European sympathies for the United States, but the European emphasis upon savagery over nobility stirred resentment among Americans. One of Jefferson's more emotional moments in Europe was his encounter with the pejorative opinions of French intellectuals concerning the American character. His *Notes on the State of Virginia* was a response to those Europeans who shared the views of the naturalist Georges Buffon that animal life in America was inferior in size and strength to that of the Old World. Jefferson's response went beyond a literary effort; Buffon received skins and skeletons of American animals sent to France at Jefferson's behest to prove the equality, if not the superiority, of life in the New World. Even more galling was the charge of the philosophe Abbé Guillaume Raynal that human life degenerated on the American continent. This observation contained aspersions on American virility as well as on American genius. Jefferson countered this assault with a spirited presentation of Indian virtues. He labored valiantly, but under obvious handicaps, in pointing out poets and artists, mathematicians and scientists, to match the products of Europe. Benjamin Franklin and David Rittenhouse were not the equals of Galileo and Newton.

The vigor of American ripostes to perceived insults to their nationality inspired more derision than respect among Europeans of this period. None was more devastating than the Reverend Sydney Smith, a Yorkshire wit who reacted to American claims to being "the greatest, the most enlightened, the most moral people upon earth" by asking rhetorically, "In the four quarters of the globe, who reads an American book? or goes to an American play? or looks at an American picture or statue?" So much for the pretensions of American nationalism. A sense of inferiority in relation to older civilizations seemed to have given rise to a hyperbolic style of self-defense that invited ridicule.

But Smith's famous article in the *Edinburgh Review*, which appeared in 1820, would have been more deflating had it appeared a generation earlier, when Barlow and Freneau were poetizing. Between 1783 and 1815 national pride expanded enormously to encompass a much larger company than a few diplomats abroad and the Hartford Wits at home. The nation, having acquired an inland empire and having faced down Britain in war, again shared its exhilaration. The very newness and freedoms of an empty land lacking oppressive government or a cultivated aristocracy, which Europeans translated as barbaric and uncultured, were the reasons for American superiority.

The Revolution had not stimulated nationalism among most Americans in the immediate postwar years. National attention was on the disarray—economic and political—that separation from Britain had brought. There was little occasion for self-congratulation. Such loyalty to country as was visible in this period was to the patriarchal figure of George Washington, and even this symbol did not emerge untarnished from the political debates. In the absence of a court, and even of a flag, Washington's services as the unifying father of his country were vital for the rallying of national sentiment. He was the Cincinnatus of America who sacrificed himself to perform services no one else could provide, and then retired rather than retain power. His was a vital function for the growth of nationalism, and yet it was incomplete. He found himself enmeshed, and ultimately damaged, by political controversy in the last years of his presidency. The Fourth of July, Independence Day, was a supplementary unifier, as toasts were drunk and cannons fired in honor of the Declaration of Independence. But as exciting as the celebrations may have been, they were as much a victory over the British by Pennsylvanians or New Yorkers as a victory by Americans.

The wave of nationalism that failed to rise in the 1780s and 1790s finally broke over America in the second war with Britain. The Francophilia that had briefly prevailed among Jeffersonians had dissipated in the disillusionment over the policies of the French Republic and in recognition of the dangers of Napoleonic imperialism. Federalist failure to exploit Francophobia fully during the Quasi-War with France in 1798–1800 reflects a deficiency in the quality of nationalism as much as it does the political power of the Jeffersonian opposition. Anglophilia, more enduring among Federalists of the Northeast, ended more gradually. For those who could not forsake British ties for reasons of custom or conviction or commerce, the consequence was isolation from most of their countrymen and, ultimately, extinction of the Federalist Party as a political entity. The majority of that party joined Republicans in a nationalism influenced by the trans-Appalachian and trans-Mississippi West. Federalists had exerted minuscule influence in 1783, and the Republican Party did not come into being until the Louisiana Purchase of 1803.

During the War of 1812, Jonathan Russell, a businessman-politician, was inspired by the *Constitution*'s victory over the British frigate *Guerrière* to burst out in a paean of praise of its commander, Isaac Hull. The event elevated Hull to Washingtonian heights:

> Yes! deathless, oh Hull, shall thy fame live
>   in story
> And cheer, in the battle, our sons on the wave—
> Through ages unborn shall the beams of
>   thy glory,
> Unclouded, illumine the march of the brave.

If such a minor figure as Hull could evoke such emotion from such an unlikely source, it is understandable that the common soldier, who was ignored after the Revolutionary War, would also receive attention. Congress finally granted pensions for revolutionary war service in 1818. American identity was no longer a problem on 4 July 1826, when the two great builders of nationalism and independence, Thomas Jefferson and John Adams, died within hours of each other on the fiftieth anniversary of the Declaration of Independence they both helped to write. A generation earlier, when Washington died, the apotheosis of the first president was still a tribute to a single man, no matter how significant the deification was in the fashioning of national unity. On Independence Day of 1826, the passing of the second and third presidents of the United States was the occasion for the nation's apotheosis of itself.

CONTINENTAL EXPANSION AND THE "YOUNG AMERICA" SPIRIT

For nationalism to flourish, it was obvious that the United States had to prove its experiment successful. The War of 1812 was one proving ground. More significant than a diplomatic success against

Britain was the spectacular rise in the national economy, sparked by population increase, territorial acquisitions, and technological changes in transportation and industry. Speaking of the period after the Treaty of Ghent, Henry Adams observed, "The continent lay before them, like an uncovered ore-bed. They could see and they even could calculate with reasonable accuracy the wealth it could be made to yield." The steady accumulation of power to the central government at the expense of the states was equated with the growth of America. Nationalism implied the denigration of sectionalism and states' rights.

The conflict between central and local governments that accompanied the rise of nationalism was not surprising. The European nation-states experienced the assertion of central power by means of powerful monarchs overcoming the separatism of feudal nobles. What distinguished the American experience from others was the special nature of the central authority; it was not personified by a president, not even George Washington. The mystical conception of a constitution blessing a union permitted the cherished American liberties to flourish.

The argument for centralizing government during the Confederation had been fought on the assumption that no other government could perform that function. States' rights might rally libertarians worried about the tyranny of rule from afar, but the veterans of the revolutionary war returning to their farms and villages were more concerned about economic depression and foreclosures on their properties than with the potential evils of a distant national government. Had there been a stronger central authority in the Confederation, revolutionary war heroes of the order of Ethan Allen, who proposed attaching Vermont to Canada, and George Rogers Clark, who considered a Spanish connection to secure Kentuckians' access to the Gulf of Mexico, would have been less tempted to join with the former British enemy and the hostile Spanish neighbor. Where the states individually or collectively as the Confederation had failed to respond to Indian or European threats in the West, the Union drove the Indians out of the Northwest, saved the nation from the British in 1812–1815, and wrested Florida from the Spanish in 1819. As the western territories entered the Union their loyalties were to the nation that welcomed them rather than to any pristine colonial commonwealth. Unlike the original thirteen states, they had been created by acts of the federal Congress.

Still, the centrifugal forces that had always been a part of the American experience had not disappeared. Such "good feeling" as existed after 1815 did not have its premise in the end of sectionalism or even states' consciousness; rather, the "American system" of Henry Clay was built on a common hostility to British economic power that would help to mesh the economies of the North, the West, and the South. If there was temporary harmony at this time, it was largely because each section had unrealistic expectations of special advantage from congressional support of tariffs or of internal improvements.

The slave-oriented South found the Union ultimately a threat both to its economy and to its society, and in the Civil War provided the greatest challenge the Union had to surmount in the nation's history. The war was considered by some as a struggle between two competing nationalisms. In the years preceding this conflict, the Union became the most vital national symbol to the North. Southern challenges on constitutional grounds became increasingly insufferable. The South's interpretations signified more than just a peculiar gloss of the Constitution; the North regarded them as a rending of the instrument of America's sovereignty and the consequent extinction of the American nation. While loyalty to a section greater than loyalty to the nation could be considered patriotism, by 1860 the majority of the country was convinced that an effective American sovereignty could be expressed only in a unified nation.

A generation earlier, Alexis de Tocqueville, that astute French visitor, wrote, "The Union is an ideal nation that exists, so to speak, only in the mind." It also existed in the heart. The passions over slavery converted it into something more than a means of achieving effective government. The Union became an object of reverence, the indispensable foundation of national values.

Daniel Webster attempted to exploit this sentiment to deflect sectional rivalry into the popular channel of xenophobia. In a direct insult to Austria in 1849, President Zachary Taylor promised recognition to Hungary if its revolution succeeded, and then, after its failure, his successor Millard Fillmore gave its leader a tumultuous welcome to America in 1852. Secretary of State Webster not only rejected Austria's subsequent protest but went out of his way to taunt its minister to the United States, Chevalier J. G. Hülsemann. He lectured the Austrian on Hungary's good sense in imitating the American Revolution. Should the

Austrians have any objection, they must reckon with the fact that "the power of this republic, at the present moment, is spread over a region, one of the richest and most fertile on the globe, and of an extent in comparison with which the possessions of the House of Hapsburg are but as a patch on the earth's surface."

This well-publicized letter struck just the chord Webster hoped to reach in Americans. The appeal to chauvinism with hyperbolic rhetoric performed an important function in 1850. It united North and South in opposition to Europe. But the forces of disunion that Webster had hoped to dissipate were stronger than those of nationalism. In even greater desperation a decade later, Secretary of State William H. Seward tried to divert the country from war by urging President Abraham Lincoln to turn over the executive powers to him so that he could save the Union by initiating war against France or Spain, or all of Europe. The president rejected the proposal, but unrealistic as it may have been in 1861 and fantastic as it has sounded to later generations, the spirit behind the plan was the same one that had propelled the American system of Henry Clay, the Mexican War maneuvers of President James K. Polk, and Daniel Webster's note to Hülsemann. Antagonism to the Old World was a staple of American nationalism, especially in times of crisis.

The traumas of sectional conflict resulted in the removal of the constitutional question from nationalism. The Union had triumphed and with it sentiments of nationalism. The sobriety with which nationalism was expressed in the middle years of the century yielded to a reassertion of the older boisterous spirits. The end of war witnessed a period of even more rapid growth in population, wealth, and power than had been seen fifty years earlier, after the Treaty of Ghent. It also revived—in exaggerated ways before the century was over—the idea of mission that had been implicit in the American self-image from the beginning: the notion that God had given America a special portion of blessings, and with it a mission to share them with less-favored peoples.

Prior to the Civil War the most vocal articulation of the American mission had accompanied crises with Spain or Britain or France over their possessions in North America. They all violated a divine plan. While the idea of providential occupation of the West antedated the annexation of Texas and the demands for Oregon—and, indeed, may be found in Jeffersonian ruminations in the 1780s—it was John L. O'Sullivan, editor of the *Democratic Review*, who in 1845 specifically charged foreign hostility and jealousy with "limiting our greatness and checking the fulfillment of our manifest destiny to overspread the continent allotted by Providence for the free development of our yearly multiplying millions." Texas, California, and Oregon—and even Upper Canada—were equated with empty land awaiting the arrival of Americans to bring it under proper cultivation.

Americans did not regard these views or the actions that followed from them as analogous to European imperialism; they were simply the natural spread of free peoples and free institutions into unoccupied space wrongly claimed by others. Although such assertions might have sounded hypocritical to hostile observers, even opponents of the Mexican War could concede that the mission to spread liberty bore marks of idealism. Frederick Merk found in expansionism a spirit that was "idealistic, self-denying, hopeful for divine favor for national aspirations, though not sure of it." So if manifest destiny was connected with the grasping for land, it was also linked to the land's improvement by peopling it with what Americans of the period considered to be a better society than could have been achieved under its original proprietors. In the midst of the Mexican War, former secretary of the Treasury Albert Gallatin defined the American mission as a great experiment in which "a representative democratic republic" had a chance to try out its ideals on a large scale. "If it failed, the last hope of the friends of mankind was lost, or indefinitely postponed; and the eyes of the world were turned towards you. Whenever real or pretended apprehension of the imminent danger of trusting people at large with power were expressed, the answer was 'Look at America.'"

In this spirit the migration of Americans to Texas or California or Oregon signified not exploitation of native peoples, or governance over unwilling subjects, but the sharing of liberties over a wider area. The growing United States had spilled its surplus population into neighboring territories that were relatively empty. When those territories were sufficiently populous, they would enter the Union, ultimately as full and equal partners of the older states. If there was conflict within the United States over their admission, this was a function of the slavery quarrels, not of a desire for imperialist control on the part of the nation.

But it was difficult to deny that the partial dismemberment of Mexico compromised the missionary spirit behind manifest destiny. The opposition of such distinguished figures as John

Quincy Adams, an authentic expansionist, and the poet James Russell Lowell helped to arouse a sense of guilt over a war that many abolitionists regarded as an act of aggression by southern slavery interests. That Mexican and Indian populations, no matter how scattered, lived in California or New Mexico gave a taste of imperialism to the fruits of American nationalism. Was manifest destiny, then, merely a mask for American conquest of a weak neighbor?

Although a repugnant element can never be expunged from nationalism, extenuating factors refine the annexation of Texas and even the ensuing war with Mexico. Manifest destiny was more than an instrument of southern interests; the pull of California had attracted New England mercantile ambitions as well. More important, it was a national rather than a sectional impulse, with a powerful England, as in the case of the Oregon quarrel, a major antagonist in 1844. The hope was that the two Canadas would sue for admission to the new and enlarged Union. O'Sullivan speculated that Canada, as easily as California, could be the next "customer."

Arrogant and self-serving as this language sounded in press, pulpit, and schools, its users could unreservedly contrast the freedom of religion and self-government in the territories under American control with the repression of a state church in Mexico and the limitations of political freedom in Canada. When the demands for annexation threatened to get out of hand, as in the pressure for the absorption of all Mexico, opponents stopped the threat effectively. Partisan fears of Mexico parceled into slave states may have been a powerful incentive for opposition, but they were fueled as well by the unpalatable prospect of governing an unassimilable population that would not participate in the American political process.

Although controversy continues to swirl about the purity of American motives in continental expansion, it does not apply to the display of nationalism in this period. It was genuine and widespread. If any emotion could have overcome the deep divisions within the Union in the middle of the nineteenth century, it was pride in American institutions and in the nation's power to proclaim them to the world. Had it not been for the slavery issue, Thomas Bailey of Stanford University speculated, "Americans would not only have swaggered more in the subsequent years but would have grasped more territories." As it was, the Young America spirit that flourished in the wake of the Mexican War expressed itself in provocations against Europe. The Revolution of 1848 was a suitable occasion for its display. George Bancroft, historian and diplomat, from his post in London expressed America's approval of the revolutions: "Can we show ourselves lukewarm, while the Old World is shaking off its chains and emancipating and enthroning the masses?"

THE AMERICAN MISSION ABROAD: IMPERIALISM AND EMPIRE

Changes that occurred later in the century provided a different gloss both to the idea of manifest destiny and to the meaning of mission. The new "manifest destiny" of the 1890s involved acquisition and control of an overseas empire. Although the older xenophobia and the civilizing mission remained, they were more strident in their tone and also more derivative of the European experience. The distinctions between European and American imperialism appeared to blur at the turn of the century. It was not that the popular nature of nationalism had altered significantly. The beer-garden simplicity with which the flag was venerated in the 1890s and the gusto with which the Spanish were rebuked for their behavior in Cuba linked Theodore Roosevelt to Davy Crockett. Finley Peter Dunne, the leading press satirist at the time of America's rise to world power, put words into the mouth of his Mr. Dooley that would have been as fitting half a century before: "'We're a great people,' said Mr. Hennessy earnestly. 'We are,' said Mr. Dooley. 'We are that. An' th' best iv it is, we know that we are.'"

What was different was a respectful interest in European imperialism and a wish by many American leaders to imitate it. As the burgeoning American economy produced enormous wealth, the instant oil, meat-packing, and rail barons sought marriage alliances with the Old World and pursued culture by bringing the French Middle Ages or Tudor England architecturally to their Rhode Island estates or New York City palaces. But they were conscious that they still lacked a sense of ideological security that European aristocrats possessed as a birthright. The spirit of Teutonic, and especially Anglo-Saxon, solidarity filled some of the needs of an insecure upper class. Although England may have remained a commercial and political rival, there was a surge of appreciation for the kinship of the two peoples that would account for the greatness of both.

The scholar-diplomats George Bancroft and John Lothrop Motley had commented earlier on the role that racial stock had in assuring a nation's greatness. Both had been students in Germany. Granting his distaste for some aspects of Prussian militarism, Bancroft claimed that it would be the instrument to win "more rapidly liberty in Europe than all that the Kossuths, Garibaldis, and Mazzinis could effect in half a century." Motley celebrated Teutonic virtues by noting that Holland's struggle with Spain in the sixteenth century "must have particular interest, for it is a portion of the records of the Anglo-Saxon race—essentially the same, whether in Friesland, England, or Massachusetts." Another diplomat, James Russell Lowell, more poet than scholar, brought the good news to England that "the duty which has been laid upon the English-speaking races, so far as we can discover, has been to carry over the great lessons of liberty combined with order. That is the great secret of civilization." In a major disquisition on democracy in 1884, Lowell had spoken of the problems that Americans encountered with the irresponsible masses in the large cities that were composed of peoples of inferior stock. America's success in overcoming these obstacles to become a great democracy could be traced to the fact that "the acorn from which it sprang was ripened on the British oak."

The only trouble with these perorations was the implication of a junior partnership for America in the racial connection. This became increasingly unacceptable to nationalists. A colonial relationship with even the best of the Old World did not fit America's self-image by the time the nineteenth century ended. America would be superior to Britain even in racism. Albert J. Beveridge of Indiana pointed out to the Senate that "God has not been preparing the English-speaking and Teutonic peoples for a thousand years for nothing but vain and idle self-contemplation and self-admiration. . . . And of all our race He has marked the American people as His chosen nation to finally lead in the redemption of the world."

For those who might not heed a divine appeal, the mandate of social Darwinism brought the same message. The transfer of Darwinian principles from a struggle among species for survival to a competition among nations moved the naturalist's theory of evolution from biology to sociology and international relations almost from the moment of its conception. Presumably the laws of nature justified power in the hands of the fittest; and in the late nineteenth century the arena for the display of national superiority lay in carving out colonial empires in Asia and Africa. For the United States to stand by and remove itself from this competition would be an admission of inferiority. Since the American continent was filled, expansion would have to take place overseas. The alternative would be both a sapping of national strength and increasing advantage to European competitors in the Darwinian struggle for greatness.

The naval historian Alfred Thayer Mahan, more than any other figure, tied together the strains of racial pride and Darwinian sanctions with the economic significance of the acquisition of colonies. Such an undertaking would solve the problems of surplus goods flowing from what appeared, after the Panic of 1893, to be an overdeveloped economic plant. It would also satisfy the defense needs of the nation, through a navy protecting routes to new colonies. Lastly, it would address the imperative of carrying the blessings of American civilization abroad.

Indeed, the American mission was ultimately the most important rationalization for imperial control. The Reverend Josiah Strong, secretary of the Evangelical Alliance and a powerful publicist for expansion, exhorted Americans to respect their sacred trust by bestowing their privileges upon other sectors of humanity. After all, "they are not proprietors, apportioning their own, but simply *trustees* or managers of God's property. . . . Our plea is not America for America's sake," he wrote in *Our Country* (1885), "but America for the world's sake." It is this eleemosynary spirit that gave meaning to President William McKinley's reluctance to leave the Philippines under Spanish control or under its own governance. In confessing his agony over the decision to annex the islands, he finally realized, "there was nothing left for us to do but to take them all, and to educate the Filipinos, and uplift and civilize and Christianize them, and by God's grace do the very best we could by them, as our fellow-men for whom Christ also died."

The gulf between McKinley's understanding of America's mission and those of the French, British, Germans, and Russians was not as wide as the gulf between McKinley's or Theodore Roosevelt's conception of mission and that of Jefferson or John Quincy Adams. The Monroe Doctrine had made it clear that America was to serve as a model for others to emulate, but not as an instrument to involve itself in the afflictions of the less fortunate. America's own system could only be corrupted by such involvement. So Adams concluded when he counseled President James Monroe not to intervene against Turkey on behalf of the admired Greek revolutionaries. But by the end of the century the combination of racial pretensions, Darwinian impulses, and putative economic imperatives had broken one great barrier of isolationism. They affected more than the special interests of navalists, businessmen, or missionaries. Even so sensitive a scholar as Frederick Jackson Turner found virtue in overseas expansion. He "rowed with the tide of the new nationalism," Ralph Gabriel noted in his *Course of American Democratic Thought,* at least for a while, as he pondered the effect of the passing of the frontier upon American democracy. It was hoped that settlement of Hawaii and the Philippines could have the same beneficial results for democracy as the settlement of Ohio and Iowa had in the past.

For Turner and for most Americans, the new manifest destiny was a mistake, an aberration of American tradition. In the wake of Filipino resistance to American occupation in 1899, William Jennings Bryan observed, "'Destiny' was not as manifest as it was a few weeks ago." Most American leaders were slower to realize this than Bryan had been. The tide of empire finally receded, but not before it had left a permanent imprint on the fabric of American nationalism, or at least had deepened indentations that had always been there. The country came to recognize the incompatibility between the governance of Iowa and the governance of the Philippines; the former was based on self-government and eventual statehood, the latter, on imperial control over unassimilable peoples. The result was the gradual disengagement from the imperial plans of 1900, and ultimate independence for those islands.

NATIVISM AND "AMERICANIZATION"

If nationalism in the twentieth century recoiled from the problems of assimilation abroad, it could not avoid those problems at home. The rise of Anglo-Saxon racism coincided with massive emigration from non–Anglo-Saxon eastern and southern Europe, which raised questions about the dilution not only of the race but also of the institutions of America. Not all the nativist reactions were hostile. Some were patronizing and even melioristic. The Daughters of the American Revolution and other patriotic societies recognized their duty to "Americanize" the foreigner, to teach him proper speech and manners as well as values. The public school would be the instrument, according to Josiah Strong, by which "the strange and dissimilar races which come to us are, in one generation, assimilated and made Americans." American Catholic and Jewish historical societies, accepting the importance of Americanization, were organized in the 1880s and 1890s to show the nation their own ties with the American past. Their objective was to justify themselves as Americans, different in background but sharing in the creation of a new people. The constitution of the American Irish Historical Society expressed the hope that "in the days to come, that lie in the womb of the future, when all the various elements that have gone and are going to make the republic great, are united in the American,—the man who in his person will represent the bravest elements of all the old races of earth,—we declare that the deeds and accomplishment of our element shall be written in the book of the new race, telling what we did and no more; giving us our rightful place by the side of the others."

Such modesty of aspiration on the part of an immigrant group and such generous impulses on the part of the patronizing older stock were balanced by less edifying side effects of the racist component in nationalism. Ethnic and religious communities vied with each other in claiming credit for contributions to the national history or character, while the Anglo-Saxon elite, under the impact of war and depression in the twentieth century, blamed immigrants for the nation's troubles. War inevitably stokes nationalist passions, and World War I was no exception. The case then was not simply undifferentiated immigrants. German-Americans were identified as enemies with dangerous attachments to the ancestral country. Such manifestations of nationalism at its worst were seen in the banning of Beethoven, the conversion of sauerkraut into liberty cabbage, and the removal of German language instruction from schools. The vehement denunciation of the "hyphenated" American by Woodrow Wilson and Theodore Roosevelt during the war assumed that hyphenation applied to the Irish and Germans, not to the British. The latter's heritage was indistinguishable from the Americans' in 1917.

The revival of the Ku Klux Klan in the 1920s, with its particularly ugly brand of national exclusiveness, was another manifestation of the Anglo-Saxon tradition translated into a self-conscious white Protestant ascendancy. Immigration restriction rather than immigrant amelioration was a consequence of this mood in the period of disillusionment that followed World War I. It is ironic that a generation later, in the aftermath of another world war, the followers of Senator Joseph McCarthy, many of them from ethnic backgrounds that could not meet the test of Americanism in the past, led a nationalist assault on the loyalty of the older elite.

In the struggle with Soviet communism after World War II, McCarthy's unprincipled attacks on putative American communists numbered among their victims not merely the principles of civil liberties but also the American eastern "establishment," mostly Anglo-Saxon, which was accused of negligence and worse in the struggle of the nation against external enemies. The emotions of the time evoked the xenophobia of earlier crises, except that the "American" embraced a wider constituency. Nonetheless, the nationalism that was demonstrated in the 1950s, as much as in the 1920s or in the 1890s, was a narrow and self-centered view of the nation's interests.

AMERICANIZING THE WORLD

Despite the many xenophobic impulses released in the name of nationalism, the missionary elements did not disappear in the twentieth century. The retreat from moral uplifting of the natives of the Caribbean or East Asia was short-lived and replaced by an attempt to uplift the entire world, not merely those regions under American governance. In both world wars American democracy became the exemplar for the world. Although Woodrow Wilson won a reputation as a supreme internationalist, seeking a new world order that would end national rivalries, his new order would be on American terms. His conception of the American mission was to disseminate those progressive values, both economic and political, that would serve America's own interests in the world. It was nothing less than the remaking of the world according to an American pattern. Wilson himself rejected a narrow distinction between nationalism and internationalism. "The greatest nationalist," he claimed, "is the man who wants his nation to be the greatest nation, and the greatest nation is the nation which penetrates to the heart of its duty and mission among the nations of the world."

In this context the mission of World War II and the Cold War was a continuation of the Wilsonian worldview. The United Nations would replicate the League of Nations by serving to help America fulfill its duty to humanity. Both the goals and the methods were clearly outlined. Nations would be freed from fear of conquest, with American military power protecting them from Nazis or communists; they would be freed from want by the application of American technology to their economies; they would be freed from ignorance by American learning spread through a Fulbright scholarship program or a Peace Corps. These were the benign purposes of the Marshall Plan and Point Four. They reflected an idealism embodied in President John F. Kennedy's inaugural address in 1961. The language in which they were expressed lacked the overt racial biases and self-satisfied smugness that had characterized many early missionary activities. The publisher Henry Luce anticipated an "American century," in which the United States would serve "as the dynamic center of ever-widening spheres of enterprise, . . . as the training center of the skillful servants of mankind, America as the Good Samaritan, really believing again that it is more blessed to give than to receive, and . . . as the powerhouse of the ideals of Freedom and Justice."

In 1967, Ronald Steel claimed that Luce's American century was in fact a Pax Americana, with very few distinctions between its dictates and those of Rome's imperialism. Whether America willed it or not, it built a world empire to serve its own economic needs; it elevated communism into a monster out of all proportion to the threat presented; it arbitrarily divided the world into Manichaean spheres of good and evil; and, in the name of altruism, it helped to turn parts of Southeast Asia into a wasteland. As Americans reflected with disillusion upon the exaggerated promises of the Truman Doctrine, undertaken in the afterglow of successes in World War II when the United States sought to extend its system throughout the world, they discovered flaws in even the most altruistic postures. Nationalism was a cover for the erosion of civil liberties identified with McCarthyism, for the corruption of government by the accretion of enormous power in the hands of the executive, and for the corresponding diminution of power in the Congress. While the crudities of American imperialism of the Theodore Roosevelt era may have been smoothed, the brutalization of the American character stemming from the anticommunist campaigns in Asia and Latin America was even more distressing.

The result in the post-Vietnam era was a decline in the nationalist spirit. The conscious abuse of the flag by many of the younger generation was a symbolic act of revenge upon a nation that, in the name of liberty, sought conquest of the world for selfish reasons. The very idea of an American mission was called into question, not simply the matter of its betrayal. The result was a retreat by both conservatives and liberals into a neoisolationist stance in the 1970s. Conservatives would turn America's attention back to its own problems, rather than waste resources on an ungrateful world. Liberals urged a less grandiose vision for America's role in the world, blaming American arrogance for troubling the peace of the world.

Both sentiments were present in American society in the last years of the twentieth century. But they were subsumed under a triumphalism that followed the end of the Cold War and implosion of the Soviet empire. President Ronald Reagan's vision of American power seemed to have been realized. Democratic capitalism was to be the model for the world. The striking victory over Saddam Hussein's Iraq in 1991 marked the nation as the world's sole superpower. That the American way of life was the ideal toward which all peoples strove—and most did envy—sparked a nationalist pride that almost effaced the memory of failure in Vietnam. But doubts about the reality of American dominance of a fractious world dimmed the optimism of those who saw the "end of history" in the demise of capitalism. The world at the turn of the twenty-first century was in as much turmoil as it had been when the Soviet Union was the nation's powerful adversary. The shortcomings of American society were also as much—or more—in evidence as in the past, as hitherto quiet minority voices were heard. David Waldstreicher in 1997 observed that Native Americans and African Americans had no reason to celebrate the national fetes that accompanied Independence Day. Nationalism seemed to many Americans to have been tainted by the realities of the nation's history. For Walter A. McDougall, hubris inhered in the familiar temptation to reform the world in the American image. There were limits not only to national virtues but also to national power.

But there is nothing unique about the present mixed emotions about American nationalism. Indeed, skepticism about nationalism is endemic in the American system. Although nationalism is dependent upon an allegiance above all others, the nature of American pluralism militates against a monistic devotion. The nation must compete for public attention. For all its flaws in the past and the present, the special qualities associated with American nationalism—an open society, a mobile society, and above all a society divinely favored—will remain a force in America as long as the nation-state system of governance prevails among the peoples of the world.

BIBLIOGRAPHY

Deutsch, Karl Wolfgang. *Nationalism and Social Communication: An Inquiry into the Foundations of Nationality.* Cambridge, Mass., 1953. Employs the techniques of the social sciences to examine nationalism.

Hayes, Carlton J. H. *Essays on Nationalism.* New York, 1926. A collection of writings by the founder of American studies in nationalism.

Kohn, Hans. *American Nationalism: An Interpretive Essay.* 2d ed. New York, 1980. Particularly useful for its insights on the American character and its relationships to nationalism.

LaFeber, Walter. *The New Empire: An Interpretation of American Expansion, 1860–1898.* Ithaca, N.Y., 1963. Presents an economic explanation of the growth of nationalism.

Levin, N. Gordon, Jr. *Woodrow Wilson and World Politics: America's Response to War and Revolution.* New York, 1968. Links American nationalism with Wilsonian internationalism.

McDougall, Walter A. *Promised Land, Crusader State: The American Encounter with the World since 1776.* Boston, 1997. Warns of the dangers that nationalist pride may bring if America overextends its reach in the world.

May, Ernest R. *American Imperialism: A Speculative Essay.* New York, 1968. Offers speculations on reasons why nationalism developed into imperialism at the end of the nineteenth century.

Merk, Frederick. *Manifest Destiny and Mission in American History: A Reinterpretation.* New York, 1963. Gives a favorable view of manifest destiny as a link between nationalism and American ideals.

Nye, Joseph S., Jr. *Bound to Lead: The Changing Nature of American Power.* New York, 1990. Reflects the pride that American leadership conveys.

Shafer, Boyd C. *Faces of Nationalism: New Realities and Old Myths.* New York, 1972. Summation of the many approaches to nationalism.

Steel, Ronald. *Pax Americana.* Rev. ed. New York, 1970. Treats nationalism and the Cold War.

Stephanson, Anders. *Manifest Destiny: American Expansion and the Empire of Right.* New York, 1995.

Van Alstyne, Richard W. *Genesis of American Nationalism.* Waltham, Mass., 1970. An examination of nationalism in the early republic.

Waldstreicher, David. *In the Midst of Perpetual Fetes: The Making of American Nationalism, 1776–1820.* Chapel Hill, 1997. Emphasizes flaws in the foundations of American nationalism.

Weinberg, Albert Katz. *Manifest Destiny: A Study of Nationalist Expansionism in American History.* Baltimore, 1935. A major revisionist statement on nineteenth-century nationalism as expressed in manifest destiny.

Zelinsky, Wilbur. *Nation into State: The Shifting Symbolic Foundations of American Nationalism.* Chapel Hill, N.C., 1988. Finds American nationalism evolving from shared national values to events glorifying the nation-state itself.

See also ANTI-IMPERIALISM; CONTINENTAL EXPANSION; IMMIGRATION; IMPERIALISM; NATIVISM; RELIGION; WILSONIAN MISSIONARY DIPLOMACY.

NATIONAL SECURITY COUNCIL

Anna Kasten Nelson

The National Security Council (NSC) has been a ubiquitous presence in the world of foreign policy since its creation in 1947. In light of the tension between the Soviet Union and the United States, policymakers felt that the diplomacy of the State Department was no longer adequate to contain the USSR. The NSC was created specifically to coordinate the various strands of national security policy among the agencies then operating under the rubric of national security. Originally, it was centered around a council dominated by the military services and the State Department and was a paper-driven organization that mostly discussed papers prepared by staff. Both President Harry Truman and President Dwight D. Eisenhower enhanced the role of the council while relying upon interdepartmental staffs for information and analysis. John F. Kennedy chose to use the NSC quite differently. He rarely called the council together, relying instead on the newly appointed national security adviser and his staff. Lyndon B. Johnson followed suit and even enhanced the role of the national security adviser and his staff while calling together the council only for its public relations value. By the presidency of Richard M. Nixon, the NSC had become the national security adviser and his staff, although the original term continued to be used to describe the effort of the president to integrate national security policy. The story of the NSC, therefore, is the story of the evolution of the organization established in 1947.

ORIGINS

For more than 150 years, presidents of the United States conducted foreign policy with the advice of a secretary of state; a small, select group of foreign service officers; and, perhaps, a personal adviser. As he directed American foreign policy during World War II, President Franklin D. Roosevelt continued this tradition through his very personal diplomacy and his reliance on friends and advisers who had served him so well during the era of the Great Depression and the New Deal. The frustrating process of resolving complex problems of strategy and diplomacy within the unstructured and chaotic Roosevelt administration led a number of wartime leaders to search for a new institutional arrangement to fulfill the postwar obligations of a world power.

Concern also centered on the elevation to the presidency after the death of Roosevelt in 1945 of the untested Harry Truman. Worried about the growing tension between the Soviet Union and the United States, many members of Roosevelt's cabinet, including Secretary of the Navy James Forrestal, assumed that the former senator from Missouri would need help from a formal council of advisers to provide the leadership necessary in the postwar period. Forrestal and his supporters began the search for a new institutional arrangement to advise the new president and provide coordination between the various military services, the State Department, and other agencies concerned with foreign affairs.

The opportunity for change unexpectedly arose when President Truman first proposed the unification of the military services, a proposal influenced by General George C. Marshall and his own experience in the Senate as chairman of a committee to investigate the national defense program. The fragmentation that had developed during World War II was now exacerbated by the development of airpower and the creation of three separate air forces, one for each service. Truman first proposed unification in December 1945 in a special message to Congress. The proposal met with hostility and protest. It was studied, debated, attacked, and revised for the next year and a half. With the support of Marshall, the army backed the plan for unification, but James Forrestal and the navy, supported by a coterie of congressional members, were adamantly opposed. The navy wanted to ensure the maintenance of its own air force and, furthermore, Forrestal was opposed to any system that would deprive the navy secretary of a seat in the cabinet and direct access to the president.

But Forrestal was also eager for the military services to be an integral part of foreign policy. He began to seek an alternative to the plan for unification, one that would integrate the decision making of the military services and the State Department without also jeopardizing the position of the navy. He called upon an old friend and former business associate, Ferdinand Eberstadt, to study and recommend an organizational system that would preserve the nation's security. The National Security Council emerged out of Eberstadt's recommendations. Eberstadt's plan emphasized coordination more than unity. The military establishment would remain decentralized but would be surrounded by several coordinating groups, the most important of which was the prototype of a coordinating body chaired by the president and composed of representatives from the State, War, and Navy Departments. Under this plan, the navy, and Forrestal, would continue to have a voice in policy.

Truman's advisers, including General Marshall, were suspicious of any congressionally imposed group that would usurp the president's power to conduct foreign policy and fulfill his duty as commander in chief. When Truman sent his proposal to Congress, a national security council was missing, made unnecessary in his view by the organization of a National Military Establishment with a unified armed services and a single secretary of defense. The navy rallied its supporters in Congress, and it appeared that after eighteen months of negotiations, unification would be defeated. Finally, to stave off defeat and achieve his goal of a unified armed services, Truman agreed to the idea of an advisory council. Meanwhile, his staff members were working on a revised draft of the original proposal. By the time they finished changing a word here and a phrase there, the precisely defined council with an executive director confirmed by the Senate had become a group purely advisory in nature, with no authoritative, statutory functions and a staff appointed at the sole discretion of the president.

Few, if any, members of Congress recognized the ramifications of the proposed National Security Council. Since it was part of the unification act, the legislation did not fall under the jurisdiction of the Senate Foreign Relations Committee but went instead to the Senate Armed Services Committee, which was concerned only with the future of the military services and gave little time to the other agencies created by the measure. The ambiguous language describing the council and its responsibilities meant that some inclusion of advice from the military services in the formation of national security policy would be considered by the president. Otherwise, the law provided little guidance to presidents and their advisers.

THE TRUMAN AND EISENHOWER YEARS

The National Security Act of 1947 established four new coordinating agencies: the National Military Establishment, the Central Intelligence Agency (CIA), the short-lived National Security Resources Board (NSRB); and the National Security Council. The statutory members of the NSC were the president; the secretaries of defense and state; the secretaries of the army, navy, and air force; and the chairman of the NSRB. Forrestal's attempt to gain the ear of the president had resulted in a membership distinctly weighted toward the military. After Forrestal was replaced, amendments to the act in 1949 eliminated the three civilian secretaries of army, navy, and air force and added the vice president to the council.

Since 1949 these four—the secretaries of state and defense, the president, and vice president—have been the core of an ever-changing set of presidential advisers. Virtually from the NSC's inception, the director of the Central Intelligence Agency and the head of the Joint Chiefs of Staff (JCS) have participated in its meetings as "advisers." Often presidents, beginning with Truman, have added the secretary of the Treasury or the director of the Bureau of the Budget (later the Office of Management and Budget) to the mix.

The ambiguity that made for successful compromise provided little guidance for actually organizing the NSC. The statute provides a council "to advise the President with respect to the integration of domestic, foreign, and military policies relating to the national security." To do this, the Council is to "assess and appraise the objectives, commitments and risks of the United States in relation to our actual and potential military power." The council has no statutory function and operates with a staff appointed at the discretion of the president. The NSC is also unique in its relation to Congress. Unlike other executive agencies created by Congress, it has no obligation to report to the legislative branch. With such a vague mandate, initial decisions concerning the NSC's structure seemed particularly important. Members of the defense group envisioned the council as part of the military establishment. It should be housed with the military, they argued, and, more importantly, the president should appoint the secretary of defense to preside over meetings in his absence. In other words, the secretary of defense rather than the secretary of state would be the principal adviser to the president on matters involving national security. Encouraged by his staff, however, Truman housed the NSC in the Executive Office Building. Furthermore, his trust in Marshall guaranteed that the secretary of state or his deputy, Robert Lovett, would sit in the chair of the presiding officer. The State Department was the key player in U.S. national security policy.

All of the NSC members agreed, for varying reasons, that the president should attend NSC meetings as seldom as possible, and Truman shared that view. But there is nothing in the legislation that indicates a president has an obligation to be present. Some supporters of the NSC felt that the presence of the president would inhibit the necessary frank exchange of views, but few presidents, including Truman, shared that opinion. The Berlin blockade brought Truman to some meetings in 1948, but it was not until the Korean War that he began to value the NSC process and depend upon NSC meetings. As Forrestal had foreseen, the very structure of the NSC made it useful as a warmaking body. It was a mechanism for bringing together the views of the diplomats, military officers, intelligence analysts, and economic prognosticators.

The war also brought home the fact that Truman's NSC system needed some repair. As a reaction to both the fall of the Chinese Nationalists and the detonation of an atomic bomb by the Soviet Union, a review of U.S. policy was begun in early 1950 that would ultimately result in NSC 68, the consummate Cold War paper. At the same time, the president mandated a review of the NSC process. But while NSC 68 was a milestone in the conduct of American foreign relations, the NSC procedural study made very little impact. The basic problem rested with Truman's reluctance to have a national security assistant. By 1950 the NSC executive-secretary had returned to private life and the president's valuable assistant, Clark Clifford, had joined a law firm. As Truman faced war in Korea and dissension at home, there was no one to coordinate policy or mediate disagreements among the various members of the NSC.

Since the end of the Truman administration, the NSC has gone through many incarnations. Each presidential candidate has heaped criticism on the system used by his predecessor and promised reform. Each president has then largely restructured the process of making national security policy. The ambiguity inherent in the creation of the NSC has allowed presidents to impose their own system on what was given to them by Congress. Because of its legislative base in the National Security Act of 1947, no president can abolish it, but several presidents, among them John F. Kennedy and Lyndon Johnson, irreparably changed it. Others, such as Richard Nixon and Ronald Reagan, reached beyond the 1947 act by stretching and manipulating the NSC for their own purposes. After more than forty years and ten presidents, several stages in the evolution of the national security process have emerged.

President Dwight D. Eisenhower came closer to implementing the NSC as it was originally conceived than any of the presidents who followed him. As he campaigned for the presidency, Eisenhower criticized what he referred to as Truman's "shadow agency." The battles of the Cold War required a stronger national security process and a revitalized NSC, he argued. Eisenhower saw the NSC as the premier coordinating agency for protecting American security. In addition, he answered the complaints against Truman by appointing a national security assistant to be the chief facilitator of a coordinated policy. But Eisenhower, like Truman, did not believe in providing the NSC with a policymaking staff in the White House. The agency had a secretariat run by an assistant, but staff work continued to be done in the various departments and agencies.

After his election, Eisenhower restructured and strengthened the NSC system by dividing the NSC process into three parts. The first of these involved the writing of the policy papers that were examined and critiqued by the council. Every agency represented on the council, plus the secretary of the Treasury and the heads of the JCS and CIA, were to choose someone on the assistant secretary level to be a member of the interdepartmental Planning Board, the substitute for the former NSC senior staff of President Truman. This group wrote the papers presented to the council and tried to resolve disagreements over policy between agencies. Each week the formal NSC meetings considered the papers, generally sent them back again, and finally approved the revised version.

Summaries of the meetings between Eisenhower and the members of the council, the second part of the process, often reveal freewheeling discussions dominated by the secretaries of state and Treasury. Few of these discussions, however, were about immediate policy matters. The council never discussed the decision to disallow funding to Egypt for the Aswan Dam, for example. Many meetings were devoted to the annual budget that the president presented to Congress. This is not a surprise, since budgets make policy. Other meetings were largely devoted to long-term or general policy issues.

Nevertheless, Eisenhower rarely missed an NSC meeting. In fact, the NSC took an inordinate amount of his time, since he would get together before the meetings with his national security adviser to go over the agenda and often had smaller meetings in the Oval Office at the conclusion of the meetings. The former army general was a man who believed in both an orderly process and planning.

The Operations Coordinating Board (OCB) was the third part of the Eisenhower national security process. Basically an interdepartmental group of deputies or assistant secretaries, the members met each week to make sure that policy decisions were coordinated and carried out. Although their task seemed straightforward, the OCB was also designed to make sure that CIA covert actions did not operate at cross-purposes with the other policy positions.

Eisenhower regarded his remade NSC as an important policy tool. Gathering together the NSC members, their numerous deputies and assistants, and the ancillary groups from the CIA and JCS, Eisenhower used the NSC as a device to keep political appointees and civil servants informed and committed to the final decisions. Everyone would have a stake in the policy if they had participated in writing the original paper and observed the discussions of the council meetings. The Eisenhower era was marked by this extensive set of meetings and the many policy papers they produced. By the president's second term, however, the designated agency representatives dreaded their participation in the NSC Planning Board meetings, and the council meetings began to sound stale. Disagreements over words and phrases replaced those of substance.

Although the work of the NSC was top secret, Eisenhower and his national security adviser were eager to talk about the orderly process behind the policies. They gained that opportunity when the Subcommittee on National Policy Machinery of the Senate Committee on Government Operations held hearings in the first six months of 1960. The committee was chaired by Senator Henry Jackson, a Democrat from Washington State, and was an effort both to discredit the administration before the presidential election and to serve as a vehicle for Jackson to enter the world of national security policy. Regardless of the motivations, it provided one of the rare glimpses into national security policymaking.

Witnesses were called from both the Truman and Eisenhower administrations. Those from the Truman administration were uniformly critical of the NSC, while Eisenhower's national security advisers not only defended their process but indicated that the NSC played a central role in making foreign policy. The NSC was, in the words of national security assistant Robert Cutler, the "top of policy hill." The impression that emerged from the subcommittee hearings was that of a passive president beholden to a paper-driven, ponderous, bureaucratic process The emphasis in these hearings on Eisenhower's extraordinary use of the council proved very damaging to him as well as to the NSC.

Eisenhower and his advisers were eager to promulgate the view that the general was a man who relied on planning procedures and the advice of NSC members rather than making policy precipitously in response to crisis. His was an orderly system that he urged his successor to follow. Unfortunately, Eisenhower's efforts to promote his NSC system failed to explain fully its value to him. Neither Eisenhower nor any other president ever made policy within the NSC structure. Policy was made in the Oval Office. Eisenhower used the complicated NSC structure to encourage a sense of participation on the part of the policymakers. Council meetings informed those at the deputy and assistant secretary level and promoted a sense of loyalty. But policy was not formulated there. Neither the Jackson subcommittee nor the incoming administration understood the duality of policymaking represented by the NSC and the Oval Office.

Ironically, Eisenhower's use of the NSC appears consistent with the original view of its creators. The NSC was a mix of State Department, Defense Department, and intelligence representatives with other participants joining the group for special projects. It was created to advise the president and met at designated intervals. There are various indications that Eisenhower was thinking about a more streamlined system by the end of his second term, but he made no changes. Although the policymaking process in the Eisenhower administration is generally given high marks, no president since Eisenhower has scheduled as many NSC meetings or participated in them as fully and as often.

THE KENNEDY AND JOHNSON YEARS

President John F. Kennedy completely dismantled the highly organized institutional NSC system, establishing arrangements more amenable to his governing style and, it would appear, to succeeding presidents. Whereas Eisenhower took his experiences as an army commander into the White House, Kennedy emerged from the much more freewheeling structure characteristic of a U.S. senator's office. Critical of Eisenhower's cautious diplomacy and reluctance to increase military budgets, Kennedy was convinced that the stolid, paper-based structure of the NSC system described in the Jackson hearings was responsible for what Kennedy perceived as the timid foreign policy that marked Eisenhower's national security policy. Both the Planning Board and OCB disappeared. The statutory council remained, but was rarely used. Yet, under Truman and Eisenhower the council was the heart of the NSC. It was here that the presidents gathered the opinions of all their advisers representing every facet of national security policy. The council was the mechanism for the widespread input of advice. After Kennedy, the NSC meant the adviser not the council.

Kennedy chose to follow the recommendation of the Jackson subcommittee and initially used the NSC as a more intimate forum for discussions with only his principal advisers. But one of his first decisions irrevocably changed the national security policymaking system. He appointed McGeorge Bundy as a national security adviser (as opposed to an assistant). Bundy, who expanded the role of facilitator and added the role of personal adviser, chose a small policy staff of a half-dozen people to work with him. For the first time, the White House had an independent national security policy staff, a step that reflected Kennedy's scorn for the bureaucratic State Department.

With fewer council meetings and more staff work, the NSC also became less of a planning group and more of an action group concerned with the events or crisis of the moment. Eisenhower administration veterans pointed out that under their system a Bay of Pigs could never have happened, since the idea would have been vetted by desk officers in the State Department, military representatives, and intelligence officials plus discussion in NSC meetings. Of course, they exaggerated the effect of the NSC system on policy. Bad policy can rarely be improved with good process and Eisenhower, for all of his dependence on procedure, began the training of the Bay of Pigs exile army. After the Cuban fiasco, Bundy and his staff were moved into offices closer to the president and the role of White House staff was strengthened by Kennedy's belief that the CIA and the JCS had misled him.

As Kennedy's national security adviser, Bundy was hardly the anonymous staffer, but he was rarely quoted in major newspapers or featured on television. He took seriously his role as presidential adviser and provided the president with staggering amounts of information, sending him home each night and weekend with reports, articles, and books to read. Kennedy rarely attended a formal meeting of the council, relying instead on smaller meetings in the Oval Office. An executive committee, or special committee, for example, was formed to manage U.S. operations in Cuba. The ExCom gained fame because of its successful work in the 1962 Cuban missile crisis.

Beginning slowly in 1961, the NSC was transformed. Aided by a White House staff, the national security adviser personally presented to the president the range of views and options that had been the function of the council during the Eisenhower administration. President Kennedy called NSC meetings for purposes of public relations. He preferred to work with the White House adviser and for the most part abandoned larger meetings. After 1961, presidents accepted the basic assumption that a White House staff and national security adviser were preferable to the unwieldy NSC meetings staffed by every department concerned with national security.

When President Kennedy was assassinated, Lyndon Johnson inherited his advisers and his reliance on the White House national security staff. Throughout his political career, Johnson had concentrated on domestic policy issues. Perhaps his insecurity in the face of the new burdens he faced accounts for his return to the practice of meeting with the National Security Council during the first year of his administration. He soon abandoned it, modifying the more informal style of Kennedy to suit his needs. Bundy continued to bring detailed information to the new president and worked to integrate policy, functions that had once been a product of the NSC system. The NSC staff remained small. Bundy had three assistants: one was detailed from the CIA, a second from the Defense Department, and a third from the Office of Science and Technology. Another staff member was an expert on foreign economic policy. The executive secretary, Bromley Smith, completed the staff. Traditionally, the persons holding the positions of executive secretary and his assistants changed with presidential administrations and the concomitant arrival of new national security advisers. But Smith was an exception and stayed on under Johnson. He was especially valuable because he had experience as an NSC staffer under both Eisenhower and Kennedy and could provide some institutional memory. He was an essential participant in the procedural work of these administrations. For example, he was responsible for the "situation room," a top secret center of communication; conferred with Bundy on agenda items for meetings; and often sat in for Bundy when he was out of town.

Despite Bundy's emphasis on process, in the Johnson White House he was regarded as an adviser as well as a facilitator. Johnson's decision to send Bundy on a fact-finding mission to Vietnam illustrates the way in which the line between the two functions began to disintegrate. Finally, Bundy and his successor, Walt W. Rostow, assumed a third role, that of presidential spokesman. As the Vietnam War hit the headlines, McGeorge Bundy became a media "star."

Bundy resigned his position in December 1965 and during the following March, Johnson chose Walt W. Rostow to replace him. Rostow, who was a member of the State Department's Policy Planning Staff at the time of the Kennedy assassination, was a man of strong opinions who was not shy in expressing them. When others in the White House began questioning Johnson's conduct of the Vietnam War, Rostow stood firmly behind the president.

After convening twenty-five NSC meetings, Johnson began replacing them with small "Tuesday lunches" attended by the secretaries of state and defense, the national security adviser, the director of the CIA, and the head of the JCS. Others were invited when issues called for additional participants. Given the amount of staff work required, these lunches combined the attributes of mini–NSC meetings and Oval Office policymaking sessions. Rather than diminish Rostow's role as national security adviser, the Tuesday lunches enhanced his position. Before each meeting Rostow discussed the agenda with participants and assembled the necessary documents, including a background paper. This was the task of a facilitator, but as Rostow readily admitted, he often added his own views. This further blurred the demarcation between facilitator and adviser. Lyndon Johnson's last years in office were dominated completely by the Vietnam War. Regardless of who attended any given Tuesday lunch, the primary topic remained the same. The president listened to friends and former colleagues in the Senate who urged him to bring the conflict to an end. Abject surrender in whatever form, however, was anathema to this proud Texan, and so he chose to act on the advice of the loyal supporters with whom he lunched each week, thus isolating the political leadership in the agencies. When the loyal members of his cabinet introduced a dose of reality and finally convinced him it was a war he could not win, the weary Johnson declined another term as president.

THE NIXON, FORD, AND CARTER YEARS

Richard Nixon promised to restore the National Security Council and blamed many of the unsuccessful foreign policies of Kennedy and Johnson on its abandonment. Nixon entered the presidency with very specific views on organizing the national security apparatus that were based on his experience in the Eisenhower administration. Soon after his election, he handed the task of reorganizing the NSC system to his national security assistant, Henry Kissinger. Although touting the changes as a return to the Eisenhower model, Nixon displayed neither trust nor regard for officials in the State Department. Seeking complete White House control of national security, he carefully chose a secretary of state, William P. Rogers, who had little foreign policy experience. Nixon's personality was so different than Eisenhower's that whereas the national security machinery was in the Eisenhower style, actual policymaking was quite different.

The NSC structure encompassed a number of interdepartmental groups representing the senior officers of an agency. Even when council meetings were in abeyance, as in the Johnson administration, these groups existed to assure presidents that they were hearing from every agency on a particular issue. During the 1960s the State Department representative had chaired each

DIALOGUE WITH MAO

On 21 February 1972, President Richard Nixon and Henry Kissinger, his assistant for national security affairs, met in China with Chairman Mao Tse-tung and Prime Minister Chou En-lai. The following are excerpts from a memorandum of that conversation.

Chairman Mao: (looking at Dr. Kissinger) He is a doctor of philosophy?

President Nixon: He is a doctor of brains.

Chairman Mao: What about asking him to be the main speaker?

President Nixon: He is an expert in philosophy.

Dr. Kissinger: I used to assign the chairman's collective [sic] writings to my classes at Harvard. . . .

Chairman Mao: [Nixon and Mao] must not monopolize the whole show. It won't do if we don't let Dr. Kissinger have a say. You have been famous about your trips to China.

Dr. Kissinger: It was the president who set the direction and worked out the plan.

President Nixon: He is a very wise assistant to say it that way. (Mao and Chou laugh.)

President Nixon: When the chairman says he voted for me, he voted for the lesser of two evils.

Chairman Mao: I like rightists. People say you are rightists, that the Republican Party is to the right. . . . I am comparatively happy when these people on the right come into power.

President Nixon: I think the important thing to note is that in America, at least at this time, those on the right can do what those on the left talk about.

Dr. Kissinger: There is another point, Mr. President. Those on the left are pro-Soviet and would not encourage a move toward the People's Republic, and in fact criticize you on those grounds.

---

of these groups. The newly organized Nixon NSC expanded these interdepartmental policy committees and added approximately 120 people to the NSC system. The principal committee was the Senior Review Group, which bore a slight resemblance to the Eisenhower NSC Planning Board. This group was on the assistant secretary level, but with Nixon's support, Kissinger came to dominate that group as well as other groups that he chaired. The president was sending a clear signal that the White House would control the agenda.

Despite Nixon's campaign oratory about restoring the Eisenhower model, this control was one among several of the profound differences between the Eisenhower NSC and the Nixon system. Quite apart from personalities, the major difference between the Eisenhower and Nixon systems was the position of the State Department within the policy process. Eisenhower's principal and trusted adviser was Secretary of State John Foster Dulles, whereas Nixon's choice for secretary of state was the inexperienced Rogers, a clear indication that the State Department would be at the periphery of the policymaking process. Nixon's national security assistant, Kissinger, shared his desire to bypass the State Department and conduct foreign policy from the White House. The NSC staff grew accordingly and a third model for the NSC system emerged: the NSC as a small State Department under the control of the president and national security adviser. A flow of paper representing the requests of the NSC for agency input continued to move, but, in contrast with previous years, the requests did not seem to matter. Agency personnel suspected that the process of making them was designed to keep them occupied while Kissinger and Nixon made policy.

As in the previous administration, frequent official NSC meetings were held early in the Nixon presidency, but the thirty-seven meetings in 1969 diminished to twenty-one in 1970 and only ten in the first two-thirds of 1971. As the NSC moved away from formal meetings, the committee system stepped into the vacuum and gained importance. While the Nixon White House tapes show an overbearing president with little respect for his national security adviser and an almost subservient Kissinger, in fact the two men were in agreement on both policy priorities and the manner in which to implement them.

Both were intent on controlling and conducting foreign policy and both were convinced of the need for secrecy.

The Nixon and post-Nixon NSC arrangements illustrate the difficulty of separating policy, process, and personality. Henry Kissinger exemplifies this problem. First as national security assistant and then as secretary of state, he insisted on full control of people and ideas. He used the diffuse NSC interdepartmental process to better accomplish his goals and bent it to his needs. Given his belief in secrecy, Kissinger often did not tell his staff what he was doing.

The results of the Nixon-Kissinger approach were mixed. They turned China policy around but failed to end the war in Vietnam. Kissinger personally began lengthy and open negotiations in the Middle East, while Nixon directed the secret intervention in Chile that resulted in the seventeen-year dictatorship of General Augusto Pinochet. Kissinger and Nixon basically took advantage of the NSC mechanism to achieve their goals, making it their handmaiden. Meanwhile, Nixon ignored Secretary of State Rogers, a pliant individual who did not try to impose his own views or those of his department. When he resigned and Kissinger took over at State, any potential conflict between the secretary and national security adviser was laid to rest.

When President Gerald Ford succeeded Nixon, he reestablished some equilibrium between the State Department and White House. National security adviser Brent Scowcroft assumed a low profile and moved to establish better relations between the State Department and the White House.

In the tradition of his predecessors, President Jimmy Carter quickly reorganized the NSC staff and stated the intention of placing more responsibility on the departments and agencies. The numerous committees of the Nixon-Ford White House were combined into two subordinate committees, the Policy Review Committee and the Special Coordination Committee. However, Carter appointed as his national security adviser a man every bit as strong willed and as opinionated as Henry Kissinger. Zbigniew Brzezinski reorganized the staff to eliminate most of the vestiges of the Kissinger years. Rather than function as a mini–State Department, his staff was to carry through the usual coordination of policy and serve as a kind of think tank for the president. Aware of the tendency of his predecessors to overshadow the secretary of state, he also assured the president, press, and public that he would cooperate with the secretaries of state and defense. The prospects for harmony seemed good, as Brzezinski and Secretary of State Cyrus Vance had served as cochairs of the Council on Foreign Relations while Secretary of Defense Harold Brown had worked with Brzezinski on the Trilateral Commission, a group to increase cooperation between the United States, western Europe, and Japan. The climate of cooperation promised smooth working relationships. Recognizing earlier problems between the NSC and the secretaries of state and defense, Carter asked for an internal study on integrating policy six months after taking office. The report, prepared by Philip Odeen, emphasized process and organization rather than personalities. In the long run, however, Carter's policy process was influenced far more by personalities than procedure.

It did not take long for Brzezinski, a dynamic man with wide-ranging interests, to become the predominant foreign policy spokesman of the Carter administration. Despite earlier plans, Carter's policy process was among the most centralized in the post–World War II era, with Brzezinski as the fulcrum. Like those of Kennedy and Johnson, it evolved into an informal structure, this time revolving around a Friday morning breakfast between Brzezinski, Vance, and Brown. Unfortunately, each man often emerged with a different interpretation of the discussion. The rivalry between the national security adviser and the secretary of state that had existed in the Nixon years took on a different cast under Carter when it became clear that Brzezinski's views on American foreign policy were quite different from those of Secretary Vance. Brzezinski, for example, sounded the death knell for détente on 28 May 1978, when he strongly attacked Soviet and Cuban activities in Africa. On 14 June, however, Vance made it clear that the White House approved of his plan to send an American diplomat to Angola for talks with the government there. Brzezinski also made it clear that negotiations over the Strategic Arms Limitation Talks (SALT) were linked to Russian meddling in Africa and its support for African revolutionaries. A more conciliatory Vance dismissed the notion of linkage between the two issues. The secretary of state also assured the House International Relations Committee that he was the only one who spoke for the president.

It was Brzezinski, however, who saw Carter several times each day and served as the liaison between the cabinet secretaries and the president.

He prepared summaries and reports of meetings and discussions held under the national security tent between the principal participants of policy meetings and did not hesitate to give his opinion or express his disagreement with Secretary Vance or Secretary of Defense Brown.

Carter, a former governor of Georgia, had very little foreign policy experience. His personal goals included improving human rights, curtailing the military, and reaching out to the Third World in Africa and Latin America. Brzezinski, on the other hand, concentrated on such traditional Cold War problems as outsmarting the Soviets and encouraging the Chinese to look to the United States to the detriment of the USSR. Carter had success in accomplishing his own goals, but as international tensions unfolded, particularly the Soviet war in Afghanistan, he was pulled between the views of Vance and Brzezinski. By the time Secretary Vance resigned in 1980, Carter had accepted the views of his national security adviser and sounded like another cold warrior. Meanwhile, foreign policy lost its coherency as the administration spoke with two voices instead of one.

To observers, the disarray in the Carter administration seemed to be one more example of a national security system out of control. The publicity generated by Brzezinski drew attention to the organization of national security in the White House and the fate of the NSC itself. Although Brzezenski's staff never reached the size of the Kissinger staff of about two hundred (of whom fifty were professionals), it was a large staff of about one hundred (of whom thirty were professionals) and, like Kissinger's staff, it was a policy staff. Meanwhile, the NSC atrophied. Only ten NSC meetings were held while Brzezenski was the national security adviser. Even the Nixon and Ford administrations had held 125 meetings in their eight years in office.

In April 1980 the Senate Foreign Relations Committee for the first time, under its chairman, Frank Church, held hearings on legislation requiring Senate confirmation of all national security advisers. Two powerful national security advisers had become major policymakers yet were free from confirmation proceedings and were not required to testify before the Foreign Relations Committee. The effort to require accountability on the part of the national security adviser was ultimately unsuccessful. A consensus existed that presidents should be allowed to pick their own advisers and organize their administrations according to their own views and personalities.

But the attempt did highlight the duality of foreign policymaking within the White House.

THE REAGAN, BUSH, AND CLINTON YEARS

President Ronald Reagan began his administration by reversing a trend and appointing a low-key national security assistant who would return to the pre-Kissinger model. Unfortunately, in an aberration from the designated use of the NSC, Reagan also used the national security system as an operating agency, with far-reaching results. Unfamiliar with and initially uninterested in national security affairs, Reagan, who had no trouble working with a triumvirate of domestic advisers, seemed unable to find the right national security person with whom to work. As a result, he had a record six national security advisers. Richard Allen, the first, was the only one since the origins of the NSC who did not have direct access to the president. Allen answered to Edwin Meese, a former Reagan associate who was now White House general counsel. He failed to gain the confidence of Meese and, despite his low profile, Allen immediately had turf battles with the intrepid secretary of state, Alexander Haig. Allen left office within a year and was followed by William Clark. Clark had no experience or background in national security policy but was close to Reagan, having served as his executive secretary when Reagan was governor of California. Someone who knew the president seemed more likely to be a successful assistant for national security. Clark was familiar with the president's work habits, goals, and governing style. He had complete access to the Oval Office, meanwhile building a strong staff of sixty-one to compensate for his own weakness. He could offer little in the way of substance, however, and resigned in 1983.

Meanwhile, the world had not waited for Reagan to find his way. Iranians, after overthrowing the shah, storming the American embassy, and taking American hostages, finally released the Americans on January 20, 1981, the day of Reagan's inauguration, but became an important anti-American and anti-Western force in the Middle East. In Central America, Reagan faced a revolutionary, left-wing government in Nicaragua. President Carter had not condoned or encouraged this new government but had chosen to accept it. Reagan and his advisers, on the other hand, saw the new Nicaraguan rulers, the Sandinistas, as partners in the Havana-Moscow nexus. Reagan assumed that Nicaragua, like Cuba, would try to export its revolution throughout Latin America. Therefore, Nicaragua was seen as a danger to U.S. interests, and so the administration began to support the military opposition to the Sandinistas, those known as contras.

Congress tied the hands of the president when it prohibited the use of funds to overthrow the Nicaraguan government. Reagan, however, was determined to rid Nicaragua of the Sandinistas and sought a different way to reach the contras. He turned to the one group outside the purview of Congress, the national security adviser and his staff. From 1983 to 1986, national security advisers Robert McFarlane and John Poindexter, who followed McFarlane in 1985, were the chief architects of the disastrous Iran-contra policy. With the help of national security staff assistants who scorned the constitutional issues involved, they devised a plan to send arms to Iran for its war against Iraq. The payment for the arms was then sent to the Nicaraguan contras.

For the first and only time in its history, the NSC became an operational agency. National security adviser McFarlane made secret trips to the Middle East while U.S. marine lieutenant colonel Oliver North, a staff assistant, coordinated the activities against the contras. Trading arms for money, the essence of what became the Iran-Contra scandal, was soon discovered and investigated, discrediting both the president and the participants. The fifth national security adviser, Frank Carlucci, a respected and experienced veteran of the Defense Department, was then called in to clean house. Finally, in 1987 General Colin Powell stepped into the position.

The Reagan interlude illustrates the failure of the NSC system when a president fails to exert leadership within the policy process. Created for battle in the Cold War, no president between Truman and Reagan entered office without a strong commitment to developing a policy process that could cope with the problems presented by the global interests of the Cold War. These presidents, cognizant of the problems posed by international responsibilities, also brought into the White House men and women who could implement their policies. As a result, the glaring deficiencies of the original 1947 legislation were invisible. The act provided the NSC with an ambiguous mandate that ignored the necessity for an adviser and staff as key participants in the making of national security policy.

Taking a cue from President Carter, Reagan included his vice president, George H. W. Bush, in many of the important national security decisions of his administration. As president, Bush—who had been ambassador to the United Nations, director of the Central Intelligence Agency, and the American representative to China—reorganized the national security process, as had previous chief executives. His national security adviser, Brent Scowcroft, and Scowcroft's deputy, Robert Gates, were at the center of the national security process, chairing the top panels of the senior officers in all the national security agencies and thus setting the agendas.

President Bush continued the use of the Principals Committee, which had been established in 1987 by Reagan. This committee was virtually the original NSC with the addition of the secretary of the Treasury, the chief of staff to the president, and the national security adviser. As was true of the NSC, the chairman of the JCS and the director of the CIA also attended, while others were invited as needed. Both Truman and Eisenhower would have recognized this group, although neither would have acquiesced to any committee of principals that did not include the president, the ultimate "principal." Instead, National Security Presidential Directive-1 noted that both President Bush and his vice president could attend any and all meetings.

Bush, like his predecessors, did not rely upon this system for making foreign policy. He valued secrecy and loyalty and relied on an unusually small set of advisers who shared similar worldviews. Bush's mini-NSC was composed of Scowcroft, Secretary of Defense Richard Cheney, and Secretary of State James Baker, who met with the president in the Oval Office. They were occasionally joined by the General Colin L. Powell, now chairman of the JCS, and Gates after his appointment as the director of the Central Intelligence Agency in September 1991. The fact that the Bush administration did not use the NSC did not diminish the role of the national security adviser. In 1991, for example, the president sent Scowcroft to the Middle East and China, not Secretary of State Baker.

Predictably, President William Clinton changed the national security process, this time by adding a broad economic element to the National Security Council. The secretary of the Treasury and the chief of the new White House Economic Council were added to the NSC as well as the ambassador to the United Nations, Madeleine K.

Albright. The Principals Committee and Deputies Committee were both retained. As usual, there were discussions in the media about relationships between national security principals, in this case Secretary of State Warren Christopher; Defense Secretary Les Aspin; and the national security adviser, Anthony Lake. But the perception of problems within the Clinton administration were partly a product of a disorganized White House and the president's initial lack of interest.

By Clinton's second term, a succession of crises had brought Clinton into the heart of foreign policy and the administration began to change. All the original players, Christopher, Aspin, and Lake, left the administration. Samuel R. Berger, Lake's deputy, became the national security adviser and Albright became the first woman to serve as secretary of state. Albright was a more colorful secretary, but, like Christopher, she apparently was relegated to traditional diplomatic tasks. She never seemed totally without influence, but the heart of the policy process remained within the gates of the White House. National security policy was again dominated by the president's staff, in particular by Sandy Berger, whose office was just steps away from the president's and for whom the president's door was always open.

When George W. Bush took office in January 2001, he quickly nominated a strong and experienced secretary of state, General Colin Powell, and moved on to nominate an equally experienced secretary of defense, Donald Rumsfeld. Under the Bush plan, the national security adviser would return to the position of facilitator, bringing information to the president and acting as a liaison officer bridging the gap between the State and Defense Departments.

CONCLUSION

No president has ever made national security policy in the National Security Council. The NSC was not created as a policymaking body but as an advisory body to the president. The Cold War brought into the policy process various agencies and groups whose views were important but rarely coordinated. Foreign policy was no longer just in the hands of the State Department. The Defense Department and the JCS, joined by the CIA and the Treasury Department, were all players on the field of U.S. global power.

Therefore, even when presidents avoided the formal structure created early in the Cold War, they found it necessary to find a substitute. Interdepartmental committees and the Committee of Principals were all created to fill this role.

The turning point in the history of the NSC came in 1961 with the election of John F. Kennedy. When Kennedy brought into the White House a national security adviser with a staff, he began an inexorable move toward a completely new process. Even though it continued to meet sporadically, after 1961 the NSC was nothing more than the president's adviser and his staff, which soon evolved into just the president's staff.

Personality has been more important to the policy process than structure. That each president uses the NSC differently is part of the received wisdom about the policy process. Every president uses the NSC differently in order to differentiate himself from his predecessor as campaign promises for new policies are subsequently translated into new processes.

Since it was created by an act of Congress, no president can abolish the NSC. For the most part, however, it has evolved beyond recognition. The interdepartmental and ad hoc committees that form the crux of agency participation bear only a slight resemblance to Truman's senior staff or Eisenhower's Planning Board, and the dominant role of the national security adviser has changed the equation since the time when chairmen set the agenda.

The effect on policy is difficult to gauge. The danger faced by most presidents has been the tendency to rely on a few loyal advisers. If they do not participate in NSC meetings or the meetings of "principals," presidents become isolated. They do not have a forum for contrary views and are remote from those who must defend and implement their policies. Nixon and Kissinger may be prime examples of this isolation, but presidents such as Johnson and George H. W. Bush also preferred selective advice.

The NSC of the 1947 statute is probably dead and certainly obsolete. The end of the Cold War and the American position as the strongest global power probably requires a different kind of national security organization in order for the president to be truly advised in this new century.

BIBLIOGRAPHY

Destler, I. M. *Presidents, Bureaucrats, and Foreign Policy: The Politics of Organizational Reform.* Princeton, N.J., 1974.

Inderfurth, Karl F., and Loch K. Johnson. *Decisions of the Highest Order: Perspectives on the National Security Council.* Pacific Grove, Calif., 1988.

Nelson, Anna Kasten. "President Truman and the Evolution of the National Security Council." *Journal of American History* 72 (September 1985): 360–378.

———. "The Importance of Foreign Policy Process: Eisenhower and the National Security Council." In Günter Bischof and Stephen E. Ambrose, eds. *Eisenhower, A Centenary Assessment.* Baton Rouge, La., 1995.

Prados, John. *Keepers of the Keys: A History of the National Security Council from Truman to Bush.* New York, 1991.

See also DECISION MAKING; DEPARTMENT OF DEFENSE; DEPARTMENT OF STATE; PRESIDENTIAL ADVISERS; PRESIDENTIAL POWER.

NATIVISM

Geoffrey S. Smith

Nativism is a construct scholars employ to explain hostility and intense opposition to an internal minority on the grounds of its imputed foreign connections. Appearing in three basic forms in American history, nativism was first characterized by antagonism toward Catholics during colonial and early national eras. Anti-Catholicism peaked from the 1830s through the 1850s, concomitant with the growing debate over slavery. This variant reflected themes popular since the Protestant Reformation, stimulated by American fears of French, Spanish, and papal threats in the New World. After the Civil War, anti-Catholic nativism became more secular, mirroring complex economic, cultural, and social upheavals and—most notably—an inchoate sense of nostalgia for a "purer" republic.

A second form of nativism, manifest in the dread of alien radicalism, emerged during the 1790s when the wars of the French Revolution embroiled the United States and threatened the republican experiment. A third manifestation of nativism, sometimes overlapping with anti-Catholicism and antiradicalism, developed during the 1840s as citizens celebrated their "manifest destiny" to bring the benefits of democracy and republican government to the Pacific. Girded by "scientific" analyses that touted Anglo-Saxon superiority against other peoples, racial nativism became crucial in the debate over imperialism at the turn of the twentieth century, underlay the incarceration of the Japanese-American minority during World War II, and remains today an important touchstone in ongoing arguments about multiculturalism, immigration, and trade.

Scholars analyze nativism in several ways. One approach, exemplified in John Higham's unsurpassed *Strangers in the Land* (1963), stresses actual, face-to-face conflicts and tensions between early settlers and subsequent arrivals. Higham underscores immigrant battles for social, political, and especially economic advancement in an individualist and competitive culture. He explores the organized nativist movements between 1860 and 1925 that resisted these newcomers, and he assesses skillfully both reality and hyperbole within nativist stereotypes, all the while focusing on the all-important sociocultural settings in which nativism has waxed and waned.

Other historians and social scientists, reflecting the long-dominant primacy of the liberal consensus (from the 1930s to the 1970s), accentuate both ideological and psychological functions of nativism as clues to understanding tensions and fault lines within national culture. Here Richard Hofstadter and David Brion Davis look to a broader definition of the term, describing nativism as a state of mind of native-born and naturalized citizens seeking to define their own Americanness by condemning real and alleged alien challenges to national values and institutions. For these historians, nativism signifies the ideology of persecuting groups, invariably bigoted, while targeted minorities emerge generally as victims.

In the last quarter of the twentieth century, cultural and social historians focused more critically upon contests for power, assessing minorities more empathetically, "from the bottom up," often attacking traditional political elites. The Vietnam War, Watergate, black and feminist drives for equality, and growing concern by many at colossal inequities in wealth and shrinking opportunity, all interact with an increasingly multicultural society and tarnished political system to undercut the very idea of legitimacy. Scholars who embrace cultural studies—much influenced by such French theorists as Jacques Derrida, Jacques Lacan, and Michel Foucault—explain battles for power and prestige between newcomers and nativist defenders of the old order by deconstructing such categories as economics, race and ethnicity, and gender and sexuality. Assessing these categories may not only allow new clarity in comprehending power relationships embedded in given contexts ("texts"), but the careful reading of evidence ("discourse") may also afford scholars a better sense of their own relationship to their realm of inquiry, indicate how the notion of "historical objectivity" invariably conveys values and requirements of dominant cultures, and supply the chance to make connections within, and between, governing and contending, often complicit, cultural paradigms. Cultural studies at its best respects history as fluid and uncontrollable (even by elites), and considers questions of cause-and-effect less important than understanding ways in which parts of the historical past (and theories like Antonio Gramsci's hegemony and complicity) fit together.

Although emerging mainly as varied forms of domestic intolerance, nativism has affected, and been affected by, United States foreign policy. On one hand, animosity toward immigrants and fear of alien influence have diverted attention from real national problems and their sources and solutions. Conversely, nativist stereotypes and images have impeded the efficient formulation and implementation of foreign policies. On several occasions, meanwhile, nativist endeavors to legitimize parochial agendas by identifying them with the nation's interests have generated crises involving the federal government. Withal, by encouraging disdain for the European concept of power politics, nativism has strengthened the nation's self-image of innocence and exceptionalism in a decadent world. Hence, the study of nativist ethnocentrism and xenophobia provides clues to aid historians in clarifying the interplay between domestic issues and foreign relations. These clues help to explain the persistence of moralism and rigidity in American diplomacy and the presence of emotionalism as an important problem for national self-interest.

Yet with the exception of the federal immigration acts of 1921 and 1924, optimistic tendencies have generally kept nativism from becoming national policy. In several cases, however, nativists achieved power sufficient to affect the nation's course. The Alien and Sedition Laws (1798) sought to stifle Jeffersonian opposition to Federalist foreign policy during the Quasi-War with France (1798–1800). But when President John Adams negotiated for peace (perhaps his most courageous accomplishment), the legislation backfired, split the Federalist Party, and helped Thomas Jefferson become elected president in 1800. During the 1850s, the Know-Nothing (or American) Party hastened disintegration of national politics when its crusade against Irish-Catholic immigrants offered citizens a choice to avoid confronting slavery, the greatest sectional crisis the nation had known. In the late nineteenth century, nativism intensified many social and economic difficulties wrought by the dislocating forces of industrialism, urbanization, and unprecedented immigration from lands nativists deemed benighted. As long as the economy remained robust, ample room existed for newcomers. But when the economy turned sour, as it did cyclically between 1870 and 1914, nativists looked more for the easy explanation—the new immigrants, of course—than they did shortcomings of the capitalist system.

The only nation that was "born in perfection and aspired to progress" (to use Hofstadter's felicitous phrase), the United States also confronted war in the twentieth century in ways that focused attention on the enemy within, the Trojan Horse that would undermine the peaceable kingdom. The United States went to war not to "muddle through" or merely win, like the British, but for moral reasons befitting its exalted (and self-anointed) global status. Messianic prophecies demand total obeisance and World War I unleashed an unprecedented campaign of repression against German Americans, foreign- and native-born Bolsheviks, socialists, anarchists, and pacifists. Wartime intolerance did not cease with the Treaty of Versailles. Indeed, the Red Scare after World War I attested not only to problems attending the failure to make the world safe for democracy, demobilization, and the emergence of the Bolshevik adversary in the Soviet Union, but also to the desire, continuing into the 1920s, to purge the nation of all cultures that did not embrace traditional Anglo-Saxon Protestant virtues. This failed effort at national purification influenced attitudes toward international cooperation, immigration, the World Court, and the Soviet Union. A similar reaction, christened "McCarthyism" after its most renowned practitioner, Senator Joseph McCarthy, exploded after World War II, and the controversy over Watergate in the early 1970s revealed a similar cleansing dynamic, albeit in inverted form, which eventually consumed the presidency of Richard M. Nixon.

EARLY FORMS OF NATIVISM

Anglo-American nativism arrived in America with the first settlers. Imbued with ideas of founding a city on a hill in the Massachusetts Bay Colony to honor God and redeem the Church of England, and harboring in Virginia a sense of commercial destiny built on racial dominion over blacks and First Nations, colonial Americans from England also nursed resentment against other white ethnicities—Irish, Dutch, German, French, and Spanish, for example, depending upon region and issues. Occasionally, as during the ethnoracial French and Indian War (1754–1763), nativist feelings burst forth. In Pennsylvania, English colonists followed Benjamin Franklin's lead in questioning local German loyalty to the crown.

After independence, the new multicultural nation faced the need to define its identity. Although the Frenchman Hector St. John de Crevecour spoke of the American as a "new" man, the Anglo-American connection died hard, if at all. With unity a key requirement for survival in a world of despotism and monarchy, many citizens expressed hostility toward European immigration—even as the new Republic became increasingly multiracial and multiethnic. This animus was understandable. Diversity heralded faction, as dangerous to a republic as the concentration of centralized power. Thomas Jefferson warned that immigrants might "warp and bias" the path of the nation and jeopardize "the freest principles of the English Constitution, with others derived from natural right and natural reason." Indeed, the American alliance with France—crucial to independence—became an albatross during the next fifteen years. The French Revolution, ironically styled in part on its American predecessor, terrified Federalist Party leaders.

The first organized expression of antiradical nativism came in 1798, when Federalist hostility exploded against both France and Jefferson's Democratic-Republicans. Influenced by Secretary of the Treasury Alexander Hamilton, whose Francophobia knew no bounds, President George Washington rejected any diplomacy that might offend Britain, at war against France since shortly after the revolution. Washington's diplomacy, therefore, aided Britain and opened a gap between Hamilton and Secretary of State Jefferson, a partisan of France. The fear of immigrants as a source of faction and corruption affected both emerging political parties in the new nation. The bipartisan Naturalization Act of 1795 required aliens to renounce earlier allegiances and disavow titles of nobility. But the more extreme Federalists—men and women of orthodox social, cultural, and religious attitudes united by their pessimistic view of human nature and aristocratic demeanor—worried lest incoming French émigrés, United Irishmen, and British radicals sow sedition and "Jacobinism" among the populace.

In fact, France did meddle in American politics, seeking to defeat Jay's Treaty in 1794 and to influence the election of 1796 in Jefferson's favor. The attachment of many immigrants to Jefferson alarmed Federalists. Democratic-Republican societies in New York and eastern Pennsylvania included recent Irish and Scots-Irish arrivals. These groups participated in the Whiskey Rebellion of 1794, led opposition to Jay's Treaty, and hence appeared connected to the intrigue of French agents like Joseph Fauchet and Pierre A. Adet. President Washington warned of this connection in his Farewell Address in 1796, but seemingly to no avail. By 1798 Federalists recalled that factionalism helped wreck the Articles of Confederation and now made the Republic vulnerable to external enemies.

The infamous XYZ affair and subsequent undeclared naval war with France presented Federalists the chance to use their control of foreign policy, in Federalist politician Theodore Sedgwick's words, "a glorious opportunity to destroy faction." Divisive issues having stimulated the lust for power in Federalists and Democratic-Republicans alike, politics now mirrored "a complete distrust of the motives and integrity, the honesty and intentions of one's political opponents." Consequently, Federalist stalwarts, moving "to crush internal opposition in the name of national security," moved to create an army and navy, to construct arsenals, and to abrogate the treaties of alliance and of amity and commerce of 1778. The more moderate wing of the party supported President John Adams's decision to seek a diplomatic solution to the crisis, but "high" Federalists became increasingly ambitious. Given reports of a pending French invasion, the hawks demanded that Adams declare war. Although the president resisted their demand, he did link his political opponents with France and hence added his voice to an outburst of nativism that momentarily diverted the Federalists from serving the national interest.

The Quasi-War generated widespread fear within Federalist circles that French spies and their internal collaborators threatened national security. Representative Harrison Gray Otis denounced "wild Irishmen" and "the turbulent and disorderly of all parts of the world" who came to the United States "with a view to disturb our own tranquility after having succeeded in the overthrow of their own governments." David Tappan, Hollis Professor of Divinity at Harvard, warned graduating seniors against infidels and impending world revolution. Congregationalist minister Jedidiah Morse called attention to the machinations of the "Bavarian Illuminati," a cabal of radical atheists who already had infiltrated American churches and schools.

The Alien and Sedition Laws, as they became known, sought to root out such subversion, and in the process destroy the Democratic-Republican opposition, slow immigrant participation in political life, and compel support for Federalist measures. These laws increased the period of residency required for citizenship, empowered the president to expel aliens suspected of activities deemed "dangerous to the peace and safety of the United States," and provided penalties for citizens who engaged in rioting, unlawful assembly, or impeding the operation of the government. The Sedition Act did not weigh exclusively against immigrants. Premised on the assumption that war would be declared, the Sedition Law aimed to gag political criticism and would expire on the last day of Adams's term. The law, rooted in the seventeenth-century British concept of seditious libel, also reflected the Federalist view that government was the master, not servant, of the people. Any critique of government was dangerous because it subverted the dignity and authority of rulers. Politics was not a popular right; it belonged "to the few, the rich, and the well-born."

Certain that Democratic-Republicans stood poised to undermine the Constitution and overturn the government, Federalist judges turned their fire on Jeffersonian editors and publicists. With stacked courts presuming guilt unless defendants proved their innocence, published criticism of elected officials became synonymous with conviction. As Jeffersonians resolutely opposed Adams's call for an accelerated defense program, they encountered the heavy hand of Federalist patriotism, which included indictment of *Philadelphia Aurora* editor William Duane and the incarcerations of Scots publicist James T. Callender, the Irish-born Vermont congressman Matthew Lyon, and Pennsylvania editor Thomas Cooper.

John Adams withstood the war cry emanating from Federalist hawks and courageously dispatched William Vans Murray, the American minister at The Hague, to France, where he signed the Treaty of Mortefontaine (1800) ending the naval conflict and abrogating the "entangling" Franco-American treaties of 1778. In the interim, as the "Black Cockade fever" raged and Federalists sought to extirpate Illuminati and other subversives, Jeffersonians mounted an effective counterattack, organizing politically and continuing to attack Adams. Jefferson and James Madison drafted the Kentucky and Virginia Resolutions, respectively, condemning the administration's violation of individual and states' rights, and the malevolence felt by many immigrant groups toward the Federalist Party became implacable. In the election of 1800, Jefferson narrowly triumphed—a victory in which Scots-Irish and Irish, Pennsylvania Germans, and New York French played a role.

The election of 1800 signified the political arrival of America's immigrants, heralded the nation's multiethnic future, and underscored the importance of public opinion—the people's right "to think freely and to speak and write what they think." With the Federalist Party in eclipse—an unintended consequence of the nativist outburst of 1798—nativism remained a potent force in New England. During the War of 1812 delegates to the Hartford Convention (1814–1815) threatened secession after denouncing the impact of the war upon their section's economy, declaring that European monarchs were "dumping" paupers on American shores, and proposing a constitutional amendment that would exclude naturalized citizens from holding civil office or serving in Congress.

THE MID-NINETEENTH CENTURY

Federalists attempted to safeguard the new nation (and their own political fortunes) against revolution by muzzling dissent and seeking to bar immigrant radicals and alien poor. These campaigns continued in the three decades before the Civil War—an era of unsettling change, disorder, and—for many Americans—uncertainty and anxiety. Jacksonian America featured the convergence of modernizing transportation and market revolutions, the emergence of liberal capitalism and government bureaucracy, as well as the concomitant growth of slavery and sectionalism and the dispossession of most Indian tribes east of the Mississippi River.

During this era, nativism became more complex, drawing its inspiration from a variety of sources. Antebellum xenophobes expressed the need for consensus at a juncture when constant and bewildering change appeared to threaten "the old landmarks of Christendom and the glorious common law of the Founding Fathers." A lack of institutional authority and standards strengthened the drive for common ideological unity. The very diversity of this period—with its myriad religious groups, faddist sects, and voluntary organizations—implied divisiveness and stimulated anxiety about the nation's future and tensions between individualism and community in a modernizing polity. Nativists took up the battle against autonomous groups combining secrecy with a demand for total loyalty. Such organizations as the Church of Jesus Christ of Latter-Day Saints, the Masonic Order, and the Roman Catholic Church troubled native-born and Protestant Americans as the antithesis of the egalitarian ideals of Jacksonian Democracy. In this era of "Pax Britannica," nativism provided worried Americans a series of contrived threats—moral equivalents of war—with which to rebuff autocratic adversaries and thus bolster the legitimacy and authority of republican institutions.

Anti-Catholicism during the Jacksonian era transferred the battle for democracy from the level of intellectual combat in the national arena to parochial politics and mob violence "where every son of liberty could strike his blow for righteousness." The Adams-Onís Treaty of 1819, concluded between John Quincy Adams and the Spanish minister Luis de Onís, struck such a symbolic blow. This "transcontinental treaty" extended American claims to the Pacific and thus "liberated" a vast expanse from a Catholic state. Four years later President James Monroe warned the European Quadruple Alliance not to intervene in the affairs of the newly independent Latin American republics. Monroe's "doctrine" was, of course, upheld by British sea power. Yet not a few Americans held to the belief that Europe's despots might attempt to reassert their power in the Western Hemisphere.

Such was the message of the artist and inventor Samuel F. B. Morse, who in 1834 warned of a Catholic plot to undermine the Republic. Echoing his father, Jedidiah Morse, in decrying the apathy of most Americans, Morse's *Foreign Conspiracy Against the Liberties of the United States* declared that the European Leopold Association, currently assisting American bishops in the Mississippi Valley, was in fact an entering wedge through which Prince Metternich of Austria and Czar Nicholas I of Russia would seize control. A year later fellow New Englander Lyman Beecher published *A Plea for the West*. A prominent minister who became president of Lane Theological Seminary in Cincinnati (with St. Louis, a stronghold of Catholicism), Beecher grasped the significance of American know-how for westward, ultimately global expansion and evangelicalization. Beecher hated demon rum, dueling, religious complacency, Unitarians, and Catholics. Unless Americans accepted God's challenge and transacted their extraordinary destiny, they could expect dreadful retribution. Either Protestant faithful would evangelize the west and the world, or the area would be captured by an institution that destroyed freedom of thought, cloaked its true atheism behind specious symbols of religiosity, generated revolution wherever it appeared, and knew no limit in its quest for riches and power. If Catholicism were not halted, Beecher averred, the republican experiment would expire in a wasteland of ignorance and infidelity.

The idea of America as a contingent experiment verging on the most abject failure provides a recurrent theme in nativist literature, linking congregationalist ministers in Federalist New England, to avatars of 1840s revivalism like Beecher, and to twentieth-century fundamentalists like Billy James Hargis and Jerry Falwell. Beecher no doubt spoke for traditional congregationalist clergy seeking to redress its loss of established power by spreading New England Protestantism westward. But the expansionist connotation of his message was clear, and alongside the influx of Irish and other Catholic immigrants, it generated concern among those unsettled by cultural change.

The immigration of the 1830s and 1840s indicated to nativists that Europe's leaders might not be able to launch navies across the Atlantic, but they could send their illiterate, destitute, and criminal elements. Perhaps because the economy recovered well from the Panic of 1837, and Europe seemed far away, anti-Catholicism did not become a staple of the Mexican War (1846–1848). That it did not underscores the marginal relationship between nativism and foreign policy at this juncture. Although observers on both sides of the debate on the war disparaged the imputed racial inferiority of the Mexican adversary, Protestant nativists never succeeded in making the conflict a religious jihad. Some southern denominations—moved by the racialism that girded slavery—did warn that the "yoke of papal oppression would be placed upon every state of the Republic" unless Mexico was crushed. But the absence of a unified anti-Catholic base was clear in the strength of other Protestant enemies, especially in northern states—including the "peculiar institution" of slavery, war generally, and the Mexican War in particular. Indeed, not a few northern Protestants scorned the threat posed by an aggressive slave-power conspiracy to extend its dominion into the western territories. Human bondage—here and now—proved more compelling than human bondage allegedly engineered by the Vatican.

More important, the cultural and social change that so alarmed Morse and Beecher had diluted Protestantism, secularized it, and stretched its basic tenets. Hence, most Americans rebuffed attempts to link Mexico with the Catholic menace. Midwestern Protestants generally held few uncertainties about the nation's future and the durability of their civilization. Mexican culture was primitive and impotent, and Mexican armies posed no threat to national safety. The historic Catholic culture of the Mississippi Valley would not halt American expansion to the Pacific.

Nevertheless, tales of Catholic atrocities persisted through the 1830s, 1840s, and 1850s, stimulating nativist imaginations (a form of ultra-Protestant pornography) and in urban and urbanizing venues making life difficult for Irish immigrants. The *Awful Disclosures of Maria Monk* (1836), which detailed lustful priests, compliant nuns, and strangled babies born of unholy wedlock, was the best known of this apocryphal confessional literature, and sold more than 130,000 copies over the next twenty years (earning the sobriquet, eventually, as the *Uncle Tom's Cabin* of the anti-Catholic crusade). For their part, Irish immigrant supporters of the Young Ireland movement spoke out in their new country against English rule and incurred violent reactions in Brooklyn, Philadelphia, and Boston, among other cities. Anti-Catholic hostility centered upon such issues as the alleged role of immigrants in urban political corruption, trusteeship, the correct version of the Bible to be used in public schools, and rivalry in labor markets. In the late 1840s more than a million immigrants—expelled by famine—arrived in America "with hatred in their hearts for the British." The new arrivals made it necessary for politicians to heed their interests, thereby transforming urban politics in several venues.

Anti-Catholicism affected but was not coeval with antebellum nativism. Xenophobes also condemned non-Catholic immigrants and native Americans whose sociopolitical affiliations or religious tenets challenged local power structures or dominant cultural ideals. In addition, numerous immigrant groups—including Scots-Irish Presbyterians in Philadelphia and German radicals in the Ohio Valley—joined the Protestant crusade, as did many native-born Catholics. Bishop John J. Hughes of New York took the lead in denouncing the radicalism of Hungarian patriot Lajos Kossuth, while Boston Irish Catholics denounced German "48ers" as "red" republicans, anarchists and despoilers of the Sabbath. In fact, between 1846 and 1855 more than a million Germans came to the United States, leaving behind revolution and potato famine, and becoming politically active in their new home. This activism, though not unified, unsettled nativists.

The arrival of three visitors in the early 1850s connected nativism with foreign relations and domestic politics more closely than any episode since the 1790s. Hungarian nationalist Lajos Kossuth fled Europe after leading a failed uprising against Austria in 1848. Attacking New York's Bishop Hughes as an agent of Habsburg despotism and warning of a Vatican conspiracy to rule the world, Kossuth sought to enlist mercenaries to return to renew Hungary's battle for independence. Kossuth captured the imagination of Americans until most realized that he might upset the delicate balance between the means and ends of foreign policy. Democratic leaders who might have aided him did not embrace his cause. And by 1852, the Whig Party had sundered along sectional lines as a result of the slavery controversy. Hence, Kossuth failed to enlist political support and had to settle for leaving behind, in the words of historian Thomas A. Bailey, "Kossuth beards, Kossuth hats, Kossuth overcoats, Kossuth cigars, the Kossuth grippe, and Kossuth County, Iowa."

The arrivals of "Father" Alessandro Gavazzi and Monsignor Gaetano Bedini early in 1853 for a time appeared to transfer the battle for Italian unification to the United States. Gavazzi was an apostate monk who took part in the rebellion of 1848, while Bedini, representing the pope on his American visit, resolutely opposed Italian unification. Gavazzi's nationalistic denunciation of Bedini for leading papal forces at the Battle of Bologna converted what had been a pleasant visit for the papal nuncio into an ordeal, as hostile crowds greeted his every appearance.

The fear of immigrants assumed political meaning during the 1850s as the slavery question slowly immobilized both parties. In 1854 the secret Order of the Star Spangled Banner transformed itself into the American Party, or "Know-Nothing" Party (as New York newspaper editor Horace Greeley dubbed them), because members claimed to know nothing about the organization. Party faithful claimed to endorse the asylum ideal—they would welcome all immigrants, except paupers and criminals—as long as the newcomers promised to abstain from politics. The initial strength and subsequent weakness of the Know-Nothings lay in their promise of an issue, the danger of immigration, that skirted the slavery dispute. Nativism in this instance was less an end in itself than a means to achieve national unity amid growing sectional crisis.

Despite its nationalist gloss, the Know-Nothings were defined mainly by sectional and local conflict. Southern Know-Nothings focused their attention primarily on the tendency of most immigrants to settle in, and augment the political clout of, northern states. Conversely, New England Know-Nothings were often reformers, and most detested slavery. This contradiction undercut the American Party, which survived only as long as the Republic avoided commitment on the slavery question. Ironically, Know-Nothing nativism served to toughen immigrant resolve and cohesion. Abraham Lincoln wooed the German vote in 1860 by seeking to learn the language, reading a German-language newspaper, and naming immigrant Germans to his cabinet.

Know-Nothing nativism also toughened the resolve of Irish Americans who, though caricatured unmercifully, began to win the battle for urban America against lower-class Protestants. Indeed, by the end of the century, the Irish would join nativists in defending the United States against the "new" immigration from southern and eastern Europe.

Yet by the end of the Civil War, nativists could show no federal legislation restricting the immigration. American religious tolerance survived the socioeconomic turmoil and mob violence of the 1830s and 1840s, the Mexican War, and the Know-Nothing movement. Until the 1880s, in fact, confidence in the nation's power to assimilate newcomers checked nativism in most regions. Even the radical Irish Fenians, who used American soil to harass British North America after the Civil War—including an "invasion" of Ontario launched from Saint Albans, Vermont, in May 1870—fell far short of involving the United States and Britain in a war to free Ireland. In short, the "free security" of the Republic, afforded by the Atlantic and Pacific and weak neighbors to the north and south, combined with a hardy strain of Anglophobia to undermine resentment against Irish immigrants. The alchemy of the melting pot, which held that Americans had only to wait a generation or two to see immigrants assimilated, dominated the national mood. Immigrants had much to offer. As Justice Oliver Wendell Holmes observed, Americans were "the Romans of the modern world, the great assimilating people."

IMMIGRATION LEGISLATION AND MORE NEWCOMERS

Until the 1880s it appeared that even the Sinophobia that flared in California in the 1850s would dissipate. Chinese laborers had proved essential in constructing the Union Pacific Railroad as it passed through the Sierra Nevada. The Fourteenth Amendment shielded the Chinese, as it did African Americans, while the Burlingame Treaty of 1868 mollified nativists by allowing Chinese who entered to provide inexpensive labor, but prevented them from becoming citizens. Economic troubles and social unrest, however, laid the basis for the Chinese Exclusion Act (1882), which proscribed immigration for a decade and marked a key change in the federal government's laissez-faire policy. The Chinese Exclusion Act codified the idea of a Yellow Peril and denied that Asians were assimilable. This legislation had a clear racial basis and hence also influenced attitudes toward the "new" southern and eastern European immigration. The historian Roger Daniels credits the law as providing "the hinge on which all American immigration policy turned." The legislation—renewed and amplified in 1884, 1888, and 1892—also influenced similar laws in Australia, Canada, and other English-speaking countries. As one senator told President Rutherford B. Hayes, they were "a cold pebble in the public stomach which cannot be digested."

The Exclusion Act and its amendments mortified China's government, which ironically practiced its own policy of ethnoracial exclusion against outsiders until Western powers in the 1840s and 1850s compelled the Chinese to treat whites as equals. China protested often against this inequality, but to no avail. With depression and social unrest increasing, Sinophobia swept the Pacific Northwest and Rocky Mountains during the 1880s. In 1885, after a local water company in Tacoma, Washington, hired Chinese to lay pipe despite high white unemployment, a riot razed Chinatown and drove Chinese residents from the city. The incident, which locals deemed a "glorious victory," resulted in China receiving from the United States an indemnity of $10,000. A year later a similar workingmen's riot in Seattle forced most of the Chinese from the city and compelled President Grover Cleveland to mobilize military force to restore order. A systematic series of arrests occurred in San Francisco and Los Angeles in 1893, and by October sixty-four Asians were in prison pending the outcome of their appeals to avoid deportation. In 1894 these difficulties were settled after Li Hung-chang informed William Bowman, the American counsel at Tientsin, that Sino-American relations were near the breaking point. Then war with Japan intervened to weaken China's position, and the Gresham-Yang Treaty of 1894 succeeded in placing exclusion and registration laws passed since 1882 on a proper treaty basis.

Resistance to newcomers who were "not like us" burgeoned between 1890 and 1920. No equivalent period in American history can match the twenty million immigrants who came to the United States. Here was the stuff of a colossal saga—given added significance by the sight of the Statue of Liberty, dedicated in October 1886 in New York's harbor, near Ellis Island, the arrival point for most immigrants. The Statue of Liberty inspired millions of newcomers, and Emma Lazarus's poem inscribed at its base promised a better tomorrow:

> Give me your tired, your poor,
> Your huddled masses yearning to breathe free,
> The wretched refuse of your teeming shore.
> Send these, the homeless, tempest-tost to me,
> I lift my lamp beside the golden door.

If the newcomers' contribution was to provide fodder for the unprecedented economic growth of this era, economic difficulties and accompanying social strife undercut the positive view of immigration many citizens held. Businessmen and reformers joined labor leaders and workingmen in arguing that immigrant gifts paled before their role in promoting domestic discord. By stressing the European origins of class conflict, critics of the American urban-industrial scene like Edwin L. Godkin, Jacob Riis, Richard T. Ely, and Josiah Strong warned of the radical portent of this immigration. Missing the deep conservatism of the great majority of newcomers from southeastern Europe, they also failed to see that new urban governments lacked requisite administrative experience to deal with their problems. According to reformers, the new immigrants were the problem, settling in cities and corrupting politics. National immunity from the ills of Europe seemed to have expired, and the melting pot seemed more a pressure cooker.

This perception gained strength as Americans sought to make sense of the intense labor-management strife of the era. The Chicago Haymarket Riot in May 1886 ushered in a decade of industrial strife and catalyzed in American minds a dread of foreign conspirators. Fearful adversaries of "long-haired, wild-eyed, bad smelling, atheistic, reckless, foreign wretches" did not distinguish between Marxists and anarchists. Indeed, patriotic citizens parceled together all varieties of immigrant radicalism and left the package in front of the house of labor.

Fears of national decay heightened after the panic of 1893 and ensuing depression. An angry agrarian crusade attacked capitalism and international finance with a cataclysmic rhetoric not designed to reassure jittery easterners. Labor discontent reached bloody pinnacles during the Homestead and Pullman strikes. As time seemed to run out, portending the end of opportunity, geography seemed to conspire. As the historian Frederick Jackson Turner told the American Historical Association in 1893, the era of the frontier—the dynamic font of individualism, liberty, and democracy—had ended. Americans would have to find something new to supplant the source of those characteristics that made the nation great.

As the center seemed incapable of holding, an assemblage of New England Brahmins—graduates of Harvard—formed the Immigration Restriction League. The league championed Anglo-Saxonism and embraced a nostalgic view of the region's homogeneous past. They pored over the works of John Fiske and John W. Burgess, who applied precepts of social Darwinism to history and politics. Cheering the Foran Act of 1885, which had prohibited European contract labor, the restrictionists gathered behind Henry Cabot Lodge of Massachusetts and developed a series of literacy tests as the best way to halt immigration. While the House passed a literacy bill five times between 1895 and 1917 (with Senate support after the first failure), presidents as distinct as Grover Cleveland, William Howard Taft, and Woodrow Wilson vetoed the legislation. Only in 1917 did Congress prevail over the veto.

In a society that questioned its ability to resolve conflicts, citizens looked for evidence of the republic's virility. The Reverend Josiah Strong expressed this anxiety in *Our Country: Its Possible Future and Its Present Crisis* (1885), which excoriated the communal disruption wrought by excessive materialism. This development threatened America's traditional Anglo-Saxon, Protestant culture in its quest to evangelize the world. As Lyman Beecher had a half-century earlier, Strong anticipated a "righteous empire" of Protestantism expanding and spreading the American way throughout the world. Not surprisingly in an era that witnessed the final relegation of America's Indians to reservations and penury and southern African Americans to Jim Crow, *Our Country* and other of Strong's writings embraced the racialist thesis that civilization would reach its zenith when Anglo-Saxons extinguished less vigorous peoples and secured international hegemony. Domestic corruption jeopardized this divine mission, made all the more imperative by the impending "final competition of races, for which the Anglo-Saxon is being schooled."

Strong advocated the mission of the United States rather than its manifest destiny. Just as Protestant Christianity would remedy domestic ills—socialism, intemperance, and the Mormon and Catholic threats—so too would Anglo-Saxon torchbearers of Protestantism carry their message to the far corners of the earth—not on the end of a sword, but through the persuasive power of example.

Pressure engendered by various domestic crises during the 1890s stimulated chauvinists and nativists alike. Richard Hofstadter's concept of a "psychic crisis" does not explain the William McKinley administration's decision for war against Spain in 1898, but by underlining the close relationship between the domestic distress of the 1890s, nativism, and the new bellicosity in American diplomacy, the construct suggests why Americans were eager for foreign adventure. During the decade the United States went to the brink of war with Italy, Chile, and Great Britain over issues peripheral to the national interest. Nativism served as a catalyst for these episodes, demonstrating its function to unify a divided nation by focusing on foreign problems and threats. In 1891 a New Orleans mob lynched eleven Italians and Italian Americans immediately after they were acquitted of the charge of murdering the city's police chief. The episode did nothing for Italian-American relations, especially when Theodore Roosevelt deemed it "a rather good thing." After Italy demanded compensation for the families of the deceased and Washington demurred, Italy cut full diplomatic relations. War talk flared among jingoists and one Georgian promised to muster a company of soldiers "to invade Rome, disperse the Mafia, and plant the stars and stripes on the dome of St. Peter's." As immigration restrictionists disparaged Italians and other southeastern Europeans and big-navy men called for an ambitious building program, President Benjamin Harrison chose the statesmanlike course and apologized to Italy. The war scare passed. But many journals observed that in the face of the threat national unity replaced sectional bickering.

A NEW CENTURY OF IMMIGRANTS

Nativism diminished at the beginning of the twentieth century. A robust national economy shielded newcomers, even as the assassination of President McKinley by Leon Czolgosz, an American-born radical, led Congress in 1903 to bar "anarchists or persons who believe or advocate the overthrow by force or violence of the Government of the United States . . . or the assassination of public officials." The nation's immigration bureaucracy grew quickly after 1900, boasting more than 1,200 workers by 1906. A year later Congress established the Immigration Commission, which in 1911 issued a huge report that popularized the distinction between the "old" and "new" immigration. The former was salutary, the latter baneful. The Immigration Commission also searched for illness at Ellis Island and on the West Coast, as bacterial and viral outbreaks—long associated with specific immigrant groups—became a means to distinguish "healthy" Americans from sickly aliens. In 1793, Philadelphians deemed an outbreak of yellow fever "Palatine Fever," to indicate German immigrant responsibility for the outbreak; in 1832 nativists attributed a cholera epidemic on the eastern seaboard to Irish-Catholic immigrants; and in 1900 the Chinese in San Francisco took the blame for an outbreak of bubonic plague. By 1907, in addition to anarchists, immigration undesirables excluded from American shores included paupers, polygamists, lepers, beggars, prostitutes, epileptics, victims of tuberculosis, those suspected of "moral turpitude," and imbeciles. Clearly the stigma of disease served to marginalize immigrants culturally and to remove them—indeed, often by quarantine—from society's mainstream. Only by embracing the consumer culture of personal cleanliness could newcomers exhibit patriotism and become American.

Nativism did flare in San Francisco in 1906, when the school board ordered the exclusion of Japanese children from that city's public schools. Regional prejudice quickly threatened to overturn President Theodore Roosevelt's Far Eastern policy. Long a bastion of racialism, California assumed its anti-Japanese stance naturally. The Japanese and Korean Exclusion League appeared in 1905, as Japan and Russia waged war in East Asia, and repeated charges made earlier against the Chinese, warning that the Japanese jeopardized not only the standard of living but also the primacy of the white race. Many nativists, including the novelist Jack London and publisher William Randolph Hearst, excoriated the Yellow Peril. Not only had Japan's strong showing in war against Russia made it a world power, but now its position of strength in the Far East threatened the self-image of the United States as a superior, Anglo-Saxon nation. Ironically, Japan itself had a long history of institutionalized xenophobia, but now showed concern over its international status. Tokyo protested this exclusion, which placed Washington in the awkward position of convincing Californians of their obligation to the Union, while at the same time seeking to secure equal treatment for citizens of a foreign power. Concerned at Japan's new strength in Asia and upset by riots in Tokyo protesting the Treaty of Portsmouth, which he helped negotiate, President Theodore Roosevelt moved to restore cordial relations with Tokyo.

His own racism notwithstanding, Roosevelt withstood opposition from the Pacific coast and Rocky Mountain regions—and from southern advocates of Jim Crow and states' rights. He warned that he would employ military force, if necessary, and sent a personal representative to San Francisco. Mayor Eugene Schmitz soon revoked the segregation order, and Roosevelt promised to work to place Japanese immigration on a treaty basis. The president also dispatched the navy's Pacific Fleet on a dramatic global voyage—after informing Tokyo not to view the move as an unfriendly act.

Roosevelt and the Japanese exchanged several diplomatic notes, which became the basis in 1907 for the so-called "Gentleman's Agreement," an executive agreement that restricted passage of Japanese laborers from Hawaii and Japan to the United States unless they had "already been in America." The arrangement, shifting Japanese migration to the United States from basically male to female, quieted but did not halt anti-Japanese agitation. Foreign-born Japanese (*Issei*) remained "aliens ineligible to citizenship," while second-generation citizens (*Nisei*) found the Fourteenth Amendment a poor guarantee of the rights of citizenship against discriminatory law and custom. After leaving office, Roosevelt himself concluded that cultural and economic conflict was inevitable in relations between Americans and Asians.

Nativism reached its apogee during and directly after World War I. Just prior to American intervention in the conflict, congressional restrictionists overcame President Woodrow Wilson's veto and passed the major recommendation the Dillingham Commission made six years earlier. The Immigration Act of 1917 barred illiterate adult immigrants; set a head tax of eight dollars per person; and excluded vagrants, alcoholics, advocates of violent revolution, and "psychopathic inferiors." Passage of a literacy test and the establishment of a barred zone in the southwest Pacific—which closed the gates to Asians not already banned by the Chinese Exclusion Act and Gentleman's Agreement—indicated that the Great War heralded a more sinister era in the history of American nativism.

WORLD WAR I AND THE 1920S

With the outbreak of war in Europe in August 1914, the geographical and political isolation—that placed foreign policy above controversy, rendered immigrant attitudes nonpolitical, facilitated assimilation, and shielded the melting pot—quickly dissipated. Foreigners who earlier solicited American support—like Edmond Genet and Lajos Kossuth—annoyed nativists, but did not change American noninterventionism. Even the wars with Mexico and Spain underlined unity. But now Europe seemed much closer. President Wilson's assurance that the United States would not intervene notwithstanding, nativism as a force for patriotism and national unity stressed conformity—targeting German Americans and political radicals. Divisive themes, like anti-Catholicism and Teutonic racism, disappeared from the nativist lexicon.

Nativism in World War I had much in common with xenophobia during the Quasi-War. The chief assertion of American nationalism, termed "100 percent Americanism" after U.S. intervention, attested to the realization of cultural and social diversity amidst crisis. First- and second-generation immigrants comprised one-third of America's population—a point made more problematic by the loss of confidence by Progressive reformers. Hence, the preparedness campaign during the period of neutrality (1914–1917) focused primarily on German immigrants. Well-organized, prosperous, and self-consciously retaining old-world customs, German Americans mobilized following the outbreak of war to block munitions shipments to belligerents and counter sensational "Hun" propaganda stories emanating from London. In January 1915 the German-American Alliance met in New York, demonstrating a great show of unity—and outraging American nativists.

This gathering coincided with Germany's announcement of submarine warfare against Britain and with German attempts to bomb American vessels and munitions plants. Soon politicians and editors condemned the apparent conspiracy, decrying "hyphenate" Americans (but never Anglo-Americans, the antiwar activist Randolph Bourne pointed out) and heeding former President Roosevelt's point that any apostasy from total allegiance smacked of "moral treason." "America for the Americans!" he thundered. "Our bitter experience should teach us for a generation . . . to crush under our heel every movement that smacks in the smallest degree of playing the German game." President Wilson's counsel at the outset that Americans "be neutral in thought as well as in deed" quickly went by the board as citizens chose sides and sought to profit from the conflict by selling matériel and munitions to the belligerents. Britain, of course, held the advantage there.

As American neutrality became increasingly pro-British, radicals and dissenters joined German immigrants as surrogate enemies for patriotic citizens. Men like Henry Cabot Lodge and Augustus Gardner, wealthy New England Brahmins, moved easily from attacking new immigrants and labor unions to alerting citizens about the dangers posed by pacifists and German Americans. Citizens organizations like the National Security League and American Defense Society competed to strengthen the military and impose unity in all areas of life. German submarine warfare and propaganda played into the hands of these grassroots patriots, whose distrust of immigrants was shared increasingly by the Wilson administration. Although the German-American Alliance forbade political activity, state and local immigrant groups continued to lobby, no doubt exacerbating the bitter feelings that peaked during the 1916 election campaign. Denouncing "that small alien element among us which puts loyalty to any foreign power before loyalty to the United States," Wilson and the Democratic Party portrayed Republican candidate Charles Evans Hughes—who refused to get involved with the hyphenate issue—as "a dupe of the Kaiser in pro-British areas, and as a Roosevelt-dominated jingo spoiling for war with Germany in areas with a large Teutonic population." The president played both sides of the nativist coin.

The mailed fist of patriotism fell even harder on German Americans once the United States entered the war. Ironically, as the Republic moved to make the world safe for democracy, American-style, patriots nearly tore up the Bill of Rights. Ethnic fidelity now became a sine qua non of foreign policy, even more so with the Russian Bolshevik Revolution of November 1917. German culture came under attack on all fronts, with hamburgers, sauerkraut, Beethoven, and German language instruction disappearing. The Department of Justice gave vigilante groups like the American Protective League carte blanche to ferret spies and saboteurs from the German-socialist-pacifist–International Workers of the World–trade unionist monolith. In Collinsville, Illinois, an area previously scarred by racial and labor-management violence, Robert Paul Praeger was lynched in April 1918. Praeger was a socialist and a radical, and his death drew little support for civil liberties. Indeed, most observers considered Praeger's hanging evidence of the inadequacy of federal legislation to suppress sedition. The *New Republic* called this argument "a species of sickening cant," but editors and politicians who disdained vigilante justice praised passage of the Sedition Act of 1918.

Nativism did not diminish with the end of the war. Indeed, the martial psychology of 1917–1918 intensified in the face of postwar domestic dislocations, the apparent menace posed by the Bolsheviks, and, most important, the sudden loss of unity and purpose fostered by war. "War is the health of the state," Randolph Bourne averred cynically, but with peace American democracy suffered anew. The Red Scare of 1919–1920 reflected anxiety at the racial violence, inflation, and economic recession attending demobilization and reconversion, as well as the appearance of new American communist parties, directed by the Moscow Comintern, and significant immigrant presence in the violent steel and textile strikes of 1919. Led by Attorney General A. Mitchell Palmer and "sustained by large numbers of business and political leaders, corporations and interest groups, several agencies of government, superpatriotic societies, and the press," federal agents targeted as security threats anarchists, communists, radical labor groups, and other citizens who had opposed the war.

The Bolshevik threat affected debate on the Treaty of Versailles and the League of Nations. Republicans and Democrats alike denounced as misguided Wilson's messianic prophecy to remake the world in the Republic's image and pointed out that Americans could never trust Old World statesmen. "Men had died," the poet Ezra Pound wrote, "for an old bitch gone in the teeth, a botched civilization." Hence, when Wilson argued that the new League of Nations would stem the Bolshevik threat, Columbia University President Nicholas Murray Butler retorted that the Versailles Treaty was "unpatriotic and un-American," an example of "subtle, half-conscious socialism." American fears peaked on 2 June 1919, when a dynamite explosion rocked Palmer's home on K Street in Washington (and blew up the perpetrator), and bombs exploded at the homes of leading citizens in eight other cities. An erstwhile Quaker with political ambitions, Palmer set out to destroy the "reds" and capture the Democratic nomination for president in 1920. He created a General Intelligence Division, led by J. Edgar Hoover, which soon amassed more than 200,000 cards detailing the character of radical organizations and publications and the case histories of more than 60,000 "dangerous radicals."

Incapacitated by a stroke, Wilson could not restrain Palmer, whose crusade soon left its mark. Within months the Palmer raids, strengthened by support from the newly formed American Legion, led to the deportation of 249 Russian immigrants whose Bolshevism was more imagined than real. The Lusk Committee in New York expelled five socialist delegates from the state legislature; business leaders fostered scare propaganda to deflect labor grievances; California prohibited Japanese from owning land; an Illinois mob turned on Italian settlers, beating them and razing their homes; and one patriot charged that Albert Einstein's theory of relativity had Bolshevik origins. Most Americans, one cynic noted, could not distinguish between Bolshevism and rheumatism, but no matter. The Soviets would provide a whipping boy for nativist patriots for the next seventy years.

When domestic conditions improved in 1920, the Red Scare collapsed—but not before Palmer himself became a victim of the episode. His presidential hopes evaporated along with the crisis. Nonetheless, World War I and the Red Scare cast a long shadow into the 1920s and beyond. Soviet-American relations were poisoned from the beginning by judgments and actions conditioned by wartime and postwar xenophobia. Bipartisan disillusionment with the politics of Europe contributed to the economic protectionism of the 1920s and also influenced the refusal of the United States to join the World Court. The linking of radicalism with disloyalty tarnished the labor movement for more than a decade. In Massachusetts, two Italian anarchists were executed after a trial that arrayed the values of the Brahmin establishment against alien radicalism. Liberals may have been outraged and transformed the defendants into martyrs after their death, but presiding Judge Webster Thayer's censure of Nicola Sacco and Bartolomeo Vanzetti as "anarchist bastards" epitomized the feelings toward southeastern Europe and radical politics held by most Americans.

Most important, the Red Scare gave the Immigration Restriction League "evidence" to show that the melting pot threatened American society and culture. The early 1920s witnessed the full flowering of Anglo-Saxon racism, part of the nostalgic drive toward Protestant Anglo-conformity that gave the decade its ambiguous cultural tone. The "roaring twenties" clashed with an "anxious twenties," in which sober citizens questioned the multicultural, interdependent, consumer-oriented future and hearkened toward a simpler past. The notion that a person's genes determined one's destiny found expression in university quotas and employment restrictions against Jews, the writings of Lothrop Stoddard and Madison Grant, the popularity of IQ tests and eugenics, and the renewal of congressional debate on immigration. Led by Albert Johnson of Washington, long an enemy of local Wobblies, congressional restrictionists overrode President Wilson's veto in early 1921 and passed legislation limiting immigration based upon nationality: the number of immigrants per year from one country could not surpass 3 percent of the total of that nationality resident in the United States in 1910. Three years later the Johnson-Reed Act closed the door to "inferior" peoples. Quotas would now reflect resident populations of 1890; after 1927 immigration would be limited to 150,000 persons annually, and Asians would be excluded. Commerce Secretary Herbert Hoover agreed, suggesting "biological and cultural grounds why there should be no mixture of Oriental and Caucasian blood." President Calvin Coolidge did not mince words. He noted in signing the bill that "America must be kept American."

If the Red Scare prevented Americans from adapting to postwar realities, it was not surprising that during the decade after the conflict many citizens wrestled with fundamental social tensions by seeking to revive the attitudes and values of an earlier era. Nativist defenders of an idealized *Gemeinschaft* ("community") culture sought to halt the intrusion of modernity. What historian John Higham called the tribal twenties exhibited a retrospective idealism, at once parochial and nationalistic, at war with urbanism, secularism, and ethnic diversity. This cultural strain drove a significant part of the populace to embrace Anglo conformity as its rejoinder to the challenges posed by modern urban-industrial America—not least its liberated women, hot films, and jazz. In the 1920 census, for the first time in the nation's history, urban residents outnumbered their rural cousins—and there would be no restoration of a preindustrial epoch. Henry Ford epitomized the cultural problem of Americans enjoying the fruits of mass production and postwar technological prowess and lamenting the sociocultural consequences of change. The father of mass production—his assembly line devastated traditional skills and his Model T automobile revolutionized travel (and also provided a bedroom on wheels and means to escape small-town surveillance)—Ford became the most notorious anti-Semite of the interwar era. A scion of the rural Midwest, he organized a "peace ship" in 1915 to halt the European war. Initially supporting Wilson's League of Nations and dunning intolerant patriots during the Red Scare, Ford met frustration at every turn.

Disillusionment and economic problems in 1920 led to Ford's espousal of an ideological anti-Semitism that ultimately caught the attention of Adolf Hitler and his Nazis. In the pages of his *Dearborn Independent,* he came to blame just about every modern problem (and personal peeve) on the Jews. The short list included gamblers, booze and cigarettes, immigrants, Bolsheviks, bankers, and unions, but the underlying peril was a sinister Jewish cabal seeking to dominate the world. *The Protocols of the Elders of Zion,* a czarist forgery in Russia in 1891, provided Ford documentation for his facile explanation of dismaying cultural trends and a dramatic symbol of the danger posed by international political cooperation.

Similar malice toward immigrants and internationalism colored the discourse of the Ku Klux Klan, reborn in 1915 and peaking eight years later with 2.3 million members. The soul of the organization, splintered into groups reflecting regional nativist animosities (against blacks in the South, Asians in the West, Catholics in the Midwest, and Jews in the Northeast), lay in America's urbanizing towns and villages—under siege from modernism, however defined. These were the same venues that gave Henry Ford his major support. Although Klan rhetoric primarily targeted these minorities, actual violence generally fell upon white, Anglo-Saxon apostates who strayed from traditional Protestant moral codes. Bootleggers, feckless husbands, and cheating wives comprised major targets for the Klan, which also prospered in urban centers in the Midwest and Southwest, reflecting demographic change wrought by World War I. Imperial Wizard Hiram W. Evans led the Klan in its "fight for Americanism," which included, among other items, support for Prohibition, immigration restriction, anti-evolution laws, and family values.

The 1920s included numerous examples of rural-minded, defensive imperialism. Yet as tribal nativists moved to prevent command of the nation's destiny from passing from Main Street to the metropolis, they affirmed the material benefits of the modernity they so grimly denounced. This contradiction mirrored a similar ambivalence in American foreign relations during the 1920s and 1930s. On one hand, Washington rejected political commitments like the League of Nations and the World Court. On the other, as William Appleman Williams and Emily Rosenberg demonstrate, apart from its protectionist tariffs, the United States proved adept internationally in economic and cultural realms, particularly in its search for markets and influence in Europe, China, Latin America, and the Middle East. Being in the world, but not of it, hearkened back to the original reason why English Puritans settled in the New World in the early seventeenth century. Now, however, this quest for what Warren I. Cohen deemed "an empire without tears" confirmed the superior morality of Americans, but did not prepare them for constructive global action in case of crisis.

Nevertheless, nativism as an organized movement triumphed with passage of the National Origins Act of 1924. The law produced a sharp decrease in the volume of European and Asian newcomers and hastened the Americanization of newcomers already present in the United States. The Great Depression that began in 1929 also advanced the assimilation process, for economic difficulties blurred cultural distinctions between ethnic groups as it sharpened class feelings in the working population. Franklin D. Roosevelt's New Deal also diminished the power of immigrant cultural and social groups by making immigrants and natives alike look to government for relief. Developments in mass communication—documentary films, Franklin Roosevelt's fireside chats and radio itself, Works Progress Administration guidebooks and chronicles—also subjected Americans to unprecedented common experience. Finally, nativist attempts to cleanse the body politic of alien growth in fact shielded minorities by sharply restricting fields open to them. With the advent of economic catastrophe in 1929, Americans directed their bitterness at the establishment—white, Anglo-Saxon, and Protestant.

Even before the depression, social scientists initiated what John Higham termed a "massive assault on racial thinking and ethnocentrism." American loathing of Nazism during the late 1930s and World War II strengthened this trend and helped prevent the sort of vicious nativism that appeared after 1916. The German-American community also remembered the indignities it encountered, and after a bitter debate on intervention in the European War, the Japanese attack on Pearl Harbor served further to unify the nation. Hence, American anti-German hatred focused not upon German immigrants and their offspring, but upon Hitler, his political hierarchy, and the Nazi doctrine of Aryan supremacy. Official policy made this distinction until the end of the war. Not surprisingly, then, anti-Catholicism and racial nativism became less important, remaining powerful only among dyed-in-the-wool Roosevelt haters.

Indeed, from the 1930s on persons who advocated old-fashioned 100 percent Americanism risked identification with European anti-Semitism and fascism. The Great Depression gave several mass leaders a name and national following. The most famous, Huey Long of Louisiana, was assassinated in 1935, after he helped defeat Washington's attempt to join the World Court. The others included Father Charles E. Coughlin, the radio priest from Royal Oak, Michigan; the spiritualist William Dudley Pelley, founder of the Silver Shirt Legion; and Fritz Kuhn, leader of the German-American Bund. These men exhibited a curiously inverted form of nativism. Father Coughlin (borrowing from Henry Ford and earlier populists and anticipating the strategy and tactics of Joseph R. McCarthy of Wisconsin) denounced treason within government circles, fingering President Herbert Hoover, Treasury Secretary Andrew W. Mellon, government bureaucrats, and ultimately the entire Roosevelt administration. Here were the real "aliens," agents of a Judeo-Bolshevik conspiracy that threatened the Republic.

WORLD WAR II AND THE EFFECTS ON NATIVISM

This charge allowed traditional targets of nativists to turn the tables on their historic adversary—the Anglo establishment. As Justus Doenecke notes, disdain for Britain and things British unified a heterogeneous group of Americans who opposed aid to Britain between 1939 and 1941. Coughlin and several other mass leaders, however, copied Hitler's anti-Semitism and anticommunism. This strategy, combined with their accusation that members of the legitimate political order were the real aliens in the United States, backfired by decade's end. Their thesis that a cabal of Anglophiles, Democratic politicians, international bankers, and Jews controlled the government gave the Roosevelt administration evidence to proclaim the existence of an internal fascist movement, to link this threat with respectable noninterventionists attempting to prevent American entrance into the war, and to strengthen presidential power over foreign affairs. In September 1941, when famed flier Charles A. Lindbergh blamed the Jews, along with Britain and Roosevelt for the nation's march toward war, he closed the circle—nativism was now perceived as un-American, and noninterventionists as minions of Hitler.

Yet if World War II did not approach the first in its violation of civil liberties, the second remains far from the "good war" portrayed in much historiography. Indeed, the racial character of the conflict figured prominently on both sides of the Pacific and revealed anew that the Republic was, in Richard Polenberg's term, "one nation, divisible." The war underlined anew the appalling treatment accorded African Americans, yet also led at long last to the postwar integration of the armed forces. The most flagrant blot on wartime civil liberties came with the incarceration of 126,000 Japanese Americans—ripped from their homes on the West Coast and transferred to "relocation" camps in the western interior. This diaspora came shortly after Pearl Harbor, when the federal government embraced the Pacific coast obsession with the Yellow Peril and accepted Lieutenant General John L. DeWitt's doctrine of "military necessity." Contrary to DeWitt's argument and popular belief, the Japanese Americans were not spies and saboteurs but a hard-working and prosperous people whose virtues did justice to Horatio Alger.

This mass relocation marked a new chapter in the history of American nativism. The Japanese Americans, who gained an official apology and partial redress in 1988 for their tribulations, were not tarred and feathered or forced to kiss the flag. For the first time, the federal government efficiently rounded them up and shipped them off to concentration camps, where—having lost their property, their jobs, and their civil and legal rights—they sat out the war behind barbed wire. The threat of Japanese-American betrayal, which girded relocation, drew support from President Roosevelt in Executive Order 9066, secured approval from Congress, and was upheld by the Supreme Court. The incarceration had unintended consequences as Japanese Americans moved eastward, and shifted their occupational emphasis from agriculture to business and the professions.

Nativism declined in importance after 1945, reflecting eroded foundations of ethnic group loyalty and changes in the basic structure of society after 1945. Religious affiliation supplanted ethnic origin as the basic means of achieving self-identity and promoting group loyalty. The memory of the Holocaust—and of the tardiness of the United States and other Allies in dealing with it—contributed in 1948 to passage of the Displaced Persons Act, which opened the gates to 400,000 Europeans. Moreover, the onset of the Cold War enabled immigrants and refugees from central and eastern Europe to move within the national consensus. Czechs, Hungarians, and Poles could be as good—or better—Americans than the white, Anglo-Saxon Protestant establishment, especially the perjured traitor, Alger Hiss, and his key character witness, Dean Acheson. In its ire against Anglophiles and intellectuals, McCarthyism both reflected and intensified the patriotism of these anticommunist Europeans.

NATIVISM'S DEATH KNELL?

In 1965, as President Lyndon Johnson sought to achieve a Great Society at home and in Southeast Asia, Congress passed an epochal immigration act that appeared to signal the death knell of nativism. Reflecting the nation's growing commitment to confronting racism, this law replaced the discriminatory national origins quotas of 1924 with an agenda based on family preference. The law exempted close relatives of persons already in the United States and limited newcomers from the Eastern Hemisphere to 170,000 persons annually and from the Western Hemisphere to 120,000 annually. Although Congress expected most immigrants to come from Europe, an upswing in Europe's economy, deteriorating conditions in Latin America, and the agonizing war in Southeast Asia produced a different outcome. In fact, the tide of immigration and refugees in 1976–1986 ranked the newcomers, in descending order of numbers: Mexico, Vietnam, the Philippines, Korea, Nationalist China (Taiwan), and Cuba. Never had the nation been more multicultural.

Nativism did not disappear, however, and in the last quarter of the twentieth century antiforeign sentiment erupted during periods of economic duress, especially in areas in which these groups settled and in contexts where political candidates like Pat Buchanan courted voters with antiforeign themes. Residents of the postindustrial rust belt seemed most sensitive to antiforeign ideas, which often emerged with antigovernment tones. For example, the downturn in the American automotive market negatively affected Asian Americans. The Ku Klux Klan and other survivalist and hate groups still sputtered along, erupting occasionally, as an unhappy underside of multicultural reality. Defenders of an older America denounced nonwhite newcomers, as their predecessors dunned immigrants in the 1840s, 1890s, and 1920s. But the nostalgic nativism at the beginning of the twenty-first century—never more than a minority position—did not hide the point that newcomers since the 1970s had often done the kinds of work that native-born Americans choose not to do. In this way newcomers continued to reap the promise of what was still the most powerful force on earth—the American dream. The terrorist plane crash into the Pentagon and the destruction of the New York World Trade Center towers on 11 September 2001, however, heralded a new chapter in nativism. Americans of Middle Eastern descent now faced uncertainty as the Republic gathered its resources to meet a new kind of threat to its national security.

BIBLIOGRAPHY

Archdeacon, Thomas J. *Becoming American: An Ethnic History.* New York, 1983. A good place to start on the history of American immigration.

Bennett, David H. *The Party of Fear: From Nativist Movements to the New Right in American History.* Rev. ed. New York, 1995. Provides a fine scholarly overview and interpretation of nativism in the nineteenth and twentieth centuries.

Bodnar, John. *The Transplanted: A History of Immigrants in Urban America.* Bloomington, Ind., 1985. Another good reference for the history of immigration.

Daniels, Roger. *Not Like Us: Immigrants and Minorities in America, 1890–1924.* Chicago, 1997. Integrates American reactions to the new immigration with policies toward African Americans, Native Americans, and other minorities. Daniels stands alone as the historian of Japanese-American relocation and redress.

Daniels, Roger, Sandra C. Taylor, and Harry H. L. Kitano, eds. *Japanese Americans: From Relocation to Redress.* Rev. ed. Seattle, 1991. A superior overview.

Davis, David Brion, ed. *The Fear of Conspiracy: Images of Un-American Subversion from the Revolution to the Present.* Ithaca, N.Y., 1970. Features a discourse and rhetoric of nativist countersubversion, including a sensitive reading of the author's construct of the paranoid style.

DeConde, Alexander. *Ethnicity, Race, and American Foreign Policy: A History.* Boston, 1992. Focuses on the rise, place, and slow decline in power of the Anglo-American majority and argues that historians often minimize the importance of British immigrants and their role in fomenting nativism against other groups. A good starting place for those wishing to further assess nativism's place in the context of foreign relations; it also has the advantage of assessing the development of racism as an integral part of the American establishment.

Doenecke, Justus D. *Storm on the Horizon: The Challenge to American Intervention, 1939–1941.* Lanham, Md., 2000. Presents a thoughtful assessment of nativist themes in American noninterventionism before World War II.

Dower, John W. *War Without Mercy: Race and Power in the Pacific War.* New York, 1986. Portrays racism on both sides of the Pacific.

Dumenil, Lynn. *The Modern Temper: American Culture and Society in the 1920s.* New York, 1995. Dumenil offers measured assessments of the wrenching cultural change of that era and regressive American reactions. Her treatment of the Klan is particularly insightful.

Higham, John. *Strangers in the Land: Patterns of American Nativism, 1860–1925.* New York, 1963. One of those few books that just gets better with time.

———. *Send These to Me: Immigrants in Urban America.* Rev. ed. Baltimore, 1984. Offers second thoughts equally significant.

Hofstadter, Richard. *The Paranoid Style in American Politics and Other Essays.* New York, 1965. Classic and problematic statement of liberal distaste for McCarthyism and the political right.

Kazin, Michael. *The Populist Persuasion: An American History.* New York, 1995. An empathic qualification of critiques of the populist skein in American history.

Knobel, Dale T. *America for the Americans: The Nativist Movement in the United States.* New York, 1996. Skillfully links nineteenth- and twentieth-century nativist themes.

Kovel, Joel. *Red Hunting in the Promised Land: Anticommunism and the Making of America.* New York, 1994. The Red Scare receives significant analysis in this work.

Kraut, Alan M. *Silent Travelers: Germs, Genes, and the "Immigrant Menace."* New York, 1994. Explores in a pathbreaking manner the virulent association in the popular mind between epidemics and immigrants.

Levin, Murray B. *Political Hysteria in America: The Democratic Capacity for Repression.* New York, 1971.

Murray, Robert K. *Red Scare: A Study in National Hysteria, 1919–1920.* Minneapolis, 1955. Still pertinent reading.

Perea, Juan F., ed. *Immigrants Out! The New Nativism and the Anti-Immigrant Impulse in the United States.* New York, 1997. Contains essays suggestive of recent themes in nativism and its postmodern meanings.

Ribuffo, Leo P. *The Old Christian Right: The Protestant Far Right from the Great Depression to the Cold War.* Philadelphia, 1983. Presents perhaps the most skillful synthesis of nativist theory, historiography, domestic culture and foreign relations.

Smith, Geoffrey S. *To Save a Nation: American Extremism, The New Deal, and the Coming of World War II.* Rev. ed. Chicago, 1992. Links the activities of the nativist mass leaders of the 1930s to political and diplomatic developments before Pearl Harbor.

See also ASYLUM; CONTINENTAL EXPANSION; IMMIGRATION; IMPERIALISM; INTERVENTION AND NONINTERVENTION; ISOLATIONISM; NATIONALISM; RACE AND ETHNICITY; RELIGION.

NAVAL DIPLOMACY

William R. Braisted

The history of American naval diplomacy may be divided into three periods that correspond to technical developments in naval warfare and with the changing situation of the United States in world affairs. During the first century of the nation's history, when the United States enjoyed considerable security provided by the oceans separating it from Europe and Asia, its naval forces were largely directed toward protecting American merchants, missionaries, and government officials in Africa, Asia, and Latin America. This involved showing the flag to induce non-European peoples to treat Americans according to European and American conceptions of civilized practice. During the period from 1890 to 1945, the diplomatic role of the navy was revolutionized by the emergence of the United States as one of the great naval powers. To its earlier responsibilities of police and protection, the "new navy" of steam and steel added the strategic objective of defending the Western Hemisphere and a good part of the Pacific against intrusion by the European powers and Japan. After 1945 the navy joined with the air and land arms to provide the element of force behind American global diplomacy when the great military powers were reduced initially to two and finally to one, the United States.

THE FIRST PERIOD: 1790–1890

To protect Americans as they moved across the seas during the early days of the Republic, the navy eventually followed the example of the British Royal Navy by establishing ships on distant stations in the Mediterranean, the Far East, the Caribbean, the southern Atlantic, the Pacific, and Africa. The ships on each station, rarely more than three to six, were too few to meet all the calls from ministers, consuls, and citizens for a show of force. Only on exceptional occasions did the navy organize a squadron for impressive display, such as the Japan expedition of 1853–1854. The station commanders were both itinerant diplomats and administrative officers who kept their ships moving individually from port to port, reported on conditions in their areas, and watched over enlistments, supplies, and ships' fitness. Before the rank of rear admiral was introduced during the Civil War, they usually were accorded the courtesy rank of commodore.

Since the Navy Department was unable to undertake detailed direction of the distant stations before the advent of electrical communications, the station commanders enjoyed broad discretion within their domains. Their instructions were generally to protect American commerce and to heed the appeals from Americans to the best of their ability. Only rarely was a navy man placed under direction of a State Department official. Indeed, in a day when American consuls were commonly merchants—and even foreigners—and when ministers were usually political appointees, naval officers were often the most reliable officials serving the United States abroad. In contrast with the independence of naval men overseas, the Navy Department in Washington was under pressure to follow the State Department's wishes. Introduction of cable and radio by the time of World War I ended most of the autonomy enjoyed by flag officers abroad.

The Mediterranean The roots of the distant-stations policy extend to the late eighteenth century, when Americans sailing to the Mediterranean were overhauled by corsairs from Algiers, Tunis, and Tripoli. The Barbary pirates assumed that non-Muslims were subject to capture and enslavement unless they were protected by treaties involving tribute payments. In response to Algerine depredations, Congress resorted to naval diplomacy in 1794 by voting to construct six frigates for a navy. Within three years, Algiers, Tunis, and Tripoli had agreed to call off their corsairs in return for monetary considerations. Thereafter, however, the navy was diverted from chastising North African potentates by the Quasi-War with France (1798–1800) and by differences with Great Britain that culminated in the War of 1812.

Once peace with Britain was restored in 1815, Congress voted for further war against the Algerine corsairs, and Commodore Stephen Decatur quickly forced a treaty on Algiers that ended tribute payments. Decatur's decisive action halted Barbary depredations, and the Navy Department provided against further outbreaks by establishing a permanent squadron in the Mediterranean. Before 1845 its ships were based at Port Mahon, Minorca.

The navy's cruising range in the Mediterranean extended eastward to Turkey, where in 1800 the frigate *George Washington* (captained by William Bainbridge) was the first American warship to call at Constantinople. After the destruction of the Turkish-Egyptian fleet at Navarino during the Greek War of Independence (1827), the Sublime Porte in 1830 finally signed a treaty of commerce with Captain James Biddle and two American commissioners that included a "separate and secret" article providing for American assistance in rebuilding the Turkish navy. Although the Senate rejected the article, President Andrew Jackson overrode the Senate's veto by sending Commodore David Porter, the first resident American representative, to Turkey with instructions to help the Turkish navy.

The Mediterranean Squadron was also a symbol of American sympathy for the liberal movements in Christian Europe. After the revolutions of 1848, American and European liberals rejoiced when the steam frigate *Mississippi* conveyed the Hungarian hero Lajos Kossuth and fifty other refugees safely to freedom. The squadron, like other distant stations, was practically disbanded during the Civil War. After it was revived in 1865 as the European Squadron, with expanded area, it provided amiable social billets for naval officers as they watched the Mediterranean and Africa fall under an order dominated by Europe.

Asia   Although the American China trade dated from the sailing of the *Empress of China* from New York for Canton in 1784, the East India Squadron gradually took shape only during some nine cruises to Asia between 1800 and 1839, six by single ships and three in pairs. Initially, the navy dispatched ships to the East Indies to protect American merchantmen on the high seas and to transport public officials such as Edmund Roberts, who negotiated treaties with Siam and Muscat in 1833. In the conflicts between China and the West that destroyed the traditional Chinese tribute system in East Asian relations, it was the diplomatic mission of the U.S. Navy to support the claims by Americans to the various rights that Britain, and later France, gained for their nationals by war. During the first Opium War between China and Britain (1839–1842), Commodore Lawrence Kearney on the frigate *Constitution* won from the governor-general at Canton what amounted to a promise of most-favored-nation treatment for Americans in China. This principle, anticipating the U.S. Open Door policy toward China, was written into the Treaty of Wanghia (1844) secured by Caleb Cushing with support from the East India Squadron. Once China was opened under the "unequal treaties," the American navy's ships on the renamed Asiatic Station, including the famed Yangtze Patrol, were important props for the vast system of interlocking foreign treaty rights, including extraterritoriality, that Chinese nationalists bitterly resented.

The most spectacular demonstration of American naval diplomacy in the nineteenth century was the expedition led by Commodore Matthew Calbraith Perry to reopen Japan after two centuries of seclusion. Planning his expedition to impress the Japanese with the wealth and power of the United States, Perry first moved up Edo (Tokyo) Bay in July 1853 with a squadron of two steam frigates towing two sloops to present letters from President Millard Fillmore and himself urging the Japanese to modify their closed-country policy. Returning seven months later with a more impressive squadron, he induced the decrepit Tokugawa shogunate to sign the Treaty of Kanagawa, which met American demands for limited intercourse. Quite unwittingly, Perry proved to be the catalyst that unleashed a furious struggle within Japan, which led within fifteen years to the full reopening of the country, the overthrow of the Tokugawa, and the great changes of the Meiji Restoration.

To Commodore Robert W. Shufeldt fell the honor of opening the hermit kingdom of Korea to Americans. Korea was historically a Chinese tributary without desire for other intercourse. The expansionist Shufeldt embarked in 1878 on a much-publicized cruise to the Far East on the USS *Ticonderoga*, during which he mediated differences between Liberia and its neighbors, investigated sites for coaling stations in Africa, negotiated with the rulers of Madagascar and Johanna (Anjouan), and introduced the U.S. Navy to the Persian Gulf.

Shufeldt's ultimate objective was to open Korea, which he sought unsuccessfully to do through the good offices of Japan. On a return trip to the Far East, he finally negotiated a Korean treaty with China's leading scholar-official, Li Hung-chang, which the Koreans signed in 1882. Although the treaty established relations between the United States and Korea, it also proved to be a further blow to the Chinese tribute system without winning secure independence for Korea.

The Americas The U.S. Navy established stations embracing waters of the Americas where, in addition to showing the flag in support of trade, it watched for alien intrusions into the hemisphere and occasionally intervened in its troubled lands. The West Indies Station, created in 1821 to run down pirates infesting the area, was expanded to form the Home Station in 1841 (the North Atlantic Station after 1865), when strained relations with Great Britain reminded the navy that American coastal shipping was defenseless against raids from overseas. The navy operated its ships in the Caribbean throughout the nineteenth century in the presence of the more powerful British navy. The Monroe Doctrine of 1823, proclaiming the American continent closed to further colonization, was initially rendered effective by tacit support from the Royal Navy. By the Clayton-Bulwer Treaty of 1850, the United States won from Great Britain the right to participate on equal terms with the latter in building an isthmian canal at a time when the U.S. Navy was not yet dominant in the Caribbean.

South of the Caribbean was the Brazil Station, established in 1826 primarily to extend protection to Americans in feuding Brazil, Argentina, and the states of the Rio de la Plata. Usually numbering from two to six ships except during a crisis with Paraguay in 1858, the Brazil Station after 1843 included some 17 million square miles north from Cape Horn to the Amazon, eastward to Cape Negro, and then south along the African coast to the Cape of Good Hope. The station was reconstituted after the Civil War as the South Atlantic Station.

Largest and probably least well defined of the stations was the Pacific Station, dating from 1818. During the early years, the few ships on station tended to cruise between Callao, Peru, and Valparaiso, Chile, with occasional runs to Panama and to the Pacific islands: the Marquesas, Tahiti, Hawaii, and others. After the cession of California by Mexico in 1848, the focus of the station shifted northward, with San Francisco serving as home port. Although it was involved in spectacular crises with Chile in 1891, when Chilean sailors clashed with sailors from the USS *Baltimore* at Valparaiso, and with Germany over Samoa in 1889 and 1899, after the Civil War the navy's primary concern on the Pacific Station was the fate of the Hawaiian Islands. It habitually kept a ship at Honolulu, gave moral support to white planters against the native monarchy, acquired naval base rights at Pearl Harbor in 1887, and provided protective cover for the movement that led to American annexation of the islands in 1898.

Africa Most lonely of the distant stations was the African Station, created in 1843 after the United States agreed in the Webster-Ashburton Treaty (1842) to cooperate with Britain in suppressing the slave trade. Whereas the Royal Navy seized 594 ships suspected of slave running between 1840 and 1848, the few American ships on station captured but nineteen suspected runners between 1843 and 1857. Moreover, since before the Civil War the United States denied British warships even a limited right to visit American merchantmen, the illicit trade found shelter under the American flag.

THE SECOND PERIOD: 1890–1945

The "old navy" of wooden ships distributed to distant stations gave way in the late nineteenth century to the "new navy" of steel that operated in a world of great powers competing for empire. Men of the new navy strove to build fleets sufficiently powerful to guarantee the United States control of the sea within an American sphere that eventually embraced most of the Western Hemisphere and the Pacific. The period from about 1890 to 1945 also embraced the navy's battleship age, during which most American naval men and many civilians looked to a fleet of battleships (capital ships) as the key instrument for assuring the hegemony of the United States within its sphere and for promoting American diplomacy. From the appearance of his first major volume on sea power in 1890, Alfred Thayer Mahan was preeminently the American naval writer who conceptualized a theory of sea power for the battleship age. Mahan was an economic determinist who held that national power derives from the flow of commerce through key maritime arteries protected by naval power. In emulation of the

British Empire, Mahan and his disciples conceived of an American naval line of empire protected by battle fleets and extending from the western Atlantic through the Caribbean and an isthmian canal to the Pacific and west.

Conspicuously absent during the battleship age was formal institutional provision for integrating American naval and diplomatic policies. President Theodore Roosevelt might himself serve as a one-man National Security Council, but the Navy Department and the State Department tended to plot their own courses with a minimum of exchange. Important for developing the naval officers' appreciation of their role in the world were such institutions as the Office of Naval Intelligence (1882), the Naval War College (1884), and the General Board (1900). Under the presidency of Admiral George Dewey, the General Board advised the secretary of the navy on a wide range of policies that touched foreign relations. The board's influence, however, gradually declined after the establishment in 1916 of the Office of Naval Operations, the navy's approach to a naval general staff. A step toward improved cooperation with the army was the creation in 1903 of the Joint Army and Navy Board, the often-ineffectual predecessor of the Joint Chiefs of Staff.

Dewey's May Day victory at the outset of the Spanish-American War (1898) was perhaps inadvertently the navy's most significant act that contributed to American political commitment in the western Pacific. By the peace with Spain, the United States gained possession of the key positions of Puerto Rico, Guam, and the Philippines, as well as control over Cuba. These island territories, together with Hawaii, Samoa, and the Panama Canal Zone (acquired in 1898, 1899, and 1903, respectively), included the prime sites for overseas bases that naval men wanted to support their imperial strategy up to World War II.

After the Spanish-American War, the navy followed a modified distant-stations policy in the Americas and the Far East while assembling its battle forces in the Atlantic and on the Asiatic Station. Although American naval men feared German aggression in the Caribbean, "the American Mediterranean," they also wanted a fleet in the Far East to support the Open Door in China. In 1906, however, all U.S. battleships were concentrated in a single battle fleet in the Atlantic, the area of the nation's greatest interests and of its vulnerability to German attack. It became a naval axiom that until the opening of the Panama Canal, the battleship fleet should be concentrated in one ocean so that its divided squadrons could not be defeated separately.

Spanish-American War to the 1920s From 1898 to World War I, the navy's Atlantic and Caribbean policies were to build a fortified isthmian canal under exclusive American control, to acquire bases for the canal's protection, and to deny the Western Hemisphere to outside aggressors. By the Hay-Pauncefote Treaty of 1901, Britain released the United States to construct a wholly American canal without restriction as to fortifications. When Colombia failed to reach quick agreement on terms for a canal in its Panama territory, the navy in 1903 afforded cover for a revolt in the isthmus. Within fifteen days a new government of independent Panama accorded the United States a ten-mile-wide canal zone in perpetuity. For Caribbean bases, the General Board by 1903 had settled on two sites: Guantánamo Bay, Cuba, close to the Windward Passage, and a lesser base farther east, probably the island of Culebra, off Puerto Rico. While determined to prevent non-American nations from acquiring bases in the region, the board wanted the United States to take no more than the navy could defend. The navy and the marines also intervened in Haiti, Santo Domingo, Cuba, Nicaragua, and elsewhere in the Caribbean in support of the roles of debt collector and policeman that the United States assumed under the Platt Amendment relating to Cuba (1901) and the Roosevelt Corollary to the Monroe Doctrine (1904), in order to obviate interference by others. During the British and German blockade of Venezuela (1902), the United States concentrated in the Caribbean, under Admiral Dewey's command, the most powerful fleet ever assembled for maneuvers, another potent reminder that other nations must keep out.

In the Far East after 1898, American naval men initially conceived of the United States as one of a half-dozen naval powers competing in China. Their planning assumed that the maritime nations (Britain, the United States, and Japan) were committed to the Open Door in China, in opposition to the continental powers (Russia, France, and Germany). In addition to a main fleet base at Subic Bay in the Philippines, the General Board wanted an advanced base on the China coast, within easy steaming range of the European bases in northern Asiatic waters.

After Japan's triumph in the Russo-Japanese War (1904–1905), the American navy's outlook in the Pacific changed radically as Japan moved from the position of sure friend to that of possible enemy. When Theodore Roosevelt ordered sixteen battleships of the Atlantic Fleet to the Pacific on the first lap of their spectacular world cruise in 1907, he was testing the navy's capacity to concentrate its power in the Pacific and reminding Japan and the world that the Pacific was an area of American naval responsibility. The navy also decided, in 1908–1909, to build its first major overseas Pacific base at Pearl Harbor rather than at Subic Bay, because the army insisted that it would be unable to hold the Philippine base against Japanese attack until the arrival of the battle fleet from the Atlantic. The navy's most important war plans on the eve of World War I were its Black Plan for defense of the Western Hemisphere against Germany and its Orange Plan for a war against Japan, precipitated by the immigration question or by Japanese aggression into China or the Philippines. Although the United States had no formal agreement with Britain, still the world's greatest naval power, there emerged before World War I a wholly informal system of naval power in which Britain built to contain the German navy while the United States strove for naval equality with Germany and decisive superiority over Britain's east Asian ally, Japan.

The ascent of Woodrow Wilson to the presidency in 1913 brought to the White House a leader determined to preserve civilian control over the conduct of foreign affairs but willing to employ the navy in war and diplomacy with utmost vigor. After the outbreak of World War I in 1914, the Wilson administration was involved in acrimonious debates with Britain and Germany in defense of the cherished American principle of freedom of the seas. The tension of the war also moved the president to support the Naval Act of 1916, directed toward a navy second to none through the construction of ten battleships and six battle cruisers. This program would provide the United States with a powerful voice in diplomacy, whatever the outcome of the war.

Upon American entry into the war, the navy joined the Allies in a coalition wholly unpremeditated in its Black Plan and Orange Plan or its building programs. Conservatives in the navy, especially on the General Board, were reluctant to halt construction of capital ships so that American shipbuilding facilities could be devoted to building desperately needed antisubmarine and merchant craft. In addition to fearing that the United States might face greatly strengthened German and Japanese navies should the allies suffer defeat, these naval conservatives apparently were uncertain what policies Britain might adopt should the allies triumph too completely. It was to allay such anxieties, and thus to promote full U.S. naval participation in the war, that President Wilson's intimate adviser, Colonel Edward M. House, unsuccessfully sought from Britain an option on five British capital ships to meet postwar contingencies. The Navy Department finally halted its capital ship program in order to provide ways for submarine destroyers, and it reached an accord with the Japanese whereby the Imperial Japanese Navy watched the Pacific while the U.S. Navy concentrated on war in the Atlantic.

The allies' naval jealousies, subdued during the war, surfaced during the Paris Peace Conference in 1919. British leaders saw President Wilson's call for freedom of the seas as a threat to the British Empire, and they strove unsuccessfully to prevent a resumption of building of American capital ships that might relegate the Royal Navy to second place. The naval advisers to the American delegation, on the other hand, opposed any division of the German navy likely to perpetuate British naval supremacy. For the American navy, however, the most significant act by the peace conference was its decision to award Germany's Pacific islands north of the equator to Japan as unfortified mandates of the League of Nations. Unfortified in Japanese hands, the islands would be open to a superior American fleet in a campaign against Japan. At the close of the war, U.S. naval representatives were prominent in the allied interventions in Russia and at Constantinople during the resurgence of Turkey under Mustafa Kemal.

The 1920s   Britain, the United States, and Japan emerged from World War I as the three great naval powers. Whereas American naval authorities watched for any new evidence that Britain might attempt to retain its naval supremacy, they held as an article of faith that any new naval construction by Britain's ally Japan was directed against the United States. The General Board stated in 1921 that the United States should maintain a navy equal to the British and twice the Japanese. If the Anglo-Japanese alliance remained, however, the board wanted a navy equal to the combined British and Japanese navies. While the navy stationed the most powerful battle forces in the United States Fleet in the Pacific to guard against Orange (Japan), the estimates of naval war planners from 1919 to 1931 also dealt with possible wars against Red (Britain) or against a Red-Orange (Anglo-Japanese) coalition.

In 1921 civilian leaders in the United States, Britain, and Japan were united in their desire to avoid a ruinous naval race and to settle numerous Pacific questions unresolved by the Paris Peace Conference. At the nine-power Washington Conference called by the United States in 1921 to consider these issues, Secretary of State Charles Evans Hughes proposed a naval holiday and a limitation on the American, British, and Japanese navies at just half the levels recommended by the General Board. Hughes's plan was incorporated in the Five-Power Naval Treaty, which limited capital ships and aircraft carriers allowed the United States, Britain, Japan, France, and Italy at a ratio of 5:5:3:1.67:1.67. At Japan's insistence, the three great naval powers also undertook, in article XIX of the treaty, to refrain from building new bases and fortifications from which their fleets could menace each other's vital territories in the Pacific. The United States thus abandoned new naval shore construction west of Hawaii, such as the proposed base on Guam that could serve the fleet in operations against Japan. The Washington naval agreements were part of a package settlement that included the Four-Power Treaty to maintain the status quo in the Pacific, the Nine-Power Treaty relating to China, and the abrogation of the Anglo-Japanese alliance.

The statesmen at Washington sought a new naval order that would provide security for the United States in the Western Hemisphere, the British Empire from the United Kingdom to Singapore, and Japan in the western Pacific. The Five-Power Naval Treaty, however, failed to limit lesser naval categories: cruisers, destroyers, and submarines. The three-power Geneva Naval Conference of 1927 broke down when British and American naval men were unable to agree on cruisers. Japan and Britain, meanwhile, built ships in the unrestricted classes more rapidly than did the United States; and Japanese naval men at the London Naval Conference of 1930 demanded a 10:10:7 ratio rather than a 10:10:6 (5:5:3) ratio in cruisers. As at Washington, the delegations at London overrode vigorous opposition from their services; and the resulting naval treaty in theory preserved the 10:10:6 ratio in heavy cruisers but in substance promised Japan higher ratios in the lesser classes through the life of the naval treaties (1936). The bitterness provoked in the Japanese navy contributed significantly to the collapse of naval limitation after 1931.

The 1930s The Washington naval system crumbled after Japan occupied Manchuria in 1931–1932. While the American and British governments were unprepared to halt Japan by force, Secretary of State Henry L. Stimson looked to the navy to deter Japanese aggression. After Japanese naval forces landed at Shanghai in 1932, Stimson publicly warned that since the Washington agreements were interdependent, a violation of a political accord, such as the Nine-Power Treaty relating to China, would nullify other Washington agreements, such as the American promise to desist from building bases in the western Pacific. The U.S. Fleet was concentrated for maneuvers off Hawaii in 1932, and Stimson induced President Herbert Hoover thereafter to retain the entire fleet in the Pacific as a warning to Japan.

Stimson's gestures proved futile. The ratio of American and Japanese naval strength in the early 1930s probably approximated 10:8, rather than 10:6, and the "fleet faction" in the Japanese navy forced the Tokyo government in 1934 to seek a common upper limit (naval parity) with the United States and Britain. The intransigent Japanese stand drove the Americans and the British to unite in defense of the 10:10:6 ratio at the preliminary and main London Naval Conferences called in 1934 and 1935 to review the naval treaties. The Japanese left the second conference, and effective naval limitation ended with the expiration of the treaties in 1936.

During the London conferences, British and U.S. naval officers established cordial relations that paved the way for increasing intimacy between their services as they faced the rising threats from Germany and Italy in Europe and from Japan after the outbreak of the China incident in 1937. Only days after Japanese aircraft sank the USS *Panay* in December 1937, President Franklin D. Roosevelt sent the navy's war plans director to London for consultations with the Admiralty during which a plan was drawn for possible joint action against Japan by an American fleet operating from Hawaii and a British fleet based in Singapore. This scheme was modified in 1939, when Britain was prevented by the Axis menace in Europe from undertaking powerful action against Japan. Admiral William D. Leahy, American chief of naval operations, then volunteered that, should a war break out in Europe to which the United States was not a party, the U.S. Fleet would assemble at Pearl Harbor to deter Japan. Should the United States be associated with Britain in war against the Axis and Japan, Leahy expected the American navy to care for the Pacific while the British navy would be responsible for the Atlantic. When war broke out in Europe in September 1939, the Joint Army and Navy Board had already begun work on five Rainbow Plans for war situations involving the United States and the European democracies against the Axis powers and Japan.

World War II   After the fall of France in June 1940, the U.S. Navy was party to a succession of measures short of war to prevent the collapse of Britain, to prepare for war in two oceans either alone or in association with the British Empire, to deter Japan in the Pacific, and to enlist Canada and the Latin American states in Western Hemisphere defense. In September 1940, Britain and the United States concluded an arrangement by which Britain granted the United States bases in British possessions in the western Atlantic in return for fifty American destroyers to be used against German submarines. This limited American naval assistance to Britain swelled in 1941, after Congress approved the lend-lease bill, American navy yards were open to British warships for repair, and the navy began patrolling the western Atlantic against German submarines.

In August 1940 representatives from the Navy Department and the Admiralty entered into urgent consultations on how the navy could best help in the war. After Japan, Germany, and Italy concluded the Berlin Pact in September 1940, the chief of naval operations, Admiral Harold R. Stark, prepared his famous Plan Dog memorandum for a two-ocean war in which British and U.S. forces would seek victory over the Axis in the Atlantic before turning to defeat Japan in the Pacific. This memorandum was the basis for the detailed ABC-1 Plan, drawn up during Anglo-American staff talks at Washington in February and March 1941. In line with this plan, the United States shifted about one-third of its battleships to the Atlantic in order to release British units for service in the Far East.

It was with gravely weakened naval forces in the Pacific that the Roosevelt administration in July 1941 finally turned to halt Japanese aggression by enlisting Britain and the Netherlands to freeze Japanese assets under their control, thereby terminating Japanese trade with the world outside East Asia. The United States and its associates thus sought to bring Japan to terms by cutting off the flow of oil and other materials vital to the Japanese economy through a distant blockade supported by naval forces divided and inferior to those of the Japanese. Facing the immobilization of their forces as their supplies ran out, Japanese leaders, including those of the Japanese navy, opted for war that closed the battleship age.

During the immediate prewar and war years, Franklin Roosevelt, as had his cousin Theodore, drew the integration of naval and diplomatic policies into his own hands. The State-War-Navy Liaison Committee established in 1938 was largely confined to Latin American affairs and lesser matters. After the president moved the Joint Army and Navy Board into the new executive offices in 1939, the military chiefs increasingly participated in foreign affairs without necessary reference to their service secretaries or even the State Department. Indeed, during World War II, the State Department repeatedly bowed to service interests; naval officers and other military men negotiated directly with foreign governments; and the military chiefs accompanied the president to summit meetings to which the secretary of state was not invited. It was only a year before the war's end that the State Department was restored somewhat to decision making in foreign affairs with the establishment of the State-War-Navy Coordinating Committee to prepare for peace. In 1942 the chief of naval operations joined with American army and air force chiefs in the Joint Chiefs of Staff, which provided institutional partners for the British chiefs in the Combined Chiefs of Staff, who determined war strategy under the watchful eyes of President Roosevelt and of British Prime Minister Winston Churchill. Cooperation with the British in coalition war was important preparation for naval men when they turned to work for what amounted to a coalition peace.

1945–1975

The thirty years following the end of World War II in 1945 witnessed political, institutional, and technological changes that revolutionized the navy's role in diplomacy. In 1945 American naval officers had not yet devised a strategy geared to the atomic bomb, to a divided world in which the United States was for a time without a naval rival, and to the passing of battleship fleets as a measure of naval and national power. Insofar as they had speculated on the postwar world, they tended to assume a return to a division of responsibility in which the U.S. Navy would dominate the western Atlantic and the Pacific while the British navy would remain supreme in Eastern Hemisphere waters: the eastern Atlantic, the Mediterranean, and the Indian Ocean. The navy's one clear objective during the war was to secure the Pacific islands that Japan had held since World War I as League of Nations mandates. The navy was soon confronted, however, by the Cold War with the Soviet Union, the Chinese communist victory on the Asian mainland in 1949, and the steady retreat by Britain to Europe that left the United States increasingly alone to deal with the supposed global menace of the Soviet Union and its allies. Moreover, whereas the navy had been the strong arm of American diplomacy through most of the nation's history, the air force emerged at the dawn of the atomic age to claim for the bombers of its Strategic Air Command the preponderant responsibility for deterring war.

The period from 1945 to 1950 was a critical one for the navy, during which the service sought meaningful roles in response to claims made by the air force in the course of the movement to organize a single Defense Department. The navy survived the unification struggle as one part of the new national security structure in which the State Department and the Defense Department were institutional equals. Under the National Defense Act of 1947 and amendments of 1949, the chief of naval operations became but one of five members of the Joint Chiefs of Staff, whose chairman conveys the chiefs' collective advice to the president, the secretary of defense, and the National Security Council. When the service secretaries lost their cabinet rank in 1949, the navy was denied separate representation on the National Security Council, the key institution responsible for integrating diplomacy and defense into national security policies. The civilian secretary of defense thereafter represented all the services in the council: the army, the navy, the air force, and, after 1978, the marines. Nevertheless, naval officers after 1945 served in unprecedented numbers in politico-military bodies concerned with foreign affairs.

While the navy thus lost its proud position as the leading force behind American diplomacy, it fought for programs of balanced defense against the claims by the air force that the threat of massive retaliation by the Strategic Air Command constituted the most effective deterrent to Soviet aggression. The navy's arguments for a variety of weapons were fully vindicated after the outbreak of the Korean War in 1950 demonstrated the effectiveness of carrier-based air and other capabilities in a limited war unsuited to massive retaliation with atomic bombs. This was a war provoked by an attack by communist North Korea on noncommunist South Korea. It was a war fought by Americans, Koreans, and allied forces under the auspices of the United Nations without a formal declaration of war. It also halted the spread of communism in Northeast Asia. The glamour of massive retaliation faded still more as the Soviet Union successfully tested an atomic device in 1949, achieved a thermonuclear explosion five years later, fired the first intercontinental ballistic missile in 1957, and launched the first artificial satellite (*Sputnik*) two months later.

To support friends and allies as well as to deter the Soviet Union, naval planners developed a transoceanic naval strategy to project the navy's power over the land and to keep the sea-lanes open. The fleets of the transoceanic navy, like the task forces of World War II, were commonly mixed forces that included two or three carriers, an amphibious marine force, and antisubmarine units. Most spectacular for display were the supercarriers, numbering fifteen in the 1960s and ranging up to 100,000 tons, whose versatile weapons could deal with local outbreaks or convey nuclear destruction to the heart of the Eurasian landmass. Responding to the Soviet Union's missile capability, the navy after 1960 also completed forty-one nuclear-powered submarines armed with Polaris and improved long-range Poseidon and Trident missiles carrying atomic warheads. The navy claimed that its mobile, seaborne forces were far more secure against Soviet attack than the land-based bombers and missiles of the air force.

Together with the army and air force, the transoceanic navy provided the American commitment of force to the multilateral regional pacts, bilateral alliances, and other arrangements through which the United States sought to organize the nations of the free world. Since western Europe seemed the most vital area to save from Soviet domination, the North Atlantic Treaty Organization (NATO), formed in 1949, assumed prime importance in American strategic planning. Through NATO the navy sought to expand its earlier "special relationship" with the British navy into a multilateral association in which the American navy provided important leadership and the largest commitment of naval force to retain control of the Atlantic and the Mediterranean. The NATO supreme commander for the Atlantic is the commander in chief of the U.S. Atlantic Fleet, based with his NATO staff at Norfolk, Virginia. The NATO powers preserve independent control of their most important naval forces, from which they contribute elements for NATO maneuvers and for a small standing force. In the Far East, when concluding peace with Japan in 1951, the United States also signed with Japan a mutual defense pact, which assured a base of operations in the western Pacific. Unlike the navies of Europe, however, the Japanese Defense Force was committed strictly to the defense of Japan.

The most visible American naval contribution to European security was the Sixth Fleet, established in the Mediterranean since 1948. In addition to its earlier role as a major segment in the maritime artery between Europe and Asia, the Mediterranean gained significance after 1945 as a deep inlet into which the United States could move naval power 2,000 miles eastward from the Atlantic, to within striking distance of the Russian homeland. It was also a sea from which the navy could support friends and allies on NATO's southern flank and in the Middle East, as well as a moat separating Europe from Africa. The United States first restored a naval presence in the Mediterranean in 1946–1947, when the Soviet Union pressed Turkey to open the Dardanelles to free movement by Soviet ships and when President Harry Truman extended assistance to Greece under the Truman Doctrine. The Sixth Fleet has commonly numbered more than fifty ships, including two supercarriers organized to meet the needs of a transoceanic navy. Its position in the Mediterranean became increasingly lonely, however, with the withdrawal of British naval power after the Suez Crisis of 1956, the spectacular buildup of Soviet naval forces in the 1960s, and the growing hostility among the Arab states that looked for Soviet aid to counter American support of Israel. In 1958, the Sixth Fleet, in response to a request from the president of Lebanon, landed a force in Beirut, which seemed to be threatened by domestic insurgency and foreign invasion.

The Seventh Fleet became the navy's Far East counterpart to the Sixth Fleet. At the close of World War II, the navy and the marines helped the Chinese Nationalists receive the Japanese surrender in eastern China, but U.S. forces withdrew from the Chinese mainland in advance of the communist victory in 1949. In January 1950, Secretary of State Dean Acheson, voicing recommendations from the Joint Chiefs of Staff, outlined an American defense perimeter in the western Pacific, extending from Alaska through Japan, for whose defense the Seventh Fleet would assume major responsibility. Acheson's omission of Korea, Taiwan, and Southeast Asia suggested that the United States was disengaging from the Asian mainland. American participation in the Korean War in 1950, however, demonstrated that the U.S. government would employ its naval and other forces to counter aggression on the mainland that threatened a key area on the American defense perimeter such as Japan, which after 1949 replaced China as the most important U.S. partner in East Asia.

The Korean War also brought the first public American commitment to the Chinese Nationalists on Taiwan, when President Truman in 1950 ordered the Seventh Fleet to interpose its power between Taiwan and the mainland, to neutralize the Taiwan Strait, and to prevent the Chinese communists and the nationalists from attacking each other across the strait. After the United States and the Chinese Nationalists signed a mutual defense treaty in 1954, the Seventh Fleet provided massive cover in 1954 for the Nationalist evacuation from the Tachen Islands and again in 1958 for Nationalist logistic operations to sustain their garrisons defending the islands of Quemoy and Matsu against Chinese communist bombardments. During the relatively placid year of 1961, the Seventh Fleet included some 125 ships and 650 aircraft based at Subic Bay, Okinawa, and Japan. When formal relations were established with the communist government in Peking in 1979, relations between Taiwan and the United States were maintained quietly on an extradiplomatic basis. The United States provided Taiwan with arms and ships, and the Seventh Fleet remained an important presence in the western Pacific. South of Taiwan lay a former colony and ally, the Philippine Islands, where the United States retained its important naval base at Subic Bay until all American naval and military facilities were returned to the Philippines in 1992.

Although the Seventh Fleet's commitments to the Southeast Asia Treaty Organization under the Manila Treaty of 1954 were unclear, the United States in 1962 landed marines in Thailand to deter communist infiltration from neighboring Laos. The fleet also fought in the Vietnam War after Congress, in the Tonkin Gulf Resolution (1964), authorized the president to employ American armed forces in defense of freedom in southeast Asia. With the winding down of the war after 1969, the Seventh Fleet resumed its station in defense of a western Pacific perimeter.

Between the normal cruising ranges of the Sixth Fleet and the Seventh Fleet, the Indian Ocean area, including the oil-rich Persian Gulf, remained free of a significant American naval presence after

1945. Responding to growing Soviet naval forces in the ocean during the 1960s, however, the navy occasionally dispatched units from the Seventh Fleet to show the flag and to participate in Central Treaty Organization maneuvers. After 1966 the navy also joined with Britain to construct a communications station, landing fields, and other amenities on the British island of Diego Garcia.

Three decades after World War II, the navy was again adjusting to major world changes as the Cold War confrontations gave way to bitter rivalry between the Soviet and Chinese communist camps, détente between the United States and the Soviet Union, and accommodations between Washington and Peking. Even as the United States and the Soviet Union moved to limit their atomic arsenals, including their seaborne missile forces, through accords at the Strategic Arms Limitation Talks, however, American naval men watched the emergence of the Soviet navy as a contender on the high seas and the spread of Soviet and Chinese influence in the Middle East, Africa, and elsewhere. The modest easing of tensions between the United States and the communist world, therefore, was followed by no lowering of the American naval guard. Indeed, the thaw in the Cold War was overshadowed in many areas of the world by the emergence of strong regional sentiment hostile to the United States and to any American naval presence. While the navy still strove to provide global force sufficient to honor security arrangements negotiated two decades earlier, when conditions were very different, it was increasingly regarded in Africa, Asia, Latin America, and even Europe as an agent of outside interference rather than as a protection.

The navy's responsibility during the Cold War, however, was not confined to the Old World. In the Western Hemisphere, Fidel Castro, after winning power in Cuba, threatened to export communism to his Latin American neighbors. President John F. Kennedy in 1961 inherited from the Eisenhower administration a Central Intelligence Agency project to support an invasion of Cuba by Cuban refugees. The consequence was the so-called Bay of Pigs incident, which was a humiliating failure, at least in part because the administration was unwilling to provide the refugees with necessary naval and air support. This was followed the next year by discovery that the Soviet Union had built in Cuba some forty-two launching pads for intermediate ballistic missiles with striking range of more than 1,000 miles. President Kennedy immediately responded by ordering the navy to establish a blockade of Cuba, described as a "quarantine," to halt arms shipments to Cuba and demanding that the Russians withdraw all missiles from the island. It seemed that nuclear war was at hand, but the Russians bowed to the president's demand in return for a promise to withdraw American missiles from Turkey.

Close on the heels of the Cuban missile crisis came war in Vietnam. There, following the withdrawal of the French from their former colony, the Americans became increasingly concerned that noncommunist South Vietnam would fall to communist North Vietnam. When President Kennedy was assassinated in November 1963, U.S. "military advisers" numbered 16,700. Large-scale U.S. intervention was sparked the following year by a clash between the American destroyer *Maddox* and several North Vietnamese torpedo boats in the Gulf of Tonkin. The U.S. Congress forthwith adopted the Tonkin Gulf Resolution, which authorized President Lyndon Johnson to take "all necessary measures to repel armed attacks against the armed forces of the United States and to prevent further aggression." The Vietnam War was an undeclared war fought without United Nations support and subject to increasing public criticism in the United States and abroad. It was also a war limited by American unwillingness to provoke serious intervention by China or the Soviet Union. Task Force 77, composed of carrier forces attached to Yankee Station in the Tonkin Gulf and Dixie Station off South Vietnam, sent strikes against North Vietnam and supported ground forces in the south. Search patrols along the southern coast sought to interrupt movement of supplies from the north to insurgent Vietcong in the south, and numerous small boats of a "brown water" patrol moved through the Mekong Delta and along other inland waters to apprehend the Vietcong. The Vietcong Tet Offensive in 1968, although itself a failure, was followed a year later by President Richard Nixon's decision to "Vietnamize" the war. The last Americans and numerous Vietnamese refugees were airlifted out of Saigon in 1975, thereby ending perhaps the most humiliating war in American history.

In 1970, when Admiral Elmo R. Zumwalt, Jr., was called from Vietnam to Washington to serve as the youngest chief of naval operations in history, the navy was in poor shape to meet the possible challenges ahead. The nation's resources had been expended on the Vietnam War, while the Soviet navy, under the leadership of Admiral Sergei G. Gorshkov, had been expanded to establish awesome capacity to operate in multiple seas.

Moreover, three years earlier, Britain had abandoned its imperial responsibilities east of Suez. To meet this situation, Zumwalt proposed a "high-low mix" by which the navy would build large numbers of less expensive "low" ships to assure "sea control" of areas where expensive "high" ships were unnecessary or would be in danger. For instance, he proposed to build a patrol frigate, half the cost and size of a destroyer, and a 17,000-ton sea control ship that would be far less expensive than the 100,000-ton supercarriers. His proposals were vigorously opposed by Admiral Hyman Rickover, the promoter of nuclear submarines and other high-tech ships, and Zumwalt's sea control ship was eventually rejected by Congress. The navy may also have suffered from the diversions that attended the resignation of President Nixon following the Watergate scandal. The decade ended with the embarrassing capture of the U.S. embassy in Tehran, Iran, by Islamic radicals and the Soviet naval ships operating out of Cam Rahn Bay in Vietnam.

1975–2000

The outlook for the navy and naval diplomacy improved with the arrival of President Ronald Reagan's energetic young secretary of the navy, John F. Lehman, Jr., who with forceful chiefs of naval operations (Admirals Thomas Hayward and James Watkins) pressed for an aggressive "maritime strategy" supported by a 600-ship navy composed of fifteen supercarriers, four battleships called back into service, 100 attack submarines, a powerful marine amphibious force, and numerous lesser craft. The program would increase by 20 percent the navy's combat ships over those in 1980. This aggressive strategy, however, did not rule out lesser actions to keep the Third World in proper order, such as the capture of the small island of Grenada (1983), a disastrous landing in Lebanon that ended with the bombing of the marine barracks in Beirut (1982–1983), clearing mines from the Red Sea, protecting Kuwaiti tankers in the Persian Gulf, denying with naval air Colonel Muammar Qaddafi's attempt to close the Gulf of Sidra (1986), the capture of Panamanian strongman General Manuel A. Noriega on charges of drug trafficking, and much more.

The decade of the 1990s was as revolutionary for the navy and naval diplomacy as had been the 1890s following the publication of Alfred Thayer Mahan's *The Influence of Sea Power on History* and the shift of the navy from wood and sail to steel and steam. The 1990s opened with the breakup of the Soviet Union, the freeing of the nations of Eastern Europe to join the Western powers, and the disappearance of the Soviet navy as a serious challenge to the U.S. Navy on the high seas. At the dawn of the twenty-first century, this left the United States claiming to be the sole superpower, NATO deprived of much of its original reason for being, and the navy in need of either a greatly revised strategy or a wholly new strategy. All this and more can be summed up by the statement that the Cold War had ended. It ended as the navy was adding such high-tech innovations as the Aegis air defense system, new Ticonderoga-class cruisers that carry long-range Tomahawk missiles, Ohio-class submarines mounting improved Trident missiles, and much more.

The navy's new strategy substituted "power from the sea" for the older "control of the sea" or "sea control." Since the majority of the world's population lives within fifty miles of the sea, the navy developed a littoral mission by which it would mount "power from the sea" to control the world's coasts as well as dispatch terrible destruction deep into the interior. The new strategy assumed that the oceans were safe and that the navy, by attacking the land "from the sea" would prepare for unopposed amphibious landings by the marines and the army.

The new era opened in early 1991 with the outbreak of the Gulf War in which Iraq attempted to annex the neighboring Persian Gulf state of Kuwait, a move that threatened the stability of the strategically vital, oil-producing region of the Middle East. Like the Korean War, the Gulf War sparked a United Nations response in which the United States provided by far the largest land and sea forces. At the height of the conflict, 130 American naval ships were joined by 50 allied ships in a multinational naval force. The marines contributed 92,000 officers and service personnel, the largest marine operation in history. The United States initially reacted by concentrating six supercarriers in the Red Sea and the Persian Gulf and enough marines to afford protection for Saudi Arabia until the arrival of reinforcements, largely army, to turn the tide and drive the Iraqis from Kuwait. The navy and the marines also assembled an amphibious force in the gulf to prevent the Iraqis from evacuating Kuwait and joining the main battle of Operation Desert Storm. After the war the navy provided forces to enforce UN punitive sanctions against Iraq.

The vital importance of this region that holds 70 percent of the world's oil reserves was reorganized in 1994 by the establishment of a new Fifth Fleet whose water areas included the Red Sea, the Persian Gulf, and the Arabian Gulf. The Fifth Fleet was subject to the Central Command, located in Tampa, Florida, whose theater of operations extended inland to Central Asia. The fleet in January 2001 comprised seventeen ships, including a carrier group, and 7,700 marines with support facilities at Bahrain within the Persian Gulf and at Diego Garcia in the Indian Ocean. The bombing of the destroyer *Cole* in Yemen in 2000 was a very sharp reminder of the religious, drug, and other terrorist groups that the navy works with others to oppose.

By far the most powerful of the American fleets on distant stations at the turn of the twenty-first century was the Seventh Fleet, whose area embraced the western Pacific, especially East Asia, and the Indian Ocean. Notwithstanding the practical disappearance of Russian naval power, the Seventh Fleet in 2001 numbered fifty-one ships, including two carriers, and 29,000 sailors and marines mostly operating out of Japanese home ports. China was probably the most unpredictable major power in the area, and the troubled relations between China and Taiwan remained potentially dangerous. The Seventh Fleet lost important shore support with the return of the Subic Bay naval base to the Philippines and British restoration of Hong Kong to China. Numerous exchanges between the American and Chinese high commands to promote understanding were seriously jeopardized by Chinese outrage following the American bombing of the Chinese embassy in Belgrade during the war in Kosovo. A port call by the U.S. cruiser *Chancellorsville* at Tsingtao in August 2000 brought public expressions from both sides that seemed to be evidence of a desire to return to stability.

With the passing of the Soviet Union, the Sixth Fleet in the Mediterranean lost one of its principal justifications. Its ships in January 2001 were down to fifteen, with no carrier representation. The eastern Mediterranean in particular included a number of potential trouble spots within the range of the navy's littoral strategy. Among these was the disintegrating Yugoslav state, which was a NATO concern, and therefore an American one. The ethnic feuds climaxed in the Kosovo war of 1999, during which American carrier air provided perhaps 50 percent of the guidance and support missions for the air force.

From 1794, when Congress voted for the construction of the first six frigates, the United States Navy was a prime support for American diplomacy as the nation's interests changed and expanded. During the nineteenth century, the navy was employed principally to show the flag on distant stations where pirates and potentates were not always respectful toward American missionaries and merchants. After 1890, as the United States came to claim the rank of a great power, the navy concentrated on building fleets to dominate the western Atlantic and the Pacific. The battleship age ended with World War II, from which the United States, Great Britain, and the Soviet Union emerged as victors. After 1945, as the British Empire gradually came to an end, the U.S. Navy's role in the Cold War was dictated by the American determination to halt the spread of Soviet power and communism. The demise of the Soviet Union left the United States and the navy committed to helping in the solution of regional problems throughout the world. The United States, as in the nineteenth century, continued to follow a sort of distant-stations policy. Although Americans would deny that they aimed to form an American empire, American power inevitably provoked such protesting acts at the end of the twentieth century as the attack on the USS *Cole* off Yemen, the demands of Okinawans that U.S. forces withdraw, and New Zealand's quest for a nuclear-free South Pacific.

BIBLIOGRAPHY

Albion, Robert G. "Distant Stations." *U.S. Naval Institute Proceedings* 80 (1954). The most useful brief survey of the distant-stations policy.

Baer, George W. *One Hundred Years of Sea Power: The U.S. Navy, 1890–1990.* Stanford, Calif., 1994. A fine general survey with much material on naval diplomacy.

Braisted, William Reynolds. *The United States Navy in the Pacific, 1897–1909.* Austin, Tex., 1958.

———. *The United States Navy in the Pacific, 1909–1922.* Austin, Tex., 1972. This and the previous volume are concerned chiefly with the navy's relation to American diplomacy in eastern Asia from the Spanish-American War through the Washington Conference.

Buckley, Thomas H. *The United States and the Washington Conference, 1921–1922.* Knoxville, Tenn., 1970. A monograph on the major naval conference following World War I.

Challener, Richard D. *Admirals, Generals, and American Foreign Policy, 1898–1914.* Princeton, N.J., 1973. A magnificently documented study of the relation of both the army and the navy to American diplomacy from the Spanish-American War to World War I.

Davis, Vincent. *The Admirals' Lobby.* Chapel Hill, N.C., 1967. Deals with institutions, planning, and politics of the navy during the twentieth century.

Field, James A., Jr. *America and the Mediterranean World, 1776-1882.* Princeton, N.J., 1969. Includes the best treatment of the navy in the Mediterranean during the distant-stations era.

Friedman, Norman. *The Fifty Year War: Conflict and Strategy in the Cold War.* Annapolis, Md., 2000. A fine survey of the Cold War by a distinguished writer on naval matters.

George, James L. *The U.S. Navy: The View from the Mid-1980s.* Boulder, Colo., 1985. A collection of essays dealing with the navy during the Reagan presidency.

Hagan, Kenneth J. *American Gunboat Diplomacy and the Old Navy, 1877–1889.* Westport, Conn., 1973. Concerns Commodore Shufeldt's cruise on the USS *Ticonderoga*.

———. *This People's Navy: The Making of American Sea Power.* New York, 1991. A fine survey with much material on naval diplomacy.

Howarth, Stephen. *To Shining Sea: A History of the United States Navy, 1775–1991.* London, 1991. A useful survey that places the navy in world affairs.

Johnson, Robert Erwin. *Thence Round Cape Horn: The Story of United States Naval Forces on Pacific Station, 1818–1923.* Annapolis, Md., 1963. The best survey of the first century of American naval diplomacy in the eastern Pacific.

O'Connor, Raymond Gish. *Perilous Equilibrium: The United States and the London Naval Conference of 1930.* Lawrence, Kans., 1962. The most complete study of the conference, based on American archival materials.

Paullin, Charles Oscar. *Diplomatic Negotiations of American Naval Officers, 1778–1883.* Baltimore, 1922. A pioneer work that has never been completely replaced.

Pelz, Stephen E. *Race to Pearl Harbor: The Failure of the Second London Naval Conference and the Onset of World War II.* Cambridge, Mass., 1974. Views the naval approach to Pearl Harbor through British, American, and Japanese sources.

Pokrant, Marvin. *Desert Storm at Sea: What the Navy Really Did.* Westport, Conn., 1999. A view of the navy in the Gulf War.

Sprout, Harold, and Margaret Sprout. *The Rise of American Naval Power, 1776–1918.* Princeton, N.J., 1946.

———. *Toward a New Order of Sea Power: American Naval Policy and the World Scene, 1918–1922.* Princeton, N.J., 1946. This work and *The Rise of American Naval Power, 1776–1918* are the classic surveys of the navy's history through the Washington Conference, including illuminating comments on naval diplomacy.

Sweetman, Jack. *American Naval History: An Illustrated Chronology of the U.S. Navy and Marine Corps, 1775–Present.* 2d ed. Annapolis, Md., 1991. Strictly a chronology of events without interpretation.

Trask, David F. *Captains and Cabinets: Anglo-American Naval Relations, 1917–1918.* Columbia, Mo., 1972. A superb multi-archival study of Anglo-American naval cooperation during World War I.

Tuleja, Thaddeus V. *Statesmen and Admirals: Quest for a Far Eastern Policy.* New York, 1963. A survey of the navy in the Far East from 1931 to 1941.

Walworth, Arthur. *Black Ships off Japan: The Story of Commodore Perry's Expedition.* New York, 1946. A good-humored account of the navy's most important diplomatic venture in the nineteenth century.

Wheeler, Gerald E. *Prelude to Pearl Harbor: The United States Navy and the Far East, 1921–1931.* Columbia, Mo., 1963. The standard study of the navy in eastern Asia during the decade before the Manchurian incident.

Zumwalt, Elmo R., Jr. *On Watch: A Memoir.* New York, 1976. A rewarding memoir by one of the most gifted American admirals of the Cold War years.

See also BLOCKADES; THE CONTINENTAL SYSTEM; EMBARGOES AND SANCTIONS; EXTRATERRITORIALITY; FREEDOM OF THE SEAS; IMPERIALISM; PROTECTORATES AND SPHERES OF INFLUENCE.

NEUTRALISM

T. Michael Ruddy

The term "neutralism" is not new to the lexicon of international relations, but in the Cold War world, divided into two competing blocs, this word assumed new meaning. For its first century and a half as a nation, the United States, under the guise of isolationism, practiced its own form of neutralism, shunning political and military involvement with the European powers and invoking its neutrality according to international law in wartime. The appeal of neutrality persisted into the 1930s, as the United States anticipated possible involvement in World War II. But those were different times. There was no Cold War, and the United States was not a superpower. While America's earlier neutralism bore a resemblance to the Cold War variety, some important distinctions set the two apart.

The Cold War, defined not only in terms of a political rivalry between the United States and Soviet Union but also in terms of a conflict between Soviet communism and Western democratic capitalism, provided the context for this new form of neutralism. This ideological rivalry dated to the time of the 1917 Russian Revolution, but during World War II, the United States and the Soviet Union put aside their ideological differences and joined in a common cause to defeat Hitler. In the aftermath of that conflict, the animosity soon resurfaced as disputes over the postwar settlement escalated. The two powers ultimately abandoned cooperation and turned to consolidating control within their respective spheres. By 1947, containment defined America's postwar policy toward the Soviet Union. The North Atlantic Treaty (1949), an alliance intended to thwart Soviet aggression, institutionalized this containment and defined the western bloc. Meanwhile, the Soviet Union was consolidating its control over the eastern bloc.

Not all European states, however, presumed that their national interests would be served by associating with this alliance system. Sweden, situated on Europe's strategically important northern flank, and Austria, bordering the Soviet bloc, are notable examples. To them, neutralism had a definite appeal. Their decision to assume an independent position created complications for U.S. foreign relations. Policymakers in Washington particularly worried that neutralism might tempt America's allies and erode the solidarity of the Atlantic alliance.

Compounding their apprehension were developments in the Third World. As the former European colonial empires slowly crumbled, many newly independent states opted for nonalignment, often with the intention of exploiting the Soviet-American rivalry to secure economic assistance from both sides. The 1955 gathering of twenty-nine nonaligned nations at Bandung, Indonesia, combined with a concerted effort by the Soviet Union to curry favor with these states, underlined the necessity for the United States to follow a well-considered approach to neutralism.

In the years after World War II, an understanding of the causes, intentions, and goals of neutralism slowly evolved within policymaking circles that would guide America's relationship with these states. The administration of President Harry Truman initially resisted neutralism, considering it a hindrance to western security. Only reluctantly, after officials realized that the neutrals would not be dissuaded from their chosen course, did Washington begin to pursue an accommodation with neutralism. The administration of President Dwight Eisenhower, despite its inflammatory rhetoric, grasped the advantages and drawbacks of this third force and endeavored to implement a policy toward neutralism that would benefit Western interests. But often Cold War considerations intruded to muddle relations with the neutrals, particularly in the Third World. Despite the more sophisticated worldview of President John F. Kennedy and his advisers, and their appreciation of the unique circumstances faced by the Third World, in practice they deviated little from the approach of their predecessors. The framework for the U.S.-neutral relationship that would survive through the Cold War was in place by the 1960s.

U.S. policy toward neutralism met with mixed results. In western Europe, the neutral states, despite their aversion to alliances, shared a common political, social, and economic heritage with the United States and its European allies. U.S. policy thus successfully fostered a relationship that to a great extent accommodated neutral interests while furthering America's Cold War goals. In the case of the Soviet bloc, Yugoslavia's adoption of neutralism offered an opportunity to weaken Soviet control within its own orbit. But contrary to the hopes of policymakers, neutralism did not spread further in the Soviet bloc. Finally, Washington often misunderstood the forces of nationalism in the Third World. America's ties to many of the former colonial powers created friction with the newly independent states and opened opportunities for the Soviet Union. The United States encouraged neutralism when it fit American interests, but opposed it when it went counter to these interests. Often, this opposition was counterproductive. It antagonized Third World nationalism and drove these states closer to the Soviet Union.

By the time the expanding conflict in Vietnam consumed America's attention in the mid-1960s, neutralism had established itself as a force to be reckoned with. As Washington struggled to extricate itself from that costly Asian war and then as it tried to reduce Cold War tensions through a détente policy, the neutrals had to be factored into the equation. The neutrals exerted an important influence, often serving as political or diplomatic bridges between the competing Cold War blocs. They recognized that it was in their interest to work toward a solution to the Cold War.

DEFINING COLD WAR NEUTRALISM

At a June 1956 news conference, when the topic of neutralism came up, President Dwight D. Eisenhower responded by noting that for 150 years the United States itself had been neutral. He then declared that "neutral" now meant avoiding any attachment to military alliances, and that "this [did] not necessarily mean . . . neutral as between right and wrong or between decay and decency." In equating America's past tradition with the neutral stance of 1956, the president exhibited a sympathy and understanding of this "third force" not always associated with his administration. The 150-year commitment to which he referred evoked two distinct but interrelated facets of how the United States defined its neutrality in the past—first, the legal status of a neutral state in time of war, and, second, the response to George Washington's admonition in his Farewell Address to "avoid entangling alliances." The traditional legal concept of neutrality, which had evolved in international law during the past century through treaty, court cases, and precedent, was codified in the Hague Conventions of 1907. These conventions recognized the legal status of a nonbelligerent state in time of war and prescribed the rights and obligations of a nation in its relations with belligerent states. During its formative years, the United States adhered to—indeed, became a champion of—these principles of neutrality. The principles of freedom of the seas and the right to trade with belligerents in time of war appealed to a fledgling nation focused on establishing its economic stability, which was so important to ensuring its viability as a nation. Even as the United States was becoming a major power in the twentieth century, it was hesitant to abandon neutrality. For three years before its 1917 entry into World War I, President Woodrow Wilson asserted America's neutral rights. And during the 1930s, encouraged particularly by a Congress and a public intent upon staying out of another conflict emerging in Europe, once again the United States declared its neutrality until events inexorably brought the country into the conflict at the end of 1941.

Besides this neutrality defined by international law, Eisenhower in his remarks also referred to another aspect of America's earlier policies that was more akin to postwar neutralism. In 1796, President George Washington in his Farewell Address warned Americans to avoid entangling alliances. At the time, war threatened to engulf Europe. The United States, which had signed an alliance with France in 1778, feared being drawn into a European conflict that did not serve its national interests. It abrogated that treaty by 1800, and for a century and a half thereafter assiduously avoided political and military entanglements with Europe.

In international affairs, America entered a period of what many historians describe as isolationism. In effect, the United States assumed a neutralist position. Yet this neutralism was not a total rejection of international involvement. The United States pursued opportunities for trade, protected in time of conflict by the neutral rights supposedly guaranteed by international law, and the independence its neutral position afforded, provided opportunities to exploit the rivalry among the European powers to America's benefit.

America's status changed dramatically after World War II. As a major power, it could not return to its former neutral position. In fact, it now confronted a neutralism, first in Europe and then in the Third World, that exhibited many of the characteristics of the neutralism it had practiced for so many years.

After World War II, the legally defined neutrality in wartime was irrelevant in the new environment of the Cold War. The more traditional European neutrals, such as Switzerland and Sweden, had used this neutrality as a basis for their status. But like earlier U.S. neutralism, this new neutralism was more political than legal. In most cases, nations that espoused neutralism did so freely. In a few notable cases, however, external pressure influenced their choice. All neutrals refused to commit to alliances and distanced themselves from the power blocs dominated by the United States and the Soviet Union. As Peter Lyon notes in his study *Neutralism,* "By neutrality is meant non-involvement in war, while by neutralism is meant non-involvement in *the* Cold War." Neutralism was a state of mind shared by a segment of Europe's and the world's population. Neutral sentiment existed in nations allied with the United States as well as in the neutral states themselves. As was the case with the United States during its early history, neutralist states determined that their national interest would best be served by not choosing sides in the great power conflict.

But Cold War neutralism, unlike that of the United States in the nineteenth century, was not isolationist. It was what political scientists call positive neutralism. Neutral states consciously exercised their status as a third force between the power blocs to further their national interests. Like the United States in the nineteenth century, this included promoting their economic and commercial cause. But positive neutralism went further. Through political involvement, especially in international organizations, neutrals exerted an influence on international affairs. They played a role as bridge-builders to span the gap between the Cold War rivals.

Neutralism presented an appealing option for those who had misgivings about subordinating their nation's sovereignty to the policies of the United States or the Soviet Union. Concern that the North Atlantic Treaty might just lead to such an eventuality at times fueled an attraction to neutralism even among some of America's traditionally closest allies. As late as 1948, political factions in Great Britain considered pursuing a "third way," which they defined as a bloc of western European states and their former colonies that would assume an independent position between the United States and the Soviet Union, to reduce British dependence on the United States. The term "neutralism" itself first came into vogue in the late 1940s in France, where it signified a state of mind that questioned whether French national interests would be served by subordinating French independence to American leadership.

The desire for U.S. economic assistance and a growing apprehension about the Soviet political and military threat ultimately trumped neutralism's appeal in Britain and France. But some of Europe's smaller states did embrace neutralism. Each of these states constructed its own distinct style of neutralism, defined in terms that served its own national interests. Switzerland and Sweden had a long tradition of neutrality that they had maintained throughout World War II and firmly guarded in the Cold War. Finland and Austria to differing degrees represented neutralism coerced. Finland, defeated and forced to deal with its victorious Soviet neighbor, tried to preserve as much of its independence as possible by signing the 1948 Treaty of Friendship, Cooperation, and Mutual Assistance, which bound it to resist any attack on the Soviet Union. Austria, like Germany occupied by the Allies after World War II, accepted the status of neutrality as a prerequisite for the 1955 Austrian State Treaty that ended the occupation of its territory and restored its autonomy.

The Soviet bloc was not immune to the appeal of neutralism. Josip Broz Tito established a communist regime in Yugoslavia, but bristled at Stalinist interference in the internal affairs of his country. When Yugoslavia was expelled from the Cominform in 1948, Tito charted a course independent of both blocs.

As neutralism took root in Europe, the dissolution of Europe's colonial empires in Africa and Asia gave rise to newly independent nations, many of which adopted a policy of nonalignment. In certain respects, nonalignment was synonymous with neutralism, for the nonaligned states eschewed commitments to either of the global power centers. But not all members of the nonaligned movement took a neutral position vis-à-vis the two blocs. Many of the twenty-nine states that attended the first meeting of the nonaligned at Bandung in 1955 tilted to one side or the other. B. K. Shrivastava, in a 1982 article titled "The United States and the Non-Aligned Movement," identified three categories of nonaligned states that had become clearly delineated by 1970: the extremists, consisting largely of Marxist and pro-Soviet countries; the conservative friends of the United States and the West; and the moderates, who wanted to maintain their distance from both the United States and the Soviet Union. Moderates, such as India and Egypt, wary both of the Soviet Union and of Western capitalist powers, their former colonial overlords, represented the true neutrals of the Third World.

As neutralism established itself in Europe and spread to Asia and Africa, U.S. policymakers had to decide whether to oppose or to pursue accommodation with that movement. Certain aspects of this phenomenon, from their viewpoint, were clearly contrary to American interests, especially the tendency for neutralism to impede the establishment of a unified opposition to Soviet advances. But neutrals, in their distrust of Soviet doctrine, also offered opportunities.

U.S. POLICY AND WESTERN EUROPEAN NEUTRALISM

After World War II, the Truman administration faced a deteriorating relationship with the Soviet Union and a Europe in dire economic straits that made it vulnerable to communist blandishments and powerless to resist potential Soviet aggression. In central Europe, the failure to establish a cooperative framework for the occupation of Germany was leading to a permanently divided German state. When the United States responded to these developments with a containment policy, it soon became clear that neutralism had the potential to undermine the unity of purpose the Truman administration deemed necessary to repel Soviet advances.

West Germany was a key factor in American policymakers' response to neutralism. With the creation of the Federal Republic in 1949 in the wake of the Berlin airlift, West Germany quickly emerged as an important component of the western European alliance, and a divided Germany became an accepted part of the Cold War landscape. To many Germans intent upon reuniting their country, however, neutralism often surfaced as a means of accomplishing this reunification. Through the years, this solution even had prominent advocates in the United States. The noted American diplomat and historian George F. Kennan, in his 1957 Reith Lectures over the BBC, called for the superpowers to disengage from Germany, which would be united and demilitarized. Throughout the Cold War, Washington consistently resisted such solutions, fearing that this would weaken Western resolve to resist the Soviet threat.

The traditional neutrals, Switzerland and Sweden, along with Finland, were particular obstacles to Western solidarity. Neutrals were more than willing to participate in postwar economic programs such as the Marshall Plan. (Finland was the notable exception. As it tried to construct a relationship with its Soviet neighbor that would preserve its national autonomy, Helsinki opted against participation so as not to antagonize the Kremlin.) Economic ties were as far as they would go, however. Political and military bonds were out of the question.

The Truman administration initially viewed neutralism with suspicion and even hostility. The advice that Secretary of State George Marshall offered to the president on the occasion of a 1948 visit by the crown prince of Sweden was typical. Marshall argued that Sweden's adherence to neutrality had "been more benefit to the Soviet Union than to the Western countries" and urged Truman to "avoid any expression of approval of the neutrality policy," since such a policy that "reveal[ed] a division among the free nations of the world [could] only serve to invite aggression."

Gradually, however, officials grudgingly conceded that it was futile to try to dissuade these neutrals and that neutralism had to be accommodated for the foreseeable future. They thus concentrated on finding a way at least indirectly to turn neutralism to the West's benefit. Washington curtailed efforts to pressure neutrals to choose between the two competing camps and moved toward a consistent, pragmatic plan to bind Europe's neutrals closer to the West, thus strengthening rather than weakening the emerging collective security.

The Eisenhower administration, despite its more confrontational public stance and expressions of intolerance for neutralism—Secretary of State John Foster Dulles called neutrality "obso-

THE EISENHOWER ADMINISTRATION AND NEUTRALISM

In the mid-1950s, Eisenhower administration public pronouncements on the issue of neutralism sometimes gave conflicting signals. Secretary of State John Foster Dulles, the administration's principal foreign policy spokesman, was consistently critical. In October 1955, speaking before an American Legion convention in Miami, he stubbornly declared that "except under very exceptional circumstances, neutrality today is an immoral and shortsighted conception." But several months later, at a June 1956 news conference, President Eisenhower took a more tolerant position. He observed that for 150 years the United States had been neutral, that in 1956 neutrality meant avoiding attachment to military alliances, and that "this does not necessarily mean . . . neutral as between right and wrong or between decay and decency." He concluded his appraisal by referring the reporters to a speech Dulles was scheduled to give the following week at Iowa State University. There, however, Dulles did not revise his assessment of neutralism but rather reiterated his intolerant stance. Dulles's hostility has been explained in different ways. It may have reflected his personal belief that there was a stark contrast between communism and democracy, and that, therefore, to take a neutral position was tantamount to choosing the former. H. W. Brands, in *The Specter of Neutralism,* offered another explanation, politics: "The secretary's sermonizing was designed to please conservatives, Republicans for the most part, who distrusted neutralists and continually threatened to block administration initiatives toward countries of the Third World." But what about Eisenhower's contrasting expression of tolerance for neutralism? The answer may lie in the behind-the-scenes deliberations of the administration. The National Security Council, responding to Nikita Khrushchev's "peaceful coexistence" campaign, was reexamining neutralism and all of its ramifications in order to construct a coherent policy toward these neutral states.

lete," "immoral," and "shortsighted"—continued and in fact institutionalized this trend. Dulles's public statements obscured an underlying realism in the administration's approach, a realism that was willing to accommodate the neutral cause if it served U.S. interests.

By the mid-1950s, a number of factors had moved neutralism to a higher priority for policymakers. Nikita Khrushchev, successor to Joseph Stalin, in 1955 proclaimed a drive for "peaceful coexistence" and backed his words with action—the return in 1956 of the port of Porkkala, which had been seized at the end of World War II, to Finland; his decision to support a neutralized Austria in return for a treaty ending its occupation; and efforts to mend relations with Yugoslavia. The United States doubted Khrushchev's sincerity and suspected that he was simply maneuvering to divide the West by encouraging neutralism. Khrushchev's actions, combined with his interest in a unified and neutralized Germany, raised some concern that the Kremlin was seeking a neutralized zone across central Europe—including Austria, Germany, and Yugoslavia—that would weaken the Western defense system. As these events unfolded in Europe, the Bandung Conference highlighted the expanding appeal of neutralism worldwide, a potential advantage for the Soviet Union.

In response to these developments, the National Security Council in 1955 asked the State Department to prepare an assessment of neutralism worldwide to aid the White House in developing an informed approach to this third force. This pivotal study established a framework for America's approach to neutralism through much of the remainder of the Cold War. For Europe, its analysis and conclusions led to a pragmatic and measured relationship with the neutral states.

The study began by making a distinction between *neutrality,* a government policy or a nation's status in foreign relations, and *neutralism,* described as "an attitude or psychological tendency." It went on to distinguish between what it called "classical" neutralism, which had always entailed a determination not to take sides in international rivalries, and a new "quasi-neutralism," a "hodge-podge of attitudes and tendencies which . . . involve[d] a disinclination to cooperate with U.S. objectives in the Cold War and in a possible hot war." Even though this new neutralism eschewed commitments to both the Soviet Union and the United States, it was more threatening to the West's interests. Soviet strategy could exploit it.

The report proceeded to list several explanations for the appeal of this new neutralist sentiment in Europe: fear of nuclear war, nationalism, negative reactions to U.S. leadership, a desire to achieve security without responsibility, pacifism, pursuit of special interests, and economic motivations. It further emphasized that this new neutralism, more than the legal government policy of neutrality or even the neutralist position some European states assumed in the Cold War, was what threatened American interests most. A government's declaring itself to be neutral, the study stressed, did not automatically mean that nation was infected with that troublesome neutralism.

This cautionary insight was fundamental to the evolution of America's relations with the neutral states. From the U.S. perspective, the litmus test for beneficial neutrality was a strong ideological identification with the West, demonstration of "solid resistance to Communist blandishments," and maintenance of a strong national defense establishment. The key neutrals in Europe fulfilled these criteria. Each for its own reasons had adopted a neutral position, but this did not necessarily translate to that damaging neutralism that threatened to undermine relations with the West. Indeed, the State Department study identified neutralist sentiment as stronger among some of America's allies than among the neutral states. These insights led the United States to understand the distinct interests and positions of the individual states.

Switzerland Switzerland, the purest of the neutrals, dated its neutrality to the sixteenth century. Its status was reinforced in the early nineteenth century by provisions of the Congress of Vienna, and it carefully maintained its neutral stance throughout World War II. After the war, Switzerland even eschewed membership in the United Nations because it determined that membership in this international organization might compromise its neutrality. Despite Switzerland's stubborn refusal to cooperate, U.S. officials took solace in the fact that Switzerland practiced an armed neutrality. There was no doubt that it would defend its territory in time of conflict. Bordered by France and Italy, Switzerland, of the four major European neutral states, was of least concern to the United States.

Sweden Sweden dated its neutrality to the Napoleonic wars at the beginning of the nineteenth century and maintained this status throughout World War II. After the war, it defined its position to be neutral in war and nonaligned in peacetime. When the United States began planning for the security for Europe, Sweden presented a particular problem. As a significant military force on Europe's northern flank, it was important to continental defense. U.S. officials understood the advantages of convincing Sweden to participate in Western defense arrangements. But as Washington negotiated the North Atlantic Treaty, Stockholm, rather than cooperating, attempted to exclude the Cold War from the Nordic region by proposing a league of armed neutrality, a Nordic Union, with its Scandinavian neighbors, Denmark and Norway. This scheme ultimately failed, and Denmark and Norway signed the North Atlantic Treaty. Sweden continued to refuse to associate itself with the Western military alliance.

Sweden's actions caused some tension with the United States, but relations improved by the early 1950s. A 1952 National Security Council policy paper on Scandinavia and Finland (NSC 121) admitted that in the near future the United States would have to accept Sweden's determination to avoid military alliances and calculate the best means to increase Sweden's contribution to Western defense. Subsequently, Sweden became an important centerpiece of a "Nordic Balance" that secured the North Atlantic alliance's northern flank. Its neutrality, furthermore, contributed to Finland's success in maintaining its neutral position.

Finland In contrast to these established neutrals, the United States confronted in Finland's situation a neutrality created out of necessity. Precariously situated on the border of the Soviet Union, the Helsinki government struggled to preserve its independence by building a relationship premised on the belief that the Kremlin's interest in Finland was strategic, not ideological. After signing a punitive peace treaty in 1947 that imposed devastating reparations and took away 11 percent of its territory, Finland agreed to a ten-year Treaty of Friendship, Cooperation, and Mutual Assistance in 1948 that required it to resist any attack on the Soviet Union through Finnish territory by Germany or any nation allied with Germany, to consult with the Soviet Union on an appropriate response in the event of attack, and to refrain from joining any alliance aimed at the Soviet Union. Finland subsequently tried to interpret and apply this pact in such a way that it could move more to a neutral position between the two blocs. Washington ultimately appreciated that Finland lacked alternatives to its chosen course, and was careful not to disrupt the delicate balance.

At times during the Eisenhower years, as Finland's economic situation improved and its independence became more secure, Washington considered the possibility that the solution crafted by Finland might serve as a model for other states bordering the Soviet Union. Secretary of State John Foster Dulles at the 1955 Geneva summit meeting between Khrushchev and Eisenhower suggested to Soviet Premier Nikolai A. Bulganin that Finland exemplified the relationship that might be acceptable to the United States for the Soviet-dominated nations of Eastern Europe. A 1959 National Security Council report titled "U.S. Policy Toward Finland" (NSC 5914/1) mirrored this suggestion when it asserted that "If Finland is able to preserve its present neutral status . . . it could serve as an example of what the United States might like to see achieved by the Soviet-dominated nations of Eastern Europe."

This appreciation of the benefits of Finnish neutralism for American foreign policy goals contrasted with later scathing assessments of the Finnish example. In a 1977 article titled "Europe: The Specter of Finlandization," the scholar Walter Laqueur coined the term "Finlandization," which from his perspective bore the negative connotation of a country willing to sacrifice its sovereignty for the sake of preserving felicitous relations with the Soviet Union. Laqueur feared that other European states might succumb to the temptation to follow Finland's example. Yet here, years before Laqueur's criticism, Dulles was offering the Finnish style of neutralism as a means of diminishing rather than enhancing Soviet control in its own sphere. Even if the Finnish situation was in no way analogous to that of the satellite states in Eastern Europe, the mere presence of this small nation resisting Soviet domination was useful as a propaganda tool for the United States.

Austria In 1955 neutral representation in western Europe expanded further as Austria joined this "third force." Austria, occupied by the Allies after the war's end, suffered through occupation and protracted treaty negotiations as the Cold War rift widened. By late 1953, Austrian officials were ready to accept neutralization as the price for regaining sovereignty. Soviet negotiators endorsed this solution at the foreign ministers' conference at Berlin in 1954, but the proposal was tabled, the victim of the continuing dispute over the status of Germany, because the neutralization of Austria could be linked to a similar solution for Germany. This was particularly unacceptable to the United States. Although Washington was willing to respect Austria's decision if it chose neutrality, Dulles articulated Washington's misgivings when he asserted that it was one thing for a nation to choose neutrality and another to have neutrality forcibly imposed. Under such circumstances, a nation could not be truly independent and sovereign.

West Germany's incorporation into NATO in 1955 removed this obstacle to a neutralized Austria. (The Soviet Union responded to West Germany's new status with the Warsaw Pact, which further solidified its control of the eastern bloc.) Austrian officials traveled to Moscow and negotiated the terms of the State Treaty of May 1955, agreeing that Austria would join no military alliances, would permit no military bases on its territory, and would practice a form of neutrality along the lines of the Swiss model. France and Britain endorsed this arrangement; the United States reluctantly agreed.

Economic and Military Assistance Each of these states traversed a different path to neutralism, and each defined its neutralism in its own distinct terms. Nevertheless, all shared an affinity with western values. This reassured U.S. officials, who employed several tactics to strengthen these ties. Economic measures figured prominently in American plans. European integration, furthermore, provided a vehicle to tie the neutrals to the West. Finally, in response to Sweden's efforts to improve its military capabilities and shore up its defensive position, covert military arrangements developed between Sweden and the United States and its NATO allies.

Economic assistance in the form of trade, loans, and credits was a particularly useful method of fostering a beneficial relationship. But economic assistance was not unrestricted; it had to address the West's Cold War interests. Switzerland and Sweden were economically sound and had healthy trade relations with the West. The United States continued to encourage this trade, but it feared the possible transfer of strategically important materials and technology by these neutrals to the Soviet bloc. In 1949, the United States and its allies had reached an agreement to restrict the transfer of strategic goods. In ongoing negotiations parallel with the establishment of the Marshall Plan, U.S. officials pressured both Switzerland and Sweden to adhere to these export controls. Both countries, reluctant to compromise their neutral status, nevertheless by 1951 informally agreed to adhere to parts of the export controls. Reflecting Sweden's strategic importance in the Nordic region, its adherence to these controls led the United States in 1952 to begin to allow Sweden to purchase selected military equipment and supplies. This made Sweden eligible for military equipment otherwise restricted to America's allies. The United States went even further in 1956 when it agreed to share some nuclear technology for peaceful purposes.

U.S. aid to Austria between 1945 and 1955, prior to the restoration of its sovereignty, amounted to an estimated $1.25 billion. Assistance continued after the State Treaty was signed in order to strengthen Austria's armed neutrality. In relations with Finland, Washington assiduously pursued an essentially hands-off political posture, intended to minimize antagonizing the Soviet Union, combined with measured economic assistance to strengthen the Finnish economy and orient it more firmly toward the west. This assistance included the sale of surplus agricultural goods as well as loans, the latter conflicting with the 1951 Battle Act, which prohibited loans to nations exporting strategic goods to the communist bloc. In the late 1950s, Eisenhower cited overriding foreign policy considerations to bypass Battle Act restrictions and ensure millions of dollars in loans to Finland. As a result, by the late 1950s, Finnish exports to and imports from the east bloc declined in relation to exports to and imports from the West.

In tandem with these economic measures, the United States exploited the steady evolution toward European integration to draw the neutrals further from the Soviet orbit, so as to reinforce rather than weaken the Western security system. Aside from any benefit integration could provide for its neutral policy, the United States recognized the value of a more tightly integrated Europe, both economically and politically. It therefore consistently encouraged Europe's movement toward cooperation, beginning with the Organization for European Economic Cooperation (OEEC), established in 1948 to coordinate Marshall Plan aid; proceeding to the European Coal and Steel Community and then the European Economic Community (EEC), which portended the possibility of a truly effective union; and refusing to rebuff the European Free Trade Association (EFTA), a tariff union created by states excluded from the EEC. Despite its interest in integration with truly effective supranational authority, the United States continued to encourage institutions like the OEEC and EFTA, which lacked that desired supranational authority, in part because these organizations provided a niche for the neutrals in the Western system. The OEEC included Sweden, Switzerland, and Austria. And when the EFTA was negotiated in 1958, U.S. officials hesitated to repudiate it, largely because it offered a haven for these three neutrals. Also, as Finland became more secure in its relationship with the Soviet Union, it began negotiations in 1959 that culminated in associate membership in this customs union in 1961.

In addition to these efforts aimed at all the neutrals, the United States and its NATO allies engaged Sweden in a covert military relationship that theoretically contradicted that nation's nonaligned posture. Soon after the promulgation of the North Atlantic Treaty, Sweden began to meet with Denmark and Norway to coordinate military cooperation and planning. These secret meetings eventually expanded to include the United States and Great Britain, and led to other areas of cooperation. Sweden in effect became an unofficial member of the Western alliance system.

The Kennedy Years   John F. Kennedy was the willing heir to this relationship with Europe's neutrals. Mirroring the findings of the 1955 neutralism study, a State Department study released in 1961 admitted that there were many variants of neutralism arising from "unique, indigenous conditions." The new administration was reassured by the fact that the European neutrals were stable nations that had proved impervious to communist influence, so Washington was content to let these favorable trends mature.

Illustrative of Kennedy's approach was his response to a visit to Washington in the fall of 1961 by Finland's President Urho Kekkonen and the subsequent "note crisis" provoked by Moscow. Finland's effort to associate with EFTA was only one of a series of cautious steps that nation had taken since 1955 to carefully establish its independence from Soviet control. On his visit to Washington, Kekkonen met with Kennedy and received a public endorsement for his country's neutral course. Soon thereafter, alarmed by Finland's expanding outreach to the West, Khrushchev sent an official note to Helsinki invoking the consultation clause of the Treaty of Friendship, Cooperation, and Mutual Assistance, a move that potentially threatened Finland's sovereignty. Although concerned about this development, Washington reacted cautiously. Bowing to Finnish wishes, Washington remained in the background and avoided escalating this incident into a Cold War confrontation. The U.S. ambassador to Finland privately reassured the Finns of America's support, then bowed to Helsinki's wish to address the crisis in its own way. After a visit to the Soviet Union, Kekkonen succeeded in defusing the crisis with Finland's independence still intact.

Britain and the EEC Despite this appreciation of neutralism, however, when neutral interests conflicted with more pressing priorities of America's Cold War policies, neutrals were the losers. A case in point was the U.S. response to Prime Minister Harold Macmillan's announcement in the spring of 1961 that Great Britain intended to apply for EEC membership. Washington encouraged Macmillan because Britain was an important force in European economic and political affairs, and would provide an Atlantic link between the European Union and the United States. But to the dismay of American officials, Macmillan also pressed for membership, either full or associate, for Britain's fellow EFTA members, including the neutrals Austria, Switzerland, and Sweden (as well as associated Finland). Although Macmillan's proposal potentially would have drawn the neutrals closer to western Europe, Washington opposed his plan because these neutrals were unwilling to accept the full political commitments required of EEC members. Their participation, therefore, would erode the supranational authority necessary for a strong union. Washington encouraged Britain's application, but pressed London to postpone its efforts on behalf of fellow EFTA members. This decision was not encouraging for the U.S.-neutrals relationship. The issue ultimately became moot when the EEC, led by France, rejected Britain's application in January 1963. Nevertheless, these events illustrated the limits of America's willingness to accommodate the interests of these neutrals.

NEUTRALISM BEYOND WESTERN EUROPE

The pragmatism evident in western Europe extended as well to U.S. policy toward neutralism worldwide, but with mixed results. In *The Specter of Neutralism,* an important study of America's early postwar relations with Yugoslavia, India, and Egypt, H. W. Brands concluded that actual American policy during the Truman and Eisenhower years, as distinct from public rhetoric, "demonstrated a pragmatic ability to deal with neutralism on its own merits. If the neutralist actions of a particular country worked to the advantage of the United States, that country deserved, and usually received, American support. If a neutralist challenged American interests, opposition was the rule." The American advantages and interests to which Brands referred were inevitably defined by the geopolitical rivalry with communism and often lacked a sophisticated understanding of the interests of the Third World states.

Although Brands's study was restricted to the Truman-Eisenhower period, his insight could for the most part extend to the Kennedy years as well. Kennedy administration pragmatism was informed by a more sophisticated understanding of Third World issues, yet Cold War interests still prevailed and affected American tolerance for neutrals. Washington offered economic assistance and encouraged social reform as means to guide these states toward democracy and, it hoped, to counter the allure of communism. Policymakers were committed to resisting Soviet influence and preferred that these countries commit to the West, but when necessary, they were willing to use neutralism as an alternative to communist expansion. Notable in this regard were the Southeast Asia states of Cambodia and Laos. In the late 1950s, as the United States slowly increased its involvement in that area of the world, these two nations, recently independent from French control, embraced neutralism in an ultimately futile attempt to keep out of the emerging conflict. While the United States preferred a Laos and Cambodia committed to the anticommunist cause, it grudgingly accepted their neutralism. Kennedy, furthermore, during his 1961 Vienna summit meeting with Khrushchev supported the neutralization of Laos.

From the end of World War II to the 1960s, neutralism brought opportunities and challenges outside western Europe. In the Soviet bloc, the United States encouraged Yugoslavia's neutralism, even in the face of congressional opposition, because this was a chance to discreetly undermine Soviet dominance. The flowering of neutralism in the Third World dictated that the United States adapt its policies, which it did with varying degrees of success, as relations with the key neutrals, India and Egypt, illustrate. In South Asia, a region on the periphery of American interests, India, the quintessential Third World neutral, vexed policymakers. Resistant to U.S. efforts to draw it into entanglements with the West, India stubbornly followed a truly independent course. But while south Asia was not critical to U.S. security interests, the Middle East with its oil and strategic geographic position was. Here, U.S.–Egyptian relations proved particularly trying.

Yugoslavia John Gaddis, in *The Long Peace,* a retrospective look at four decades of the Cold War, argues that from as early as the middle of 1947, the United States had pursued a "multifaceted strategy aimed at driving a wedge between Moscow and its ideological allies throughout the world." Nowhere was this wedge strategy more evident than in relations with Yugoslavia. After World War II, Josip Broz Tito had imposed a Marxist regime. But, although committed to building a communist regime internally, he chafed under Stalin's attempts to impose tighter control over the eastern bloc. Stalin could not tolerate Tito's separate road to communism because Tito's neutralism conflicted with Soviet domination of the communist movement. Their dispute culminated with Stalin labeling Tito a deviationist and expelling Yugoslavia from the Cominform in June 1948. Without abandoning his commitment to communism, Tito then adopted nonalignment to address his nation's best interests.

The break left Yugoslavia desperate for economic assistance. The United States, quick to recognize the opportunity Tito's defection offered, stepped in to fill the vacuum left by his former Soviet benefactor. U.S. officials anticipated that, if successful, Tito's independent brand of communism might spread not only in Eastern Europe but also among communist states elsewhere, perhaps even China. Of added benefit was Yugoslavia's military strength. Tito commanded a force of thirty divisions that could potentially be turned against the Soviet Union in case of attack. In pursuit of these ends, the Truman administration adopted a low-key public approach, both to divert congressional opposition to support of a communist regime and to avoid the impression that the United States was responsible for Tito's defection, thus lending credence to Stalin's charges that Tito was selling out to the West. The United States extended aid and credits, including a $20 million loan from the Export-Import Bank, and lifted trade restrictions on many items, including some munitions. In the aftermath of North Korea's invasion of South Korea in 1950, Washington offered further military assistance through the Mutual Defense Assistance Act.

As its defection became more permanent, Yugoslavia also figured in plans for the military containment of the Soviet Union. In February 1953, negotiations between Yugoslavia and Greece and Turkey, endorsed by the United States, resulted in the Balkan Pact, a friendship treaty providing for consultation and coordination of defense planning. Within a year, this pact evolved into a military alliance. The agreement enhanced Tito's international standing, but it never fulfilled expectations of closer collaboration with the West. For Tito, carefully guarding his nonaligned position, never abandoned the option of resuming relations with the Soviet Union. Following Stalin's death, formal relations were restored in 1955, after Khrushchev recognized Yugoslavia's independent road to communism. In that same year, Tito enhanced his neutral credentials by joining India and Egypt as a principal sponsor of the Bandung Conference. Despite Tito's machinations, the Eisenhower administration continued America's cautious support for Yugoslavia throughout the 1950s, seeing his independence as a beneficial break in the monolithic control that the Soviet Union exerted over the eastern bloc.

The Kennedy administration likewise willingly accepted Yugoslavia's neutralism as an alternative to Soviet influence. It tolerated Tito's independent initiatives even when they challenged Western interests. In September 1961, for example, Tito hosted a conference of nonaligned states in Belgrade. There, he played a leading role in pressing the nonaligned agenda that promoted, among other things, peaceful coexistence and condemnation of colonialism. His tilt toward the Soviet Union on certain issues addressed at this meeting irritated U.S. officials, especially when he failed to condemn the recent Soviet decision to resume nuclear testing, but blamed the capitalist bloc for the recent crisis in Germany surrounding the construction of the Berlin Wall. But Washington still pursued amicable relations.

The Third World If the advantages of a neutral heretic in the Soviet bloc seemed obvious and led to a straightforward policy, appropriately addressing nonalignment among the former European colonies proved more problematic. The 1955 neutralism study commissioned by Eisenhower's

National Security Council had also examined the phenomenon of neutralism in the Near East and Far East. Like European neutrals, Third World neutrals wanted to remain independent of the competing power blocs. But the study stressed that in the developing world anticolonialism and nationalism were closely intertwined with neutralism, creating a more complex set of circumstances. Furthermore, these newly independent nations had little international experience and had very little power in international relations. However pragmatic and insightful these observations were, in application U.S. policy was less effective in the Third World. Cold War concerns often gave priority to global considerations, which tended to obfuscate officials' interpretations of the motives and actions taken by these nonaligned neutrals. Strained relations often resulted.

World War II hastened the demise of the former colonial empires. During the war, the U.S. government had signaled some sympathy for the plight of these colonies. The Atlantic Charter (1941), a statement of wartime aims signed by President Franklin Roosevelt and British Prime Minister Winston Churchill, had called for self-determination of all people, a reference in part to peoples under colonial rule. But political developments after the war soon complicated America's relationship with these former colonial possessions. As one former colony after another achieved independence, the United States was distracted by events in Europe. By the time the communist victory in China and, more significantly, the outbreak of the Korean War finally compelled America to turn its attention to the Third World, it encountered a rising tide of nationalism, resentful of years of colonial domination and determined to establish an independent position. Marxism appealed to many Third World nationalists, and the Soviet Union and People's Republic of China competed for influence. On one level, Khrushchev's call for "peaceful coexistence" was a blatant attempt to associate the Soviet Union with the cause of these newly independent states. The United States thus found itself in an awkward position. Not only were the former colonial powers some of its most valued European allies, but communism's appeal in the Third World aroused fears of the expansion of Soviet influence. The two prominent Third World neutrals, India and Egypt, illustrate the problems the United States faced in forging a successful relationship under these circumstances.

After India achieved independence in 1947, its first prime minister, Jawaharlal Nehru, crafted a foreign policy designed to steer clear of military involvements and to maintain an independent role in international affairs. Nehru's India was a democratic state that adopted the Marxist model of economic reform, thereby triggering suspicion among some policymakers. In contrast to Washington's global perspective, Nehru's outlook was decidedly regional. Given India's desperate economic state, his first priority was to improve the lot of his people. To accomplish this, he was open to economic assistance regardless of whether it came from the East or the West.

The Truman administration from the start encouraged India's effort to establish itself as a viable independent state. As Dennis Merrill notes in *Bread and the Ballot: The United States and India's Economic Development, 1947–1963*, "United States policy toward India abounded with contradictions." But, according to Merrill, it was guided by several goals: to prevent India from succumbing to communism and the increasing influence of the Soviet Union; to draw India into the Western alliance, tap its raw materials, and make it a reliable military ally; and to make India a model for noncommunist development in the Third World and an Asian "counterweight" to the People's Republic of China.

India, which from the beginning not only espoused neutralism but also acted in a neutral fashion, confounded American officials. Nehru's criticism of American policies, including Washington's refusal to recognize Communist China and its support for what he characterized as French aggression in Indochina, created friction. When the Korean War broke out, India supported early UN resolutions condemning the invasion and sanctioning UN actions to repulse the North Korean forces, at the same time that it strove to mediate an end to the conflict. By the latter stages of the war, the United States found it convenient to use Indian diplomats as a conduit to convey its positions to the Soviet Union. After the armistice was signed, India chaired the Neutral Nations Repatriation Committee.

India's marginal importance to America's global strategy partially explained both America's measured response to its nonalignment policies even when they were detrimental to U.S. interests, and also why economic assistance to this poor country was slow in coming. But once it began, it steadily expanded during the Eisenhower years and reached its zenith during the Kennedy administration, peaking in 1962 at $465.5 million.

Good relations engendered by this aid, however, were often negated by the incompatibility of Washington's global goals with India's more regional interests. Nowhere was this more evident than in New Delhi's reaction to U.S. relations with Pakistan, a Muslim state established in 1947, at the time of India's independence, and a state engaged in an ongoing conflict with India over control of the state of Kashmir. In contrast to India's neutralism, Pakistan became a willing participant in America's containment efforts, which led the Eisenhower administration to view Pakistan as a barrier to Soviet expansion in the Middle East and as a potential bridge to Muslim populations there. In 1954, Washington concluded a mutual defense assistance agreement with Pakistan. Soon thereafter, Pakistan became a member of the Southeast Asia Treaty Organization. (Washington had previously tried to persuade India to join, but was rebuffed.) Then, in 1955, Pakistan joined NATO members Turkey and Great Britain in the Baghdad Pact (in 1959 renamed the Central Treaty Organization). While these maneuvers served America's global interests, they strained relations with India. Nehru not only was wary of bringing the Cold War rivalry to the Asian continent, but he feared the advantage American military assistance gave to his regional foe.

The Kennedy administration, more sensitive to India's interests, appointed the prominent economist and confidant of the president, John Kenneth Galbraith, as ambassador in 1961, signaling an interest in improving relations. Galbraith promoted expanded assistance to India and counseled acceptance of its nonaligned foreign policy. When the People's Republic of China attacked India in 1962 over disputed border areas, the United States provided India with necessary military aid. The United States now saw India as a counterweight to the growing influence of Communist China in that area of the world. India accepted U.S. assistance, but still resisted any commitment that would draw it into the Cold War. Washington continued to pursue improved relations, but India never achieved priority status.

In contrast to India, Egypt, located in the Middle East, a region rich in oil and strategically situated in the eastern Mediterranean, became a serious concern for American policy. Gamal Abdel Nasser rose to power in 1954, two years after a military coup had deposed King Farouk. Nasser rapidly established himself as a leader of the nonaligned movement and became a hero to the cause of Arab nationalism. Prior to the early 1950s, the Middle East seemed safely in the Western camp. And for a time after the coup, U.S. relations with Egypt were cordial. Washington promoted an Anglo-Egyptian base treaty that ended British occupation of the Suez Canal zone and expressed willingness to provide Cairo with both economic and military aid. But relations gradually deteriorated. U.S. commitments to Israel and its determination to deter the advance of Soviet influence in the region proved increasingly incompatible with the course Nasser chose to follow.

Nasser, whose country for years had endured British rule, adopted a form of neutralism intent on preventing domination by both the West and the Soviet Union. He resisted Western influence and rebuffed U.S. attempts to get Egypt to join a Middle East Defense Organization, an effort to expand the Western alliance system into the eastern Mediterranean. At the same time, while he willingly cooperated with the Soviet Union when it served his purposes, he guarded against letting this cooperation turn to subservience. To Nasser and fellow Arab neutralists, opposition to the State of Israel was part and parcel of this policy. They opposed Zionism not only because Israel occupied Arab lands, but also because the former imperial powers supported Zionism. They saw Zionism as a tool of Western imperialism.

The neutral Nasser, like Nehru, willingly accepted aid from both the Soviet Union and the United States. He recognized that the West was a more reliable source of aid, but he was wary of any assistance that threatened his independence of action. Thus, his independent neutralism increasingly ran counter to American interests. Nasser refused to join the Baghdad Pact in 1955, so Washington turned to Iraq, long one of Egypt's adversaries. Later, when Nasser requested military supplies after some serious border skirmishes with the Israelis in the Gaza Strip, Washington rejected his request. In response, Nasser turned to Czechoslovakia for arms, evoking vehement objections from Washington. While his actions were consistent with his neutral strategy, Secretary of State John Foster Dulles condemned him for opening opportunities for the expansion of Soviet influence.

Dulles's handling of the Aswan Dam project antagonized Nasser even further. In 1955, the United States, Great Britain, and the World Bank offered a financial package to fund this ambitious project intended to provide irrigation and other benefits for Egypt's economic improvement. However, Dulles made this offer contingent on Egypt's abandoning closer ties with the Soviet Union.

When Nasser continued to negotiate with the Kremlin for a better offer to build the dam, refused to rescind his arms deal with Czechoslovakia, and then extended diplomatic recognition to the People's Republic of China in 1956, Dulles rescinded his offer, prompting Nasser to nationalize the Suez Canal in order to use the fees collected to finance the dam.

Dulles created a self-fulfilling prophecy. The United States worried that neutralism provided opportunities for the Soviet Union in the Middle East. Washington's response to Nasser's neutralism resulted in the spread of Soviet influence and damaged American prestige. In October 1956, when Israel invaded Egypt, and Britain and France in a coordinated move occupied the Suez Canal under the pretext of protecting it, the United States found itself at odds with its major allies in Europe. The United States was forced to join with the Soviet Union in calling for a cease-fire and the withdrawal of all foreign forces from Egypt.

Washington added to the damage by suspending aid to Egypt and freezing Egyptian assets. U.S. officials could not shake the fear that Nasser was a pawn of the Soviet Union. The 1957 Eisenhower Doctrine, which assured American support for Middle Eastern nations threatened by external aggression, was intended to contain the spread of Soviet communism. But Arab allies of Nasser interpreted it as an attempt to contain his nationalist movement. In 1958, Nasser accepted Soviet aid for the construction of the Aswan Dam and welcomed Soviet advisers, who remained in Egypt until Nasser's successor, Anwar Sadat, expelled them in 1972.

Beginning in 1959, relations improved as Eisenhower once more made Egypt eligible for food aid. By 1960, the United States provided two-thirds of Egypt's grain imports. And in October 1962, the Kennedy administration reached a $432 million aid deal with Egypt. But these steps could not totally mend the damage done to U.S. prestige by the events of the mid-1950s. Uneasy relations with Nasser continued, especially after he signed another arms agreement with the Soviet Union in June 1963.

THE UNITED NATIONS, VIETNAM, AND DÉTENTE

By the mid-1960s, Cold War neutralism had matured as a distinct force in international affairs. As the Vietnam conflict monopolized America's attention, neutral states both in Europe and in the Third World became more assertive and outspoken. The two blocs that defined the Cold War ever so slowly succumbed to a new international order. The appeal of neutralism threatened to challenge America's control over the western bloc at the same time that the Soviet Union met with only limited success in wooing the neutrals. Harto Hakovirta, in an article titled "The Soviet Union and the Varieties of Neutrality in Western Europe," observed that "at the height of the Cold War in the 1940s and 1950s, a tendency toward absolute alliance was dominant; but, starting roughly in 1963, the direction seemed to reverse itself. Cold-war structures began to crumble, and the United States gradually lost control over its West European partners."

The United Nations provided a major forum for neutrals to voice their concerns. The composition of that organization changed significantly in the years after the end of World War II as its membership expanded to include newly independent Asian and African states, many of which embraced nonalignment. In 1964, these states formed a caucus, the Group of Seventy-seven (the number of members would increase in subsequent years), that, constituting a two-thirds majority, could effectively control the General Assembly. Although these new states resisted Soviet efforts to assume a role of leadership, they could often count on Soviet support. In contrast to the immediate postwar years, the United States no longer dominated the United Nations, and faced criticism and opposition from the membership.

Neutrals in the United Nations became increasingly outspoken on many issues—the need to reduce Cold War tensions, colonialism, and, importantly, nuclear proliferation. As early as 1961, neutrals took up the cause of nuclear disarmament. In that year, Swedish Foreign Minister Bo Östen Unden, addressing the General Assembly, called upon the nonnuclear members to band together to pressure the nuclear powers to reduce their armaments. Later, in a noteworthy success in the crusade to reduce the spread of nuclear weapons, neutral states played a role in the promulgation of the 1968 Nuclear Non-Proliferation Treaty. The terms of this treaty, after initially being negotiated by the Soviet Union and the United States, were revised and then submitted to the UN General Assembly by an eighteen-nation disarmament committee. In addition to five representatives each from the Western and Eastern blocs, eight neutral states were represented on this committee.

While the United States welcomed support for attempts to curtail the arms race, on some issues its interests were pitted against the neutral position. America's strong support for Israel and its intervention in Vietnam are prominent examples. Vietnam particularly exposed the United States to charges of being an imperialist power bent on pursuing its own ends, with no consideration for the Third World countries trying to overcome their years under colonialism. As opposition to American involvement grew, Sweden and India stood out among critics of that war.

By words and deeds, Sweden made its opposition known. In 1966, citing its commitment to freedom of speech and assembly, the Swedish government ignored Washington's protests and permitted the Bertrand Russell War Crimes Tribunal, made up of a long list of prominent critics of American policy, to meet in Stockholm. Sweden also granted asylum to draft dodgers and military deserters. The numbers seeking safe haven grew significantly in the late 1960s. Prime Minister Olof Palme further strained U.S.–Swedish relations when in December 1972 he likened the massive Christmas bombing of North Vietnam to past Nazi atrocities. Most damaging to U.S.–Swedish relations, in 1969 Sweden became the first Western nation to extend full diplomatic recognition to North Vietnam. Presidents Lyndon Johnson and Richard Nixon both threatened, but did not follow through on, economic sanctions.

Prime Minister Indira Gandhi of India incurred the wrath of the Johnson administration in 1966 when she publicly condemned U.S. bombing of North Vietnam, prompting Washington to postpone needed agricultural aid to her country. This, combined with the continued U.S. support for Pakistan, put a real strain on U.S.–Indian relations.

In Europe, the United States feared a weakening of the Western alliance and a drift toward neutralism among its allies. Following the 1962 Cuban missile crisis, the United States, chastened by the possibility of nuclear annihilation, gradually adopted détente to reduce tensions with the Soviet bloc. Beginning in 1969, President Richard Nixon and his national security adviser (and later secretary of state), Henry Kissinger, made détente the cornerstone of their foreign policy. As their efforts probed the possibility that the divide between the two superpowers might be narrowed, Willy Brandt, foreign minister of West Germany from 1966 to 1969 and chancellor from 1969 to 1974, pursued his own form of détente, *Ostpolitik,* an independent effort by West Germany to resolve the differences with East Germany and the Soviet Union. Between 1970 and 1972, his diplomatic efforts led to treaties with Poland and the Soviet Union, and ultimately normalization of relations with East Germany.

Brandt's *Ostpolitik* in many respects coincided with Nixon's quest to improve relations with the Soviet Union. But Kissinger feared that *Ostpolitik* represented a drift toward neutralism and the possible resurgence of German nationalism. He worried that it might create fissures in the Western alliance, give the advantage to the Soviet Union, and consequently hinder the détente at the superpower level that he and Nixon were so intent upon pursuing. While the United States could not oppose *Ostpolitik,* its support for these initiatives was lukewarm.

As détente changed the dynamics of the Cold War, neutral states in Europe willingly assumed a role as bridge-builders between the competing blocs. They helped facilitate the resolution of Cold War disputes. Beginning in 1969, Helsinki and Vienna provided the settings for arms control negotiations that resulted in the first Strategic Arms Limitations Treaty in 1972. More significant, Finland played a prominent role in encouraging negotiations in the Conference on Security and Cooperation in Europe (1975). Jussi Hanhimäki, in his study *Scandinavia and the United States: An Insecure Friendship,* characterized the role of Finland, along with its Scandinavian neighbors including Sweden, as that of "midwives, providing the services and the medium needed for the conclusion of the agreements." He conceded that the agreements would not have come about without Brandt's *Ostpolitik,* Nixon's efforts at détente, and the Soviet desire for recognition of the postwar borders. But with its commitment to bridge-building, neutral Finland was a valuable vehicle for fostering and moving these negotiations forward.

By the 1980s, great strides had been made in narrowing the chasm created by the Cold War. Although this trend would experience setbacks during the early years of Ronald Reagan's presidency, when Reagan returned to confrontational politics of the earlier Cold War, and although consequently the U.S.-neutral relationship would decline, with Mikhail Gorbachev's rise to power in the Soviet Union, the momentum spawned by détente resumed in the late 1980s. Likewise, the interest of neutrals in reducing nuclear armaments and easing East-West tensions increasingly coincided with Reagan administration policy. Washington welcomed neutral support. Through the Conference on Security and Cooperation in Europe and other means, neutrals worked to maintain the momentum of improving relations between the two superpowers. Just as the neutrals had played a role in the events of the era of détente, so as bridge builders they served America's policy interests and facilitated the exchanges leading to the end of the Cold War.

With the end of the Cold War, neutralism effectively became an anachronism. Nevertheless, for nearly five decades, it was a third force that American policy had with varying degrees of success addressed in its rivalry with the Soviet Union. U.S. policy that became established during the first two decades of the Cold War for the most part successfully steered a course that, with relatively few exceptions, preserved a good relationship with Europe's neutrals—if not promoting, at least not hindering—America's Cold War goals. This success to a large extent was attributable to the fact that Europe's neutrals shared political, economic, and cultural values and interests with the United States. Relations with Third World neutrals were more troublesome. Anticolonial feelings and the growing tide of nationalism that U.S. policymakers often misunderstood and resisted, strained relationships and opened opportunities for the Soviet Union. Cold War perspectives and global concerns regularly obfuscated policymakers' appreciation of the Third World neutral position, and the Soviet Union often stepped in to exploit the situation.

BIBLIOGRAPHY

Annals of the American Academy of Political and Social Sciences 32 (1965). Entire volume devoted to articles on various aspects of neutralism.

Brands, H. W. "Redefining the Cold War: American Policy Toward Yugoslavia, 1948–1960." *Diplomatic History* 11 (1987): 41–53.

———. *The Specter of Neutralism: The United States and the Emergence of the Third World, 1947–1960.* New York, 1989. Essential work examining the origins of U.S. policy through case studies of three Third World nations.

———. *India and the United States: The Cold Peace.* Boston, 1990.

Brecher, Michael. "Neutralism: An Analysis." *International Journal* 17 (1961–1962): 224–236.

Deák, Francis. "Neutrality Revisited." In Wolfgang Friedmann, Louis Henkin, and Oliver Lissitzyn, eds. *Transnational Law in a Changing Society.* New York, 1972.

Gabriel, Jürg Martin. *The American Conception of Neutrality After 1941.* New York, 1988.

Gaddis, John Lewis. *The Long Peace: Inquiries into the History of the Cold War.* New York and Oxford, 1987.

Gehler, Michael, and Rolf Steininger, eds. *The Neutrals and the European Integration, 1945–1995.* Vienna, 2000.

Hahn, Peter L. *The United States, Great Britain, and Egypt, 1945–1956: Strategy and Diplomacy in the Early Cold War.* Chapel Hill, N.C., 1991.

Hakovirta, Harto. "The Soviet Union and the Varieties of Neutrality in Western Europe." *World Politics* 35 (1983): 563–585.

———. *East-West Conflict and European Neutrality.* New York and Oxford, 1988.

Hanhimäki, Jussi M. "The First Line of Defence or a Springboard for Disintegration? European Neutrals in American Foreign Policy, 1945–61." *Diplomacy and Statecraft* 7 (1996): 378-403. A valuable synthesis of U.S. policy toward Europe's neutrals.

———. *Scandinavia and the United States: An Insecure Friendship.* New York, 1997.

Hess, Gary R. "Accommodation and Discord: The United States, India, and the Third World." *Diplomatic History* 16 (1992): 1–22.

Karsh, Efraim. *Neutrality and the Small States.* London, 1988.

Kissinger, Henry. *The White House Years.* Boston and Toronto, 1979.

Krüzel, Joseph, and Michael H. Haltzel, eds. *Between the Blocs: Problems and Prospects for Europe's Neutral and Nonaligned Countries.* Washington, D.C., and Cambridge, U.K., 1989.

Laqueur, Walter. "Europe: The Specter of Finlandization." *Commentary* 64 (1977): 37–41.

Lees, Lorraine. *Keeping Tito Afloat: The United States, Yugoslavia, and the Cold War.* University Park, Pa., 1997.

Logevall, Fredrik. "The Swedish-American Conflict over Vietnam." *Diplomatic History* 17 (1993): 421–445.

Lyon, Peter. "Neutrality and the Emergence of the Concept of Neutralism." *Review of Politics* 22 (1960): 255–265. A brief synthesis of the theory and meaning of neutralism.

———. *Neutralism.* Leicester, U.K., 1963. A useful work defining neutralism and its roots.

Maurer, Pierre. "The United States-Yugoslav Relations: A Marriage of Convenience." *Studia Diplomatica* (1985): 429–451.

McMahon, Robert J. *The Cold War on the Periphery: The United States, India, and Pakistan.* New York, 1994.

Merrill, Dennis. *Bread and the Ballot: The United States and India's Economic Development, 1947–1963.* Chapel Hill, N.C., 1990.

Papacosma, S. Victor, and Mark R. Rubin, eds. *Europe's Neutral and Nonaligned States: Between NATO and the Warsaw Pact.* Wilmington, Del., 1989.

Shrivastava, B. K. "The United States and the Non-Aligned Movement." In K. P. Misra, ed. *Non-Alignment Frontiers and Dynamics.* New Delhi, 1982.

See also COLD WAR EVOLUTION AND INTERPRETATIONS; COLD WAR ORIGINS; FOREIGN AID; ISOLATIONISM; NEUTRALITY.

NEUTRALITY

Thom M. Armstrong

The term "neutrality" is generally used to designate the legal status under international law of a sovereign state that seeks to avoid involvement in an armed conflict between belligerent states, protect its rights, and exercise its responsibilities as a neutral. Consequently, a neutral state under international law or practice asserts that it has the right to remain at peace and prohibit sovereign acts by belligerents within its jurisdiction, and also a responsibility to treat belligerents impartially. Customary international law, treaties, and relevant domestic legislation confirm such rights and responsibilities. A nation's sovereignty extends to its territory, its ships on the high seas, and the air space above its territory. These principles were, for the most part, reconfirmed in the late twentieth century by the Third United Nations Conference on the Law of the Sea (UNCLOS III) from 1972 to 1982. After reviewing the entire historical body of law related to maritime issues, the conference produced the UN Convention on the Law of the Sea. Among other things, the convention established the breadth of territorial seas and economic zones and guaranteed traditional rights of navigation on the high seas as well as overflight.

Neutral states may engage in all legal international intercourse; therefore, neutrality is not synonymous with isolation, nor should it be confused with neutralism or nonalignment, terms that refer to peacetime foreign policies of nations desiring to remain detached from conflicting interests of other nations or power groups. This concept of neutrality has its origins in western Europe after the rise of independent states following the Peace of Westphalia at the close of the Thirty Years' War in 1648.

Respect for, and acceptance of, neutrality as having any bearing in international law or practice developed slowly during the seventeenth and eighteenth centuries. At the time, Europe was in a state of anarchy and neutrals' rights were limited to what was acceptable to belligerents. The little advancement that did occur was largely the result of rivalry among states for trade and territory in the New World. Spain and Portugal's attempts to divide the New World between themselves, establish a monopoly of trade and colonization there, and close the seas to other nations was soon challenged by early writers on international law. In 1608 Hugo Grotius advanced the doctrine that since the seas could not be occupied, they could not become the property of any person or nation. Like the air, the seas were therefore the common property of all men. Although Spain and Portugal accepted this doctrine somewhat begrudgingly, it was firmly established by the end of the seventeenth century, and the notion of neutrality started to evolve among nations.

In general, restraints on trade revolved around the laws of blockade, the definition of contraband of war, the principle that free ships make free goods, and the right of neutrals to trade between the ports of belligerents. In all of these situations, the restraints on neutrals resulted from the obvious desire of belligerents to prevent their enemies from receiving war materials or other goods that may be needed in war. The law of blockade was an outgrowth of the law of siege in land warfare. Governments acknowledged the practice that a city or a place effectively besieged could be legally cut off from all outside help. When this principle was applied to ports, a blockade had to be effective in order for it to be legal; however, it was difficult, particularly during the age of sail, to seal a port completely. No precise definition of effectiveness was ever found, although an attempt was made in some commercial treaties to establish that a blockaded port had to be sufficiently guarded so as to render a ship "in imminent danger of capture" if it attempted to run the blockade.

The laws governing contraband of war have a long history. Under a late medieval code, *Conso-*

lato del Mare, all goods destined for an enemy, in belligerent or other ships, were subject to seizure. Early in the seventeenth century, commercial treaties started to distinguish between contraband and noncontraband. The earliest example of this was the Anglo-Dutch Treaty of Southampton in 1625. Ordinarily, such treaties contained lists of goods under both categories, but uniformity in such lists was difficult, except that obvious materials of war were always considered contraband. The idea that free ships make free goods was associated with the issue of contraband. In essence, the concept meant that a ship's nationality determined the status of its cargo, and that enemy goods on a neutral ship, excepting contraband, would not be subject to capture on the high seas.

THE EIGHTEENTH CENTURY

By the time of the American Revolution, a considerable body of customary law existed relative to the rights of neutrals, derived from European commercial treaties and the writings of jurists. Although the law was quite nebulous because it lacked uniformity in practice or means of enforcement, it nonetheless provided a basis for American policy.

A basic tenet of early American foreign policy was to remain free from European conflicts. Known as the Doctrine of the Two Spheres, the Massachusetts Bay Colony had indirectly asserted it in 1644. There were two aspects to this doctrine. One was that a European nation might restrict the trade of its colonials to the mother country although allowing trade between its metropolitan citizens and other metropolitan areas. The other was that wars in Europe between colonial powers would not extend to their colonials and, conversely, those conflicts between their colonies would not spread to Europe. The doctrine failed, for all practical purposes, under the pressures of colonial wars, but the Doctrine of the Two Spheres (the belief that the United States' destiny could be separate from Europe's) was advanced in the Continental Congress's debates over the question of independence. Clearly, this argument is evident in Thomas Paine's influential pamphlet *Common Sense* (1776) Americans saw themselves as victims of British mercantile policy. As long as the colonies were linked to the mother country, they would be drawn inevitably into Britain's wars, ones in which the colonies had no real interest. If they had been allowed to trade freely without restrictions, they would have flourished.

In June 1776 the Continental Congress appointed a committee to draft a declaration of independence and one to develop a plan of government, while also appointing a third committee, chaired by John Adams, to pen a model treaty for the conduct of foreign relations. The committee that worked on the model treaty studied the commercial treaties of Europe and drew from them the provisions on neutral rights that were most likely to be accepted by European nations in commercial relations with the United States.

The Model Treaty of 1776 represented a liberal interpretation of neutral rights. The list of contraband was restricted and short. The treaty called for free trade between countries at war and acceptance of the principle that free ships make free goods. The subsequent treaty of amity and commerce with France, a companion to the treaty of alliance of 1778, contained provisions that Americans had espoused in the model treaty. The United States then sought to make similar treaties with other European nations. When Catherine the Great of Russia issued a declaration of the rights of neutrals in 1780 and called for the formation of the Armed Neutrality to enforce those rights, Americans were optimistic. Although in principle Spain, Holland, and other neutral nations accepted the tenets of the declaration, Holland was the only other country with whom the United States signed a formal treaty during the Revolutionary War. Following the end of the war, the United States signed treaties of amity and commerce with Sweden in 1783, Prussia in 1785, and Morocco in 1787.

Although the United States signed commercial treaties with several nations following the Treaty of Paris (1783), it did not succeed in concluding similar treaties with Britain or Spain, two major maritime powers. Under the terms of the Treaty of Paris, Britain had recognized the independence of the United States, even though she treated the fledgling nation with disdain and did not even fully respect the commercial provisions of the treaty to which she had agreed. Although subjected at times to inconveniences, annoyances, and insults, American trade with Great Britain was nonetheless lucrative. No serious problems arose until the outbreak of war between Britain and France in 1793. The wars of the French Revolution and Napoleon would seriously threaten America's ability to remain neutral, although the United States sought measures to ensure against becoming involved militarily while at the same time promoting its commercial interests.

The American desire to remain free from European affairs and to stay neutral in European wars was associated with the goal of protecting American neutral rights. One of the reasons for the establishment of a stronger central government under the Constitution of 1787 was a desire to retaliate against British restrictions on American trade. This desire increased as Britain seized enemy goods on American ships and impressed sailors, alleged to be British citizens, serving on American merchant and naval vessels. Both practices violated the principle that free ships make free goods, that a nation's sovereignty applied also to its ships on the high seas. The official nationality of an impressed seaman was irrelevant. The fact that Congress would most likely retaliate against high-handed British measures in defense of national honor alarmed many who felt that the United States might be drawn into the war on the side of revolutionary France.

The American position during the French revolutionary wars was complicated by the fact that the United States had treaties of commerce and alliance with France dating back to 1778. In a technical sense, these treaties violated the Doctrine of the Two Spheres, as well as the principle of impartial treatment of a neutral toward a belligerent. However, the treaties had been consummated during the desperate days of the American Revolution, when doctrine was expendable if necessary to gain alliances that might help secure independence from Great Britain. Under the treaty of alliance, the United States guaranteed to France its territories in America, a provision that the French might invoke if their possessions were attacked. Under the treaty of commerce, the United States would allow French warships and privateers to enter American ports and sell their prizes, something denied to France's enemies. From the French perspective, this enabled them to outfit privateers in American ports. Concerned that the terms of the French alliance might drag the fledgling republic into the European conflagration, President George Washington, with the encouragement of his anti-French secretary of the treasury, Alexander Hamilton, sought to pursue a neutral course. This was much to the chagrin of the president's pro-French and anti-British secretary of state, Thomas Jefferson. On 22 April 1793 the president issued his Neutrality Proclamation. In doing so, Washington advised that the United States should "with sincerity and good faith adopt and pursue a conduct friendly and impartial toward the belligerent powers." Although the federal courts already had jurisdiction under an act of 24 September 1789 to deal with cases involving international law, Congress nonetheless passed the Neutrality Act of 5 June 1794, giving the courts additional authority.

A test of the terms of the Franco-American treaties came in 1793, when "Citizen" Edmond Genêt, minister to the United States of the French Girondin revolutionary government, arrived in the country in April and was warmly received by the American people. Genêt's activities, however, soon caused the Washington administration considerable consternation. The terms of the 1778 treaty with France, Genêt argued, allowed for the outfitting of French privateers in American ports in order to prey upon British merchant ships. Having arrived in the United States with little money, Genêt also had been instructed to prevail upon the Washington administration for repayment of the American revolutionary war debt owed to France. This money would be used in recruiting American sailors and in funding privateering operations against British shipping. Washington and Hamilton both opposed payment and viewed the outfitting of French privateers as a violation of American neutrality. Even Jefferson, while sympathetic to the French, believed that the United States had to prohibit them from using American ports for hostile purposes.

Ultimately, Genêt's activities convinced Washington to request his recall, and in February 1794 Genêt's successor, Joseph Fauchet, arrived in Philadelphia. A change in the French government that brought the Jacobins into power caused Genêt, who would probably have been executed upon his return to France, to request political asylum from Washington, who granted it. Washington's demand for Genêt's recall had prompted the French government to ask for the corresponding recall of the American minister to France, Gouverneur Morris, whose involvement in French politics had irritated the French revolutionary government. Washington had sent U.S. Supreme Court chief justice John Jay on a special mission to England, causing the French to fear an Anglo-American rapprochement in spite of the 1778 Franco-American treaty. In an attempt to allay French fears and suspicions, Washington appointed James Monroe of Virginia, a well-known pro-French Jeffersonian, to replace Morris as American minister to France.

In seeking to reduce tensions between the United States and Great Britain, Jay's mission to London secured a treaty of commerce and navigation. Jay's Treaty of 19 November 1794 was, in some ways, more remarkable for what it did not contain than what it included. For the first time, Great Britain had signed a commercial treaty, though limited in scope, with an independent United States. Most lacking in the treaty, however, was any reference to the British practice of impressing American seamen. On the principle that free ships make free goods, Jay conceded an important neutral point. When terms of the treaty leaked out, Americans, especially Jeffersonian Republicans, denounced it. To many, including the French, the treaty was viewed as a betrayal of the French alliance and a pro-British move by a Federalist administration. In response, the French renewed their seizure of American merchant vessels, intervened in American politics, and laid the groundwork for the reestablishment of a French empire in North America. Despite the treaty's limitations, and with mixed feelings, President Washington signed it. One of the indirect consequences of the treaty was a new settlement with Spain in the form of Pinckney's Treaty of October 1795. Fearing that Jay's Treaty foreshadowed an Anglo-American alliance that would threaten Spanish territories in North America, Spain acquiesced to most American demands. It agreed to a narrowed list of contraband, the right to trade with belligerents except under conditions of an effective blockade, and acceptance of the principle that free ships make free goods.

Jay's Treaty not only had a significant impact on American foreign relations; it was also important to American domestic politics. Reaction to the treaty contributed to the development of formal political parties in the United States: Republicans, who were basically pro-French, and Federalists, who were basically pro-British. When details of Jay's Treaty became known to the French, they were convinced that the Federalist administration was pro-British and was repudiating its obligations to its revolutionary war ally. On 2 July 1796 the French government announced that it would treat neutral powers the way the British treated them; namely, France would renew its seizure of American merchant vessels. When Republican James Monroe, who had replaced Gouverneur Morris as minister to France, suggested that Federalists like Washington and Adams would be thrown out of office in the election of 1796, the president recalled him. The Directory, the new French government, determined that it would not receive another American minister plenipotentiary until its grievances had been resolved.

Efforts to resolve the issues between the two countries produced the notorious XYZ Affair, in which French officials sought to bribe an American delegation for the mere privilege of meeting with them. In response to this perceived insult Congress, during the summer of 1798, declared all treaties with France abrogated. President John Adams, who had succeeded George Washington, was authorized to employ the navy to protect American merchant ships from French spoliation in the Atlantic Ocean. Additionally, American merchant vessels were authorized to arm themselves for defensive purposes and to seize French armed vessels if attacked. On 2 March 1799, Congress created the Department of the Navy.

THE NINETEENTH CENTURY

The so-called Quasi-War with France lasted until 1801. President Adams wisely took advantage of a change in the French government and negotiated the Convention of 1800, destroying his chances at reelection in 1796. Many Federalists, including Hamilton, who sought a war with France and an Anglo-American rapprochement, felt betrayed by Adams. The convention abrogated the 1778 alliance with France, but retained the commercial provisions and liberal definition of neutral rights characteristic of the earlier commercial treaty. This agreement, together with the Peace of Amiens (1802) that temporarily ended the European war, enabled the United States to pursue a course independent of the European conflict while at the same time maintaining its neutral rights. Under the provisions of the Convention of 1800, the interdiction on American trade pertaining to all countries except Great Britain and France was removed, and the president was authorized to permit trade with the two great powers if they should cease violating the neutral trade of the United States. However, with the resumption of war between Great Britain and France, and its expansion by 1805 with the formation of the Third Coalition against Napoleon, each side sought to gain advantage by shutting off the other's trade. In this deadly duel between the leading belligerents, neutral rights were once again neither recognized or respected.

In 1805, in the case of the *Essex*, a British admiralty court ruled that the practice by which American ships carried goods from French colonies to France, with only a brief stop in an American port, did not constitute a broken voyage but, in reality, was a continuous voyage. Thus, French goods were not neutralized and were therefore subject to seizure. Consequently, Britain passed a series of orders in council designed to impose a blockade of all ports controlled by France, thereby forcing American vessels to go first to Great Britain, pay fees, and allow their goods to be subject to search and seizure. France retaliated with its Berlin and Milan Decrees, placing an embargo on all trade with Britain, and ordering the seizure of all ships that had paid the fees demanded by the Orders in Council, arguing that neutral vessels which did so were no longer neutral but British, and thus liable to seizure. Subsequent decrees also allowed for the arrest of American ships in ports controlled by France and the confiscation of their cargoes. These and subsequent acts and other retaliatory measures by both belligerents, although primarily directed toward each other, nonetheless violated American rights and severely threatened American trade with Europe and its colonies. Lacking effective military and naval power to protect its shipping, the United States attempted through negotiations with Britain, and peaceable economic coercion directed at both Britain and France, to force both belligerents to respect American neutral rights. The Monroe-Pinkney Treaty (1806) with Britain failed to achieve guarantees for American neutral rights. In fact, so unsatisfactory was the treaty that President Thomas Jefferson refused even to submit it to the Senate for ratification.

Calculating that American trade was essential to the British, and to a lesser extent to the French, the United States employed coercive measures, beginning with the Non-Importation Act of 1806. This measure prohibited certain British manufactures from being exported to the United States. In 1807 Jefferson imposed the Embargo Act, a measure that prohibited American ships from leaving American ports. Although many American merchant vessels failed to adhere to the embargo, particularly as time elapsed and it failed to achieve its objectives, the embargo still severely restricted American trade, caused a depression, and produced intense political and sectional feelings in the country. In 1809 British minister David Erskine negotiated the Erskine Agreement with the United States, and President Madison prematurely lifted the embargo. When the treaty reached England, it was repudiated by the British government and Madison, somewhat humiliated, was forced to reimpose the embargo.

In 1809, under severe economic and political pressures, the Madison administration replaced the Embargo and the Non-Importation Act with a watered-down version of the embargo known as the Non-Intercourse Act. This measure opened trade to the world, except for Britain, France, and their possessions. In 1810 the Non-Intercourse Act was replaced by Macon's Bill No. 2, which reopened trade with even Britain and France, but stipulated that if one belligerent rescinded its restrictive measures, the United States would then impose nonintercourse against the other. When Napoleon's government implied that it was rescinding the Continental Decrees against American commerce, Madison jumped at the promise on face value when, in reality, France continued to seize American ships and cargoes. As Britain refused to rescind its orders in council when evidence confirmed that France had not actually stopped violating American neutral rights, Madison issued a proclamation, backed by the Non-Importation Act of 1811, prohibiting British goods from being imported into the United States.

Although the United States resented both Great Britain and France, the issues with the British were more long-standing and had greater impact. Many factors contributed to the War of 1812 with Britain, but certainly violation of American neutral rights, impressment of American seamen, and defense of national honor were major contributing factors. The war ended with neither belligerent achieving its expressed purposes. However, the establishment of peace and the conclusion of an Anglo-American treaty of commerce, as well as an agreement to limit naval armaments on the Great Lakes and to settle boundary and fisheries disputes, launched a new relationship between the two nations. After the Treaty of Ghent of 1814, which ended the war with Britain, and the conclusion of the Napoleonic Wars in 1815, there were no major maritime wars for the rest of the century. Thus ended an epoch in the American struggle for neutral rights.

A new phase in the American policy of neutrality was brought about by revolutions in the colonies of Spanish America. Officially, the United States did not play a role in these revolutions and was not particularly concerned about them until such time as any had established permanent governments and therefore warranted recognition as independent states. However, when it looked like one or more European powers might assist Spain in restoring its American empire, President James

Monroe in 1823 issued a message to Congress, largely written by Secretary of State John Quincy Adams, that came to be known as the Monroe Doctrine. In essence, Monroe's message was a reaffirmation of the Doctrine of the Two Spheres. It also announced that while the United States would refrain from involvement in European affairs, it opposed any further European colonization of the Western Hemisphere, an extension of Europe's political systems to American states, or efforts to interfere in their internal affairs. Although Congress did not confirm the Monroe Doctrine and there was no occasion that developed immediately to test it, it became a cornerstone of American foreign policy and a justification for future acts that attempted to establish U.S. hegemony in the Western Hemisphere in the decades to follow.

From 1823 until the American Civil War, the United States had no serious problems regarding neutrality. It officially maintained a neutral position during the Texas War for Independence (1835–1836) and the Canadian Uprising of 1837. During the Mexican War (1846–1848) the United States was able to establish an effective, and therefore legal, blockade of Mexican ports. When the Crimean War broke out in 1854, Britain and France agreed to a set of principles that were later codified and proclaimed by the leading European nations as the Declaration of Paris of 1856. This declaration acknowledged the long-standing American position that free ships make free goods, and that a blockade must be effective to be legal. It also contained the principles that noncontraband goods on enemy ships should be free from capture and that privateers should not be commissioned. As the United States was unwilling to surrender its right to commission privateers, and as it hoped to secure an additional agreement that all private property except contraband would be free, it failed to endorse the declaration. Ironically, after the outbreak of the American Civil War in 1861, the United States agreed to adhere to the declaration if its provisions were applied to the Confederacy. This offer was rejected by such nations as Britain and France.

The beginning of the Civil War saw the United States in an anomalous situation regarding its position on neutrality. War was not declared against the Confederacy, nor was belligerent status accorded it. Rather, the administration of Abraham Lincoln considered Union military operations to be a police action against rebellious citizens. Given this view, when Lincoln proclaimed a blockade of Confederate ports on 19 April 1861, it was a domestic action and did not have to be effective in order to be legal. However, when Britain declared neutrality on 13 May 1861, it in effect granted the Confederacy belligerent status that, among other things, meant Britain would consider a blockade of Confederate ports subject to the usual rules of international law. Since the United States did not have sufficient naval power to make the blockade effective until later in the war, the Confederate government, while also pursuing diplomatic recognition, hoped that European nations would challenge the blockade's legality. This did not occur, however, largely because Great Britain concluded that its long-term interests would be best served by accepting the Union interpretation of a blockade's effectiveness. Before the end of the war, Confederate trade with Europe was almost completely stifled because of superior Union naval strength and the capture of major Confederate ports.

In addition to its position on blockade, the United States adopted the doctrine of continuous voyage, a principle taken from British prize law: a ship carrying contraband goods for a belligerent could be captured on the high seas in voyage from a neutral port to another neutral port whenever such a port was only a way station and not the ultimate destination of the cargo. The adoption and use of this doctrine by the United States established a precedent in American policy that was useful to Britain and the Allies in their conflict with the Central Powers when the United States was still a neutral state prior to its entry into World War I.

One incident occurred during the Civil War that caused the British to assert their rights as a neutral. This was the *Trent* affair of 8 November 1861, when an American naval vessel on the high seas stopped a British mail steamer, the *Trent*. On board were two Confederate diplomats on their way to England. The ship was boarded and the two diplomats were arrested and sent to prison in Boston. News of this violation of British neutral rights produced an immediate response from the British government, which demanded the release of the Confederates and an apology. For a short time there was even talk of war as the British undertook preparations. On the American side, with no desire for war with Britain given its preoccupation with the challenges of civil war, Secretary of State William H. Seward acquiesced to British demands and conflict was averted.

Aside from the *Trent* affair, the most significant conflict over neutral rights and duties during the Civil War was the construction and outfitting of warships (designed to be commerce raiders). This was significant primarily in relations between the United States and Britain, whose laws permitted—as did international law—the sale of merchant ships to belligerents, but prohibited the sale of warships. The Confederacy sought to circumvent this prohibition by having vessels built ostensibly as merchant ships, but constructed in such a way so as to be easily converted into warships at sea or in a Confederate port. The most notorious case, albeit not the only one, was the Confederate cruiser *Alabama*. The United States contended that Great Britain had failed to live up to its obligations as a neutral by allowing the *Alabama* to leave British waters. The British government asserted that the *Alabama* was a merchant vessel until it was significantly altered and equipped with naval armament in a Confederate port. This controversy continued throughout the Civil War, and was not resolved until the Treaty of Washington in 1871. In addition to the United States being awarded $15.5 million by an international tribunal, the significance of the treaty was in the concession by Great Britain that a neutral had an obligation to use "due diligence" in preventing a ship from being built "in whole or in part" as a warship for a belligerent. Although only signatories were bound by the treaty, the principle was subsequently incorporated in a convention on the rights and duties of neutrals at the Second Hague Conference (1907), the difference being that the imprecise rule of "due diligence" was changed to the obligation of a neutral to use the "means at its disposal."

THE TWENTIETH CENTURY

During the years between the American Civil War and the outbreak of World War I, the United States experienced no serious problems connected with its own neutral rights. While promoting its strategic interests, the United States failed in one situation to adhere strictly to its obligations as a neutral nation and to live up to its treaty obligations. During the Panamanian Revolution of 1903, the United States departed from its neutral position by preventing the landing in Panama of Colombian troops attempting to suppress the revolution. In the same action, the United States violated its treaty obligations with Colombia in a 1846 treaty that pledged the United States to guarantee the "rights of sovereignty and property" of Colombia over the Isthmus of Panama. In 1921 the United States compensated Colombia for its loss of Panama.

At the Second Hague Conference, the United States sought to secure an agreement on the rights and duties of neutrals that included the principle that had been advocated by the United States since 1784: that noncontraband neutral private property was exempt from capture. Although the conference adopted a convention on neutral rights, so many significant issues remained unresolved, such as the one of private property, that a separate meeting of the major maritime powers was organized to consider those issues. They met in London in 1908, and the following year issued the Declaration of London. The declaration provided for the most extensive and, as far as neutrals were concerned, the most liberal rules governing neutral trade that had ever been achieved. Although they did not prohibit the capture of private property, they did enumerate an extensive list of free goods and limited the principle of continuous voyage to absolute contraband. Universal acceptance of the declaration would have benefited neutral trade with belligerents, and it would have assisted those belligerents who would have profited from such trade. However, it would have restricted other belligerents in the exercise of rights previously recognized under generally acceptable rules of international law. Consequently, Britain rejected the Declaration of London, and as universal ratification was not achieved, the United States did not ratify the treaty, although the Senate had consented to it.

When World War I began the United States, under President Woodrow Wilson, issued a declaration of neutrality on 4 August 1914. Issues concerning American neutral rights arose most seriously with Britain and Germany. The British did not establish a traditional close blockade of German ports. Rather, it gradually expanded the contraband list to include goods that could be used to manufacture war materials and those that would be of significant value to the German war effort. The British also made extensive use of the doctrine of continuous voyage. The United States protested British maritime practices; however, Britain possessed a basis in international law for its policies. No precise lists of contraband had ever been universally accepted. The idea that some materials on a free list might become contraband had been a feature of treaties since the seventeenth century. During the American Civil War, the United States had added naval stores and "articles of like character with those specifically enumerated" to the contraband list. The doctrine of continuous voyage was also firmly based in international practice and had been sanctioned by the United States during the Civil War. Even under the Declaration of London (1909), in which the principle of continuous voyage was limited to absolute contraband, the legal extension of such contraband was admitted. Although the United States might have protested the extremes to which Britain carried its maritime policies, it had no solid basis in international law to deny their validity, nor did it grant to the Allies rights prohibited to the Central Powers. General American sympathy for the Allied cause, plus ties of culture and economics, precluded the United States from forcefully defending its neutral rights, or engaging in retaliation as it had during the Napoleonic Wars. Furthermore, Germany's reliance upon the submarine, which caused not only property damage but also the loss of lives, came for most Americans to overshadow any actions by Great Britain.

The conflict between the United States and Germany stemmed largely from German insistence upon the use of unrestricted submarine warfare. The United States did not oppose a German blockade of Allied ports if the blockade were proclaimed and effective, nor did it deny the right of Germany to stop neutral ships on the high seas and to seize both the cargo and the ship if it carried contraband. In an attempt to break the tightening of the British blockade and deny the British supplies from across the Atlantic, Germany—in a proclamation of 4 February 1915—declared a war zone in the waters around Britain, including the English Channel. Germany threatened to sink all merchant vessels, including neutrals, without warning or providing for the safety of passengers and crew. The United States replied on 10 March 1915 that if American ships were so destroyed or American lives lost, this would be "an indefensible violation of neutral rights" and that it would "take any steps it might be necessary to take to safeguard American lives and property."

Although early attacks on American ships prompted protests from the United States, it was not until the sinking of the British liner *Lusitania* on 7 May 1915, with the loss of 1,198 lives, including 128 Americans, that the American government vehemently protested. In the first *Lusitania* note from the Wilson government to Germany, the United States insisted that German submarines stop firing on merchant vessels. In a second *Lusitania* note, the United States threatened direct action if Germany did not stop its unrestricted use of the submarine against merchant vessels. In a conciliatory reply and an offer for compensation, Germany sought to defuse the situation with the United States. However, on 19 August 1915 the British liner *Arabic* was sunk, claiming two Americans. To stave off possible American retaliation, Germany issued the so-called *Arabic* Pledge, a promise that submarines would not attack passenger ships without providing warning and making provisions to rescue passengers and crews. In March 1916 a German submarine torpedoed the French liner *Sussex,* resulting in the injury of two Americans. From the American perspective, this appeared to be a violation of the *Arabic* Pledge and Wilson threatened to break off diplomatic relations. The German government once again tried to assuage the Americans by reaffirming the *Arabic* Pledge.

Germany had failed to achieve military victory by the summer of 1916. With serious political and social problems developing at home, and the German high command concerned about the will of the German people to continue the war, a last major all-out offensive on the western front was planned for the spring of 1917. In a desperate gamble designed to deprive the Allies of vital foodstuffs and materials, the German government resumed unrestricted submarine warfare on 1 February 1917, fully aware that this was likely to bring the United States into the war on the side of the Allies. The United States broke off diplomatic relations with Germany. Following the sinking of several U.S. ships by German submarines in March, the United States declared war on Germany on 6 April 1917. Several factors contributed to American entry into the war, but preservation of neutral rights was a key one.

By the end of World War I, President Wilson had determined that in the interests of humanity, as well as national security, a new approach to world peace was necessary. He was able to convince most of the major statesmen in the world to accept this need and the Covenant of the League of Nations was the outcome. The signatories to the covenant agreed "to preserve as against external aggression the territorial integrity and existing political independence of all Members of the League." If a member of the league resorted to war in disregard of its obligations under the covenant, then members of the league would prohibit all trade and financial relations with the covenant-violating state. Furthermore, nonmembers of the league would also be required to abide by these sanctions. Thus, the traditional rights of neutrals to trade with belligerents would be prohibited. However, when Japan violated the Covenant in 1931 by invading Manchuria, and Italy followed in 1935 with its invasion of Abyssinia, the league failed to impose sanctions at all in the first case, and only partially and ineffectively in the second. The league system of collective security collapsed. The extent to which American refusal to join the league contributed to the failure of the League of Nations failure is debatable.

In the twenty years after World War I, the United States rejected the League of Nations, pursued nationalistic economic policies, promoted naval arms limitations, and signed feeble and useless pacts, such as the Kellogg-Briand Pact of 1928 and the London Naval Treaties of 1930 and 1936. At the same time it focused overwhelmingly on domestic affairs and displayed apparent indifference to the moral and political disintegration of world order. When the specter of another world war arose, the nation naively sought to isolate itself from world affairs and pursued safety in the abandonment of its once-cherished neutral rights, for which it had fought two foreign wars. American neutrality had never meant simply noninvolvement in world affairs. Rather, it meant the determination to support the rights of its people under rules of international law that, in turn, would contribute to the civilized conduct of nations.

This reversal of America's traditional policy was accomplished through a series of congressional neutrality acts commencing in 1935 and reaching their most comprehensive form in the Neutrality Act of 1937. Believing that American insistence upon its historical defense of neutral rights, along with the greed of bankers and arms merchants, had helped to suck the United States into World War I, Congress passed legislation that in essence repudiated traditional American views of neutral rights. Under these acts, if the president determined that a "state of war" existed among two or more foreign states, American citizens were prohibited from exporting arms, munitions, or implements of war to belligerents or to neutrals for transshipment to belligerents, or to a state where civil strife existed. The selling of securities or making of loans was prohibited, as was travel by American citizens on belligerent ships. American merchant vessels were not to be armed, and they were prohibited from carrying materials of war. Nonprohibited goods could be sold to belligerents, provided the title to them was transferred before being transported abroad. By renouncing its historical interpretation of neutral rights, so the thinking went, the United States could hope to escape being drawn into another foreign war.

Commensurate with this "new neutrality" policy, the United States moved to strengthen relations with Latin American nations. The Neutrality Act of 1937 specifically exempted Latin American states from its application in case of war between one or more of them and a non-American state. In a series of conferences between the United States and Latin America, beginning at Buenos Aires in 1936, the American republics agreed to preserve their neutrality and to act in concert in the event of any threat to their safety or independence. However, when war broke out in Europe and the United States began to alter its neutrality policies, it acted independently of its Latin American neighbors. During World War II some Latin American states that remained neutral referred to their status as "nonbelligerency," a term without precise meaning in international law, but in reality an extension of commercial rights to the United States not accorded to other belligerents.

The "new neutrality" policy failed for many reasons. In actuality, under President Franklin D. Roosevelt the United States was not about to stand idly by and let the world be dominated by the aggressors who had signed the Tripartite Pact. Presidential acts as well as congressional measures eroded the new policy. President Roosevelt refused to recognize that a state of war existed between Japan and China, or between Russia and Finland. In the destroyers-for-bases deal of 1940, he sold or traded World War I–vintage warships to Great Britain, and extended the Monroe Doctrine to include the mid-Atlantic. In 1939 Congress repealed the arms embargo provisions of the Neutrality Act of 1937, cut trade with Japan, and passed the Lend-Lease Act of 1941, which in effect made the United States an unofficial ally of the nations opposing the Axis. By the end of October 1941, a virtual state of war existed between Germany and the United States, with President Roosevelt convinced that formal war would break out over some incident in the Atlantic between the two countries. However, as Japan was bent upon establishing its "greater East Asia co-prosperity sphere," Roosevelt—in an effort to pressure the

Japanese to relinquish their conquests in China and Southeast Asia—ultimately cut off all exports to Japan. Convinced that the United States meant to strangle Japan, its government in 1941 undertook plans to attack and, if possible, destroy the American Pacific fleet. When the attack on Pearl Harbor came on 7 December 1941, followed in quick succession with an American declaration of war on the Japanese Empire and German and Italian declarations of war on the United States, history witnessed the end of the United States as a neutral nation, at least in a traditional sense.

Prior to the formal conclusion of World War II, the United States reversed its traditional policy for the second time since 1920 by playing the leading role in establishing the United Nations. While the Charter of the United Nations differed significantly from the Covenant of the League of Nations, its impact on the concept of neutrality was basically the same. The Security Council of the United Nations was assigned the primary responsibility for world peace and for taking action against a state deemed to have threatened the peace of the world. Such action could be in the form of economic sanctions, which have had the effect of eroding the historical rights of neutrals.

Because of the preeminent political, economic, and military position of the United States in world affairs since the end of World War II, the nation was involved in numerous armed conflicts, some of which, like Vietnam, were protracted, even though war was never declared. The United States intervened, covertly and overtly, throughout the world where it felt its interests, or its vision of a desirable world order, was threatened, with little regard to concepts of neutral rights. In other situations, such as in the Korean War or the Persian Gulf War, the United States operated under the umbrella of the United Nations. Neutrality, a cornerstone of American foreign policy since before the establishment of the republic, was no longer relevant. Although there were some in the United States who hoped the country could once again return to an independent, neutral position in the world, President Harry S. Truman and other policymakers pursued international economic and military policies that were essential for the promotion of international trade, expansion of democratic ideals, prevention of another postwar depression, and stopping the spread of communism.

The wartime conferences at Yalta and Potsdam, followed by a series of Council of Foreign Ministers' meetings, were characterized by mutual suspicion and mistrust, and foreshadowed the rivalry that would come to be called the Cold War. Although the Western powers were already skeptical of Soviet intentions in territories they had liberated in Eastern Europe, the issue over Iran gave cause for Western alarm. In late 1945 a communist-orchestrated revolution broke out in the oil-rich region of Azerbaijan in northern Iran, particularly when the Soviets sent troops and arms to assist the revolutionaries. In addition, the Soviets failed to pull out of Iran in March 1946, as they had agreed previously. Although the Soviets withdrew in May after receiving minor concessions from Iran, their actions in the Near East, commensurate with increasing tensions in Eastern Europe, helped convince Truman that Soviet leader Joseph Stalin meant no good. Winston Churchill's Iron Curtain speech in March 1946, a United States decision against a loan to the Soviets, the termination of German reparations to the USSR from the American occupation zone in Germany, American promotion of the Baruch Plan to control atomic weapons testing and development, and other issues concerning Germany heightened the feelings of mistrust between the Western powers and the Soviets.

The United States was anything but neutral in the Greek civil war and was extremely concerned about Soviet pressure on Turkey. If successful there, the Soviets would gain access to the Persian Gulf, the Mediterranean, and the oil-rich Middle East. Western Europe would most likely collapse and the British Mediterranean barrier to Soviet expansion and influence would be breached if Greece and Turkey fell.

Fighting had broken out in Greece in December 1944 between rightists, who tended to support the return of the monarchist government in exile, and communists. Under the terms of an uneasy truce reached at Varkiza in February 1946, an election was to be held to determine the form of government, and then another election was to take place for a constituent assembly. However, in the days before the election the conservative government repressed the opposition to the monarchy. By the time the election was to occur in March, both the British and the Americans had reneged on the procedures agreed to at Varkiza. Although a general election and plebiscite were held, the communists boycotted them. The results seemingly indicated support for the return of the king. These actions set off a civil war that was largely internal in origin. Many Americans, however, assumed it was Soviet coordinated, and by the spring of 1947 the situation seemed critical.

The gravity of the Greek situation, coinciding as it did with Soviet demands on Turkey and the notification by Britain in the fall of 1947 that it could no longer afford to maintain its commitments to Greece and Turkey, compelled President Truman to act. The result was what became known as the Truman Doctrine, the provisions of which were enumerated before a joint session of Congress on 12 March 1947. In addressing Congress, Truman stated "that it must be the policy of the United States to support free peoples who are resisting attempted subjugation by armed minorities or by outside pressures." The Truman Doctrine, although initially directed at Greece and Turkey, had as its primary goal the "containment" of communism. The Truman Doctrine represented a watershed in American history. This policy it represented became the justification for American intervention, covertly and overtly, in the internal affairs of nations throughout the world, and it formed the basis for the establishment of regional security treaties that were directed against the Soviet Union and its perceived allies. The United States sought to contain communism in Europe through such measures as the Truman Doctrine, the Marshall Plan, and the formation of NATO, and virtually every other part of the world witnessed American interventions calculated to stop communism's spread.

In Asia the United States' major concern was China. As World War II came to an end, civil war in China between the nationalist armies under Chiang Kai-shek, and the communists under Mao Zedong, resumed. Each side hoped to secure territory and supplies by accepting the surrender of Japanese troops in China and Manchuria. Although outwardly encouraging talks between the two rival factions, the United States nonetheless moved its troops and transported nationalist soldiers into key eastern and northern Chinese cities in order to accept the Japanese surrender. In northern China and Manchuria, fighting broke out between the two groups. The communists were assisted by the Soviets in Manchuria, and the nationalists were assisted by the Americans. Although American lend-lease assistance to its other allies had ended, it was continued in the case of China. In January 1946 it seemed that there was a glimmer of hope when President Truman sent General George C. Marshall to China as a special envoy to get the two sides to talk. The truce, however, proved illusory as each side maneuvered to gain the upper hand. The resulting civil war was one of the most bitter and devastating in modern history. In the end, Chiang Kai-shek could not command the same level of popular support as Mao and the communists proclaimed victory in October 1949, with Chiang fleeing to Taiwan. The "loss" of China subjected the Truman administration to severe political criticism for not doing enough for China. In the final analysis, short of an all-out effort to support the Nationalists, nothing could have been done to prevent their defeat. Also, for Truman the most important foreign policy priority was shoring up Europe against Soviet threats. The thirty-year treaty of alliance negotiated by Mao and the Soviet Union in 1950 was further evidence to many Americans that worldwide communism was being orchestrated by the Soviets. As far as China was concerned, American efforts to contain communism had failed.

For the United States, intervention in Asian affairs would prove extremely frustrating. Under the umbrella of the United Nations, the Cold War suddenly became a hot war with the eruption of the Korean conflict in 1950, and at the beginning of the twenty-first century the peace between North and South Korea remained precarious. In Vietnam, the United States—influenced by the domino theory and convinced of its ability to impose an outcome because of its superior strength—foolishly involved itself in what was essentially a civil war in Vietnam. For two decades the United States was caught up in a quagmire that, in the end, witnessed consolidation of the country by the communists. What the United States had tried so hard to prevent came about anyway.

In the Western Hemisphere, the United States did not hesitate to intervene in the internal affairs of governments closer to its borders than those of Asia, Europe, the Middle East, or Africa. In countries such as Nicaragua, the United States supported right-wing dictators including General Anastasio Somoza. In Chile the Central Intelligence Agency played a significant role in a coup that saw the overthrow and subsequent death of the popularly elected Marxist president Salvador Allende, who was succeeded by the anticommunist and repressive General Augusto Pinochet. The United States openly intervened in Guatemala, the Dominican Republic, and other countries because of the belief that American interests were greatly threatened by governments that included communists or suspected communists. However, the stakes were never so high as they were in Cuba, first with the Bay of Pigs invasion in 1961, then with the Cuban Missile Crisis of October 1962, which saw the world come to the brink of nuclear war as the Americans and Soviets stared down each other.

In the last decades of the twentieth century, the United States did not hesitate to continue intervening in the internal affairs of numerous nations around the word. However, there have been occasions where it sought to maintain the outward appearance of neutrality, particularly in the case of the Iran-Iraq War (1980–1988). This war threatened to drag in other nations in a geopolitically sensitive part of the world. Passage through the Persian Gulf was threatened, which in turn posed a serious threat to oil interests. While the Soviet Union shrewdly tried to cater to both sides, the United States claimed it was neutral in the conflict. Clearly there was no love lost with Iran, what with the Iran hostage crisis still fresh in Americans' minds, and relations with Iraq had only recently improved after the State Department removed Iraq from the official list of nations that sanctioned terrorism. Although publicly opposed to arms sales to Iraq, the United States nonetheless sent a large quantity of arms and supplies to Iraq's ruler, Saddam Hussein. As the administration of President Ronald Reagan became more involved in the Middle East, its preference for Iraq over Iran became evident. Ironically, in the subsequent Gulf War of 1991, the United States under President George H. W. Bush put together a United Nations coalition of forty-eight countries against Hussein.

It may be premature to suggest that the concept of neutrality has come full circle since the Treaty of Westphalia and that the historical rights of neutrals under international law no longer exist. Conceivably, a war could take place in which the United Nations would not interfere and belligerents and neutrals would assert their traditional rights. However, given the realities of the modern world, particularly since the end of World War II, and the proliferation of nuclear weapons, this does not seem to be a likely prospect. In the years since 1941, the traditional concept of American neutrality seems to have been irreversibly transformed.

BIBLIOGRAPHY

Bernath, Stuart L. *Squall Across the Atlantic: American Civil War Prize Cases and Diplomacy.* Berkeley, Calif., 1970. A superb monograph that examines the doctrine of continuous voyage.

Borchard, Edwin M., and William P. Lange. *Neutrality for the United States.* 2d ed. New Haven, Conn., 1940. Focuses on the issues involving American neutrality during the 1930s.

Bowman, Albert Hall. *The Struggle for Neutrality: Franco-American Diplomacy During the Federalist Era.* Knoxville, Tenn., 1974. An excellent account of the early problems with France, particularly from the French perspective.

Dallek, Robert. *Franklin D. Roosevelt and American Foreign Policy, 1932–1945.* New York, 1979. In this comprehensive account of Roosevelt's diplomacy, the president fares well given the constraints under which he operated.

DeConde, Alexander. *Entangling Alliance: Politics and Diplomacy Under George Washington.* Durham, N.C., 1958. One of the standard works on politics and diplomacy during the Washington administration, it examines European-American conflicts over neutrality.

———. *The Quasi-War: The Politics and Diplomacy of the Undeclared War with France, 1797–1801.* New York, 1966. The most authoritative work on the subject.

Devlin, Patrick. *Too Proud to Fight: Woodrow Wilson's Neutrality.* New York, 1975. Considerable attention is given to the legal problems of neutrality.

Divine, Robert A. *The Illusion of Neutrality.* Chicago, 1962. A scholarly survey of the origins and consequences of the Neutrality Acts of 1935 to 1939.

Drummond, Donald F. *The Passing of American Neutrality, 1937–1941.* Ann Arbor, Mich., 1955. A good overview of the history of American neutrality, with an emphasis on the forces and events that transformed American policy between 1937 and 1941.

Fenwick, Charles G. *International Law.* 4th ed. New York, 1965. A good general survey of the principles of international law.

Gilbert, Felix. *To the Farewell Address: Ideas of Early American Foreign Policy.* Princeton, N.J., 1961.

Horsman, Reginald. *The Causes of the War of 1812.* Philadelphia, 1962.

Jessup, Philip C., et al. *Neutrality: Its History, Economics, and Law.* 4 vols. New York, 1936. The most authoritative and detailed study on the history of neutrality up to its publication date.

Link, Arthur S. *Wilson*. 5 vols. Princeton, N.J., 1947–1965. The most comprehensive study of Woodrow Wilson, whose neutrality policies are explored in volumes 3 through 5.

May, Ernest R. *The World War and American Isolation, 1914–1917*. 2d ed. Chicago, 1966.

Meecham, J. Lloyd. *The United States and Inter-American Security, 1889–1960*. Austin, Tex., 1961. Includes accounts of American efforts to secure a unified neutrality policy and hemispheric security with Latin America prior to and during World War II.

Ørvik, Nils. *The Decline of Neutrality, 1914–1941*. Oslo, Norway, 1953.

Pares, Richard. *Colonial Blockade and Neutral Rights, 1739–1763*. Oxford, 1938. Although an older work, it has relevance for understanding eighteenth-century maritime law.

Perkins, Bradford. *Prologue to War: England and the United States, 1805–1812*. Berkeley, Calif., 1961. A fine study of Anglo-American conflicts that led to the War of 1812.

———. *Castlereagh and Adams: England and the United States, 1812–1823*. Berkeley, Calif., 1964. Examines the Anglo-American conflict over neutral rights.

Porter, David L. *The Seventy-sixth Congress and World War II, 1939–1940*. Columbia, Mo., and London, 1979. Examines the role of Congress in enacting neutrality revision.

Savelle, Max. *The Origins of American Diplomacy: The International History of Angloamerica, 1492–1763*. New York, 1967. The most detailed examination of European treaties and agreements that helped shape early American foreign policy relative to the Doctrine of the Two Spheres.

Trefousse, Hans J. *Germany and American Neutrality, 1939–1941*. New York, 1951. A study of the German response to American neutrality policies prior to U.S. entry into World War II.

See also ARMED NEUTRALITIES; BLOCKADE; CIVIL WAR DIPLOMACY; THE CONTINENTAL SYSTEM; DOCTRINES; EMBARGOES AND SANCTIONS; FREEDOM OF THE SEAS; INTERNATIONAL LAW; NAVAL DIPLOMACY; TREATIES.

NORTH ATLANTIC TREATY ORGANIZATION

Klaus Larres

The North Atlantic Treaty Organization (NATO) was founded on 4 April 1949 in Washington, D.C. On behalf of the United States, the North Atlantic Treaty was signed by Dean Acheson, secretary of state throughout President Harry S. Truman's second term. The founding members of the Atlantic alliance consisted of the United States, United Kingdom, France, Canada, Norway, Denmark, Iceland, Belgium, the Netherlands, Luxembourg, Portugal, and Italy. The U.S. Senate ratified the treaty on 21 July 1949 by a vote of 82 to 13; it entered into force on 14 August 1949. By joining the North Atlantic pact, the Truman administration turned its back on the many voices in the American political establishment and the country at large that favored a return to the political isolationism of the interwar years. After all, isolationists were able to go as far back as George Washington's Farewell Address, in which he admonished his fellow Americans to beware of the Europeans and "to have with them as little political connection as possible." But U.S. membership in the United Nations in 1945 had indicated that the country intended to stay involved in international political affairs. Subsequently, the 1947–1948 Marshall Plan made clear that the United States felt it was in its national interest to use its massive economic and financial resources to help in the reconstruction of Europe. This, it was hoped, would stabilize the old continent, prevent it from becoming once again a hotbed of nationalist fervor and civil war and, not least, make it immune to the forces of international communism. But even after the European Recovery Program (ERP) had been announced, it was still a major step to enter into a close military association. By committing the United States to NATO and thus to a formal and long-lasting entangling military alliance in peacetime, the North Atlantic Treaty of April 1949 marked, as Lawrence Kaplan put it, a "radical transformation in American foreign policy."

It is unlikely that this almost revolutionary development in U.S. political thinking would have come about without the Cold War and the global ideological and political power struggle with the Soviet Union. With the signing of the North Atlantic Treaty the United States indicated its willingness—after much prodding by the United Kingdom and other leading European nations—to accede to the role of protector of western Europe. The Truman administration clearly hoped that with the help of both the Marshall Plan and NATO, U.S. influence, and indeed its example, would help the countries of the old continent to integrate their political and above all economic and military systems in a peaceful and stabilizing way. It was expected that eventually a united and federally organized Europe would evolve in a manner similar to the development of the United States 150 years previously.

One should not credit the leading U.S. politicians of the day and organs like the State Department's Policy Planning Staff too much with a visionary long-term strategy: much came about by default and by means of ad hoc reactions to unexpected developments. Still, quite a few elements of a coherent and well-considered strategy can be detected in American foreign policy after World War II. Much thought was for example dedicated to the perennial German question. It was hoped that the unification of the European continent would defuse the German problem by incorporating this large and potentially still powerful and economically important country into a peaceful and fully integrated European system.

In view of the perceived military threat from the Soviet Union and the weakness of the Western world in terms of conventional warfare capabilities, America's unrivaled nuclear security umbrella was initially gladly accepted by all members. In fact, possession of the atomic bomb and Washington's apparent willingness to use this weapon if necessary in response to an attack on any NATO member was the basis for Washington's hegemonic position in the Atlantic alliance. NATO allowed the United States to carve out a clear sphere of interest for itself. Washington's overwhelming military and also economic and political strength as well as its supremacy within NATO and the Western alliance enabled the United States to form what in the 1960s came to be called bluntly "the American Empire." In the 1970s and 1980s, when Europe's important role in the early Cold War and the creation of NATO was belatedly recognized, many historians began to refer to Washington's dominance somewhat more benevolently as an "empire by invitation." Yet the existence of American hegemony was disputed by very few European observers. Americans, however, often tended to regard their country's superiority in the Western alliance as the realization of Thomas Jefferson's well-meaning "empire of liberty." While to some extent Washington's role as a benign but still vastly powerful and at times quite autocratic leader rested on its economic strength and its political influence, primarily it was American dominance of NATO that furnished it with formidable global importance.

This explains why both the Bush and the Clinton administrations strongly objected to any thoughts of abandoning NATO after the end of the Cold War in 1989–1991. The largely unchallenged American dominance of NATO was the most important and most powerful tool at the disposal of the United States to maintain its influence in Europe and beyond. More than a decade later this was still the case. In view of the increasingly frequent economic and trade as well as political and strategic disagreements in transatlantic relations in the early twenty-first century, Washington's efforts to bolster NATO and turn it into one of its main pillars of influence in the contemporary world was hardly surprising. NATO still provided the United States with a crucial instrument of global leadership. Moreover, in the aftermath of the entirely unexpected terrorist bombing of the World Trade Center in New York City and the Pentagon in Washington, D.C., in September 2001, NATO would also serve as the instrument that was able to provide the United States with crucial military and logistic help and indeed much needed political and moral support in the war against international terrorism.

CREATION OF NATO

The establishment of NATO in April 1949 rested upon a European and in particular a British initiative. As John Lewis Gaddis has written, it was "as explicit an invitation as has ever been extended from smaller powers to a great power to construct an empire and include them within it." However, in the circumstances of the times, considerations about American empire building and American dominance played a rather minor role. The Europeans were looking for military protection and economic and military aid to ensure their survival as democratic states. Some American observers have therefore concluded that the western Europeans deviously "entrapped" the United States. This is unjustified. The American political establishment of the time—both the Democratic administration and, until the election of 1948, the Republican leadership of Congress—realized very well that putting a stop to Soviet expansionist encroachments and maintaining democratic states with a liberal economic order on the European continent were very much in the national interest of the United States.

Yet, admittedly, without strenuous European attempts to persuade the Truman administration to come to the rescue of the European nation-states, American involvement might never have come about. What proved to be decisive for American support in both the economic and military sphere was evidence of European willingness to help themselves. This was Washington's condition for providing financial aid under the Marshall Plan and joining the European nations in talks about setting up a North Atlantic defensive alliance.

In the immediate aftermath of World War II, American policymakers, and in particular Secretary of State James Byrnes, were hopeful that some kind of modus vivendi could be found with Stalin's Soviet Union. Yet, this soon proved to be impossible. In March 1946, in Fulton, Missouri, Winston Churchill spoke of the iron curtain that was descending "from Stettin in the Baltic to Trieste in the Adriatic." A month before this well-publicized event, the U.S. diplomat George Kennan had already sent his influential Long Telegram from the Moscow embassy to Washington warning about Soviet expansionist intentions. As a result of these efforts, in the course of 1946 the foreign policy elite in Washington and American public opinion were becoming rather critical of Stalin's activities. It was a slow process, however, and the turning point only came in 1947. The tightening of Moscow's grip on the states of Eastern Europe, frequent difficulties with Moscow's ambitions in Turkey, Greece, and elsewhere, and increasingly tense East-West relations in occupied Germany made many contemporaries slowly aware of the apparently irreconcilable nature of Soviet and Western political aims. Of great importance was the ever more apparent economic weakness of Britain and the unsustainable nature of the country's long-standing imperial role. Crucially significant also was the state of near starvation and the considerable political and economic instability of much of western Europe. This propelled the United States into action.

In the Truman Doctrine of 12 March 1947, the United States declared that it would respond to the British request to assume responsibility for the support of the anticommunist forces in Greece and Turkey. Moreover, much less to Britain's liking, Truman also promised American support for the worldwide fight against international communism. Three months later, Secretary of State George Marshall, Acheson's predecessor, announced the European Recovery Program (ERP) in his speech at Harvard University on 5 June. The Marshall Plan was meant to provide economic assistance to the states of western Europe to enable them to withstand the onslaught of communist fifth columns. Otherwise communism's ideological temptations might well have held a tremendous attraction for the peoples of Europe who lacked food, housing, and heating fuel.

It was Washington's intention to stabilize and reconstruct the continent with the help of generous economic and financial aid. American policymakers recognized that only a united western Europe at peace with itself would be able to create a common front against the military and ideological threat from the Soviet Union. Only such a Europe would ensure the reconciliation of Germany with the countries of the Western world while avoiding tendencies toward neutralism and defeatism. Underlying America's postwar vision was the assumption that only a fully integrated, stable, and economically viable Europe would develop into a peaceful and democratic continent. The lessons from America's own past as well as the country's federalist structure were to serve as the model to achieve a single European market. This would prevent economic nationalism, lead to European prosperity, and form a truly free and multilateral transatlantic economic system.

It also was expected that in due course this strategy would have the advantage of making unnecessary the continuation of American economic aid to western Europe. Active American governmental support and interference were always regarded as temporary. It was hoped that European reconstruction would close the dollar gap, permit the convertibility of European currencies, allow the Europeans to export to the United States, and, not least, create a huge market for U.S. exporters. The latter would be important in avoiding the predicted domestic American recession. Washington therefore stipulated that most of the goods purchased with Marshall Plan aid had to be bought in the United States.

In his speech at Harvard, Marshall had spelled out that while the United States would give generous economic aid, the initiative for proposals on how best to make use of this aid for reconstruction and economic revival had to come from the Europeans themselves. British foreign secretary Ernest Bevin realized this; he regarded Marshall's offer as "a life-line to sinking men" to avert "the looming shadow of catastrophe" over western Europe. Together with his French counterpart Georges Bidault, he organized an international conference in Paris in June and July 1947. The conference led to the formation of the Committee of European Economic Cooperation and to the acceptance of decisive American economic and political involvement in the internal affairs of the countries of western Europe. Eventually, in April 1948, the European Recovery Program was set up and a new European Payments Union and the Organization for European Economic Cooperation (OEEC) were established. The latter was the organ responsible for the distribution of Marshall Plan aid to sixteen European nations and the western zones of Germany. Due to European disagreements and contrary to its original intention, Washington decided to become a direct participant in the running of the OEEC.

The Soviet Union, however, declined to accept the liberal-capitalist economic conditions Washington imposed as a precondition for participation in the ERP. Moreover, Moscow prevented Eastern European states like Poland and Czechoslovakia from accepting U.S. aid. According to some historians, the Soviet Union's self-exclusion may well have been a result secretly hoped for in Washington, as the United States had no interest in using American taxpayers' money to support the economic reconstruction of the communist world. Be this as it may, the nonparticipation of Eastern Europe meant that the Marshall Plan and the OEEC contributed to the widening of the economic, ideological, and political gulf in postwar Europe.

Although Marshall's speech was received with a great deal of hope in Europe, throughout

1947 and most of 1948 fear of a military invasion from the East stalked the western part of the continent. The spirit of the times was characterized by despondency and fatalism. Not only were Greece, France, and Italy, with their large communist parties, on the brink of civil war, but East-West relations in Germany, with the eastern zone firmly controlled by Stalin's lieutenants, were becoming ever icier. Questions such as reparations, four-power control of Germany's industrial heartland (the Ruhr Valley), and the desirability of the reestablishment of a central and united state were among the most contested.

It was the collapse of the London foreign ministers conference in December 1947 over disagreements regarding the future of Germany and the February 1948 communist coup and subsequent purges in Czechoslovakia that were decisive. These moved the United States toward participation in an Atlantic defense organization. In early 1948 both Ernest Bevin and Georges Bidault impressed on American leaders the urgency of the situation. Ever since he had become British foreign secretary in July 1945, it had been Bevin's primary aim to persuade the United States to remain committed to the security and well-being of the European continent. But in the absence of a lasting U.S. commitment to Europe, Bevin, in response to a French initiative, had signed the Treaty of Dunkirk on 4 March 1947. It established an Anglo-French bilateral military alliance with an anticipated duration of fifty years; the formal aim of the treaty was the prevention of renewed German militarism. Yet for both Britain and France the Dunkirk treaty represented merely a second-best solution as it did not involve the United States.

Shortly after the collapse of the foreign ministers conference, Bevin explained his idea of a Western union to Marshall and Bidault, who both heartily endorsed a new political and defensive agreement among Britain, France, and the Benelux countries. Bevin insisted, however, on the need for American assistance and participation in a loose and flexible "spiritual federation of the West." He told Marshall that the "salvation of the West depends on the formation of some form of union, formal or informal in character, in Western Europe, backed by the United States and the [British] Dominions." During an impressive speech in the House of Commons on 22 January 1948, Bevin officially proposed the establishment of a western European union; he did not hesitate to spell out that such a treaty would be directed against the threat posed to western Europe by the Soviet Union. The impact of the communist coup in Czechoslovakia in February and increasing Soviet intransigence over Berlin, which by June had led to the Berlin blockade crisis, confirmed the importance of Bevin's pronouncements.

On 17 March 1948 a treaty for European economic, political, cultural, and military cooperation with a duration of fifty years was signed in Brussels. Participants of this multilateral treaty, the anti-German tone of which was much milder than that of the Dunkirk treaty, were Britain, France, and the three Benelux countries. Unlike the Dunkirk treaty arrangements, the Brussels Treaty Organization (BTO) could be enlarged to include other members. The values of self-help and cooperation were emphasized in the treaty to impress the United States and, indeed, President Truman warmly welcomed the new organization. Nevertheless, the United States still needed to be persuaded to accept a European security commitment. Truman's enthusiastic welcome of the BTO and his unusual decision to maintain conscription in time of peace were hopeful signs.

Almost immediately after the Brussels treaty was concluded, top-secret Pentagon talks between Britain and the United States and Canada about the setting up of a North Atlantic defense organization took place. It is unlikely that these talks would have taken place without the prior formation of the BTO. However, the establishment of transatlantic military cooperation was still viewed in terms of cooperation between the BTO and the United States; neither American membership in the BTO nor the creation of a new treaty organization was yet envisaged.

Shortly after the Pentagon talks, from July 1948 to March 1949 the BTO and the United States and Canada entered into drawn-out negotiations for the establishment of some sort of Atlantic security organization. The aim of the talks was the achievement of a unanimous decision rather than merely a majority vote. Still, the Truman administration remained cautious. As Lawrence Kaplan has explained, opposition to the establishment of a joint American-European military alliance came from three major camps in the United States.

First, there was the still formidable opposition from isolationists who suspected that America was being asked to pull the European chestnuts out of the fire. These largely emotional and psychological pressures were difficult to satisfy. The administration, and in particular Secretary Acheson, embarked on a major effort of persuasion to win over as many isolationists in Congress as possible by, for example, emphasizing the harmony of interests between the UN Charter and the NATO treaty. But due to congressional pressure, and much to the dislike of the Europeans, Article 5 of the North Atlantic charter, in which an attack on one member was regarded as an attack on all and would lead to a joint war effort, had to be expressed much more vaguely than originally anticipated. Thus, not the Soviet Union or any other potential enemy but the U.S. Congress would in fact decide whether or not the United States would become involved in a war. Essentially, this was the result of the Vandenberg Resolution passed by the Senate in early June 1948. On the whole, however, the compromise achieved by Arthur Vandenberg, the influential Republican senator and chairman of the Senate Foreign Relations Committee, only slightly diluted the North Atlantic Treaty. However, when article 5 was invoked for the very first time after the terrorist bombing of the World Trade Center and the Pentagon on 11 September 2001, it occurred in an entirely unforeseen way and for a totally unexpected reason. During the Cold War it had always been expected that the United States would have to come to the aid of European countries to defend them against a Soviet invasion. But in September 2001, article 5 was invoked by NATO Secretary General Lord Robertson and the North Atlantic Council on the request of the U.S. administration to obtain NATO's political and military support in the fight against international terrorism.

Secondly, the Joint Chiefs of Staff and the U.S. military in general were more than doubtful whether the country had the resources to build up a transatlantic military alliance. Indeed, the Joint Chiefs feared that the resources Congress would be able to make available to the American military services would be greatly reduced if Washington decided to rearm the Europeans. Whether or not European rearmament went ahead, in view of Stalin's conventional superiority, the West would be helpless if faced with a Soviet invasion of Europe. Eventually, however, the Joint Chiefs realized that the proposed Mutual Defense Assistance Program would actually enable them to enlarge and modernize the equipment available to the army, navy, and air force. Moreover, the administration's willingness to listen to the military and to agree to rule out the right of any of the future NATO members to automatic military assistance greatly pleased the Joint Chiefs. Instead, bilateral agreements with each member were made the precondition for offering U.S. military aid to western Europe.

Thirdly, supporters of the United Nations and Roosevelt's "one world" concept feared that an "entangling alliance" would revive the despised and dangerous balance-of-power concept of pre–World War II days. Although they recognized that the Soviet Union's veto in the Security Council made any use of the United Nations for Western defense purposes difficult, if not impossible, the envisaged alliance appeared to ignore the United Nations altogether. This was a poor precedent that might well threaten to undermine the United Nations fatally. The Truman administration therefore invoked the UN Charter as much as possible in the articles of the North Atlantic Treaty, although they realized, as Kaplan writes, "that there was a basic incompatibility between the treaty and the charter." During the strenuous efforts to sell the North Atlantic Treaty to the country, the administration pretended that NATO was a regional organization of the United Nations (chapter 8, article 53). Wisely, however, no reference to this effect was included in the text of the treaty. After all, regional organizations were obliged to report to the UN Security Council, which would have given Moscow an unacceptable element of influence on NATO.

During the many months of negotiations between the Brussels Treaty Organization and the United States and Canada many other issues became controversial. For example, the question of whether the new organization should be only a strategic or also a political alliance was contentious. In the end, and largely on the insistence of Canada, the envisaged organization was also given a political and ideological role rather than a mere military function. Thus, article 2 emphasized the necessity of economic and social cooperation between the member states, and article 8 stated that no member state should enter into any obligations that conflicted with NATO—in other words, no member state was allowed to go communist. Also, the role of Germany, and how to restrain and integrate Germany into the Western world, was extensively and successfully discussed. At the London conference in the spring of 1948, the three Western allies were therefore able to agree on the radical step of setting up a separate West German state.

Of particular importance were questions of NATO membership, coverage, and duration. Eventually it was decided that there should be no different categories of membership; countries were either participants or not. For strategic and political reasons it was decided to interpret the term "North Atlantic" loosely. For example, the Algerian departments of France were accepted as being covered by NATO, and countries such as Italy and Portugal (and later Greece and Turkey) were of such strategic importance that they needed to become involved. This meant for example that Antonio Salazar's Portugal, which was hardly a democratic country, was allowed to join. Yet, Spain only became a member in 1982, after the death of fascist dictator Francisco Franco. For largely strategic reasons, Portugal (including the Portuguese Azores) and Italy as well as Norway, Denmark (including Danish Greenland), and Iceland were allowed to accede to NATO in April 1949. They had not participated in the negotiations between the BTO, the United States, and Canada.

By September–October 1948 it had become clear that a new unified alliance would be created rather than a defensive agreement between the Brussels Treaty Organization and a North American organization, as had been envisaged in the Pentagon talks. Most importantly, at around the same time it became obvious that the United States would be a definite member of the new North Atlantic alliance. While the Europeans expected above all to benefit from NATO by means of American protection and military aid, Washington hoped that the existence of NATO would convince the Soviet Union to restrain its expansionist ambitions. Not least the United States expected that due to American participation, the North Atlantic alliance would help to overcome the outdated balance-of-power concept that had dominated European politics for centuries. NATO was therefore meant to contribute decisively to the establishment of a peaceful, stable, and prosperous continent.

NATO CONSTRUCTION AND REARMAMENT

After the establishment of the North Atlantic alliance in 1949, almost immediately two important organs for the running of NATO were set up under article 9 of the treaty: the North Atlantic Council and the Defense Committee. The first council meeting in September 1949 in Washington and the subsequent meetings in late 1949 and early 1950 decided that for the time being the organizational structure of the Brussels Treaty Organization was to be adopted for NATO's use. In addition, the establishment of a united command with a supreme commander and Council of Deputies was also agreed upon. The most important NATO institutions for the next few years were the five regional planning groups (including the Western European Regional Planning Group consisting of the five BTO nations); the Military Committee, consisting of the chiefs of staff of the member states with a standing group based in the Pentagon; and a general three-nation standing group of NATO's most crucial members, the United States, Britain, and France. Thus by 1950 a relatively well-integrated alliance structure was taking shape.

It was much more difficult, however, to design a strategic and military concept that would turn NATO from a paper tiger into a real collaborative transatlantic alliance. NATO's first strategic concept was adopted in January 1950, with the United States being mostly responsible for strategic bombing issues, the United Kingdom for naval warfare matters, and the continental Europeans for tactical air warfare issues and the provision of ground troops. However, differences soon surfaced regarding American ideas about the defense of Europe. During the first few years of NATO the U.S. Joint Chiefs of Staff were so pessimistic about the availability of Western military resources that the American defense plans for Europe essentially consisted of the withdrawal of U.S. troops to the Pyrenees and Britain. It was hoped that it might be possible to reconquer the continent at a later stage. Not surprisingly, the Europeans were less than impressed; they insisted on a defense of Europe at the Rhine or ideally at the Elbe. Thus, in May 1950 the Medium Term Defense Plan (MTDP) that took European sensitivities into account was agreed upon. Still, the plan was based largely on the optimistic prognosis that more than ninety divisions and eight thousand planes would be available by 1954. This was highly unrealistic but NATO essentially believed that no Soviet invasion was to be expected in the foreseeable future (1954 was regarded as the danger year). Further, it was assumed that the American atomic monopoly would provide immunity from attack, whatever the availability and readiness of Western conventional forces on the continent. There was great fear that any strenuous rearmament effort by the Europeans would irreparably damage the economic and social reconstruction of the continent.

The explosion of an atomic bomb by the Soviet Union in August 1949 undermined this confident belief in the American atomic umbrella. After all, the Western alliance had expected that Moscow would not be able to develop atomic weapons for a considerable number of years. Yet, much to the consternation of politicians in Washington, by mid-September firm scientific evidence was available that a Soviet explosion had indeed taken place. Britain was only able to embark on its first atomic test explosion in 1952, and it took France until 1960 to develop an atomic device. Although it was considered unlikely that the Soviet Union would be able to rival Washington's growing atomic arsenal for a significant period of time, the Truman administration decided to go ahead with the building of a hydrogen bomb.

In the course of 1950 the U.S. government began to doubt whether the resources allocated to the defense of the Western world were sufficient. The result was the controversial document NSC 68, which reflected the increasing militarization of the Cold War. Subsequently, Washington's belief in the necessity of making more radical efforts to rearm the countries of western Europe (including the new West German state) and to expand and modernize America's conventional and nuclear forces was strengthened by the outbreak of war in Korea, which was regarded as another Western failure in Asia after the loss of China to the communists in 1949. In June 1950 communist North Korean forces invaded South Korea, the American protectorate. Parallels were drawn with the precarious position of divided Germany in Europe. It was clear that the envisaged MTDP program was grossly inadequate. Under the impact of the Korean War the huge American and allied rearmament program called for by NSC 68 was signed into law by President Truman. In addition, and despite strong French opposition during the Western head of government conference in September 1950 in Washington, the United States firmly insisted on the rearmament of the new West German state. West German forces as well as the territory of West Germany were needed for the forward defense of the European continent.

Eventually, a compromise was achieved by means of the Pleven Plan, which was based on the recently conceived European Coal and Steel Community (ECSC) for the integration of the French and German coal and steel industries. Both plans were the brainchild of the influential French businessman and civil servant Jean Monnet. Instead of an independent German army, navy, air force, and general staff, French Prime Minister René Pleven proposed the creation of a multinational European army under the umbrella of a European Defense Community (EDC), which, as Acheson expressed it, would be closely "interlocked" with (and presumably subordinate to) NATO. Approximately ten German divisions would be integrated with other countries' forces at the regimental level to form mixed European divisions that would remain under the command of non-German EDC member states. To make the difficult task of rearming the Germans more palatable to West German Chancellor Konrad Adenauer, who would face enormous domestic opposition, he was offered sovereignty for the Federal Republic as a reward. The EDC solution also envisaged the establishment of a European minister of defense, an assembly, and a council of ministers as well as a common defense budget. The persuasive skills of NATO's first allied supreme commander and World War II hero Dwight D. Eisenhower helped to convince the Truman administration that the EDC project was a sensible way of obtaining West German rearmament without antagonizing the other European countries too much. Fears of the reestablishment of Hitler's Wehrmacht were still widespread. Consequently, Washington regarded the realization of the EDC as of vital importance. It was believed that the European army would cement the Western alliance and lead to the establishment of lasting Franco-German friendship, thus strengthening NATO's coherence and preventing future European civil wars.

Although the EDC treaty was signed in May 1952, ratification was a difficult affair. President Eisenhower and Secretary of State John Foster Dulles, who succeeded Truman and Acheson in January 1953, were unable to pressure Paris into ratifying the treaty. Ultimately, in the absence of Britain, which was prepared to cooperate with the EDC but not to join it, fear of German dominance of the EDC led the French parliament not to go ahead with the ratification of the EDC treaty in late August 1954. With the exception of the outbreak of the Korean War, this was the most severe crisis of the Atlantic alliance to date. NATO was thrown into turmoil. Washington was particularly shocked. After all, the U.S. administration had hoped that the establishment of the EDC might enable Washington to reduce both its financial and troop commitments to Europe. Instead, the rearmament and sovereignty of the Federal Republic of Germany, as well as the European integration process and the coherence and military buildup of NATO, had to be reconsidered from scratch.

The British managed to come to the rescue. During two rapidly convened conferences in London and Paris in September and October 1954, and by way of an earlier whirlwind journey through the European capitals, Foreign Secretary Anthony Eden was able to convince his partners to agree to West German membership in NATO on a nondiscriminatory basis. Eventually, French agreement was won after the negotiation of Bonn's prior admission to the Western European Union (WEU). This was the renamed Brussels Treaty Organization of 1948. By way of West German WEU membership, France and the other member states were to receive a veto over the rearmament and arms procurement activities of the Federal Republic. Eden had also announced during the London conference that despite British sovereignty concerns, his country would not withdraw its Rhine army and tactical air force based in West Germany without the agreement of its WEU partners. As long as U.S. troops remained on the continent, the British would also be prepared to make a European commitment. The "great debate" of 1951 in Washington between the administration and isolationists in Congress about further troop commitments in Europe had already resulted in the dispatch of four additional American divisions to Europe.

Thus, the WEU solution to control German rearmament and London and Washington's commitment to continue deploying troops on the European continent were decisive in persuading France to cease its opposition to West German membership in NATO. Both German rearmament and the unity of the Western alliance had been preserved. Yet the WEU never developed a life of its own. It is fair to say that the development of a European defense identity and a European pillar of NATO—as had been envisaged with the explicit agreement of the United States by means of the EDC—therefore did not commence before the 1980s and 1990s. With the exception of France and despite the occasional crisis in transatlantic security relations, throughout most of the Cold War the western Europeans placidly accepted American predominance in NATO and thus the buildup of the American empire. While Britain believed it could rely on the "special relationship" with the United States to maintain its influence, the West Germans, at the front line of the Cold War, felt too dependent on the American security umbrella to oppose this strongly. Only the French were prepared to challenge American hegemony in Europe.

At the Lisbon North Atlantic Council conference in February 1952, agreement had been reached on a substantial military and political reorganization of NATO. That structure was largely still in place in the early twenty-first century. With regard to the military organization of the alliance, most of the regional planning groups were abolished. Instead, the standing group of the Military Committee would oversee SHAPE (Supreme Headquarters Allied Powers Europe), commanded by SACEUR (Supreme Allied Command Europe). An Atlantic command (Supreme Allied Command Atlantic, SACLANT) and an English Channel command were established on the same level of responsibility, which included planning issues. SHAPE, which was essentially modeled on the Brussels Treaty Organization headquarters near Paris and took over many of its administrative units, was clearly the most important command. It was subdivided into four geographical commands: Northern Europe, Central Europe, Southern Europe, and the Mediterranean. While the supreme commanders for Europe and the Atlantic were Americans, the Channel Command was headed by a Briton; all the command posts reported directly to the standing group in Washington. Unlike the failed European Defense Community, in NATO the vast majority of troops were national forces; NATO only mixed nationalities at the various command headquarters.

The Lisbon conference also approved a new political structure. A civilian secretary general (who would always be a European) was to be appointed. The secretary general was to be responsible to the Council of Ministers and in charge of an international secretariat that had responsibility for financial and economic planning and for military production issues. The Council of Deputies was to be replaced by permanent representatives at the ambassadorial level who assumed responsibility when the Council of Ministers was not sitting; their meetings would be chaired by the secretary general. Moreover, despite British protests it was decided to move NATO headquarters from London to outside Paris where it would be closer to SHAPE.

The conference also approved the first enlargement of NATO, which led to the admission of Greece and Turkey in 1952. Both countries were of great strategic importance to NATO's southern rim and contributed more than twenty-five valuable divisions. The western Europeans reiterated their willingness to make huge rearmament efforts in the conventional field so that ninety-six well-equipped divisions (including the West German contingents) would be available by 1954. However, economic and financial realities in western Europe would prevent the achievement of these ambitious and quite unrealistic military goals. With respect to domestic opinion and the obvious limits on the tax burden that could be imposed, no country was willing to adhere to the Lisbon goals.

Still, by 1955 NATO had already expanded its membership twice, had become a much more integrated military alliance with a clear political dimension, and had also seriously attempted to tackle its military weakness. However, it was still in no position to rival the forces at the disposal of the Soviet Union.

CONSOLIDATION

After the Austrian peace treaty in April and the admission of West Germany to NATO in May 1955, the Geneva Four-Power Summit in July inaugurated the first thaw in East-West relations. Although neither the summit conference nor the subsequent Geneva foreign ministers' conference managed to solve any of the many outstanding Cold War problems, the two meetings led to a more relaxed international climate. It appeared to be possible to contain the Cold War in Europe peacefully and agree to disagree, something that was soon called "peaceful coexistence."

Although East-West relations deteriorated temporarily when the Soviet Union invaded Hungary in late 1956, the almost simultaneous Anglo-French-Israeli attack on Egypt to reverse nationalization of the Suez Canal shook the Western alliance to its foundations. American anger at not having been consulted and Washington's fear that the British-French action would open the doors of the Middle East to the Soviet Union (as it did) led to the first occasion when the United States and the Soviet Union sided against two western European countries. An American-inspired run on the pound sterling and the effective imposition of an oil embargo on Britain by President Eisenhower had the desired result. Britain gave notice to the French that they would have to withdraw from Egypt, an action that caused a great deal of anti-British resentment in Paris. The Suez crisis made it clear that Britain and France, who still retained a good deal of global influence, were not able to embark on independent international action without the approval and support of the United States. Thus the crisis symbolized the decline of western Europe to the status of a mere satellite continent.

After the Suez crisis American preponderance within the Western alliance, both in its political and strategic dimension, could no longer be doubted. The Europeans increasingly became reactive members who criticized and complained while most constructive initiatives originated in Washington. This was evident during the long Berlin crisis of 1958–1963, which led to a quite unexpected escalation of the Cold War and to the building of the Berlin Wall in August 1961. The Berlin crisis and in particular the October 1962 Cuban missile crisis brought the world close to nuclear war. The August 1963 limited test ban treaty between the United States, the United Kingdom, the Soviet Union, and any other state that wished to join was one of the lessons drawn from the missile crisis. Another was the installation of a "hot line" between Washington and Moscow.

Despite the increasing Cold War marginalization of Europe in the second half of the 1950s and during the 1960s, European alliance members played a subordinate but still significant role with regard to the development of NATO's strategic concepts. However, most initiatives came from the United States. Shortly after taking office the Eisenhower administration realized that the conventional force goals as agreed at Lisbon would either remain unrealistic or, if implemented, would undermine American and European economic competitiveness and social well-being. Thus, Washington invented vague concepts with names such as "long haul," "massive retaliation," and "new look," which would obscure the fact that the alliance was unable to develop as quickly and as intensively as originally envisaged.

Although the European alliance members were very critical of the increased reliance on nuclear containment, there was very little they could do. While always prepared to criticize American proposals, NATO's European members were not prepared to put more of their own scarce resources into developing their conventional forces. The only concept they partially agreed with was the "long haul" idea, which essentially consisted of the insight that the frantic rearmament efforts of the Korean War and Lisbon conference era could not be sustained for financial and psychological reasons; the plan was therefore to be stretched out over a longer period of time. However, "massive retaliation" and the "new look," as first outlined in NSC document 162/2 in late 1953, were very different matters. Because the envisaged conventional rearmament goals were unrealistic and because the production of atomic weapons appeared to be a lot cheaper than conventional warfare methods, the Eisenhower administration intended to focus NATO's strategy on nuclear containment. U.S. officials argued that fear of an American atomic response would prevent any Soviet attack on the countries of the Western alliance. Moreover, getting "greater bang for the buck," as Eisenhower's secretary of defense expressed it, would ensure the maintenance of healthy Western economies and budgets.

The increasing reliance on nuclear diplomacy meant that NATO would have no choice but to respond with atomic weapons if, for example, the Soviet Union invaded West Germany. NATO was all but incapable of retaliating to a communist attack with conventional weapons. Instead it would rely on the so-called "trip-wire" idea: once the Soviet Union attacked Europe and the U.S. soldiers stationed there, Washington's Strategic Air Command would be activated. The implications of such a scenario were most disconcerting for the West Germans and their European neighbors. The Joint Chiefs of Staff Admiral William Radford's 1956 suggestion, as leaked to the *New York Times*, that the United States needed to reduce U.S. troops in Europe to two million by the withdrawal of 800,000 soldiers from the continent, gave rise to great concern. Moreover, the greater the arsenal of intercontinental nuclear weapons at the disposal of the Soviet Union, the larger the question mark in the minds of European leaders about whether or not Washington would be prepared to run the risk of inviting a Soviet attack on American territory by coming to the aid of Europe.

This became a realistic concern in 1957, when Moscow sent *Sputnik*, the first space satellite, into orbit and also managed to launch the first intercontinental ballistic missile. American cities, and not merely European ones, could now be reached by Soviet nuclear bombs. Soon politicians were talking about a "missile gap" to the detriment of the West; this dominated the U.S. election campaign of 1960, although it soon became known that Nikita Khrushchev had been vastly exaggerating the Soviet Union's nuclear capabilities. Still, *Sputnik* contributed to the fact that the U.S. government was more than ever in favor of "burden sharing" within the alliance. While the United States would be responsible for enhanced nuclear containment, Washington expected the western Europeans to provide for the cost-intensive conventional means of defending the European continent from any Soviet invasion. However, much to the irritation of the United States, the Europeans were both unwilling and economically unable to dedicate the expected resources to the defense of the Western alliance.

American politicians also became increasingly uneasy about the military implications of "massive retaliation." In the last few years of the Eisenhower administration and in particular with the advent of the Kennedy administration in January 1961, U.S. officials considered plans for replacing this doctrine with a new NATO strategy. Initially, they developed the concept of a shield force, which would include troops equipped with tactical nuclear weapons as well as conventional arms. The administration attempted to persuade Congress that nuclear sharing with the NATO allies, in particular with Britain, was essential for maintaining NATO's credibility. In 1958 this resulted in the repeal of the 1946 McMahon Act, which had forbidden the sharing of nuclear secrets with either friend or foe. In late 1962 it also helped British prime minister Harold Macmillan argue his case with President Kennedy that the canceled Skybolt missile be replaced with American Polaris missiles that the British could equip with their own nuclear warheads. The French were offered a similar deal but turned it down. Under President Charles de Gaulle, France would later insist on military independence.

A new strategic concept, "flexible response," was eventually adopted in 1967. It was meant to allow NATO to respond to an invasion by the Soviet Union with a range of escalating options: use of conventional weapons, use of small tactical atomic weapons, and only finally initiation of a full-scale nuclear war. But this also was a controversial concept. The European NATO allies generally feared that a Soviet and eastern European attack at multiple locations and by multiple means would still give the Western alliance no option but to embark on escalating the conflict into a nuclear counterattack. Moreover, the question remained: Who would decide the use of nuclear weapons by NATO and would the European members be able to influence Washington's decision? As Ian Thomas has recognized, the issues were "command and control" of NATO's nuclear forces. A compromise solution had already been found with the so-called dual key arrangements for the use of intercontinental ballistic missiles; the host nations had to give their agreement to the use of these weapons. However, Britain and other European nations were concerned about whether in a sudden emergency the United States would wait for the agreement of the Europeans. After all, despite the looming threat of a global nuclear war during the Cuban missile crisis, the Americans had not bothered to consult with the Europeans; even the British had hardly been informed. Thus, the anxieties of the Europeans that they might be dragged into a nuclear confrontation with the Soviet Union against their will dominated the early to mid-1960s.

American ideas about the establishment of a multilateral force (MLF), put forth in early 1963, were a reaction to this. Although originally developed during the Eisenhower years, the Kennedy administration argued that the MLF would lead to greater alliance cooperation and transatlantic military transparency. It would create an integrated nuclear force similar to the existing integrated conventional forces and thus increase NATO military efficiency. Washington also hoped to integrate British and French nuclear forces into the MLF and thereby defuse the discussion about the creation of German-owned nuclear forces and Germany's participation in nuclear decision making.

The MLF was to consist of twenty-five ships, to be jointly owned, financed, controlled, and manned by the entire alliance; each ship would be equipped with eight Polaris missiles. In military circles it was technologically and organizationally a very controversial concept, and many experts doubted its military usefulness. However, the Kennedy administration appeared to believe that the MLF could be used to overcome the deep dissatisfaction within the alliance with regard to NATO's nuclear strategy. It would continue full American control over the deployment and use of nuclear weapons while giving the Europeans the impression that they were participating in nuclear decision making. At the same time, the MLF concept had the advantage of preventing the further proliferation of nuclear weapons within the alliance. Despite strong German support for the MLF (and strong French and British opposition; London even proposed its own equally flawed Atlantic Nuclear Force concept), by 1965 the Johnson administration had withdrawn the idea. Instead, Washington was now in favor of creating a nuclear planning group within NATO.

By then France's increasing uneasiness about American dominance of and strategy for the alliance was rapidly posing a severe threat to the unity and coherence of NATO. Paris doubted the U.S. commitment to nuclear deterrence if America's own national interest (that is, U.S. territory) was not threatened. Moreover, many in France argued that multilateral nuclear deterrence would contribute to the prevention of nuclear war. Thus, for French nuclear strategy the existence of NATO was counterproductive and not necessary at all. In addition, De Gaulle viewed American predominance in NATO and talk of an Atlantic community with ever greater suspicion. Not without justification he believed that Washington intended to prevent the development of independent nuclear forces within NATO and to keep individual alliance members as subordinate as possible.

In early March 1966 President Lyndon Johnson was informed that France would leave NATO's Integrated Military Command (IMC) and that all NATO forces and NATO headquarters had to depart France by April 1967. This led to another severe crisis within NATO, yet by late 1967 the alliance had resettled in Brussels, and no lasting damage to the unity of the remaining NATO IMC members had occurred.

NATO AND DÉTENTE

After the Cuban missile crisis in 1962, East-West détente was widely seen as the only option to ensure the world's long-term survival. Washington became increasingly interested in East-West détente and pushed NATO in the same direction. As early as May 1964, President Johnson had spoken of the need for "building bridges," and in October 1966 he advanced the idea of "peaceful engagement" with the countries of the Eastern bloc. The Harmel Report, approved by NATO member states in December 1967, spoke explicitly of the Western aim "to further a détente in East-West relations." However, it was made clear that any détente would have to be based on NATO's and the West's cherished policy of strength. During the NATO Council of Ministers meeting in Reykjavik in June 1968, all NATO members emphasized their willingness to embark upon East-West negotiations regarding troop reductions in Europe. In fact, Washington hoped that NATO would become one of the instruments driving détente; in an era of lessening threat perception it would help to give the Atlantic alliance a new sense of purpose. It would also discourage the European allies from pursuing bilateral policies of détente, as for example the French and especially the West Germans were doing.

Washington's readiness in the late 1960s and early 1970s to use NATO as a vehicle for embarking upon détente with the Soviet Union, thus giving in to European calls for a relaxation of the Cold War, was strongly influenced by American economic and financial problems. Some commentators began speaking of relative American decline and the end of the American century. This was symbolized by Richard Nixon's termination in 1971 of the 1944 Bretton Woods economic system by his sudden suspension of the dollar's convertibility into gold, which resulted in the free floating of international currencies and an effective devaluation of the dollar. Simultaneously, the president imposed a 10 percent protective tariff on imported goods. These measures were solely dictated by domestic economic requirements in the United States, and any negative economic consequences for its European allies were disregarded. America's problems were largely due to the costs of the Vietnam War, the lingering burden of financing the domestic Great Society programs of the 1960s, and the relative overvaluation of the dollar, which helped European and Japanese exports. The European Community's imposition of quotas, exchange controls, and import licenses on goods from outside the community as well as its protectionist common agricultural policy (CAP), inaugurated in 1966 also, contributed to America's ever-larger budget deficit. The United States had not only accumulated a considerable balance-of-payments deficit, but from 1971 it also had a considerable trade deficit as well as inflationary problems, rising unemployment, and almost stagnant wages; further, the position of the dollar, the world's leading reserve currency, was weakening. Transatlantic relations were becoming increasingly difficult, and this included relations within NATO.

America's relative economic and financial decline, in combination with global détente and the accompanying perception that the military threat from the Warsaw Pact was receding, decisively contributed to undermining the Nixon administration's commitment to the European continent and, to some extent, to NATO. Congress had also grown increasingly skeptical about the benefits of America's involvement in Europe. During the 1970s, Senator Mike Mansfield introduced eight amendments for U.S. troop reductions in Europe. Within the administration, it was the national security adviser Henry Kissinger, a keen student of nineteenth-century European power politics, who insisted on basing America's relations with its western European allies on a purely bilateral nation-state basis within the Atlantic framework. Establishing a united and federal Europe, as the creators of NATO originally had envisaged, was now seen as counterproductive for Washington's hegemony in the Western world. In Kissinger's realist worldview, it was unlikely that "Europe would unite in order to share *our* burdens or that it would be content with a subordinate role once it had the means to implement its own views." Kissinger even recognized that once "Europe had grown economically strong and politically united, Atlantic cooperation could not be an American enterprise in which consultations elaborated primarily American designs."

However, as far as public rhetoric was concerned, the Nixon administration continued speaking out in favor of a united federal Europe with a large single market, fully integrated into the Atlantic system. It was still assumed in Washington that a united Europe would share "the burdens and obligations of world leadership" with the United States. In particular, the Nixon White House favored the envisaged expansion of the European Community. It hoped that Britain's entry and the revival of the Anglo-American "special relationship" would lead to an improvement in transatlantic relations and within NATO. Yet on the whole Nixon and Kissinger were not prepared to accept the growing maturity of Europe and the realities of a more pluralistic and interdependent world. The Nixon administration still expected a largely docile Europe. As far as East-West relations and the NATO alliance were concerned, Washington certainly wished to be in full control. *Ostpolitik*, West Germany's fairly independent variant of détente, was therefore only grudgingly accepted by the U.S. administration. Nixon and Kissinger disliked the independence and confidence with which the West Germans proceeded with *Ostpolitik* and competed with Washington's own strategy of superpower détente.

By 1973 Kissinger realized that transatlantic relations were in urgent need of revision and repair. To the anger of the European Community countries who had not been consulted, he grandly announced the "Year of Europe." The Nixon administration had been largely occupied with the Vietnam War and the development of détente with China and the Soviet Union during its first years in office, and the "Year of Europe" was Kissinger's attempt to improve U.S.–EC relations inside and outside NATO while safeguarding Washington's leadership role. Kissinger proposed a new Atlantic Charter and did not hesitate to emphasize that the United States had global responsibilities while the EC countries only had to deal with regional problems. Moreover, he insisted on a greater degree of military burden-sharing, arguing that only Europe's economic contribution would guarantee the continued functioning of America's security umbrella. The so-called Nixon Doctrine of 1970 had emphasized that America's allies ought to assume more of the burden of defending themselves.

The linkage between economic and security concerns led to severe difficulties between Washington and the western Europeans. Kissinger, however, managed to persuade the Europeans to agree to a clause in the new Atlantic Declaration, signed in June 1974, stating that Washington should be consulted before the EC countries arrived at important decisions that impacted on transatlantic issues. Thus, American ideas of the nature of the transatlantic relationship had largely won the day. In practice, however, allied relations remained tense. Severe friction occurred during the Yom Kippur War of October 1973 when Washington wholeheartedly backed Israel and many European countries hesitated to do so. The European Community was much more dependent on Middle Eastern oil than the United States, and many countries (like France, the United Kingdom, and West Germany) had strong economic links with the Arab countries in the region. Thus the war and the energy question were closely connected with both security and economic prosperity.

American-European differences with respect to the Year of Europe and the Yom Kippur War pushed the European Community into developing more sophisticated processes of cooperation, not least in order to resist pressure to fall in line with American wishes. The 1973 Declaration on European Identity was influential in gradually leading to a tentative common European foreign policy. It encouraged EC members to use the instrument of European Political Cooperation (EPC), created in 1970, to ensure that foreign policy positions would be coordinated among all EC countries. In 1968 the informal Eurogroup of EC defense ministers had been founded to discuss European defense cooperation. In late 1970 this led to the launch of the European Defense Improvement Program (EDIP) to build up NATO's infrastructure and national European forces. But as some authors have argued, this may have been less a demonstration of European independence in defense matters than an attempt to impress the United States with Europeans' willingness to help themselves. Thus, most authors view the 1970s as a "dark age" for both transatlantic relations and European integration. The two oil crises and the accompanying economic recession (best characterized by the term "stagflation"), as well as the expansion of the European Community from six to nine countries with the addition of the United Kingdom, Ireland, and Denmark on 1 January 1973, caused a severe, long-lasting crisis of adaptation within Europe.

It certainly weakened the ability of the European member states of NATO to embark on any decisive initiatives to reform the problem-ridden alliance. However, "the disarray of Europe" worked to the benefit of the United States. Washington was able to insist on the importance of the Atlantic framework and regain, as Alfred Grosser says, "its position as the leading power among the partners who were unified only when under its direction." Still, under Nixon and Kissinger an important reevaluation of U.S.–EC relations inside and outside NATO had taken place. Washington had begun to look after its own economic and political interests much more than before. It was no longer prepared to accept unilateral disadvantages in the hope of obtaining vaguely defined benefits in the long run. But it was still not prepared to accept western European emancipation from American tutelage.

The rising tide of Eurocommunism in southern Europe (particularly in Italy, France, and Spain) worried the United States much more than it did the Europeans. Despite the Eurocommunists' independence from Moscow and their ambition to democratize their party structures, Washington feared that NATO might not survive the international developments of the 1970s. Greece withdrew from NATO in August 1974 in view of the West's ambiguous attitude toward the Turkish invasion of Cyprus after the Greek-inspired coup. The ruling military regime in Athens had hoped to unite the island with Greece and thus improve their plummeting domestic popularity.

From the mid- to late 1970s the western and eastern Europeans cautiously began to diverge from the policies pursued by their masters in Moscow and Washington. With hindsight it seems that the European nations became gradually aware again of their common European identity and their shared interests in world affairs. In fact, the greater the respective difficulties with Washington and Moscow appeared, the more united the European countries became. Serious problems in superpower cooperation in the mid-1970s—for example, the prolonged MBFR arms control talks regarding conventional armaments in Geneva and Vienna beginning in 1972 and the SALT II negotiations during the Carter administration—as well as the strengthening of the American neoconservative movement in the 1970s appeared to foreshadow a new hostile phase in the Cold War. European public opinion and many western European politicians refused to go along with this. Yet European politicians also felt the need to ensure that the United States remained committed to Europe. They were torn between opposition to a policy of renewed East-West tension and the awareness that the American security umbrella was still vital for the protection of the European continent.

TENSION, DÉTENTE, AND THE END OF THE COLD WAR

Détente climaxed in the first half of the 1970s. Nixon's visits to Moscow and Beijing, the Berlin Treaty of 1971–1972, the 1972 Basic Treaty between the two German states, and the Helsinki Accord of 1975 appeared to prove the vitality of East-West détente. But there was increasing domestic American opposition to détente; the growing number of neoconservatives were firmly opposed, for example, to the Helsinki conference. Many on the right of the political spectrum in the United States viewed Western acceptance of the postwar borders in Europe by means of the Helsinki Final Act as a substantial defeat of the West. Soviet ratification of the human rights accord, an element that may well have contributed to the unraveling of the Soviet empire a decade later, was seen as unimportant.

When President Jimmy Carter took office in 1977, he embarked on a human rights crusade. He viewed NATO as more than just a military and political alliance; to him NATO ought to contribute to a more humane development of international politics and create a more just world. This antagonized the Soviet Union and led to much increased tension in East-West relations. When the Soviets invaded Afghanistan in December 1979, détente was all but over. Carter turned into a full-blown cold warrior, not least in order to increase his chances for reelection in 1980. The U.S. government boycotted the Olympic Games in Moscow in 1980 and the president refused to let the SALT II Treaty proceed for ratification in the Senate (where it probably would have been defeated).

However, in 1977 Carter made three important proposals that were accepted by NATO at the North Atlantic Council meeting in May 1978 and indicated the alliance's enduring mistrust of Moscow. The first proposal argued that Western policy should continue to be based on the Harmel Report: détente had to be pursued on the basis of strength. The second proposal referred to the standardization of military equipment and to the necessity of making further progress with integrating NATO at the operational level. The third proposal, which developed into the Long-Term Defense Program (LTDP), indicated that détente had not overcome the arms race. In view of continued Soviet expansion of its offensive capabilities, NATO's defenses also needed to be strengthened, particularly in the area of conventional weapons. NATO's long-term nuclear needs were to be discussed by the Nuclear Planning Group. Although most European countries wholeheartedly approved of the LTDP, the renewed outbreak of Cold War tension after the Afghanistan invasion worried the Europeans. The simultaneous continuation of détente in Europe became a serious problem for the coherence of NATO and America's dominant position within the alliance.

Soon the belief, widespread in the United States, that the Soviet Union was in fact attempting to obtain military and nuclear superiority under the guise of arms control agreements also began to worry a number of European NATO countries such as West Germany and Britain. It eventually led to NATO's "dual track" rearmament decision of December 1979. The dual track strategy consisted of the attempt to negotiate with Moscow for the reduction or even elimination of the Kremlin's intermediate-range SS-20 missiles, which were targeted at western Europe, by 1983. If this should prove impossible, as was in fact the case, equivalent U.S. weapons (464 cruise missiles and 108 Pershing missiles) would be deployed in western European countries: the Pershings in West Germany and the cruise missiles in the United Kingdom, Italy, Holland, and Belgium. Among the European peoples this decision was severely criticized. In Bonn it contributed to the downfall of the Helmut Schmidt government and its replacement by the center-right government of Helmut Kohl in 1982. It also caused many domestic upheavals in France and Italy and led to the rapid development of a European-wide peace movement. The latter largely benefited the new left-leaning, pacifist, and environmental Green parties across western Europe, which were particularly strong in West Germany, France, and the Benelux countries. After all, while European countries had to agree to the deployment of the new nuclear missiles in their countries, negotiations with the Soviet Union, if they were to take place, would be a bilateral affair between Moscow and Washington. It would exclude the Europeans—including the United Kingdom and France, whose nuclear weapons might also be affected by any negotiated solution—from having any input.

By the early 1980s America's political elite was increasingly dominated by anticommunist ideology, which eventually culminated in the election of President Ronald Reagan in late 1980. Reagan did not hesitate to go back to the days of intensive Cold War first experienced in the 1950s and early 1960s. However, Washington habitually failed to consult or even inform its European allies.

When Ronald Reagan entered the White House he was intent on reimposing America's leadership on transatlantic relations. The European Community's much stronger economic position and greater political confidence as well as the era of détente with the Soviet Union were simply ignored by Reagan as if these developments had never taken place. Thus, under Reagan, even more so than under Carter, economic as well as security issues and severely differing perceptions regarding the East-West conflict affected the transatlantic alliance. Reagan went on the offensive to implement NATO's "dual track" decision and undermine the European peace movements by attempting to sell the alliance as a harbinger of peace. At the same time, the reassertion of America's leadership of NATO and the concurrent attempt to increase America's global prestige were at the heart of Reagan's foreign policy. Reagan also did not hesitate to employ anticommunist rhetoric. Much to the despair of the European NATO allies, Reagan did not appear to be interested in rescuing what was left of East-West détente. Among European leaders only British Prime Minister Margaret Thatcher supported Reagan's hard-line approach.

Reagan, like Thatcher, was not interested in supporting the creation of a supranational Europe. In fact, his new policy of strength toward Moscow precluded a reassessment of Washington's relations with its allies. With regard to Reagan's policy toward the Soviet Union, however, it is useful to differentiate between his first and second terms in office; from 1984 to 1985 the president embarked upon a less hard-line approach toward the USSR. Although this helped to improve Washington's relations with its allies to a considerable degree, Reagan still expected the Europeans to follow America's hegemonic lead without questioning any of its policies. Thus, in terms of transatlantic relations, a deliberate policy of arrogant rather than benign neglect can be observed throughout Reagan's terms in office. Early in his presidency, for example, the administration talked casually of developing capabilities for fighting nuclear war and the possibility of entering into tactical nuclear exchanges with the Soviet Union. Such exchanges would of course have taken place over European territory, destroying much of the continent in the process. The same apparent willingness to distance himself from European security concerns appeared to apply to the president's enthusiasm regarding the development of the Strategic Defense Initiative (SDI). If this project ever were to come to fruition it purportedly would make the United States immune to nuclear attacks by the Soviet Union, while in all likelihood such protection would not be available to the Europeans.

Reagan's negotiations with Soviet secretary general Mikhail Gorbachev in Reykjavik in October 1986 almost led to the elimination of all ballistic missiles in East and West and the tabling of plans for the eradication of all nuclear weapons in the foreseeable future. Although such a development would have dramatically affected the future of the European continent, the president never consulted the Europeans but drew the lesson that only a united NATO front would convince the Soviets to make concessions. The same unilateral approach was applied when Gorbachev surprised Western leaders by accepting the United States' "zero-zero" INF proposal in December 1987, which foresaw the removal of all intermediate-range missiles from Europe. Reagan's 1988 proposal to modernize NATO's short-range nuclear Lance missiles in Europe to counter Moscow's still existing conventional strength in Europe also occurred without much consultation with America's NATO allies.

The Reagan administration's disinterest in consulting the Europeans can also be observed with respect to economic issues. The European Community's, and in particular West Germany and France's, increasing trade with East Germany, the Soviet Union, the developing world, and certain Arab nations was viewed with a combination of suspicion and envy in Washington. Reagan attempted to restrain the competition of the EC countries, and he did not hesitate to explain the rationale of American trade policy with the help of NATO and transatlantic security arguments, which usually resulted in the development of severe economic conflicts. Such crises emerged, for example, in connection with the proposed European gas pipeline deal with Moscow. Reagan's controversial trade sanctions on the Soviet Union in the wake of the declaration of martial law in Poland in December 1981 ensured that transatlantic relations deteriorated further.

As usual, the European Community was ready to compromise as far as security and political issues were concerned, fully realizing that reasonable transatlantic relations and a functioning NATO alliance were still the indispensable pillars of the Cold War world. From November 1983, after the negotiations with Moscow within NATO's dual track framework had failed, most EC countries went along with the deployment of new intermediate-range missiles in the face of very hostile peace movements in many countries. Indeed, the deployment of the missiles even reassured some European governments that the Reagan administration did not intend to "decouple" from the European continent. Eventually the EC countries compromised over SDI and agreed to the imposition of sanctions (though largely symbolic ones) on Moscow after the Polish crisis of late 1981.

With regard to important economic issues the European Community was much less disposed to compromise. Regarding the envisaged gas pipeline to Moscow, the EC countries were adamant in their refusal to be browbeaten by the American attempt to undermine the deal; for example, they forbade the employment of American companies and technology in the construction of the pipeline. Reagan's attempts to impose what in effect amounted to extraterritorial sanctions on European companies who were willing to participate led to an outcry. Eventually Reagan had no option but to quietly give in.

Overall, Reagan's economic and financial policies showed yet again that the European Community was helpless in the face of unilateral American policies, forced to react to decisions that had been taken in Washington. Thus, as John Peterson has argued, "the precarious dependence of European economies on decisions taken by a fundamentally unsympathetic U.S. administration pushed the EC countries towards closer co-operation." The European Community under commission president Jacques Delors began developing plans for a Single European Market (SEM) to liberate itself from overwhelming American influence on western Europe's economic and financial fate. It intended to develop a fully free and integrated internal European market by 1992 and to design a common European currency system for implementation shortly thereafter. The French-led, though rather short-lived, revival of the Western European Union (WEU) in 1984 helped to contribute to the development of new ideas for creating a genuine common European foreign and defense policy, as later articulated in the Maastricht Treaty of 1991. In 1988 a Franco-German brigade was founded. This was expanded to corps level three years later; it had the dual purpose of making sure that Germany would remain committed to European integration and of strengthening Europe's military capacities. America's economic and financial predicament, made worse by a rapid decline of the dollar's value in the second half of the 1980s, seemed to indicate the possibility of U.S. troop withdrawals from Europe for financial reasons. The unilateral actions of Gorbachev regarding the reduction of nuclear and conventional armaments and the winding down of the Cold War also appeared to make this a distinct possibility for political reasons.

The Reagan administration viewed these moves toward an economically and politically more integrated and independent Europe with great suspicion. Despite its own protectionist and discriminatory trade policies, it did not hesitate to speak of a "Fortress Europe" and was deeply disturbed by European protectionist measures. By the end of the Reagan years it appeared that not much was left of America's vision for the European continent as it had been developed in the late 1940s and 1950s. The Reagan administration certainly had not been willing to deal constructively with the attempt of its European allies to emancipate themselves a little from American preponderance.

NATO AND THE POST–COLD WAR WORLD

By the late 1980s it became clear that the Cold War was about to end. In April 1988 Gorbachev announced the Soviet Union's withdrawal from Afghanistan. In December, speaking before the UN General Assembly, he offered to withdraw half a million troops and thousands of tanks from eastern Europe, which subsequently he did. Gorbachev's wide-reaching proposals—his domestic reform policy, his suggestion for a strategic arms reduction treaty (START) and a ban on chemical weapons as well as his agreement to the INF treaty—turned him into an immensely popular person in western Europe. NATO leaders were confused and feared for the relevance of the Western alliance. The North Atlantic Council summit in Brussels in May 1989, NATO's fortieth anniversary, therefore reiterated the common values and interests among all NATO members and announced a "Design for Cooperation."

One of the alliance's earliest tasks had been the reconciliation of France and Germany, and now NATO was meant to become the forum for overcoming the division of Europe, creating a free and united Europe, and integrating the eastern Europeans under a common European roof. Under American leadership this was NATO's counteroffensive to Gorbachev's talk about overcoming the Cold War by creating a common European house. This conception appealed to the Europeans and worried the United States. After all, it seemed to indicate that Washington's participation in a new post–Cold War framework for Europe was not really required. In more practical terms, the Brussels summit also envisaged the creation of a European security identity and the strengthening of transatlantic ties. Thus, NATO intended to remain relevant for the dialogue within the Western alliance. In view of Soviet disarmament moves, the modernization of the Lance missiles was postponed to 1992 and ultimately shelved. NATO also made proposals for the radical scaling down of conventional and short-range missiles on both sides of the Iron Curtain. President George H. W. Bush believed that the alliance should go "beyond containment."

Thanks in considerable part to Bush, Western triumphalism was avoided when the Berlin Wall was breached in November 1989. It was also Bush and his secretary of state, James Baker, who attempted to support Gorbachev and his increasingly beleaguered position in Russian domestic politics. In close cooperation with West German Chancellor Kohl and his foreign minister, Hans-Dietrich Genscher, Washington skillfully used the "two-plus-four" talks in 1990 and subtle diplomacy with Gorbachev to ensure that a unified Germany would remain a member of NATO. This was also the desire, if not the condition, of Thatcher and French President François Mitterrand, who both had initially attempted to prevent unification. By the time of German unification in October 1990 the issue had been resolved. The newly united state was both a member of NATO and the European Community, and a compromise had been reached for the position of East Germany. Until the last Russian troops had left the former German Democratic Republic by the summer of 1994, no NATO troops were to be based there. Large amounts of money went to the former Soviet Union to pay for the rehousing of the soldiers as the Russian government claimed officially. The all-German army was to be reduced to 350,000 (the old West German army consisted of just under 500,000 troops).

During NATO's first two post–Cold War summits, in London in May 1990 and in Rome in November 1991, the alliance attempted to devise a new strategic concept and ensure that NATO would be relevant after the East-West conflict had come to an end. It was emphasized that NATO's role was based on mutual values and trust and was meant to improve peace and cooperation. During the Cold War, NATO still did not exclude a nuclear first strike if necessary. Now the importance of nuclear weapons was scaled down. The alliance announced the elimination of all short-range nuclear forces. Henceforth NATO would focus on a more flexible approach to crisis management at a much lower level; during the London summit the NATO Rapid Reaction Corps (RRC) was created. It was recognized that NATO would no longer have to concentrate on repulsing a sweeping Soviet invasion of the European mainland but would have to focus on much lower-scale emergency situations. Thus, a wider role for NATO was found that would ensure that the alliance remained relevant for the crises of the post–Cold War world.

This new and already fairly open-ended conception was expanded further at the Rome summit. NATO expressed the desire to be at the center of all major European institutions—the European Community, the Western European Union, the Conference on Security and Cooperation in Europe, and the Council of Europe—to ensure transatlantic unity as well as intra-European cooperation. The alliance also expressed the opinion that it felt responsible for the security of the eastern part of the continent, its former enemies. Thus by late 1991, NATO had turned itself into a global crisis management instrument for the post–Cold War era. At the same time, it continued emphasizing its key role for solving conflicts among NATO members and with regard to transatlantic relations in a wider sense.

Perhaps one of the most important decisions at the Rome summit was the establishment of the North Atlantic Cooperation Council (NACC), which was a forum of consultation of the defense and foreign ministers of the eastern European states, including the Soviet successor states. It would enable them to participate in strategic planning, disarmament, and crisis management discussions with the alliance. With the help of the NACC, NATO also believed that it was called upon to contribute to the democratization processes in eastern Europe. The January 1994 "Partnership for Peace" (PfP) concept built on the NACC. While the former Warsaw Pact countries were not (yet) allowed to join NATO, the vague and wide-ranging Partnership for Peace as well as the 1997 political cooperation agreement were clearly regarded as stepping stones to NATO membership for many eastern European countries, though not for Russia. Indeed, the April 1999 admission of the former Warsaw Pact members Poland, Hungary, and the Czech Republic was greatly resented in Moscow. The intention to grant NATO membership to former parts of the Soviet Union like the Baltic states, Russia's so-called "near abroad," was perceived as even more humiliating and a severe potential threat to Russia's national security. While attempting to placate Russia as much as possible, however, NATO was unwilling to give Moscow an effective veto over its enlargement process.

The decisive event that convinced the world that NATO was still relevant to the post–Cold War era was the Gulf War of 1991. NATO itself was not a participant in the war, caused by Iraq's invasion of Kuwait, but U.S., British, and French contingents drew on NATO operational resources. In view of the failure of western European countries to provide an effective and united response to the crisis, the successful reversal of the conquest of Kuwait appeared to justify NATO's military and political crisis management techniques. It also meant that NATO members, and the Western public, became gradually used to the out-of-area activities of the alliance.

In response to the dire European performance during the Gulf War, at the Maastricht summit in late 1991 the EC countries decided to further develop the Western European Union in order to build up a Common Foreign and Security Policy. In early 1992 the Eurocorps (initially called the Franco-German corps) was meant to be the core of a new European army. This awakened American anxieties about whether or not the European Union was in the process of building up a serious rival to NATO. It also appeared to challenge the long-term future of America's engagement on the European continent. However, it was soon revealed that this was not the case. The European role in the wars in the former Yugoslavia was frequently characterized by military incompetence and political disunity, as well as financial and political unwillingness to assume a more prominent role in the Balkans. Thus, NATO's activities in the former Yugoslavia relied on American resources. Initially, NATO's performance (in the form of the Implementation Force, IFOR) was less than impressive during the wars of succession in Yugoslavia that began in 1991. In the war in Bosnia it was characterized by much hesitation and exaggerated caution. But in 1995–1996 the alliance embarked on its largest military operation ever and excelled in its effective cooperation. The Dayton Peace Agreement of November–December 1995 was largely due to NATO's belated but ultimately successful bombing campaign against the Serbs. NATO, it appeared, was still greatly relevant. In the absence of any united European military effort and an effective United Nations, NATO was indeed the only organization available to achieve such a task. Moreover, it was the United States that had contributed overwhelmingly to the alliance's military effort and provided it with forceful leadership.

This was also the case in the Kosovo war of 1999. After a hesitant and often ill-conceived strategy to oppose Slobodan Milosevic's ethnic cleansing of the Serbian province, only the employment of NATO's (and Washington's) overwhelming resources and a forceful American-led bombing campaign seemed to impress the Serbian leader. But it may well have been the threat to employ ground troops, which the Europeans had been pressing for against strong opposition by the Clinton administration, that convinced Milosevic to withdraw from Kosovo. However, NATO's bombing campaign led to the deterioration of relations with Russia and China, and even NATO countries like Greece were less than impressed by NATO's activities in the Kosovo war, which had not been sanctioned by the United Nations.

NATO's involvement in the wars in the Balkans at the turn of the century and the alliance's careful crisis management and disarmament role in Macedonia in 2001 decisively contributed to NATO's new confidence and rediscovered sense of importance. While NATO took the credit for the defeat of Serbia in Kosovo, the poor performance of the European NATO allies catapulted France, the United Kingdom, and other countries into making renewed efforts to build up a European military force. By late 2001 these efforts, though not the intention, had largely petered out. The economic difficulties of the global recession of 2001 and a persistent high rate of unemployment in Europe were welcome excuses for not dedicating an increased share of the national budgets to build up military resources and capabilities. Washington resented this but did appreciate that a European rival to NATO was no longer on the horizon. Even the right-wing administration of George W. Bush had no intention of returning to isolationism and leaving the European continent. In fact, in 2001, as in 1949, NATO was still the most important American instrument for maintaining Washington's involvement in European affairs. This in turn contributed significantly to the ability of the United States to continue playing such a dominant global role.

At the beginning of the twenty-first century, there was widespread perception among both Western politicians and Western public opinion that NATO was still of great relevance. While in the years immediately after the end of the Cold War and German unification many critical voices could be heard that questioned the necessity of NATO's further existence once the Soviet threat had disappeared, in the course of the 1990s this strand of thinking lost support. NATO's on-the-whole not unsuccessful peacemaking activities in the former Yugoslavia decisively contributed to this. In view of an ineffective and divided United Nations, it was increasingly NATO that was seen as a factor of stability in the post–Cold War world. Although the presence of American NATO troops on the European continent was regarded as much less crucial after the disappearance of the Soviet Union than during the Cold War, on the whole, both Washington and the various European countries still viewed them as a constructive force for good. They still gave the United States an important political and military voice in intra-European squabbles and contributed an element of psychological security to latent French fears about the rise of a too powerful Germany. For the United States, its troops in Europe made global military activities in the Balkans and elsewhere logistically easier. But perhaps most important, they provided Washington with a crucial, albeit expensive, symbol of its global reach and worldwide power and influence. Perhaps surprisingly, most European countries were keen on the continuation of America's military presence in Europe. By the early years of the twenty-first century, the Western public's hostility to NATO, which could be frequently observed during the Cold War, had almost disappeared, and most eastern European nations were keen on joining NATO as soon as possible. Even Russia indicated that it would like to become a member. While this posed the question of whether NATO would make itself redundant once most of Europe had joined the alliance, this was not the way it was viewed in Brussels or indeed in Washington and most European capitals. NATO, it was argued, was the primary factor of stability in the post–Cold War world. The alliance appeared to be here to stay for a significant period of time.

Yet NATO was also faced with a great number of new challenges. There were increasingly heated transatlantic difficulties in political, military, and, perhaps most importantly, economic and trade areas. NATO's crisis management capability was persistently challenged by the enduring civil wars in the former Yugoslavia and elsewhere. The enlargement of the alliance posed further serious problems, antagonizing Russia and also the countries who would be left outside. Increasing the number of NATO members also complicated organizational, operational, and indeed financial dimensions of NATO. George W. Bush's declaration to develop a missile defense shield to protect the United States (and perhaps its allies) from nuclear attacks by so-called rogue states, a scheme similar to Reagan's ultimately unrealistic SDI program, exposed great rifts within NATO. Most European NATO members strongly opposed Bush's scheme; it was regarded as technologically untested and prohibitively expensive. The missile defense scheme also appeared to be politically destabilizing as it threatened to undermine relations with countries such as Russia and China and to lead to a new arms race. The terrorist attack on America's financial and political centers in New York and Washington, D.C., in September 2001 demonstrated however that unprecedented terrorist attacks that could not be prevented by even the most sophisticated antimissile scheme were to be feared more than attacks from foreign states. It threatened to undermine relations with countries such as Russia and China and to lead to a new arms race.

Despite these problems, it was thought that for the foreseeable future reasonable transatlantic relations would be maintained. In all likelihood European Union member states would reluctantly agree to continue accepting American predominance within NATO. Ultimately, however, the latter will be influenced by American flexibility and willingness to enter into a constructive dialogue with its allies. During the Cold War, American unilateralism always caused great resentment and proved damaging to the alliance. In the post–Cold War world Washington's European NATO allies were even more unlikely than before to accept this. Yet, American unilateralism may well have been profoundly undermined by the terrorist bombing of American cities in September 2001. Asking for the invocation of article 5 of the NATO treaty was an indication that the Bush administration hoped to fight the war against terrorism with the help of multilateralism and close cooperation with the NATO allies. While the United States will still, and quite justifiably in view of its powerful military and economic potential, demand a clear leadership role, it can be expected that this new kind of war can only be successfully fought with the help of a common cooperative effort.

BIBLIOGRAPHY

Barnett, Richard J. *The Alliance: America, Europe, Japan, Makers of the Postwar World.* New York, 1983.

Baylis, John. *The Diplomacy of Pragmatism: Britain and the Formation of NATO, 1942–1949.* Basingstoke, U.K., 1992.

Calleo, David. *The Atlantic Fantasy: The U.S., NATO, and Europe.* Baltimore, 1970.

Cornish, Paul. *Partnership in Crisis: The U.S., Europe, and the Fall and Rise of NATO.* London, 1997.

Di Nolfo, Ennio, ed. *The Atlantic Pact Forty Years Later: A Historical Appraisal.* Berlin, 1991. Essays published on the occasion of NATO's fortieth anniversary in 1989.

Duffield, John S. *Power Rules: The Evolution of NATO's Conventional Force Posture.* Stanford, Calif., 1995. See for the development of NATO's conventional and nuclear strategies.

Gregory, Shaun. *Nuclear Command and Control in NATO: Nuclear Weapons Operations and the Strategy of Flexible Response.* Basingstoke, U.K., 1996.

Heller, Francis H., and John R. Gillingham, eds. *NATO: The Founding of the Atlantic Alliance and the Integration of Europe.* New York, 1992.

Heuser, Beatrice. *NATO, Britain, France, and the FRG: Nuclear Strategies and Forces for Europe, 1949–2000.* Basingstoke, U.K., 1997.

Ireland, Timothy P. *Creating the Entangling Alliance: The Origins of the North Atlantic Treaty Organization.* London, 1981.

Kaplan, Lawrence S. *The United States and NATO: The Formative Years.* Lexington, Ky., 1984.

———. *NATO and the United States: The Enduring Alliance.* Updated ed. New York and Toronto, 1994.

———. *The Long Entanglement: NATO's First Fifty Years.* Westport, Conn., 1999. A useful collection of the author's journal articles on NATO.

Kaplan, Lawrence S., ed. *American Historians and the Atlantic Alliance.* Kent, Ohio, 1991. The very different views of American historians on NATO.

Martin, Pierre, and Mark R. Brundy, eds. *Alliance Politics: Kosovo and NATO's War: Allied Force or Forced Allies?* Basingstoke, U.K., 2001.

Mattox, Gale A., and Arthur R. Rachwald, eds. *Enlarging NATO: The National Debates.* Boulder, Colo., 2001.

Menon, Anand. *France, NATO, and the Limits of Independence, 1981–1997: The Politics of Ambivalence.* Basingstoke, U.K., and New York, 2000. Covers France's ambiguous attitude toward U.S. domination of NATO.

Norton, Augustus R., comp. *NATO: A Bibliography and Resource Guide.* New York and London, 1985.

Osgood, Robert E. *NATO: The Entangling Alliance.* Chicago, 1962. One of the first and a still useful scholarly books dealing with the creation of NATO.

Sandler, Todd M., and Keith Hartely. *The Political Economy of NATO: Past, Present and Into the Twenty-First Century.* Cambridge and New York, 1999.

Schmidt, Gustav, ed. *A History of NATO.* New York, 2001. One of the best overviews of the history of NATO by a plethora of experts, based on conferences held on NATO's fiftieth anniversary in 1999.

Schwartz, David N. *NATO's Nuclear Dilemmas.* Washington, D.C., 1983. See for the development of NATO's conventional and nuclear strategies.

Smith, Mark. *NATO Enlargement During the Cold War: Strategy and System in the Western Alliance.* Basingstoke, U.K., 2000.

Thomas, Ian Q. R. *The Promise of Alliance: NATO and the Political Imagination.* Lanham, Md.,

1997. A highly interest approach to the history of NATO with a focus on the organization's political culture and its political dimensions and goals.

Williams, Geoffrey Lee, and Barkley Jared Jones. *NATO and the Transatlantic Alliance in the Twenty-First Century: The Twenty-Year Crisis.* Basingstoke, U.K., 2001.

Yost, David S. *NATO Transformed: The Alliance's New Role in International Security.* Washington, D.C., 1998.

See also ALLIANCES, COALITIONS, AND ENTENTES; BALANCE OF POWER; COLD WAR ORIGINS; COLLECTIVE SECURITY; CONTAINMENT; INTERNATIONAL ORGANIZATION; POST–COLD WAR POLICY; SUMMIT CONFERENCES.

NUCLEAR STRATEGY AND DIPLOMACY

Kenneth J. Hagan and Elizabeth Skinner

On 6 August 1945 a single atomic bomb (A-bomb) dropped from an American B-29 bomber, named *Enola Gay* after the pilot's mother, leveled the Japanese city of Hiroshima and killed well over 80,000 residents. Three days later a second bomb smashed Nagasaki, exterminating 60,000 inhabitants. Emperor Hirohito forced the Supreme War Council to allow the government to sue for peace. Although World War II ended in the convulsive birth of the atomic age, the fiery climax failed to validate the putative war-winning efficacy of "strategic bombing." On 8 August the Soviet Union had broken its neutrality in the Pacific and declared war against Japan. News that the Red Army was sweeping across Manchuria caused greater alarm in official Japan than the latest episodes in a relentless American aerial campaign that in previous months included the fire-bombing of Japanese cities at the cost of more than 300,000 lives.

President Harry S. Truman justified history's first use of an atomic weapon on the grounds of military necessity. By the middle of 1945 the United States had dismembered Japan's overseas empire, blockaded its home islands, and razed a total of 178 square miles in sixty-six cities targeted with incendiary bombs. Still, Japan had refused to meet the long-standing American demand for unconditional surrender, a stipulation reiterated in July 1945 at the Potsdam Conference of Allied chiefs of state. Thus, short of some deus ex machina, an American invasion of Japan proper seemed inescapable. Its advocates, the strategic planners of the U.S. Army, recognized that fatalistic and suicidal Japanese resistance would "make the invasion of their homeland a horrendously costly endeavor." The disputed estimates of potential U.S. Army and Marine Corps casualties have ranged from the tens of thousands to more than 500,000. These figures do not reflect the inevitably heavy naval losses to kamikaze and midget submarine suicide attacks. Truman understandably chose to seek a cheaper victory through the shock of atomic bombing.

Devastating though it was to Japan, the atomic bombing of Hiroshima and Nagasaki had more significance for the future than for ending World War II. By 1945 twentieth-century warfare had witnessed the introduction of several revolutionary weapons systems characterized by horrifying destructiveness—the machine gun, the tank, the strategic bomber, and the submarine—but none of these remotely approached the nuclear bomb in transforming strategy and diplomacy. In the nuclear age, for the first time in history, armies and navies were no longer the principal objects at immediate risk in warfare. With their soldiers untouched and still waiting to engage the enemy, nations now could be obliterated in their entirety—populations, cities, societies. In his magisterial book *The American Way of War* (1973), Russell Weigley observed, "A strong strategy of annihilation could now be so complete that the use of . . . atomic weapons could no longer serve 'for the object of war,' unless the object of war was to transform the enemy's country into a desert." After August 1945, it therefore became the prime objective of the statesmen of the great powers to repudiate Carl von Clausewitz's famous dictum that war is merely "a continuation of policy by other means." The "other means" no longer could include the unlimited warfare symbolized by the American Civil War and the eastern front of World War II.

Despite fundamentally opposed political philosophies and almost universal pessimistic expectation, the leaders of the United States and Soviet Union grimly and steadfastly refrained from using the ultimate weapons in their arsenals during the half century between Hiroshima and the sociopolitical implosion of the USSR in 1991. Time and again, Soviet and American heads of state substituted statecraft for warfare as they patched together agreements aimed at curtailing

>
>
> ## HIROSHIMA: A MILITARY TARGET
>
> "The world will note that the first atomic bomb was dropped on Hiroshima, a military base. That was because we wished in the first instance to avoid, in so far as possible, the killing of civilians."
>
> — *President Harry S. Truman, 9 August 1945* —

the enlargement of one another's stockpiles of nuclear weapons. Time and again, after seeming to establish a numerical ceiling, one or the other superpower—but usually the United States—would make an "end run" around the existing agreements with a technological breakthrough in delivery vehicles or nuclear warheads. Then the game began again. Amid mutual recriminations, Soviet and American negotiators stitched together another diplomatic limit governing the nature and quantity of weapons in their arsenals. The number grew to uncountable thousands, but not one nuclear weapon was ever actually launched at the opponent and detonated in anger.

The noted Cold War historian John L. Gaddis has described the Soviet-American era of nuclear restraint as "The Long Peace," and Arthur M. Schlesinger, Jr., has suggested that "nukes" be awarded the Nobel Peace Prize. Gaddis falls somewhat short of the mark, and Schlesinger seems facetious, but each was trying to encapsulate the magnitude of a phenomenal achievement, one without precedent and probably without sequel. The sobering reality is that in the 1990s nuclear strategy and diplomacy entered a new epoch, one in which the inexorable proliferation of "weapons of mass destruction" among second- and third-tier states posed unforeseen and highly complex challenges to the major powers' desire to avoid actual use of such weapons in combat.

THE FUTILE STRATEGY OF ATOMIC MONOPOLY

Historians today agree that ending World War II dominated the president's thinking in the summer of 1945. However, for many years "revisionists" contended that Truman's desire to practice what the scholar Gar Alperovitz aptly called "atomic diplomacy" strongly affected his decision to authorize the nuclear attack on Japan. According to this thesis, Truman sought to influence Soviet policy by dramatically proving that the United States possessed an unprecedentedly destructive weapon that American leaders were willing to use against an enemy. With one awesome stroke Truman could show his mettle as a tough warrior, end the war, depreciate the Soviet Union's claim to share in the occupation of Japan, and discourage Soviet communism's expansion into Europe and Asia. Overstated though it was, the Alperovitz thesis described one very real rationale for dropping the atomic bombs on Japan, and Truman certainly anticipated that a great geopolitical advantage would accrue to the United States from its atomic monopoly. What he did not foresee was the vehement reaction of Soviet Premier Joseph Stalin, who interpreted the atomic bombing as an anti-Soviet action disruptive to the postwar balance of power. No matter how unrealistic it was in the first place, any lingering hope of Soviet-American harmony in the early postwar world was doomed on 6 August 1945.

In a radio address delivered the day Nagasaki was bombed, President Truman elaborated the fundamental tenet of his postwar nuclear policy. Because the atomic bomb "is too dangerous to be loose in a lawless world," he warned, "Great Britain and the United States, who have the secret of its production, do not intend to reveal the secret until means have been found to control the bomb so as to protect ourselves and the rest of the world from the danger of total destruction." It soon became obvious that in the minds of American policymakers, "control" connoted some kind of global inspection system.

At first, prospects for negotiating the international regulation of atomic weapons appeared deceptively bright. In December 1945 the foreign ministers of the United States, Great Britain, and the Soviet Union met in Moscow. They jointly proposed the creation of an atomic energy commission responsible to the United Nations Security Council, where a veto precluded any action abhorrent to one of the five permanent members. The guidelines for the proposed commission also included the inspections demanded by President Truman.

On 24 January 1946 the General Assembly voted unanimously to form the UN Atomic Energy Commission (UNAEC) precisely as envisioned by the three foreign ministers. In June the commission met to forge the machinery for controlling atomic weapons. The American delegate, Bernard Baruch, immediately derailed the negotiations by introducing the concept of an International Atomic Development Authority that would operate independently of the Security Council. This autonomous body would have the power to punish, possibly by atomic attack, any nation that violated its pledge not to construct nuclear weapons. In a single sentence that broke the Moscow agreement, Baruch tersely explained the American rejection of the Security Council as the ultimate punitive agency of the United Nations: "There must be no veto to protect those who violate their solemn agreements not to develop or use atomic energy for destructive purposes."

Baruch's astringent tone reflected the views of a president increasingly worried by the deterioration of American relations with the Soviet Union. During the spring of 1946 the Soviet Union and the United States had failed to agree about the admission of Soviet satellite states to the United Nations, the composition of the Security Council's military arm, and the future of Germany. Moreover, Truman was upset by Soviet penetration of Iran and Manchuria, the latter an area of historic interest to the United States. According to the official historians of the U.S. Atomic Energy Commission, the president recalled the Manchurian crisis of 1931 and 1932, reasoning that if Secretary of State Henry L. Stimson had been able to threaten the use of force at that time, World War II would have been avoided. For all of these reasons, Truman decided that the veto rendered the Security Council impotent against any transgression by the Soviet Union.

By the middle of 1946 the Soviet Union had also shifted its position on the international regulation of nuclear weapons. Five days after Baruch spoke, the Soviet delegate, Andrei Gromyko, addressed the UN Atomic Energy Commission. Ignoring the American's remarks, Gromyko proposed a multilateral treaty binding the signatories to destroy "all stocks of atomic weapons whether in a finished or unfinished condition" within three months. The Russian made no provision for inspections to ensure compliance, thus rendering his proposal utterly unacceptable to an American president who refused to "throw away our gun until we are sure the rest of the world can't arm against us."

Truman was not the only senior American to favor the threatening metaphor of a gun. In September 1945, at a reception held during a London meeting of the foreign ministers of the United States, Soviet Union, and England, Secretary of State James F. Byrnes chided Soviet Foreign Minister Vyacheslav M. Molotov, "If you don't cut all this stalling and let us get down to work, I am going to pull an atomic bomb out of my hip pocket and let you have it." This crude sortie into atomic diplomacy led to what the historian Gregg Herkin has described as Molotov's "reverse atomic psychology." The durable old Bolshevik made several dismissive jokes of his own, the import of which was to let the United States know that Byrnes "could not use the threat of the bomb to gain political concessions from the Soviet Union."

As hope for the international control of atomic weapons waned at the United Nations, the Truman administration began to shape a coherent nationalistic nuclear policy. The domestic political impediments were formidable. Congress was demanding sharply reduced postwar military expenditures and rapid demobilization of all branches of the armed forces. The army, for example, shrank from more than eight million men to fewer than two million in nine months. In this postwar environment, Truman won approval only for establishment of the Strategic Air Command (SAC) in March 1946 and a test of the effectiveness of atomic weapons against ships at Bikini atoll later in the year.

Watchful waiting characterized American foreign policy immediately after the failure of the Baruch plan. Then, beginning in February 1947, a series of crises swept the noncommunist world. Britain's announcement of its inability to continue to sustain anticommunist forces in Greece and Turkey elicited an immediate promise of aid from President Truman, the first formal step toward the policy of containment. For sixteen months international tension mounted; in June 1948 it reached a peak with a Soviet blockade of land routes to West Berlin.

American nuclear diplomacy during that year and a half focused more directly on Great Britain than on the Soviet Union. In highly secret wartime agreements, Prime Minister Winston Churchill and President Franklin D. Roosevelt, with the approval of the Belgian government-in-exile, had apportioned the rich Belgian Congo (Democratic Republic of Congo) uranium ore reserves to Britain and the United States on an equal basis. At Quebec, in 1943, they also had agreed that neither nation would use atomic weapons in war without the consent of the other. By mid-1947 policymakers in Washington viewed these two agreements as detrimental to the United States. In order to enlarge its nuclear arsenal, the United States needed more than half of the annual supply of the Congo's ore. To exercise full control over its own foreign and military policies, Washington had to eliminate London's voice in the use of atomic weapons. Britain finally agreed to these American demands in December 1947, receiving in exchange the promise of technical aid in the search for peaceful uses for atomic energy.

The military facet of Anglo-American nuclear interdependence manifested itself in the early weeks of the Berlin blockade (June 1948–May 1949), when the British permitted the newly autonomous U.S. Air Force to deploy to England three squadrons of B-29 bombers, which may have been modified to carry atomic bombs. This deployment was the first forward staging of American strategic airpower since World War II. It complemented the growing emphasis on military aviation within the United States, as evidenced by appointment of the aggressive General Curtis E. LeMay to head SAC, accelerated development of long-range atomic bombers, and agitation in Congress and the new Department of Defense for a seventy-combat-group air force. The American search for overseas air bases to encircle the Soviet Union and threaten it with nuclear attack began in earnest with the creation of the North Atlantic Treaty Organization (NATO) in 1949.

In August 1949 the Soviet Union successfully detonated an atomic bomb, ending the American nuclear monopoly fifteen years earlier than anticipated by Washington. Secretary of State Dean Acheson, Secretary of Defense Louis Johnson, and members of the powerful Congressional Joint Committee on Atomic Energy pleaded with President Truman to counter the Soviet technological surge by building a hydrogen bomb. The outgoing chairman of the Atomic Energy Commission (AEC), David Lilienthal, openly expressed the fear of such scientists as J. Robert Oppenheimer that it was morally wrong for the United States to base its foreign policy on "a weapon of genocide." But other equally prominent scientists, notably the nuclear physicists Ernest O. Lawrence and Edward Teller, argued the Soviet Union would surely try to outflank the American preponderance in fission weapons by developing a fusion weapon, or H-bomb, as quickly as possible. The only way for the United States to retain overall predominance in nuclear weapons technology was through creation of the hydrogen bomb, which Truman ordered in January 1950. He simultaneously directed a thoroughgoing reassessment of American foreign and military policy by the State Department, Department of Defense, and National Security Council (NSC). By April, Paul Nitze of the State Department had written NSC 68, a blueprint for the future that Truman approved in September.

NSC 68 was a stark document whose authors attributed to Moscow a "fundamental design" of completely subverting or forcibly destroying the governments and societies of the non-Soviet world and replacing them with "an apparatus and structure subservient to and controlled from the Kremlin." Only the United States had the potential to thwart Russian expansionism and ultimately "foster a fundamental change in the nature of the Soviet system." But successful containment would require that America increase its own political, economic, and military power and aid its allies in strengthening themselves. To ensure maximum American strength, NSC 68 discouraged seeking a negotiated control of atomic energy because agreement "would result in a relatively greater disarmament of the United States than of the Soviet Union." Looking ahead to 1954, when the Soviet Union presumably would possess a substantial atomic stockpile of its own, NSC 68 postulated a time of maximum danger during which the Soviet Union could lay waste the British Isles, destroy the communications centers of western Europe, or devastate "certain vital centers of the United States and Canada."

This suspicious and bellicose attitude permeated the highest levels of the executive branch when the advent of the Korean War in June 1950 loosened congressional constraints on massive military expenditures. President Truman immediately sought and obtained supplemental appropriations for the defense budget. By 1952 he had nearly quadrupled annual military spending, which had averaged about $15 billion since 1946. Although the president allocated a great deal of the hugely expanded sum to Korea and the buildup of conventional forces for NATO, the increase also made possible an exponential enlargement of the American capacity to wage nuclear war.

Truman moved on several fronts. First, he accelerated production of a hydrogen bomb. In theory, H-bombs can have unlimited explosive power, and their deadly radiation effects vastly exceed those of atomic, or fission, bombs such as those unleashed on Hiroshima and Nagasaki. The Atomic Energy Commission successfully tested a fusion device on 1 November 1952. A viable hydrogen bomb was added to the American stockpile in 1956, a year after the Soviets had developed their own practicable H-bomb. The second most important item on President Truman's atomic agenda was multiplication of fission weapons. Discovery of rich uranium deposits in the American Southwest and construction of several plutonium-producing reactors contributed to this atomic proliferation, but the big breakthrough in sources came with the determination in 1951 that the amount of fissionable material required for a bomb could be cut in half by surrounding the nuclear core with a neutron shield. The new abundance of fissionable substances permitted a third advance, the creation of "tactical" nuclear weapons. General Omar N. Bradley, chairman of the Joint Chiefs of Staff, had publicly advocated this step in October 1949. Speaking as a soldier challenging the congressional popularity of the Strategic Air Command, Bradley argued that wars were won on battlefields, not by destruction of cities and factories. If Soviet armies massed to invade western Europe, tactical nuclear weapons could devastate them. Only in that manner could the thin divisions of NATO defeat a numerically superior foe.

Bradley won the endorsement of key nuclear physicists and congressmen. By the fall of 1951, Representative Henry Jackson of Washington State, a member of the Joint Committee on Atomic Energy, was urging an annual expenditure of between $6 and $10 billion for tactical nuclear weapons. Under this pressure, the Atomic Energy Commission moved energetically. In March 1953 it exploded a fifteen-kiloton device amid simulated battlefield conditions. Two months earlier, at President Dwight D. Eisenhower's inaugural parade, the army had displayed a cannon capable of firing nuclear projectiles.

The Truman administration and Congress created many highly sophisticated delivery systems for new weapons. The very high-altitude, all-jet B-52 Stratofortress bomber with a range of 7,000 miles was beginning to take shape as the principal strategic aircraft of the future. As a stopgap measure, to replace the piston-driven B-29 strategic bomber of World War II, Truman acquired bases from America's allies for the intermediate-range, six-jet-engine Boeing B-47. Congress allotted funds for the first aircraft carrier capable of launching jet-powered nuclear bombers, the Forrestal-class supercarrier with a flight deck nearly 1,000 feet long. The Atomic Energy Commission and Westinghouse designed a reactor to fuel some of the new aircraft carriers, but nuclear propulsion of submarines had the navy's highest priority thanks to the unrelenting vigor of one naval officer, Hyman G. Rickover. In June 1952 the keel was laid for a nuclear-propelled prototype, the USS *Nautilus* (SSN-571). It would signal "underway on nuclear power" on 17 January 1955.

At a rapid pace, the U.S. Navy fashioned and deployed two distinct types of nuclear-fueled submarines. The "attack boat," or SSN, came first. It was intended for the classic submarine role of striking ships or other submarines with torpedoes. Five years after Truman left office, Chief of Naval Operations Arleigh E. Burke prodded Congress to fund the first nuclear-driven, ballistic-missile-launching submarine (SSBN). Armed with ballistic missiles of ever-increasing range—first Polaris (1,200 nautical miles), later Poseidon (2,500 nm), finally Trident (4,000 nm)—this truly revolutionary weapons system aimed warheads at cities and other targets deep inland. It guaranteed the navy a permanent place in the strategic or nuclear "triad" of weaponry intended to deter Soviet attacks on the United States, or to launch a devastating retaliatory strike if deterrence failed.

Truman did not intend these weapons for limited war, but of necessity he had to consider the employment of atomic weaponry in the darkest days of the Korean War. On 30 November 1950, as Chinese troops swept General Douglas MacArthur's vastly outnumbered soldiers and marines south from the Yalu River, the president held a press conference. In answering a question about possibly dropping the atomic bomb on North Korea or China, he said, "There has always been active consideration of its use." He immediately added, "I don't want to see it used. It is a terrible weapon, and it should not be used on innocent men, women, and children who have nothing to do with this military aggression." But the doomsday alarm had been sounded. John Hersey, author of the widely read book *Hiroshima*, wrote, "There were glaring headlines in Paris.... Big headlines in Finland gave the impression that MacArthur had already received the go-ahead. In Vienna, the story had the lead in all the morning papers except the Soviet army sheet."

A thoroughly aroused House of Commons dispatched Prime Minister Clement Attlee to Washington to determine exactly what Truman was contemplating. At an extended series of high-level meetings in early December, the president attempted to mollify the Briton with the prayer that "world conditions would never call for the use of the atomic bomb." But he would not categorically rule out use of the bomb if the UN position deteriorated radically and MacArthur was in danger of being driven off the Korean peninsula. As it was, the UN forces stemmed the tide and the front was gradually stabilized roughly along the thirty-eighth parallel of north latitude, the original dividing line between North and South Korea.

General MacArthur has been popularly condemned for advocating the use of atomic weapons, as indeed he did. In December 1952 he told his former protégé, president-elect Dwight D. Eisenhower, "I would have dropped between 30 and 50 atomic bombs." But contemplation of a nuclear war in Korea was widespread in Washington between 1950 and 1953. The Joint Chiefs of Staff fantasized about implanting a cordon sanitaire north of the Yalu River with cobalt 60, a highly radioactive residue derived from reprocessed plutonium. Always eager to be involved in a bombing campaign, General Curtis LeMay, head of SAC, thought his airmen were well qualified to drop nuclear bombs because of their "intimate knowledge" of atomic weaponry. He almost got his chance. According to the historian Stanley Sandler, B-36s armed with nuclear weapons were deployed to Okinawa in June 1952 to induce the Chinese to sign an armistice. Across town from the Joint Chiefs of Staff, Representative Albert Gore, Sr., a member of the Joint Committee on Atomic Energy, believed radiating a large strip of the Chinese-Korean border was "morally justifiable" since Korea had become "a meat grinder of American manhood." In the supercharged atmosphere of early Cold War Washington, there was abundant domestic support for a nuclear war in Korea. The "buck" stopped with the president, as Harry Truman said it always did.

The American commander in chief refrained from authorizing atomic warfare against Korea or China partly out of belief that the Korean War was a Soviet feint and that the real communist attack would come in Europe, in which case the United States would need all of its nearly 300 atomic warheads. Moreover, by using atomic weapons the United States could spark North Korean retaliation against Pusan or other South Korean cities with Soviet-supplied atomic bombs. British disapproval and the racist implications of again employing the ultimate weapon against an Asian people contributed to Truman's restraint. Atomic diplomacy also helped stay his hand. In the opinion of one veteran of the Korean War, the historian Stanley Weintraub, Truman realized that if the bomb were used in Korea without producing "decisive results, it would lose credibility as a Cold War deterrent." The president therefore accepted a stalemate in conventional warfare in Korea while simultaneously fathering what Atomic Energy Commission chairman Gordon Dean described in September 1952 as "a complete 'family' of atomic weapons, for use not only by strategic bombers, but also by ground support aircraft, armies, and navies."

A STRATEGY OF OVERKILL

Dwight D. Eisenhower, who succeeded Truman in January 1953, warmly embraced this monstrous "family." The new Republican president's conservative economic advisers demanded a balanced budget, and reduction of swollen defense expenditures was an obvious step in that direction. Complementing this fiscal orthodoxy was Eisenhower's conviction that Soviet leaders hoped their military challenge would force the United States into what he called "an unbearable security burden leading to economic disaster.... Communist guns, in this sense, have been aiming at an economic target no less than a military target." He abandoned NSC 68's conception of a time of maximum danger and began planning a less costly strategy for the "long haul." Throughout his two terms (1953–1961), Eisenhower limited annual defense spending to about $40 billion. He sought to deter communist aggression with an array of nuclear weapons rather than a large army. His strategic mainstay was SAC, supplemented by the navy's carrier-based atomic bombers and its new fleet of submarines (SSBNs) armed with the Polaris ballistic missile. By the late 1950s, SAC was flying 1,500 intermediate-range B-47 jet bombers from domestic and foreign air bases, and the intercontinental B-52 heavy bomber became operational, the first of a final total of 500. If deterrence or tactical nuclear weapons failed to prevent a Red Army sweep through western Europe—or if the Soviet air force dropped nuclear bombs on the United States—Eisenhower would employ his strategic airpower to destroy Soviet Russia.

Until 1957, when the Soviet Union demonstrated its technological sophistication by launching the *Sputnik* satellite and an intercontinental ballistic missile (ICBM) with a range of about

3,500 nautical miles, American policymakers generally considered a Soviet ground attack upon western Europe the most likely form of overt aggression. To cope with a Red Army advance in Europe, or a communist military offensive anywhere else, the Eisenhower administration adopted an asymmetrical strategy. On 12 January 1954, in a speech before the Council on Foreign Relations in New York, Secretary of State John Foster Dulles stated that to meet communist aggression the United States would "depend primarily upon a great capacity to retaliate, instantly, by means and at places of our choosing." This public pronouncement of the doctrine of "massive retaliation" capped an intensive high-level review of American strategy begun the previous May. As early as October 1953, Eisenhower had approved NSC 162/2, a paper attempting to reconcile deterrence with reduced defense spending. The solution, labeled the "New Look," was to equip U.S. troops in Europe with tactical nuclear weapons whose destructiveness would permit him to reduce "the big, expensive army he had inherited from Truman."

To preclude bankrupting the U.S. economy with military spending, Eisenhower planned to shrink the army from twenty to fourteen combat divisions by mid-1957. He would arm this leaner army with atomic artillery and short-range, air-breathing missiles carrying nuclear warheads. In February 1954 he induced Congress to amend the Atomic Energy Act to permit divulging information about operational characteristics of American nuclear weapons to NATO allies. By December 1954 he had persuaded NATO strategists to assume that tactical nuclear weapons would be used in any future conflict with the Red Army. American General Lauris Norstad, NATO's supreme commander, succinctly summarized the new strategy in January 1956. The threat to use tactical nuclear weapons would "link the lowest and highest levels of violence and reinforce the credibility of the Western deterrent."

Although the rhetoric of massive retaliation usually did not discriminate between geographic areas, Eisenhower did have a different plan to meet aggression beyond Europe and the Western Hemisphere. If a noncommunist Asian nation were attacked, he intended to place the primary burden of defense upon that country's ground troops. The U.S. Navy's fiercely mobile aircraft carriers could be rushed into the arena, and in extreme cases the marines might be landed for finite periods. Nuclear airpower conceivably

MASSIVE RETALIATION

"Local defense will always be important. But there is no local defense which alone will contain the mighty land power of the Communist world. Local defenses must be reinforced by the further deterrent of massive retaliatory power. A potential aggressor must know that he cannot always prescribe battle conditions that suit him. . . .

"The way to deter aggression is for the free community to be willing and able to respond vigorously at places and with means of its own choosing."

— *Secretary of State John Foster Dulles at the Council on Foreign Relations, New York City, 12 January 1954* —

might be brought to bear, but only selectively. As Secretary of State Dulles said in a news conference on 18 July 1956, "In the case of a brush-fire war, we need not drop atomic bombs over vast populated areas." It might suffice merely to vaporize key military and industrial installations.

Abstract bombast about massive retaliation notwithstanding, in only three instances did Eisenhower actually warn other governments that the United States was prepared to launch a nuclear attack if its demands were not met. In April 1953 the Korean armistice talks between the communist Chinese and Americans had bogged down over the question of exchanging prisoners of war. At Dulles's behest, neutral India cautioned China that if peace did not come soon, the United States would resort to nuclear warfare. The two sides quickly agreed on international supervision of the repatriation of captured troops. Shortly thereafter, as the French position in Indochina disintegrated, Washington warned Beijing that direct military intervention in support of the communist Vietminh would be met with an American atomic attack on China. Finally, on 20 March 1955, as the communist Chinese bombarded the Nationalist-held islands of Quemoy and Matsu, Dulles publicly speculated about possible American use of "new and powerful weapons of precision, which can utterly destroy military targets without endangering unrelated civilian centers." This foolhardy boast sent shivers around the world, especially throughout Asia, where national leaders recalled ruefully that the only atomic bombs dropped so far had fallen on an Asian people. Eisenhower, who was privately determined to defend the islands with nuclear weapons if necessary, gradually realized that he could not rattle the nuclear sword without arousing global apprehension. According to the scholar Gordon H. Chang, communist China's conciliation had contributed significantly to ending the crisis, but at the cost of Beijing's realization that it would have to build a nuclear force to counter modern-day American gunboat diplomacy in the western Pacific.

The Soviets at the same time were providing additional stimulus for American reconsideration of the doctrine of limited nuclear warfare. They had detonated a hydrogen device in August 1953, unveiled the intercontinental turboprop Bear bomber (Tu-95) in 1954, and displayed the all-jet, long-range Bison bomber (M-4) in 1955. That year they also added a functional hydrogen bomb to their arsenal. Eisenhower's response was to build an extensive radar network and multiply the air force's interceptor wings. But the successful Soviet test of an intercontinental ballistic missile in the summer of 1957, coupled with the October *Sputnik* satellite launch, made these defenses prematurely obsolete. The United States suddenly was exposed to a potential Soviet thermonuclear delivery system against which existing countermeasures were powerless. For the first time, all-out nuclear war would inevitably entail widespread death and destruction within the United States. Since it was impossible to ensure that escalation could be avoided once nuclear weapons of any sort were used anywhere in the world, the threat to use them thereafter must be restricted to crises involving areas absolutely essential to the United States: noncommunist Europe and the Western Hemisphere.

The stage was set for a policy of containment resting on conventional forces that the next president would adopt under the slogan of "flexible response." But Eisenhower's reluctance to spend large sums on defense prevented him from rebuilding or enlarging the army. For the same reasons of fiscal prudence, he also steadfastly resisted public and congressional pressure to disperse SAC aircraft more widely, to begin a crash program of ballistic missile development, or to spend tens of billions of dollars on fallout shelters. In August 1958, when the Department of Defense and some scientists warned him that discontinuation of

FLEXIBLE RESPONSE

"The National Military Program of Flexible Response should contain at the outset an unqualified renunciation of reliance on the strategy of Massive Retaliation. It should be made clear that the United States will prepare itself to respond anywhere, any time, with weapons and forces appropriate to the situation."

— General Maxwell D. Taylor,
The Uncertain Trumpet,
New York, 1960 —

nuclear testing would endanger further evolution of American tactical nuclear weapons, Eisenhower overrode their objections and announced a moratorium on atmospheric testing.

The sophistication of American aviation technology made restraint possible. Beginning in August 1955, the United States regularly flew extremely high-altitude reconnaissance aircraft over the Soviet Union. Dubbed U-2s, these glider-like jets soared above the reach of Soviet air defenses. They returned with photographs proving that the Soviet Union had not built a massive offensive nuclear striking force, despite the technological capacity to do so. The sluggishness of Soviet production permitted Eisenhower to proceed at a measured pace with deployment of ICBMs and intermediate-range ballistic missiles (IRBMs), including the submarine-launched Polaris. Eisenhower also could accurately describe Democratic presidential candidate John Kennedy's alleged "missile gap" as a "fiction." What Eisenhower could not do was win Soviet acquiescence to any form of inspections. Negotiations in the United Nations for the limitation of nuclear armaments therefore remained deadlocked throughout his presidency.

AT THE GATES OF ARMAGEDDON

President John F. Kennedy may have been perpetrating what one observer called a "pure election fraud," but it is more likely that as a candidate he decried the fictitious and nonexistent missile gap because he agreed with the militant representatives and senators in the Democratic Party who disliked Eisenhower's tightly controlled defense spending. In any event, upon becoming president in January 1961, Kennedy admitted that a gap in nuclear weapons indeed existed, but it was favorable to the United States. At that time the United States possessed at least 200 operational strategic missiles of varying range, while the Soviet Union probably had no more than sixteen. Despite this substantial nuclear advantage in missiles alone, in February 1961 Kennedy requested congressional permission to strengthen America's deterrent forces by accelerating the acquisition of second-generation, solid-propellant, land-based ICBMs and nuclear-powered submarines armed with longer-range Polaris ballistic missiles. In a clear reversal of Eisenhower's fiscal conservatism, Kennedy decided to "develop the force structure necessary to our military requirements without regard to arbitrary or predetermined budget ceilings."

The new president also reversed his predecessor by enlarging the nonnuclear, or conventional, forces of the United States. In the summer of 1961, Kennedy seized on Soviet Premier Nikita Khrushchev's bellicosity about the American presence in Berlin to extract from Congress a $3.2 billion supplement to the defense budget. With these funds he increased the armed services by 300,000 men and sent 40,000 more troops to Europe. This deployment underscored Kennedy's commitment to "flexible response," a strategy resting largely on nonnuclear weaponry. He refined the electronic "fail-safe" devices designed to prevent accidental firing of tactical nuclear weapons, discouraged planning that envisioned the use of such weapons, and retarded their technological evolution. These restrictions hampered NATO, which remained numerically inferior to the Red Army, by denying to the alliance the equalizing potential of clean and extremely low-yield tactical nuclear weapons. Thus, massive retaliation remained the only real deterrent to a Soviet military thrust into western Europe; and as the Soviets enhanced their ability to devastate the United States in any strategic nuclear exchange, the ghoulish doctrine became increasingly less reassuring to the NATO countries and less credible to the Soviet Union.

One reason for the Soviet nuclear buildup of the 1960s was the ambiguity of American strategy. From the beginning of the Kennedy presidency, Secretary of Defense Robert S. McNamara insisted on maintaining clear strategic nuclear superiority over the Soviet Union. With Kennedy's concurrence, McNamara increased the number of American ICBMs from about 200 to 1,000, completed the construction of forty-one submarines carrying 656 Polaris missile launchers, oversaw the development of the multiple independently targetable reentry vehicle (MIRV), and kept a large percentage of SAC B-52s in a constant state of alert. Some of these measures, notably the conversion to MIRVs, came late in the decade, but the trend was apparent in 1961. Equally obvious was the possibility that a huge increase in the American stockpile would create a "first strike" capability with which the United States could preemptively attack and destroy the Russian nuclear striking force, thus making Soviet retaliation largely ineffective if not altogether impossible. The Soviets had lived with fears of an American nuclear bombing offensive since 1945, but nuclear-tipped ballistic missiles were virtually impossible to intercept. Kennedy's multiplication of those weapons thus deepened old apprehensions. As if to allay suspicion, on 26 March 1961 the president promised, "Our arms will never be used to strike the first blow in any attack."

Despite Kennedy's reassurance that the United States would not strike first, Khrushchev announced in August 1961 that he was breaking the three-year-old moratorium on nuclear testing in the atmosphere. Worried by the dangers of radioactive fallout, Kennedy at first resorted to underground testing. In April 1962 he resumed atmospheric testing in order to evaluate sophisticated new warheads and to prevent the Soviet Union from scoring a technological breakthrough that would eliminate the American nuclear superiority. Khrushchev then sought a cheap and quick adjustment to the strategic imbalance by placing 900-mile medium-range ballistic missiles (MRBMs) in Cuba. He also hoped to enhance his fading image as a supporter of overseas communist regimes, especially Fidel Castro's Cuban dictatorship, thereby answering hard-liners in Moscow and Beijing who deplored his efforts to ease tensions with the West. In this manner, reinvigoration of the strategic arms race in 1961 led to the Cold War's most dangerous nuclear war scare.

On 14 October 1962, American U-2 reconnaissance aircraft photographed the Cuban missile sites while they were still under construction. For one week the Kennedy administration debated its response, finally settling upon a naval "quarantine" of further shipments of offensive missiles. As he announced his decision to the world on 22 October, President Kennedy also warned that if ballistic missiles were launched from Cuba against any country in the Western Hemisphere, the United States would counter with a "full retaliatory response upon the Soviet Union." While massing troops in Florida for a possible invasion of Cuba, the president insisted that the Soviet Union remove the missiles already on the island. The face-off lasted for another week and was highlighted by an intense debate among the president's most senior advisers over whether to offer a contingent palliative to the Soviet Union: removal of the fifteen American Jupiter IRBMs based in Turkey. Obsolete by the time they became operational in 1962, the Jupiters already "were supposed to be replaced by submarine-launched Polaris missiles." Moscow nonetheless found their presence on the southern Soviet border extremely provocative and destabilizing. Evan Thomas, a meticulous student of the administration, sums up the situation: "President Kennedy was not inalterably opposed to swapping the Jupiters, but he thought it would be foolish to publicly offer right away to trade them." His brother, Attorney General Robert F. Kennedy, therefore privately assured Soviet Ambassador Anatoly Dobrynin that once the Cuban crisis passed, the American missiles would be withdrawn. For the rest of his life, Robert Kennedy feared the political repercussions of his intervention. Dobrynin claimed Robert Kennedy told him that "some day—who knows?—he might run for president, and his prospects could be damaged if this secret deal about the missiles in Turkey were to come out." The dour Robert was as much a political animal as was his glamorous brother.

Khrushchev capitulated and removed the Soviet missiles from Cuba because he feared losing control of the situation. Castro was beseeching the Soviet leader to launch a nuclear attack to stave off an American invasion of Cuba. In Washington, President Kennedy was under equally extreme pressure to take military action. A post-crisis outburst by the air force chief of staff expressed the attitude of the Joint Chiefs of Staff. General Curtis LeMay, who had masterminded the firebombing of Japan and the atomic bombing of Hiroshima and Nagasaki, shouted at the president: "We lost! We ought to just go in there today and knock 'em off." The president knew better. He had risked Armageddon because he regarded the Russian MRBMs as an unacceptable challenge to American strategic superiority and an immediate danger to the nation's security. The missiles were gone; he had achieved his strategic goal, and not incidentally thwarted Republican critics in a congressional election year. Most Americans probably agreed with him in 1962, but with the passage of time the ultimate gamble seems increasingly less defensible. "In retrospect," the strategic analyst Norman Friedman concluded soon after the Cold War ended, "it is difficult to understand why Soviet weapons in Cuba were worth a global war."

The Cuban missile crisis reverberated throughout the 1960s. The continental European members of NATO were shaken by the unilateral way in which the United States went to the brink of nuclear conflagration without consulting its allies. French President Charles de Gaulle reaffirmed his determination to reduce European economic and military dependence upon the United States. In January 1963 he vetoed British entry into the Common Market on the grounds that British membership would make the association "appear as a colossal Atlantic community under American domination and direction." Simultaneously he rejected Kennedy's plan for a multilateral nuclear force (MLF) as a transparent scheme to give the impression of multinational authority while in fact preserving the American veto over NATO's nuclear strategy. To end France's subservience to the United States, De Gaulle gradually immunized his military units from unquestioning subordination to the NATO command, and he ordered the removal of the alliance's headquarters from French soil as of April 1967. To document great power status in the nuclear age, he forged a French atomic striking force, the *force de frappe*. Britain at the same time was building its own strategic nuclear arsenal, but because of the special Anglo-American relationship it faced far fewer developmental obstacles. Kennedy simply provided the Royal Navy with Polaris missiles.

The impact of the missile crisis on Soviet-American relations was tragically paradoxical. On the one hand, the humiliating Soviet retreat strengthened the militants in the Kremlin who favored increased defense expenditures. They resolved that in the future the Soviet Union would deal with the United States as a nuclear equal. On the other hand, leaders in both countries were chastened by having faced nuclear annihilation. They installed a Teletype link, or "hot line," between the White House and the Kremlin to minimize misunderstanding during acute crises. Even in the midst of capitulating, on 29 October 1962, Khrushchev set the tone for further accommodation: "We should like to continue the exchange of views on the prohibition of atomic and thermonuclear weapons, general disarmament, and other problems relating to the relaxation of international tension." For some months Kennedy hesitated. Then, on 10 June 1963, in a speech at American University he made a passionate appeal for peace as "the necessary rational end of rational men." Coupled with various Anglo-American diplomatic initiatives, Kennedy's speech broke the impasse in superpower negotiations. Within weeks Britain, the Soviet Union, and the United States signed the Limited Test Ban Treaty, which prohibited testing nuclear weapons in outer space, in the atmosphere, or under water. The treaty fell short of Kennedy's original goal for a comprehensive test ban that would have preserved American technological superiority by slowing or preventing improvements to the Soviet arsenal. Nevertheless, the U.S. arms control and disarmament director, William C. Foster, reminded Congress that half a loaf was better than none. With the limited test ban, he said, "improvements in yield-to-weight ratios would come more slowly through laboratory work alone. Some weapons effects phenomena would remain unsettled or undiscovered by both sides. . . . In general, our present nuclear advantages would last for a considerably longer period." In September the Senate ratified the Limited Test Ban Treaty by a vote of 80 to 19.

A MAD, MAD WORLD

Two months after Senate ratification of the treaty, on 22 November 1963, President Kennedy was assassinated in Dallas, Texas. The unspeakable tragedy abruptly ended any possibility of subsequent nuclear weapons agreements between himself and Khrushchev. The new president, Lyndon B. Johnson, was focused foremost on ramming through Congress the domestic reforms he advertised as the "Great Society." For continuity and simplicity he kept Kennedy's foreign policy and national security advisers in place, including Secretary of Defense McNamara.

McNamara continued to espouse a variant of the old Dulles doctrine of deterring a Soviet attack through the threat of massive retaliation, a strategic premise not wholly shared by Moscow's leaders. As the secretary of defense explained in his "posture statement" of January 1964, the United States was building a nuclear force of such superiority that it could "ensure the destruction, singly or in combination, of the Soviet Union, communist China, and the communist satellites as national societies." In addition, it could "destroy their war making capability so as to limit . . . damage to this country and its allies." The inconsistency of this statement is patent: there can be no need to destroy an enemy's nuclear arsenal if its entire nation has already been obliterated. But underlying what appeared to be a logical lapse was the dawning and extremely reluctant acknowledgment in Washington of the "difficulties of appreciably limiting damage to the United States and its allies." By 1964, as the strategic historian John Newhouse observed, "the recognition that the United States was in the autumn of its strategic supremacy had set in." The immediate upshot was an unresolved debate about whether nuclear missiles should be "counter-force" weapons targeted only against the Soviet Union's ICBMs and other military assets, or "counter-value" weapons targeted against major Soviet industrial centers and their populations.

A counter-force strategy was preferable for reasons of humanity if nothing else, but the possibility of a counter-value assault by a desperate nuclear power could never be altogether ruled out. The counter-value strategy enjoyed disconcertingly wide theoretical appeal. It lay firmly in the mainstream of the "strategic bombing" doctrines of the Italian theorist Guilio Douhet, who wrote approvingly in 1921, "A complete breakdown of the social structure cannot but take place in a country subjected to this kind of merciless pounding from the air." The army general William "Billy" Mitchell adapted Douhet to the American experience in the 1920s and 1930s, and in World War II the U.S. Army Air Forces had adopted these draconian concepts of annihilating the enemy and its urban-industrial infrastructure. The theories had helped to rationalize the decision to drop the first atomic bombs on Japan in 1945.

In this confused environment, both the United States and the Soviet Union began to design nuclear weapons and delivery systems that could withstand a nuclear first strike and mount a crushing retaliatory strike. The United States led in deployment of such innovative systems as hardened silos, submarine-launched ballistic missiles (SLBMs) of ever-increasing range, new generations of heavy bombers, and MIRVs (a MIRV consisted of several relatively small but highly accurate warheads atop a single ICBM, each destined for an independently preprogrammed target). Toward the end of the decade the ability to cripple the Soviet nuclear arsenal in a gargantuan strike seemed to be coming within America's reach. By 1968 the United States had deployed 1,054 ICBMs to the Soviets' 858, and the U.S. lead in the other indices of nuclear superiority was equally daunting.

Owing to this preponderance and to the enormous fiscal drain that the Vietnam War levied on defense resources, the pace of the United States buildup of strategic weapons actually began to level off at the height of the arms race in 1965. At the same time, the Soviet Union initiated a massive expansion of its strategic forces in an attempt to achieve parity with the United States. Finally conceding that the goal of limiting damage in a nuclear exchange had become unattainable, strategists in Washington began to use the term "assured destruction" in describing the standoff between the two nuclear powers. McNamara himself became convinced that neither further arms buildups nor the visionary antiballistic missile defense system (ABM) could guarantee Americans the security they craved. He began to search for a new formula for strategic stability. The answer was found in a 1946 book entitled *The Absolute Weapon,* in which America's preeminent strategist, Bernard Brodie, argued for nuclear equality between the United States and the Soviet Union. "Neither we nor the Russians," Brodie and his coauthors presciently wrote, "can expect to feel even reasonably safe unless an atomic attack by one were certain to unleash a devastating atomic counterattack by the other." McNamara now adopted this proposition, and it became enshrined in a telling acronym unfairly ascribed to him: MAD, for "mutual assured destruction." The converted secretary made it his mission to proselytize the American and Soviet leadership.

In 1967, U.S. leaders discovered that the Soviet Union was deploying a protective ABM system around Moscow. McNamara anxiously sought to avoid a reactionary massive increase in America's offensive nuclear forces. He persuaded President Johnson to bring up ABM defenses at the summit meeting with Soviet Prime Minister Alexei Kosygin in June 1967 at Glassboro, New Jersey. When Johnson was unable to convince Kosygin that antiballistic missile defenses would only trigger an offensive nuclear arms race, McNamara tried to explain the administration's reasoning to the prime minister. The secretary of defense described at length the action-reaction dynamic he foresaw if the Soviet Union persisted in deploying antimissile shields, and he insisted that the only way to prevent an endless arms race was to limit or even eliminate these embryonic protective systems. This reasoning infuriated Kosygin, who found the idea of abandoning defensive weapons in favor of offensive weapons to be irresponsible and immoral. His premises differed fundamentally from McNamara's. Like other Soviet leaders, Kosygin based his thinking on the cruel lessons of World War II, during which the Soviet Union suffered cataclysmic devastation at the hands of Hitler's invading armies. The imperative "never again" informed all Soviet military planning. For Kosygin, McNamara's proposal to abandon missile defenses was a direct invitation to a reprise of national disaster. Kerry Kartchner, an American disarmament negotiator, observed critically, "there is little evidence that McNamara took actual Soviet strategic thinking about nuclear weapons into account, either in determining what was required to deter Soviet leaders, or how the Soviet Union might react to American deployment of ABMs." McNamara also appeared hypocritical, because as spokesman for the Johnson administration he had testified before Congress in favor of a limited Sentinel ABM system intended to protect cities and ICBM silos from destruction in a Soviet nuclear attack.

By late 1967, McNamara's days in power were nearing their end. He and others within the Johnson administration were belatedly realizing that the parasitical war in Vietnam was unwinnable, and they soon faced incontrovertible evidence that their strategy for waging limited war had failed. The communist Vietnamese Tet offensive of January 1968 broke America's will to fight and precipitated McNamara's resignation as secretary of defense. It also induced Lyndon Johnson to withdraw from the presidential race. In November, Republican Richard M. Nixon was elected president. He inherited only one undeniably positive nuclear policy achievement from the Johnson administration: the multilateral Treaty on the Nonproliferation of Nuclear Weapons (NPT), signed by the Soviet Union and more than fifty other nations in 1968 and ratified by the United States in 1969.

The Nonproliferation Treaty set up a two-tiered "regime" that divided the world into nuclear haves and have-nots. The United States, Soviet Union, France, Britain, and China were designated "nuclear weapons states" by virtue of the fact that they had tested nuclear weapons before 1968. All other parties to the treaty, officially designated as "non-nuclear weapon states," joined with the understanding that they would not seek to import or develop nuclear technology or materials for military purposes. The International Atomic Energy Agency (IAEA), which had been founded by the United Nations in 1957, was given the task of verifying treaty compliance through an elaborate inventory procedure including on-site inspections at regular intervals. The five so-called weapons states were exempt from all such controls, but they were expected to honor the regime out of self-interest. Even so, France and China were dissatisfied and did not ratify the accord until 1992.

During the treaty negotiations, India led the nonaligned states in opposing the treaty's codification of elite status for the weapons states. The principal sop that the five nuclear-armed signatories conceded to the nonnuclear weapons states was the provision to share nonweapon nuclear technology "in good faith." New Delhi strongly objected to the absence of a provision for the enforcement of this obligation. In the end, several important countries, including India, Pakistan, and Israel, refused to sign the treaty; they remained beyond negotiated global nuclear controls. Such a treaty was a thin reed of hope for nonproliferation, as Richard Nixon well knew.

A COOPERATIVE BALANCE OF TERROR

Unscrupulous and devious in many ways, President Nixon was the consummate realist in foreign policy, especially when guided and prodded by his national security affairs adviser, the German émigré and former Harvard professor Henry A. Kissinger. Upon learning that the Soviets were rapidly approaching nuclear parity with the United States, the new president sensibly abandoned the quixotic search for American superiority in nuclear weapons systems and accepted the concept of parity or "sufficiency." He simultaneously made the decision to expand ABM defenses in the name of damage limitation, citing not only the danger from the Soviet Union but also from the People's Republic of China, which recently had joined the special weapons club by testing and deploying a nuclear weapon. Unlike Sentinel, however, the new Nixon Safeguard system was designed exclusively to protect Minuteman ICBM silos. The administration made public its decision that, in light of the Soviet Union's burgeoning offensive nuclear capability, limiting damage to civilian targets no longer was possible. The United States could only hope to preserve a retaliatory capability, the existence of which would deter an opponent from striking first. To further underscore his tough-mindedness and enhance the American retaliatory arsenal, Nixon installed more MIRVs on U.S. ICBMs.

Considering himself to be in a position of diplomatic strength, President Nixon entered into the Strategic Arms Limitation Talks (SALT) negotiations with the Soviet Union in November 1969. The Soviets, for their part, were now willing to negotiate because they were drawing abreast of the United States in numbers of ICBMs, if not in MIRVed warheads. A rough de facto nuclear parity had been achieved, and each side sought to freeze it in order to avoid the astronomical expense of building elaborate ABM systems, which existing technology could not make fully effective. The cost of the Vietnam War was driving American fiscal prudence; the chronic inefficiency of the Soviet economy was inspiring Moscow's circumspection. The two sides, however, were unable to reach any agreement and the SALT I discussions dragged on until the spring of 1972.

Fruition came at a summit in Moscow on 26 May 1972, when the Soviet Union and the United States agreed by treaty to curtail deployment of ABMs. Delegates of the two superpowers also initialed a five-year interim agreement freezing offensive strategic nuclear weapons systems at their existing levels. In essence, the United States conceded to the Soviet Union an advantage in large missiles with horrifically destructive warheads, and the Soviet Union yielded to the United States the countervailing advantage in MIRVs. "What are 3,000 MIRVs among friends?" Henry Kissinger joked, but he later regretted that he had not pondered "the implications of a MIRVed world more thoughtfully."

The ABM Treaty likewise failed to prohibit further development of new delivery systems, such as the supersonic intercontinental B-1 bomber to replace the B-52, longer-range Trident SLBMs to replace the Polaris-Poseidon system, and nuclear-tipped cruise missiles. Maintenance of nuclear parity at the 1972 level, therefore, gave the United States the chance to capitalize on its technological supremacy to make an end run on the Soviets. With characteristic insight and cynicism, Kissinger quipped, "The way to use this freeze is for us to catch up." The Senate showed its appreciation for the advantages of the ABM

Treaty by approving it with an overwhelming vote: 88 to 2. A joint congressional resolution endorsed the five-year moratorium on development of new offensive strategic nuclear weapons.

Nixon's acceptance of atomic equality did not deter him from relying on nuclear weapons in his conduct of foreign and military policy. For example, during the 1973 Yom Kippur War in the Middle East, he authorized a full alert of American strategic forces to forestall intervention by Soviet airborne troops. Similarly, as he progressively reduced the size of the U.S. Army, he permitted his advisers to revive plans for using tactical, or battlefield, nuclear weapons. In January 1971, when speaking about the American defense posture from 1972 through 1976, Secretary of Defense Melvin B. Laird said: "For those levels in the deterrent spectrum below general nuclear war, the forces to deter Soviet and Chinese adventures clearly must have an adequate war-fighting capability, both in limited nuclear and conventional options."

Hoping to capitalize on the success of the ABM Treaty, Nixon ordered new negotiations with the Soviet Union. SALT II opened with promise in November 1972 but soon foundered for several reasons: the scandal of the Watergate burglary and the forced resignation of Nixon in August 1974, Soviet-American disagreements over technical issues, and the objections of militants like Senator Henry Jackson who cried for the restoration of nuclear superiority.

THE LIMITS OF DÉTENTE

The new president, Republican Gerald R. Ford, initially retained Kissinger as both secretary of state and national security affairs adviser, but the old diplomatic wizardry had dissipated. The secretary of state and Soviet Ambassador Anatoly Dobrynin met frequently and maneuvered endlessly for an advantage in arms control negotiations, warily proposing to limit weapons in which the other side had superiority while protecting their own favorites. In the interminable horse-trading, the United States claimed that the supersonic Soviet Backfire bomber (Tu-26) should be included in any new limitations agreements; the Soviets demanded inclusion of American nuclear-armed, ground-hugging, nonballistic cruise missiles. Technological strides kept raising the ante: the Soviet Union was perfecting the triple-MIRVed SS-20 IRBM, a terrifying threat to NATO; the United States was readying highly accurate Pershing IRBMs for NATO deployment and completing the Trident SSBN, with ballistic missiles that had a range of 4,000 nautical miles. Since neither side would yield, the dimming hopes for SALT II were bequeathed to the new Democratic administration of James Earl Carter in January 1977. When Carter took office, the U.S. nuclear inventory stood at 8,500 nuclear warheads in comparison with 5,700 in 1972, and the Soviet count had nearly doubled in the same period. If moderation of the nuclear balance of terror was the benchmark, the Nixon-Kissinger policy of détente had failed miserably.

President Jimmy Carter thought détente was worse than a failure. He believed U.S. strategic potency actually had diminished under Republicans Nixon and Ford: "We've been outtraded in almost every instance." The Naval Academy graduate and former nuclear submariner was perpetually torn between the "mailed fist" of his hawkish national security affairs adviser, Zbigniew Brzezinski, and the "dove's coo" of his temperate and cautious secretary of state, Cyrus R. Vance. The president played off China against the Soviet Union, lectured Moscow on its policy toward Jews and dissident intellectuals, and at the same time tried to reignite the stalled SALT II talks. Soviet Ambassador Dobrynin lamented, "President Carter continued to attack us in public, in public, in public. Always in public."

Two months after Carter's inauguration, Secretary of State Vance flew to Moscow with a proposal to revive the SALT process by radically reducing the number of deployed ICBMs, not surprisingly the nuclear category in which the Soviets held the lead. Initially rebuffed, Vance persevered until Carter and Soviet President Leonid Brezhnev signed the SALT II treaty at a summit meeting in Vienna in June 1979. For the first time, each superpower accepted numerical equality with the other in total nuclear delivery vehicles. The total number of MIRVed launchers for each side was set at 1,200, and the quantity of MIRVs per missile was also fixed. Moscow and Washington promised to allow on-site verification of compliance by representatives from the other side, an unprecedented step forward. Excluded from the agreement were several new high-technology weapons systems: the American MX ("missile experimental"), an improved ICBM that could deliver ten MIRVs to targets 7,000 miles distant from the launch site; the Trident-II SLBM with MIRVed ballistic missiles almost twice the weight of their predecessors; the nonballistic, nuclear-armed cruise missile; and the supersonic Soviet Backfire bomber with a threatening range of 5,500 miles.

This qualified success fell victim to domestic critics and to Soviet-American disputes over hegemony throughout the world. Paul Nitze, the bellicose author of NSC 68, protested against SALT II. He said it was "time for the United States to stand up and not be a patsy." Senator Henry Jackson, always a patron of the arms industry and an intransigent foe of conciliation, complained that SALT II sanctified an imbalance in which the Soviet Union could destroy American land-based nuclear retaliatory forces in a preemptive first strike. In contrast, doves faulted the treaty because it was not comprehensive enough.

The objectors might have scuttled the pact regardless of international affairs, but in the fall of 1979 they were aided immeasurably by Carter's accusation that the Soviets were infiltrating a combat brigade into Cuba. The president vainly attempted to placate his critics and to warn the Soviets. He proclaimed a five-year military expansion program focused on European-based intermediate and cruise missiles, and his personal rage at the Soviet invasion of Afghanistan in December of that year led him to withdraw SALT II from the Senate. Discredited by a wide variety of foreign policy failures, most notably the Iranian hostage crisis (1979–1981), Carter lost the 1980 election to Ronald Reagan, a charismatic movie actor and former governor of California.

TAMING THE EVIL EMPIRE

Pledging to "make America great again," President Reagan carried enough Republican candidates on his popular coattails to win control of the Senate for his party. Reelected by a landslide vote in 1984, he was superbly well positioned to maintain a contentious posture vis-à-vis the Soviet Union, which he denounced with ideological fervor as an "evil empire." He and a kaleidoscopically shifting cast of senior advisers perceived a mortal U.S. disadvantage in strategic armament. The deficit arose primarily from the Soviet Union's greater aggregate "throw-weight," that is, the sheer tonnage of destructive power its missiles could deliver to targets in the United States and NATO countries. This simplistic measure of relative capability was used by the Reagan administration to warn of a "window of vulnerability" through which the United States could be devastated by a preemptive Soviet first strike.

To redress the Soviet Union's ostensible "margin of superiority," Reagan instructed the Pentagon to disregard budgetary restrictions and request whatever weapons it wanted. He goaded Congress to fund accelerated development and deployment of the B-1 bomber, the neutron bomb, the B-2 "stealth bomber," the Trident-II SLBM, the MX and cruise missiles, and mobile Minuteman ICBM launching sites. Thus fortified, President Reagan, Secretary of State George P. Shultz, and Secretary of Defense Caspar W. "Cap" Weinberger undertook arms-reduction talks with the Soviet Union. The Reagan cohort would extort Soviet concessions by using the revived arms race to strain the creaking Soviet economy.

The Reagan administration soon was managing several approaches to strategic security in the wake of the inherited SALT II failure: a rapid buildup of strategic and conventional capabilities; negotiations in 1981 to limit intermediate-range nuclear forces (INF); the opening of talks on a Strategic Arms Reduction Treaty (START) in 1982; and research into space-based antiballistic missile defenses. The Strategic Defense Initiative (SDI), announced in March 1983 and derisively dubbed "Star Wars" by its opponents after the hit science-fiction movie, was an ambitious scheme to put laser-firing satellites into low orbit around the earth. These "killer satellites," assisted by a complex system of ground-based tracking radars, would intercept and destroy ICBMs at the height of their trajectory outside the earth's atmosphere. The program was projected to cost hundreds of billions of dollars, and it relied on future development of problematical new technologies. Domestic opposition based on cost, feasibility, and SDI's contravention of the ABM Treaty remained strong throughout Reagan's presidency.

In 1981, Reagan had suggested a "zero sum" option for tactical nuclear weapons that the Soviet Union promptly rejected. The president promised that NATO would refrain from deploying any American cruise missiles if the Soviet Union eliminated the ballistic missiles it had aimed at western Europe, including existing systems that had never been on the negotiating table before. This suggestion that the Soviet Union scrap extant missiles to preclude American deployment of systems that as yet were in the planning stage dumbfounded Soviet leaders. In November 1983 they broke off the INF discussions.

The U.S. arms buildup continued during a two-year hiatus in negotiations, as did NATO's planning for deployment of intermediate-range

>
>
> ## THE EVIL EMPIRE
>
> "So, in your discussions of the nuclear freeze proposals, I urge you to beware the temptation of pride—the temptation of blithely declaring yourselves above it all and label both sides equally at fault, to ignore the facts of history and the aggressive impulses of an evil empire, to simply call the arms race a giant misunderstanding and thereby remove yourself from the struggle between right and wrong and good and evil."
>
> — *Remarks by President Ronald Reagan, 8 March 1983, at the annual convention of the National Association of Evangelicals in Orlando, Florida* —

nuclear weapons in Europe. The inhabitants of NATO nations and other European countries did not wholeheartedly accept the alliance's decision to place additional U.S. tactical nuclear forces in Europe as counters to Soviet SS-20s, SS-5s, and SS-4s. Street protests erupted in the Federal Republic of Germany and the Netherlands, while parliaments and citizens across Europe reacted with alarm. Any Soviet attempt to turn these apparent fissures in NATO to negotiating advantage was foredoomed by a rapid succession of top leaders in Moscow. President Brezhnev had died in 1982, his successor, Yuri Andropov, in 1984, and Andropov's heir a year later.

Negotiations based on versions of Reagan's 1981 zero sum languished until Mikhail Gorbachev became the new secretary general of the Communist Party in March 1985. Relatively young at age fifty-four, and refreshingly dynamic in contrast with the typical Soviet apparatchik, Gorbachev was absolutely determined to liberalize the Soviet political system (*glasnost*), reform the economy (*perestroika*), and reduce expenditures for arms, especially nuclear missile systems. According to Michael K. Deaver, who served as Ronald Reagan's personal adviser for twenty years, the president sensed in Gorbachev a kindred spirit. "With Gorbachev, Reagan could do business, and business they would do, eliminating entire classes of nuclear weapons and paving the way for the literal collapse of arguably the greatest enemy we have ever faced." In three separate summit meetings between 1985 and 1987, this unique rapport greatly facilitated negotiations—up to a point. At the October 1986 meeting in Reykjavík, Iceland, the two heads of state came tantalizingly close to agreement on sweeping reductions in nuclear armaments and withdrawal of all American IRBMs from Europe. But things came unstuck when Gorbachev told Reagan, "All this depends, of course, on your giving up SDI." The president reacted with extreme defensiveness, and the meeting collapsed.

START was paralyzed, but all was not lost. The less glamorous INF talks had been revived by Reagan and Gorbachev, and in 1987 the two superpowers signed a treaty that for the first time eliminated an entire class of existing weapons. On-site inspections would verify the elimination of all Soviet and American land-based, intermediate-range, nuclear-armed ballistic missiles. There is debate as to how much the treaty actually lowered the nuclear threat. Both the Soviet and American intermediate-range nuclear forces by that time were becoming obsolete, and each side already was working on new systems. The INF treaty's successful conclusion, on the other hand, signaled that the two powers were ready to resume cooperation in arms control, and that they recognized a mutual need to maintain strategic stability. Gorbachev deserves credit for his flexibility and imagination in breaking the stalemate. He understood that he could not hope to match a U.S. arms buildup when his own domestic economy was on the verge of implosion. Reagan, too, deserves plaudits. In May 1988 he won Senate approval of the INF treaty by a vote of 93 to 5. Six months later, Reagan's phenomenal popularity helped elect his understudy to the presidency.

GENTLY INTO THAT GOOD NIGHT

A former Central Intelligence Agency director and ambassador to China, Vice President George H. W. Bush succeeded Reagan in January 1989. President Bush's one-term administration inherited a tentatively cooperative relationship with the Soviet Union, the moribund START I negotiations, and a well-funded research and development program for strategic missile defense. Gorbachev, meanwhile, had been proceeding with unprecedented reforms in the Soviet Union and its satellite states. As he cut the Soviet military by 500,000 men and reduced Red Army troop levels in Eastern Europe, public demonstrations demanding freedom from communist rule spread from the shipyards of Gdansk to the coffee shops of East Berlin. A totally unpredictable unraveling had begun. In November 1989 the Berlin Wall was literally dismantled by crowds of young people fed up with the economic and political sterility of the communist system. The destruction of the emblem of East-West division shook the Soviet Union to its core, but somehow in the midst of chaos Gorbachev managed to reach out to the new government in Washington. For its part, the Bush administration sharply slowed Reagan's very costly force buildup and began to reconfigure the planned missile defense architecture that had been created to support SDI. Eventually, the president would attempt to modify the ABM Treaty, but first he and Gorbachev sought to revitalize the START process, a casualty of the Reagan-Gorbachev contretemps over SDI. Meeting in Washington, D.C., in June 1990, Bush and Gorbachev initialed a trade pact and opened negotiations for deeper cuts in strategic weapons.

A year later, in July 1991, they met in Moscow to sign the START I treaty. The new accord reduced and limited total numbers of warheads rather than delivery systems. This was a breakthrough for arms control, although a cap of 4,900 ballistic-missile warheads does seem phantasmagorical. The approach had political appeal as a tool for both leaders to demonstrate to their constituents their seriousness about reducing the threat of nuclear war. It is equally true, however, that the dissolution of the Soviet Union and the Warsaw Pact within six months of each other made the enormous size of the U.S. nuclear arsenal a political and economic liability more than a security asset. American strategic planners began to calculate the level of weapons actually needed to ensure the security of the United States in a world order no longer defined by nuclear bipolarity.

START I was Gorbachev's diplomatic swan song. On the evening of 25 December 1991, the hammer and sickle was lowered from the Kremlin's flagstaff for the last time, and the Soviet Union ceased to be. Boris Yeltsin, who had been outmaneuvering Gorbachev for primacy within the Soviet Union, became president of the new Russian Federation. Bush preferred to work with the less volatile Gorbachev, but in a typically pedestrian aside he said, "You dance with who is on the dance floor." The American pragmatist and the Russian usurper contrived to sign the SALT II agreement just before Bush left office in January 1993. It reduced the total of nuclear warheads to between 3,000 and 3,500 for each side. All MIRVed missiles were to be eliminated by the year 2003.

No matter how comprehensive, Russian-American cooperation was no longer a sufficient guarantee of nuclear security, as both Yeltsin and Bush realized. In the last decade of the twentieth century, Russia and the United States suddenly encountered a new and unprecedented danger of attack by "rogue states" equipped with nuclear missiles. It was common knowledge that Iraq and Iran had used chemical weapons against one another during their eight-year war (1980–1988), and it had been estimated in 1990 that the Iraqis were "perhaps one year away from deploying a nuclear device." During the Gulf War of 1991, Iraq brazenly launched short-range Scud missiles to terrorize Saudis in Riyadh and Israelis in Tel Aviv, and American-designed Patriot missiles performed marginally as counters to the Scuds. Subsequent arms-elimination inspections by the United Nations exposed an extensive and sophisticated Iraqi network of nuclear, biological, and chemical weapons installations. Iraq and other so-called rogue states could no longer be discounted as insignificant to the international nuclear calculus. Something had to be done to ensure that the American homeland remained invulnerable to missile attack by minor powers possessing weapons of mass destruction.

President Bush reacted to the alarm with a new missile defense concept called Global Protection Against Limited Strikes. Bearing the friendly acronym GPALS, the innovation of 1991 showed that the proponents of Reagan's "Star Wars" had never really gone away. Like SDI before it, GPALS would take nuclear warfare into space, initially with space-based sensors but eventually to include actual missile interceptors in earth orbit. To allow testing and deployment of these new systems, the administration formally proposed changes to the 1972 ABM Treaty. Suddenly divested of its sacrosanct character, the treaty would remain under siege for the rest of the twentieth century and into the twenty-first.

LOOSE NUKES, SUCCESSOR STATES, ROGUES, AND FRIENDS

Throughout the tenure of Democratic President William Jefferson Clinton, Europe was experiencing a political reordering of a magnitude not witnessed since the signing of the Versailles Treaty in 1919. As a component of the continental reconfiguration, Clinton inherited from George H. W. Bush a wide array of unresolved nuclear issues. Some of them dated well back into the Cold War. Others were of recent vintage, the by-products of the disappearance of one of the Cold War's two principal protagonists and the global hegemonic ambitions of the self-proclaimed "one remaining superpower." Foremost among these dark bequests was the precipitous proliferation of nuclear weapons.

When the Soviet Union broke up, U.S. strategists were appalled to see the largest foreign nuclear arsenal suddenly scattered among four unstable, economically weak, and potentially antagonistic successor states: Russia, Kazakhstan, Ukraine, and Belarus. Simply by declaring their independence, Ukraine and Kazakhstan became the third- and fourth-largest nuclear powers in the world. Russia, with U.S. concurrence, quickly declared itself the legal heir to the Soviet Union and the inheritor of its treaty obligations. Russia therefore became the only legitimate nuclear weapons power among the four successor states, according to the provisions of the Nonproliferation Treaty of 1968, and it joined the United States in insisting that the other three disarm as soon as possible. Belarus, Ukraine, and Kazakhstan took the first hesitant step in this direction in May 1992 when they signed the Lisbon Protocol to the START I Treaty. This action made them parties to what was originally a bilateral agreement. They further pledged to adhere to the 1968 Nonproliferation Treaty as nonnuclear weapons states, a move that would codify their acquiescence to the global nuclear order and put their civilian nuclear assets under the safeguards of the International Atomic Energy Agency.

The Clinton administration and Congress provided some monetary assistance to the Soviet Union's successor states for their transition to nonnuclear status. One means of aid, the Cooperative Threat Reduction Act (CTR)—also known as Nunn-Lugar—advanced $1.5 billion to the four struggling nations. With this aid, Russia would bring its strategic weapons inventory into compliance with START I limitations; the other three states would dismantle their segments of the former Soviet nuclear arsenal and sequester all weapons materials in Russia for indefinite safekeeping. Under CTR, President Clinton promised to purchase 500 metric tons of highly enriched Russian uranium for $12 billion over a twenty-year period. More immediately, in 1994 American technicians mounted a top-secret operation, code-named "Sapphire," which spirited 600 tons of weapons-grade uranium out of Kazakhstan. The objective was to keep this unprotected stockpile beyond the reach of Iran's nuclear weapons fabricators.

CTR attracted sharp criticism from some members of Congress for failing to focus narrowly on disarmament and for not adequately verifying destruction of nuclear weapons in Russia. Moscow, for its part, complained that most of the CTR money went to pay American contractors rather than to helping Russian firms develop the expertise to eliminate nuclear weapons. However, as one of the act's sponsors, Senator Richard G. Lugar, pointed out, the fact that most of the CTR appropriations remained in the United States was an essential selling point for the American people and Congress: "Eighty-four percent of Nunn-Lugar funds have been awarded to American firms to carry out dismantlement operations in the former Soviet Union. There are no blank checks to Moscow." As with the early Cold War's Marshall Plan, U.S. industry stood to profit from critical European instability.

Clinton supplemented the monetary inducements with diplomacy, but each of the three non-Russian nuclear-armed descendants of the Soviet Union presented unique impediments to the negotiation of nuclear disarmament. Belarus, highly Russified and sporadically ambivalent about independence, was the most readily compliant of the three; it also was the most lightly armed of them. Ukraine and Kazakhstan were tougher nuts to crack.

Bitterness against the former Soviet regime ran deep in Ukraine. Despite repeated assurances to George H. W. Bush's secretary of state, James A. Baker III, and to others concerning their intention to give up their nuclear arsenal, Ukraine's leaders stalled negotiations on assistance and delayed ratification of the Lisbon Protocol. By 1993 it was clear that Ukraine was working to establish positive control—the ability to launch—over its strategic arsenal. Ukrainian technicians already had gained negative control, which meant that President Leonid Kravchuk could prevent a missile launch by Moscow from Ukrainian soil if Russian President Boris Yeltsin should neglect to consult Kiev beforehand. Kiev's negotiators sought three main benefits from any agreement to disarm: attention and respect from the international community, money, and security guarantees from the remaining nuclear weapons states. Their intransigence delayed the Supreme Rada's ratification of START I until February 1994, and of the NPT until December of that year. Ultimately, Kiev simply had to acknowledge that it could not afford, either financially or politically, to maintain a nuclear arsenal in the face of intense international pressure.

Kazakhstan trod a path somewhere between the acquiescence of Belarus and the hard line of Ukraine. Security guarantees figured prominently in the negotiations of Alma-Ata (Almaty) with Russia and the West over disarmament. Located at the juncture of Russia, China, India, and the Middle East, Kazakhstan feared losing its nuclear deterrent without acquiring the compensating umbrella of a powerful ally. While the United States stopped short of giving positive guarantees that it would intervene if Kazakhstan were attacked, it did help to alleviate the Kazakhstani parliament's apprehensions when it joined Russia and the other weapons states in guaranteeing Kazakhstan, Ukraine, and Belarus that they would never be attacked with nuclear weapons. After holding out along with Ukraine as long as possible, Kazakhstan reluctantly faced up to the realization that it had neither the fiscal resources nor the expertise to maintain, much less use, its weapons. The Supreme Council of Kazakhstan ratified START I and the Lisbon Protocol on 23 July 1992 and, finally, the Nonproliferation Treaty as a nonnuclear state on 13 December 1993.

With Russia, nuclear matters were more complicated. When Clinton entered office in January 1993, the implementation of START I was under way and ratification of START II seemed imminent, but serious obstacles soon arose on both sides of the Atlantic. American opponents to START II raised the fear that swift action on arms reductions could leave the United States vulnerable if political instability in Russia should lead to a breakdown in bilateral arms control cooperation. An attempted parliamentary coup against President Yeltsin in October 1993 and the gradual deterioration of Yeltsin's ability to govern reinforced these concerns. Aside from the geostrategic relationship, domestic political maneuvering between the Republican-led Congress and the Democratic White House kept START II off the Senate's agenda for the better part of a year, until a quid pro quo on legislative priorities could be worked out between them. The U.S. Senate finally ratified START II by a large margin on 26 January 1996.

Strong opposition to key provisions of the treaty arose in the Russian Duma, whose members were sensitive to the changes in the U.S.–Russian strategic relationship and distressed over Russia's uncertain status as a world power. If Russia were to give up its MIRVed warheads, opponents to START II argued, it would be forced to invest in the creation of a new single-warhead ICBM force, an expenditure it could not afford, or lose its superpower status. Others believed that START II already was outdated and that negotiations should move directly to START III, as a means of bringing the U.S. arsenal down to the level at which Russian strategic forces probably would find themselves anyway. START III, it also was hoped, would eliminate objectionable features of START II, such as the provision that the United States would keep half its MIRVed SLBMs while Russia would have to eliminate all its MIRVed ICBMs.

The increase in NATO's membership, first proposed by Clinton in 1994, dealt another serious blow to prospects for the Duma's ratification of START II. Enlargement of the pact would be "the most fateful error of American policy in the entire post–Cold War era," according to George F. Kennan, the "father" of the 1947 containment policy who was still alive and writing in the 1990s. The grand master of American political-strategic thinking predicted that such a move would inflame hard-line nationalism within Russia, damage Russia's nascent democracy, and shift bilateral relations back to a Cold War status. Within Russia, analysts argued that expansion of NATO, juxtaposed with the downsizing of Russia's conventional forces, would force Moscow to rely even more heavily on its strategic arsenal. To calm this apprehension, the Russian Federation and NATO signed the 1997 Founding Act on Mutual Relations, Cooperation, and Security. They promised to build "a lasting and inclusive peace in the Euro-Atlantic area on the principles of democracy and cooperative security," and they proclaimed "the beginning of a fundamentally new relationship between NATO and Russia." While it did not satisfy the concerns of many who opposed expansion, the Founding Act did mitigate the damage enough for Moscow and Washington to continue cooperation on other issues. In 1997 Presidents Yeltsin and Clinton agreed to coordinate the START II and START III processes, with implementation of both to be complete by 31 December 2007.

Ratification of START II, and the START III talks themselves, unfortunately were soon paralyzed by the brouhaha over U.S. national missile defenses and the status of the ABM Treaty. This controversy, in turn, stemmed from the serious setbacks to nonproliferation that characterized the 1990s. The United States and Russia had been working feverishly to contain the threat of uncontrolled nuclear arsenals in the former Soviet Union at the same time that North Korea, Pakistan, and India were demonstrating their intention to crash the five-member Nonproliferation Treaty nuclear club at all costs.

The first eruption occurred in early 1993, when North Korea violated its signatory obligations to the treaty by refusing to allow International Atomic Energy Agency inspections of nuclear waste sites. Agency inspectors had found radioactive evidence suggesting that North Korea was separating plutonium from reactor waste in direct violation of the Nonproliferation Treaty. North Korean President Kim Il Sung accused the United States and South Korea of using the inspectors to spy on North Korea's military facilities and of planning to launch a "nuclear war" against the North as part of a joint military exercise, "Team Spirit." Tensions mounted throughout the spring of 1993. In March, Pyongyang threatened to withdraw from the Nonproliferation Treaty, while the United States sought sanctions through the United Nations to force North Korea to back down. At one point, the Pentagon raised the possibility of a preventive strike against the suspected facilities. Fearing an attack upon themselves as the U.S. allies geographically closest to North Korea, Tokyo and Seoul were urging Washington to consider diplomatic solutions that would avoid "cornering" Pyongyang. China and Russia also refused to support U.S. efforts to force North Korean compliance with the International Atomic Energy Agency regime. A second war on the Korean peninsula, perhaps employing nuclear weapons, began to seem possible.

Pyongyang began to moderate its position eighteen months later, however, after Kim Il Sung's son, Kim Jong Il, succeeded his father as president. In October 1994 the Clinton administration and North Korea signed an accord known as the Agreed Framework pledging that North Korea would receive light-water reactors, which do not produce plutonium, and economic aid in exchange for free and full inspections of its declared nuclear facilities. Under the accord both sides agreed to make efforts to normalize their economic and political relations. As a further concession, Secretary of Defense William J. Perry canceled Exercise Team Spirit. U.S. public opinion, however, remained strongly opposed to providing any economic support for the "rogue nation," so financing for the assistance was arranged through an international consortium of private and governmental agencies from Japan, South Korea, and the United States. These imposed inhibitions on North Korea's nuclear aspirations did not last.

On 31 August 1998, North Korea rocketed a three-stage Taep'o-dong ballistic missile over Japan's main island of Honshu. Western intelligence attributed to the missile a surprising range of between 3,800 and 5,900 kilometers. This extended reach constituted remarkable progress in five years for the North Korean missile program, from the 500 kilometer-range Nodong-1 in 1993. It sparked American fears that North Korea might be working on an intercontinental ballistic missile to bring the western United States under threat of nuclear attack. More likely, North Korea's motives for unveiling the Taep'o-dong in such a dramatic fashion had as much to do with political posturing as with aggressive concepts of national security. Just before the test, North Korea's leaders indicated that they would halt the missile program if the United States lifted economic sanctions and compensated them for lost missile sales. There also were solid indications that North Korea's nuclear weapons program, halted under the Agreed Framework, had been put back on track in reaction to U.S. failure to provide the light-water reactors it promised in 1994.

The Taep'o-dong missile launch was not the only setback to Clinton's hopes for halting the diffusion of nuclear weapons in 1998. In May of that year India announced that it had detonated five nuclear devices at its testing range in the Thar Desert near Pakistan's border. The subcontinent had been problematic for the international nonproliferation regime ever since India's refusal to sign the Nonproliferation Treaty in 1968. India had become a de facto, but undeclared, nuclear power in 1974, when Prime Minister Indira Gandhi authorized what Indian officials characterized as a "peaceful nuclear explosion." Governance of India's nuclear program was tightly held by its civilian leaders, to the almost complete exclusion of the Indian military. Since 1974, India had chosen to rely on an ambiguous "existential deterrent" policy toward its declared enemy, Pakistan, and toward its arch-rival, China. Although India clearly possessed the capability to deploy warheads, none were placed on delivery vehicles or deployed at launch sites; nor was their existence officially conceded.

Upon India's announcement of the tests in 1998, the United States and the United Nations immediately launched efforts to persuade Pakistan, long suspected of having a rudimentary nuclear capability, not to test in reaction to India. All threats and pleas failed, and Pakistan conducted six tests of its own within a month. With tensions between the two adversaries already soaring due to a chronic Islamic insurgency in Kashmir, world attention swung to the subcontinent as the next possible site for a nuclear war. In this quarter, the United States and United Nations faced a dilemma quite different from that posed by North Korea. The largest democracy in the world and a challenger to China for hegemony in South Asia, India was not constrained by the nonproliferation or safeguards conventions. Moreover, India's people and their political leaders had in the past proved remarkably resistant to threats or attempts at coercion regarding their nuclear status. Pakistan for its part was able to depend upon a close relationship with China to sustain its nuclear defense program in the face of international opprobrium.

UN Security Council Resolution 1172 of 6 June 1998, which had been sponsored by the five permanent members of the Security Council, demanded an immediate end to testing by New Delhi and Islamabad and called on the two countries to reopen negotiations over disputed territories. It enjoined them to sign the 1996 Comprehensive Test Ban Treaty (CTBT) and the Nonproliferation Treaty of 1968 as nonnuclear weapons states. In the United States, the Glenn Resolution to the Arms Export Control Act of 1998 legally required President Clinton to impose sanctions on both countries in response to the tests. Military and financial aid was restricted, but commercial intercourse continued without impediment.

International opinion was divided on the utility of sanctions as a means to coerce India or Pakistan. Many analysts thought such attempts were more likely to harden than soften the resolve of the two countries' leaders, given the overwhelming domestic approval of the tests. There was the additional risk of intensifying Pakistan's political instability by disrupting an already unsteady economy and strengthening the hand of its military in political affairs. Finally, vigorous anti-American factions in both countries resented what they regarded as Washington's interference in their bilateral affairs, while each state was highly suspicious of the other's relations with the United States. This atmosphere limited Washington's ability to influence either government, particularly in the area of arms control. Clinton and the U.S. Congress therefore gradually eased or waived many of the Glenn Resolution's prohibitions, and the administration's diplomats continued to encourage nuclear prudence on the part of India and Pakistan. Unfortunately, the Nonproliferation Treaty and International Atomic Energy Agency safeguards regimes made no provision for admitting new weapons states or for safeguarding the nuclear facilities of states that lacked official treaty nonweapon status. This hiatus left Pakistan and India in a nonproliferation limbo, and their civilian nuclear assets remained beyond international oversight.

The dramatic proliferation of nuclear weapons technology and missile arsenals, together with the bombing of the World Trade Center by a group of international terrorists in 1993, the April 1995 Oklahoma City bombing, and simultaneous car bomb attacks on the U.S. embassies in Tanzania and Kenya in August 1998, left Americans feeling uncomfortably vulnerable in an increasingly hostile and unpredictable world. Interest was revived in a total ban on testing nuclear weapons. First broached during the Kennedy presidency, the idea remained moribund until the 1990s, when it again gained currency as the most obvious means to halt nuclear weapons proliferation and arms races. In 1996 the UN General Assembly had formulated the Comprehensive Test Ban Treaty and disseminated it for signature. President Clinton, one of the first heads of state to sign, characterized the treaty as the "longest sought, hardest fought prize in arms control history." He submitted the treaty to the Senate for approval, confident he would be able to cite its ratification as one of the chief foreign policy victories of his presidency. His confidence was premature. Chairman of the Senate Foreign Relations Committee Jesse Helms, a Republican from North Carolina, with the full support of Republican Majority Leader Trent Lott, saw the treaty as a golden opportunity to thwart Clinton. They let it die in committee without a single hearing. In light of U.S. senatorial obstinacy, other governments began to question the wisdom of forgoing their right to test. By 1998 few countries had ratified the pact, and hope for a comprehensive test ban faded.

In retrospect, the monumental dangers of the Cold War's bipolar nuclear standoff had been manageable, and decades of arms control negotiations had made the likelihood of war between the two superpowers appear increasingly remote. In the afterglow of the Cold War and the disappearance of the Soviet Union, Americans were faced with a world full of apparent enemies against whom the tremendous U.S. nuclear deterrent was impotent. The threat of massive retaliation simply could not be used to deter terrorists, not only because their provenance usually was unclear, but also because it was politically untenable and morally unjustifiable to carry out such a lopsided exchange.

The function of the nuclear deterrent in the post–Cold War world became a subject of intense concern, and the topical center of gravity within U.S. security and policymaking circles began to shift from nonproliferation to counterproliferation. A search was begun for promising new technologies to defend U.S. territory and citizens against possible attack. As the threat of rogue states armed with weapons of mass destruction became a favorite subject of national security debates within Washington, Ronald Reagan's "Star Wars" concept began a relentless comeback.

President Clinton gave missile defenses a lower priority than had George H. W. Bush, but he continued a modest developmental program. The Strategic Defense Initiative Organization metamorphosed into the Ballistic Missile Defense Organization, with a much smaller budget than its predecessor had enjoyed. Drawing lessons from the Gulf War of 1991, Clinton shifted the program's concentration from strategic to regional or "theater" defense. Theater missile defenses (TMD) were seen by critics in both the United States and Russia as an attempted end run around the ABM Treaty, even though the treaty did not specifically cover TMD. Some TMD hardware could easily be reconfigured to counter strategic as well as tactical ballistic missiles, opponents argued. They predicted that development of TMD would induce Russia to build up rather than reduce its strategic arsenal, thus undoing the historic achievements of arms control negotiations and agreements. In 1993 the Clinton administration sought to alleviate these concerns by negotiating a "line of demarcation" between strategic and theater defenses based on Article 6 of the ABM Treaty, which forbade giving an ABM "capability" to non-ABM defense systems. This approach met with powerful opposition from the newly elected Senate Republican majority in 1994. The Republicans insisted that the Russians should not have a "veto" over the future of American missile defenses, as they did under the ABM Treaty.

Caught between these conflicting factions, Clinton worked directly with Yeltsin to fashion language that would evade both the legal triggers of the treaty and the political guns of the U.S. Senate. The result was a joint statement by the two presidents issued in May 1995. It paved the way for negotiating a demarcation agreement, recognized the validity of TMD in principle, and reaffirmed the importance of the ABM Treaty to the bilateral relationship. The negotiations themselves were complex. The current parties to the ABM Treaty—the United States, Russia, Belarus, Ukraine, and Kazakhstan—had to hammer out a common interpretation of interceptor range and velocity, flight-testing, space- and land-based sensors, and other arcane technical issues within the parameters of the treaty before they could reach agreement on what any signatory actually was allowed to do with its missile defenses.

Meanwhile, the controversy in the United States over a national missile defense continued to evoke strong reactions from powerful international friends and potential adversaries. China and Russia were the most vociferous in their condemnation of what they viewed as a unilaterally destabilizing course of action. European and Asian allies asked whether the United States was attempting to withdraw behind a "Fortress America" defensive bulwark that would leave them facing potential threats without a credible deterrent. Having gotten itself entangled in some future overseas adventure, their argument went, the United States could retreat without fear of reprisal, leaving its allies exposed as defenseless targets for the missiles of disgruntled adversaries. The Clinton administration disingenuously countered that, on the contrary, a United States free from the fear of retaliation would be more willing, not less, to come to the aid of its allies in a nuclear emergency. This was a ghostly reprise of the American assertions that in the early 1960s had led a skeptical Charles de Gaulle to form a French nuclear *force de frappe* and to withdraw from NATO strategic planning. De Gaulle knew in the 1960s, as European leaders knew in the 1990s, that there was only a negative answer to the question, "Would the Americans really be willing to trade Washington for, say, Paris?"

To appease a dubious Russia, the Clinton administration in 1999 proposed that the two countries cooperate in the development of national missile defense systems. Before any real progress could be made, in December 2000, Yeltsin abdicated and was succeeded by the former secret police (KGB) officer Vladimir Putin.

The new Russian president warned Clinton that abrogation of the ABM Treaty would force Russia to reconsider all of its treaty obligations with the United States, including the pending ratification of START II. Clinton vacillated. He had signed the 1999 National Missile Defense Act calling for an effective missile defense system as soon as one was technologically feasible, but he deferred a final decision to deploy one and passed that hot potato to his successor. Putin in the meantime was doing his best to keep the United States committed to bilateral strategic arms control and to salvage the ABM Treaty. Strong lobbying by the Russian president persuaded the Duma to ratify START II in April 2000. The desperate gesture's futility would be demonstrated soon after President Clinton left office.

YIELDING TO THE NEW ORDER

George W. Bush, the son of Clinton's predecessor, entered the White House in January 2001 as a strange amalgam of neoisolationist and latter-day cold warrior. Lacking his father's lifetime of exposure to world affairs or to politics beyond Texas, Bush had very rarely traveled overseas. From the first days of his administration he showed an alarming tendency to discount the stabilizing results of a half century's patient negotiation, especially the thirty-year-old ABM Treaty. His most senior advisers were men and women with broad foreign policy expertise and extensive experience in managing the national security apparatus. Richard Cheney, the vice president, had been secretary of defense at the time of the Gulf War; Secretary of Defense Donald Rumsfeld had held the same office under President Reagan; General Colin Powell, the secretary of state, was a former national security adviser who had been chairman of the Joint Chiefs of Staff during the Gulf War. Bush's national security adviser, Condoleezza Rice, was a newcomer to high office but she brought to the Oval Office an intimate academic familiarity with the military and foreign policy of Soviet Russia. On balance, these counselors were aggressive and combative veterans of the Cold War; they were not inclined to dissuade the president from attacking the ABM Treaty as obsolete in a world of nuclear-armed rogue states, or from pushing the eastward expansion of NATO regardless of the objections of Russia.

Bush immediately made it clear that creation of a missile defense system would command his highest priority. At the same time, he began distancing himself from the traditionally close strategic and arms control relationship the United States had maintained with Russia since Nixon's presidency. In the earliest days of his administration Bush warned that if Russia refused to negotiate changes to the ABM Treaty the United States might abrogate the pact. He further suggested that the United States would make future changes to its strategic arsenal on a unilateral basis. This autarchy would free the United States from the need to negotiate missile defenses in tandem with arms reductions, thereby decoupling Russian and American strategic interests for the first time in more than fifty years.

Early in 2001 the éminence grise of the Republican foreign policy establishment, Henry Kissinger, weighed in on the side of the opponents of the ABM Treaty, which had been negotiated when he was President Nixon's national security adviser. In a book entitled *Does America Need a Foreign Policy?* Kissinger quite remarkably traced the treaty's origins to congressional and bureaucratic opposition to an ABM defense system that, he claimed, was what President Nixon had preferred. Kissinger said the opponents of Nixon's antiballistic missile program used the same arguments as were being used in 2001 to discredit President Bush's national and theater missile defense proposals. In Kissinger's version, the Cassandras incoherently predicted that a ballistic missile defense program "would not work; that it would work so well as to be destabilizing; that it would weaken the Atlantic Alliance by decoupling the defense of the United States from that of Europe; that it would drive the Soviet Union into intransigence and an arms race."

Kissinger and others who would scrap the ABM Treaty in order to construct antiballistic missile systems postulated that regardless of any treaty, the United States and Russia would not attack one another because each side had far more than enough nuclear weapons to obliterate its rival. On the other side of the debate was Thomas L. Friedman, the foreign correspondent of the *New York Times*. A strategic thinker who believed that "the information revolution and [economic] globalization" were radically transforming international relations, Friedman vigorously denounced Kissinger and "the Bush team's latest version of a high-tech missile defense shield." It was "an idea that, so far, doesn't work, [and] shows every possibility of unraveling the complex web of arms control and diplomatic initiatives that have kept the peace for 50 years."

President Bush met Vladimir Putin, the president of the Russian Federation, for the first time in Slovenia in June 2001. Bush said he looked his counterpart in the eye, liked what he saw, and invited him to his ranch in Texas. Some naive columnists were quick to herald a breakthrough and a revitalization of Russian American relations. But prudent skeptics wondered whether real Russian-American harmony could be established or persist given the substantive differences dividing the two countries. Asked about the U.S.–Russian relationship in May 2000, the deputy chairman of the defense committee of the Russian Duma, Alexei Arbatov, replied without hesitation, "There are a lot of very bad feelings, bad expectations, suspicions and mistrust. A lot of those are not justified, some are, unfortunately, justified. Russia sees itself as now being an opponent of the United States. . . . Russia is willing to compete . . . in important areas such as the post-Soviet states, the Balkans, the issue of ballistic missile defenses and strategic offenses [sic]."

Another pertinent question to consider when assessing Russian-American relations in the first decade of the twenty-first century was whether the relationship between the two should really remain the central thread of American nuclear strategy and diplomacy. The United States might bill itself as the "one remaining superpower" in 2001, but the People's Republic of China was a nascent great power with potentially unlimited geopolitical ambitions and energy. Vociferous in denouncing the Bush administration's plans to build missile defenses as destabilizing, China shrugged off American accusations that it was benefiting from the ABM Treaty while the United States lay exposed to missile attacks by powers other than Russia. Beijing continued to vilify the United States as a "rogue hegemon" whose self-aggrandizement threatened the security of the rest of the world. At the same time, China modernized its own nuclear and conventional forces and opened mutual defense discussions with Russia. President Putin of Russia, seeking a counterweight to U.S. power, turned eagerly to China, where he found enthusiasm for cooperation in arms and technology transfers. A Sino-Russian voting alliance in the UN Security Council became less and less far-fetched, but this was not the most ominous development. Alexei Arbatov warned, "Russia certainly views China as its present partner. . . . [F]or the nearest and medium-term future, China is perceived as much closer to Russia on international security issues than the United States and the West in general."

In mid-2001 it was hard to see how the emergence of a Sino-Russian bloc could do other than increase the Bush administration's resolve to abandon the ABM Treaty and go it alone with nuclear missile defenses. In July of that year a missile-borne "kill vehicle" dramatically intercepted a Minuteman II warhead 144 miles above the Pacific Ocean. The highly orchestrated test convinced credulous proponents of Star Wars "that we can hit a bullet with a bullet." Less than a week later, at a summit in the Kremlin, the presidents of Russia and China jointly condemned George W. Bush's national missile defense and his intended abrogation of the ABM Treaty as threats to the security of their countries. For the first time in fifty years, Beijing and Moscow concluded a treaty of friendship and mutual cooperation. This rapprochement between America's two former major antagonists was a far cry from the benign "new world order" that the first President Bush had proclaimed at the end of the Cold War.

CONCLUSION

The world has turned round many times since Harry S. Truman permitted the U.S. Army Air Forces to drop atomic bombs on Japan. Having borne the full moral responsibility for opening the age of nuclear warfare, he courageously repudiated advisers who would have him repeat the macabre performance in Korea or China. His five-star successor, Dwight D. Eisenhower, constructed a magnificent nuclear armory and resolutely refused to use a single weapon in the inventory, despite the proclivity of his secretary of state for saber-rattling warnings of imminent Armageddon. After the bone-chilling scare of John F. Kennedy's Cuban missile crisis, a long period of mature Soviet-American nuclear diplomacy and restraint settled over Washington and Moscow. The well-understood rules of the nuclear-diplomatic road did not become obsolete until the dissolution of the Soviet Union in 1991. Thereafter, the restless new nuclear powers and a freshly assertive China cast the most ominous shadows over the future. It would take extraordinary American statesmanship to steer a safe course through a world of revanchist states armed with weapons of mass destruction. George H. W. Bush, William Jefferson Clinton, and George W. Bush were only the first of a long line of American presidents who would face a challenge for which the Cold War's nuclear policy offered precious little direct guidance.

BIBLIOGRAPHY

Alperovitz, Gar. *Atomic Diplomacy: Hiroshima and Potsdam.* New York, 1965. The classic formulation of the revisionists' questions about the motives behind the atomic bombing of Japan. See also the author's revised edition (London and Boulder, Colo., 1994), in which, after reconsidering the evidence, he reasserts his earlier thesis.

Arbatov, Alexei. "Arbatov on U.S.–Russian Arms Reduction." Proliferation Brief 3, no. 16 (18 May 2000) of the Carnegie Endowment for International Peace. A pithy analysis of Russia's decision to ratify START II, by the deputy chairman of the Duma defense committee.

Bernstein, Barton J. "Roosevelt, Truman and the Atomic Bomb, 1941–1945: A Reinterpretation." *Political Science Quarterly* 90 (spring 1975): 23–69. A prominent Cold War revisionist defends the Truman administration for dropping the bomb and refutes some of the Alperovitz criticism.

Bertsch, Gary K., and William C. Potter, eds. *Dangerous Weapons, Desperate States: Russia, Belarus, Kazakhstan, and Ukraine.* New York, 1999. An exhaustive study of export controls and the danger of illegal transfer of nuclear materials in the four nuclear successor states to the Soviet Union.

Brodie, Bernard, ed. *The Absolute Weapon: Atomic Power and World Order.* New York, 1946. The scholarly argument for a balance of terror by the American master of military strategy.

Burdick, Eugene, and Harvey Wheeler. *Fail-Safe.* New York, 1962. Two political scientists resort to fiction to explain what would happen if SAC lost control of any of its aircraft and the superpowers had to choose which cities to offer up in a mutual sacrifice to prevent all-out nuclear war.

Chang, Gordon H. "To the Nuclear Brink: Eisenhower, Dulles and the Quemoy-Matsu Crisis." *International Security* 12, no. 4 (spring 1988): 96–122. President Eisenhower took the United States closer to nuclear war with China in 1955 than has been imagined.

Cirincione, Joseph, ed. *Repairing the Regime: Preventing the Spread of Weapons of Mass Destruction.* New York, 2000. Papers from the premier annual conference on controlling the spread of weapons of mass destruction.

Dawisha, Adeed, and Karen Dawisha, eds. *The Making of Foreign Policy in Russia and the New States of Eurasia.* Armonk, N.Y., 1995. A glimpse into the complexities facing American policymakers in their dealings with the remains of the Soviet Union.

Deaver, Michael K. *A Different Drummer: My Thirty Years with Ronald Reagan.* New York, 2001. An insider's frightening view of Reagan's mind and diplomacy.

Drew, S. Nelson, ed. *NSC-68: Forging the Strategy of Containment, with Analyses by Paul H. Nitze.* Washington, D.C., 1996. The document itself, accompanied by a post-hoc exegesis by the principal author.

Fitzgerald, Frances. *Way Out There in the Blue: Reagan, Star Wars, and the End of the Cold War.* New York, 2000. Antimissile defense systems thoroughly debunked with literary lucidity, by one of the great political and social critics of the late twentieth century.

Friedman, Norman. *The Fifty-Year War: Conflict and Strategy in the Cold War.* Annapolis, Md., 2000. A technologically oriented analyst's comprehensive account of the strategy and diplomacy of the Cold War.

Friedman, Thomas L. *The Lexus and the Olive Tree: Understanding Globalization.* New York, 2000. Businessmen, not bombers, hold the key to the world's future according to a leading opponent of visionary missile defense systems.

Gaddis, John L. *Strategies of Containment: A Critical Appraisal of Postwar American National Security Policy.* New York, 1982. Ideas formulated during strategy seminars at the Naval War College just after the Vietnam War.

———. *The United States and the End of the Cold War: Implications, Reconsiderations, Provocations.* New York, 1992. Some projections about "where we may be going" written at the very end of the Cold War, as the Soviet Union was dissolving.

———. *We Now Know: Rethinking Cold War History.* New York, 1997. The distinguished conservative blames Stalin for the Cold War, credits Khrushchev with a victory in the Cuban missile crisis, and chastises revisionists for interpretive flexibility.

Herkin, Gregg. *The Winning Weapon: The Atomic Bomb and the Cold War, 1945–1950.* New York, 1980. A finely balanced assessment of atomic diplomacy in practice.

Hersey, John. *Hiroshima.* New York, 1946. The classic conscience-shattering account of six who survived the bombing.

Hewlett, Richard G., and Oscar E. Anderson, Jr. *A History of the Atomic Energy Commission: The New World, 1939–1946*. University Park, Pa., 1962. The first of two volumes of the history of the AEC written with unflagging precision and based on the agency's documents.

Hewlett, Richard G., and Francis Duncan. *A History of the Atomic Energy Commission: Atomic Shield, 1947–1952*. University Park, Pa., 1969. The second volume of the AEC's history.

———. *Nuclear Navy, 1946–1962*. Chicago and London, 1974. An extremely detailed study of Admiral Hyman Rickover's struggle for a nuclear-powered submarine, the first step toward the Polaris system.

Holloway, David. *Stalin and the Bomb: The Soviet Union and Atomic Energy, 1939–1956*. New Haven, Conn., 1994. A full account of how Stalin instantly perceived the atomic bombing of Japan as an anti-Soviet act disrupting the international balance of power.

Huntington, Samuel P. *The Common Defense: Strategic Programs in National Politics*. New York, 1961. A superior survey of 1945–1960 by a pioneer in the study of strategy.

Isaacson, Walter, and Evan Thomas. *The Wise Men: Six Friends and the World They Made*. New York, 1986. The makers of policy and strategy in thought, deed, and camaraderie from World War II through Vietnam.

Kaplan, Morton A. *S.A.L.T.: Problems and Prospects*. Morristown, N.J., 1973. A glimpse of the intricacies of arms limitations by a distinguished observer.

Kartchner, Kerry M. *Negotiating START: Strategic Arms Reduction Talks and the Quest for Strategic Stability*. New Brunswick, N.J., 1992. One of the best in-depth analyses of U.S. and Soviet-Russian policies and positions in the first START negotiations.

Kaufman, Robert G. *Henry M. Jackson: A Life in Politics*. Seattle, Wash., 2000. A highly sympathetic and comprehensive scholarly biography of the "senator from Boeing."

Kegley, Charles W., Jr., and Eugene R. W. Wittkopf, eds. *The Nuclear Reader: Strategy, Weapons, War.* New York, 1985. A variety of views from the American perspective on such crucial topics as MAD and civil defense.

Kissinger, Henry. *Does America Need a Foreign Policy?: Towards a Diplomacy for the 21st Century*. New York, 2001. A plea for admission to George W. Bush's inner circle, made at the price of disavowing his own ABM Treaty.

Kolodziej, Edward A. *The Uncommon Defense and Congress, 1945–1963*. Columbus, Ohio, 1966. A good summary of the military arguments presented to Congress each year.

LaFeber, Walter. *America, Russia, and the Cold War, 1945–1973*. 3d ed. New York, 1976. A careful portrait of the diplomatic context shaping nuclear policies by one of America's preeminent diplomatic historians.

Lavoy, Peter R., Scott D. Sagan, and James J. Wirtz, eds. *Planning the Unthinkable: How New Powers Will Use Nuclear, Biological and Chemical Weapons*. Ithaca, N.Y., 2000. This ground-breaking work seeks to explain why different actors want to obtain unconventional weapons and how they intend to use them. Case studies of six states and a chapter on terrorists.

Lodal, Jan. *The Price of Dominance: The New Weapons of Mass Destruction and Their Challenge to American Leadership*. New York, 2001. Warning that complacency is unwarranted, the author proposes a comprehensive post–Cold War nuclear strategy for the United States.

Mandelbaum, Michael, ed. *The Other Side of the Table: The Soviet Approach to Arms Control*. New York, 1990. Excellent dissection of the Soviet Union's motivations and reasoning by an internationally recognized scholar.

McCullough, David. *Truman*. New York, 1992. A Pulitzer Prize–winning biography.

Messer, Robert L. *The End of an Alliance: James F. Byrnes, Roosevelt, and the Origins of the Cold War.* Chapel Hill, N.C., 1982. Documents the belligerency of the Truman cold warriors and casts doubt on the diplomatic efficacy of verbal bluster.

Mueller, John. *Retreat from Doomsday: The Obsolescence of Major War.* New York, 1989. Advances the dubious thesis that historical conditions other than the advent of nuclear warfare account for the elimination of major war as a serious policy option.

Myrdal, Alva. *The Game of Disarmament: How the United States and Russia Run the Arms Race*. New York, 1976. A critical analysis of the arms race from the perspective of an advocate of disarmament.

Newhouse, John. *Cold Dawn: The Story of SALT*. Washington, D.C., 1989. A detailed and fascinating account of the first attempt to control the nuclear arms race through bilateral negotiations.

———. "The Missile Defense Debate." *Foreign Affairs* 80, no. 4 (July/August 2001): 97–109. The master of the subject again opposes an American missile defense system as technologically and politically impractical.

Pape, Robert A. *Bombing to Win: Air Power and Coercion in War.* Ithaca, N.Y., 1996. Thoughtful and critical evaluation of the utility of nuclear and nonnuclear strategic bombing as an instrument of policy.

Paret, Peter, ed. *Makers of Modern Strategy: From Machiavelli to the Nuclear Age.* Princeton, N.J., 1986. A grand survey by authors who believe in wars of annihilation.

Paterson, Thomas G., J. Garry Clifford, and Kenneth J. Hagan. *American Foreign Relations. Vol. 2: A History Since 1895.* 5th ed. Boston, 2000. This revisionist but balanced survey contains at least one succinct paragraph on every major episode in Soviet-American nuclear relations.

Rhodes, Richard. *The Making of the Atomic Bomb.* New York, 1986. Every aspect of the creation and use of the first atomic bombs.

———. *Dark Sun: The Making of the Hydrogen Bomb.* New York, 1995.

Rotblat, Joseph, ed. *Security, Cooperation, and Disarmament: The Unfinished Agenda for the 1990s.* Proceedings of the Forty-sixth Pugwash Conference on Science and World Affairs, 2–7 September, 1996, in Lahti, Finland. London, 1998. A group of experts from twenty countries debate a broad array of issues facing the world, including nuclear arms control and disarmament. Valuable for its sometimes widely divergent points of view.

Sapolsky, Harvey M. *The Polaris System Development: Bureaucratic and Programmatic Success in Government.* Cambridge, Mass., 1972. A provocative explanation of why and how strategic weapons systems are built.

Schelling, Thomas C. *Arms and Influence.* New Haven, Conn., 1966. The argument for practicing coercive nuclear diplomacy or atomic blackmail by an originator of deterrence theory.

Schroeer, Dietrich. *Science, Technology, and the Nuclear Arms Race.* New York, 1984. A stunning integration of the technical and political components of the nuclear arms race by a nuclear physicist concerned about the loss of life that would attend a nuclear war.

Sherry, Michael S. *The Rise of American Air Power: The Creation of Armageddon.* New Haven, Conn., 1987. Strategic bombing in the context of the historical evolution of theory.

Sherwin, Martin J. *A World Destroyed: The Atomic Bomb and the Grand Alliance.* New York, 1975. Persuasively argues the pros and cons of bombing Hiroshima and Nagasaki and criticizes the strategic doctrine of unconditional surrender.

Stimson, Henry L. "The Decision to Use the Atomic Bomb." *Harper's* (February 1947). The orthodox position on the use of the atomic bomb in 1945 by one of the participants in the decision making.

Takaki, Ronald. *Hiroshima: Why America Dropped the Atomic Bomb.* New York, 1995. A Japanese American finds Truman fully responsible, but with understandable military justification.

Thomas, Evan. *Robert Kennedy: His Life.* New York, 2000. A balanced look at the pivotal role the president's brother played in defusing the Cuban missile crisis.

Trachtenburg, Marc. *A Constructed Peace: The Making of the European Settlement, 1945–1963.* Princeton, N.J., 1999. Contends that Germany, not Soviet-American nuclear accommodation, held the key to global peace in the Cold War.

Van Cleave, William R., and S. T. Cohen. *Nuclear Weapons, Policies, and the Test Ban Issue.* New York, 1987. A conservative view that is critical of test-ban agreements.

Walsh, James, ed. *The Future Role of United States' Nuclear Weapons.* Defense and Arms Control Studies Program Working Paper. Cambridge, Mass., August 1994. Experts from the U.S. arms control community gathered in February 1994 to discuss the present and future of the U.S. nuclear arsenal and U.S. strategic policy.

Weigley, Russell F. *The American Way of War: A History of United States Military Strategy and Policy.* New York, 1973. The ageless and classic study of the American strategy of annihilation.

Weintraub, Stanley. *MacArthur's War: Korea and the Undoing of an American Hero.* New York, 2000. Puts MacArthur's advocacy of using atomic weapons in the Korean War into national perspective.

Weir, Gary E. *Forged in War: The Naval Industrial Complex and American Submarine Construction, 1940–1961.* Washington, D.C., 1993. A superb historian puts Rickover into context.

Wirtz, James J., and Jeffrey A. Larsen, eds. *Rockets' Red Glare: Missile Defenses and World Politics.* Boulder, Colo., 2002. Generally favorable analyses by U.S. experts of the arguments for development of a national missile defense. A wealth of historical and technical information for those unfamiliar with the issue.

York, Herbert. *Race to Oblivion: A Participant's View of the Arms Race.* New York, 1970. Disturbing criticism by a disillusioned nuclear scientist who was present at the creation.

Zubok, Vladislav, and Constantine Pleshakov. *Inside the Kremlin's Cold War: From Stalin to Khrushchev.* Cambridge, Mass., 1996. Superb and readable discussion of the other side's nuclear diplomacy from Soviet sources opened after the Cold War.

See also ARMS CONTROL AND DISARMAMENT; ARMS TRANSFERS AND TRADE; BALANCE OF POWER; COLD WAR EVOLUTION AND INTERPRETATIONS; COLD WAR ORIGINS; COLD WARRIORS; COLD WAR TERMINATION; COLLECTIVE SECURITY; CONGRESSIONAL POWER; CONTAINMENT; DETERRENCE; DOCTRINES; IDEOLOGY; INTERNATIONAL ORGANIZATION; MILITARY-INDUSTRIAL COMPLEX; NORTH ATLANTIC TREATY ORGANIZATION; OUTER SPACE; POST–COLD WAR POLICY; POWER POLITICS; PRESIDENTIAL POWER; SCIENCE AND TECHNOLOGY; SUMMIT CONFERENCES; SUPERPOWER DIPLOMACY; TREATIES.

ISBN 0-684-80659-2

90000